HENRY ADAMS

HENRY ADAMS

HISTORY OF THE
UNITED STATES OF AMERICA
DURING THE ADMINISTRATIONS OF
THOMAS JEFFERSON

THE LIBRARY OF AMERICA

The paper used in this publication meets the
minimum requirements of the American National Standard
for Information Sciences—Permanence of Paper for
Printed Library Materials, ANSI Z39.48-1984.

Distributed to the trade in the United States
and Canada by the Viking Press.

Published outside North America by the Press Syndicate
of the University of Cambridge,
The Pitt Building, Trumpington Street, Cambridge CB2 IRP, England.
ISBN O 521 32483 I

Library of Congress Catalog Card Number: 85-23098
For cataloging information, see end of volume.
ISBN 0-940450-34-8
———
First Printing

Manufactured in the United States of America

EARL N. HARBERT
WROTE THE NOTES AND SELECTED
THE TEXTS FOR THIS VOLUME

Grateful acknowledgement is made to the National Endowment for the Humanities and the Ford Foundation for their generous financial support of this series.

Contents

Each section has its own table of contents.

HISTORY OF
THE UNITED STATES
OF AMERICA

DURING THE FIRST ADMINISTRATION OF

THOMAS JEFFERSON

1801–1805

Contents

MAPS

Chapter I

ACCORDING to the census of 1800, the United States of America contained 5,308,483 persons. In the same year the British Islands contained upwards of fifteen millions; the French Republic, more than twenty-seven millions. Nearly one fifth of the American people were negro slaves; the true political population consisted of four and a half million free whites, or less than one million able-bodied males, on whose shoulders fell the burden of a continent. Even after two centuries of struggle the land was still untamed; forest covered every portion, except here and there a strip of cultivated soil; the minerals lay undisturbed in their rocky beds, and more than two thirds of the people clung to the seaboard within fifty miles of tide-water, where alone the wants of civilized life could be supplied. The centre of population rested within eighteen miles of Baltimore, north and east of Washington. Except in political arrangement, the interior was little more civilized than in 1750, and was not much easier to penetrate than when La Salle and Hennepin found their way to the Mississippi more than a century before.

A great exception broke this rule. Two wagon-roads crossed the Alleghany Mountains in Pennsylvania,—one leading from Philadelphia to Pittsburg; one from the Potomac to the Monongahela; while a third passed through Virginia southwestward to the Holston River and Knoxville in Tennessee, with a branch through the Cumberland Gap into Kentucky. By these roads and by trails less passable from North and South Carolina, or by water-ways from the lakes, between four and five hundred thousand persons had invaded the country beyond the Alleghanies. At Pittsburg and on the Monongahela existed a society, already old, numbering seventy or eighty thousand persons, while on the Ohio River the settlements had grown to an importance which threatened to force a difficult problem on the union of the older States. One hundred and eighty thousand whites, with forty thousand negro slaves, made Kentucky the largest community west of the mountains; and about ninety thousand whites and fourteen thousand slaves were scattered over Tennessee. In the territory north of the Ohio less progress had been made. A New England colony existed at Marietta; some fifteen thousand people were gathered at Cincinnati; half-way between the two, a small town had grown up at Chillicothe, and other villages or straggling cabins were to be found elsewhere; but the whole Ohio territory contained only forty-five thousand inhabitants. The entire population, both free and slave, west of the mountains, reached not yet half a million; but already they were partly disposed to think themselves, and the old thirteen States were not altogether unwilling to consider them, the germ of an independent empire, which was to find its outlet, not through the Alleghanies to the seaboard, but by the Mississippi River to the Gulf.

Nowhere did eastern settlements touch the western. At least one hundred miles of mountainous country held the two regions everywhere apart. The shore of Lake Erie, where alone contact seemed easy, was still unsettled. The Indians had been pushed back to the Cuyahoga River, and a few cabins were built on the site of Cleveland; but in 1800, as in 1700, this intermediate region was only a portage where emigrants and merchandise were transferred from Lake Erie to the Muskingum and Ohio valleys. Even western New York remained a wilderness: Buffalo was not laid out; Indian titles were not extinguished; Rochester did not exist; and the county of Onondaga numbered a population of less than eight thousand. In 1799 Utica contained fifty houses, mostly small and temporary. Albany was still a Dutch city, with some five thousand inhabitants; and the tide of immigration flowed slowly through it into the valley of the Mohawk, while another stream from Pennsylvania, following the Susquehanna, spread toward the Genesee country.

The people of the old thirteen States, along the Atlantic seaboard, thus sent westward a wedge-shaped mass of nearly half a million persons, penetrating by the Tennessee, Cumberland, and Ohio rivers toward the western limit of the Union. The Indians offered sharp resistance to this invasion, exacting life for life, and yielding only as their warriors perished. By the close of the century the wedge of white settlements, with its apex at Nashville and its flanks covered by the Ohio and Tennessee rivers, nearly split the Indian country in halves. The northern half—consisting of the later States of Wisconsin, Michigan, Illinois, Indiana, and one third of Ohio—contained Wyandottes and Shawanese, Miamis, Kickapoos, and other tribes, able to send some five thousand warriors to hunt or fight. In the southern half, powerful confederacies of Creeks, Cherokees, Chickasaws, and Choctaws lived and hunted where the States of Mississippi, Alabama, and the western parts of Georgia, Tennessee, and Kentucky were to extend; and so weak was the State of Georgia, which claimed the southwestern territory for its own, that a well-concerted movement of Indians might without much difficulty have swept back its white population of one hundred thousand toward the ocean or across the Savannah River. The Indian power had been broken in halves, but each half was still terrible to the colonists on the edges of their vast domain, and was used as a political weapon by the Governments whose territory bounded the Union on the north and south. The governors-general of Canada intrigued with the northwestern Indians, that they might hold in check any aggression from Washington; while the Spanish governors of West Florida and Louisiana maintained equally close relations with the Indian confederacies of the Georgia territory.

With the exception that half a million people had crossed the Alleghanies and were struggling with difficulties all their own, in an isolation like that of Jutes or Angles in the fifth century, America, so far as concerned physical problems, had changed little in fifty years. The old landmarks remained nearly where they stood before. The same bad roads and difficult rivers, connecting the same small towns, stretched into the same forests in 1800 as when the armies of Braddock and Amherst pierced the western and northern wilderness, except that these roads extended a few miles farther from the seacoast. Nature was rather man's master than his servant, and the five million Americans struggling with the untamed continent seemed hardly more competent to their task than the beavers and buffalo which had for countless generations made bridges and roads of their own.

Even by water, along the seaboard, communication was as

slow and almost as irregular as in colonial times. The wars in Europe caused a sudden and great increase in American shipping employed in foreign commerce, without yet leading to general improvement in navigation. The ordinary sea-going vessel carried a freight of about two hundred and fifty tons; the largest merchant ships hardly reached four hundred tons; the largest frigate in the United States navy, the "line-of-battle ship in disguise," had a capacity of fifteen hundred and seventy-six tons. Elaborately rigged as ships or brigs, the small merchant craft required large crews and were slow sailers; but the voyage to Europe was comparatively more comfortable and more regular than the voyage from New York to Albany, or through Long Island Sound to Providence. No regular packet plied between New York and Albany. Passengers waited till a sloop was advertised to sail; they provided their own bedding and supplies; and within the nineteenth century Captain Elias Bunker won much fame by building the sloop "Experiment," of one hundred and ten tons, to start regularly on a fixed day for Albany, for the convenience of passengers only, supplying beds, wine, and provisions for the voyage of one hundred and fifty miles. A week on the North River or on the Sound was an experience not at all unknown to travellers.

While little improvement had been made in water-travel, every increase of distance added to the difficulties of the westward journey. The settler who after buying wagon and horses hauled his family and goods across the mountains, might buy or build a broad flat-bottomed ark, to float with him and his fortunes down the Ohio, in constant peril of upsetting or of being sunk; but only light boats with strong oars could mount the stream, or boats forced against the current by laboriously poling in shallow water. If he carried his tobacco and wheat down the Mississippi to the Spanish port of New Orleans, and sold it, he might return to his home in Kentucky or Ohio by a long and dangerous journey on horseback through the Indian country from Natchez to Nashville, or he might take ship to Philadelphia, if a ship were about to sail, and again cross the Alleghanies. Compared with river travel, the sea was commonly an easy and safe highway. Nearly all the rivers which penetrated the interior were unsure, liable to be made dangerous by freshets, and both dangerous and impassable by drought; yet such as they were, these streams made the main paths of traffic. Through the mountainous gorges of the Susquehanna the produce of western New York first found an outlet; the Cuyahoga and Muskingum were the first highway from the Lakes to the Ohio; the Ohio itself, with its great tributaries the Cumberland and the Tennessee, marked the lines of western migration; and every stream which could at high water float a boat was thought likely to become a path for commerce. As General Washington, not twenty years earlier, hoped that the brawling waters of the Cheat and Youghiogheny might become the channel of trade between Chesapeake Bay and Pittsburg, so the Americans of 1800 were prepared to risk life and property on any streamlet that fell foaming down either flank of the Alleghanies. The experience of mankind proved trade to be dependent on water communications, and as yet Americans did not dream that the experience of mankind was useless to them.

If America was to be developed along the lines of water communication alone, by such means as were known to Europe, Nature had decided that the experiment of a single republican government must meet extreme difficulties. The valley of the Ohio had no more to do with that of the Hudson, the Susquehanna, the Potomac, the Roanoke, and the Santee, than the valley of the Danube with that of the Rhone, the Po, or the Elbe. Close communication by land could alone hold the great geographical divisions together either in interest or in fear. The union of New England with New York and Pennsylvania was not an easy task even as a problem of geography, and with an ocean highway; but the union of New England with the Carolinas, and of the seacoast with the interior, promised to be a hopeless undertaking. Physical contact alone could make one country of these isolated empires, but to the patriotic American of 1800, struggling for the continued existence of an embryo nation, with machinery so inadequate, the idea of ever bringing the Mississippi River, either by land or water, into close contact with New England, must have seemed wild. By water, an Erie Canal was already foreseen; by land, centuries of labor could alone conquer those obstacles which Nature permitted to be overcome.

In the minds of practical men, the experience of Europe left few doubts on this point. After two thousand years of public labor and private savings, even despotic monarchs, who employed the resources of their subjects as they pleased, could in 1800 pass from one part of their European dominions to another little more quickly than they might have done in the age of the Antonines. A few short canals had been made, a few bridges had been built, an excellent post-road extended from Madrid to St. Petersburg; but the heavy diligence that rumbled from Calais to Paris required three days for its journey of one hundred and fifty miles, and if travellers ventured on a trip to Marseilles they met with rough roads and hardships like those of the Middle Ages. Italy was in 1800 almost as remote from the north of Europe as when carriage-roads were first built. Neither in time nor in thought was Florence or Rome much nearer to London in Wordsworth's youth than in the youth of Milton or Gray. Indeed, such changes as had occurred were partly for the worse, owing to the violence of revolutionary wars during the last ten years of the eighteenth century. Horace Walpole at his life's close saw about him a world which in many respects was less civilized than when as a boy he made the grand tour of Europe.

While so little had been done on the great highways of European travel, these highways were themselves luxuries which furnished no sure measure of progress. The post-horses toiled as painfully as ever through the sand from Hamburg to Berlin, while the coach between York and London rolled along an excellent road at the rate of ten miles an hour; yet neither in England nor on the Continent was the post-road a great channel of commerce. No matter how good the road, it could not compete with water, nor could heavy freights in great quantities be hauled long distances without extravagant cost. Water communication was as necessary for European commerce in 1800 as it had been for the Phœnicians and Egyptians; the Rhine, the Rhone, the Danube, the Elbe, were still the true commercial highways, and except for government post-roads, Europe was as dependent on these rivers in the eighteenth century as in the thirteenth. No certainty could be offered of more rapid progress in the coming century than in the past; the chief hope seemed to lie in the construction of canals.

While Europe had thus consumed centuries in improving paths of trade, until merchandise could be brought by canal a few score miles from the Rhone to the Loire and Seine, to the Garonne and the Rhine, and while all her wealth and energy had not yet united the Danube with other river systems, America was required to construct, without delay, at least three great roads and canals, each several hundred miles long, across mountain ranges, through a country not yet inhabited, to points where no great markets existed,—and this under constant peril of losing her political union, which could not even by such connections be with certainty secured. After this should be accomplished, the Alleghanies must still remain between the eastern and western States, and at any known rate of travel Nashville could not be reached in less than a fortnight or three weeks from Philadelphia. Meanwhile the simpler problem of bringing New England nearer to Virginia and Georgia had not advanced even with the aid of a direct ocean highway. In becoming politically independent of England, the old thirteen provinces developed little more commercial intercourse with each other in proportion to their wealth and population than they had maintained in colonial days. The material ties that united them grew in strength no more rapidly than the ties which bound them to Europe. Each group of States lived a life apart.

Even the lightly equipped traveller found a short journey no slight effort. Between Boston and New York was a tolerable highway, along which, thrice a week, light stage-coaches carried passengers and the mail, in three days. From New York a stage-coach started every week-day for Philadelphia, consuming the greater part of two days in the journey; and the road between Paulus Hook, the modern Jersey City, and Hackensack, was declared by the newspapers in 1802 to be as bad as any other part of the route between Maine and Georgia. South of Philadelphia the road was tolerable as far as Baltimore, but between Baltimore and the new city of Washington it meandered through forests; the driver chose the track which seemed least dangerous, and rejoiced if in wet seasons he reached Washington without miring or upsetting his wagon. In the Northern States, four miles an hour was the average speed for any coach between Bangor and Baltimore. Beyond the Potomac the roads became steadily worse, until south of Petersburg even the mails were carried on horseback. Except for a stage-coach which plied between Charleston and Savannah, no public conveyance of any kind was mentioned in the three southernmost States.

The stage-coach was itself a rude conveyance, of a kind still familiar to experienced travellers. Twelve persons, crowded into one wagon, were jolted over rough roads, their bags and parcels, thrust inside, cramping their legs, while they were protected from the heat and dust of mid-summer and the intense cold and driving snow of winter only by leather flaps buttoned to the roof and sides. In fine, dry weather this mode of travel was not unpleasant, when compared with the heavy vehicles of Europe and the hard English turnpikes; but when spring rains drew the frost from the ground the roads became nearly impassable, and in winter, when the rivers froze, a serious peril was added, for the Susquehanna or the North River at Paulus Hook must be crossed in an open boat,—an affair of hours at best, sometimes leading to fatal accidents. Smaller annoyances of many kinds were habitual. The public, as a rule, grumbled less than might have been expected, but occasionally newspapers contained bitter complaints. An angry Philadelphian, probably a foreigner, wrote in 1796 that, " with a few exceptions, brutality, negligence, and filching are as naturally expected by people accustomed to travelling in America, as a mouth, a nose, and two eyes are looked for in a man's face." This sweeping charge, probably unjust, and certainly supported by little public evidence, was chiefly founded on the experience of an alleged journey from New York:—

"At Bordentown we went into a second boat where we met with very sorry accommodation. This was about four o'clock in the afternoon. We had about twenty miles down the Delaware to reach Philadelphia. The captain, who had a most provoking tongue, was a boy about eighteen years of age. He and a few companions despatched a dozen or eighteen bottles of porter. We ran three different times against other vessels that were coming up the stream. The women and children lay all night on the bare boards of the cabin floor. . . . We reached Arch Street wharf about eight o'clock on the Wednesday morning, having been about sixteen hours on a voyage of twenty miles."

In the Southern States the difficulties and perils of travel were so great as to form a barrier almost insuperable. Even Virginia was no exception to this rule. At each interval of a few miles the horseman found himself stopped by a river, liable to sudden freshets, and rarely bridged. Jefferson in his frequent journeys between Monticello and Washington was happy to reach the end of the hundred miles without some vexatious delay. "Of eight rivers between here and Washington," he wrote to his Attorney-General in 1801, "five have neither bridges nor boats."

Expense caused an equally serious obstacle to travel. The usual charge in the Northern States was six cents a mile by stage. In the year 1796, according to Francis Baily, President of the Royal Astronomical Society, three or four stages ran daily from Baltimore to Philadelphia, the fare six dollars, with charges amounting to two dollars and a quarter a day at the inns on the road. Baily was three days in making the journey. From Philadelphia to New York he paid the same fare and charges, arriving in one day and a half. The entire journey of two hundred miles cost him twenty-one dollars. He remarked that travelling on the main lines of road in the settled country was about as expensive as in England, and when the roads were good, about as rapid. Congress allowed its members six dollars for every twenty miles travelled. The actual cost, including hotel expenses, could hardly have fallen below ten cents a mile.

Heavy traffic never used stage routes if it could find cheaper. Commerce between one State and another, or even between the seaboard and the interior of the same State, was scarcely possible on any large scale unless navigable water connected them. Except the great highway to Pittsburg, no road served as a channel of commerce between different regions of the country. In this respect New England east of the

Connecticut was as independent of New York as both were independent of Virginia, and as Virginia in her turn was independent of Georgia and South Carolina. The chief value of inter-State communication by land rested in the postal system; but the post furnished another illustration of the difficulties which barred progress. In the year 1800 one general mail-route extended from Portland in Maine to Louisville in Georgia, the time required for the trip being twenty days. Between Portsmouth in New Hampshire and Petersburg in Virginia the contracts required a daily service, except Sundays; between Petersburg and Augusta the mail was carried thrice a week. Branching from the main line at New York, a mail went to Canandaigua in ten days; from Philadelphia another branch line went to Lexington in sixteen days, to Nashville in twenty-two days. Thus more than twenty thousand miles of post-road, with nine hundred post-offices, proved the vastness of the country and the smallness of the result; for the gross receipts for postage in the year ending Oct. 1, 1801, were only $320,000.

Throughout the land the eighteenth century ruled supreme. Only within a few years had the New Englander begun to abandon his struggle with a barren soil, among granite hills, to learn the comforts of easier existence in the valleys of the Mohawk and Ohio; yet the New England man was thought the shrewdest and most enterprising of Americans. If the Puritans and the Dutch needed a century or more to reach the Mohawk, when would they reach the Mississippi? The distance from New York to the Mississippi was about one thousand miles; from Washington to the extreme southwestern military post, below Natchez, was about twelve hundred. Scarcely a portion of western Europe was three hundred miles distant from some sea, but a width of three hundred miles was hardly more than an outskirt of the United States. No civilized country had yet been required to deal with physical difficulties so serious, nor did experience warrant conviction that such difficulties could be overcome.

If the physical task which lay before the American people had advanced but a short way toward completion, little more change could be seen in the economical conditions of American life. The man who in the year 1800 ventured to hope for a new era in the coming century, could lay his hand on no statistics that silenced doubt. The machinery of production showed no radical difference from that familiar to ages long past. The Saxon farmer of the eighth century enjoyed most of the comforts known to Saxon farmers of the eighteenth. The eorls and ceorls of Offa and Ecgbert could not read or write, and did not receive a weekly newspaper with such information as newspapers in that age could supply; yet neither their houses, their clothing, their food and drink, their agricultural tools and methods, their stock, nor their habits were so greatly altered or improved by time that they would have found much difficulty in accommodating their lives to that of their descendants in the eighteenth century. In this respect America was backward. Fifty or a hundred miles inland more than half the houses were log-cabins, which might or might not enjoy the luxury of a glass window. Throughout the South and West houses showed little attempt at luxury; but even in New England the ordinary farmhouse was hardly so well built, so spacious, or so warm as that of a well-to-do contemporary of Charlemagne. The cloth which the farmer's family wore was still homespun. The hats were manufactured by the village hatter; the clothes were cut and made at home; the shirts, socks, and nearly every other article of dress were also home-made. Hence came a marked air of rusticity which distinguished country from town,—awkward shapes of hat, coat, and trousers, which gave to the Yankee caricature those typical traits that soon disappeared almost as completely as coats of mail and steel head-pieces. The plough was rude and clumsy; the sickle as old as Tubal Cain, and even the cradle not in general use; the flail was unchanged since the Aryan exodus; in Virginia, grain was still commonly trodden out by horses. Enterprising gentlemen-farmers introduced threshing-machines and invented scientific ploughs; but these were novelties. Stock was as a rule not only unimproved, but ill cared for. The swine ran loose; the cattle were left to feed on what pasture they could find, and even in New England were not housed until the severest frosts, on the excuse that exposure hardened them. Near half a century afterward a competent judge asserted that the general treatment of cows in New

England was fair matter of presentment by a grand jury. Except among the best farmers, drainage, manures, and rotation of crops were uncommon. The ordinary cultivator planted his corn as his father had planted it, sowing as much rye to the acre, using the same number of oxen to plough, and getting in his crops on the same day. He was even known to remove his barn on account of the manure accumulated round it, although the New England soil was never so rich as to warrant neglect to enrich it. The money for which he sold his wheat and chickens was of the Old World; he reckoned in shillings or pistareens, and rarely handled an American coin more valuable than a large copper cent.

At a time when the wealth and science of London and Paris could not supply an article so necessary as a common sulphur-match, the backwardness of remote country districts could hardly be exaggerated. Yet remote districts were not the only sufferers. Of the whole United States New England claimed to be the most civilized province, yet New England was a region in which life had yet gained few charms of sense and few advantages over its rivals. Wilson, the ornithologist, a Pennsylvania Scotchman, a confirmed grumbler, but a shrewd judge, and the most thorough of American travellers, said in 1808: "My journey through almost the whole of New England has rather lowered the Yankees in my esteem. Except a few neat academies, I found their schoolhouses equally ruinous and deserted with ours; fields covered with stones; stone fences; scrubby oaks and pine-trees; wretched orchards; scarcely one grain-field in twenty miles; the taverns along the road dirty, and filled with loungers brawling about lawsuits and politics; the people snappish and extortioners, lazy, and two hundred years behind the Pennsylvanians in agricultural improvements." The description was exaggerated, for Wilson forgot to speak of the districts where fields were not covered with stones, and where wheat could be grown to advantage. Twenty years earlier, Albert Gallatin, who knew Pennsylvania well, having reached Hartford on his way to Boston, wrote: "I have seen nothing in America equal to the establishments on the Connecticut River." Yet Wilson's account described the first general effect of districts in the New England States, where agriculture was backward and the country poor. The houses were thin wooden buildings, not well suited to the climate; the churches were unwarmed; the clothing was poor; sanitary laws were few, and a bathroom or a soil-pipe was unknown. Consumption, typhoid, scarlet fever, diphtheria, and rheumatic fevers were common; habits of drinking were still a scourge in every family, and dyspepsia destroyed more victims than were consumed by drink. Population increased slowly, as though the conditions of life were more than usually hard. A century earlier, Massachusetts was supposed to contain sixty thousand inhabitants. Governor Hutchinson complained that while the other colonies quadrupled their numbers, Massachusetts failed to double its population in fifty years. In 1790 the State contained 378,000 people, not including the province of Maine; in 1800 the number rose to 423,000, which showed that a period of more rapid growth had begun, for the emigration into other States was also large.

A better measure of the difficulties with which New England struggled was given by the progress of Boston, which was supposed to have contained about eighteen thousand inhabitants as early as 1730, and twenty thousand in 1770. For several years after the Revolution it numbered less than twenty thousand, but in 1800 the census showed twenty-five thousand inhabitants. In appearance, Boston resembled an English market-town, of a kind even then old-fashioned. The footways or sidewalks were paved, like the crooked and narrow streets, with round cobblestones, and were divided from the carriage way only by posts and a gutter. The streets were almost unlighted at night, a few oil-lamps rendering the darkness more visible and the rough pavement rougher. Police hardly existed. The system of taxation was defective. The town was managed by selectmen, the elected instruments of town-meetings whose jealousy of granting power was even greater than their objection to spending money, and whose hostility to city government was not to be overcome.

Although on all sides increase of ease and comfort was evident, and roads, canals, and new buildings, public and private, were already in course of construction on a scale before unknown, yet in spite of more than a century and a half of incessant industry, intelligent labor, and pinching economy

Boston and New England were still poor. A few merchants enjoyed incomes derived from foreign trade, which allowed them to imitate in a quiet way the style of the English mercantile class; but the clergy and the lawyers, who stood at the head of society, lived with much economy. Many a country clergyman, eminent for piety and even for hospitality, brought up a family and laid aside some savings on a salary of five hundred dollars a year. President Dwight, who knew well the class to which he belonged, eulogizing the life of Abijah Weld, pastor of Attleborough, declared that on a salary of two hundred and twenty dollars a year Mr. Weld brought up eleven children, besides keeping a hospitable house and maintaining charity to the poor.

On the Exchange a few merchants had done most of the business of Boston since the peace of 1783, but six mail-coaches a week to New York, and occasional arrivals from Europe, or the departure of a ship to China, left ample leisure for correspondence and even for gossip. The habits of the commercial class had not been greatly affected by recent prosperity. Within ten or fifteen years before 1800 three Banks had been created to supply the commercial needs of Boston. One of these was a branch Bank of the United States, which employed there whatever part of its capital it could profitably use; the two others were local Banks, with capital of $1,600,000, toward which the State subscribed $400,000. Altogether the banking capital of Boston might amount to two millions and a half. A number of small Banks, representing in all about two and a half millions more, were scattered through the smaller New England towns. The extraordinary prosperity caused by the French wars opened to Boston a new career. Wealth and population were doubling; the exports and imports of New England were surprisingly large, and the shipping was greater than that of New York and Pennsylvania combined; but Boston had already learned, and was to learn again, how fleeting were the riches that depended on foreign commerce, and conservative habits were not easily changed by a few years of accidental gain.

Of manufactures New England had many, but none on a large scale. The people could feed or clothe themselves only by household industry; their whale-oil, salt fish, lumber, and rum were mostly sent abroad; but they freighted coasters with turners' articles, home-made linens and cloths, cheese, butter, shoes, nails, and what were called Yankee Notions of all sorts, which were sent to Norfolk and the Southern ports, and often peddled from the deck, as goods of every sort were peddled on the flat-boats of the Ohio. Two or three small mills spun cotton with doubtful success; but England supplied ordinary manufactures more cheaply and better than Massachusetts could hope to do. A tri-weekly mail and a few coasting sloops provided for the business of New England with domestic ports. One packet sloop plied regularly to New York.

The State of New York was little in advance of Massachusetts and Maine. In 1800 for the first time New York gained the lead in population by the difference between 589,000 and 573,000. The valuation of New York for the direct tax in 1799 was $100,000,000; that of Massachusetts was $84,000,000. New York was still a frontier State, and although the city was European in its age and habits, travellers needed to go few miles from the Hudson in order to find a wilderness like that of Ohio and Tennessee. In most material respects the State was behind New England; outside the city was to be seen less wealth and less appearance of comfort. The first impression commonly received of any new country was from its inns, and on the whole few better tests of material condition then existed. President Dwight, though maintaining that the best old-fashioned inns of New England were in their way perfect, being in fact excellent private houses, could not wholly approve what he called the modern inns, even in Connecticut; but when he passed into New York he asserted that everything suffered an instant change for the worse. He explained that in Massachusetts the authorities were strict in refusing licenses to any but respectable and responsible persons, whereas in New York licenses were granted to any one who would pay for them,—which caused a multiplication of dram-shops, bad accommodations, and a gathering of loafers and tipplers about every tavern porch, whose rude appearance, clownish manners, drunkenness, swearing, and obscenity confirmed the chief of Federalist clergymen in his belief that democracy had an evil influence on morals.

Far more movement was to be seen, and accumulation was more rapid than in colonial days; but little had yet been done for improvement, either by Government or by individuals, beyond some provision for extending roads and clearing watercourses behind the advancing settlers. If Washington Irving was right, Rip Van Winkle, who woke from his long slumber about the year 1800, saw little that was new to him, except the head of President Washington where that of King George had once hung, and strange faces instead of familiar ones. Except in numbers, the city was relatively no farther advanced than the country. Between 1790 and 1800 its population rose from 33,000 to 60,000; and if Boston resembled an old-fashioned English market-town, New York was like a foreign seaport, badly paved, undrained, and as foul as a town surrounded by the tides could be. Although the Manhattan Company was laying wooden pipes for a water supply, no sanitary regulations were enforced, and every few years—as in 1798 and 1803—yellow fever swept away crowds of victims, and drove the rest of the population, panic stricken, into the highlands. No day-police existed; constables were still officers of the courts; the night-police consisted of two captains, two deputies, and seventy-two men. The estimate for the city's expenses in 1800 amounted to $130,000. One marked advantage New York enjoyed over Boston, in the possession of a city government able to introduce reforms. Thus, although still mediæval in regard to drainage and cleanliness, the town had taken advantage of recurring fires to rebuild some of the streets with brick sidewalks and curbstones. Travellers dwelt much on this improvement, which only New York and Philadelphia had yet adopted, and Europeans agreed that both had the air of true cities: that while Boston was the Bristol of America, New York was the Liverpool, and Philadelphia the London.

In respect to trade and capital, New York possessed growing advantages, supplying half New Jersey and Connecticut, a part of Massachusetts, and all the rapidly increasing settlements on the branches of the Hudson; but no great amount of wealth, no considerable industry or new creation of power was yet to be seen. Two Banks, besides the branch Bank of the United States, supplied the business wants of the city, and employed about the same amount of capital in loans and discounts as was required for Boston. Besides these city institutions but two other Banks existed in the State,—at Hudson and at Albany.

The proportion of capital in private hands seemed to be no larger. The value of exports from New York in 1800 was but $14,000,000; the net revenue on imports for 1799 was $2,373,000, against $1,607,000 collected in Massachusetts. Such a foreign trade required little capital, yet these values represented a great proportion of all the exchanges. Domestic manufactures could not compete with foreign, and employed little bank credit. Speculation was slow, mostly confined to lands which required patience to exchange or sell. The most important undertakings were turnpikes, bridges such as Boston built across the Charles, or new blocks of houses; and a canal, such as Boston designed to the Merrimac, overstrained the resources of capital. The entire banking means of the United States in 1800 would not have answered the stock-jobbing purposes of one great operator of Wall Street in 1875. The nominal capital of all the Banks, including the Bank of the United States, fell short of $29,000,000. The limit of credit was quickly reached, for only the richest could borrow more than fifteen or twenty thousand dollars at a time, and the United States Government itself was gravely embarrassed whenever obliged to raise money. In 1798 the Secretary of the Treasury could obtain five million dollars only by paying eight per cent interest for a term of years; and in 1814 the Government was forced to stop payments for the want of twenty millions.

The precise value of American trade was uncertain, but in 1800 the gross exports and imports of the United States may have balanced at about seventy-five million dollars. The actual consumption of foreign merchandise amounted perhaps to the value of forty or fifty million dollars, paid in wheat, cotton, and other staples, and by the profits on the shipping employed in carrying West India produce to Europe. The amount of American capital involved in a trade of fifty millions, with credits of three, six, and nine months, must have been small, and the rates of profit large.

As a rule American capital was absorbed in shipping or

agriculture, whence it could not be suddenly withdrawn. No stock-exchange existed, and no broker exclusively engaged in stock-jobbing, for there were few stocks. The national debt, of about eighty millions, was held abroad, or as a permanent investment at home. States and municipalities had not learned to borrow. Except for a few banks and insurance offices, turn-pikes, bridges, canals, and land-companies, neither bonds nor stocks were known. The city of New York was so small as to make extravagance difficult; the Battery was a fashionable walk, Broadway a country drive, and Wall Street an uptown residence. Great accumulations of wealth had hardly begun. The Patroon was still the richest man in the State. John Jacob Astor was a fur-merchant living where the Astor House after-ward stood, and had not yet begun those purchases of real estate which secured his fortune. Cornelius Vanderbilt was a boy six years old, playing about his father's ferry-boat at Staten Island. New York city itself was what it had been for a hundred years past,—a local market.

As a national capital New York made no claim to consid-eration. If Bostonians for a moment forgot their town-meet-ings, or if Virginians overcame their dislike for cities and pavements, they visited and admired, not New York, but Phil-adelphia. "Philadelphia," wrote the Duc de Liancourt, "is not only the finest city in the United States, but may be deemed one of the most beautiful cities in the world." In truth, it surpassed any of its size on either side of the Atlantic for most of the comforts and some of the elegancies of life. While Bos-ton contained twenty-five thousand inhabitants and New York sixty thousand, the census of 1800 showed that Philadel-phia was about the size of Liverpool,—a city of seventy thou-sand people. The repeated ravages of yellow fever roused there a regard for sanitary precautions and cleanliness; the city, well paved and partly drained, was supplied with water in wooden pipes, and was the best-lighted town in America; its market was a model, and its jail was intended also for a model,—although the first experiment proved unsuccessful, because the prisoners went mad or idiotic in solitary confine-ment. In and about the city flourished industries considerable for the time. The iron-works were already important; paper and gunpowder, pleasure carriages and many other manufactures, were produced on a larger scale than elsewhere in the Union. Philadelphia held the seat of government until July, 1800, and continued to hold the Bank of the United States, with its capital of ten millions, besides private banking capital to the amount of five millions more. Public spirit was more active in Pennsylvania than in New York. More roads and canals were building; a new turnpike ran from Philadelphia to Lancaster, and the great highway to Pittsburg was a more important artery of national life than was controlled by any other State. The exports of Pennsylvania amounted to $12,000,000, and the custom-house produced $1,350,000. The State contained six hundred thousand inhabitants,—a population somewhat larger than that of New York.

Of all parts of the Union, Pennsylvania seemed to have made most use of her national advantages; but her progress was not more rapid than the natural increase of population and wealth demanded, while to deal with the needs of America, man's resources and his power over Nature must be increased in a ratio far more rapid than that which governed his numbers. Nevertheless, Pennsylvania was the most encouraging spectacle in the field of vision. Baltimore, which had suddenly sprung to a population and commerce greater than those of Boston, also offered strong hope of future improvement; but farther South the people showed fewer signs of change.

The city of Washington, rising in a solitude on the banks of the Potomac, was a symbol of American nationality in the Southern States. The contrast between the immensity of the task and the paucity of means seemed to challenge suspicion that the nation itself was a magnificent scheme like the federal city, which could show only a few log-cabins and negro quarters where the plan provided for the traffic of London and the elegance of Versailles. When in the summer of 1800 the government was transferred to what was regarded by most persons as a fever-stricken morass, the half-finished White House stood in a naked field overlooking the Potomac, with two awkward Department buildings near it, a single row of brick houses and a few isolated dwellings within sight, and nothing more; until across a swamp, a mile and a half away, the shapeless, unfinished Capitol was seen, two wings without a body, ambitious enough in design to make more grotesque the nature of its surroundings. The conception proved that the United States understood the vastness of their task, and were willing to stake something on their faith in it. Never did hermit or saint condemn himself to solitude more consciously than Congress and the Executive in removing the government from Philadelphia to Washington: the discontented men clustered together in eight or ten boarding-houses as near as possible to the Capitol, and there lived, like a convent of monks, with no other amusement or occupation than that of going from their lodgings to the Chambers and back again. Even private wealth could do little to improve their situation, for there was nothing which wealth could buy; there were in Washington no shops or markets, skilled labor, commerce, or people. Public efforts and lavish use of public money could alone make the place tolerable; but Congress doled out funds for this national and personal object with so sparing a hand, that their Capitol threatened to crumble in pieces and crush Senate and House under the ruins, long before the building was complete.

A government capable of sketching a magnificent plan, and willing to give only a half-hearted pledge for its fulfilment; a people eager to advertise a vast undertaking beyond their present powers, which when completed would become an object of jealousy and fear,—this was the impression made upon the traveller who visited Washington in 1800, and mused among the unraised columns of the Capitol upon the destiny of the United States. As he travelled farther south his doubts were strengthened, for across the Potomac he could detect no sign of a new spirit. Manufactures had no existence. Alexandria owned a bank with half a million of capital, but no other was to be found between Washington and Charleston, except the branch Bank of the United States at Norfolk, nor any industry to which loans and discounts could safely be made. Virginia, the most populous and powerful of all the States, had a white population of 514,000, nearly equal to that of Pennsylvania and New York, besides about 350,000 slaves. Her energies had pierced the mountains and settled the western territory before the slow-moving Northern people had torn themselves from the safer and more comfortable life by the seaboard; but the Virginia ideal was patriarchal, and an American continent on the Virginia type might reproduce the virtues of Cato, and perhaps the eloquence of Cicero, but was little likely to produce anything more practical in the way of modern progress. The Shenandoah Valley rivalled Pennsylvania and Connecticut in richness and skill of husbandry; but even agriculture, the favorite industry in Virginia, had suffered from the competition of Kentucky and Tennessee, and from the emigration which had drawn away fully one hundred thousand people. The land was no longer very productive. Even Jefferson, the most active-minded and sanguine of all Virginians,— the inventor of the first scientific plough, the importer of the first threshing-machine known in Virginia, the experimenter with a new drilling-machine, the owner of one hundred and fifty slaves and ten thousand acres of land, whose negroes were trained to carpentry, cabinet-making, house-building, weaving, tailoring, shoe-making,— claimed to get from his land no more than six or eight bushels of wheat to an acre, and had been forced to abandon the more profitable cultivation of tobacco. Except in a few favored districts like the Shenandoah Valley, land in Virginia did not average eight bushels of wheat to an acre. The cultivation of tobacco had been almost the sole object of land-owners, and even where the lands were not exhausted, a bad system of agriculture and the force of habit prevented improvement.

The great planters lavished money in vain on experiments to improve their crops and their stock. They devoted themselves to the task with energy and knowledge; but they needed a diversity of interests and local markets, and except at Baltimore these were far from making their appearance. Neither the products, the markets, the relative amount of capital, nor the machinery of production had perceptibly changed. "The Virginians are not generally rich," said the Duc de Liancourt, "especially in net revenue. Thus one often finds a well-served table, covered with silver, in a room where for ten years half the window panes have been missing, and where they will be missed for ten years more. There are few houses in a passable state of repair, and of all parts of the establishment those best cared for are the stables." Wealth reckoned in slaves or land was plenty; but the best Virginians, from President Washington downward, were most outspoken in their warnings against the Virginia system both of slavery and agriculture.

The contrast between Virginia and Pennsylvania was the subject of incessant comment.

"In Pennsylvania," said Robert Sutcliffe, an English Friend who published travels made in 1804–1806, "we meet great numbers of wagons drawn by four or more fine fat horses, the carriages firm and well made, and covered with stout good linen, bleached almost white; and it is not uncommon to see ten or fifteen together travelling cheerfully along the road, the driver riding on one of his horses. Many of these come more than three hundred miles to Philadelphia from the Ohio, Pittsburg, and other places, and I have been told by a respectable Friend, a native of Philadelphia, that more than one thousand covered carriages frequently come to Philadelphia market. . . . The appearance of things in the Slave States is quite the reverse of this. We sometimes meet a ragged black boy or girl driving a team consisting of a lean cow and a mule; sometimes a lean bull or an ox and a mule; and I have seen a mule, a bull, and a cow each miserable in its appearance, composing one team, with a half-naked black slave or two riding or driving as occasion suited. The carriage or wagon, if it may be called such, appeared in as wretched a condition as the team and its driver. Sometimes a couple of horses, mules, or cows would be dragging a hogshead of tobacco, with a pivot or axle driven into each end of the hogshead, and something like a shaft attached, by which it was drawn or rolled along the road. I have seen two oxen and two slaves pretty fully employed in getting along a single hogshead; and some of these come from a great distance inland."

In the middle of these primitive sights, Sutcliffe was startled by a contrast such as Virginia could always show. Between Richmond and Fredericksburg,—

"In the afternoon, as our road lay through the woods, I

was surprised to meet a family party travelling along in as elegant a coach as is usually met with in the neighborhood of London, and attended by several gayly dressed footmen."

The country south of Virginia seemed unpromising even to Virginians. In the year 1796 President Washington gave to Sir John Sinclair his opinion upon the relative value of American lands. He then thought the valley of Virginia the garden of America; but he would say nothing to induce others to settle in more southern regions.

"The uplands of North and South Carolina and Georgia are not dissimilar in soil," he wrote, "but as they approach the lower latitudes are less congenial to wheat, and are supposed to be proportionably more unhealthy. Towards the seaboard of all the Southern States, and farther south more so, the lands are low, sandy, and unhealthy; for which reason I shall say little concerning them, for as I should not choose to be an inhabitant of them myself, I ought not to say anything that would induce others to be so. . . . I understand that from thirty to forty dollars per acre may be denominated the medium price in the vicinity of the Susquehanna in the State of Pennsylvania, from twenty to thirty on the Potomac in what is called the Valley, . . . and less, as I have noticed before, as you proceed southerly."

Whatever was the cause, the State of North Carolina seemed to offer few temptations to immigrants or capital. Even in white population ranking fifth among the sixteen States, her 478,000 inhabitants were unknown to the world. The beautiful upper country attracted travellers neither for pleasure nor for gain, while the country along the sea-coast was avoided except by hardy wanderers. The grumbling Wilson, who knew every nook and corner of the United States, and who found New England so dreary, painted this part of North Carolina in colors compared with which his sketch of New England was gay. "The taverns are the most desolate and beggarly imaginable; bare, bleak, and dirty walls, one or two old broken chairs and a bench form all the furniture. The white females seldom make their appearance. At supper you sit down to a meal the very sight of which is sufficient to deaden the most eager appetite, and you are surrounded by half-a-dozen dirty, half-naked blacks, male and female, whom any man of common scent might smell a quarter of a mile off. The house itself is raised upon props four or five feet, and the space below is left open for the hogs, with whose charming vocal performance the wearied traveller is serenaded the whole night long." The landscape pleased him no better,— "immense solitary pine savannahs through which the road winds among stagnant ponds; dark, sluggish creeks of the color of brandy, over which are thrown high wooden bridges without railings," crazy and rotten.

North Carolina was relatively among the poorest States. The exports and imports were of trifling value, less than one tenth of those returned for Massachusetts, which were more than twice as great as those of North Carolina and Virginia together. That under these conditions America should receive any strong impulse from such a quarter seemed unlikely; yet perhaps for the moment more was to be expected from the Carolinas than from Virginia. Backward as these States in some respects were, they possessed one new element of wealth which promised more for them than anything Virginia could hope. The steam-engines of Watt had been applied in England to spinning, weaving, and printing cotton; an immense demand had risen for that staple, and the cotton-gin had been simultaneously invented. A sudden impetus was given to industry; land which had been worthless and estates which had become bankrupt acquired new value, and in 1800 every planter was growing cotton, buying negroes, and breaking fresh soil. North Carolina felt the strong flood of prosperity, but South Carolina, and particularly the town of Charleston, had most to hope. The exports of South Carolina were nearly equal in value to those of Massachusetts or Pennsylvania; the imports were equally large. Charleston might reasonably expect to rival Boston, New York, Philadelphia, and Baltimore. In 1800 these cities still stood, as far as concerned their foreign trade, within some range of comparison; and between Boston, Baltimore, and Charleston, many plausible reasons could be given for thinking that the last might have the most brilliant future. The three towns stood abreast. If Charleston had but about eighteen thousand inhabitants, this was the number reported by Boston only ten years before, and was five thousand more than Baltimore then boasted. Neither Boston nor Baltimore saw about them a vaster region to supply, or so profitable a staple to export. A cotton crop of two hundred thousand pounds sent abroad in 1791 grew to twenty millions in 1801, and was to double again by 1803. An export of fifty thousand bales was enormous, yet was only the beginning. What use might not Charleston, the only considerable town in the entire South, make of this golden flood?

The town promised hopefully to prove equal to its task. Nowhere in the Union was intelligence, wealth, and education greater in proportion to numbers than in the little society of cotton and rice planters who ruled South Carolina; and they were in 1800 not behind— they hoped soon to out-strip—their rivals. If Boston was building a canal to the Merrimac, and Philadelphia one along the Schuylkill to the Susquehanna, Charleston had nearly completed another which brought the Santee River to its harbor, and was planning a road to Tennessee which should draw the whole interior within reach. Nashville was nearer to Charleston than to any other seaport of the Union, and Charleston lay nearest to the rich trade of the West Indies. Not even New York seemed more clearly marked for prosperity than this solitary Southern city, which already possessed banking capital in abundance, intelligence, enterprise, the traditions of high culture and aristocratic ambition, all supported by slave-labor, which could be indefinitely increased by the African slave-trade.

If any portion of the United States might hope for a sudden and magnificent bloom, South Carolina seemed entitled to expect it. Rarely had such a situation, combined with such resources, failed to produce some wonderful result. Yet as Washington warned Sinclair, these advantages were counter-balanced by serious evils. The climate in summer was too relaxing. The sun was too hot. The sea-coast was unhealthy, and at certain seasons even deadly to the whites. Finally, if history was a guide, no permanent success could be prophesied for a society like that of the low country in South Carolina, where some thirty thousand whites were surrounded by a dense mass of nearly one hundred thousand negro slaves. Even Georgia, then only partially settled, contained sixty thousand slaves and but one hundred thousand whites. The cotton States might still argue that if slavery, malaria, or summer heat barred civilization, all the civilization that was ever known must have been blighted in its infancy; but although the future of South Carolina might be brilliant, like that of other oligarchies in which only a few thousand freemen took part, such a development seemed to diverge far from the path likely to be followed by Northern society, and bade fair to increase and complicate the social and economical difficulties with which Americans had to deal.

A probable valuation of the whole United States in 1800 was eighteen hundred million dollars, equal to $328 for each human being, including slaves; or $418 to each free white. This property was distributed with an approach to equality, except in a few of the Southern States. In New York and Philadelphia a private fortune of one hundred thousand dollars was considered handsome, and three hundred thousand was great wealth. Inequalities were frequent; but they were chiefly those of a landed aristocracy. Equality was so far the rule that every white family of five persons might be supposed to own land, stock, or utensils, a house and furniture, worth about two thousand dollars; and as the only considerable industry was agriculture, their scale of life was easy to calculate,—taxes amounting to little or nothing, and wages averaging about a dollar a day.

Not only were these slender resources, but they were also of a kind not easily converted to the ready uses required for rapid development. Among the numerous difficulties with which the Union was to struggle, and which were to form the interest of American history, the disproportion between the physical obstacles and the material means for overcoming them was one of the most striking.

Chapter II

THE GROWTH of character, social and national,—the formation of men's minds,—more interesting than any territorial or industrial growth, defied the tests of censuses and surveys. No people could be expected, least of all when in infancy, to understand the intricacies of its own character, and rarely has a foreigner been gifted with insight to explain what natives did not comprehend. Only with diffidence could the best-informed Americans venture, in 1800, to generalize on the subject of their own national habits of life and thought. Of all American travellers President Dwight was the most experienced; yet his four volumes of travels were remarkable for no trait more uniform than their reticence in regard to the United States. Clear and emphatic wherever New England was in discussion, Dwight claimed no knowledge of other regions. Where so good a judge professed ignorance, other observers were likely to mislead; and Frenchmen like Liancourt, Englishmen like Weld, or Germans like Bülow, were almost equally worthless authorities on a subject which none understood. The newspapers of the time were little more trustworthy than the books of travel, and hardly so well written. The literature of a higher kind was chiefly limited to New England, New York, and Pennsylvania. From materials so poor no precision of result could be expected. A few customs, more or less local; a few prejudices, more or less popular; a few traits of thought, suggesting habits of mind,—must form the entire material for a study more important than that of politics or economics.

The standard of comfort had much to do with the standard of character; and in the United States, except among the slaves, the laboring class enjoyed an ample supply of the necessaries of life. In this respect, as in some others, they claimed superiority over the laboring class in Europe, and the claim would have been still stronger had they shown more skill in using the abundance that surrounded them. The Duc de Liancourt, among foreigners the best and kindest observer, made this remark on the mode of life he saw in Pennsylvania:—

"There is a contrast of cleanliness with its opposite which to a stranger is very remarkable. The people of the country are as astonished that one should object to sleeping two or three in the same bed and in dirty sheets, or to drink from the same dirty glass after half a score of others, as to see one neglect to wash one's hands and face of a morning. Whiskey diluted with water is the ordinary country drink. There is no settler, however poor, whose family does not take coffee or chocolate for breakfast, and always a little salt meat; at dinner, salt meat, or salt fish, and eggs; at supper again salt meat and coffee. This is also the common regime of the taverns."

An amusing, though quite untrustworthy Englishman named Ashe, who invented an American journey in 1806, described the fare of a Kentucky cabin: —

"The dinner consisted of a large piece of salt bacon, a dish of hominy, and a tureen of squirrel broth. I dined entirely on the last dish, which I found incomparably good, and the meat equal to the most delicate chicken. The Kentuckian eat nothing but bacon, which indeed is the favorite diet of all the inhabitants of the State, and drank nothing but whiskey, which soon made him more than two-thirds drunk. In this last practice he is also supported by the public habit. In a country, then, where bacon and spirits form the favorite summer repast, it cannot be just to attribute entirely the causes of infirmity to the climate. No people on earth live with less regard to regimen. They eat salt meat three times a day, seldom or never have any vegetables, and drink ardent spirits from morning till night. They have not only an aversion to fresh meat, but a vulgar prejudice that it is unwholesome. The truth is, their stomachs are depraved by burning liquors, and they have no appetite for anything but what is high-flavored and strongly impregnated by salt."

Salt pork three times a day was regarded as an essential part of American diet. In the "Chainbearer," Cooper described what he called American poverty as it existed in 1784. "As for bread," said the mother, "I count that for nothing. We always have bread and potatoes enough; but I hold a family to be in a desperate way when the mother can see the bottom of the pork-barrel. Give me the children that 's raised on good sound pork afore all the game in the country. Game 's good as a relish, and so 's bread; but pork is the staff of life. . . My children I calkerlate to bring up on pork."

Many years before the time to which Cooper referred, Poor Richard asked: "Maids of America, who gave you bad teeth?" and supplied the answer: "Hot soupings and frozen apples." Franklin's question and answer were repeated in a wider sense by many writers, but none was so emphatic as Volney: —

"I will venture to say," declared Volney, "that if a prize were proposed for the scheme of a regimen most calculated to injure the stomach, the teeth, and the health in general, no better could be invented than that of the Americans In the morning at breakfast they deluge their stomach with a quart of hot water, impregnated with tea, or so slightly with coffee that it is mere colored water; and they swallow, almost without chewing, hot bread, half baked, toast soaked in butter, cheese of the fattest kind, slices of salt or hung beef, ham, etc., all which are nearly insoluble. At dinner they have boiled pastes under the name of puddings, and the fattest are esteemed the most delicious; all their sauces, even for roast beef, are melted butter; their turnips and potatoes swim in hog's lard, butter, or fat; under the name of pie or pumpkin, their pastry is nothing but a greasy paste, never sufficiently baked. To digest these viscous substances they take tea almost instantly after dinner, making it so strong that it is absolutely bitter to the taste, in which state it affects the nerves so powerfully that even the English find it brings on a more obstinate restlessness than coffee. Supper again introduces salt meats or oysters. As Chastellux says, the whole day passes in heaping indigestions on one another; and to give tone to the poor, relaxed, and wearied stomach, they drink Madeira, rum, French brandy, gin, or malt spirits, which complete the ruin of the nervous system."

An American breakfast never failed to interest foreigners, on account of the variety and abundance of its dishes. On the main lines of travel, fresh meat and vegetables were invariably served at all meals; but Indian corn was the national crop, and Indian corn was eaten three times a day in another form as salt pork. The rich alone could afford fresh meat. Ice-chests were hardly known. In the country fresh meat could not regularly be got, except in the shape of poultry or game; but the hog cost nothing to keep, and very little to kill and preserve. Thus the ordinary rural American was brought up on salt pork and Indian corn, or rye; and the effect of this diet showed itself in dyspepsia.

One of the traits to which Liancourt alluded marked more distinctly the stage of social development. By day or by night, privacy was out of the question. Not only must all men travel in the same coach, dine at the same table, at the same time, on the same fare, but even their beds were in common, without distinction of persons. Innkeepers would not understand that a different arrangement was possible. When the English traveller Weld reached Elkton, on the main road from Philadelphia to Baltimore, he asked the landlord what accommodation he had. "Don't trouble yourself about that," was the reply; "I have no less than eleven beds in one room alone." This primitive habit extended over the whole country from Massachusetts to Georgia, and no American seemed to revolt against the tyranny of innkeepers.

"At New York I was lodged with two others, in a back room on the ground floor," wrote, in 1796, the Philadelphian whose complaints have already been mentioned. "What can be the reason for that vulgar, hoggish custom, common in America, of squeezing three, six, or eight beds into one room?"

Nevertheless, the Americans were on the whole more neat than their critics allowed. "You have not seen the Americans," was Cobbett's reply, in 1819, to such charges; "you have not seen the nice, clean, neat houses of the farmers of Long Island, in New England, in the Quaker counties of Pennsylvania; you have seen nothing but the smoke-dried ultra-montanians." Yet Cobbett drew a sharp contrast between the laborer's neat cottage familiar to him in Surrey and Hampshire, and the "shell of boards" which the American occupied, "all around him as barren as a sea-beach." He added, too, that "the example of neatness was wanting;" no one taught it by showing its charm. Felix de Beaujour, otherwise not an enthusiastic American, paid a warm compliment to the country in this single respect, although he seemed to have the cities chiefly in mind:

> "American neatness must possess some very attractive quality, since it seduces every traveller; and there is no one of them who, in returning to his own country, does not wish to meet again there that air of ease and neatness which rejoiced his sight during his stay in the United States."

Almost every traveller discussed the question whether the Americans were a temperate people, or whether they drank more than the English. Temperate they certainly were not, when judged by a modern standard. Every one acknowledged that in the South and West drinking was occasionally excessive; but even in Pennsylvania and New England the universal taste for drams proved habits by no means strict. Every grown man took his noon toddy as a matter of course; and although few were seen publicly drunk, many were habitually affected by liquor. The earliest temperance movement, ten or twelve years later, was said to have had its source in the scandal caused by the occasional intoxication of ministers at their regular meetings. Cobbett thought drinking the national disease; at all hours of the day, he said, young men, "even little boys, at or under twelve years of age, go into stores and tip off their drams." The mere comparison with England proved that the evil was great, for the English and Scotch were among the largest consumers of beer and alcohol on the globe.

In other respects besides sobriety American manners and morals were subjects of much dispute, and if judged by the diatribes of travellers like Thomas Moore and H. W. Bülow, were below the level of Europe. Of all classes of statistics, moral statistics were least apt to be preserved. Even in England, social vices could be gauged only by the records of criminal and divorce courts; in America, police was wanting and a divorce suit almost, if not quite, unknown. Apart from some coarseness, society must have been pure; and the coarseness was mostly an English inheritance. Among New Englanders, Chief-Justice Parsons was the model of judicial, social, and religious propriety; yet Parsons, in 1808, presented to a lady a copy of "Tom Jones," with a letter calling attention to the adventures of Molly Seagrim and the usefulness of describing vice. Among the social sketches in the "Portfolio" were many allusions to the coarseness of Philadelphia society, and the manners common to tea-parties. "I heard from married ladies," said a writer in February, 1803, " whose station as mothers demanded from them a guarded conduct,—from young ladies, whose age forbids the audience of such conversation, and who using it modesty must disclaim,—indecent allusions, indelicate expressions, and even at times immoral innuendoes. A loud laugh or a coarse exclamation followed each of these, and the young ladies generally went through the form of raising their fans to their faces."

Yet public and private records might be searched long, before they revealed evidence of misconduct such as filled the press and formed one of the commonest topics of conversation in the society of England and France. Almost every American family, however respectable, could show some victim to intemperance among its men, but few were mortified by a public scandal due to its women.

If the absence of positive evidence did not prove American society to be as pure as its simple and primitive condition implied, the same conclusion would be reached by observing the earnestness with which critics collected every charge that could be brought against it, and by noting the substance of the whole. Tried by this test, the society of 1800 was often coarse and sometimes brutal, but, except for intemperance, was moral. Indeed, its chief offence, in the eyes of Europeans, was dulness. The amusements of a people were commonly a fair sign of social development, and the Americans were only beginning to amuse themselves. The cities were small and few in number, and the diversions were such as cost little and required but elementary knowledge. In New England, although the theatre had gained a firm foothold in Boston, Puritan feelings still forbade the running of horses.

"The principal amusements of the inhabitants," said Dwight, "are visiting, dancing, music, conversation, walking,

riding, sailing, shooting at a mark, draughts, chess, and unhappily, in some of the larger towns, cards and dramatic
exhibitions. A considerable amusement is also furnished in
many places by the examination and exhibitions of the superior schools; and a more considerable one by the public
exhibitions of colleges. Our countrymen also fish and hunt.
Journeys taken for pleasure are very numerous, and are a
very favorite object. Boys and young men play at foot-ball,
cricket, quoits, and at many other sports of an athletic cast,
and in the winter are peculiarly fond of skating. Riding in
a sleigh, or sledge, is also a favorite diversion in New
England."

President Dwight was sincere in his belief that college com-
mencements and sleigh-riding satisfied the wants of his people; he looked upon whist as an unhappy dissipation, and
upon the theatre as immoral. He had no occasion to condemn
horse-racing, for no race-course was to be found in New England. The horse and the dog existed only in varieties little
suited for sport. In colonial days New England produced one
breed of horses worth preserving and developing,—the Nar-
ragansett pacer; but, to the regret even of the clergy, this animal almost disappeared, and in 1800 New England could
show nothing to take its place. The germ of the trotter and
the trotting-match, the first general popular amusement,
could be seen in almost any country village, where the owners
of horses were in the habit of trotting what were called
scratch-races, for a quarter or half a mile from the door of the
tavern, along the public road. Perhaps this amusement had
already a right to be called a New-England habit, showing
defined tastes; but the force of the popular instinct was not
fully felt in Massachusetts, or even in New York, although
there it was given full play. New York possessed a race-course,
and made in 1792 a great stride toward popularity by importing the famous stallion "Messenger" to become the source of
endless interest for future generations; but Virginia was the
region where the American showed his true character as a
lover of sport. Long before the Revolution the race course
was commonly established in Virginia and Maryland; English
running-horses of pure blood—descendants of the Darley

Arabian and the Godolphin Arabian—were imported, and racing became the chief popular entertainment. The long Revolutionary War, and the general ruin it caused, checked the habit and deteriorated the breed; but with returning prosperity Virginia showed that the instinct was stronger than ever. In 1798 "Diomed," famous as the sire of racers, was imported into the State, and future rivalry between Virginia and New York could be foreseen. In 1800 the Virginia race-course still remained at the head of American popular amusements.

In an age when the Prince of Wales and crowds of English gentlemen attended every prize-fight, and patronized Tom Crib, Dutch Sam, the Jew Mendoza, and the negro Molyneux, an Englishman could hardly have expected that a Virginia race-course should be free from vice; and perhaps travellers showed best the general morality of the people by their practice of dwelling on Virginia vices. They charged the Virginians with fondness for horse-racing, cock-fighting, betting, and drinking; but the popular habit which most shocked them, and with which books of travel filled pages of description, was the so-called rough-and-tumble fight. The practice was not one on which authors seemed likely to dwell; yet foreigners like Weld, and Americans like Judge Longstreet in "Georgia Scenes," united to give it a sort of grotesque dignity like that of a bull-fight, and under their treatment it became interesting as a popular habit. The rough-and-tumble fight differed from the ordinary prize-fight, or boxing-match, by the absence of rules. Neither kicking, tearing, biting, nor gouging was forbidden by the law of the ring. Brutal as the practice was, it was neither new nor exclusively Virginian. The English travellers who described it as American barbarism, might have seen the same sight in Yorkshire at the same date. The rough-and-tumble fight was English in origin, and was brought to Virginia and the Carolinas in early days, whence it spread to the Ohio and Mississippi. The habit attracted general notice because of its brutality in a society that showed few brutal instincts. Friendly foreigners like Liancourt were honestly shocked by it; others showed somewhat too plainly their pleasure at finding a vicious habit which they could consider a natural product of democratic society. Perhaps the description written by Thomas Ashe showed best not only the ferocity of the fight but also the antipathies of the writer, for Ashe had something of the artist in his touch, and he felt no love for Americans. The scene was at Wheeling. A Kentuckian and a Virginian were the combatants.

"Bulk and bone were in favor of the Kentuckian; science and craft in that of the Virginian. The former promised himself victory from his power; the latter from his science. Very few rounds had taken place or fatal blows given, before the Virginian contracted his whole form, drew up his arms to his face, with his hands nearly closed in a concave by the fingers being bent to the full extension of the flexors, and summoning up all his energy for one act of desperation, pitched himself into the bosom of his opponent. Before the effects of this could be ascertained, the sky was rent by the shouts of the multitude; and I could learn that the Virginian had expressed as much beauty and skill in his retraction and bound, as if he had been bred in a menagerie and practised action and attitude among panthers and wolves. The shock received by the Kentuckian, and the want of breath, brought him instantly to the ground. The Virginian never lost his hold. Like those bats of the South who never quit the subject on which they fasten till they taste blood, he kept his knees in his enemy's body; fixing his claws in his hair and his thumbs on his eyes, gave them an instantaneous start from their sockets. The sufferer roared aloud, but uttered no complaint. The citizens again shouted with joy."

Ashe asked his landlord whether this habit spread down the Ohio.

"I understood that it did, on the left-hand side, and that I would do well to land there as little as possible. . . . I again demanded how a stranger was to distinguish a good from a vicious house of entertainment. 'By previous inquiry, or, if that was impracticable, a tolerable judgment could be formed from observing in the landlord a possession or an absence of ears.' "

The temper of the writer was at least as remarkable in this description as the scene he pretended to describe, for Ashe's

Travels were believed to have been chiefly imaginary; but no one denied the roughness of the lower classes in the South and Southwest, nor was roughness wholly confined to them. No prominent man in Western society bore himself with more courtesy and dignity than Andrew Jackson of Tennessee, who in 1800 was candidate for the post of major-general of State militia, and had previously served as Judge on the Supreme Bench of his State; yet the fights in which he had been engaged exceeded belief.

Border society was not refined, but among its vices, as its virtues, few were permanent, and little idea could be drawn of the character that would at last emerge. The Mississippi boatman and the squatter on Indian lands were perhaps the most distinctly American type then existing, as far removed from the Old World as though Europe were a dream. Their language and imagination showed contact with Indians. A traveller on the levee at Natchez, in 1808, overheard a quarrel in a flatboat near by:—

"I am a man; I am a horse; I am a team," cried one voice; "I can whip any man in all Kentucky, by God!" "I am an alligator," cried the other; "half man, half horse; can whip any man on the Mississippi, by God!" "I am a man," shouted the first; "have the best horse, best dog, best gun, and handsomest wife in all Kentucky, by God!" "I am a Mississippi snapping-turtle," rejoined the second; "have bear's claws, alligator's teeth, and the devil's tail; can whip *any* man, by God!"

And on this usual formula of defiance the two fire-eaters began their fight, biting, gouging, and tearing. Foreigners were deeply impressed by barbarism such as this, and orderly emigrants from New England and Pennsylvania avoided contact with Southern drinkers and fighters; but even then they knew that with a new generation such traits must disappear, and that little could be judged of popular character from the habits of frontiersmen. Perhaps such vices deserved more attention when found in the older communities, but even there they were rather survivals of English low-life than products of a new soil, and they were given too much consequence in the tales of foreign travellers.

This was not the only instance where foreigners were struck by what they considered popular traits, which natives rarely noticed. Idle curiosity was commonly represented as universal, especially in the Southern settler who knew no other form of conversation: —

"Frequently have I been stopped by one of them," said Weld, "and without further preface asked where I was from, if I was acquainted with any news, where bound to, and finally my name. 'Stop, Mister! why, I guess now you be coming from the new State?' 'No, sir.' 'Why, then, I guess as how you be coming from Kentuck?' 'No, sir.' 'Oh, why, then, pray now where might you be coming from?' 'From the low country.' 'Why, you must have heard all the news, then; pray now, Mister, what might the price of bacon be in those parts?' 'Upon my word, my friend, I can't inform you.' 'Ay, ay; I see, Mister, you be'ent one of us. Pray now, Mister, what might your name be?'"

Almost every writer spoke with annoyance of the inquisitorial habits of New England and the impertinence of American curiosity. Complaints so common could hardly have lacked foundation, yet the Americans as a people were never loquacious, but inclined to be somewhat reserved, and they could not recognize the accuracy of the description. President Dwight repeatedly expressed astonishment at the charge, and asserted that in his large experience it had no foundation. Forty years later, Charles Dickens found complaint with Americans for taciturnity. Equally strange to modern experience were the continual complaints in books of travel that loungers and loafers, idlers of every description, infested the taverns, and annoyed respectable travellers both native and foreign. Idling seemed to be considered a popular vice, and was commonly associated with tippling. So completely did the practice disappear in the course of another generation that it could scarcely be recalled as offensive; but in truth less work was done by the average man in 1800 than in aftertimes, for there was actually less work to do. "Good country this for lazy fellows," wrote Wilson from Kentucky; "they plant corn, turn their pigs into the woods, and in the autumn feed upon corn and pork. They lounge about the rest of the year." The roar of the steam-engine had never been heard in the land, and the carrier's wagon was three weeks between Philadelphia and Pittsburg. What need for haste when days counted for so little? Why not lounge about the tavern when life had no better amusement to offer? Why mind one's own business when one's business would take care of itself?

Yet however idle the American sometimes appeared, and however large the class of tavern loafers may have actually been, the true American was active and industrious. No immigrant came to America for ease or idleness. If an English farmer bought land near New York, Philadelphia, or Baltimore, and made the most of his small capital, he found that while he could earn more money than in Surrey or Devonshire, he worked harder and suffered greater discomforts. The climate was trying; fever was common; the crops ran new risks from strange insects, drought, and violent weather; the weeds were annoying; the flies and mosquitoes tormented him and his cattle; laborers were scarce and indifferent; the slow and magisterial ways of England, where everything was made easy, must be exchanged for quick and energetic action; the farmer's own eye must see to every detail, his own hand must hold the plough and the scythe. Life was more exacting, and every such man in America was required to do, and actually did, the work of two such men in Europe. Few English farmers of the conventional class took kindly to American ways, or succeeded in adapting themselves to the changed conditions. Germans were more successful and became rich; but the poorer and more adventurous class, who had no capital, and cared nothing for the comforts of civilization, went West, to find a harder lot. When, after toiling for weeks, they reached the neighborhood of Genessee or the banks of some stream in southern Ohio or Indiana, they put up a rough cabin of logs with an earthen floor, cleared an acre or two of land, and planted Indian corn between the tree-stumps,— lucky if, like the Kentuckian, they had a pig to turn into the woods. Between April and October, Albert Gallatin used to say, Indian corn made the penniless immigrant a capitalist. New settlers suffered many of the ills that would have afflicted an army marching and fighting in a country of dense forest and swamp, with one sore misery besides,—that whatever trials the men endured, the burden bore most heavily upon the women and children. The chance of being shot or scalped by Indians was hardly worth considering when compared with the certainty of malarial fever, or the strange disease called milk-sickness, or the still more depressing homesickness, or the misery of nervous prostration, which wore out generation after generation of women and children on the frontiers, and left a tragedy in every log-cabin. Not for love of ease did men plunge into the wilderness. Few laborers of the Old World endured a harder lot, coarser fare, or anxieties and responsibilities greater than those of the Western emigrant. Not merely because he enjoyed the luxury of salt pork, whiskey, or even coffee three times a day did the American laborer claim superiority over the European.

A standard far higher than the average was common to the cities; but the city population was so small as to be trifling. Boston, New York, Philadelphia, and Baltimore together contained one hundred and eighty thousand inhabitants; and these were the only towns containing a white population of more than ten thousand persons. In a total population of more than five millions, this number of city people, as Jefferson and his friends rightly thought, was hardly American, for the true American was supposed to be essentially rural. Their comparative luxury was outweighed by the squalor of nine hundred thousand slaves alone.

From these slight notices of national habits no other safe inference could be drawn than that the people were still simple. The path their development might take was one of the many problems with which their future was perplexed. Such few habits as might prove to be fixed, offered little clew to the habits that might be adopted in the process of growth, and speculation was useless where change alone could be considered certain.

If any prediction could be risked, an observer might have been warranted in suspecting that the popular character was likely to be conservative, for as yet this trait was most marked, at least in the older societies of New England, Pennsylvania, and Virginia. Great as were the material obstacles in the path of the United States, the greatest obstacle of all was in the human mind. Down to the close of the eighteenth century no change had occurred in the world which warranted practical men in assuming that great changes were to come. Afterward, as time passed, and as science developed man's capacity to control Nature's forces, old-fashioned conservatism vanished from society, reappearing occasionally, like the stripes on a mule, only to prove its former existence; but during the eighteenth century the progress of America, except in political paths, had been less rapid than ardent reformers wished, and the reaction which followed the French Revolution made it seem even slower than it was. In 1723 Benjamin Franklin landed at Philadelphia, and with his loaf of bread under his arm walked along Market Street toward an immortality such as no American had then conceived. He died in 1790, after witnessing great political revolutions; but the intellectual revolution was hardly as rapid as he must, in his youth, have hoped.

In 1732 Franklin induced some fifty persons to found a subscription library, and his example and energy set a fashion which was generally followed. In 1800 the library he founded was still in existence; numerous small subscription libraries on the same model, containing fifty or a hundred volumes, were scattered in country towns; but all the public libraries in the United States—collegiate, scientific, or popular, endowed or unendowed—could hardly show fifty thousand volumes, including duplicates, fully one third being still theological.

Half a century had passed since Franklin's active mind drew the lightning from heaven, and decided the nature of electricity. No one in America had yet carried further his experiments in the field which he had made American. This inactivity was commonly explained as a result of the long Revolutionary War; yet the war had not prevented population and wealth from increasing, until Philadelphia in 1800 was far in advance of the Philadelphia which had seen Franklin's kite flying among the clouds.

In the year 1753 Franklin organized the postal system of the American colonies, making it self-supporting. No record was preserved of the number of letters then carried in proportion to the population, but in 1800 the gross receipts for postage were $320,000, toward which Pennsylvania contributed most largely,—the sum of $55,000. From letters the Government received in gross $290,000. The lowest rate of letter postage was then eight cents. The smallest charge for letters carried more than a hundred miles was twelve and a half cents. If on an average ten letters were carried for a dollar, the whole number of letters was 2,900,000,—about one a year for every grown inhabitant.

Such a rate of progress could not be called rapid even by conservatives, and more than one stanch conservative thought it unreasonably slow. Even in New York, where foreign influence was active and the rewards of scientific skill were comparatively liberal, science hardly kept pace with wealth and population.

Noah Webster, who before beginning his famous dictionary edited the "New York Commercial Advertiser," and wrote on all subjects with characteristic confidence, complained of the ignorance of his countrymen. He claimed for the New Englanders an acquaintance with theology, law, politics, and light English literature; "but as to classical learning, history (civil and ecclesiastical), mathematics, astronomy, chemistry, botany, and natural history, excepting here and there a rare instance of a man who is eminent in some one of these branches, we may be said to have no learning at all, or a mere smattering." Although defending his countrymen from the criticisms of Dr. Priestley, he admitted that "our learning is superficial in a shameful degree, . . . our colleges are disgracefully destitute of books and philosophical apparatus, . . . and I am ashamed to own that scarcely a branch of science can be fully investigated in America for want of books, especially original works. This defect of our libraries I have experienced myself in searching for materials for the History of Epidemic Diseases. . . . As to libraries, we have no such things. There are not more than three or four tolerable libraries in America, and these are extremely imperfect. Great numbers of the most valuable authors have not found their way across the Atlantic."

This complaint was made in the year 1800, and was the more significant because it showed that Webster, a man equally at home in Philadelphia, New York, and Boston, thought his country's deficiencies greater than could be excused or explained by its circumstances. George Ticknor felt at least equal difficulty in explaining the reason why, as late as 1814, even good schoolbooks were rare in Boston, and a copy of Euripides in the original could not be bought at any book-seller's shop in New England. For some reason, the American mind, except in politics, seemed to these students of literature in a condition of unnatural sluggishness; and such complaints were not confined to literature or science. If Americans agreed in any opinion, they were united in wishing for roads; but even on that point whole communities showed an indifference, or hostility, that annoyed their contemporaries. President Dwight was a somewhat extreme conservative in politics and religion, while the State of Rhode Island was radical in both respects; but Dwight complained with bitterness unusual in his mouth that Rhode Island showed no spirit of progress. The subject of his criticism was an unfinished turnpike-road across the State.

"The people of Providence expended upon this road, as we are informed, the whole sum permitted by the Legislature. This was sufficient to make only those parts which I have mentioned. The turnpike company then applied to the Legislature for leave to expend such an additional sum as would complete the work. The Legislature refused. The principal reason for the refusal, as alleged by one of the members, it is said, was the following: that turnpikes and the establishment of religious worship had their origin in Great Britain, the government of which was a monarchy and the inhabitants slaves; that the people of Massachusetts and Connecticut were obliged by law to support ministers and pay the fare of turnpikes, and were therefore slaves also; that if they chose to be slaves they undoubtedly had a right to their choice, but that free-born Rhode Islanders ought never to submit to be priest-ridden, nor to pay for the privilege of travelling on the highway. This demonstrative reasoning prevailed, and the road continued in the state which I have mentioned until the year 1805. It was then completed, and free-born Rhode Islanders bowed their necks to the slavery of travelling on a good road."

President Dwight seldom indulged in sarcasm or exaggeration such as he showed in this instance; but he repeated only matters of notoriety in charging some of the most democratic communities with unwillingness to pay for good roads. If roads were to exist, they must be the result of public or private enterprise; and if the public in certain States would neither construct roads nor permit corporations to construct them, the entire Union must suffer for want of communication. So strong was the popular prejudice against paying for the privilege of travelling on a highway that in certain States, like Rhode Island and Georgia, turnpikes were long unknown, while in Virginia and North Carolina the roads were little better than where the prejudice was universal.

In this instance the economy of a simple and somewhat rude society accounted in part for indifference; in other cases, popular prejudice took a form less easily understood. So general was the hostility to Banks as to offer a serious obstacle to enterprise. The popularity of President Washington and the usefulness of his administration were impaired by his support of a national bank and a funding system. Jefferson's hostility to all the machinery of capital was shared by a great majority of the Southern people and a large minority in the North. For seven years the New York legislature refused to charter the first banking company in the State; and when in 1791 the charter was obtained, and the Bank fell into Federalist hands, Aaron Burr succeeded in obtaining banking privileges for the Manhattan Company only by concealing them under the pretence of furnishing a supply of fresh water to the city of New York.

This conservative habit of mind was more harmful in America than in other communities, because Americans needed more than older societies the activity which could alone partly compensate for the relative feebleness of their means compared with the magnitude of their task. Some instances of sluggishness, common to Europe and America, were hardly credible. For more than ten years in England the steam-engines of Watt had been working, in common and successful use, causing a revolution in industry that threatened to drain the world for England's advantage; yet Europe during a generation left England undisturbed to enjoy the monopoly of steam. France and Germany were England's rivals in commerce and manufactures, and required steam for

self-defence; while the United States were commercial allies
of England, and needed steam neither for mines nor manufactures, but their need was still extreme. Every American knew
that if steam could be successfully applied to navigation, it
must produce an immediate increase of wealth, besides an ultimate settlement of the most serious material and political
difficulties of the Union. Had both the national and State
Governments devoted millions of money to this object, and
had the citizens wasted, if necessary, every dollar in their
slowly filling pockets to attain it, they would have done no
more than the occasion warranted, even had they failed; but
failure was not to be feared, for they had with their own eyes
seen the experiment tried, and they did not dispute its success. For America this question had been settled as early as
1789, when John Fitch—a mechanic, without education or
wealth, but with the energy of genius—invented engine and
paddles of his own, with so much success that during a whole
summer Philadelphians watched his ferry-boat plying daily
against the river current. No one denied that his boat was
rapidly, steadily, and regularly moved against wind and tide,
with as much certainty and convenience as could be expected
in a first experiment; yet Fitch's company failed. He could
raise no more money; the public refused to use his boat or to
help him build a better; they did not want it, would not believe in it, and broke his heart by their contempt. Fitch struggled against failure, and invented another boat moved by a
screw. The Eastern public still proving indifferent, he wandered to Kentucky, to try his fortune on the Western waters.
Disappointed there, as in Philadelphia and New York, he
made a deliberate attempt to end his life by drink; but the
process proving too slow, he saved twelve opium pills from
the physician's prescription, and was found one morning
dead.

Fitch's death took place in an obscure Kentucky inn, three
years before Jefferson, the philosopher president, entered the
White House. Had Fitch been the only inventor thus neglected, his peculiarities and the defects of his steamboat
might account for his failure; but he did not stand alone. At
the same moment Philadelphia contained another inventor,
Oliver Evans, a man so ingenious as to be often called the

American Watt. He, too, invented a locomotive steam-engine which he longed to bring into common use. The great services actually rendered by this extraordinary man were not a tithe of those he would gladly have performed, had he found support and encouragement; but his success was not even so great as that of Fitch, and he stood aside while Livingston and Fulton, by their greater resources and influence, forced the steamboat on a sceptical public.

While the inventors were thus ready, and while State legislatures were offering mischievous monopolies for this invention, which required only some few thousand dollars of ready money, the Philosophical Society of Rotterdam wrote to the American Philosophical Society at Philadelphia, requesting to know what improvements had been made in the United States in the construction of steam-engines. The subject was referred to Benjamin H. Latrobe, the most eminent engineer in America, and his Report, presented to the Society in May, 1803, published in the Transactions, and transmitted abroad, showed the reasoning on which conservatism rested.

"During the general lassitude of mechanical exertion which succeeded the American Revolution," said Latrobe, "the utility of steam-engines appears to have been forgotten; but the subject afterward started into very general notice in a form in which it could not possibly be attended with much success. A sort of mania began to prevail, which indeed has not yet entirely subsided, for impelling boats by steam-engines. . . . For a short time a passage-boat, rowed by a steam-engine, was established between Bordentown and Philadelphia, but it was soon laid aside. . . . There are indeed general objections to the use of the steam-engine for impelling boats, from which no particular mode of application can be free. These are, first, the weight of the engine and of the fuel; second, the large space it occupies; third, the tendency of its action to rack the vessel and render it leaky; fourth, the expense of maintenance; fifth, the irregularity of its motion and the motion of the water in the boiler and cistern, and of the fuel-vessel in rough water; sixth, the difficulty arising from the liability of the paddles or oars to break if light, and from the weight, if made strong. Nor have I ever heard of an instance, verified by other testimony than that of the inventor, of a speedy and agreeable voyage having been performed in a steamboat of any construction. I am well aware that there are still many very respectable and ingenious men who consider the application of the steam-engine to the purpose of navigation as highly important and as very practicable, especially on the rapid waters of the Mississippi, and who would feel themselves almost offended at the expression of an opposite opinion. And perhaps some of the objections against it may be obviated. That founded on the expense and weight of the fuel may not for some years exist in the Mississippi, where there is a redundance of wood on the banks; but the cutting and loading will be almost as great an evil."

Within four years the steamboat was running, and Latrobe was its warmest friend. The dispute was a contest of temperaments, a divergence between minds, rather than a question of science; and a few visionaries such as those to whom Latrobe alluded—men like Chancellor Livingston, Joel Barlow, John Stevens, Samuel L. Mitchill, and Robert Fulton—dragged society forward. What but scepticism could be expected among a people thus asked to adopt the steamboat, when as yet the ordinary atmospheric steam-engine, such as had been in use in Europe for a hundred years, was practically unknown to them, and the engines of Watt were a fable? Latrobe's Report further said that in the spring of 1803, when he wrote, five steam-engines were at work in the United States,—one lately set up by the Manhattan Water Company in New York to supply the city with water; another in New York for sawing timber; two in Philadelphia, belonging to the city, for supplying water and running a rolling and slitting mill; and one at Boston employed in some manufacture. All but one of these were probably constructed after 1800, and Latrobe neglected to say whether they belonged to the old Newcomen type, or to Watt's manufacture, or to American invention; but he added that the chief American improvement on the steam-engine had been the construction of a wooden boiler, which developed sufficient power to work the Philadelphia pump at the rate of twelve strokes, of six feet, per minute. Twelve strokes a minute, or one stroke every five seconds, though not a surprising power, might have answered its purpose, had not the wooden boiler, as Latrobe admitted, quickly decomposed, and steam-leaks appeared at every bolt-hole.

If so eminent and so intelligent a man as Latrobe, who had but recently emigrated in the prime of life from England, knew little about Watt, and nothing about Oliver Evans, whose experience would have been well worth communicating to any philosophical society in Europe, the more ignorant and unscientific public could not feel faith in a force of which they knew nothing at all. For nearly two centuries the Americans had struggled on foot or horseback over roads not much better than trails, or had floated down rushing streams in open boats momentarily in danger of sinking or upsetting. They had at length, in the Eastern and Middle States, reached the point of constructing turnpikes and canals. Into these undertakings they put sums of money relatively large, for the investment seemed safe and the profits certain. Steam as a locomotive power was still a visionary idea, beyond their experience, contrary to European precedent, and exposed to a thousand risks. They regarded it as a delusion.

About three years after Latrobe wrote his Report on the steam-engine, Robert Fulton began to build the boat which settled forever the value of steam as a locomotive power. According to Fulton's well-known account of his own experience, he suffered almost as keenly as Fitch, twenty years before, under the want of popular sympathy: —

"When I was building my first steamboat at New York," he said, according to Judge Story's report, "the project was viewed by the public either with indifference or with contempt as a visionary scheme. My friends indeed were civil, but they were shy. They listened with patience to my explanations, but with a settled cast of incredulity upon their countenances. I felt the full force of the lamentation of the poet, —

'Truths would you teach, or save a sinking land,
All fear, none aid you, and few understand.'

As I had occasion to pass daily to and from the building-yard while my boat was in progress, I have often loitered unknown near the idle groups of strangers gathering in little circles, and heard various inquiries as to the object of this new vehicle. The language was uniformly that of scorn, or sneer, or ridicule. The loud laugh often rose at my expense; the dry jest; the wise calculation of losses and expenditures; the dull but endless repetition of the Fulton Folly. Never did a single encouraging remark, a bright hope, or a warm wish cross my path."

Possibly Fulton and Fitch, like other inventors, may have exaggerated the public apathy and contempt; but whatever was the precise force of the innovating spirit, conservatism possessed the world by right. Experience forced on men's minds the conviction that what had ever been must ever be. At the close of the eighteenth century nothing had occurred which warranted the belief that even the material difficulties of America could be removed. Radicals as extreme as Thomas Jefferson and Albert Gallatin were contented with avowing no higher aim than that America should reproduce the simpler forms of European republican society without European vices; and even this their opponents thought visionary. The United States had thus far made a single great step in advance of the Old World,—they had agreed to try the experiment of embracing half a continent in one republican system; but so little were they disposed to feel confidence in their success, that Jefferson himself did not look on this American idea as vital; he would not stake the future on so new an invention. "Whether we remain in one confederacy," he wrote in 1804, "or form into Atlantic and Mississippi confederations, I believe not very important to the happiness of either part." Even over his liberal mind history cast a spell so strong, that he thought the solitary American experiment of political confederation "not very important" beyond the Alleghanies.

The task of overcoming popular inertia in a democratic society was new, and seemed to offer peculiar difficulties. Without a scientific class to lead the way, and without a wealthy class to provide the means of experiment, the people of the United States were still required, by the nature of their problems, to become a speculating and scientific nation. They could do little without changing their old habit of mind, and without learning to love novelty for novelty's sake. Hitherto their timidity in using money had been proportioned to the scantiness of their means. Henceforward they were under every inducement to risk great stakes and frequent losses in order to win occasionally a thousand fold. In the colonial state they had naturally accepted old processes as the best, and European experience as final authority. As an independent people, with half a continent to civilize, they could not afford to waste time in following European examples, but must devise new processes of their own. A world which assumed that what had been must be, could not be scientific; yet in order to make the Americans a successful people, they must be roused to feel the necessity of scientific training. Until they were satisfied that knowledge was money, they would not insist upon high education; until they saw with their own eyes stones turned into gold, and vapor into cattle and corn, they would not learn the meaning of science.

Chapter III

WHETHER THE United States were to succeed or fail in their economical and political undertakings, the people must still develop some intellectual life of their own, and the character of this development was likely to interest mankind. New conditions and hopes could hardly fail to produce a literature and arts more or less original. Of all possible triumphs, none could equal that which might be won in the regions of thought if the intellectual influence of the United States should equal their social and economical importance. Young as the nation was, it had already produced an American literature bulky and varied enough to furnish some idea of its probable qualities in the future, and the intellectual condition of the literary class in the United States at the close of the eighteenth century could scarcely fail to suggest both the successes and the failures of the same class in the nineteenth.

In intellectual tastes, as in all else, the Union showed well-marked divisions between New England, New York, Pennsylvania, and the Southern States. New England was itself divided between two intellectual centres,—Boston and New Haven. The Massachusetts and Connecticut schools were as old as the colonial existence; and in 1800 both were still alive, if not flourishing.

Society in Massachusetts was sharply divided by politics. In 1800 one half the population, represented under property qualifications by only some twenty thousand voters, was Republican. The other half, which cast about twenty-five thousand votes, included nearly every one in the professional and mercantile classes, and represented the wealth, social position, and education of the Commonwealth; but its strength lay in the Congregational churches and in the cordial union between the clergy, the magistracy, the bench and bar, and respectable society throughout the State. This union created what was unknown beyond New England,—an organized social system, capable of acting at command either for offence or defence, and admirably adapted for the uses of the eighteenth century.

Had the authority of the dominant classes in Massachusetts

depended merely on office, the task of overthrowing it would have been as simple as it was elsewhere; but the New England oligarchy struck its roots deep into the soil, and was supported by the convictions of the people. Unfortunately the system was not and could not be quickly adapted to the movement of the age. Its starting-point lay in the educational system, which was in principle excellent; but it was also antiquated. Little change had been made in it since colonial times. The common schools were what they had been from the first; the academies and colleges were no more changed than the schools. On an average of ten years, from 1790 to 1800, thirty-nine young men annually took degrees from Harvard College; while during the ten years, 1766–1776, that preceded the Revolutionary War, forty-three bachelors of arts had been annually sent into the world, and even in 1720–1730 the average number had been thirty-five. The only sign of change was that in 1720–1730 about one hundred and forty graduates had gone into the Church, while in 1790–1800 only about eighty chose this career. At the earlier period the president, a professor of theology, one of mathematics, and four tutors gave instruction to the under-graduates. In 1800 the president, the professor of theology, the professor of mathematics, and a professor of Hebrew, created in 1765, with the four tutors did the same work. The method of instruction had not changed in the interval, being suited to children fourteen years of age; the instruction itself was poor, and the discipline was indifferent. Harvard College had not in eighty years made as much progress as was afterward made in twenty. Life was quickening within it as within all mankind,—the spirit and vivacity of the coming age could not be wholly shut out; but none the less the college resembled a priesthood which had lost the secret of its mysteries, and patiently stood holding the flickering torch before cold altars, until God should vouchsafe a new dispensation of sunlight.

Nevertheless, a medical school with three professors had been founded in 1783, and every year gave degrees to an average class of two doctors of medicine. Science had already a firm hold on the college, and a large part of the conservative clergy were distressed by the liberal tendencies which the governing body betrayed. This was no new thing. The college always stood somewhat in advance of society, and never joined heartily in dislike for liberal movements; but unfortunately it had been made for an instrument, and had never enjoyed the free use of its powers. Clerical control could not be thrown off, for if the college was compelled to support the clergy, on the other hand the clergy did much to support the college; and without the moral and material aid of this clerical body, which contained several hundred of the most respected and respectable citizens, clad in every town with the authority of spiritual magistrates, the college would have found itself bankrupt in means and character. The graduates passed from the college to the pulpit, and from the pulpit attempted to hold the college, as well as their own congregations, facing toward the past. "Let us guard against the insidious encroachments of *innovation*," they preached,—"that evil and beguiling spirit which is now stalking to and fro through the earth, seeking whom he may destroy." These words were spoken by Jedediah Morse, a graduate of Yale in 1783, pastor of the church at Charlestown, near Boston, and still known in biographical dictionaries as "the father of American geography." They were contained in the Election Sermon of this worthy and useful man, delivered June 6, 1803; but the sentiment was not peculiar to him, or confined to the audience he was then addressing,—it was the burden of a thousand discourses enforced by a formidable authority.

The power of the Congregational clergy, which had lasted unbroken until the Revolution, was originally minute and inquisitory, equivalent to a police authority. During the last quarter of the century the clergy themselves were glad to lay aside the more odious watchfulness over their parishes, and to welcome social freedom within limits conventionally fixed; but their old authority had not wholly disappeared. In country parishes they were still autocratic. Did an individual defy their authority, the minister put his three-cornered hat on his head, took his silver-topped cane in his hand, and walked down the village street, knocking at one door and another of his best parishioners, to warn them that a spirit of license and of French infidelity was abroad, which could be repressed only by a strenuous and combined effort. Any man once placed under this ban fared badly if he afterward came before a bench of magistrates. The temporal arm vigorously supported the ecclesiastical will. Nothing tended so directly to make respectability conservative, and conservatism a fetich of respectability, as this union of bench and pulpit. The democrat had no caste; he was not respectable; he was a Jacobin,—and no such character was admitted into a Federalist house. Every dissolute intriguer, loose-liver, forger, false-coiner, and prison-bird; every hair-brained, loud-talking demagogue; every speculator, scoffer, and atheist,—was a follower of Jefferson; and Jefferson was himself the incarnation of their theories.

A literature belonging to this subject exists,—stacks of newspapers and sermons, mostly dull, and wanting literary merit. In a few of them Jefferson figured under the well-remembered disguises of Puritan politics: he was Ephraim, and had mixed himself among the people; had apostatized from his God and religion; gone to Assyria, and mingled himself among the heathen; "gray hairs are here and there upon him, yet he knoweth not;" or he was Jeroboam, who drave Israel from following the Lord, and made them sin a great sin. He had doubted the authority of revelation, and ventured to suggest that petrified shells found embedded in rocks fifteen thousand feet above sea-level could hardly have been left there by the Deluge, because if the whole atmosphere were condensed as water, its weight showed that the seas would be raised only fifty-two and a half feet. Sceptic as he was, he could not accept the scientific theory that the ocean-bed had been uplifted by natural forces; but although he had thus instantly deserted this battery raised against revelation, he had still expressed the opinion that a universal deluge was *equally* unsatisfactory as an explanation, and had avowed preference for a profession of ignorance rather than a belief in error. He had said, "It does me no injury for my neighbors to say there are twenty gods, or no god," and that all the many forms of religious faith in the Middle States were "good enough, and sufficient to preserve peace and order." He was notoriously a deist; he probably ridiculed the doctrine of total depravity; and he certainly would never have part or portion in the blessings of the New Covenant, or be saved because of grace.

No abler or more estimable clergyman lived than Joseph

Buckminster, the minister of Portsmouth, in New Hampshire, and in his opinion Jefferson was bringing a judgment upon the people.

"I would not be understood to insinuate," said he in his sermon on Washington's death, "that contemners of religious duties, and even men void of religious principle, may not have an attachment to their country and a desire for its civil and political prosperity,—nay, that they may not even expose themselves to great dangers, and make great sacrifices to accomplish this object; but by their impiety . . . they take away the heavenly defence and security of a people, and render it necessary for him who ruleth among the nations in judgment to testify his displeasure against those who despise his laws and contemn his ordinances."

Yet the congregational clergy, though still greatly respected, had ceased to be leaders of thought. Theological literature no longer held the prominence it had enjoyed in the days of Edwards and Hopkins. The popular reaction against Calvinism, felt rather than avowed, stopped the development of doctrinal theology; and the clergy, always poor as a class, with no weapons but their intelligence and purity of character, commonly sought rather to avoid than to challenge hostility. Such literary activity as existed was not clerical but secular. Its field was the Boston press, and its recognized literary champion was Fisher Ames.

The subject of Ames's thought was exclusively political. At that moment every influence combined to maintain a stationary condition in Massachusetts politics. The manners and morals of the people were pure and simple; their society was democratic; in the worst excesses of their own revolution they had never become savage or bloodthirsty; their experience could not explain, nor could their imagination excuse, wild popular excesses; and when in 1793 the French nation seemed mad with the frenzy of its recovered liberties, New England looked upon the bloody and blasphemous work with such horror as religious citizens could not but feel. Thenceforward the mark of a wise and good man was that he abhorred the French Revolution, and believed democracy to be its cause. Like Edmund Burke, they listened to no argument: "It is a

vile, illiberal school, this French Academy of the sans-cu-
lottes; there is nothing in it that is fit for a gentleman to
learn." The answer to every democratic suggestion ran in a
set phrase, "Look at France!" This idea became a monomania
with the New England leaders, and took exclusive hold of
Fisher Ames, their most brilliant writer and talker, until it
degenerated into a morbid illusion. During the last few
months of his life, even so late as 1808, this dying man could
scarcely speak of his children without expressing his fears of
their future servitude to the French. He believed his alarms
to be shared by his friends. "Our days," he wrote, "are made
heavy with the pressure of anxiety, and our nights restless
with visions of horror. We listen to the clank of chains, and
overhear the whispers of assassins. We mark the barbarous
dissonance of mingled rage and triumph in the yell of an infuriated mob; we see the dismal glare of their burnings, and
scent the loathsome steam of human victims offered in sacrifice." In theory the French Revolution was not an argument
or a proof, but only an illustration, of the workings of divine
law; and what had happened in France must sooner or later
happen in America if the ignorant and vicious were to govern
the wise and good.

The bitterness against democrats became intense after the
month of May, 1800, when the approaching victory of Jefferson was seen to be inevitable. Then for the first time the
clergy and nearly all the educated and respectable citizens of
New England began to extend to the national government
the hatred which they bore to democracy. The expressions of
this mixed antipathy filled volumes. "Our country," wrote
Fisher Ames in 1803, "is too big for union, too sordid for
patriotism, too democratic for liberty. What is to become of
it, he who made it best knows. Its vice will govern it, by
practising upon its folly. This is ordained for democracies."
He explained why this inevitable fate awaited it. "A democracy cannot last. Its nature ordains that its next change shall
be into a military despotism,—of all known governments
perhaps the most prone to shift its head, and the slowest to
mend its vices. The reason is that the tyranny of what is called
the people, and that by the sword, both operate alike to debase and corrupt, till there are neither men left with the spirit

to desire liberty, nor morals with the power to sustain justice. Like the burning pestilence that destroys the human body, nothing can subsist by its dissolution but vermin." George Cabot, whose political opinions were law to the wise and good, held the same convictions. "Even in New England," wrote Cabot in 1804, " where there is among the body of the people more wisdom and virtue than in any other part of the United States, we are full of errors which no reasoning could eradicate, if there were a Lycurgus in every village. We are democratic altogether, and I hold democracy in its natural operation to be the government of the worst."

Had these expressions of opinion been kept to the privacy of correspondence, the public could have ignored them; but so strong were the wise and good in their popular following, that every newspaper seemed to exult in denouncing the people. They urged the use of force as the protection of wisdom and virtue. A paragraph from Dennie's "Portfolio," reprinted by all the Federalist newspapers in 1803, offered one example among a thousand of the infatuation which possessed the Federalist press, neither more extravagant nor more treasonable than the rest:—

"A democracy is scarcely tolerable at any period of national history. Its omens are always sinister, and its powers are unpropitious. It is on its trial here, and the issue will be civil war, desolation, and anarchy. No wise man but discerns its imperfections, no good man but shudders at its miseries, no honest man but proclaims its fraud, and no brave man but draws his sword against its force. The institution of a scheme of policy so radically contemptible and vicious is a memorable example of what the villany of some men can devise, the folly of others receive, and both establish in spite of reason, reflection, and sensation."

The Philadelphia grand jury indicted Dennie for this paragraph as a seditious libel, but it was not more expressive than the single word uttered by Alexander Hamilton, who owed no small part of his supremacy to the faculty of expressing the prejudices of his followers more tersely than they themselves could do. Compressing the idea into one syllable, Hamilton, at a New York dinner, replied to some democratic sentiment by striking his hand sharply on the table and saying, "Your people, sir,—your people is a great *beast!*"

The political theories of these ultra-conservative New Englanders did not require the entire exclusion of all democratic influence from government. "While I hold," said Cabot, "that a government altogether popular is in effect a government of the populace, I maintain that no government can be relied on that has not a material portion of the democratic mixture in its composition." Cabot explained what should be the true portion of democratic mixture: "If no man in New England could vote for legislators who was not possessed in his own right of two thousand dollars' value *in land*, we could do something better." The Constitution of Massachusetts already restricted the suffrage to persons "having a freehold estate within the commonwealth of an annual income of three pounds, or any estate of the value of sixty pounds." A further restriction to freeholders whose estate was worth two thousand dollars would hardly have left a material mixture of any influence which democrats would have recognized as theirs.

Meanwhile even Cabot and his friends Ames and Colonel Hamilton recognized that the reform they wished could be effected only with the consent of the people; and firm in the conviction that democracy must soon produce a crisis, as in Greece and Rome, in England and France, when political power must revert to the wise and good, or to the despotism of a military chief, they waited for the catastrophe they foresaw. History and their own experience supported them. They were right, so far as human knowledge could make them so; but the old spirit of Puritan obstinacy was more evident than reason or experience in the simple-minded, overpowering conviction with which the clergy and serious citizens of Massachusetts and Connecticut, assuming that the people of America were in the same social condition as the contemporaries of Catiline and the adherents of Robespierre, sat down to bide their time until the tempest of democracy should drive the frail government so near destruction that all men with one voice should call on God and the Federalist prophets for help. The obstinacy of the race was never better shown than when, with the sunlight of the nineteenth century bursting upon them, these resolute sons of granite and ice turned their faces from the sight, and smiled in their sardonic way at the folly or wickedness of men who could pretend to believe the world improved because henceforth the ignorant and vicious were to rule the United States and govern the churches and schools of New England.

Even Boston, the most cosmopolitan part of New England, showed no tendency in its educated classes to become American in thought or feeling. Many of the ablest Federalists, and among the rest George Cabot, Theophilus Parsons, and Fisher Ames, shared few of the narrower theological prejudices of their time, but were conservatives of the English type, whose alliance with the clergy betrayed as much policy as religion, and whose intellectual life was wholly English. Boston made no strong claim to intellectual prominence. Neither clergy, lawyers, physicians, nor literary men were much known beyond the State. Fisher Ames enjoyed a wider fame; but Ames's best political writing was saturated with the despair of the tomb to which his wasting body was condemned. Five years had passed since he closed his famous speech on the British Treaty with the foreboding that if the treaty were not carried into effect, "even I, slender and almost broken as my hold upon life is, may outlive the government and constitution of my country." Seven years more were to pass in constant dwelling upon the same theme, in accents more and more despondent, before the long-expected grave closed over him, and his warning voice ceased to echo painfully on the air. The number of his thorough-going admirers was small, if his own estimate was correct. "There are," he said, "not many, perhaps not five hundred, even among the Federalists, who yet allow themselves to view the progress of licentiousness as so speedy, so sure, and so fatal as the deplorable experience of our country shows that it is, and the evidence of history and the constitution of human nature demonstrate that it must be." These five hundred, few as they were, comprised most of the clergy and the State officials, and overawed large numbers more.

Ames was the mouthpiece in the press of a remarkable group, of which George Cabot was the recognized chief in wisdom, and Timothy Pickering the most active member in national politics. With Ames, Cabot, and Pickering, joined in confidential relations, was Theophilus Parsons, who in the year 1800 left Newburyport for Boston. Parsons was an abler man than either Cabot, Ames, or Pickering, and his influence was great in holding New England fast to an independent course which could end only in the overthrow of the Federal constitution which these men had first pressed upon an unwilling people; but though gifted with strong natural powers, backed by laborious study and enlivened by the ready and somewhat rough wit native to New England, Parsons was not bold on his own account; he was felt rather than seen, and although ever ready in private to advise strong measures, he commonly let others father them before the world.

These gentlemen formed the Essex Junto, so called from the county of Essex where their activity was first felt. According to Ames, not more than five hundred men fully shared their opinions; but Massachusetts society was so organized as to make their influence great, and experience foretold that as the liberal Federalists should one by one wander to the Democratic camp where they belonged, the conservatism of those who remained would become more bitter and more absolute as the Essex Junto represented a larger and larger proportion of their numbers.

Nevertheless, the reign of old-fashioned conservatism was near its end. The New England Church was apparently sound; even Unitarians and Baptists were recognized as parts of one fraternity. Except a few Roman and Anglican bodies, all joined in the same worship, and said little on points of doctrinal difference. No one had yet dared to throw a firebrand into the temple; but Unitarians were strong among the educated and wealthy class, while the tendencies of a less doctrinal religious feeling were shaping themselves in Harvard College. William Ellery Channing took his degree in 1798, and in 1800 was a private tutor in Virginia. Joseph Stevens Buckminster, thought by his admirers a better leader than Channing, graduated in 1800, and was teaching boys to construe their Latin exercises at Exeter Academy. Only the shell of orthodoxy was left, but respectable society believed this shell to be necessary as an example of Christian unity and a safeguard against more serious innovations. No one could fail to see that the public had lately become restive under its antiquated

discipline. The pulpits still fulminated against the fatal tolerance which within a few years had allowed theatres to be
opened in Boston, and which scandalized God-fearing men
by permitting public advertisements that "Hamlet" and
"Othello" were to be performed in the town founded to protest against worldly pageants. Another innovation was more
strenuously resisted. Only within the last thirty years had
Sunday travel been allowed even in England; in Massachusetts and Connecticut it was still forbidden by law, and the
law was enforced. Yet not only travellers, but inn-keepers and
large numbers of citizens connived at Sunday travel, and it
could not long be prevented. The clergy saw their police authority weakening year by year, and understood, without
need of many words, the tacit warning of the city congregations that in this world they must be allowed to amuse themselves, even though they were to suffer for it in the next.

The longing for amusement and freedom was a reasonable
and a modest want. Even the young theologians, the Buck-
minsters and Channings, were hungry for new food. Boston
was little changed in appearance, habits, and style from what
it had been under its old king. When young Dr. J. C. Warren
returned from Europe about the year 1800, to begin practice
in Boston, he found gentlemen still dressed in colored coats
and figured waistcoats, short breeches buttoning at the knee,
long boots with white tops, ruffled shirts and wristbands, a
white cravat filled with what was called a "pudding," and for
the elderly, cocked hats, and wigs which once every week
were sent to the barber's to be dressed,—so that every Saturday night the barbers' boys were seen carrying home piles
of wig-boxes in readiness for Sunday's church. At evening
parties gentlemen appeared in white small-clothes, silk stockings and pumps, with a colored or white waistcoat. There
were few hackney-coaches, and ladies walked to evening entertainments. The ancient minuet was danced as late as 1806.
The waltz was not yet tolerated.

Fashionable society was not without charm. In summer
Southern visitors appeared, and admired the town, with its
fashionable houses perched on the hillsides, each in its own
garden, and each looking seaward over harbor and islands.
Boston was then what Newport afterward became, and its

only rival as a summer watering-place in the North was Ball-ston, whither society was beginning to seek health before finding it a little farther away at Saratoga. Of intellectual amusement there was little more at one place than at the other, except that the Bostonians devoted themselves more seriously to church-going and to literature. The social instinct took shape in varied forms, but was highly educated in none; while the typical entertainment in Boston, as in New York, Philadelphia, and Charleston, was the state dinner,—not the light, feminine triviality which France introduced into an amusement-loving world, but the serious dinner of Sir Robert Walpole and Lord North, where gout and plethora waited behind the chairs; an effort of animal endurance.

There was the arena of intellectual combat, if that could be called combat where disagreement in principle was not tolerated. The talk of Samuel Johnson and Edmund Burke was the standard of excellence to all American society that claimed intellectual rank, and each city possessed its own circle of Federalist talkers. Democrats rarely figured in these entertainments, at least in fashionable private houses. "There was no exclusiveness," said a lady who long outlived the time; "but I should as soon have expected to see a cow in a drawing-room as a Jacobin." In New York, indeed, Colonel Burr and the Livingstons may have held their own, and the active-minded Dr. Mitchill there, like Dr. Eustis in Boston, was an agreeable companion. Philadelphia was comparatively cosmopolitan; in Baltimore the Smiths were a social power; and Charleston, after deserting Federal principles in 1800, could hardly ignore Democrats; but Boston society was still pure. The clergy took a prominent part in conversation, but Fisher Ames was the favorite of every intelligent company; and when Gouverneur Morris, another brilliant talker, visited Boston, Ames was pitted against him.

The intellectual wants of the community grew with the growing prosperity; but the names of half-a-dozen persons could hardly be mentioned whose memories survived by intellectual work made public in Massachusetts between 1783 and 1800. Two or three local historians might be numbered, including Jeremy Belknap, the most justly distinguished. Jedediah Morse the geographer was well known; but not a

poet, a novelist, or a scholar could be named. Nathaniel Bow-
ditch did not publish his "Practical Navigator" till 1800, and
not till then did Dr. Waterhouse begin his struggle to introduce vaccination. With the exception of a few Revolutionary
statesmen and elderly clergymen, a political essayist like
Ames, and lawyers like Samuel Dexter and Theophilus Parsons, Massachusetts could show little that warranted a reputation for genius; and, in truth, the intellectual prominence of
Boston began as the conservative system died out, starting
with the younger Buckminster several years after the century
opened.

The city was still poorer in science. Excepting the medical
profession, which represented nearly all scientific activity,
hardly a man in Boston got his living either by science or art.
When in the year 1793 the directors of the new Middlesex
Canal Corporation, wishing to bring the Merrimac River to
Boston Harbor, required a survey of an easy route not thirty
miles long, they could find no competent civil engineer in
Boston, and sent to Philadelphia for an Englishman named
Weston, engaged on the Delaware and Schuylkill Canal.

Possibly a few Bostonians could read and even speak
French; but Germany was nearly as unknown as China, until
Madame de Staël published her famous work in 1814. Even
then young George Ticknor, incited by its account of German
university education, could find neither a good teacher nor a
dictionary, nor a German book in the shops or public libraries
of the city or at the college in Cambridge. He had discovered
a new world.

Pope, Addison, Akenside, Beattie, and Young were still the
reigning poets. Burns was accepted by a few; and copies of a
volume were advertised by book-sellers, written by a new
poet called Wordsworth. America offered a fair demand for
new books, and anything of a light nature published in England was sure to cross the ocean. Wordsworth crossed with
the rest, and his "Lyrical Ballads" were reprinted in 1802, not
in Boston or New York, but in Philadelphia, where they were
read and praised. In default of other amusements, men read
what no one could have endured had a choice of amusements
been open. Neither music, painting, science, the lecture-
room, nor even magazines offered resources that could rival

what was looked upon as classical literature. Men had not the alternative of listening to political discussions, for stump-speaking was a Southern practice not yet introduced into New England, where such a political canvass would have terrified society with dreams of Jacobin license. The clergy and the bar took charge of politics; the tavern was the club and the forum of political discussion; but for those who sought other haunts, and especially for women, no intellectual amusement other than what was called "belles-lettres" existed to give a sense of occupation to an active mind. This keen and innovating people, hungry for the feast that was almost served, the Walter Scotts and Byrons so near at hand, tried meanwhile to nourish themselves with husks.

Afraid of Shakspeare and the drama, trained to the standards of Queen Anne's age, and ambitious beyond reason to excel, the New Englanders attempted to supply their own wants. Massachusetts took no lead in the struggle to create a light literature, if such poetry and fiction could be called light. In Connecticut the Muses were most obstinately wooed; and there, after the Revolutionary War, a persistent effort was made to give prose the form of poetry. The chief of the movement was Timothy Dwight, a man of extraordinary qualities, but one on whom almost every other mental gift had been conferred in fuller measure than poetical genius. Twenty-five years had passed since young Dwight, fresh from Yale College, began his career by composing an epic poem, in eleven books and near ten thousand lines, called "The Conquest of Canaan." In the fervor of patriotism, before independence was secured or the French Revolution imagined, he pictured the great Hebrew leader Joshua preaching the Rights of Man, and prophesying the spread of his "sons" over America:—

"Then o'er wide lands, as blissful Eden bright,
  Type of the skies, and seats of pure delight,
  Our sons with prosperous course shall stretch their sway,
  And claim an empire spread from sea to sea;
  In one great whole th' harmonious tribes combine,
  Trace Justice' path, and choose their chiefs divine;
  On Freedom's base erect the heavenly plan,
  Teach laws to reign, and save the Rights of Man.

> Then smiling Art shall wrap the fields in bloom,
> Fine the rich ore, and guide the useful loom;
> Then lofty towers in golden pomp arise,
> Then spiry cities meet auspicious skies;
> The soul on Wisdom's wing sublimely soar,
> New virtues cherish and new truths explore;
> Through Time's long tract our name celestial run,
> Climb in the east and circle with the sun;
> And smiling Glory stretch triumphant wings
> O'er hosts of heroes and o'er tribes of kings."

A world of eighteenth-century thought, peopled with personifications, lay buried in the ten thousand lines of President Dwight's youthful poem. Perhaps in the year 1800, after Jefferson's triumph, Dwight would have been less eager that his hero should save the Rights of Man; by that time the phrase had acquired a flavor of French infidelity which made it unpalatable to good taste. Yet the same Jeffersonian spirit ran through Dwight's famous national song, which was also written in the Revolutionary War:—

> "Columbia, Columbia, to glory arise,
>   The queen of the world and child of the skies!
>
>   .   .   .   .   .
>
> Thy heroes the rights of mankind shall defend,
> And triumph pursue them, and glory attend.
>
>   .   .   .   .   .
>
> While the ensigns of union in triumph unfurled
> Hush the tumult of war and give peace to the world."

"Peace to the world" was the essence of Jeffersonian principles, worth singing in something better than jingling metre and indifferent rhyme; but President Dwight's friends in 1800 no longer sang this song. More and more conservative as he grew older, he published in 1797 an orthodox "Triumph of Infidelity," introduced by a dedication to Voltaire. His rebuke to mild theology was almost as severe as that to French deism:—

> "There smiled the smooth divine, unused to wound
> The sinner's heart with Hell's alarming sound."

His poetical career reached its climax in 1794 in a clerical Connecticut pastoral in seven books, called "Greenfield Hill." Perhaps his verses were not above the level of the Beatties and Youngs he imitated; but at least they earned for President Dwight no mean reputation in days when poetry was at its lowest ebb, and made him the father of a school.

One quality gave respectability to his writing apart from genius. He loved and believed in his country. Perhaps the uttermost depths of his nature were stirred only by affection for the Connecticut Valley; but after all where was human nature more respectable than in that peaceful region? What had the United States then to show in scenery and landscape more beautiful or more winning than that country of meadow and mountain? Patriotism was no ardent feeling among the literary men of the time, whose general sentiment was rather expressed by Cliffton's lines:—

> "In these cold shades, beneath these shifting skies,
>   Where Fancy sickens, and where Genius dies,
>   Where few and feeble are the Muse's strains,
>   And no fine frenzy riots in the veins,
>   There still are found a few to whom belong
>   The fire of virtue and the soul of song."

William Cliffton, a Pennsylvania Friend, who died in 1799 of consumption, in his twenty-seventh year, knew nothing of the cold shades and shifting skies which chilled the genius of European poets; he knew only that America cared little for such genius and fancy as he could offer, and he rebelled against the neglect. He was better treated than Wordsworth, Keats, or Shelley; but it was easy to blame the public for dulness and indifference, though readers were kinder than authors had a right to expect. Even Cliffton was less severe than some of his contemporaries. A writer in the "Boston Anthology," for January, 1807, uttered in still stronger words the prevailing feeling of the literary class:—

> "We know that in this land, where the spirit of democracy is everywhere diffused, we are exposed as it were to a poisonous atmosphere, which blasts everything beautiful in nature, and corrodes everything elegant in art; we know

that with us 'the rose-leaves fall ungathered,' and we believe that there is little to praise and nothing to admire in most of the objects which would first present themselves to the view of a stranger."

Yet the American world was not unsympathetic toward Cliffton and his rivals, though they strained prose through their sieves of versification, and showed open contempt for their audience. Toward President Dwight the public was even generous; and he returned the generosity with parental love and condescension which shone through every line he wrote. For some years his patriotism was almost as enthusiastic as that of Joel Barlow. He was among the numerous rivals of Macaulay and Shelley for the honor of inventing the stranger to sit among the ruins of St. Paul's; and naturally America supplied the explorer who was to penetrate the forest of London and indulge his national self-complacency over ruined temples and towers.

> "Some unknown wild, some shore without a name,
>   In all thy pomp shall then majestic shine
>   As silver-headed Time's slow years decline.
>   Not ruins only meet th' inquiring eye;
>   Where round yon mouldering oak vain brambles twine,
>   The filial stem, already towering high,
> Erelong shall stretch his arms and nod in yonder sky."

From these specimens of President Dwight's poetry any critic, familiar with the time, could infer that his prose was sensible and sound. One of the few books of travel which will always retain value for New Englanders was written by President Dwight to describe his vacation rambles; and although in his own day no one would have ventured to insult him by calling these instructive volumes amusing, the quaintness which here and there gave color to the sober narrative had a charm of its own. How could the contrast be better expressed between volatile Boston and orthodox New Haven than in Dwight's quiet reproof, mixed with paternal tenderness? The Bostonians, he said, were distinguished by a lively imagination, ardor, and sensibility; they were "more like the Greeks

than the Romans;" admired where graver people would only
approve; applauded or hissed where another audience would
be silent; their language was frequently hyperbolical, their
pictures highly colored; the tea shipped to Boston was destroyed,—in New York and Philadelphia it was stored; education in Boston was superficial, and Boston women showed
the effects of this misfortune, for they practised accomplish-
ments only that they might be admired, and were taught from
the beginning to regard their dress as a momentous concern.

Under Dwight's rule the women of the Connecticut Valley
were taught better; but its men set to the Bostonians an example of frivolity without a parallel, and they did so with the
connivance of President Dwight and under the lead of his
brother Theodore. The frivolity of the Hartford wits, as they
were called, was not so light as that of Canning and the
"Anti Jacobin," but had it been heavier than the "Conquest
of Canaan" itself, it would still have found no literary rivalry
in Boston. At about the time when Dwight composed his
serious epic, another tutor at Yale, John Trumbull, wrote a
burlesque epic in Hudibrastic verse, "McFingal," which his
friend Dwight declared to be not inferior to "Hudibras" in
wit and humor, and in every other respect superior. When
"Hudibras" was published, more than a hundred years before,
Mr. Pepys remarked: "It hath not a good liking in me,
though I had tried but twice or three times reading to bring
myself to think it witty." After the lapse of more than another
century, the humor of neither poem may seem worth imitation; but to Trumbull in 1784 Butler was a modern classic, for
the standard of taste between 1663 and 1784 changed less than
in any twenty years of the following century. "McFingal" was
a success, and laid a solid foundation for the coming school
of Hartford wits. Posterity ratified the verdict of Trumbull's
admirers by preserving for daily use a few of his lines quoted
indiscriminately with Butler's best:—

> "What has posterity done for us?"

> "Optics sharp it needs, I ween,
> To see what is not to be seen."

> "A thief ne'er felt the halter draw
> With good opinion of the law."

Ten years after the appearance of "McFingal," and on the strength of its success, Trumbull, Lemuel Hopkins, Richard Alsop, Theodore Dwight, Joel Barlow, and others began a series of publications, "The Anarchiad," "The Echo," "The Guillotine," and the like, in which they gave tongue to their wit and sarcasm. As Alsop described the scene,—

> "Begrimed with blood where erst the savage fell,
> Shrieked the wild war-whoop with infernal yell,
> The Muses sing; lo, Trumbull wakes the lyre.
>
> .   .   .   .
>
> Majestic Dwight, sublime in epic strain,
> Paints the fierce horrors of the crimson plain;
> And in Virgilian Barlow's tuneful lines
> With added splendor great Columbus shines."

Perhaps the Muses would have done better by not interrupting the begrimed savage; for Dwight, Trumbull, Alsop, and Hopkins, whatever their faults, were Miltonic by the side of Joel Barlow. Yet Barlow was a figure too important in American history to be passed without respectful attention. He expressed better than any one else that side of Connecticut character which roused at the same instant the laughter and the respect of men. Every human influence twined about his career and lent it interest; every forward movement of his time had his sympathy, and few steps in progress were made which he did not assist. His ambition, above the lofty ambition of Jefferson, made him aspire to be a Connecticut Mæcenas and Virgil in one; to patronize Fulton and employ Smirke; counsel Jefferson and contend with Napoleon. In his own mind a figure such as the world rarely saw,—a compound of Milton, Rousseau, and the Duke of Bridgewater,— he had in him so large a share of conceit, that tragedy, which would have thrown a solemn shadow over another man's life, seemed to render his only more entertaining. As a poet, he undertook to do for his native land what Homer had done for Greece and Virgil for Rome, Milton for England and Camoens for Portugal,—to supply America with a great epic, without which no country could be respectable; and his "Vision of Columbus," magnified afterward into the

"Columbiad," with a magnificence of typography and illustration new to the United States, remained a monument of his
ambition. In this vision Columbus was shown a variety of
coming celebrities, including all the heroes of the Revolutionary War:—

> "Here stood stern Putnam, scored with ancient scars,
>   The living records of his country's wars;
> Wayne, like a moving tower, assumes his post,
>   Fires the whole field, and is himself a host;
> Undaunted Stirling, prompt to meet his foes,
>   And Gates and Sullivan for action rose;
> Macdougal, Clinton, guardians of the State,
>   Stretch the nerved arm to pierce the depth of fate;
> Moultrie and Sumter lead their banded powers;
> Morgan in front of his bold riflers towers,
>   His host of keen-eyed marksmen, skilled to pour
> Their slugs unerring from the twisted bore;
> No sword, no bayonet they learn to wield,
> They gall the flank, they skirt the battling field,
> Cull out the distant foe in full horse speed,
> Couch the long tube and eye the silver bead,
> Turn as he turns, dismiss the whizzing lead,
> And lodge the death-ball in his heedless head."

More than seven thousand lines like these furnished constant pleasure to the reader, the more because the "Columbiad" was accepted by the public in a spirit as serious as that
in which it was composed. The Hartford wits, who were bitter Federalists, looked upon Barlow as an outcast from their
fold, a Jacobin in politics, and little better than a French atheist in religion; but they could not deny that his poetic gar-
ments were of a piece with their own. Neither could they
without great ingratitude repudiate his poetry as they did his
politics, for they themselves figured with Manco Capac, Mon-
tezuma, Raleigh, and Pocahontas before the eyes of Columbus; and the world bore witness that Timothy Dwight,
"Heaven in his eye and rapture on his tongue," tuned his
"high harp" in Barlow's inspired verses. Europe was as little
disposed as America to cavil; and the Abbé Grégoire assured

Barlow in a printed letter that this monument of genius and typography would immortalize the author and silence the criticisms of Pauw and other writers on the want of talent in America.

That the "Columbiad" went far to justify those criticisms was true; but on the other hand it proved something almost equivalent to genius. Dwight, Trumbull, and Barlow, whatever might be their differences, united in offering proof of the boundless ambition which marked the American character. Their aspirations were immense, and sooner or later such restless craving was sure to find better expression. Meanwhile Connecticut was a province by itself, a part of New England rather than of the United States. The exuberant patriotism of the Revolution was chilled by the steady progress of democratic principles in the Southern and Middle States, until at the election of Jefferson in 1800 Connecticut stood almost alone with no intellectual companion except Massachusetts, while the breach between them and the Middle States seemed to widen day by day. That the separation was only superficial was true; but the connection itself was not yet deep. An extreme Federalist partisan like Noah Webster did not cease working for his American language and literature because of the triumph of Jeffersonian principles elsewhere; Barlow became more American when his friends gained power; the work of the colleges went on unbroken; but prejudices, habits, theories, and laws remained what they had been in the past, and in Connecticut the influence of nationality was less active than ten, twenty, or even thirty years before. Yale College was but a reproduction of Harvard with stricter orthodoxy, turning out every year about thirty graduates, of whom nearly one fourth went into the Church. For the last ten years the number tended rather to diminish than to increase.

Evidently an intellectual condition like that of New England could not long continue. The thoughts and methods of the eighteenth century held possession of men's minds only because the movement of society was delayed by political passions. Massachusetts, and especially Boston, already contained a younger generation eager to strike into new paths, while forcibly held in the old ones. The more decidedly the college graduates of 1800 disliked democracy and its habits of thought, the more certain they were to compensate for political narrowness by freedom in fields not political. The future direction of the New England intellect seemed already suggested by the impossibility of going further in the line of President Dwight and Fisher Ames. Met by a barren negation on that side, thought was driven to some new channel; and the United States were the more concerned in the result because, with the training and literary habits of New Englanders and the new models already established in Europe for their guidance, they were likely again to produce something that would command respect.

Chapter IV

BETWEEN New England and the Middle States was a gap like that between Scotland and England. The conceptions of life were different. In New England society was organized on a system,—a clergy in alliance with a magistracy; universities supporting each, and supported in turn,—a social hierarchy, in which respectability, education, property, and religion united to defeat and crush the unwise and vicious. In New York wisdom and virtue, as understood in New England, were but lightly esteemed. From an early moment no small number of those who by birth, education, and property were natural leaders of the wise and virtuous, showed themselves ready to throw in their lot with the multitude. Yet New York, much more than New England, was the home of natural leaders and family alliances. John Jay, the governor; the Schuylers, led by Philip Schuyler and his son-in-law Alexander Hamilton; the Livingstons, led by Robert R. Livingston the chancellor, with a promising younger brother Edward nearly twenty years his junior, and a brother-in-law John Armstrong, whose name and relationship will be prominent in this narrative, besides Samuel Osgood, Morgan Lewis, and Smith Thompson, other connections by marriage with the great Livingston stock; the Clintons, headed by Governor George Clinton, and supported by the energy of De Witt his nephew, thirty years of age, whose close friend Ambrose Spencer was reckoned as one of the family; finally, Aaron Burr, of pure Connecticut Calvinistic blood, whose two active lieutenants, William P. Van Ness and John Swartwout, were socially well connected and well brought up,—all these Jays, Schuylers, Livingstons, Clintons, Burrs, had they lived in New England, would probably have united in the support of their class, or abandoned the country; but being citizens of New York they quarrelled. On one side Governor Jay, General Schuyler, and Colonel Hamilton were true to their principles. Rufus King, the American minister in London, by birth a New Englander, adhered to the same connection. On the other hand, George Clinton, like Samuel Adams in Boston, was a Republican by temperament, and his protest against the Constitution made him leader of the Northern Republicans long before Jefferson was mentioned as his rival. The rest were all backsliders from Federalism,—and especially the Livingston faction, who, after carefully weighing arguments and interests, with one accord joined the mob of free-thinking democrats, the "great beast" of Alexander Hamilton. Aaron Burr, who prided himself on the inherited patrician quality of his mind and manners, coldly assuming that wisdom and virtue were powerless in a democracy, followed Chancellor Livingston into the society of Cheetham and Paine. Even the influx of New Englanders into the State could not save the Federalists; and in May, 1800, after a sharp struggle, New York finally enrolled itself on the side of Jefferson and George Clinton.

Fortunately for society, New York possessed no church to overthrow, or traditional doctrines to root out, or centuries of history to disavow. Literature of its own it had little; of intellectual unity, no trace. Washington Irving was a boy of seventeen wandering along the banks of the river he was to make famous; Fenimore Cooper was a boy of eleven playing in the primitive woods of Otsego, or fitting himself at Albany for entrance to Yale College; William Cullen Bryant was a child of six in the little village of Cummington, in western Massachusetts.

Political change could as little affect the educational system as it could affect history, church, or literature. In 1795, at the suggestion of Governor Clinton, an attempt had been made by the New York legislature to create a common-school system, and a sum of fifty thousand dollars was for five years annually applied to that object; but in 1800 the appropriation was exhausted, and the thirteen hundred schools which had been opened were declining. Columbia College, with a formidable array of unfilled professorships, and with fifteen or twenty annual graduates, stood apart from public affairs, although one of its professors, Dr. Samuel L. Mitchill, gave scientific reputation to the whole State. Like the poet Barlow, Mitchill was a universal genius,—a chemist, botanist, naturalist, physicist, and politician, who, to use the words of a shrewd observer, supported the Republican party because Jefferson was its leader, and supported Jefferson because he was a philosopher. Another professor of Columbia College, Dr. David Hosack, was as active as Dr. Mitchill in education, although he contented himself with private life, and did not, like Mitchill, reach the dignity of congressman and senator.

Science and art were still less likely to be harmed by a democratic revolution. For scientific work accomplished before 1800 New York might claim to excel New England; but the result was still small. A little botany and mineralogy, a paper on the dispute over yellow fever or vaccination, was the utmost that medicine could show; yet all the science that existed was in the hands of the medical faculty. Botany, chemistry, mineralogy, midwifery, and surgery were so closely allied that the same professor might regard them all as within the range of his instruction; and Dr. Mitchill could have filled in succession, without much difficulty, every chair in Columbia College as well as in the Academy of Fine Arts about to be established. A surgeon was assumed to be an artist. The Capitol at Washington was designed, in rivalry with a French architect, by Dr. William Thornton, an English physician, who in the course of two weeks' study at the Philadelphia Library gained enough knowledge of architecture to draw incorrectly an exterior elevation. When Thornton was forced to look for some one to help him over his difficulties, Jefferson could find no competent native American, and sent for Latrobe. Jefferson considered himself a better architect than either of them, and had he been a professor of materia medica at Columbia College, the public would have accepted his claim as reasonable.

The intellectual and moral character of New York left much to be desired; but on the other hand, had society adhered stiffly to what New England thought strict morals, the difficulties in the path of national development would have been increased. Innovation was the most useful purpose which New York could serve in human interests, and never was a city better fitted for its work. Although the great tide of prosperity had hardly begun to flow, the political character of city and State was already well defined in 1800 by the election which made Aaron Burr vice-president of the United States, and brought De Witt Clinton into public life as Burr's rival. De Witt Clinton was hardly less responsible than Burr himself for lowering the standard of New York politics, and indirectly that of the nation; but he was foremost in creating the Erie Canal. Chancellor Livingston was frequently charged with selfishness as great as that of Burr and Clinton; but he built the first steamboat, and gave immortality to Fulton. Ambrose Spencer's politics were inconsistent enough to destroy the good name of any man in New England; but he became a chief-justice of ability and integrity. Edward Livingston was a defaulter under circumstances of culpable carelessness, as the Treasury thought; but Gallatin, who dismissed him from office, lived to see him become the author of a celebrated code of civil law, and of the still more celebrated Nullification Proclamation. John Armstrong's character was so little admired that his own party could with difficulty be induced to give him high office; yet the reader will judge how Armstrong compared in efficiency of public service with the senators who distrusted him.

New York cared but little for the metaphysical subtleties of Massachusetts and Virginia, which convulsed the nation with spasms almost as violent as those that, fourteen centuries before, distracted the Eastern Empire in the effort to establish the double or single nature of Christ. New York was indifferent whether the nature of the United States was single or multiple, whether they were a nation or a league. Leaving this class of questions to other States which were deeply interested in them, New York remained constant to no political theory. There society, in spite of its aristocratic mixture, was democratic by instinct; and in abandoning its alliance with New England in order to join Virginia and elect Jefferson to the Presidency, it pledged itself to principles of no kind, least of all to Virginia doctrines. The Virginians aimed at maintaining a society so simple that purity should suffer no danger, and corruption gain no foothold; and never did America witness a stranger union than when Jefferson, the representative of ideal purity, allied himself with Aaron Burr, the Livingstons and Clintons, in the expectation of fixing the United States in a career of simplicity and virtue. George Clinton indeed, a States-rights Republican of the old school, understood and believed the Virginia doctrines; but as for Aaron Burr, Edward Livingston, De Witt Clinton, and Ambrose Spencer, —young men whose brains were filled with dreams of a different sort,—what had such energetic democrats to do with the plough, or what share had the austerity of Cato and the simplicity of Ancus Martius in their ideals? The political partnership between the New York Republicans and the Virginians was from the first that of a business firm; and no more curious speculation could have been suggested to the politicians of 1800 than the question whether New York would corrupt Virginia, or Virginia would check the prosperity of New York.

In deciding the issue of this struggle, as in every other issue that concerned the Union, the voice which spoke in most potent tones was that of Pennsylvania. This great State, considering its political importance, was treated with little respect by its neighbors; and yet had New England, New York, and Virginia been swept out of existence in 1800, democracy could have better spared them all than have lost Pennsylvania. The only true democratic community then existing in the eastern States, Pennsylvania was neither picturesque nor troublesome. The State contained no hierarchy like that of New England; no great families like those of New York; no oligarchy like the planters of Virginia and South Carolina. "In Pennsylvania," said Albert Gallatin, "not only we have neither Livingstons nor Rensselaers, but from the suburbs of Philadelphia to the banks of the Ohio I do not know a single family that has any extensive influence. An equal distribution of property has rendered every individual independent, and there is among us true and real equality." This was not all. The value of Pennsylvania to the Union lay not so much in the democratic spirit of society as in the rapidity with which it turned to national objects. Partly for this reason the State made an insignificant figure in politics. As the nation grew, less and less was said in Pennsylvania of interests distinct from those of the Union. Too thoroughly democratic to fear democracy, and too much nationalized to dread nationality, Pennsylvania became the ideal American State, easy, tolerant, and contented. If its soil bred little genius, it bred still less treason. With twenty different religious creeds, its practice could not be narrow, and a strong Quaker element made it humane. If the American Union succeeded, the good sense, liberality, and democratic spirit of Pennsylvania had a right to claim credit for the result; and Pennsylvanians could afford to leave power and patronage to their neighbors, so long as their own interests were to decide the path of administration.

The people showed little of that acuteness which prevailed to the eastward of the Hudson. Pennsylvania was never smart, yet rarely failed to gain her objects, and never committed serious follies. To politics the Pennsylvanians did not take kindly. Perhaps their democracy was so deep an instinct that they knew not what to do with political power when they gained it; as though political power were aristocratic in its nature, and democratic power a contradiction in terms. On this ground rested the reputation of Albert Gallatin, the only Pennsylvanian who made a mark on the surface of national politics. Gallatin's celebrated financial policy carried into practice the doctrine that the powers of government, being necessarily irresponsible, and therefore hostile to liberty, ought to be exercised only within the narrowest bounds, in order to leave democracy free to develop itself without interference in its true social, intellectual, and economical strength. Unlike Jefferson and the Virginians, Gallatin never hesitated to claim for government all the powers necessary for whatever object was in hand; but he agreed with them in checking the practical use of power, and this he did with a degree of rigor which has been often imitated but never equalled. The Pennsylvanians followed Gallatin's teachings. They indulged in endless factiousness over offices, but they never attempted to govern, and after one brief experience they never rebelled. Thus holding abstract politics at arm's length, they supported the national government with a sagacious sense that their own interests were those of the United States.

Although the State was held by the New Englanders and Virginians in no high repute for quickness of intellect, Philadelphia in 1800 was still the intellectual centre of the nation. For ten years the city had been the seat of national government, and at the close of that period had gathered a more agreeable society, fashionable, literary, and political, than could be found anywhere, except in a few capital cities of Europe. This Quaker city of an ultra-democratic State startled travellers used to luxury, by its extravagance and display. According to the Duc de Liancourt, writing in 1797, —

"The profusion and luxury of Philadelphia on great days, at the tables of the wealthy, in their equipages, and the dresses of their wives and daughters, are extreme. I have seen balls on the President's birthday where the splendor of the rooms and the variety and richness of the dresses did not suffer in comparison with Europe; and it must be acknowledged that the beauty of the American ladies has the advantage in the comparison. The young women of Philadelphia are accomplished in different degrees, but beauty is general with them. They want the ease and fashion of French women, but the brilliancy of their complexion is infinitely superior. Even when they grow old they are still handsome; and it would be no exaggeration to say, in the numerous assemblies of Philadelphia it is impossible to meet with what is called a plain woman. As to the young men, they for the most part seem to belong to another species."

For ten years Philadelphia had attracted nearly all the intelligence and cultivation that could be detached from their native stocks. Stagnation was impossible in this rapid current of men and ideas. The Philadelphia press showed the effect of such unusual movement. There Cobbett vociferated libels against democrats. His career was cut short by a blunder of his own; for he quitted the safe field of politics in order to libel the physicians, and although medical practice was not much better than when it had been satirized by Le Sage some eighty years before, the physicians had not become less sensitive. If ever medical practice deserved to be libelled, the bleeding which was the common treatment not only for fevers but for consumption, and even for old age, warranted all that could be said against it; but Cobbett found to his cost that the Pennsylvanians were glad to bleed, or at least to seize the opportunity for silencing the libeller. In 1800 he returned to England; but the style of political warfare in which he was so great a master was already established in the Philadelphia press. An Irish-American named Duane, who had been driven from England and India for expressing opinions too liberal for the time and place, came to Philadelphia and took charge of the opposition newspaper, the "Aurora," which became in his hands the most energetic and slanderous paper in America. In the small society of the time libels rankled, and Duane rivalled Cobbett in the boldness with which he slandered. Another point of resemblance existed between the two men. At a later stage in his career Duane, like Cobbett, disregarded friend as well as foe; he then attacked all who offended him, and denounced his party leaders as bitterly as he did his opponents; but down to the year 1800 he reserved his abuse for his enemies, and the "Aurora" was the nearest approach to a modern newspaper to be found in the country.

Judged by the accounts of his more reputable enemies, Duane seemed beneath forbearance; but his sins, gross as they were, found abettors in places where such conduct was less to be excused. He was a scurrilous libeller; but so was Cobbett; so was William Coleman, who in 1801 became editor of the New York "Evening Post" under the eye of Alexander Hamilton; so was the refined Joseph Dennie, who in the same year established at Philadelphia the "Portfolio," a weekly paper devoted to literature, in which for years to come he was to write literary essays, diversified by slander of Jefferson. Perhaps none of these habitual libellers deserved censure so much as Fisher Ames, the idol of respectability, who cheered on his party to vituperate his political opponents. He saw no harm in showing "the knaves," Jefferson and Gallatin, "the cold-thinking villains who lead, ' whose black blood runs temperately bad,' " the motives of "their own base hearts. . . . The vain, the timid, and trimming must be made by examples to see that scorn smites and blasts and withers like lightning the knaves that mislead them." Little difference could be seen between the two parties in their use of such weapons, except that democrats claimed a right to slander opponents because they were monarchists and aristocrats, while Federalists thought themselves bound to smite and wither with scorn those who, as a class, did not respect established customs.

Of American newspapers there was no end; but the education supposed to have been widely spread by eighteenth-century newspapers was hardly to be distinguished from ignorance. The student of history might search forever these storehouses of political calumny for facts meant to instruct the public in any useful object. A few dozen advertisements of shipping and sales; a marine list; rarely or never a price-list, unless it were European; copious extracts from English newspapers, and long columns of political disquisition,— such matter filled the chief city newspapers, from which the smaller sheets selected what their editors thought fit. Reporters and regular correspondents were unknown. Information of events other than political—the progress of the New York or Philadelphia water-works, of the Middlesex Canal, of Fitch's or Fulton's voyages, or even the commonest details of a Presidential inauguration—could rarely be found in the press. In such progress as newspapers had made Philadelphia took the lead, and in 1800 was at the height of her influence. Not until 1801 did the extreme Federalists set up the "Evening Post" under William Coleman, in New York, where at about the same time the Clinton interest put an English refugee named Cheetham in charge of their new paper, the "American Citizen and Watchtower," while Burr's friends established the "Morning Chronicle," edited by Dr. Peter Irving. Duane's importance was greatly reduced by this outburst of journalism in New York, and by the rise of the "National Intelligencer" at Washington, semi-official organ of Jefferson's administration. After the year 1800 the "Aurora" languished; but between 1795 and 1800 it was the leading newspaper of the United States, and boasted in 1802 of a circulation of four thousand copies, at least half of which its rivals declared to be imaginary.

Although Philadelphia was the literary as well as the political capital of America, nothing proved the existence of a highly intellectual society. When Joseph Dennie, a graduate of Harvard College, quitted Boston and established his "Portfolio" in Philadelphia in 1801, he complained as bitterly as the Pennsylvanian Cliffton against the land "where Genius sickens and where Fancy dies;" but he still thought Philadelphia more tolerable than any other city in the United States. With a little band of literary friends he passed his days in defying the indifference of his countrymen. "In the society of Mr. Dennie and his friends at Philadelphia I passed the few agreeable moments which my tour through the States afforded me," wrote in 1804 the British poet whom all the world united in calling by the familiar name of Tom Moore. "If I

did not hate as I ought the rabble to which they are opposed,
I could not value as I do the spirit with which they defy it;
and in learning from them what Americans *can be*, I but see
with the more indignation what Americans *are*."

"Yet, yet forgive me, O you sacred few,
   Whom late by Delaware's green banks I knew;
   Whom, known and loved, through many a social eve
   'T was bliss to live with, and 't was pain to leave.
   Oh, but for *such*, Columbia's days were done!
   Rank without ripeness, quickened without sun,
   Crude at the surface, rotten at the core,
   Her fruits would fall before her spring were o'er."

If Columbia's days were to depend on *"such,"* they were
scarcely worth prolonging, for Dennie's genius was but the
thin echo of an English classicism thin at its best. Yet Moore's
words had value, for they gave a lifelike idea of the "sacred
few" who sat with him, drinking deep, and reviling America
because she could not produce poets like Anacreon and artists
like Phidias, and still more because Americans cared little for
Addisonian essays. An adventurer called John Davis, who
published in London a book of American travels, mentioned
in it that he too met the Philadelphia authors. "Dennie passed
his mornings in the shop of Mr. Dickens, which I found the
rendezvous of the Philadelphia sons of literature,—Blair
[Linn], author of a poem called the 'Powers of Genius;' Ingersoll, known by a tragedy of which I forget the title; Stock,
celebrated for his dramatic criticisms." C. J. Ingersoll did in
fact print a tragedy called "Edwy and Elgiva," which was
acted in 1801, and John Blair Linn's "Powers of Genius" appeared in the same year; but Dennie's group boasted another
member more notable than these. Charles Brockden Brown,
the first American novelist of merit, was a Philadelphian.
Davis called upon Brown. "He occupied a dismal room in a
dismal street. I asked him whether a view of Nature would
not be more propitious to composition, or whether he should
not write with more facility were his window to command
the prospect of the Lake of Geneva. 'Sir,' said he, 'good pens,
thick paper, and ink well diluted would facilitate my compo-

sition more than the prospect of the broadest expanse of water or mountains rising against the clouds.' "

Pennsylvania was largely German and the Moravians were not without learning, yet no trace of German influence showed itself in the educated and literary class. Schiller was at the end of his career, and Goethe at the zenith of his powers; but neither was known in Pennsylvania, unless it might be by translations of the "Robbers" or the "Sorrows of Werther." As for deeper studies, search in America would be useless for what was rare or unknown either in England or France. Kant had closed and Hegel was beginning his labors; but the Western nations knew no more of German thought than of Egyptian hieroglyphics, and America had not yet reached the point of understanding that metaphysics apart from theology could exist at all. Locke was a college text-book, and possibly a few clergymen had learned to deride the idealism of Berkeley; but as an interest which concerned life, metaphysics, apart from Calvinism, had no existence in America, and was to have none for another generation. The literary labors of Americans followed easier paths, and such thought as prevailed was confined within a narrow field,—yet within this limit Pennsylvania had something to show, even though it failed to please the taste of Dennie and Moore.

Not far from the city of Philadelphia, on the banks of the Schuylkill, lived William Bartram, the naturalist, whose "Travels" through Florida and the Indian country, published in 1791, were once praised by Coleridge, and deserved reading both for the matter and the style. Not far from Bartram, and his best scholar, was Alexander Wilson, a Scotch poet of more than ordinary merit, gifted with a dogged enthusiasm, which in spite of obstacles gave to America an ornithology more creditable than anything yet accomplished in art or literature. Beyond the mountains, at Pittsburg, another author showed genuine and original qualities. American humor was not then so marked as it afterward became, and good-nature was rarer; but H. H. Brackenridge set an example of both in a book once universally popular throughout the South and West. A sort of prose "Hudibras," it had the merit of leaving no sting, for this satire on democracy was written by a democrat and published in the most democratic community of America.

"Modern Chivalry" told the adventures of a militia captain, who riding about the country with a raw Irish servant, found this red-headed, ignorant bog-trotter, this Sancho Panza, a much more popular person than himself, who could only with difficulty be restrained from becoming a clergyman, an Indian chief, a member of the legislature, of the philosophical society, and of Congress. At length his employer got for him the appointment of excise officer in the Alleghanies, and was gratified at seeing him tarred and feathered by his democratic friends. "Modern Chivalry" was not only written in good last-century English, none too refined for its subject, but was more thoroughly American than any book yet published, or to be published until the "Letters of Major Jack Downing" and the "Georgia Scenes" of forty years later. Never known, even by title, in Europe, and little enjoyed in the seaboard States, where bog-trotters and weavers had no such prominence, Judge Brackenridge's book filled the place of Don Quixote on the banks of the Ohio and along the Mississippi.

Another man whose literary merits were not to be overlooked, had drifted to Philadelphia because of its varied attractions. If in the last century America could boast of a poet who shared some of the delicacy if not the grandeur of genius, it was Philip Freneau; whose verses, poured out for the occasion, ran freely, good and bad, but the bad, as was natural, much more freely than the good. Freneau proved his merit by an experience unique in history. He was twice robbed by the greatest English poets of his day. Among his many slight verses were some pleasing lines called "The Indian Burying Ground": —

> "His bow for action ready bent,
>   And arrows with a head of stone,
>   Can only mean that life is spent,
>   And not the finer essence gone.
>
> "By midnight moons, o'er moistening dews,
>   In vestments for the chase arrayed,
>   The hunter still the deer pursues,
>   The hunter and the deer, — a shade."

The last line was taken by the British poet Campbell for his

own poem called "O'Connor's Child," and Freneau could afford to forgive the theft which thus called attention to the
simple grace of his melody; but although one such compliment might fall to the lot of a common man, only merit could
explain a second accident of the same kind. Freneau saw a
greater genius than Campbell borrow from his modest capital. No one complained of Walter Scott for taking whatever
he liked wherever he chose, to supply that flame of genius
which quickened the world; but Freneau had the right to
claim that Scott paid him the highest compliment one poet
could pay to another. In the Introduction to the third canto
of "Marmion" stood and still stands a line taken directly from
the verse in Freneau's poem on the Heroes of Eutaw:—

"They took the spear—but left the shield."

All these men—Wilson, Brackenridge, Freneau—were
democrats, and came not within the Federalist circle where
Moore could alone see a hope for Columbia; yet the names
of Federalists also survived in literature. Alexander Graydon's
pleasant Memoirs could never lose interest. Many lawyers,
clergymen, and physicians left lasting records. Dallas was
bringing out his reports; Duponceau was laboring over juris-
prudence and languages; William Lewis, William Rawle, and
Judge Wilson were high authorities at the bar; Dr. Wistar was
giving reputation to the Philadelphia Medical School, and the
famous Dr. Physic was beginning to attract patients from far
and near as the best surgeon in America. Gilbert Stuart, the
best painter in the country, came to Philadelphia, and there
painted portraits equal to the best that England or France
could produce,—for Reynolds and Gainsborough were dead,
and Sir Thomas Lawrence ruled the fashion of the time. If
Franklin and Rittenhouse no longer lived to give scientific
fame to Philadelphia, their liberal and scientific spirit survived. The reputation of the city was not confined to America, and the accident that made a Philadelphian, Benjamin
West, President of the Royal Academy in succession to Sir
Joshua Reynolds, was a tacit compliment, not undeserved, to
the character of the American metropolis.
There manners were milder and more humane than else-

where. Societies existed for lessening the hardships of the unfortunate. A society labored for the abolition of slavery
without exciting popular passion, although New York contained more than twenty thousand slaves, and New Jersey
more than twelve thousand. A society for alleviating the miseries of prisons watched the progress of experiments in the
model jail, which stood alone of its kind in America. Elsewhere the treatment of criminals was such as it had ever been.
In Connecticut they were still confined under-ground, in the
shafts of an abandoned copper-mine. The Memoirs of Stephen Burroughs gave some idea of the prisons and prison
discipline of Massachusetts. The Pennsylvania Hospital was
also a model, for it contained a department for the insane, the
only one of the sort in America except the Virginia Lunatic
Asylum at Williamsburg. Even there the treatment of these
beings, whom a later instinct of humanity thought peculiarly
worthy of care and lavish expenditure, was harsh enough,—
strait-jackets, whippings, chains, and dark-rooms being a part
of the prescribed treatment in every such hospital in the
world; but where no hospitals existed, as in New England,
New York, and elsewhere, the treatment was apt to be far
worse. No horror of the Middle Ages wrung the modern conscience with a sense of disgust more acute than was felt in
remembering the treatment of the insane even within recent
times. Shut in attics or cellars, or in cages outside a house,
without warmth, light, or care, they lived in filth, with nourishment such as was thrown to dogs. Philadelphia led the way
in humanitarian efforts which relieved man from incessant
contact with these cruel and coarsening associations.

The depth of gratitude due to Pennsylvania as the model
democratic society of the world was so great as to risk over-
estimating what had been actually done. As yet no common-
school system existed. Academies and colleges were indifferent. New Jersey was no better provided than Pennsylvania.
The Englishman Weld, a keen if not a friendly critic, visited
Princeton,—

> "A large college," he said, "held in much repute by the
> neighboring States. The number of students amounts to
> upwards of seventy; from their appearance, however, and

the course of studies they seem to be engaged in, like all the other American colleges I ever saw, it better deserves the title of a grammar-school than of a college. The library which we were shown is most wretched, consisting for the most part of old theological books not even arranged with any regularity. An orrery contrived by Mr. Rittenhouse stands at one end of the apartment, but it is quite out of repair, as well as a few detached parts of a philosophical apparatus enclosed in the same glass-case. At the opposite end of the room are two small cupboards which are shown as the museum. These contain a couple of small stuffed alligators and a few singular fishes in a miserable state of preservation, from their being repeatedly tossed about."

Philadelphia made no claim to a wide range of intellectual interests. As late as 1811, Latrobe, by education an architect and by genius an artist, wrote to Volney in France,—

"Thinking only of the profession and of the affluence which it yields in Europe to all who follow it, you forget that I am an engineer in America; that I am neither a mechanic nor a merchant, nor a planter of cotton, rice, or tobacco. You forget—for you know it as well as I do—that with us the labor of the hand has precedence over that of the mind; that an engineer is considered only as an overseer of men who dig, and an architect as one that watches others who hew stone or wood."

The labor of the hand had precedence over that of the mind throughout the United States. If this was true in the city of Franklin, Rittenhouse, and West, the traveller who wandered farther toward the south felt still more strongly the want of intellectual variety, and found more cause for complaint.

Chapter V

BETWEEN Pennsylvania and Virginia stretched no barrier of mountains or deserts. Nature seemed to mean that the northern State should reach toward the Chesapeake, and embrace its wide system of coasts and rivers. The Susquehanna, crossing Pennsylvania from north to south, rolled down wealth which in a few years built the city of Baltimore by the surplus of Pennsylvania's resources. Any part of Chesapeake Bay, or of the streams which flowed into it, was more easily accessible to Baltimore than any part of Massachusetts or Pennsylvania to New York. Every geographical reason argued that the Susquehanna, the Potomac, and the James should support one homogeneous people; yet the intellectual difference between Pennsylvania and Virginia was already more sharply marked than that between New England and the Middle States.

The old Virginia society was still erect, priding itself on its resemblance to the society of England, which had produced Hampden and Chatham. The Virginia gentleman, wherever met, was a country gentleman or a lawyer among a society of planters. The absence of city life was the sharpest characteristic of Virginia, even compared with South Carolina. In the best and greatest of Virginians, the virtues which always stood in most prominence were those of the field and farm, — the simple and straightforward mind, the notions of courage and truth, the absence of mercantile sharpness and quickness, the rusticity and open-handed hospitality, which could exist only where the struggle for life was hardly a struggle at all. No visitor could resist the charm of kindly sympathy which softened the asperities of Virginian ambition. Whether young Albert Gallatin went there, hesitating between Europe and America, or the still younger William Ellery Channing, with all New England on his active conscience, the effect was the same: —

"I blush for my own people," wrote Channing from Richmond in 1799, " when I compare the selfish prudence of a Yankee with the generous confidence of a Virginian.

Here I find great vices, but greater virtues than I left behind me. There is one single trait which attaches me to the
people I live with more than all the virtues of New England,—they *love money less* than we do; they are more dis-
interested; their patriotism is not tied to their purse-strings.
Could I only take from the Virginians their sensuality and
their slaves, I should think them the greatest people in the
world. As it is, with a few great virtues, they have innumerable vices."

Even forty years afterward, so typical a New Englander as the
poet Bryant acknowledged that " whatever may be the comparison in other respects, the South certainly has the advantage over us in point of manners." Manners were not all their
charm; for the Virginians at the close of the eighteenth century were inferior to no class of Americans in the sort of education then supposed to make refinement. The Duc de
Liancourt bore witness:—

"In spite of the Virginian love for dissipation, the taste
for reading is commoner there among men of the first class
than in any other part of America; but the populace is perhaps more ignorant there than elsewhere."

Those whom Liancourt called "men of the first class" were
equal to any standard of excellence known to history. Their
range was narrow, but within it they were supreme. The traditions of high breeding were still maintained, and a small
England, much as it existed in the time of the Commonwealth, was perpetuated in the Virginia of 1800. Social position was a birthright, not merely of the well born, but of the
highly gifted. Nearly all the great lawyers of Virginia were of
the same social stock as in New England,—poor and gifted
men, welcomed into a landed aristocracy simple in tastes and
genial in temper. Chief-Justice Marshall was such a man, commanding respect and regard wherever he was seen,—perhaps
most of all from New Englanders, who were least familiar
with the type. George Mason was an ideal republican,—a
character as strong in its way as Washington or Marshall.
George Wythe the Chancellor stood in the same universal esteem; and even his young clerk Henry Clay, "the mill-boy of

the slashes," who had lately left Chancellor Wythe's office to set up one of his own at Lexington in Kentucky, inherited that Virginia geniality which, as it ripened with his years, made him an idol among Northern and Western multitudes who knew neither the source nor secret of his charm. Law and politics were the only objects of Virginian thought; but within these bounds the Virginians achieved triumphs. What could America offer in legal literature that rivalled the judicial opinions of Chief-Justice Marshall? What political essay equalled the severe beauty of George Mason's Virginia Bill of Rights? What single production of an American pen reached the fame of Thomas Jefferson's Declaration of Independence? "The Virginians are the best orators I ever heard," wrote the young Channing; although Patrick Henry, the greatest of them all, was no longer alive.

Every one admitted that Virginia society was ill at ease. In colonial days it rested on a few great props, the strongest being its close connection with England; and after this had been cut away by the Revolutionary War, primogeniture, the Church, exemption of land from seizure for debt, and negro slavery remained to support the oligarchy of planters. The momentum given by the Declaration of Independence enabled Jefferson and George Wythe to sweep primogeniture from the statute book. After an interval of several years, Madison carried the law which severed Church from State. There the movement ended. All the great Virginians would gladly have gone on, but the current began to flow against them. They suggested a bill for emancipation, but could find no one to father it in the legislature, and they shrank from the storm it would excite.

President Washington, in 1796, in a letter already quoted, admitted that land in Virginia was lower in price than land of the same quality in Pennsylvania. For this inferiority he suggested, among other reasons, the explanation that Pennsylvania had made laws for the gradual abolition of slavery, and he declared nothing more certain than that Virginia must adopt similar laws at a period not remote. Had the Virginians seen a sure prospect that such a step would improve their situation, they would probably have taken it; but the slave-owners were little pleased at the results of reforms already effected, and they were in no humor for abolishing more of their old institutions. The effects of disestablishing the Church were calculated to disgust them with all reform. From early times the colony had been divided into parishes, and each parish owned a church building. The system was the counterpart of that established in New England. The church lands, glebes, and endowments were administered by the clergyman, wardens, and vestry. Good society in Virginia recognized no other religion than was taught in this branch of English episcopacy. "Sure I am of one thing," was the remark in the Virginia legislature of an old-fashioned Federalist, with powdered hair, three-cornered hat, long queue, and white top-boots,—"Sure I am of one thing, that no *gentleman* would choose any road to heaven but the Episcopal." Every plantation was attached to a parish, and the earliest associations of every well-bred man and woman in Virginia were connected with the Church service. In spite of all this, no sooner had Madison and his friends taken away the support of the State than the Church perished. They argued that freedom of religion worked well in Pennsylvania, and therefore must succeed in Virginia; but they were wrong. The Virginia gentry stood by and saw their churches closed, the roofs rot, the aisles and pews become a refuge for sheep and foxes, the tombstones of their ancestry built into strange walls or turned into flagging to be worn by the feet of slaves. By the year 1800, Bishop Madison found his diocese left so nearly bare of clergy and communicants that after a few feeble efforts to revive interest he abandoned the struggle, and contented himself with the humbler task of educating boys at the ancient College of William and Mary in the deserted colonial capital of Williamsburg. There the English traveller Weld visited him about the year 1797, and gave a curious picture of his establishment:—

"The Bishop," he said, "is president of the college, and has apartments in the buildings. Half-a-dozen or more of the students, the eldest about twelve years old, dined at his table one day that I was there. Some were without shoes or stockings, others without coats. During dinner they constantly rose to help themselves at the sideboard. A couple of dishes of salted meat and some oyster-soup formed the whole of the dinner."

Such a state of society was picturesque, but not encouraging. An aristocracy so lacking in energy and self-confidence was a mere shell, to be crushed, as one might think, by a single vigorous blow. Nevertheless, Jefferson and Madison, after striking it again and again with the full force of Revolutionary violence, were obliged to desist, and turned their reforming axes against the Church and hierarchy of New England. There they could do nothing but good, for the society of New England was sound, whatever became of the Church or of slavery; but in Virginia the gap which divided gentry from populace was enormous; and another gap, which seemed impassable, divided the populace from the slaves. Jefferson's reforms crippled and impoverished the gentry, but did little for the people, and for the slaves nothing.

Nowhere in America existed better human material than in the middle and lower classes of Virginians. As explorers, adventurers, fighters,—wherever courage, activity, and force were wanted,—they had no equals; but they had never known discipline, and were beyond measure jealous of restraint. With all their natural virtues and indefinite capacities for good, they were rough and uneducated to a degree that shocked their own native leaders. Jefferson tried in vain to persuade them that they needed schools. Their character was stereotyped, and development impossible; for even Jefferson, with all his liberality of ideas, was Virginian enough to discourage the introduction of manufactures and the gathering of masses in cities, without which no new life could grow. Among the common people, intellectual activity was confined to hereditary commonplaces of politics, resting on the axiom that Virginia was the typical society of a future Arcadian America. To escape the tyranny of Cæsar by perpetuating the simple and isolated lives of their fathers was the sum of their political philosophy; to fix upon the national government the stamp of their own idyllic conservatism was the height of their ambition.

Debarred from manufactures, possessed of no shipping, and enjoying no domestic market, Virginian energies necessarily knew no other resource than agriculture. Without church, university, schools, or literature in any form that required or fostered intellectual life, the Virginians concentrated their thoughts almost exclusively upon politics; and this concentration produced a result so distinct and lasting, and in character so respectable, that American history would lose no small part of its interest in losing the Virginia school.

No one denied that Virginia, like Massachusetts, in the War of Independence, believed herself competent to follow independently of other provinces whatever path seemed good. The Constitution of Virginia did not, like that of Massachusetts, authorize the governor to "be the commander-in-chief of the army and navy," in order "to take and surprise, by all ways and means whatsoever, all and every such person or persons (with their ships, arms, ammunition, and other goods) as shall in a hostile manner invade or attempt the invading, conquering, or annoying this Commonwealth;" but although Massachusetts expressed the power in language more detailed, Virginia held to its essence with equal tenacity. When experience showed the necessity of "creating a more perfect union," none of the great States were unanimous for the change. Massachusetts and New York were with difficulty induced to accept the Constitution of 1787. Their final assent was wrung from them by the influence of the cities and of the commercial class; but Virginia contained no cities and few merchants. The majority by which the State Convention of Virginia, after an obstinate contest, adopted the Constitution, was influenced by pure patriotism as far as any political influence could be called pure; but the popular majority was probably hostile to the Constitution, and certainly remained hostile to the exercise of its powers. From the first the State took an attitude of opposition to the national government, which became more and more decided, until in 1798 it found expression in a formal announcement, through the legislature and governor, that the limit of further obedience was at hand. The General Assembly adopted Resolutions promising support to the government of the United States in all measures warranted by the Constitution, but declaring the powers of the federal government "no further valid than they are authorized by the grants enumerated in that compact; and that in case of a deliberate, palpable, and dangerous exercise of other powers, not granted by said compact, the States who are parties thereto have the right, and are in duty bound, to interpose, for arresting the progress of the evil and for maintaining within their respective limits the authorities, rights, and liberties appertaining to them."

Acting immediately on this view, the General Assembly did interpose by declaring certain laws, known as the Alien and Sedition Laws, unconstitutional, and by inviting the other States to concur, in confidence "that the necessary and proper measures will be taken by each for co-operating with this State in maintaining unimpaired the authorities, rights, and liberties reserved to the States respectively or to the people."

These Virginia Resolutions, which were drawn by Madison, seemed strong enough to meet any possible aggression from the national government; but Jefferson, as though not quite satisfied with these, recommended the Kentucky legislature to adopt still stronger. The draft of the Kentucky Resolutions, whether originally composed or only approved by him, representing certainly his own convictions, declared that " where powers are assumed which have not been delegated a nullification of the Act is the rightful remedy," and "that every State has a natural right, in cases not within the compact, to nullify of their own authority all assumptions of power by others within their limits." Jefferson did not doubt "that the co-States, recurring to their natural right in cases not made federal, will concur in declaring these acts void and of no force, and will each take measures of its own for providing that neither these acts, nor any others of the federal government not plainly and intentionally authorized by the Constitution, shall be exercised within their respective territories."

In the history of Virginia thought, the personal opinions of Jefferson and Madison were more interesting, if not more important, than the official opinion of State legislatures. Kentucky shrank from using language which seemed unnecessarily violent, but still declared, with all the emphasis needed, that the national government was not "the exclusive or final judge of the extent of the powers delegated to itself, since that would have made its discretion, and not the Constitution, the measure of its powers," but that each party had an equal right to judge for itself as to an infraction of the compact, and the proper redress; that in the case of the Alien and Sedition Laws the compact had been infringed, and that these Acts, being unconstitutional and therefore void, "may tend to drive these States into revolution and blood;" finally, the State of Kentucky called for an expression of sentiment from other States, like Virginia not doubting "that the co-States, recurring to their natural right in cases not made federal, will concur in declaring these Acts void and of no force."

These famous Resolutions of Virginia and Kentucky, historically the most interesting of all the intellectual products of the Virginia school, were adopted in 1798 and 1799. In 1800, Jefferson their chief author was chosen President of the United States, and Madison became his Secretary of State. Much discussion then and afterward arose over the Constitutional theory laid down by Virginia and Kentucky, and thus apparently adopted by the Union; but in such cases of disputed powers that theory was soundest which was backed by the strongest force, for the sanction of force was the most necessary part of law. The United States government was at that time powerless to enforce its theories; while, on the other hand, Virginia had all the power necessary for the object desired. The Republican leaders believed that the State was at liberty to withdraw from the Union if it should think that an infraction of the Constitution had taken place; and Jefferson in 1798 preferred to go on by way of Resolution rather than by way of Secession, not because of any doubt as to the right, but because, "if we now reduce our Union to Virginia and North Carolina, immediately the conflict will be established between those two States, and they will end by breaking into their simple units." In other letters he explained that the Kentucky Resolutions were intended "to leave the matter in such a train as that we may not be committed absolutely to push the matter to extremities, and yet may be free to push as far as events will render prudent." Union was a question of expediency, not of obligation. This was the conviction of the true Virginia school, and of Jefferson's opponents as well as his supporters; of Patrick Henry, as well as John Taylor of Caroline and John Randolph of Roanoke.

The Virginia and Kentucky Resolutions, giving form to ideas that had not till then been so well expressed, left a permanent mark in history, and fixed for an indefinite time the direction and bounds of Virginia politics; but if New England could go no further in the lines of thought pursued by Fisher Ames and Timothy Dwight, Virginia could certainly expect no better results from those defined by Jefferson and Madison. The science of politics, if limited by the Resolutions of Virginia and Kentucky, must degenerate into an enumeration of powers reserved from exercise. Thought could find little room for free development where it confined its action to narrowing its own field.

This tendency of the Virginia school was the more remarkable because it seemed little suited to the tastes and instincts of the two men who gave it expression and guided its course. By common consent Thomas Jefferson was its intellectual leader. According to the admitted standards of greatness, Jefferson was a great man. After all deductions on which his enemies might choose to insist, his character could not be denied elevation, versatility, breadth, insight, and delicacy; but neither as a politician nor as a political philosopher did he seem at ease in the atmosphere which surrounded him. As a leader of democracy he appeared singularly out of place. As reserved as President Washington in the face of popular familiarities, he never showed himself in crowds. During the last thirty years of his life he was not seen in a Northern city, even during his Presidency; nor indeed was he seen at all except on horseback, or by his friends and visitors in his own house. With manners apparently popular and informal, he led a life of his own, and allowed few persons to share it. His tastes were for that day excessively refined. His instincts were those of a liberal European nobleman, like the Duc de Liancourt, and he built for himself at Monticello a château above contact with man. The rawness of political life was an incessant torture to him, and personal attacks made him keenly unhappy. His true delight was in an intellectual life of science and art. To read, write, speculate in new lines of thought, to keep abreast of the intellect of Europe, and to feed upon Homer and Horace, were pleasures more to his mind than any to be found in a public assembly. He had some knowledge of mathematics, and a little acquaintance with classical art; but he fairly revelled in what he believed to be beautiful, and his writings often betrayed subtile feeling for artistic form,—a sure mark of intellectual sensuousness. He shrank from whatever was rough or coarse, and his yearning for sympathy was almost feminine. That such a man should have ventured upon the stormy ocean of politics was surprising, the more because he was no orator, and owed nothing to any magnetic influence of voice or person. Never effective in debate, for seventeen years before his Presidency he had not appeared in a legislative body except in the chair of the Senate. He felt a nervous horror for the contentiousness of such assemblies, and even among his own friends he sometimes abandoned for the moment his strongest convictions rather than support them by an effort of authority.

If Jefferson appeared ill at ease in the position of a popular leader, he seemed equally awkward in the intellectual restraints of his own political principles. His mind shared little in common with the provincialism on which the Virginia and Kentucky Resolutions were founded. His instincts led him to widen rather than to narrow the bounds of every intellectual exercise; and if vested with political authority, he could no more resist the temptation to stretch his powers than he could abstain from using his mind on any subject merely because he might be drawn upon ground supposed to be dangerous. He was a deist, believing that men could manage their own salvation without the help of a state church. Prone to innovation, he sometimes generalized without careful analysis. He was a theorist, prepared to risk the fate of mankind on the chance of reasoning far from certain in its details. His temperament was sunny and sanguine, and the atrabilious philosophy of New England was intolerable to him. He was curiously vulnerable, for he seldom wrote a page without exposing himself to attack. He was superficial in his knowledge, and a martyr to the disease of omniscience. Ridicule of his opinions and of himself was an easy task, in which his Federalist opponents delighted, for his English was often confused, his assertions inaccurate, and at times of excitement he was apt to talk with indiscretion; while with all his extraordinary versatility of character and opinions, he seemed during his entire life to breathe with perfect satisfaction nowhere except in the liberal, literary, and scientific air of Paris in 1789.

Jefferson aspired beyond the ambition of a nationality, and embraced in his view the whole future of man. That the United States should become a nation like France, England, or Russia, should conquer the world like Rome, or develop a typical race like the Chinese, was no part of his scheme. He wished to begin a new era. Hoping for a time when the world's ruling interests should cease to be local and should become universal; when questions of boundary and nationality should become insignificant; when armies and navies should be reduced to the work of police, and politics should consist only in non-intervention,—he set himself to the task of governing, with this golden age in view. Few men have dared to legislate as though eternal peace were at hand, in a world torn by wars and convulsions and drowned in blood; but this was what Jefferson aspired to do. Even in such dangers, he believed that Americans might safely set an example which the Christian world should be led by interest to respect and at length to imitate. As he conceived a true American policy, war was a blunder, an unnecessary risk; and even in case of robbery and aggression the United States, he believed, had only to stand on the defensive in order to obtain justice in the end. He would not consent to build up a new nationality merely to create more navies and armies, to perpetuate the crimes and follies of Europe; the central government at Washington should not be permitted to indulge in the miserable ambitions that had made the Old World a hell, and frustrated the hopes of humanity.

With these humanitarian ideas which passed beyond the bounds of nationality, Jefferson held other views which seemed narrower than ordinary provincialism. Cities, manufactures, mines, shipping, and accumulation of capital led, in his opinion, to corruption and tyranny.

"Generally speaking," said he, in his only elaborate work, the Notes on Virginia, "the proportion which the aggregate of the other classes of citizens bears in any State to that of its husbandmen is the proportion of its unsound to its healthy parts, and is a good enough barometer whereby to measure its degree of corruption. . . . Those who labor in the earth are the chosen people of God if ever he had a chosen people, whose breasts he has made his peculiar deposit for substantial and genuine virtue."

This doctrine was not original with Jefferson, but its application to national affairs on a great scale was something new in the world, and the theory itself clashed with his intellectual instincts of liberality and innovation.

A school of political thought, starting with postulates like these, was an interesting study, and would have been more interesting had Jefferson's friends undertaken to develop his ideas in the extent he held them. Perhaps this was impossible. At all events, Madison, although author of the Virginia Resolutions, showed little earnestness in carrying out their principles either as a political or as a literary task; and John Taylor of Caroline, the only consistent representative of the school, began his writings only when political power had established precedents inconsistent with their object.

With such simple conceptions as their experience gave them in politics, law, and agriculture, the Virginians appeared to be satisfied; and whether satisfied or not, they were for the time helpless to produce other literature, science, or art. From the three States lying farther south, no greater intellectual variety could be expected. In some respects North Carolina, though modest in ambition and backward in thought, was still the healthiest community south of the Potomac. Neither aristocratic like Virginia and South Carolina, nor turbulent like Georgia, nor troubled by a sense of social importance, but above all thoroughly democratic, North Carolina tolerated more freedom of political action and showed less family and social influence, fewer vested rights in political power, and less tyranny of slaveholding interests and terrors than were common elsewhere in the South. Neither cultivated nor brilliant in intellect, nor great in thought, industry, energy, or organization, North Carolina was still interesting and respectable. The best qualities of the State were typified in its favorite representative, Nathaniel Macon.

The small society of rice and cotton planters at Charleston, with their cultivated tastes and hospitable habits, delighted in whatever reminded them of European civilization. They were travellers, readers, and scholars; the society of Charleston compared well in refinement with that of any city of its size in the world, and English visitors long thought it the most agreeable in America. In the southern wilderness which stretched from the Appomattox to the St. Mary's, Charleston was the only oasis. The South Carolinians were ambitious for other distinctions than those which could be earned at the bar or on the plantation. From there Washington Allston went to study at Harvard College, and after taking his degree in the same class with young Buckminster, sailed in the same year, 1800, for Europe with his friend Malbone, to learn to express in color and form the grace and dignity of his imagination. In South Carolina were felt the instincts of city life. During two or three weeks of the winter, the succession of dinners, balls, and races at Charleston rivalled the gayety of Philadelphia itself; and although the city was dull during the rest of the year, it was not deserted even in the heat of summer, for the sea-breeze made it a watering-place, like Boston, and the deadly fevers sure to kill the white man who should pass a night on one bank of the Ashley River were almost unknown on the other. In the summer, therefore, the residents remained or returned; the children got their schooling, and business continued. For this reason South Carolina knew less of the country hospitality which made Virginia famous; city life had the larger share in existence, although in the hot weather torpor and languor took the place of gayety. In certain respects Charleston was more Northern in habits than any town of the North. In other warm countries, the summer evening was commonly the moment when life was best worth living; music, love-making, laughter, and talk turned night into day; but Charleston was Puritanic in discipline. Every night at ten o'clock the slamming of window-blinds and locking of doors warned strangers and visitors to go not only to their houses, but to their beds. The citizens looked with contempt on the gayety of Spanish or Italian temper. Beneath all other thoughts, the care of the huge slave population remained constant. The streets were abandoned at an early hour to the patrol, and no New England village was more silent.

Confident as the Carolinian was in the strength of the

slave-system, and careless as he seemed and thought himself to be on that account, the recent fate of St. Domingo gave him cause for constant anxiety; but even without anxiety, he would have been grave. The gentry of the lower country belonged to the same English class which produced the gentry of Virginia and Massachusetts. The austerity of the Puritan may have been an exaggerated trait, but among the Middletons, Pinckneys, Rutledges, and Lowndeses the seriousness of the original English stock was also not without effect in the habit of their minds. They showed it in their treatment of the slave-system, but equally in their churches and houses, their occupations and prejudices, their races and sports, the character of their entertainments, the books they read, and the talk at their tables. No gentleman belonged to any church but the Anglican, or connected himself with trade. No court departed from the practice and precedents of English law, however anomalous they might be. Before the Revolution large numbers of young men had been educated in England, and their influence was still strong in the society of Charleston. The younger generation inherited similar tastes. Of this class the best-known name which will appear in this narrative was that of William Lowndes; and no better example could be offered of the serious temper which marked Carolinian thought, than was given by the career of this refined and highly educated gentleman, almost the last of his school.

Charleston was more cosmopolitan than any part of Virginia, and enjoyed also a certain literary reputation on account of David Ramsay, whose works were widely read; and of Governor Drayton, whose "Letters written during a Tour through the Northern and Eastern States," and "View of South Carolina," gave an idea of the author as well as of the countries he described. Charleston also possessed a library of three or four thousand well-selected books, and maintained a well-managed theatre. The churches were almost as strictly attended as those in Boston. The fashionable wine-party was even more common, and perhaps the guests took pride in drinking deeper than they would have been required to do in New York or Philadelphia.

Politics had not mastered the thought of South Carolina so completely as that of Virginia, and the natural instincts of

Carolinian society should have led the gentry to make common cause with the gentry of New England and the Middle States against democratic innovations. The conservative side in politics seemed to be that which no Carolinian gentleman could fail to support. The oligarchy of South Carolina, in defiance of democratic principles, held the political power of the State, and its interests could never harmonize with those of a theoretic democracy, or safely consent to trust the national government in the hands of Jefferson and his friends, who had founded their power by breaking down in Virginia an oligarchy closely resembling that of the Carolinian rice-planters. Yet in 1800 enough of these gentlemen, under the lead of Charles Pinckney, deserted their Northern friends, to secure the defeat of the Federalist candidates, and to elect Jefferson as President. For this action, no satisfactory reason was ever given. Of all States in the Union, South Carolina, under its actual system of politics, was the last which could be suspected of democratic tendencies.

Such want of consistency seemed to show some peculiarity of character. Not every educated and privileged class has sacrificed itself to a social sentiment, least of all without understanding its object. The eccentricity was complicated by another peculiar element of society. In South Carolina the interesting union between English tastes and provincial prejudices, which characterized the wealthy planters of the coast, was made more striking by contrast with the character of the poor and hardy yeomanry of the upper country. The seriousness of Charleston society changed to severity in the mountains. Rude, ignorant, and in some of its habits half barbarous, this population, in the stiffness of its religious and social expression, resembled the New England of a century before rather than the liberality of the Union. Largely settled by Scotch and Irish emigrants, with the rigid Presbyterian doctrine and conservatism of their class, they were democratic in practice beyond all American democrats, and were more conservative in thought than the most aristocratic Europeans. Though sharply divided both socially and by interest from the sea-coast planters, these up-country farmers had one intellectual sympathy with their fellow-citizens in Charleston,—a sympathy resting on their common dislike for change, on the

serious element which lay at the root of their common characters; and this marriage of two widely divergent minds produced one of the most extraordinary statesmen of America.
In the year 1800 John Caldwell Calhoun, a boy of eighteen,
went from the upper country to his brother-in-law's academy
in Georgia. Grown nearly to manhood without contact with
the world, his modes of thought were those of a Connecticut
Calvinist; his mind was cold, stern, and metaphysical; but he
had the energy and ambition of youth, the political fervor of
Jeffersonian democracy, and little sympathy with slavery or
slave-owners. At this early age he, like many other Republicans, looked on slavery as a "scaffolding," to be taken down
when the building should be complete. A radical democrat,
less liberal, less cultivated, and much less genial than Jefferson, Calhoun was the true heir to his intellectual succession;
stronger in logic, bolder in action. Upon him was to fall the
duty of attempting to find for Carolina an escape from the
logical conclusions of those democratic principles which Jefferson in 1800 claimed for his own, but which in the full
swing of his power, and to the last day of his life, he shrank
from pressing to their results.

Viewed from every side by which it could be approached,
the society of South Carolina, more than that of any other
portion of the Union, seemed to bristle with contradictions.
The elements of intellectual life existed without a sufficient
intellectual atmosphere. Society, colonial by origin and dependent by the conditions of its existence, was striving to exist without external support. Whether it would stand or fall,
and whether, either standing or falling, it could contribute
any new element to American thought, were riddles which,
with so many others, American history was to answer.

Chapter VI

NEARLY EVERY foreign traveller who visited the United States during these early years, carried away an impression sober if not sad. A thousand miles of desolate and dreary forest, broken here and there by settlements; along the seacoast a few flourishing towns devoted to commerce; no arts, a provincial literature, a cancerous disease of negro slavery, and differences of political theory fortified within geographical lines,—what could be hoped for such a country except to repeat the story of violence and brutality which the world already knew by heart, until repetition for thousands of years had wearied and sickened mankind? Ages must probably pass before the interior could be thoroughly settled; even Jefferson, usually a sanguine man, talked of a thousand years with acquiescence, and in his first Inaugural Address, at a time when the Mississippi River formed the Western boundary, spoke of the country as having "room enough for our descendants to the hundredth and thousandth generation." No prudent person dared to act on the certainty that when settled, one government could comprehend the whole; and when the day of separation should arrive, and America should have her Prussia, Austria, and Italy, as she already had her England, France, and Spain, what else could follow but a return to the old conditions of local jealousies, wars, and corruption which had made a slaughter-house of Europe?

The mass of Americans were sanguine and self-confident, partly by temperament, but partly also by reason of ignorance; for they knew little of the difficulties which surrounded a complex society. The Duc de Liancourt, like many critics, was struck by this trait. Among other instances, he met with one in the person of a Pennsylvania miller, Thomas Lea, "a sound American patriot, persuading himself that nothing good is done, and that no one has any brains, except in America; that the wit, the imagination, the genius of Europe are already in decrepitude;" and the duke added: "This error is to be found in almost all Americans,—legislators, administrators, as well as millers, and is less innocent there." In the year 1796 the House of Representatives debated whether to insert

in the Reply to the President's Speech a passing remark that
the nation was "the freest and most enlightened in the
world,"—a nation as yet in swaddling-clothes, which had neither literature, arts, sciences, nor history; nor even enough
nationality to be sure that it was a nation. The moment was
peculiarly ill-chosen for such a claim, because Europe was on
the verge of an outburst of genius. Goethe and Schiller, Mo-
zart and Haydn, Kant and Fichte, Cavendish and Herschel
were making way for Walter Scott, Wordsworth, and Shelley,
Heine and Balzac, Beethoven and Hegel, Oersted and Cuvier,
great physicists, biologists, geologists, chemists, mathemati-
cians, metaphysicians, and historians by the score. Turner was
painting his earliest landscapes, and Watt completing his latest
steam-engine; Napoleon was taking command of the French
armies, and Nelson of the English fleets; investigators, reformers, scholars, and philosophers swarmed, and the influence of enlightenment, even amid universal war, was working
with an energy such as the world had never before conceived.
The idea that Europe was in her decrepitude proved only ignorance and want of enlightenment, if not of freedom, on the
part of Americans, who could only excuse their error by
pleading that notwithstanding these objections, in matters
which for the moment most concerned themselves Europe
was a full century behind America. If they were right in thinking that the next necessity of human progress was to lift the
average man upon an intellectual and social level with the
most favored, they stood at least three generations nearer
than Europe to their common goal. The destinies of the
United States were certainly staked, without reserve or escape,
on the soundness of this doubtful and even improbable principle, ignoring or overthrowing the institutions of church, aristocracy, family, army, and political intervention, which long
experience had shown to be needed for the safety of society.
Europe might be right in thinking that without such safe-
guards society must come to an end; but even Europeans
must concede that there was a chance, if no greater than one
in a thousand, that America might, at least for a time, succeed. If this stake of temporal and eternal welfare stood on
the winning card; if man actually should become more virtuous and enlightened, by mere process of growth, without

church or paternal authority; if the average human being could accustom himself to reason with the logical processes of Descartes and Newton!—what then?

Then, no one could deny that the United States would win a stake such as defied mathematics. With all the advantages of science and capital, Europe must be slower than America to reach the common goal. American society might be both sober and sad, but except for negro slavery it was sound and healthy in every part. Stripped for the hardest work, every muscle firm and elastic, every ounce of brain ready for use, and not a trace of superfluous flesh on his nervous and supple body, the American stood in the world a new order of man. From Maine to Florida, society was in this respect the same, and was so organized as to use its human forces with more economy than could be approached by any society of the world elsewhere. Not only were artificial barriers carefully removed, but every influence that could appeal to ordinary ambition was applied. No brain or appetite active enough to be conscious of stimulants could fail to answer the intense incentive. Few human beings, however sluggish, could long resist the temptation to acquire power; and the elements of power were to be had in America almost for the asking. Reversing the old-world system, the American stimulant increased in energy as it reached the lowest and most ignorant class, dragging and whirling them upward as in the blast of a furnace. The penniless and homeless Scotch or Irish immigrant was caught and consumed by it; for every stroke of the axe and the hoe made him a capitalist, and made gentlemen of his children. Wealth was the strongest agent for moving the mass of mankind; but political power was hardly less tempting to the more intelligent and better-educated swarms of American-born citizens, and the instinct of activity, once created, seemed heritable and permanent in the race.

Compared with this lithe young figure, Europe was actually in decrepitude. Mere class distinctions, the *patois* or dialect of the peasantry, the fixity of residence, the local costumes and habits marking a history that lost itself in the renewal of identical generations, raised from birth barriers which paralyzed half the population. Upon this mass of inert matter rested the Church and the State, holding down activity of thought.

Endless wars withdrew many hundred thousand men from production, and changed them into agents of waste; huge debts, the evidence of past wars and bad government, created interests to support the system and fix its burdens on the laboring class; courts, with habits of extravagance that shamed common-sense, helped to consume private economies. All this might have been borne; but behind this stood aristocracies, sucking their nourishment from industry, producing nothing themselves, employing little or no active capital or intelligent labor, but pressing on the energies and ambition of society with the weight of an incubus. Picturesque and entertaining as these social anomalies were, they were better fitted for the theatre or for a museum of historical costumes than for an active workshop preparing to compete with such machinery as America would soon command. From an economical point of view, they were as incongruous as would have been the appearance of a mediæval knight in helmet and armor, with battle-axe and shield, to run the machinery of Arkwright's cotton-mill; but besides their bad economy they also tended to prevent the rest of society from gaining a knowledge of its own capacities. In Europe, the conservative habit of mind was fortified behind power. During nearly a century Voltaire himself—the friend of kings, the wit and poet, historian and philosopher of his age—had carried on, in daily terror, in exile and excommunication, a protest against an intellectual despotism contemptible even to its own supporters. Hardly was Voltaire dead, when Priestley, as great a man if not so great a wit, trying to do for England what Voltaire tried to do for France, was mobbed by the people of Birmingham and driven to America. Where Voltaire and Priestley failed, common men could not struggle; the weight of society stifled their thought. In America the balance between conservative and liberal forces was close; but in Europe conservatism held the physical power of government. In Boston a young Buckminster might be checked for a time by his father's prayers or commands in entering the path that led toward freer thought; but youth beckoned him on, and every reward that society could offer was dangled before his eyes. In London or Paris, Rome, Madrid, or Vienna, he must have sacrificed the worldly prospects of his life.

Granting that the American people were about to risk their future on a new experiment, they naturally wished to throw aside all burdens of which they could rid themselves. Believing that in the long run interest, not violence, would rule the world, and that the United States must depend for safety and success on the interests they could create, they were tempted to look upon war and preparations for war as the worst of blunders; for they were sure that every dollar capitalized in industry was a means of overthrowing their enemies more effective than a thousand dollars spent on frigates or standing armies. The success of the American system was, from this point of view, a question of economy. If they could relieve themselves from debts, taxes, armies, and government interference with industry, they must succeed in outstripping Europe in economy of production; and Americans were even then partly aware that if their machine were not so weakened by these economies as to break down in the working, it must of necessity break down every rival. If their theory was sound, when the day of competition should arrive, Europe might choose between American and Chinese institutions, but there would be no middle path; she might become a confederated democracy, or a wreck.

Whether these ideas were sound or weak, they seemed self-evident to those Northern democrats who, like Albert Gallatin, were comparatively free from slave-owning theories, and understood the practical forces of society. If Gallatin wished to reduce the interference of government to a minimum, and cut down expenditures to nothing, he aimed not so much at saving money as at using it with the most certain effect. The revolution of 1800 was in his eyes chiefly political, because it was social; but as a revolution of society, he and his friends hoped to make it the most radical that had occurred since the downfall of the Roman empire. Their ideas were not yet cleared by experience, and were confused by many contradictory prejudices, but wanted neither breadth nor shrewdness.

Many apparent inconsistencies grew from this undeveloped form of American thought, and gave rise to great confusion in the different estimates of American character that were made both at home and abroad.

That Americans should not be liked was natural; but that

they should not be understood was more significant by far. After the downfall of the French republic they had no right to expect a kind word from Europe, and during the next twenty years they rarely received one. The liberal movement of Europe was cowed, and no one dared express democratic sympathies until the Napoleonic tempest had passed. With this attitude Americans had no right to find fault, for Europe cared less to injure them than to protect herself. Nevertheless, observant readers could not but feel surprised that none of the numerous Europeans who then wrote or spoke about America seemed to study the subject seriously. The ordinary traveller was apt to be little more reflective than a bee or an ant, but some of these critics possessed powers far from ordinary; yet Talleyrand alone showed that had he but seen America a few years later than he did, he might have suggested some sufficient reason for apparent contradictions that perplexed him in the national character. The other travellers—great and small, from the Duc de Liancourt to Basil Hall, a long and suggestive list—were equally perplexed. They agreed in observing the contradictions, but all, including Talleyrand, saw only sordid motives. Talleyrand expressed extreme astonishment at the apathy of Americans in the face of religious sectarians; but he explained it by assuming that the American ardor of the moment was absorbed in money-making. The explanation was evidently insufficient, for the Americans were capable of feeling and showing excitement, even to their great pecuniary injury, as they frequently proved; but in the foreigner's range of observation, love of money was the most conspicuous and most common trait of American character. "There is, perhaps, no civilized country in the world," wrote Félix de Beaujour, soon after 1800, "where there is less generosity in the souls, and in the heads fewer of those illusions which make the charm or the consolation of life. Man here weighs everything, calculates everything, and sacrifices everything to his interest." An Englishman named Fearon, in 1818, expressed the same idea with more distinctness: "In going to America, I would say generally, the emigrant must expect to find, not an economical or cleanly people; not a social or generous people; not a people of enlarged ideas; not a people of liberal opinions, or

toward whom you can express your thoughts free as air; not
a people friendly to the advocates of liberty in Europe; not a
people who understand liberty from investigation and principle; not a people who comprehend the meaning of the words
'honor' and 'generosity.'" Such quotations might be multiplied almost without limit. Rapacity was the accepted explanation of American peculiarities; yet every traveller was
troubled by inconsistencies that required explanations of a
different kind. "It is not in order to hoard that the Americans
are rapacious," observed Liancourt as early as 1796. The extravagance, or what economical Europeans thought extravagance, with which American women were allowed and
encouraged to spend money, was as notorious in 1790 as a
century later; the recklessness with which Americans often
risked their money, and the liberality with which they used it,
were marked even then, in comparison with the ordinary European habit. Europeans saw such contradictions, but made
no attempt to reconcile them. No foreigner of that day—neither poet, painter, nor philosopher—could detect in American life anything higher than vulgarity; for it was something
beyond the range of their experience, which education and
culture had not framed a formula to express. Moore came to
Washington, and found there no loftier inspiration than any
Federalist rhymester of Dennie's school.

"Take Christians, Mohawks, democrats and all,
    From the rude wigwam to the Congress hall,—
    From man the savage, whether slaved or free,
    To man the civilized, less tame than he:
    'T is one dull chaos, one unfertile strife
    Betwixt half-polished and half-barbarous life;
    Where every ill the ancient world can brew
    Is mixed with every grossness of the new;
    Where all corrupts, though little can entice,
    And nothing 's known of luxury but vice."

Moore's two small volumes of Epistles, printed in 1807, contained much more so-called poetry of the same tone,—poetry
more polished and less respectable than that of Barlow and
Dwight; while, as though to prove that the Old World knew

what grossness was, he embalmed in his lines the slanders
which the Scotch libeller Callender invented against Jefferson:—

> "The weary statesman for repose hath fled
> From halls of council to his negro's shed;
> Where, blest, he woos some black Aspasia's grace,
> And dreams of freedom in his slave's embrace."

To leave no doubt of his meaning, he explained in a footnote
that his allusion was to the President of the United States;
and yet even Moore, trifler and butterfly as he was, must have
seen, if he would, that between the morals of politics and
society in America and those then prevailing in Europe, there
was no room for comparison,—there was room only for
contrast.

Moore was but an echo of fashionable England in his day.
He seldom affected moral sublimity; and had he in his wan-
derings met a race of embodied angels, he would have sung
of them or to them in the slightly erotic notes which were so
well received in the society he loved to frequent and flatter.
His remarks upon American character betrayed more temper
than truth; but even in this respect he expressed only the
common feeling of Europeans, which was echoed by the Federalist society of the United States. Englishmen especially indulged in unbounded invective against the sordid character of
American society, and in shaping their national policy on this
contempt they carried their theory into practice with so much
energy as to produce its own refutation. To their astonishment and anger, a day came when the Americans, in defiance
of self-interest and in contradiction of all the qualities ascribed to them, insisted on declaring war; and readers of this
narrative will be surprised at the cry of incredulity, not un-
mixed with terror, with which Englishmen started to their
feet when they woke from their delusion on seeing what they
had been taught to call the meteor flag of England, which
had burned terrific at Copenhagen and Trafalgar, suddenly
waver and fall on the bloody deck of the "Guerriere." Fearon
and Beaujour, with a score of other contemporary critics,
could see neither generosity, economy, honor, nor ideas of

any kind in the American breast; yet the obstinate repetition of these denials itself betrayed a lurking fear of the social forces whose strength they were candid enough to record. What was it that, as they complained, turned the European peasant into a new man within half an hour after landing at New York? Englishmen were never at a loss to understand the poetry of more prosaic emotions. Neither they nor any of their kindred failed in later times to feel the "large excitement" of the country boy, whose "spirit leaped within him to be gone before him," when the lights of London first flared in the distance; yet none seemed ever to feel the larger excitement of the American immigrant. Among the Englishmen who criticised the United States was one greater than Moore,—one who thought himself at home only in the stern beauty of a moral presence. Of all poets, living or dead, Wordsworth felt most keenly what he called the still, sad music of humanity; yet the highest conception he could create of America was not more poetical than that of any Cumberland beggar he might have met in his morning walk:—

> "Long-wished-for sight, the Western World appeared;
> And when the ship was moored, I leaped ashore
> Indignantly,   resolved to be a man,
> Who, having o'er the past no power, would live
> No longer in subjection to the past,
> With abject mind—from a tyrannic lord
> Inviting penance, fruitlessly endured.
> So, like a fugitive whose feet have cleared
> Some boundary which his followers may not cross
> In prosecution of their deadly chase,
> Respiring, I looked round. How bright the sun,
> The breeze how soft! Can anything produced
> In the Old World compare, thought I, for power
> And majesty, with this tremendous stream
> Sprung from the desert? And behold a city
> Fresh, youthful, and aspiring! . . .
>   Sooth to say,
> On nearer view, a motley spectacle
> Appeared, of high pretensions—unreproved
> But by the obstreperous voice of higher still;

Big passions strutting on a petty stage,
Which a detached spectator may regard
Not unamused. But ridicule demands
Quick change of objects; and to laugh alone,
. . . in the very centre of the crowd
To keep the secret of a poignant scorn,
                              . . . is least fit
For the gross spirit of mankind."

Thus Wordsworth, although then at his prime, indulging in
what sounded like a boast that he alone had felt the sense
sublime of something interfused, whose dwelling is the light
of setting suns, and the round ocean, and the living air, and
the blue sky, and in the mind of man,—even he, to whose
moods the heavy and the weary weight of all this unintelligible world was lightened by his deeper sympathies with nature
and the soul, could do no better, when he stood in the face
of American democracy, than "keep the secret of a poignant
scorn."

Possibly the view of Wordsworth and Moore, of Weld,
Dennie, and Dickens was right. The American democrat possessed little art of expression, and did not watch his own emotions with a view of uttering them either in prose or verse;
he never told more of himself than the world might have assumed without listening to him. Only with diffidence could
history attribute to such a class of men a wider range of
thought or feeling than they themselves cared to proclaim. Yet
the difficulty of denying or even ignoring the wider range was
still greater, for no one questioned the force or the scope of
an emotion which caused the poorest peasant in Europe to
see what was invisible to poet and philosopher,—the dim
outline of a mountain-summit across the ocean, rising high
above the mist and mud of American democracy. As though
to call attention to some such difficulty, European and American critics, while affirming that Americans were a race without illusions or enlarged ideas, declared in the same breath
that Jefferson was a visionary whose theories would cause the
heavens to fall upon them. Year after year, with endless itera-
tion, in every accent of contempt, rage, and despair, they
repeated this charge against Jefferson. Every foreigner and

Federalist agreed that he was a man of illusions, dangerous to society and unbounded in power of evil; but if this view of his character was right, the same visionary qualities seemed also to be a national trait, for every one admitted that Jefferson's opinions, in one form or another, were shared by a majority of the American people.

Illustrations might be carried much further, and might be drawn from every social class and from every period in national history. Of all presidents, Abraham Lincoln has been considered the most typical representative of American society, chiefly because his mind, with all its practical qualities, also inclined, in certain directions, to idealism. Lincoln was born in 1809, the moment when American character stood in lowest esteem. Ralph Waldo Emerson, a more distinct idealist, was born in 1803. William Ellery Channing, another idealist, was born in 1780. Men like John Fitch, Oliver Evans, Robert Fulton, Joel Barlow, John Stevens, and Eli Whitney were all classed among visionaries. The whole society of Quakers belonged in the same category. The records of the popular religious sects abounded in examples of idealism and illusion to such an extent that the masses seemed hardly to find comfort or hope in any authority, however old or well established. In religion as in politics, Americans seemed to require a system which gave play to their imagination and their hopes.

Some misunderstanding must always take place when the observer is at cross-purposes with the society he describes. Wordsworth might have convinced himself by a moment's thought that no country could act on the imagination as America acted upon the instincts of the ignorant and poor, without some quality that deserved better treatment than poignant scorn; but perhaps this was only one among innumerable cases in which the unconscious poet breathed an atmosphere which the self-conscious poet could not penetrate. With equal reason he might have taken the opposite view,—that the hard, practical, money-getting American democrat, who had neither generosity nor honor nor imagination, and who inhabited cold shades where fancy sickened and where genius died, was in truth living in a world of dream, and acting a drama more instinct with poetry than all the avatars of the East, walking in gardens of emerald and rubies, in ambition already ruling the world and guiding Nature with a kinder and wiser hand than had ever yet been felt in human history. From this point his critics never approached him,—they stopped at a stone's throw; and at the moment when they declared that the man's mind had no illusions, they added that he was a knave or a lunatic. Even on his practical and sordid side, the American might easily have been represented as a victim to illusion. If the Englishman had lived as the American speculator did,—in the future,—the hyperbole of enthusiasm would have seemed less monstrous. "Look at my wealth!" cried the American to his foreign visitor. "See these solid mountains of salt and iron, of lead, copper, silver, and gold! See these magnificent cities scattered broadcast to the Pacific! See my cornfields rustling and waving in the summer breeze from ocean to ocean, so far that the sun itself is not high enough to mark where the distant mountains bound my golden seas! Look at this continent of mine, fairest of created worlds, as she lies turning up to the sun's never-failing caress her broad and exuberant breasts, overflowing with milk for her hundred million children! See how she glows with youth, health, and love!" Perhaps it was not altogether unnatural that the foreigner, on being asked to see what needed centuries to produce, should have looked about him with bewilderment and indignation. "Gold! cities! cornfields! continents! Nothing of the sort! I see nothing but tremendous wastes, where sickly men and women are dying of home-sickness or are scalped by savages! mountain-ranges a thousand miles long, with no means of getting to them, and nothing in them when you get there! swamps and forests choked with their own rotten ruins! nor hope of better for a thousand years! Your story is a fraud, and you are a liar and swindler!"

Met in this spirit, the American, half perplexed and half defiant, retaliated by calling his antagonist a fool, and by mimicking his heavy tricks of manner. For himself he cared little, but his dream was his whole existence. The men who denounced him admitted that they left him in his forest-swamp quaking with fever, but clinging in the delirium of death to the illusions of his dazzled brain. No class of men could be required to support their convictions with a steadier faith, or pay more devotedly with their persons for the mistakes of their judgment. Whether imagination or greed led them to describe more than actually existed, they still saw no more than any inventor or discoverer must have seen in order to give him the energy of success. They said to the rich as to the poor, "Come and share our limitless riches! Come and help us bring to light these unimaginable stores of wealth and power!" The poor came, and from them were seldom heard complaints of deception or delusion. Within a moment, by the mere contact of a moral atmosphere, they saw the gold and jewels, the summer cornfields and the glowing continent. The rich for a long time stood aloof,—they were timid and narrow-minded; but this was not all,—between them and the American democrat was a gulf.

The charge that Americans were too fond of money to win the confidence of Europeans was a curious inconsistency; yet this was a common belief. If the American deluded himself and led others to their death by baseless speculations; if he buried those he loved in a gloomy forest where they quaked and died while he persisted in seeing there a splendid, healthy, and well-built city, —no one could deny that he sacrificed wife and child to his greed for gain, that the dollar was his god, and a sordid avarice his demon. Yet had this been the whole truth, no European capitalist would have hesitated to make money out of his grave; for, avarice against avarice, no more sordid or meaner type existed in America than could be shown on every 'Change in Europe. With much more reason Americans might have suspected that in America Englishmen found everywhere a silent influence, which they found nowhere in Europe, and which had nothing to do with avarice or with the dollar, but, on the contrary, seemed likely at any moment to sacrifice the dollar in a cause and for an object so illusory that most Englishmen could not endure to hear it discussed. European travellers who passed through America noticed that everywhere, in the White House at Washington and in log-cabins beyond the Alleghanies, except for a few Federalists, every American, from Jefferson and Gallatin down to the poorest squatter, seemed to nourish an idea that he was doing what he could to overthrow the tyranny which the past had fastened on the human mind. Nothing was easier than to laugh at the ludicrous expressions of this simple-minded conviction, or to cry out against its coarseness, or grow angry with its prejudices; to see its nobler side, to feel the beatings of a heart underneath the sordid surface of a gross humanity, was not so easy. Europeans seemed seldom or never conscious that the sentiment could possess a noble side, but found only matter for complaint in the remark that every American democrat believed himself to be working for the overthrow of tyranny, aristocracy, hereditary privilege, and priesthood, wherever they existed. Even where the American did not openly proclaim this conviction in words, he carried so dense an atmosphere of the sentiment with him in his daily life as to give respectable Europeans an uneasy sense of remoteness.

Of all historical problems, the nature of a national character is the most difficult and the most important. Readers will be troubled, at almost every chapter of the coming narrative, by the want of some formula to explain what share the popular imagination bore in the system pursued by government. The acts of the American people during the administrations of Jefferson and Madison were judged at the time by no other test. According as bystanders believed American character to be hard, sordid, and free from illusion, they were severe and even harsh in judgment. This rule guided the governments of England and France. Federalists in the United States, knowing more of the circumstances, often attributed to the democratic instinct a visionary quality which they regarded as sentimentality, and charged with many bad consequences. If their view was correct, history could occupy itself to no better purpose than in ascertaining the nature and force of the quality which was charged with results so serious; but nothing was more elusive than the spirit of American democracy. Jefferson, the literary representative of the class, spoke chiefly for Virginians, and dreaded so greatly his own reputation as a visionary that he seldom or never uttered his whole thought. Gallatin and Madison were still more cautious. The press in no country could give shape to a mental condition so shadowy. The people themselves, although millions in number, could not have expressed their finer instincts had they tried, and might not have recognized them if expressed by others.

In the early days of colonization, every new settlement represented an idea and proclaimed a mission. Virginia was founded by a great, liberal movement aiming at the spread of English liberty and empire. The Pilgrims of Plymouth, the Puritans of Boston, the Quakers of Pennsylvania, all avowed a moral purpose, and began by making institutions that consciously reflected a moral idea. No such character belonged to the colonization of 1800. From Lake Erie to Florida, in long, unbroken line, pioneers were at work, cutting into the forests with the energy of so many beavers, and with no more express moral purpose than the beavers they drove away. The civilization they carried with them was rarely illumined by an idea; they sought room for no new truth, and aimed neither at creating, like the Puritans, a government of saints, nor, like the Quakers, one of love and peace; they left such experiments behind them, and wrestled only with the hardest problems of frontier life. No wonder that foreign observers, and even the educated, well-to-do Americans of the sea-coast, could seldom see anything to admire in the ignorance and brutality of frontiersmen, and should declare that virtue and wisdom no longer guided the United States! What they saw was not encouraging. To a new society, ignorant and semi-barbarous, a mass of demagogues insisted on applying every stimulant that could inflame its worst appetites, while at the same instant taking away every influence that had hitherto helped to restrain its passions. Greed for wealth, lust for power, yearning for the blank void of savage freedom such as Indians and wolves delighted in,—these were the fires that flamed under the caldron of American society, in which, as conservatives believed, the old, well-proven, conservative crust of religion, government, family, and even common respect for age, education, and experience was rapidly melting away, and was indeed already broken into fragments, swept about by the seething mass of scum ever rising in greater quantities to the surface.

Against this Federalist and conservative view of democratic tendencies, democrats protested in a thousand forms, but never in any mode of expression which satisfied them all, or explained their whole character. Probably Jefferson came nearest to the mark, for he represented the hopes of science as well as the prejudices of Virginia; but Jefferson's writings may be searched from beginning to end without revealing the whole measure of the man, far less of the movement. Here and there in his letters a suggestion was thrown out, as though by chance, revealing larger hopes,—as in 1815, at a moment of despondency, he wrote: "I fear from the experience of the last twenty-five years that morals do not of necessity advance hand in hand with the sciences." In 1800, in the flush of triumph, he believed that his task in the world was to establish a democratic republic, with the sciences for an intellectual field, and physical and moral advancement keeping pace with their advance. Without an excessive introduction of more recent ideas, he might be imagined to define democratic progress, in the somewhat affected precision of his French philosophy: "Progress is either physical or intellectual. If we can bring it about that men are on the average an inch taller in the next generation than in this; if they are an inch larger round the chest; if their brain is an ounce or two heavier, and their life a year or two longer,—that is progress. If fifty years hence the average man shall invariably argue from two ascertained premises where he now jumps to a conclusion from a single supposed revelation,—that is progress! I expect it to be made here, under our democratic stimulants, on a great scale, until every man is potentially an athlete in body and an Aristotle in mind." To this doctrine the New Englander replied, "What will you do for moral progress?" Every possible answer to this question opened a chasm. No doubt Jefferson held the faith that men would improve morally with their physical and intellectual growth; but he had no idea of any moral improvement other than that which came by nature. He could not tolerate a priesthood, a state church, or revealed religion. Conservatives, who could tolerate no society without such pillars of order, were, from their point of view, right in answering, "Give us rather the worst despotism of Europe,—there our souls at least may have a chance of salvation!" To their minds vice and virtue were not relative, but fixed terms. The Church was a divine institution. How could a ship hope to reach port when the crew threw overboard sails, spars, and compass, unshipped their rudder, and all the long day thought only of eating and drinking. Nay, even should the new experiment succeed in a worldly sense, what was a man profited if he gained the whole world, and lost his own soul? The Lord God was a jealous God, and visited the sins of the parents upon the children; but what worse sin could be conceived than for a whole nation to join their chief in chanting the strange hymn with which Jefferson, a new false prophet, was deceiving and betraying his people: "It does me no injury for my neighbor to say there are twenty Gods or no God!"

On this ground conservatism took its stand, as it had hitherto done with success in every similar emergency in the world's history, and fixing its eyes on moral standards of its own, refused to deal with the subject as further open to argument. The two parties stood facing opposite ways, and could see no common ground of contact.

Yet even then one part of the American social system was proving itself to be rich in results. The average American was more intelligent than the average European, and was becoming every year still more active-minded as the new movement of society caught him up and swept him through a life of more varied experiences. On all sides the national mind responded to its stimulants. Deficient as the American was in the machinery of higher instruction; remote, poor; unable by any exertion to acquire the training, the capital, or even the elementary text-books he needed for a fair development of his natural powers,—his native energy and ambition already responded to the spur applied to them. Some of his triumphs were famous throughout the world; for Benjamin Franklin had raised high the reputation of American printers, and the actual President of the United States, who signed with Franklin the treaty of peace with Great Britain, was the son of a small farmer, and had himself kept a school in his youth. In both these cases social recognition followed success; but the later triumphs of the American mind were becoming more and more popular. John Fitch was not only one of the poorest, but one of the least-educated Yankees who ever made a name; he could never spell with tolerable correctness, and his life ended as it began,—in the lowest social obscurity. Eli

Whitney was better educated than Fitch, but had neither wealth, social influence, nor patron to back his ingenuity. In the year 1800 Eli Terry, another Connecticut Yankee of the same class, took into his employ two young men to help him make wooden clocks, and this was the capital on which the greatest clock-manufactory in the world began its operations. In 1797 Asa Whittemore, a Massachusetts Yankee, invented a machine to make cards for carding wool, which "operated as if it had a soul," and became the foundation for a hundred subsequent patents. In 1790 Jacob Perkins, of Newburyport, invented a machine capable of cutting and turning out two hundred thousand nails a day; and then invented a process for transferring engraving from a very small steel cylinder to copper, which revolutionized cotton-printing. The British traveller Weld, passing through Wilmington, stopped, as Liancourt had done before him, to see the great flour-mills on the Brandywine. "The improvements," he said, " which have been made in the machinery of the flour-mills in America are very great. The chief of these consist in a new application of the screw, and the introduction of what are called elevators, the idea of which was evidently borrowed from the chain-pump." This was the invention of Oliver Evans, a native of Delaware, whose parents were in very humble life, but who was himself, in spite of every disadvantage, an inventive genius of the first order. Robert Fulton, who in 1800 was in Paris with Joel Barlow, sprang from the same source in Pennsylvania. John Stevens, a native of New York, belonged to a more favored class, but followed the same impulses. All these men were the outcome of typical American society, and all their inventions transmuted the democratic instinct into a practical and tangible shape. Who would undertake to say that there was a limit to the fecundity of this teeming source? Who that saw only the narrow, practical, money-getting nature of these devices could venture to assert that as they wrought their end and raised the standard of millions, they would not also raise the creative power of those millions to a higher plane? If the priests and barons who set their names to Magna Charta had been told that in a few centuries every swine-herd and cobbler's apprentice would write and read with an ease such as few kings could then command, and reason with better logic than any university could then practise, the priest and baron would have been more incredulous than any man who was told in 1800 that within another five centuries the ploughboy would go a-field whistling a sonata of Beethoven, and figure out in quaternions the relation of his furrows. The American democrat knew so little of art that among his popular illusions he could not then nourish artistic ambition; but leaders like Jefferson, Gallatin, and Barlow might without extravagance count upon a coming time when diffused ease and education should bring the masses into familiar contact with higher forms of human achievement, and their vast creative power, turned toward a nobler culture, might rise to the level of that democratic genius which found expression in the Parthenon; might revel in the delights of a new Buonarotti and a richer Titian; might create for five hundred million people the America of thought and art which alone could satisfy their omnivorous ambition.

Whether the illusions, so often affirmed and so often denied to the American people, took such forms or not, these were in effect the problems that lay before American society: Could it transmute its social power into the higher forms of thought? Could it provide for the moral and intellectual needs of mankind? Could it take permanent political shape? Could it give new life to religion and art? Could it create and maintain in the mass of mankind those habits of mind which had hitherto belonged to men of science alone? Could it physically develop the convolutions of the human brain? Could it produce, or was it compatible with, the differentiation of a higher variety of the human race? Nothing less than this was necessary for its complete success.

Chapter VII

T HE MAN who mounted the steps of the Capitol, March 4, 1801, to claim the place of an equal between Pitt and Bonaparte, possessed a character which showed itself in acts; but person and manner can be known only by contemporaries, and the liveliest description was worth less than a moment of personal contact. Jefferson was very tall, six feet two-and-a-half inches in height; sandy-complexioned; shy in manner, seeming cold; awkward in attitude, and with little in his bearing that suggested command. Senator Maclay of Pennsylvania described him in 1790, when he had returned from France to become Secretary of State, and appeared before a Committee of the Senate to answer questions about foreign relations.

"Jefferson is a slender man," wrote the senator;[1] "has rather the air of stiffness in his manner. His clothes seem too small for him. He sits in a lounging manner, on one hip commonly, and with one of his shoulders elevated much above the other. His face has a sunny aspect. His whole figure has a loose, shackling air. He had a rambling, vacant look, and nothing of that firm collected deportment which I expected would dignify the presence of a secretary or minister. I looked for gravity, but a laxity of manner seemed shed about him. He spoke almost without ceasing; but even his discourse partook of his personal demeanor. It was loose and rambling; and yet he scattered information wherever he went, and some even brilliant sentiments sparkled from him."

Maclay was one of the earliest members of the Republican party, and his description was not unfriendly. Augustus Foster, Secretary of the British Legation, described Jefferson as he appeared in 1804:[2] —

"He was a tall man, with a very red freckled face, and gray neglected hair; his manners good-natured, frank, and rather friendly, though he had somewhat of a cynical

[1] Sketches of Debate in the First Senate, by William Maclay, p. 212.
[2] The Quarterly Review (London, 1841), p. 24.

expression of countenance. He wore a blue coat, a thick gray-colored hairy waistcoat, with a red under-waistcoat lapped over it, green velveteen breeches with pearl buttons, yarn stockings, and slippers down at the heels,—his appearance being very much like that of a tall, large-boned farmer."

In the middle of the seventeenth century the celebrated Cardinal de Retz formed a judgment of the newly-elected Pope from his remark, at a moment when minds were absorbed in his election, that he had for two years used the same pen. "It is only a trifle," added De Retz, "but I have often observed that the smallest things are sometimes better marks than the greatest." Perhaps dress could never be considered a trifle. One of the greatest of modern writers first made himself famous by declaring that society was founded upon *cloth*, and Jefferson, at moments of some interest in his career as President, seemed to regard his peculiar style of dress as a matter of political importance, while the Federalist newspapers never ceased ridiculing the corduroy small-clothes, red-plush waistcoat, and sharp-toed boots with which he expressed his contempt for fashion.

For eight years this tall, loosely built, somewhat stiff figure, in red waistcoat and yarn stockings, slippers down at the heel, and clothes that seemed too small for him, may be imagined as Senator Maclay described him, sitting on one hip, with one shoulder high above the other, talking almost without ceasing to his visitors at the White House. His skin was thin, peeling from his face on exposure to the sun, and giving it a tettered appearance. This sandy face, with hazel eyes and sunny aspect; this loose, shackling person; this rambling and often brilliant conversation, belonged to the controlling influences of American history, more necessary to the story than three-fourths of the official papers, which only hid the truth. Jefferson's personality during these eight years appeared to be the government, and impressed itself, like that of Bonaparte, although by a different process, on the mind of the nation. In the village simplicity of Washington he was more than a king, for he was alone in social as well as in political pre-eminence. Except the British Legation, no house in Washington was open to general society; the whole mass of politicians, even the Federalists, were dependent on Jefferson and "The Palace" for amusement; and if they refused to go there, they "lived like bears, brutalized and stupefied."[1]

Jefferson showed his powers at their best in his own house, where among friends as genial and cheerful as himself his ideas could flow freely, and could be discussed with sympathy. Such were the men with whom he surrounded himself by choice, and none but such were invited to enter his Cabinet. First and oldest of his political associates was James Madison, about to become Secretary of State, whose character also described itself, and whose personality was as distinct as that of his chief. A small man, quiet, somewhat precise in manner, pleasant, fond of conversation, with a certain mixture of ease and dignity in his address, Madison had not so much as Jefferson of the commanding attitude which imposed respect on the world. "He has much more the appearance of what I have imagined a Roman cardinal to be," wrote Senator Mills of Massachusetts in 1815.[2] An imposing presence had much to do with political influence, and Madison labored under serious disadvantage in the dryness of his personality. Political opponents of course made fun of him. "As to Jemmy Madison,— oh, poor Jemmy!—he is but a withered little apple-john," wrote Washington Irving in 1812, instinctively applying the Knickerbocker view of history to national concerns.

"In his dress," said one who knew him,[3] "he was not at all eccentric or given to dandyism, but always appeared neat and genteel, and in the costume of a well-bred and tasty old-school gentleman. I have heard in early life he sometimes wore light-colored clothes; but from the time I first knew him . . . never any other color than black, his coat being cut in what is termed dress-fashion; his breeches short, with buckles at the knees, black silk stockings, and shoes with strings, or long fair top-boots when out in cold weather, or when he rode on horseback, of which he was fond. . . . He wore powder on his hair, which was

[1] The Quarterly Review (London, 1841), p. 23.
[2] Massachusetts Historical Society's Proceedings, vol. xix. 1881–1882.
[3] Grigsby's Convention of 1776, p. 85.

dressed full over the ears, tied behind, and brought to a point above the forehead, to cover in some degree his baldness, as may be noticed in all the likenesses taken of him."

Madison had a sense of humor, felt in his conversation, and detected in the demure cast of his flexile lips, but leaving no trace in his published writings. Small in stature, in deportment modest to the point of sensitive reserve, in address simple and pleasing, in feature rather thoughtful and benevolent than strong, he was such a man as Jefferson, who so much disliked contentious and self-asserting manners, loved to keep by his side. Sir Augustus Foster liked Mr. Madison, although in 1812 Madison sent him out of the country:—

"I thought Mr. Jefferson more of a statesman and man of the world than Mr. Madison, who was rather too much the disputatious pleader; yet the latter was better informed, and moreover a social, jovial, and good-humored companion, full of anecdote, sometimes rather of a loose description, but oftener of a political and historical interest. He was a little man with small features, rather wizened when I saw him, but occasionally lit up with a good-natured smile. He wore a black coat, stockings with shoes buckled, and had his hair powdered, with a tail."

The third aristocrat in this democratic triumvirate was Albert Gallatin, marked by circumstances even more than by the President's choice for the post of Secretary of the Treasury. Like the President and the Secretary of State, Gallatin was born and bred a gentleman; in person and manners he was well fitted for the cabinet-table over which Jefferson presided. Gallatin possessed the personal force which was somewhat lacking in his two friends. His appearance impressed bystanders with a sense of strength. His complexion was dark; his eyes were hazel and full of expression; his hair black, and like Madison he was becoming bald. From long experience, at first among the democrats of western Pennsylvania, and afterward as a leader in the House of Representatives, he had lost all shyness in dealing with men. His long prominent nose and lofty forehead showed character, and his eyes expressed humor. A slight foreign accent betrayed his Genevan origin.

Gallatin was also one of the best talkers in America, and perhaps the best-informed man in the country; for his laborious mind had studied America with infinite care, and he retained so much knowledge of European affairs as to fit him equally for the State Department or the Treasury. Three more agreeable men than Jefferson, Madison, and Gallatin were never collected round the dinner-table of the White House; and their difference in age was enough to add zest to their friendship; for Jefferson was born in 1743, Madison in 1751, and Gallatin in 1761. While the President was nearly sixty years old, his Secretary of the Treasury had the energy and liberality of forty.

Jefferson was the first President inaugurated at Washington, and the ceremony, necessarily simple, was made still simpler for political reasons. The retiring President was not present at the installation of his successor. In Jefferson's eyes a revolution had taken place as vast as that of 1776; and if this was his belief, perhaps the late President was wise to retire from a stage where everything was arranged to point a censure upon his principles, and where he would have seemed, in his successor's opinion, as little in place as George III. would have appeared at the installation of President Washington. The collapse of government which marked the last weeks of February, 1801, had been such as to leave of the old Cabinet only Samuel Dexter of Massachusetts, the Secretary of the Treasury, and Benjamin Stoddert of Maryland, the Secretary of the Navy, still in office. John Marshall, the late Secretary of State, had been appointed, six weeks before, Chief-Justice of the Supreme Court.

In this first appearance of John Marshall as Chief-Justice, to administer the oath of office, lay the dramatic climax of the inauguration. The retiring President, acting for what he supposed to be the best interests of the country, by one of his last acts of power, deliberately intended to perpetuate the principles of his administration, placed at the head of the judiciary, for life, a man as obnoxious to Jefferson as the bitterest New England Calvinist could have been; for he belonged to that class of conservative Virginians whose devotion to President Washington, and whose education in the common law, caused them to hold Jefferson and his theories in antipathy. The new President and his two Secretaries were political philanthropists, bent on restricting the powers of the national government in the interests of human liberty. The Chief-Justice, a man who in grasp of mind and steadiness of purpose had no superior, perhaps no equal, was bent on enlarging the powers of government in the interests of justice and nationality. As they stood face to face on this threshold of their power, each could foresee that the contest between them would end only with life.

If Jefferson and his two friends were the most aristocratic of democrats, John Marshall was of all aristocrats the most democratic in manners and appearance.

"A tall, slender figure," wrote Joseph Story in 1808,[1] "not graceful or imposing, but erect and steady. His hair is black, his eyes small and twinkling, his forehead rather low; but his features are in general harmonious. His manners are plain yet dignified, and an unaffected modesty diffuses itself through all his actions. His dress is very simple yet neat; his language chaste, but hardly elegant; it does not flow rapidly, but it seldom wants precision. In conversation he is quite familiar, but is occasionally embarrassed by a hesitancy and drawling. . . . I love his laugh, it is too hearty for an intriguer; and his good temper and unwearied patience are equally agreeable on the bench and in the study."

The unaffected simplicity of Marshall's life was delightful to all who knew him, for it sprang from the simplicity of his mind. Never self-conscious, his dignity was never affected by his situation. Bishop Meade,[2] who was proud of the Chief-Justice as one of his flock, being in a street near Marshall's house one morning between daybreak and sunrise, met the Chief-Justice on horseback, with a bag of clover-seed lying before him, which he was carrying to his little farm at seed-time. Simple as American life was, his habits were remarkable for modest plainness; and only the character of his mind, which seemed to have no flaw, made his influence irresistible upon all who were brought within its reach.

Nevertheless this great man nourished one weakness. Pure

[1] Life of Story, i. 166.
[2] Old Churches of Virginia, ii. 222.

in life; broad in mind, and the despair of bench and bar for the unswerving certainty of his legal method; almost idolized by those who stood nearest him, and loving warmly in return,—this excellent and amiable man clung to one rooted prejudice: he detested Thomas Jefferson. He regarded with quiet, unspoken, but immovable antipathy the character and doings of the philosopher standing before him, about to take the oath to preserve, protect, and defend the Constitution. No argument or entreaty affected his conviction that Jefferson was not an honest man. "By weakening the office of President he will increase his personal power," were Marshall's words, written at this time;[1] "the morals of the author of the letter to Mazzei cannot be pure." Jefferson in return regarded Marshall with a repugnance tinged by a shade of some deeper feeling, almost akin to fear. "The judge's inveteracy is profound," he once wrote,[2] "and his mind of that gloomy malignity which will never let him forego the opportunity of satiating it on a victim."

Another person, with individuality not less marked, took the oath of office the same day. When the Senate met at ten o'clock on the morning of March 4, 1801, Aaron Burr stood at the desk, and having duly sworn to support the Constitution, took his seat in the chair as Vice-President. This quiet, gentlemanly, and rather dignified figure, hardly taller than Madison, and dressed in much the same manner, impressed with favor all who first met him. An aristocrat imbued in the morality of Lord Chesterfield and Napoleon Bonaparte, Colonel Burr was the chosen head of Northern democracy, idol of the wards of New York city, and aspirant to the highest offices he could reach by means legal or beyond the law; for as he pleased himself with saying, after the manner of the First Consul of the French Republic, "Great souls care little for small morals." Among the other party leaders who have been mentioned,—Jefferson, Madison, Gallatin, Marshall,— not one was dishonest. The exaggerations or equivocations that Jefferson allowed himself, which led to the deep-rooted conviction of Marshall that he did not tell the truth and must therefore be dangerous, amounted to nothing when com-

[1] Marshall to Hamilton, Jan. 1, 1801; Hamilton's Works, vi. 502.
[2] Jefferson to Gallatin, Sept. 27, 1810; Gallatin's Writings, i. 492.

pared with the dishonesty of a corrupt man Had the worst political charges against Jefferson been true, he would not have been necessarily corrupt. The self-deception inherent in every struggle for personal power was not the kind of immorality which characterized Colonel Burr. Jefferson, if his enemies were to be believed, might occasionally make misstatements of fact; yet he was true to the faith of his life, and would rather have abdicated his office and foregone his honors than have compassed even an imaginary wrong against the principles he professed. His life, both private and public, was pure. His associates, like Madison, Gallatin, and Monroe, were men upon whose reputations no breath of scandal rested. The standard of morality at Washington, both in private society and in politics, was respectable. For this reason Colonel Burr was a new power in the government; for being in public and in private life an adventurer of the same school as scores who were then seeking fortune in the antechambers of Bonaparte and Pitt, he became a loadstone for every other adventurer who frequented New York or whom the chances of politics might throw into office. The Vice-President wielded power, for he was the certain centre of corruption.

Thus when the doors of the Senate chamber were thrown open, and the new President of the United States appeared on the threshold; when the Vice-President rose from his chair, and Jefferson sat down in it, with Aaron Burr on his right hand and John Marshall on his left, the assembled senators looked up at three men who profoundly disliked and distrusted each other.

John Davis, one of many Englishmen who were allowed by Burr to attach themselves to him on the chance of some future benefit to be derived from them, asserted in a book of American travels published in London two years afterward, that he was present at the inauguration, and that Jefferson rode on horseback to the Capitol, and after hitching his horse to the palings, went in to take the oath. This story, being spread by the Federalist newspapers, was accepted by the Republicans and became a legend of the Capitol. In fact Davis was not then at Washington, and his story was untrue. Afterward as President, Jefferson was in the habit of going on horseback, rather than in a carriage, wherever business called him, and the Federalists found fault with him for doing so. "He makes it a point," they declared,[1] "when he has occasion to visit the Capitol to meet the representatives of the nation on public business, to go on a single horse, which he leads into the shed and hitches to a peg." Davis wished to write a book that should amuse Englishmen, and in order to give an air of truth to invention, he added that he was himself present at the ceremony. Jefferson was then living as Vice-President at Conrad's boarding-house, within a stone's throw of the Capitol. He did not mount his horse only to ride across the square and dismount in a crowd of observers. Doubtless he wished to offer an example of republican simplicity, and he was not unwilling to annoy his opponents; but the ceremony was conducted with proper form.

Edward Thornton, then in charge of the British Legation at Washington, wrote to Lord Grenville, then Foreign Secretary in Pitt's administration, a despatch enclosing the new President's Inaugural Address, with comments upon its democratic tendencies; and after a few remarks on this subject, he added:[2] —

"The same republican spirit which runs through this performance, and which in many passages discovers some bitterness through all the sentiments of conciliation and philanthropy with which it is overcharged, Mr. Jefferson affected to display in performing the customary ceremonies. He came from his own lodgings to the House where the Congress convenes, and which goes by the name of the Capitol, on foot, in his ordinary dress, escorted by a body of militia artillery from the neighboring State, and accompanied by the Secretaries of the Navy and the Treasury, and a number of his political friends in the House of Representatives. He was received by Mr. Burr, the Vice-President of the United States, who arrived a day or two ago at the seat of government, and who was previously admitted this morning to the chair of the Senate; and was afterward complimented at his own lodgings by the very few foreign

[1] Evening Post, April 20, 1802.
[2] Thornton to Grenville, March 4, 1801; MSS. British Archives.

agents who reside at this place, by the members of Congress, and other public officials."

Only the north wing of the Capitol had then been so far completed as to be occupied by the Senate, the courts, and the small library of Congress. The centre rose not much above its foundations; and the south wing, some twenty feet in height, contained a temporary oval brick building, commonly called the "Oven," in which the House of Representatives sat in some peril of their lives, for had not the walls been strongly shored up from without, the structure would have crumbled to pieces. Into the north wing the new President went, accompanied by the only remaining secretaries, Dexter and Stoddert, and by his friends from the House. Received by Vice-President Burr, and seated in the chair between Burr and Marshall, after a short pause Jefferson rose, and in a somewhat inaudible voice began his Inaugural Address.

Time, which has laid its chastening hand on many reputations, and has given to many once famous formulas a meaning unsuspected by their authors, has not altogether spared Jefferson's first Inaugural Address, although it was for a long time almost as well known as the Declaration of Independence; yet this Address was one of the few State Papers which should have lost little of its interest by age. As the starting-point of a powerful political party, the first Inaugural was a standard by which future movements were measured, and it went out of fashion only when its principles were universally accepted or thrown aside. Even as a literary work, it possessed a certain charm of style peculiar to Jefferson, a flavor of Virginia thought and manners, a Jeffersonian ideality calculated to please the ear of later generations forced to task their utmost powers in order to carry the complex trains of their thought.

The chief object of the Address was to quiet the passions which had been raised by the violent agitation of the past eight years. Every interest of the new Administration required that the extreme Federalists should be disarmed. Their temper was such as to endanger both Administration and Union; and their power was still formidable, for they controlled New England and contested New York. To them, Jefferson turned: —

"Let us unite with one heart and one mind," he entreated; "let us restore to social intercourse that harmony and affection without which liberty and even life itself are but dreary things. And let us reflect, that, having banished from our land that religious intolerance under which mankind so long bled and suffered, we have yet gained little if we countenance a political intolerance as despotic, as wicked, and capable of as bitter and bloody persecutions. During the throes and convulsions of the ancient world, during the agonizing spasms of infuriated man, seeking through blood and slaughter his long-lost liberty, it was not wonderful that the agitation of the billows should reach even this distant and peaceful shore; that this should be more felt and feared by some than by others; that this should divide opinions as to measures of safety. But every difference of opinion is not a difference of principle. We are all Republicans, we are all Federalists."

The Federalist newspapers never ceased laughing at the "spasms" so suddenly converted into "billows," and at the orthodoxy of Jefferson's Federalism; but perhaps his chief fault was to belittle the revolution which had taken place. In no party sense was it true that all were Republicans or all Federalists. As will appear, Jefferson himself was far from meaning what he seemed to say. He wished to soothe the great body of his opponents, and if possible to win them over; but he had no idea of harmony or affection other than that which was to spring from his own further triumph; and in representing that he was in any sense a Federalist, he did himself a wrong.

"I know, indeed," he continued, "that some honest men fear that a republican government cannot be strong; that this government is not strong enough. But would the honest patriot, in the full tide of successful experiment, abandon a government which has so far kept us free and firm, on the theoretic and visionary fear that this government, the world's best hope, may by possibility want energy to preserve itself? I trust not. I believe this, on the contrary, the strongest government on earth. I believe it is the only one where every man, at the call of the laws, would fly to the standard of the law, and would meet invasions of the public order as his own personal concern. Sometimes it is said that man cannot be trusted with the government of himself. Can he then be trusted with the government of others? Or have we found angels in the forms of kings to govern him? Let history answer this question!"

That the government, the world's best hope, had hitherto kept the country free and firm, in the full tide of successful experiment, was a startling compliment to the Federalist party, coming as it did from a man who had not been used to compliment his political opponents; but Federalists, on the other hand, might doubt whether this government would continue to answer the same purpose when administered for no other avowed object than to curtail its powers. Clearly, Jefferson credited government with strength which belonged to society; and if he meant to practise upon this idea, by taking the tone of "the strongest government on earth" in the face of Bonaparte and Pitt, whose governments were strong in a different sense, he might properly have developed this idea at more length, for it was likely to prove deeply interesting. Moreover, history, if asked, must at that day have answered that no form of government, whether theocratic, autocratic, aristocratic, democratic, or mixed, had ever in Western civilization lasted long, without change or need of change. History was not the witness to which Republicans could with entire confidence appeal, even against kings.

The Address next enumerated the advantages which America enjoyed, and those which remained to be acquired:—

"With all these blessings, what more is necessary to make us a happy and prosperous people? Still one thing more, fellow-citizens,—a wise and frugal government, which shall restrain men from injuring one another, which shall leave them otherwise free to regulate their own pursuits of industry and improvement, and shall not take from the mouth of labor the bread it has earned. This is the sum of good government, and this is necessary to close the circle of our felicities."

A government restricted to keeping the peace, which

should raise no taxes except for that purpose, seemed to be simply a judicature and a police. Jefferson gave no development to the idea further than to define its essential principles, and those which were to guide his Administration. Except the Kentucky and Virginia Resolutions of 1798, this short passage was the only official gloss ever given to the Constitution by the Republican party; and for this reason students of American history who would understand the course of American thought should constantly carry in mind not only the Constitutions of 1781 and of 1787, but also the Virginia and Kentucky Resolutions, and the following paragraph of Jefferson's first Inaugural Address:—

"I will compress them," said the President, "within the narrowest compass they will bear, stating the general principle, but not all its limitations. Equal and exact justice to all men, of whatever state or persuasion, religious or political; peace, commerce, and honest friendship with all nations, entangling alliances with none; the support of the State governments in all their rights, as the most competent administrations for our domestic concerns and the surest bulwarks against anti-republican tendencies; the preservation of the general government in its whole Constitutional vigor, as the sheet-anchor of our peace at home and safety abroad; a jealous care of the right of election by the People,—a mild and safe corrective of abuses which are lopped by the sword of revolution where peaceable remedies are unprovided; absolute acquiescence in the decisions of the majority,—the vital principle of republics, from which there is no appeal but to force, the vital principle and immediate parent of despotism; a well-disciplined militia,— our best reliance in peace and for the first moments of war, till regulars may relieve them; the supremacy of the civil over the military authority; economy in the public expense, that labor may be lightly burdened; the honest payment of our debts, and sacred preservation of the public faith; encouragement of agriculture, and of commerce as its handmaid; the diffusion of information, and arraignment of all abuses at the bar of public reason; freedom of religion, freedom of the press, and freedom of person under the protection of the *habeas corpus*; and trial by juries impartially selected;—these principles form the bright constellation which has gone before us and guided our steps through an age of revolution and reformation. The wisdom of our sages and the blood of our heroes have been devoted to their attainment; they should be the creed of our political faith, the text of civic instruction, the touchstone by which to try the services of those we trust; and should we wander from them in moments of error or alarm, let us hasten to retrace our steps and to regain the road which alone leads to peace, liberty, and safety."

From the metaphors in which these principles appeared as a constellation, a creed, a text, a touchstone, and a road, the world learned that they had already guided the American people through an age of revolution. In fact, they were mainly the principles of President Washington, and had they been announced by a Federalist President, would have created little remonstrance or surprise. In Jefferson's mouth they sounded less familiar, and certain phrases seemed even out of place.

Among the cardinal points of republicanism thus proclaimed to the world was one in particular, which as a maxim of government seemed to contradict cherished convictions and the fixed practice of the Republican party. "Absolute acquiescence" was required "in the decisions of the majority,—the vital principle of republics, from which there is no appeal but to force, the vital principle and immediate parent of despotism." No principle was so thoroughly entwined in the roots of Virginia republicanism as that which affirmed the worthlessness of decisions made by a majority of the United States, either as a nation or a confederacy, in matters which concerned the exercise of doubtful powers. Not three years had passed since Jefferson himself penned the draft of the Kentucky Resolutions, in which he declared[1] "that in cases of an abuse of the delegated powers, the members of the general government being chosen by the people, a change by the people would be the Constitutional remedy; but where powers are assumed which have not been delegated, a nullification of the act is the rightful remedy; that every State has a natural

[1] Jefferson's Works, ix. 469.

right, in cases not within the compact, to nullify of their own authority all assumptions of power by others within their limits; that without this right they would be under the dominion, absolute and unlimited, of whosoever might exercise this right of judgment for them." He went so far as to advise that every State should forbid, within its borders, the execution of any act of the general government "not plainly and intentionally authorized by the Constitution;" and although the legislatures of Kentucky and Virginia softened the language, they acted on the principle so far as to declare certain laws of the United States unconstitutional, with the additional understanding that whatever was unconstitutional was void. So far from accepting with "absolute acquiescence" the decisions of the majority, Jefferson and his followers held that freedom could be maintained only by preserving inviolate the right of every State to judge for itself what was, and what was not, lawful for a majority to decide.

What, too, was meant by the words which pledged the new Administration to preserve the general government "in its whole Constitutional vigor"? The two parties were divided by a bottomless gulf in their theories of Constitutional powers; but until the precedents established by the Federalists should be expressly reversed, no one could deny that those precedents, to be treated as acts of the majority with absolute acquiescence, were a measure of the vigor which the President pledged himself to preserve. Jefferson could not have intended such a conclusion; for how could he promise to "preserve" the powers assumed in the Alien and Sedition laws, which then represented the whole vigor of the general government in fact if not in theory, when he had himself often and bitterly denounced those powers, when he had been a party to their nullification, and when he and his friends had actually prepared to resist by arms their enforcement? Undoubtedly Jefferson meant no more than to preserve the general government in such vigor as in his opinion was Constitutional, without regard to Federalist precedents; but his words were equivocal, and unless they were to be defined by legislation, they identified him with the contrary legislation of his predecessors. In history and law they did so. Neither the Alien nor the Sedition Act, nor any other Federalist precedent, was ever declared unconstitutional by any department of the general government; and Jefferson's pledge to preserve that government in its full Constitutional vigor was actually redeemed with no exception or limitation on the precedents established. His intention seemed to be different; but the sweeping language of his pledge was never afterward restricted or even more exactly defined while he remained in power.

Hence arose a sense of disappointment for future students of the Inaugural Address. A revolution had taken place; but the new President seemed anxious to prove that there had been no revolution at all. A new experiment in government was to be tried, and the philosopher at its head began by pledging himself to follow in the footsteps of his predecessors. Americans ended by taking him at his word, and by assuming that there was no break of continuity between his ideas and those of President Washington; yet even at the moment of these assurances he was writing privately in an opposite sense. In his eyes the past was wrong, both in method and intention; its work must be undone and its example forgotten. His conviction of a radical difference between himself and his predecessors was expressed in the strongest language. His predecessors, in his opinion, had involved the government in difficulties in order to destroy it, and to build up a monarchy on its ruins. "The tough sides of our Argosie," he wrote two days after his inauguration,[1] "have been thoroughly tried. Her strength has stood the waves into which she was steered with a view to sink her. We shall put her on her Republican tack, and she will now show by the beauty of her motion the skill of her builders." "The Federalists," said he at one moment,[2] " wished for everything which would approach our new government to a monarchy; the Republicans, to preserve it essentially republican. . . . The real difference consisted in their different degrees of inclination to monarchy or republicanism." "The revolution of 1800," he wrote many years afterward,[3] " was as real a revolution in the principles of our government as that of 1776 was in its form."

[1] Jefferson to J. Dickinson, March 6, 1801; Works, iv. 365.
[2] Jefferson's Works, ix. 480.
[3] Jefferson to Roane, Sept. 6, 1819; Works, vii. 133.

Not, therefore, in the Inaugural Address, with its amiable professions of harmony, could President Jefferson's full view of his own reforms be discovered. Judged by his inaugural addresses and annual messages, Jefferson's Administration seemed a colorless continuation of Washington's; but when seen in the light of private correspondence, the difference was complete. So strong was the new President's persuasion of the monarchical bent of his predecessors, that his joy at obtaining the government was mingled with a shade of surprise that his enemies should have handed to him, without question, the power they had so long held. He shared his fears of monarchy with politicians like William B. Giles, young John Randolph, and many Southern voters; and although neither Madison nor Gallatin seemed to think monarchists formidable, they gladly encouraged the President to pursue a conservative and conciliatory path. Jefferson and his Southern friends took power as republicans opposed to monarchists, not as democrats opposed to oligarchy. Jefferson himself was not in a social sense a democrat, and was called so only as a term of opprobrium. His Northern followers were in the main democrats; but he and most of his Southern partisans claimed to be republicans, opposed by secret monarchists.

The conflict of ideas between Southern republicanism, Northern democracy, and Federal monarchism marked much of Jefferson's writing; but especially when he began his career as President his mind was filled with the conviction that he had wrung power from monarchy, and that in this sense he was the founder of a new republic. Henceforward, as he hoped, republicanism was forever safe; he had but to conciliate the misguided, and give an example to the world, for centralization was only a monarchical principle. Nearly twenty years passed before he woke to a doubt on this subject; but even then he did not admit a mistake. In the tendency to centralization he still saw no democratic instinct, but only the influence of monarchical Federalists "under the pseudo-republican mask."[1]

The republic which Jefferson believed himself to be founding or securing in 1801 was an enlarged Virginia,—a society

[1] Jefferson to Judge Johnson, June 12, 1823; Works, vii. 293.

to be kept pure and free by the absence of complicated interests, by the encouragement of agriculture and of commerce as its handmaid, but not of industry in a larger sense. "The agricultural capacities of our country," he wrote long afterward,[1] "constitute its distinguishing feature; and the adapting our policy and pursuits to that is more likely to make us a numerous and happy people than the mimicry of an Amsterdam, a Hamburg, or a city of London." He did not love mechanics or manufactures, or the capital without which they could not exist.[2] "Banking establishments are more dangerous than standing armies," he said; and added, "that the principle of spending money to be paid by posterity, under the name of funding, is but swindling futurity on a large scale." Such theories were republican in the Virginia sense, but not democratic; they had nothing in common with the democracy of Pennsylvania and New England, except their love of freedom, and Virginia freedom was not the same conception as the democratic freedom of the North.

In 1801 this Virginia type was still the popular form of republicanism. Although the Northern democrat had already developed a tendency toward cities, manufactures, and "the mimicry of an Amsterdam, a Hamburg, or a city of London," while the republican of the South was distinguished by his dislike of every condition except that of agriculture, the two wings of the party had so much in common that they could afford to disregard for a time these divergencies of interest; and if the Virginians cared nothing for cities, banks, and manufactures, or if the Northern democrats troubled themselves little about the dangers of centralization, they could unite with one heart in overthrowing monarchy, and in effecting a social revolution.

Henceforward, as Jefferson conceived, government might act directly for the encouragement of agriculture and of commerce as its handmaid, for the diffusion of information and the arraignment of abuses; but there its positive functions stopped. Beyond that point only negative action remained,— respect for States' rights, preservation of constitutional powers, economy, and the maintenance of a pure and simple

---

[1] Jefferson to W. H. Crawford, June 20, 1816; Works, vii. 6.
[2] Jefferson to John Taylor, May 28, 1816; Works, vi. 608.

society such as already existed. With a political system which would not take from the mouth of labor the bread it had earned, and which should leave men free to follow whatever paths of industry or improvement they might find most profitable, "the circle of felicities" was closed.

The possibility of foreign war alone disturbed this dream. President Washington himself might have been glad to accept these ideas of domestic politics, had not France, England, and Spain shown an unequivocal wish to take advantage of American weakness in arms in order to withhold rights vital to national welfare. How did Jefferson propose to convert a government of judiciary and police into the strongest government on earth? His answer to this question, omitted from the Inaugural Address, was to be found in his private correspondence and in the speeches of Gallatin and Madison as leaders of the opposition. He meant to prevent war. He was convinced that governments, like human beings, were on the whole controlled by their interests, and that the interests of Europe required peace and free commerce with America. Believing a union of European Powers to be impossible, he was willing to trust their jealousies of each other to secure their good treatment of the United States. Knowing that Congress could by a single act divert a stream of wealth from one European country to another, foreign Governments would hardly challenge the use of such a weapon, or long resist their own overpowering interests. The new President found in the Constitutional power "to regulate commerce with foreign nations" the machinery for doing away with navies, armies, and wars.

During eight years of opposition the Republican party had matured its doctrines on this subject. In 1797, in the midst of difficulties with France, Jefferson wrote:[1] —

"If we weather the present storm, I hope we shall avail ourselves of the calm of peace to place our foreign connections under a new and different arrangement. We must make the interest of every nation stand surety for their justice, and their own loss to follow injury to us, as effect

[1] Jefferson to Edward Rutledge, June 24, 1797; Works, iv. 189.

follows its cause. As to everything except commerce, we ought to divorce ourselves from them all."

A few months before the inauguration, he wrote in terms more general:[1] —

"The true theory of our Constitution is surely the wisest and best, that the States are independent as to everything within themselves, and united as to everything respecting foreign nations. Let the general government be reduced to foreign concerns only, and let our affairs be disentangled from those of all other nations, except as to commerce, which the merchants will manage the better the more they are left free to manage for themselves, and our general government may be reduced to a very simple organization and a very unexpensive one, — a few plain duties to be performed by a few servants."

Immediately after the inauguration the new President explained his future foreign policy to correspondents, who, as he knew, would spread his views widely throughout both continents. In a famous letter to Thomas Paine,[2] —a letter which was in some respects a true inaugural address, — Jefferson told the thought he had but hinted in public. "Determined as we are to avoid, if possible, wasting the energies of our people in war and destruction, we shall avoid implicating ourselves with the Powers of Europe, even in support of principles which we mean to pursue. They have so many other interests different from ours that we must avoid being entangled in them. We believe we can enforce those principles as to ourselves by peaceable means, now that we are likely to have our public councils detached from foreign views." A few days later, he wrote to the well-known Pennsylvania peacemaker, Dr. Logan, and explained the process of enforcing against foreign nations "principles as to ourselves by peaceable means." "Our commerce," said he,[3] "is so valuable to them, that they will be glad to purchase it, when the only price we ask is to do us justice. I believe we have in our own

[1] Jefferson to Gideon Granger, Aug. 13, 1800; Works, iv. 330.
[2] Jefferson to Thomas Paine, March 18, 1801; Works, iv. 370.
[3] Jefferson's Writings (Ford), viii. 23.

hands the means of peaceable coercion; and that the moment they see our government so united as that we can make use of it, they will for their own interest be disposed to do us justice."

To Chancellor Livingston, in September, 1801,[1] the President wrote his views of the principles which he meant to pursue: "Yet in the present state of things," he added, "they are not worth a war; nor do I believe war the most certain means of enforcing them. Those peaceable coercions which are in the power of every nation, if undertaken in concert and in time of peace, are more likely to produce the desired effect."

That these views were new as a system in government could not be denied. In later life Jefferson frequently asserted, and took pains to impress upon his friends, the difference between his opinions and those of his Federalist opponents. The radical distinction lay in their opposite conceptions of the national government. The Federalists wished to extend its functions; Jefferson wished to exclude its influence from domestic affairs: —

"The people," he declared in 1821,[2] "to whom all authority belongs, have divided the powers of government into two distinct departments, the leading characters of which are foreign and domestic; and they have appointed for each a distinct set of functionaries. These they have made coordinate, checking and balancing each other, like the three cardinal departments in the individual States, — each equally supreme as to the powers delegated to itself, and neither authorized ultimately to decide what belongs to itself or to its coparcener in government. As independent, in fact, as different nations, a spirit of forbearance and compromise, therefore, and not of encroachment and usurpation, is the healing balm of such a Constitution."

In the year 1824 Jefferson still maintained the same doctrine, and expressed it more concisely than ever: —

"The federal is in truth our foreign government, which department alone is taken from the sovereignty of the sep-

[1] Jefferson to R. R. Livingston, Sept. 9, 1801; Works, iv. 408.
[2] Jefferson to Judge Roane, June 27, 1821; Works, vii. 212.

arate States."[1] "I recollect no case where a question simply between citizens of the same State has been transferred to the foreign department, except that of inhibiting tenders but of metallic money, and *ex post facto* legislation."[2]

These expressions, taken together, partly explain why Jefferson thought his assumption of power to be "as real a revolution in the principles of our government as that of 1776 was in its form." His view of governmental functions was simple and clearly expressed. The national government, as he conceived it, was a foreign department as independent from the domestic department, which belonged to the States, as though they were governments of different nations. He intended that the general government should "be reduced to foreign concerns only;" and his theory of foreign concerns was equally simple and clear. He meant to enforce against foreign nations such principles as national objects required, not by war, but by "peaceable coercion" through commercial restrictions. "Our commerce is so valuable to them that they will be glad to purchase it, when the only price we ask is to do us justice."

The history of his Administration will show how these principles were applied, and what success attended the experiment.

[1] Jefferson to Robert J. Garnett, Feb. 14, 1824; Works, vii. 336.
[2] Jefferson to Edward Livingston, April 4, 1824; Works, vii. 342.

Chapter VIII

IN 1801, and throughout Jefferson's Administration, the Cabinet consisted of five heads of department,—the Secretaries of State, of the Treasury, of the Army, and of the Navy, with the Attorney-General. The law business of the government being light, the Attorney-General was frequently absent, and, indeed, was not required to reside permanently at Washington. Rather the official counsel of government than a head of department, he had no clerks or office-room, and his salary was lower than that of his colleagues. The true Cabinet consisted of the four secretaries; and the true government rested in still fewer hands, for it naturally fell within the control of the officers whose responsibility was greatest,—the President, the Secretary of State, and the Secretary of the Treasury.

Simple as such a system was, Jefferson found that months elapsed before his new Cabinet could be organized and set at work. Although Madison was instantly nominated and confirmed as Secretary of State, some weeks passed before he arrived in Washington and assumed his duties. Gallatin was supposed to be in danger of rejection by the Senate, and his nomination as Secretary of the Treasury was therefore postponed till the next session. This delay was not allowed to prevent his taking charge of the office; but he was obliged first to make the long journey to his residence on the Monongahela, in southwestern Pennsylvania, in order to arrange his affairs and bring his family to Washington. During the interval between the inauguration and the meeting of his completed Cabinet, Jefferson was left without means of governing. For Attorney-General he selected Levi Lincoln, a lawyer of Worcester County in Massachusetts, who had been recently elected to fill a vacancy in the House of Representatives, and, being on the spot, was useful in acting as Secretary of State, or in any other capacity in which the services of a secretary were required. For the War Department the President chose Henry Dearborn, a resident of the District of Maine, then a part of Massachusetts. With such assistance as Lincoln and Dearborn could give, and with the aid of Samuel

Dexter the Federalist Secretary of the Treasury, and Benjamin Stoddert the Federalist Secretary of the Navy, who consented to remain for a time, Jefferson slowly set his Administration in motion.

The Navy Department seemed likely to baffle the President's utmost efforts. The appointment was intended for Robert R. Livingston of New York, who refused; then it was offered to Samuel Smith of Maryland, a prominent member of Congress; but General Smith was a merchant, and declined to abandon his business. Next, the place was pressed upon John Langdon of New Hampshire, although New England already supplied two members of the Cabinet. Langdon refusing, the President wrote to William Jones of Philadelphia, a member of the next Congress, who declined. Meanwhile Benjamin Stoddert became weary of waiting, and Samuel Smith consented to perform the duties in order to give the President time for further search. At the end of March, Jefferson left Washington to pass the month of April at Monticello, and on his return, May 1, the Navy Department was still unfilled. Not until July did General Smith succeed in escaping the burden of his temporary duties. Then the President abandoned the attempt to place a man of public importance in the position, and allowed Samuel Smith to substitute in his place his brother Robert, a Baltimore lawyer, whose fitness for naval duties was supposed to consist chiefly in the advice and aid which Samuel would supply.

The appointment of Robert Smith, July 15, completed the Cabinet. Of its five members, only two—Madison and Gallatin—were much known beyond their States. Neither Dearborn nor Lincoln was so strong, either in political or social connections or in force of character, as greatly to affect the course of the Cabinet, and both were too honest to thwart it.

"General Dearborn is a man of strong sense, great practical information on all the subjects connected with his department, and is what is called a man of business. He is not, I believe, a scholar; but I think he will make the best Secretary of War we have as yet had. Mr. Lincoln is a good lawyer, a fine scholar, a man of great discretion and sound judgment, and of the mildest and most amiable manners. He has never, I should think from his manners, been out of his own State, or mixed much with the world, except on business. Both are men of 1776, sound and decided Republicans; both are men of the strictest integrity; and both, but Mr. Lincoln principally, have a great weight of character to the Eastward with both parties."[1]

Thus Gallatin, March 12, before his own appointment, estimated the characters of his two New England colleagues. The confidence reposed in them was justified by the result. Neither Dearborn nor Lincoln showed remarkable powers, but the work they had to do was done without complaint or objection. No charge of dishonesty, of intrigue, or of selfish ambition was made against them; and they retired from office at last with as much modesty as they showed in entering it, after serving Jefferson faithfully and well.

In some respects Robert Smith was better suited than either Dearborn or Lincoln for a seat in Jefferson's Cabinet. The Smiths were strong not only in Maryland, but also in Virginia, being connected by marriage with Wilson Cary Nicholas, one of the most influential Republican politicians of the State, whose relations with Jefferson were intimate. Robert Smith was a Baltimore gentleman, easy and cordial, glad to oblige and fond of power and show, popular in the navy, yielding in the Cabinet, but as little fitted as Jefferson himself for the task of administering with severe economy an unpopular service. The navy was wholly Federalist in tendencies and composition. The Republican party had always denounced this Federalist creation; and that a navy caused more dangers than it prevented or corrected, was one of the deepest convictions that underlay the policy of Jefferson, Madison, and Gallatin. In theory they had no use for a sea-going navy; at the utmost they wanted only coast and harbor defences, sloops-of-war and gunboats. During the four years of the last Administration, of a total expenditure averaging about $11,000,000 per annum, not less than $2,500,000 had been annually spent on the navy. The public debt itself required only about $4,500,000, and the army less than $3,000,000.

[1] Life of Gallatin, p. 276.

Economies in the debt were impossible; on the contrary, a mass of deferred annuities was to be met, and some provision must be made for more rapid discharge of the principal. Economies in the civil list were equally impossible; for the Federalists had there wasted little money, and salaries were low. The army and navy could alone be cut down; and since the Western people required regular troops for their defence against the Indians, the most radical reformers hardly ventured to recommend that the army should be reduced much below an aggregate of three thousand rank-and-file. The navy, on the other hand, was believed to be wholly superfluous, and Jefferson was anxious to lay up all the larger ships, especially the frigates.

"I shall really be chagrined," he wrote from Monticello in April,[1] "if the water in the Eastern Branch will not admit our laying up the whole seven there in time of peace, because they would be under the immediate eye of the department, and would require but one set of plunderers to take care of them. As to what is to be done when everything shall be disposed of according to law, it shall be the subject of conversation when I return. It oppresses me by night and by day, for I do not see my way out of the difficulty. It is the department I understand the least, and therefore need a person whose complete competence will justify the most entire confidence and resignation."

Robert Smith was certainly not such a person as Jefferson described, and his appointment, however suitable in other respects, was not likely to attain the object which Jefferson had at heart.

Hardly was the Navy Department thus bestowed, and the new Cabinet, toward the middle of July, completely organized for the work that was still to be defined, when another annoyance distracted the President's attention from the main objects of his policy. The government had been, for eight years, in the hands of Federalist partisans. If, as Jefferson declared in his Inaugural Address, "we are all Republicans, we are all Federalists;" if differences of opinion were not differ-

[1] Jefferson to S. Smith, April 17, 1801; Jefferson MSS.

ences of principle; if he seriously wished all Americans to "re-store to social intercourse that harmony and affection without which liberty and even life itself are but dreary things,"—he could afford to make few removals for party reasons. On the other hand, if, as he privately declared and as was commonly believed, the actual office-holders were monarchists at heart, and could not be trusted to carry the new Republican princi-ples into practice, the public welfare required great changes. For the first time in national experience, the use of patronage needed some definite regulation.

The most skilful politician must have failed in the attempt to explain that a revolution had been made which ought to satisfy every one, by methods which no one had an excuse for opposing. Jefferson was embarrassed, not so much by the pa-tronage, as by the apparent inconsistency between his profes-sions and his acts concerning it. At first he hoped to make few removals, and these only for misconduct or other suffi-cient cause. "Of the thousands of officers in the United States," he wrote to Dr. Rush,[1] "a very few individuals only, probably not twenty, will be removed; and these only for doing what they ought not to have done." As these removals began, the outcry of the Federalists grew loud, until the Pres-ident thought himself obliged to defend his course. The oc-casion was furnished by the State of Connecticut, where the necessity for a change in office-holders was proved by the temper of the office-holding class. "The spirit in that State," wrote Madison,[2] July 10, "is so perverse that it must be rec-tified by a peculiar mixture of energy and delicacy." The spirit of which Madison complained was illustrated, only three days before, by an oration delivered July 7, at New Haven, by Theodore Dwight. The government, said Dwight, which had been established under the auspices of Washington was the sport of popular commotion, adrift without helm or compass in a turbid and boisterous ocean.

"The great object of Jacobinism, both in its political and moral revolution, is to destroy every trace of civilization in the world, and to force mankind back into a savage

[1] Jefferson to Dr. Rush, March 24, 1801; Works, iv. 382.
[2] Madison to W. C. Nicholas, July 10, 1801; Nicholas MSS.

state. . . . That is, in plain English, the greatest villain in the community is the fittest person to make and execute the laws. Graduated by this scale, there can be no doubt that Jacobins have the highest qualifications for rulers. . . . We have now reached the consummation of democratic blessedness. We have a country governed by blockheads and knaves; the ties of marriage with all its felicities are severed and destroyed; our wives and daughters are thrown into the stews; our children are cast into the world from the breast and forgotten; filial piety is extinguished, and our surnames, the only mark of distinction among families, are abolished. Can the imagination paint anything more dreadful on this side hell?"

In the fervor of his representation, Dwight painted what he believed was to happen as though it had actually come to pass. He and his friends, at least, felt no doubt of it. Madison could hardly be blamed for thinking this spirit perverse; and the President was as little to be censured for wishing to rectify it. Elizur Goodrich, a person who was quite in the same way of thinking, was Collector of New Haven. Jefferson removed him, and appointed an old man named Bishop, whose son had made himself conspicuous by zealous republicanism in a community where zeal in such a cause was accounted a social crime. A keen remonstrance was drawn up, signed by New Haven merchants, and sent to the President. Couched, as Madison said, "in the strongest terms that decorum would tolerate," this vigorous paper was in effect a challenge, for it called on the President to proclaim whether he meant to stand by the conciliatory professions of his Inaugural Address, or on his private convictions; and Jefferson was not slow to accept the challenge, in order to withdraw himself from an embarrassing position which was rapidly rousing discontent among his friends. He wrote a reply to the New Haven remonstrants, in which, without going so far as to assert that to the victors belonged the spoils, he contented himself with claiming that to the victors belonged half the spoils. Without abandoning his claim to establish harmony, he appealed to the necessity under which he was placed by the duty of doing justice to his friends.

"If a due participation of office," he said,[1] "is a matter of right, how are vacancies to be obtained? Those by death are few; by resignation, none. Can any other mode than that of removal be proposed? This is a painful office, but it is made my duty, and I meet it as such."

The Federalists found much material for ridicule in these expressions, which were certainly open to criticism; but the chief objection was that they admitted an unwilling surrender to the demands of office-seekers.

"It would have been to me a circumstance of great relief had I found a moderate participation of office in the hands of the majority. I would gladly have left to time and accident to raise them to their just share. But their total exclusion calls for prompter corrections. I shall correct the procedure, but that done, disdain to follow it, shall return with joy to that state of things when the only questions concerning a candidate shall be: Is he honest? Is he capable? Is he faithful to the Constitution?"   .

With a degree of deference to his critics which was perhaps unnecessary, and was certainly unfortunate, Jefferson characterized the officials who were to be first removed. "I proceed in the operation," he said, " with deliberation and inquiry, that it may injure the best men least, and effect the purposes of justice and public utility with the least private distress; that it may be thrown, as much as possible, on delinquency, on oppression, on intolerance, on ante-Revolutionary adherence to our enemies." Language so mild soothed and conciliated hundreds of voters who were glad to meet Jefferson's advances, but at the cost of increasing the anger felt by the great mass of Federalists for professions which they believed to be deceptive. For this result Jefferson was probably prepared, but he could hardly have intended that his letter should, by a common accident of politics, serve to create ill-feeling in his own party.

Rules which might suit New England conveyed quite another impression elsewhere. While Jefferson professed tenderness to New England in order to undermine a Federalist

[1] Writings of Jefferson (Ford), viii. 67–70.

majority, nothing of the sort was needed in other States of the Union. New York and Pennsylvania had grown used to the abuse of political patronage, and no sooner had the Republicans wrested these two States from Federalist hands than they rooted out all vestige of Federalist influence. Governor McKean, in Pennsylvania, was arbitrary enough; but when George Clinton, elected Governor of New York in the spring of 1801, came into power, the State government showed no disposition to imitate Jefferson's delicacy or his professions. August 8, 1801, a few weeks after the New Haven letter was written, Governor Clinton called a meeting of the Council which, under the Constitution of New York, had charge of the State patronage. Young De Witt Clinton and his friend Ambrose Spencer controlled this Council, and they were not persons who affected scruple in matters of political self-interest. They swept the Federalists out of every office even down to that of auctioneer, and without regard to appearances, even against the protests of the Governor, installed their own friends and family connections in power.

Had this been all, Jefferson might have ignored it. The difficulties he encountered in New York were caused not so much by the removal of Federalists, as by unwillingness to appoint Republicans. Jefferson did not like the Clintons, but he liked Aaron Burr still less.

The character of Burr was well understood by the party leaders on both sides long before 1800. The Virginians twice refused to vote for him as Vice-President before they were induced to do so in that year. Jefferson himself recorded that he considered Burr as for sale between 1790 and 1800; he even added that the two parties bid against each other in the latter year for the prize. "He was told by Dayton in 1800 he might be Secretary at War; but this bid was too late; his election as Vice-President was then foreseen."[1] According to this view, the Virginians bought him; but they had no sooner done so than they prayed to be delivered from their bargain; and De Witt Clinton undertook to deliver them, with a tacit understanding, at least on his part, that in 1808 the Virginians must reckon with him for the debt.

[1] Jefferson's Anas; Works, ix. 207.

Not, therefore, Federalists alone were victims of the scandal in New York. The exhibition of selfish intrigue which centred in New York politics was calculated to startle Jefferson from his confidence in human nature. Burr's overthrow was a matter of offices and public patronage; no principle of reform or pure motive in any person was involved in it. The New York Republicans were divided into three factions, represented by the Clinton, Livingston, and Burr interests; and among them was so little difference in principle or morals, that a politician as honest and an observer as keen as Albert Gallatin inclined to Burr as the least selfish of the three.[1] The Vice-President was popular in the city of New York, and to some extent in the country districts throughout the State. Bad as his morality was understood to be, he had at that time committed no offence that warranted ostracism; but from the moment of Governor Clinton's accession to power, he was pursued and persecuted by the whole Clinton interest.

Burr, aware of the dislike and jealousy with which the Clintons regarded him, had until then depended for a counterbalance on the Livingston interest, of which General Armstrong in the Senate and Edward Livingston in the House were the representatives at Washington; in alliance with them and in accord with Gallatin, he parcelled out the federal patronage of the State. His chief anxiety was to provide offices for his two friends, John Swartwout and Matthew L. Davis; and he succeeded in obtaining for the first the marshalship of New York, for the second a promise of the supervisorship. No sooner did the news of this arrangement reach the ears of De Witt Clinton than he remonstrated, and in a few days drew from President Jefferson a letter addressed to Governor Clinton, which in effect surrendered Burr into the hands of his enemies. "The following arrangement," wrote the President,[2] May 17, " was agreed on by Colonel Burr and some of your senators and representatives,—David Gelston, collector; Theodorus Bailey, naval officer; and M. L. Davis, supervisor." Objections had been made. Would Governor Clinton express his opinion?

In a short time Burr found that the President showed no

[1] Gallatin to Jefferson, Sept. 14, 1801; Adams's Gallatin, p. 288.
[2] Jefferson's Writings (Ford), viii. 53.

alacrity for the removal of Federalist officials in New York. Neither Bailey nor Davis was appointed. Bailey, hitherto a friend of Burr, withdrew from his candidacy under a promise, as was supposed, of the postmastership; and Davis was pressed by Burr for the post of naval officer, then held by a Federalist named Rogers, who was charged with adhesion to the British during the Revolution. Within six weeks after Jefferson's letter to Governor Clinton, Burr caught the rumor of some secret understanding, and wrote angrily to Gallatin,[1] —

"Strange reports are here in circulation respecting secret machinations against Davis. . . . This thing has, in my opinion, gone too far to be now defeated. . . . Davis is too important to be trifled with."

His remonstrances fell on deaf ears. No entreaty, even from Gallatin himself, could thenceforward induce the President to open his mouth on the subject. After waiting two months longer, Davis resorted to the desperate expedient of seeking a personal interview; and early in September undertook the long journey to Monticello, furnished with a strong letter from Gallatin, and supported by a private letter which was stronger still:[2] —

"I dislike much," wrote the Secretary in this remarkable paper, "the idea of supporting a section of Republicans in New York, and mistrusting the great majority because that section is supposed to be hostile to Burr, and he is considered as the leader of that majority. A great reason against such policy is that the reputed leaders of that section, — I mean the Livingstons generally, and some broken remnants of the Clintonian party who hate Burr, —. . . are so selfish and so uninfluential that they never can obtain their great object, the State government, without the assistance of what is called Burr's party, and will not hesitate a moment to bargain for that object with him and his friends, granting in exchange their support for anything he or they may want out of the State. . . . I do not know that there is hardly a man who meddles with politics in New York who

[1] Burr to Gallatin, June 28, 1801; Adams's Gallatin, p. 283.
[2] Gallatin to Jefferson, Sept. 14, 1801; Adams's Gallatin, p. 288.

does not believe that Davis's rejection is owing to Burr's recommendation."

Gallatin was not in the secret. Although he was the only Cabinet representative of the Middle States, his advice was neither asked nor followed. Jefferson had decided to let De Witt Clinton have his way, but he explained his intentions neither to Gallatin, Burr, nor to Davis. In reply to Gallatin's remonstrance, he wrote back from Monticello:[1] "Mr. Davis is now with me. He has not opened himself. When he does, I shall inform him that nothing is decided, nor can be till we get together at Washington."

That nothing had been decided was not only, as Burr called it,[2] a "commonplace" answer, but was also incorrect. Everything had been decided; and by the time Davis, amid the jeers of the press, rejoined Burr in New York, the results of the Clinton intrigue had become visible. While Jefferson withheld from Burr all sign of support, De Witt Clinton and Ambrose Spencer, acting in unison with the President, detached the Livingstons from Burr's interest. The Chancellor was already provided for. Too important to be overlooked, he was offered and had accepted the mission to France even before the inauguration.[3] Edward Livingston, Burr's friend, was made mayor of New York,—an office then in the gift of the Council, and supposed to be worth ten thousand dollars a year.[4] He also received from Jefferson the appointment of district attorney. The chief-justice and two of the Supreme Court judges were of the Livingston connection. The secretary of state was another of the family, and General Armstrong, one of the senators in Congress, still another. In various meetings of the Council of Appointment during the summer and autumn, the State and city offices were taken from the Federalists and divided between the Clintons and Livingstons, until the Livingstons were gorged; while Burr was left to beg from Jefferson the share of national patronage which De Witt Clinton had months before taken measures to prevent his obtaining.

[1] Jefferson to Gallatin; Adams's Gallatin, p. 289.
[2] Burr to Gallatin, March 5, 1802; Adams's Gallatin, p. 289.
[3] Jefferson to Livingston, Feb. 24, 1801; Jefferson's Works, iv. 360.
[4] Hammond's Political History, i. 180.

That Jefferson and De Witt Clinton expected and intended to drive Burr from the party was already clear to Burr and his friends as early as September, 1801, when Matthew L. Davis forced himself into Jefferson's house at Monticello, while Burr watched the tactics of De Witt Clinton's Council of Appointment. On both sides the game was selfish, and belonged rather to the intrigues of Guelfs and Ghibellines in some Italian city of the thirteenth century than to the pure atmosphere of Jefferson's republicanism. The disgust of Gallatin was deep; but he knew too well the nature of New York politics to care greatly whether Burr or Clinton were to rule, and he was anxious only to stop the use of federal patronage in the interests of party intrigue. The New Haven letter had not pleased him. Within a fortnight after that letter was written, he sent to the President[1] the draft of a Treasury Circular which would not only have stopped the removal of inferior officers, but would have shut them out from active politics. Jefferson declined to approve it. He insisted that one half the tide-waiters and other employees should be changed before he should interfere. Gallatin replied that this had already been done. "The number of removals is not great, but in importance they are beyond their number. The supervisors of all the violent party States embrace all the collectors. Add to that the intended change in the post-office, and you have in fact every man in office out of the seaports." Still Jefferson hung back, and declared that it would be a poor manoeuvre to revolt tried friends in order to conciliate moderate Federalists.[2] He could not follow his true instincts; for the pressure upon him, although trifling when compared with what he thus helped to bring on his successors, was more than he could bear. In New York Governor Clinton protested in vain against the abuse of patronage, and from Pennsylvania Governor McKean wrote:[3] "The thirst for office is immoderate; it has become an object of serious attention, and I wish I knew how to check it." The scandalous proceedings of the New York Council of Appointment sharpened the tone of Gallatin, who declared that they disgraced the Republican cause, and

[1] Gallatin to Jefferson, July 25, 1801; Gallatin's Works, i. 28.
[2] Jefferson to Gallatin, August 14, 1801; Gallatin's Works, i. 36.
[3] McKean to Jefferson, August 10, 1801; Jefferson MSS.

sank the Administration itself to a level with its predecessor.[1] With all this, the only removal in New York which
Jefferson resolutely resisted, was that of the supposed Revolutionary Tory whose place was asked for Matthew L. Davis
by Vice-President Burr.

No other member of the Cabinet offered active support to
Gallatin in this struggle against the use of federal patronage.
Madison concurred with the President in thinking the proposed Treasury Circular premature.[2] Nevertheless the Secretary of State made no changes in the bureaus of his
department, although these were full of zealous Federalists.
Not even the chief clerk, Jacob Wagner, was removed, as bitter a Federalist as any in the United States, whose presence in
the office was a disadvantage if not a danger to the Government. When Duane came to Washington, after the New York
removals had begun, and urged sweeping measures of change,
he was coldly received at the State and Treasury departments,[3] which gave him contracts for supplying paper, but
declined to give him offices; and Duane returned to Philadelphia bearing toward Madison and Gallatin a grudge which he
never forgot, and which, like that of Burr, was destined in
due time to envenom a party schism.

Although these disputes over patronage seemed to require
more of the President's thoughts than were exacted by the
study of general policy, the task of government was not severe. After passing the month of April at Monticello, Jefferson was able to rest there during the months of August and
September, leaving Washington July 30. During six months,
from April to October, he wrote less than was his custom,
and his letters gave no clear idea of what was passing in his
mind. In regard to his principles of general policy he was
singularly cautious.

"I am sensible," he wrote, March 31,[4] "how far I should
fall short of effecting all the reformation which reason
could suggest and experience approve, were I free to do

---

[1] Gallatin to Jefferson, Sept. 12, 1801; Gallatin's Works, i. 47.
[2] Jefferson to Gallatin, July 26, 1801; Gallatin's Works, i. 29. Gallatin to Jefferson, Sept. 18, 1804; Gallatin's Works, i. 208.
[3] Gallatin to Jefferson, August 17, 1801; Gallatin's Works, i. 38.
[4] Jefferson to Walter Jones, March 31, 1801; Works, iv. 392.

whatever I thought best; but when we reflect how difficult it is to move or inflect the great machine of society, how impossible to advance the notions of a whole people suddenly to ideal right, we see the wisdom of Solon's remark,—that no more good must be attempted than the nation can bear, and that all will be chiefly to reform the waste of public money, and thus drive away the vultures who prey upon it, and improve some little on old routines."

"Levees are done away," he wrote to Macon;[1] "the first communication to the next Congress will be, like all subsequent ones, by message, to which no answer will be expected; the diplomatic establishment in Europe will be reduced to three ministers; the army is undergoing a chaste reformation; the navy will be reduced to the legal establishment by the last of this month; agencies in every department will be revised; we shall push you to the utmost in economizing."

His followers were not altogether pleased with his moderation of tone. They had expected a change of system more revolutionary than was implied by a pledge to do away with the President's occasional receptions and his annual speech to Congress, to cut off three second-rate foreign missions, to chasten the army, and to execute a Federalist law about the navy, or even to revise agencies. John Randolph wrote, July 18, to his friend Joseph Nicholson, a member from Maryland:[2] "In this quarter we think that the great work is only begun, and that without a substantial reform we shall have little reason to congratulate ourselves on the mere change of men."

The task of devising what Randolph called a substantial reform fell almost wholly upon Gallatin, who arrived in Washington, May 13, and set himself to the labor of reducing to a system the theories with which he had indoctrinated his party. Through the summer and autumn he toiled upon this problem, which the President left in his hands. When October arrived, and the whole Cabinet assembled at length in Washington, under the President's eye, to prepare business

[1] Jefferson to Macon, May 14, 1801; Works, iv. 396.
[2] Adams's Randolph, p. 51.

for the coming session, Gallatin produced his scheme. First, he required common consent to the general principle that payment of debt should take precedence of all other expenditure. This axiom of Republicanism was a party dogma too well settled to be disputed. Debt, taxes, wars, armies, and navies were all pillars of corruption; but the habit of mortgaging the future to support present waste was the most fatal to freedom and purity. Having fixed this broad principle, which was, as Gallatin afterward declared, the principal object of bringing him into office,[1] a harder task remained; for if theory required prompt payment of the debt, party interest insisted with still greater energy on reduction of taxes; and the revenue was not sufficient to satisfy both demands. The customs duties were already low. The highest *ad valorem* rate was twenty per cent; the average was but thirteen. Reduction to a lower average, except in the specific duties on salt, coffee, and sugar, was asked by no one; and Gallatin could not increase the rates even to relieve taxation elsewhere. Whatever relief the party required must come from another source.

The Secretary began by fixing the limits of his main scheme. Assuming four Administrations, or sixteen years, as a fair allowance of time for extinguishing the debt, he calculated the annual sum which would be required for the purpose, and found that $7,300,000 applied every year to the payment of interest and principal would discharge the whole within the year 1817. Setting aside $7,300,000 as an annual fund to be devoted by law to this primary object, he had to deal only with such revenue as should remain.

The net receipts from customs he calculated at $9,500,000 for the year, and from lands and postage at $450,000; or $9,950,000 in all. Besides this sum of less than ten million dollars, internal taxes, and especially the tax on whiskey-stills, produced altogether about $650,000; thus raising the income to $10,600,000, or $3,300,000 in excess of the fund set apart for the debt.

If taxation were to be reduced at all, political reasons required that the unpopular excise should come first in order of

[1] Life of Gallatin, p. 270.

reduction; but if the excise were abolished, the other internal taxes were not worth retaining. Led by the wish to relieve government and people from the whole system of internal taxation, Gallatin consented to sacrifice the revenue it produced. After thus parting with internal revenue to the amount of $650,000, and setting aside $7,300,000 for the debt, he could offer to the other heads of departments only $2,650,000 for the entire expenses of government. Gallatin expected the army to be supported on $930,000, while the navy was to be satisfied with $670,000,—a charge of less than thirty-three cents a head on the white population.

Of all standards by which the nature of Jeffersonian principles could be gauged, none was so striking as this. The highest expenditure of the Federalists in 1799, when preparing for war with France and constructing a navy and an army, was six million dollars for these two branches. Peace with France being made in 1800, the expenses of army and navy would naturally fall to a normal average of about three million dollars. At a time when the population was small, scattered, and surrounded by enemies, civilized and savage; when the Mississippi River, the Gulf region, and the Atlantic coast as far as the St. Mary's were in the hands of Spain, which was still a great power; when English frigates were impressing American seamen by scores, and Napoleon Bonaparte was suspected of having bought Louisiana; when New York might be ransomed by any line-of-battle ship, and not a road existed by which a light field-piece could be hauled to the Lakes or to a frontier fort,—at such a moment, the people could hardly refuse to pay sixty cents apiece for providing some protection against dangers which time was to prove as serious as any one then imagined them to be. Doubtless the republican theory required the States to protect their own coasts and to enforce order within their own jurisdiction; but the States were not competent to act in matters which concerned the nation, and the immense territory, the Lakes, and the Mississippi and Mobile rivers, belonged within the exclusive sphere of national government.

Gallatin cut down by one half the natural estimate. That he should have done this was not surprising, for he was put in office to reduce debt and taxation, not to manage the army and navy; but he could hardly have expected that all his colleagues should agree with him,—yet his estimates were accepted by the Cabinet without serious objection, and adopted as a practical scale of governmental expenditure. Encouraged by the announcement of peace in Europe, the Secretaries of War and of the Navy consented to reduce their establishments to suit Gallatin's plans, until the entire expense of both branches for the future was to be brought within $1,900,000; while Gallatin on his side made some concessions which saved his estimates from error. The army bore the brunt of these economies, and was reduced to about three thousand men. The navy was not so great a sufferer, and its calculated reductions were less certain.

Gallatin's scheme partially warranted the claim which Jefferson in his old age loved to put forward, that he had made a revolution in the principles of the government. Yet apart from the question of its success, its rigor was less extreme than it appeared to be. Doubtless, such excessive economy seemed to relieve government of duties as well as responsibilities. Congress and the Executive appeared disposed to act as a machine for recording events, without guiding or controlling them. The army was not large enough to hold the Indians in awe; the navy was not strong enough to watch the coasts; and the civil service was nearly restricted to the collection and disbursement of revenue. The country was at the mercy of any Power which might choose to rob it, and the President announced in advance that he relied for safety upon the soundness of his theory that every foreign country felt a vital interest in retaining American commerce and the use of American harbors. All this was true, and the experiment might be called revolutionary, considering the condition of the world; nevertheless there were shades of difference in the arguments on which it rested. Even Jefferson wavered in asserting the permanence of the system, while Gallatin avowedly looked forward to the time when diminished debt and increasing resources would allow wider scope of action. Viewed from this standpoint, the system was less rigid than it seemed, since a period of not more than five or six years was needed to obtain Gallatin's object.

By an unlucky chance the system never became fully estab lished. The first step in foreign affairs taken by the new Administration plunged it into difficulties which soon forced Congress to reimpose taxation to the full amount of the internal taxes. Jefferson had not been three months in power before he found himself, by no fault of his own or of his predecessors, at war with a country against which he was forced to use in his own defence some of those frigates, the construction of which had been vehemently resisted by his party, and which he was anxious only to leave under the care of a score of marines at the Navy Yard in the Eastern Branch of the Potomac. From time immemorial the northern coast of Africa had been occupied by a swarm of pirates who played a dramatic part in the politics and literature of Europe. They figured in the story of Don Quixote as in the lies of Scapin, and enlivened with picturesque barbarism the semi civilization of European habits and manners through centuries of slow growth. The four Barbary Powers, Morocco, Algiers, Tunis, and Tripoli, lived by black-mail. So little sense of common interest had the nations of Europe, that they submitted to the demands of these petty Mahometan despots, and paid yearly sums of money, or an equivalent in ships, arms, or warlike stores, in return for which the Barbary Powers permitted them to trade with the ports on the coast and protected their ships and men. The European consuls at Algiers, Tunis, and Tripoli intrigued to impose heavier conditions on rival commerce. Following the established custom, the United States had bought treaties with all four Powers, and had during the past ten years appropriated altogether more than two million dollars for the account of ransoms, gifts, and tribute. The treaty with Tripoli, negotiated in 1796, had been observed about three years and a half. The Pacha received under it from the United States Government $83,000 in cash and presents. He suddenly demanded more, and when his demand was refused, May 14, 1801, he ordered the consular flagstaff to be cut down, which was his formal declaration of war.

The conduct of the Dey of Algiers was almost as threatening to peace as that of the Pacha of Tripoli; for the Dey compelled Captain Bainbridge to put his frigate, the "George

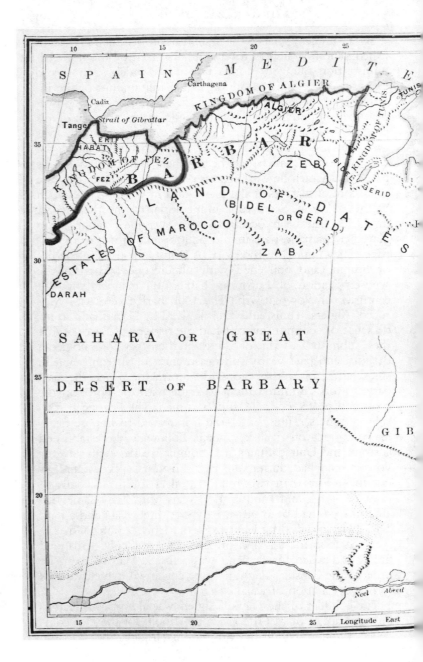

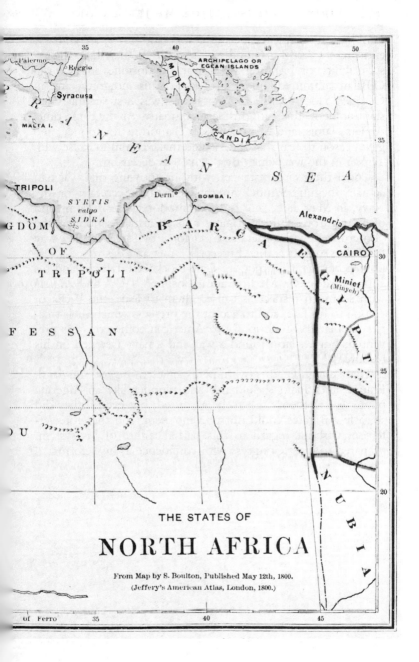

THE STATES OF

NORTH AFRICA

From Map by S. Boulton, Published May 12th, 1800.

(Jeffery's American Atlas, London, 1800.)

Washington," under Algerine colors and carry an embassy and presents to the Grand Sultan. Rather than take the responsibility of bringing on a war, Bainbridge and Consul O'Brian submitted, under protest, to this indignity; and in October, 1800, the United States flag was first seen at Constantinople in this extraordinary company. At the same time, Algiers, Tunis, and Morocco were clamorous for money, and gave reason to fear that they would make common cause with Tripoli in the war which the Pacha was declaring.

Under these circumstances, without knowing that war had actually begun, Samuel Smith, as acting Secretary of the Navy, in May, 1801, sent out Commodore Dale in command of a squadron of three frigates and an armed schooner, the "Enterprise," with orders to meet force by force. On her way to Malta, August 1, the "Enterprise" met and destroyed a Tripolitan corsair. Commodore Dale blockaded Tripoli; and his appearance in the Mediterranean inspired Tunis and Algiers with so much respect as caused them to leave the Pacha of Tripoli to his fate, and to accept the presents which their treaties stipulated. Much injury to American commerce was prevented; but Gallatin found a war and a navy fastened on his resources.

That enlightened governments like those of England, France, and Spain should rob and plunder like an Algerine pirate was in theory not to be admitted; but even if they did so, a few frigates could not prevent them, and therefore Jefferson, without regard to this partial failure of his system, prepared to meet Congress with confidence in his reforms.

Chapter IX

PRESIDENT WASHINGTON began his administration by addressing Congress in a speech, which Congress answered; and the precedent established by him in 1790 was followed by his successor. The custom was regarded by the opposition as an English habit, tending to familiarize the public with monarchical ideas, and Jefferson gave early warning that he should address Congress in a message, which would require no answer. In after times the difference between oral and written communications as signs of monarchy or republicanism became less self-evident; but the habit of writing to Congress was convenient, especially to Presidents who disliked public speaking, and Jefferson's practice remained the rule. The Federalists naturally regarded the change as a reproof, and never admitted its advantages. The Republicans also missed some of the conveniences of the old system. John Randolph, eight years afterward, seemed to regret that the speech had been abandoned:[1] —

> "The answer to an Address, although that answer might finally contain the most exceptionable passages, was in fact the greatest opportunity which the opposition to the measures of the Administration had of canvassing and sifting its measures. . . . This opportunity of discussion of the answer to an Address, however exceptionable the answer might be when it had received the last seasoning for the Presidential palate, did afford the best opportunity to take a review of the measures of the Administration, to canvass them fully and fairly, without there being any question raised whether the gentleman was in order or not; and I believe the time spent in canvassing the answer to a speech was at least as well spent as a great deal that we have expended since we discontinued the practice."

President Jefferson did not assign political reasons for changing the custom. "I have had a principal regard," he

[1] Annals of Congress, May 26, 1809, XI. Congress, Part I. p. 92.

said,[1] "to the convenience of the legislature, to the economy of their time, to their relief from the embarrassment of immediate answers on subjects not yet fully before them, and to the benefits thence resulting to the public affairs." With this preamble, he sent his message.

Jefferson's first Annual Message deserved study less for what it contained than for what it omitted. If the scope of reform was to be measured by the President's official recommendations, party spirit was likely to find little excuse for violence. The Message began by announcing, in contrast with the expectations of Republicans, that while Europe had returned to peace the United States had begun a war, and that a hostile cruiser had been captured "after a heavy slaughter of her men." The Federalist wits made fun of the moral which the President added to soften the announcement of such an event: "The bravery exhibited by our citizens on that element will, I trust, be a testimony to the world that it is not the want of that virtue which makes us seek their peace, but a conscientious desire to direct the energies of our nation to the multiplication of the human race, and not to its destruction." The idea seemed a favorite one with the President, for he next congratulated Congress on the results of the new census, which, he said, "promises a duplication in little more than twenty-two years. We contemplate this rapid growth and the prospect it holds up to us, not with a view to the injuries it may enable us to do to others in some future day, but to the settlement of the extensive country still remaining vacant within our limits, to the multiplications of men susceptible of happiness, educated in the love of order, habituated to self-government, and valuing its blessings above all price."

Just and benevolent as this sentiment might be, Jefferson rarely invented a phrase open to more perversion than when he thus announced his party's "conscientious desire to direct the energies of our nation to the multiplication of the human race." Perhaps his want of a sense of humor prevented his noticing this slip of the tongue which the English language had no precise word to describe; perhaps he intended the phrase rather for a European than for an American audience;

[1] Letter to the President of the Senate, Dec. 8, 1801.

in any case, such an introduction to his proposed reforms, in the eyes of opponents, injured their dignity and force. As he approached the reforms themselves, the manner in which he preferred to present them was characteristic. As in his Inaugural Address, he showed skill in selecting popular ground.

"There is reasonable ground of confidence," he said, "that we may now safely dispense with all the internal taxes, . . . and that the remaining sources of revenue will be sufficient to provide for the support of government, to pay the interest on the public debts, and to discharge the principals within shorter periods than the laws or the general expectation had contemplated. War, indeed, and untoward events may change this prospect of things, and call for expenses which the imposts could not meet; but sound principles will not justify our taxing the industry of our fellow-citizens to accumulate treasure for wars to happen we know not when, and which might not perhaps happen but from the temptations offered by that treasure."

Assuming that "the States themselves have principal care of our persons, our property, and our reputation, constituting the great field of human concerns," the Message maintained that the general government was unnecessarily complicated and expensive, and that its work could be better performed at a smaller cost.

"Considering the general tendency," it said, "to multiply offices and dependencies, and to increase expense to the ultimate term of burden which the citizen can bear, it behooves us to avail ourselves of every occasion which presents itself for taking off the surcharge, that it never may be seen here that, after leaving to labor the smallest portion of its earnings on which it can subsist, government shall itself consume the residue of what it was instituted to guard."

No one could deny that these sentiments were likely to please a majority of citizens, and that they announced principles of government which, if not new, were seldom or never put into practice on a great scale. As usual in such cases, the objections came from the two classes who stood at the extremes of the political movement. The Federalists denied that they had ever asked "to accumulate treasures for wars." They asked for cannon and muskets in the armories; for timber and ship-stores in the navy-yards; for fortifications to defend New York, and for readiness to resist attack. Gallatin's economies turned on the question whether the national debt or the risk of foreign aggression were most dangerous to America. Freedom from debt and the taxation which debt entailed was his object, not in order to save money, but to prevent corruption. He was ready to risk every other danger for the short time required. "Eight years hence," he afterward wrote,[1] " we shall, I trust, be able to assume a different tone; but our exertions at present consume the seeds of our greatness, and retard to an indefinite time the epoch of our strength." The epoch of strength once reached, Gallatin had no objection to tax, and tax freely, for any good purpose, even including ships-of-the-line. "Although I have been desirous," he wrote some four years later,[2] "that the measure might at least be postponed, I have had no doubt for a long time that the United States would ultimately have a navy." Nothing in his political theories prevented his spending money on defensive armaments or internal improvements or any other honest object, provided he had the money to spend.

The Federalists disagreed with Gallatin rather on a question of fact than of principle. They asserted that the country could not safely disarm; Gallatin, on the other hand, thought that for a few years military helplessness might be risked without too much danger. Time could alone decide which opinion was correct; but in this issue the Federalists could see no suggestion such as Jefferson made, that "sound principles will not justify our taxing the industry of our fellow-citizens to accumulate treasures for wars to happen we know not when." If this was the true principle of government, and if the hands of Congress were to be tied so fast that no provision could ever be made for national defence except in actual presence of war, this "sound principle" should have been announced, according to Federalist theories, not as a detail of administration but as a constitutional amendment.

[1] Gallatin to Jefferson, Aug. 16, 1802; Works, i. 88.
[2] Gallatin to Jefferson, Sept. 12, 1805; Works, i. 253.

In this opinion the true Virginia school probably con curred. Economy for its own sake was not the chief object of that class of men, and any reform on such narrow ground was not wholly to their taste. Even they were well aware at the moments when they complained most of extravagance that the United States, compared with any powerful European government, had always been a model of economy,—and indeed the most obvious criticism of the system was that economy had been its only extravagance. In the year 1800, when expenses were swollen to their highest point, in consequence of a *quasi* war with France, the disbursements reached about $11,500,000, of which the sum of $4,578,000 was on account of public debt. The running expenses of the government, including the creation of an army and a navy, did not then exceed $7,000,000, or about $1.30 a head to each inhabitant. The average annual expenditure for the past ten years had been about $9,000,000,—a smaller sum than Jefferson ever succeeded in spending. This example of economy was enough to strike the imagination of any observer; and still greater parsimony, even though it should reduce the running expenses by one half, could do no more than strengthen the same impression, or at most create an idea that republican government was too economical for its own safety. This was no revolution such as the Virginians wished to effect. They aimed at restricting power even more than at relieving taxation.

The Message put economy in the place of principle in dealing with patronage, while in regard to constitutional powers it ignored the existence of a problem. In this silence, which for the first time since 1787 fell on the lips of those who had hitherto shown only jealousy of government; in this alacrity with which Republicans grasped the powers which had, as they affirmed, made "monocrats" of their old opponents,—a European would have seen the cynicism of conscious selfishness. Certain phrases in the Constitution had been shown by experience to be full of perils, and were so well established by precedent in their dangerous meaning as to be susceptible only of excision. The clause which gave Congress sweeping power to make all laws which a majority might think "necessary and proper" for carrying the Constitution into effect, was, as settled by precedents, fatal not only to the theory of

States-rights, but to the doctrine of strict construction on which American liberties were supposed to rest. The war and treaty making powers, with their undefined and therefore unlimited consequences, were well understood. These loopholes for the admission of European sovereignty into the citadel of American liberty were seen in 1800 as clearly as when the children and grandchildren of the Southern statesmen broke up the Union because they feared the consequences of centralization. Yet Jefferson called no man's attention to the danger, took no step toward averting it, but stretched out his hand to seize the powers he had denounced.

Even in regard to the Judiciary, the most dangerous part of the system, he recommended no legislation but for the apparent purpose of saving money.

"The judiciary system of the United States," continued the Message, "and especially that portion of it recently erected, will of course present itself to the contemplation of Congress; and that they may be able to judge of the proportion which the institution bears to the business it has to perform, I have caused to be procured from the several States, and now lay before Congress, an exact statement of all the causes decided since the first establishment of the Courts, and of those which were depending when additional Courts and Judges were brought in to their aid."

That he should have shown no anxiety to limit the vague powers of Legislature and Executive was less surprising, because these powers were henceforward to remain in the hands of his own party; but the Judiciary was in the hands of Federalists, whose constitutional theories were centralization itself. The essence of Virginia republicanism lay in a single maxim: THE GOVERNMENT SHALL NOT BE THE FINAL JUDGE OF ITS OWN POWERS. The liberties of America, as the Republican party believed, rested in this nutshell; for if the Government, either in its legislative, executive, or judicial departments, or in any combination of them, could define its own powers in the last resort, then its will, and not the letter of the Constitution, was law. To this axiom of republicanism the Federalist Judiciary opposed what amounted to a flat negative. Chief-Justice Marshall and his colleagues meant to interpret the Constitution as seemed to them right, and they admitted no appeal from their decision.

The question how to deal with the Judiciary was, therefore, the only revolutionary issue before the people to be met or abandoned; and if abandoned then, it must be forever. No party could claim the right to ignore its principles at will, or imagine that theories once dropped could be resumed with equal chance of success. If the revolution of 1800 was to endure, it must control the Supreme Court. The object might be reached by constitutional amendment, by impeachment, or by increasing the number of judges. Every necessary power could be gained by inserting into the United States Constitution the words of the Constitution of Massachusetts, borrowed from English constitutional practice, that judges might be removed by the President on address by both Houses of the Legislature. Federalists were certain to denounce both object and means as revolutionary and dangerous to public repose; but such an objection could carry little weight with men who believed themselves to have gained power for no other purpose than to alter, as Jefferson claimed, the principles of government. Serious statesmen could hardly expect to make a revolution that should not be revolutionary.

Had Jefferson overlooked the danger, costly as the oversight was, it might cause no surprise; but he perceived it clearly, and in private denounced it with as much keenness as though he already knew what was to be judged "necessary and proper" for the purposes of a government which, as Virginians foresaw, would in the end interpret its own powers. "They have retired into the Judiciary as a stronghold," cried he in the same breath with which he talked to Congress only of economy.[1] "There the remains of federalism are to be preserved and fed from the Treasury; and from that battery all the works of republicanism are to be beaten down and erased." Some twenty years afterward Jefferson awoke to see his prophecy come true, and he then threw responsibility on the Constitution.

"The nation declared its will," he said,[2] "by dismissing

[1] Jefferson to J. Dickinson, Dec. 19, 1801; Works, iv. 424.
[2] Jefferson to Roane, Sept. 6, 1819; Works, vii. 133.

functionaries of one principle and electing those of another in the two branches, executive and legislative, submitted to their election. Over the judiciary department the Constitution had deprived them of their control. That, therefore, has continued the reprobated system; and although new matter has occasionally been incorporated into the old, yet the leaven of the old mass seems to assimilate to itself the new; and after twenty years' confirmation of the federated system by the voice of the nation, declared through the medium of elections, we find the Judiciary, on every occasion, still driving us into consolidation."

Such was the fact; and when Jefferson spoke of "the leaven of the old mass," he meant Chief-Justice Marshall, who had won a slow, certain victory over States-rights, and had thrust powers on the national government which, if Jefferson were right, must end in corrupting and destroying it. Whose was the fault? Was it true that the Constitution deprived the people of their control over the Judiciary? Even if it were so, did not Jefferson for years control with autocratic power the strength necessary for altering the Constitution? When at last, four years before his death, the impending certainty of defeat forced itself on Jefferson's mind, he made what amounted to a confession of his oversight, and withdrew the apology which threw blame on the Constitution: "Before the canker is become inveterate,—before its venom has reached so much of the body politic as to get beyond control,—remedy should be applied. Let the future appointments of judges be for four or six years, and renewable by the President and Senate."[1] If this could be done, as his words implied, in 1822 under the Presidency of James Monroe, when J. Q. Adams, Calhoun, Clay, and Andrew Jackson were each in his own way laboring to consolidate a nation still hot with the enthusiasm of foreign war, why was it not attempted in 1801, when a word from Jefferson would have decided the action of his party?

If this were all, some explanation of the President's silence might be offered; for in 1801–1802 his majority in the Senate was small, and only a political leader as bold as Andrew Jackson would have dared to risk his popularity on such a ven-

[1] Jefferson to W. T. Barry, July 2, 1822; Works, vii. 256.

ture. The judges held office for life; the Constitution required for amendment two thirds of the Senate and three fourths of the States; any violent shock might have thrown Connecticut and Massachusetts into open secession; but these objections to a revolution in constitutional law did not apply to partisan Federalist legislation. Why did not Jefferson officially invite Congress to confirm the action of Virginia and Kentucky by declaring the Alien and Sedition Laws to be unconstitutional and null as legislative precedents? In the absence of such a declaratory act, the Republican party left on the statute book the precedent established by those laws, which had expired only by limitation. Had the Alien and Sedition Laws been alone in dispute, the negligence might have seemed acciden- tal; but the statute-book contained another Federalist law, aimed against States-rights, which had roused alarm on that account. The Judiciary Act of 1789, the triumph of Federalist centralization, had conferred on the Supreme Court jurisdic- tion over the final judgment of State courts in cases where the powers of the general government had been "drawn in ques- tion" and the decision was unfavorable to them. This conces- sion of power to the Supreme Court,—a concession often alleged to be more dangerous to the States than the "neces- sary and proper" clause itself,—was believed to be dictated by a wish to make the State judiciaries inferior courts of the central government, because the powers of the general gov- ernment might be "drawn in question" in many ways and on many occasions, and thus the authority of the State courts made contemptible. Chief-Justice Marshall achieved one of his greatest triumphs by causing Judge Story, a republican raised to the bench in 1811 for the purpose of contesting his author- ity, to pronounce in 1816 the opinion of the court in the case of Martin *vs.* Hunter's Lessee, by which the Virginia Court of Appeals was overruled upon the question of constitution- ality raised by the State court in regard to Section 25 of the Judiciary Act. Such a result would hardly have happened had the Republicans in 1801 revised the laws which they consid- ered unconstitutional; but with what propriety could Virginia in 1816 assert the unconstitutionality of a law which she had for fifteen years possessed the power to repeal, without mak- ing an attempt or expressing a wish to exercise it?

Whatever was the true cause of the inaction, it was certainly intentional. President Jefferson wished to overthrow the Federalists and annihilate the last opposition before attempting radical reforms. Confident that States-rights were safe in his hands, he saw no occasion to alarm the people with legislation directed against past rather than future dangers. His party acquiesced, but not without misgivings. John Taylor of Caroline, most consistent of the States-rights school, thought that reforms should have been made. John Randolph, eight years afterward, expressed his opinion with characteristic frankness:—

"You know very well," he said,[1] addressing Speaker Varnum, "that there were many of us, and I was one, who thought that at the commencement of Mr. Jefferson's administration it would be proper for us to pass a sort of declaratory Act on the subject of the Sedition Law; . . . but on this subject, as well as the reduction of the army below its then standard, as on some others, I had the honor, or dishonor as some might esteem it, to be in the minority. I had thought that we ought to have returned the fines of all those who suffered under the law; . . . but you know that it was said that we came in as reformers; that we should not do too much; that we should go on little by little; that we should fire minute-guns, I think was the expression,—which produced no other effect, that I ever found, than the keeping up a spirit of irritation."

Speaker Macon, Joseph Nicholson, and William B. Giles were probably among those who held the same opinion, and were overruled by the Northern democrats. They never quite forgave Madison, to whose semi-Federalist influence they ascribed all Jefferson's sins. Distrust of Madison was natural, for neither Virginian nor New Englander understood how Madison framed the Constitution and wrote the "Federalist" with the same hand which drafted the Virginia Resolutions of 1798; but Jefferson himself would have been last to admit the correctness of such an explanation. He could point to the sentence of his Inaugural Address which pledged him to "the preservation of the general government in its whole constitutional vigor." If in redeeming the pledge he preserved vigor that his friends deemed unconstitutional, his own habits of mind, not Madison's semi-Federalist tendencies, explained the error.

Another reason partly accounted for the President's silence. In theory the Executive received its instructions from the Legislature. Upon no point had the Republican party, when in opposition, laid more stress than on the necessity of reducing Executive influence. President Washington's personal authority, even more than the supposed monarchical tendencies of his successor, inspired anger, if not terror, in the minds of his opponents. Jefferson wished to avoid this error, and to restore the true constitutional theory to its place in practice. His recommendations were studiously restrained, and the Federalists were so far silenced that they could only say with Chief-Justice Marshall, "By weakening the office of President, he will increase his personal power." The concluding sentences of the Message expressed in a few words the two leading ideas which Jefferson wished most to impress on the people, —his abnegation of power and his wish for harmony:—

> "Nothing shall be wanting on my part to inform, as far as in my power, the legislative judgment, nor to carry that judgment into faithful execution. The prudence and temperance of your discussions will promote, within your own walls, that conciliation which so much befriends rational conclusion, and by its example will encourage among our constituents that progress of opinion which is tending to unite them in object and in will. That all should be satisfied with any one order of things is not to be expected, but I indulge the pleasing persuasion that the great body of our citizens will cordially concur in honest and disinterested efforts, which have for their object to preserve the General and State governments in their constitutional form and equilibrium; to maintain peace abroad, and order and obedience to the laws at home; to establish principles and practices of administration favorable to the security of liberty and property, and to reduce expenses to what is necessary for the useful purposes of government."

Chapter X

HONEST AS Jefferson undoubtedly was in his wish to diminish executive influence, the task was beyond his powers. In ability and in energy the Executive overshadowed Congress, where the Republican party, though strong in numbers and discipline, was so weak in leadership, especially among the Northern democrats, that the weakness almost amounted to helplessness. Of one hundred and five members, thirty-six were Federalists; of the sixty-nine Republicans, some thirty were Northern men, from whom the Administration could expect little more than votes. Boston sent Dr. Eustis; from New York came Dr. Samuel L. Mitchill,—new members both; but two physicians, or even two professors, were hardly competent to take the place of leaders in the House, or to wield much influence outside. The older Northern members were for the most part men of that respectable mediocrity which followed where others led. The typical Northern democrat of that day was a man disqualified for great distinction by his want of the habits of leadership; he was obliged, in spite of his principles, to accept the guidance of aristocrats like the Livingstons, Clintons, and Burrs, or like Gallatin, Jefferson, John Randolph, and the Smiths, because he had never been used to command, and could not write or speak with perfect confidence in his spelling and grammar, or enter a room without awkwardness. He found himself ill at ease at the President's dinner-table; he could talk only upon subjects connected with his district, and he could not readily accustom himself to the scale of national affairs. Such men were thrust aside with more or less civility by their leaders, partly because they were timid, but chiefly because they were unable to combine under the lead of one among themselves. The moment true democrats produced a leader of their own, they gave him the power inherent in leadership, and by virtue of this power he became an aristocrat, was admitted into the circle of Randolphs and Clintons, and soon retired to an executive office, a custom-house or a marshalship; while the never-failing succession of democratic Congressmen from the North continued to act as before at the command of some aristocratic Virginian or educated gentleman from the city of New York.

Owing to this peculiarity, the Northern democrats were and always remained, in their organization as a party, better disciplined than their opponents. Controlling the political power of New York, New Jersey, and Pennsylvania, they wielded it as they were bid. Their influence was not that of individuality, but of mass; they affected government strongly and permanently, but not consciously; their steady attraction served to deflect the Virginia compass several degrees from its supposed bearings; but this attraction was commonly mechanical. Jefferson might honestly strip himself of patronage, and abandon the receptions of other Presidents; he might ride every day on horseback to the Capitol in "overalls of corduroy, faded, by frequent immersions in soapsuds, from yellow to a dull white," and hitch his horse in the shed,—he alone wielded power. The only counterpoise to his authority was to be found among his Southern equals and aristocratic Northern allies, whose vantage-ground was in the United States Senate or at the head of State governments; but the machinery of faction was not yet well understood. In the three former Administrations, the House had been the most powerful part of the body politic, and the House was ill-suited for factious purposes. The Senate was not yet a favorite place for party leaders to fortify themselves in power; its debates were rarely reported, and a public man who quitted the House for the Senate was thrown into the background rather than into prominence. In 1803 De Witt Clinton resigned a seat there in order to become mayor of New York. In the same year Theodorus Bailey resigned the other seat, in order to become postmaster of New York, leaving the State unrepresented. While senators had not yet learned their power, representatives were restrained by party discipline, which could be defied only by men so strong as to resist unpopularity. As long as this situation lasted, Jefferson could not escape the exercise of executive influence even greater than that which he had blamed in his predecessors.

The House chose for Speaker Nathaniel Macon, a typical, homespun planter, honest and simple, erring more often in his grammar and spelling than in his moral principles, but knowing little of the world beyond the borders of Carolina. No man in American history left a better name than Macon; but the name was all he left. An ideal Southern republican, independent, unambitious, free from intrigue, true to his convictions, a kindly and honorable man, his influence with President Jefferson was not so great as that of some less respectable and more busy politicians.

The oldest members of much authority were William B. Giles of Virginia, and Samuel Smith of Maryland. In the characters of both these men was something which, in spite of long service and fair abilities, kept them subordinate. Whether on account of indolence or temper, restlessness or intrigue, they seldom commanded the full weight to which their service entitled them. Speaker Macon, in appointing his standing committees, passed over both in order to bring forward a young favorite of his own,—a Virginian barely twenty-eight years old, whose natural quickness of mind and faculty for ready speaking gave him prominence in a body of men so little marked by ability as was the Seventh Congress. During several years the Federalist newspapers never wearied of gibing at the long lean figure, the shrill voice and beardless face of the boyish Republican leader, among whose peculiarities of mind and person common shrewishness seemed often to get the better of intense masculine pride. Besides his natural abilities and his superior education, the young man had the advantage of belonging to the most widely-connected of all Virginia families; and this social distinction counted for everything in a party which, although reviled as democratic, would be led by no man without birth and training. Incomprehensible to New England Federalists, who looked on him as a freak of Nature; obnoxious to Northern democrats, who groaned in secret under his insane spur and curb; especially exasperating to those Southern Republicans whose political morality or whose manners did not suit him,—Randolph, by his independence, courage, wit, sarcasm, and extreme political orthodoxy, commanded strong influence among the best Virginians of the States-rights school. More than half the Virginia delegation belonged to the same social and political caste; but none of them could express so well as Randolph the mixture of contradictory theories, the breadth and narrowness, the aspirations and ignorance, the genius and prejudices of Virginia.

The experiment of placing Randolph at the head of the Ways and Means Committee was hazardous; and to support him the Speaker put as second member their friend Joseph Nicholson of Maryland, while General Smith retained his old place at the head of the Committee on Commerce, and Giles was quite neglected. The Federalists even in their reduced condition, numbering barely one third of the House, still overmatched the majority in debate. Randolph, Nicholson, Samuel Smith, and Giles were hardly equal to Bayard, Griswold, Dana, John Cotton Smith, and John Rutledge.

No member of the House wielded serious influence over the President, or represented with authority the intentions of the party; and although in the Senate the Republicans were stronger in ability, they were weaker in numbers, and therefore more inclined to timidity. The ablest of the Republican senators was a new man, John Breckinridge of Kentucky, another Virginia aristocrat, chiefly known as the putative father of the Kentucky Resolutions of 1798. Breckinridge was bold enough to support any policy that the Administration would consent to impose; but he was new to the Senate, and, like Randolph, had yet to win the authority of a leader against a strong Federalist opposition.

The business of the first session of the Seventh Congress quickly took shape in two party struggles on the lines marked out by the Message; and the same caution which made the Message disappointing as a declaration of principles, affected the debates and laws. Although the Federalists offered challenge after challenge, charging the majority with revolutionary schemes which no honest democrat needed to deny, the Republicans, abiding carefully for the most part within the defences selected by the President, seemed unwilling to avow the legitimate objects of their acts. The two measures over which the struggle took place were not so important as to touch the foundations of government, unless they were parts of more sweeping changes to come. They required the overthrow of two Federalist creations, but not expressly of any Federalist principle. They abolished the internal taxes and the circuit courts, but touched no vital power of government.

Resistance to the abolition of taxes was impossible after the promise which the President's Message held out. The Federalists themselves had made peace with France, and hostilities between France and England had ceased. For the first time in ten years no danger of foreign war was apparent, and if the Administration offered to effect economies in the public service, Congress could hardly deny that economies were possible. The opposition preferred not to question the estimates, but to rival the Government in zeal for reduction of taxes; and on this point they argued with some force that although the *ad valorem* duties were low,—averaging about thirteen per cent,—the specific duties on necessaries of life like salt and sugar, tea and coffee, amounted to fifty and a hundred per cent; and reduction of these would surely give more relief than would be afforded by repealing the tax on whiskey,—a proper object of taxation,—or the stamp-duty, which was one of the best and cheapest taxes on the list. The majority replied that to abolish the internal revenue system was to diminish by one half the Executive patronage. Forcible as this reasoning was, it did not convince the Federalist leaders in the House, who insisted upon moving amendments. The majority became irritated; a Kentucky member advised that the Federalists should be left unanswered, and their motions voted down. A Republican caucus decided to adopt for a time this course; and the next day, Jan. 25, 1802, when a New York Federalist called for returns in regard to the stamp-tax, the House by a vote of fifty-four to thirty-four bluntly refused the information. Such motions were usually adopted by courtesy, and the Federalists, in their twelve years of rule, were rarely accused of a course so high-handed as that of the new majority. James A. Bayard, of Delaware, who led the Federalists, instantly called up another motion of the same class. After he had spoken in its favor, John Randolph rose and ordered the clerk to read an extract from Gallatin's report. No other reply was offered. One Federalist member after another remonstrated against this tyranny of silence; but not a member of the majority spoke, and the returns were refused by a vote of fifty-seven to thirty-seven. Immediately John Rutledge called up a third resolution of the same nature, and Samuel Dana of Connecticut made a sensation long remembered, by quoting to the majority the remark, then quite new, of Bonaparte to Sieyès: "That dumb legislature will immortalize your name."

Neither in the Senate nor in the House did Gallatin's financial schemes meet with serious question; they were accepted without change, and embodied in legislation evidently the work of the secretary's own hand. So cautious was Gallatin, that notwithstanding the assertions of the President's Message, he would not make himself responsible for the repeal of internal taxes, but left his colleagues of the War and Navy to pledge themselves to John Randolph for economies to the amount of $600,000, which the event proved to be not wholly practicable. Dearborn and Robert Smith in good faith gave to Randolph the required pledges, and Congress gladly acted upon them. The internal taxes were swept away, and with them one half the government patronage; while a sinking fund was organized, by means of which the public debt, amounting to a nominal capital of about $80,000,000, was to be paid off in sixteen years.

This financial legislation was the sum of what was accomplished by Congress toward positive reform. The whole of Jefferson's theory of internal politics, so far as it was embodied in law, rested in the Act making an annual appropriation of $7,300,000 for paying interest and capital of the public debt; and in the Act for repealing the internal taxes. In these two measures must be sought the foundation for his system of politics abroad and at home, as this system has been described; for his policy flowed in a necessary channel as soon as these measures were adopted.

Great as the change was which under the guise of economy Congress thus quietly effected, —a change which in Jefferson's intention was to substitute commercial restrictions in the place of armaments, for purposes of national defence,— so skilfully was it done that the Federalists could muster only twenty-four votes against it. Jefferson succeeded in carrying his preliminary measures through Congress without meeting, or even raising, the question of their ultimate objects and practical scope; but this manner of dealing with a free people had disadvantages, for it caused them to adopt a system which they did not wholly understand, and were not fully prepared to carry out. A few Virginians knew what Jefferson meant; a clique of members in the House and Senate might have foretold every step in the movement of Government: but the Northern and Western democrats thought only of economy, and accepted the President's partial reasoning as sufficient; while the Federalists, although they saw the truth more clearly, could not oblige the Administration to enter into a full and candid discussion, which, without affecting the result, would have educated the public and saved much misunderstanding in the future.

The Federalists, left to an issue involving mere details of taxation, wasted their strength on a subordinate point. Perhaps their exertions were not wholly wasted, for their outcries may have had some effect in persuading the majority that the new reforms were extreme; but in reality the opposition resisted feebly the vital financial scheme, and exerted all its energies against the second and less serious Administration measure,—the repeal of the Judiciary Act of 1801.

The previous history of the Judiciary Act belonged to the administration of Jefferson's predecessor and to the records of the Federalist party. Before 1801 the Supreme Court consisted of six justices, who held two terms a year at Washington, and twice a year rode their circuits, each justice then sitting in association with a district judge. The system pleased no one. The justices, men of age and dignity, complained that they were forced twice a year, in the most trying seasons and through the roughest country, to ride hundreds of miles on horseback " with the agility of post-boys;" the lawyers found fault because the errors of the inferior court were corrected by the judges who had made them; the suitors were annoyed by the delays and accidents inevitable to such journeys and such judges. In the last year of Federalist power a new arrangement was made, and the Judiciary Act of 1801 reduced the Supreme Court to five judges, who were fixed at Washington, while their circuit duties were transferred to a new class of circuit judges, eighteen in number. Twenty-three districts were divided into six circuits, and the circuit judges sat independently of the district judges, as well as of the Supreme Bench. This separation of the machinery of the District, Circuit, and Supreme Courts caused a multiplication of judicial

offices and an increased annual expense of some thirty thousand dollars.

No sooner did this Bill become law, Feb. 13, 1801, than the
Federalists used their last moments of power to establish
themselves in the posts it created. In Jefferson's words, they
retreated into the Judiciary as a stronghold. They filled the
new courts as well as the vacancies on the old bench with safe
men, at whose head, as Chief-Justice of the Supreme Court,
was placed the Secretary of State, John Marshall. That Jefferson should have been angry at this manoeuvre was natural;
but, apart from greed for patronage, the Federalists felt
bound to exclude Republicans from the bench, to prevent the
overthrow of those legal principles in which, as they believed,
national safety dwelt. Jefferson understood the challenge, and
was obliged to accept or decline it.

On one ground alone could the President and his party
fully meet the issue thus offered. They had sought and won
popularity on the principle of States-rights. The Judiciary Act
of 1789, even more than its supplement of 1801, was notoriously intended to work against the object they had most at
heart. The effect of both these Acts was, in their belief, to
weaken the State judiciaries and to elevate the national judiciary at their expense, until the national courts should draw
to themselves all litigation of importance, leaving the State
courts without character or credit. From their point of view,
the whole judiciary system should be remodelled, with the
purpose of reversing this centralizing movement; and that
such a reform must begin with the Supreme Court was too
evident for discussion. The true question for Congress to consider was not so much the repeal of the Judiciary Act of 1801,
as the revision of that which had set in motion the whole
centripetal machine in 1789.

Jefferson's Message, as has been shown, offered to Congress an issue quite different, at least in appearance.

"The judiciary system of the United States,"—so his
words ran,—"and especially that portion of it recently
erected, will of course present itself to the contemplation
of Congress; and that they may be able to judge of the
proportion which the institution bears to the business it

has to perform, I have caused to be procured from the several States, and now lay before Congress, an exact statement of all the causes decided since the first establishment of the courts, and of those which were depending when additional courts and judges were brought in to their aid."

From the true Virginia standpoint, the fewer the causes the less danger. What the Virginians feared most was the flow of business to the national courts; and Jefferson's statistics tended only to show that as yet the new courts had done no harm, inasmuch as they had little to do. Their abolition on the ground of economy would still leave the Judiciary establishment of 1789 untouched, merely in order to lop off an excrescence which might be restored whenever increase of business should require it,—and which Jefferson's argument in a manner pledged him in such an event to re-establish.

The contradictions in Jefferson's character have always rendered it a fascinating study. Excepting his rival Alexander Hamilton, no American has been the object of estimates so widely differing and so difficult to reconcile. Almost every other American statesman might be described in a parenthesis. A few broad strokes of the brush would paint the portraits of all the early Presidents with this exception, and a few more strokes would answer for any member of their many cabinets; but Jefferson could be painted only touch by touch, with a fine pencil, and the perfection of the likeness depended upon the shifting and uncertain flicker of its semi-transparent shadows. Of all the politicians and writers of that day, none could draw portraits with a sharper outline than Hamilton, whose clear-cut characterizations never failed to fix themselves in the memory as distinctly as his own penetrating features were fixed in Ceracchi's marble or on Trumbull's canvas; and Hamilton's contrasted portraits of Jefferson and Burr, drawn in an often-quoted letter written to Bayard in January, 1801, painted what he believed to be the shifting phase of Jefferson's nature.

"Nor is it true," he said,[1] "that Jefferson is zealot enough to do anything in pursuance of his principles which will

[1] Hamilton to Bayard, Jan. 15, 1801; Hamilton's Works, vi. 419.

contravene his popularity or his interest. He is as likely as any man I know to temporize, to calculate what will be likely to promote his own reputation and advantage; and the probable result of such a temper is the preservation of systems, though originally opposed, which, being once established, could not be overturned without danger to the person who did it. To my mind, a true estimate of Mr. Jefferson's character warrants the expectation of a temporizing rather than a violent system."

Never was a prophecy more quickly realized. Jefferson's suggestion that the new Judiciary was unnecessary because it had not enough business to keep it fully employed, although by implication admitting that more business would justify its creation, became at once the doctrine of his party. Jan. 8, 1802, Breckinridge undertook the task of moving in the Senate the repeal of the Act; and his argument closely followed the President's suggestion, that the new courts, being unnecessary and therefore improper, might and should be abolished. The Federalists took the ground that the Constitution secured to the judges their office during good behavior, and that to destroy the office was as distinct a violation of the compact as to remove the judge. Thus from the beginning the debate was narrowed to a technical issue. On the one side was seen an incessant effort to avoid the broader issues which the Federalists tried to force; on the other side, a certain dramatic folding of robes, a theatrical declamation over the lay-figure which Federalists chose to declare a mangled and bleeding Constitution. Gouverneur Morris of New York, whose oratory was apt to verge on the domain of melodrama, exceeded himself in lamentations over the grave of the Constitution:--

"Cast not away this only anchor of our safety. I have seen its progress. I know the difficulties through which it was obtained. I stand in the presence of Almighty God and of the world, and I declare to you that if you lose this charter, never, no, never will you get another! We are now, perhaps, arrived at the parting point. Here, even here, we stand on the brink of fate. Pause! pause! For Heaven's sake, pause!"

If ever a party had paused, it was the Republicans. The progress of what Gouverneur Morris, with characteristic rhetoric, called the "anchor," was thus far arrested only in appearance; and there were already symptoms that the Virginians had reached not only the limit of their supposed revolutionary projects, but also of their influence, and that they were themselves anxious to go no farther. Signs of trouble appeared among the Northern democrats, and sharp hints were given that the Virginians might expect revolt, not so much against their principles as against their patronage. Vice-President Burr did not appear in Washington until six weeks of the session had passed; and when he took the chair of the Senate, Jan. 15, 1802, the Virginians had every reason to expect that he would show them no kindness. Under the affected polish and quiet of his manner, he nursed as bitter a hatred as his superficial temper could feel against the whole Virginia oligarchy. Any suggestion that Burr held scruples of conscience in regard to the Federalist judiciary would border on satire, for Burr's conscience was as elastic as his temper; but he made grave inquiries as to the law, and hinted doubts calculated to alarm the Virginians. Had he been content to affect statesmanship, Breckinridge could have afforded to ignore his demonstrations; but the behavior of General Armstrong, the democratic senator from New York, and the accidental absence of Senator Bradley of Vermont unexpectedly threw into Burr's hands the power to do mischief. Armstrong failed to appear at Washington, and his vote was lost. Breckinridge's motion for a committee of inquiry was carried, January 19, only by fifteen against thirteen votes; and no sooner had his committee, with all practicable speed, reported a Bill for the repeal of the Judiciary Act of 1801, than it appeared that the Senate was tied, fifteen to fifteen, with Armstrong and Bradley absent, and the Vice-President controlling the fate of the Bill. Burr lost no time in giving a first warning to the Virginians. Dayton of New Jersey, a Federalist, but an intimate friend of the Vice-President, moved January 27 to recommit the Bill to a select committee, and Burr's casting vote carried the motion.

That Breckinridge and his friends were angry at this check

need not be said; but they were forced to wait several days for Bradley's return, before Breckinridge could move and obtain, February 2, the discharge of the special committee, and recover control of the Bill. Burr was never given another opportunity to annoy his party by using his casting vote; but meanwhile symptoms of hesitation appeared among the Northern democrats, even more significant than the open insubordination of Burr. On the day when Breckinridge succeeded in discharging the special committee, Senator Ross of Pennsylvania presented a memorial from the Philadelphia Bar, declaring their conviction that the actual Circuit Court was a valuable institution, which could not be abolished without great public inconvenience; and this memorial was enforced by a letter in strong terms, signed by A. J. Dallas, Jefferson's own district attorney, and by the Republican Attorney-General of Pennsylvania, Governor McKean's son. The behavior of Senator Armstrong raised a fear that the Livingstons were not to be depended upon; and hardly had the Bill passed the Senate, February 3, by a vote of sixteen to fifteen, than Armstrong resigned his post in order to let De Witt Clinton take it. In the House, Dr. Eustis of Boston, alone among the Republicans, opposed the repeal; but the tone of the debate and of the press showed that few Northern democrats cared to risk the odium of a genuine assault on the authority of the Supreme Court.

Another and still sharper hint was soon given to the Virginians. At the moment when the Bill coming before the House roused there an acrimonious debate, in which the Federalists assumed a tone that exasperated and alarmed their opponents, the anniversary of Washington's birthday occurred. The Federalist Congressmen were accustomed to give, February 22, what was called a banquet,—a practice which verged so closely on monarchism that Jefferson made a secret of his own birthday, for fear that his followers should be misled by the example into making him a monocrat against his will. Either at Burr's secret instigation, or in a spirit of mischief, the Federalists this year, on the pretence that they had voted for Burr as President only a year before, invited him to their banquet.

"We knew," wrote Bayard to Hamilton,[1] "the impression which the coincidence of circumstances would make upon a certain great personage; how readily that impression would be communicated to the proud and aspiring lords of the Ancient Dominion; and we have not been mistaken as to the jealousy we expected it would excite through the party."

In the middle of the feast the door opened, and the Vice-President, courteous and calm as though he were taking the chair of the Senate, entered and took a seat of honor at the table. His appearance was expected, and roused no surprise; but to the startled amusement of the Federalists he presently rose and pronounced a toast: "The union of all honest men!"

This dramatic insult, thus flung in the face of the President and his Virginia friends, was the more significant to them because they alone understood what it meant. To the world at large the toast might seem innocent; but the Virginians had reason to know that Burr believed himself to have been twice betrayed by them, and that his union of honest men was meant to gibbet them as scoundrels. They had no choice but to resent it. Henceforward the party could not contain both him and them. Within a few days De Witt Clinton's newspaper, the "American Citizen," began the attack, and its editor Cheetham henceforward pursued Burr with a vindictiveness which perplexed and divided the Northern democrats, who had no great confidence in Clinton. What was of far more consequence, Duane and the Philadelphia "Aurora," after a moment's hesitation, joined in the hue-and-cry.

[1] Bayard to Hamilton, April 12, 1802; Hamilton's Works, vi. 539.

Chapter XI

THE BILL REPEALING the new Judiciary Act, having passed the Senate, February 3, was taken into consideration by the House, in Committee of the Whole, February 4, and caused the chief debate of the session. By common consent Giles and Bayard were accepted as the champions of the two parties, and their speeches were taken as the official arguments on either side. The men were equal to their tasks. For ten years William Branch Giles had been the most active leader of the extreme Republicans. A Virginian, born in 1762, he began his career as a Member of Congress in 1791, by opposing the creation of a national bank. In 1793 he distinguished himself by an attack on Secretary Hamilton, charging him with peculation. In 1796 he led the opposition to Jay's Treaty. After opposing Washington's administration with consistency and severity during six years, he retired from Congress in 1798 in order to oppose Washington's successor with more effect in the legislature of Virginia. With James Madison, John Taylor of Caroline, and Wilson Cary Nicholas, he had taken an active part in the Resolutions of 1798, and his remarks in the debate of December, 1798, showed that he carried the extreme conclusions of the Virginia school to their extreme practical consequences.[1] He "said that the measures of our present government tended to the establishment of monarchy, limited or absolute. . . . If . . . the government were a social compact, he pronounced monarchy to be near at hand, the symptoms and causes of which he particularly pointed out; and concluded that the State legislatures alone, at this time, prevented monarchy." In language perfectly intelligible to his friends he hinted that his party "had no arms, but they would find arms." Even men naturally benevolent, like Jefferson, could rarely resist the conviction that the objects of political opponents were criminal, but Giles exceeded every prominent partisan on either side by the severity of his imputations. As late as June, 1801, he wrote from Richmond to President Jefferson:[2] "The ejected party is now almost uni-

[1] The Virginia Report of 1799–1800, etc. Richmond, 1850, pp. 143–148.
[2] Giles to Jefferson, June 1, 1801. Hamilton's History, vii. 585 n.

versally considered as having been employed, in conjunction
with Great Britain, in a scheme for the total destruction of
the liberties of the people." No man in the Union was more
cordially detested by the Federalists; and even between parties
that held each other in little or no respect, few men of so
much eminence were so little respected as Giles. The dislike
and distrust were mutual. Giles's nature was capable of no
pleasure greater than that of exasperating his Federalist opponents; and he rarely enjoyed a better opportunity for irritation than on Feb. 18, 1802, when, with a great majority
behind him, and with the consciousness of triumph attained,
he broke into the dull debate on the Judiciary Bill.

Both sides were weary of the narrow question whether
Congress had the power to remove Judges by legislation.
Whether such a power existed or not, every one knew that
the Republican majority meant to use it, and the Federalists
were chiefly anxious to profit by the odium they could attach
to its abuse. The Federalists, in a character new to them,
posed as the defenders of the Constitution against sacrilegious
attacks; while the Republicans, for the first time in their history as a party, made light of constitutional objections, and
closed their ears to warnings in which they had themselves
hitherto found their chief rhetorical success. With Giles's appearance on the floor the tedious debate started into virulence. He began by insinuating motives, as though he were
still discussing the Alien and Sedition Laws in the Virginia
legislature of 1798: "A great portion of the human mind," he
began, "has been at all times directed toward monarchy as the
best form of government to enforce obedience and insure the
general happiness; whereas another portion of the human
mind has given a preference to the republican form as best
calculated to produce the same end." On this difference of
opinion the two parties had been founded, the one wishing
"to place in executive hands all the patronage it was possible
to create for the purpose of protecting the President against
the full force of his constitutional responsibility to the people;" the other contending "that the doctrine of patronage
was repugnant to the opinions and feelings of the people;
that it was unnecessary, expensive, and oppressive; and that
the highest energy the government could possess would flow

from the confidence of the mass of the people, founded upon their own sense of their common interest." Thus patronage, or in other words the creation of partial interests for the protection and support of government, had become the guiding principle of the Federalists. For this purpose the debt was funded; under cover of an Indian war, an army was created; under cover of an Algerine war, a navy was built; to support this system, taxation was extended; and finally, by availing itself of French depredations on commerce, the Administration succeeded in pushing all the forms of patronage to an extreme. When the people at last rebelled, and the Federalists saw themselves in danger, "it was natural for them to look out for some department of the government in which they could intrench themselves in the event of an unsuccessful issue in the election, and continue to support those favorite principles of irresponsibility which they could never consent to abandon."

Whatever amount of truth was contained in these charges against the Federalists, they had the merit of consistency; they reaffirmed what had been the doctrine of the party when in opposition; what Jefferson was saying in private, and what was a sufficient argument not so much against the circuit judges as against the Federalist Judiciary altogether; but the position seemed needlessly broad for the support of the technical argument by which Giles proved the power of Congress in regard to the measure under discussion:—

"On one side it is contended that the office is the vested property of the judge, conferred on him by his appointment, and that his good behavior is the consideration of his compensation; so long, therefore, as his good behavior exists, so long his office must continue in consequence of his good behavior; and that his compensation is his property in virtue of his office, and therefore cannot be taken away by any authority whatever, although there may be no service for him to perform. On the other it is contended that the good behavior is not the consideration upon which the compensation accrues, but services rendered for the public good; and that if the office is to be considered as a property, it is a property held in trust for the benefit of the people, and must therefore be held subject to that condition of which Congress is the constitutional judge."

Assuming that the latter view was correct, Giles gave his reasons for holding that the new Judiciary should be abolished; and the subject led him into a history of the circumstances under which the Act passed, at the moment when the House of Representatives was in permanent session, "in the highest paroxysm of party rage," disputing over the choice between Jefferson and Burr as President. He charged that members of the legislature who voted for the law " were appointed to offices, not indeed created by the law, the Constitution having wisely guarded against an effect of that sort, but to judicial offices previously created by the removal, or what was called the promotion, of judges from the offices they then held to the offices newly created, and supplying their places by members of the legislature who voted for the creation of the new offices." He showed that the business of the courts "is now very much declined, and probably will decline still more."

> "Under the view of the subject thus presented, he considered the late courts as useless and unnecessary, and the expense therefore was to him highly objectionable. He did not consider it in the nature of a compensation, for there was no equivalent rendition of service. He could not help considering it as a tribute for past services; as a tribute for the zeal displayed by these gentlemen in supporting principles which the people had denounced."

Such arguments, if good for the new circuit courts, were still stronger in their application to the Supreme Court itself. Giles affirmed that the "principles advanced in opposition . . . go to the establishment of a permanent corporation of individuals invested with ultimate censorial and controlling power over all the departments of the government, over legislation, execution, and decision, and irresponsible to the people." He believed that these principles were "in direct hostility with the great principle of representative government." Undoubtedly these principles, if they existed anywhere, were strongest, not in the circuit, but in the Supreme Court; and if any judge was to be set aside because his appointment might be considered as a reward for zeal displayed in supporting "principles which the people had denounced," Chief-Justice Marshall, the person most likely to exercise "ultimate censorial and controlling power over all the departments of government," was peculiarly subject to suspicion and removal. To no man had the last President been more indebted, and to no one had he been more grateful.

Only incidentally, at the close of his speech, Giles advanced a final, and in his mind fatal, objection to the new courts, "because of their tendency to produce a gradual demolition of State Courts." Of all arguments this seemed to be the most legitimate, for it depended least on the imputation of evil motives to the Congress which passed the Act. No one need be supposed criminal for wishing, as was often admitted, to bring justice to every man's door; and as little need any one be blamed for wishing to maintain or to elevate the character of his State Judiciary. Parties might honestly and wisely differ, and local interests might widely diverge in a matter so much depending upon circumstances; but no argument seemed to satisfy Giles unless it carried an implication of criminality against his opponents.

Giles's speech was such as an orator would select to answer, and James Asheton Bayard could fairly claim the right to call himself an orator. Born in Philadelphia, in 1767, Bayard was five years younger than Giles, and had followed the opposite path in politics. Without being an extreme Federalist, he had been since 1796 a distinguished member of the Federalist party in Congress, and had greatly contributed to moderate the extravagances of his friends. In the style of personality which Giles affected, Bayard was easily a master. Virulence against virulence, aristocracy had always the advantage over democracy; for the aristocratic orator united distinct styles of acrimony, and the style of social superiority was the most galling. Giles affected democratic humility to the last, and partly for that reason never became a master even of invective; while John Randolph, finding the attitude of a democrat unsuited for his rhetoric, abandoned it, and seemed to lose his mental balance in the intoxication of his recovered social superiority. Giles's charges, by an opposite illusion, seemed to crawl; his contempt resembled fear; his democratic virtues crouched before the aristocratic insolence they reproved. Bayard appeared to carry with him the sympathy of all that was noble in human character when, taking the floor as Giles sat down, he turned on the Virginian with a dignity of retort which, whatever might be its value as argument, cut the deeper because its justice could not be denied.

Jefferson's administration was not yet a year old; the Federalists had twelve long years abounding in mistakes and misfortunes to defend, and Giles's arraignment embraced the whole. Bayard accepted the challenge, and his speech, too historical for compression, varied between long periods of defence and brief intervals of attack. The defence belonged to past history; the attack concerned the actual moment, and need alone be noticed here. He began by refusing belief that Giles ever seriously felt the fear of monarchy he expressed; he was led by other motives:—

"I pray to God I may be mistaken in the opinions I entertain as to the designs of gentlemen to whom I am opposed. Those designs I believe hostile to the powers of this government. State pride extinguishes a national sentiment. Whatever power is taken from this government is given to the States. The ruins of this government aggrandize the States. There are States which are too proud to be controlled, whose sense of greatness and resource renders them indifferent to our protection, and induces a belief that if no general government existed, their influence would be more extensive and their importance more conspicuous. There are gentlemen who make no secret of an extreme point of depression to which the government is to be sunk. To that point we are rapidly progressing."

The charge was certainly emphatic, and deserved as clear an answer from Giles as Bayard gave to the charge of monarchical tendencies. On the constitutional point involved in the Bill before the House, Bayard was equally distinct:—

"The point on which I rely is that you can do no act which impairs the independence of a judge. When gentlemen assert that the office may be vacated notwithstanding the incumbency of a judge, do they consider that they beg the very point which is in controversy? The office cannot be vacated without violating the express provision of the Constitution in relation to the tenure. . . . The second plain, unequivocal provision on this subject is that the compensation of the judge shall not be diminished during the time he continues in office. This provision is directly levelled at the power of the legislature: they alone could reduce the salary. Could this provision have any other design than to place the judge out of the power of Congress? You cannot reduce a part of the compensation, but you may extinguish the whole. What is the sum of this notable reasoning? You cannot remove the judge from the office, but you may take the office from the judge; you cannot take the compensation from the judge, but you may separate the judge from the compensation. If your Constitution cannot resist reasoning like this, then indeed is it waste paper."

When Bayard reached Giles's favorite doctrine that patronage was a Federalist system, and the charge that two senators who voted for the Judiciary Act of 1801 were rewarded by the offices vacated in consequence of promotions to circuit judgeships, he produced a true oratorical sensation by a retort that sank deep into the public memory: —

"The case to which I refer carries me once more to the scene of the Presidential election. I should not have introduced it into this debate, had it not been called up by the honorable member from Virginia. In that scene I had my part; it was a part not barren of incident, and which has left an impression which cannot easily depart from my recollection. I know who were rendered important characters, either from the possession of personal means or from the accident of political situation. And now, Sir, let me ask the honorable member what his reflections and belief will be when he observes that every man on whose vote the event of the election hung has since been distinguished by presidential favor. I fear, Sir, I shall violate the decorum of parliamentary proceeding in the mentioning of names, but I hope the example which has been set me will be admitted as an excuse. Mr. Charles Pinckney of South Carolina was not a member of the House, but he was one of the most active, efficient, and successful promoters of the election of the present chief magistrate. It was well ascertained that the votes of South Carolina were to turn the equal balance of the scales. The zeal and industry of Mr. Pinckney had no bounds; the doubtful politics of South Carolina were decided, and her votes cast in the scale of Mr. Jefferson. Mr. Pinckney has since been appointed Minister Plenipotentiary to the Court of Madrid,—an appointment as high and honorable as any within the gift of the Executive. I will not deny that this preferment is the reward of talents and services, although, Sir, I have never yet heard of the talents or services of Mr. Charles Pinckney. In the House of Representatives I know what was the value of the vote of Mr. Claiborne of Tennessee; the vote of a State was in his hands. Mr. Claiborne has since been raised to the high dignity of Governor of the Mississippi Territory. I know how great, and how greatly felt, was the importance of the vote of Mr. Linn of New Jersey. The delegation of the State consists of five members; two of the delegation were decidedly for Mr. Jefferson, two were decidedly for Mr. Burr. Mr. Linn was considered as inclining to one side, but still doubtful; both parties looked up to him for the vote of New Jersey. He gave it to Mr. Jefferson; and Mr. Linn has since had the profitable office of supervisor of his district conferred upon him. Mr. Lyon of Vermont was in this instance an important man; he neutralized the vote of Vermont; his absence alone would have given the vote of a State to Mr. Burr. It was too much to give an office to Mr. Lyon,—his character was low; but Mr. Lyon's son has been handsomely provided for in one of the Executive offices. I shall add to the catalogue but the name of one more gentleman, Mr. Edward Livingston of New York. I knew well—full well I knew—the consequence of this gentleman. His means were not limited to his own vote; nay, I always considered more than the vote of New York within his power. Mr. Livingston has been made the Attorney for the District of New York; the road of preferment has been opened to him, and his brother has been raised to the distinguished place of Minister Plenipotentiary to the French Republic."

Such charges would have caused little feeling at any subsequent period, but the Republican party was the first opposition that gained power in the United States, and hitherto it had believed in its own virtue. Such a state of things could never occur again, for only a new country could be inexperienced in politics; but the cynical indifference with which Europe looked on while patriots were bought, was as yet unknown to Jefferson's friends. They were honest; they supposed themselves to have crushed a corrupt system, and to have overthrown in especial the influence of Executive patronage upon Congress. Men like Gallatin, Giles, Randolph, Macon, Nicholson, Stanford, and John Taylor of Caroline listened to Bayard's catalogue of Executive favors as though it were a criminal indictment. They knew that he might have said more, had he been deeper in Executive secrets. Not only had he failed to include all the rewards given to Jefferson's friends, but he omitted the punishments inflicted on those who were believed to be Jefferson's enemies. He did not know that Theodorus Bailey, another of Burr's friends who had voted for Jefferson, was soon to be made postmaster of New York, while Burr himself was not only refused the appointment of Matthew L. Davis, but was to be condemned without a trial.

The acrimony which Giles's tongue thus threw into the debate continued to the end of the session, but had no deeper effect than to make the majority cautious. They were content to show that the Constitution did not expressly forbid the act they meant to perform. In truth the legality of the act depended on the legitimacy of the motive. Of all the root-and-branch Virginians, John Randolph was perhaps the most extreme; and his speech of February 20 laid down an honest principle of action. "It is not on account of the paltry expense of the establishment that I want to put it down," he protested; and with still more energy he said, "I am free to declare that if the intent of this Bill is to get rid of the judges, it is a perversion of your power to a base purpose; it is an unconstitutional act."

As a matter of expediency and public convenience, no one seriously denied that the Federalists were altogether in the right. The introduction of railways and steamboats greatly altered the problem of judicial organization; but no system could have been better adapted to its time and purposes than that of 1801. The only solid argument brought against it was that it attained its object too completely, bringing Federal justice to every man's door, and removing every difficulty or objection to suing in Federal courts. There was truth in the complaint that it thus placed the State judiciaries at a disadvantage. Beyond and above this, the controversy involved another question of far-reaching consequences which the Republicans were too timid to avow. A true democrat might have said openly that he wanted an elective judiciary, or would have insisted that the whole judiciary must be made subject to removal by the legislature. In neither of these opinions was anything disgraceful or improper; yet such was the dread of Federalist and conservative outcry, that although many of the Republican speakers went to the verge of the avowal, none dared make the issue.

Their timidity cost the Virginians dear. They knew, and never ceased to complain, that power grew mechanically; and only their want of experience excused them for over-confidence in the strength of their own virtue. They saw that the only part of Federalist centralization still remaining beyond their control was the judiciary; and they knew that if the judiciary were allowed to escape them in their first fervor of Republican virtue, they never could grapple with it after their own hands had learned the use of centralized power and felt the charm of office. Instead of acting, they temporized, threatened without daring to strike, and were made to appear like secret conspirators, planning what they feared to avow.

The repeal of the Judiciary Act passed the House, March 3, by a party vote of fifty-nine to thirty-two; but the Federalists were far from feeling themselves beaten. They had measured the strength of the majority, and felt that the revolutionary impulse was exhausted. As the Federalists grew bolder, the Republicans grew more timid. They passed a supplementary Judiciary Act, to quiet complaint and to prevent the Supreme

Court from holding its customary autumn term, lest Marshall should declare the abolition of the circuit courts unconstitutional. The evidences of timidity were not confined to judiciary measures. On no subject had the Republicans expressed stronger convictions than against the navy; yet when Michael Leib of Pennsylvania, in the heat of the judiciary debate, moved for a committee to consider the question of abolishing the navy, his motion was allowed to lie on the table until Roger Griswold, an extreme Connecticut Federalist, called it up, March 5, in a spirit of defiance. The House sustained Griswold, and took up the Resolution; whereat Leib withdrew his own motion, and evaded the issue he had challenged. In regard to another Federalist creation which had been the subject of Republican attacks, a similar failure occurred. The mint cost nearly as much as the circuit courts, and accomplished less. Since its foundation it had coined, in gold, silver, and copper, only $3,000,000, at a cost of nearly $300,000; while a gold or silver coin of the United States was still a rare sight. The Republican party when in opposition had opposed the mint as a monarchical institution,—unnecessary, expensive, and symbolic of centralized power. Giles accordingly moved, January 29, that the Act under which it existed should be repealed. In a speech, February 8, he avowed his hostility to the establishment from the beginning; he thought none but self-supporting establishments should exist. "There is a difference," said he, "between this and other countries. Other nations need to coin their own money; it is not with them the general but the partial good; it is aggrandizement of individuals, the trappings of royalty. Here, it is true, you established a mint, you have raised armies and fleets, to create an Executive influence; but what do the people say now? They send men here now to govern, who shall not govern for themselves but for the people." This was party doctrine. John Randolph adopted it in principle, asserting that nineteen-twentieths of the silver in circulation was Spanish-milled dollars or their parts, and that sovereignty was no more affected by using foreign coin than by using foreign cordage or cannon. The House accepted these views; Giles brought in his Bill for abolishing the mint; and after a short debate the House passed it, April 26, without a division. On the same day the Senate, quietly, without discussion or a call of yeas and nays, rejected it.

Perhaps the limit of Virginian influence was shown with most emphasis in the fate of a fugitive-slave Bill reported Dec. 18, 1801, by a committee of which Joseph Nicholson was chairman. The Bill imposed a fine of five hundred dollars on any one who should employ a strange negro without advertising in two newspapers a description of the man. Every free negro in the North must under this law carry about him a certificate of his freedom. To this sweeping exercise of a "centralized despotism" the Northern democrats objected, and, with only half-a-dozen exceptions, voted against it, although Bayard and several Southern Federalists joined Giles, Michael Leib, and John Randolph in its support. The Bill was rejected, January 18, by a vote of forty-six to forty-three.

Before the session closed, sensible Federalists were reassured, and the Administration was glad to repose on such triumphs as had been won.

"The President's party in Congress," wrote Bayard to Hamilton,[1] "is much weaker than you would be led to judge from the printed state of the votes. Here we plainly discern that there is no confidence, nor the smallest attachment prevails among them. The spirit which existed at the beginning of the session is entirely dissipated; a more rapid and radical change could not have been anticipated. An occasion is only wanting for Virginia to find herself abandoned by all her auxiliaries, and she would be abandoned upon the ground of her inimical principles to an efficient federal government."

The general legislation of the year showed no partisan character. A naturalization law was adopted, re-establishing the term of five years' residence as a condition of citizenship,—a measure recommended by the annual Message. A new apportionment Act was passed, fixing the ratio of Congressional representation at one member for 33,000 citizens. During the next ten years the House was to consist of one hundred and

[1] Bayard to Hamilton, April 25, 1802; Hamilton's Works, vi. 534.

forty-one members. The military peace establishment was fixed at three regiments, one of artillery and two of infantry, comprising in all about three thousand men, under one brigadier-general. By Sections 26 and 27 of the Act, approved March 16, 1802, the President was authorized to establish a corps of engineers, to be stationed at West Point in the State of New York, which should constitute a military academy; and the Secretary of War was authorized to procure the necessary apparatus for the institution. Great as the influence of this new establishment was upon the army, its bearing on the general education of the people was still greater, for the government thus assumed the charge of introducing the first systematic study of science in the United States.

Perhaps the most important legislation of the year was an Act approved April 30, which authorized the people of Ohio to form a Constitution and enter the Union; for not only was the admission of Ohio a formidable increase of power to the Northern democracy, but Gallatin inserted into the law a contract, which bound the State and nation to set aside the proceeds of a certain portion of the public lands for the use of schools and for the construction of roads between the new State and the seaboard. This principle, by which education and internal improvements were taken under the protection of Congress, was a violation of States-rights theories, against which, in after years, the strict constructionists protested; but in this first year of their sway Gallatin and the Northern democrats were allowed to manage their own affairs without interference. John Randolph would not vote for the admission of a new State, but Giles and Nicholson gave their votes for the bill, which passed without a murmur.

Gallatin's influence carried another point, more annoying to the Southern Republicans, although less serious. After years of wrangling, Georgia surrendered to the United States government all right and title to the territory which was afterward to become the States of Alabama and Mississippi. This immense region, shut from the Gulf of Mexico by the Spaniards, who owned every river-mouth, was inhabited by powerful Indian tribes, of whom the Georgians stood in terror. The Creeks and Cherokees, Choctaws and Chickasaws, owned the land, and were wards of the United States government. No one could say what was the value of Georgia's title, for it depended on her power to dispossess the Indians; but however good the title might be, the State would have been fortunate to make it a free gift to any authority strong enough to deal with the Creeks and Cherokees alone. In the year 1795, ignoring the claims of the national government, the Georgia Legislature sold its rights over twenty million acres of Indian land to four land-companies for the gross sum of five hundred thousand dollars. With one exception, every member of the Legislature appeared to have a pecuniary interest in the transaction; yet no one could say with certainty that the title was worth more than half a million dollars, or indeed was worth anything to the purchasers, unless backed by the power of the United States government, which was not yet the case. Nevertheless, the people of Georgia, like the people of Massachusetts and Pennsylvania, being at the moment in the fever of land-speculation, partly because they thought the land too cheap, partly because they believed their representatives to have been bribed, rose in anger against their Legislature and elected a new one, which declared the sales "null and void," burned the Yazoo Act, as it was called, in the public square of Louisville, and called a State Convention which made the repealing Act a part of the Constitution.

This series of measures completed the imbroglio. No man could say to whom the lands belonged. President Washington interposed on the part of the central government; the Indians quietly kept possession; hundreds of individuals in the Eastern States who had bought land-warrants from the Yazoo companies, claimed their land; while Georgia ignored President Washington, the Indians, the claimants, and the law, insisting that as a sovereign State she had the right to sell her own land, and to repudiate that sale for proper cause. In this case the State maintained that the sale was vitiated by fraud.

Doubtless the argument had force. If a sovereign State had not the power to protect itself from its own agents, it had, in joining the Union, entered into a relation different from anything hitherto supposed. Georgia put the utmost weight on the Rescinding Act as a measure of States-rights, and the true Virginia school made common cause with Georgia. Republicans who believed in the principles of 1798 considered the maintenance of the Rescinding Act a vital issue.

At length Congress took the matter in hand. Madison, Gallatin, and Levi Lincoln were appointed commissioners to make a settlement; and Senator James Jackson, the anti-Yazoo leader, supported by his colleague Senator Baldwin and by Governor Milledge, met them on behalf of Georgia,—a formidable array of high officials, whose whole authority was needed to give their decision weight. April 24, 1802, they reached a settlement so liberal to Georgia that Jackson and his associates took the risk of yielding more than they liked to concede. The western boundary was fixed to please the State; an immediate cession of land was obtained from the Indians, and the United States undertook to extinguish at their own expense, as early as they could reasonably do it, the Indian title to all lands within the limits of Georgia; the sum of $1,250,000 was to be paid to the State from the first net proceeds of land-sales; the ceded territory was to be admitted as a State, with slavery, whenever its population should reach sixty thousand; and in consideration for these advantages the Georgians unwillingly agreed that five million acres should be set aside for the purpose of compromising claims. The commissioners did not venture to affirm the legality of the Yazoo sale, but, while expressing the opinion that "the title of the claimants cannot be supported," declared that "the interest of the United States, the tranquillity of those who may hereafter inhabit that territory, and various equitable considerations which may be urged in favor of most of the present claimants, render it expedient to enter into a compromise on reasonable terms." With this concession to the principle of States-rights, the Georgians were appeased, and the commissioners hoped that all parties would be satisfied. The brunt of the negotiation fell upon Gallatin; but Madison found no difficulty in giving his support to the compromise.

These two measures greatly affected the Government and increased its power. The admission of Ohio into the Union gave two more senators to the Administration, and the acquisition of the southwestern territory relieved it from an annoying conflict of authority. Jefferson was henceforward better able to carry out his humane policy toward the Indians,—a

policy which won him praise from some of his bitterest enemies; while Gallatin turned his energies toward developing
the public-land system, in which he had, when in opposition,
taken active interest. The machinery of government worked
more easily every day.

Chapter XII

WHEN THE SESSION of Congress closed, May 3, the Administration was left to administer a system greatly reduced in proportions. In Jefferson's own words, he had "put the ship on her republican tack," where she was to show by the beauty of her motion the skill of her builders. Nothing remained, with respect to internal politics, but to restore harmony by winning recalcitrant New England, a task which he confidently hoped to accomplish within the course of the year. "If we are permitted," he wrote,[1] in October, 1801, "to go on so gradually in the removals called for by the Republicans, as not to shock or revolt our well-meaning citizens who are coming over to us in a steady stream, we shall completely consolidate the nation in a short time, — excepting always the royalists and priests." So hopeful was he of immediate success, that he wrote to his French correspondent, Dupont de Nemours,[2] in January, 1802: "I am satisfied that within one year from this time, were an election to take place between two candidates, merely Republican and Federal, where no personal opposition existed against either, the Federal candidate would not get the vote of a single elector in the United States." To revolutionize New England, he concentrated Executive influence, and checked party spirit. He began by placing two Massachusetts men in his Cabinet; before long he appointed as Postmaster-General an active Connecticut politician, Gideon Granger. The Postmaster-General was not then a member of the Cabinet, but his patronage was not the less important. Granger and Lincoln carried on a sapper's duty of undermining and weakening the Federalists' defences, while the Republican party refrained from acts that could rouse alarm.

Although in cooler moments Jefferson was less sanguine, he still so far miscalculated the division between himself and New England, that when the spring elections showed less increase than he expected in the Republican vote, he could not

[1] Jefferson to Peter Carr, Oct. 25, 1801; Jefferson MSS.
[2] Jefferson to M. Dupont, Jan. 18, 1802; Jefferson MSS.

explain the cause of his error. "I had hoped," he wrote,[1] in April, 1802, "that the proceedings of this session of Congress would have rallied the great body of citizens at once to one opinion; but the inveteracy of their quondam leaders has been able, by intermingling the grossest lies and misrepresentations, to check the effect in some small degree until they shall be exposed." Nevertheless, he flattered himself that the work was practically done.[2] "In Rhode Island the late election gives us two to one through the whole State. Vermont is decidedly with us. It is said and believed that New Hampshire has got a majority of Republicans now in its Legislature, and wanted a few hundreds only of turning out their Federal governor. He goes assuredly the next trial. Connecticut is supposed to have gained for us about fifteen or twenty per cent since the last election; but the exact issue is not yet known here, nor is it certainly known how we shall stand in the House of Representatives of Massachusetts; in the Senate there we have lost ground. The candid Federalists acknowledge that their party can never more raise its head." This was all true; he had won also in national politics a triumph that warranted confidence. "Our majority in the House of Representatives has been about two to one; in the Senate, eighteen to fifteen. After another election it will be of two to one in the Senate, and it would not be for the public good to have it greater. A respectable minority is useful as censors; the present one is not respectable, being the bitterest remains of the cup of Federalism rendered desperate and furious by despair."

Jefferson resembled all rulers in one peculiarity of mind. Even Bonaparte thought that a respectable minority might be useful as censors; but neither Bonaparte nor Jefferson was willing to agree that any particular minority was respectable. Jefferson could not persuade himself to treat with justice the remnants of that great party which he himself, by opposition not more "respectable" than theirs, had driven from power and "rendered desperate and furious by despair." Jefferson prided himself on his services to free-thought even more than on those he had rendered to political freedom: in the political

[1] Jefferson to Cæsar A. Rodney, April 24, 1802; Jefferson's Writings (Ford), viii. 147.
[2] Jefferson to Joel Barlow, May 3, 1802; Works, iv. 437.

field he had many rivals, but in the scientific arena he stood, or thought he stood, alone. His relations with European philosophers afforded him deep enjoyment; and in his Virginian remoteness he imagined his own influence on thought, abroad and at home, to be greater than others supposed it. His knowledge of New England was so slight that he readily adopted a belief in the intolerance of Puritan society toward every form of learning; he loved to contrast himself with his predecessor in the encouragement of science, and he held that to break down the theory and practice of a state-church in New England was necessary not only to his own complete triumph, but to the introduction of scientific thought. Had he known the people of New England better, he would have let them alone; but believing that Massachusetts and Connecticut were ruled by an oligarchy like the old Virginia tobacco-planters, with no deep hold on the people, he was bent upon attacking and overthrowing it. At the moment when he was thus preparing to introduce science into New England by political methods, President Dwight, the head of New England Calvinism, was persuading Benjamin Silliman to devote his life to the teaching of chemistry in Yale College.[1] Not long afterward, the Corporation of Harvard College scandalized the orthodox by electing as Professor of Theology, Henry Ware, whose Unitarian sympathies were notorious. All three authorities were working in their own way for the same result; but Jefferson preferred to work through political revolution, — a path which the people of New England chose only when they could annoy their rulers. To effect this revolution from above, to seduce the hesitating, harass the obstinate, and combine the champions of free-thought against the priests, was Jefferson's ardent wish. Soon after his inauguration he wrote to Dr. Priestley,[2] —

"Yours is one of the few lives precious to mankind, and for the continuance of which every thinking man is solicitous. Bigots may be an exception. What an effort, my dear sir, of bigotry, in politics and religion, have we gone through! The barbarians really flattered themselves they

[1] Life of Benjamin Silliman, i. 90–96.
[2] Jefferson to Priestley, March 21, 1801; Works, iv. 373.

should be able to bring back the times of Vandalism, when ignorance put everything into the hands of power and priestcraft. All advances in science were proscribed as innovations. They pretended to praise and encourage education, but it was to be the education of our ancestors. We were to look backwards, not forwards, for improvement,— the President himself declaring, in one of his Answers to Addresses, that we were never to expect to go beyond them in real science. This was the real ground of all the attacks on you. Those who live by mystery and *charlatanerie*, fearing you would render them useless by simplifying the Christian philosophy,—the most sublime and benevolent, but most perverted, system that ever shone on man,—endeavored to crush your well-earned and well-deserved fame."

Who was it that lived "by mystery and *charlatanerie?*" Some three years before, in the excitement of 1798, Jefferson wrote to his friend John Taylor of Caroline his opinion of the New Englanders, with the serious air which sometimes gave to his occasional exaggerations the more effect of humor because no humor was intended:[1] —

"Seeing that we must have somebody to quarrel with, I had rather keep our New England associates for that purpose than to see our bickerings transferred to others. They are circumscribed within such narrow limits, and their population so full, that their numbers will ever be the minority; and they are marked, like the Jews, with such a perversity of character as to constitute, from that circumstance, the natural division of our parties. A little patience, and we shall see the reign of witches pass over, their spells dissolved, and the people recovering their true sight, restoring their government to its true principles."

The letters to Priestley and Taylor gave comparatively mild expression of this dislike for New Englanders and Jews. Another letter, written at the same time with that to Priestley, spoke more plainly:[2] —

[1] Jefferson to John Taylor, June 1, 1798; Works, iv. 247.
[2] Jefferson to Moses Robinson, March 23, 1801; Works, iv. 379.

"The Eastern States will be the last to come over, on account of the dominion of the clergy, who had got a smell of union between Church and State, and began to indulge reveries which can never be realized in the present state of science. If, indeed, they could have prevailed on us to view all advances in science as dangerous innovations, and to look back to the opinions and practices of our forefathers instead of looking forward for improvement, a promising groundwork would have been laid; but I am in hopes their good sense will dictate to them that since the mountain will not come to them, they had better go to the mountain; that they will find their interest in acquiescing in the liberty and science of their country; and that the Christian religion, when divested of the rags in which they have enveloped it, and brought to the original purity and simplicity of its benevolent institutor, is a religion of all others most friendly to liberty, science, and the freest expansion of the human mind."

If the New England Calvinists ever laughed, one might suppose that they could have found in this letter, had it been published, material for laughter as sardonic as the letter itself. Their good sense was not likely then to dictate, their interest certainly would not induce them to believe, that they had best adopt Jefferson's views of the "benevolent institutor" of Christianity; and Jefferson, aware of the impossibility, regarded his quarrel with them as irreconcilable. "The clergy," he wrote again, a few weeks later,[1] "who have missed their union with the State, the Anglo-men who have missed their union with England, and the political adventurers who have lost the chance of swindling and plunder in the waste of public money, will never cease to bawl on the breaking up of their sanctuary." Of all these classes the clergy alone were mortal enemies. "Of the monarchical Federalists," he wrote to his attorney-general,[2] "I have no expectations; they are incurables, to be taken care of in a mad-house if necessary, and on motives of charity." The monarchical Federalists, as he chose to call them, were the Essex Junto,—George Cabot,

[1] Jefferson to Gideon Granger, May 3, 1801; Works, iv. 395.
[2] Jefferson to Levi Lincoln, Aug. 26, 1801; Works, iv. 406.

Theophilus Parsons, Fisher Ames, Timothy Pickering, Stephen Higginson, and their followers; but it was not with them or their opinions that Jefferson was angriest. "The 'Palladium,' " he went on, "is understood to be the clerical paper, and from the clergy I expect no mercy. They crucified their Saviour, who preached that their kingdom was not of this world; and all who practise on that precept must expect the extreme of their wrath. The laws of the present day withhold their hands from blood, but lies and slander still remain to them."

This was strong language. When Jefferson cried that law alone withheld the hands of the New England clergy from taking his blood, his words were not wholly figures of speech. He had fought a similar battle in Virginia, and still felt its virulence. What was more to the purpose, every politician could see that his strategy was correct. The New England church was the chief obstacle to democratic success, and New-England society, as then constituted, was dangerous to the safety of the Union. Whether a reform could be best accomplished by external attack, or whether Massachusetts and Connecticut had best be left in peace to work out their own problems, was a matter of judgment only. If Jefferson thought he had the power to effect his object by political influence, he could hardly refuse to make the attempt, although he admitted that his chance of success in Connecticut was desperate. "I consider Rhode Island, Vermont, Massachusetts, and New Hampshire," he wrote to Pierpont Edwards, of Connecticut,[1] "as coming about in the course of this year, . . . but the nature of your government being a subordination of the civil to the ecclesiastical power, I consider it as desperate for long years to come. Their steady habits exclude the advances of information, and they seem exactly where they were when they separated from the Saints of Oliver Cromwell; and there your clergy will always keep them if they can. You will follow the bark of Liberty only by the help of a tow-rope."

Expecting no mercy from the clergy, Jefferson took pains to show that they were to look for no mercy from him. At the moment he began the attempt to "completely consolidate

[1] Jefferson to Pierpont Edwards, July 21, 1801; Jefferson's Writings (Ford), viii. 74.

the nation," he gave what amounted to a formal notice that with the clergy he would neither make peace nor accept truce. A few days after announcing in his Inaugural Address, "We are all Republicans—we are all Federalists," and appealing for harmony and affection in social intercourse, Jefferson wrote a letter to the famous Thomas Paine, then at Paris waiting for means of conveyance to America. A sloop-of-war, the "Maryland," was under orders for Havre to carry the ratification of the new treaty with France, and the President made his first use of the navy to pay a public compliment to Paine.

"You expressed a wish," he wrote,[1] "to get a passage to this country in a public vessel. Mr. Dawson is charged with orders to the captain of the 'Maryland' to receive and accommodate you with a passage back, if you can be ready to depart at such short warning. . . . I am in hopes you will find us returned generally to sentiments worthy of former times. In these it will be your glory to have steadily labored, and with as much effect as any man living. That you may long live to continue your useful labors, and to reap their reward in the thankfulness of nations, is my sincere prayer. Accept assurances of my high esteem and affectionate attachment."

The sentiments in which Paine gloried "to have steadily labored," so far as they were recent, chiefly consisted in applause of the French Revolution, in libels on President Washington and his successor, and in assaults on the Christian religion. Whether he was right or wrong need not be discussed. Even though he were correct in them all, and was entitled to higher respect than any which Jefferson could show him, he was at that time regarded by respectable society, both Federalist and Republican, as a person to be avoided, a character to be feared. Among the New England churches the prejudice against him amounted to loathing, which epithets could hardly express. Had Jefferson written a letter to Bonaparte applauding his "useful labors" on the 18th Brumaire, and praying that he might live long to continue them, he would not have excited in the minds of the New

[1] Jefferson to Thomas Paine, March 18, 1801; Works, iv. 370.

England Calvinists so deep a sense of disgust as by thus seeming to identify himself with Paine. All this was known to him when he wrote his letter; he knew too that Paine would be likely to make no secret of such a compliment; and even if Paine held his tongue, the fact of his return in a national vessel must tell the story.

Jefferson's friends took a tone of apology about the letter to Paine, implying that he acted without reflection. They treated the letter as a formal civility, such as might without complaint have been extended to Gates or Conway or Charles Lee,[1]—a reminiscence of Revolutionary services which implied no personal feeling. Had Jefferson meant no more than this, he would have said only what he meant. He was not obliged to offer Paine a passage in a ship-of-war; or if he felt himself called upon to do so, he need not have written a letter; or if a letter must be written, he might have used very cordial language without risking the charge of applauding Paine's assaults on Christianity, and without seeming to invite him to continue such "useful labors" in America. No man could express more delicate shades of sympathy than Jefferson when he chose. He had smarted for years under the lashing caused by his Mazzei letter, and knew that a nest of hornets would rise about him the moment the "Maryland" should arrive; yet he wrote an assurance of his "high esteem and affectionate attachment" to Paine, with a "sincere prayer" that he might "long live to continue" his "useful labors." These expressions were either deceptive, or they proved the President's earnestness and courage. The letter to Paine was not, like the letter to Mazzei, a matter of apology or explanation. Jefferson never withdrew or qualified its language, or tried to soften its effect. "With respect to the letter," he wrote[2] to Paine in 1805, "I never hesitated to avow and to justify it in conversation. In no other way do I trouble myself to contradict anything which is said." Believing that the clergy would have taken his blood if the law had not restrained them, he meant to destroy their church if he could; and he gave them fair notice of his intention.

Although the letter to Paine was never explained away,

[1] Randall's Jefferson, ii. 643.
[2] Jefferson to Paine, June 5, 1805; Works, iv. 582.

other expressions of the President seemed to contradict the spirit of this letter, and these the President took trouble to explain. What had he meant by his famous appeal in behalf of harmony and affection in social intercourse, " without which liberty and even life itself are but dreary things"? What was to become of the still more famous declaration, "We are all Republicans—we are all Federalists"? Hardly had he uttered these words than he hastened to explain them to his friends. "It was a conviction," he wrote to Giles,[1] "that these people did not differ from us in principle which induced me to define the principles which I deemed orthodox, and to urge a reunion on those principles; and I am induced to hope it has conciliated many. I do not speak of the desperadoes of the quondam faction in and out of Congress. These I consider as incurables, on whom all attentions would be lost, and therefore will not be wasted; but my wish is to keep their flock from returning to them." He intended to entice the flock with one hand and to belabor the shepherds with the other. In equally clear language he wrote to Governor McKean of Pennsylvania:[2] —

> "My idea is that the mass of our countrymen, even of those who call themselves Federalist, are Republican. They differ from us but in a shade of more or less power to be given to the Executive or Legislative organ. . . . To restore that harmony which our predecessors so wickedly made it their object to break up, to render us again one people acting as one nation,—should be the object of every man really a patriot. I am satisfied it can be done, and I own that the day which should convince me to the contrary would be the bitterest of my life."

This motive, he said, had dictated his answer to the New Haven remonstrants,—a paper, he added, which "will furnish new texts for the monarchists; but from them I ask nothing: I wish nothing but their eternal hatred."

The interest of Jefferson's character consisted, to no small extent, in these outbursts of temper, which gave so lively a

[1] Jefferson to W. B. Giles, March 23, 1801; Works, iv. 382.
[2] Jefferson to Governor McKean, July 24, 1801; Jefferson's Writings (Ford), viii. 78.

tone to his official, and still more to his private, language. The avowal in one sentence of his duty as a patriot to restore the harmony which his predecessors (one of whom was President Washington) had "so wickedly made it their object to break up," and the admission that the day of his final failure would be the bitterest of his life, contrasted strangely with his wish, in the next sentence, for the eternal hatred of a class which embraced most of the bench and bar, the merchants and farmers, the colleges and the churches of New England! In any other man such contradictions would have argued dishonesty. In Jefferson they proved only that he took New England to be like Virginia,—ruled by a petty oligarchy which had no sympathies with the people, and whose artificial power, once broken, would vanish like that of the Virginia church. He persuaded himself that if his system were politically successful, the New England hierarchy could be safely ignored. When he said that all were Republicans and all Federalists, he meant that the churches and prejudices of New England were, in his opinion, already so much weakened as not to be taken into his account.

At first the New Englanders were half inclined to believe his assurances. The idea of drawing a line between the people on one side and the bulk of their clergy, magistrates, political leaders, learned professions, colleges, and land-owners on the other did not occur to them, and so thoroughly Virginian was this idea that it never came to be understood; but when they found Jefferson ejecting Federalists from office and threatening the clergy with Paine, they assumed, without refined analysis, that the President had deliberately deceived them. This view agreed with their previous prejudices against Jefferson's character, and with their understanding of the Mazzei letter. Their wrath soon became hot with the dry white heat peculiar to their character. The clergy had always hated Jefferson, and believed him not only to be untruthful, but to be also a demagogue, a backbiter, and a sensualist. When they found him, as they imagined, actually at work stripping not only the rags from their religion, but the very coats from their backs, and setting Paine to bait them, they were beside themselves with rage and contempt.

Thus the summer of 1802, which Jefferson's hopes had

painted as the term of his complete success, was marked by an outburst of reciprocal invective and slander such as could not be matched in American history. The floodgates of calumny were opened. By a stroke of evil fortune Jefferson further roused against himself the hatred of a man whose vileness made him more formidable than the respectability of New England could ever be. James Thompson Callender, a Scotch adventurer compared with whom the Cobbetts, Duanes, Cheethams, and Woods who infested the press were men of moral and pure life, had been an ally of Jefferson during the stormy days of 1798, and had published at Richmond a volume called "The Prospect before us," which was sufficiently libellous to draw upon him a State prosecution, and a fine and some months' imprisonment at the rough hands of Judge Chase. A few years later the Republicans would have applauded the sentence, and regretted only its lightness. In 1800 they were bound to make common cause with the victim. When Jefferson became President, he pardoned Callender, and by a stretch of authority returned to him the amount of his fine. Naturally Callender expected reward. He hastened to Washington, and was referred to Madison. He said that he was in love, and hinted that to win the object of his affection nothing less than the post-office at Richmond was necessary for his social standing.[1] Meeting with a positive refusal, he returned to Richmond in extreme anger, and became editor of a newspaper called "The Recorder," in which he began to wage against Jefferson a war of slander that Cobbett and Cheetham would have shrunk from. He collected every story he could gather, among overseers and scandal-mongers, about Jefferson's past life,—charged him with having a family of negro children by a slave named Sally; with having been turned out of the house of a certain Major Walker for writing a secret love-letter to his wife; with having swindled his creditors by paying debts in worthless currency, and with having privately paid Callender himself to write "The Prospect before us," besides furnishing materials for the book. Disproof of these charges was impossible. That which concerned Black Sally, as she was called, seems to have rested on a confusion

[1] Madison to Monroe, June 1, 1801; Madison's Works, ii. 173.

of persons which could not be cleared up; that relating to
Mrs. Walker had a foundation of truth, although the parties
were afterward reconciled;[1] that regarding the payment of
debt was true in one sense, and false only in the sense which
Callender gave it; while that which referred to "The Prospect
before us" was true enough to be serious. All these charges
were welcomed by the Federalist press, reprinted even in the
New York "Evening Post," and scattered broadcast over New
England. There men's minds were ready to welcome any tale
of villany that bore out their theory of Jefferson's character;
and, at the most critical moment, a mistake made by himself
went far to confirm their prejudice.

Jefferson's nature was feminine; he was more refined than
many women in the delicacy of his private relations, and even
men as shameless as Callender himself winced under attacks
of such a sort. He was sensitive, affectionate, and, in his own
eyes, heroic. He yearned for love and praise as no other great
American ever did. He hated the clergy chiefly because he
knew that from them he could expect neither love nor praise,
perhaps not even forbearance. He had befriended Callender
against his own better judgment, as every party leader befriended party hacks, not because the leaders approved them,
but because they were necessary for the press. So far as license
was concerned, "The Prospect before us" was a mild libel
compared with Cobbett's, Coleman's, and Dennie's cataracts
of abuse; and at the time it was written, Callender's character
was not known and his habits were still decent. In return for
kindness and encouragement, Callender attempted an act of
dastardly assassination, which the whole Federalist press
cheered. That a large part of the community, and the part
socially uppermost, should believe this drunken ruffian, and
should laugh while he bespattered their President with his
filth, was a mortification which cut deep into Jefferson's heart.
Hurt and angry, he felt that at bottom it was the old theological hatred in Virginia and New England which sustained this
mode of warfare; that as he had flung Paine at them, they
were flinging Callender at him. "With the aid of a lying ren-
egade from Republicanism, the Federalists have opened all

[1] Madison to Monroe, April 20, 1803; Madison's Writings, ii. 181.

their sluices of calumny," he wrote;[1] and he would have done wisely to say no more. Unluckily for him, he undertook to contradict Callender's assertions.

James Monroe was Governor of Virginia. Some weakness in Monroe's character caused him more than once to mix in scandals which he might better have left untouched. July 7, 1802, he wrote to the President, asking for the facts in regard to Jefferson's relations with Callender. The President's reply confessed the smart of his wound:[2] —

> "I am really mortified at the base ingratitude of Callender. It presents human nature in a hideous form. It gives me concern because I perceive that relief which was afforded him on mere motives of charity, may be viewed under the aspect of employing him as a writer."

He explained how he had pitied Callender, and repeatedly given him money.

> "As to myself," he continued, "no man wished more to see his pen stopped; but I considered him still as a proper object of benevolence. The succeeding year [1800] he again wanted money to buy paper for another volume. I made his letter, as before, the occasion of giving him another fifty dollars. He considers these as proofs of my approbation of his writings, when they were mere charities, yielded under a strong conviction that he was injuring us by his writings."

Unfortunately, Jefferson could not find the press-copies of his letters to Callender, and let Monroe send out these apologies without stopping to compare them with his written words. No sooner had the Republican newspapers taken their tone from Monroe, and committed themselves to these assertions of fact, than Callender printed the two letters which Jefferson had written to him,[3] which proved that not only had Jefferson given him at different times some two hundred dollars, but had also supplied information, of a harmless nature, for "The Prospect before us," and under an injunction of secrecy had encouraged Callender to write. His words were

---

[1] Jefferson to R. R. Livingston, Oct. 10, 1802; Works, iv. 448.
[2] Jefferson to Monroe, July 15 and 17, 1802; Works, iv. 444–447.
[3] The Recorder, September–October, 1802.

not to be explained away: "I thank you for the proof-sheets you enclosed me; such papers cannot fail to produce the best effect."[1]

No man who stood within the circle of the President's intimates could be perplexed to understand how this apparent self-contradiction might have occurred. Callender was neither the first nor the last to take advantage of what John Randolph called the "easy credulity" of Jefferson's temper. The nearest approach Jefferson could make toward checking an over-zealous friend was by shades of difference in the strength of his encouragement. To tell Callender that his book could not fail to produce the best effect was a way of hinting that it might do harm; and, however specious such an excuse might seem, this language was in his mind consistent with a secret wish that Callender should not write. More than one such instance of this kindly prevarication, this dislike for whatever might seem harsh or disobliging, could be found in Jefferson's correspondence.

A man's enemies rarely invent specious theories of human nature in order to excuse what they prefer to look upon as falsehood and treason. July 17, 1803, Callender was drowned in some drunken debauch; but the Federalists never forgot his calumnies, or ceased ringing the changes on the President's self-contradictions,—and throughout New England the trio of Jefferson, Paine, and Callender were henceforward held in equal abhorrence. That this prejudice did not affect Jefferson's popular vote was true, but it seriously affected his social relations; and it annoyed and mortified him more than coarser men could understand, to feel in the midst of his utmost popularity that large numbers of his worthiest fellow-citizens, whose respect he knew himself to deserve, despised him as they did the vermin they trod upon.

In the ferment of the Callender scandal, October 29, Paine arrived from Europe. Unable to come by the "Maryland," he had waited a year, and then appeared at Baltimore. The Republican newspapers made the same blunder in regard to Paine which they had made in regard to Callender,—they denied at first that he had been invited to return in a Govern-

---

[1] Jefferson to Callender, Oct. 6, 1799; Jefferson MSS.

ment ship, or that Jefferson had written him any such letter as was rumored, and they were altogether perplexed to know how to deal with so dangerous an ally, until the President invited Paine to the White House and gave him all the support that political and social influence could command. In a few days the "National Intelligencer," Jefferson's more than semi-official organ, published the first of a series of letters addressed by Paine to the American people; and no one could longer doubt what kind of "useful labors" Jefferson had invited him to continue. Fourteen years of absence had not abated the vigor of that homely style which once roused the spirits of Washington's soldiers; and age lent increased virulence to powers of invective which had always been great. His new series of letters overflowed with abuse of the Federalists, and bristled with sarcasms on the Federalist Presidents. Unfortunately for Jefferson's object Paine had exhausted the effect of such weapons, which resemble the sting of a bee lost in the wound it makes. The bee dies of her own mutilation. Paine, too, was dying from the loss of his sting. Only once in any man's career could he enjoy the full pleasure of saying, as Paine said to President Washington: "You are treacherous in private friendship, and a hypocrite in public life." To repeat it in other forms, to fumble and buzz about a wound meant to be deadly, was to be tiresome and ridiculous. Paine, too, was no longer one of a weak minority struggling for freedom of speech or act; he represented power, and was the mouthpiece of a centralized Government striking at the last remnants of Puritan independence. The glory of wounding Cæsar on his throne was one thing; that of adding one more stab to his prostrate body was another. Paine's weapon no longer caused alarm. The Federalist newspapers were delighted to reprint his letters, and to hold the President responsible for them. The clergy thundered from their pulpits. The storm of recrimination raged with noisy violence amid incessant recurrence to the trio of godless ruffians,—Jefferson, Paine, and Callender; but the only permanent result was to leave a fixed prejudice in the New England mind,—an ineradicable hatred for President Jefferson, in due time to bear poisonous fruit.

The summer of 1802 was a disappointment to Jefferson. He had hoped for better things. The time-servers and those voters whose love of nationality was stronger than their local interests or personal prejudices were for the most part drawn over to the Administration,—even Boston and Salem chose Republican Congressmen; yet Massachusetts as a whole was still Federalist, and of course, as the Federalists became fewer, the extreme wing became more influential in the party. The Essex Junto were still far from control, but they succeeded better than the moderate Federalists in holding their own. Thus these three influences in Massachusetts had nearly reached an equilibrium, and Jefferson was at a loss to understand why the growth of his popularity had been checked. He saw that provincial jealousies were strengthened, and this consequence of isolation he chose to look upon as its cause. Even an ode of the Massachusetts poet Thomas Paine, whose better-known name of Robert Treat Paine recorded the political passions which caused him to petition for the change, served to console Jefferson for the partial defeat of his consolidating schemes. Paine's refrain ran,—

"Rule, New England! New England rules and saves!"

and this echo of Virginia sentiments in 1798, this shadowy suggestion of a New England Confederacy, jarred on the President's ear. Toward autumn he wrote to his friend Langdon, of New Hampshire:[1]—

"Although we have not yet got a majority into the fold of Republicanism in your State, yet one long pull more will effect it. We can hardly doubt that one twelve-month more will give an executive and legislature in that State whose opinions may harmonize with their sister States,—unless it be true, as is sometimes said, that New Hampshire is but a satellite of Massachusetts. In this last State the public sentiment seems to be under some influence additional to that of the clergy and lawyers. I suspect there must be a leaven of State pride at seeing itself deserted by the public opinion, and that their late popular song of 'Rule, New England,' betrays one principle of their present variance from the Union. But I am in hopes they will in time discover that the shortest road to rule is to join the majority."

[1] Jefferson's Writings (Ford), viii. 160.

The struggle was full of interest; for if Jefferson had never yet failed to break down every opponent, from King George III. to Aaron Burr, the New England oligarchy for near two hundred years were a fatal enemy to every ruler not of their own choice, from King Charles I. to Thomas Jefferson.

Had the clergy and lawyers, the poets and magistrates of Massachusetts been the only troublesome element with which Jefferson had to deal, the task of the Republican party would have been simple; but virulent as party feeling was in New England during the summer of 1802, a feud broke out in New York which took a darker hue. Vice-President Burr, by his birthday toast to the "Union of honest men" and by his vote on the Judiciary Bill, flung down a challenge to the Virginians which De Witt Clinton, on their behalf, hastened to take up. With a violence that startled uninitiated bystanders, Cheetham in his "American Citizen" flung one charge after another at Burr: first his Judiciary vote; then his birthday toast; then the suppression of a worthless history of the last Administration written by John Wood, another foreign adventurer, whose book Burr bought in order, as Cheetham believed, to curry favor with the New England Federalists; finally, with the rhetorical flourish of an American Junius, Cheetham charged that Burr had tried to steal the Presidency from Jefferson in February, 1801, when the House of Representatives was divided. All the world knew that not Cheetham, but De Witt Clinton thus dragged the Vice-President from his chair, and that not Burr's vices but his influence made his crimes heinous; that behind De Witt Clinton stood the Virginia dynasty, dangling Burr's office in the eyes of the Clinton family, and lavishing honors and money on the Livingstons. All this was as clear to Burr and his friends as though it were embodied in an Act of Congress. No one ever explained why Burr did not drag De Witt Clinton from his ambush and shoot him, as two years later he shot Alexander Hamilton with less provocation. At midsummer the city was startled by the report that John Swartwout the marshal, one of Burr's intimates, had charged Clinton with attacking the Vice-President from personal and selfish motives; that Clinton had branded Swartwout as a liar, a scoundrel, and a villain; that they had met at Weehawken, where, after lodging two bullets in his opponent, Clinton had flung down his pistol at the sixth shot, swearing that he would have no more to do with the bloody business. Among the stories current was one that Clinton had expressed regret at not having Swartwout's *principal* before his pistol. Swartwout, wounded as he was, returned directly to Burr's house. In the face of all this provocation, the Vice-President behaved with studied caution and reserve. Never in the history of the United States did so powerful a combination of rival politicians unite to break down a single man as that which arrayed itself against Burr; for as the hostile circle gathered about him, he could plainly see not only Jefferson, Madison, and the whole Virginia legion, with Duane and his "Aurora" at their heels; not only De Witt Clinton and his whole family interest, with Cheetham and his "Watchtower" by their side; but—strangest of companions—Alexander Hamilton himself joining hands with his own bitterest enemies to complete the ring.

Under the influence of these personal hatreds, which raged from the Penobscot to the Potomac, American politics bade fair to become a faction-fight. The President proposed no new legislation; he had come to the end of his economies, and was even beginning to renew expenditures; he had no idea of amending the Constitution or reconstructing the Supreme Court; he thought only of revolutionizing the State governments of New England.[1] "The path we have to pursue is so quiet, that we have nothing scarcely to propose to our Legislature,"—so he wrote a few days before Congress was to meet. "If we can prevent the government from wasting the labors of the people under the pretence of taking care of them, they must become happy." The energy of reform was exhausted, the point of departure no longer in sight; the ever-increasing momentum of a governmental system required constant care; and with all this, complications of a new and unexpected kind began, which henceforward caused the chief interest of politics to centre in foreign affairs.

[1] Jefferson to Dr. Cooper, Nov. 29, 1802; Works, iv. 453.

Chapter XIII

MOST PICTURESQUE of all figures in modern history, Napoleon Bonaparte, like Milton's Satan on his throne of state, although surrounded by a group of figures little less striking than himself, sat unapproachable on his bad eminence; or, when he moved, the dusky air felt an unusual weight. His conduct was often mysterious, and sometimes so arbitrary as to seem insane; but later years have thrown on it a lurid illumination. Without the mass of correspondence and of fragmentary writings collected under the Second Empire in not less than thirty-two volumes of printed works, the greatness of Napoleon's energies or the quality of his mind would be impossible to comprehend. Ambition that ground its heel into every obstacle; restlessness that often defied common-sense; selfishness that eat like a cancer into his reasoning faculties; energy such as had never before been combined with equal genius and resources; ignorance that would have amused a school-boy; and a moral sense which regarded truth and falsehood as equally useful modes of expression,—an unprovoked war or secret assassination as equally natural forms of activity,—such a combination of qualities as Europe had forgotten since the Middle Ages, and could realize only by reviving the Eccelinos and Alberics of the thirteenth century, had to be faced and overawed by the gentle optimism of President Jefferson and his Secretary of State.

As if one such character were not riddle enough for any single epoch, a figure even more sinister and almost as enigmatical stood at its side. On the famous 18th Brumaire, the 9th November, 1799, when Bonaparte turned pale before the Five Hundred, and retired in terror from the hall at St. Cloud, not so much his brother Lucien, or the facile Sieyès, or Barras, pushed him forward to destroy the republic, but rather Talleyrand, the ex-Bishop of Autun, the Foreign Secretary of the Directory. Talleyrand was most active in directing the *coup d'état*, and was chiefly responsible for the ruin of France.[1] Had he profited by his exile in America, he would have turned to Moreau rather than to Bonaparte; and some

[1] M. de Talleyrand, par Sainte-Beuve, p. 70.

millions of men would have gone more quietly to their graves. Certainly he did not foresee the effects of his act; he had not meant to set a mere soldier on the throne of Saint Louis. He betrayed the republic only because he believed the republic to be an absurdity and a nuisance, not because he wanted a military despotism. He wished to stop the reign of violence and scandal, restore the glories of Louis XIV., and maintain France in her place at the head of civilization. To carry out these views was the work of a lifetime. Every successive government was created or accepted by him as an instrument for his purposes; and all were thrown aside or broke in his hands. Superior to Bonaparte in the breadth and steadiness of his purpose, Talleyrand was a theorist in his political principles; his statecraft was that of the old *régime*, and he never forgave himself for having once believed in a popular revolution.

This was the man with whom Madison must deal, in order to reach the ear of the First Consul. In diplomacy, a more perplexing task could scarcely be presented than to fathom the policy which might result from the contact of a mind like Talleyrand's with a mind like Bonaparte's. If Talleyrand was an enigma to be understood only by those who lived in his confidence, Bonaparte was a freak of nature such as the world had seen too rarely to comprehend. His character was misconceived even by Talleyrand at this early period; and where the keenest of observers failed to see through a mind he had helped to form, how were men like Jefferson and Madison, three thousand miles away, and receiving at best only such information as Chancellor Livingston could collect and send them every month or six weeks,—how were they, in their isolation and ignorance, to solve a riddle that depended on the influence which Talleyrand could maintain over Bonaparte, and the despotism which Bonaparte could establish over Talleyrand?

Difficult as this riddle was, it made but a part of the problem. France had no direct means of controlling American policy. Within the last four years she had tried to dictate, and received severe discipline. If France was a political factor of the first class in Jefferson's mind, it was not because of her armies or fleets, or her almost extinguished republican character, or her supposed friendship for Jefferson's party in its struggle with Anglican federalism. The 18th Brumaire severed most of these sentimental ties. The power which France wielded over American destinies sprang not from any direct French interest or fear of French arms, but from the control which Napoleon exercised over the Spanish government at Madrid. France alone could not greatly disturb the repose of Jefferson; but France, acting through Spain on the hopes and fears of the Southern States, exercised prodigious influence on the Union.

Don Carlos IV. reigned at Madrid,—a Bourbon, but an ally of the French republic, and since the 18th Brumaire a devoted admirer of the young Corsican who had betrayed the republic. So far as Don Carlos was king of Spain only, his name meant little to Americans; but as an American ruler his empire dwarfed that of the United States. From the sources of the Missouri and Mississippi to the borders of Patagonia, two American continents acknowledged his rule. From the mouth of the St. Mary's, southward and westward, the shores of Florida, Louisiana, Texas, and Mexico were Spanish; Pensacola, Mobile, and New Orleans closed all the rivers by which the United States could reach the gulf. The valley of the Ohio itself, as far as Pittsburg, was at the mercy of the King of Spain; the flour and tobacco that floated down the Mississippi, or any of the rivers that fell into the Gulf, passed under the Spanish flag, and could reach a market only by permission of Don Carlos IV. Along an imaginary line from Fernandina to Natchez, some six hundred miles, and thence northward on the western bank of the Mississippi River to the Lake of the Woods, some fourteen hundred miles farther, Spanish authority barred the path of American ambition. Of all foreign Powers Spain alone stood in such a position as to make violence seem sooner or later inevitable even to the pacific Jefferson; and every Southern or Western State looked to the military occupation of Mobile, Pensacola, and New Orleans as a future political necessity.

By a sort of tacit agreement, the ordinary rules of American politics were admitted not to apply to this case. To obtain Pensacola, Mobile, and New Orleans, the warmest States-rights champions in the South, even John Taylor of Caroline and John Randolph of Roanoke, were ready to employ every instrument of centralization. On the Southern and Western States this eagerness to expel Spain from their neighborhood acted like a magnet, affecting all, without regard to theories or parties. The people of Kentucky, Tennessee, and Georgia could not easily admit restrictions of any sort; they were the freest of the free; they felt keenly their subjection to the arbitrary authority of a king,—and a king of Spain. They could not endure that their wheat, tobacco, and timber should have value only by sufferance of a Spanish official and a corporal's guard of Spanish soldiers at New Orleans and Mobile. Hatred of a Spaniard was to the Tennesseean as natural as hatred of an Indian, and contempt for the rights of the Spanish government was no more singular than for those of an Indian tribe. Against Indians and Spaniards the Western settler held loose notions of law; his settled purpose was to drive both races from the country, and to take their land.

Between the Americans and the Spaniards no permanent friendship could exist. Their systems were at war, even when the nations were at peace. Spain, France, and England combined in maintaining the old colonial system; and Spain, as the greatest owner of American territory, was more deeply interested than any other Power in upholding the rule that colonies belonged exclusively to the mother country, and might trade only with her. Against this exclusive system, although it was one with which no foreign Power had the legal right to meddle, Americans always rebelled. Their interests required them to maintain the principles of free-trade; and they persuaded themselves that they had a natural right to sell their produce and buy their home cargoes in the best market, without regard to protective principles. Americans were the professional smugglers of an age when smuggling was tolerated by custom. Occasionally the laws were suddenly enforced, and the American trader was ruined; but in war times the business was comparatively safe and the profits were large. Naturally Americans wanted the right to do always what they did by sufferance as neutrals; and they were bent not only upon gaining foothold on the Gulf of Mexico, but on forcing Spain and England to admit them freely to their colonial ports. To do these two things they needed to do more. That the vast and inert mass of Spanish possessions in America must ultimately be broken up, became the cardinal point of their foreign policy. If the Southern and Western people, who saw the Spanish flag flaunted every day in their faces, learned to hate the Spaniard as their natural enemy, the Government at Washington, which saw a wider field, never missed an opportunity to thrust its knife into the joints of its unwieldy prey. In the end, far more than half the territory of the United States was the spoil of Spanish empire, rarely acquired with perfect propriety. To sum up the story in a single word, Spain had immense influence over the United States; but it was the influence of the whale over its captors,—the charm of a huge, helpless, and profitable victim.

Throughout the period of Spain's slow decomposition, Americans took toward her the tone of high morality. They were ostensibly struggling for liberty of commerce; and they avowed more or less openly their wish to establish political independence and popular rights throughout both continents. To them Spain represented despotism, bigotry, and corruption; and they were apt to let this impression appear openly in their language and acts. They were persistent aggressors, while Spain, even when striking back, as she sometimes timidly did, invariably acted in self-defence. That the Spaniards should dread and hate the Americans was natural; for the American character was one which no Spaniard could like, as the Spanish character had qualities which few Americans could understand. Each party accused the other of insincerity and falsehood; but the Spaniards also charged the Americans with rapacity and shamelessness. In their eyes, United States citizens proclaimed ideas of free-trade and self-government with no other object than to create confusion, in order that they might profit by it.

With the characters of English and French rulers—of George III. and Bonaparte, Pitt, Canning, Castlereagh, and Talleyrand—Americans were more or less familiar. The face and mind of King George III. were almost as well known to them as those of George Washington. Of Spaniards and Spanish rulers Americans knew almost nothing; yet Spanish weaknesses were to enrich the Union with more than half a continent from the ruin of an empire which would hardly have felt the privation had it been the chief loss the Spanish Crown was forced to suffer.

Europe could show no two men more virtuous in their private lives than King George III. of England and King Charles IV. of Spain. If personal purity was a test of political merit, these two rulers were the best of kings. Had George III. been born a Spanish prince, he might perhaps have grown into another Charles IV.; and Don Carlos was a kind of Spanish George. Every morning throughout the whole year King Charles rose at precisely five o'clock and heard Mass.[1] Occasionally he read a few minutes in some book of devotion, then breakfasted and went to his workrooms, where the most skilful gunsmiths in his kingdom were always busy on his hunting weapons. His armory was a part of his court; the gunsmiths, joiners, turners, and cabinet-makers went with him from Madrid to Aranjuez, and from Aranjuez to La Granja. Among them he was at his ease; taking off his coat, and rolling his shirt-sleeves up to the shoulder, he worked at a dozen different trades within the hour, in manner and speech as simple and easy as the workmen themselves. He was skilful with his tools, and withal a dilettante in his way, capable of enjoying not only the workmanship of a gunlock, but the beauties of his glorious picture-gallery,—the "Feconditá" of Titian, and the "Hilanderas" of Velasquez.

From his workshops he went to his stables, chatted familiarly with the grooms, and sometimes roughly found fault with them. After this daily duty was done, he received the Queen and the rest of his family, who came to kiss his hand,—a ceremony which took some ten minutes; after which, precisely at noon, he sat down to dinner. He dined alone, eat enormously, and drank only water. "Find if you can," said the Spaniards, "another king who never got out of his bed later than five o'clock; never drank wine, coffee, or liqueur; and in his whole life never so much as looked at any woman but his wife!" After dinner, every day at one o'clock, except when court etiquette interfered, King Charles set out, no matter what might be the weather, and drove post with guards and six coaches of companions to the ground where

[1] Alquier to Talleyrand, 26 Vendémiaire, An ix. (Oct. 18, 1800); Archives des Aff. Étr. MSS.

he was to shoot. Three hundred men drove the game toward him; seven hundred men and five hundred horses were daily occupied in this task of amusing him. The expenses were enormous; but the King was one of the best shots in Europe, and his subjects had reason to be grateful that his ambition took so harmless a path as the destruction of vast swarms of game.

From this sport he returned toward evening, and always found the Queen and the Court waiting his arrival. For some fifteen minutes he chatted with them; then his ministers were admitted, each separately presenting his business, while the Queen was present; and about half an hour was thus devoted to the welfare of many million subjects scattered in several continents. Cabinet councils were rare at this court, and no other council or assembly for legislative or executive purposes was imagined. Business disposed of, Don Carlos took his violin, which was as dear to him as his gun,—although in playing he gave himself no trouble to keep time with the other musicians, but played faster or slower, without apparent consciousness. After music he sat down to cards, and played ombre with two old courtiers, who for fifteen years had been required to perform this daily service; and he regularly went to sleep with the cards in his hand. Almost as regularly the other players, as well as the lookers-on, went to sleep also, and aroused themselves only when the major-domo came to announce supper. This meal at an end, the King gave his orders for the next day, and at eleven o'clock went to bed.

Such, word for word, was the official account of the Spanish court given by the French minister at Madrid to his Government in the year 1800; but it told only half the story. Charles was a religious man, and strictly observed all the fasts of the Church. To rouse in his mind an invincible repugnance against any individual, one had only to say that such a person had no religion. He held the priesthood in deep respect; his own character was open and frank; he possessed the rare quality of being true at any cost to his given word; he was even shrewd in his way, with a certain amount of common-sense; but with all this he was a nullity, and his career was that of a victim. Far above all distinctions of rank or class, the King was alone in Spain, as isolated as an Eastern idol; even the great nobles who in the feudal theory stood next to him, and should have been his confidential advisers, appeared to have no more influence than ploughboys. So extreme was this isolation, even for the traditions of Spanish etiquette, that the Court believed it to be intentionally encouraged by the Queen, Doña Maria Luisa de Parma, who was supposed to have many reasons for keeping her husband under watch. The society of Madrid was never delicate in such matters, nor was there a court in Europe which claimed to be free from scandal; but hardened as Europe was to royal license, Queen Luisa became notorious from Madrid to Petersburg. Her conduct was the common talk of Spain, and every groom and chambermaid about the royal palaces had the list of the Queen's lovers at their tongue's end; yet Don Carlos shut his eyes and ears. Those who knew him best were first to reject the idea that this conduct was the mere blindness of a weak mind. Charles's religion, honor, personal purity, and the self-respect of a king of Spain made it impossible for him to believe ill of one who stood toward him in such a relation. Never for a moment was he known to swerve in his loyalty.

Of all supposed facts in history, scandal about women was the commonest and least to be trusted. Queen Luisa's character may have been good, notwithstanding the gossip of diplomats and courtiers; but her real or supposed vices, and her influence over the King had much to do with the fate of Louisiana. Sooner or later, no doubt, Louisiana must have become a part of the American Union; but if court intrigues had little to do with actual results, they had, at least in Spain, everything to do with the way in which results were reached. At the court of Madrid the Queen was, in some respects, more influential than the King, and a man who was supposed to be one of the Queen's old lovers exercised the real authority of both.

In the year 1792 King Charles, then in his forty-fifth year, suddenly raised to the post of his prime minister a simple gentleman of his guard, Don Manuel Godoy, barely twenty-five years old. The scandalous chronicle of the court averred that two of the Queen's children bore on their faces incontrovertible evidence of their relation to Godoy. From 1792 until 1798 he was prime minister; he conducted a war with France, and made a treaty which procured for him the remarkable title of the Principe de la Paz,—the Prince of Peace. In 1798 he retired from office, but retained his personal favor. In 1800 he was not a minister, nor did even the scandal-mongers then charge him with improper relations with the Queen, for all were agreed that the Queen had found another lover. The stories of the palace were worthy of Saint-Simon. The King himself was far from refined in manners or conversation, and gave even to his favors some of the roughness of insults. If a servant suffered from any personal infirmity, he was forced to hear cruel derision from the King's lips; while the commonest of royal jokes was to slap courtiers and grooms on the back with a violence that brought tears into their eyes, followed by shouts of royal laughter and by forced smiles from the victim. This roughness of manner was not confined to the King. Most of the stories told about the Queen would not bear repeating, and, whether true or false, reflected the rottenness of a society which could invent or believe them; but among the many tales echoed by the gentlemen and ladies who were nearest her chamber was one worthy of Gil Blas, and as such was officially reported to Talleyrand and Bonaparte. The Queen's favorite in the year 1800 was a certain Mallo, whom she was said to have enriched, and who, according to the women of the bed-chamber, beat her Majesty in return as though she were any common Maritornes. One day in that year, when the Prince of Peace had come to San Ildefonso to pay his respects to the King, and as usual was having his interview in the Queen's presence, Charles asked him a question: "Manuel," said the King, " what is this Mallo? I see him with new horses and carriages every day. Where does he get so much money?" "Sire," replied Godoy, "Mallo has nothing in the world; but he is kept by an ugly old woman who robs her husband to pay her lover." The King shouted with laughter, and turning to his wife, said: "Luisa, what think you of that?" "Ah, Charles!" she replied; "do you not know that Manuel is always joking?"

Europe rang with such stories, which were probably as old as the tales of folk-lore, but none the less characterized the moral condition of Spain. Whatever had been Godoy's relations with the Queen they had long ceased, yet the honors, the wealth, and the semi-royal position of the Prince of Peace still scandalized the world. According to the common talk of Madrid, his riches and profligacy had no limits; his name was a by-word for everything that was shameless and corrupt. A young man, barely thirty-three years old, on whose head fortune rained favors, in an atmosphere of corruption, was certainly no saint; yet this creature, Manuel Godoy, reeking with vice, epitome of the decrepitude and incompetence of Spanish royalty, was a mild, enlightened, and intelligent minister so far as the United States were concerned, capable of generosity and of courage, quite the equal of Pitt or Talleyrand in diplomacy, and their superior in resource. In the eyes of Spain, Godoy may have been the most contemptible of mortals; but American history cannot estimate his character so low.

Godoy negotiated the treaty of 1795 with the United States, and did it in order to redress the balance which Jay's treaty with England disturbed.[1] The Spanish treaty of 1795 never received the credit it deserved; its large concessions were taken as a matter of course by the American people, who assumed that Spain could not afford to refuse anything that America asked, and who resented the idea that America asked more than she had a right to expect. Fearing that the effect of Jay's treaty would throw the United States into the arms of England at a moment when Spain was about to declare war, Godoy conceded everything the Americans wanted. His treaty provided for a settlement of the boundary between Natchez and New Orleans; accepted the principle of "free ships, free goods," so obnoxious to England; gave a liberal definition of contraband such as Jay had in vain attempted to get from Lord Grenville; created a commission to settle the claims of American citizens against Spain on account of illegal captures in the late war; granted to citizens of the United States for three years the right to deposit their merchandise at New Orleans without paying duty; and pledged the King of Spain to continue this so-called *entrepôt*, or "right of deposit," at the same place if he found it not injurious to his interests, or if it were so, to assign some similar place of deposit on another part of the banks of the Mississippi.

This treaty came before the Senate at the same time with

[1] Mémoires du Prince de la Paix, iii. 36–38.

that which Jay negotiated with Lord Grenville; and in the midst of the bitter attacks made upon the British instrument, not a voice was raised against the Spanish. Every one knew that it was the most satisfactory treaty the United States had yet negotiated with any foreign Power; and if Frederick the Great of Prussia deserved praise for the liberality of his treaty of 1785,—a liberality which implied no concessions and led to no consequences,—King Charles IV. had right to tenfold credit for the settlement of 1795.

If the Americans said but little on the subject, they felt the full value of their gain. Doubtless they grumbled because the Spanish authorities were slow to carry out the provisions of the treaty; but they had reason to know that this was not the fault of Godoy. Had France been as wisely directed as Spain, no delay would have occurred; but the French Directory resented the course taken by the United States in accepting Jay's treaty, and being angry with America, they turned a part of their wrath against Godoy. Before his American treaty was known to the world, Spain was driven to declare war against England, and thenceforth became an almost helpless appendage to France. The French government not only tried to prevent the delivery of the Spanish forts on the Mississippi, but, in defiance of law, French privateers made use of Spanish ports to carry on their depredations against American commerce; and scores of American vessels were brought into these ports and condemned by French consuls without right to exercise such a jurisdiction, while the Spanish government was powerless to interfere. In the end, Godoy's want of devotion to the interests of France became so evident that he could no longer remain prime minister. In March, 1798, he announced to King Charles that one of two measures must be chosen,—either Spain must prepare for a rupture with France, or must be guided by a new ministry. His resignation was accepted, and he retired from office. Fortunately for the United States, the last days of his power were marked by an act of friendship toward them which greatly irritated Talleyrand. March 29, 1798, the Spanish posts on the eastern bank of the Mississippi were at last delivered to the United States government; and thus Godoy's treaty of 1795 was faithfully carried out.

Chapter XIV

IN JULY, 1797, eight months before Godoy's retirement from power at Madrid, Talleyrand became Minister for Foreign Affairs to the French Directory. If the Prince of Peace was a man of no morals, the ex-Bishop of Autun was one of no morality. Colder than Pitt, and hardly less corrupt than Godoy, he held theories in regard to the United States which differed from those of other European statesmen only in being more aggressive. Chateaubriand once said, "When M. Talleyrand is not conspiring, he traffics." The epigram was not an unfair description of Talleyrand's behavior toward the United States. He had wandered through America in the year 1794, and found there but one congenial spirit. "Hamilton avait deviné l'Europe," was his phrase: Hamilton had felt by instinct the problem of European conservatives. After returning from America and obtaining readmission to France, Talleyrand made almost his only appearance as an author by reading to the Institute, in April, 1797, a memoir upon America and the Colonial System.[1] This paper was the clew to his ambition, preparing his return to power by laying the foundation for a future policy. The United States, it said, were wholly English, both by tastes and by commercial necessity; from them France could expect nothing; she must build up a new colonial system of her own,—but "to announce too much of what one means to do, is the way not to do it at all." In October Bonaparte announced a part of it in sending to the Directory the Treaty of Campo Formio as a step, he wrote,[2] to the destruction of England, and "the re-establishment of our commerce and our marine."

France still coveted Louisiana, the creation of Louis XIV., whose name it bore, which remained always French at heart, although in 1763 France ceded it to Spain in order to reconcile the Spanish government to sacrifices in the treaty of Paris. By the same treaty Florida was given by Spain to England, and remained twenty years in English hands, until the close of the Revolutionary War, when the treaty of 1783 restored it to

[1] Mémoire, etc., lu à l'Institut National le 15 Germinal, An v. (April 4, 1797).
[2] Correspondance, iii. 390.

Spain. The Spanish government of 1783, in thus gaining possession of Florida and Louisiana together, aimed at excluding
the United States, not France, from the Gulf. Indeed, when
the Count de Vergennes wished to recover Louisiana for
France, Spain was willing to return it, but asked a price
which, although the mere reimbursement of expenses, exceeded the means of the French treasury, and only for that
reason Louisiana remained a Spanish province. After Godoy's
war with France, at the Peace of Bâle the French Republic
again tried to obtain the retrocession of Louisiana, but in
vain. Nevertheless some progress was made, for by that
treaty, July 22, 1795, Spain consented to cede to France the
Spanish, or eastern, part of St. Domingo,—the cradle of her
Transatlantic power, and the cause of yearly deficits to the
Spanish treasury. Owing to the naval superiority of England,
the French republic did not ask for immediate possession.
Fearing Toussaint Louverture, whose personal authority in
the French part of the island already required forbearance,
France retained the title, and waited for peace. Again, in 1797,
Carnot and Barthelemy caused the Directory to offer the
King of Spain a magnificent bribe for Louisiana.[1] They proposed to take the three legations just wrung from the Pope,
and joining them with the Duchy of Parma, make a principality for the son of the Duke of Parma, who had married a
daughter of Don Carlos IV. Although this offer would have
given his daughter a splendid position, Charles refused it, because he was too honest a churchman to share in the spoils
of the Church.

These repeated efforts proved that France, and especially
the Foreign Office, looked to the recovery of French power
in America. A strong party in the Government aimed at restoring peace in Europe and extending French empire abroad.
Of this party Talleyrand was, or aspired to be, the head; and
his memoir, read to the Institute in April and July, 1797, was
a cautious announcement of the principles to be pursued in
the administration of foreign affairs which he immediately
afterward assumed.

July 24, 1797, commissioners arrived from the United States

[1] Mémoires du Prince de la Paix, iii. 23.

to treat for a settlement of the difficulties then existing between the two countries; but Talleyrand refused to negotiate
without a gift of twelve hundred thousand francs,—amounting to about two hundred and fifty thousand dollars. Two of
the American commissioners, in the middle of April, 1798, returned home, and war seemed inevitable.

Thus the month of April, 1798, was a moment of crisis in
American affairs. Talleyrand had succeeded in driving Godoy
from office, and in securing greater subservience from his successor, Don Mariano Luis de Urquijo, who had been chief
clerk in the Foreign Department, and who acted as Minister
for Foreign Affairs. Simultaneously Talleyrand carried his
quarrel with the United States to the verge of a rupture; and
at the same time Godoy's orders compelled Governor Gayoso
of Louisiana to deliver Natchez to the United States. The actual delivery of Natchez was hardly yet known in Europe; and
the President of the United States at Philadelphia had but
lately heard that the Spaniards were fairly gone, when Talleyrand drafted instructions for the Citizen Guillemardet, whom
he was sending as minister to Madrid. These instructions offered a glimpse into the heart of Talleyrand's policy.[1]

"The Court of Madrid," said he, "ever blind to its own
interests, and never docile to the lessons of experience, has
again quite recently adopted a measure which cannot fail to
produce the worst effects upon its political existence and
on the preservation of its colonies. The United States have
been put in possession of the forts situated along the Mississippi which the Spaniards had occupied as posts essential
to arrest the progress of the Americans in those countries."

The Americans, he continued, meant at any cost to rule
alone in America, and to exercise a preponderating influence
in the political system of Europe, although twelve hundred
leagues of ocean rolled between.

"Moreover, their conduct ever since the moment of their
independence is enough to prove this truth: the Americans
are devoured by pride, ambition, and cupidity; the mer-

[1] Instructions données au Citoyen Guillemardet, Prairial, An vi. (May 20–
June 19, 1798); Archives des Aff. Étr. MSS.

cantile spirit of the city of London ferments from Charleston to Boston, and the Cabinet of St. James directs the
Cabinet of the Federal Union."

Chateaubriand's epigram came here into pointed application. Down to the moment of writing this despatch, Talleyrand had for some months been engaged in trafficking with
these Americans, who were devoured by cupidity, and whom
he had required to pay him two hundred and fifty thousand
dollars for peace. He next conspired.

"There are," he continued, "no other means of putting
an end to the ambition of the Americans than that of shutting them up within the limits which Nature seems to have
traced for them; but Spain is not in a condition to do this
great work alone. She cannot, therefore, hasten too quickly
to engage the aid of a preponderating Power, yielding to it
a small part of her immense domains in order to preserve
the rest."

This small gratuity consisted of the Floridas and Louisiana.

"Let the Court of Madrid cede these districts to France,
and from that moment the power of America is bounded
by the limit which it may suit the interests and the tranquillity of France and Spain to assign her. The French Republic, mistress of these two provinces, will be a wall of
brass forever impenetrable to the combined efforts of England and America. The Court of Madrid has nothing to
fear from France."

This scheme was destined to immediate failure, chiefly
through the mistakes of its author; for not only had Talleyrand, a few weeks before, driven the United States to reprisals, and thus sacrificed what was left of the French colonies in
the West Indies, but at the same moment he aided and encouraged young Bonaparte to carry a large army to Egypt,
with the idea, suggested by the Duc de Choiseul many years
before, that France might find there compensation for the loss
of her colonies in America. Two years were consumed in re-
trieving these mistakes. Talleyrand first discovered that he
could not afford a war with the United States; and even at

the moment of writing these instructions to his minister at Madrid, he was engaged in conciliating the American commissioner who still remained unwillingly at Paris. The unexpected revelation by the United States government of his demands for money roused him, May 30, to consciousness of his danger. He made an effort to recover his lost ground.[1] "I do not see what delay I could have prevented. I am mortified that circumstances have not rendered our progress more rapid." When Gerry coldly refused to hear these entreaties, and insisted upon receiving his passport, Talleyrand was in genuine despair. "You have not even given me an opportunity of proving what liberality the executive Directory would use on the occasion."[2] He pursued Gerry with entreaties to use his influence on the President for peace; he pledged himself that no obstacle should be put in the path of negotiation if the American government would consent to renew it. At first the Americans were inclined to think his humility some new form of insult; but it was not only real, it was unexampled. Talleyrand foresaw that his blunder would cost France her colonies, and this he could bear; but it would also cost himself his office, and this was more than he could endure. His fears proved true. A year later, July 20, 1799, he was forced to retire, with little hope of soon recovering his character and influence, except through subservience to some coming adventurer.

Thus occurred a delay in French plans. By a sort of common agreement among the discontented factions at Paris, Bonaparte was recalled from Egypt. Landing at Fréjus early in October, 1799, a month afterward, November 9, he effected the *coup d'état* of the 18th Brumaire. He feared to disgust the public by replacing Talleyrand immediately in the office of foreign minister, and therefore delayed the appointment. "The place was naturally due to Talleyrand," said Napoleon in his memoirs,[3] "but in order not too much to shock public opinion, which was very antagonistic to him, especially on account of American affairs, Reinhard was kept in office for a short time." The delay was of little consequence, for internal

[1] Talleyrand to E. Gerry, June 27, 1798; State Papers, ii. 215.
[2] Talleyrand to E. Gerry, July 12, 1798; Ibid. 219.
[3] Correspondance de Napoléon Premier, xxx. 330.

reorganization preceded the establishment of a new foreign policy; and Talleyrand was in no haste to recall the blunders of his first experiment.

Although Talleyrand had mismanaged the execution of his plan, the policy itself was a great one. The man who could pacify Europe and turn the energies of France toward the creation of an empire in the New World was the more sure of success because, in the reactionary spirit of the time, he commanded the sympathies of all Europe in checking the power of republicanism in its last refuge. Even England would see with pleasure France perform this duty, and Talleyrand might safely count upon a tacit alliance to support him in curbing American democracy. This scheme of uniting legitimate governments in peaceful combination to crush the spirit of license ran through the rest of Talleyrand's political life, and wherever met, whether in France, Austria, or England, was the mark of the school which found its ablest chief in him.

The first object of the new policy was to restore the peace of Europe; and the energy of Bonaparte completed this great undertaking within two years after the 18th Brumaire. France was at variance with the United States, Great Britain, and Austria. Peace with Austria could be obtained only by conquering it; and after passing a winter in organizing his government, Bonaparte sent Moreau to attack the Austrians on the line of the Danube, while he himself was to take command in Italy. As yet diplomacy could not act with effect; but early in the spring, March 1, 1800, before campaigning began, new American commissioners reached Paris, rather as dictators than as suppliants, and informed Talleyrand that the President of the United States was still ready to take him at his word. They were received with marked respect, and were instantly met by French commissioners, at whose head was Joseph Bonaparte, the First Consul's brother. While their negotiations were beginning, Bonaparte left Paris, May 20, crossed the Alps, and wrung from the Austrians, June 14, a victory at Marengo, while Moreau on the Danube pressed from one brilliant success to another. Hurrying back to Paris, July 2, Bonaparte instantly began the negotiations for peace with Austria; and thus two problems were solved.

Yet Talleyrand's precipitation in pledging France to prompt

negotiation with the United States became a source of annoyance to the First Consul, whose shrewder calculation favored
making peace first with Europe, in order to deal with America
alone, and dictate his own terms. His brother Joseph, who
was but an instrument in Napoleon's hands, but who felt a
natural anxiety that his first diplomatic effort should succeed,
became alarmed at the First Consul's coldness toward the
American treaty, and at the crisis of negotiation, when failure
was imminent, tried to persuade him that peace with the
United States was made necessary by the situation in Europe.
Napoleon met this argument by one of his characteristic rebuffs. "You understand nothing of the matter," he said;[1]
"within two years we shall be the masters of the world."
Within two years, in fact, the United States were isolated.
Nevertheless Joseph was allowed to have his way. The First
Consul obstinately refused to admit in the treaty any claim of
indemnity for French spoliations on American commerce;
and the American commissioners as resolutely refused to
abandon the claim. They in their turn insisted that the new
treaty should abrogate the guaranties and obligations imposed on the United States government by the old French
treaty of alliance in 1778; and although Bonaparte cared nothing for the guaranty of the United States, he retained this
advantage in order that he might set it off against the claims.
Thus the negotiators were at last obliged to agree, by the
second article of the treaty, that these two subjects should be
reserved for future negotiation; and Sept. 30, 1800, the Treaty
of Morfontaine, as Joseph Bonaparte wished to call it, was
signed. It reached America in the confusion of a presidential
election which threatened to overthrow the government; but
the Senate voted, Feb. 3, 1801, to ratify it, with the omission
of the second article. The instrument, with this change, was
then sent back to Paris, where Bonaparte in his turn set terms
upon his ratification. He agreed to omit the second article, as
the Senate wished, "provided that by this retrenchment the
two States renounced the respective pretensions which are the
object of the said article." The treaty returned to America
with this condition imposed upon it, and Jefferson sub-

[1] Mémoires de Miot de Melito, i. 288.

mitted it to the Senate, which gave its final approval Dec. 19, 1801.

Thus Bonaparte gained his object, and won his first diplomatic success. He followed an invariable rule to repudiate debts and claims wherever repudiation was possible. For such demands he had one formula:[1] "Give them a very civil answer,—that I will examine the claim, etc.; but of course one never pays that sort of thing." In this case he meant to extinguish the spoliation claims; and nothing could be more certain than that he would thenceforward peremptorily challenge and resist any claim, direct or indirect, founded on French spoliations before 1800, and would allege the renunciation of Article II. in the treaty of Morfontaine as his justification. Equally certain was it that he had offered, and the Senate had approved his offer, to set off the guaranties of the treaty of alliance against the spoliation claims,—which gave him additional reason for rejecting such claims in future. The United States had received fair consideration from him for whatever losses American citizens had suffered.

Meanwhile the First Consul took action which concerned America more closely than any of the disputes with which Joseph Bonaparte was busied. However little admiration a bystander might feel for Napoleon's judgment or morals, no one could deny the quickness of his execution. Within six weeks after the battle of Marengo, without waiting for peace with the United States, England, or Austria, convinced that he held these countries in the hollow of his hand, he ordered[2] Talleyrand to send a special courier to the Citizen Alquier, French minister at Madrid, with powers for concluding a treaty by which Spain should retrocede Louisiana to France, in return for an equivalent aggrandizement of the Duchy of Parma. The courier was at once despatched, and returned with a promptitude and success which ought to have satisfied even the restlessness of Bonaparte. The Citizen Alquier no sooner received his orders than he went to Señor Urquijo, the Spanish Secretary for Foreign Relations, and passing abruptly over the well-worn arguments in favor of retrocession, he bluntly told Urquijo to oppose it if he dared.

[1] Gallatin's Writings, ii. 490.
[2] Correspondance, vi. 415; Bonaparte to Talleyrand, July 22, 1800.

" 'France expects from you,' I said to him,[1] 'what she asked in vain from the Prince of Peace. I have dispersed the prejudice which had been raised against you in the mind of the French government. You are to-day distinguished by its esteem and its consideration. Do not destroy my work; do not deprive yourself of the only counterpoise which you can oppose to the force of your enemies. The Queen, as you know, holds by affection as much as by vanity to the aggrandizement of her house; she will never forgive you if you oppose an exchange which can alone realize the projects of her ambition,—for I declare to you formally that your action will decide the fate of the Duke of Parma, and should you refuse to cede Louisiana you may count on getting nothing for that Prince. You must bear in mind, too, that your refusal will necessarily change my relations with you. Obliged to serve the interests of my country and to obey the orders of the First Consul, who attaches the highest value to this retrocession, I shall be forced to receive for the first time the offers of service that will inevitably be made to me; for you may be sure that your enemies will not hesitate to profit by that occasion to increase their strength—already a very real force—by the weight of the French influence; they will do what you will not do, and you will be abandoned at once by the Queen and by us.' "

Urquijo's reply measured the degradation of Spain:

" 'Eh! who told you that I would not give you Louisiana? But we must first have an understanding, and you must help me to convince the King.' "

At this reply, which sounded like Beaumarchais' comedies, Alquier saw that his game was safe. "Make yourself easy on that score," he replied; "the Queen will take that on herself." So the conference ended.

Alquier was right. The Queen took the task on herself, and Urquijo soon found that both King and Queen were anxious to part with Louisiana for their daughter's sake. They received the offer with enthusiasm, and lavished praises upon

[1] Alquier to Talleyrand, 19 Thermidor, An viii. (Aug. 7, 1800); Archives des Aff. Étr. MSS.

Bonaparte. The only conditions suggested by Urquijo were that the new Italian principality should be clearly defined, and that Spain should be guaranteed against the objections that might be made by other Governments.

Meanwhile Bonaparte reiterated his offer on a more definite scale. August 3, immediately after the interview with Urquijo, Alquier put the first demand on record in a note important chiefly because it laid incidental stress on Talleyrand's policy of restraining the United States:[1]

"The progress of the power and population of America, and her relations of interest always maintained with England, may and must some day bring these two powers to concert together the conquest of the Spanish colonies. If national interest is the surest foundation for political calculations, this conjecture must appear incontestable. The Court of Spain will do, then, at once a wise and great act if it calls the French to the defence of its colonies by ceding Louisiana to them, and by replacing in their hands this outpost of its richest possessions in the New World."

Before this note was written, the First Consul had already decided to supersede Alquier by a special agent who should take entire charge of this negotiation. July 28 he notified Talleyrand[2] that General Berthier, Bonaparte's right hand in matters of secrecy and importance, was to go upon the mission. Talleyrand drafted the necessary instructions,[3] which were framed to meet the fears of Spain lest the new arrangement should cause complications with other Powers; and toward the end of August Berthier started for Madrid, carrying a personal letter of introduction from the First Consul to King Charles[4] and the *projet* of a treaty of retrocession drawn by Talleyrand. This *projet* differed in one point from the

[1] Note adressée par l'Ambassadeur da la République, etc., 15 Thermidor, An viii. (Aug. 3, 1800); Archives des Aff. Étr. MSS.

[2] Correspondance, vi. 426; Bonaparte to Talleyrand, 9 Thermidor, An viii. (July 28, 1800).

[3] Rapport au Premier Consul, 6 Fructidor, An viii. (Aug. 24, 1800); Archives des Aff. Étr MSS.

[4] Correspondance, vi. 445.

scheme hitherto put forward, and, if possible, was still more alarming to the United States.[1]

"The French Republic," it ran, "pledges itself to procure for the Duke of Parma in Italy an aggrandizement of territory to contain at least one million inhabitants; the Republic charges itself with procuring the consent of Austria and the other States interested, so that the Duke may be put in possession of his new territory at the coming peace between France and Austria. Spain on her side pledges herself to retrocede to the French Republic the colony of Louisiana, with the same extent it actually has in the hands of Spain, and such as it should be according to the treaties subsequently passed between Spain and other States. Spain shall further join to this cession that of the two Floridas, eastern and western, with their actual limits."

Besides Louisiana and the two Floridas, Spain was to give France six ships of war, and was to deliver the provinces to France whenever the promised territory for the Duke of Parma should be delivered by France to Spain. The two Powers were further to make common cause against any person or persons who should attack or threaten them in consequence of executing their engagement.

In the history of the United States hardly any document, domestic or foreign, to be found in their archives has greater interest than this *projet*; for from it the United States must trace whatever legal title they obtained to the vast region west of the Mississippi. The treaties which followed were made merely in pursuance of this engagement, with such variations as seemed good for the purpose of carrying out the central idea of restoring Louisiana to France.

That the recovery of colonial power was the first of all Bonaparte's objects was proved not only by its being the motive of his earliest and most secret diplomatic step, but by the additional evidence that every other decisive event in the next three years of his career was subordinated to it. Berthier hastened to Madrid, and consumed the month of September,

[1] Instructions au Général Berthier, 8 Fructidor, An viii. (Aug. 26, 1800); Projet de Traité préliminaire et secret, 10 Fructidor, An viii. (Aug. 28, 1800); Archives des Aff. Étr. MSS.

1800, in negotiations. Eager as both parties were to conclude their bargain, difficulties soon appeared. So far as these concerned America, they rose in part from the indiscretion of the French Foreign Office, which announced the object of Berthier's mission in a Paris newspaper, and thus brought on Urquijo a demand from the American minister at Madrid for a categorical denial. Urquijo and Alquier could silence the attack only by denials not well calculated to carry conviction. This was not all. Alquier had been told to ask for Louisiana; Berthier was instructed to demand the Floridas and six ships of war in addition. The demand for the Floridas should have been made at first, if Bonaparte expected it to be successful. King Charles was willing to give back to France a territory which was French in character, and had come as the gift of France to his father; but he was unwilling to alienate Florida, which was a part of the national domain. Urquijo told Berthier[1] that "for the moment the King had pronounced himself so strongly against the cession of any portion whatever of Florida as to make it both useless and impolitic to talk with him about it;" but he added that, "after the general peace, the King might decide to cede a part of the Floridas between the Mississippi and the Mobile, on the special demand which the First Consul might make for it." Berthier was embarrassed, and yielded.

Thus at last the bargain was put in shape. The French government held out the hope of giving Tuscany as the equivalent for Louisiana and six seventy-fours. If not Tuscany, the three legations, or their equivalent, were stipulated. The suggestion of Tuscany delighted the King and Queen. Thus far the secret was confined to the parties directly interested; but after the principle had been fixed, another person was intrusted with it. The Prince of Peace was suddenly called to the Palace by a message marked "luego, luego, luego!"—the sign of triple haste.[2] He found Don Carlos in a paroxysm of excitement; joy sparkled in his eyes. "Congratulate me," he cried, "on this brilliant beginning of Bonaparte's relations with Spain! The Prince-presumptive of Parma, my son-in-law

---

[1] Rapport à l'Empereur, 28 Brumaire, An xiii. (Nov. 19, 1804); Archives des Aff. Étr. MSS.

[2] Mémoires, iii. 20, 55.

and nephew, a Bourbon, is invited by France to reign, on the delightful banks of the Arno, over a people who once spread their commerce through the known world, and who were the controlling power of Italy,—a people mild, civilized, full of humanity; the classical land of science and art!" The Prince of Peace could only offer congratulations; his opinion was asked without being followed, and a few days later the treaty was signed.[1]

On the last day of September, 1800, Joseph Bonaparte signed the so-called Treaty of Morfontaine, which restored relations between France and the United States. The next day, October 1, Berthier signed at San Ildefonso the treaty of retrocession, which was equivalent to a rupture of the relations established four-and-twenty hours earlier. Talleyrand was aware that one of these treaties undid the work of the other. The secrecy in which he enveloped the treaty of retrocession, and the pertinacity with which he denied its existence showed his belief that Bonaparte had won a double diplomatic triumph over the United States.

Moreau's great victory at Hohenlinden, December 3, next brought Austria to her knees. Joseph Bonaparte was sent to Lunéville in Lorraine, and in a few weeks negotiated the treaty which advanced another step the cession of Louisiana. The fifth article of this treaty, signed Feb. 9, 1801, deprived the actual Grand Duke of his Grand Duchy, and established the young Duke of Parma in Tuscany. To complete the transaction, Lucien Bonaparte was sent as ambassador to Madrid.

Lucien had the qualities of his race. Intelligent, vivacious, vain, he had been a Jacobin of the deepest dye; and yet his hands were as red with the crime of the 18th Brumaire as those of his brother Napoleon. Too troublesome at Paris to suit the First Consul's arbitrary views, he was sent to Spain, partly to remove him, partly to flatter Don Carlos IV. The choice was not wise; for Lucien neither could nor would execute in good faith the wishes of his dictatorial brother, and had no idea of subordinating his own interests to those of the man whose blunders on the 18th Brumaire, in his opinion, nearly cost the lives of both, and whose conduct since had

[1] Traité préliminaire et secret, Oct. 1, 1800; Recueil de Traités de la France, par De Clercq, i. 411.

turned every democrat in France into a conspirator. To make the selection still more dangerous, Lucien had scarcely reached Madrid before Urquijo was sent into retirement and Godoy restored to power in some anomalous position of general superintendence, supporting the burden, but leaving to Don Pedro Cevallos the title of Foreign Secretary. The secret of this restoration was told by Godoy himself with every appearance of truth.[1] The King insisted on his return, because Godoy was the only man who could hold his own against Bonaparte; and at that moment Bonaparte was threatening to garrison Spain with a French army, under pretence of a war with Portugal. The measure showed that Charles IV. was not wanting in shrewdness, for Godoy was well suited to deal with Lucien. He was more subtle, and not less corrupt.

Lucien's first act was to negotiate a new treaty closing the bargain in regard to Parma and Tuscany. Here Godoy offered no resistance. The Prince of Parma was created King of Tuscany, and the sixth article provided that the retrocession of Louisiana should at once be carried out. This treaty was signed at Madrid, March 21, 1801. The young King and Queen of Tuscany—or, according to their title, of Etruria—were despatched to Paris. Lucien remained to overlook the affair of Portugal. To the extreme irritation of Napoleon, news soon came that the Prince of Peace had signed at Badajos, June 5, 1801, a treaty with Portugal, to which Lucien had put his name as ambassador of France, and which baffled Napoleon's military designs in the Peninsula.

Lucien, with inimitable effrontery, wrote to his brother two days later:[2] "For the treaty of Tuscany I have received twenty good pictures out of the Gallery of the Retiro for my gallery, and diamonds to the value of one hundred thousand crowns have been set for me. I shall receive as much more for the Peace of Portugal." Two hundred thousand crowns and twenty pictures from the Retiro, besides flattery that would have turned the head of Talleyrand himself, were what Lucien acknowledged receiving; but there was reason to believe that this was not all, and that the Prince of Peace gorged him with spoil, until he carried back to France wealth which made him

[1] Mémoires, iii. 76–78.
[2] Lucien Bonaparte et ses Mémoires, Th. Jung, ii. 104.

the richest member of his family, and gave him an income of sixty or eighty thousand dollars a year. Godoy paid this price to save Spain for seven years.

The treaty of Badajos into which Godoy thus drew Lucien not only checked Napoleon's schemes, but came on the heels of other reverses which threatened to place the First Consul in an awkward position, unless he should hasten the general pacification to which he was tending. The assassination of his ally, the Czar Paul I. March 23, 1801, cost him the aid of Russia, as Godoy's return to power cost him the control of Spain. A few days after Paul's murder, April 9, 1801, Nelson crushed the Danish fleet at Copenhagen, and tore Denmark from his grasp. More serious than all, the fate of the French army which Bonaparte had left in Egypt could not be long delayed, and its capitulation would give a grave shock to his credit. All these reasons forced the First Consul to accept the check he had received from Godoy and Lucien, and to hasten peace with England; but he yielded with a bad grace. He was furious with Godoy.[1] "If this prince, bought by England, draws the King and Queen into measures contrary to the honor and interests of the republic, the last hour of the Spanish monarchy will have sounded." So he wrote to Talleyrand in anger at finding himself checked, and Talleyrand instructed Lucien accordingly.[2] Within a fortnight Bonaparte sent orders to London which rendered peace with England certain;[3] and without waiting to hear further, acting at length on the conviction that nothing could be gained by delay, he ordered Talleyrand to demand of the Court of Spain the authority to take possession of Louisiana.[4]

Supple and tenacious as any Corsican, Godoy's temper was perfect and his manners charming; he eluded Bonaparte with the skill and coolness of a picador. After causing the First Consul to stumble and fall on the very threshold of Portugal, Godoy kept Louisiana out of his control. As the affair then

[1] Correspondance, vii. 190; Bonaparte to Talleyrand, 21 Messidor, An ix. (July 10, 1801).

[2] Lucien Bonaparte, Jung, ii. 466.

[3] Correspondance, vii. 200; Note à remettre à Lord Hawkesbury, 4 Thermidor, An ix. (July 23, 1801).

[4] Ibid.; Bonaparte to Talleyrand, 8 Thermidor, An ix. (July 27, 1801).

stood, surrender of Louisiana except at the sword's point would have been inexcusable. The young King of Etruria had been entertained at Paris by the First Consul with a patronizing hospitality that roused more suspicion than gratitude; he had been sent to Italy, and had there been told that he possessed a kingdom and wore a crown,—but French armies occupied the territory; French generals administered the government; no foreign Power recognized the new kingdom, and no vestige of royal authority went with the royal title. Godoy and Cevallos gave it to be understood that they did not consider the First Consul to have carried out his part of the bargain in such a sense as to warrant Charles IV. in delivering Louisiana. They were in the right; but Bonaparte was angrier than ever at their audacity, and drafted with his own hand the note which Talleyrand was to send in reply.[1]

> "It is at the moment when the First Consul gives such strong proofs of his consideration for the King of Spain, and places a prince of his house on a throne which is fruit of the victories of French arms, that a tone is taken toward the French Republic such as might be taken with impunity toward the Republic of San Marino. The First Consul, full of confidence in the personal character of his Catholic Majesty, hopes that from the moment he is made aware of the bad conduct of some of his ministers, he will look to it, and will recall them to the sentiments of esteem and consideration which France does not cease to entertain for Spain. The First Consul will never persuade himself that his Catholic Majesty wishes to insult the French people and their Government at the moment when these are doing so much for Spain. This would suit neither his heart nor his loyalty, nor the interest of his crown."

In a note written the same day to Talleyrand,[2] Bonaparte spoke in a still stronger tone of the "misérable" who was thus crossing his path, and he ordered that Lucien should let the King and Queen know "that I am long-suffering, but that

[1] Correspondance, vii. 225; Projets de Notes, 27 Thermidor, An ix. (15 Aug. 1801).

[2] Correspondance, vii. 226; Talleyrand to Saint Cyr, 16 Frimaire, An x. (6 Dec. 1801); Lucien Bonaparte, Jung, ii. 468.

already I am warmly affected by this tone of contempt and deconsideration which is taken at Madrid; and that if they continue to put the republic under the necessity either of enduring the shame of the outrages publicly inflicted on it, or of avenging them by arms, they may see things they do not expect."

Nevertheless Godoy held his ground, well aware that the existence of Spain was at stake, but confident that concession would merely tempt encroachment. History might render what judgment it would of Godoy's character or policy,— with this moral or political question the United States had nothing to do; but Bonaparte's hatred of Godoy and determination to crush him were among the reasons why Louisiana fell at a sudden and unexpected moment into the hands of Jefferson, and no picture of American history could be complete which did not show in the background the figures of Bonaparte and Godoy, locked in struggle over Don Carlos IV.

Chapter XV

FORTUNATELY FOR the Prince of Peace, the world contained at that moment one man for whom Bonaparte entertained more hatred and contempt, and whom he was in still more haste to crush. The policy which Talleyrand had planned, and into which he had drawn the First Consul, could not be laid aside in order to punish Spain. On the contrary, every day rendered peace with England more necessary, and such a peace was inconsistent with a Spanish war. That Bonaparte felt no strong sympathy with Talleyrand's policy of peace in Europe and peaceful development abroad, is more than probable; but he was not yet so confident of his strength as to rely wholly on himself,—he had gone too far in the path of pacification to quit it suddenly for one of European conquest and dynastic power. He left Godoy and Spain untouched, in order to rebuild the empire of France in her colonies. Six weeks after he had threatened war on Charles IV., his agent at London, Oct. 1, 1801, signed with Lord Hawkesbury preliminary articles of peace which put an end to hostilities on the ocean. No sooner did Bonaparte receive the news[1] than he summoned his brother-in-law Leclerc to Paris. Leclerc was a general of high reputation, who had married the beautiful Pauline Bonaparte and was then perhaps the most promising member of the family next to Napoleon himself. To him, October 23, Napoleon entrusted the command of an immense expedition already ordered to collect at Brest, to destroy the power of Toussaint Louverture and re-establish slavery in the Island of St. Domingo.[2]

The story of Toussaint Louverture has been told almost as often as that of Napoleon, but not in connection with the history of the United States, although Toussaint exercised on their history an influence as decisive as that of any European ruler. His fate placed him at a point where Bonaparte needed absolute control. St. Domingo was the only centre from

[1] Correspondance, vii. 279; Bonaparte to Berthier, 16 Vendémiaire, An x (Oct. 8, 1801).

[2] Correspondance, vii. 298. Bonaparte to Berthier, 1 Brumaire, An x. (23 Oct. 1801).

which the measures needed for rebuilding the French colonial system could radiate. Before Bonaparte could reach Louisiana he was obliged to crush the power of Toussaint.

The magnificent Island of St. Domingo was chiefly Spanish. Only its western end belonged by language as well as by history to France; but this small part of the island, in the old days of Bourbon royalty, had been the most valuable of French possessions. Neither Martinique nor Guadeloupe compared with it. In 1789, before the French Revolution began, nearly two thirds of the commercial interests of France centred in St. Domingo;[1] its combined exports and imports were valued at more than one hundred and forty million dollars; its sugar, coffee, indigo, and cotton supplied the home market, and employed in prosperous years more than seven hundred ocean-going vessels, with seamen to the number, it was said, of eighty thousand. Paris swarmed with creole families who drew their incomes from the island, among whom were many whose political influence was great; while, in the island itself, society enjoyed semi-Parisian ease and elegance, the natural product of an exaggerated slave-system combined with the manners, ideas, and amusements of a French proprietary caste.

In 1789 the colony contained about six hundred thousand inhabitants, five sixths of whom were full-blooded negroes held in rigid slavery. Of the eighty or hundred thousand free citizens, about half were mulattoes, or had some infusion of negro blood which disqualified them from holding political power. All social or political privileges were held by forty or fifty thousand French creoles, represented by the few hundred planters and officials who formed the aristocracy of the island. Between the creoles and the mulattoes, or mixed-breeds, existed the jealousy sure to result from narrow distinctions of blood marking broad differences in privilege. These were not the only jealousies which raged in the colony; for the creoles were uneasy under the despotism of the colonial system, and claimed political rights which the home government denied. Like all colonists of that day, in the quiet of their plantations they talked of independence, and thought with envy of their

[1] Pamphile de Lacroix, Mémoires, ii. 277.

neighbors in South Carolina, who could buy and sell where they pleased.

When in 1789 France burst into a flame of universal liberty, the creoles of St. Domingo shared the enthusiasm so far as they hoped to gain by it a relaxation of the despotic colonial system; but they were alarmed at finding that the mulattoes, who claimed to own a third of the land and a fourth of the personalty in the colony, offered to make the Republic a free gift of one fifth of their possessions on condition of being no longer subjected to the creole tyranny of caste. The white and mulatto populations were thus brought into collision. The National Assembly of France supported the mulattoes. The creoles replied that they preferred death to sharing power with what they considered a bastard and despicable race. They turned royalists. Both parties took up arms, and in their struggle with each other they at length dropped a match into the immense powder-magazine upon which they both lived. One August night in the year 1791 the whole plain of the north was swept with fire and drenched with blood. Five hundred thousand negro slaves in the depths of barbarism revolted, and the horrors of the massacre made Europe and America shudder.

For several years afterward the colony was torn by convulsions; and to add another element of confusion, the Spaniards and English came in, hoping to effect its conquest. Feb. 4, 1794, the National Assembly of France took the only sensible measure in its power by proclaiming the abolition of slavery; but for the moment this step only embroiled matters the more. Among its immediate results was one of great importance, though little noticed at the time. A negro chief, who since the outbreak had become head of a royalist band in Spanish pay, returned, in April, 1794, within French jurisdiction and took service under the Republic. This was Toussaint Louverture, whose father, the son of a negro chief on the slave-coast of Africa, had been brought to St. Domingo as a slave. Toussaint was born in 1746. When he deserted the Spanish service, and with some four thousand men made the sudden attack which resulted in clearing the French colony of Spanish troops, he was already forty-eight years old.

Although Toussaint was received at once into the French

service, not until more than a year later, July 23, 1795, did the National Convention recognize his merits by giving him the commission of brigadier-general. Within less than two years, in May, 1797, he was made General-in-Chief, with military command over the whole colony. The services he rendered to France were great, and were highly rewarded. His character was an enigma. Hated by the mulattoes with such vindictiveness as mutual antipathies and crimes could cause, he was liked by the whites rather because he protected and flattered them at the expense of the mulattoes than because they felt any love for him or his race. In return they flattered and betrayed him. Their praise or blame was equally worthless; yet to this rule there were exceptions. One of the best among the French officers in St. Domingo, Colonel Vincent, was deep in Toussaint's confidence, and injured his own career by obstinate attempts to intervene between Bonaparte and Bonaparte's victim. Vincent described Toussaint, in colors apparently unexaggerated, as the most active and indefatigable man that could be imagined,—one who was present everywhere, but especially where his presence was most needed; while his great sobriety, his peculiar faculty of never resting, of tiring out a half-dozen horses and as many secretaries every day; and, more than all, his art of amusing and deceiving all the world,—an art pushed to the limits of imposture,—made him so superior to his surroundings that respect and submission to him were carried to fanaticism.[1]

Gentle and well-meaning in his ordinary relations, vehement in his passions, and splendid in his ambition, Toussaint was a wise, though a severe, ruler so long as he was undisturbed; but where his own safety or power was in question he could be as ferocious as Dessalines and as treacherous as Bonaparte. In more respects than one his character had a curious resemblance to that of Napoleon,—the same abnormal energy of body and mind; the same morbid lust for power, and indifference to means; the same craft and vehemence of temper; the same fatalism, love of display, reckless personal courage, and, what was much more remarkable, the same occasional acts of moral cowardice. One might suppose that

[1] Vie de Toussaint, par Saint-Remy, p. 322.

Toussaint had inherited from his Dahomey grandfather the qualities of primitive society, but if this was the case, the conditions of life in Corsica must have borne some strong resemblance to barbarism, because the rule of inheritance which applied to Toussaint should hold good for Bonaparte. The problem was the more interesting because the parallelism roused Napoleon's anger, and precipitated a conflict which had vast influence on human affairs. Both Bonaparte and Louverture were the products of a revolution which gave its highest rewards to qualities of energy and audacity. So nearly identical were the steps in their career, that after the 18th Brumaire Toussaint seemed naturally to ape every action which Bonaparte wished to make heroic in the world's eyes. There was reason to fear that Toussaint would end in making Bonaparte ridiculous; for his conduct was, as it seemed to the First Consul, a sort of negro travesty on the consular *régime*.

When the difficulties between France and America became serious, after Talleyrand's demand for money and sweeping attacks upon American commerce, Congress passed an Act of June 13, 1798, suspending commercial relations with France and her dependencies. At that time Toussaint, although in title only General-in-Chief, was in reality absolute ruler of St. Domingo. He recognized a general allegiance to the French Republic, and allowed the Directory to keep a civil agent— the Citizen Roume—as a check on his power; but in fact Roume was helpless in his hands. Toussaint's only rival was Rigaud, a mulatto, who commanded the southern part of the colony, where Jacmel and other ports were situated. Rigaud was a perpetual danger to Louverture, whose safety depended on tolerating no rival. The Act of Congress threatened to create distress among the blacks and endanger the quiet of the colony; while Rigaud and the French authority would be strengthened by whatever weakened Louverture. Spurred both by fear and ambition, Toussaint took the character of an independent ruler. The United States government, counting on such a result, had instructed its consul to invite an advance; and, acting on the consul's suggestion, Toussaint sent to the United States an agent with a letter to the President[1]

---

[1] Toussaint to President Adams, 16 Brumaire, An vii. (Nov. 6, 1798); MSS. State Department Archives.

containing the emphatic assurance that if commercial intercourse were renewed between the United States and St. Domingo it should be protected by every means in his power.
The trade was profitable, the political advantages of neutral-
izing Toussaint were great; and accordingly the President obtained from Congress a new Act, approved Feb. 9, 1799,
which was intended to meet the case. He also sent a very able
man—Edward Stevens—to St. Domingo, with the title of
Consul-General, and with diplomatic powers. At the same
time the British Ministry despatched General Maitland to the
same place, with orders to stop at Philadelphia and arrange a
general policy in regard to Toussaint. This was rapidly done.
Maitland hurried to the island, which he reached May 15,
1799, within a month after the arrival of Stevens. Negotiations
followed, which resulted, June 13, in a secret treaty[1] between
Toussaint and Maitland, by which Toussaint abandoned all
privateering and shipping, receiving in return free access to
those supplies from the United States which were needed to
content his people, fill his treasury, and equip his troops.

To this treaty Stevens was not openly a party; but in Toussaint's eyes he was the real negotiator, and his influence had
more to do with the result than all the ships and soldiers at
Maitland's disposal. Under this informal tripartite agreement,
Toussaint threw himself into the arms of the United States,
and took an enormous stride toward the goal of his ambition,—a crown.

Louverture had waited only to complete this arrangement
before attacking Rigaud. Then the fruits of his foreign policy
ripened. Supplies of every kind flowed from the United States
into St. Domingo; but supplies were not enough. Toussaint
began the siege of Jacmel,—a siege famous in Haytian history. His position was hazardous. A difficult war in a remote
province, for which he could not bring the necessary supplies
and materials by land; a suspicious or hostile French agent
and government; a population easily affected by rumors and
intrigues; finally, the seizure by English cruisers of a flotilla
which, after his promise to abandon all shipping, was bringing
his munitions of war along the coast for the siege,—made

[1] Treaty of June 13, 1799; MSS. State Department Archives.

Toussaint tremble for the result of his civil war. He wrote once more to the President,[1] requesting him to send some frigates to enforce the treaty by putting an end to all trade with the island except such as the treaty permitted. Stevens again came to his assistance. The United States frigate, "General Greene," was sent to cruise off Jacmel in February and March, 1800, and was followed by other vessels of war. Rigaud's garrison was starved out; Jacmel was abandoned; and Rigaud himself, July 29, 1800, consented to quit the country.

Toussaint's gratitude was great, and his confidence in Stevens unbounded. Even before the fall of Jacmel, Stevens was able to inform Secretary Pickering that Toussaint was taking his measures slowly but certainly to break connection with France.[2] "If he is not disturbed, he will preserve appearances a little longer; but as soon as France interferes with this colony, he will throw off the mask and declare it independent." Hardly was Rigaud crushed, when the first overt act of independence followed. Toussaint imprisoned Roume, and on an invitation from the municipalities assumed the civil as well as military authority, under the title of governor. In announcing to his Government that this step was to be taken, Stevens added:[3] "From that moment the colony may be considered as forever separated from France. Policy perhaps may induce him to make no open declaration of independence before he is compelled." A few days afterward Toussaint took the Napoleonic measure of seizing by force the Spanish part of the island, which had been ceded to France by the treaty of Bâle five years before, but had not yet been actually transferred In thus making war on the ally of France, Toussaint had no other motive, as Stevens explained,[4] than to prevent the French government from getting a footing there. Bonaparte had given a new Constitution to France after the 18th Brumaire. Toussaint, after the deposition of Roume, which was his *coup d'état* and 18th Brumaire, gave a new Constitution to St. Domingo in the month of May, 1801, by which he not

---

[1] Toussaint to President Adams, Aug. 14, 1799; MSS. State Department Archives.

[2] Stevens to Pickering, Feb. 13, 1800; MSS. State Department Archives.

[3] Stevens to Pickering, April 19, 1800; MSS. State Department Archives.

[4] Ibid.

only assumed all political power for life, but also ascribed to himself the right of naming his own successor. Bonaparte had not yet dared to go so far, although he waited only another year, and meanwhile chafed under the idea of being imitated by one whom he called a "gilded African."

Perhaps audacity was Louverture's best policy; yet no wise man would intentionally aggravate his own dangers by unnecessary rashness, such as he showed in Bonaparte's face. He was like a rat defying a ferret; his safety lay not in his own strength, but in the nature of his hole. Power turned his head, and his regular army of twenty thousand disciplined and well-equipped men was his ruin. All his acts, and much of his open conversation, during the years 1800 and 1801, showed defiance to the First Consul. He prided himself upon being "First of the Blacks" and "Bonaparte of the Antilles." Warning and remonstrance from the Minister of Marine in France excited only his violent anger.[1] He insisted upon dealing directly with sovereigns, and not with their ministers, and was deeply irritated with Bonaparte for answering his letters through the Minister of Marine. Throwing one of these despatches aside unopened, he was heard to mutter before all his company the words, *"Ministre! . . . valet! . . ."*[2] He was right in the instinct of self-assertion, for his single hope lay in Bonaparte's consent to his independent power; but the attack on Spanish St. Domingo, and the proclamation of his new Constitution, were unnecessary acts of defiance.

When Jefferson became President of the United States and the Senate confirmed the treaty of Morfontaine, had Louverture not lost his balance he would have seen that Bonaparte and Talleyrand had out-manœuvred him, and that even if Jefferson were not as French in policy as his predecessor had been hostile to France, yet henceforth the United States must disregard sympathies, treat St. Domingo as a French colony, and leave the negro chief to his fate. England alone, after the month of February, 1801, stood between Toussaint and Bonaparte. Edward Stevens, who felt the storm that was in the air, pleaded ill-health and resigned his post of consul-general. Jefferson sent Tobias Lear to Cap Français in Stevens's place,

[1] Stevens to Pickering, May 24, 1800; MSS. State Department Archives.
[2] Pamphile de Lacroix, Mémoires, ii. 52.

and Lear's first interview showed that Toussaint was beginning to feel Talleyrand's restraints. The freedom he had enjoyed was disappearing, and he chafed at the unaccustomed limitations. He complained bitterly that Lear had brought him no personal letter from the President; and Lear in vain explained the custom of the Government, which warranted no such practice in the case of consuls. "It is because of my color!" cried Toussaint.[1] Justice to President Jefferson and a keener sense of the diplomatic situation would have shown him that such a letter could not be written by the President consistently with his new relations of friendship toward France; and in fact almost the first act of Pichon, on taking charge of the French Legation in Washington after the treaty, was to remonstrate against any recognition of Toussaint, and to cause Lear's want of diplomatic character which offended Louverture.[2]

Rarely has diplomacy been used with more skill and energy than by Bonaparte, who knew where force and craft should converge. That in this skill mendacity played a chief part, need hardly be repeated. Toussaint was flattered, cajoled, and held in a mist of ignorance, while one by one the necessary preparations were made to prevent his escape; and then, with scarcely a word of warning, at the First Consul's order the mist rolled away, and the unhappy negro found himself face to face with destruction. The same ships that brought news of the preliminary treaty signed at London brought also the rumor of a great expedition fitting at Brest and the gossip of creole society in Paris, which made no longer a secret that Bonaparte meant to crush Toussaint and restore slavery at St. Domingo. Nowhere in the world had Toussaint a friend or a hope except in himself. Two continents looked on with folded arms, more and more interested in the result, as Bonaparte's ripening schemes began to show their character. As yet President Jefferson had no inkling of their meaning. The British government was somewhat better informed, and perhaps Godoy knew more than all the rest; but none of them grasped the whole truth, or felt their own dependence on Toussaint's

[1] Lear to Madison, July, 1801; MSS. State Department Archives.
[2] Pichon to Decrès, 18 Fructidor, An ix. (Sept. 5, 1801); Archives de la Marine, MSS.

courage. If he and his blacks should succumb easily to their fate, the wave of French empire would roll on to Louisiana and sweep far up the Mississippi; if St. Domingo should resist, and succeed in resistance, the recoil would spend its force on Europe, while America would be left to pursue her democratic destiny in peace.

Bonaparte hurried his preparations. The month of October, 1801, saw vast activity in French and Spanish ports, for a Spanish squadron accompanied the French fleet. Not a chance was to be left for Toussaint's resistance or escape. To quiet English uneasiness, Bonaparte dictated to Talleyrand a despatch explaining to the British government the nature of the expedition.[1] "In the course which I have taken of annihilating the black government at St. Domingo," he said, "I have been less guided by considerations of commerce and finance than by the necessity of stifling in every part of the world every kind of germ of disquiet and trouble; but it could not escape me that St. Domingo, even after being reconquered by the whites, would be for many years a weak point which would need the support of peace and of the mother country; . . . that one of the principal benefits of peace, at the actual moment, for England was its conclusion at a time when the French government had not yet recognized the organization of St. Domingo, and in consequence the power of the blacks; and if it had done so, the sceptre of the new world would sooner or later have fallen into the hands of the blacks."

No such explanations were given to the United States, perhaps because no American minister asked for them. Livingston landed at Lorient November 12, the day before Bonaparte wrote these words; Leclerc's expedition sailed from Brest November 22; and Livingston was presented to the First Consul in the diplomatic audience of December 6. Caring nothing for Toussaint and much for France, Livingston did not come prepared to find that his own interests were the same with those of Toussaint, but already by December 30 he wrote to Rufus King: "I know that the armament, destined in the first instance for Hispaniola, is to proceed to Louisiana provided Toussaint makes no opposition."

[1] Correspondance, vii. 319; Bonaparte to Talleyrand, 22 Brumaire, An x. (Nov. 13, 1801).

While the First Consul claimed credit with England for in-tending to annihilate the black government and restore slav-ery at St. Domingo, he proclaimed to Toussaint and the negroes intentions of a different kind. He wrote at last a letter to Toussaint, and drew up a proclamation to the inhabitants of the island, which Leclerc was to publish. "If you are told," said this famous proclamation,[1] "that these forces are destined to ravish your liberty, answer: The Republic has given us lib-erty, the Republic will not suffer it to be taken from us!" The letter to Toussaint was even more curious, when considered as a supplement to that which had been written to the British government only five days before. "We have conceived esteem for you," wrote Bonaparte to the man he meant to destroy,[2] "and we take pleasure in recognizing and proclaiming the great services you have rendered to the French people. If their flag floats over St. Domingo, it is to you and to the brave blacks that they owe it." Then, after mildly disapproving cer-tain of Toussaint's acts, and hinting at the fatal consequences of disobedience, the letter continued: "Assist the Captain-General [Leclerc] with your counsels, your influence, and your talents. What can you desire?—the liberty of the blacks? You know that in all the countries where we have been, we have given it to the peoples who had it not." In order to quiet all alarms of the negroes on the subject of their freedom, a pledge still more absolute was given in what Americans might call the Annual Message sent to the French Legislature a week afterward. "At St. Domingo and at Guadeloupe there are no more slaves. All is free there; all will there remain free."[3]

A few days afterward Leclerc's expedition sailed; and the immense fleet, with an army of ten thousand men and all their equipments, arrived in sight of St. Domingo at the close of January, 1802. Toussaint was believed to have watched them from a look-out in the mountains while they lay for a day making their preparations for combined action. Then Leclerc sailed for Cap Français, where Christophe commanded. After

---

[1] Correspondance, vii. 315; Proclamation, 17 Brumaire, An x. (Nov. 8, 1801).
[2] Ibid., 322; Bonaparte to Toussaint, 27 Brumaire, An x. (Nov. 18, 1801).
[3] Ibid., 327; Exposé de la situation de la République, 1 Frimaire, An x. (Nov. 22, 1801).

a vain attempt to obtain possession of the town as a friend, he was obliged to attack. February 5 Christophe set the place in flames, and the war of races broke out.

The story of this war, interesting though it was, cannot be told here. Toussaint's resistance broke the force of Bonaparte's attack. Although it lasted less than three months, it swept away one French army, and ruined the industry of the colony to an extent that required years of repair. Had Toussaint not been betrayed by his own generals, and had he been less attached than he was to civilization and despotic theories of military rule, he would have achieved a personal triumph greater than was won by any other man of his time. His own choice was to accept the war of races, to avoid open battle where his troops were unequal to their opponents, and to harass instead of fighting in line. He would have made a war of guerillas, stirred up the terror and fanaticism of the negro laborers, put arms into their hands, and relied on their courage rather than on that of his army. He let himself be overruled. "Old Toussaint," said Christophe afterward, "never ceased saying this, but no one would believe him. We had arms; pride in using them destroyed us."[1] Christophe, for good reasons, told but half the story. Toussaint was not ruined by a few lost battles, but by the treachery of Christophe himself and of the other negro generals. Jealous of Toussaint's domination, and perhaps afraid of being sent to execution like Moyse—the best general officer in their service—for want of loyalty to his chief, Christophe, after one campaign, April 26, 1802, surrendered his posts and forces to Leclerc without the knowledge and against the orders of Toussaint. Then Louverture himself committed the fatal mistake of his life, which he of all men seemed least likely to commit,—he trusted the word of Bonaparte. May 1, 1802, he put himself in Leclerc's hands in reliance on Leclerc's honor.

Surprising as such weakness was in one who had the sensitiveness of a wild animal to danger,—Leclerc himself seemed to be as much surprised that the word of honor of a French soldier should be believed as any bystander at seeing the negro believe it,—the act had a parallel in the weakness

[1] Pamphile de Lacroix, Mémoires, ii. 228.

which led Bonaparte, twelve years afterward, to mount the deck of the "Bellerophon," and without even the guaranty of a pledge surrender himself to England. The same vacillations and fears, the same instinct of the desperate political gambler, the same cowering in the face of fate, closed the active lives of both these extraordinary men. Such beings should have known how to die when their lives were ended. Toussaint should have fought on, even though only to perish under the last cactus on his mountains, rather than trust himself in the hands of Bonaparte.

The First Consul's orders to Leclerc were positive, precise, and repeated.[1] "Follow exactly your instructions," said he, "and the moment you have rid yourself of Toussaint, Christophe, Dessalines, and the principal brigands, and the masses of the blacks shall be disarmed, send over to the continent all the blacks and mulattoes who have played a *rôle* in the civil troubles. . . . Rid us of these gilded Africans, and we shall have nothing more to wish."[2] With the connivance and at the recommendation of Christophe, by a stratagem such as Bonaparte used afterward in the case of the Duc d'Enghien and of Don Carlos IV., Toussaint was suddenly arrested, June 10, 1802, and hurried on ship-board. Some weeks later he was landed at Brest; then he disappeared. Except a few men who were in the secret, no one ever again saw him. Plunged into a damp dungeon in the fortress of Joux, high in the Jura Mountains on the Swiss frontier, the cold and solitude of a single winter closed this tropical existence. April 7, 1803, he died forgotten, and his work died with him. Not by Toussaint, and still less by Christophe or Dessalines, was the liberty of the blacks finally established in Hayti, and the entrance of the Mississippi barred to Bonaparte.

The news of Leclerc's success reached Paris early in June,[3] and set Bonaparte again in motion. Imagining that the blacks were at his mercy, orders were at once issued to provide for restoring them to slavery. The truth relating to this part of the subject, habitually falsified or concealed by Bonaparte and

[1] Correspondance, vii. 413; Bonaparte to Leclerc, 25 Ventôse, An x. (March 16, 1802).

[2] Ibid., 503, 504; Bonaparte to Leclerc, 12 Messidor, An x. (July 1, 1802).

[3] Moniteur, 24 Prairial, An x. (June 13, 1802).

his admirers,[1] remained hidden among the manuscript records of the Empire; but the order to restore slavery at Guadeloupe was given, June 14, by the Minister of the Marine to General Richepanse, who commanded there, and on the same day a similar instruction was sent to General Leclerc at St. Domingo, in each case leaving the general to act according to his discretion in the time and manner of proceeding.

"As regards the return of the blacks to the old *régime*," wrote the Minister to General Leclerc,[2] "the bloody struggle out of which you have just come victorious with glory commands us to use the utmost caution. Perhaps we should only entangle ourselves in it anew if we wished precipitately to break that idol of liberty in whose name so much blood has flowed till now. For some time yet vigilance, order, a discipline at once rural and military, must take the place of the positive and pronounced slavery of the colored people of your colony. Especially the master's good usage must reattach them to his rule. When they shall have felt by comparison the difference between a usurping and tyrannical yoke and that of the legitimate proprietor interested in their preservation, then the moment will have arrived for making them return to their original condition, from which it has been so disastrous to have drawn them."

[1] Correspondance, xxx. 535; Notes sur St. Domingue.
[2] Decrès to Leclerc, 25 Prairial, An x. (June 14, 1802); Archives de la Marine, MSS. Cf. Revue Historique, "Napoléon Premier et Saint Domingue," Janvier–Février, 1884.

Chapter XVI

SIMULTANEOUSLY WITH the order to restore slavery at Guadeloupe and St. Domingo, Bonaparte directed his Minister of Marine to prepare plans and estimates for the expedition which was to occupy Louisiana. "My intention is to take possession of Louisiana with the shortest delay, and that this expedition be made in the utmost secrecy, under the appearance of being directed on St. Domingo."[1] The First Consul had allowed Godoy to postpone for a year the delivery of Louisiana, but he would wait no longer. His Minister at Madrid, General Gouvion St.-Cyr, obtained at length a promise that the order for the delivery of Louisiana should be given by Charles IV. to the First Consul on two conditions: first, that Austria, England, and the dethroned Grand Duke of Tuscany should be made to recognize the new King of Etruria; second, that France should pledge herself "not to alienate the property and usufruct of Louisiana, and to restore it to Spain in case the King of Tuscany should lose the whole or the greater part of his estates."

To these demands Talleyrand immediately replied in a letter of instructions to Gouvion St -Cyr, which was destined to a painful celebrity.[2] After soothing and reassuring Spain on the subject of the King of Etruria, this letter came at last to the required pledge in regard to Louisiana: —

> "Spain wishes that France should engage herself not to sell or alienate in any manner the property or enjoyment of Louisiana. Her wish in this respect perfectly conforms with the intentions of the French government, which parted with it in 1762 only in favor of Spain, and has wished to recover it only because France holds to a possession which once made part of French territory. You can declare in the name of the First Consul that France will never alienate it."

St.-Cyr accordingly gave a formal written pledge in the

[1] Correspondance, vii. 485; Bonaparte to Decrès, 15 Prairial, An x. (June 4, 1802).

[2] Talleyrand to Gouvion St.-Cyr, 30 Prairial, An x. (June 19, 1802); Archives des Aff. Étr., MSS.

name of the First Consul that France would never alienate Louisiana.[1]

Even yet the formal act of delivery was delayed. Bonaparte gave orders[2] that the expedition should be ready to sail in the last week of September; but the time passed, and delays were multiplied. For once the First Consul failed to act with energy. His resources were drained to St. Domingo as fast as he could collect them,[3] and the demands of the colonies on his means of transportation exceeded his supply of transports. The expedition to Louisiana was postponed, but, as he hoped, only to give it more scope.

From the time of Berthier's treaty of retrocession, Bonaparte had tried to induce the King of Spain to part with the Floridas; but Charles IV. refused to talk of another bargain. In vain Bonaparte wrote to the young King of Etruria, offering to give him Parma, Piacenza, and Guastalla, if Don Carlos would add Florida to Louisiana.[4] When at length the King signed at Barcelona, October 15, the order which delivered Louisiana to France, Bonaparte pressed more earnestly than ever for the Floridas. Talleyrand made a report on the subject, dissuading him from acquiring more than West Florida.[5]

"West Florida," he wrote, "suffices for the desired enlargement of Louisiana; it completes the retrocession of the French colony, such as it was given to Spain; it carries the eastern boundary back to the river Appalachicola; it gives us the port of Pensacola, and a population which forms more than half that of the two Floridas. By leaving East Florida to Spain we much diminish the difficulties of our relative position in regard to the United States,—dif-

[1] St.-Cyr to Don Pedro Cevallos, 23 Messidor, An x. (July 12, 1802). Yrujo to Madison, Sept. 4, 1803. State Papers, ii. 569.

[2] Correspondance, viii. 5; Bonaparte to Decrès, 6 Fructidor, An x. (Aug. 24, 1802).

[3] Ibid., 112; Bonaparte to Leclerc, 6 Frimaire, An xi. (Nov. 27, 1802).

[4] Ibid., 12; Bonaparte to the King of Tuscany, 11 Fructidor, An x. (Aug. 29, 1802).

[5] Rapport au Premier Consul; Frimaire, An xi. (November, 1802); Archives des Aff. Étr., MSS.

ficulties little felt to-day, but which some day may become of the gravest importance."

Bonaparte did not follow this advice. On the death of the Duke of Parma he wrote with his own hand to the King of Spain, offering the old family estate of Parma as a gift for the King of Tuscany, in return for which France was to receive the Floridas.[1] The Queen, as before, favored the exchange, and all her influence was exerted to effect it; but Godoy was obstinate in evading or declining the offer, and after months of diplomatic effort Bonaparte received at last, toward the end of January, 1803, a despatch from General Beurnonville, his new representative at Madrid, announcing that the Prince of Peace, with the aid of the British Minister John Hookham Frere, had succeeded in defeating the scheme.[2]

"The Prince told me that the British Minister had declared to him, in the name of his Government, that his Britannic Majesty, being informed of the projects of exchange which existed between France and Spain, could never consent that the two Floridas should become an acquisition of the Republic; that the United States of America were in this respect of one mind with the Court of London; and that Russia equally objected to France disposing of the estates of Parma in favor of Spain, since the Emperor Alexander intended to have them granted as indemnity to the King of Sardinia. In imparting to me this proceeding of the British Minister, the Prince had a satisfied air, which showed how much he wished that the exchange, almost agreed upon and so warmly desired by the Queen, may not take place "

Europe would have acted more wisely in its own interest by offering Bonaparte every inducement to waste his strength on America. Had England, Spain, and Russia united to give him Florida on his own terms, they would have done only what was best for themselves. A slight impulse given to the

[1] Correspondance, viii. 111; Bonaparte to the King of Spain, 6 Frimaire, An xi. (Nov. 27, 1802).

[2] Beurnonville to Talleyrand, 27 Nivôse, An xi. (Jan. 17, 1803); Archives des Aff. Étr., MSS.

First Consul would have plunged him into difficulties with the United States from which neither France nor the United States could have easily escaped. Both Godoy and the Emperor Alexander would have done well to let French blood flow without restraint in St. Domingo and on the Mississippi, rather than drown with it the plains of Castile and Smolensk.

Although the retrocession of Louisiana to France had been settled in principle by Berthier's treaty of Oct. 1, 1800, six months before Jefferson came into office, the secret was so well kept that Jefferson hardly suspected it. He began his administration by anticipating a long period of intimate relations with Spain and France. In sending instructions to Claiborne as governor of the Mississippi Territory,—a post of importance, because of its relations with the Spanish authority at New Orleans,—President Jefferson wrote privately,[1]—

> "With respect to Spain, our disposition is sincerely amicable, and even affectionate. We consider her possession of the adjacent country as most favorable to our interests, and should see with an extreme pain any other nation substituted for them."

Disposed to be affectionate toward Spain, he assumed that he should stand in cordial relations with Spain's ally, the First Consul. Convinced that the quarrels of America with France had been artificially created by the monarchical Federalists, he believed that a policy of open confidence would prevent such dangers in the future. The First Consul would naturally cultivate his friendship, for every Federalist newspaper had for years proclaimed Jefferson as the head of French influence in America, and every Republican newspaper had branded his predecessors as tools of Great Britain. In spite of the 18th Brumaire, Jefferson had not entirely lost faith in Bonaparte, and knew almost nothing of his character or schemes. At the moment when national interest depended on prompt and exact information, the President withdrew half his ministers from Europe, and paid little attention to the agents he retained. He took diplomatic matters into his own hands, and

[1] Jefferson to W. C. C. Claiborne, July 13, 1801; Jefferson MSS.

meant to conduct them at Washington with diplomatists under his personal influence,—a practice well suited to a power
superior in will and force to that with which it dealt, but one
which might work badly in dealing with Bonaparte. When
Chancellor Livingston, the new minister to Paris, sailed for
France, Jefferson wrote him a private letter[1] in regard to the
appointment of a new French minister at Washington. Two
names had been suggested,—La Forest and Otto. Neither of
these was quite satisfactory; some man would be preferred
whose sympathies should be so entire as to make reticences
and restraints unnecessary. The idea that Jefferson could put
himself in Bonaparte's hands without reticence or restraint
belonged to old theories of opposition,—a few months dispelled it; and when he had been a year in office, he wrote
again to Livingston, withdrawing the objection to La Forest
and Otto. "When I wrote that letter," said he,[2] "I did not
harbor a doubt that the disposition on that side the water was
as cordial as I knew ours to be." He had discovered his
mistake,—"the dispositions now understood to exist there
impose of themselves limits to the openness of our
communications."

Even before Livingston sailed, the rumors of the retrocession of Louisiana had taken such definite shape[3] that, in June,
1801, Secretary Madison instructed the ministers at London,
Paris, and Madrid on the subject. These instructions were
remarkable for their mildness.[4] No protest was officially
ordered against a scheme so hostile to the interests of the
Union. On the contrary, Livingston was told, in September,
1801, that if he could obtain West Florida from France, or by
means of French influence, "such a proof on the part of
France of good-will toward the United States would contribute to reconcile the latter" to seeing Bonaparte at New Orleans. Even after Rufus King, the United States minister at
London, sent home a copy of Lucien Bonaparte's treaty of

[1] Jefferson to R. R. Livingston, Aug. 28, 1801; Jefferson's Writings (Ford),
viii. 85.
[2] Ibid., viii. 138.
[3] Rufus King to Madison, June 1, 1801; State Papers, ii. 509.
[4] Madison to Pinckney, June 9, 1801; Madison to Livingston, Sept. 28, 1801;
State Papers, ii. 510.

Madrid, in which the whole story was told,[1] this revelation, probably managed by Godoy in order to put the United States and England on their guard, produced no immediate effect. Jefferson yielded with reluctance to the conviction that he must quarrel with Bonaparte. Had not Godoy's delays and Toussaint's resistance intervened, ten thousand French soldiers, trained in the school of Hoche and Moreau, and commanded by a future marshal of France, might have occupied New Orleans and St. Louis before Jefferson could have collected a brigade of militia at Nashville.

By the spring of 1802 Jefferson became alive to the danger. He then saw what was meant by the French expedition against Toussaint. Leclerc had scarcely succeeded, Feb. 5, 1802, in taking possession of the little that Christophe left at Cap Français, when his difficulties of supply began. St. Domingo drew its supplies chiefly from the United States. Toussaint's dependence on the American continent had been so complete as to form one of the chief complaints of French merchants. General Leclerc disliked the United States,—not without reason, since the Government of that country, as was notorious, had done its utmost to punish France, and had succeeded beyond expectation. Leclerc was a soldier,—severe, impatient, quick to take offence, and also quick to forget it. He knew that he could expect no sympathy from Americans, and he found that all the supplies in St. Domingo were American property. Of course the owners asked extortionate prices; and had Leclerc paid them, he would within six weeks have seen his harbors glutted with goods from Baltimore and New York. Instead of doing this, he seized them, and insulted the American shipmasters and merchants. By the month of March the newspapers of the United States were filled with stories of Leclerc's arbitrary and violent conduct. He was reported as saying that the Americans were no better than Arabs; and one of his general officers was said to have told Lear, the American consul-general, that they were the scum of nations. Cargoes were taken without payment, American shipmasters were seized and imprisoned for offences unknown to the law; while Lear was notified that no consul could be received in

---

[1] Rufus King to Madison, Nov. 20, 1801; State Papers, ii. 511.

St. Domingo as a colony of France, and that he must quit the island within a fortnight. No protest availed against such summary discipline. Lear obeyed; and returning to Madison at Washington, told him of American property confiscated and American citizens in prison.

Madison sent for Pichon, then in charge of the French legation at Washington pending the appointment of a minister. Pichon was a relic of the French republic; he had been long in the United States, and felt little apparent sympathy with the consular *régime* or its plans. At Madison's request, Pichon undertook to interfere, and wrote to Leclerc letter upon letter of remonstrance.[1] America, he said, could either feed or famish the French army: "Experience proves it; our colonies were brought into revolt only by our unlucky misunderstanding with her; through her alone can we raise them up again." Leclerc resented the tone of these letters, and wrote to Bonaparte that Pichon was a scoundrel and a wretch, with whom he would hold no further relations;[2] but before Leclerc's letter could have arrived, the First Consul had already ordered[3] Talleyrand to rebuke the *chargé* at Washington for his American officiousness. Pichon's diplomatic career was closed; he retired into private life as soon as the new minister arrived, but meanwhile his remonstrances were not without effect upon Leclerc, whose anger rarely became vindictive.

The conduct of Leclerc in expelling Lear and imprisoning American shipmasters because munitions of war were found among the cargoes lying in the ports of Toussaint, first opened President Jefferson's eyes to the situation into which he was drifting; but other evidences were not wanting that Bonaparte was no friend of the United States. Talleyrand's conduct was almost as exasperating as when he provoked reprisals four years before. Chancellor Livingston reached France about Nov. 10, 1801, just in time to see Leclerc's expedition sail. He was met by private assurances that Louisiana

---

[1]Pichon to Leclerc, 29 Ventôse–11 Messidor, An x. (March 20–June 30, 1802); Archives de la Marine, MSS.

[2]Leclerc to Bonaparte, 17 Prairial, An x. (June 6, 1802); Archives Nationales, MSS.

[3]Correspondance, vii. 508; Bonaparte to Talleyrand, 15 Messidor, An x. (July 4, 1802).

and the Floridas had been bought by France, and he went to Talleyrand with inquiries.[1] The imperturbable Talleyrand looked him in the face and denied the fact. "It had been a subject of conversation," he said, "but nothing concluded." At that moment Rufus King was sending from London the text of Lucien Bonaparte's treaty, dated eight months before, which fixed the details of the retrocession. President Jefferson received at the same instant Talleyrand's explicit denial and the explicit proof that Talleyrand was trying to deceive him. Jefferson soon satisfied himself that Talleyrand's conduct rested on a system; and he became angrier with every act of the French foreign minister. Livingston, naturally somewhat suspicious and fretful, soon became restive under the treatment he received; for his notes and remonstrances were left equally without answer or attention, whether they related to Louisiana or to the debts due by the Government of France to American citizens. As Livingston grew hot, and Leclerc's temper burst into violence, Madison became irritable, and by the month of May had reached the point of saying that if such conduct should continue, "the worst events are to be apprehended."[2]

The President himself then intervened. A French gentleman, Dupont de Nemours, happened to be in the United States on the point of returning to France. Dupont's name was then as well and honorably known in France as that of his descendants was to become in the annals of the United States. To him Jefferson turned as a medium of unofficial communication with the First Consul. He enclosed to Dupont a letter addressed to Livingston on the Louisiana affair, which he requested Dupont to read, and, after reading, to seal.

"I wish you to be possessed of the subject," he wrote,[3] "because you may be able to impress on the Government of France the inevitable consequences of their taking possession of Louisiana; and though, as I here mention, the

[1] Livingston to Madison, Dec. 10, 1801; Livingston to King, Dec. 30; King to Madison, Nov. 20; State Papers, ii. 511, 512.

[2] Madison to Livingston, May 1, 1802; State Papers, ii. 516.

[3] Jefferson to Dupont de Nemours, April 25, 1802; Works, iv. 435.

cession of New Orleans and the Floridas to us would be a palliation, yet I believe it would be no more, and that this measure will cost France, and perhaps not very long hence, a war which will annihilate her on the ocean, and place that element under the despotism of two nations,—which I am not reconciled to the more because my own would be one of them."

This idea was still more strongly expressed in the enclosure to Livingston, which Dupont was to read, in order that he might communicate its sense to Bonaparte:[1] —

"The day that France takes possession of New Orleans fixes the sentence which is to restrain her forever within her low-water mark. It seals the union of two nations, who in conjunction can maintain exclusive possession of the ocean. From that moment we must marry ourselves to the British fleet and nation. . . . Will not the amalgamation of a young and thriving nation continue to that enemy the health and force which are at present so evidently on the decline? And will a few years' possession of New Orleans add equally to the strength of France?"

Dupont was to impress on the First Consul the idea that if he should occupy Louisiana, the United States would wait "a few years," until the next war between France and England, but would then make common cause with England. Even a present cession of New Orleans and the Floridas to the United States, though it would remove the necessity of an immediate advance to England, would not prevent the risk of a quarrel with France, so long as France should hold the west bank of the Mississippi. To obviate such a quarrel was the object of Dupont's unofficial mission. "If you can be the means of informing the wisdom of Bonaparte of all its consequences, you have deserved well of both countries."

As though to alarm Bonaparte were not task enough for any one man, Jefferson suggested that it would be well to hoodwink Talleyrand.

"There is another service you can render. I am told that

[1] Jefferson to Livingston, April 18, 1802; Works, iv. 431.

Talleyrand is personally hostile to us. This, I suppose, has been occasioned by the X. Y. Z. history; but he should consider that that was the artifice of a party willing to sacrifice him to the consolidation of their power. This nation has done him justice by dismissing them."

To do Talleyrand justice was impossible; but his reflections on the letter which Dupont was tacitly authorized to show him could hardly have been just to Jefferson. With the X. Y. Z. history, as Jefferson called it, fresh in Talleyrand's mind, — an instance of his venality so notorious that it had cost him his office, and so outrageous that even his associates of the 18th Brumaire had not at first ventured to reappoint him, — hostility to the United States had become with him a personal as well as a political passion. Accustomed to the penetrating candor of his own untroubled avowals, he read these words of Jefferson, announcing that an American President had been dismissed from office in order to do him justice: —

"This nation has done him justice by dismissing them; those in power are precisely those who disbelieved that story, and saw in it nothing but an attempt to deceive our country. We entertain toward him personally the most friendly dispositions. As to the government of France, we know too little of the state of things there to understand what it is, and have no inclination to meddle in their settlement. Whatever government they establish, we wish to be well with it."

Talleyrand must have known enough of the American character to feel that a Republican President could not seriously mean to represent his own election as an act of national justice to a venal French politician; in his eyes, the letter could have seemed to show only simple-mindedness. One point needed no analysis of character. Jefferson said that he did not know what sort of government the 18th Brumaire created, or care to meddle in its affairs; he wished to be well with it, and in any case should not go to war until England did so. Dupont remonstrated against the nature of the message. "A young soldier," he wrote back,[1] " whose ministers can keep

[1] Dupont to Jefferson, April 30, 1802; Jefferson MSS.

their places only by perpetually flattering his military pride, will be much more offended than touched by this reasoning; and if this be all that is advanced, we may regard the negotiation as a failure." To make its chances worse, it crossed the ocean at the same time with the news that Toussaint had submitted, and that no obstacle to the immediate occupation of Louisiana remained. Dupont talked in vain. Bonaparte answered only by pressing Spain for the Floridas, and demanding possession of New Orleans.

Thus far American diplomacy was not successful; Jefferson's efforts were no more effective than Madison's more cautious suggestions. As the summer began, the President watched anxiously the course of events at St. Domingo, and found consolation there for the baseness of Callender and the assaults on Paine at home. "Though I take for granted," he wrote to Governor McKean,[1] "that the colonization of Louisiana is a settled point, yet I suspect they must be much stronger in St. Domingo before they can spare troops to go there. What has been called a surrender of Toussaint to Leclerc, I suspect was in reality a surrender of Leclerc to Toussaint."

The seizure of Toussaint and his disappearance from the island, which occurred as Jefferson wrote this letter, overthrew its hopeful theories; but before long, reports began to arrive in the United States that Leclerc had met with a new disaster, so terrible as to surpass the horrors even of St. Domingo history. The first French army, of seventeen thousand men, had been consumed in the task of subjecting the negroes. A second army was next swept away by yellow fever. In the middle of September, 1802, Leclerc wrote to the First Consul that of twenty-eight thousand three hundred men sent to St. Domingo, four thousand remained fit for service.[2] "Add to our losses that of five thousand sailors, and the occupation of St. Domingo has cost us till now twenty-four thousand men, and we are not yet definitely masters of it." He was depending on Toussaint's generals and army for his support against an insurrection of the laborers, who were

[1] Jefferson to Governor McKean, June 14, 1802; Jefferson MSS.
[2] Leclerc to Bonaparte, 29 Fructidor, An x. (Sept. 16, 1802); Archives Nationales, MSS.

maddened by the rumor that slavery had been restored at Guadeloupe, and was soon to be re-established at St. Domingo. Nothing could be more discouraging than Leclerc's letters:[1]—

"I have no false measure to reproach myself with, Citizen Consul; and if my position, from being a very good one, has become very bad, it is necessary to blame here only the malady which has destroyed my army, the premature re-establishment of slavery at Guadeloupe, and the newspapers and letters from France, which speak only of slavery. Here is my opinion on this country. We must destroy all the negroes in the mountains, men and women, keeping only infants less than twelve years old; we must also destroy half those of the plain, and leave in the colony not a single man of color who has worn an epaulette. Without this the colony will never be quiet; and at the beginning of every year, especially after murderous seasons like this, you will have a civil war, which will shake your hold on the country. In order to be master of St. Domingo, you must send me twelve thousand men without losing a single day."

Besides these twelve thousand men and twelve hundred thousand dollars in specie, Leclerc required five thousand more men in the following summer. "If you cannot send the troops I demand, and for the season I point out, St. Domingo will be forever lost to France."

Long afterward, at St. Helena, Napoleon wrote comments[2] on the causes of his disaster at St. Domingo, severely blaming his brother-in-law Leclerc for failing to carry out his orders to arrest and send to Europe all the black generals, as he sent Toussaint. Napoleon's rule in politics, and one which cost him dear, was to disregard masses and reckon only on leaders. Toussaint came within a step of achieving the greatest triumph of his age. Had he been true to himself and his color, and had he hidden himself for a few months in the mountains, he need not have struck a blow in order to drive Bonaparte's generals back to Europe; the yellow fever and the

[1] Leclerc to Bonaparte, 15 Vendémiaire, An xi. (Oct. 7, 1802); Archives Nationales, MSS.
[2] Correspondance, xxx. 534.

blind despair of the negro laborers would have done the work alone. Bonaparte's theory in regard to the negro chiefs was an illusion. Christophe, Dessalines, Maurepas, and all Toussaint's chief officers served Leclerc faithfully till they saw his case to be hopeless. "Dessalines is at this moment the butcher of the blacks," wrote Leclerc Sept. 16, 1802, in the midst of insurrections; "Christophe has so maltreated them as to be execrated by them." The negro chiefs were traitors to both sides; and if not arrested by Leclerc, they deserved to be shot by their own people. While they helped to exterminate the black laboring class, Leclerc sent home reports that might have frozen the blood of any man less callous than Bonaparte:[1] —

"The decrees of General Richepanse [at Guadeloupe] circulate here, and do much harm. The one which restores slavery, in consequence of being published three months too soon, will cost many men to the army and colony of St. Domingo. . . . I get news of a bloody combat sustained by General Boyer at the Gros Morne. The rebels were exterminated; fifty prisoners were hung. These men die with incredible fanaticism,—they laugh at death; it is the same with the women. The rebels of Moustique have attacked and carried Jean Rabel; it should have been retaken by this time. This fury is the work of General Richepanse's proclamation and of the inconsiderate talk of the colonists."

As the insurrection spread, and the fever reduced Leclerc's European force, the black generals and troops began to desert. Shooting was useless; drowning had no effect. No form of terror touched them. "Few colonial troops remain with me," wrote Leclerc in almost his last letter. "A battalion of the Eleventh Colonial, which had been joined with the Legion of the Cape, having furnished a number of deserters, 176 men of this battalion were embarked at Jacmel for Port Republican. Of this number 173 strangled themselves on the way, the Chef de Bataillon at their head. There you see the men

[1] Leclerc to Decrès, 21 Thermidor, An x. (Aug. 9, 1802); Archives de la Marine, MSS.

we have to fight!"[1] At length the report came that Leclerc himself had succumbed. Worn by anxieties, exertions, and incessant fever, he followed his army to the grave.

News of Leclerc's death, Nov. 1, 1802, and of the hopelessness of Bonaparte's schemes against St. Domingo, reached the Government at Washington nearly at the same time with other news which overshadowed this. The people of the United States expected day by day to hear of some sudden attack, from which as yet only the dexterity of Godoy and the disasters of Leclerc had saved them. Although they could see only indistinctly the meaning of what had taken place, they knew where to look for the coming stroke, and in such a state of mind might easily exaggerate its importance. A few days before Congress met, the Western post brought a despatch from Governor Claiborne at Natchez announcing that the Spanish Intendant, Don Juan Ventura Morales, had forbidden the Americans to deposit their merchandise at New Orleans, as they had a right to do under the treaty of 1795.[2]

No one doubted that although the attack might come from a Spanish Intendant, the real party with whom America had to deal was not Spain, but France. The secret papers of the French government show what was said, but hardly believed at the time, that the First Consul was not directly responsible for the act; but they also prove that the act was a consequence of the retrocession. The colonial system of Spain was clumsy and disconnected. Viceroys, governors, commandants, intendants, acted in Mexico, Cuba, New Orleans, Peru, everywhere without relation to each other. At New Orleans the Governor, Don Juan de Salcedo, was powerless to control the Intendant, Don Juan Ventura Morales, and no authority nearer than Madrid could decide between them. The *entrepôt*, or right of deposit, not only prevented the Spanish Intendant from imposing duties on American produce, but also covered a large amount of smuggling which further diminished the revenue. The Intendant, who had charge of the revenues, and was partly responsible for the large deficit which every year drained the resources of Spain to Louisiana, was forced to

[1] Leclerc to Bonaparte, 15 Vendémiaire, An xi. (Oct. 7, 1802); Archives Nationales, MSS.

[2] Despatch of W. C. C. Claiborne, Oct. 29, 1802; State Papers, ii. 470.

hear the complaints of the Treasury at Madrid, continually asking him to find a remedy, and at last, in one of its despatches, letting slip the remark that "after all, the right of deposit was only for three years." The treaty of 1795 had in fact stipulated that the King of Spain would "permit the citizens of the United States, for the space of three years from this time, to deposit their merchandise and effects in the port of New Orleans, and to export them from thence, without paying any other duty than a fair price for the hire of the stores; and his Majesty promises either to continue this permission if he finds during that time that it is not prejudicial to the interests of Spain, or if he should not agree to continue it there, he will assign to them on another part of the banks of the Mississippi an equivalent establishment."

According to the explanation given by Morales to Laussat,[1] the new French prefect whom Bonaparte sent to receive possession of Louisiana, the Spaniard acted on his own responsibility, in what he believed to be the interests of the colony, and within the stipulations of the treaty. Thinking that the retrocession offered a chance, which might never recur, for reopening a question which had been wrongly decided, Morales, defying the opposition and even the threats of Governor Salcedo, proclaimed the right of deposit to be at an end. He reasoned that Spain as a result of peace with England had shut her colonial ports to strangers, and this measure, so far as it included Louisiana, was illusory so long as the right of deposit should exist. The right had been granted for three years from 1795; and if the practice had been permitted to continue after these three years expired, it might have been owing, not to the treaty, but to the general privileges granted to neutrals during the war; and as for the Americans, it was their own fault not to have looked more carefully to their rights at the close of the three years, when they should have secured the continuation or the promised substitute. As Spain was about to lose Louisiana in any case, Morales remarked that she need not trouble herself about the quarrel he was making with the United States; while the French republic took Louisiana as it actually stood under the treaties, and

[1] Laussat to Decrès, 29 Germinal, An xi. (April 19, 1803); Archives de la Marine, MSS.

ought therefore to be glad of whatever improved the actual situation, or opened the path to negotiations more advantageous. This view of the matter, as Morales presented it, was the more interesting because it was in the spirit of Talleyrand's plans, and reversed Godoy's policy.

The rumor that Spain had closed the Mississippi roused varied sensations as it spread eastward. Tennessee and Kentucky became eager for war. They knew that Morales's act was a foretaste of what they were to expect from France; and they might well ask themselves how many lives it would cost to dislodge a French army once fortified on the lower Mississippi. The whole power of the United States could not at that day, even if backed by the navy of England, have driven ten thousand French troops out of Louisiana. On the contrary, a vigorous French officer, with a small trained force and his Indian allies, could make Claiborne uneasy for the safety of his villages at Natchez and Vicksburg. No one could foresee what might be the effect of one or two disastrous campaigns on the devotion of the Western people to the Government at Washington. The existence of the Union and the sacrifice of many thousand lives seemed, in the opinion of competent judges, likely to be risked by allowing Bonaparte to make his position at New Orleans impregnable.

The New England Federalists were satisfied that President Jefferson must either adopt their own policy and make war on France, or risk a dissolution of the Union. They had hardly dared hope that democracy would so soon meet what might prove to be its crisis. They too cried for war, and cared little whether their outcry produced or prevented hostilities, for the horns of Jefferson's dilemma were equally fatal to him. All eyes were bent on the President, and watched eagerly for some sign of his intentions.

Chapter XVII

AFTER THE LETTERS sent to Europe by Dupont de Nemours in May, neither the President nor the Secretary of State again stirred before the meeting of Congress in December. The diplomacy of 1800 was slow. Nearly six months were required to decide upon a policy, write to Europe, receive a reply, and decide again upon an answer. An entire year was needed for taking a new line of action, and ascertaining its chances of success. In October, Madison wrote to Livingston that the President still waited to learn the impression produced at Paris by Dupont.[1] Livingston, on his side, had been active and unsuccessful. The President again wrote to him, by the October packet, a letter which would have perplexed any European diplomatist.[2]

"We shall so take our distance between the two rival nations," said Jefferson, "as, remaining disengaged till necessity compels us, we may haul finally to the enemy of that which shall make it necessary. We see all the disadvantageous consequences of taking a side, and shall be forced into it only by a more disagreeable alternative; in which event we must countervail the disadvantages by measures which will give us splendor and power, but not as much happiness as our present system. We wish, therefore, to remain well with France; but we see that no consequences, however ruinous to them, can secure us with certainty against the extravagance of her present rulers. . . . No matter at present existing between them and us is important enough to risk a breach of peace,—peace being indeed the most important of all things for us, except the preserving an erect and independent attitude."

"Peace is our passion!" This phrase of President Jefferson, taken from a letter written a few months later,[3] expressed his true policy. In spite of his frequent menaces, he told Livingston in October, 1802, that the French occupation of Louisiana

[1] Madison to Livingston, Oct. 15, 1802; State Papers, ii. 525.
[2] Jefferson to Livingston, Oct. 10, 1802; Works, iv. 447.
[3] Jefferson to Sir John Sinclair, June 30, 1803; Works, iv. 490.

was not "important enough to risk a breach of peace." Within a week after this letter was written, New Orleans was closed to American commerce, and a breach of peace seemed unavoidable. Down to that time the Executive had done nothing to check Napoleon. The President had instructed his agents at Paris and Madrid to obtain, if they could, the cession of New Orleans and West Florida, and had threatened an alliance with England in case this request were refused; but England was at peace with France, and Bonaparte was not likely to provoke another war until he should be able to defend Louisiana. So far as any diplomatic action by the United States government was concerned, Madison and Jefferson might equally well have written nothing; and when news arrived that the Mississippi was closed, alarming as the situation became, no new action was at first suggested. The President was contented to accept the assistance of the Spanish and French representatives at Washington.

In Jefferson's domestic as well as in his political household Don Carlos Martinez de Yrujo,—created in 1802 Marquis of Casa Yrujo,—the minister of Spain, was thoroughly at home, for he had a double title to confidence, and even to affection. His first claim was due to his marriage with a daughter of Governor McKean of Pennsylvania, whose importance in the Republican party was great. His second claim was political. Some years earlier he had so exasperated Timothy Pickering, then Secretary of State, as to provoke a demand for his recall. One of President Jefferson's first diplomatic acts was to ask from the Spanish government that Yrujo should be allowed to remain at Washington; and Godoy, who knew even better than Jefferson the character and merits of Yrujo, readily granted the favor.

Thus Yrujo was doubly and trebly attached to the Administration. Proud as a typical Spaniard should be, and mingling an infusion of vanity with his pride; irascible, headstrong, indiscreet as was possible for a diplomatist, and afraid of no prince or president; young, able, quick, and aggressive; devoted to his King and country; a flighty and dangerous friend, but a most troublesome enemy; always in difficulties, but in spite of fantastic outbursts always respectable,—Yrujo needed only the contrast of characters such as those of

Pickering or Madison to make him the most entertaining figure in Washington politics. He had become an American in language, family, and political training. He loved the rough-and-tumble of democratic habits, and remembered his diplomatic dignity only when he could use it as a weapon against a secretary of state. If he thought the Government to need assistance or warning, he wrote communications to the newspapers in a style which long experience had made familiar to the public and irritating to the Government whose acts he criticised. For natural reasons the American Executive, which never hesitated to use the press without limit for its own purposes, held it indecorous that a foreign minister should attempt to affect public opinion. The example of Genet was regarded as a proof even more than a warning that such action was highly improper; but from Yrujo's point of view, as from Genet's, the question of decorum was ridiculous in a country which prided itself on the absence of etiquette, and the only question he cared to consider was whether the press answered his purpose. His success could be best measured by the exasperation it caused to the tempers of Pickering and Madison.

Yrujo felt no love for Bonaparte, and no wish to serve his ends. At this moment of anxiety, stepping forward to assist the President, he asserted that there was no cause for alarm;[1] that the act of Morales was not authorized by the King of Spain, but rose from some excess of zeal or mistaken interpretation of the treaty on the part of the Intendant; and that a packet-boat should be instantly sent to New Orleans to inquire the reasons of the measure. His letter to the Intendant was in reality extremely sharp,—"a veritable diatribe," according to Laussat, the new French prefect, to whom Morales showed it. Yrujo pointed out the fatal consequences of Morales's conduct, and the ground it gave to United States citizens for claiming indemnity for their commercial losses.[2] At the same time Madison instructed Charles Pinckney at Madrid to inform the Spanish government that the President expected it to lose not a moment in countermanding the order

[1] Yrujo to Madison, Nov. 27, 1802; MSS. State Department Archives.
[2] Yrujo to Morales, Nov. 26, 1802; Gayarré, History of Louisiana, iii. 576.

of Morales, and in repairing every damage that might result from it.[1]

There the matter rested until December 6, when Congress met. Even at so exciting a moment, senators were slow in arriving at Washington, and a week passed before a quorum was formed. Not till December 15 could the Annual Message be read. No message could be more pacific in tone. The President discussed everything except the danger which engrossed men's minds. He talked of peace and friendship, of law, order, and religion, of differential duties, distressed seamen, the blockade of Tripoli, Georgia lands, Indian treaties, the increase in revenue, "the emancipation of our posterity from that mortal canker" a national debt, "by avoiding false objects of expense;" he said that no change in the military establishment was deemed necessary, but that the militia might be improved; he regretted that the behavior of the Barbary Powers rendered a small squadron still necessary to patrol the Mediterranean, but at the same time he strongly urged Congress to take measures for laying up the whole navy, by constructing a large dry-dock on the Eastern Branch, where the seven frigates might be stowed away side by side under cover, and kept from decay or expense. All these subjects he touched in a spirit of peace and good-will toward mankind; but when he came to the question of Louisiana, about which he had written so many alarming letters to Europe, he spoke in a tone of apparent indifference. "The cession of the Spanish province of Louisiana to France," he said, "which took place in the course of the late war, will, if carried into effect, make a change in the aspect of our foreign relations which will doubtless have a just weight in any deliberations of the Legislature connected with that subject." No allusion was made to the closure of the Mississippi.

Nothing could more disconcert the war party than this manner of ignoring their existence. Jefferson afterward explained that his hope was to gain time; but he could not more effectually have belittled his Federalist enemies than by thus telling them that a French army at New Orleans would "make a change in the aspect of our foreign relations." This manner

[1] Madison to Pinckney, Nov. 27, 1802; State Papers, ii. 527.

of treating Congress was the more dexterous, because if the President did not at once invite the Legislature to realize the alarming state of foreign affairs, he abstained only in order to carry out other tactics. Two days after the Message was read, December 17, John Randolph, the Administration leader in the House, moved for the papers relating to the violated right of deposit. Great curiosity was felt to know what course the President meant to take.

"However timid Mr. Jefferson may be," wrote Pichon to Talleyrand,[1] "and whatever price he may put on his pacific policy, one cannot foresee precisely what his answer will be. . . . I find in general a bad temper as regards us; and I cannot help seeing that there is a tendency toward adopting an irrevocably hostile system. This circumstance will be decisive for Mr. Jefferson. If he acts feebly, he is lost among his partisans; it will be then the time for Mr. Burr to show himself with advantage."

Thornton watched with equal anxiety the movement which promised to throw the United States into the arms of England. He expected as little as Pichon that the President would act with energy, but he hoped that the situation would force him into taking a side.[2]

"From the language of his ministers, and from the insinuations of some members of the Federal party, it will not be, I doubt, such a measure of vigor as would place the country on a commanding ground in the negotiation with Spain, or eventually with France; and the latter persons have some of them designated it to me as likely to be a very foolish thing."

Five days passed before Jefferson answered the call of the House; and when he did so, he sent papers which might have been prepared in five minutes, for most of them had been long printed in the newspapers.[3] In communicating these documents, the President added that he had not lost a mo-

---

[1] Pichon to Talleyrand, 2 Nivôse, An xi. (Dec. 22, 1802); Archives des Aff Étr., MSS.

[2] Thornton to Lord Hawkesbury, Jan. 3, 1803; MSS. British Archives.

[3] Message of Dec. 22, 1802; State Papers, ii. 469.

ment in causing every step to be taken which the occasion claimed from him; but he did not say what these steps were. A week later he sent another document, which he requested the House to return without publication;[1] it was a letter which Governor Claiborne had received from Governor Salcedo, denying responsibility for the Intendant's act, and asserting that it was not authorized by the Spanish government. The House shut its doors and debated a week. Then it reopened its doors, and announced to the world that by a party vote of fifty to twenty-five, the following resolution had been adopted:[2] —

"Adhering to that humane and wise policy which ought ever to characterize a free people, and by which the United States have always professed to be governed; willing at the same time to ascribe this breach of compact to the unauthorized misconduct of certain individuals rather than to a want of good faith on the part of his Catholic Majesty; and relying with perfect confidence on the vigilance and wisdom of the Executive, — they will wait the issue of such measures as that department of the Government shall have pursued for asserting the rights and vindicating the injuries of the United States."

Strenuously as the President exerted himself to stifle the warlike feeling in Congress, his influence did not extend far enough to check the same feeling elsewhere. Successful in Washington, he found himself exposed to an alarming pressure from the West. One State legislature after another adopted resolutions which shook the ground under his feet. Eighteen months had passed since the seriousness of Napoleon's schemes became known to him, but as yet he had done nothing that could be construed as an attempt to represent the demands of the western country; all his ingenuity had, in fact, been exerted to evade these demands. The West wanted troops at Natchez, to seize New Orleans at the first sign of a French occupation; but the use of force at that stage was not in Jefferson's thoughts. To quiet Kentucky and Tennessee without satisfying them was a delicate matter; but, delicate as

[1] Message of Dec. 30, 1802; State Papers, ii. 471.
[2] Resolutions of Jan. 7, 1803; Annals of Congress, 1802–1803, p. 339.

it was, Jefferson succeeded in doing it. He explained his plan in a letter to Monroe, written at the moment when everything depended on Monroe's aid:[1] —

"The agitation of the public mind on occasion of the late suspension of our right of deposit at New Orleans is extreme. In the western country it is natural, and grounded on honest motives; in the seaports it proceeds from a desire for war, which increases the mercantile lottery; in the Federalists generally, and especially those of Congress, the object is to force us into war if possible, in order to derange our finances; or if this cannot be done, to attach the western country to them as their best friends, and thus get again into power. Remonstrances, memorials, etc., are now circulating through the whole of the western country, and signed by the body of the people. The measures we have been pursuing, being invisible, do not satisfy their minds. Something sensible, therefore, has become necessary."

This sensible, or rather this tangible, measure was the appointment of a minister extraordinary to aid Livingston in buying New Orleans and the Floridas. The idea was adopted after the secret debate in the House. As Madison wrote soon afterward to Livingston,[2] "such has been the impulse given to the public mind" by these debates and by the press, "that every branch of the government has felt the obligation of taking the measures most likely not only to re-establish our present rights, but to promote arrangements by which they may be enlarged and more effectually secured." According to this view, the impulse of Congress and the Press alone made the Executive feel its obligation. For more than a year the Executive had known the danger and had done nothing; being obliged to do something, its first object was to avoid doing too much.

Accordingly, General Smith of Maryland, Jan. 11, 1803, carried the House again into secret session, and moved to appropriate two million dollars "to defray any expenses which may be incurred in relation to the intercourse between the United States and foreign nations." The next day a committee re-

[1] Jefferson to Monroe, Jan. 13, 1803; Works, iv. 453.
[2] Madison to Livingston, Jan. 18, 1803; State Papers, ii. 529.

ported, through Joseph Nicholson, in favor of appropriating the money, with a view to purchasing West Florida and New Orleans.[1] The Report argued that there was no alternative between purchase and war. Meanwhile, January 11, the President sent to the Senate the name of James Monroe as minister extraordinary to France and Spain to help Livingston and Pinckney in "enlarging and more effectually securing our rights and interests in the river Mississippi and in the territories eastward thereof."

The nomination was approved by the Senate January 13; and without losing a moment, Jefferson wrote to Monroe, explaining the reasons which made his course necessary:[2] —

"The measure has already silenced the Federalists here. Congress will no longer be agitated by them; and the country will become calm as fast as the information extends over it. All eyes, all hopes, are now fixed on you; and were you to decline, the chagrin would be universal, and would shake under your feet the high ground on which you stand with the public. Indeed, I know nothing which would produce such a shock; for on the event of this mission depend the future destinies of this Republic. If we cannot, by a purchase of the country, insure to ourselves a course of perpetual peace and friendship with all nations, then, as war cannot be distant, it behooves us immediately to be preparing for that course, without however hastening it; and it may be necessary, on your failure on the Continent, to cross the Channel. We shall get entangled in European politics; and, figuring more, be much less happy and prosperous."

With infinite pertinacity Jefferson clung to his own course. He deserved success, although he hardly expected to win it by means of Monroe, whom he urged to go abroad, as his letter implied, not so much to purchase New Orleans, as to restore political quiet at home. For the purchase of New Orleans, Livingston was fully competent; but the opposition at home, as Jefferson candidly wrote to him,[3] were pressing

[1] Report of Jan. 12, 1803; Annals of Congress, 1802–1803, pp. 371–374.
[2] Jefferson to Monroe, Jan. 13, 1803; Works, iv. 453.
[3] Jefferson to Livingston, Feb. 3, 1803; Works, iv. 460.

their inflammatory resolutions in the House so hard that "as a remedy to all this we determined to name a minister extraordinary to go immediately to Paris and Madrid to settle this matter. This measure being a visible one, and the person named peculiarly popular with the western country, crushed at once and put an end to all further attempts on the Legislature. From that moment all has been quiet." The quiet was broken again, soon after this letter was written, by a sharp attack in the Senate. Ross of Pennsylvania, White of Delaware, and Gouverneur Morris of New York, assailed the Administration for the feebleness of its measures. In private, Jefferson did not deny that his measures were pacific, and that he had no great confidence in Monroe's success; he counted rather on Bonaparte's taking possession of New Orleans and remaining some years on the Mississippi.[1]

> "I did not expect he would yield until a war took place between France and England; and my hope was to palliate and endure, if Messrs. Ross, Morris, etc., did not force a premature rupture, until that event. I believed the event not very distant, but acknowledge it came on sooner than I had expected."

"To palliate and endure" was therefore the object of Jefferson's diplomacy for the moment. Whether the Western States could be persuaded to endure or to palliate the presence of a French army at New Orleans was doubtful; but Jefferson's success in controlling them proved his personal authority and political skill. Meanwhile the interest and activity of the little diplomatic world at Washington increased. Monroe accepted his appointment and came for his instructions. Every one was alive with expectation. As public opinion grew more outspoken, the President was obliged to raise his tone. He talked with a degree of freedom which seemed more inconsistent than it really was with his radical policy of peace. With Thornton he was somewhat cautious.[2] Immediately after Monroe's nomination, Thornton asked the President whether he intended to let the new envoy pass to England and converse with British ministers about the free navigation of the

[1] Jefferson to Dr. Priestley, Jan. 29, 1804; Works, iv. 524.
[2] Thornton to Lord Hawkesbury, Jan. 31, 1803; MSS. British Archives.

Mississippi,—a right to which Great Britain, as well as the United States, was entitled by treaty.

"The inquiry was somewhat premature, and I made it with some apology. Mr. Jefferson replied, however, unaffectedly, that at so early a stage of the business he had scarcely thought himself what it might be proper to do, that I might be assured the right would never be abandoned by this country; that he wished earnestly for a tranquil and pacific recognition and confirmation of it; that on the whole he thought it very probable that Mr. Monroe might cross the Channel. He reiterated to me with additional force the resolution of the country never to abandon the claim of the free navigation,—which indeed cannot be without dissevering the Western States from the Union,— declaring that should they be obliged at last to resort to force, *they would throw away the scabbard.*"

Thornton added that the President still hoped the French would not for some time take possession of Louisiana, and rested his hope on the demand which the Island of St. Domingo would create for every soldier that could be spared; but he also talked of building gunboats for the navigation of the Mississippi.

"In the mean time," continued Thornton, "the country seems in general well satisfied with the resolution taken by the House and the measure adopted by himself; and, what is more important, authentic information is received that the people of Kentucky will wait with patience the result of the steps which the executive government may think it right to take, without recurring, as was apprehended would be the case to force, for the assertion of their claims. The President regards this circumstance (with great justice, it appears to me) as the surest pledge of the continuance of his authority, and as the death-blow of the Federal party."

Upon Pichon the Government concentrated its threats, and Pichon sent to Talleyrand cry after cry of distress:—

"It is impossible to be more bitter than this Government is at the present posture of affairs and at the humiliating

attitude in which our silence about Louisiana places them.
. . . Mr. Jefferson will be forced to yield to necessity his
pretensions and scruples against a British alliance. I noticed
at his table that he redoubled his civilities and attentions to
the British *chargé*. I should also say that he treats me with
much consideration and politeness, in spite of the actual
state of affairs."

No sooner had Monroe been confirmed by the Senate, than
Secretary Madison sent for Pichon and asked him to do what
he could for the success of Monroe's mission.[1] At ample
length he explained that the undivided possession of New Orleans and West Florida was a necessity for the American settlements on the upper Mississippi and Mobile rivers, and that
Monroe was instructed to obtain the whole territory east of
the Mississippi, including New Orleans, at a price not exceeding two or three million dollars. This part of the Secretary's
argument was simple; but not content with this, "he entered
into details to prove that New Orleans had no sort of interest
for us, that its situation was acknowledged to be bad, the
choice of it was due to accident, and we might very soon
build a city on the opposite bank." He argued further that the
true policy of France required her to make the river her
boundary against the United States; for "the United States
had no interest in seeing circumstances rise which should
eventually lead their population to extend itself on the right
bank. In point of fact, was it not evident that since these em-
igrations tended to weaken the State and to slacken the concentration of its forces, sound policy ought not to encourage
them? In spite of affinities in manners and language, no colony beyond the river could exist under the same government,
but would infallibly give birth to a separate State having in
its bosom germs of collision with the East, the easier to develop in proportion to the very affinities between the two empires." The Secretary ended by hinting that should the First
Consul not be persuaded by these suggestions, "it might
happen that the conduct of France would decide political
combinations which, getting the upper hand of all these

[1] Pichon to Talleyrand, 4 Pluviôse, An xi. (Jan. 24, 1803); Archives des Aff.
Étr., MSS.

considerations, would tend to produce results no doubt disagreeable to the United States, but certainly still more so to
France and her allies."

Pichon was a sore trial to the moderate amount of patience
which Bonaparte possessed. Instead of hinting to Madison
that these arguments would have more weight if the President
proposed to support them by acts such as a military First
Consul was accustomed to respect, Pichon wrote melancholy
accounts of his situation to Talleyrand. The Americans, he
said, were throwing themselves into the arms of England;
they thought they held the balance of power between France
and Great Britain, and meant to make the nation which
should force them into war regret the inconsiderate act; the
States of New York, Virginia, Maryland, and Pennsylvania,
either through their legislatures or their governors, had energetically announced their readiness to risk everything to maintain the dignity and rights of the nation; Madison refused to
do business, on the ground that Talleyrand's want of attention
to Livingston required reprisals; the Secretary of the Treasury
talked of war; a public dinner had been given to Monroe, at
which General Smith offered the toast, "Peace, if peace is
honorable; war, if war is necessary!" the President was open
in denouncing Bonaparte's ambition; Monroe who had talked
long with Pichon, used language even more startling than
that of the President or the Cabinet:—

> "He did not conceal from me that if his negotiation
> failed, the Administration had made up its mind to act with
> the utmost vigor, and to receive the overtures which En-
> gland was incessantly making. He repeated to me several
> times that I could only imperfectly imagine the extent of
> those overtures, and that if the tie were once made between
> the two States, they would not stop half way."[1]

If Monroe made such an assertion as Pichon reported, he
carried his diplomacy beyond the line of truthfulness; for although Thornton, without instructions, had offered one or
two suggestions of concert, England had made no overture.
Monroe's own instructions rested on the opposite principle,

[1] Pichon to Talleyrand, 29 Pluviôse, An xi. (Feb. 17, 1803); Archives des Aff.
Étr., MSS.

—that England was to receive, not to make, overtures. Jefferson wished only to create the impression that disaster impended over France if she persevered in closing the Mississippi. He spoke clearly to this effect in a letter written to Dupont at the time he was alarming Pichon:—

"Our circumstances are so imperious as to admit of no delay as to our course, and the use of the Mississippi so indispensable that we cannot hesitate one moment to hazard our existence for its maintenance. If we fail in this effort to put it beyond the reach of accident, we see the destinies we have to run, and prepare at once for them."[1]

Alarmed by such language, Pichon volunteered to imitate Yrujo and write a letter to the future French prefect whose arrival at New Orleans was expected, urging him to raise the interdict on American commerce.[2] Madison was pleased with the offer, and in return communicated to Pichon a despatch just received from Livingston, which announced that Talleyrand had consented to speak, so far as to promise that France would strictly observe in Louisiana the treaties which existed between America and Spain. "I quickly saw, by the rapidity with which this news circulated in the two houses of Congress, the salutary effect it produced. On all sides I was talked with, and the Administration is sincerely satisfied by it." Small as the favor was, the Administration had reason to be grateful, as it served for the moment to pacify Kentucky and Tennessee.

The months of January and February passed. Not until spring came, and the Seventh Congress was about to expire, did Monroe receive his instructions and prepare to sail. The nature of these instructions was so remarkable as to deserve a moment of study.[3]

They were framed to provide for three contingencies. Should the French government be willing to sell New Orleans and the Floridas, the President would bid high rather

[1] Jefferson to Dupont, Feb. 1, 1803; Works, iv. 456.
[2] Pichon to Talleyrand, 24 Pluviôse, An xi. (Feb. 12, 1803); Archives des Aff. Étr., MSS.
[3] Instructions to Livingston and Monroe, March 2, 1803; State Papers, ii. 540.

than lose the opportunity. Should France refuse to cede any territory whatever, even the site for a town, the two commissioners were to content themselves with securing the right of deposit, with such improvements as they could obtain. Should Bonaparte deny the right of deposit also, the commissioners were to be guided by instructions specially adapted to the case. For New Orleans and West Florida Monroe and Livingston were to offer any sum within ten million dollars, commercial privileges for ten years in the ceded ports, incorporation of the inhabitants on an equal footing with citizens without unnecessary delay, and, if absolutely necessary, a guaranty of the west bank of the Mississippi.

These were the main ideas of Monroe's instructions. In brief, they offered to admit the French to Louisiana without condition. Bonaparte could have regarded nothing in these instructions as hostile to his own plans, and could have satisfied every demand by giving the United States, in the terms of the Spanish treaty, a place of deposit anywhere on the banks of the Mississippi, or by merely allowing American vessels to pass up and down the river.[1] In private, Jefferson professed preference for Natchez over New Orleans as the seat of American trade.[2] He made no secret of his intention to put off the day of forcible resistance until the national debt should be reduced and the Mississippi Valley filled with fighting men.

The tenor of these expressions seemed inconsistent with that of his letters by Dupont. After telling Bonaparte that[3] "the cession of New Orleans and the Floridas to us would be a palliation," but no more, to the presence of France on the west bank, which would "cost France, and perhaps not very long hence, a war which will annihilate her on the ocean," then within a year to guarantee France forever in possession of the west bank,—had an air of vacillation. After telling Dupont again in February that if the United States failed to put the use of the Mississippi beyond the reach of accident, they should see the destinies they had to run, and at once prepare for them; then within a month to admit Bonaparte to possession of all Spanish rights at New Orleans, without guaranty

[1] Madison to Monroe, April 20, 1803; Madison's Writings, ii. 181.
[2] Jefferson to Hugh Williamson, April 30, 1803; Works, iv. 483.
[3] Jefferson to Dupont, April 25, 1802; Works, iv. 435.

of any kind for putting the use of the river beyond accident,—looked like fear. The instructions contained one positive expression: "The United States cannot remain satisfied,
nor the Western people be kept patient, under the restrictions
which the existing treaty with Spain authorizes." This
sentence introduced only a moderate request: "Should it be
impossible to procure a complete jurisdiction over any convenient spot whatever, it will only remain to explain and improve the present right of deposit by adding thereto the
express privilege of holding real estate for commercial purposes, of providing hospitals, of having consuls residing
there," and other commercial agents. Even this moderate condition was not an ultimatum. Madison required only that the
Spanish treaty of 1795 should be respected, and this had already been promised by Talleyrand.

In truth the inconsistency was more apparent than real. Jefferson explained to the French government that the war he
had in his mind was a contingent result. While assuring Dupont that if he failed to put the use of the Mississippi beyond
the reach of accident he should prepare for war, he added in
italics an explanation:[1] —

> "Not but that we shall still endeavor to go on in peace
> and friendship with our neighbors as long as we can, *if our
> rights of navigation and deposit are respected*; but as we fore
> see that the caprices of the local officers and the abuse of
> those rights by our boatmen and navigators, which neither
> government can prevent, will keep up a state of irritation
> which cannot long be kept inactive, we should be crimi
> nally improvident not to take at once eventual measures for
> strengthening ourselves for the contest."

The essence and genius of Jefferson's statesmanship lay in
peace. Through difficulties, trials, and temptations of every
kind he held fast to this idea, which was the clew to whatever
seemed inconsistent, feeble, or deceptive in his administration. Yielding often, with the suppleness of his nature, to the
violence of party, he allowed himself to use language which
at first sight seemed inconsistent, and even untruthful; but

[1] Jefferson to Dupont, Feb. 1, 1803; Works, iv. 456.

such concessions were momentary: the unswerving intent could always be detected under every superficial disguise; the consistency of the career became more remarkable on account of the seeming inconsistencies of the moment. He was pliant and yielding in manner, but steady as the magnet itself in aim. His manœuvres between the angry West and the arbitrary First Consul of France offered an example of his political method. He meant that there should be no war. While waiting to hear the result of Monroe's mission he wrote to an English correspondent a letter[1] which expressed his true feelings with apparent candor:—

"We see . . . with great concern the position in which Great Britain is placed, and should be sincerely afflicted were any disaster to deprive mankind of the benefit of such a bulwark against the torrent which has for some time been bearing down all before it. But her power and prowess by sea seem to render everything safe in the end. Peace is our passion, and wrongs might drive us from it. We prefer trying *every* other just principle, right and safety, before we would recur to war."

[1] Jefferson to Sir John Sinclair, 30 June, 1803; Works, iv. 490.

Chapter I

CONGRESS EXPIRED; Monroe set sail March 8, 1803; Washington relapsed into silence; and the President and his Cabinet waited alone in the empty village, triumphing for the moment over their difficulties. Although a French prefect was actually in New Orleans, and the delivery of Louisiana to Bonaparte might from day to day be expected, not an additional soldier stood on the banks of the Mississippi, and the States of Kentucky and Tennessee were as quiet as though their flat-boats still floated down to New Orleans. A month passed before Madison or Jefferson again moved. Then the President asked his Cabinet[1] what Monroe should do in case France, as he expressed it, "refused our rights." He proposed an alliance with England, and suggested three inducements which might be offered to Great Britain: "1. Not to make a separate peace. 2. To let her take Louisiana. 3. Commercial privileges." The Cabinet unanimously rejected the second and third concessions, but Dearborn and Lincoln were alone in opposing the first; and a majority agreed to instruct Monroe and Livingston, "as soon as they find that no arrangements can be made with France, to use all possible procrastination with them, and in the mean time enter into conferences with the British government, through their ambassador at Paris, to fix principles of alliance, and leave us in peace till Congress meets; and prevent war till next spring."

Madison wrote the instructions. If the French government, he said,[2] should meditate hostilities against the United States, or force a war by closing the Mississippi, the two envoys were to invite England to an alliance, and were to negotiate a treaty stipulating that neither party should make peace or truce without consent of the other. Should France deny the right of deposit without disputing the navigation, the envoys

---

[1] Cabinet Memoranda of Mr. Jefferson, April 8, 1803; Jefferson's Writings (Ford), i. 298.

[2] Madison to Livingston and Monroe, April 18 and 20, 1803; State Papers, ii. 555.

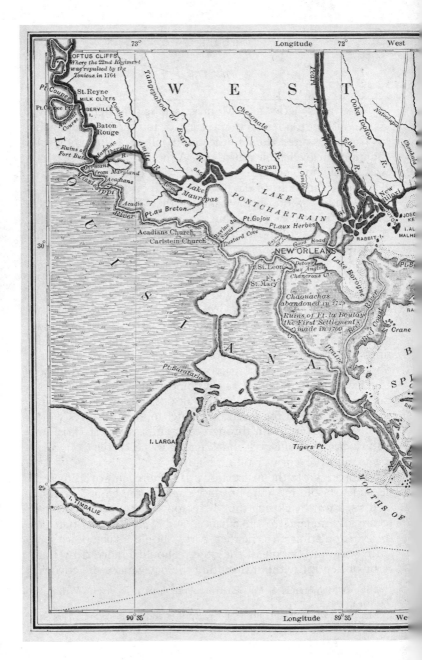

LOFTUS CLIFFS
*Where the 22nd Regiment
was repulsed by the
Tonicas in 1764*

Pt. Coupee
Pt. Coupee Ft.   IBERVILLE
St. Reyne
MILK CLIFFS

Baton
Rouge

Ruins of Manshac
Fort But—   *Iberville* R.

Germans
from Maryland
Acadians

W   E   S   T

Tangepahoa or Bears

Chesonate R.

LAKE
PONTCHARTRAIN

LAKE
Maurepas

Lake
Maurepas

Bryan

Pt. Gojou
Pt. aux Herbes

Acadia
River
Pt. au Breton

Acadians Church
Carlstein Church

Ravine de
Sœur
Mustard Cove

Guard Road

RABBIT I.

NEW ORLEANS

Ft. St. Leon
Ft.
St. Mary

Detour
aux Anglois
Chancrons C.

Lake Borgne

Pt. B

I. AL
MALHE

*Chaouachas
abandoned in 172*
Ruins of Ft. la Boulaye
*the First Settlement
made in 1700*

Crane

L   O   U   I   S   I   A   N   A

Pt. Barataria

I. LARGA

Tigers Pt.

MOUTHS OF

I. TIMBALIE

SPI

B

New
Biloxi

JOSE
KE

Ooka toqoo
Natoolupa

Ohoolata

Chata

East

Pearl

Bird Coast Key

Prairie

SP

30°

29°

were to make no positive engagement, but should let Congress decide between immediate war or further procrastination.

At no time in Talleyrand's negotiations had the idea of war against the United States been suggested. Of his intentions in this respect alone he had given positive assurances.[1] Above all things both he and the First Consul feared a war with the United States. They had nothing to gain by it. Madison's instructions therefore rested on an idea which had no foundation, and which in face of the latest news from Europe was not worth considering; yet even if intended only for use at home, the instructions were startling enough to warrant Virginians in doubting their authenticity. The late Administration, British in feeling as it was supposed to be, had never thought an alliance with England necessary even during actual hostilities with France, and had not hesitated to risk the chances of independent action. Had either of Jefferson's predecessors instructed American ministers abroad, in case of war with France, to bind the United States to make no peace without England's consent, the consequence would have been an impeachment of the President, or direct steps by Virginia, Kentucky, and North Carolina, as in 1798, tending to a dissolution of the Union. Such an alliance, offensive and defensive, with England contradicted every principle established by President Washington in power or professed by Jefferson in opposition. If it was not finesse, it was an act such as the Republicans of 1798 would have charged as a crime.

While Madison was writing these instructions, he was interrupted by the Marquis of Casa Yrujo,[2] who came in triumph to say that his Government had sent out a brigantine especially to tell the President that the right of deposit would be restored and continued till another agreement or equivalent place could be fixed upon.[3] Yrujo was instructed to thank the President for his friendly, prudent, and moderate conduct during the excitement. He sent to New Orleans the positive order of King Charles IV. to the Intendant Morales, that the

[1] Livingston to Madison, Nov. 11, 1802; State Papers, ii. 526.
[2] State Papers, ii. 556.
[3] Yrujo to Madison, Notes of April 19 and 20, 1803; MSS. State Department Archives.

right of deposit should be immediately restored; the western people were told that their produce might go down the river as before, and thus the last vestige of anxiety was removed. In face of this action by Godoy, and of the war evidently at hand between France and England, the success of the peace policy was assured. These events in some degree explained the extraordinary nature of the new instructions of April, 1803.

Monroe was then already at Paris. In order to make clear the situation in which he found himself, the sequence of events in Europe needs to be understood.

Bonaparte's expedition to Louisiana was to have sailed at the end of September, 1802.[1] A general of division, three generals of brigade, five battalions of infantry, two companies of artillery, sixteen pieces of cannon, and three thousand muskets were to be collected at Dunkirk for shipment; but as fast as regiments could be named they were consumed by the fiery furnace of St. Domingo. Nevertheless, all the orders and arrangements were gradually made. Victor was to command the forces in Louisiana; Laussat was to be prefect, charged with the civil administration. Both received elaborate written instructions; and although Victor could not sail without ships or troops, Laussat was sent on his way.

These instructions, which were never published, had extreme value for the decision of disputes which were to perturb American politics for the next twenty years. Although Victor was forced to wait in Holland for the expedition he commanded, a copy of his instructions was given to Laussat, and served to regulate his conduct as long as he remained in office. Decrès, the Minister of Marine, was the author of this paper, which unfolded the purpose that had guided France in recovering, and was to control her in administering, this vast possession. Nothing could be simpler, clearer, or more consistent with French policy than this document, which embodied so large a part of Talleyrand's political system.

The instructions began, as was natural, by a careful definition of the new province. After reciting the terms of the retrocession according to the Third Article of Berthier's Treaty, Decrès fixed the boundaries of the territory which Victor, on

[1] Bonaparte to Decrès, 6 Fructidor, An x. (Aug. 24, 1802); Correspondance, viii. 4.

the part of the French republic, was to receive from the Marquis of Somoruelos, the Captain-General of Cuba.[1]

"The extent of Louisiana," he said, "is well determined on the south by the Gulf of Mexico. But bounded on the west by the river called Rio Bravo from its mouth to about the 30° parallel, the line of demarcation stops after reaching this point, and there seems never to have been any agreement in regard to this part of the frontier. The farther we go northward, the more undecided is the boundary. This part of America contains little more than uninhabited forests or Indian tribes, and the necessity of fixing a boundary has never yet been felt there. There also exists none between Louisiana and Canada."

In this state of things the captain-general would have to relieve the most remote Spanish garrisons, in order to establish possession; in other respects he would be guided only by political and military interests. The western and northern boundary was of less consequence than the little strip which separated New Orleans from Mobile; and to this point the instructions specially called Victor's attention. Quoting the treaty of 1763 between Spain, Great Britain, and France, when Florida was to become a British possession, Decrès fixed its terms as still binding upon all the interested parties.

" 'It is agreed,' " said the seventh article of this treaty, " 'that in future the boundaries between the States of his Most Christian Majesty and those of his Britannic Majesty shall be irrevocably fixed by a line drawn down the middle of the Mississippi River from its source to the River Iberville, and from there by a line down the middle of that river and of the lakes Maurepas and Pontchartrain to the sea. New Orleans and the island on which it stands shall belong to France.' Such is still to-day the eastern limit of Louisiana. All to the east and north of this limit makes part of the United States or of West Florida."

Nothing could be clearer. Louisiana stretched from the

[1] Instructions secrètes pour le Capitaine-Général de la Louisiane, approuvées par le Premier Consul le 5 Frimaire, An xi. (Nov. 26, 1802); Archives de la Marine, MSS.

Iberville to the Rio Bravo; West Florida from the Iberville to the Appalachicola. The retrocession of Louisiana by Spain to France could restore only what France had ceded to Spain in 1762. West Florida had nothing to do with the cession of 1762 or the retrocession of 1800, and being Spanish by a wholly different title could not even be brought in question by the First Consul, much as he wanted Baton Rouge, Mobile, and Pensacola. Victor's orders were emphatic:—

> "There is therefore no obscurity as to our boundary on this side any more than as to that of our allies; and although Florida belongs to Spain, Spain's right of property in this quarter will have as much interest for the Captain-General of Louisiana as though Florida were a French possession."

After thus establishing the boundary, as far as possible, in every direction, the minister treated at some length of the English claim to navigation on the Mississippi, and at last reached the general subject of the relation between Louisiana and the world about it,—the subject in which Jefferson would have found acute interest:—

> "The system of this, as of all our other colonies, should be to concentrate its commerce in the national commerce; it should have in particular the aim of establishing its relations with our Antilles, so as to take the place, in these colonies, of the American commerce for all the objects whose import and export is permitted to them. The captain-general should especially abstain from every innovation favorable to strangers, who should be restricted to such communications as are absolutely indispensable to the prosperity of Louisiana and to such as are explicitly determined by the treaties."

Commercial relations with the Spanish colonies were to be encouraged and extended as much as possible, while the utmost caution was to be observed toward the United States:—

> "From what has been said of Louisiana and the adjacent States, it is clear that the republic of France, being master of both banks at the mouth of the Mississippi, holds the

key to its navigation. This navigation is nevertheless a matter of the highest importance for the western States of the Federal Government. . . . This is enough to show with what jealousy the Federal Government will see us take possession of Louisiana. Whatever may be the events which this new part of the continent has to expect, the arrival of the French forces should be marked there by the expression of sentiments of great benevolence for these new neighbors."

Expression of benevolent sentiments was a pleasing duty; but it was not to interfere with practical measures, both defensive and offensive:—

"The greatest circumspection will be required in directing the colonial administration. A little local experience will soon enable you to discern the sentiments of the western provinces of the Federal Government. It will be well to maintain sources of intelligence in that country, whose numerous, warlike, and sober population may present you a redoubtable enemy. The inhabitants of Kentucky especially should fix the attention of the captain-general. . . . He must also fortify himself against them by alliance with the Indian nations scattered to the east of the river. The Chibackas, Choctaws, Alabamas, Creeks, etc., are represented as being entirely devoted to us. . . . He will not forget that the French government wishes peace; but that if war takes place, Louisiana will certainly become the theatre of hostilities. . . . The intention of the First Consul is to raise Louisiana to a degree of strength which will allow him in time of war to abandon it to its own resources without anxiety; so that enemies may be forced to the greatest sacrifices merely in attempting to attack it."

In these instructions not a word could be found which clashed with Jefferson's pacific views; and partly for that reason they were more dangerous to the United States than if they had ordered Victor to seize American property on the Mississippi and occupy Natchez with his three thousand men. Victor was instructed, in effect, to tamper with every adventurer from Pittsburg to Natchez; buy up every Indian tribe in the Georgia and Northwestern Territory; fortify every bluff on the western bank from St. Louis to New Orleans; and in a few years create a series of French settlements which would realize Madison's "sound policy" of discouraging the United States from colonizing the west bank.

Fortified by these instructions, the Citizen Laussat set sail Jan. 12, 1803, and in due time arrived at New Orleans. Victor labored in Holland to put his ships and supplies in a condition to follow. As Laussat sailed, another step was taken by the French government. General Bernadotte, a very distinguished republican officer, brother-in-law of Joseph Bonaparte, was appointed minister at Washington.[1] The First Consul had his own reasons for wishing to remove Bernadotte, as he meant to remove Moreau; and Washington was a place of indirect banishment for a kinsman whose character was to be feared. Bernadotte's instructions[2] were signed by Talleyrand Jan. 14, 1803, the day after Monroe was confirmed as special envoy to France by the Senate at Washington, and while Laussat was still on the French coast. Although Bonaparte had been obliged to withdraw a part of Victor's force, he still intended that the expedition should start at once with two thousand men;[3] and its departure was to be so timed that Bernadotte should reach Washington as Victor and his troops reached New Orleans. Their instructions were on one point identical. News of the closure of the Mississippi by Morales had reached Paris, and had already caused an official protest by Livingston, when Talleyrand drew up the instructions to Bernadotte: —

"Louisiana being soon to pass into our hands, with all the rights which have belonged to Spain, we can only with pleasure see that a special circumstance has obliged the Spanish Administration to declare formally [*constater*] its right to grant or to refuse at will to the Americans the privilege of a commercial *entrepôt* at New Orleans; the difficulty of maintaining this position will be less for us than

[1] Livingston to Madison, Feb. 18, 1803; State Papers, ii. 533.
[2] Talleyrand to Bernadotte, 24 Nivôse, An xi. (Jan. 14, 1803); Archives des Aff. Étr., MSS.
[3] Correspondance, viii. 145; Bonaparte to Decrès, 28 Frimaire, An xi. (Dec. 19, 1802).

that of establishing it. . . . Yet in any discussion that may arise on this subject, and in every discussion you may have to sustain, the First Consul wishes you to be informed of his most positive and pronounced desire to live in good understanding with the American government, to cultivate and to improve for the advantage of American commerce the relations of friendship which unite the two peoples. No one in Europe wishes the prosperity of that people more than he. In accrediting you to its Government he has given it a peculiar mark of his good disposition; he doubts not that you will make every effort to bind closer the ties which exist between the two nations. In consequence of the firm intention which the First Consul has shown on this subject, I must recommend you to take every care to avoid whatever might alter our relations with that nation and its Government. The agents of the French republic in the United States should forbid themselves whatever might even remotely lead to a rupture. In ordinary communication, every step should show the benevolent disposition and mutual friendship which animate the chiefs and all the members of the two Governments; and when any unforeseen difficulty rises which may in any degree whatever compromise their good understanding, the simplest and most effectual means of preventing all danger is to refer its solution to the inquiry and direct judgment of the two Governments."

Talleyrand's language was more elaborate, but not clearer, than that which Bonaparte himself used to Victor.[1]

"I have no need to tell you," the First Consul wrote, "with what impatience the Government will wait for news from you in order to settle its ideas in regard to the pretensions of the United States and their usurpations over the Spaniards. What the Government may think proper to do must not be judged in advance until you have rendered an account of the state of things. Every time you perceive that the United States are raising pretensions, answer that no one has an idea of this at Paris (*que l'on n'a aucune idée de*

[1] Correspondance, viii. 146; Bonaparte to Victor, 25 Frimaire, An xi. (Dec. 16, 1802).

cela à Paris); but that you have written, and that you are expecting orders."

These were the ideas held by the government of France at the moment when Jefferson nominated Monroe as a special envoy to buy New Orleans and West Florida. Jefferson's hopes of his success were small; and Livingston, although on the spot and eager to try the experiment, could only write:[1] "Do not absolutely despair." Whatever chance existed of obtaining New Orleans seemed to lie in the possibility that Addington's peaceful administration in England might be driven into some act contrary to its vital interests; and even this chance was worth little, for so long as Bonaparte wanted peace, he could always keep it. England was thoroughly weary of war; and proved it by patiently looking on while Bonaparte, during the year, committed one arbitrary act after another, which at any previous time would have been followed by an instant withdrawal of the British minister from Paris.

On the other hand, the world could see that Bonaparte was already tired of peace; his *rôle* of beneficent shopkeeper disgusted him, and a new war in Europe was only a question of months. In such a case the blow might fall on the east bank of the Rhine, on Spain, or on England. Yet Bonaparte was in any case bound to keep Louisiana, or return it to Spain. Florida was not his to sell. The chance that Jefferson could buy either of these countries, even in case of a European war, seemed so small as hardly to be worth considering; but it existed, because Bonaparte was not a man like other men, and his action could never be calculated in advance.

The news that Leclerc was dead, that his army was annihilated, St. Domingo ruined, and the negroes more than ever beyond control, reached Paris and was printed in the "Moniteur" Jan. 7, 1803, in the same active week when Bernadotte, Laussat, and Victor were ordered from France to America, and Monroe was ordered from America to France. Of all the events of the time, Leclerc's death was the most decisive. The colonial system of France centred in St. Domingo. Without that island the system had hands, feet, and even a head, but

[1] Livingston to Madison, Dec. 20, 1802; State Papers, ii. 528.

no body. Of what use was Louisiana, when France had clearly lost the main colony which Louisiana was meant to feed and fortify? The new ruler of France was not unused to failure. More than once he had suddenly given up his dearest plans and deserted his oldest companions when their success was hopeless. He had abandoned Paoli and Corsica with as little compunction as afterward he abandoned the army and the officers whom he led to Egypt. Obstinate in pursuing any object which led to his own advancement, he was quick to see the moment when pursuit became useless; and the difficulties that rose in his path toward colonial empire were quite as great as those which had driven him to abandon Corsica and Egypt. Not only had the island of St. Domingo been ruined by the war, its plantations destroyed, its labor paralyzed, and its population reduced to barbarism, so that the task of restoring its commercial value had become extremely difficult; but other and greater objections existed to a renewal of the struggle. The army dreaded service in St. Domingo, where certain death awaited every soldier; the expense was frightful; a year of war had consumed fifty thousand men and money in vast amounts, with no other result than to prove that at least as many men and as much money would be still needed before any return could be expected for so lavish an expenditure. In Europe war could be made to support war; in St. Domingo peace alone could but slowly repair some part of this frightful waste.

Leclerc was succeeded at St. Domingo by General Rochambeau, a son of the Comte de Rochambeau, who twenty years before had commanded the French corps which enabled Washington to capture Cornwallis at Yorktown. A brave officer, but known to be little fit for administration, Rochambeau was incompetent for the task that fell on him. Leclerc had warned the Government that in case of his own retirement he had no officer fit to replace him,—least of all Rochambeau, who was next in rank. Rochambeau wrote to inform the First Consul that thirty-five thousand men must be sent to save the island.[1] Without a new commander-in-chief of the highest ability, a new army was useless; and meanwhile Rochambeau

[1] Rochambeau to Decrès, 16 Frimaire, An xi. (Dec. 7, 1802); Archives de la Marine, MSS.

was certain to waste the few thousand acclimated soldiers who should form its nucleus.

The First Consul found himself in a difficult and even dangerous situation. Probably the colonial scheme had never suited his tastes, and perhaps he had waited only until he should be firm in power in order to throw off the tutelage of Talleyrand; but the moment had arrived when his tastes coincided with policy. A second failure at St. Domingo would destroy his own credit, and disgust both the army and the public. Abandonment of the island was equally hazardous; for it required the abandonment of French traditions and a confession of failure. Retirement from St. Domingo was impossible, except under cover of some new enterprise; and as Europe stood, no other enterprise remained for France to undertake which would not lead her armies across the Rhine or the Pyrenees. For this undertaking Bonaparte was not yet ready; but even had he been so, it would have offered no excuse for abandoning the colonies. The ocean would still have been open, and St. Domingo within easy reach.

Only one resource remained. Bonaparte told no one his plans; but he was not a man to hesitate when decision was needed. From the day when news of Leclerc's death arrived, during the first week of January, 1803, the First Consul brooded over the means of abandoning St. Domingo without appearing to desert intentionally a policy dear to France. Talleyrand and Decrès were allowed to go on as before; they gave instructions to Bernadotte, and hurried the preparations of Victor, whom the ice and snow of Holland and the slowness of the workmen held motionless; they prepared a reinforcement of fifteen thousand men for Rochambeau, and Bonaparte gave all the necessary orders for hastening the departure of both expeditions. As late as February 5, he wrote to Decrès that fifteen thousand men had been, or were about to be, sent to St. Domingo, and that fifteen thousand more must be ready to sail by the middle of August.[1] Yet his policy of abandoning the colonial system had been already decided; for on January 30 the "Moniteur" produced Sebastiani's famous Report on the military condition of the East,—a

[1] Correspondance, viii. 201; Bonaparte to Decrès, 16 Pluviôse, An xi. (Feb. 5, 1803).

publication which could have no other object than to alarm England.[1]

Livingston was quick to see the change of policy; but although he understood as much as was known to any one, he could not count with certainty on the result.[2] Not even Joseph and Lucien knew what was in their brother's mind. Talleyrand seems to have been elaborately deceived; even as late as February 19 he was allowed to instruct General Beurnonville, the French ambassador at Madrid, to express "the warm satisfaction which the last acts of sovereignty exercised by the King of Spain in Louisiana have given to the First Consul."[3] The last act of sovereignty exercised by Spain in Louisiana had been the closure of the Mississippi. Before Beurnonville could obey this order, Godoy, hastening to anticipate possible interference from France, promised Pinckney, February 28, that the *entrepôt* should be restored. King Charles's order of restitution bore date March 1, 1803; Beurnonville's note, urging the King to sustain Morales, bore date March 4, and March 10 Don Pedro Cevallos replied to Talleyrand's congratulation in a tone so evasive as to show that Godoy was again deceiving the First Consul.[4] Cevallos did not say that the right of deposit had ten days before been restored; he contented himself with mentioning the reasons alleged by Morales for his act, adding at the close the empty assurance that "in every way his Majesty prizes highly the applause of the French government." In January, only a few weeks before, Godoy had told Beurnonville, with unconcealed satisfaction, that Bonaparte should not have Florida, — although without Florida the town of New Orleans was supposed to be of little value. In February he snatched away what he could of New Orleans by replacing the Americans in all their privileges there.

Livingston plied the French officials with arguments and memorials; but he might have spared himself the trouble, for

[1] Lucien Bonaparte et ses Mémoires, Th. Jung, ii. 165, *n.*; Lanfrey's Napoleon, ii. 495.

[2] Livingston to Madison, Feb. 18, 1803; State Papers, ii. 533.

[3] Beurnonville to Talleyrand, 15 Ventôse, An xi. (March 6, 1803); Archives des Aff. Étr., MSS.

[4] Cevallos to Beurnonville, March 10, 1803; Archives des Aff. Étr., MSS.

Bonaparte's policy was already fixed. The First Consul acted with the rapidity which marked all his great measures. England at once took Sebastiani's Report as a warning, and began to arm. February 20 Bonaparte sent to the Corps Législatif his Annual Report, or Message, which spoke of Great Britain in language that could not be disregarded; finally, March 12, Livingston saw a melodramatic spectacle which transfixed him with surprise and excitement.[1] The scene was at Madame Bonaparte's drawing-room; the actors were Bonaparte and Lord Whitworth, the British ambassador. "I find, my Lord, your nation want war again!" said the First Consul. "No, sir," replied Whitworth; " we are very desirous of peace." *"I must either have Malta or war!"* rejoined Bonaparte. Livingston received these words from Lord Whitworth himself on the spot; and returning at once to his cabinet, wrote to warn Madison. Within a few days the alarm spread through Europe, and the affairs of St. Domingo were forgotten.

Bonaparte loved long-prepared transformation-scenes. Such a scene he was preparing, and the early days of April, 1803, found the actors eagerly waiting it. All the struggles and passions of the last two years were crowded into the explosion of April. At St. Domingo, horror followed fast on horror. Rochambeau, shut in Port au Prince,—drunken, reckless, surrounded by worthless men and by women more abandoned still, wallowing in the dregs of the former English occupation and of a half-civilized negro empire,—waged as he best could a guerilla war, hanging, shooting, drowning, burning all the negroes he could catch; hunting them with fifteen hundred bloodhounds bought in Jamaica for something more than one hundred dollars each; wasting money, squandering men; while Dessalines and Christophe massacred every white being within their reach. To complete Bonaparte's work, from which he wished to turn the world's attention, high among the Jura Mountains, where the ice and snow had not yet relaxed their grip upon the desolate little Fortress and its sunless casemate, in which for months nothing but Toussaint's cough had been heard, Commander Amiot wrote a brief

---

[1] Livingston to Madison, March 12, 1803; State Papers, ii. 547.

military Report to the Minister of Marine:[1] "On the 17th [April 7], at half-past eleven o'clock of the morning, on taking him his food, I found him dead, seated on his chair near his fire." According to Tavernier, doctor of medicine and *chirurgien* of Pontarlier, who performed the autopsy, pleuro-pneumonia was the cause of Toussaint's death.

Toussaint never knew that St. Domingo had successfully resisted the whole power of France, and that had he been truer to himself and his color he might have worn the crown that became the play-thing of Christophe and Dessalines; but even when shivering in the frosts of the Jura, his last moments would have glowed with gratified revenge, had he known that at the same instant Bonaparte was turning into a path which the negroes of St. Domingo had driven him to take, and which was to lead him to parallel at St. Helena the fate of Toussaint himself at the Château de Joux. In these days of passion, men had little time for thought; and the last subject on which Bonaparte thereafter cared to fix his mind was the fate of Toussaint and Leclerc. That the "miserable negro," as Bonaparte called him, should have been forgotten so soon was not surprising; but the prejudice of race alone blinded the American people to the debt they owed to the desperate courage of five hundred thousand Haytian negroes who would not be enslaved.

If this debt was due chiefly to the negroes, it was also in a degree due to Godoy and to Spain. In the new shifting of scenes, Godoy suddenly found himself, like Toussaint eighteen months before, face to face with Bonaparte bent on revenge. No one knew better than Godoy the dangers that hung over him and his country. Aware of his perils, he tried, as in 1795, to conciliate the United States by a course offensive to France. Not only did he restore the *entrepôt* at New Orleans, but he also admitted the claims for damages sustained by American citizens from Spanish subjects in the late war, and through Don Pedro Cevallos negotiated with Pinckney a convention which provided for a settlement of these claims.[2] Although he refused to recognize in this convention the spo-

---

[1] Amiot to Decrès, 19 Germinal, An xi. (April 9, 1803); Archives de la Marine, MSS.

[2] Claims Convention, Aug. 11, 1802; State Papers, ii. 476.

liations made by Frenchmen within Spanish jurisdiction, and insisted that these were in their nature claims against France which Spain was not morally bound to admit, he consented to insert an article copied from the expunged Article II. of the treaty of Morfontaine, reserving to the United States the right to press these demands at a future time.

So well pleased was Jefferson with the conduct of Spain and the Spanish ministers, that not a complaint was made of ill treatment; and even the conduct of Morales did not shake the President's faith in the friendliness of King Charles. No doubt he mistook the motives of this friendliness, for Spain had no other object than to protect her colonies and commerce on the Gulf of Mexico, and hoped to prevent attack by conciliation; while Madison imagined that Spain might be induced by money to part with her colonies and admit the United States to the Gulf. In this hope he instructed Pinckney,[1] in case he should find that Louisiana had not been retroceded to France, to offer a guaranty of Spanish territory west of the Mississippi as part of the consideration for New Orleans and the Floridas. The offer was made with a degree of cordiality very unlike the similar offer to France, and was pressed by Pinckney so zealously that at last Cevallos evaded his earnestness by a civil equivocation.

"The system adopted by his Majesty," said he,[2] "not to dispossess himself of any portion of his States, deprives him of the pleasure of assenting to the cessions which the United States wish to obtain by purchase. . . . The United States can address themselves to the French government to negotiate the acquisition of territories which may suit their interest."

Cevallos knew that Bonaparte had bound himself formally never to alienate Louisiana, and in referring Pinckney to France he supposed himself safe. Pinckney, on the other hand, prided himself on having helped to prevent France from gaining Florida as well as Louisiana, and was anxious to secure West Florida for his own credit; while he had no idea that Louisiana could be obtained at all.

[1] Madison to Pinckney, May 11, 1802; State Papers, ii. 517.
[2] Cevallos to Pinckney, May 4, 1803; State Papers, ii. 557.

Yet nearly a week before this note was written Louisiana had become American property. So completely was Godoy deceived, that when April arrived and he saw Spain again about to be dragged into unknown perils, he never divined that he was to be struck in America; his anxieties rose from fear that Spain might be dragged into a new war in Europe, in subservience to France. He could expect to escape such a war only by a quarrel with Napoleon, and he knew that a war with Napoleon was a desperate resource.

In London statesmanship had an easier game, and played it at first simply and coolly. Rufus King watched it with anxious eyes. He wished to escape from the duty of expressing a diplomatic policy which he might not approve, to a Government which had other and heavier tasks than that of listening to his advice or warnings. The British Ministry behaved well to America; for their advices from Thornton led them to hope that the United States would, if properly supported, seize Louisiana and accept war with Bonaparte. "If you can obtain Louisiana,—well!" said Addington to Rufus King;[1] "if not, we ought to prevent its going into the hands of France."

[1] Rufus King to Madison, April 2, 1803; State Papers, ii. 551.

Chapter II

Monroe arrived in sight of the French coast April 7, 1803; but while he was still on the ocean, Bonaparte without reference to him or his mission, opened his mind to Talleyrand in regard to ceding Louisiana to the United States. The First Consul a few days afterward repeated to his Finance Minister, Barbé Marbois,[1] a part of the conversation with Talleyrand; and his words implied that Talleyrand opposed Bonaparte's scheme, less because it sacrificed Louisiana than because its true object was not a war with England, but conquest of Germany. "He alone knows my intentions," said Bonaparte to Marbois. "If I attended to his advice, France would confine her ambition to the left bank of the Rhine, and would make war only to protect the weak States and to prevent any dismemberment of her possessions; but he also admits that the cession of Louisiana is not a dismemberment of France." In reality, the cession of Louisiana meant the overthrow of Talleyrand's influence and the failure of those hopes which had led to the coalition of the 18th Brumaire.

Easter Sunday, April 10, 1803, arrived, and Monroe was leaving Havre for Paris, when Bonaparte, after the religious ceremonies of the day at St. Cloud, called to him two of his ministers, of whom Barbé Marbois was one.[2] He wished to explain his intention of selling Louisiana to the United States; and he did so in his peculiar way. He began by expressing the fear that England would seize Louisiana as her first act of war. "I think of ceding it to the United States. I can scarcely say that I cede it to them, for it is not yet in our possession. If, however, I leave the least time to our enemies, I shall only transmit an empty title to those republicans whose friendship I seek. They ask of me only one town in Louisiana; but I already consider the colony as entirely lost; and it appears to me that in the hands of this growing Power it will be more useful to the policy, and even to the commerce, of France than if I should attempt to keep it."

To this appeal the two ministers replied by giving two

[1] History of Louisiana, Barbé Marbois, p. 277.
[2] Ibid., p. 263.

opposite opinions. Marbois favored the cession, as the First Consul probably expected him to do; for Marbois was a republican who had learned republicanism in the United States, and whose attachment to that country was secured by marriage to an American wife. His colleague, with equal decision, opposed the scheme. Their arguments were waste of breath. The First Consul said no more, and dismissed them; but the next morning, Monday, April 11, at daybreak, summoning Marbois, he made a short oration of the kind for which he was so famous:[1] —

"Irresolution and deliberation are no longer in season; I renounce Louisiana. It is not only New Orleans that I cede; it is the whole colony, without reserve. I know the price of what I abandon. I have proved the importance I attach to this province, since my first diplomatic act with Spain had the object of recovering it. I renounce it with the greatest regret; to attempt obstinately to retain it would be folly. I direct you to negotiate the affair. Have an interview this very day with Mr. Livingston."

The order so peremptorily given was instantly carried out; but not by Marbois. Talleyrand, in an interview a few hours afterward, startled Livingston with the new offer.[2]

"M. Talleyrand asked me this day, when pressing the subject, whether we wished to have the whole of Louisiana. I told him no; that our wishes extended only to New Orleans and the Floridas; that the policy of France, however, should dictate (as I had shown in an official note) to give us the country above the River Arkansas, in order to place a barrier between them and Canada. He said that if they gave New Orleans the rest would be of little value, and that he would wish to know 'what we would give for the whole.' I told him it was a subject I had not thought of, but that I supposed we should not object to twenty millions [francs], provided our citizens were paid. He told me that this was too low an offer, and that he would be glad if I would reflect upon it and tell him to-morrow. I told

[1] Marbois's Louisiana, p. 274.
[2] Livingston to Madison, April 11, 1803; State Papers, ii. 552.

him that as Mr. Monroe would be in town in two days, I would delay my further offer until I had the pleasure of introducing him. He added that he did not speak from authority, but that the idea had struck him."

The suddenness of Bonaparte's change disconcerted Livingston. For months he had wearied the First Consul with written and verbal arguments, remonstrances, threats,—all intended to prove that there was nothing grasping or ambitious in the American character; that France should invite the Americans to protect Louisiana from the Canadians; that the United States cared nothing for Louisiana, but wanted only West Florida and New Orleans,—"barren sands and sunken marshes," he said; "a small town built of wood; . . . about seven thousand souls;" a territory important to the United States because it contained "the mouths of some of their rivers," but a mere drain of resources to France.[1] To this rhapsody, repeated day after day for weeks and months, Talleyrand had listened with his imperturbable silence, the stillness of a sceptical mind into which such professions fell meaningless; until he suddenly looked into Livingston's face and asked: "What will you give for the whole?" Naturally Livingston for a moment lost countenance.

The next day, Tuesday, April 12, Livingston, partly recovered from his surprise, hung about Talleyrand persistently, for his chance of reaping alone the fruit of his labors vanished with every minute that passed. Monroe had reached St. Germain late Monday night, and at one o'clock Tuesday afternoon descended from his postchaise at the door of his Paris hotel.[2] From the moment of his arrival he was sure to seize public attention at home and abroad. Livingston used the interval to make one more effort with Talleyrand:[3] —

"He then thought proper to declare that his proposition was only personal, but still requested me to make an offer; and upon my declining to do so, as I expected Mr. Monroe the next day, he shrugged up his shoulders and changed

[1] Livingston to Talleyrand, Jan. 10, 1803; Livingston to Bonaparte, Feb. 27, 1803; State Papers, ii. 531, 539.
[2] Memoir of James Monroe, 1828; Colonel Mercer's Journal, p. 55.
[3] Livingston to Madison, April 13, 1803; State Papers, ii. 552.

the conversation. Not willing, however, to lose sight of it, I told him I had been long endeavoring to bring him to some point, but unfortunately without effect; and with that view had written him a note which contained that request. . . . He told me he would answer my note, but that he must do it evasively, because Louisiana was not theirs. I smiled at this assertion, and told him that I had seen the treaty recognizing it. . . . He still persisted that they had it in contemplation to obtain it, but had it not."

An hour or two afterward came a note from Monroe announcing that he would wait upon Livingston in the evening. The two American ministers passed the next day together,[1] examining papers and preparing to act whenever Monroe could be officially presented. They entertained a party at dinner that afternoon in Livingston's apartments, and while sitting at table Livingston saw Barbé Marbois strolling in the garden outside. Livingston sent to invite Marbois to join the party at table. While coffee was served, Marbois came in and entered into conversation with Livingston, who began at once to tell him of Talleyrand's "extraordinary conduct." Marbois hinted that he knew something of the matter, and that Livingston had better come to his house as soon as the dinner company departed. The moment Monroe took leave, Livingston acted on Marbois's hint, and in a midnight conversation the bargain was practically made. Marbois told a story, largely of his own invention, in regard to the First Consul's conduct on Easter Sunday, three days before. Bonaparte mentioned fifty million francs as his price for Louisiana; but as Marbois reported the offer to Livingston, Bonaparte said: "Well! you have charge of the Treasury. Let them give you one hundred millions of francs, and pay their own claims, and take the whole country." The American claims were estimated at about twenty-five millions, and therefore Marbois's price amounted to at least one hundred and twenty-five million francs.

Yet twenty-four or twenty-five million dollars for the whole west bank of the Mississippi, from the Lake of the Woods to the Gulf of Mexico, and indefinitely westward, was not an

[1] Livingston to Madison, April 13, 1803; State Papers, ii. 552, 544.

extortionate price, especially since New Orleans was thrown into the bargain, and indirect political advantages which could not be valued at less than the cost of a war, whatever it might be. Five million dollars were to be paid in America to American citizens, so that less than twenty millions would come to France. Livingston could hardly have been blamed for closing with Marbois on the spot, especially as his instructions warranted him in offering ten millions for New Orleans and the Floridas alone; but Livingston still professed that he did not want the west bank. "I told him that the United States were anxious to preserve peace with France; that for that reason they wished to remove them to the west side of the Mississippi; that we would be perfectly satisfied with New Orleans and the Floridas, and had no disposition to extend across the river; that of course we would not give any great sum for the purchase. . . . He then pressed me to name the sum." After a little more fencing, Marbois dropped at once from one hundred millions to sixty, with estimated claims to the amount of twenty millions more. "I told him that it was vain to ask anything that was so greatly beyond our means; that true policy would dictate to the First Consul not to press such a demand; that he must know it would render the present government unpopular." The conversation closed by Livingston's departure at midnight with a final protest: "I told him that I would consult Mr. Monroe, but that neither he nor I could accede to his ideas on the subject." Then he went home; and sitting down to his desk wrote a long despatch to Madison, to record that without Monroe's help he had won Louisiana. The letter closed with some reflections:—

"As to the quantum, I have yet made up no opinion. The field open to us is infinitely larger than our instructions contemplated, the revenue increasing, and the land more than adequate to sink the capital, should we even go the sum proposed by Marbois,—nay, I persuade myself that the whole sum may be raised by the sale of the territory west of the Mississippi, with the right of sovereignty, to some Power in Europe whose vicinity we should not fear. I speak now without reflection and without having seen Mr. Monroe, as it was midnight when I left the Treasury

Office, and it is now near three o'clock. It is so very important that you should be apprised that a negotiation is actually opened, even before Mr. Monroe has been presented,
in order to calm the tumult which the news of war will
renew, that I have lost no time in communicating it. We
shall do all we can to cheapen the purchase; but my present
sentiment is that we shall buy."

A week was next passed in haggling over the price.[1] Livingston did his utmost to beat Marbois down, but without
success. Meanwhile he ran some risk of losing everything; for
when Bonaparte offered a favor suitors did well to waste no
time in acceptance. A slight weight might have turned the
scale; a divulgence of the secret, a protest from Spain, a moment of irritation at Jefferson's coquetry with England or at
the vaporings of the American press, a sudden perception of
the disgust which every true Frenchman was sure sooner or
later to feel at this squandering of French territory and enterprise,—any remonstrance that should stir the First Consul's
pride or startle his fear of posterity, might have cut short the
thread of negotiation. Livingston did not know the secrets of
the Tuileries, or he would not have passed time in cheapening
the price of his purchase. The voice of opposition was silenced in the French people, but was still so high in Bonaparte's family as to make the Louisiana scheme an occasion
for scenes so violent as to sound like the prelude to a tragedy.

One evening when Talma was to appear in a new *rôle*, Lucien Bonaparte, coming home to dress for the theatre, found
his brother Joseph waiting for him.[2] "Here you are at last!"
cried Joseph; "I was afraid you might not come. This is
no time for theatre-going; I have news for you that will give
you no fancy for amusement. The General wants to sell
Louisiana."

Lucien, proud of having made the treaty which secured the
retrocession, was for a moment thunderstruck; then recovering confidence, he said, "Come, now! if he were capable of
wishing it, the Chambers would never consent."

"So he means to do without their consent," replied Joseph.

[1] Livingston to Madison, April 17, 1803; State Papers, ii. 554.
[2] Lucien Bonaparte et ses Mémoires, Th. Jung, ii. 121–192.

"This is what he answered me, when I said to him, like you, that the Chambers would not consent. What is more, he added that this sale would supply him the first funds for the war. Do you know that I am beginning to think he is much too fond of war?"

History is not often able to penetrate the private lives of famous men, and catch their words as they were uttered. Although Lucien Bonaparte's veracity was not greatly superior to that of his brother Napoleon, his story agreed with the known facts. If his imagination here and there filled in the gaps of memory,—if he was embittered and angry when he wrote, and hated his brother Napoleon with Corsican passion, these circumstances did not discredit his story, for he would certainly have told the truth against his brother under no other conditions. The story was not libellous, but Napoleonic; it told nothing new of the First Consul's character, but it was honorable to Joseph, who proposed to Lucien that they should go together and prevent their brother from committing a fault which would rouse the indignation of France, and endanger his own safety as well as theirs.

The next morning Lucien went to the Tuileries; by his brother's order he was admitted, and found Napoleon in his bath, the water of which was opaque with mixture of *eau de Cologne*. They talked for some time on indifferent matters. Lucien was timid, and dared not speak until Joseph came. Then Napoleon announced his decision to sell Louisiana, and invited Lucien to say what he thought of it.

"I flatter myself," replied Lucien, "that the Chambers will not give their consent."

"You flatter yourself!" repeated Napoleon in a tone of surprise; then murmuring in a lower voice, "that is precious, in truth!" (*c'est précieux, en vérité!*)

"And I too flatter myself, as I have already told the First Consul," cried Joseph.

"And what did I answer?" said Napoleon warmly, glaring from his bath at the two men.

"That you would do without the Chambers."

"Precisely! That is what I have taken the great liberty to tell Mr. Joseph, and what I now repeat to the Citizen Lucien,—begging him at the same time to give me his opinion about it, without taking into consideration his paternal tenderness for his diplomatic conquest." Then, not satisfied with irony, he continued in a tone of exasperating contempt: "And now, gentlemen, think of it what you will; but both of you go into mourning about this affair,—you, Lucien, for the sale itself; you, Joseph, because I shall do without the consent of any one whomsoever. Do you understand?"

At this Joseph came close to the bath, and rejoined in a vehement tone: "And you will do well, my dear brother, not to expose your project to parliamentary discussion; for I declare to you that if necessary I will put myself first at the head of the opposition which will not fail to be made against you."

The First Consul burst into a peal of forced laughter, while Joseph, crimson with anger and almost stammering his words, went on: "Laugh, laugh, laugh, then! I will act up to my promise; and though I am not fond of mounting the tribune, this time you will see me there!"

Napoleon, half rising from the bath, rejoined in a serious tone: "You will have no need to lead the opposition, for I repeat that there will be no debate, for the reason that the project which has not the fortune to meet your approval, conceived by me, negotiated by me, shall be ratified and executed by me alone, do you comprehend?—by me, who laugh at your opposition!"

Hereupon Joseph wholly lost his self-control, and with flashing eyes shouted: "Good! I tell you, General, that you, I, and all of us, if you do what you threaten, may prepare ourselves soon to go and join the poor innocent devils whom you so legally, humanely, and especially with such justice, have transported to Sinnamary."

At this terrible rejoinder Napoleon half started up, crying out: "You are insolent! I ought—" then threw himself violently back in the bath with a force which sent a mass of perfumed water into Joseph's flushed face, drenching him and Lucien, who had the wit to quote, in a theatrical tone, the words which Virgil put into the mouth of Neptune reproving the waves,—

"*Quos ego . . .*"

Between the water and the wit the three Bonapartes re-

covered their tempers, while the valet who was present, overcome by fear, fainted and fell on the floor. Joseph went home
to change his clothes, while Lucien remained to pass through
another scene almost equally amusing. A long conversation
followed after the First Consul's toilet was finished. Napoleon
spoke of St. Domingo. "Do you want me to tell you the
truth?" said he. "I am to-day more sorry than I like to confess
for the expedition to St. Domingo. Our national glory will
never come from our marine." He justified what he called, in
jest at Lucien, his "Louisianicide," by the same reasons he
gave to Marbois and Talleyrand, but especially by the necessity of providing funds for the war not yet declared. Lucien
combated his arguments as Joseph had done, until at last he
reached the same point. "If, like Joseph, I thought that this
alienation of Louisiana without the assent of the Chambers
might be fatal to me,—to me alone,—I would consent to run
all risks in order to prove the devotion you doubt; but it is
really too unconstitutional and—"

"Ah, indeed!" burst out Napoleon with another prolonged,
forced laugh of derisive anger. "You lay it on handsomely!
Unconstitutional is droll from you. Come now, let me alone!
How have I hurt your Constitution? Answer!"

Lucien replied that the intent to alienate any portion whatever of territory belonging to the Republic without the consent of the Chambers was an unconstitutional project. "In a
word, the Constitution—"

"Go about your business!" broke in the guardian of the
Constitution and of the national territory. Then he quickly
and vehemently went on: "Constitution! unconstitutional!
republic! national sovereignty!—big words! great phrases!
Do you think yourself still in the club of St. Maximin? We
are no longer there, mind that! Ah, it becomes you well,
Sir Knight of the Constitution, to talk so to me! You had
not the same respect for the Chambers on the 18th Brumaire!"

Nothing exasperated Lucien more than any allusion to the
part he took in the *coup d'état* of the 18th Brumaire, when he
betrayed the Chamber over which he presided. He commanded himself for the moment; but when Napoleon went
on to say with still more contempt, "I laugh at you and your

national representation," Lucien answered coldly, "I do not laugh at you, Citizen Consul, but I know well what I think about it."

"*Parbleu!*" said Napoleon, "I am curious to know what you think of me: say it, quick!"

"I think, Citizen Consul, that having given your oath to the Constitution of the 18th Brumaire into my own hands as President of the Council of Five Hundred, seeing you despise it thus, if I were not your brother I would be your enemy."

"My enemy! ah, I would advise you! My enemy! That is a trifle strong!" cried Napoleon, advancing as though to strike his younger brother. "You my enemy! I would break you, look, like this box!" And so saying he flung his snuff-box violently on the floor.

In these angry scenes both parties knew that Napoleon's bravado was not altogether honest. For once, Lucien was in earnest; and had his brother left a few other men in France as determined as he and his friend Bernadotte, the First Consul would have defied public opinion less boldly. Joseph, too, although less obstinate than his brothers, was not easily managed. According to Lucien there were further scenes between them, at one of which Joseph burst into such violence that the First Consul took refuge in Josephine's room. These stories contained nothing incredible. The sale of Louisiana was the turning-point in Napoleon's career; no true Frenchman forgave it. A second betrayal of France, it announced to his fellow conspirators that henceforward he alone was to profit by the treason of the 18th Brumaire.

Livingston and Monroe knew nothing of all this; they even depended upon Joseph to help their negotiation. Monroe fell ill and could not act. Over the negotiation of the treaty has always hung a cloud of mystery such as belonged to no other measure of equal importance in American history. No official report showed that the commissioners ever met in formal conference; no protocol of their proceedings, no account of their discussions, no date when their agreement was made, was left on record. Both the treaty itself and the avowals of Livingston gave evidence that at the end all parties acted in haste. If it were not for a private memorandum by Monroe,—not sent to the Government, but preserved among his private papers,—the course of negotiation could not be followed.

A fortnight passed after Monroe's arrival without advancing matters a step. This period of inaction seems to have been broken by the First Consul. April 23 he drew up a "*Projet* of a Secret Convention,"[1] which he gave to Marbois and which set forth that to prevent misunderstandings about the matters of discussion mentioned in Articles II. and V. of the Morfontaine treaty, and also to strengthen friendly relations, the French republic was to cede its rights over Louisiana; and "in consequence of the said cession, Louisiana, its territory, and its proper dependencies shall become part of the American Union, and shall form successively one or more States on the terms of the Federal Constitution;" in return the United States were to favor French commerce in Louisiana, and give it all the rights of American commerce, with perpetual *entre pôts* at six points on the Mississippi, and a corresponding perpetual right of navigation; further, they were to assume all debts due to American citizens under the treaty of Morfontaine; and, finally, were to pay a hundred million francs to France. With this *projet* Marbois went by appointment, at two o'clock, April 27, to Monroe's lodgings, where the three gentlemen had an informal meeting, of which no other record is known to exist than Monroe's memoranda.[2] Monroe himself was too unwell to sit at the table, and reclined on a sofa throughout the discussion. Marbois produced Bonaparte's *projet*, and after admitting that it was hard and unreasonable, presented a substitute of his own which he thought the First Consul would accept.

Livingston tried to give precedence to the claims; he wanted to dispose of them first, in case the cession should fail; but after pressing the point as far as he could, he was overruled by Monroe, and Livingston took Marbois's project for consideration. The two American commissioners passed a day in working over it. Livingston drafted a claims convention, and it was drawn, as he thought, " with particular attention."[3] Monroe thought differently. "My colleague took Mr.

[1] Correspondance, viii. 289.

[2] Monroe's Memoranda, Monroe MSS., State Department Archives.

[3] Livingston to Madison, May 3, 1804; MSS. State Department Archives.

Marbois's project with him, and brought me one, very loosely drawn, founded on it."[1] Monroe made a draft of his own which was certainly not creditable to his legal or diplomatic skill, and which began by adopting an oversight contained in Bonaparte's draft, according to which the cancelled Article II. of the treaty of Morfontaine was made a foundation of the new convention.[2] "We called on Mr. Marbois the 29th, and gave him our project, which was read to him and discussed. We proposed to offer fifty millions to France, and twenty millions on account of her debt to the citizens of the United States, making seventy in the whole." Marbois replied that he would proceed only on the condition that eighty millions were accepted as the price. Then at last the American commissioners gave way; and with this change Marbois took their *projet* for reference to the First Consul the next morning.

The 30th of April was taken by Marbois for consultation with the First Consul. May 1 Monroe was presented at the Tuileries, and dined there with Livingston; but Bonaparte said nothing of their business, except that it should be settled. The same evening the two envoys had a final discussion with Marbois. "May 2, we actually signed the treaty and convention for the sixty million francs to France, in the French language; but our copies in English not being made out, we could not sign in our language. They were however prepared, and signed in two or three days afterward. The convention respecting American claims took more time, and was not signed till about the 8th or 9th." All these documents were antedated to the 30th April.[3]

The first object of remark in this treaty was the absence of any attempt to define the property thus bought and sold. "Louisiana with the same extent that is now in the hands of Spain, and that it had when France possessed it, and such as it should be after the treaties subsequently entered into between Spain and other States,"—these words, taken from Berthier's original treaty of retrocession, were convenient for

[1] Monroe's Memoranda, Monroe MSS., State Department Archives.
[2] Draft of Convention in Monroe's writing, Monroe MSS., State Department Archives.
[3] State Papers, ii. 507–509.

France and Spain, whose governments might be supposed to know their own boundaries; but all that the United States government knew upon the subject was that Louisiana, as France possessed it, had included a part of Florida and the whole Ohio Valley as far as the Alleghany Mountains and Lake Erie. The American commissioners at first insisted upon defining the boundaries, and Marbois went to the First Consul with their request. He refused.[1] "If an obscurity did not already exist, it would perhaps be good policy to put one there." He intentionally concealed the boundary he had himself defined, a knowledge of which would have prevented a long and mortifying dispute. Livingston went to Talleyrand for the orders given by Spain to the Marquis of Somoruelo, by France to Victor and Laussat. "What are the eastern bounds of Louisiana?" asked Livingston. "I do not know," replied Talleyrand; "you must take it as we received it." "But what did you mean to take?" urged Livingston. "I do not know," repeated Talleyrand. "Then you mean that we shall construe it our own way?" "I can give you no direction. You have made a noble bargain for yourselves, and I suppose you will make the most of it," was the final reply of Talleyrand. Had Livingston known that Victor's instructions, which began by fixing the boundaries in question, were still in Talleyrand's desk, the answer would have been the same.

One point alone was fixed,—the Floridas were not included in the sale; this was conceded on both sides. In his first conversation with Marbois, Livingston made a condition that France should aid him in procuring these territories from Spain.[2] "I asked him, in case of purchase, whether they would stipulate that France would never possess the Floridas, and that she would aid us to procure them, and relinquish all right that she might have to them. He told me that she would go thus far." Several days later, Marbois repeated this assurance to Monroe, saying that the First Consul authorized him, besides offering Louisiana, "to engage his support of our claim to the Floridas with Spain."[3] Yet when the American commissioners tried to insert this pledge into the treaty, they

[1] Marbois, Louisiana, pp. 283, 286.
[2] Livingston to Madison, April 13, 1803; State Papers, ii. 552.
[3] Monroe to Madison, April 19, 1803; State Department Archives.

failed. Bonaparte would give nothing but a verbal promise to use his good offices with Spain.

Besides the failure to dispose of these two points, which were in reality but one, the treaty contained a positive provision, Article III., taken from Bonaparte's *projet*, with slight alteration, that "the inhabitants of the ceded territory shall be incorporated in the Union of the United States, and admitted as soon as possible, according to the principles of the Federal Constitution, to the enjoyment of all the rights, advantages, and immunities of citizens of the United States." On republican principles of the Virginian school, only the States themselves could by a new grant of power authorize such an incorporation. Article III. violated Madison's instructions, which forbade the promise.[1] "To incorporate the inhabitants of the hereby-ceded territory with the citizens of the United States," said these instructions, "being a provision which cannot now be made, it is to be expected, from the character and policy of the United States, that such incorporation will take place without unnecessary delay." The provision, which Madison said could not be made, was nevertheless made by Livingston and Monroe.

Embarrassing as these omissions or provisions were, they proved not so much that the treaty was carelessly drawn, as that the American negotiators were ready to stipulate whatever was needed for their purpose. Other portions of the treaty were not to be defended on that excuse. The price stipulated for Louisiana was sixty million francs, in the form of United States six-per-cent bonds, representing a capital of $11,250,000. Besides this sum of eleven and a quarter million dollars, the United States government was to assume and pay the debts due by France to American citizens, estimated at twenty million francs, or, at the same rate of exchange, $3,750,000,—making fifteen million dollars in all as the price to be paid. Livingston himself drew the claims convention with what he supposed to be particular attention; but it was modified by Monroe, and still further altered by Marbois. "The moment was critical; the question of peace or war was in the balance; and it was important to come to a conclusion

[1] Madison to Livingston and Monroe, March 2, 1803; State Papers, ii. 540.

before either scale preponderated. I considered the convention as a trifle compared with the other great object," avowed Livingston; "and as it had already delayed us many days, I was ready to take it under any form."[1] The claims convention was not signed till nearly a week after the signature of the treaty of cession. The form in which Livingston took it showed that neither he nor Monroe could have given careful attention to the subject; for not only did the preamble declare that the parties were acting in compliance with Article II. of the treaty of Morfontaine,—an Article which had been formally struck out by the Senate, cancelled by Bonaparte, and the omission ratified by the Senate and President since Livingston's residence at Paris; not only did the claims specified fail to embrace all the cases provided for by the treaty of 1800, which this convention was framed to execute; not only were the specifications arbitrary, and even self-contradictory,—but the estimate of twenty million francs was far below the amount of the claims admitted in principle; no rule of apportionment was provided, and, worst of all, the right of final decision in every case was reserved to the French government. The meaning of this last provision might be guessed from the notorious corruption of Talleyrand and his band of confidential or secret agents.

Doubtless Livingston was right in securing his main object at any cost; but could he have given more time to his claims convention, he would perhaps have saved his own reputation and that of his successor from much stain, although he might have gained no more than he did for his Government. In the two conventions of 1800 and 1803 the United States obtained two objects of the utmost value,—by the first, a release from treaty obligations which, if carried out, required war with England; by the second, the whole west bank of the Mississippi River and the island of New Orleans, with all the incidental advantages attached. In return for these gains the United States government promised not to press the claims of its citizens against the French government beyond the amount of three million seven hundred and fifty thousand dollars, which was one fourth part of the price paid for Louisiana.

[1] Livingston to Madison, May 3, 1804; View of the Claims, etc., by a Citizen of Baltimore, p. 75.

The legitimate claims of American citizens against France amounted to many million dollars; in the result, certain favored claimants received three million seven hundred and fifty thousand dollars less their expenses, which reduced the sum about one half.

The impression of diplomatic oversight was deepened by the scandals which grew out of the distribution of the three million seven hundred and fifty thousand dollars which the favored claimants were to receive. Livingston's diplomatic career was poisoned by quarrels over this money.[1] That the French government acted with little concealment of venality was not matter of surprise; but that Livingston should be officially charged by his own associates with favoritism and corruption,—"imbecility of mind and a childish vanity, mixed with a considerable portion of duplicity,"—injured the credit of his Government; and the matter was not bettered when he threw back similar charges on the Board of Commissioners, or when at last General Armstrong, coming to succeed him, was discredited by similar suspicions. Considering how small was the amount of money distributed, the scandal and corruption surpassed any other experience of the national government.

Livingston's troubles did not end there. He could afford to suffer some deduction from his triumph; for he had achieved the greatest diplomatic success recorded in American history. Neither Franklin, Jay, Gallatin, nor any other American diplomatist was so fortunate as Livingston for the immensity of his results compared with the paucity of his means. Other treaties of immense consequence have been signed by American representatives,—the treaty of alliance with France; the treaty of peace with England which recognized independence; the treaty of Ghent; the treaty which ceded Florida; the Ashburton treaty; the treaty of Guadalupe Hidalgo,—but in none of these did the United States government get so much for so little. The annexation of Louisiana was an event so portentous as to defy measurement; it gave a new face to politics, and ranked in historical importance next to the Declaration of Independence and the adoption of the Con-

---

[1] View of the Claims, etc., by a Citizen of Baltimore. 1829.

stitution,—events of which it was the logical outcome; but as a matter of diplomacy it was unparallelled, because it cost almost nothing.

The scandalous failure of the claims convention was a trifling drawback to the enjoyment of this unique success; but the success was further embittered by the conviction that America would give the honor to Monroe. Virginia was all-powerful. Livingston was unpopular, distrusted, not liked even by Madison; while Monroe, for political reasons, had been made a prominent figure. Public attention had been artifically drawn upon his mission; and in consequence, Monroe's name grew great, so as almost to overshadow that of Madison, while Livingston heard few voices proclaiming his services to the country. In a few weeks Livingston began to see his laurels wither, and was forced to claim the credit that he thought his due. Monroe treated him less generously than he might have done, considering that Monroe gained the political profit of the success.[1] Acknowledging that his own share was next to nothing in the negotiation, he still encouraged the idea that Livingston's influence had been equally null. This view was doubtless correct, but if universally applied in history, would deprive many great men of their laurels. Monroe's criticism helped only to diminish the political chances of a possible rival who had no Virginia behind him to press his preferment and cover his mistakes.

[1] Livingston to Madison, Nov. 15, 1803; State Papers, ii. 573. Diary of John Quincy Adams, v. 433. Memoir of James Monroe, 1828.

Chapter III

WHEN MARBOIS took the treaty to the First Consul, Bonaparte listened to its provisions with lively interest; and on hearing that twenty millions were to be employed in paying claims,—a use of money which he much disliked,—he broke out: "Who authorized you to dispose of the money of the State? I want to have these twenty millions paid into the Treasury. The claimants' rights cannot come before our own."[1] His own *projet* had required the Americans to assume these claims,—which was, in fact, the better plan. Marbois's alteration turned the claims into a French job. Perhaps Bonaparte was not averse to this; for when Marbois reminded him that he had himself fixed the price at fifty millions, whereas the treaty gave him sixty, and settled the claims besides,—"It is true," he said; "the negotiation leaves me nothing to wish. Sixty millions for an occupation that will not perhaps last a day! I want France to have the good of this unexpected capital, and to employ it in works of use to her marine." On the spot he dictated a decree for the construction of five canals. This excellent use of the money seemed inconsistent with Lucien's remark that it was wanted for war,—but the canals were never built or begun; and the sixty millions were spent, to the last centime, in preparations for an impracticable descent on England.

Yet money was not the inducement which caused Bonaparte to sell Louisiana to the United States. The Prince of Peace would at any time have given more money, and would perhaps have been willing, as he certainly was able, to pay it from his private means rather than allow the United States to own Louisiana. In other respects, the sale needed explanation, since it contradicted the First Consul's political theories and prejudices. He had but two rooted hatreds. The deeper and fiercer of these was directed against the republic,—the organized democracy, and what he called ideology, which Americans knew in practice as Jeffersonian theories; the second and steadier was his hatred of England as the chief barrier to his military omnipotence. The cession of Louisiana to the United

[1] Marbois's Louisiana, pp. 311, 312.

States contradicted both these passions, making the ideologists supreme in the New World, and necessarily tending in the end to strengthen England in the Old. Bonaparte had been taught by Talleyrand that America and England, whatever might be their mutual jealousies, hatred, or wars, were socially and economically one and indivisible. Barely ten years after the Revolutionary War had closed, and at a time when the wounds it made were still raw, Talleyrand remarked: "In every part of America through which I have travelled, I have not found a single Englishman who did not feel himself to be an American; not a single Frenchman who did not find himself a stranger." Bonaparte knew that England held the monopoly of American trade, and that America held the monopoly of democratic principles; yet he did an act which was certain to extend British trade and fortify democratic principles.

This contradiction was due to no change in Bonaparte's opinions; these remained what they were. At the moment when talking to Marbois about "those republicans whose friendship I seek," he was calculating on the chance that his gift would one day prove their ruin. "Perhaps it will also be objected to me," he said,[1] "that the Americans may in two or three centuries be found too powerful for Europe; but my foresight does not embrace such remote fears. Besides, we may hereafter expect rivalries among the members of the Union. The confederations that are called perpetual last only till one of the contracting parties finds it to its interest to break them. . . . It is to prevent the danger to which the colossal power of England exposes us that I would provide a remedy." The colossal power of England depended on her navy, her colonies, and her manufactures. Bonaparte proposed to overthrow it by shattering beyond repair the colonial system of France and Spain; and even this step was reasonable compared with what followed. He expected to check the power of England by giving Louisiana to the United States,—a measure which opened a new world to English commerce and manufactures, and riveted England's grasp on the whole American continent, inviting her to do

[1] Marbois's Louisiana, p. 276.

what she afterward did,—join hands with the United States in revolutionizing Mexico and South America in her own interests. As though to render these results certain, after extending this invitation to English commerce and American democracy, Bonaparte next invited a war with England, which was certain to drive from the ocean every ship belonging to France or Spain,—a war which left even the United States at England's mercy.

Every detail that could explain Bonaparte's motives becomes interesting in a matter so important to American history. Certain points were clear. Talleyrand's colonial and peace policy failed. Resting on the maintenance of order in Europe and the extension of French power in rivalry with the United States and England in America, it was a statesmanlike and honorable scheme, which claimed for the Latin races what Louis XIV. tried to gain for them; but it had the disadvantage of rousing hostility in the United States, and of throwing them into the arms of England. For this result Talleyrand was prepared. He knew that he could keep peace with England, and that the United States alone could not prevent him from carrying out his policy. Indeed, Madison in his conversation with Pichon invited such action, and Jefferson had no means of resisting it; but from the moment when St. Domingo prevented the success of the scheme, and Bonaparte gained an excuse for following his own military instincts, the hostility of the United States became troublesome. President Jefferson had chiefly reckoned on this possibility as his hope of getting Louisiana; and slight as the chance seemed, he was right.

This was, in effect, the explanation which Talleyrand officially wrote to his colleague Decrès, communicating a copy of the treaty, and requesting him to take the necessary measures for executing it.[1]

"The wish to spare the North American continent the war with which it was threatened, to dispose of different points in dispute between France and the United States of America, and to remove all the new causes of misunder-

[1] Talleyrand to Decrès, 4 Prairial, An xi. (May 24, 1803); Archives des Aff. Étr., MSS.

standing which competition and neighborhood might have produced between them; the position of the French colonies; their want of men, cultivation, and assistance; in fine, the empire of circumstances, foresight of the future, and the intention to compensate by an advantageous arrangement for the inevitable loss of a country which war was going to put at the mercy of another nation,—all these motives have determined the Government to pass to the United States the rights it had acquired from Spain over the sovereignty and property of Louisiana."

Talleyrand's words were always happily chosen, whether to reveal or to conceal his thoughts. This display of reasons for an act which he probably preferred to condemn, might explain some of the First Consul's motives in ceding Louisiana to the United States, but it only confused another more perplexing question. Louisiana did not belong to France, but to Spain. The retrocession had never been completed; the territory was still possessed, garrisoned, and administered by Don Carlos IV.; until actual delivery was made, Spain might yet require that the conditions of retrocession should be rigorously performed. Her right in the present instance was complete, because she held as one of the conditions precedent to the retrocession a solemn pledge from the First Consul never to alienate Louisiana. The sale of Louisiana to the United States was trebly invalid: if it were French property, Bonaparte could not constitutionally alienate it without the consent of the Chambers; if it were Spanish property, he could not alienate it at all; if Spain had a right of reclamation, his sale was worthless. In spite of all these objections the alienation took place; and the motives which led the First Consul to conciliate America by violating the Constitution of France were perhaps as simple as he represented them to be; but no one explained what motives led Bonaparte to break his word of honor and betray the monarchy of Spain.

Bonaparte's evident inclination toward a new war with England greatly distressed King Charles IV. Treaty stipulations bound Spain either to take part with France in the war, or to pay a heavy annual subsidy; and Spain was so weak that either alternative seemed fatal. The Prince of Peace would have liked to join England or Austria in a coalition against Bonaparte; but he knew that to this last desperate measure King Charles would never assent until Bonaparte's hand was actually on his crown; for no one could reasonably doubt that within a year after Spain should declare an unsuccessful war on France, the whole picturesque Spanish court—not only Don Carlos IV. himself and Queen Luisa, but also the Prince of Peace, Don Pedro Cevallos, the Infant Don Ferdinand, and the train of courtiers who thronged La Granja and the Escorial—would be wandering in exile or wearing out their lives in captivity. To increase the complication, the young King of Etruria died May 27, 1803, leaving an infant seated upon the frail throne which was sure soon to disappear at the bidding of some military order countersigned by Berthier.

In the midst of such anxieties, Godoy heard a public rumor that Bonaparte had sold Louisiana to the United States; and he felt it as the death-knell of the Spanish empire. Between the energy of the American democracy and the violence of Napoleon whom no oath bound, Spain could hope for no escape. From New Orleans to Vera Cruz was but a step; from Bayonne to Cadiz a winter campaign of some five or six hundred miles. Yet Godoy would probably have risked everything, and would have thrown Spain into England's hands, had he been able to control the King and Queen, over whom Bonaparte exercised the influence of a master. On learning the sale of Louisiana, the Spanish government used language almost equivalent to a rupture with France. The Spanish minister at Paris was ordered to remonstrate in the strongest terms against the step which the First Consul had taken behind the back of the King his ally.[1]

"This alienation," wrote the Chevalier d'Azara to Talleyrand, "not only deranges from top to bottom the whole colonial system of Spain, and even of Europe, but is directly opposed to the compacts and formal stipulations agreed upon between France and Spain, and to the terms of the cession in the treaty of Tuscany; and the King my master brought himself to give up the colony only on con-

[1] D'Azara to Talleyrand, June 6, 1803; Archives des Aff. Étr., MSS.

dition that it should at no time, under no pretext, and in no manner, be alienated or ceded to any other Power."

Then, after reciting the words of Gouvion St.-Cyr's pledge, the note continued: —

"It is impossible to conceive more frankness or loyalty than the King has put into his conduct toward France throughout this affair. His Majesty had therefore the right to expect as much on the part of his ally, but unhappily finds himself deceived in his hopes by the sale of the said colony. Yet trusting always in the straightforwardness and justice of the First Consul, he has ordered me to make this representation, and to protest against the alienation, hoping that it will be revoked, as manifestly contrary to the treaties and to the most solemn anterior promises."

Not stopping there, the note also insisted that Tuscany should be evacuated by the French troops, who were not needed, and had become an intolerable burden, so that the country was reduced to the utmost misery. Next, King Charles demanded that Parma and Piacenza should be surrendered to the King of Etruria, to whom they belonged as the heir of the late Duke of Parma. Finally, the note closed with a complaint even more grave in substance than any of the rest: —

"The King my master could have wished also a little more friendly frankness in communicating the negotiations with England, and especially in regard to the dispositions of the Northern courts, guarantors of the treaty of Amiens; but as this affair belongs to negotiations of another kind, the undersigned abstains for the moment from entering into them, reserving the right to do so on a better occasion."

Beurnonville, the French minister at Madrid, tried to soothe or silence the complaints of Cevallos; but found himself only silenced in return. The views of the Spanish secretary were energetic, precise, and not to be met by argument.[1] "I

[1] Beurnonville to Talleyrand, 24 Prairial, An xi. (June 13, 1803); Archives des Aff. Étr., MSS.

have not been able to bring M. Cevallos to any moderate, conciliatory, or even calm expression," wrote Beurnonville to Talleyrand; "he has persistently shown himself inaccessible to all persuasion." The Prince of Peace was no more manageable than Cevallos: "While substituting a soft and pliant tone for the sharpest expressions, and presenting under the appearance of regret what had been advanced to me with the bitterness of reproach, the difference between the Prince's conduct and that of M. Cevallos is one only in words." Both of them said, what was quite true, that the United States would not have objected to the continued possession of Louisiana by Spain, and that France had greatly exaggerated the dispute about the *entrepôt*.

"The whole matter reduces itself to a blunder (*gaucherie*) of the Intendant," said Cevallos; "it has been finally explained to Mr. Jefferson, and friendship is restored. On both sides there has been irritation, but not a shadow of aggression; and from the moment of coming to an understanding, both parties see that they are at bottom of one mind, and mutually very well disposed toward each other. Moreover, it is quite gratuitous to assume that Louisiana is so easy to take in the event of a war, either by the Americans or by the English. The first have only militia,—very considerable, it is true, but few troops of the line; while Louisiana, at least for the moment, has ten thousand militia-men, and a body of three thousand five hundred regular troops. As for the English, they cannot seriously have views on a province which is impregnable to them; and all things considered, it would be no great calamity if they should take it. The United States, having a much firmer hold on the American continent, should they take a new enlargement, would end by becoming formidable, and would one day disturb the Spanish possessions. As for the debts due to Americans, Spain has still more claim to an arrangement of that kind; and in any case the King, as Bonaparte must know, would have gladly discharged all the debts contracted by France, and perhaps even a large instalment of the American claim, in order to recover an old domain of the crown. Finally, the intention which led the King to give his consent to the exchange of Louisiana was completely deceived. This intention had been to interpose a strong dyke between the Spanish colonies and the American possessions; now, on the contrary, the doors of Mexico are to stay open to them."

To these allegations, which Beurnonville called "insincere, weak, and ill-timed," Cevallos added a piece of evidence which, strangely enough, was altogether new to the French minister, and reduced him to confusion: it was Gouvion St.-Cyr's letter, pledging the First Consul never to alienate Louisiana.

When Beurnonville's despatch narrating these interviews reached Paris, it stung Bonaparte to the quick, and called from him one of the angry avowals with which he sometimes revealed a part of the motives that influenced his strange mind. Talleyrand wrote back to Beurnonville, June 22, a letter which bore the mark of the First Consul's hand.

"In one of my letters," he began,[1] "I made known to you the motives which determined the Government to give up Louisiana to the United States. You will not conceal from the Court of Madrid that one of the causes which had most influence on this determination was discontent at learning that Spain, after having promised to sustain the measures taken by the Intendant of New Orleans, had nevertheless formally revoked them. These measures would have tended to free the capital of Louisiana from subjection to a right of deposit which was becoming a source of bickerings between the Louisianians and Americans. We should have afterward assigned to the United States, in conformity to their treaty with Spain, another place of deposit, less troublesome to the colony and less injurious to its commerce; but Spain put to flight all these hopes by confirming the privileges of the Americans at New Orleans,—thus granting them definitively local advantages which had been at first only temporary. The French government, which had reason to count on the contrary assurance given in this regard by that of Spain, had a right to feel surprise at this

[1] Talleyrand to Beurnonville, 3 Messidor, An xi. (June 22, 1803); Archives des Aff. Étr., MSS.

determination; and seeing no way of reconciling it with the commercial advantages of the colony and with a long peace between the colony and its neighbors, took the only course which actual circumstances and wise prevision could suggest."

These assertions contained no more truth than those which Cevallos had answered. Spain had not promised to sustain the Intendant, nor had she revoked the Intendant's measures after, but before, the imagined promise; she had not confirmed the American privileges at New Orleans, but had expressly reserved them for future treatment. On the other hand, the restoration of the deposit was not only reconcilable with peace between Louisiana and the United States, but the whole world knew that the risk of war rose from the threat of disturbing the right of deposit. The idea that the colony had become less valuable on this account was new. France had begged for the colony with its American privileges, and meaning to risk the chances of American hostility; but if these privileges were the cause of selling the colony to the Americans, and if, as Talleyrand implied, France could and would have held Louisiana if the right of deposit at New Orleans had been abolished and the Americans restricted to some other spot on the river-bank, fear of England was not, as had been previously alleged, the cause of the sale. Finally, if the act of Spain made the colony worthless, why was Spain deprived of the chance to buy it back?

The answer was evident. The reason why Bonaparte did not keep his word to Don Carlos IV. was that he looked on Spain as his own property, and on himself as representing her sovereignty. The reasons for which he refused to Spain the chance to redeem the colony, were probably far more complicated. The only obvious explanation, assuming that he still remembered his pledge, was a wish to punish Spain.

After all these questions were asked, one problem still remained. Bonaparte had reasons for not returning the colony to Spain; he had reasons, too, for giving it to the United States,—but why did he alienate the territory from France? Fear of England was not the true cause. He had not to learn how to reconquer Louisiana on the Danube and the Po. At one time or another Great Britain had captured nearly all the French colonies in the New World, and had been forced not only to disgorge conquests, but to abandon possessions; until of the three great European Powers in America, England was weakest. Any attempt to regain old ascendency by conquering Louisiana would have thrown the United States into the hands of France; and had Bonaparte anticipated such an act, he should have helped it. That Great Britain should waste strength in conquering Louisiana in order to give it to the United States, was an idea not to be gravely argued. Jefferson might, indeed, be driven into an English alliance in order to take Louisiana by force from France or Spain; but this danger was slight in itself, and might have been removed by the simple measure of selling only the island of New Orleans, and by retaining the west bank, which Jefferson was ready to guarantee. This was the American plan; and the President offered for New Orleans alone about half the price he paid for all Louisiana.[1] Still, Bonaparte forced the west bank on Livingston. Every diplomatic object would have been gained by accepting Jefferson's *projet* of a treaty, and signing it without the change of a word. Spain would have been still in some degree protected; England would have been tempted to commit the mistake of conquering the retained territory, and thereby the United States would have been held in check; the United States would have gained all the stimulus their ambition could require for many years to come; and what was more important to Bonaparte, France could not justly say that he had illegally and ignobly sold national territory except for a sufficient and national object.

The real reasons which induced Bonaparte to alienate the territory from France remained hidden in the mysterious processes of his mind. Perhaps he could not himself have given the true explanation of his act. Anger with Spain and Godoy had a share in it, as he avowed through Talleyrand's letter of June 22; disgust for the sacrifices he had made, and impatience to begin his new campaigns on the Rhine,—possibly a wish to show Talleyrand that his policy could never be revived, and that he had no choice but to follow into Germany,—had still

---

[1] Madison to Livingston and Monroe, March 2, 1803; State Papers, ii. 543.

more to do with the act. Yet it is also reasonable to believe that the depths of his nature concealed a wish to hide forever the monument of a defeat. As he would have liked to blot Corsica, Egypt, and St. Domingo from the map, and wipe from human memory the record of his failures, he may have taken pleasure in flinging Louisiana far off, and burying it forever from the sight of France in the bosom of the only government which could absorb and conceal it.

For reasons of his own, which belonged rather to military and European than to American history, Bonaparte preferred to deal with Germany before crossing the Pyrenees; and he knew that meanwhile Spain could not escape. Godoy on his side could neither drag King Charles into a war with France, nor could he provide the means of carrying on such a war with success. Where strong nations like Austria, Russia, and Prussia were forced to crouch before Bonaparte, and even England would have been glad to accept tolerable terms, Spain could not challenge attack. The violent anger that followed the sale of Louisiana and the rupture of the peace of Amiens soon subsided. Bonaparte, aware that he had outraged the rights of Spain, became moderate. Anxious to prevent her from committing any act of desperation, he did not require her to take part in the war, but even allowed her stipulated subsidies to run in arrears; and although he might not perhaps regret his sale of Louisiana to the United States, he felt that he had gone too far in shaking the colonial system. At the moment when Cevallos made his bitterest complaints, Bonaparte was least disposed to resent them by war. Both parties knew that so far as Louisiana was concerned, the act was done and could not be undone; that France was bound to carry out her pledge, or the United States would take possession of Louisiana without her aid. Bonaparte was willing to go far in the way of conciliation, if Spain would consent to withdraw her protest.

Of this the American negotiators knew little. Through such complications, of which Bonaparte alone understood the secret, the Americans moved more or less blindly, not knowing enemies from friends. The only public man who seemed ever to understand Napoleon's methods was Pozzo di Borgo, whose ways of thought belonged to the island society in which both had grown to manhood; and Monroe was not skilled in the diplomacy of Pozzo, or even of Godoy. Throughout life, Monroe was greatly under the influence of other men. He came to Paris almost a stranger to its new society, for his only relations of friendship had been with the republicans, most of whom Bonaparte had sent to Cayenne. He found Livingston master of the situation, and wisely interfered in no way with what Livingston did. The treaty was no sooner signed than he showed his readiness to follow Livingston further, without regard to embarrassments which might result.

When Livingston set his name to the treaty of cession, May 2, 1803, he was aware of the immense importance of the act. He rose and shook hands with Monroe and Marbois. "We have lived long," said he; "but this is the noblest work of our lives." This was said by the man who in the Continental Congress had been a member of the committee appointed to draft the Declaration of Independence; and it was said to Monroe, who had been assured only three months before, by President Jefferson of the grandeur of his destinies in words he could hardly have forgotten:[1] "Some men are born for the public Nature, by fitting them for the service of the human race on a broad scale, has stamped them with the evidences of her destination and their duty." Monroe was born for the public, and knew what destiny lay before him; while in Livingston's mind New York had thenceforward a candidate for the Presidency whose claims were better than Monroe's. In the cup of triumph of which these two men then drank deep, was yet one drop of acid. They had been sent to buy the Floridas and New Orleans. They had bought New Orleans; but instead of Florida, so much wanted by the Southern people, they had paid ten or twelve million dollars for the west bank of the Mississippi. The negotiators were annoyed to think that having been sent to buy the east bank of the Mississippi, they had bought the west bank instead; that the Floridas were not a part of their purchase. Livingston especially felt the disappointment, and looked about him for some way to retrieve it.

Hardly was the treaty signed, when Livingston found what

[1] Jefferson to Monroe, Jan. 13, 1803; Works, iv. 455.

he sought. He discovered that France had actually bought West Florida without knowing it, and had sold it to the United States without being paid for it. This theory, which seemed at first sight preposterous, became a fixed idea in Livingston's mind. He knew that West Florida had not been included by Spain in the retrocession, but that on the contrary Charles IV. had repeatedly, obstinately, and almost publicly rejected Bonaparte's tempting bids for that province. Livingston's own argument for the cession of Louisiana had chiefly rested on this knowledge, and on the theory that without Mobile New Orleans was worthless. He recounted this to Madison in the same letter which announced Talleyrand's offer to sell:[1] —

"I have used every exertion with the Spanish Ambassador and Lord Whitworth to prevent the transfer of the Floridas, . . . and unless they [the French] get Florida, I have convinced them that Louisiana is worth little."

In the preceding year one of the French ministers had applied to Livingston "to know what we understand in America by Louisiana;" and Livingston's answer was on record in the State Department at Washington:[2] "Since the possession of the Floridas by Britain and the treaty of 1762, I think there can be no doubt as to the precise meaning of the terms." He had himself drafted an article which he tried to insert in Marbois's *projet*, pledging the First Consul to interpose his good offices with the King of Spain to obtain the country east of the Mississippi. As late as May 12, Livingston wrote to Madison:[3] "I am satisfied that . . . if they [the French] could have concluded with Spain, we should also have had West Florida." In his next letter, only a week afterward, he insisted that West Florida was his:[4]

"Now, sir, the sum of this business is to recommend to you in the strongest terms, after having obtained the possession that the French commissary will give you, to insist

[1] Livingston to Madison, April 11, 1803; State Papers, ii. 552.
[2] Ibid., July 30, 1802; State Papers, ii. 519.
[3] Ibid., May 12, 1803; State Papers, ii. 557.
[4] Ibid., May 20, 1803; State Papers, ii. 561.

upon this as a part of your right, and to take possession at
all events to the River Perdido. I pledge myself that your
right is good."

The reasoning on which he rested this change of opinion
was in substance the following: France had, in early days,
owned nearly all the North American continent, and her
province of Louisiana had then included Ohio and the watercourses between the Lakes and the Gulf, as well as West Florida, or a part of it. This possession lasted until the treaty of
peace, Nov. 3, 1762, when France ceded to England not only
Canada, but also Florida and all other possessions east of the
Mississippi, except the Island of New Orleans. Then West
Florida by treaty first received its modern boundary at the
Iberville. On the same day France further ceded to Spain the
Island of New Orleans and all Louisiana west of the Mississippi. Not a foot of the vast French possessions on the continent of North America remained in the hands of the King
of France; they were divided between England and Spain.
The retrocession of 1800 was made on the understanding
that it referred to this cession of 1762. The province of Louisiana which had been ceded was *retro*-ceded, with its treaty-
boundary at the Iberville. Livingston knew that the understanding between France and Spain was complete; yet on examination he found that it had not been expressed in words
so clearly but that these words could be made to bear a different meaning. Louisiana was retroceded, he perceived,
" with the same extent that it now has in the hands of Spain,
and that it had when France possessed it, and such as it
should be according to the treaties subsequently entered into
between Spain and other States." When France possessed
Louisiana it included Ohio and West Florida: no one could
deny that West Florida was in the hands of Spain; therefore
Bonaparte, in the absence of negative proof, might have
claimed West Florida, if he had been acute enough to know
his own rights, or willing to offend Spain,—and as all Bonaparte's rights were vested in the United States, President Jefferson was at liberty to avail himself of them.
The ingenuity of Livingston's idea was not to be disputed;
and as a ground for a war of conquest it was as good as some

of the claims which Bonaparte made the world respect. As a diplomatic weapon, backed as Napoleon would have backed it by a hundred thousand soldiers, it was as effective an instrument as though it had every attribute of morality and good faith; and all it wanted, as against Spain, was the approval of Bonaparte. Livingston hoped that after the proof of friendship which Bonaparte had already given in selling Louisiana to the United States, he might without insuperable difficulty be induced to grant this favor. Both Marbois and Talleyrand, under the First Consul's express orders, led him on. Marbois did not deny that Mobile might lie in Louisiana, and Talleyrand positively denied knowledge that Laussat's instructions contained a definition of boundaries. Bonaparte stood behind both these agents, telling them that if an obscurity did not exist about the boundary they should make one. Talleyrand went so far as to encourage the pretensions which Livingston hinted: "You have made a noble bargain for yourselves," said he, "and I suppose you will make the most of it." This was said at the time when Bonaparte was still intent on punishing Spain.

Livingston found no difficulty in convincing Monroe that they had bought Florida as well as Louisiana.[1]

"We consider ourselves so strongly founded in this conclusion, that we are of opinion the United States should act on it in all the measures relative to Louisiana in the same manner as if West Florida was comprised within the Island of New Orleans, or lay to the west of the River Iberville."

Livingston expected that "a little force,"[2] as he expressed himself, might be necessary.

"After the explanations that have been given here, you need apprehend nothing from a decisive measure; your minister here and at Madrid can support your claim, and the time is peculiarly favorable to enable you to do it without the smallest risk at home. . . . The moment is so fa-

[1] Livingston and Monroe to Madison, June 7, 1803; State Papers, ii. 563–565.
[2] Livingston to Madison, May 20, 1803; Nov. 15, 1803; State Papers, ii. 561, 573.

vorable for taking possession of that country that I hope it has not been neglected, even though a little force should be necessary to effect it. Your minister must find the means to justify it."

A little violence added to a little diplomacy would answer the purpose. To use the words which "Aristides" Van Ness was soon to utter with striking effect, the United States ministers to France "practised with unlimited success upon the Livingston maxim,—

'Rem facias, rem
Si possis recte; si non, quocunque modo, REM.' "

Chapter IV

I̶N THE EXCITEMENT of this rapid and half-understood foreign drama, domestic affairs seemed tame to the American
people, who were busied only with the routine of daily life.
They had set their democratic house in order. So short and
easy was the task, that the work of a single year finished it.
When the President was about to meet Congress for the second time, he had no new measures to offer.[1] "The path we
have to pursue is so quiet that we have nothing scarcely to
propose to our legislature." The session was too short for severe labor. A quorum was not made until the middle of December, 1802; the Seventh Congress expired March 4, 1803.
Of these ten weeks, a large part was consumed in discussions
of Morales's proclamation and Bonaparte's scheme of colonizing Louisiana.

On one plea the ruling party relied as an excuse for inactivity and as a defence against attack. Their enemies had said and
believed that the democrats possessed neither virtue nor ability enough to carry on the government; but after eighteen
months of trial, as the year 1803 began, the most severe Federalist could not with truth assert that the country had yet
suffered in material welfare from the change. Although the
peace in Europe, after October, 1801, checked the shipping
interests of America, and although France and Spain, returning to the strictness of their colonial system, drove the American flag from their harbors in the Antilles, yet Gallatin at the
close of the first year of peace was able to tell Congress[2] that
the customs revenue, which he had estimated twelve months
before at $9,500,000, had brought into the Treasury
$12,280,000, or much more than had ever before been realized
in a single year from all sources of revenue united. That the
Secretary of the Treasury should miscalculate by one third the
product of his own taxes was strange; but Gallatin liked to
measure the future, not by a probable mean, but by its lowest
possible extreme, and his chief aim was to check extravagance

[1] Jefferson to Thomas Cooper, Nov. 29, 1802; Works, iv. 452.
[2] Report of the Secretary of the Treasury, Dec. 16, 1802. Annals of Congress, 1802–1803, 1276.

in appropriations for objects which he thought bad. His caution increased the popular effect of his success. Opposition became ridiculous when it persisted in grumbling at a system which, beginning with a hazardous reduction of taxes, brought in a single year an immense increase in revenue. The details of Gallatin's finance fretted the Federalists without helping them.

The Federalists were equally unlucky in finding other domestic grievances. The removals from office did not shock the majority. The Judiciary was not again molested. The overwhelming superiority of the democrats was increased by the admission of Ohio, Nov. 29, 1802. No man of sense could deny that the people were better satisfied with their new Administration than they ever had been with the old. Loudly as New England grumbled, the Federalists even there steadily declined in relative strength; while elsewhere an organized body of opposition to the national government hardly existed. From New York to Savannah, no one complained of being forced to work for national objects; South Carolina as well as Virginia was pleased with the power she helped to sway.

Here and there might be found districts in which Federalism tried to hold its own; but the Federalism of Delaware and Maryland was not dangerous, and even in Delaware the Federalist champion Bayard was beaten by Cæsar A. Rodney in his contest for the House, and was driven to take refuge in the Senate. Pennsylvania, New York, Virginia, and North Carolina were nearly unanimous; and beyond the mountains democracy had its own way without the trouble of a discussion. Federalism was already an old-fashioned thing; a subject of ridicule to people who had no faith in forms; a halfway house between the European past and the American future. The mass of Americans had become democratic in thought as well as act; not even another political revolution could undo what had been done. As a democrat, Jefferson's social success was sweeping and final; but he was more than a democrat,—and in his other character, as a Virginia republican of the States-rights school, he was not equally successful.

In the short session of 1802—1803 many signs proved that

the revolution of 1800 had spent its force, and that a reaction was at hand. Congress showed no eagerness to adopt the President's new economies, and dismissed, with silence almost contemptuous, his scheme for building at Washington a large dry-dock in which the navy should be stored for safety and saving. The mint was continued by law for another five years, and twenty thousand dollars were quietly appropriated for its support. Instead of reducing the navy, Congress decided to build four sixteen-gun brigs and fifteen gunboats, and appropriated ninety-six thousand dollars for the brigs alone. The appropriation of two millions as a first instalment toward paying for New Orleans and Florida was another and a longer stride in the old Federalist path of confidence in the Executive and liberality for national objects. The expenditure for 1802, excluding interest on debt, was $3,737,000. Never afterward in United States history did the annual expenditure fall below four millions. The navy, in 1802, cost $915,000; never afterward did it cost less than a million.

The reaction toward Federalist practices was more marked in the attitude of the Executive than in that of Congress. If Jefferson's favorite phrase was true,—that the Federalist differed from the Republican only in the shade more or less of power to be given the Executive,—it was hard to see how any President could be more Federalist than Jefferson himself. A resolution to commit the nation without its knowledge to an indissoluble British alliance, was more than Washington would have dared take; yet this step was taken by the President, and was sustained by Madison, Gallatin, and Robert Smith as fairly within the limits of the Constitution. In regard to another stretch of the treaty-making power, they felt with reason the gravest doubts. When the President and Cabinet decided early in January, 1803, to send Monroe with two million dollars to buy New Orleans and Florida, a question was instantly raised as to the form in which such a purchase could be constitutionally made. Attorney-General Lincoln wished to frame the treaty or convention in such language as to make France appear not as adding new territory to the United States, but as extending already existing territory by an alteration of its boundary. He urged this idea upon the President in a letter written the day of Monroe's nomination to the Senate.[1]

"If the opinion is correct," said he, "that the general government when formed was predicated on the then existing *United* States, and such as could grow out of them, and out of them only; and that its authority is constitutionally limited to the people composing the several political State societies in that Union, and such as might be formed out of them,—would not a direct independent purchase be extending the executive power farther, and be more alarming, and improvable by the opposition and the Eastern States, than the proposed indirect mode?"

Jefferson sent this letter to Gallatin, who treated it without favor.[2]

"If the acquisition of territory is not warranted by the Constitution," said he, "it is not more legal to acquire for one State than for the United States. . . . What could, on his construction, prevent the President and Senate, by treaty, annexing Cuba to Massachusetts, or Bengal to Rhode Island, if ever the acquirement of colonies should become a favorite object with governments, and colonies should be acquired? But does any constitutional objection really exist? . . . To me it would appear, (1) that the United States, as a nation, have an inherent right to acquire territory; (2) that whenever that acquisition is by treaty, the same constituted authorities in whom the treaty-making power is vested have a constitutional right to sanction the acquisition."

Gallatin not only advanced Federal doctrine, but used also what the Virginians always denounced as Federalist play on words. "The United States as a nation" had an inherent right to do whatever the States in union cared to do; but the Republican party, with Jefferson, Madison, and Gallatin at their head, had again and again maintained that the United States *government* had the inherent right to do no act whatever, but was the creature of the States in union; and its acts, if not

[1] Lincoln to Jefferson, Jan. 10, 1803; Jefferson MSS.
[2] Gallatin to Jefferson, Jan. 13, 1803; Gallatin's Works, i. 112.

resulting from an expressly granted power, were no acts at all, but void, and not to be obeyed or regarded by the States. No foreigner, not even Gallatin, could master the theory of Virginia and New England, or distinguish between the nation of States in union which granted certain powers, and the creature at Washington to which these powers were granted, and which might be strengthened, weakened, or abolished without necessarily affecting the nation. Whether the inability to grasp this distinction was a result of clearer insight or of coarser intelligence, the fact was the same; and on this point, in spite of his speech on the Alien and Sedition Acts, Gallatin belonged to the school of Hamilton, while both were of one mind with Dallas. The chief avowed object of Jefferson's election had been to overthrow the reign of this school. No Virginian could be expected within two short years to adopt the opinions of opponents who had been so often branded as "monocrats," because of acting on these opinions. Although the Attorney-General's advice was not followed, the negotiation for New Orleans was begun on the understanding that the purchase, if made, would be an inchoate act which would need express sanction from the States in the shape of an amendment to the Constitution.

There the matter rested. At the moment of Monroe's appointment, the President, according to his letters, had little hope of quick success in the purchase of territory. His plan was to "palliate and endure," unless France should force a war upon him; the constitutional question could wait, and it was accordingly laid aside. Yet the chief ambition of Southern statesmen in foreign affairs was to obtain the Floridas and New Orleans; and in effecting this object they could hardly escape establishing a serious precedent. Already Jefferson had ordered his ministers at Paris to buy this territory, although he thought the Constitution gave him no power to do so; he was willing to increase the national debt for this purpose, even though a national debt was a "mortal canker;" and he ordered his minister, in case Bonaparte should close the Mississippi, to make a permanent alliance with England, or in his own words to "marry ourselves to the British fleet and nation," as the price of New Orleans and Florida. Jefferson foresaw and accepted the consequences of the necessity; he repeatedly referred to them and deprecated them in his letters; but the territory was a vital object, and success there would, as he pointed out, secure forever the triumph of his party even in New England.

"I believe we may consider the mass of the States south and west of Connecticut and Massachusetts as now a consolidated body of Republicanism,"—he wrote to Governor McKean in the midst of the Mississippi excitement.[1] "In Connecticut, Massachusetts, and New Hampshire there is still a Federal ascendency; but it is near its last. If we can settle happily the difficulties of the Mississippi, I think we may promise ourselves smooth seas during our time." What he rightly feared more than any other political disaster was the risk of falling back to the feelings of 1798 and 1799, "when a final dissolution of all bonds, civil and social, appeared imminent."[2] With zeal which never flagged, Jefferson kept up his struggle with the New England oligarchy, whose last move alarmed him. So sensitive was the President, that he joined personally in the fray that distracted New England; and while waiting for news from Monroe, he wrote a defence of his own use of patronage, showing, under the assumed character of a Massachusetts man, that a proportionate division of offices between the two parties would, since the Federalists had so much declined in numbers, leave to them even a smaller share of Federal offices than they still possessed. This paper he sent to Attorney-General Lincoln,[3] to be published in the Boston "Chronicle;" and there, although never recognized, it appeared.

Had the Federalists suspected the authorship, they would have fallen without mercy upon its arguments and its inserted compliment to "the tried ability and patriotism of the present Executive;" but the essay was no sooner published than it was forgotten. The "Chronicle" of June 27, 1803, contained Jefferson's argument founded on the rapid disappearance of the Federalist party; the next issue of the "Chronicle," June 30, contained a single headline, which sounded the death-knell of Federalism altogether: "Louisiana ceded to the United

[1] Jefferson to Governor McKean, Feb. 19, 1803; Jefferson MSS.
[2] Jefferson to Colonel Hawkins, Feb. 18, 1803; Works, iv. 565.
[3] Jefferson's Writings (Ford), viii. 234.

States!" The great news had arrived; and the Federalist orators of July 4, 1803, set about their annual task of foreboding the ruin of society amid the cheers and congratulations of the happiest society the world then knew.

The President's first thought was of the Constitution. Without delay he drew up an amendment, which he sent at once to his Cabinet.[1] "The province of Louisiana is incorporated with the United States and made part thereof," began this curious paper; "the rights of occupancy in the soil and of self-government are confirmed to the Indian inhabitants as they now exist." Then, after creating a special Constitution for the territory north of the 32d parallel, reserving it for the Indians until a new amendment to the Constitution should give authority for white ownership, the draft provided for erecting the portion south of latitude 32° into a territorial government, and vesting the inhabitants with the rights of other territorial citizens.

Gallatin took no notice of this paper, except to acknowledge receiving it.[2] Robert Smith wrote at some length, July 9, dissuading Jefferson from grafting so strange a shoot upon the Constitution.[3]

> "Your great object is to prevent emigrations," said he, "excepting to a certain portion of the ceded territory. This could be effectually accomplished by a constitutional prohibition that Congress should not erect or establish in that portion of the ceded territory situated north of latitude 32° any new state or territorial government, and that they should not grant to any people excepting Indians any right or title whatever to any part of the said portion of the said territory."

Of any jealousy between North and South which could be sharpened by such a restriction of northern and extension of southern territory, Jefferson was unaware. He proposed his amendment in good faith as a means of holding the Union together by stopping its too rapid extension into the wilderness.

[1] Jefferson's Writings (Ford), viii. 241.
[2] Gallatin to Jefferson, July 9, 1803; Works, i. 127.
[3] Jefferson's Writings (Ford), viii. 241.

Coldly as his ideas were received in the Cabinet, Jefferson did not abandon them. Another month passed, and a call was issued for a special meeting of Congress October 17 to provide the necessary legislation for carrying the treaty into effect. As the summer wore away, Jefferson imparted his opinions to persons outside the Cabinet. He wrote, August 12, to Breckinridge of Kentucky a long and genial letter. Congress, he supposed,[1] after ratifying the treaty and paying for the country, "must then appeal to *the nation* for an additional article to the Constitution approving and confirming an act which the nation had not previously authorized. The Constitution has made no provision for our holding foreign territory, still less for incorporating foreign nations into our Union. The Executive, in seizing the fugitive occurrence which so much advances the good of their country, have done an act beyond the Constitution. The Legislature, in casting behind them metaphysical subtleties and risking themselves like faithful servants, must ratify and pay for it, and throw themselves on their country for doing for them unauthorized what we know they would have done for themselves had they been in a situation to do it."

Breckinridge—whose Kentucky Resolutions, hardly five years before, declared that unconstitutional assumptions of power were the surrender of the form of government the people had chosen, and the replacing it by a government which derived its powers from its own will—might be annoyed at finding his principles abandoned by the man who had led him to father them; and surely no leader who had sent to his follower in one year the draft of the Kentucky Resolutions could have expected to send in another the draft of the Louisiana treaty. "I suppose they must then appeal to *the nation*" were the President's words; and he underscored this ominous phrase. "We shall not be disavowed by the nation, and their act of indemnity will confirm and not weaken the Constitution by more strongly marking out its lines." The Constitution, in dealing with the matter of amendments, made no reference to the nation; the word itself was unknown to the Constitution, which invariably spoke of the *Union* wherever

[1] Jefferson to Breckinridge, Aug. 12, 1803; Works, iv. 498.

such an expression was needed; and on the Virginia theory Congress had no right to appeal to the nation at all, except as a nation of States, for an amendment. The language used by Jefferson was the language of centralization, and would have been rejected by him and his party in 1798 or in 1820.

On the day of writing to Breckinridge the President wrote in a like sense to Paine; but in the course of a week despatches arrived from Paris which alarmed him. Livingston had reason to fear a sudden change of mind in the First Consul, and was willing to hasten the movements of President and Congress. Jefferson took the alarm, and wrote instantly to warn Breckinridge and Paine that no whisper of constitutional difficulties must be heard:[1] —

> "I wrote you on the 12th instant on the subject of Louisiana and the constitutional provision which might be necessary for it. A letter received yesterday shows that nothing must be said on that subject which may give a pretext for retracting, but that we should do *sub silentio* what shall be found necessary. Be so good, therefore, as to consider that part of my letter as confidential."

He gave the same warning to his Cabinet:[2] "I infer that the less we say about constitutional difficulties the better; and that what is necessary for surmounting them must be done *sub silentio.*"

He then drew up a new amendment, which he sent to the members of his Cabinet.[3] The July draft was long, elaborate, and almost a new Constitution in itself; the August draft was comparatively brief. "Louisiana as ceded by France to the United States is made a part of the United States. Its white inhabitants shall be citizens, and stand, as to their rights and obligations, on the same footing with other citizens of the United States in analogous situations." The whole country north of the Arkansas River was reserved for Indians until another amendment should be made; and as an afterthought

---

[1] Jefferson's Writings (Ford), viii. 245.
[2] Jefferson to Madison, Aug. 18, 1803; to R. Smith, Aug. 23; Jefferson MSS.
[3] Jefferson to Madison, Aug. 25; to Lincoln, Aug. 30, 1803; Works, iv. 501–505; to Gallatin, Aug. 23, 1803; Gallatin's Works, i. 144.

Florida was to be admitted as a part of the United States "whenever it may be rightfully obtained."

These persistent attempts to preserve his own consistency and that of his party were coldly received. Jefferson found himself alone. Wilson Cary Nicholas, a prominent supporter of the Virginia Resolutions in 1798 and a senator of the United States in 1803, had a long conversation with the President, and in the early days of September wrote him a letter which might have come from Theodore Sedgwick or Roger Griswold in the days of Jay's treaty, when Federalist notions of prerogative ran highest.

> "Upon an examination of the Constitution," wrote Nicholas,[1] "I find the power as broad as it could well be made (Sect. 3, Art. IV.), except that new States cannot be formed out of the old ones without the consent of the State to be dismembered; and the exception is a proof to my mind that it was not intended to confine the Congress in the admission of new States to what was then the territory of the United States. Nor do I see anything in the Constitution that limits the treaty-making power, except the general limitations of the other powers given to the government, and the evident objects for which the government was instituted."

Had Nicholas reasoned thus in 1798 he would have been a Federalist, as he seemed conscious, for he went on to say: "I am aware that this is to us delicate ground, and perhaps my opinions may clash with the opinions given by our friends during the discussion of the British treaty." Nevertheless he argued that if this treaty was unconstitutional, all other treaties were open to the same objection, and the United States government in such a case could make no treaty at all. Finally, he begged the President to avoid giving an opinion on the subject: "I should think it very probable if the treaty should be declared by you to exceed the constitutional authority of the treaty-making power, it would be rejected by the Senate, and if that should not happen, that great use would be made with the people of a wilful breach of the Constitution."

[1] W. C. Nicholas to Jefferson, Sept. 3, 1803; Jefferson MSS.

Such reasoning in the mouths of Virginia Republicans, who had asked and gained office by pledging themselves to their people against the use of implied powers, marked a new epoch. From them the most dangerous of all arguments, the *reductio ad absurdum*, was ominous. What right had they to ask whether any constitutional grant was less complete than the people might have wished or intended? If the Constitution were incomplete or absurd, not the government, but the people of the States who had made it were the only proper authority to correct it. Otherwise, as Nicholas had so often pointed out, their creature would become their tyrant, as had been the law of politics from the beginning.

Jefferson was distressed to find himself thus deserted by his closest friends on an issue which he felt to be vital. The principle of strict construction was the breath of his political life. The Pope could as safely trifle with the doctrine of apostolic succession as Jefferson with the limits of Executive power. If he and his friends were to interpret the treaty-making power as they liked, the time was sure to come when their successors would put so broad an interpretation on other powers of the government as to lead from step to step, until at last Virginia might cower in blood and flames before the shadowy terror called the war-power. With what face could Jefferson then appear before the tribunal of history, and what position could he expect to receive?

All this he felt in his kindly way; and with this weight on his mind he wrote his reply to Nicholas.[1] Beginning with the warning that Bonaparte could not be trusted, and that Congress must act with as little debate as possible, particularly as respected the constitutional difficulty, he went on: —

"I am aware of the force of the observations you make on the power given by the Constitution to Congress to admit new States into the Union without restraining the subject to the territory then constituting the United States. But when I consider that the limits of the United States are precisely fixed by the treaty of 1783, that the Constitution expressly declares itself to be made for the United States, . . . I do not believe it was meant that [Congress] might

[1] Jefferson to W. C. Nicholas, Sept. 7, 1803; Works, iv. 505.

receive England, Ireland, Holland, etc., into it,— which would be the case on your construction. . . . I had rather ask an enlargement of power from the nation, where it is found necessary, than to assume it by a construction which would make our powers boundless. Our peculiar security is in the possession of a written Constitution. Let us not make it a blank paper by construction. I say the same as to the opinion of those who consider the grant of the treaty-making power as boundless. If it is, then we have no Constitution."

From the Virginia standpoint nothing could be better said. Jefferson in this letter made two points clear: the first was that the admission of Louisiana into the Union without express authority from the States made blank paper of the Constitution; the second was that if the treaty-making power was equal to this act, it superseded the Constitution. He entertained no doubts on either point, and time sustained his view; for whether he was right or wrong in law, the Louisiana treaty gave a fatal wound to "strict construction," and the Jeffersonian theories never again received general support. In thus giving them up, Jefferson did not lead the way, but he allowed his friends to drag him in the path they chose. The leadership he sought was one of sympathy and love, not of command; and there was never a time when he thought that resistance to the will of his party would serve the great ends he had in view. The evils which he foresaw were remote: in the hands of true Republicans the Constitution, even though violated, was on the whole safe; the precedent, though alarming, was exceptional. So it happened that after declaring in one sentence the Constitution at an end if Nicholas had his way, Jefferson in the next breath offered his acquiescence in advance:—

"I confess I think it important in the present case to set an example against broad construction by appealing for new power to the people. If, however, our friends shall think differently, certainly I shall acquiesce with satisfaction, confiding that the good sense of our country will correct the evil of construction when it shall produce ill effects."

With these words Jefferson closed his mouth on this subject forever. Although his future silence led many of his friends to think that he ended by altering his opinion, and by admitting that his purchase of Louisiana was constitutional, no evidence showed the change; but rather one is led to believe that when in later life he saw what he called the evils of construction grow until he cried against them with violence almost as shrill as in 1798, he felt most strongly the fatal error which his friends had forced him to commit, and which he could neither repudiate nor defend. He had declared that he would acquiesce with satisfaction in making blank paper of the Constitution.

A few weeks later, Oct. 17, 1803, Congress met. The President's Message had little to say of domestic affairs. The Kaskaskia Indians had sold their territory to the United States, the revenue had again exceeded the estimate, more than three millions of debt had been paid within the year. Much was said about war in Europe and the rights and duties of neutrals, about gunboats which were no longer needed, and about the unsettled boundary in Maine and at the Lake of the Woods, but not a word about the constitutional difficulties raised by the Louisiana treaty. "With the wisdom of Congress it will rest," said Jefferson, "to take those ulterior measures which may be necessary for the immediate occupation and temporary government of the country, for its incorporation into our Union, for rendering the change of government a blessing to our newly adopted brethren, for securing to them the rights of conscience and of property, for confirming to the Indian inhabitants their occupancy and self-government." These were the points of his proposed amendment; but he gave no sign of his opinion that Congress was incompetent to deal with them, and that the Senate was equally incompetent to make the treaty valid.

There were good reasons for silence. Not only were Livingston's letters alarming, but the Marquis of Casa Yrujo, the friend and benefactor of the Administration, sent to Madison one protest after another against the sale of Louisiana.[1] He quoted St.-Cyr's letter of July, 1802, which bound France not

[1] Yrujo to Madison, Sept. 4, Sept. 27, Oct. 12, 1803; State Papers, ii. 569, 570.

to alienate the province, and he declared that France had never carried out the conditions of contract in regard to Tuscany, and therefore could not rightfully treat Louisiana as her own. A probable war with Spain stared Jefferson in the face, even if Bonaparte should raise no new difficulties. The responsibility for a mistake was great, and no one could blame Jefferson if he threw his burden on Congress.

Chapter V

IF PRESIDENT JEFFERSON and Secretary Madison, who wrote the Resolutions of 1798, acquiesced, in 1803, in a course of conduct which as Jefferson believed made blank paper of the Constitution, and which, whether it did so or not, certainly made waste paper of the Virginia and Kentucky Resolutions, no one could expect that their followers would be more consistent or more rigid than themselves. Fortunately, all the more prominent Republicans of 1798 had been placed in office by the people as a result of popular approval, and were ready to explain their own views. In the Senate sat John Breckinridge of Kentucky, supposed to be the author of the Kentucky Resolutions, and known as their champion in the Kentucky legislature. From Virginia came John Taylor of Caroline, the reputed father of the Virginia Resolutions, and the soundest of strict constructionists. Twenty years later, his "Construction Construed" and "New Views of the Constitution" became the text-books of the States-rights school. His colleague was Wilson Cary Nicholas, who had also taken a prominent part in supporting the Virginia Resolutions, and whose devotion to the principles of strict construction was beyond doubt. One of the South Carolina senators was Pierce Butler; one of those from North Carolina was David Stone; Georgia was represented by Abraham Baldwin and James Jackson,—stanch States-rights Republicans all. In the House a small coterie of States-rights Republicans controlled legislation. Speaker Macon was at their head; John Randolph, chairman of the Ways and Means Committee, was their mouthpiece. Joseph H. Nicholson of Maryland, and Cæsar A. Rodney of Delaware, supported Randolph on the committee; while two of President Jefferson's sons-in-law, Thomas Mann Randolph and John W. Eppes, sat in the Virginia delegation. Both in Senate and House the Southern Republicans of the Virginia school held supremacy; their power was so absolute as to admit no contest; they were at the flood of that tide which had set in three years before. In the Senate they controlled twenty-five votes against nine; in the House, one hundred and two against thirty-nine. Virginia ruled the

United States, and the Republicans of 1798 ruled Virginia. The ideal moment of Republican principles had arrived.

This moment was big with the fate of theories. Other debates of more practical importance may have frequently occurred,—for in truth whatever the decision of Congress might have been, it would in no case have affected the result that Louisiana was to enter the Union; and this inevitable result overshadowed all theory,—but no debate ever took place in the Capitol which better deserved recollection.

Of extraordinary ability Congress contained but little, and owing to the meagre character of the reports, appeared to contain even less than it actually possessed; but if no one rose to excellence either of logic or rhetoric, the speakers still dealt with the whole subject, and rounded the precedent with all the argument and illustration that a future nation could need. Both actions and words spoke with decision and distinctness till that time unknown in American politics.

The debate began first in the House, where Gaylord Griswold of New York, Oct. 24, 1803, moved for such papers as the Government might possess tending to show the value of the title to Louisiana as against Spain. Under the lead of John Randolph the House refused the call. That this decision clashed with the traditions of the Republican party was proved by the vote. With a majority of three to one, Randolph succeeded in defeating Griswold only by fifty-nine to fifty-seven; while Nicholson, Rodney, Varnum of Massachusetts, and many other stanch Republicans voted with the Federalists.

The next day the House took up the motion for carrying the treaty into effect. Griswold began again, and without knowing it repeated Jefferson's reasoning. The framers of the Constitution, he said, "carried their ideas to the time when there might be an extended population; but they did not carry them forward to the time when an addition might be made to the Union of a territory equal to the whole United States, which additional territory might overbalance the existing territory, and thereby the rights of the present citizens of the United States be swallowed up and lost." The power to admit new States referred only to the territory existing when the Constitution was framed; but this right, whatever it might be, was vested in Congress, not in the Executive. In promising to admit Louisiana as a State into the Union, the treaty assumed for the President power which in any case could not have been his. Finally, the treaty gave to French and Spanish ships special privileges for twelve years in the port of New Orleans; while the Constitution forbade any preference to be given, by any regulation of commerce or revenue, to the ports of one State over those of another.

John Randolph next rose. Just thirty years old, with a sarcasm of tone and manner that overbore remonstrance, and with an authority in the House that no one contested, Randolph spoke the voice of Virginia with autocratic distinctness. His past history was chiefly marked by the ardor with which, from 1798 to 1800, he had supported the principles of his party and encouraged resistance to the national government. He had gone beyond Jefferson and Madison in willingness to back their theories by force, and to fix by a display of Virginia power the limit beyond which neither Executive, Congress, nor Judiciary should pass. Even then he probably cared little for what he called the "parchment barriers" of the Constitution: in his mind force was the real balance,—force of State against force of Union; and any measure which threatened to increase the power of the national government beyond that of the State, was sure of his enmity. A feather might turn the balance, so nice was the adjustment; and Randolph again and again cried with violence against feathers.

In the Louisiana debate, Randolph spoke in a different tone. The Constitution, he said, could not restrict the country to particular limits, because at the time of its adoption the boundary was unsettled on the northeastern, northwestern, and southern frontiers. The power to settle disputes as to limits was indispensable; it existed in the Constitution, had been repeatedly exercised, and involved the power of extending boundaries.

This argument was startling in the mouth of one who had helped to arm the State of Virginia against a moderate exercise of implied powers. Randolph asserted that the right to annex Louisiana, Texas, Mexico, South America, if need be, was involved in the right to run a doubtful boundary line between the Georgia territory and Florida. If this power existed in the government, it necessarily devolved on the Executive as the organ for dealing with foreign States. Thus Griswold's first objection was answered.

Griswold objected in the second place that the treaty made New Orleans a favored port. "I regard this stipulation," replied Randolph, "as a part of the price of the territory. It was a condition which the party ceding had a right to require, and to which we had a right to assent. The right to acquire involves the right to give the equivalent demanded." Randolph did not further illustrate this sweeping principle of implied power.

After the subject had been treated by speakers of less weight, Roger Griswold of Connecticut took the floor. So long as his party had been in office, the vigor of the Constitution had found no warmer friend than he; but believing New England to have fallen at the mercy of Virginia, he was earnest to save her from the complete extinction which he thought near at hand. Griswold could not deny that the Constitution gave the power to acquire territory: his Federalist principles were too fresh to dispute such an inherent right; and Gouverneur Morris, as extreme as Federalist as himself, whose words had been used in the Constitution, averred that he knew in 1788 as well as he knew in 1803, that all North America must at length be annexed, and that it would have been Utopian to restrain the movement.[1] This was old Federalist doctrine, resting on "inherent rights," on nationality and broad construction,—the Federalism of President Washington, which the Republican party from the beginning denounced as monarchical. Griswold would not turn his back on it; he still took a liberal view of the power, and even stretched it beyond reasonable shape to accord with Morris's idea. "A new territory and new subjects," said he, "may undoubtedly be obtained by conquest and by purchase; but neither the conquest nor the purchase can incorporate them into the Union. They must remain in the condition of colonies, and be governed accordingly." This claim gave the central government despotic power over its new purchase; but it declared that a treaty which pledged the nation to admit the

[1] Morris to H. W. Livingston, Nov. 25, 1803. Writings of Gouverneur Morris, iii. 185.

people of Louisiana into the Union must be invalid, because it assumed that "the President and Senate may admit at will any foreign nation into this copartnership without the consent of the States,"—a power directly repugnant to the principles of the compact. In substance, Griswold maintained that either under the war power or under the treaty-making power the government could acquire territory, and as a matter of course could hold and govern that territory as it pleased,—despotically if necessary, or for selfish objects; but that the President and Senate could not admit a foreign people into the Union, as a State. Yet to this, the treaty bound them.

To meet this attack the Republicans put forward their two best men,—Joseph H. Nicholson of Maryland, and Cæsar A. Rodney of Delaware. The task was difficult, and Nicholson showed his embarrassment at the outset. "Whether the United States," said he, "as a sovereign and independent empire, has a right to acquire territory is one thing; but whether they can admit that territory into the Union upon an equal footing with the other States is a question of a very different nature." He refused to discuss this latter issue; in his opinion it was not before the House.

This flinching was neither candid nor courageous; but it was within the fair limits of a lawyer's if not of a statesman's practice, and Nicholson at least saved his consistency. On the simpler question, whether "a sovereign nation," as he next said, "had a right to acquire new territory," he spoke with as much emphasis as Roger Griswold and Gouverneur Morris, and he took the same ground. The separate States had surrendered their sovereignty by adopting the Constitution; "the right to declare war was given to Congress; the right to make treaties, to the President and Senate. Conquest and purchase alone are the means by which nations acquire territory." Griswold was right, then, in the ground he had taken; but Nicholson, not satisfied with gaining his point through the treaty-making power, which was at least express, added: "The right must exist somewhere: it is essential to independent sovereignty." As it was prohibited to the States, the power was necessarily vested in the United States.

This general implication, that powers inherent in sovereignty which had not been expressly reserved to the States were vested in the national government, was not more radical centralization than Nicholson's next point. The treaty gave to the port of New Orleans a decided preference over all other ports of the United States, although the Constitution said that no preference should be given to the ports of one State over those of another. To this objection Nicholson replied that Louisiana was not a State. "It is a territory purchased by the United States in their confederate capacity, and may be disposed of by them at pleasure. It is in the nature of a colony whose commerce may be regulated without any reference to the Constitution." The new territory, therefore, was in the nature of a European colony; the United States government might regulate its commerce without regard to the Constitution, give its population whatever advantages Congress might see fit, and use it to break down New England—or slavery.

With the fecund avowal that Louisiana must be governed by Congress at pleasure without reference to the Constitution, Nicholson sat down; and Cæsar Rodney took the floor,—an able and ingenious lawyer, who came to the House with the prestige of defeating the Federalist champion Bayard. If Randolph and Nicholson, like the mouse in the fable nibbling at the cords which bound the lion of Power, had left one strand still unsevered, the lion stood wholly free before Rodney ended. He began by appealing to the "general welfare" clause,—a device which the Republican party and all States-rights advocates once regarded as little short of treason. "I cannot perceive," said he, " why within the fair meaning of this general provision is not included the power of increasing our territory, if necessary for the general welfare or common defence." This argument in such a mouth might well have sent a chill to the marrow of every Republican of 1798; but this was not the whole. He next invoked the "necessary and proper" clause, even at that early time familiar to every strict constructionist as one of the most dangerous instruments of centralization. "Have we not also vested in us every power necessary for carrying such a treaty into effect, in the words of the Constitution which give Congress the authority to 'make all laws which shall be necessary and proper for carrying into execution the foregoing powers, and all other powers vested by this Constitution in the government of the United States or in any department or officer thereof'?"

One more point was affirmed by Rodney. Gaylord Griswold had maintained that the territory mentioned in the Constitution was the territory existing in 1789. Rodney denied it. Congress, he said, had express power to "make all needful rules and regulations" respecting any and all territory; it had no need to infer this power from other grants. As for the special privilege of trade accorded to New Orleans, it violated in no way the Constitution; it was indirectly a benefit to all the States, and a preference to none.

The Northern democrats also supported these views; but the opinions of Northern democrats on constitutional questions carried little weight. Neither among them nor among Southern Republicans did any member question what Randolph, Nicholson, and Rodney had said. Macon sat silent in his chair, while John Randolph closed the debate. As though he could not satisfy himself with leaving a doubt as to the right of Government to assume what powers it wanted, Randolph took this moment to meet Roger Griswold's assertion that the United States government could not lawfully incorporate Great Britain or France into the Union. Randolph affirmed that, so far as the Constitution was concerned, this might be done. "We cannot because we cannot."

The reply was disingenuous, but decisive. The question was not whether the States in union could lawfully admit England or France into the Union, for no one denied that the States could do what they pleased. Griswold only affirmed that the people of the States had never delegated to John Randolph or Thomas Jefferson, or to a majority of the United States Senate, the right to make a political revolution by annexing a foreign State. Jefferson agreed with Griswold that they had not; if they had, "then we have no Constitution" was his comment. Yet not a voice was raised in the Administration party against Randolph's views. After one day's debate, ninety Republicans supported Randolph with their votes, and twenty-five Federalists alone protested. Of these twenty-five, not less than seventeen were from New England.

A week afterward, Nov. 2, 1803, the Senate took up the subject. After several speeches had been made without touching deeply the constitutional difficulty, Senator Pickering of Massachusetts took the floor, and in a few words stated the extreme New England doctrine. Like Griswold and Gouverneur Morris, he affirmed the right of conquest or of purchase, and the right to govern the territory so acquired as a dependent province; but neither the President nor Congress could incorporate this territory in the Union, nor could the incorporation lawfully be effected even by an ordinary amendment to the Constitution. "I believe the assent of each individual State to be necessary for the admission of a foreign country as an associate in the Union, in like manner as in a commercial house the consent of each member would be necessary to admit a new partner into the company." With his usual skill in saying what was calculated to annoy,—a skill in which he had no superior,—he struck one truth which no other eyes would see. "I believe that this whole transaction has been purposely wrapped in obscurity by the French government. The boundary of Louisiana, for instance, on the side of Florida is in the treaty really unintelligible; and yet nothing was more easy to define."

Pickering was followed by Dayton of New Jersey, and he by the celebrated John Taylor of Caroline, the senator from Virginia, whose Resolutions of 1798, with echoes which were to ring louder and louder for sixty years to come, had declared "deep regret that a spirit has in sundry instances been manifested by the federal government to enlarge its powers by forced constructions of the constitutional charter which defines them; and that indications have appeared of a design to expound certain general phrases . . . so as to consolidate the States by degrees into one sovereignty." In purchasing Louisiana, the United States government had done an act identical with the despotic acts of consolidated European governments,—it had bought a foreign people without their consent and without consulting the States, and had pledged itself to incorporate this people in the Union. Colonel Taylor's argument, so far as it went, supported the act; and although it evaded, or tried to evade, the most difficult points of objection, it went as far as the farthest in the path of forced construction. On the right to acquire territory, Taylor took the ground taken by Joseph Nicholson in the House,—he inferred it from the war and treaty powers: "If the means of acquiring and the right of holding are equivalent to the right of acquiring territory, then this right merged from the separate States to the United States, as indispensably annexed to the treaty-making power and the power of making war." This part of the Federalist scheme he adopted without a murmur; but when he came to the next inevitable step, he showed the want of courage often felt by honest men trying to be untrue to themselves. This territory which the Washington government could acquire by conquest or treaty,—what was its status? Could the Washington government "dispose of" it, as the government was expressly permitted to dispose of the territory it already held under the Constitution; or must Louisiana be governed extra-constitutionally by "inherent powers," as Griswold maintained; or ought Congress to ask for new and express authority from the States? Taylor took the first position. The treaty-making power, he said, was not defined; it was competent to acquire territory. This territory by the acquisition became a part of the Union, a portion of the territories of the United States, and might be "disposed of" by Congress without an amendment to the Constitution. Although Taylor differed with Jefferson on this point, no objection could be made to the justice of his opinion except that it left the true dispute to be settled by mere implication. The power of the government over the territory had no limits, so far as Colonel Taylor defined it; yet it either could or could not admit the new territory as a State. If it could, the government could alter the original compact by admitting a foreign country as a State; if it could not, either the treaty was void, or government must apply to the people of the States for new powers.

Uriah Tracy of Connecticut replied to Taylor in a speech which was probably the best on his side of the question. His opposition to the purchase was grounded on a party reason: "The relative strength which this admission gives to a Southern and Western interest is contradictory to the principles of our original Union." The President and Senate had no power to make States, and the treaty was void.

"I have no doubt but we can obtain territory either by

conquest or compact, and hold it, even all Louisiana and a thousand times more if you please, without violating the Constitution. We can hold territory; but to admit the inhabitants into the Union, to make citizens of them, and States, by treaty, we cannot constitutionally do; and no subsequent act of legislation, or even ordinary amendment to our Constitution, can legalize such measures. If done at all, they must be done by universal consent of all the States or partners to our political association; and this universal consent I am positive can never be obtained to such a pernicious measure as the admission of Louisiana,—of a world, and such a world, into our Union. This would be absorbing the Northern States, and rendering them as insignificant in the Union as they ought to be, if by their own consent the measure should be adopted."

Tracy's speech was answered by Breckinridge of Kentucky, who had induced the Kentucky legislature, only five years before, to declare itself determined "tamely to submit to undelegated, and consequently unlimited, powers in no man or body of men on earth;" and to assert further that submission to the exercise of such powers "would be to surrender the form of government we have chosen, and to live under one deriving its powers from its own will, and not from our authority." When he came to deal with the same question in a new form, he glided with extreme delicacy over the thin ice of the Constitution. His answer to Tracy was an admission. He pointed out that the Federalist argument carried centralization further than it was carried by this treaty. "By his construction," said Breckinridge, "territories and citizens are considered and held as the property of the government of the United States, and may consequently be used as dangerous engines in the hands of the government against the States and people." This was true. The Federalists maintained that such territory could be held only as property, not as part of the Union; and the consequences of this doctrine, if granted, were immense. Breckinridge argued that the admission by treaty of a foreign State was less dangerous, and therefore more constitutional, than such ownership of foreign territory. The conclusion was not perfectly logical, and was the less so because he denied the power in neither case. "Could we not," he went on, quoting from Tracy's speech, "incorporate in the Union some foreign nation containing ten millions of inhabitants,—Africa, for instance,—and thereby destroy our government? Certainly the thing would be possible if Congress would do it and the people consent to it. . . . The true construction must depend on the manifest import of the instrument and the good sense of the community." What then had become of the old Republican principle that acts of undelegated authority were no acts at all? Or had the States really delegated to the President and two thirds of the Senate the right to "destroy our government"? If Breckinridge had expressed these ideas in his Kentucky Resolutions, American history would have contained less dispute as to the meaning of States-rights and the powers of the central government; but Breckinridge himself would have then led the Federalist, not the Republican party.

Breckinridge's speech was followed by one from Pickering's colleague, the young senator from Massachusetts, son of John Adams, the Federalist President whom Jefferson had succeeded. The Federalist majority in Massachusetts was divided; one portion followed the lead of the Essex Junto, the other and larger part yielded unwillingly to the supremacy of Alexander Hamilton and George Cabot. When in the spring of 1803 both seats of Massachusetts in the United States Senate became by chance vacant at once, the Essex Junto wished to choose Timothy Pickering for the long term. The moderate Federalists set Pickering aside, elected John Quincy Adams, then thirty-six years old, for the long term, and allowed Pickering to enter the Senate only as junior senator to a man more than twenty years younger than himself, whose father had but three years before dismissed Pickering abruptly and without explanation from his Cabinet. Neither of the senators owned a temper or character likely to allay strife. The feud between them was bitter and life-long. From the moment of their appearance in the Senate they took opposite sides.

Pickering held with Tracy, Griswold, and all the extreme Federalists that the treaty was void, and that the admission of Louisiana as a State without the separate consent of each State in the Union was a rupture of the compact, which broke the tie and left each State free to act independently of the rest. His colleague was as decided in favor of the Louisiana purchase as Pickering and Tracy were opposed to it; but he too agreed that the treaty was outside of the Constitution, and he urged the Senate to take this view. He believed that even Connecticut would approve of admitting Louisiana if the Southern majority had the courage to try the experiment. "I firmly believe, if an amendment to the Constitution, amply sufficient for the accomplishment of everything for which we have contracted, shall be proposed, as I think it ought, it will be adopted by the legislature of every State in the Union." This was in effect the view which Jefferson had pressed upon his Cabinet and friends.

Then came Wilson Cary Nicholas. Five years before, in the Virginia legislature, Nicholas had spoken and voted for the Resolutions moved by his colleague, John Taylor of Caroline. He then said that if the principle were once established that Congress had a right to use powers not expressly delegated, "the tenure by which we hold our liberty would be entirely subverted: instead of rights independent of human control, we must be content to hold by the courtesy and forbearance of those whom we have heretofore considered as the servants of the people." Instead of using the same language in 1803, he accepted his colleague's views as to the extent of the treaty-making power, and added reasoning of his own. If the spirit of New England Calvinism contained an element of self-deceit, Virginia metaphysics occasionally ran into slippery evasion, as the argument of Nicholas showed. He evaded a straightforward opinion on every point at issue. The treaty-making power was undefined, he thought, but not unlimited; the general limitations of the Constitution applied to it, not the special limitations of power; and of course the treaty must be judged by its conformity with the general meaning of the compact. He then explained away the apparent difficulties in the case. "If the third article of the treaty," said he, "is an engagement to incorporate the territory of Louisiana into the Union of the United States and to make it a State, it cannot be considered as an unconstitutional exercise of the treaty-making power, for it will not be asserted by any rational man that the territory is incorporated as a State by the treaty itself." This incorporation was stipulated to be done "according to the principles of the Constitution," and the States might do it or not, at their discretion: if it could not be done constitutionally, it might be done by amendment.

Nothing could be more interesting than to see the discomfort with which the champions of States-rights tossed themselves from one horn to the other of the Federalist dilemma. The Federalists cared little on which horn their opponents might choose to impale themselves, for both were equally fatal. Either Louisiana must be admitted as a State, or must be held as territory. In the first case the old Union was at an end; in the second case the national government was an empire, with "inherent sovereignty" derived from the war and treaty-making powers,—in either case the Virginia theories were exploded. The Virginians felt the embarassment, and some of them, like Nicholas, tried to hide it in a murmur of words and phrases; but the Republicans of Kentucky and Tennessee were impatient of such restraint, and slight as it was, thrust it away. The debate was closed by Senator Cocke of Tennessee, who defied opposition. "I assert," said he, "that the treaty-making powers in this country are competent to the full and free exercise of their best judgment in making treaties without limitation of power."

On this issue the vote was taken without further discussion, and by twenty-six to five the Senate passed the bill. Pickering of Massachusetts, Tracy and Hillhouse of Connecticut, and the two senators Wells and White from Delaware, were alone in opposition.

The result of these debates in the Senate and House decided only one point. Every speaker, without distinction of party, agreed that the United States government had the power to acquire new territory either by conquest or by treaty; the only difference of opinion regarded the disposition of this territory after it was acquired. Did Louisiana belong to the central government at Washington, or to the States? The Federalists maintained that the central government, representing the States in union, might, if it pleased, as a consequence of its inherent sovereignty, hold the rest of America in its possession and govern it as England governed Jamaica or as Spain was governing Louisiana, but without the consent of the States could not admit such new territory into the Union. The Republicans seemed rather inclined to think that new territory acquired by war or conquest would become at once a part of the general territory mentioned in the Constitution, and as such might be admitted by Congress as a State, or otherwise disposed of as the general welfare might require, but that in either case neither the people nor the States had anything to do with the matter. At bottom, both doctrines were equally fatal to the old status of the Union. In one case the States, formed or to be formed, east of the Mississippi had established a government which could hold the rest of the world in despotic control, and which bought a foreign people as it might buy cattle, to rule over them as their owner; in the other case, the government was equally powerful, and might besides admit the purchased or conquered territory into the Union as States. The Federalist theory was one of empire, the Republican was one of assimilation; but both agreed that the moment had come when the old Union must change its character. Whether the government at Washington could possess Louisiana as a colony or admit it as a State, was a difference of no great matter if the cession were to hold good; the essential point was that for the first time in the national history all parties agreed in admitting that the government could govern.

Chapter VI

HARDLY WAS it decided that the government had an inherent right to acquire territory and annex foreign States, when the next question forced itself on Congress for settlement,—What were the powers of Congress over the new territory?

Three paths were open. The safest was to adopt an amendment of the Constitution admitting Louisiana into the Union and extending over it the express powers of Congress as they had applied to the old territory of the United States. The second course was to assume that the new territory became, by the fact of acquisition, assimilated to the old, and might be "disposed of" in the same way. The third was to hold it apart as a peculiar estate, and govern it, subject to treaty stipulations, by an undefined power implied in the right to acquire,—on the principle that government certainly had the right to govern what it had the right to buy.

The first plan, which was in effect Jefferson's original idea, preserved the theory of the Constitution as far as was possible; but the Republicans feared the consequences with France and Spain of throwing a doubt on the legality of the treaty. Another reason for their activity lay in the peculiarities of their character as a party. The Northern democrats, never strict constructionists, knew and cared little for the dogmas of their Southern allies. The Southern Republicans, especially those of the Virginia school, were honest in their jealousy of the central government; but as a class they were impatient of control and unused to self-restraint: they liked to do their will, and counted so surely on their own strength and honesty of purpose that they could not feel the need of a curb upon their power. None of them moved. The only man in Congress who showed a sincere wish to save what could be preserved of the old constitutional theory was Senator Adams of Massachusetts, who called upon Madison October 28, before the debate, to ask whether the Executive intended, through any member of either House, to propose an amendment of the Constitution to carry the treaty into effect.[1] Madison talked to him openly, and expressed ideas which as far as they went were the same with those of Jefferson. For his own part, said Madison, had he been on the floor of Congress he should have seen no difficulty in acknowledging that the Constitution had not provided for such a case as this; that it must be estimated by the magnitude of the object; and that those who had agreed to it must rely upon the candor of their country for justification. Probably, when the immediate pressure of special legislation was past, the matter would be attended to; and if he should have any agency in concerting the measure, he would request its mover to consult Senator Adams. There for a month the matter rested, while Congress adopted its special legislation.

At length, November 25, Senator Adams, becoming impatient, called again on the Secretary of State, with the draft of an amendment which he meant to propose. Madison thought it too comprehensive, and suggested a simple declaration to meet the special case: "Louisiana is hereby admitted into this Union." On the same day Adams accordingly moved for a committee, but could not obtain a seconder. The Senate unanimously refused even the usual civility of a reference. No more was ever heard of amending the Constitution.

With almost unanimous consent Louisiana was taken into the Union by the treaty-making power, without an amendment. This point being fixed, Congress had also to determine whether the new territory should be governed by authority drawn from the power of acquisition, or whether it should be merged in the old territory which Congress had express right to "dispose of" and regulate at will.

By an act of sovereignty as despotic as the corresponding acts of France and Spain, Jefferson and his party had annexed to the Union a foreign people and a vast territory, which profoundly altered the relations of the States and the character of their nationality. By similar acts they governed both. Jefferson, in his special Message of October 23, requested Congress to make "such temporary provisions . . . as the case may require." A select committee, Randolph being chairman, immediately reported a Bill, emanating from the Executive.

[1] Documents relating to New England Federalism, pp. 156, 157; Diary of J. Q. Adams, i. 267.

"It was a startling Bill," was the criticism[1] of a man who shared in much legislation, "continuing the existing Spanish government; putting the President in the place of the King of Spain; putting all the territorial officers in the place of the King's officers, and placing the appointment of all these officers in the President alone without reference to the Senate. Nothing could be more incompatible with our Constitution than such a government,—a mere emanation of Spanish despotism, in which all powers, civil and military, legislative, executive, and judicial, were in the Intendant General, representing the King; and where the people, far from possessing political rights, were punishable arbitrarily for presuming to meddle with political subjects."

The Federalists immediately objected that the powers conferred on the President by this bill were unconstitutional. The Republicans replied, in effect, that the Constitution was made for States, not for territories. Rodney explained the whole intent of his party in advocating the bill: "It shows that Congress have a power in the territories which they cannot exercise in the States, and that the limitations of power found in the Constitution are applicable to States and not to territories."[2] John Randolph defended the assumption of power on the ground of necessity, and maintained that the government of the United States, with respect to this territory, possessed the powers of European sovereignty: "Gentlemen will see the necessity of the United States taking possession of this country in the capacity of sovereigns, in the same extent as that of the existing government of the province." The Bill passed Congress by a party vote, and was approved by Jefferson, October 31,[3] without delay.

The Act of October 31 was a temporary measure rather for taking possession of the territory than for governing it. Four weeks later, Senator Breckinridge moved for a committee to prepare a territorial form of government for Louisiana. Two senators of the States-rights school,—Jackson and Baldwin of Georgia,—besides Breckinridge and J. Q. Adams, were ap-

[1] Examination of the Decision of the Supreme Court in the case of Dred Scott. By Thomas H. Benton, p. 55.
[2] Annals of Congress, 1803–1804, p. 514.
[3] Act of October 31, 1803. Annals of Congress, 1803–1804. App. p. 1245.

pointed on this committee; and they reported, December 30, a Bill that settled the principle on which the new territory should be governed.

Breckinridge's Bill divided the purchased country at the 33d parallel, the line which afterward divided the State of Arkansas from the State of Louisiana. The country north of that line was named the District of Louisiana, and, after some dispute, was subjected to the territorial government of the Indiana Territory, consisting of a governor, secretary, and judges without a legislature, all controlled by the Ordinance of 1787. This arrangement implied that Congress considered the new territory as assimilated to the old, and "disposed of" it by the same constitutional power.

The northern district contained few white inhabitants, and its administrative arrangements chiefly concerned Indians; but the southern district, which received the name "Territory of Orleans," included an old and established society, numbering fifty thousand persons. The territory of Ohio numbered only forty-five thousand persons by the census of 1800, while the States of Delaware and Rhode Island contained less than seventy thousand. The treaty guaranteed that "the inhabitants of the ceded territory shall be incorporated in the Union of the United States, and admitted as soon as possible, according to the principles of the Federal Constitution, to the enjoyment of all the rights, advantages, and immunities of citizens of the United States; and in the mean time they shall be maintained and protected in the free enjoyment of their liberty, property, and the religion which they profess."

Breckinridge's Bill, which was probably drawn by Madison in co-operation with the President, created a territorial government in which the people of Louisiana were to have no share. The governor and secretary were to be appointed by the President for three years; the legislative council consisted of thirteen members to be appointed by the President without consulting the Senate, and was to be convened and prorogued by the governor as he might think proper. The judicial officers, also appointed by the President, were to hold office for four years, instead of the usual term of good behavior. The right to a jury trial was restricted to cases where the matter in controversy exceeded twenty dollars, and to capital cases in criminal prosecutions. The slave-trade was restricted by threefold prohibitions: 1. No slave could be imported from abroad; 2. No slave could be brought into the territory from the Union who had been imported from abroad since May 1, 1798; 3. No slave could be introduced into the territory, "directly or indirectly," except by an American citizen "removing into said territory for actual settlement, and being, at the time of such removal, *bona fide* owner of such slave,"—the penalty being three hundred dollars fine and the slave's freedom.

This Bill seemed to set the new Territory apart, as a peculiar estate, to be governed by a power implied in the right to acquire it. The debate which followed its introduction into the Senate was not reported, but the Journal mentioned that Senator Adams, Jan. 10, 1804, moved three Resolutions, to the effect that no constitutional power existed to tax the people of Louisiana without their consent, and carried but three voices with him in support of the principle.[1] Other attempts were made to arrest the exercise of arbitrary power without better success, and the Bill passed the Senate, Feb. 18, 1804, after six weeks consideration, by a vote of twenty to five.

Few gaps in the parliamentary history of the Union left so serious a want as was caused by the failure to report the Senate debate on this Bill; but the report of the House debate partly supplied the loss, for the Bill became there a target for attack from every quarter. Michael Leib, one of the extreme Pennsylvania democrats, began by objecting to the power given to the governor over the Louisiana legislature as "royal." His colleague, Andrew Gregg, objected altogether to the appointment of the council by the President. Varnum of Massachusetts denounced the whole system, and demanded an elective legislature. Matthew Lyon, who represented Kentucky, compared Jefferson to Bonaparte. "Do we not owe something on this score to principle?" he asked. Speaker Macon took the same ground. George W. Campbell of Tennessee was more precise. "It really establishes a complete despotism," he said; "it does not evince a single trait of liberty; it does not confer one single right to which they are entitled under the treaty; it does not extend to them the benefits of the

[1] Diary of J. Q. Adams (Jan. 10, 1804), i. 287.

Federal Constitution, or declare when, hereafter, they shall receive them." On the other hand Dr. Eustis, of Boston, took the ground that a despotism was necessary: "I am one of those who believe that the principles of civil liberty cannot suddenly be engrafted on a people accustomed to a regimen of a directly opposite hue." In contradiction to the language of the treaty and the principles of his party, he went on to say that the people of Louisiana had no rights: "I consider them as standing in nearly the same relation to us as if they were a conquered country." Other speakers supported him. The Louisianians, it was said, had shed tears when they saw the American flag hoisted in place of the French; they were not prepared for self-government. When the treaty was under discussion, the speakers assumed that the people of Louisiana were so eager for annexation as to make an appeal to them useless; when they were annexed, they were so degraded as not to be worth consulting.

The House refused to tolerate such violation of principle, and by the majority of seventy-four to twenty-three struck out the section which vested legislative powers in the President's nominees. John Randolph did not vote; but his friend Nicholson and the President's son-in-law, Thomas Mann Randolph, were in the minority. By fifty-eight to forty-two the House then adopted an amendment which vested legislative powers, after the first year, in an elective council; by forty-four to thirty-seven the restriction on jury trials was rejected; the Act was then limited to two years; and so altered it passed the House March 17, 1804, several Republicans recording their votes against it to the end.

When the Bill, thus amended, came back to the Senate, that body, March 20, summarily disagreed with all the changes made by the House except the limitation of time, which the Senate further reduced to one year. This change reconciled the House, not very cheerfully, to recede, and March 23 the Bill, as it passed the Senate, became law by a vote of fifty-one to forty-five. With the passage of this Act and its twin statute for collecting duties in the ceded territory, the precedent was complete. Louisiana received a government in which its people, who had been solemnly promised all the rights of American citizens, were set apart, not as citizens, but as subjects lower in the political scale than the meanest tribes of Indians, whose right to self-government was never questioned.

By these measures the Executive and the Legislature recorded their decision in regard to the powers of government over national territory. The Judiciary was not then consulted; but twenty-five years afterward, in the year 1828, Chief-Justice Marshall was in his turn required to give an opinion, and he added the final authority of the Supreme Court to the precedent. With characteristic wisdom he claimed for the government both the constitutional and the extra-constitutional powers in question. The case concerned the rights of inhabitants of Florida, who he said—

> "Do not participate in political power; they do not share in the government till Florida shall become a State. In the mean time Florida continues to be a territory of the United States, governed by virtue of that clause in the Constitution which empowers Congress 'to make all needful rules and regulations respecting the territory or other property belonging to the United States.' Perhaps the power of governing a territory belonging to the United States which has not, by becoming a State, acquired the means of self-government, may result necessarily from the fact that it is not within the jurisdiction of any particular State, and is within the power and jurisdiction of the United States. The right to govern may be the inevitable consequence of the right to acquire territory. Whichever may be the source whence the power is derived, the possession of it is unquestioned."[1]

The effect of such a precedent on constitutional principles was certain to be great. A government competent to interpret its own powers so liberally in one instance, could hardly resist any strong temptation to do so in others. The doctrines of "strict construction" could not be considered as the doctrines of the government after they had been abandoned in this leading case by a government controlled by strict constructionists. The time came at last when the opponents of centralization were obliged to review their acts and to discover the source of their mistakes. In 1856 the Supreme Court was

[1] American Insurance Company and Others *v.* Canter (January Term, 1828), 1 Peter's Reports, 511–546.

again required to pronounce an opinion, and found itself confronted by the legislation of 1803–1804 and the decision of Chief-Justice Marshall in 1828. Chief-Justice Taney and his associates, in the case of Dred Scott, then reviewed the acts of Jefferson and his friends in 1803–1804, and pronounced upon them the final judgment of the States-rights school.

Chief-Justice Taney affirmed the right of the government to buy Louisiana and to govern it, but not to govern it as a part of the old territory over which the Constitution gave Congress unlimited power. Louisiana was governed, according to Marshall's dictum, by a power which was "the inevitable consequence of the right to acquire territory,"—a power limited by the general purposes of the Constitution, and therefore not extending to a colonial system like that of Europe. Territory might thus be acquired; but it was acquired in order to become a State, and not to be held as a colony and governed by Congress with absolute authority; citizens who migrated to it "cannot be ruled as mere colonists dependent upon the will of the general government, and to be governed by any laws it may think proper to impose." The chief-justice dwelt on this point at much length; the federal government, he said, "cannot, when it enters a territory of the United States, put off its character and assume discretionary or despotic powers which the Constitution has denied it."

Even this emphatic opinion, which implied that all the Louisiana legislation was unconstitutional, did not satisfy Justice Campbell, a Georgian, who represented the ultimate convictions of the strict constructionists. Campbell reviewed the national history in search of evidence "that a consolidated power had been inaugurated, whose subject comprehended an empire, and which had no restriction but the discretion of Congress." He held that the Constitution had been plainly and repeatedly violated; "and in reference to the precedent of 1804, the wisest statesmen protested against it, and the President more than doubted its policy and the power of the government." The Court, he said, could not undertake to conquer their scruples as the President and Congress had done. "They acknowledge that our peculiar security is in the possession of a written Constitution, and they cannot make it blank paper by construction."

This sneer at President Jefferson was almost the last official expression of strict-constructionist principles. Of its propriety the Court itself was the best judge, but its historical interest could not be denied.

If Justice Campbell and Chief-Justice Taney were right, according to the tenets of their school the legislation of 1803–1804 was plainly unconstitutional. In that case, by stronger reasoning the treaty itself was unconstitutional and void from the beginning; for not only did Jefferson's doubts to which Campbell alluded refer to the treaty and not to the legislation, but the treaty was at least equally responsible with the laws for making, in 1803, a situation which required what Campbell denounced,—"the supreme and irresistible power which is now claimed for Congress over boundless territories, the use of which cannot fail to react upon the political system of the States to its subversion."

With the law the story need not concern itself, but the view of American history thus suggested was peculiarly interesting. If the chief-justice and his associate expressed correctly the opinions of the strict-constructionist school, the government had at some time been converted from a government of delegated powers into a sovereignty. Such was the belief of Campbell's political friends. Four years after the Dred Scott decision was declared, the State of South Carolina, in Convention, issued an "Address to the People of the Slave-holding States," justifying its act of secession from the Union.

> "The one great evil," it declared, "from which all other evils have flowed, is the overthrow of the Constitution of the United States. The government of the United States is no longer the government of confederated republics, but of a consolidated democracy. It is no longer a free government, but a despotism."

If the strict constructionists held this opinion, they necessarily believed that at some moment in the past the government must have changed its character. The only event which had occurred in American history so large in its proportions, so permanent in its influence, and so cumulative in its effects as to represent such a revolution was the Louisiana purchase;

and if the Louisiana purchase was to be considered as having done what the Federalists expected it to do,—if it had made a new constitution and a government of sovereign powers,—the strict constructionists were not only consenting parties to the change, they were its authors.

From every point of view, whether Justice Campbell and the secession convention of South Carolina were right or wrong in their historical judgment, the Louisiana purchase possessed an importance not to be ignored. Even in 1804 the political consequences of the act were already too striking to be overlooked. Within three years of his inauguration Jefferson bought a foreign colony without its consent and against its will, annexed it to the United States by an act which he said made blank paper of the Constitution; and then he who had found his predecessors too monarchical, and the Constitution too liberal in powers,—he who had nearly dissolved the bonds of society rather than allow his predecessor to order a dangerous alien out of the country in a time of threatened war,—made himself monarch of the new territory, and wielded over it, against its protests, the powers of its old kings. Such an experience was final; no century of slow and half-understood experience could be needed to prove that the hopes of humanity lay thenceforward, not in attempting to restrain the government from doing whatever the majority should think necessary, but in raising the people themselves till they should think nothing necessary but what was good.

Jefferson took a different view. He regarded, or wished to regard, the Louisiana treaty and legislation as exceptional and as forming no precedent. While he signed the laws for governing the territory, he warmly objected to the establishment of a branch bank of the United States at New Orleans. "This institution is one of the most deadly hostility existing against the principles and form of our Constitution," he wrote to Gallatin;[1] "ought we to give further growth to an institution so powerful, so hostile?" Gallatin was clear that the business of the Treasury required such aid, and Jefferson again acquiesced. Gallatin was also allowed and encouraged to

[1] Jefferson to Gallatin, Dec. 13, 1803; Works, iv. 518.

enforce the restrictions on the importation of slaves into Louisiana.[1] "It seems that the whole Cabinet," wrote the French
chargé to his government, "put the utmost weight on this
prohibition. Mr. Jefferson is earnestly bent on maintaining it,
and his Secretary of the Treasury takes the severest measures
to insure its execution."

As though the annexation of Louisiana alone made not
enough change in the old established balances of the Constitution, Congress took up another matter which touched the
mainspring of the compact. A new Presidential election was
at hand. The narrow escape of 1800 warned the party in
power not again to risk society by following the complicated
arrangements of 1788. In the convention which framed the
Constitution no single difficulty was more serious than that
of compromising the question of power between the large
and small States. Delaware, New Jersey, Rhode Island, Maryland, and Connecticut were well aware that the large States
would take the lion's share of power and patronage; they
knew that except by accident no citizen of theirs could ever
reach the Presidency; and as accident alone could give the
small States a chance, accident was to them a thing of value.
Whatever tended to make their votes decisive was an additional inducement with them to accept the Constitution. The
Vice-presidency, as originally created, more than doubled
their chance of getting the Presidency, and was invented
chiefly for this purpose; but this was not all. As the number
of electoral votes alone decided between President and Vice-
president, a tie-vote was likely often to occur; and such a tie
was decided by the House of Representatives, where another
bribe was intentionally offered to the small States by giving
the election to the State delegations voting as units, so that
the vote of Delaware weighed as heavily as the vote of Pennsylvania.

The alarm caused by Burr's rivalry with Jefferson in February, 1801, satisfied the Republican party that such a door to
intrigue ought not to be left open. Oct. 17, 1803, before the
Louisiana treaty was taken up, an amendment to the Constitution was moved by friends of the Administration in the

[1] Pichon to Talleyrand, 16 Fructidor, An xii. (Sept. 3, 1804); Archives des
Aff. Étr., MSS.

House. This, which took shape at length as the Twelfth Amendment, obliged the members of the electoral college to distinguish in their ballots the persons voted for as President and Vice-president.

Slight as this change might appear, it tended toward centralizing powers hitherto jealously guarded. It swept away one of the checks on which the framers had counted to resist majority rule by the great States. Lessening the influence of the small States, and exaggerating the office of President by lowering the dignity of Vice-president, it made the processes of election and government smoother and more efficient, — a gain to politicians, but the result most feared by the States-rights school. The change was such as Pennsylvania or New York might naturally want; but it ran counter to the theories of Virginia Republicans, whose jealousy of Executive influence had been extreme.

Roger Griswold said with prophetic emphasis:[1] —

> "The man voted for as Vice-president will be selected without any decisive view to his qualifications to administer the government. The office will generally be carried into the market to be exchanged for the votes of some large States for President; and the only criterion which will be regarded as a qualification for the office of Vice-president will be the temporary influence of the candidate over the electors of his State. . . . The momentary views of party may perhaps be promoted by such arrangements, but the permanent interests of the country are sacrificed."

Griswold held that true reform required abolition of the office; and in this opinion his old enemy John Randolph warmly agreed. In the Senate, had the question risen as a new one, perhaps a majority might have favored abolition, for the results of retaining the office were foreseen; but the discussion was hampered by the supposed popular will and by express votes of State legislatures, and Congress felt itself obliged to follow a prescribed course. The amendment was adopted by the usual party vote; and the Federalists thenceforward were able to charge Jefferson and his party with

[1] Dec. 8, 1803; Annals of Congress, 1803–1804, p. 751.

responsibility not only for stripping the small States of an advantage which had made part of their bargain, but also for putting in the office of President, in case of vacancies, men whom no State and no elector intended for the post.

Chapter VII

THE EXTRAORDINARY success which marked Jefferson's foreign relations in the year 1803 was almost equally conspicuous in domestic affairs. The Treasury was as fortunate as the Department of State. Gallatin silenced opposition. Although the customs produced two millions less than in 1802, yet when the Secretary in October, 1803, announced his financial arrangements, which included the purchase-money of fifteen million dollars for Louisiana, he was able to provide for all his needs without imposing a new tax. The treaty required the issue of six-per-cent bonds for eleven million two hundred and fifty thousand dollars, redeemable after fifteen years. These were issued; and to meet the interest and sinking fund Gallatin added from his surplus an annual appropriation of seven hundred thousand dollars to his general fund; so that the discharge of the whole debt would take place within the year 1818, instead of eighteen months earlier, as had been intended. New Orleans was expected to provide two hundred thousand dollars a year toward the interest. Of the remaining four millions, the Treasury already held half, and Gallatin hoped to provide the whole from future surplus, which he actually did.

This was ideal success. On a sudden call, to pay out four million dollars in hard money, and add seven hundred thousand dollars to annual expenditure, without imposing a tax, and with a total revenue of eleven millions, was a feat that warranted congratulations. Yet Gallatin's success was not obtained without an effort. As usual, he drew a part of his estimated surplus from the navy. He appealed to Jefferson to reduce the navy estimates from nine hundred thousand to six hundred thousand dollars.[1]

"I find that the establishment now consists of the 'Constitution,' the 'Philadelphia,' each 44, and five small vessels, all of which are now out, and intended to stay the whole year, as the crew is enlisted for two years. In my opinion

[1] Remarks on the Message, Gallatin's Writings, i. 156; Gallatin to Jefferson, Oct. 6, 1803; ibid., i. 162.

one half of the force,—namely, one frigate and two or three small vessels,—were amply sufficient."

Jefferson urged the reduction,[1] and Secretary Smith consented. The navy estimates were reduced to six hundred and fifty thousand dollars, and on the strength of this economy Gallatin made his calculation. As he probably foresaw, the attempt failed. Whether in any case Smith could have effected so great a retrenchment was doubtful; but an event occurred which made retrenchment impossible.

The war with Tripoli dragged tediously along, and seemed no nearer its end at the close of 1803 than eighteen months before. Commodore Morris, whom the President sent to command the Mediterranean squadron, cruised from port to port between May, 1802, and August, 1803, convoying merchant vessels from Gibraltar to Leghorn and Malta, or lay in harbor and repaired his ships, but neither blockaded nor molested Tripoli; until at length, June 21, 1803, the President called him home and dismissed him from the service. His successor was Commodore Preble, who Sept. 12, 1803, reached Gibraltar with the relief-squadron which Secretary Gallatin thought unnecessarily strong. He had the "Constitution," of 44 guns, and the "Philadelphia," of 38; the four new brigs just built,—the "Argus" and the "Syren," of 16 guns, the "Nautilus" and the "Vixen," of 14 guns; and the "Enterprise," of 12. With this force Preble set energetically to work.

Tripoli was a feeble Power, and without much effort could be watched and blockaded; but if the other governments on the coast should make common cause against the United States, the task of dealing with them was not so easy. Morocco was especially dangerous, because its ports lay on the ocean, and could not be closed even by guarding the Straits. When Preble arrived, he found Morocco taking part with Tripoli. Captain Bainbridge, who reached Gibraltar in the "Philadelphia" August 24, some three weeks before Preble arrived, caught in the neighborhood a Moorish cruiser of 22 guns with an American brig in its clutches. Another American brig had just been seized at Mogador. Determined to stop this peril at the outset, Preble united to his own

[1] Jefferson to R. Smith, Oct. 10, 1803; Jefferson MSS.

squadron the ships which he had come to relieve, and with this combined force,—the "Constitution," 44; the "New York," 36; the "John Adams," 28; and the "Nautilus," 14,—sending the "Philadelphia" to blockade Tripoli, he crossed to Tangiers October 6, and brought the Emperor of Morocco to reason. On both sides prizes and prisoners were restored, and the old treaty was renewed. This affair consumed time; and when at length Preble got the "Constitution" under way for the Tripolitan coast, he spoke a British frigate off the Island of Sardinia, which reported that the "Philadelphia" had been captured October 21, more than three weeks before.

The loss greatly embarrassed Preble. The "Philadelphia" was, next to the "Constitution," his strongest ship. Indeed he had nothing else but his own frigate and small brigs of two and three hundred tons; but the accident was such as could not fail sometimes to happen, especially to active commanders. Bainbridge, cruising off Tripoli, had chased a Tripolitan cruiser into shoal water, and was hauling off, when the frigate struck on a reef at the mouth of the harbor. Every effort was made without success to float her; but at last she was surrounded by Tripolitan gunboats, and Bainbridge struck his flag. The Tripolitans, after a few days' work, floated the frigate, and brought her under the guns of the castle. The officers became prisoners of war, and the crew, in number three hundred or more, were put to hard labor.

The affair was in no way discreditable to the squadron. Morris had been recalled in disgrace for over-caution, and Bainbridge was required to be active. The Tripolitans gained nothing except the prisoners; for at Bainbridge's suggestion Preble, some time afterward, ordered Stephen Decatur, a young lieutenant in command of the "Enterprise," to take a captured Tripolitan craft re-named the "Intrepid," and with a crew of seventy-five men to sail from Syracuse, enter the harbor of Tripoli by night, board the "Philadelphia," and burn her under the castle guns. The order was literally obeyed. Decatur ran into the harbor at ten o'clock in the night of Feb. 16, 1804, boarded the frigate within half gun-shot of the Pacha's castle, drove the Tripolitan crew overboard, set the ship on fire, remained alongside until the flames were beyond control, and then withdrew without losing a man, while the Tripolitan gunboats and batteries fired on him as rapidly as want of discipline and training would allow. Gallant and successful as the affair was, it proved only what was already well known, that the Tripolitans were no match for men like Decatur and his companions; and it left Preble, after losing in the "Philadelphia" nearly one third of his force, still strong enough to do the work that needed to be done.

The frigate had been built by the citizens of Philadelphia, and given to the government in 1799. So far as the ship was concerned, the loss was not much regretted, for the Republicans when in opposition had strenuously opposed the building of frigates, and still considered them a danger rather than a defence. Although the "Philadelphia" was the newest ship in the service, a companion to the "Constellation," the "Congress," and the "Chesapeake," she was never replaced; two 18-gun brigs, the "Hornet" and the "Wasp," were constructed instead of one 38-gun frigate; and these were the last sea-going vessels built under Jefferson's administration. The true annoyance was not that a frigate had been lost, but that the captivity and enslavement of the crew obliged Government to rescue them and to close the war, by a kind of expenditure which the Republican party disliked.

Bainbridge's report of his capture, which had happened at the end of October, 1803, was sent to Congress March 20, 1804, in the last week of the session. The President sent with it a brief Message recommending Congress to increase the force and enlarge expenses in the Mediterranean. As Gallatin never willingly allowed his own plans for the public service to be deranged, Congress adopted a new means for meeting the new expense. Although the Treasury held a balance of $1,700,000, Gallatin would not trench upon this fund, but told Randolph, who was Chairman of the Ways and Means Committee, that the specie in the Treasury could not be safely reduced below that amount.[1] He informed Joseph Nicholson that $150,000 was the utmost sum he could spare. The sum wanted was $750,000 per annum. A Bill was introduced which imposed an additional duty of 2½ per cent on all

---

[1] Speech of John Randolph, March 22, 1804; Annals of Congress, 1803–1804, p. 1221.

imports that paid duty *ad valorem*. These imports had been divided, for purposes of revenue, into three classes, taxed respectively 12½, 15, and 20 per cent; the increase raised them to 15, 17½, and 22½ per cent. The average *ad valorem* duty was before about 13½; the additional tax raised it above 16 per cent; and the Republicans preferred this method of raising money as in every way better than the system of internal taxation. After imposing the additional duty of 2½ per cent,—a duty intended to produce about $750,000,— the Bill made of it a separate Treasury account, to be called the "Mediterranean Fund," which was to last only as long as the Mediterranean war should last, when the 2½ per cent duty was to cease three months after a general peace.

The Mediterranean Fund was meant as a protest against loose expenditure,—a dike against the impending flood of extravagance. The Mediterranean war was the first failure of President Jefferson's theory of foreign relations, and the Mediterranean Fund was the measure of the error in financial form. No reproach henceforward roused more ill temper among Republicans than the common charge that their elaborate financial precautions and formalities were a deception, and that the Mediterranean Fund was meant to conceal a change of principle and a return to Federalist practices. Even in the first words of the debate, Roger Griswold told them that their plausible special fund was "perfectly deceptive," and amounted to nothing. John Randolph retaliated by declaring that the Republican government consisted of men who never drew a cent from the people except when necessity compelled it; and Griswold could not assert, though he might even then foresee, that for ten years to come, Randolph would denounce the extravagance and waste of the men whom he thus described.

The annexation of Louisiana, the constitutional amendment in regard to the Vice-presidency, the change of financial practices foreshadowed by the Mediterranean Fund, were signs of reaction toward nationality and energy in government. Yet the old prejudices of the Republican party had not yet wholly lost their force. Especially the extreme wing, consisting of men like John Randolph and W. B. Giles, thought that a substantial reform should be attempted. Increase of power encouraged them to act. The party, stimulated by its splendid success and irresistible popularity, at length, after long hesitation, prepared for a trial of strength with the last remnant of Federalism,—the Supreme Court of the United States.

A year of truce between Congress and the Supreme Court had followed the repeal of the Judiciary Act. To prevent Chief-Justice Marshall and his associates from interfering with the new arrangements, Congress in abolishing the circuit courts in 1801 took the strong measure of suspending for more than a year the sessions of the Supreme Court itself. Between December, 1801, and February, 1803, the court was not allowed to sit. Early in February, 1803, a few days before the Supreme Court was to meet, after fourteen months of separation, President Jefferson sent an ominous Message to the House of Representatives.

"The enclosed letter and affidavits," he said,[1] "exhibiting matter of complaint against John Pickering, district judge of New Hampshire, which is not within executive cognizance, I transmit them to the House of Representatives, to whom the Constitution has confided a power of instituting proceedings of redress if they shall be of opinion that the case calls for them."

The enclosed papers tended to show that Judge Pickering, owing to habits of intoxication or other causes, had become a scandal to the bench, and was unfit to perform his duties. At first sight the House of Representatives might not understand what it had to do with such a matter; but the President's language admitted no doubt of his meaning. The Constitution said that the House of Representatives "shall have the sole power of impeachment;" and "all civil officers of the United States shall be removed from office on impeachment for, and conviction of, treason, bribery, or other high crimes and misdemeanors." Jefferson's Message officially announced to the House the President's opinion that Judge Pickering's conduct was a misdemeanor within the reach of impeachment.

[1] Message of Feb. 3, 1803; Annals of Congress, 1802–1803, p. 460.

The House referred the Message to a committee of five, controlled by Joseph Nicholson and John Randolph. A fortnight later, Nicholson reported a resolution ordering the impeachment; and before the session closed, the House, by a vote of forty-five to eight, adopted his report, and sent Nicholson and Randolph to the bar of the Senate to impeach Judge Pickering of high crimes and misdemeanors. March 3, 1803, the last day of the session, the two members delivered their message.

Precisely as the House, by the President's invitation, was about to impeach Judge Pickering, the Supreme Court, through the Chief-Justice's mouth, delivered an opinion which could be regarded in no other light than as a defiance. Chief-Justice Marshall's own appointment had been one of those made by the last President between Dec. 12, 1800, and March 4, 1801, which Jefferson called an "outrage on decency,"[1] and which, except as concerned life offices, he held to be "nullities." His doctrine that all appointments made by a retiring President were nullities, unless made with the consent of the President elect, rested on the argument that the retiring President was no longer selecting his own but his successor's agents. Perhaps it involved also the favorite idea that the election of 1800 was something more than a change of Presidents,—that it was a real revolution in the principle of government. Any theory was sufficient for the Executive, but executive theories did not necessarily bind the Judiciary. Among the nominations which, like the appointment of Marshall, were obnoxious to Jefferson, was that of William Marbury as justice of the peace for five years for the District of Columbia. The nomination was sent to the Senate March 2, 1801, and was approved the next day, a few hours before Jefferson took his oath of office. The commission, regularly made out, signed by the President, countersigned by John Marshall the acting Secretary of State, and duly sealed, was left with other documents on the table in the State Department, where it came into the possession of Attorney-General Lincoln, acting as President Jefferson's Secretary of State. Jefferson, having decided that late appointments were nullities,

[1] Jefferson to General Knox, March 27, 1801; Works, iv. 386.

retained Marbury's commission. Marbury, at the December term of 1801, moved the Supreme Court for a Rule to Secretary Madison to show cause why a mandamus should not issue commanding him to deliver the document. The Rule was duly served, and the case argued in December, 1801; but the Judiciary Act having suspended for fourteen months the sessions of the Supreme Court, the Chief-Justice did not deliver his opinion until Feb. 24, 1803.[1]

The strongest admirers of Marshall admitted that his manner of dealing with this case was unusual. Where a judgment was to turn on a question of jurisdiction, the Court commonly considered that point as first and final. In the case of Marbury the Court had no original jurisdiction, and so decided; but instead of beginning at that point and dismissing the motion, the Court began by discussing the merits of the case, and ruled that when a commission had been duly signed and sealed the act was complete, and delivery was not necessary to its validity. Marbury's appointment was complete; and as the law gave him the right to hold for five years, independent of the Executive, his appointment was not revocable: "To withhold his commission, therefore, is an act deemed by the Court not warranted by law, but violative of a legal vested right."

This part of the decision bore the stamp of Marshall's character. The first duty of law, as he understood it, was to maintain the sanctity of pledged word. In his youth society had suffered severely from want of will to enforce a contract. The national government, and especially the judiciary, had been created to supply this want by compelling men to perform their contracts. The essence of the opinion in Marbury's case was that the Executive should be held to the performance of a contract, all the more because of his personal repugnance. Marshall ruled that Marbury had to his commission a vested legal right of which the Executive could not deprive him; and although the Court could not intermeddle with the prerogatives of the Executive, it might and would command a head of department to perform a duty not depending on Executive discretion, but on particular Acts of Congress and the general

[1] Cranch's Reports, i. 153.

principles of law. The mandamus might issue, but not from the Supreme Court, which had appellate jurisdiction only. In other words, if Marbury chose to apply for the mandamus to Judge Cranch and the District Court, he might expect the success of his application.

The decision in Marbury's case naturally exasperated Jefferson; but the chief-justice knew the point beyond which he could not go in asserting the jurisdiction of his court, and was content to leave the matter as it stood. Marbury never applied for the mandamus in the court below. The opinion in the case of Marbury and Madison was allowed to sleep, and its language was too guarded to furnish excuse for impeachment; but while the President was still sore under the discourtesy of Marshall's law, another member of the Supreme Bench attacked him in a different way. If one judge in the United States should have known the peril in which the judiciary stood, it was Justice Samuel Chase of Maryland, who had done more than all the other judges to exasperate the democratic majority. His overbearing manners had twice driven from his court the most eminent counsel of the circuit; he had left the bench without a quorum in order that he might make political speeches for his party; and his contempt for the popular will was loudly expressed. In the cases of Fries and Callender, in 1800, he had strained the law in order to convict for the government; and inasmuch as his energy was excess of zeal, for conviction was certain, he had exposed himself to the charge of over-officiousness in order to obtain the chief-justice's chair, which was given to Marshall. That he was not impeached after the change of administration proved the caution of the Republican party; but by this neglect Congress seemed to have condoned his old offences, or at least had tacitly consented to let their punishment depend on the judge's future good behavior.

Unluckily Chase's temper knew no laws of caution. He belonged to the old class of conservatives who thought that judges, clergymen, and all others in authority should guide and warn the people. May 2, 1803, barely two months after Marshall's defiance of the President in Marbury's case and the impeachment of Pickering, Justice Chase addressed the grand jury at Baltimore on the democratic tendencies of their local and national government.[1]

"Where law is uncertain, partial, or arbitrary," he said; " where justice is not impartially administered to all; where property is insecure, and the person is liable to insult and violence without redress by law,—the people are *not free*, whatever may be their form of government. To this situation I greatly fear we are fast approaching. . . . The late alteration of the Federal judiciary by the abolition of the office of the sixteen circuit judges, and the recent change in our State Constitution by the establishing of universal suffrage, and the further alteration that is contemplated in our State judiciary (if adopted) will in my judgment take away all security for property and personal liberty. The independence of the national judiciary is already shaken to its foundation, and the virtue of the people alone can restore it. . . . Our republican Constitution will sink into a mobocracy,—the worst of all possible governments. . . . The modern doctrines by our late reformers, that all men in a state of society are entitled to enjoy equal liberty and equal rights, have brought this mighty mischief upon us; and I fear that it will rapidly progress until peace and order, freedom and property, shall be destroyed."

At the moment of Justice Chase's outburst to the Baltimore grand jury, the President was at Washington deeply interested in the Louisiana business, and unaware that on the day when Chase delivered his tirade Livingston and Monroe in Paris were signing their names to a treaty which put the Administration beyond danger from such attacks. When he saw in the newspapers a report of what had been said from the bench at Baltimore, he wrote to Joseph Nicholson, in whose hands already lay the management of Pickering's impeachment:[2] —

"You must have heard of the extraordinary charge of Chase to the grand jury at Baltimore. Ought this seditious and official attack on the principles of our Constitution and on the proceedings of a State to go unpunished; and to

[1] Annals of Congress, 1804–1805, pp. 673–676.
[2] Jefferson to Nicholson, May 13, 1803; Works, iv. 486.

whom so pointedly as yourself will the public look for the necessary measures? I ask these questions for your consideration; for myself, it is better that I should not interfere."

"Non intervention," according to Talleyrand, "is a word used in politics and metaphysics, which means very nearly the same thing as intervention." The event proved that non-intervention was wise policy; but Jefferson was somewhat apt to say that it was better he should not interfere in the same breath with which he interfered. The warning that he could not officially interfere seemed to imply that the quarrel was personal; for in the case of Pickering he had interfered with decision. If this was his view, the success of any attack upon Chase would be a gain to him, and he was so ordering as to make failure a loss only to those who undertook it. Nicholson, hot-headed though he was, did not enter readily into this hazardous venture. He reflected upon it all summer, and consulted the friends on whose support he depended. Macon wrote to him a letter of unusual length,[1] suggesting grave doubts whether a judge ought to be impeached for expressing to a grand jury political opinions which every man was at liberty to hold and express elsewhere, and closed by announcing the conviction that if any attempt were made to impeach, Nicholson ought not to be the leader. In this opinion Macon was evidently right, for Chase's friends could not fail to suggest that Nicholson was to be rewarded by an appointment to Chase's vacant seat on the Supreme Bench; but the House of Representatives contained no other leader whose authority, abilities, and experience warranted him in taking so prominent a part, unless it were John Randolph.

A worse champion than Randolph for a difficult cause could not be imagined. Between him and Jefferson little sympathy existed. Randolph had quarrelled with the branch of his family to which Jefferson was closely allied; and his private feelings stood in the way of personal attachment. His intimates in Congress were not chiefly Virginians, but men like Macon of North Carolina, Joseph Bryan of Georgia, and Nicholson of Maryland,—independent followers of Virginia doctrine, who owned no personal allegiance to Jefferson. That

[1] Macon to Nicholson, Aug. 6, 1803; Nicholson MSS.

the President should have been willing to let such a man take entire responsibility for an impeachment was natural; but had Jefferson directed the step, he would never have selected Randolph to manage a prosecution on which the fate of his principles closely depended. Randolph was no lawyer; but this defect was a trifling objection compared with his greater unfitness in other respects. Ill-balanced, impatient of obstacles, incapable of sustained labor or of methodical arrangement, illogical to excess, and egotistic to the verge of madness, he was sparkling and formidable in debate or on the hustings, where he could follow the wayward impulse of his fancy running in the accustomed channels of his thought; but the qualities which helped him in debate were fatal to him at the bar.

Such was the origin of a measure which did more to define the character of the government than any other single event in Jefferson's first administration, except the purchase of Louisiana. Randolph threw himself into the new undertaking; for he sincerely believed in the justice of his cause, and was alive to the danger of leaving the Supreme Court in the hands of Marshall and men of his stamp who were determined to consolidate the government. Yet the chance of obtaining a conviction, on a charge no stronger than that of the Baltimore address, was so slight as to incline Randolph against risking it; and he decided to insure success by putting the cases of Fries and Callender in the foreground.

This was not easily done. Pickering's impeachment had been brought before the House by a Message from the President; but in Chase's case the President preferred not to take part. Randolph was forced to escape the difficulty by an awkward manœuvre. During the autumn and early winter of 1803 Congress was busy with Louisiana legislation, and had no leisure for other matters; but soon after the new year Randolph rose and said[1] that in the course of the last session Mr. Smilie of Pennsylvania had made some statements in regard to Justice Chase's conduct which seemed to call for notice, but that want of time had precluded action. Finding his attention thus drawn to the matter, Randolph gravely continued, he had felt it his duty to investigate Smilie's charges; and having con-

[1] Jan. 5, 1804; Annals of Congress, 1803–1804, p. 805.

vinced himself that ground for impeachment existed, he asked the House to appoint a committee of inquiry. Such an introduction of a great constitutional struggle was not imposing; but party discipline was at its highest point, and after some vigorous Federalist resistance Randolph carried his motion by a vote of eighty-one to forty. Three Northern democrats voted with the Federalists; and although the defection seemed not serious so far as concerned the scientific Dr. Samuel L. Mitchill, whose political principles were liberal enough at all times, some importance even then attached to the vote of John Smith of New York, who was about to enter the Senate and to act as one of Chase's judges.

Meanwhile Judge Pickering's trial began. The Senate, "sitting as a Court of Impeachments," listened while Nicholson, Randolph, Rodney, and six or seven other Republican members "exhibited the grand inquest of the nation." The character of a court was taken in all the forms of summons. The Secretary of the Senate signed, and the Sergeant-at-Arms served, the summons to Judge Pickering, while the witnesses were regularly subpœnaed by the Secretary, "to appear before the Senate of the United States in their capacity of a Court of Impeachments," and the subpœnas were served by the marshals of the district courts.

Judge Pickering was ordered to appear on the 2d of March, 1804; but when the day arrived, and the Senate was assembled, with the managers in attendance, John Pickering's name was three times called without an answer. Vice-President Burr then submitted to the Senate a petition from Jacob Pickering, son of the impeached judge, praying the court to postpone the trial that he might have time to collect evidence with the view of showing that when the alleged crimes were committed, and two years before as well as ever since, the judge was wholly deranged, incapable of transacting any kind of business which required the exercise of reason, and therefore incapable of corruption of judgment, no subject of impeachment, and amenable to no tribunal for his actions. With this petition a letter from Robert G. Harper was laid before the court, requesting to be allowed to appear on the part of the petitioner in support of the petition. Harper, having been invited to a seat within the bar, asked whether he might be heard, not as counsel for Judge Pickering, who being insane could give no authority for the purpose, but as agent for the petitioner, to ask a postponement.

The question threw all parties into agitation. The managers instantly protested that Harper in such a character could not be heard. The senators retired for consultation, and debated all day without coming to a decision. The impeaching party dreaded the alternative to which the proof of insanity must force them,—of saying either that an insane man was responsible, or that a man mentally irresponsible might still be guilty of "high crimes and misdemeanors" for purposes of impeachment. Senator Jackson of Georgia, who had always the merit of speaking with candor, avowed the fear that presently Judge Chase's friends would come and pretend that he too was mad;[1] but he could not, even with Breckinridge's help, carry his point. The Northern democrats flinched. Six of them and three Southern senators voted with the Federalists, and admitted Harper in his volunteer character.

Harper put in his testimony, which was decisive in regard to the insanity; but when he rose to do so, the managers retired, saying that they considered themselves under no obligation to discuss a preliminary question raised by an unauthorized third party. The Senate went on with its session. The managers were obliged to maintain that insanity was no bar to impeachment, and the Northern democrats were forced to accept the doctrine.[2]

This view of impeachment, so far as concerned the judiciary, had strong arguments in its favor. Although the Constitution made judges' tenure of office dependent on their good behavior, it provided no other means than that of impeachment for their removal. Even in England and in Massachusetts, judges could be removed by the joint action of Legislature and Executive; but this was not the case under the Constitution of the United States. If insanity or any other misfortune was to bar impeachment, the absurdity followed that unless a judge committed some indictable offence the people were powerless to protect themselves. Even Federalists

[1] Diary of J. Q. Adams, i. 299.
[2] Ibid., i. 301–302. Pickering to George Cabot, Jan. 29, 1804; Pickering to Theodore Lyman, Feb. 11, 1804; New England Federalism, pp. 340, 344.

might reasonably assume that the people had never placed themselves in such a situation, but that in making their judges subject to impeachment for misdemeanors they had meant to extend the scope of impeachment, and to include within it all cases of misbehavior which might require a removal from office for the good of the public service.

This ground was fairly taken by the impeachers, though not formally expressed. When Harper had put in his evidence and retired, the Senate sent again for the managers, who occupied one day in supplying evidence, and then left their case without argument in the hands of the court. The Senate found itself face to face with an issue beyond measure delicate, which had never been discussed, but from which escape was impossible. Acquittal of Pickering would probably be fatal to the impeachment of Chase, and would also proclaim that the people could not protect themselves from misbehavior in their judicial servants. On the other hand, conviction would violate the deep principle of law and justice that an insane man was not responsible for his acts, and not amenable to any earthly tribunal. Virginians like Randolph and Wilson Cary Nicholas, or John Breckinridge, were ready to make a precedent which should fix the rule that impeachment need not imply criminality, and might be the equivalent to removal by address. The Northern democrats were not unwilling to accept this view; but their consciences revolted against saying "guilty" where no guilt was implied or proved.

To escape this objection a compromise was proposed and adopted. The Federalists would have forced senators to say in their final vote that Judge Pickering was "guilty" or "not guilty" of high crimes and misdemeanors. Senator Anderson of Tennessee eluded this challenge by moving for a yea-and-nay vote on the question whether Pickering was guilty "as charged." The nine Federalists alone opposed his motion, which was at length adopted by a majority of two to one. By a vote of nineteen to seven Judge Pickering was declared "guilty as charged" in the articles of impeachment; and by a vote of twenty to six the Senate resolved that he ought to be removed from office.

Two of the Federalist senators refused to vote, on the ground that the proceedings were irregular; Senator Bradley of Vermont, Senator Armstrong of New York, and Senator Stone of North Carolina tacitly protested by absenting themselves. In a Senate of thirty-four members only twenty-six voted, and only nineteen voted for conviction. So confused, contradictory, and irregular were these proceedings that Pickering's trial was never considered a sound precedent. That an insane man could be guilty of crime, and could be punished on *ex parte* evidence, without a hearing, with not even an attorney to act in his behalf, seemed such a perversion of justice that the precedent fell dead on the spot. Perhaps, from the constitutional point of view, a more fatal objection was that in doing what the world was sure to consider an arbitrary and illegal act, the Virginians failed to put on record the reasons which led them to think it sound in principle. In the Louisiana purchase they had acted in a way equally arbitrary, but they had given their reasons for thinking themselves in the right. In Pickering's case not a word was publicly spoken on either side; a plainly extra-constitutional act was done without recording the doctrine on which it rested.

The Republicans showed no hesitation. John Randolph's orders were obeyed without open protest. Senator Bradley of Vermont talked strongly in private against them; Senator Armstrong of New York would not support them; barely half the Senate voted in their favor; but Randolph forced his party forward without stopping to see how well his steps were taken, or how far he was likely to go. As though to intimidate the Senate, March 6, the day after the managers were defeated on the vote to hear Harper, Randolph reported to the House a resolution ordering the impeachment of Justice Chase. March 12, the day when the Senate voted Pickering guilty, the House took up Randolph's report, and the majority, without debate, voted by seventy-three to thirty-two that Chase should be impeached. Not a Republican ventured to record a vote in the negative. The next morning Randolph again appeared at the bar of the Senate, and announced that the House of Representatives would in due time exhibit articles of impeachment against Samuel Chase.

Chapter VIII

As THE YEAR 1804 began, with Louisiana annexed, the Electoral Amendment secured, and the impeachments in prospect, the Federalists in Congress wrought themselves into a dangerous state of excitement. All agreed that the crisis was at hand; democracy had nearly reached its limit; and, as Justice Chase said from the bench, peace and order, freedom and property, would soon be destroyed. They discussed in private what should be done; and among the New Englanders almost all the men of weight were found to favor the policy of at least saving New England. Of the six Federalist senators from the Eastern States,—Plumer and Olcott of New Hampshire, Pickering and Adams of Massachusetts, Tracy and Hillhouse of Connecticut,—all but Olcott and Adams thought a dissolution of the Union inevitable.[1] Among the Federalist members of the House, Roger Griswold of Connecticut was the most active; he too was convinced that New England must protect herself. Samuel Hunt of New Hampshire, and Calvin Goddard of Connecticut held the same opinion. Indeed, Pickering declared that he did not know "one reflecting Nov-Anglian" who held any other.

In the month of January, 1804, despair turned into conspiracy. Pickering, Tracy, Griswold, Plumer, and perhaps others of the New England delegation, agreed to organize a movement in their States for a dissolution of the Union. They wrote to their most influential constituents, and sketched a plan of action. In a letter to George Cabot, Pickering recounted the impending dangers:[2]—

"By the Philadelphia papers I see that the Supreme Court judges of Pennsylvania are to be hurled from their seats, on the pretence that in punishing one Thomas Passmore for a contempt they acted illegally and tyrannically. I presume that Shippen, Yates, and Smith are to be removed by the Governor, on the representation of the Legislature. And

[1] New England Federalism, pp. 106, 146, 342, 352; Plumer's Life of Plumer, pp. 284–311.

[2] Pickering to George Cabot, Jan. 29, 1804; Lodge's Cabot, p. 337.

when such grounds are taken in the National and State legislatures to destroy the rights of the judges, whose rights can be safe? Why destroy *them*, unless as the prelude to the destruction of every influential Federalist and of every man of considerable property who is not of the reigning sect? New judges, of characters and tempers suited to the object, will be the selected ministers of vengeance."

A separation, Pickering inferred, had become necessary; but when and how was it to be effected?

"If Federalism is crumbling away in New England, there is no time to be lost, lest it should be overwhelmed and become unable to attempt its own relief; its last refuge is New England, and immediate exertion perhaps its only hope. It must begin in Massachusetts. The proposition would be welcomed in Connecticut; and could we doubt of New Hampshire? But New York must be associated; and how is her concurrence to be obtained? She must be made the centre of the confederacy. Vermont and New Jersey would follow of course, and Rhode Island of necessity. Who can be consulted, and who will take the lead? The legislatures of Massachusetts and Connecticut meet in May, and of New Hampshire in the same month, or June. The subject has engaged the contemplation of many. The Connecticut gentlemen have seriously meditated upon it. . . . Tracy has written to several of his most distinguished friends in Connecticut, and may soon receive their answers. R. Griswold, examining the finances, has found that the States above mentioned, to be embraced by the Northern confederacy, now pay as much or more of the public revenues as would discharge their share of the public debts due those States and abroad, leaving out the millions given for Louisiana."

Roger Griswold wrote a few weeks afterward to Oliver Wolcott in similar terms:[1] —

"The project which we had formed was to induce, if possible, the legislatures of the three New England States who

---

[1] Roger Griswold to Oliver Wolcott, March 11, 1804; Hamilton's History of the Republic, vii. 781; New England Federalism, p. 354.

remain Federal to commence measures which should call
for a reunion of the Northern States. The extent of those
measures, and the rapidity with which they shall be followed up, must be governed by circumstances. The magnitude and jealousy of Massachusetts would render it
necessary that the operation should be commenced there.
If any hope can be created that New York will ultimately
support the plan, it may perhaps be supported."

The first action, said he, must come from the Legislature of
Massachusetts, which was not yet elected, but would meet
early in June. Connecticut and New Hampshire were to follow; and to Pickering's sanguine mind the Northern Confederacy seemed already established. "The people of the East,"
he said, "cannot reconcile their habits, views, and interests
with those of the South and West. The latter are beginning
to rule with a rod of iron."

Pickering knew that the Federalist majority in Massachusetts was none too great. The election in May, four months
later, showed a Federalist vote of 30,000 against a Republican
minority of 24,000, while in the Legislature Harrison Gray
Otis was chosen Speaker by 129 votes to 103. Pickering knew
also that his colleague, Senator Adams, was watching his
movements with increasing ill-will, which Pickering lost no
chance to exasperate. Nothing could be more certain than
that at the first suggestion of disunion Senator Adams and
the moderate Federalists would attack the Essex Junto with
the bitterness of long-suppressed hatred; and if they could not
command fourteen votes in the Legislature and three thousand in the State, a great change must have occurred since the
year before, when they elected Adams to the Senate for the
long term over Pickering's head. Pickering concealed his
doings from his colleague; but Tracy was not so cautious.
Adams learned the secret from Tracy; and the two senators
from Massachusetts drew farther and farther apart, in spite of
the impeachments, which tended to force them together.

The Essex Junto, which sent Pickering to Washington, and
to which he appealed for support, read his letter with evident
astonishment. George Cabot, Chief-Justice Parsons, Fisher
Ames, and Stephen Higginson, who were the leaders con-

sulted,[1] agreed that the scheme was impracticable; and Cabot, as gently as possible, put their common decision into words.

"All the evils you describe," he said,[2] "and many more, are to be apprehended; but I greatly fear that a separation would be no remedy, because the source of them is in the political theories of our country and in ourselves. A separation at some period not very remote may probably take place,—the first impression of it is even now favorably received by many; but I cannot flatter myself with the expectation of essential good to proceed from it while we retain maxims and principles which all experience, and I may add reason too, pronounce to be impracticable and absurd. Even in New England, where there is among the body of the people more wisdom and virtue than in any other part of the United States, we are full of errors which no reasoning could eradicate if there were a Lycurgus in every village. We are democratic altogether; and I hold democracy in its natural operation to be the government of the worst.

"There is no energy in the Federal party, and there could be none manifested without great hazard of losing the State government. Some of our best men in high stations are kept in office because they forbear to exert any influence, and not because they possess right principles. They are permitted to have power if they will not use it. . . . I incline to the opinion that the essential alterations which may in future be made to amend our form of government will be the consequences only of great suffering or the immediate effects of violence. If we should be made to feel a very great calamity from the abuse of power by the National Administration, we might do almost anything; but it would be idle to talk to the deaf, to warn the people of distant evils. By this time you will suppose I am willing to do nothing but submit to fate. I would not be so understood. I am convinced we cannot do what is wished; but we can do much, if we work with Nature (or the course of things), and not against her. A separation is now impracticable, because we do not feel the necessity or utility of it. The same

[1] Cabot to Pickering, March 7, 1804; New England Federalism, p. 353.
[2] Cabot to Pickering, Feb. 14, 1804; Lodge's Cabot, p. 341.

separation then will be unavoidable when our loyalty to the Union is generally perceived to be the instrument of debasement and impoverishment. If it is prematurely attempted, those few only will promote it who discern what is hidden from the multitude."

Cabot's letter, more clearly than any writing of Alexander Hamilton himself, expressed the philosophy and marked the tactics of their school. Neither Cabot nor Hamilton was a lively writer, and the dust which has gathered deep on their doctrines dulls whatever brilliancy they once possessed; but this letter showed why Cabot was considered the wisest head in his party, to whose rebuke even Hamilton was forced to bow. For patient and willing students who have groped in search of the idea which, used by Hamilton and Jefferson, caused bitterer feeling and roused deeper terrors than civil war itself, Cabot's long and perhaps pedantic letter on the policy of disunion was full of meaning. "We shall go the way of all governments wholly popular,—from bad to worse,—until the evils, no longer tolerable, shall generate their own remedies." Democracy must end in a crisis, experience and reason pronounced it impracticable and absurd, Nature would in due time vindicate her own laws; and when the inevitable chaos should come, then conservative statesmanship could set society on a sound footing by limiting the suffrage to those citizens who might hold in their own right two thousand dollars value in land. Meanwhile disunion would be useless, and the attempt to bring it about would break up the Federalist party. "A war with Great Britain manifestly provoked by our rulers" was the only chance which Cabot foresaw of bringing the people of New England to a dissolution of the Union.

Pickering was not so intelligent as Cabot, Parsons, and Ames; his temper was harsher than theirs; he was impatient of control, and never forgot or wholly forgave those who forced him to follow another course than the one he chose. Cabot's letter showed a sense of these traits; for though it was in the nature of a command or entreaty to cease discussing disunion, if the Federalist party in Massachusetts were to be saved, it was couched in gentle language, and without affecting a tone of advice suggested ideas which ought to guide Federalists in Congress. Pickering was to wait for the crisis. Inaction was easy; and even though the crisis should be delayed five or ten years,—a case hardly to be supposed,— no step could be taken without a blunder before the public should be ready for it. With this simple and sound principle to guide them, conservatives could not go wrong. Cabot there left the matter.

Such gentleness toward a man of Pickering's temper was a mistake, which helped to cost the life of one whom conservatives regarded as their future leader in the crisis. Pickering was restive under the sense that his friends preferred other counsellors; whereas his experience and high offices, to say nothing of his ability, entitled him, as he thought, to greater weight in the party than Hamilton, Cabot, or Rufus King. Backed by Tracy, Griswold, and other men of standing, Pickering felt able to cope with opposition. His rough sense and democratic instincts warned him that the fine-drawn political theories of George Cabot and Theophilus Parsons might end in impotence. He could see no reason why Massachusetts, once corrupted, might not wallow in democratic iniquities with as much pleasure as New York or Pennsylvania; and all that was worth saving might be lost before her democracy would consent to eat the husks of repentance and ask forgiveness from the wise and good. Cabot wanted to wait a few months or years until democracy should work out its own fate; and whenever the public should yearn for repose, America would find her Pitt and Bonaparte combined in the political grasp and military genius of Alexander Hamilton. Pickering, as a practical politician, felt that if democracy were suffered to pull down the hierarchy of New England, neither disunion nor foreign war, nor "a very great calamity" of any kind, could with certainty restore what had once been destroyed.

Cabot's argument shook none of Pickering's convictions; but the practical difficulty on which the home Junto relied was fatal unless some way of removing it could be invented. During the month of February, 1804, when the impeachment panic was at its height in Congress, Pickering, Tracy, and Plumer received letter after letter from New England, all telling the same story. The eminent Judge Tapping Reeve, of Connecticut, wrote to Tracy:[1] "I have seen many of our friends; and all that I have seen and most that I have heard from believe that we must separate, and that this is the most favorable moment." He had heard only one objection,—that the country was not prepared; but this objection, which meant that the disunionists were a minority, was echoed from all New England. The conspirators dared not openly discuss the project. "There are few among my acquaintance," wrote Pickering's nephew, Theodore Lyman,[2] "with whom I could on that subject freely converse; there may be more ready than I am aware of." Plumer found a great majority of the New Hampshire Federalists decidedly opposed. Roger Griswold, toward the end of the session, summed up the result in his letter to Oliver Wolcott:—

"We have endeavored during this session to rouse our friends in New England to make some bold exertions in that quarter. They generally tell us that they are sensible of the danger, that the Northern States must unite; but they think the time has not yet arrived. Prudence is undoubtedly necessary; but when it degenerates into procrastination it becomes fatal. Whilst we are waiting for the time to arrive in New England, it is certain the democracy is making daily inroads upon us, and our means of resistance are lessening every day. Yet it appears impossible to induce our friends to make any decisive exertions. Under these circumstances I have been induced to look to New York."

The representatives of the wise and good looked at politics with eyes which saw no farther than those of the most profligate democrat into the morality of the game. Pickering enjoyed hearing himself called "honest Tim Pickering," as though he were willing to imply a tinge of dishonesty in others, even in the Puritan society of Wenham and Salem. Griswold was to the end of his life a highly respected citizen of Connecticut, and died while governor of the State. That both these worthy men should conspire to break up the Union implied to their minds no dishonesty, because they both held

[1] Tapping Reeve to Uriah Tracy, Feb. 7, 1804; Lodge's Cabot, p. 442.
[2] Theodore Lyman to Pickering, Feb. 29, 1804; Lodge's Cabot, p. 446.

that the Republican majority had by its illegal measures already destroyed the Constitution which they had sworn to support; but although such casuistry might excuse in their own consciences the act of conspiracy, neither this reasoning nor any other consistent with self-respect warranted their next step. Griswold's remark that the procrastination of New England had led him to look to New York was not quite candid; his plan had from the first depended on New York. Pickering had written to Cabot at the outset, "She must be made the centre of the confederacy." New York seemed, more than New England, unfit to be made the centre of a Northern confederacy, because there the Federalist party was a relatively small minority. If Massachusetts and Connecticut showed fatal apathy, in New York actual repulsion existed; the extreme Federalists had no following. To bring New York to the Federalism of Pickering and Griswold, the Federalist party needed to recover power under a leader willing to do its work. The idea implied a bargain and an intrigue on terms such as in the Middle Ages the Devil was believed to impose upon the ambitious and reckless. Pickering and Griswold could win their game only by bartering their souls; they must invoke the Mephistopheles of politics, Aaron Burr.

To this they had made up their minds from the beginning. Burr's four years of office were drawing to a close. The Virginians had paid him the price he asked for replacing them in power; and had it been Shylock's pound of flesh, they could not have looked with greater care to see that Burr should get neither more nor less, even in the estimation of a hair, than the exact price they had covenanted to pay. In another year the debt would be discharged, and the Virginians would be free. Burr had not a chance of regaining a commanding place among Republicans, for he was bankrupt in private and public character. In New York the Clintons never ceased their attacks, with the evident wish to drive him from the party. Cheetham, after publishing in 1802 two heavy pamphlets, a "Narrative" and a "View," attempted in 1803 to crush him under the weight of a still heavier volume, containing "Nine Letters on the Subject of Aaron Burr's Political Defection." Nov. 16, 1803, the "Albany Register" at length followed Cheetham's lead; and nearly all the other democratic newspapers followed the "Register," abandoning Burr as a man who no longer deserved confidence.

Till near the close of 1803 the Vice-President held his peace. The first sign that he meant energetic retaliation was given by an anonymous pamphlet,[1] which won the rare double triumph of political and literary success, in which ability and ill temper seemed to have equal shares. The unexpected appearance of "Aristides" startled New York. This attack recalled the scandal which Alexander Hamilton had created four years before by his pamphlet against his own President. "Aristides" wrote with even more bitterness than Hamilton, and the ferocity of his assault on the personal and political characters of the Republican leaders made the invectives of Hamilton and Cheetham somewhat tame; but the scandal in each case was due not so much to personalities of abuse as to breaches of confidence. "Aristides" furnished to the enemies of the Clintons and Livingstons an arsenal of poisoned weapons; but what was more to the purpose, his defence of Burr was strong. That it came directly from the Vice-President was clear; but the pamphlet showed more literary ability than Burr claimed, and the world was at a loss to discover who could be held responsible for its severities. Cheetham tried in vain to pierce the incognito. Not till long afterward was "Aristides" acknowledged by Burr's most intimate friend, William Peter Van Ness.

An attempt to separate what was just from what was undeserved in Van Ness's reproaches of the Clintons and Livingstons would be useless. The Clintons and Livingstons, however unprincipled they might be, could say that they were more respectable than Burr; but though this were true so far as social standing was concerned, they could not easily show that as a politician the Vice-President was worse than his neighbors. The New England Federalists knew well that Burr was not to be trusted, but they did not think much worse of him than they thought of De Witt Clinton, or John Armstrong, or Edward Livingston, at this moment removed from office by Jefferson for failing to account for thirty thousand dollars due to the United States Treasury. As a politician Burr

[1] An Examination of the various Charges against Aaron Burr, by Aristides. December, 1803.

had played fast and loose with all parties; but so had most of his enemies. Seeing that he was about to try another cast of the dice, all the political gamblers gathered round to help or hurt his further fortunes; and Van Ness might fairly have said that in the matter of principle or political morality, none of them could show clean hands.

Although Vice-President until March, 1805, Burr announced that he meant to offer himself as a candidate for the post of governor of New York in April, 1804. At the same time Governor Clinton privately gave warning of his own retirement. De Witt Clinton was annoyed at his uncle's conduct, and tried to prevent the withdrawal by again calling Jefferson to his aid and alarming him with fear of Burr.

"A certain gentleman was to leave this place yesterday morning," wrote De Witt to the President.[1] "He has been very active in procuring information as to his probable success for governor at the next election. This, I believe, is his intention at present, although it is certain that if the present Governor will consent to be a candidate, he will prevail by an immense majority. . . . Perhaps a letter from you may be of singular service."

Jefferson declined to interfere, putting his refusal on the ground of Burr's candidacy.

"I should think it indeed a serious misfortune," was his reply,[2] "should a change in the administration of your government be hazarded before its present principles be well established through all its parts; yet on reflection you will be sensible that the delicacy of my situation, considering who may be competitors, forbids my intermeddling even so far as to write the letter you suggest. I can therefore only brood in silence over my secret wishes."

No real confidence ever existed between Jefferson and the Clintons. A few days after these letters were written, "Aristides" betrayed the secret that Governor Clinton, in the spring of 1800, declared Jefferson to be "an accommodating trimmer, who would change with times and bend to circum-

[1] De Witt Clinton to Jefferson, Nov. 26, 1803; Jefferson MSS.
[2] Jefferson's Writings (Ford), viii. 282.

stances for the purposes of personal promotion." This revelation by "Aristides," supported by the names of persons who
heard the remark, forced Governor Clinton into an awkward
denial of the charge, and led to an exchange of letters[1] and to
professions of confidence between him and Jefferson; but
time showed that neither the Governor nor his nephew loved
the Virginians more than they were loved by Burr.

The threads of intrigue drew together, as they were apt to
do before a general election. The last week in January came.
Three days before Senator Pickering wrote his conspiracy letter to George Cabot, a letter which implied co-operation with
Burr in making him governor of New York, Burr asked for a
private interview with Jefferson, and formally offered him the
choice between friendship or enmity. The President thought
the conversation so curious that he made a note of it.

> "He began," said Jefferson,[2] "by recapitulating summar-
> ily that he had come to New York a stranger, some years
> ago; that he found the country in possession of two rich
> families,—the Livingstons and Clintons; . . . that since,
> those great families had become hostile to him and had ex-
> cited the calumnies which I had seen published; that in this
> Hamilton had joined, and had even written some of the
> pieces against him. . . He observed, he believed it would
> be for the interest of the Republican cause for him to re-
> tire,— that a disadvantageous schism would otherwise take
> place; but that were he to retire, it would be said he shrank
> from the public sentence, which he would never do; that
> his enemies were using my name to destroy him, and some-
> thing was necessary from me to prevent and deprive them
> of that weapon,—some mark of favor from me which
> would declare to the world that he retired with my con-
> fidence."

Jefferson, with many words but with his usual courtesy,
intimated that he could not appoint the Vice-President to an
Executive office; and Burr then united his intrigues with
those of Pickering and Griswold. Thenceforth his chance of
retaining power depended on the New York election; and his

[1] Jefferson to Governor Clinton, Dec. 31, 1803; Works, iv. 520.
[2] The Anas, Jan. 26, 1804; Works, ix. 204.

success in this election depended on the Federalists. Before George Cabot had yet written his answer to Pickering's questions, Pickering could no longer resist the temptation to act.

The effect of what passed at Washington was instantly felt at Albany. Toward the middle of February, about three weeks after Jefferson had civilly rejected the Vice-President's advances, Burr's friends in the New York legislature announced that they should hold a caucus February 18, and nominate him as candidate for governor. The Federalists at once called a preliminary caucus to decide whether they should support Burr. Alexander Hamilton, who happened to be engaged in law business at Albany, Feb. 16, 1804, attended the Federal caucus, and used his influence in favor of the regular Clinton candidate against Burr's pretensions. The drift of his argument was given in an abstract of reasons which he drew up for the occasion.[1] Unfortunately the strongest of these reasons was evidently personal; the leadership of Hamilton would not tolerate rivalry from Burr. Hamilton pointed out that Burr's elevation by the Federalists of New York would present him as their leader to the Federalists of New England, and would assist him to disorganize New England if so disposed; that there "the ill-opinion of Jefferson, and jealousy of the ambition of Virginia, is no inconsiderable prop of good opinions; but these causes are leading to an opinion that a dismemberment of the Union is expedient. It would probably suit Mr. Burr's views to promote this result, — to be the chief of the Northern portion; and placed at the head of the State of New York, no man would be more likely to succeed."

If the Union was to be severed, Hamilton was the intended chief of the Northern portion; but he wanted no severance that should leave the germs of the democratic disease. His philosophy was that of George Cabot, William Pitt, and Talleyrand; he waited for the whole country to come to its senses and restore sound principles, that democracy might everywhere die out or be stifled. Burr's methods were democratic, and would perpetuate in a Northern confederacy the vices of the Union; they would break up the conservative strength without weakening democracy. Within a few days the danger

[1] Hamilton's Works, vii. 851.

which Hamilton foresaw came to pass. Burr's little band of friends in the Legislature, Feb. 18, 1804, set him in nomination; and a large majority of Federalists, in defiance of Hamilton's entreaties, meant to vote for him.

As the situation became clearer, Hamilton's personal feeling became public. While at Albany, February 16, he dined with John Tayler, and at table talked of the political prospect. One of the company, Dr. Charles D. Cooper, an active partisan, wrote an account of the conversation to a certain Mr. Brown near Albany: "General Hamilton and Judge Kent have declared, in substance, that they looked upon Mr. Burr to be a dangerous man, and one who ought not to be trusted with the reins of government." The letter was printed, and went the rounds of the press. As it roused some question and dispute, Cooper wrote again: "I could detail to you a still more despicable opinion which General Hamilton has expressed of Mr. Burr." This letter also was printed; the "Albany Register" of April 24 contained the correspondence.

The news of Burr's nomination reached Washington at the moment when Pickering and Tracy received answers to their disunion scheme; and it served to keep them steady to their plan. The Federalists, who professed to consider Hamilton their leader, seldom followed his advice; but on this occasion they set him somewhat unkindly aside. Too much in awe of Hamilton to say directly to his face that he must be content with the place of Burr's lieutenant, they wrote letters to that effect which were intended for his eye.

Of all Federalist leaders, moderate and extreme, Rufus King, who had recently returned from London, stood highest in the confidence of his party. He was to be the Federalist candidate for Vice-President; he had mixed in none of the feuds which made Hamilton obnoxious to many of his former friends; and while King's manners were more conciliatory, his opinions were more moderate, than those of other party leaders. To him Pickering wrote, March 4, 1804, in a tone of entreaty:—

"I am disgusted with the men who now rule, and with their measures. At some manifestations of their malignancy I am shocked. The cowardly wretch at their head, while like a Parisian revolutionary monster prating about humanity, would feel an infernal pleasure in the utter destruction of his opponents."

After avowing his hopes of disunion, Pickering next touched the New York election:[1] —

"The Federalists here in general anxiously desire the election of Mr. Burr to the chair of New York, for they despair of a present ascendency of the Federalist party. Mr. Burr alone, we think, can break your democratic phalanx, and we anticipate much good from his success. Were New York detached, as under his administration it would be, from the Virginia influence, the whole Union would be benefited. Jefferson would then be forced to observe some caution and forbearance in his measures. And if a separation should be deemed proper, the five New England States, New York, and New Jersey would naturally be united."

Rufus King was as cautious as Pickering was indiscreet. He acknowledged this letter in vague terms of compliment,[2] saying that Pickering's views "ought to fix the attention of the real friends of liberty in this quarter of the Union, and the more so as things seem to be fast advancing to a crisis." Even King's cool head was possessed with the thought which tormented Hamilton, Cabot, Ames, Pickering, Griswold, and Tracy,—the crisis which was always coming, and which, in the midst of peace, plenty, and contentment such as a tortured world had seldom known, overhung these wise and virtuous men like the gloom of death.

A week later Roger Griswold followed Pickering's example by writing to another of Hamilton's friends, Oliver Wolcott, who apparently sent the letter to Hamilton.[3] A Congressional caucus, February 25, nominated George Clinton as the Republican candidate for Vice-President by sixty-five votes against forty-one,—Burr's friends absenting themselves. This nomination showed some division between the Northern and

---

[1] Pickering to Rufus King, March 4, 1804; Lodge's Cabot, p. 447.

[2] Rufus King to Pickering, March 9, 1804; Lodge's Cabot, p. 450.

[3] Roger Griswold to Oliver Wolcott, March 11, 1804; Hamilton's History, vii. 781; New England Federalism, p. 354.

Southern democrats; but Griswold rightly argued that nothing could be done in Congress,—the formation of a Northern interest must begin at home, and must find its centre of union in Burr. The arguments for this course were set forth with entire candor.

"I have wished to ascertain," wrote Griswold, "the views of Colonel Burr in relation to the general government; but having had no intimacy with him myself, and finding no one on the spot calculated, or indeed authorized, to require an explanation, I have obtained but little information. He speaks in the most bitter terms of the Virginia faction, and of the necessity of a union at the northward to resist it; but what the ultimate objects are which he would propose, I do not know. It is apparent that his election is supported in New York on the principle of resisting Virginia and uniting the North; and it may be presumed that the support given to him by Federal men would tend to reconcile the feelings of those democrats who are becoming dissatisfied with their Southern masters. But it is worthy of great consideration whether the advantage gained in this manner will not be more than counterbalanced by fixing on the Northern States a man in whom the most eminent of our friends will not repose confidence. If Colonel Burr is elevated in New York to the office of governor by the votes of Federalism, will he not be considered, and must he not in fact become, the head of the Northern interest? His ambition will not suffer him to be second, and his office will give him a claim to the first rank."

Having proposed this question, Griswold argued it as one in which the interests of New York must yield to the larger interests behind, and decided that "unpleasant as the thing may be," Burr's election and consequent leadership of the Federalist party was "the only hope which at this time presents itself of rallying in defence of the Northern States. . . . What else can we do? If we remain inactive, our ruin is certain. Our friends will make no attempts alone. By supporting Mr. Burr we gain some support, although it is of a doubtful nature, and of which, God knows, we have cause enough to be jealous. In short, I see nothing else left for us."

Had this been all, though it was a rude blow to Hamilton, it might have passed as a difference of opinion on a point of party policy; but Griswold's object in writing these excuses was to explain that he had already done more, and had even entered into personal relations with Colonel Burr in view of a bargain. What this bargain was to be, Griswold explained: —

"I have engaged to call on the Vice-President as I pass through New York. The manner in which he gave me the invitation appeared to indicate a wish to enter upon some explanation. He said he wished very much to see me, and to converse, but his situation in this place did not admit of it, and he begged me to call on him at New York. This took place yesterday in the library. Indeed, I do not see how he can avoid a full explanation with Federal men. His prospects must depend on the union of the Federalists with his friends, and it is certain that his views must extend much beyond the office of governor of New York. He has the spirit of ambition and revenge to gratify, and can do but little with his 'little band' alone."

Even George Cabot deserted Hamilton, and wrote from Boston to Rufus King a long letter, in the tone of indolent speculation which irritated restless fighters like Pickering and Griswold:[1] —

"An *experiment* has been suggested by some of our friends, to which I object that it is impracticable, and if practicable would be ineffectual. The thing proposed is obvious and natural; but it would now be thought too bold, and would be fatal to its advocates as public men; yet the time *may* soon come when it will be demanded by the people of the North and East, and then it will unavoidably take place."

He explained his favorite thesis,—the last resource of failing protestants,—that things must be worse before they were better; but closed by wishing success to Burr. "I should rejoice to see Burr win the race in your State, but I cannot

[1] George Cabot to Rufus King, March 17, 1804; Lodge's Cabot, p. 345.

approve of aid being given him by any of the *leading* Federalists."

Ten days later, March 27, Congress adjourned; and thenceforward the intrigue centred about Burr and Hamilton in New York. No sooner did Griswold reach that city, on his way from Washington to Connecticut, than he kept his engagement with Burr, and in a conversation, April 4, Burr cautiously said[1] that in his present canvass "he must go on democratically to obtain the government; that if he succeeded, he should administer it in a manner that would be satisfactory to the Federalists. In respect to the affairs of the nation, Burr said that the Northern States must be governed by Virginia, or govern Virginia, and that there was no middle course; that the democratic members of Congress from the East were in this sentiment,—some of those from New York, some of the leaders in Jersey, and likewise in Pennsylvania." Further than this he would not go; and Griswold contented himself with such vague allurements.

On the other hand, Rufus King's library was the scene of grave dissensions. There Pickering went, April 8, to urge his scheme of disunion, and retired on the appearance of his colleague, Senator Adams, who for the first and last time in his life found himself fighting the battle of Alexander Hamilton, whom he disliked as decidedly as Pickering professed to love him. As the older senator left the house at his colleague's entrance, King said to Adams:[2] "Colonel Pickering has been talking to me about a project they have for a separation of the States and a Northern Confederacy; and he has also been this day talking of it with General Hamilton. Have you heard anything of it at Washington?" Adams replied that he had heard much, but not from Colonel Pickering. "I disapprove entirely of the project," said King; "and so, I am happy to tell you, does General Hamilton."

The struggle for control between Hamilton and the conspirators lasted to the eve of the election,—secret, stifled, mysterious; the intrigue of men afraid to avow their aims, and seeming rather driven by their own passions than guided by the lofty and unselfish motives which ought to inspire those

[1] Hamilton's History, vii. 787; King's Life of Rufus King, iv. 356.
[2] New England Federalism, p. 148.

whom George Cabot emphatically called the *best*! The result was a drawn battle. Hamilton prevented leading Federalists from open committal of the party, but he could not prevent the party itself from voting for Burr. The election took place April 25, 1804; and although Burr succeeded in carrying to the Federalists a few hundred voters in the city of New York, where his strength lay, giving him there a majority of about one hundred in a total vote of less than three thousand, he polled but about twenty-eight thousand votes in the State against thirty-five thousand for the Clinton candidate. The Federalists gained nothing by supporting him; but only a small portion of the party refused him their aid.

The obstinacy of Pickering and Griswold in pressing Burr on the party forced Hamilton to strain his strength in order to prevent what he considered his own humiliation. That all Hamilton's doings were known to Burr could hardly be doubted. When the election closed, a new era in Burr's life began. He was not a vindictive man, but this was the second time Hamilton had stood in his way and vilified his character. Burr could have no reason to suppose that Hamilton was deeply loved; for he knew that four fifths of the Federal party had adopted his own leadership when pitted against Hamilton's in the late election, and he knew too that Pickering, Griswold, and other leading Federalists had separated from Hamilton in the hope of making Burr himself the chief of a Northern confederacy. Burr never cared for the past,—the present and future were his only thought; but his future in politics depended on his breaking somewhere through the line of his personal enemies; and Hamilton stood first in his path, for Hamilton would certainly renew at every critical moment the tactics which had twice cost Burr his prize.

Pickering and Griswold saw their hopes shattered by the result of the New York election. They gained at the utmost only an agreement to hold a private meeting of leading Federalists at Boston in the following autumn;[1] and as Hamilton was to be present, he probably intended to take part only in order to stop once for all the intrigues of these two men. Such an assemblage, under the combined authority of Cabot,

[1] Life of Plumer, p. 299.

King, and Hamilton, could not have failed to restore discipline.

Nearly two months passed after the New York election, when, on the morning of June 18, William P. Van Ness, not yet known as "Aristides," appeared in Hamilton's office. He brought a note from Vice-President Burr, which enclosed newspaper-cuttings containing Dr. Cooper's report of Hamilton's "despicable" opinion of Burr's character. The paragraph, Burr said, had but very recently come to his knowledge. "You must perceive, sir, the necessity of a prompt and unqualified acknowledgment or denial of the use of any expression which would warrant the assertions of Dr. Cooper." General Hamilton took two days to consider the subject; and then replied in what Burr thought an evasive manner, but closed with two lines of defiance: "I trust on more reflection you will see the matter in the same light with me; if not, I can only regret the circumstance, and must abide the consequences."[1]

These concluding words were the usual form in which men expressed themselves when they intended to accept a challenge to a duel. At first sight, no sufficient reason for accepting a challenge was shown by Hamilton's letter, which disavowed Dr. Cooper's report so far as Burr was warranted in claiming disavowal. Hamilton might without impropriety have declined to give further satisfaction. In truth, not the personal but the political quarrel drew him into the field; he knew that Burr meant to challenge, not the man, but the future political chief, and that an enemy so bent on rule must be met in the same spirit. Hamilton fought to maintain his own right to leadership, so rudely disputed by Burr, Pickering, and Griswold. He devoted some of his moments before the duel to the task of explaining, in a formal document, that he fought only to save his political influence.[2] "The ability to be in future useful, whether in resisting mischief or effecting good, in those crises of our public affairs which seem likely to happen, would probably be inseparable from a conformity with public prejudice in this particular."

Always the crisis! Yet this crisis which brought Hamilton

[1] Hamilton's History, vii. 806.
[2] Hamilton's History, vii. pp. 816–819.

in July to the duelling-ground at Weehawken was not the same as that which Pickering and Griswold had so lately tried to create. Pickering's disunion scheme came to a natural end on Burr's defeat in April. The legislatures of the three Federalist States had met and done nothing; all chance of immediate action was lost, and all parties, including even Pickering and Griswold, had fallen back on their faith in the "crisis"; but the difference of opinion between Hamilton and the New Englanders was still well defined. Hamilton thought that disunion, from a conservative standpoint, was a mistake; nearly all the New Englanders, on the contrary, looked to ultimate disunion as a conservative necessity. The last letter which Hamilton wrote, a few hours before he left his house for the duelling-ground, was a short and earnest warning against disunion, addressed to Theodore Sedgwick, one of the sternest Massachusetts Federalists of Pickering's class.[1]

> "Dismemberment of our empire," said Hamilton, "will be a clear sacrifice of great positive advantages, without any counterbalancing good; administering no relief to our real disease, which is *democracy*,—the poison of which, by a subdivision, will only be the more concentred in each part, and consequently the more virulent."

The New Englanders thought this argument unsound, as it certainly was; for a dissolution of the American Union would have struck a blow more nearly fatal to democracy throughout the world than any other "crisis" that man could have compassed. Yet the argument showed that had Hamilton survived, he would probably have separated from his New England allies, and at last, like his friends Rufus King and Oliver Wolcott, would have accepted the American world as it was.

The tragedy that actually happened was a fitter ending to this dark chapter than any tamer close could have been. Early on the morning of July 11, in the brilliant sunlight of a hot summer, the two men were rowed to the duelling-ground across the river, under the rocky heights of Weehawken, and were placed by their seconds face to face. Had Hamilton acted with the energy of conviction, he would have met Burr

---

[1] Hamilton to Sedgwick, July 10, 1804; Works, vi. 567.

in his own spirit; but throughout this affair Hamilton showed want of will. He allowed himself to be drawn into a duel, but instead of killing Burr he invited Burr to kill him. In the paper Hamilton left for his justification, he declared the intention to throw away his first fire. He did so. Burr's bullet passed through Hamilton's body. The next day he was dead.

As the news spread, it carried a wave of emotion over New England, and roused everywhere sensations strangely mixed. In New York the Clinton interest, guided by Cheetham, seized the moment to destroy Burr's influence forever. Cheetham affected to think the duel a murder, procured Burr's indictment, and drove him from the State. Charges were invented to support this theory, and were even accepted as history. In the South and West, on the other hand, the duel was considered as a simple "affair of honor," in which Burr appeared to better advantage than his opponent. In New England a wail of despair arose. Even the clergy, though shocked that Hamilton should have offered the evil example of duelling, felt that they had lost their champion and sword of defence. "In those crises of our public affairs which seemed likely to happen," Hamilton's genius in council and in the field had been their main reliance; he was to be their Washington, with more than Washington's genius,—their Bonaparte, with Washington's virtues. The whole body of Federalists, who had paid little regard to Hamilton's wishes in life, went into mourning for his death, and held funeral services such as had been granted to no man of New England birth. Orators, ministers, and newspapers exhausted themselves in execration of Burr. During the whole summer and autumn, undisturbed by a breath of discord or danger, except such as their own fears created, they bewailed their loss as the most fatal blow yet given to the hopes of society.

The death of Hamilton cleared for a time the murky atmosphere of New York and New England politics. Pickering and Griswold, Tracy and Plumer, and their associates retired into the background. Burr disappeared from New York, and left a field for De Witt Clinton to sacrifice in his turn the public good to private ambition. The bloody feuds of Burr's time never again recurred. The death of Hamilton and the Vice-President's flight, with their accessories of summer-morning sunlight on rocky and wooded heights, tranquil river, and distant city, and behind all, their dark background of moral gloom, double treason, and political despair, still stand as the most dramatic moment in the early politics of the Union.

Chapter IX

PRESIDENT JEFFERSON was told from day to day of the communications that passed between Burr and the Connecticut Federalists. Of all members of the Government, the most active politician was Gideon Granger, the Postmaster-General, whose "intimacy with some of those in the secret," as Jefferson afterward testified, gave him "opportunities of searching into their proceedings."[1] Every day during this period Granger made a confidential report to the President; and at the President's request Granger warned De Witt Clinton of Burr's intrigues with the Federalists. What passed in Rufus King's library and in Burr's private room seemed known at once by Granger, and was reported within a few days to Jefferson, who received the news with his innate optimism, warranted by experience.[2]

"It will be found in this, as in all other similar cases, that crooked schemes will end by overwhelming their authors and coadjutors in disgrace, and that he alone who walks strict and upright, and who in matters of opinion will be contented that others should be as free as himself, and acquiesce when his opinion is fairly overruled, will attain his object in the end."

If Jefferson and his Virginia friends in 1798, when their own opinions were overruled, had expressed the idea of acquiescence as strongly, the nation might perhaps have been saved the necessity of proving later the truth of his words; but Jefferson could afford to treat with contempt the coalition between Burr and Pickering, because, as he wisely said, it had no cohesive force to hold it together, no common principle on which to rest. When Burr's defeat in April and Hamilton's death in July dissolved the unnatural connection, Jefferson let the secret die; he wanted no scandal. He stood a little in awe of the extreme Federalists, whom he called incurables, and was unwilling to exasperate them without an object.

The Administration had every reason to rejoice that Burr's

[1] Jefferson to Granger, March 9, 1814; Works, vi. 329.
[2] Jefferson to Granger, April 16, 1804; Works, iv. 542.

431

factious influence in the State of New York was at an end; for other causes of anxiety gave the President more personal annoyance. The strength of the Republican party lay in the alliance between Virginia and Pennsylvania. So long as these two central States, with their forty members of Congress, remained harmonious, nothing could shake Jefferson's power; but any discord which threatened his control of Pennsylvania caused him anxiety. Hardly had Burr's schism been checked in New York by a succession of measures as energetic as De Witt Clinton could persuade Jefferson to adopt, when a schism, that threatened greater mischief, broke out in Pennsylvania.

In this State no social hierarchy existed such as governed New England, nor were rich families with political followings to be found there, as in New York; but instead, Duane's "Aurora" shone without break or bar over one broad democratic level. Duane was represented in Congress by Michael Leib; while over the State Legislature his influence was complete. In Jefferson's Cabinet Pennsylvania was represented by Gallatin, who had little sympathy with the "Aurora," and began his administration of the finances by resisting Duane's demand for Federal patronage.

"The thirst for offices," to use Gallatin's own words,[1] "too much encouraged by Governor McKean's first measures, created a schism in Philadelphia as early as 1802. Leib, ambitious, avaricious, envious, and disappointed, blew up the flame, and watched the first opportunity to make his cause a general one. The vanity, the nepotism, and the indiscretion of Governor McKean afforded the opportunity. Want of mutual forbearance among the best-intentioned and most respectable Republicans has completed the schism. Duane, intoxicated by the persuasion that he alone had overthrown Federalism, thought himself neither sufficiently rewarded nor respected; and possessed of an engine which gives him an irresistible control over public opinion, he easily gained the victory for his friends."

In the spring of 1803 the "Aurora" began to attack Gallatin

[1] Gallatin to Badollet, Oct. 25, 1805; Adams's Gallatin, p. 331.

and Madison, under cover of devotion to the President; and from this beginning Duane went on to quarrel with Governor McKean and Alexander J. Dallas, the district attorney.

The impeachment of Judge Pickering in Congress followed and in some degree imitated an impeachment by the Pennsylvania Legislature of Judge Addison, one of the five president judges of the Common Pleas. With the help of Dallas and Governor McKean, the Legislature in January, 1803, removed Judge Addison; then, inspired by Randolph's attack on Justice Chase, they turned against their Supreme Court,—at one sweep impeaching three of the judges, and addressing the Governor for the removal of H. H. Brackenridge, the fourth, because he insisted on making common cause with his associates. The alleged ground of impeachment was the arbitrary committal of a suitor for contempt of court; the real motive seemed rather to be a wish for legal reforms such as society was too unskilful to make for itself, and lawyers were slow to begin. Throughout America the bar was a sort of aristocracy, conservative to a degree that annoyed reformers of every class. Jefferson and his party raised one Republican lawyer after another to the bench, only to find that when their professions of political opinion were tested in legal form, the Republican judge rivalled Marshall in the Federalist and English tendencies of his law. The bar chose to consider the prejudice of society against their caste unreasonable; but the bar was itself somewhat unreasonable to require that an untrained and ill-led body of country farmers and local politicians should say precisely what legal reform they wanted, or know exactly what was practicable.

No sooner did the Pennsylvania Legislature begin to pull in pieces the judicial system of the State, and persecute the legal profession, than Dallas, McKean, and all the educated leaders of the Republican party broke from the mass of their followers, and attempted to check their violence. Governor McKean stopped with his veto certain measures which the Legislature had approved, and he declined to remove Judge Brackenridge when the Legislature asked him to do so. Dallas became counsel for the impeached judges. Duane and Leib raged against McKean and Dallas; a large majority of Pennsylvania Republicans followed the "Aurora;" Gallatin lost control over his State, and saw himself threatened, like his friend Dallas, with ostracism; while the outside world, roused by the noise of this faction-fight, asked what it meant, and could not understand the answer. The Federalists alone professed to explain the mystery which perplexed people less wise than themselves; they had said from the beginning that the democrats had neither virtue nor understanding to carry on the government, and must bring about a crisis at last.

After the excitement of Burr's intrigues and Hamilton's death subsided, leaving the politics of New York in comparative repose, the autumn elections in Pennsylvania began to disturb Jefferson's temper.

"Thank Heaven!" wrote Dallas to Gallatin, in October,[1] "our election is over! The violence of Duane has produced a fatal division. He seems determined to destroy the Republican standing and usefulness of every man who does not bend to his will. He has attacked me as the author of an address which I never saw till it was in the press. He menaces the Governor; you have already felt his lash; and I think there is reason for Mr. Jefferson himself to apprehend that the spirit of Callender survives."

A struggle took place over the re-election of Leib to Congress, which the "Aurora" carried by a few hundred votes. Republicans of Dallas's kind, who would not support Leib, were nicknamed "Quids" by Duane, after the *tertium quid*, which was worth not even a name. At least three fourths of the Republican party followed the "Aurora," and left the "Quids" in the solitude of deserted leaders.

Jefferson's social relations were wholly with Gallatin, McKean, and Dallas, but his political strength depended on the popular vote, which followed Duane and Leib. At one moment he wanted to reason with Duane, but by Gallatin's advice gave up this idea. At length he temporized, became neutral, and left Gallatin and Dallas to their own resources.

"I see with infinite pain," he wrote to Dr. Logan,[2] "the bloody schism which has taken place among our friends in

---

[1] Dallas to Gallatin, Oct. 16, 1804; Adams's Gallatin, p. 326.
[2] Jefferson to Dr. Logan, May 11, 1805; Works, iv. 575.

Pennsylvania and New York, and will probably take place in other States. The main body of both sections mean well, but their good intentions will produce great public evil. The minority, whichever section shall be the minority, will end in coalition with the Federalists and some compromise of principle. Republicanism will thus lose, and royalism gain, some portion of that ground which we thought we had rescued to good government."

The idea that "royalism" could in any case gain support among the factions of Pennsylvania democrats was one which could have occurred only to Jefferson, who saw monarchy, as the New Englanders saw Antichrist, in every man who opposed him in politics. Apart from this trick of words, Jefferson's theory of his own duties failed to satisfy his followers. Dallas was disgusted at the situation in which he found himself left.

"It is obvious to me,"[1] he wrote to Gallatin soon after the schism broke out, "that unless our Administration take decisive measures to discountenance the factious spirit that has appeared; unless some principle of political cohesion can be introduced into our public councils as well as at our elections; and unless men of character and talents can be drawn from professional and private pursuits into the legislative bodies of our governments, Federal and State,—the empire of Republicanism will moulder into anarchy, and the labor and hope of our lives will terminate in disappointment and wretchedness. . . . At present we are the slaves of men whose passions are the object of all their actions,— I mean your Duanes, Cheethams, Leibs, etc. They have the press in their power; and though we may have virtue to assert the liberty of the press, it is too plain that we have not spirit enough to resist the tyranny of the printers."

This last sharp sentence aimed at the President, who displeased Dallas by showing too evident a wish not to offend Duane. "The duty of an upright Administration," Jefferson told Dr. Logan,[2] "is to pursue its course steadily, to know

[1] A. J. Dallas to Gallatin, Jan. 16, 1805; Adams's Gallatin, p. 327.
[2] Jefferson to Dr. Logan, May 11, 1805; Works, iv. 575.

nothing of these family dissensions, and to cherish the good principles of both parties." Had the President followed this duty in the case of Burr, the triumph of De Witt Clinton and Cheetham would have been more difficult than it was; but the President feared Burr the less because Burr's newspaper, the "Morning Chronicle," was respectable, while the "Aurora" was unscrupulous, and to cherish Duane's principles, whether good or bad, was the only way of escaping the lash of his tongue. Jefferson chose the path of caution in refusing to sustain Dallas and the "Quids" against the party and the Legislature; but during the rest of his term he was forced to endure Duane's attachment, and to feel that Madison and Gallatin were sacrificed to his own safety. Duane never hesitated to assert that he was in Jefferson's confidence and was acting in his interests,[1] and commonly he or some of his friends could show a recent letter in the President's handwriting which gave color to their assertion.

The Pennsylvania schism was not serious. Governor McKean and Dallas were alarmed when they saw the democratic system blundering in its rude way, without taking sound advice or heeding trained lawyers; but only the Federalists believed in a crisis. Society went undisturbed to its daily duties in spite of Duane's outcries and Dallas's grumbling. The only result of the Pennsylvania schism was to check the aggressive energy of the democratic movement by alarming a few of the older leaders and causing them to halt. From the day of Jefferson's inauguration this tendency toward reaction had begun, and it developed in party schisms which could not fail to hurry the process. The symptom, however unpleasant to old political leaders such as Jefferson, McKean, and Dallas, who liked the quiet enjoyment of power, was healthy for society at large; but no one could fail to be struck by the contrast which in this respect was offered by the two great sections of the country. While the mobile, many-sided, restless democracy of New England, New York, and Pennsylvania exhibited its faults, and succeeded, with much personal abuse, in thrusting out the elements foreign to its character which retarded its movement, the society of the Southern States was

[1] Dallas to Gallatin, April 4, 1805; April 21, 1811; Adams's Gallatin, pp. 333, 439.

classically calm. Not a breath disturbed the quiet which brooded over the tobacco and cotton fields between the Potomac and Florida. A Presidential election was taking place, but the South saw only one candidate. The State legislatures quietly chose electors to vote for Jefferson and Clinton. From the St. Mary's to the Potomac and the Ohio, every electoral voice was given to Jefferson. With some surprise the public learned that Maryland gave two of eleven votes to C. C. Pinckney, who received also the three votes of Delaware. This little State even went back on its path, repudiated Cæsar A. Rodney, and returned to its favorite Bayard, who was sent by a handsome majority to his old seat in the House of Representatives. Broken for an instant only by this slight check, the tide of democratic triumph swept over the States of Pennsylvania, New Jersey, and New York, and burst upon Connecticut as though Jefferson's hope of dragging even that State from its moorings were at length to be realized. With difficulty the Connecticut hierarchy held its own; and with despair after the torrent passed by, it looked about and found itself alone. Even Massachusetts cast 29,310 votes for Jefferson, against 25,777 for Pinckney.

Rarely was a Presidential election better calculated to turn the head of a President, and never was a President elected who felt more keenly the pleasure of his personal triumph. At the close of four years of administration, all Jefferson's hopes were fulfilled. He had annihilated opposition. The slanders of the Federalist press helped to show that he was the idol of four fifths of the nation. He received one hundred and sixty two of one hundred and seventy-six electoral votes, while in 1801 he had but seventy-three in one hundred and thirty-eight; and in the Ninth Congress, which was to meet in December, 1805, barely seven out of thirty-four senators, and twenty-five out of one hundred and forty-one representatives, would oppose his will. He described his triumph, in language studiously modest, in a letter to Volney:[1] —

"The two parties which prevailed with so much violence when you were here are almost wholly melted into one. At the late Presidential election I have received one hundred

[1] Jefferson to Volney, Feb. 8, 1805; Works, iv. 573.

and sixty-two votes against fourteen only. Connecticut is still Federalist by a small majority, and Delaware on a poise, as she has been since 1775, and will be till Anglomany with her yields to Americanism. Connecticut will be with us in a short time. Though the people in mass have joined us, their leaders had committed themselves too far to retract. Pride keeps them hostile; they brood over their angry passions, and give them vent in the newspapers which they maintain. They still make as much noise as if they were the whole nation."

Such success might have turned the head of any philosopher that ever sat on a throne. Easily elated, unwilling to forebode trouble, devoid of humor, and unable to see himself in any but the heroic light, President Jefferson basked in the sunshine of popularity and power as though it were no passing warmth such as had led scores of kings into disaster, but shone by virtue of some democratic law which rested on truth that could never change. The White House was filled with an atmosphere of adulation. Flattery, gross as any that man could ask, was poured into the President's ear, but was as nothing compared with the more subtle flattery of the popular vote. No friend stopped him to ask how such a miraculous success had been brought about. Four years had not passed since Jefferson and his party had clamored against attempts to give energy to government; and no one could ever forget that they claimed and received power from the people in order to defend States-rights, restrict Executive influence, and correct strained constructions of the Constitution. Who upheld States-rights in 1804, and complained of Executive influence and strained constructions? Certainly not Jefferson or his friends, but the monarchical Federalists, who were fit inmates for an asylum. Whenever Jefferson had occasion to discuss the aims and opinions of the two parties, he did not allude to the principles set forth in 1798; not a word was said of "strict construction." The only theories opposed to his own which he could see in the political horizon were those of a few hundred conservatives of the colonial epoch.

"What, in fact," he wrote,[1] "is the difference of principle

[1] Jefferson to J. F. Mercer, Oct. 9, 1804; Works, iv. 563.

between the two parties here? The one desires to preserve an entire independence of the executive and legislative branches on each other and the dependence of both on the same source,—the free election of the people. The other party wishes to lessen the dependence of the Executive and of one branch of the Legislature on the people, some by making them hold for life, some hereditary, and some even for giving the Executive an influence by patronage or corruption over the remaining popular branch, so as to reduce the elective franchise to its minimum "

After nearly four years of Executive authority more complete than had ever before been known in American history, Jefferson could see in himself and in his principles only a negation of Executive influence. What had become of the old radical division of parties,—the line between men who wished the national government to exercise inherent powers of sovereignty and those who held to a strict observance of powers expressly delegated by the people of the States?

Jefferson said with truth that the two old parties were almost wholly melted into one; but in this fusion his own party had shown even more willingness than its opponents to mix its principles in a useful, but not noble, amalgam. His own protests in regard to the Louisiana purchase and the branch bank at New Orleans were recorded. With such evidence on their side, the moderate Federalists who in the election of 1804 gave to Jefferson the nineteen electoral votes of Massachusetts and the seven of New Hampshire, could claim that they had altered no opinion they ever held; that the government had suffered no change in principle from what it had been under President Washington; that not a Federalist measure, not even the Alien and Sedition laws, had been expressly repudiated; that the national debt was larger than it had ever been before, the navy maintained and energetically employed, the national bank preserved and its operations extended; that the powers of the national government had been increased to a point that made blank paper of the Constitution as heretofore interpreted by Jefferson, while the national territory, vastly more than doubled in extent, was despotically enlarged and still more despotically ruled by the President and Congress, in the teeth of every political profession the Republican party had ever made. Had this been the work of Federalists, it would have been claimed as a splendid triumph of Federalist principles; and the good sense of New England was never better shown than when Massachusetts and New Hampshire flung aside their prejudices and told Jefferson that they accepted his inaugural pledge to be a Federalist as they were Republicans.

Every Federalist who came over and every State that joined the majority weakened the relative influence of Virginia, and helped to dilute the principles of the pure Virginia school. The new democrats in New England, New York, and Ohio were Federalists in disguise, and cared nothing for fine-spun constitutional theories of what government might or might not do, provided government did what they wanted. They feared no corruption in which they were to have a part. They were in secret jealous of Virginia, and as devoted as George Cabot and Stephen Higginson to the interests of commerce and manufactures. A majority of the Northern democrats were men of this kind. Their dislike of Federalists was a social rather than political feeling, for Federalist manners seemed to them a wilful impertinence; but the Varnums and Crowninshields of Massachusetts cared as little as De Witt Clinton or Aaron Burr for the notions of Speaker Macon and John Randolph. As orators and leaders the Northern democrats made a poor figure beside the Virginians; but their votes weighed more and more heavily with every succeeding Congress, and both Randolph and Macon were becoming suspicious that these votes were too apt to be cast against the wishes of Virginia.

The second session of the Eighth Congress met on the first Monday in November, as provided by a law passed in view of Judge Chase's impeachment. The President's Message, sent to Congress Nov. 8, 1804, was as usual toned to cheerful harmony. The income had reached eleven millions and a half of dollars; more than three million six hundred thousand dollars of the public debt had been discharged within the year, more than twelve millions since 1801; and the revenue was still increasing. Difficulties had risen with foreign nations, but no disturbance of the peace was to be expected. The Indians were quiet. Gunboats were in course of construction. No increase of the army was called for. Congress had only to inquire whether anything remained to be done for the public good.

The Federalists were reduced to showing that Jefferson's political success had not chastened his style; for the Message contained a number of sentences that exaggerated his peculiar faults of expression:—

"The war which was lighted up in Europe a little before our last meeting has not yet extended its flames to other nations, nor been marked by the calamities which sometimes stain the footsteps of war."

The Federalists reasonably objected to the figure of a war which not only extended flames but also made footsteps and marked them by calamities which stained. Jefferson went on to say that he had bought from the Delaware Indians the country between the Wabash and the Ohio:—

"This acquisition is important not only for its extent and fertility, but as fronting three hundred miles on the Ohio, and near half that on the Wabash. The produce of the settled country descending those rivers will no longer pass in view of the Indian frontier but in a small portion, and with the cession heretofore made by the Kaskaskias nearly consolidates our possessions north of the Ohio in a very respectable breadth from Lake Erie to the Mississippi."

Produce passing in view of a frontier in a portion and consolidating possessions in a breadth did not suit fastidious Federalists; nor were they satisfied with the President's closing exhortation, requesting the Legislature to inquire "whether laws are provided in all cases where they are wanting." They enjoyed their jests at Jefferson's literary style; but with the public the matter of the Message was more weighty than its manner. No kind of criticism had less political value than that wasted on the style of a public document.

Yet one thing was certainly wanting in this Message. No hint was given that Congress stood in danger of overstepping the limits of its powers, or would do well to return within them. This silence was not accidental; it marked the moment of separation between Jefferson and the old Republicans of 1798. Speaker Macon, John Randolph, and Joseph Nicholson soon showed that they meant to take no such view of their duties.

Hardly had legislation begun, when Randolph, November 26, made a report against the remission of duties on books imported for the use of schools and colleges. The Constitution, he said, was a grant of limited powers for general objects; its leading feature was an abhorrence of exclusive privileges; impost must be uniform; if Congress could exempt one class of the people from taxes, they might exempt other classes; and although the practice had been different, and philosophical apparatus for the use of schools was actually exempt by law, he believed that law to be unconstitutional. The doctrine, which if carried to its ultimate conclusions would have left hardly a tax on the statute-book, was accepted by the same House which had supported Randolph in defending the Louisiana purchase by arguments that, in President Jefferson's opinion, left no Constitution at all. Two days afterward Randolph repeated the lesson, and his friends Macon and Nicholson came to his support. A Bill was before the House authorizing the corporation of Georgetown to construct a dam or causeway from Mason's Island to the shore of the Potomac, in order to scour the channel and improve navigation. Randolph affirmed that the Potomac was the joint property of Maryland and Virginia, over which Congress had no right to legislate; that the Bill authorized the corporation of Georgetown to lay a tax which would be unequal and oppressive, because all Georgetown property would not be equally benefited by deepening the harbor; and finally, "he hoped a prompt rejection of the Bill would serve as a general notice to the inhabitants of the District to desist from their daily and frivolous applications to Congress." Macon, Nicholson, and a number of the Virginians spoke earnestly in the same sense. "So long as I have the honor of a seat in the House," said Nicholson, "I will hold up my hands against any measure like the present, which would go to affect the rights of any of the States. If Congress have a right to interfere in the least with the free navigation of the Potomac, they have a right to stop it altogether." In reply to these exhortations the

House passed the Bill by a vote of sixty-six to thirty-eight; and more than enough Republicans voted for it to have passed it without Federalist help.

The reason for this sudden decline of Randolph's influence was not far to seek. He was undertaking to act without concert with the President. While he and his friends argued on the States-rights theory at one end of Pennsylvania Avenue, Jefferson at the other end said openly, to Federalists and Republicans alike, that such arguments were mere metaphysical subtleties which ought to have no weight.[1] The next subject in debate left no longer a doubt of the cleft opening between the old Republicans of 1798 and the Republicans of the future, with Jefferson and Madison at their head. That Randolph had determined to fight for control of the party and for the principles upon which it had come into office was clear; but the reason for the suddenness and violence of his emotion was found in the once famous story of the Yazoo Claims, which from his youth acted on his passionate temper with the force of a point of honor.

As already told, Congress seemed about to settle these claims as early as April, 1802, when the six commissioners made their Report.[2] John Randolph and his friends were then supreme Dec. 30, 1803, a few days before the Federalists were startled by Randolph's demand for the impeachment of Judge Chase, the Northern democrats and the friends of Madison were surprised by a Resolution offered by Randolph excluding claimants under the Georgia grants of 1795 from any share in the proposed settlement. A few weeks later, Feb. 20, 1804, Randolph withdrew this Resolution, in order to introduce a series of declaratory Resolves, which, after reciting the story of the Georgia grants, affirmed the right of Georgia to rescind them, and forbade the appropriation of money to the settlement of claims derived from them. March 7, 1804, he made a long and earnest speech on the subject; and after a sharp struggle in a House nearly equally divided, he succeeded in defeating action on the Bill. On the final vote of postponement, March 12, 1804, he carried fifteen members of the Virginia delegation with him. Of the three Republicans from

[1] Diary of J. Q. Adams (Jan. 11, 1805), i. 331.
[2] See p. 207.

Virginia who rejected his lead, one was John G. Jackson, brother-in-law of the Secretary of State.

From that moment Randolph's energies quickened in sympathy with old Republican principles; and when he returned to Congress in November, 1804, he and his friends began at once to take extreme ground as champions of States-rights. He lost no chance of enforcing his theories, whether in regard to exemptions from taxes, or in denying to government power to improve navigation within the District of Columbia, or in reproving the people of Georgetown for proposing to lay a general tax on their property for the betterment of their river front. He found the Administration opposed to him. "Mere metaphysical subtleties," said Jefferson. The influence of Madison was strong in favor of the Yazoo Compromise, and the Northern democrats supported the Secretary. A struggle for supremacy was imminent, and its consequences were soon felt. The impeachment of Judge Chase was Randolph's measure, and received no support from Madison. The Yazoo Compromise was Madison's measure, and its defeat was Randolph's passionate wish.

The three branches of government were likely to be at variance on a point of deep concern. No one who knew Chief-Justice Marshall could doubt that he, and the Supreme Bench with him, would hold that the State of Georgia was bound by its contract with the Land Companies. The Administration had taken the ground that the State was not bound in law, but that the United States should nevertheless make an equitable compromise with the claimants. Randolph was bent on forcing Congress to assert that a State had the right to repudiate its own acts where it was evident that these acts were against common morality or public interest; and that its decision in such a case should be final. The conflict was embittered by the peculiarities of Randolph's character. In his eyes, when such questions of honor were involved, every man who opposed him seemed base. Unfortunately the New England Mississippi Company secured the services of Gideon Granger, the Postmaster-General, as their agent; and Randolph's anger became intense when, at the close of the year 1804, he saw the Postmaster-General on the floor of the House openly lobbying for the passage of the Bill.

At length, at the end of January, 1805, the House went into committee on the Georgia claims, and Randolph for the first time displayed the full violence of his temper. Hitherto as a leader he had been at times arrogant; but from this moment he began the long series of personal assaults which made him famous, as though he were the bully of a race course, dispensed from regarding ordinary rules of the ring, and ready at any sudden impulse to spring at his enemies, gouging, biting, tearing, and rending his victims with the ferocity of a rough-and-tumble fight. The spectacle was revolting, but terrific; and until these tactics lost their force by repetition, few men had the nerve and quickness to resist them with success.

"Past experience has shown," he cried, "that this is one of those subjects which pollution has sanctified." He treated the majority of the House as corruptionists, "As if animated by one spirit, they perform all their evolutions with the most exact discipline, and march in a firm phalanx directly up to their object. Is it that men combined to effect some evil purpose, acting on previous pledge to each other, are ever more in unison than those who, seeking only to discover truth, obey the impulse of that conscience which God has placed in their bosoms?" He fell upon Granger: "Millions of acres are easily digested by such stomachs. Goaded by avarice, they buy only to sell, and sell only to buy. The retail trade of fraud and imposture yields too small and slow a profit to gratify their cupidity. They buy and sell corruption in the gross." He hinted that the Administration was to blame: "Is it come to this? Are heads of executive departments to be brought into this House, with all the influence and patronage attached to them, to extort from us now what was refused at the last session of Congress?" He closed by asserting that this was the spirit of Federalism, and that Republicans who yielded to it were false to their party: "Of what consequence is it that a man smiles in your face, holds out his hand, and declares himself the advocate of those political principles to which you are also attached, when you see him acting with your adversaries upon other principles which the voice of the nation has put down, and which I did hope were buried, never to rise again in this section of the globe?" He maintained that the Federalist administrations had done no act so corrupt: "If Congress shall determine to sanction this fraud upon the public, I trust in God we shall hear no more of the crimes and follies of the former Administration. For one, I promise that my lips upon this subject shall be closed in eternal silence. I should disdain to prate about the petty larcenies of our predecessors after having given my sanction to this atrocious public robbery."

The tirade could have no other result than a personal quarrel and a party schism. Madison and the Administration had done nothing to deserve the attack, and of course could not trust Randolph again. The question whether the claimants had rights which the government would do well to compromise was for the law to decide, and was ultimately settled by Chief-Justice Marshall in their favor. The question of morality, in regard to sanctioning fraud, though a much wider issue, was not to be settled *ex parte*, but must abide by the answer to the question of law. Only the States-rights difficulty remained; and even on that delicate ground, although the right of Georgia to repudiate her own pledges under the plea of her own corruption were conceded, the States-rights theory could not insist that this act must bind other States, or affect any sovereignty except that which was directly involved. After the property in question had been sold to the United States government, Georgia need not prevent the purchaser from doing what it would with its own. Randolph could not make States-rights serve his whole purpose in the argument, and was obliged to rely on the charge of sanctioning corruption and fraud,—a charge irrelevant to the claim of innocent third parties like the New Englanders, unless he could prove their complicity, which was not in his power.

Randolph's harangue struck at the credit of Madison; and the conduct of the Postmaster-General in acting as claim-agent cast a shadow of corruption over the whole government. Madison's friends were obliged to take up the challenge; and his brother-in-law, John G. Jackson of Virginia, replied to Randolph in a speech which was thought to bear evident marks of Madison's hand. Some of Jackson's retorts carried a sting. Randolph had dwelt much on the silence and discipline of the majority. "When unprincipled men," said he,

"acquire the ascendency, they act in concert and are silent."
"Silence and concert, then," retorted Jackson, "are to him
proofs of corrupt motive. Is this always a correct position?
Does the gentleman recollect that measures were adopted a
few years past without discussion, by my political friends in
conjunction with him, who were *silent and united*?" Throughout Jackson's speech ran a tone of irritating disregard for his
colleague, " whose influence in this House is equal to the rapacity of the speculator whose gigantic grasp has been described by him as extending from the shores of Lake Erie to
the mouth of the Mobile." Whether Madison meant it or not,
an impression prevailed in the House that in Jackson's speech
the Secretary of State took up Randolph's challenge with a
defiance equally strong.

Randolph returned to his charges, attacking Granger bitterly, but not yet venturing to take the single step that remained to create a Virginia feud; he left Jackson and Madison
alone. He bore with something like patience the retorts which
his violence drew upon him, and his self-esteem made him
proof to the insults of democrats like Matthew Lyon, who
thanked his Creator "that he gave me the face of a man, not
that of an ape or a monkey, and that he gave me the heart of
a man also." After a long and ill-tempered debate, Feb. 2,
1805, Randolph closed by an allusion to Madison and Gallatin
which implied hesitation. "When I first read their Report, I
was filled with unutterable astonishment, finding men in
whom I had and still have the highest confidence recommend
a measure which all the facts and all the reasons they had
collected opposed and unequivocally condemned." Prudence
restrained him from making a final breach with Madison; and
perhaps he was the more cautious because he felt the danger
of pressing too far his influence over Virginia sentiment
which to this point supported his opposition. When the
House divided, a majority of sixty-three to fifty-eight sustained the compromise, and ordered the committee of claims
to report a Bill; but in the minority Randolph found by his
side every Republican member of the Virginia delegation except two, one of whom was Jackson. Even the two sons-in-
law of President Jefferson voted against the Yazoo claims. So
strong was the current of opinion in Virginia, that Senator

Giles went about Washington[1] asserting that Jefferson himself would lose an election there if he were known to favor the compromise, and that Jackson would certainly be defeated. For the moment Randolph might fairly suppose that in a contest for supremacy with the Secretary of State, his own hold on Virginia was stronger than Madison's. In spite of the majority against him, he succeeded in postponing action on the Bill.

Perhaps his temper was further restrained by another motive. The trial of Judge Chase was near at hand. Within a few days after the close of the Yazoo debate, Randolph was to open the case for the managers before the Senate; and he had reason to fear that the Northern democrats were beginning to doubt the wisdom of this Virginia scheme.

[1] Diary of J. Q. Adams (Feb. 1, 1805), i. 343.

Chapter X

THE SCHISMS which characterized the last year of President Jefferson's first term increased the difficulty of convicting Justice Chase. Burr was still Vice-President, and was sure not only to preside at the trial, but also, unless conciliated, to encourage rebellion against the Virginians. He had warm friends even in the Senate; and he was observed to cultivate close social relations with John Smith, the senator from Ohio, whose vote was likely to be necessary for conviction. Although the two senators from New York were no friends of Burr, one of them, Dr. Samuel L. Mitchill, was known to oppose impeachment; and not only he, but also his colleague, another John Smith, when members of the House, voted against Randolph's motion for a committee of inquiry. Senator Bradley of Vermont privately talked with earnestness against the Pickering impeachment, and never favored that of Chase. His colleague, Israel Smith, shared his doubts. Twenty-three votes were required to convict, and the Republicans had but twenty-five senators against nine Federalists. A defection of three Republican senators would be fatal; but the votes of at least five were in doubt.

Randolph's attack on the Yazoo Republicans and on the friends of Madison took from them all desire to strengthen his influence; while, as though to complicate confusion, his assault on his own party was cheered by Duane and the "Aurora," until the Pennsylvania schism seemed about to join with a Virginia schism for the overthrow of the judiciary in the first place, and of Madison and Gallatin afterward. A collapse of the Republican party was to be feared. In the success of impeachment, the interests of Duane and Randolph were closely connected, and Duane controlled Pennsylvania as Randolph ruled Virginia. Everything tended to show that Chase's conviction would add to the power already in the hands of these two men; and hands less fitted to guide a government or less trusted by moderate Republicans could hardly be found in either party.

Duane's support of Randolph was the warmer because his own attack on the judiciary failed. The Pennsylvania judges were brought to trial in January, 1805. The managers for the Legislature, knowing no law themselves and unable to persuade any competent Pennsylvania lawyer to act as counsel, sent for Cæsar A. Rodney from Delaware to conduct the case. So important did Randolph and Nicholson at Washington think the success of the Pennsylvania impeachment, that at the end of December, 1804, they allowed Rodney to drop his work as member of Congress and manager of Chase's trial, in order to hurry to Lancaster and do battle with Dallas, Jefferson's district attorney, who was defending the judges. After a long struggle, Jan. 28, 1805, the Senate at Lancaster came to a vote, and Rodney was beaten. Thirteen senators declared the judges guilty,—three less than the required two thirds.

This defeat of the impeachers occurred the day before Randolph attacked Granger and the Yazoo claims in Congress. During the week that preceded Chase's trial, Randolph's bad management or ill-luck seemed accumulating disasters on his head. He roused needless hatred against himself in Congress; his alliance with Duane was unsuccessful; he exhausted his strength in fighting the Yazoo Bill, and was in no condition of mind or body to meet the counsel of Judge Chase.

Neither the Administration nor his Virginia friends failed to support Randolph. They made efforts to conciliate Burr, whose opposition to the impeachment was most feared. Jefferson appointed J. B. Prevost of New York, Burr's stepson, a judge of the Superior Court at New Orleans; James Brown, who married Mrs. Burr's sister, was made secretary to the Louisiana Territory and sent to govern St. Louis, solely on Burr's recommendation; James Wilkinson, one of Burr's most intimate friends and general-in-chief of the army, was made governor of the Louisiana Territory,—an appointment directly opposed to Jefferson's theories about the union of civil and military authority.[1] Besides these conciliatory compliments the President repeatedly invited Burr to dinner, and treated him with more attention than ever before;[2] both Madison and Gallatin kept up friendly relations with him; while Senator Giles of Virginia drew an Address to Governor Bloomfield of New Jersey, and caused it to be signed by all

[1] Jefferson to General Smith, May 4, 1806; Works, v. 13.
[2] Life of Plumer, p. 330.

the senators who could be induced to let their names be used, requesting that a *nolle prosequi* should be entered on the indictment against Burr found by the grand jury of Bergen county.

The Virginians closed their quarrels for the moment in order to support the impeachment. William B. Giles, who came to the Senate in place of Wilson Cary Nicholas, acted as Randolph's representative in shaping the Senate's rules.[1] He canvassed its members, and dealt with those who doubted, laboring earnestly and openly to bring senators to the Virginia standpoint, as fixed by him in a speech intended to serve as guide in framing rules for the proceedings about to begin. This speech, made Dec. 20, 1804,[2] maintained that the Constitution put no limit on impeachment, but said only that the Senate should try *all* impeachments; and therefore, while any civil officer convicted of treason, bribery, or other high crimes and misdemeanors should be removed from office, in all other cases not enumerated the Senate might at its discretion remove, disqualify, or suspend the officer. Thus Judge Pickering had been removed, said Giles, though undoubtedly insane and incapable of committing any crime or of making his defence. "So the assumption of power on the part of the Supreme Court in issuing their process to the office of the Secretary of State, directing the Executive how a law of the United States should be executed, and the right which the courts have assumed to themselves of reviewing and passing upon the Acts of the Legislature in other cases," were matter of impeachment. In arguing this thesis Giles was obliged to take the ground that the Senate was not a court, and ought to discard all analogy with a court of justice;[3] impeachment need imply no criminality or corruption, and removal was nothing more than a notice to the impeached officer that he held opinions dangerous to the State, and that his office must be put in better hands. He induced the Senate to strike out the word "court" where it occurred in the proposed rules;[4] and at length went so far as to deny that the secretary of the

[1] Diary of J. Q. Adams (Nov. 29, 30, 1804), i. 318.
[2] Boston Centinel, Jan. 9, 1805.
[3] Diary of J. Q. Adams (Dec. 21, 1804), i. 322.
[4] Ibid. (Dec. 24, 1804), i. 324, 325.

Senate could administer the oath to witnesses, or that the Senate had power to authorize the secretary to administer such an oath, but must send for a magistrate competent for the purpose. Unfortunately for him, the impeachment of Judge Pickering was a precedent directly opposed to this doctrine. He was compelled to submit while the Senate unwillingly took the forms of a court.

Giles's view of impeachment, which was the same with that of Randolph, had the advantage of being clear and consistent. The opposite extreme, afterward pressed by Luther Martin and his associate counsel for the defence, restricted impeachment to misdemeanors indictable at law,—a conclusion not to be resisted if the words of the Constitution were to be understood in a legal sense. Such a rule would have made impeachment worthless for many cases where it was likely to be most needed; for comparatively few violations of official duty, however fatal to the State, could be brought within this definition. Giles might have quoted Madison in support of the broader view; and if Madison did not understand the Constitution, any other Virginian might be excused for error. So far back as the year 1789, when Congress began to discuss the President's powers, Madison said: "I contend that the wanton removal of meritorious officers would subject him to impeachment and removal from his own high trust." Such a misdemeanor was certainly not indictable, and could not technically be brought within the words of the Constitution; it was impeachable only on Giles's theory.

The Senate became confused between these two views, and never knew on what theory it acted. Giles failed to take from its proceedings the character of a court of justice; but though calling itself a court of justice, it would not follow strict rules of law. The result was a nondescript court, neither legal nor political, making law and voting misdemeanors for itself as it went, and stumbling from one inconsistency to another.

The managers added to the confusion. They put forward no steady theory of their own as to the nature of impeachment; possibly differing in opinion, they intentionally allotted different lines of argument to each. In opening the case, Feb. 20, 1805, one of the managers, George W. Campbell of Tennessee, took the ground that "misdemeanor" in the

Constitution need imply no criminality. "Impeachment," said he, "according to the meaning of the Constitution, may fairly be considered a kind of inquest into the conduct of an officer merely as it regards his office. . . . It is more in the nature of a civil investigation than of a criminal prosecution." Such seemed to be the theory of the managers and of the House; for although the articles of impeachment reported by Randolph in March, 1804, had in each case alleged acts which were inspired by an evil intent to oppress the victim or to excite odium against the Government, and were at least misdemeanors in the sense of misbehavior, Randolph at the last moment slipped into the indictment two new articles, one of which alleged no evil intent at all, while both alleged, at worst, errors in law such as every judge in the United States had committed. Article V. charged that Chase had issued a *capias* against Callender, when the law of Virginia required a summons to appear at the next court. Article VI. charged that he had, "with intent to oppress," held Callender for trial at once, contrary to the law of Virginia. Every judge on the Supreme Bench had ruled that United States courts were not bound to follow the processes of the State courts; Chief-Justice Marshall himself, as Giles threatened, must be the first victim if such an offence were a misdemeanor in constitutional law.

That a judge was impeachable for a mistake in declaring the law seemed therefore to be settled, so far as the House and its managers could decide the point. Judge Chase's counsel assumed that this principle, which had been so publicly proclaimed, was seriously meant; and one after another dwelt on the extravagance of the doctrine that a civil officer should be punished for mere error of judgment. In reply, Joseph H. Nicholson, Randolph's closest ally, repudiated the theory on which he had himself acted in Pickering's case, and which Giles, Randolph, and Campbell pressed; he even denied having heard such ground taken as that an impeachment was a mere inquest of office:—

"For myself, I am free to declare that I heard no such position taken. If declarations of this kind have been made, in the name of the managers I here disclaim them. We do contend that this is a criminal prosecution for offences committed in the discharge of high official duties, and we now support it,—not merely for the purpose of removing an individual from office, but in order that the punishment inflicted on him may deter others from pursuing the baneful example which has been set them."

The impeachment, then, was a criminal prosecution, and the Senate was a criminal court; yet no offence was charged which the law considered a misdemeanor, while error of judgment, with no imputed ill-intent, was alleged as a crime.

Staggering under this load of inconsistencies, uncertain what line of argument to pursue, and ignorant whether the Senate would be ruled by existing law or invent a system of law of its own, the managers, Feb. 9, 1805, appeared in the Senate chamber to open their case and produce their witnesses. Upon the popular imagination of the day the impeachment of Warren Hastings had taken deep hold. Barely ten years had passed since the House of Lords rendered its judgment in that famous case; and men's minds were still full of associations with Westminster Hall. The impeachment of Judge Chase was a cold and colorless performance beside the melodramatic splendor of Hastings's trial; but in the infinite possibilities of American democracy, the questions to be decided in the Senate chamber had a weight for future ages beyond any that were then settled in the House of Lords. Whether Judge Chase should be removed from the bench was a trifling matter; whether Chief-Justice Marshall and the Supreme Court should hold their power and principles against this combination of States-rights conservatives and Pennsylvania democrats was a subject for grave reflection. Men who did not see that the tide of political innovation had long since turned, and that the French revolution was no longer raging, were consumed with anxiety for the fate of Chase, and not wholly without reason; for had Marshall been a man of less calm and certain judgment, a single mistake by him might easily have prostrated the judiciary at the feet of partisans.

By order of the Vice-President the Senate chamber was arranged in accordance with his ideas of what suited so grave an occasion. His own chair stood, like that of the chief-justice in the court-room, against the wall, and on its right and left crimson benches extended like the seats of associate judges, to accommodate the thirty-four senators, who were all present. In front of the Vice-President, on the right, a box was assigned to the managers; on the left, a similar box was occupied by Justice Chase and his counsel. The rest of the floor was given to members of the House, foreign ministers, and other official persons. Behind these a new gallery was erected especially for ladies, and at each end of this temporary gallery boxes were reserved for the wives and families of public officers. The upper and permanent gallery was public. The arrangement was a mimic reproduction of the famous scene in Westminster Hall; and the little society of Washington went to the spectacle with the same interest and passion which had brought the larger society of London to hear the orations of Sheridan and Burke.

Before this audience Justice Chase at last appeared with his array of counsel at his side, — Luther Martin, Robert Goodloe Harper, Charles Lee, Philip Barton Key, and Joseph Hopkinson. In such a contest weakness of numbers was one element of strength; for the mere numbers of Congressmen served only to rouse sympathy for the accused. The contest was unequal in another sense, for the intellectual power of the House was quite unable on the field of law to cope with the half-dozen picked and trained champions who stood at the bar. Justice Chase alone was a better lawyer than any in Congress; Luther Martin could easily deal with the whole box of managers; Harper and Lee were not only lawyers, but politicians; and young Hopkinson's genius was beyond his years.

In the managers' box stood no lawyer of corresponding weight. John Randolph, who looked upon the impeachment as his personal act, was not only ignorant of law, but could not work by legal methods. Joseph H. Nicholson and Cæsar A. Rodney were more formidable; but neither of them would have outweighed any single member of Chase's counsel. The four remaining managers, all Southern men, added little to the strength of their associates. John Boyle of Kentucky lived to become chief-justice of that State, and was made district judge of the United States by a President who was one of the Federalist senators warmly opposed to the impeachment.

George Washington Campbell of Tennessee lived to be a senator, Secretary of the Treasury, and minister to Russia. Peter Early of Georgia became a judge on the Supreme Bench of his own State. Christopher Clark of Virginia was chosen only at the last moment to take the place of Roger Nelson of Maryland, who retired. None of them rose much above the average level of Congress; and Chase's counsel grappled with them so closely, and shut them within a field so narrow, that no genius could have found room to move. From the moment that the legal and criminal character of impeachment was conceded, Chase's counsel dragged them hither and thither at will.

Feb. 9, 1805, the case was opened by John Randolph. Randolph claimed to have drawn all the articles of impeachment with his own hand. If any one understood their character, it was he; and the respondent's counsel naturally listened with interest for Randolph's explanation or theory of impeachment, and for the connection he should establish between his theory and his charges. These charges were numerous, but fell under few heads. Of the eight articles which Randolph presented, the first concerned the judge's conduct at the trial of John Fries for treason in Philadelphia in 1800; the five following articles alleged a number of offences committed during the trial of James Thompson Callender for libel at Richmond in that year; Article VII. charged as a misdemeanor the judge's refusal, in the same year, to dismiss the grand jury in Delaware before indicting a seditious printer; finally, Article VIII. complained of the judge's harangue to the grand jury at Baltimore in May, 1803, which it characterized as "highly indecent, extra-judicial, and tending to prostitute the high judicial character with which he was invested to the low purpose of an electioneering partisan."

Serious as some of these charges certainly were,—for in the case of Callender, even more than in that of Fries, Chase's temper had led him to strain, if not to violate, the law,— none of the articles alleged an offence known to the statute-books or the common law; and Randolph's first task was to show that they could be made the subject of impeachment, that they were high crimes and misdemeanors in the sense of the Constitution, or that in some sense they were impeachable. Instead of arguing this point, he contented himself by declaring the theory of the defence to be monstrous. His speech touched the articles, one by one, adding little to their force, but piling one mistake on another in its assertions of fact and assumptions of law.

Ten days passed in taking evidence before the field was cleared and the discussion began. Then, Feb. 20, 1805, Early and Campbell led for the managers in arguments which followed more or less closely in Randolph's steps, inferring criminality in the accused from the manifest tenor of his acts. Campbell ventured to add that he was not obliged to prove the accused to have committed any crime known to the law,—it was enough that he had transgressed the line of official duty with corrupt motives; but this timid incursion into the field of the Constitution was supported by no attempt at argument. "I lay it down as a settled rule of decision," said he, "that when a man violates a law or commits a manifest breach of his duty, an evil intent or corrupt motive must be presumed to have actuated his conduct."

Joseph Hopkinson opened for the defence. Friends and enemies joined in applauding the vigor of this young man's attack. The whole effort of Chase's counsel was to drive the impeachers within the limits of law, and compel them to submit to the restrictions of legal methods. Hopkinson struck into the heart of the question. He maintained that under the Constitution no judge could be lawfully impeached or removed from office for any act or offence for which he could not be indicted; "misdemeanor," he argued, was a technical term well understood and defined, which meant the violation of a public law, and which, when occurring in a legal instrument like the Constitution, must be given its legal meaning. After stating this proposition with irresistible force, he dealt with Article I. of the impeachment, which covered the case of Fries, and shook it to pieces with skill very unlike the treatment of Early and Campbell. Barton Key next rose, and dealt with Articles II., III., and IV., covering part of Callender's case; he was followed by Charles Lee, who succeeded in breaking down Randolph's interpolated Articles V. and VI. Then Luther Martin appeared on the scene, and the audience felt that the managers were helpless in his hands.

This extraordinary man—"unprincipled and impudent Federalist bulldog," as Jefferson called him—revelled in the pleasure of a fight with democrats. The bar of Maryland felt a curious mixture of pride and shame in owning that his genius and vices were equally remarkable. Rough and coarse in manner and expression, verbose, often ungrammatical, commonly more or less drunk, passionate, vituperative, gross, he still had a mastery of legal principles and a memory that overbalanced his faults, an audacity and humor that conquered illwill. In the practice of his profession he had learned to curb his passions until his ample knowledge had time to give the utmost weight to his assaults. His argument at Chase's trial was the climax of his career; but such an argument cannot be condensed in a paragraph. Its length and variety defied analysis within the limits of a page, though its force made other efforts seem unsubstantial.

Martin covered the same ground that his associates had taken before him, dwelling earnestly on the contention that an impeachable offence must be also indictable. Harper followed, concluding the argument for the defence, and seeming to go beyond his associates in narrowing the field of impeachment; for he argued that it was a criminal prosecution, which must be founded on some wilful violation of a known law of the land,—a line of reasoning which could end only in requiring the violation of an Act of Congress. This theory did not necessarily clash with that of Martin. No hesitation or inconsistency was shown on the side of the defence; every resource of the profession was used with energy and skill.

The managers then put forward their best pleaders; for they had need of all their strength. Nicholson began by disavowing the idea that impeachment was a mere inquest of office; this impeachment was, he said, a criminal prosecution intended not merely to remove, but to punish, the offender. On the other hand, he maintained that since judges held their commissions during good behavior, and could be removed only by impeachment, the Constitution must have intended that any act of misbehavior should be considered a misdemeanor. He showed the absurdities which would rise from construing the Constitution in a legal sense. His argument, though vigorous and earnest, and offering the advantages of a plausible compromise between two extreme and impracticable doctrines, yet evidently strained the language of the Constitution and disregarded law. As Nicholson himself said, he discarded legal usage: "In my judgment the Constitution of the United States ought to be expounded upon its own principles, and foreign aid ought never to be called in. Our Constitution was fashioned after none other in the known world; and if we understand the language in which it is written, we require no assistance in giving it a true exposition." He wanted a construction "purely and entirely American." In the mouth of a strict constructionist this substitution of the will of Congress for the settled rules of law had as strange a sound as Luther Martin could have wished, and offered another example of the instinct, so striking in the Louisiana debate, which not even Nicholson, Randolph, or Jefferson himself could always resist.

Rodney, the same day, followed Nicholson; and as though not satisfied with his colleague's theory, did what Nicholson, in the name of all the managers, had a few hours before expressly disclaimed,—he adopted and pressed Giles's theory of impeachment with all the precision of language he could command. Nicholson seemed content to assume impeachment as limited to "treason, bribery, or other high crimes and misdemeanors;" but in his view misbehavior might be construed as a misdemeanor in a "purely and entirely American" sense. Rodney was not satisfied with this argument, and insisted that the Constitution imposed no limit on impeachment.

"Is there a word in the whole sentence," he asked, "which expresses an idea, or from which any fair inference can be drawn, that no person shall be impeached but for 'treason, bribery, or other high crimes and misdemeanors?' . . . From the most cursory and transient view of this passage I submit with due deference that it must appear very manifest that there are other cases than those here specified for which an impeachment will lie and is the proper remedy."

The judges held their offices during good behavior; the instant a judge should behave ill his office became forfeited. To ascertain the fact "officially, or rather judicially," impeachment was provided; the authority of the Senate was therefore coextensive with the complaint.

Rodney stated this principle broadly, but did not rest upon it; on the contrary, he accepted the respondent's challenge, and undertook to show that Chase had been guilty of crimes and misdemeanors in the technical sense of the term. Probably he was wise in choosing this alternative; for no one could doubt that his constitutional doctrine was one into which Chase's counsel were sedulously trying to drive him. If Rodney was right, the Senate was not a court of justice, and should discard judicial forms. Giles had seen this consequence of the argument, and had acted upon it, until beaten by its inevitable inconsistencies; at least sixteen senators were willing to accept the principle, and to make of impeachment an "official, or rather judicial," inquest of office. Judge Chase's counsel knew also that some half-dozen Republican senators feared to allow a partisan majority in the Senate to decide, after the fact, that such or such a judicial opinion had forfeited the judge's seat on the bench. This practice could end only in making the Senate, like the House of Lords, a court of last appeal. Giles threatened to impeach Marshall and the whole Supreme Court on Rodney's theory; and such a threat was as alarming to Dr. Mitchill of New York, or Senator Bradley of Vermont, as it was to Pickering and Tracy.

When Rodney finished, the theory of impeachment was more perplexed than ever, and but one chance remained to clear it. All the respondent's counsel had spoken in their turn; all the managers had expounded their theories: John Randolph was to close. Randolph was an invalid, overwhelmed by work and excitement, nervous, irritable, and not to be controlled. When he appeared in the box, Feb. 27, 1805, he was unprepared; and as he spoke, he not only made his usual long pauses for recollection, but continually complained of having lost his notes, of his weakness, want of ability, and physical as well as moral incompetence. Such expressions in the mouths of other men might have passed for rhetoric; but Randolph's speech showed that he meant all he said. He too undertook to answer the argument of Luther Martin, Harper, and Hopkinson on the nature of impeachment; but he an-

swered without understanding it, calling it "almost too absurd for argument," "a monstrous pretension," "a miserable
quibble," but advancing no theory of his own, and supporting neither Campbell's, Nicholson's, nor Rodney's opinion.
After a number of arguments which were in no sense answers,
he said he would no longer worry the good sense of the
Court by combating such a claim,—a claim which the best
lawyers in America affirmed to be sound, and the two ablest
of the managers had exhausted themselves in refuting.

Randolph's closing speech was overcharged with vitupera-
tion and with misstatements of fact and law, but was chiefly
remarkable on account of the strange and almost irrational
behavior of the speaker. Randolph's tall, thin figure, his penetrating eyes and shrill voice, were familiar to the society of
Washington, and his violence of manner in the House only a
short time before, in denouncing Granger and the Yazoo
men, had prepared his audience for some eccentric outburst;
but no one expected to see him, " with much distortion of
face and contortion of body, tears, groans, and sobs," break
down in the middle of his self-appointed task, and congratulate the Senate that this was "the last day of my sufferings and
of yours."[1]

The next day the Senate debated the form of its final judgment.[2] Bayard moved that the question should be put: "Is
Samuel Chase guilty or not guilty of a high crime or misdemeanor as charged in the article just read?" The point was
vital; for if this form should be adopted, the Senate returned
to the ground it had deserted in the case of Judge Pickering,
and every senator would be obliged to assert that Chase's acts
were crimes. At this crisis Giles abandoned the extreme impeachers. He made a speech repeating his old argument, and
insisting that the House might impeach and the Senate convict not only for other than indictable offences, but for other
than high crimes and misdemeanors; yet since in the present
case the charges were avowedly for high crimes and misdemeanors, he was willing to take the question as Bayard proposed it, protesting meanwhile against its establishment as a
precedent. Bayard's Resolution was adopted March 1, a few

[1] Diary of J. Q. Adams (Feb. 27, 1805), i. 359.
[2] Ibid., i. 361, 362.

moments before the hour of half-past twelve, which had been appointed for pronouncing judgment.

The Senate chamber was crowded with spectators when Vice-President Burr took the chair and directed the secretary to read the first article of impeachment. Every member of the Senate answered to his name. Tracy of Connecticut, prostrated by recent illness, was brought on a couch and supported to his seat, where his pale face added to the serious effect of the scene. The first article, which concerned the trial of Fries, was that on which Randolph had founded the impeachment, and on which the managers had thrown perhaps the greatest weight. As the roll was called, Senator Bradley of Vermont, first of the Republican members, startled the audience by saying "Not Guilty." Gaillard of South Carolina, and, to the astonishment of every one, Giles, the most ardent of impeachers, repeated the same verdict. These three defections decided the result; but they were only the beginning. Jackson of Georgia, another hot impeacher, came next; then Dr. Mitchill, Samuel Smith of Maryland, and in quick succession all the three Smiths of New York, Ohio, and Vermont. A majority of the Senate declared against the article, and the overthrow of the impeachers was beyond expectation complete.

On the second article the acquittal was still more emphatic; but on the third the impeachers rallied,—Giles, Jackson, and Samuel Smith returned to their party, and for the first time a majority appeared for conviction. Yet even with this support, the impeachers were far from obtaining the required twenty-three votes; the five recalcitrant Northern democrats stood firm; Gaillard was not to be moved, and Stone of North Carolina joined him:—the impeachers could muster but eighteen votes. They did no better on the fourth article. On the fifth,—Randolph's interpolated charge, which alleged no evil intent,—every member of the Senate voted "Not Guilty;" on the sixth, which was little more than a repetition of the fifth, only four senators could be found to condemn, and on the seventh, only ten. One chance of conviction remained, the eighth article, which covered the judge's charge to the grand jury at Baltimore in 1803. There lay the true cause of impeachment; yet this charge had been least pressed and least defended. The impeachers brought out their whole strength in its support; Giles, Jackson, Samuel Smith, and Stone united in pronouncing the judge guilty: but the five Northern democrats and Gaillard held out to the last, and the managers saw themselves deserted by nearly one fourth of the Republican senators. Nineteen voices were the utmost that could be induced to sustain impeachment.

The sensation was naturally intense; and yet the overwhelming nature of the defeat would have warranted an excitement still greater. No one understood better the meaning of Chase's acquittal than John Randolph, whose authority it overthrew. His anger showed itself in an act which at first alarmed and then amused his enemies. Hurrying from the Senate chamber to the House, he offered a Resolution for submitting to the States an amendment to the Constitution: "The judges of the Supreme and all other courts of the United States shall be removed by the President on the joint address of both Houses of Congress." His friend Nicholson, as though still angrier than Randolph, moved another amendment,—that the legislature of any State might, whenever it thought proper, recall a senator and vacate his seat. These resolutions were by a party vote referred to the next Congress.

Randolph threatened in vain; the rod was no longer in his hands. His overthrow before the Senate was the smallest of his failures. The Northern democrats talked of him with disgust; and Senator Cocke of Tennessee, who had voted "Guilty" on every article of impeachment except the fifth, told his Federalist colleagues in the Senate that Randolph's vanity, ambition, insolence, and dishonesty, not only in the impeachment but in other matters, were such as to make the acquittal no subject for regret.[1] Madison did not attempt to hide his amusement at Randolph's defeat. Jefferson held himself studiously aloof. To Jefferson and men of his class Randolph seems to have alluded, in a letter written a few weeks later, as "whimsicals," who "advocated the leading measures of their party until they were nearly ripe for execution, when they hung back, condemned the step after it was taken, and on most occasions affected a glorious neutrality."[2] Even Giles

[1] Diary of J. Q. Adams (March 1, 1805), i. 364.
[2] Randolph to Nicholson, April 30, 1805; Adams's Randolph, p. 157.

turned hostile. He not only yielded to the enemies of Randolph in regard to the form of vote to be taken on the impeachment, and fairly joined them in the vote on the first article, but he also aided in offering Randolph a rebuke on another point connected with the impeachment.

In the middle of the trial, February 15, Randolph reported to the House, and the House quickly passed, a Bill appropriating five thousand dollars for the payment of the witnesses summoned by the managers. When this Bill came before the Senate, Bayard moved to amend it by extending its provisions to the witnesses summoned by Judge Chase. The point was delicate; for if the Senate was a court, and impeachment a criminal procedure, this court should follow the rules that guided other judicial bodies; and every one knew that no court in America or in Christendom obliged the State, as a prosecutor, to pay the witnesses of the accused. After the acquittal, such a rule was either equivalent to telling the House that its charges against Chase were frivolous and should never have been presented, or it suggested that the trial had been an official inquiry into the conduct of an officer, and not a criminal procedure at law. The Republicans might properly reject the first assumption, the Federalists ought to resist the second; yet when Bayard's amendment came to a vote, it was unanimously adopted.[1] The House disagreed; the Senate insisted, and Giles led the Senate, affirming that he had drawn the form of summons, and that this form made no distinction between the witnesses for one party and the other. The argument was not decisive, for the court records showed at once by whom each witness was called; but Giles's reasoning satisfied the Senate, and led to his appointment, March 3, with Bradley, an enemy of impeachment, as conferrees to meet Randolph, Nicholson, and Early on the part of the House. They disagreed; and Randolph, with his friends, felt that Giles and the Senate had inflicted on them a grievous insult. The Report of the conference committee was received by the House at about seven o'clock on the evening of March 3, when the Eighth Congress was drawing its last breath. Randolph, who reported the disagreement, moved that the

[1] Diary of J. Q. Adams (March 2, 1805), i. 367.

House adhere; and having thus destroyed the Bill, he next moved that the Clerk of the House should be directed to pay the witnesses, or any other expense certified by the managers, from the contingent fund. He would have carried his point, although it violated every financial profession of the Republican party, but that the House was thin, and the Federalists, by refusing to vote, prevented a quorum. At half-past nine o'clock on Sunday night, the 3d of March, 1805, the Eighth Congress came to an end in a scene of total confusion and factiousness.

The failure of Chase's impeachment was a blow to the Republican party from which it never wholly recovered. Chief-Justice Marshall at length was safe; he might henceforward at his leisure fix the principles of Constitutional law. Jefferson resigned himself for the moment to Randolph's overthrow; but the momentary consolations passed away, and a life-long disappointment remained. Fifteen years later his regret was strongly expressed:—

"The Judiciary of the United States," mourned the old ex-President,[1] "is the subtle corps of sappers and miners constantly working underground to undermine the foundations of our confederated fabric. They are construing our Constitution from a co-ordination of a general and special government to a general and supreme one alone. . . . Having found from experience that impeachment is an impracticable thing, a mere scarecrow, they consider themselves secure for life; they skulk from responsibility; . . . an opinion is huddled up in conclave, perhaps by a majority of one, delivered as if unanimous, and with the silent acquiescence of lazy or timid associates, by a crafty chief-judge who sophisticates the law to his mind by the turn of his own reasoning."

The acquittal of Chase proved that impeachment was a scarecrow; but its effect on impeachment as a principle of law was less evident. No point was decided. The theory of Giles, Randolph, and Rodney was still intact, for it was not avowedly applied to the case. The theory of Judge Chase's

[1] Jefferson to Thomas Ritchie, Dec. 25, 1820; Works, vii. 192.

counsel—that an impeachable offence must be also indictable, or even a violation of some known statute of the United
States—was overthrown neither by the argument nor by the
judgment. So far as Constitutional law was concerned, President Jefferson himself might still be impeached, according to
the dictum of Madison, for the arbitrary removal of a useful
tide-waiter, and Chief-Justice Marshall might be driven from
the bench, as Giles wished, for declaring the Constitution to
be above the authority of a statute; but although the acquittal
of Chase decided no point of law except his innocence of high
crimes or misdemeanors, as charged in the indictment, it
proved impeachment to be "an impracticable thing" for partisan purposes, and it decided the permanence of those lines
of Constitutional development which were a reflection of the
common law. Henceforward the legal profession had its own
way in expounding the principles and expanding the powers
of the central government through the Judiciary.

Chapter XI

THE LOUISIANA TREATY, signed in May, 1803, was followed by two years of diplomatic activity. The necessary secrecy of diplomacy gave to every President the power to involve the country without its knowledge in dangers which could not be afterward escaped, and the Republican party neither invented nor suggested means by which this old evil of irresponsible politics could be cured; but of all Presidents, none used these arbitrary powers with more freedom and secrecy than Jefferson. His ideas of Presidential authority in foreign affairs were little short of royal. He loved the sense of power and the freedom from oversight which diplomacy gave, and thought with reason that as his knowledge of Europe was greater than that of other Americans, so he should be left to carry out his policy undisturbed.

Jefferson's overmastering passion was to obtain West Florida. To this end two paths seemed open. If he chose to conciliate, Yrujo was still ready to aid; and Spain stood in such danger between England and France that Godoy could not afford to throw the United States into the hands of either. If Jefferson wished the friendship of Spain, he had every reason to feel sure that the Prince of Peace would act in the same spirit in which he had negotiated the treaty of 1795 and restored the right of deposit in 1802. In this case Florida must be let alone until Spain should be willing to cede, or the United States be ready for war.

On the other hand, the President might alienate Spain and grasp at Florida. Livingston and Monroe warmly urged this policy, and were in fact its authors. Livingston's advice would by itself have had no great weight with Jefferson or Madison, but they believed strongly in Monroe; and when he made Livingston's idea his own, he gave it weight. Monroe had been sent abroad to buy Florida; he had bought Louisiana. From the Potomac to the Mississippi, every Southern man expected and required that by peace or war Florida should be annexed to the Union; and the annexation of Louisiana made that of Florida seem easy. Neither Monroe, Madison, nor Jefferson could resist the impulse to seize it.

Livingston's plan has been described. He did not assert that Spain had intended to retrocede Florida to France, or that France had claimed it as included in the retrocession. He knew the contrary; and tried in vain to find some one willing to say that the country to the Perdido ought to be included in the purchase. He made much of Marbois's cautious encouragement and Talleyrand's transparent manœuvres; but he was forced at last to maintain that Spain had retroceded West Florida to France without knowing it, that France had sold it to the United States without suspecting it, that the United States had bought it without paying for it, and that neither France nor Spain, although the original contracting parties, were competent to decide the meaning of their own contract. Believing that Bonaparte was pledged to support the United States in their effort to obtain West Florida, Livingston was anxious only to push Spain to the utmost. Talleyrand allowed him to indulge in these dreams. "I have obtained from him," wrote Livingston to Madison,[1] "a positive promise that this government shall aid any negotiation that shall be set on foot" for the purchase of East Florida; while as for Florida west of the Perdido, "the moment is so favorable for taking possession of that country, that I hope it has not been neglected, even though a little force should be necessary to effect it. Your minister must find the means to justify it."

When the letters written by Livingston and Monroe in May, 1803, reached Washington, they were carefully studied by the President, fully understood, and a policy quickly settled. When Jefferson wrote to Senator Breckinridge his ideas on the unconstitutionality of the purchase, he spoke with equal clearness on the course he meant to pursue toward Spain in order to obtain Florida:[2] —

"We have some claims to extend on the sea-coast westwardly to the Rio Norte or Bravo, and, better, to go eastwardly to the Rio Perdido, between Mobile and Pensacola, the ancient boundary of Louisiana. These claims will be a subject of negotiation with Spain; and if as soon as she is at war we push them strongly with one hand, holding out

[1] Livingston to Madison, Nov. 15, 1803; State Papers, ii. 573, 574.
[2] Jefferson to Breckinridge, Aug. 12, 1803; Works, iv. 498.

a price with the other, we shall certainly obtain the Floridas, and all in good time."

This was not Livingston's plan, but something quite distinct from it. Livingston and Monroe wanted the President
to seize West Florida, and negotiate for East Florida. Jefferson
preferred to negotiate for West Florida and to leave East Florida alone for the time.

Madison had already instructed[1] the minister at Madrid
that the Floridas were not included in the treaty, "being, it
appears, still held by Spain," and that the negotiation for their
purchase would be conducted by Monroe at Madrid. Instructions of the same date were instantly sent to Monroe,[2] urging
him to pursue the negotiation for Florida, although owing to
the large drain made on the Treasury, and to the "manifest
course of events," the government was not disposed to make
sacrifices for the sake of obtaining that country. "Your inquiries may also be directed," wrote Madison, "to the question
whether any, and how much, of what passes for West Florida
be fairly included in the territory ceded to us by France."

The idea that West Florida could be claimed as a part of
the Louisiana purchase was a turning-point in the second Administration of Jefferson. Originating in Minister Livingston's
mind, it passed from him to Monroe; and in a few weeks the
President declared the claim substantial.[3] As the summer of
1803 closed, Jefferson's plan became clear. He meant to push
this claim, in connection with other claims, and to wait the
moment when Spain should be dragged into the war between
France and England.

These other claims were of various degrees of merit, and
involved France as well as Spain. During the *quasi* war between the United States and France, before Jefferson came
into power, American commerce in Spanish waters suffered
severely from two causes. The first consisted in captures made
by Spanish cruisers, and condemnations decided in Spanish
courts; the second was due to captures made by French cruisers, and condemned by French consuls in Spanish ports, or

[1] Madison to Pinckney, July 29, 1803; State Papers, ii. 614.
[2] Madison to Monroe, July 29, 1803; State Papers, ii. 626.
[3] Jefferson to Madison, Aug. 25, 1803; Works, iv. 501.

by courts of appeal in France, without regard to the rights or dignity of Spain. With much trouble, in August, 1802, at the time when Europe and America were waiting for the end of Leclerc's struggle with the negroes and fevers of St. Domingo, Pinckney succeeded in persuading the Prince of Peace to let the claims for Spanish depredations go before a commission for settlement; but Godoy obstinately refused to recognize the claims for French depredations, taking the ground that Spain was in no way responsible for them, had never in any way profited by them, and had no power at the time they occurred to prevent them; that France, and France alone, had committed the offence, and should pay for it.

Pinckney resisted this reasoning as energetically as possible; but when Cevallos offered to sign a convention covering the Spanish depredations, and reserving the Franco-Spanish claims for future discussion, Pinckney properly decided to accept an offer which secured for his fellow-citizens five or ten millions of money, and which left the other claim still open.[1] The convention of Aug. 11, 1802, was sent to the Senate Jan. 11, 1803, in the excitement that followed Morales's withdrawal of the *entrepôt* at New Orleans. The Senate deferred action until the last moment of the session; and then, March 3, 1803, after Nicholson and Randolph had appeared at the bar to impeach Judge Pickering, Pinckney's claims convention was taken up, and the nine Federalists were allowed to defeat it by the absence of Republican senators. The majority reconsidered the vote and postponed the whole subject till the next session. Thus, owing to the action of Federalist senators, when Jefferson in the following summer, after buying Louisiana, looked about for the means of buying Florida, he found these classes of claims, aggregating as he supposed between five and ten million dollars, ready to his hand. Monroe was promptly ordered to insist upon treating both classes alike, and setting both of them against the proposed purchase of Florida. "On the subject of these claims you will hold a strong language," said Madison.[2]

A third class of claims could be made useful for the same purpose. Damages had been sustained by individuals in the

[1] Pinckney to Madison, Aug. 15, 1802; State Papers, ii. 482.
[2] Madison to Monroe, July 29, 1803; State Papers, ii. 626.

violation of their right of deposit at New Orleans in the autumn of 1802.

"A distinction, however, is to be made," wrote Madison, "between the positive and specific damages sustained by individuals and the general injuries accruing from that breach of treaty. The latter could be provided for by a gross and vague estimate only, and need not be pressed as an indispensable condition. The claim however may be represented as strictly just, and a forbearance to insist on it as an item in the valuable considerations for which the cession [of Florida] is made. Greater stress may be laid on the positive and specific damages capable of being formally verified by individuals; but there is a point beyond which it may be prudent not to insist, even here, especially as the incalculable advantage accruing from the acquisition of New Orleans will diffuse a joy throughout the western country that will drown the sense of these little sacrifices. Should no bargain be made on the subject of the Floridas, our claims of every sort are to be kept in force."

The President had not then decided to claim West Florida as included in the Louisiana purchase, and he conceived of no reason which should make Spain cling the more closely to Florida on account of the loss of New Orleans.

The news of the Louisiana purchase reached Washington early in July, 1803; Madison wrote his instructions to Monroe at the end of the same month; Jefferson announced his policy to Breckinridge in August. This was the harvest season of his life. His theories were proved sound; his system of government stood in successful rivalry with that of Bonaparte and Pitt; and he felt no doubt that his friendship was as vital to England, France, and Spain as all the armies and navies of the world. In the midst of this enjoyment, September 4, he was suddenly told by the Marquis of Casa Yrujo that he had bought stolen goods, and that Spain as the rightful owner protested against the sale.[1]

Notwithstanding this strong measure, doubtless taken in obedience to orders, Yrujo was still true to his old friendship.

[1] Yrujo to Madison, Sept. 4 and 27, 1803; State Papers, ii. 569.

On hearing of the cession, he did again what he had done eight months before, in the excitement about the *entrepôt* at New Orleans,—he tried to smooth difficulties and quiet alarms.

"The ports of Florida," he wrote to Don Pedro Cevallos,[1] "as they would make it easy for us to annoy greatly the American commerce in case of a war, would in like degree furnish the Americans, if the Americans should possess them, the same means of annoying ours, and of carrying on an immense contraband trade from them, especially from Pensacola and Mobile, with our provinces in the Gulf of Mexico. This last is the chief evil which in my opinion will result from the acquisition of Louisiana by the Americans, and can only be diminished by numerous, watchful, and active revenue-cutters. For the rest I do not look on the alienation of Louisiana as a loss for Spain. That colony cost us much, and produced us very little."

In short, Louisiana could not be defended by Spain, while as a part of the United States it would certainly weaken, and probably dissolve, the Union. As for the protest, he told[2] his Government, even before he received Madison's reply, that nothing would come of it.

As late as Nov. 5, 1803, Yrujo continued to write in the same tone to his Government.

"The information I have received from trustworthy persons," he said,[3] "in regard to the disposition in which General Victor was coming here, and the spirit of restlessness and almost of rapine which reigned among many of the officials in his army, leave me no doubt that the military colony of the French in Louisiana would have been in reality a worse neighbor than the Americans for us. Things have now taken such a turn, that in my humble opinion if we are to lose Louisiana, the choice whether that colony shall fall into the power of one nation rather than another is not worth the expense and trouble of a war, provided we

[1] Yrujo to Cevallos, Aug. 3, 1803; MSS. Spanish Archives.
[2] Yrujo to Cevallos, Sept. 12, 1803; MSS. Spanish Archives.
[3] Yrujo to Cevallos, Nov. 5, 1803; MSS. Spanish Archives.

preserve the Floridas. . . . I am convinced that this Government knows perfectly the national interests, and to promote them will follow in this respect a course of conduct which in proportion as it better suits our own, should inspire us with greater confidence."

Yrujo acted the part of a true friend to both countries, in trying by such arguments to reconcile his Government to the loss of Louisiana; but there were limits to his good-will. He held that Spain could not afford to part with Florida. Yrujo went to the extreme of concession when he reconciled his Government to the loss of New Orleans, and nothing would reconcile him to the further loss of Mobile and Pensacola. Only on the theory that Spanish America was already ruined by the cession of Louisiana could Yrujo argue in favor of selling Florida.

On receiving Yrujo's protests of September 4 and 27, Jefferson's first feeling was of anger. He sent a strong body of troops to Natchez. "The Government of Spain," he wrote to Dupont de Nemours,[1] "has protested against the right of France to transfer, and it is possible she may refuse possession, and that may bring on acts of force; but against such neighbors as France there and the United States here, what she can expect from so gross a compound of folly and false faith is not to be sought in the book of wisdom." The folly of such conduct might be clear, but the charge of false faith against Spain for protesting against being deprived of her rights, seemed unjust, especially in the mouth of Jefferson, who meant to claim West Florida under a Franco-Spanish treaty which was acknowledged by all parties to have transferred Louisiana alone.

Only a week before this letter was written, the scheme of seizing West Florida had been publicly avowed by John Randolph on the floor of the House. Randolph's speech of October 24, in language as offensive to Spain as was possible in the mouth of a responsible leader, asserted, as a fact admitting no doubt, that West Florida belonged to the United States.[2] "We have not only obtained the command of the mouth of

---

[1] Jefferson to Dupont, Nov. 1, 1803; Works, iv. 508.
[2] Annals of Congress, 1803–1804, p. 415.

the Mississippi, but of the Mobile, with its widely extended branches; and there is not now a single stream of note rising within the United States and falling into the Gulf of Mexico which is not entirely our own, the Appalachicola excepted." In a second speech the next day, he reiterated the statement even more explicitly and in greater detail.[1] The Republican press echoed the claim. Jefferson and Madison encouraged the manœuvre until they could no longer recede, and pushed inquiries in every direction,[2] without obtaining evidence that West Florida was, or ever had been, a part of the government of Louisiana. They even applied to Laussat,[3] the mortified and angry French commissioner whom Bonaparte had sent to receive possession of New Orleans; and Laussat, to the annoyance of Talleyrand and Godoy, told the truth,—that the Iberville and the Rio Bravo were the boundaries fixed by his instructions, and therefore that West Florida was not a part of the purchase, but that Texas was.

Notwithstanding John Randolph's official declaration, when the time came for the delivery of Louisiana the Spanish governor, Dec. 20, 1803, peacefully surrendered the province to Laussat; Laussat handed it in due form to Claiborne; and Claiborne received it without asking for West Florida, or even recording a claim for it. That this silence was accidental no one pretended. The acquiescence in Spanish authority was so implicit that Madison three months afterward, at a time when both Executive and Legislature were acting on the theory that West Florida was in Louisiana, found himself obliged to explain the cause of conduct and contradictions so extraordinary. He wrote[4] to Livingston at Paris that the President had for several reasons preferred to make no demand for West Florida,—

"First, because it was foreseen that the demand would not only be rejected by the Spanish authority at New Orleans, which had in an official publication limited the cession westwardly by the Mississippi and the Island of

[1] Annals of Congress, 1803–1804, p. 440.
[2] Jefferson to William Dunbar, March 13, 1804; Works, iv. 537.
[3] Madison to Livingston, Jan. 31, 1804; State Papers, ii. 574.
[4] Madison to Livingston, March 31, 1804; State Papers, ii. 575.

New Orleans, but it was apprehended, as has turned out, that the French commissioner might not be ready to support the demand, and might even be disposed to second the Spanish opposition to it; secondly, because in the latter of these cases a serious check would be given to our title, and in either of them a premature dilemma would result between an overt submission to the refusal and a resort to force; thirdly, because mere silence would be no bar to a plea at any time that a delivery of a part, particularly of the seat of the government, was a virtual delivery of the whole."

The President's silence at New Orleans was the more conspicuous because, at the moment when the province of Louisiana was thus delivered with such boundaries as Spain chose to define, Congress was legislating for Florida as an integral part of the Union John Randolph's official assertion that Mobile belonged to the United States under the treaty of cession, was made in the last part of October, 1803, soon after Congress met. About a month later, November 30, he introduced a Bill nominally for giving effect to the laws of the United States within the ceded territory. After much debate and disagreement this Bill at length passed both Houses, and Feb. 24, 1804, received the President's signature. The fourth section directed that the territories ceded to the United States by the treaty, "and also all the navigable waters, rivers, creeks, bays, and inlets lying within the United States, which empty into the Gulf of Mexico east of the River Mississippi, shall be annexed to the Mississippi district, and shall, together with the same, constitute one district, to be called the 'District of Mississippi.' " This provision was remarkable, because, as every one knew, no creeks, bays, or inlets lying within the United States emptied into the Gulf. The Act by its eleventh section authorized the President, " whenever he shall deem it expedient, to erect the shores, waters, and inlets of the Bay and River of Mobile, and of the other rivers, creeks, inlets, and bays emptying into the Gulf of Mexico east of the said River Mobile, and west thereof to the Pascagoula, inclusive, into a separate district, and to establish such place within the same as he shall deem expedient, to be the port of entry and delivery for such district." This section gave the President power of peace and war, for had he exercised it, the exercise must have been an act of war; and John Randolph's previous declarations left no doubt as to the meaning in which he, who reported the Bill, meant it to be understood.

By this time Yrujo was boiling with such wrath as a Spaniard alone could imagine or express. His good-will vanished from the moment he saw that to save Florida he must do battle with President, Secretary of State, Congress, and people. One insult had followed another with startling rapidity. The President's *pêle-mêle*, of which the story will be told hereafter, wounded him personally. The cold reception of his protest against the Louisiana cession; the captiousness of Madison's replies to his remonstrances; the armed seizure of New Orleans with which he was threatened; the sudden disregard of his friendship and great services; the open eagerness of the Government to incite Bonaparte to plunder and dismember Spain; the rejection of the claims convention in March, and its sudden approval by the Senate in January, as though to obtain all the money Spain was willing to give before taking by force territory vital to her empire; and above all, the passage of this law annexing the Floridas without excuse or explanation,—all these causes combined to change Yrujo's ancient friendship into hatred.

In the midst of the complicated legislation about Louisiana, while the Mobile Act was under discussion, Jefferson sent to the Senate, Dec. 21, 1803, the correspondence about the Spanish claims, and among the rest an adverse opinion which Yrujo had obtained from five prominent American lawyers on an abstract case in regard to the Franco-Spanish spoliations. Madison was particularly annoyed by this legal opinion, and thought it should bring these five gentlemen within the penalties of the law passed Jan. 30, 1799, commonly known as Logan's Act. Senator Bradley of Vermont moved for a committee, which reported in favor of directing the President to institute proceedings against Jared Ingersoll, William Rawle, J. B. McKean, Peter S. Duponceau, and Edward Livingston,—five lawyers whose legal, social, and political character made a prosecution as unwise in politics as it was doubtful in law. The Senate having at the moment too many prosecutions already on its hands, let Senator Bradley's Report lie unnoticed, and soon afterward confirmed the claims convention by a vote of eighteen to eight,[1] — barely two thirds, the least factious of the Federalists joining the majority, and by this unpartisan act causing in the end more embarrassment to the party in power than the most ingenious factiousness could have plotted. Madison, in the midst of his measures for pressing the acquisition of Florida, sent the ratified claims convention to Madrid. The period fixed for ratification had long since expired, and the attitude of the United States toward Florida had altered the feelings and interests of Spain; but either Madison was unaware of the change, or he wished to embarrass Godoy. He added in his letter to Pinckney,[2] "It was judged best, on the whole, no longer to deprive that class of our citizens who are comprehended in the convention of the benefit of its provisions;" but although consenting to take what Spain was willing to give, he spoke with contempt of the Spanish argument against the Franco-Spanish claims, and insisted that these should be pressed without relaxation. He even complained that Yrujo, in taking the opinion of American lawyers, had failed in respect to the United States government and his own.[3]

Madison seemed unconscious that Yrujo could have any just cause of complaint, or that his Government could resent the tone and temper of President and Congress. The passage of the Bill which made Mobile a collection district and a part of the Mississippi territory gave Yrujo the chance to retaliate. About a fortnight after the President had signed this law, Yrujo one morning entered the State Department with the printed Act in his hand, and overwhelmed Madison with reproaches, which he immediately afterward supported by a note[4] so severe as to require punishment, and so able as to admit of none. He had at first, he said, regarded as "an atrocious libel" on the United States government the assertion that it had made a law which usurped the rights of Spanish sovereignty; yet such was the case. He gave a short and clear

[1] Journal of Executive Sessions, Jan. 9, 1804.
[2] Madison to Pinckney, Jan. 31, 1804; State Papers, ii. 614.
[3] Madison to Pinckney, Feb. 6, 1804; State Papers, ii. 615.
[4] Yrujo to Madison, March 7, 1804; MSS. State Department Archives.

abstract of the evidence which refuted the claim to West Florida, and closed by requesting that the law be annulled.

Madison could neither maintain the law nor annul it; he
could not even explain it away. Gallatin told the President six
months afterward,[1] that "the public mind is altogether unprepared for a declaration that the terms and object of the Mobile Act had been misunderstood by Spain; for every writer,
without a single exception, who has written on the subject
seems to have understood the Act as Spain did; it has been
justified by our friends on that ground." Yet Jefferson was not
prepared to maintain and defend the Act in its full assertions
of authority, after accepting Louisiana without asking for
West Florida. Madison wrote a letter of complaint to Livingston at Paris,[2] explaining, as already quoted, the reasons
which had induced the President to make no demand for
West Florida before ascertaining the views and claiming the
interposition of the French government.

> "In this state of things," said he, "it was deemed proper
> by Congress, in making the regulations necessary for the
> collection of revenue in the ceded territory, and guarding
> against the new danger of smuggling into the United States
> through the channels opened by it, to include a provision
> for the case of West Florida by vesting in the President a
> power which his discretion might accommodate to events."

This interpretation of the law was not in harmony with the
law itself or with Randolph's speeches; but Madison hastened
to turn from this delicate subject in order to bring another
complaint against Yrujo.

> "The Act had been many weeks depending in Congress
> with these sections, word for word, in it; . . . it must in
> all probability have been known to the Marquis d'Yrujo in
> an early stage of its progress; if it was not, it marks much
> less of that zealous vigilance over the concerns of his sov-
> ereign than he now makes the plea for his intemperate con-
> duct. For some days, even after the Act was published in
> the Gazette of this city, he was silent. At length, however,

[1] Gallatin to Jefferson, October, 1804; Gallatin's Works, i. 211.
[2] Madison to Livingston, March 31, 1804; State Papers, ii. 575.

he called at the office of State, with the Gazette in his hand, and entered into a very angry comment."

The Spanish minister's subsequent notes had been written with "a rudeness which no government can tolerate;" but his conduct was chiefly of importance "as it urges the expediency of cultivating the disposition of the French government to take our side of the question."

The President came to Madison's relief. By a proclamation issued a few weeks afterward, reciting the terms of the Act of Congress in regard to the Bay and River of Mobile, he declared all these "shores, waters, inlets, creeks, and rivers, lying *within the boundaries of the United States*," to be a collection district, with Fort Stoddert for its port of entry.[1] The italics were a part of the proclamation, and suggested that such could not have been the intent of Congress, because no part of the shores or waters of Mobile Bay, or of the other bays east of Mobile, lay within the boundaries of the United States. The evasion was a divergence from the words of the Act unwarranted by anything in the context; and to give it authority, Jefferson, in spite of Gallatin's remonstrance, declared in his next Annual Message that the Mobile Act had been misunderstood on the part of Spain.[2]

[1] Proclamation of May 30, 1804; State Papers, ii. 583.
[2] Message of Nov. 8, 1804. Annals of Congress, 1804–1805, p. 11.

Chapter XII

THOUGH YRUJO's language was strong, and his anonymous writings in the press were indiscreet, he had, down to the summer of 1804, laid himself open to no just official censure; for whatever the Secretary of State might think, no one could seriously blame a foreign minister for obtaining the best legal advice in America on an abstract question of international law. The protests with which Yrujo contented himself, vigorous as they were, could neither be disavowed by his Government nor answered by Madison. Had he stopped there, his triumph would have been signal; but fortunately for Madison, the Spaniard, with all the high qualities of his nation, had also its weaknesses, besides having the love of intrigue inherent in diplomacy. Yrujo was in his political training more American than Spanish. At home in Philadelphia, son-in-law to Governor McKean, and well acquainted with the methods of party politics, he burned to counteract the influence of the Administration press, and had no other means of doing so than by acting on Federalist editors. As no one but himself knew even a part of the truth about the Spanish imbroglio, he was obliged to be the channel for conveying his own information to the public; and from time to time Madison read in opposition newspapers anonymous letters which bore plain marks of Yrujo's peculiar style. He had already published a pamphlet on the Louisiana cession. After his hot protest against the Mobile Act, in March, 1804, the Spanish minister left Washington, without taking leave of the Secretary of State. At length his indiscretions enabled Madison to enjoy the pleasure of seeing him keenly mortified.

Among other Federalist newspapers in Philadelphia was one called the "Political Register," edited by a man named Jackson. In September, 1804, six months after the passage-at-arms over the Mobile Act, Yrujo, then in Philadelphia, asked for an interview with Jackson, and urged him to oppose the course which the President had taken against Spain. "If you will consent," he said, "to take elucidations on the subject from me, I will furnish them, and I will make you any acknowledgment." He charged the Administration with wishing for war, and with intriguing for a rebellion among the Spaniards of West Florida.

That Yrujo or any other diplomatic agent was quite ready to use money, if by doing so he could obtain objects necessary for his purposes, need not be doubted,—although corruption of this kind in the affairs of the United States has left few traces even on the most secret diplomatic records of England, France, and Spain. In the ethical code of diplomacy the offer of money to an editor for inserting information was no offence, but discovery was fatal; and for this reason perhaps Yrujo told the truth when he afterward said that the use of money was not in his mind. Had he meant to bribe, he would not have exposed himself to detection, or put himself, without need, in the hands of a person over whom he held no power. Nevertheless, his blunder deserved the punishment which quickly followed.

A few days after his interview with Jackson, Yrujo left Philadelphia to visit Jefferson at Monticello. Sept. 20, 1804, immediately after his departure, Jackson printed an affidavit narrating the attempt which Yrujo had made upon his virtue, and detailing every expression of the minister which could do him most injury. As though to make Yrujo's position still more mortifying, Jackson sent this affidavit to President Jefferson ten days or more before publishing it; and when Yrujo, ignorant of the betrayal, after passing Madison's door at Montpelier without the courtesy of stopping to inquire for the Secretary's health,[1] at last reached Monticello, not only his host, but every one except himself, had heard of the diplomatic scandal to which he was a party.

Jefferson received his visitor with the usual hospitality, and said not a word on the subject. Being obliged to return to Washington, the President left Yrujo, two days later, under the protection of his daughter Mrs. Randolph, and set out to meet his Cabinet on the last day of the month at the Federal city. Madison was delayed at Montpelier, and could not attend the Cabinet meeting, but wrote a few days afterward:[2]—

[1] Pichon to Talleyrand, 18 Brumaire, An xiii. (Nov. 9, 1804); Archives des Aff. Étr., MSS.

[2] Madison to Jefferson, Oct. 2, 1804; Jefferson MSS.

"Jackson, I find, has lost no time in giving publicity to the affair between him and Yrujo. What course the latter will take, remains to be seen. Should circumstances of any kind be thought to urge a close of the business with him, or any other arrangement with respect to it, why might not one of the other secretaries, or even Mr. Wagner, be made a channel of your sentiments and determinations? . . . Should the door be shut against further communication [through] Yrujo, and Pinckney's situation at Madrid not be contradicted, a direct communication with Cevallos appears to be the next resource."

Already Madison flattered himself with the hope that he was to be relieved from relations with the Spaniard, whose continuance at Washington he had asked as a favor from Don Carlos IV. only three years before.

Jefferson's delicacy and hospitality were worthy of a great lord of Spain, and did honor to his innate kindliness; but they put Yrujo in an attitude so mortifying, that when he returned to Washington and learned what had taken place in his absence, he was overcome with shame at finding himself charged with calumniating his host at the moment of claiming his hospitality. He immediately prepared a counter-statement and took it to the President, who replied that the matter was one which should properly belong to Madison. Yrujo then printed his letter in the "National Intelligencer," where Madison first saw it. For the moment the matter went no further; but Madison was fixed in his purpose of effecting Yrujo's recall, and when in the following spring he instructed his minister at Madrid to ask this favor, he alleged the affair of Jackson among the reasons which justified his request.

Pichon, who was in charge of the French legation, cordially disliked Yrujo, and did nothing to help him against Madison, although the relations between Spain and France were those of close alliance; but Madison next suffered a severe loss in the removal of Pichon, and in the arrival, Nov. 23, 1804, of the first minister sent by France to the United States since the departure of Adet in President Washington's time. The new appointment was not a happy one. Pichon had carried friendliness so far as on several serious questions to take sides with the United States government against his own, and had fallen into disfavor with Napoleon in consequence. The new minister was little likely to repeat this blunder. Napoleon liked military discipline in all things; and he sent as his minister to Washington a former general of the Republic, Louis Marie Turreau, best known for the extreme severities he was charged with having inflicted on the Vendeans in 1794. Like most of the republican generals, including even Moreau and Bernadotte, Turreau accepted the *coup d'état* of the 18th Brumaire, and was for private reasons anxious to obtain some position far removed from France. According to his own story, he had during the Vendean war been so unfortunate as to be saved from death, in a moment of extreme danger, by a woman's self-sacrifice. In token of his gratitude he married his preserver; but from that time his life became a long regret. His wife's temper was terrible; his own was querulous and morbidly depressed. Although he could speak no English, had no diplomatic experience and little taste for general society, he sought the post of minister resident at Washington in order to escape his wife. To his extreme annoyance, she followed him to America; and Washington resounded with the scandal of their quarrels, which reached the extremity of pitched battles. He wrote to his friends in the French Foreign Office that he was almost mad with mortification and despair.

Such a minister was not happily chosen for the difficult task on hand; but Bonaparte loaded him with other burdens, of a kind even more embarrassing to a diplomatist. At best, the position of a French minister in America was not agreeable. The mere difference in habits, manners, amusements, and the want of a thousand luxuries and pleasures such as made Paris dear to every Frenchman, rendered Washington a place of exile. Perhaps nothing but fear of the guillotine could have reconciled even republican Frenchmen to staying in a country where, in the words of Talleyrand, there was no Frenchman who did not feel himself a stranger; but if this were true while France was a republic fighting the battles of American democracy, it became doubly true after Bonaparte had crushed French liberties and made himself the foremost enemy of republican ideas. Turreau arrived at Washington about six months before Bonaparte took the title of Emperor; and he found that as representative of Napoleon I. he could never hope for a friend in the United States, unless it were among a few bankrupt adventurers, who to retrieve their broken fortunes would have liked to see an 18th Brumaire at New Orleans, which should give an imperial crown and the mines of Mexico to Aaron Burr and his troop of embryo dukes and marshals.

As though to embarrass his representative to the utmost, Bonaparte deprived him of the only means by which he could win even the venal respect of a money-making people. At one stroke the First Consul had annulled and sent to protest all the drafts drawn under Rochambeau's orders by the fiscal administrator of St. Domingo.[1] His avowed reason was that every bill of exchange or draft on the public treasury which did not purport to rest on the authority of a letter from the minister authorizing the expenditure, should not be paid. The true reason was that he had determined to waste no more money on St. Domingo, but to sacrifice his army there under cover of a war with England, which required all the means then at his disposal. Rochambeau's expenditures were becoming wild; but thus far his drafts on the Treasury were regularly drawn. They had been taken in good faith throughout the West Indies and in every commercial city on the American seaboard; they rested on the national credit of France, and their repudiation destroyed French credit in America, public and private. Before Turreau sailed for his post, the credit of his Government was at an end in the United States. Not only had the drafts drawn in St. Domingo been refused payment, but Pichon's had also suffered the same fate; and neither the new minister nor his consuls could find a man in Baltimore, Philadelphia, or New York to advance money on their official signatures. Turreau complained bitterly to Talleyrand of the penury and mortification to which he was condemned. In one

[1] Note du Premier Consul, 2 Floréal, An xi. (April 22, 1803); Correspondance, viii. 288.

of his despatches[1] he reported that at a tavern in Baltimore one of the French agents, not known to be such, was offered French government paper at fifty per cent discount, and at the same time five per cent premium for drafts on the British government. "In short, we are brought to such a state of affairs that private discredit follows the discredit of the nation, and I experience it for my own individual drafts."

Owing to these circumstances, Turreau declared that his position was hardly tolerable; but even apart from such matters, he found a formidable legacy of diplomatic difficulties left by Pichon to be settled. The question of trade with St. Domingo, of boundary on both sides of Louisiana, the Spanish imbroglio, the unpaid claims on France, and the repudiated drafts negotiated by Pichon in the United States, were all matters which Turreau was required to master and manage; but none of them gave him more trouble than the personal quarrel between his colleague Yrujo and the Secretary of State.

Yrujo's affair with Major Jackson occurred in September, 1804, and Turreau, reaching Washington in the following November, was soon obliged to take part in Yrujo's feuds. Not only the tone of his instructions, but the increasing certainty that Spain must side with France in the war against England, obliged him to make common cause with the Spanish minister, who came from Philadelphia to Washington in order to invoke his services. The result was told in a despatch to Talleyrand:[2] —

"Following your instructions and the request of M. d'Yrujo, I consented to an interview with him at Mr. Madison's. . . . I had no trouble in perceiving from the outset of the conversation that Mr. Madison and M. d'Yrujo cordially detested each other, and in the discussion that their passions took the place of reason and law."

This discussion naturally turned on the question of West Florida; and unfortunately for Madison, Turreau's instruc-

[1] Turreau to Talleyrand, 23 Floréal, An xiii. (May 13, 1805); Archives des Aff. Étr., MSS.

[2] Turreau to Talleyrand, 6 Pluviôse, An xii. (Jan. 27, 1805); Archives des Aff. Étr., MSS.

tions on that point were emphatic in support of Spain. Turreau was obliged to enter the lists in defence of Yrujo's position.

"I mixed in the discussion only in order to represent to Mr. Madison, who is unwilling to stop at the treaty of 1762, that in general the last conventions were those which ought to guide in negotiations; otherwise, if each party invoked the antecedent ones in favor of his system, we should be forced to go back to the Deluge to find the primitive title. 'But, General!' replied Mr. Madison, ' we have a map which probably carries to the Perdido the eastern limit of Louisiana!'—'I should be curious to see it, sir; the more, because I have one which includes Tennessee and Kentucky in Louisiana. You will agree that maps are not titles.' The Secretary of State closed this session, which lasted two long hours, by saying that if Spain had always conducted herself toward the United States as well as France had done, the difficulties would not have taken place. I did not think myself called upon to appear very grateful for this kind of cajolery."

Turreau did not want keenness of insight; and this early experience gave him no high respect either for Madison or for the American system of government. His despatch explained that the dispute was in great part due to the fact that the Louisiana purchase had been made a battle-ground in the Presidential election just ended; that the opposition, by depreciating its importance, had driven the party in power to exaggerate its value; and that the Administration, to assure itself of victory, had committed itself to the policy of obtaining Florida by one means or another, till it could no longer recede. Yrujo's indiscretions had helped to make it impossible for Jefferson to withdraw with dignity from his position.

"For the rest," continued Turreau, "I have made every effort to reconcile M. d'Yrujo with the Secretary of State, and if I have not succeeded, it is the fault of the latter. He is dry (*sec*), spiteful (*haineux*), passionate; and his private resentments, still more than political difference, will long keep him apart from M. d'Yrujo. Nevertheless, as I am on very good terms with Mr. Madison, whom I was about to ask to dine with me, I sent my first aide-de-camp to ask him whether he would be pleased to meet the Spanish minister at dinner; and in consequence of his very civil and even obliging answer, I had them together at my table, where I again attempted a reconciliation. M. d'Yrujo would have agreed to it; but the Secretary of State cannot forgive."

Finally, Turreau called Talleyrand's attention to the question whether it was for the interest of France and Spain that Yrujo should be kept at Washington: —

"Doubtless the Government here wishes for his recall, and regards this step as the duty of the Court at Madrid, the more because Mr. Pinckney has been recalled; but ought the Spanish minister to be changed because the American government wishes it? This point deserves attention. These people here have been well spoiled; it is time to send them back to their proper place."

The quarrel with Yrujo was the more unfortunate because it happened at a moment when Charles Pinckney, the American minister at Madrid, showed extreme want of discretion. The President had not intended to leave Pinckney unassisted. After the conclusion of the Louisiana treaty, in May, 1803, Madison supposed that Monroe, in obedience to his instructions, would go at once to Madrid and take the negotiation from Pinckney's hands.[1] For reasons that will hereafter appear, Monroe decided against this step, and went to London instead. On learning the change of plan, Madison warned Pinckney[2] to make no propositions to the Spanish government, which was not yet in a humor to receive them with favor. Pinckney, restive under restraint, managed to keep up an appearance of diplomatic activity that greatly vexed the Secretary of State. Madison complained[3] to the President that his minister at Madrid teased the Spanish government on the

---

[1] Madison to Monroe, July 29, 1803; State Papers, ii. 626. Madison to Pinckney, July 29, 1803; State Papers, ii. 614.

[2] Madison to Pinckney, Oct. 12, 1803; State Papers, ii. 570.

[3] Madison to Jefferson, April 9, 1804; Jefferson MSS.

subject of Florida, which he had been ordered not to touch without the presence or the advice of Monroe; forbidden to make but permitted to accept offers, he was continually offering to accept; while Livingston at Paris, equally restive under the imposed authority of Monroe, could not resist the temptation to stimulate Pinckney and offer advice both to France and Spain. Madison's complaints were well founded; but when he wrote in this sense to Jefferson, he had not begun to appreciate the full measure of diplomatic activity which his minister at Madrid was capable of displaying.

Yrujo always managed to embarrass the American government without seriously committing his own; but Pinckney showed no such forbearance, and by the close of the year 1804 drew Madison into a mortifying position. He began his activity in July, 1803, immediately after hearing that Monroe had given up the proposed visit to Madrid, and had gone to London. Without waiting to learn how this change of plan and the purchase of Louisiana might affect the President's views toward Spain, Pinckney, to use his own words,[1] "pushed the new propositions respecting our claims in that positive and decided manner which the circumstances of Europe and the particular situation of Spain seemed to me to warrant." Cevallos contented himself with parrying this attack by giving to Pinckney the written opinion obtained by Yrujo from the five American lawyers in support of his argument that the United States, by their treaty with France of Sept. 30, 1800, had renounced their right to demand indemnity for losses sustained from French cruisers.[2]

Both parties next appealed to the French ambassador at Madrid. The Prince of Peace, though irritated by the sale of Louisiana, quickly saw that his only chance of retaining Florida was to conciliate Bonaparte; and Pinckney, who knew that the French ambassador at Madrid had been instructed to support Monroe in negotiating for Florida, counted on the same aid in order to maintain a threatening attitude. The result was soon seen. Pinckney, disturbed by the news of Yrujo's protest against the sale of Louisiana, turned to the French

[1] Pinckney to Madison, Aug. 2, 1803; State Papers, ii. 597.
[2] Cevallos to Pinckney, Aug. 23, 1803; State Papers, ii. 604.

ambassador for advice.[1] Beurnonville accordingly wrote to
Talleyrand for instructions; but Talleyrand had already sent to
the Spanish embassy at Paris a note of sharp remonstrance
against the protest.[2] Beurnonville, learning this, asked the
Prince of Peace for explanations; and Godoy hastened to assure him that Bonaparte might be at ease on this score, for
orders had been sent to New Orleans to surrender the province without opposition, and already Yrujo had been instructed to change his tone at Washington.[3] Soon afterward
Cevallos formally notified Pinckney that the King renounced
his opposition to the cession of Louisiana.[4] In due time Yrujo
sent to the State Department a formal note to the same
effect.[5]

At the cost of recognizing the Louisiana cession, Godoy
pacified Bonaparte, who stood in need of Spanish support.
From that moment Pinckney begged in vain for help from
the French ambassador at Madrid, although the need of aid
increased from day to day. Just as his first and least important
point, the withdrawal of Yrujo's protest, was gained at Madrid, the Government at Washington created new difficulties
about his path. At the moment when Beurnonville, Talleyrand, and Pinckney wrung from King Charles his adhesion to
the Louisiana treaty, the Senate at Washington, Jan. 9, 1804,
ratified the Spanish claims convention, which had been negotiated by Pinckney nearly eighteen months before, and had
been held an entire year under consideration by the Senate.
The last article of this convention provided, as usual with
such instruments, that it should have no effect until ratified
by both parties, and that the ratifications should be exchanged
as soon as possible. So far from performing its part of the
contract, the Senate had at one moment refused to ratify at
all, and after reconsidering this refusal, had delayed ratification an entire year, until the relations of the two parties had

[1] Beurnonville to Talleyrand, 18 Nivôse, An xii. (Jan. 9, 1804); Archives des
Aff. Étr., MSS.
[2] Talleyrand to D'Hervas, 12 Nivôse, An xii. (Jan. 3, 1804); Archives des
Aff. Étr., MSS.
[3] Beurnonville to Talleyrand, 21 Nivôse, An xii. (Jan. 12, 1804); Archives des
Aff. Étr., MSS.
[4] Cevallos to Pinckney, Feb. 10, 1804; State Papers, ii. 583.
[5] Yrujo to Madison, May 15, 1804; State Papers, ii. 583.

been wholly changed. The idea that the King of Spain was bound to ratify in his turn, implied excessive confidence in his good-nature; but Madison, in sending the ratified treaty to Pinckney, suggested no suspicion that Charles IV. might have changed his mind, and gave not a hint to Pinckney of the course to be followed in such a contingency. The Mobile Act had not yet become law, and Yrujo was waiting for its signature by the President before waking Madison from his dreams of doing what he pleased with Spanish property.

Early in February, 1804, Madison sent these new instructions to Pinckney, inclosing the ratified treaty, and instructing him in effect to press the reserved claims for French spoliations in Spanish ports. The despatch reached Pinckney in May, and he went at once to Cevallos for the ratification. To his great annoyance Cevallos made difficulties. During the discussion, Cevallos received from Yrujo a copy of the Mobile Act, which he sent to Pinckney May 31, with a demand for explanations. Pinckney replied in a tone little short of dictatorial.[1]

"Permit me on this subject to remind your Excellency," said he, "that on the first intelligence being received of the cession of Louisiana, I communicated verbally to your Excellency and the Prince of Peace the contents of an official letter I had received from Mr. Livingston and Mr. Monroe, informing me that they considered a great part of West Florida, as so called by the English, as included. Such letter could not have been written officially to me by them without their having been so informed by the French plenipotentiary and government."

Pinckney urged that the two subjects should be kept separate. "Do not show the United States that you have no confidence either in their honor or justice,—qualities on which they value themselves more than on power or wealth."

Unfortunately Pinckney's note obliged Spain to show want of confidence in the "honor or justice" of the United States, unless indeed she meant to acquiesce in losing Florida as well as Louisiana. Pinckney next appealed to the French ambas-

[1] Pinckney to Cevallos, June 1, 1804; State Papers, ii. 618.

sador for help.[1] "I took the course of giving Mr. Pinckney an obliging but vague answer," said Beurnonville, writing for instructions to Talleyrand. Cevallos, on his side, wrote to Admiral Gravina, the Spanish ambassador at Paris, instructing him to remonstrate with Talleyrand against Pinckney's conduct. After a month's delay, Cevallos, in answer to Pinckney's letters, sent a sharp note,[2] offering to ratify the convention on three conditions,—one being that the reserved claim for French spoliations should be abandoned, and another that the Mobile Act should be revoked.

Without waiting for further instructions, or even consulting Monroe at London, Pinckney next wrote to Cevallos a letter which surpassed all indiscretions that Madison could have imagined. Requesting Cevallos "merely to answer this question," whether ratification was refused except on the conditions specified, he added:[3] —

> "I wish to have your Excellency's answer as quickly as possible, as on Tuesday I send a courier with circular letters to all our consuls in the ports of Spain, stating to them the critical situation of things between Spain and the United States, the probability of a speedy and serious misunderstanding, and directing them to give notice thereof to all our citizens; advising them so to arrange and prepare their affairs as to be able to move off within the time limited by the treaty, should things end as I now expect. I am also preparing the same information for the commander of our squadron in the Mediterranean, for his own notice and government, and that of all the American merchant-vessels he may meet."

Cevallos immediately answered[4] that as he could not comprehend the motive for "breaking out in the decisions, not to say threats," of this letter, or how it was possible that Pinckney could have the authority of his government for such conduct, he should by the King's order transfer the negotiation

[1] Beurnonville to Talleyrand, 18 Prairial, An xii. (June 7, 1804); Archives des Aff. Étr., MSS.
[2] Cevallos to Pinckney, July 2, 1804; State Papers, ii. 619.
[3] Pinckney to Cevallos, July 5, 1804; State Papers, ii. 620.
[4] Cevallos to Pinckney, July 8, 1804; State Papers, ii. 620.

to Washington. Pinckney rejoined by despatching his circular letter, which created a panic in the Mediterranean. He then informed Cevallos that so soon as his affairs could be arranged, he should send for his passports and quit Madrid.[1]

Although this step was in the highest degree improper, Pinckney had some excuse for his conduct. Left without instructions in the face of an emergency which might have been foreseen at Washington, he argued that his government, which had officially annexed West Florida, meant to support its acts with a strong hand. He thought that the issue presented by Cevallos was such as the President was bound to take up, and he knew that the only chance of carrying the points which the President had at heart was in energetic action. For three years he had watched the peremptory tone of France and England at Madrid, and had been assured by the common voice of his diplomatic colleagues that threats alone could extort action from the Spanish government. He had seen the Prince of Peace, after resorting to one subterfuge after another, repeatedly forced to cower before the two great robbers who were plundering Spain, and he explained to Madison the necessity of imitating their example if the President meant that Spain should cower before the United States. Perhaps he felt that Godoy looked on the President at Washington as the jackal of Bonaparte, and he may have wished to prove that America could act alone. His eager ambition to make himself as important as the representatives of France and England in the eyes of Europe might imply vanity, but rested also on logic.

The first result of this energetic tone was not what Pinckney had hoped. Cevallos was outwardly unmoved; Pinckney's violence only caused him to lay aside that courtesy which was the usual mark of Spanish manners. His official notes were in outward form still civil enough, but in two or three conversations Pinckney listened to a series of remarks as blunt as though Lord Harrowby were the speaker. Pinckney reported to Madison the tenor of these rough rejoinders.[2] Cevallos told him that the Americans, ever since their independence, had been receiving the most pointed proofs of friendship and

[1] Pinckney to Cevallos, July 14, 1804; State Papers, ii. 621.
[2] Pinckney to Madison, July 20, 1804; MSS. State Department Archives.

generosity from Spain, who, as was well known, received no benefit from them, — on the contrary, their commerce was extremely injurious to Spain; the Spanish government had ten times more trouble with them than with any other nation, and for his part, he did not wish to see the trade with the United States extended. Spain had nothing to fear from the United States, and had heard with contempt the threats of senators like Ross and Gouverneur Morris. The Americans had no right to expect much kindness from the King; in the purchase of Louisiana they had paid no attention to his repeated remonstrances against the injustice and nullity of that transaction, whereas if they had felt the least friendship they would have done so. They were well known to be a nation of calculators, bent on making money and nothing else; the French, and probably in the result all the nations having possessions in the West Indies, would be materially injured by them, for without a doubt it was entirely owing to the United States that St. Domingo was in its present situation.

Pinckney received[1] at the same time what he called secret intelligence on which he could implicitly rely, that Cevallos meant to create indefinite delays to the ratification, for Yrujo had written that neither these nor the French spoliation claims, nor West Florida, would induce the American government to depart from its pacific system. France had indeed gone to the point of advising and even commanding Spain to relinquish her claim on Louisiana, and this was the reason why Spain had so quietly given it up; but in regard to the spoliations, France preferred not to see them paid, as the more money Spain paid America the less she could pay France, and France knew as well as Spain how little serious was the American government in the idea of abandoning its neutrality.

Pinckney having done his worst, found himself in a position extremely awkward. Although he threatened to leave Spain, and proclaimed that he meant soon to demand his passports, he did not venture to take this last step without instructions. Cevallos, excessively perplexed by his conduct, could not conceive that he should act thus without some

[1] Pinckney to Madison, July 20, 1804; MSS. State Department Archives.

definite authority. Boldly as Cevallos talked, he was in truth greatly alarmed by the idea of war. The French representative at Madrid wrote to Talleyrand that Pinckney had terrified the secretary beyond reason:[1] —

"The difficulty of making himself understood by M. de Cevallos in a language with which he is not familiar, excites Mr. Pinckney to fly out in terms beyond moderation and proper civility. He positively threatens war, and loudly announces his resolution shortly to demand his passports. The truth is that he is preparing to depart, and finds himself almost deprived of power to remain, not only in consequence of his personal altercation with the minister, but also of the care with which he has taken the public into his confidence. . . . M. de Cevallos seems to me to be quite seriously alarmed at the results this may have."

Ten days later the Frenchman reported that Cevallos was more uneasy than ever.[2]

" 'If the Emperor,' added M. de Cevallos, 'would but say a word, and let the United States understand that he is not pleased at seeing them abuse the advantages which they owe to their strength and to the nearness of their resources over an ally of France, this would reconcile all difficulties, and save his Majesty the necessity of exacting satisfaction for an insult which is as good as inflicted.' "

The Frenchman, having no instructions, contented himself with suggesting that the Emperor had more pressing matters on hand. " 'So,' said M. de Cevallos, 'France will have caused our actual misunderstanding with our neighbors, and we are to expect no service from her influence!' "

While Cevallos thus invoked the aid of France, the news of Pinckney's war slowly crossed the Atlantic. No sooner did it arrive than Yrujo in the middle of October, shortly after his attempt to seduce the patriotism of Major Jackson, wrote to

[1] Vandeul to Talleyrand, 7 Thermidor, An xii. (July 26, 1804); Archives des Aff. Étr., MSS.
[2] Vandeul to Talleyrand, 18 Thermidor, An xii. (Aug. 6, 1804); Archives des Aff. Étr., MSS.

the Secretary of State a formal letter,[1] repeating what had already been said to Pinckney at Madrid. Madison's reply was studiously moderate and conciliatory.[2] He explained as best he could the offensive language of the Mobile Act, and announced that a special minister would soon reach Madrid, to hasten the adjustment of all territorial disputes; he deprecated the demand for an abandonment of the French claims, and argued that such a condition of ratification was not supported by international law; he urged Yrujo to give assurances of an unqualified ratification, but he said not a word about Pinckney's performances, and gave it to be understood that Pinckney would be recalled. A few days afterward he wrote to Monroe, ordering him in haste to Spain. "The turn which our affairs at Madrid have taken renders it expedient in the judgment of the President that you should proceed thither without delay."[3] In another letter, written at nearly the same time, he was more explicit:[4] —

"Pinckney's recall has been asked by the Spanish government, and a letter of leave goes to him. I suspect he will not return in good humor. I could not permit myself to flatter him, and truth would not permit me to praise him. He is well off in escaping reproof, for his agency has been very faulty as well as feeble."

The first attempts to overawe Spain had failed. Pinckney, not disavowed but ignored, fell into the background; and once more Monroe stepped forward to rescue the Administration. When these instructions were written, he had already reached Paris on his way to Madrid; but Madison, undeterred by Pinckney's disaster, still persisted in advising him to place his main reliance "in a skilful appeal to the fears of Spain."[5]

[1] Yrujo to Madison, Oct. 13, 1804; State Papers, ii. 624.
[2] Madison to Yrujo, Oct. 15, 1804; State Papers, ii. 625.
[3] Madison to Monroe, Oct. 26, 1804; State Papers, ii. 631.
[4] Madison to Monroe, Nov. 9, 1804; Works, ii. 208.
[5] Ibid.

Chapter XIII

HARDLY WAS the Louisiana treaty sent to America in May, 1803, when Monroe began preparations for a journey to Madrid. The outbreak of temper with which Godoy and Cevallos received the news that Spain had been secretly deprived of Louisiana, caused Bonaparte to feel that further maltreatment of his ally was for the moment unwise; and he interposed a sudden veto on Monroe's journey. "With respect to Florida, this is not the time to pursue that object," said he, when Monroe came to take leave.[1] The Consul Cambacérès echoed the warning: "You must not go to Spain at present; it is not the time; you had better defer it." The Third Consul Lebrun spoke in the same tone. Monroe took the advice, and abandoned the journey to Madrid. In July he crossed the Channel to London, and Aug. 17, 1803, was duly presented to George III. as the successor of Rufus King, who had already returned to America. Livingston remained at Paris to manage the relations with Napoleon.

In spite of success that should have filled his cup of ambition to overflowing, Livingston was far from satisfied. Neither the President nor the Secretary of State liked him; and to the latter he was a possible rival, who might become dangerous if the authority of President Jefferson, which was Madison's great support, should wane, and should New York claim the presidency from Virginia. Monroe distrusted Livingston, believing him to grasp at the whole credit of the Louisiana treaty, and to be intriguing to withdraw the Florida negotiation from Monroe's hands by causing its transfer from Madrid to Paris.[2] The Secretary of State was perpetually annoyed by his minister. Sometimes Livingston experimented on Spain, sometimes on England. At one moment he sent to the First Consul an indiscreet memorial that brought a remonstrance from the British government; at another he fell into a virulent quarrel with the American claims commissioners under the Louisiana treaty. His claims convention was admitted to be full of mistakes which he did not

[1] Monroe to Madison, July 20, 1803; MSS. State Department Archives.
[2] Monroe's Memoranda, Monroe MSS., State Department Archives.

himself attempt to defend, while the American consul at Paris declared that his conduct in regard to certain claims was dictated by blind and insatiable vanity, if not by corrupt and criminal motives.[1]

Mistakes cost Livingston little serious annoyance; but although he could afford to disregard British complaints or Consul Skipwith's abuse, or even the severe criticisms of the claims commissioners, he must have had more than human patience to sit quiet under the superiority of Monroe. He knew that whatever diplomatic credit was due for the Louisiana negotiation rightly belonged to him, and that Monroe had no claim to any part of it, except that of supporting and approving what was already accomplished; yet he saw the Administration and the public attribute the chief honor to his rival. He showed his wounded self-esteem in protests and statements to which the world was deaf. His old Federalist friends took malicious pleasure in telling him that his triumph had offended the vanity of Jefferson.[2]

Consoling himself with the reflection that he should insist on returning to America in the autumn of 1804, Livingston endured these annoyances as he best could, and found in the society of Robert Fulton and Joel Barlow the hope of greater fame and profit than political distinctions could possibly bring. While he watched and encouraged Fulton's experiments with the steamboat, clouds gathered more and more thickly round his diplomatic path. The First Consul had never inspired him with much confidence; but after the rupture of the Peace of Amiens, in May, 1803, Bonaparte's acts became more and more alarming to every Republican. He passed the autumn of 1803 in preparations for a descent on England. He next effected, in February, 1804, the arrest, trial, and banishment of Moreau. The seizure and arbitrary execution of the Duc d'Enghien followed a month afterward, and finally, in May, 1804, the proclamation of the Empire.

In the midst of these events Livingston received from home the letter already quoted, in which Madison told the story of the Mobile Act, and complained of Yrujo's violent conduct. "The correspondence is chiefly of importance," said the

[1] Skipwith to Madison, Feb. 21, 1804; State Department Archives.
[2] Gouverneur Morris to Livingston, Nov. 28, 1803; Sparks's Morris, iii. 188.

Secretary of State, "as it urges the expediency of cultivating the disposition of the French government to take our side of the question." Livingston was personally rather inclined to the opposite course. He had little faith in obtaining favors from the Emperor, and no disposition to place the United States in the attitude of begging for them; but he had not the chief share in shaping action. A few weeks after receiving these instructions, when he heard of the *quasi* war which Pinckney in July declared at Madrid, Livingston was already expecting the arrival of his successor, General Armstrong, in the autumn.

The news from Spain reaching London, startled Monroe from his repose. As soon as he could make ready, Oct. 8, 1804, placing his legation in charge of a secretary, Monroe left London. While he waited in Paris to sound the disposition of Talleyrand, General Armstrong arrived to relieve Livingston. Thus it happened that three American ministers—Monroe, Livingston, and Armstrong—met at Paris in November, 1804, to cope with Talleyrand, in whose hands lay the decision of Jefferson's quarrel with Spain.

The question to be decided was whether the United States government should disregard its obligations to Napoleon and act independently, or whether the President should defer to the opinion of Talleyrand and to the Emperor's will. The story of diplomatic adventure, which has so often an interest beyond what could be supposed possible from the contact of three or four quiet and elderly gentlemen meeting about a green table, or writing letters inordinately long, owes that interest in most cases to a hope or a despair, to a mystery or an elucidation; but Monroe's labors at that time offered little mystery, and less hope. Although he did not know all that was happening behind the diplomatic curtain, he knew enough to be aware that his negotiation for Florida, on the ground chosen by the President, was hopeless.

Three months had passed since Cevallos made his appeal to Talleyrand for help. "If the Emperor would but say a word," Cevallos urged;[1] "if he would make the United States understand that he will not be pleased at seeing them abuse their

[1] Vandeul to Talleyrand, July 26 and Aug. 6, 1804; Archives des Aff. Étr., MSS.

advantages,"—this would put an end to insults like the Mobile Act and Pinckney's threats. Talleyrand's answer could not be doubtful. Angry with Jefferson, Madison, Monroe, and Livingston for their attack on West Florida, into which his own and his master's finessing had drawn them; still angrier with Pinckney for the burlesque of Napoleonic manners with which he alarmed the government of Spain; hostile at heart to Bonaparte's ultimate schemes against the Spanish empire, but determined that if Spain were to be plundered France should have the booty; willing to repay a part of the humiliation and disappointment which the United States had twice inflicted upon him,— the instant the Spanish ambassador at Paris brought the Mobile Act to his notice, Talleyrand assured him with emphasis that the Emperor would formally oppose such pretensions on the part of the United States;[1] and when Pinckney's conduct was reported to him, with the request that the Emperor would instruct his minister at Washington to act in concert with Yrujo in order to prevent a rupture, Talleyrand hastened to meet the wish of the Spanish government.

Cevallos made other requests. After narrating the history of Pinckney's claims convention, he touched briefly on the claim for French spoliations which the Americans so warmly urged against Spain, and he asserted that Lucien Bonaparte had given an assurance that these claims were covered by the Franco-American treaty of 1800, and therefore could not be pressed against Spain. He complained that Pinckney had used "language the most gross, the most insulting, and, so to speak, the most audacious and menacing." He called attention to the dangers which would result from allowing the boundary of Louisiana to be extended toward either Florida or Mexico; and he begged "that orders might be sent to the French commissioner Laussat in Louisiana, enjoining him to restrain the pretensions of the Americans regarding the limits of that province, and not to show himself favorable to the wishes of the Americans, as there is reason to suspect him of doing, according to his correspondence with the Spanish commissioner."

[1] Gravina to Talleyrand, July 24, 1804; Archives des Aff. Étr., MSS. Cevallos to Monroe and Pinckney, 16 Feb. 1805; State Papers, ii. 643.

Laussat's offence consisted in telling the American commissioners that his instructions fixed the Rio Bravo as the western boundary of Louisiana. Cevallos made no protest to Talleyrand against the truth of Laussat's statement. He tacitly admitted that Laussat was right; but he invited Talleyrand to join in depriving the United States of Texas, which the United States had bought, and the price of which they had paid to France. That Godoy should conspire for this purpose was natural, for he had no reason to respect the Louisiana cession, and he had pledged his honor in no way to the United States; but that he should ask Napoleon to deprive the United States of property which Napoleon himself had bought from Spain and sold to the United States, and for which he had received some millions of coin for his personal objects and ambitions, showed that the Prince of Peace understood the characters of Bonaparte and Talleyrand.

Talleyrand, who held that Bonaparte had made a mistake in selling Louisiana to the United States, and who looked upon himself as having no responsibility for the transaction, was glad to restrict what he thought the evil that had been done. Taking the complaints of Spain to the Emperor, he received permission to do what Spain requested; and during the month of August he sent from the Foreign Office a series of documents that disposed for the time of any hopes still nourished by Jefferson's diplomacy.

These three papers were too important to be forgotten. French diplomatic writings were models of concise, impassive clearness, contrasting with the diffuse and argumentative, if not disputatious, style which sometimes characterized American and Spanish official correspondence. These three short letters offered examples of French methods. The first was addressed to General Turreau at Washington, and concerned the boundaries of Louisiana toward the west:[1] —

"If the Mississippi and the Iberville trace with precision the eastern boundary of that colony, it has less precise limits to the westward. No river, no chain of mountains, separates it from the Spanish possessions; and between the last

[1] Talleyrand to Turreau (No. 99), 20 Thermidor, An xii. (Aug. 8, 1804); Archives des Aff. Étr., MSS.

settlements of Louisiana and the first of those in the Spanish colonies are frequently to be found intervals so great as
to make a line of demarcation difficult to agree upon. So
Spain already appears to fear that the United States, who
show an intention of forcing back the western limits of
Louisiana, may propose to advance in this direction to the
ocean, and establish themselves on that part of the American coast which lies north of California."

Turreau was directed to divert the United States government from the idea of extension toward the west and northwest in any manner that might annoy Spain. He was to
employ means of persuasion and friendly influence for this
purpose, rather than to act officially; all official action being
reserved for objects directly interesting France.

The second document[1] was also addressed to Turreau, but
was more decided in tone, as though the Emperor himself
had dictated its language. After a brief allusion to Pinckney's
claims convention and the American theory that Spain was
responsible for French spoliations which she had not prevented, Talleyrand continued:—

"That convention, made under date of Aug. 11, 1802, is
posterior by — months to that which France concluded
with the United States, the 8th Vendemiaire, An ix. (30
Sept. 1800), and which declared that no indemnity should
be given for prizes made by either of the two Powers. This
Article ought to leave the Americans no hope that prizes
made against them on Spanish shores would be excepted
and paid for; it would be useless for them to suppose that
it is Spain from whom they seek these indemnities: Spain,
who would have only the advances to pay, would afterward
recur to France for reimbursement. It is, then, upon France
that this charge would ultimately fall; and as we are relieved
by the convention of Sept. 30, 1800, from every kind of
debt relating to prizes, we can only with some surprise see
the United States seeking to obtain from another government a part of the indemnities which they had decidedly
renounced in their convention with France. Spain had

[1] Talleyrand to Turreau (No. 101), 27 Thermidor, An xii. (Aug. 15, 1804);
Archives des Aff. Étr., MSS.

doubtless lost sight of these considerations, and had not in view this convention of ours, when her plenipotentiary signed that of Aug. 11, 1802, which the United States now require her to ratify. Circumstances which have since taken place have, fortunately, furnished Spain with an occasion for retracing the false step she took in signing this convention. The Federal government, which by different acts relative to the Floridas has violated the sovereign rights of Spain, and which for more than eighteen months has refused to ratify its convention with her, has lost the right to complain because the Court of Madrid now imitates its refusal, and insists upon making such modifications in this treaty as the lapse of time may make it think necessary and better suited to its rights and dignity."

After sending these instructions to Turreau, the French Minister for Foreign Relations next turned to Spain, and wrote a note intended to reassure Cevallos. The peculiar interest of this document lay in the spirit it showed toward the United States. Cevallos had invited an understanding as to the boundaries of Louisiana to be alleged against the United States. These boundaries, defined eighteen months before in the secret instructions for Victor, a copy of which was given to Laussat, declared the Rio Bravo to be the western limit of Louisiana:[1] "Bounded on the west by the river called Rio Bravo, from the mouth of this stream up to the 30th parallel, beyond this point the line of demarcation ceases to be traced, and it seems that there has never been an agreement as to this part of the frontier." That Laussat meant to act on these instructions was proved by his language to Governor Claiborne and General Wilkinson.[2] "M. Laussat confidentially signified" to these two American commissioners that the territory "did not comprehend any part of West Florida; adding at the same time that it extended westwardly to the Rio Bravo, otherwise called Rio del Norte." Although Cevallos had remonstrated against the indiscretion of this statement, he had not sug-

---

[1] Instructions secrètes pour le Capitaine-Général de la Louisiane, approuvées par le Premier Consul le 5 Frimaire, An xi. (Nov. 26, 1802), Archives de la Marine, MSS.

[2] Madison to Livingston, March 31, 1804; State Papers, ii. 575.

gested that Laussat was in error;[1] he merely invited Talleyrand to check a subordinate officer, in order to limit
American pretensions. In accordance with this hint, Talleyrand marked for the Spanish government the line it was to
take in resisting the American claim to territory for which
France had received the purchase money.

After defining the eastern boundary of Florida as fixed by
treaty at the Iberville and the Mississippi rivers, the French
minister instructed the Spanish government as follows:[2] —

"The western limit of Louisiana not having been fixed in
a manner equally precise by the treaties which preceded
that of March 21, 1801, nor by that treaty itself, the uncertainty which prevailed in regard to the direction of its frontiers has necessarily continued since the cession made to the
United States. France could not even take upon herself to
indicate to the United States what ought to be that precise
limit, for fear of wounding on this point the pretensions of
one or the other Power directly interested in this question.
It would have become the object of negotiation between
his Imperial and his Catholic Majesties. To-day it can be
treated only between Spain and the United States. Nevertheless, as the Americans derive their rights from France, I
have been enabled to express to his Imperial Majesty's minister plenipotentiary near the United States the chief bases
on which the Emperor would have planted himself in the
demand for a demarcation of boundaries. Starting from the
Gulf of Mexico, we should have sought to distinguish between settlements that belong to the kingdom of Mexico,
and settlements that had been formed by the French or by
those who succeeded them in this colony. This distinction
between settlements formed by the French or by the Spaniards would have been made equally in ascending north-
wards. All those which are of French foundation would
have belonged to Louisiana; and since European settlements in the interior are rare and scattered, we might have

[1] Cf. Memoir upon the Negotiations between Spain and the United States
of America. By Don Louis de Onis, Madrid, 1820. Washington, 1821; pp. 146,
147.

[2] Talleyrand to Gravina, 12 Fructidor, An xii. (Aug. 30, 1804); Archives des
Aff. Étr., MSS.

imagined direct lines drawn from one to the other to connect them; and it is to the west of this imaginary line that
the boundary between Louisiana and the Spanish possessions would have been traced at such distance and in such
direction as France and Spain should have agreed. The
great spaces which sometimes exist between the last French
settlements and the last Spanish missions might have left
still some doubts on the direction of the boundary to be
traced between them, but with the views of friendship and
conciliation which animate their Majesties, these difficulties
would have been soon smoothed away."

Such were, according to Talleyrand, the conciliatory intentions which should have animated his Imperial Majesty. They
were widely different from the positive instructions formally
approved by the First Consul Nov. 26, 1802, which ordered
Victor and Laussat to consider the Rio Bravo as the boundary
of their command. The difference was the whole province of
Texas.

On another point Talleyrand reassured the Spanish government.

"In any case," said he, "the Court of Madrid would appear to have no ground for the fear it shows that the
United States may make use of their possession of Louisiana in order to form settlements on the northwest coast of
America. Whatever boundary may be agreed upon between
Spain and the United States, the line will necessarily be so
far removed from the western coast of America as to relieve
the Court of Madrid from any anxiety on that score."

Yet no one knew better than Talleyrand the instincts of the
American people, and their ambition to use the entire continent for their experiments! He knew that the First Consul, by
his instructions to Laussat, had given, so far as he could, the
authority of both French and Spanish governments to the
claim of the United States that Louisiana stretched westwardly to the Rio Bravo, and on the northwest indefinitely to
a line yet to be fixed. He knew that Laussat, who hated the
Spaniards more than he did the Americans, had betrayed the
secret. If Talleyrand hoped to repress American ambition, he

must have calculated on the effects of force or fear, or he must have been overwhelmed by the immensity of the scale on which the Americans were acting. The doctrine of contiguity, on which the United States could rest their most plausible claim to Oregon, was as valid then as it ever afterward became; and if Talleyrand did not appreciate it, Godoy proved himself the more sagacious statesman.

By Sept. 1, 1804, these precautionary measures were completed, and Talleyrand could wait for the coming of Monroe and Armstrong. About the middle of October Monroe appeared in Paris. His instructions, sent from Washington before the news of Pinckney's extravagances had reached America, obliged him to insist upon the right to West Florida as "a *sine quâ non*, and no price to be given for it;"[1] to insist, also, upon the right to Texas, but with a border-land to be kept unsettled for thirty years; and to offer two million dollars for East Florida beyond the Perdido. The Cabinet then for the first time decided to commit itself to the doctrine that West Florida was a part of the Louisiana purchase,[2] alleging as its ostensible reason, not so much the abstract justice of the title, as the wish to avoid acknowledging Spanish land-grants made in Florida since the Louisiana cession.

> "It is indispensable," wrote Madison, April 15, 1804, "that the United States be not precluded from such a construction [of the treaty],—first, because they consider the right as well founded; secondly and principally, because it is known that a great proportion of the most valuable lands between the Mississippi and the Perdido have been granted by Spanish officers since the cession was made by Spain. These illicit speculations cannot otherwise be frustrated than by considering the territory as included in the cession made by Spain."

The hope that Spain might submit to these concessions rested on the belief that she could not afford to quarrel with the United States. Foreseeing that she must soon be drawn into the war with England, the President from the first looked

---

[1] Jefferson to Madison, July 5, 1804; Works, iv. 550.

[2] Madison to Monroe, April 15, 1804; State Papers, ii. 627. Madison to Monroe and Pinckney, July 8, 1804; State Papers, ii. 630.

forward to that event, believing that the same reasons which as he supposed had forced Bonaparte to cede Louisiana, must reconcile Spain to the cession of Florida.

"Should she be engaged in the war," wrote Madison to Monroe, "or manifestly threatened with that situation, she cannot fail to be the more anxious for a solid accommodation on all points with the United States, and the more willing to yield, for that purpose, to terms which, however proper in themselves, might otherwise be rejected by her pride and misapplied jealousy."

The first part of this calculation was realized even before Monroe quitted London. Oct. 1, 1804, a British squadron seized the Spanish treasure-ships on their voyage from America; and no one doubted that Spain must declare war. She did so a few weeks later, December 12, before Monroe reached Madrid. The effect of this new disaster on what Madison called her "misapplied jealousy" remained to be seen.

The only published record of Monroe's stay in Paris is contained in a note dated Nov. 8, 1804, which he persuaded Livingston to convey to Talleyrand. Although Livingston's temper was peculiar, and his diplomacy under ordinary circumstances restless, he was well acquainted with the men who governed France; and he had little faith in another man's ability to do what he had himself attempted in vain. That Livingston should be jealous of Monroe's presence in Paris was natural; for the American minister at London was not accredited to the Emperor, and his interference could do nothing but harm to the actual minister at Paris. When asked to act as medium for Monroe's proposed communications with Talleyrand, Livingston made objections. Not until Armstrong arrived, about November 1, did the ministers agree upon the terms of the note, and send it to its address. Monroe had then been one month absent from London.

Nothing could be more courteous than the tone of Monroe's letter, which ignored Pinckney's conduct, and breathed a spirit of benevolence.[1] The object of writing was to ask the Emperor's good offices in support of the negotiation to be

---

[1] Monroe to Talleyrand, Nov. 8, 1804; State Papers, ii. 634.

opened at Madrid; and in order to reach this end, Monroe touched on the story of his present mission, recounting the causes of the previous quarrel with Spain, and alluding to West Florida, the spoliation claims, the claims for damages rising from Morales's occlusion of the Mississippi, and to the Mobile Act, which, as Monroe admitted, was intended to authorize the taking immediate possession of Florida. The only offensive idea suggested in the note was that the Spanish occupation of Florida implied an aggression against the United States, " which tends to provoke hostility and lead to war."

The note combining the diplomacy of three ministers was sent; and the three diplomatists waited in fear of what would follow, dreading nothing so much as Talleyrand's answer. They had reason to know that it would be unfavorable, and that at least on the question of West Florida Talleyrand had already committed himself against the United States. They were told, too, that on reading their note Napoleon showed great irritation. Besides this, they had other causes of alarm. Within three days after Monroe's arrival at Paris, Marbois, his best friend among Napoleon's ministers, told him that the question was one of money:[1] "Such was the situation of Spain at this time, that he was persuaded if we would make her suitable pecuniary accommodations we might succeed." M. Hauterive, another gentleman within the circle of government, soon afterward repeated the remark: "Spain must cede territory; the United States must pay money." Care was taken to let Monroe understand that once this principle should be agreed upon, France would cause the negotiation to be transferred to Paris. Armstrong soon afterward wrote to Madison, alluding to the story in regard to the Emperor:[2] —

"This country has determined to convert the negotiation into a job, and to draw from it advantages merely pecuniary to herself, or, in other language, to her agents. It is this venality that explains her present reserve, the degree of excitement displayed by the Emperor on reading the note, and the marked incivility with which Mr. Monroe was treated by Talleyrand. Since his departure, repeated inti-

[1] Monroe to Madison, Dec. 16, 1804; MSS. State Department Archives.
[2] Armstrong to Madison, Dec. 24, 1804; MSS. State Department Archives.

mations have been given to me that if certain persons could be sufficiently gratified, the negotiation should be transferred hither, and brought to a close with which we should have no reason to find fault."

Monroe, though honest as any man in public life, and more courageous in great emergencies than some of his friends or rivals, was commonly not quick at catching an idea, nor did he see it at last from a great elevation; but in this instance the idea was thrust so persistently into his face, that had he been blind he could not have missed it. Nothing could more clearly explain his situation than the language of the diary in which he recorded, for the President's benefit, the daily course of his conduct.

"No other alternative," he explained,[1] "presented itself to me than to abandon the object and return to London, or to submit to the terms which it was sufficiently well understood France was willing to accept, and seemed in some measure to dictate, which amounted to this: that we should create a new loan of about seventy millions of livres, and transfer the same to Spain, who would immediately pass them over to France, in consideration of which we should be put in possession of the disputed territory, under stipulations which should provide for the adjustment of the ultimate right there, and reimbursement of the money by instalment in seven years."

"To submit to the terms proposed was altogether out of the question," continued Monroe. Having led his Government to take the ground that West Florida had already been bought, he could not enter into a negotiation to buy it a second time. His instructions made this point a *sine quâ non* of negotiation. Recognizing that under these circumstances further effort was useless, or in his own words that no other alternative presented itself but to abandon the object and return to London, Monroe intimated to Talleyrand that he meant not only to pay no money, but also to negotiate in spite of Napoleon; and started for Madrid.

[1] Diary at Aranjuez, April 22, 1805; MSS. State Department Archives.

"I did not hesitate," he wrote home,[1] "in many informal communications, the substance of which I was persuaded were made known to those in power, to declare most solemnly that I would sanction no measure which contemplated a payment of money to Spain in any transaction we might have with her in the affair,—by which was meant, by creation of stock or otherwise which took the money from our people; that neither the state of things between the parties, the example of France in a similar case, or my instructions, permitted it. These conversations were with a person who possessed the confidence of certain persons in power, as well as my own, though they were not of a nature to compromit either party. That circumstance enabled me to speak with the utmost freedom, and perhaps to say things which it might have been difficult to press directly in the same manner to the parties themselves."

In thus defying France, Monroe, if he resembled European diplomatists, must have aimed at giving his Government an opportunity to break with the Emperor and to proceed against Florida by means of force. That he should have still hoped for success in negotiating at Madrid was hardly possible. Armstrong thought his chance desperate.[2]

"Mr. Monroe has no doubt communicated to you," he wrote to the Secretary of State, "the motives which induced him to leave England in prosecution of his mission to Spain, and while here to attempt to draw from this Government some new declaration in support of our construction of the late treaty. With this view a note was prepared and transmitted through Livingston, the receipt of which was acknowledged by Mr. Talleyrand with a promise that 'an answer should be given to it as soon as the Emperor should have signified his will on the subject.' Having waited nearly a month, and no answer being given, having some reason to believe that any declaration from this Court now would be less favorable than those already made, and fearful lest something might be lost at Madrid, while nothing could be gained here, he set out on the 8th instant for

[1] Monroe to Madison, Dec. 16, 1804; MSS. State Department Archives.
[2] Armstrong to Madison, Dec. 24, 1804; MSS. State Department Archives.

Spain. I have but little hope, however, that he will be able to do more than fulfil the forms of his mission."

Armstrong preferred, as he expressed it, "an effort (which cannot fail) to do the business at home." He had already discovered that the Emperor was personally irritated with the Americans, that he took no pains to conceal it, and that this irritation was a cause of his reserve.

"I have employed every means in my power to ascertain the cause of this cause, and have learned from a person sufficiently near him to know the fact, that this temper originated in representations made by Leclerc and others from St. Domingo; that it has since been kept alive by the incident of the war in that country, the trade carried on between it and the United States, the freedom with which he is treated in our press, the matrimonial connection of Jerome, and, above all, the support which principles he wishes to extinguish in France receive from the progressing prosperity of the United States."

With Napoleon in this frame of mind; with Godoy and Cevallos in a humor far worse; and with Talleyrand in such a temper as not to allow of his treating Monroe with civility, — the American plenipotentiary departed to Madrid, hoping that something might occur to overcome his difficulties. During his journey, Charles IV. declared war against England. This long-foreseen event, which should have brought Spain to terms with the United States, in fact threw her only at the feet of Napoleon. Henceforward every offence to Spain was an offence to France, which the Emperor was the more bound to resent because by treaty he must regard a war upon Charles IV. as a war upon himself.

Talleyrand was not vindictive, but he had been twice mortified by the failure of his policy toward America. If his callous cheek could burn, it was still red with the blow which the last President of the United States had struck it; and no waters of oblivion could drown in his memory the cry of distress with which he had then begged for mercy. He had been again overthrown by the present President, and obliged to sell Louisiana, turn his back on the traditions of France, and shut

up his far-reaching mind within the limit of his master's artillery politics. Day by day he saw more clearly that soldiership,
and not statecraft, was to guide the destinies of France, and
that the new *régime* was but revolution without ideas. He had
probably begun already to feel that the presence of his coldly
silent face was becoming irksome to a will which revolted at
the memory of a remonstrance. Talleyrand was corrupt,—
perhaps he thought himself more corrupt than he was; but
his political instincts were sounder than his private morality.
He was incarnate conservatism; but he was wider-minded and
more elevated in purpose than Napoleon. He had no faith in
Napoleon's methods, and was particularly hostile to his projects against Spain; but in respect to Monroe and his mission,
Talleyrand's ideas coincided with those of the Emperor; and
when two such men marked out a victim, his chance of escape
was small.

Talleyrand was not to blame that Monroe's note remained
unanswered before Monroe left Paris. About ten days after
receiving it Talleyrand made to the Emperor a report on
the subject, so cool and clear as to read like a mathematical
demonstration.[1]

> "The United States," he began, "who wish to negotiate
> at Madrid under the auspices of France for the acquisition
> of Florida, have acquired little title to the good offices of
> the Emperor by the sharpness of tone and the want of ci-
> vility (*égards*) with which they have conducted themselves
> toward Spain."

After enumerating the threats and aggressions of the
United States government against Spain during the last three
years, the report disposed of the American claims, one by
one, in few words. First, the spoliations, which had been formally abandoned by treaty; second, the claim for losses rising
from the interruption of *entrepôt* at New Orleans, which
"should be terminated by the treaty of cession,—the acquisition of an immense country might throw out of view some
anterior losses;" finally, the claim to West Florida,—a species
of attack on the Emperor's dignity and good faith which

---

[1] Rapport à l'Empereur, 28 Brumaire, An xii. (Nov. 19, 1804); Archives des
Aff. Étr., MSS.

merited some expression of his displeasure. To support this view, Talleyrand related the history of the French negotiation for West Florida and its failure, commenting on the manner in which the Americans had fabricated their claim, and coming at last to a conclusion studiously moderate, and evidently in harmony with the views of Hauterive as expressed to Monroe. Talleyrand rarely wrote such papers with his own hand; probably they were drawn up under his directions by Hauterive, or some other subordinate of the Office, in the form of suggestions rather than advice.

"According to such evidence, no one can suppose the United States to be convinced of the justice of their rights; and we are warranted in thinking that the Federal government, as a result of confidence in its own strength, of its ambition, and its ascendency in America, raises pretensions to a part of Florida in order to show itself afterward more exacting toward Spain. The Emperor will feel that justice requires him not to recognize such pretensions. If he should assist by his good offices an arrangement between the United States and Spain, he would wish good faith and impartiality for its base.

"Only in case the United States should desist from their unjust pretensions to West Florida, and return to the forms of civility and decorum,—from which in their relations with each other governments should never depart,—could the Emperor allow himself to second at the Court of Madrid the project of acquisition of the two Floridas. Then perhaps the Emperor might think that this country is less suited to Spain now that it is separated from her other colonies, and that it is better suited to the United States because a part of their Western rivers cross the Floridas before flowing into the Gulf of Mexico; and finally, that Spain may see in her actual situation, and in the expenses entailed on her by the war, some motives for listening to the offers of the Federal government."

Talleyrand had great need to insist on "the forms of civility and decorum from which governments should never depart"! Perhaps Talleyrand already foresaw the scene, said to have occurred some two years later, when Napoleon violently denounced him to his face as "a silk stocking stuffed with filth," and the minister coldly retaliated by the famous phrase, "Pity that so great a man should be so ill brought up!" The task of teaching manners to Jefferson was not Napoleon's view of his own functions in the world. He probably gave more attention to the concluding lines of the report, which suggested that he should decide whether a Spanish colony, made worthless by an arbitrary act of his own, could be usefully employed in sustaining his wars.

This report, dated Nov. 19, 1804, lay some weeks in the Emperor's hands. Monroe left Paris for Madrid December 8, and still no answer had been sent to his note. He wrote from Bordeaux, December 16, a long and interesting letter to Madison, and resumed his journey. He could hardly have crossed the Bidassoa when Armstrong received from Talleyrand, December 21, the long-expected answer,[1] which by declaring the claim to West Florida emphatically unfounded struck the ground from under Monroe's feet, and left him to repent at leisure his defiance of Talleyrand's advice. Under the forms of perfect courtesy, this letter contained both sarcasm and menace. Talleyrand expressed curiosity to learn the result of Monroe's negotiation: --

"This result his Imperial Majesty will learn with real interest. He saw with pain the United States commence their difficulties with Spain in an unusual manner, and conduct themselves toward the Floridas by acts of violence which, not being founded in right, could have no other effect but to injure the lawful owner. Such an aggression gave the more surprise to his Majesty because the United States seemed in this measure to avail themselves of their treaty with France as an authority for their proceedings, and because he could scarcely reconcile with the just opinion which he entertains of the wisdom and fidelity of the Federal government a course of proceedings which nothing can authorize toward a Power which has long occupied, and still occupies, one of the first ranks in Europe."

Madison and Monroe, as well as Jefferson, in the course of

---

[1] Talleyrand to Armstrong, Dec. 21, 1804; State Papers, ii. 635.

their diplomacy had many mortifications to suffer; but they rarely received a reprimand more keen than this. Yet its sharpness was so delicately covered by the habitual forms of Talleyrand's diplomacy that Americans, who were accustomed to hear and to use strong language, hardly felt the wound it was intended to inflict. After hearing Yrujo denounce an act of their government as an "atrocious libel," they were not shocked to hear Talleyrand denounce the same act as one of violence which nothing could authorize. The force of Talleyrand's language was more apparent to Godoy than to Madison, for it bore out every expression of Yrujo and Cevallos. The Prince of Peace received a copy of Talleyrand's note at the moment when Monroe, after almost a month of weary winter travel, joined Pinckney, who had for six months been employed only in writing letter after letter begging for succor and support. Don Pedro Cevallos, with this public pledge in his hand, and with secret French pledges covering every point of the negotiation in his desk, could afford to meet with good humor the first visit of the new American plenipotentiary.

Pinckney's humiliation was extreme. After breaking off relations with Cevallos and pledging himself to demand his passports and to leave Spain, he had been reduced to admit that his Government disavowed him; and not only was he obliged to remain at Madrid, but also to sue for permission to resume relations with Cevallos. The Spanish government good-naturedly and somewhat contemptuously permitted him to do so; and he was only distressed by the fear that Monroe might refuse to let him take part in the new negotiation, for he was with reason confident that Monroe would be obliged to follow in his own footsteps,—that the United States could save its dignity and influence only by war.

At the beginning of the new year, Jan. 2, 1805, Monroe entered Madrid to snatch Florida from the grasp of Spain and France. The negotiation fell chiefly within Jefferson's second term, upon which it had serious results. But while Monroe, busy at Madrid with a quarrel which could lead only to disappointment or war, thus left the legation at London for eight months to take care of itself, events were occurring which warned President Jefferson that the supreme test of his principles was near at hand, and that a storm was threatening from the shores of Great Britain compared with which all other dangers were trivial.

Chapter XIV

FOR EIGHTEEN YEARS after 1783 William Pitt guided England through peace and war with authority almost as absolute as that of Don Carlos IV. or Napoleon himself. From him and from his country President Jefferson had much to fear and nothing to gain beyond a continuance of the good relations which President Washington, with extreme difficulty, had succeeded in establishing between the two peoples. So far as England was concerned, this understanding had been the work of Pitt and Lord Grenville, who rather imposed it on their party than accepted it as the result of any public will. The extreme perils in which England then stood inspired caution; and of this caution the treaty of 1794 was one happy result. So long as the British government remained in a cautious spirit, America was safe; but should Pitt or his successors throw off the self-imposed restraints on England's power, America could at the utmost, even by a successful war, gain nothing materially better than a return to the arrangements of 1794.

The War of Independence, which ended in the definitive treaty of 1783, naturally left the English people in a state of irritation and disgust toward America; and the long interregnum of the Confederation, from 1783 to 1789, allowed this disgust to ripen into contempt. When at length the Constitution of 1789 restored order in the American chaos, England felt little faith in the success of the experiment. She waited for time to throw light on her interests.

This delay was natural; for American independence had shattered into fragments the commercial system of Great Britain, and powerful interests were combined to resist further concession. Before 1776 the colonies of England stretched from the St. Lawrence to the Mississippi, and across the Gulf of Mexico to the coast of South America, mutually supporting and strengthening each other. Jamaica and the other British islands of the West Indies drew their most necessary supplies from the Delaware and the Hudson. Boston and New York were in some respects more important to them than London itself. The timber, live-stock, and provisions which came from the neighboring continent were essential to the existence of the West Indian planters and negroes. When war cut off these supplies, famine and pestilence followed. After the peace of 1783 even the most conservative English statesmen were obliged to admit that the strictness of their old colonial system could not be maintained, and that the United States, though independent, must be admitted to some of the privileges of a British colony. The government unwillingly conceded what could not be refused, and the West Indian colonists compelled Parliament to relax the colonial system so far as to allow a restricted intercourse between their islands and the ports of the United States. The relaxation was not a favor to the United States,—it was a condition of existence to the West Indies; not a boon, but a right which the colonists claimed and an Act of Parliament defined.[1]

The right was dearly paid for. The islands might buy American timber and grain, but they were allowed to make return only in molasses and rum. Payment in sugar would have been cheaper for the colonists, and the planters wished for nothing more earnestly than to be allowed this privilege; but as often as they raised the prayer, English shipowners cried that the navigation laws were in peril, and a chorus of familiar phrases filled the air, all carrying a deep meaning to the English people. "Nursery of seamen" was one favorite expression; "Neutral frauds" another; and all agreed in assuming that at whatever cost, and by means however extravagant, the navy must be fed and strengthened. Under the cover of supporting the navy any absurdity could be defended; and in the case of the West Indian trade, the British shipowner enjoyed the right to absurdities sanctioned by a century and a half of law and custom. The freight on British sugars belonged of right to British shippers, who could not be expected to surrender of their own accord, in obedience to any laws of political economy, a property which was the source of their incomes. The colonists asked permission to refine their own sugar; but their request not only roused strong opposition from the shipowners who wanted the bulkier freight, but started the home sugar-refiners to their feet, who proved by Acts of

[1] 28 George III. c. 6.

Parliament that sugar-refining was a British and not a colonial right. The colonist then begged a reduction of the heavy duty on sugar; but English country gentlemen cried against a measure which might lead to an increase of the income-tax or the imposition of some new burden on agriculture. In this dilemma the colonists frankly said that only their weakness, not their will, prevented them from declaring themselves independent, like their neighbors at Charleston and Philadelphia.

Even when the qualified right of trade was conceded, the colonists were not satisfied; and the concession itself laid the foundation of more serious changes. From the moment that American produce was admitted to be a necessity for the colonists, it was clear that the Americans must be allowed a voice in the British system. Discussion whether the Americans had or had not a right to the colonial trade was already a long step toward revolution. One British minister after another resented the idea that the Americans had any rights in the matter; yet when they came to practical arrangements the British statesmen were obliged to concede that they were mistaken. From the necessity of the case, the Americans had rights which never could be successfully denied. Parliament struggled to prevent the rebel Americans from sharing in the advantages of the colonial system from which they had rebelled; but unreasonable as it was that the United States should be rewarded for rebellion by retaining the privileges of subjects, this was the inevitable result. Geography and Nature were stronger than Parliament and the British navy.

At first Pitt hoped that the concession to the colonists might entail no concession to the United States; while admitting a certain hiatus in the colonial system, he tried to maintain the navigation laws in their integrity. The admission of American produce into the West Indies was no doubt an infraction of the protectionist principle on which all the civilized world, except America, founded its economical ideas; but in itself it was not serious. To allow the flour, potatoes, tobacco, timber, and horses of the American continent to enter the harbors of Barbadoes and Jamaica; to allow in turn the molasses and rum of the islands to be sent directly to New York and Boston,—harmed no one, and was advantageous to all parties, so long as British ships were employed to carry on the trade. At first this was the case. The Act of Parliament allowed only British subjects, in British-built ships, to enter colonial ports with American produce. Whether the United States government would long tolerate such legislation without countervailing measures was a question which remained open for a time, while the system itself had a chance to prove its own weakness. The British shipping did not answer colonial objects. Again and again the colonists found themselves on the verge of starvation; and always in this emergency the colonial governors threw open their ports by proclamation to American shipping, while with equal regularity Parliament protected the governors by Acts of Indemnity. To this extent the navigation system suffered together with the colonial system, but in theory it was intact. Ministry, Parliament, and people clung to the navigation laws as their ark of safety; and even the colonists conceded that although they had a right to eat American wheat and potatoes, they had no right to eat those which came to them in the hold of a Marblehead schooner.

Such a principle, however convenient to Great Britain, was not suited to the interests of New England shippers. In peace their chances were comparatively few, and the chief diplomatic difficulties between European governments and the United States had their source in the American attempt to obtain legal recognition of trade which America wished to maintain with the colonies; but in war the situation changed, and more serious disputes occurred. Then the French and Spanish West Indian ports were necessarily thrown open to neutral commerce, because their own ships were driven from the ocean by the superiority of the British navy. Besides the standing controversy about the admission of American produce to British islands, the British government found itself harassed by doubts to what extent it might safely admit the Americans into the French or Spanish West Indies, and allow them to carry French property, as though their flag were competent to protect whatever was under it. Granting that an article like French sugar might be carried in a neutral vessel, there were still other articles, called contraband, which ought not to be made objects of neutral commerce; and England was obliged to define the nature of contraband. She was also forced to make free use of the right of blockade. These delicate questions were embittered by another and more serious quarrel. The European belligerents claimed the right to the military service of their subjects, and there was no doubt that their right was perfect. In pursuance of the claim they insisted upon taking their seamen from American merchant-vessels wherever met on the high seas. So far as France was concerned, the annoyance was slight; but the identity of race made the practice extremely troublesome as concerned England.

At the outbreak of the French wars, Nov. 6, 1793, the British government issued instructions directing all British armed vessels to seize every neutral ship they should meet, loaded with the produce of a French colony or carrying supplies for its use.[1] These orders were kept secret for several weeks, until the whole American commerce with the Antilles, and all American ships found on the ocean, laden in whole or in part with articles of French colonial produce or for French colonial use, were surprised and swept into British harbors, where they were condemned by British admiralty courts, on the ground known as the "Rule of the War of 1756,"—that because trade between the French colonies and the United States was illegal in peace, it was illegal in war. From the point of view in which European Powers regarded their colonies, much could be said in support of this rule. A colony was almost as much the property of its home government as a dockyard or a military station. France and Spain could hardly complain if England chose to treat the commerce of such government-stations as contraband; but a rule which might perhaps be applied by European governments to each other worked with great injustice when applied to the United States, who had no colonies, and made no attempt to build up a navy or support an army by such means. Taken in its broadest sense, the European colonial system might be defined by the description which the best of British commentators gave to that of England,[2]—a "policy pursued for rendering the foreign trade of the whole world subservient to the increase of her shipping and navigation." American Inde-

[1] Additional Instructions of Nov. 6, 1793; State Papers, i. 430.
[2] Reeves's Law of Shipping and Navigation, part ii. chap. iii.

pendence was a protest against this practice; and the first great task of the United States was to overthrow and destroy the principle, in order to substitute freedom of trade. America naturally objected to becoming a martyr to the rules of a system which she was trying to revolutionize.

When these British instructions of Nov. 26, 1793, became known in the United States, the Government of President Washington imposed an embargo, threatened retaliation, and sent Chief-Justice Jay to London as a last chance of maintaining peace. On arriving there, Jay found that Pitt had already voluntarily retreated from his ground, and that new Orders, dated Jan. 8, 1794, had been issued, exempting from seizure American vessels engaged in the direct trade from the United States to the French West Indies. In the end, the British government paid the value of the confiscated vessels. The trade from the United States to Europe was not interfered with; and thus American ships were allowed to carry French colonial produce through an American port to France, while Russian or Danish ships were forbidden by England to carry such produce to Europe at all, although their flags and harbors were as neutral as those of the United States. America became suddenly a much favored nation, and the enemies of England attributed this unexpected kindness to fear. In truth it was due to a natural mistake. The British Treasury calculated that the expense and trouble of carrying sugar and coffee from Martinique or St. Domingo to Boston, of landing it, paying duties, re-embarking it, receiving the drawback, and then carrying it to Bordeaux or Brest, would be such as to give ample advantages to English vessels which could transship more conveniently at London. The mistake soon became apparent. The Americans quickly proved that they could under these restrictions carry West Indian produce to Europe not only more cheaply than British ships could do it, but almost as quickly; while it was a positive advantage on the return voyage to make double freight by stopping at an American port. The consequence of this discovery was seen in the sudden increase of American shipping, and was largely due to the aid of British seamen, who found in the new service better pay, food, and treatment than in their own, and comparative safety from the press-gang and the lash. At the close of the century the British flag seemed in danger of complete exclusion from the harbors of the United States. In 1790 more than 550 British ships, with a capacity of more than 115,000 tons, had entered inward and outward, representing about half that number of actual vessels; in 1799 the custom-house returns showed not 100 entries, and in 1800 about 140, representing a capacity of 40,000 tons. In the three years 1790–1792, the returns showed an average of some 280 outward and inward entries of American ships with a capacity of 54,000 tons; in 1800 the entries were 1,057, with a capacity of 236,000 tons. The Americans were not only beginning to engross the direct trade between their own ports and Europe, but were also rapidly obtaining the indirect carrying-trade between the West Indies and the European continent, and even between one European country and another. The British government began to feel seriously uneasy. At a frightful cost the people of England were striving to crush the navies and commerce of France and Spain, only to build up the power of a dangerous rival beyond the ocean.

Doubtless the British government would have taken measures to correct its mistake, if the political situation had not hampered its energies. Chief-Justice Jay, in 1794, negotiated a treaty with Lord Grenville which was in some respects very hard upon the United States, but was inestimably valuable to them, because it tied Pitt's hands and gave time for the new American Constitution to acquire strength. Ten years of steady progress were well worth any temporary concessions, even though these concessions exasperated France, and roused irritation between her and the United States which in 1798 became actual hostility. The prospect that the United States would become the ally of England was so fair that Pitt dared not disturb it. His government was in a manner forced to give American interests free play, and to let American shipping gain a sudden and unnatural enlargement. His liberality was well paid. For a moment France drove the United States to reprisals; and as the immediate consequence, St. Domingo became practically independent, owing to the support given by the United States to Toussaint. Even the reconciliation of France with America effected by Bonaparte and Talleyrand in 1800 did not at first redress the balance. Not till the Peace of

Amiens, in 1802, did France recover her colonies; and not till a year later did Bonaparte succeed, by the sacrifice of Louisiana, in bringing the United States back to their old attitude of jealousy toward England.

Nevertheless, indications had not been wanting that England was aware of the advantage she had given to American commerce, and still better of the advantages which had been given it by Nature. All the Acts of Parliament on the statute-book could not prevent the West Indies from being largely dependent on the United States; yet the United States need not be allowed the right to carry West Indian produce to France,—a right which depended only on so-called international law, and was worthless unless supported by the stronger force. A new Order was issued, Jan. 25, 1798, which admitted European neutrals to enemies' colonies, and allowed them to bring French colonial produce to England or to their own ports. This Order was looked upon as a side-blow at American shipping, which was not allowed the same privilege of sailing direct from the Antilles to Europe. The new Order was justified on the ground that the old rule discriminated in favor of American merchants, whose competition might be injurious to the commercial interests of England [1]

Further than this the British government did not then go; on the contrary, it officially confirmed the existing arrangement. The British courts of admiralty conformed closely to the rules of their political chiefs. Sir William Scott, better known as Lord Stowell, whose great reputation as a judge was due to the remarkable series of judgments in which he created a new system of admiralty law, announced with his usual clearness the rules by which he meant to be guided. In the case of the "Emmanuel," in November, 1799, he explained the principle on which the law permitted neutrals to carry French produce from their own country to France. "By importation," he said, "the produce became part of the national stock of the neutral country; the inconveniences of aggravated delay and expense were a safeguard against this right becoming a special convenience to France or a serious abridgement of belligerent rights." Soon afterward, in the case of the

[1] Appendix to 4 Robinson, 6.

"Polly," April 29, 1800, he took occasion to define what he meant by importation into a neutral country. He said it was not his business to decide what was universally the test of a *bona fide* importation; but he was strongly disposed to hold that it would be sufficient if the goods were proved to have been landed and the duties paid; and he did accordingly rule that such proof was sufficient to answer the fair demands of his court.

Rufus King, then American minister in London, succeeded in obtaining from Pitt an express acceptance of this rule as binding on the government. On the strength of a report[1] from the King's Advocate, dated March 16, 1801, the British Secretary of State notified the American minister that what Great Britain considered as the general principle of colonial trade had been relaxed in a certain degree in consideration of the present state of commerce. Neutrals might import French colonial produce, and convey it by re-exportation to France. Landing the goods and paying the duties in America legalized the trade, even though these goods were at once re-shipped and forwarded to France on account of the same owners.

With this double guaranty Jefferson began his administration, and the American merchants continued their profitable business. Not only did they build and buy large numbers of vessels, and borrow all the capital they could obtain, but doubtless some French and Spanish merchants, besides a much greater number of English, made use of the convenient American flag. The Yankees exulted loudly over the decline of British shipping in their harbors; the British masters groaned to see themselves sacrificed by their own government; and the British admirals complained bitterly that their prize-money was cut off, and that they were wearing out their lives in the hardest service, in order to foster a commerce of smugglers and perjurers, whose only protection was the flag of a country that had not a single line-of-battle ship to fly it.

Yet President Jefferson had reason to weigh long and soberly the pointed remark with which the King's Advocate began his report,—that the general principle with respect to

---

[1] Advocate-General's Report, March 16, 1801; State Papers, ii. 491.

the colonial trade had been to a certain extent relaxed in consideration of the present state of commerce. No doubt the British pretension, as a matter of international law, was outrageous. The so-called rule of 1756 was neither more nor less than a rule of force; but when was international law itself anything more than a law of force? The moment a nation found itself unable to show some kind of physical defence for its protection, the wisdom of Grotius and Bynkershoek could not prevent it from being plundered; and how could President Jefferson complain merely because American ships were forbidden by England to carry French sugars to France, when he looked on without a protest while England and France committed much greater outrages on every other country within their reach?

President Jefferson believed that the United States had ample means to resist any British pretension. As his letters to Paine and Logan showed, he felt that European Powers could be controlled through the interests of commerce.[1] He was the more firmly convinced by the extraordinary concessions which Pitt had made, and by the steady encouragement he gave to the American merchant. Jefferson felt sure that England could not afford to sacrifice a trade of some forty million dollars, and that her colonies could not exist without access to the American market. What need to spend millions on a navy, when Congress, as Jefferson believed, already grasped England by the throat, and could suffocate her by a mere turn of the wrist!

This reasoning had much in its favor. To Pitt the value of the American trade at a time of war with France and Spain was immense; and when taken in connection with the dependence of the West Indian colonies on America, it made a combination of British interests centring in the United States which much exceeded the entire value of all England's other branches of foreign commerce. Its prospective value was still greater if things should remain as they were, and if England should continue to undersell all rivals in articles of general manufacture. England could well afford to lose great sums of money in the form of neutral freights rather than drive Con-

[1] See p. 145.

gress to a protective system which should create manufactures of cotton, woollen, and iron. These were motives which had their share in the civility with which England treated America; and year by year their influence should naturally have increased.

Of all British markets the American was the most valuable; but next to the American market was that of the West Indies. In some respects the West Indian was of the two the better worth preserving. From head to foot the planters and their half-million negroes were always clad in cottons or linens made by the clothiers of Yorkshire, Wiltshire, or Belfast. Every cask and hoop, every implement and utensil, was supplied from the British Islands. The sailing of a West Indian convoy was "an epoch in the diary of every shop and warehouse throughout the Kingdom."[1] The West Indian colonies employed, including the fisheries, above a thousand sail of shipping and twenty-five thousand seamen. While America might, and one day certainly would, manufacture for herself, the West Indies could not even dream of it; there the only profitable or practicable industry was cultivation of the soil, and the chief article of cultivation was the sugar-cane. Rival industries to those of Great Britain were impossible; the only danger that threatened British control was the loss of naval supremacy or the revolt of the negroes.

A great majority of British electors would certainly have felt no hesitation in deciding, as between the markets of the United States and of the West Indies, that if a choice must be made, good policy required the government to save at all hazards the West Indies. Both as a permanent market for manufactures and as a steady support for shipping, the West Indian commerce held the first place in British interests. This fact needed to be taken into account by the United States government before relying with certainty on the extent to which Great Britain could be controlled by the interests involved in the American trade. At the most critical moment all Jefferson's calculations might be upset by the growth of a conviction in England that the colonial system was in serious danger; and to make this chance stronger, another anxiety

[1] Thoughts on Commerce and Colonies, by Charles Bosanquet.

was so closely connected with it as to cause incessant alarm in the British mind.

The carrying-trade between the French West Indies and Europe which had thus fallen into American hands, added to the natural increase of national exports and imports, required a large amount of additional shipping; and what was more directly hostile to English interests, it drew great numbers of British sailors into the American merchant-service. The desertion of British seamen and the systematic encouragement offered to deserters in every seaport of the Union were serious annoyances, which the American government was unable to excuse or correct. Between 1793 and 1801 they reached the proportions of a grave danger to the British service. Every British government packet which entered the port of New York during the winter before Jefferson's accession to power lost almost every seaman in its crew; and neither people nor magistrates often lent help to recover them. At Norfolk the crew of a British ship deserted to an American sloop-of-war, whose commander, while admitting the fact, refused to restore the men, alleging his construction of official orders in his excuse.[1] In most American harbors such protection as the British shipmaster obtained sprang from the personal goodwill of magistrates, who without strict legal authority consented to apply, for the benefit of the foreign master, the merchant-shipping law of the United States; but in one serious case even this voluntary assistance was stopped by the authority of a State government.

This interference was due to the once famous dispute over Jonathan Robbins, which convulsed party politics in America during the heated election of 1800. Thomas Nash, a boatswain on the British frigate "Hermione," having been ringleader in conspiracy and murder on the high seas, was afterward identified in the United States under the name and with the papers of Jonathan Robbins of Danbury, in Connecticut. On a requisition from the British minister, dated June 3, 1799, he was delivered under the extradition clause of Jay's treaty, and was hung. The Republican party, then in opposition, declared that Robbins, or Nash, was in their

[1] Thornton to Grenville, March 7, 1801; MSS. British Archives.

belief an American citizen whose surrender was an act of base subservience to Great Britain. An effigy of Robbins hanging to a gibbet was a favorite electioneering device at public meetings. The State of Virginia, having a similar grievance of its own, went so far as to enact a law[1] which forbade, under the severest penalties, any magistrate who acted under authority of the State to be instrumental in transporting any person out of its jurisdiction. As citizens of the Union, sworn to support the Constitution, such magistrates were equally bound with the Federal judges to grant warrants of commitment, under the Twenty-seventh Article of Jay's treaty, against persons accused of specified crimes. The Virginia Act directly contravened the treaty; while indirectly it prevented magistrates from granting warrants against deserters and holding them in custody, so that every English vessel which entered a Virginia port was at once abandoned by her crew, who hastened to enter the public or private ships of the United States.[2]

The captain of any British frigate which might happen to run into the harbor of New York, if he went ashore, was likely to meet on his return to the wharf some of his boat's crew strolling about the town, every man supplied with papers of American citizenship. This was the more annoying, because American agents in British ports habitually claimed and received the benefit of the British law; while so far as American papers were concerned, no pretence was made of concealing the fraud, but they were issued in any required quantity, and were transferred for a few dollars from hand to hand.

Not only had the encouragement to desertion a share in the decline of British shipping in American harbors, but it also warranted, and seemed almost to render necessary, the only countervailing measure the British government could employ. Whatever happened to the merchant-service, the British navy could not be allowed to suffer. England knew no conscription for her armies, because for centuries she had felt no need of general military service; but at any moment she might compel her subjects to bear arms, if circumstances required it. Her necessities were greater on the ocean. There,

[1] Act of Jan. 21, 1801, Statutes at Large of Virginia, New Series, ii. 302.
[2] Thornton to Grenville, June 1, 1802; MSS. British Archives.

from time immemorial, a barbarous sort of conscription, known as impressment, had been the ordinary means of supplying the royal navy in emergencies; and every seafaring man was liable to be dragged at any moment from his beer-cellar or coasting-vessel to man the guns of a frigate on its way to a three-years' cruise in the West Indies or the Mediterranean. Mere engagement in a foreign merchant-service did not release the British sailor from his duty. When the captain of a British frigate overhauled an American merchant-vessel for enemy's property or contraband of war, he sent an officer on board who mustered the crew, and took out any seamen whom he believed to be British. The measure, as the British navy regarded it, was one of self-protection. If the American government could not or would not discourage desertion, the naval commander would recover his men in the only way he could. Thus a circle of grievances was established on each side. Pitt's concessions to the United States irritated the British navy and merchant-marine, while they gave great profits to American shipping; the growth of American shipping stimulated desertions from the British service to the extent of injuring its efficiency; and these desertions in their turn led to a rigorous exercise of the right of impressment. To find some point at which this vicious circle could be broken was a matter of serious consequence to both countries, but most so to the one which avowed that it did not mean to protect its interests by force.

Great Britain could have broken the circle by increasing the pay and improving the condition of her seamen; but she was excessively conservative, and the burdens already imposed on her commerce were so great that she could afford to risk nothing. In the face of a combined navy like that of Spain and France, her control of the seas at any given point, such as the West Indies, was still doubtful; and in the face of American competition, her huge convoys suffered under great disadvantage. Conscious of her own power, she thought that the United States should be first to give way. Had the American government been willing to perform its neutral obligations strictly, the circle might have been broken without much trouble; but the United States wished to retain their advantage, and preferred to risk whatever England might do rather than discourage desertion, or enact and enforce a strict naturalization law, or punish fraud. The national government was too weak to compel the States to respect neutral obligations, even if it had been disposed to make the attempt.

The practice of impressment brought the two governments to a deadlock on an issue of law. No one denied that every government had the right to command the services of its native subjects, and as yet no one ventured to maintain that a merchant-ship on the high seas could lawfully resist the exercise of this right; but the law had done nothing to define the rights of naturalized subjects or citizens. The British government might, no doubt, impress its own subjects; but almost every British sailor in the American service carried papers of American citizenship, and although some of these were fraudulent, many were genuine. The law of England, as declared from time out of mind by every generation of her judges, held that the allegiance of a subject was indefeasible, and therefore that naturalization was worthless. The law of the United States, as declared by Chief-Justice Ellsworth in 1799, was in effect the same;[1] he held that no citizen could dissolve the compact of protection and defence between himself and society without the consent or default of the community. On both sides the law was emphatic to the point that naturalization could not bind the government which did not consent to it; and the United States could hardly require England to respect naturalization papers which the Supreme Court of the United States declared itself unable to respect in a similar case. Nevertheless, while courts and judges declare what the law is or ought to be, they bind only themselves, and their decisions have no necessary effect on the co-ordinate branches of government. While the judges laid down one doctrine in Westminster Hall, Parliament laid down another in St. Stephen's chapel; and no one could say whether the law or the statute was final. The British statute-book contained Acts of Parliament as old as the reign of Queen Anne[2] to encourage the admission of foreign seamen into the British navy, offering them naturalization as an inducement. American legisla-

---

[1] Trial of Isaac Williams, Hartford, 1799; Wharton's State Trials, 653. Shanks v. Dupont, 3 Peters, 242.
[2] 6 Anne, c. 20.

tion went not quite so far, but by making naturalization easy it produced worse results. A little perjury, in no wise unsafe, was alone required in order to transform British seamen into American citizens; and perjury was the commonest commodity in a seaport. The British government was forced to decide whether papers so easily obtained and transferred should be allowed to bar its claims on the services of its subjects, and whether it could afford to become a party to the destruction of its own marine, even though the United States should join with France and carry on endless war.

That there were some points which not even the loss of American trade would bring England to concede was well known to Jefferson; and on these points he did not mean to insist. Setting the matter of impressment aside, the relations between England and America had never been better than when the new President took office March 4, 1801. The British government seemed earnest in conciliation, and lost no opportunity of showing its good-will. Under the Sixth Article of Jay's treaty, a commission had been appointed to settle long-standing debts due to British subjects, but held in abeyance by State legislation in contravention of the treaty of 1783. After long delays the commission met at Philadelphia and set to work, but had made little progress when the two American commissioners, with the President's approval, in the teeth of the treaty which created the Board, refused to accept its decisions, and seceded. This violent measure was not taken by the Administration without uneasiness, for England might reasonably have resented it; but after some further delay the British government consented to negotiate again, and at last accepted a round sum of three million dollars in full discharge of the British claim. This was a case in which England was the aggrieved party; she behaved equally well in other cases where the United States were aggrieved. Rufus King complained that her admiralty courts in the West Indies and at Halifax were a scandal; in deference to his remonstrances these courts were thoroughly reformed by Act of Parliament. The vice-admiralty court at Nassau condemned the American brigantine "Leopard," engaged in carrying Malaga wine from the United States to the Spanish West Indies. The American minister complained of the decision, and within three days the King's Advocate reported in his favor.[1] The report was itself founded on Sir William Scott's favorable decision in the case of the "Polly." Soon afterward the American minister complained that Captain Pellew, of the "Cleopatra," and Admiral Parker had not effectually restrained their subordinates on the American station; both officers were promptly recalled. Although the Ministry had not yet consented to make any arrangement on the practice of impressment, Rufus King felt much hope that they might consent even to this reform; meanwhile Lord Grenville checked the practice, and professed a strong wish to find some expedient that should take its place.

There was no reason to doubt the sincerity of the British Foreign Office in wishing friendship. Its policy was well expressed in a despatch written from Philadelphia by Robert Liston, the British minister, shortly before he left the United States to return home:[2] —

"The advantages to be ultimately reaped from a perseverance in the line of conduct which Great Britain has adopted for the last four years appear to my mind to be infallible and of infinite magnitude; the profitable consequences of a state of hostility, small and uncertain. I have been pleasing my imagination with looking forward to the distant spectacle of all the northern continent of America covered with friendly though not subject States, consuming our manufactures, speaking our language, proud of their parent State, attached to her prosperity. War must bring with it extensive damage to our navigation, the probable loss of Canada, and the *world* behind it, the propagation of enmity and prejudices which it may be impossible to eradicate. The system of the American government does not strike me, with the near view I have of it, as being in so perilous a situation as is imagined in Europe. I am willing to avoid political prophecies, but I confess I think it will get on well enough if the country remains in peace; and if they go to war, the fabric may acquire strength. God forbid that it should be to our detriment, and to the triumph of our enemies!"

[1] Rufus King to Madison, April 12, 1801; State Papers, ii. 490.
[2] Liston to Grenville (private), May 7, 1800; MSS. British Archives.

Chapter XV

FEBRUARY 4, 1801, one month before the inauguration of President Jefferson, Pitt suddenly retired from office, and was succeeded by a weak ministry, in which Mr. Addington, afterward Lord Sidmouth, took the post vacated by Pitt. No event could have been happier for the prospects of President Jefferson, who might fairly count upon Addington's weakness to prevent his interference in American affairs.

Knowing himself to be universally regarded as the friend and admirer of France, Jefferson was the more anxious not to be classed by the British government among the enemies of England. Even before he was inaugurated, he took occasion to request Edward Thornton, the British *chargé*,—

> "With great earnestness, to assure his Majesty's government that it should experience during his administration as cordial and sincere acts of friendship as had ever been received under that of his predecessors. I am aware," said the President elect, "that I have been represented as hostile to Great Britain, but this has been done only for electioneering purposes, and I hope henceforward such language will be used no longer. I can appeal to all my past conduct that in everything in which I have been engaged relatively to England, I have always been guided by a liberal policy. I wish to be at the head of affairs no longer than while I am influenced by such sentiments of equal liberality toward all nations. There is nothing to which I have a greater repugnance than to establish distinctions in favor of one nation against another."

The day after his inauguration he returned to the subject:—

> "There is nothing I have more, or I may say so much, at heart as to adjust happily all differences between us, and to cultivate the most cordial harmony and good understanding. The English government is too just, I am persuaded, to regard newspaper trash, and the assertions contained in them that I am a creature of France and an enemy of Great

533

Britain. For *republican* France I may have felt some interest; but that is long over; and there is assuredly nothing in the present government of that country which could naturally incline me to show the smallest undue partiality to it at the expense of Great Britain, or indeed of any other country."[1]

Thornton felt no great confidence in the new President's protests, and thought it possible that Jefferson had "on this, as he seems to have done on many late public occasions, taxed his imagination to supply the deficiency of his feelings." All Englishmen were attached to the Federalist and New England interest; they could not understand that Virginia should be a safer friend than Massachusetts. Yet in truth Jefferson never was more serious than when he made these professions. The Southern republicans had nothing to gain from a quarrel with England; they neither wished for Canada, nor aspired to create shipping or manufactures: their chief antagonist was not England, but Spain. The only Power which could seriously injure them was Great Britain; and the only injury they could inflict in return was by conquering Canada for the benefit of Northern influence, or by building up manufactures which they disliked, or by cutting off their own markets for tobacco and cotton. Nothing warranted a belief that men like Jefferson, Madison, and Gallatin would ever seek a quarrel with England.

The British Ministry soon laid aside any doubts they might have felt on the subject. Lord Grenville, who retired with Pitt, was succeeded as Foreign Secretary by Lord Hawkesbury, afterward better known as Lord Liverpool. The new Ministry negotiated for peace with Bonaparte. Oct. 1, 1801, the preliminaries were signed, and the world found itself again in a sort of repose, broken only by the bloody doings at St. Domingo and Guadeloupe. England returned, like France and Spain, to the rigor of the colonial system. The customs entries of New York, Boston, and Philadelphia rapidly diminished in number; American shipping declined; but Madison was relieved from the burden of belligerent disputes,

[1] Thornton to Grenville, March 7, 1801; MSS. British Archives.

which had been the chief anxiety of his predecessors in the State Department.

Yet peace did not put an end to all difficulties. Rufus King continued to negotiate in London in regard to the outstanding British debts, twice recognized by treaty, yet still unpaid by the United States; in regard to the boundary of Maine and that of the extreme northwest territory at the source of the Mississippi; and finally, in regard to impressments; while Edward Thornton at Washington complained that, in spite of peace and the decline of American shipping, encouragement was still offered to the desertion of British seamen in every port of the United States,—in fact that this means was systematically used to prevent British shipping from entering American ports in competition with the shipping of America. When Madison alleged that the national government had no share in such unfriendly conduct, Thornton thrust under his eyes the law of Virginia,—a law enacted by President Jefferson's political friends in his political interests,— which forbade, under penalty of death, any magistrate of Virginia to be instrumental in surrendering deserters or criminals, even in cases where they were bound by treaty to do so. Madison could not deny that this legislation was contrary to a treaty right which the United States government was bound to enforce. He admitted that American shipmasters and consuls in British ports habitually asked the benefit of the British law, and received it; but he could hold out only a remote hope that mutual legislation might solve the difficulty by applying the merchant-seamen laws of the two countries reciprocally. In conversation with Thornton he lamented, with every appearance of sincerity and candor, the deficiency of the existing laws, and did not dispute that Great Britain could hardly be blamed for refusing the surrender of seamen on her side; but when Thornton asked him to order the return of a man who under aggravated circumstances had deserted from the British ship-of-war "Andromache" in the port of Norfolk, and had been immediately engaged on the United States revenue cutter there, Madison replied in a note coldly reiterating the fact, with which both parties were already acquainted, that neither the law of nations nor the provisions of any treaty enjoined the mutual restitution of seamen. This recognized formula, under which governments commonly express a refusal to act, was understood by Thornton as equivalent to an avowal that the new Administration, controlled by Virginians, would not venture, even in the future emergency of a demand for extradition under treaty, to risk the displeasure of Virginia.[1] Desertion, therefore, received no discouragement from the United States government; on the contrary, deserters, known to be such, were received at once into the national service, and their surrender refused. Under such circumstances the British government was not likely to be more accommodating than the American.

As the summer of 1802 approached, President Jefferson drew into closer and more confidential relations with Thornton. During the Federalist rule the two countries were never on more affectionate terms. At London Rufus King and Christopher Gore received courteous attention from Lord Hawkesbury. At Washington, Thornton's intimacy at the White House roused the jealousy and alarm of Pichon. As Bonaparte's projects against Louisiana disclosed themselves, and as Leclerc's first successes at St. Domingo opened the French path to New Orleans, Jefferson began to pay sudden and almost eager court to Thornton, who was a little embarrassed by the freedom with which the President denounced the First Consul. The preliminary articles of peace between France and England had been signed Oct. 1, 1801; but the treaty of Amiens, which made these articles definitive, was signed only March 25, 1802. Addington was naturally anxious that the peace should be maintained; indeed, no one could doubt that the existence of his Ministry depended on maintaining it. Thornton had no instructions which warranted him in intriguing against the First Consul, or in making preparations for a new war; and yet hardly was the treaty of Amiens made public, when President Jefferson began to talk as though England were still at war, and it were only a question of time when the United States must become her ally. The Louisiana question excited him. In April he wrote his

[1] Thornton to Hawkesbury, Oct. 25 and Nov. 26, 1802; MSS. British Archives.

letters to Dupont and Livingston. At about the same time he took Thornton into his confidence.

"I have had many occasions since it was first started," wrote Thornton,[1] "of conversing freely with Mr. Jefferson on this topic, which is indeed peculiarly interesting to him, and his reflections on which he utters with perhaps too little caution to persons who are not disposed to think very favorably of any change of sentiments with respect to France. He not only regards the cession of Louisiana and New Orleans as a certain cause of future war between the two countries, but makes no scruple to say that if the force of the United States should be unable to expel the French from those settlements, they must have recourse to the assistance of other Powers, meaning unquestionably Great Britain. With regard to France and the person who is at the head of its government, whether in consequence of the projected cession of Louisiana or of the little account which seems to be made of the United States as well at Paris as by French officers in other parts of the world, Mr. Jefferson speaks in very unqualified terms of the usurpation of Bonaparte, of the arbitrary nature and spirit of his government, of his love of flattery and vain pomp, features, according to Mr. Jefferson, which indicate the frivolous character of his mind rather than a condescension to the taste of the French people. The presses in America devoted to the President's Administration make use of the same language; and without pretending to say that this party is cured of its bitterness against Great Britain, I can safely venture to assure your Lordship that its predilection for France scarcely exists even in name."

After the stoppage of the *entrepôt* at New Orleans, when public opinion seemed intent on driving Jefferson into the war with France which he had predicted, Thornton found himself and his government in favor at Washington. The Republicans were even better disposed than the Federalists. Jefferson was willing to abolish between England and America the discriminating duties on shipping which the New En-

[1] Thornton to Hawkesbury, July 3, 1802; MSS. British Archives.

gland Federalists had imposed, and which they still wished to
maintain for use in the disputed West Indian trade. He told
Thornton that he could no doubt carry the repeal of these
countervailing duties through Congress over the heads of the
opposition,[1] "but he wished it to be adopted in consequence
of their own conviction, rather than by a contrary conduct to
afford them the least ground for asserting that the Southern
States were carrying into execution their scheme of ruin
against the navigation and commerce of their Eastern brethren." Jefferson was rapidly becoming the friend and confidant
of England. Thornton, naturally delighted with his own success, and with the mortifications and anxieties of Yrujo and
Pichon, went so far as to urge his government to help the
views of the United States against Louisiana:[2] —

"I should hope, my Lord, that by having some share in
the delivery of this Island of New Orleans to the United
States, which it will be impossible to keep from them
whenever they choose to employ force, his Majesty's government may hereafter attach still more this country to our
interests, and derive all the advantage possible from the intercourse with that important part of the world. A very
great change has gradually taken place in the opinions of
all ranks in this government in favor of Great Britain,
which has struck observers more likely to be impartial than
myself. A sense of a common interest has a great share in
the change; but the conduct of France in all her relations
has not failed to produce its full effect; and I find men,
formerly the most vehement in their politics, asserting in
the most unqualified terms the necessity of a union among
all the members of the civilized world to check her encroachments and to assure the general tranquillity."

A few days later the President nominated Monroe to act
with Livingston and Pinckney in an attempt to purchase New
Orleans. This step, which was openly avowed to be the alternative and perhaps the antecedent of war with France,
brought Thornton into still more confidential relations with
the Government. Finding that the Secretary of State was as

[1] Thornton to Hawkesbury, Dec. 31, 1802; MSS. British Archives.
[2] Thornton to Hawkesbury, Jan. 3, 1803; MSS. British Archives.

cautious as the President was talkative, Thornton carried on an active intercourse with the latter. He first offered to detain the British government packet for Monroe's use; but it was found that a month or two of delay would be necessary. Then, without instructions from his Government, Thornton took a bolder step:[1] —

"This state of things has naturally excited a sentiment of common interest, and has encouraged me to enter with more freedom into the subject, as well with the President as with Mr. Madison, than I should otherwise have thought right, without being acquainted with the views of his Majesty's government. Under this impression, I ventured, immediately after the nomination and before the first arrival of Mr. Monroe, to inquire of the President whether it was his intention to let him pass over to England, and hold any conversation with his Majesty's ministers upon the general question of the free navigation of the Mississippi. The inquiry was somewhat premature, and I made it with some apology. Mr. Jefferson replied, however, unaffectedly, that at so early a stage of the business he had scarcely thought himself what it might be proper to do; . . . that, on the whole, he thought it very probable that Mr. Monroe might cross the Channel. . . . Some time after Mr. Monroe's arrival, actuated by the same view, I mentioned to Mr. Jefferson that it would give me pleasure to furnish the former with an introduction to his Majesty's ambassador at Paris, as it would afford me the occasion of making Lord Whitworth acquainted with the nature of the object in dispute between this country, France, and Spain, and would give to Mr. Monroe, if he were disposed of himself, or were instructed by his Government to seek it, a more ready pretext for opening himself to his Lordship, and of keeping him apprised of the progress and turn of the negotiation. Mr. Jefferson seemed pleased with this offer, and said he was sure Mr. Monroe would accept it with great thankfulness."

Madison talked less freely than his chief, and contented

[1] Thornton to Hawkesbury, Jan. 31, 1803; MSS. British Archives.

himself with explaining to the British representative that the views of the Government in sending Monroe to France were limited to the hope of inducing the First Consul by money, or other means of persuasion, to cede in Louisiana a place of deposit over which the United States might have absolute jurisdiction. He did not tell Thornton of the decision made by the Cabinet, and the instructions given to Monroe, April 18, 1803, to offer terms of alliance with England in case the First Consul should make war;[1] but the tone of cordiality in Government and people, both in public and private, in New York, Boston, and Philadelphia, as in the South and West, was gratifying to British pride, and would have been still more so had not the community somewhat too openly avowed the intention of leaving England, if possible, to fight alone. At the first news of the approaching rupture between France and England, this wish began to appear so plainly that Thornton was staggered by it. The Americans took no trouble to conceal the hope that England would have to fight their battles for them.[2]

"The manifest advantage that such a state of things is calculated to give to their negotiation with France, and which is already sensibly felt in the altered tone and conduct of the French government, . . . will sufficiently account for their wishes and for this belief. But possessing the same opinion of the encroachments of France, and of the barrier which Great Britain alone places between her and the United States, and actuated, as I really believe they are, by sincere wishes for our success, I am afraid they begin to see more clearly that in a state of war we are effectually fighting their battles, without the necessity of their active interference; and they recur once more to the flattering prospect of peace and a lucrative neutrality."

In this state of doubt President Jefferson continued his intimate relations with Thornton.

"He expressed himself very freely," wrote Thornton, May 30, 1803, "on the contemptible and frivolous conduct, as he

[1] See p. 301.
[2] Thornton to Hawkesbury, May 30, 1803; MSS. British Archives.

termed it, of a Government that could alter its language so entirely on the prospect of an approaching rupture with another nation,—which he acknowledged instantly, on my mention of it, had been the case toward Mr. Livingston."

Jefferson attributed Bonaparte's returning courtesy to fear rather than to foresight. Thornton himself began to feel the danger that Bonaparte, after all, might outwit him. He revised his opinion about Louisiana. England, he saw, had the strongest motives for wishing France to keep that province.

"The most desirable state of things," he wrote, "seems to be that France should become mistress of Louisiana, because her influence in the United States would be by that event lost forever, and she could only be dispossessed by a concert between Great Britain and America in a common cause, which would produce an indissoluble bond of union and amity between the two countries."

This cordiality between England and the United States lasted without interruption until midsummer. Pichon complained, as has been shown, of the attentions paid to Thornton by the President.[1] "I remarked at table that he redoubled his courtesies and attentions toward the British *chargé.*" The dinner was in the month of January; in the following June Pichon wrote that the President had begun to accept the idea of seeing the British at New Orleans:[2]—

"Mr. Jefferson told me a few days ago that he was engaged in letting that Power know that her presence there would be seen with regret; but I perceive that, little by little, people are familiarizing themselves with this eventuality, as their fears increase in regard to us. They are so convinced that England sees more and more her true interests in relation to the United States, and is resolved to conciliate them, that they have no doubt of her lending herself to some arrangement. What they fear most is that, as the price of this accommodation, she may require the United

[1] Pichon to Talleyrand, 8 Pluviôse, An xi. (Jan. 28, 1803); Archives des Aff. Étr., MSS.

[2] Pichon to Talleyrand, 14 Prairial, An xii. (June 3, 1803); Archives des Aff. Étr., MSS.

States to take an active part in the indispensable war; and this is what they ardently wish to avoid."

Until July 3, 1803, the relations between President Jefferson's government and that of Great Britain were so cordial as to raise a doubt whether the United States could avoid becoming an ally of England, and taking part in the war with France. Suddenly came the new convulsion of Europe.

"It was on the third of this month," wrote Pichon July 7, 1803, "the eve of the anniversary of Independence, that we received two pieces of news of the deepest interest for this country,—that of the rupture between France and England, proclaimed by the latter on May 16, and that of the cession of Louisiana and New Orleans, made by us on April 30."[1]

The next day, when Pichon attended the usual reception at the White House, he found himself received in a manner very different from that to which he had been of late accustomed.

The two events, thus coming together, were sure to affect seriously the attitude of the United States toward England. Not only did Jefferson no longer need British aid, but he found himself in a position where he could afford with comparative freedom to insist upon his own terms of neutrality. He had always felt that Great Britain did not sufficiently respect this neutrality; he never failed to speak of Jay's treaty in terms of vehement dislike; and he freely avowed his intention of allowing all commercial treaties to expire. The relation between these treaties and the rights of neutrality was simple. Jefferson wanted no treaties which would prevent him from using commercial weapons against nations that violated American neutrality; and therefore he reserved to Congress the right to direct commerce in whatever paths the Government might prefer.

"On the subject of treaties," he wrote,[2] "our system is to have none with any nation, as far as can be avoided. The treaty with England has therefore not been renewed, and

[1] Pichon to Talleyrand, 18 Messidor, An xii. (July 7, 1803); Archives des Aff. Étr., MSS.
[2] Jefferson to Mazzei, July 18, 1804; Works, iv. 552.

all overtures for treaty with other nations have been declined. We believe that with nations, as with individuals,
dealings may be carried on as advantageously, perhaps
more so, while their continuance depends on a voluntary
good treatment, as if fixed by a contract, which, when it
becomes injurious to either, is made by forced constructions to mean what suits them, and becomes a cause of war
instead of a bond of peace."

Such a system was best suited to the strongest nations, and
to those which could control their dealings to most advantage. The Administration believed that the United States
stood in this position.

The President and Secretary Madison were inclined to assert authority in their relations with foreign Powers. Even so
early as the preceding February, before Monroe sailed for Europe, Madison told Pichon of this intention.[1] "He added,"
wrote Pichon to Talleyrand, "that if war should be renewed,
as seemed probable, the United States would be disposed to
take a higher tone than heretofore, that Europe had put their
spirit of moderation to proofs that would be no longer endured." Immediately after hearing of the Louisiana cession,
Pichon wrote that the same spirit continued to animate the
Government.[2] "It is certain that they propose to cause the
neutrality of the United States to be more exactly respected
by the belligerent Powers than in the last war. The Government has often shown its intentions in this respect, from the
time when everything pointed to an infallible rupture between us and England." President Jefferson, while avowing a
pacific policy, explained that his hopes of peace were founded
on his power to affect the interests of the belligerents. At the
same moment when Pichon wrote thus to Talleyrand, the
President wrote to the Earl of Buchan:[3] —

"My hope of preserving peace for our country is not
founded in the Quaker principle of non-resistance under

[1] Pichon to Talleyrand, 1 Ventôse, An xi. (Feb. 20, 1803); Archives des Aff.
Étr., MSS.
[2] Pichon to Talleyrand, 18 Messidor, An xii. (July 7, 1803); Archives des Aff.
Étr., MSS.
[3] Jefferson to Earl of Buchan, July 10, 1803; Works, iv. 493.

every wrong, but in the belief that a just and friendly conduct on our part will procure justice and friendship from others. In the existing contest, each of the combatants will find an interest in our friendship."

He was confident that he could control France and England:[1] "I do not believe we shall have as much to swallow from them as our predecessors had."

The Louisiana question being settled, the field was clear for the United States to take high ground in behalf of neutral rights; and inevitably the first step must be taken against England. No one denied that thus far the administration of Addington had behaved well toward the United States. Rufus King brought to America at the same time with news of the Louisiana treaty, or had sent shortly before, two conventions by which long-standing differences were settled. One of these conventions disposed of the old subject of British debts,—the British government accepting a round sum of six hundred thousand pounds on behalf of the creditors.[2] The other created two commissions for running the boundary line between Maine and Nova Scotia, and between the Lake of the Woods and the Mississippi River.[3] King went so far as to express the opinion that had he not been on the eve of his departure, he might have succeeded in making some arrangement about impressments; and he assured Gallatin that the actual Administration in England was the most favorable that had existed or could exist for the interests of the United States; its only misfortune was its weakness.[4] The conduct of the British government in regard to Louisiana proved the truth of King's assertion. Not only did it offer no opposition to the sale, but it lent every possible assistance to the transfer; and under its eye, with its consent, Alexander Baring made the financial arrangements which were to furnish Bonaparte with ten million American dollars to pay the preliminary expenses of an invasion of England.

Nevertheless, if the United States government intended to take a high tone in regard to neutral rights, it must do so

[1] Jefferson to General Gates, July 11, 1803; Works, iv. 494.
[2] State Papers, ii. 382.
[3] State Papers, ii. 584.
[4] Gallatin to Jefferson, Aug. 18, 1803; Gallatin's Works, i. 140.

from the beginning of the war. Aware that success in regard to England, as in regard to Spain, depended on asserting at the outset, and maintaining with obstinacy, the principles intended to be established, the President and Secretary Madison lost no time in causing their attitude to be clearly understood. An opportunity of asserting this authoritative tone was given by the appearance of a new British minister at Washington; and thus it happened that at the time when the Secretary of State was preparing for his collision with the Marquis of Casa Yrujo and the Spanish empire, he took on his hands the more serious task of curbing the pretensions of Anthony Merry and the King of England.

Chapter XVI

O NE OF ADDINGTON'S friendly acts was the appointment of Anthony Merry as British minister to the United States. For this selection Rufus King was directly responsible. Two names were mentioned to him by the Foreign Office as those of the persons entitled to claim the place; one was that of Merry, the other was that of Francis James Jackson.

"As I have had the opportunity of knowing both these gentlemen during my residence here," wrote Minister King to Secretary Madison,[1] "it was not without some regret that I heard of the intention to appoint Mr. Jackson in lieu of Mr. Merry. From this information I have been led to make further inquiry concerning their reputations, and the result has proved rather to increase than to lessen my solicitude. Mr. Jackson is said to be positive, vain, and intolerant. He is moreover filled with English prejudices in respect to all other countries, and as far as his opinions concerning the United States are known, seems more likely to disserve than to benefit a liberal intercourse between them and his own country. On the other hand, Mr. Merry appears to be a plain, unassuming, and amiable man, who having lived for many years in Spain is in almost every point of character the reverse of Mr. Jackson, who were he to go to America would go for the sake of present employment and with the hope of leaving it as soon as he could receive a similar appointment in Europe; while Mr. Merry wishes for the mission with the view of obtaining what he believes will prove to be an agreeable and permanent residence."

In deference to Rufus King's wishes or for some other reason Merry received the appointment. Doubtless he came to America in the hope of finding a "permanent residence," as King remarked; but it could hardly be agreeable, as he hoped. He was a thorough Englishman, with a wife more English than himself. He was not prepared for the isolation of the so-called Federal City, and he did not expect to arrive at a

---

[1] King to Madison, April 10, 1802; MSS. State Department Archives.

moment when the United States government, pleased with having curbed Bonaparte, was preparing to chasten Spain and to discipline England.

Landing at Norfolk from a ship of war Nov. 4, 1803, Merry was obliged to hire a vessel to carry himself and his belongings to Washington, where, after a tempestuous voyage, he at last arrived, November 26. Possibly Mr. and Mrs. Merry, like other travellers, would have grumbled even though Washington had supplied them with Aladdin's palace and Aladdin's lamp to furnish it; but the truth was not to be denied that the Federal City offered few conveniences, and was better suited for members of Congress, who lived without wives in boarding-houses, than for foreign ministers, with complaining wives, who were required to set up large establishments and to entertain on a European scale.

"I cannot describe to you," wrote Merry privately,[1] "the difficulty and expense which I have to encounter in fixing myself in a habitation. By dint of money I have just secured two small houses on the common which is meant to become in time the city of Washington. They are mere shells of houses, with bare walls and without fixtures of any kind, even without a pump or well, all which I must provide at my own cost. Provisions of any kind, especially vegetables, are frequently hardly to be obtained at any price. So miserable is our situation."

Had these been the worst trials that awaited the new British minister, he might have been glad to meet them; for when once surmounted, they favored him by preventing social rivalry. Unfortunately he met more serious annoyances. Until his arrival, Yrujo was the only minister of full rank in the United States; and Yrujo's intimate relations at the White House had given him family privileges. For this reason the Spanish minister made no struggle to maintain etiquette, but living mostly in Philadelphia disregarded the want of what he considered good manners at Washington, according to which he was placed on the same social footing with his own secretary of legation. Yet Yrujo, American in many respects,

[1] Merry to Hammond, Dec. 7, 1803; MSS. British Archives.

belonged to the school of Spanish diplomacy which had for
centuries studied points of honor. He might well have made
with his own mouth the celebrated retort which one of his
predecessors made to Philip II., who reproached him with
sacrificing an interest to a ceremony: "How a ceremony? Your
Majesty's self is but a ceremony!" Although Yrujo submitted
to Jefferson, he quarrelled with Pichon on this point, for Pichon was only a secretary in charge of the French legation. In
November, 1803, Yrujo's friendship for Jefferson was cooling,
and he waited the arrival of Merry in the hope of finding a
champion of diplomatic rights. Jefferson, on the other hand,
waited Merry's arrival in order to establish, once for all, a
new social code; and that there might be no misunderstanding, he drafted with his own hand the rules which were to
control Executive society,—rules intended to correct a tendency toward monarchical habits introduced by President
Washington.

In 1801 on coming into power Jefferson announced that he
would admit not the smallest distinction that might separate
him from the mass of his fellow-citizens. He dispensed with
the habit of setting apart certain days and hours for receiving
visits of business or curiosity, announcing that he would on
any day and at any hour receive in a friendly and hospitable
manner those who should call upon him.[1] He evidently
wished to place the White House on the footing of easy and
generous hospitality which was the pride of every Virginia
gentleman. No man should be turned away from its doors;
its table, liberal and excellent, should be filled with equal
guests, whose self-respect should be hurt by no artificial rules
of precedence. Such hospitality cost both time and money;
but Washington was a petty village, society was very small,
and Jefferson was a poor economist. He entertained freely
and handsomely.

"Yesterday I dined with the President," wrote Senator
Plumer of New Hampshire, Dec. 25, 1802.[2] "His rule is to
have about ten members of Congress at a time. We sat
down to the table at four, rose at six, and walked imme-

[1] Thornton to Hawkesbury, Dec. 9, 1801; MSS. British Archives.
[2] Life of William Plumer, p. 245.

diately into another room and drank coffee. We had a very good dinner, with a profusion of fruits and sweetmeats. The wine was the best I ever drank, particularly the champagne, which was indeed delicious. I wish his French politics were as good as his French wines."

So long as this manner of life concerned only the few Americans who were then residents or visitors at Washington, Jefferson found no great difficulty in mixing his company and disregarding precedence. Guests accommodated themselves to the ways of the house, took care of their own comfort, went to table without special request, and sat wherever they found a vacant chair; but foreigners could hardly be expected at first to understand what Jefferson called the rule of pell-mell. Thornton and Pichon, being only secretaries of legation, rather gained than lost by it; but Yrujo resented it in secret; and all eyes were turned to see how the new British minister would conduct himself in the scramble.

A month afterwards the President drew up the Code which he called "Canons of Etiquette to be observed by the Executive,"[1] and which received the approval of the Cabinet. Foreign ministers, he said, were to pay the first visit to the "ministers of the nation;" their wives were to receive the first visit from the wives of "national ministers." No grades among diplomatic members were to give precedence; "all are perfectly equal, whether foreign or domestic, titled or untitled, in or out of office." Finally, "to maintain the principle of equality, or of *pêle-mêle*, and prevent the growth of precedence out of courtesy, the members of the Executive will practise at their own houses, and recommend an adherence to, the ancient usage of the country, —of gentlemen in mass giving precedence to the ladies in mass in passing from one apartment where they are assembled into another." Such, according to Rufus King, whose aid was invoked on this occasion, was the usage in London.[2]

Merry duly arrived in Washington, and was told by Madison that the President would receive his letter of credence Nov. 29, according to the usual formality. At the appointed

[1] Jefferson's Works, ix. 454.
[2] King to Madison, 22 Dec., 1803; MSS. State Department Archives.

hour the British minister, in diplomatic uniform, as was required in the absence of any hint to the contrary, called upon Madison, and was taken to the White House, where he was received by the President. Jefferson's manner of receiving guests was well known, although this was the first occasion on which he had given audience to a new foreign minister. Among several accounts of his appearance at such times, that of Senator Plumer was one of the best.

"In a few moments after our arrival," said the senator, writing two years before Merry's mishap,[1] "a tall, high-boned man came into the room. He was dressed, or rather undressed, in an old brown coat, red waistcoat, old corduroy small-clothes much soiled, woollen hose, and slippers without heels. I thought him a servant, when General Varnum surprised me by announcing that it was the President."

The "Evening Post," about a year later, described him as habitually appearing in public "dressed in long boots with tops turned down about the ankles like a Virginia buck; overalls of corduroy faded, by frequent immersions in soap suds, from yellow to a dull white; a red single-breasted waistcoat; a light brown coat with brass buttons, both coat and waistcoat quite threadbare; linen very considerably soiled; hair uncombed and beard unshaven." In truth the Virginia republicans cared little for dress. "You know that the Virginians have some pride in appearing in simple habiliments," wrote Joseph Story in regard to Jefferson, "and are willing to rest their claim to attention upon their force of mind and suavity of manners." Indeed, "Virginia carelessness" was almost a proverb.[2]

On the occasion of Merry's reception, the President's chief offence in etiquette consisted in the slippers without heels. No law of the United States or treaty stipulation forbade Jefferson to receive Merry in heelless slippers, or for that matter in bare feet, if he thought proper to do so. Yet Virginia gentlemen did not intentionally mortify their guests; and perhaps Madison would have done better to relieve the President of such a suspicion by notifying Merry beforehand that he

[1] Life of William Plumer, p. 242.
[2] Life of Joseph Story, pp. 151, 158.

would not be expected to wear full dress. In that case the British minister might have complimented Jefferson by himself appearing in slippers without heels.

A card of invitation was next sent, asking Mr. and Mrs. Merry to dine at the White House, December 2. Such an invitation was in diplomatic usage equivalent to a command, and Merry at once accepted it. The new minister was then told that he must call on the heads of departments. He remonstrated, saying that Liston, his predecessor, had been required to make the first visit only to the Secretary of State; but he was told, in effect, that what had been done under the last Administration was no rule for the present one. Merry acquiesced, and made his calls. These pin-thrusts irritated him; but he was more seriously inconvenienced by the sudden withdrawal of diplomatic privileges by the Senate, although Vice-President Burr took occasion to explain that the Senate's action was quite unconnected with the President's "canons of etiquette," and was in truth due to some indiscretion of Yrujo in the House of Representatives.

Meanwhile the President took an unusual step. When two countries were at war, neutral governments commonly refrained from inviting the representative of one belligerent to meet the representative of the other, unless on formal occasions where the entire diplomatic body was invited, or in crowds where contact was not necessary. Still more rarely were such incongruous guests invited to an entertainment supposed to be given in honor of either individual. No one knew this rule better than Jefferson, who had been himself four years in diplomatic service at Paris, besides being three years Secretary of State to President Washington at Philadelphia. He knew that the last person whom Merry would care to meet was Pichon, the French *chargé*; yet he not only invited Pichon, but pressed him to attend. The Frenchman, aware that Merry was to be mortified by the etiquette of the dinner, and watching with delight the process by which Jefferson, day after day, took a higher tone toward England, wrote an account of the affair to Talleyrand.[1] He said:—

---

[1] Pichon to Talleyrand, 15 Pluviôse, An xii. (Feb. 5, 1804); Archives des Aff. Étr., MSS.

"I was invited to this dinner. I had learned from the President what was the matter (*ce qui en était*), when I went to tell him that I was going for some days to Baltimore, where I was called by the affairs of the frigate 'La Poursuivante.' The President was so obliging as to urge my return in order to be present with Mme. Pichon at the dinner (*Le Président eut l'honnêteté de me presser de revenir pour être au diner*). I came back here, although business required a longer stay at Baltimore. Apart from the reason of respect due to the President, I had that of witnessing what might happen (*j'avais celle de connaître ce qui se passerait*)."

Pichon accordingly hurried back from Baltimore, especially at the President's request, in order to have the pleasure of seeing Jefferson humiliate his own guest in his own house.

Pichon was gratified by the result. At four o'clock on the afternoon of Dec. 2, 1803, this curious party assembled at the White House,—Mr. and Mrs. Merry, the Marquis Yrujo and his American wife, M. Pichon and his American wife, Mr. and Mrs. Madison, and some other persons whose names were not mentioned. When dinner was announced, the President offered his hand to Mrs. Madison and took her to table, placing her on his right. Mme. Yrujo took her seat on his left.

"Mrs. Merry was placed by Mr. Madison below the Spanish minister, who sat next to Mrs. Madison. With respect to me," continued the British minister in his account of the affair,[1] "I was proceeding to place myself, though without invitation, next to the wife of the Spanish minister, when a member of the House of Representatives passed quickly by me and took the seat, without Mr. Jefferson's using any means to prevent it, or taking any care that I might be otherwise placed. . .

"I will beg leave to intrude a moment longer on your Lordship's time," continued Merry's report, "by adding to this narrative that among the persons (none of those who were of this country were the principal officers of the government except Mr. Madison) whom the President selected for a dinner which was understood to be given to me, was

[1] Merry to Hawkesbury, Dec. 6, 1803; MSS. British Archives.

M. Pichon the French *chargé d'affaires*. I use the word *se-lected*, because it could not be considered as a diplomatic dinner, since he omitted to invite to it the Danish *chargé d'affaires*, who, with the Spanish minister, form the whole body."

Merry's report was brief; but Yrujo, who also made an official report to his Government, after mentioning the neglect shown to Merry before dinner, added a remark that explained the situation more exactly:[1] —

"I observed immediately the impression that such a proceeding of the President must have on Mr. and Mrs. Merry; and their resentment could not but be increased at seeing the manifest, and in my opinion studied, preference given by the President throughout to me and my wife over him and Mrs. Merry."

There the matter might have rested, had not Madison carried the new "canons" beyond the point of endurance. December 6, four days after the dinner at the White House, the British minister was to dine with the Secretary of State. Pichon and Yrujo were again present, and all the Cabinet with their wives. Yrujo's report described the scene that followed.

"I should observe," said he, "that until then my wife and I had enjoyed in the houses of Cabinet ministers the precedence of which we had been deprived in the President's house; but on this day the Secretary of State too altered his custom, without informing us beforehand of his resolution, and took to table the wife of the Secretary of the Treasury. This unexpected conduct produced at first some confusion, during which the wife of the British minister was left without any one giving her his hand, until her husband advanced, with visible indignation, and himself took her to table."

Even Pichon, though pleased to see the British minister humbled, felt his diplomatic pride a little scandalized at this proceeding. He admitted that it was an innovation, and added, —

[1] Yrujo to Cevallos, Feb. 7, 1804; MSS. Spanish Archives.

"There is no doubt that Mr. Madison in this instance wished to establish in his house the same formality as at the President's, in order to make Mr. Merry feel more keenly the scandal he had made; but this incident increased it."

The scandal which Merry had made consisted in saying that he believed his treatment at the White House was a premeditated insult against his country. Madison's course took away any remaining doubt on the subject in his mind. Merry became bitter. He wrote home informally:[1] —

"On this occasion, also, the *pas* and the preference in every respect was taken by, and given to, the wives of the Secretaries of the Departments (a set of beings as little without the manners as without the appearance of gentlewomen), the foreign ministers and their wives being left to take care of themselves. In short the latter are now placed here in a situation so degrading to the countries they represent, and so personally disagreeable to themselves, as to have become almost intolerable. The case yesterday was so marked and so irritating that I determined to hand Mrs. Merry myself to the table, and to place ourselves wherever we might conveniently find seats."

Merry then received an official explanation that Jefferson invariably gave precedence to the wives of his Cabinet ministers, and that he made no exceptions in favor of foreigners in his rule of *pêle-mêle*.[2] Merry notified Lord Hawkesbury to that effect. He did not fail to point out the signs which indicated to him that these proceedings were but part of a general plan intended to press on the British government. In truth, the whole issue lay in the question whether that intent influenced Jefferson's behavior.

A sort of civil war ensued in the little society of Washington, in which the women took prominent part, and Mrs. Merry gave back with interest the insults she considered herself to have received. The first serious evil was an alliance between Merry and Yrujo, the two men whom Jefferson had

---

[1] Merry to Hammond, Dec. 7, 1803; MSS. British Archives.
[2] Madison to Monroe, 19 Jan., 1804. Madison MSS., State Department Archives. Merry to Hawkesbury, 30 Jan., 1804. MSS. British Archives.

most interest in keeping apart. Pichon wrote home a lively account of the hostilities that followed.[1]

"M. Yrujo, who is vanity itself, blew the flame more vigorously than ever. . . . He concerted reprisals with Mr. Merry, and it was agreed that whenever they should entertain the secretaries and their wives, they should take none of them to table, but should give their hands to their own wives. This resolution was carried out at a dinner given some days afterward by M. Yrujo. Mr. and Mrs. Merry were next invited by the Secretary of the Navy. Mrs. Merry refused; yet this minister, a very well-bred man (*homme fort poli*), had so arranged things as to give her his hand. Apparently what had taken place at Mr. Madison's was thought harsh (*dur*), and it was wished to bring Mr. and Mrs. Merry back to a reconciliation. The Cabinet took up the question, as reported in the newspaper of which I sent you an extract, and it was resolved that hereafter the President should give his hand to the lady who might happen to be nearest him, and that there should be no precedence. Mr. Merry was invited to a tea by the Secretary of War and by the Secretary of the Treasury. To avoid all discussion he wholly refused the first, and after accepting the second he did not come. Finally, New Year's Day gave another occasion for scandal. On this day, as on the Fourth of July, it is the custom to call upon the President; and even the ladies go there. This year neither Mme. Yrujo nor Mrs. Merry went, and the Marquis took care to answer every one who inquired after his wife's health, that she was perfectly well. Since then Washington society is turned upside down; all the women are to the last degree exasperated against Mrs. Merry; the Federal newspapers have taken up the matter, and increased the irritation by sarcasms on the Administration and by making a burlesque of the facts, which the Government has not thought proper to correct. The arrival of M. Bonaparte with his wife in the midst of all this explosion has furnished Mr. Merry with new griefs. The President asked M. and Mme. Bonaparte to dinner, and gave his

[1] Pichon to Talleyrand, 15 Pluviôse, An xii. (Feb. 5, 1804); Archives des Aff. Étr., MSS.

hand to Madame. There was, however, this difference between the two cases,— the President had invited on this
day, besides myself and Mme. Pichon, only the two Messrs.
Smith and their wives, who are of Mme. Bonaparte's family. But when Mr. Merry heard of it, he remarked that
Mme. Bonaparte had on this occasion taken precedence of
the wife of the Secretary of the Navy. . . I am aware,"
continued the delighted Pichon, "that with tact on the part
of Mr. Jefferson he might have avoided all these scandals."

The British minister wrote to Lord Hawkesbury a brief account of his reception, closing with the remark:[1] —

"Under these circumstances, my Lord, I have thought it
advisable to avoid all occasions where I and my wife might
be exposed to a repetition of the same want of distinction
toward us until I shall have received authority from you to
acquiesce in it, by a signification of his Majesty's pleasure
to that effect."

Accordingly, when the President invited the two ministers
to dine at the White House without their wives, they replied
that they could not accept the invitation until after receiving
instructions from their Governments. Jefferson regarded this
concerted answer as an insult.[2] He too lost his temper so far
as to indulge in sharp comments, and thought the matter important enough to call for explanation. In a private letter to
Monroe, dated Jan. 8, 1804, he wrote:[3] —

"Mr. Merry is with us, and we believe him to be personally as desirable a character as could have been sent us; but
he is unluckily associated with one of an opposite character
in every point. She has already disturbed our harmony extremely. He began by claiming the first visit from the national ministers. He corrected himself in this; but a
pretension to take precedence at dinner, etc., over all others
is persevered in. We have told him that the principle of

[1] Merry to Hawkesbury, Dec. 31, 1803; MSS. British Archives.
[2] Pichon to Talleyrand, 27 Pluviôse, An xii. (Feb. 13, 1804); Archives des
Aff. Étr., MSS.
[3] Jefferson to Monroe, Jan. 8, 1804; Jefferson's Writings (Ford), viii. 286.
Cf. Madison to Monroe, 16 Feb. 1804. Madison's Works, ii. 195–199.

society as well as of government with us is the equality of
the individuals composing it, that no man here would
come to a dinner where he was to be marked with inferiority to any other; that we might as well attempt to force
our principle of equality at St. James's as he his principle of
precedence here. I had been in the habit when I invited
female company (having no lady in my family) to ask one
of the ladies of the four Secretaries to come and take care
of my company, and as she was to do the honors of the
table I handed her to dinner myself. That Mr. Merry might
not construe this as giving them a precedence over Mrs.
Merry I have discontinued it, and here as in private houses
the *pêle-mêle* practice is adhered to. They have got Yrujo to
take a zealous part in the claim of precedence. It has excited
generally emotions of great contempt and indignation (in
which the members of the Legislature participate sensibly)
that the agents of foreign nations should assume to dictate
to us what shall be the laws of our society. The consequence will be that Mr. and Mrs. Merry will put themselves
into coventry, and that he will lose the best half of his usefulness to his nation,—that derived from a perfectly familiar and private intercourse with the Secretaries and myself.
The latter, be assured, is a virago, and in the short course
of a few weeks has established a degree of dislike among all
classes which one would have thought impossible in so
short a time. . . . With respect to Merry, he appears so
reasonable and good a man that I should be sorry to lose
him as long as there remains a possibility of reclaiming him
to the exercise of his own dispositions. If his wife perse-
veres she must eat her soup at home, and we shall endeavor
to draw him into society as if she did not exist."

Of all American hospitality none was so justly famous as
that of Virginia. In this State there was probably not a white
man, or even a negro slave, but would have resented the
charge that he was capable of asking a stranger, a foreigner, a
woman, under his roof, with the knowledge that he was
about to inflict what the guest would feel as a humiliation.
Still less would he have selected his guest's only enemy, and
urged him to be present for the purpose of witnessing the

slight. Reasons of state sometimes gave occasion for such practices, but under the most favorable conditions the tactics were unsafe. Napoleon in the height of his power insulted queens, browbeat ambassadors, trampled on his ministers, and made his wife and servants tremble; but although these manners could at his slightest hint be imitated by a million soldiers, until Europe, from Cadiz to Moscow, cowered under his multiplied brutality, the insults and outrages recoiled upon him in the end. Jefferson could not afford to adopt Napoleonic habits. His soldiers were three thousand in number, and his own training had not been that of a successful general; he had seven frigates, and was eager to lay them up in a single dry-dock. Peace was his passion.

To complicate this civil war in the little society of Washington, Jerome Bonaparte appeared there, and brought with him his young wife, Elizabeth Patterson, of Baltimore. Jerome married this beautiful girl against the remonstrances of Pichon; but after the marriage took place, not only Pichon, but also Yrujo and Jefferson, showed proper attention to the First Consul's brother, who had selected for his wife a niece of the Secretary of the Navy, and of so influential a senator as General Smith. Yet nothing irritated Napoleon more than Jerome's marriage. In some respects it was even more objectionable to him than that of Lucien, which gave rise to a family feud. Pichon suspected what would be the First Consul's feelings, and wrote letter after letter to clear himself of blame. In doing so he could not but excite Napoleon's anger against American society, and especially against the family of his new sister-in-law.

"It appears, Citizen Minister," wrote Pichon to Talleyrand,[1] "that General Smith, who in spite of the contrary assurances he has given me, has always had this alliance much at heart, has thrown his eyes on the mission to Paris as a means of appeasing (*ramener*) the First Consul. He has long since aimed at the diplomatic career, for which he is little qualified; this motive and the near return of Mr. Livingston have decided his taste. For some time there has

[1] Pichon to Talleyrand, 30 Pluviôse, An xii. (Feb. 16, 1804); Archives des Aff. Étr., MSS.

been much question of this nomination among the friends of General Smith. There is also question of promoting, on the part of the First Consul, for minister to this country, a selection which should be connected with the other. It is thought that the appointment of M. Jerome Bonaparte would be an honorable mode of leaving the First Consul's brother time to have his fault forgotten, and of preparing his return to favor."

Such readiness among Jefferson's advisers to court the favors of the young First Consul was sure not to escape the eyes of the embittered Federalists. Pichon's account, although sharp in allusions to General Smith's "vanity," was mild compared with the scorn of the New Englanders. Apparently the new matrimonial alliance was taken seriously by prominent Republican leaders. One of the Massachusetts senators mentioned in his diary[1] a "curious conversation between S. Smith, Breckinridge, Armstrong, and Baldwin, about 'Smith's nephew, the First Consul's brother.' Smith swells upon it to very extraordinary dimensions." Pichon openly spoke of the whole family connection, including both Robert and Samuel Smith, and even Wilson Cary Nicholas, as possessed with "an inconceivable infatuation" for the match; "it was really the young man who was seduced." Nothing that Pichon could say affected them. Senator J. Q. Adams remarked: "the Smiths are so elated with their supposed elevation by this adventure, that one step more would fit them for the discipline of Dr. Willis,"—the famous English expert in mental diseases.[2]

The President and his friends might not know enough of Napoleon's character to foresee the irritation which such reports would create in his mind, but they were aware of the contrast between their treatment of Jerome Bonaparte and their slights to Anthony Merry. Had they felt any doubt upon the subject, the free comments of the British minister and his wife would have opened their eyes. In truth, no doubt existed. Washington society was in a manner ordered to pro-

[1] Diary of J. Q. Adams (Jan. 7, 1804), i. 284.
[2] Ibid.

scribe the Merrys and Yrujo, and pay court to Jerome and the Smiths.

Had this been all, the matter would have ended in a personal quarrel between the two envoys and the two Virginians, with which the public would have had no concern. Jefferson's "canons of etiquette" would in such a case have had no further importance than as an anecdote of his social habits. The seriousness of Jefferson's experiments in etiquette consisted in the belief that they were part of a political system which involved a sudden change of policy toward two great Powers. The "canons" were but the social expression of an altered feeling which found its political expression in acts marked by equal disregard of usage. The Spanish minister had already reason to know what he might expect; for six weeks before Merry's dinners John Randolph proclaimed in the House that West Florida belonged to the United States, and within the week that preceded Merry's reception, he brought in the Bill which authorized the President to annex Mobile. After such a proceeding, no diplomatist would have doubted what meaning to put upon the new code of Republican society. Merry's arrival, at the instant of this aggression upon Spain, was the signal for taking toward England a higher tone.

Merry could not fail to see what lay before him. From the President, notwithstanding heelless slippers and "canons of etiquette," the British minister heard none but friendly words. After the formal ceremony of delivering the letter of credence was over,—

> "He desired me to sit down," wrote Merry,[1] "when we conversed for some time on general affairs. The sentiments which he expressed respecting those of Europe appeared very properly to be by no means favorable to the spirit of ambition and aggrandizement of the present ruler in France, or to the personal character in any respect of the First Consul, and still less so to his conduct toward all nations."

From this subject the President passed to Spanish affairs and to the Spanish protest against the Louisiana cession,

[1] Merry to Hawkesbury, Dec. 6, 1803; MSS. British Archives.

founded on Bonaparte's pledge never to alienate that province.

"This circumstance," continued Merry, "as well as the resistance altogether which Spain had unexpectedly brought
forward in words, Mr. Jefferson considered as highly ridiculous, and as showing a very pitiful conduct on her part,
since she did not appear to have taken any measures to support it either by preparation of defence on the spot, or by
sending there a force to endeavor to prevent the occupation
of the country by the troops of the United States. He concluded by saying that possession of it would, at all events,
be taken."

If Merry did not contrive, after his dinner at the White
House, to impart this conversation to his colleagues Yrujo
and Pichon, he must have been a man remarkably free from
malice. Meanwhile he had his own affairs to manage, and
Madison was not so forbearing as the President. Merry's first
despatch announced to his Government that Madison had already raised his tone. Without delay the matter of impressments was brought into prominence. The "pretended"
blockade of Martinique and Guadeloupe was also strongly
characterized.

"It is proper for me to notice," said Merry in his report
of these remonstrances,[1] "that Mr. Madison gave great
weight to them by renewing them on every occasion of my
seeing him, and by his expressing that they were matters
upon which this Government could not possibly be silent
until a proper remedy for the evil should be applied by his
Majesty's government. His observations were, however,
made with great temper, and accompanied with the strongest assurances of the disposition of this Government to
conciliate, and to concur in whatever means could be devised which should not be absolutely derogatory to their
independence and interests, to establish principles and rules
which should be satisfactory to both parties. . . . But, my
Lord, while it is my duty to do justice to Mr. Madison's
temperate and conciliatory language, I must not omit to

[1] Merry to Hawkesbury, Dec. 6, 1803; MSS. British Archives.

observe that it indicated strongly a design on the part of this Government to avail themselves of the present conjuncture by persisting steadily in their demands of redress of their pretended grievances, in the hope of obtaining a greater respect to their flag, and of establishing a more convenient system of neutral navigation than the interests of the British empire have hitherto allowed his Majesty to concur in."

The British government was aware that its so-called right of impressment and its doctrine of blockade rested on force, and could not be maintained against superior force; but this consciousness rendered England only the more sensitive in regard to dangers that threatened her supremacy. Knowing that the United States would be justified in declaring war at any moment, Great Britain looked uneasily for the first symptoms of retaliation. When Madison took so earnest a tone, Merry might reasonably expect that his words would be followed by acts.

These shocks were not all that the new British minister was obliged to meet at the threshold of his residence in Washington. At the moment when he was, as he thought, socially maltreated, and when he was told by Madison that America meant to insist on her neutral rights, he learned that the Government did not intend to ratify Rufus King's boundary convention. The Senate held that the stipulations of its fifth article respecting the Mississippi might embarrass the new territory west of the river. King had not known of the Louisiana cession when he signed the Treaty; and the Senate, under the lead of General Smith,[1] preferred to follow its own views on the subject, as it had done in regard to the second article of the treaty with France, Sept. 30, 1800, and as it was about to do in regard to Pinckney's claims convention, Aug. 11, 1802, with Spain. Merry was surprised to find that Madison, instead of explaining the grounds of the Senate's hesitation, or entering into discussion of the precise geographical difficulty, contented himself with a bald statement of the fact. The British minister thought that this was not the most courteous way of dealing with a treaty negotiated after a full ac-

[1] Diary of J. Q. Adams (Oct. 31, 1803), i. 269.

quaintance with all the circumstances, and he wrote to his Government to be on its guard:[1] —

"Notwithstanding Mr. Madison's assurances to the contrary, I have some reason to suspect that ideas of encroachment on his Majesty's just rights are entertained by some persons who have a voice in deciding upon the question of the ratification of this convention, not to say that I have much occasion to observe, from circumstances in general, that there exists here a strong impression of the consequences which this country is supposed to have acquired by the recent additions to the territory of the United States, as well as by the actual situation of affairs in Europe."

In view of the Mobile Act, introduced into Congress by Randolph on behalf of the government a week before this letter was written, Merry's suspicions could hardly be called unreasonable. A like stretch of authority applied to the northwest territory would have produced startling results.

Merry's suspicions that some assault was to be made upon England were strengthened when Madison, December 5, in pursuance of a call from the Senate, sent a list of impressments reported to the Department during the last year. According to this paper the whole number of impressments was forty-six, — three of which were made by France and her allies; while of the forty-three made by Great Britain twenty-seven of the seamen were not American citizens. Of the entire number, twelve were stated to have had American papers; and of the twelve, nearly half were impressed on land within British jurisdiction. The grievance, serious as it was, had not as yet reached proportions greater than before the Peace of Amiens. Merry drew the inference that Jefferson's administration meant to adopt stronger measures than had hitherto been thought necessary. He soon began to see the scope which the new policy was to take.

Dec. 22, 1803, Madison opened in a formal conference the diplomatic scheme which was the outcome of these preliminary movements.[2] Beginning with a repetition of complaints in regard to impressments, and dwelling upon the great irri-

[1] Merry to Hawkesbury, Dec. 6, 1803; MSS. British Archives.
[2] Merry to Hawkesbury, Dec. 31, 1803; MSS. British Archives.

tation created by such arbitrary acts, the secretary next remonstrated against the extent given to the law of blockade by British cruisers in the West Indies, and at length announced that the frequent repetition of these grievances had rendered it necessary for the United States to take immediate steps to find a remedy for them. Instructions would therefore be shortly sent to Monroe at London to negotiate a new convention on these subjects. The American government would wish that its flag should give complete protection to whatever persons might be under it, excepting only military enemies of the belligerent. Further, it would propose that the right of visiting ships at sea should be restrained; that the right of blockade should be more strictly defined, and American ships be allowed, in consideration of the distance, to clear for blockaded ports on the chance of the blockade being removed before they arrived; and finally that the direct trade between the West Indies and Europe should be thrown open to American commerce without requiring it to pass through a port of the United States.

In return Madison offered to the British government the unconditional surrender of deserters by sea and land, together with certain precautions against the smuggling of articles contraband of war.

Although Madison pressed the necessity of an immediate understanding on these points, he did so in his usual temperate and conciliatory manner; while Merry frankly avowed that he could give no hopes of such propositions being listened to. He did this the more decisively because Congress seemed about to take the matter of impressments into its own hands, and was already debating a Bill for the protection of seamen by measures which tended to hostilities. Madison disavowed responsibility for the legislation, although he defended it in principle.[1] Merry contented himself for the time by saying that if the United States government sought their remedy in municipal law, the matter would immediately cease to be a subject of negotiation.

Thus, in one short month, the two governments were brought to what the British minister supposed to be the verge

---

[1] Merry to Hawkesbury, Jan. 20, 1804; Jan. 30, 1804; MSS. British Archives.

of rupture. That any government should take so well-considered a position without meaning to support it by acts, was not probable. Acts of some kind, more or less hostile in their nature, were certainly intended by the United States government in case Great Britain should persist in contempt for neutral rights; the sudden change of tone at Washington left no doubt on this point. Edward Thornton, who had not yet been transferred to another post, wrote in consternation to the Foreign Office, fearing that blame might be attached to his own conduct while in charge of the legation:[1] —

"When I compare the complexion of Mr. Merry's correspondence with that of my own, particularly during the course of the last summer, before the intelligence of the Louisiana purchase reached this country, I can scarcely credit the testimony of my own senses in examining the turn which affairs have taken, and the manifest ill-will discovered toward us by the Government at the present moment. . . . I believe that the simple truth of the case is, after all, the circumstance . . . that a real change has taken place in the views of this Government, which may be dated from the first arrival of the intelligence relative to the Louisiana purchase, and which has since derived additional force and acrimony from the opinion that Great Britain cannot resist, under her present pressure, the new claims of the United States, and now, from the necessity they are under of recurring to the influence of France in order to support their demands against Spain. . . . The cession of Louisiana, notwithstanding that the circumstances under which it was made ought to convince the vainest of men that he was not the sole agent in the transaction, has elevated the President beyond imagination in his own opinion; and I have no doubt that he thinks of securing himself at the next election by having to boast of concessions and advantages derived from us, similar to those he has gained from France,—that is, great in appearance, and at a comparatively insignificant expense."

From such premises, the conclusion, so far as concerned

[1] Thornton to Hammond, Jan. 29, 1804; MSS. British Archives.

England, was inevitable; and Thornton agreed with Merry in affirming it without reserve:—

"Everything, as it relates to this government, now depends on our firmness. If we yield an iota without a real and perfect equivalent (not such imaginary equivalents as Mr. Madison mentions to Mr. Merry), we are lost."

Chapter XVII

WHATEVER OBJECTS the President and the Secretary of State may have expected to gain by their change of tone in the winter of 1803–1804 toward Spain and England, they must have been strangely free from human passions if they were unconscious of making at least two personal enemies upon whose ill-will they might count. If they were unaware of giving their victims cause for bitterness,—or if, as seemed more probable, they were indifferent to it,—the frequent chances of retaliation which the two ministers enjoyed soon showed that in diplomacy revenge was not only sweet but easy. Even the vehement Spanish hatred felt by Yrujo for Madison fell short of the patient Anglo-Saxon antipathy rooted in the minds of the British minister and his wife. When Yrujo, in March, 1804, burst into the State Department with the Mobile Act in his hand and denounced Madison to his face as party to an "infamous libel," he succeeded in greatly annoying the secretary without violating Jefferson's "canons of etiquette." Under the code of republican manners which the President and his secretary had introduced, they could not fairly object to anything which Yrujo might choose to say or do. Absolute equality and "the rule of *pêle-mêle*" reached their natural conclusion between such hosts and guests in freedom of language and vehemence of passion. What might have been Merry's feelings or conduct had he met with more cordiality and courtesy was uncertain; but the mortifications of his first month at Washington embittered his temper, and left distinct marks of acrimony in the diplomacy of America and England, until war wiped out the memory of reciprocal annoyances. The Spaniard's enmity was already a peril to Madison's ambition, and one which became more threatening every day; but the Englishman's steady resentment was perhaps more mischievous, if less noisy. The first effect of Jefferson's tactics was to ally the British minister with Yurjo; the second bound him to Senator Pickering and Representative Griswold; the third united his fortunes with those of Aaron Burr. Merry entered the path of secret conspiracy; he became the confidant of all the intriguers in Washington, and gave to their intrigues the support of his official influence.

The Federalists worked mischievously to widen the breach between the British minister and the President. They encouraged Merry's resentment. Late in January, nearly two months after the first *pêle-mêle*, Madison officially informed Merry for the first time that the President meant to recognize no precedence between foreign ministers, but that all, even including secretaries of legation in charge, were to be treated with perfect equality, or what Madison termed "a complete pell-mell," and would be received, even at their first audience, with no more ceremony than was practised toward any other individual. Merry replied that this notice should have been given to him on his arrival, and that he could not acquiesce in it without instructions. He then wrote to his Government,[1] —

> "I have now but too much reason to fear, what I did not at first suspect, that the marked inattention toward me of the present Administration of this country has been a part of their unfriendly disposition toward his Majesty and toward the nation which I have the honor to represent."

At the same moment, in January and February, 1804, Pickering and Griswold were plotting their New England confederacy. Merry was taken by them into the secret, and gave them aid. The Senate, February 9, voted to strike out the fifth article of Rufus King's boundary convention, and to approve the other articles, which provided for fixing the disputed boundary-line of Maine, New Hampshire, and Vermont. Merry wrote to his Government that the object of cancelling the fifth article was to deprive Great Britain of her treaty-right to navigate the Mississippi:[2] —

> "It is hardly necessary for me to point out to your Lordship that the other articles of the convention are of great importance to the Eastern States of America, which are much interested in the immediate settlement of the eastern boundary. I am led to believe from the language of some of the members of this State [Massachusetts] that their anxiety on this head is so great that the rejection of those

[1] Merry to Hawkesbury, Jan. 30, 1804; MSS. British Archives.
[2] Merry to Hawkesbury, March 1, 1804; MSS. British Archives.

articles by his Majesty would, as having been occasioned by the exclusion on the part of this government of the fifth article, prove to be a great exciting cause to them to go forward rapidly in the steps which they have already commenced toward a separation from the Southern part of the Union. The members of the Senate have availed themselves of the opportunity of their being collected here to hold private meetings on this subject, and I learn from them that their plans and calculations respecting the event have been long seriously resolved. They think that whenever it shall take place it will happen suddenly, yet with quietness and the universal concurrence of the people. Although it does not appear to be their opinion that any external secret agency would accelerate the moment, they naturally look forward to Great Britain for support and assistance whenever the occasion shall arrive."

As the summer of 1804 came on, Merry's despatches grew more sombre. He reported that at Norfolk twelve British ships were detained at one time in consequence of the desertion of their seamen, several of whom had entered the United States service on the frigates which were under orders for Tripoli. Six British seamen having deserted at Charleston and re-enlisted in the same way, Merry remonstrated. He was told that the seamen, having voluntarily enlisted in the United States service, could not be restored, because the British government never restored American seamen who had voluntarily enlisted. Merry could only reply that the British government did not knowingly enlist deserters. On the other hand, Madison remonstrated in "high language," "accompanied even with some degree of menace," against the conduct of Captain Bradley of the frigate "Cambrian," one of the British squadron cruising off Sandy Hook, for taking a British seaman out of a British vessel within American jurisdiction. Merry added that in contrast to this strictness toward England the authorities had allowed the officers of the French frigate "La Poursuivante," at Baltimore, to send armed parties on shore at night for the purpose of seizing French seamen, one of whom they had actually taken by force from a Spanish vessel lying at the wharf.

"From this government having brought into such serious discussion objects which would certainly have passed unnoticed had they occurred in relation to the King's enemies, his Majesty's ministers may be led to suspect that such a resolution has been dictated by some hostile design," wrote Merry, with increasing solemnity; "but it is proper for me to observe that . . . I cannot persuade myself that they will dare to provoke hostilities with his Majesty, at least before Mr. Jefferson's re-election to the Presidency shall have taken place."[1]

Merry made a representation to Madison on impressments; but his arguments did not satisfy the secretary. "This specimen of Merry shows him to be a mere diplomatic pettifogger," wrote Madison privately to the President.[2]

Merry's temper was in this stage of ever-increasing irritability, when an event occurred which gave him, as it seemed, a chance to gratify his resentments. After the adjournment of Congress in March the British minister heard nothing from Pickering and Griswold. Early in June he wrote home that the democrats were carrying all the elections:[3] —

"In addition to this triumph of the reigning party, there have lately appeared in the prints of this country, which are generally made the instruments of the measures of all parties, publications of the discovery that has been made of secret meetings held at this place by some of the Federal members during the last sitting of Congress for the purpose of consulting upon the important point of the separation of the Eastern from the Southern States, which publications seem to have imposed a complete silence upon the Federal adherents."

A few weeks afterward, July 11, occurred the duel between Burr and Hamilton. Merry had no relations with Hamilton, and felt no peculiar interest in his fate; but he had become intimate with Burr at Washington, and watched his career with the curiosity which was the natural result of their com-

[1] Merry to Harrowby, July 18, 1804; MSS. British Archives.
[2] Madison to Jefferson, Aug. 28, 1804; Jefferson MSS.
[3] Merry to Hawkesbury, June 2, 1804; MSS. British Archives.

mon hatred of Jefferson. July 21 Burr fled from New York, and a few days afterward reached Philadelphia, where Merry was passing the summer. While there, Burr sent one of his friends—an Englishman named Williamson—to the British minister with a startling message, which Merry immediately transmitted to his Government:[1]—

"I have just received an offer from Mr. Burr, the actual Vice-President of the United States (which situation he is about to resign), to lend his assistance to his Majesty's government in any manner in which they may think fit to employ him, particularly in endeavoring to effect a separation of the western part of the United States from that which lies between the Atlantic and the mountains, in its whole extent. His proposition on this and other subjects will be fully detailed to your Lordship by Colonel Williamson, who has been the bearer of them to me, and who will embark for England in a few days. It is therefore only necessary for me to add that if after what is generally known of the profligacy of Mr. Burr's character, his Majesty's minister should think proper to listen to his offer, his present situation in this country, where he is now cast off as much by the democratic as by the Federal party, and where he still preserves connections with some people of influence, added to his great ambition and spirit of revenge against the present Administration, may possibly induce him to exert the talents and activity which he possesses with fidelity to his employers."

Meanwhile a change of ministry occurred in England. Pitt returned to power, representing a state of feeling toward America very different from that which prevailed under the mild rule of Addington. Subordinates were quick to feel such changes in the temper of their superiors. Every British officer knew that henceforth he had behind him an energetic government, which required vigorous action in maintaining what it claimed as British rights. Merry felt the new impulse like the rest; but Pitt's return acted most seriously on the naval service. After the renewal of the war in May, 1803, a small British

---

[1] Merry to Harrowby, Aug. 6, 1804; MSS. British Archives.

squadron cruised off Sandy Hook, keeping a sharp look-out for French frigates in New York Harbor, and searching every merchant-vessel for enemy's property. During the summer of 1804 this annoyance became steadily greater, until the port of New York was almost blockaded, and every vessel that sailed out or in was liable not only to be stopped and searched, but to lose some part of its crew by impressment. The British ministry did indeed instantly recall Captain Bradley of the "Cambrian" for violating American jurisdiction, and gave strict orders for the lenient exercise of belligerent rights; but all the more it showed the intention of insisting upon the submission of America to such rules as England should prescribe. The President, already in trouble with Spain, began to feel the double peril; but Congress pressed him forward, and even while busy with the trial of Judge Chase it found time for two measures which greatly disturbed the British envoy.

The first of these measures was an "Act for the more effectual preservation of peace in the ports and harbors of the United States." Under this law any United States marshal, on the warrant of any United States judge, was bound to board any British or other foreign ship-of-war lying in American waters, and seize every person charged with having violated the peace. If the marshal should be resisted, or if surrender was not made, he must call in the military power, and compel surrender by force of arms. If death should ensue, he should be held blameless; but the resisting party should be punished as for felonious homicide. Further, the President was authorized to interdict at will the ports of the United States to all or any armed vessels of a foreign nation; and to arrest and indict any foreign officer who should come within the jurisdiction after committing on the high seas "any trespass or tort, or any spoliation, on board any vessel of the United States, or any unlawful interruption or vexation of trading-vessels actually coming to or going from the United States."

Such laws were commonly understood in diplomacy as removing the subject in question from the field of negotiation, preliminary to reprisals and war. The Act was passed with little debate in the last hours of the session, in the midst of the confusion which followed the acquittal of Judge Chase. Merry immediately called on the Secretary of State, and asked him for some assurance that might serve to quiet the apprehensions which his Government would feel on reading the Act.[1] Madison could give none, except that the President would probably not exercise for the present his discretionary powers. As for the words, "any trespass or tort," Madison frankly avowed "he could not but confess they were meant to imply the impressment of any individual whatsoever from on board an American vessel, the exercise of which pretended right on the part of his Majesty's officers was a matter, he said, which the sense of the people at large would never allow the government of this country to acquiesce in."

To this announcement Merry replied in substance that the right was one which would certainly never be abandoned by his Government; and there the matter rested at the close of Jefferson's first term. Madison assured the British minister that the authority granted to the President by Congress over foreign ships of war in American waters would not at present be enforced. He went even a step further toward conciliation. The Legislature of Virginia was induced quietly to modify the Act which had hitherto offered so much encouragement to the desertion of British seamen.[2]

The second threatening measure was a Resolution of the Senate, March 2, 1805, calling upon the Secretary of State for such Acts of the British Parliament as imposed heavier duties on the exportation of merchandise to the United States than on similar goods exported to the nations of Europe. Such an export duty upon merchandise for the United States and the West Indies had in fact been imposed by Parliament some two years before; and this Resolution foreshadowed some commercial retaliation by Congress.

While sending to his Government these warnings to expect from Jefferson's second administration a degree of hostility more active than from the first, Merry suggested means of giving the United States occupation that should induce them to leave England alone. A new element of conspiracy disclosed itself to the British minister.

[1] Merry to Harrowby, March 4, 1805; MSS. British Archives.
[2] Merry to Harrowby, March 29, 1805; MSS. British Archives.

Under the Louisiana treaty of cession, the United States government had promised that "the inhabitants of the ceded territory shall be incorporated in the Union of the United States, and admitted as soon as possible, according to the principles of the Federal Constitution, to the enjoyment of all the rights, advantages, and immunities of citizens of the United States." This pledge had been broken. The usual display of casuistry had been made to prove that the infraction of treaty was no infraction at all; but the more outspoken Republicans avowed, as has been already shown, that the people of Louisiana could not be trusted, or in the commoner phrase that they were unfit for self-government, and must be treated as a conquered race until they learned to consider themselves American citizens.

The people of New Orleans finding themselves in a position of dependence, which, owing chiefly to their hatred of Governor Claiborne, seemed more irritating than their old Spanish servitude, sent three representatives to Washington to urge upon Congress the duty of executing the treaty. Messieurs Sauvé, Derbigny, and Destréhan accordingly appeared at Washington, and in December, 1804, presented a remonstrance so strong that Government was greatly embarrassed to deal with it.[1] Any reply that should repudiate either the treaty obligation or the principles of American liberty and self-government was out of the question; any reply that should affirm either the one or the other was fatal to the system established by Congress in Louisiana. John Randolph, on whose shoulders the duty fell, made a report on the subject. "It is only under the torture," said he, "that this article of the treaty of Paris can be made to speak the language ascribed to it by the memorialists;" but after explaining in his own way what the article did not mean, he surprised his audience by admitting in effect that the law of the last session was repugnant to the Constitution, and that the people of Louisiana had a right to self-government.[2] Senator Giles said in private that Randolph's report was "a perfect transcript of Ran-

[1] Remonstrance of the People of Louisiana, Dec. 31, 1804; Annals of Congress, 1804–1805, Appendix, p. 1597.

[2] Report of Committee, Jan. 25, 1805; Annals of Congress, 1804–1805, p. 1014.

dolph's own character; it began by setting the claims of the Louisianians at defiance, and concluded with a proposal to give them more than they asked."[1]

Under these influences the three delegates from the creole society succeeded in getting, not what they asked, but a general admission that the people of Louisiana had political rights, which Congress recognized by an Act, approved March 2, 1805, to the extent of allowing them to elect a General Assembly of twenty-five representatives, and of promising them admission into the Union whenever their free inhabitants should reach the number of sixty thousand. Considering that the people of Louisiana were supposed to be entitled to "*all* the rights, advantages, and immunities of citizens," Messieurs Sauvé, Derbigny, and Destréhan thought the concession too small, and expressed themselves strongly on the subject. Naturally the British minister, as well as other ill affected persons at Washington, listened eagerly to the discontent which promised to breed hostility to the Union.

"The deputies above mentioned," wrote Merry to his Government,[2] "who while they had any hopes of obtaining the redress of their grievances had carefully avoided giving any umbrage or jealousy to the Government by visiting or holding any intercourse with the agents of foreign Powers at this place, when they found that their fate was decided, although the law had not as yet passed, no longer abstained from communicating with those agents, nor from expressing very publicly the great dissatisfaction which the law would occasion among their constituents,—going even so far as to say that it would not be tolerated, and that they would be obliged to seek redress from some other quarter; while they observed that the opportunity they had had of obtaining a correct knowledge of the state of things in this country, and of witnessing the proceedings of Congress, afforded them no confidence in the stability of the Union, and furnished them with such strong motives to be dissatisfied with the form and mode of government as to make them regret extremely the connection which they had been

[1] Diary of J. Q. Adams (Feb. 1, 1805), i. 342.
[2] Merry to Harrowby, (No. 14), March 29, 1805; MSS. British Archives.

forced into with it. These sentiments they continued to ex-press till the moment of their departure from hence, which took place the day after the close of the session."

Another man watched the attitude of the three delegates with extreme interest. Aaron Burr, March 4, 1805, ceased to hold the office of Vice-president. Since the previous August he had awaited the report of his friend Colonel Williamson, who entered into conferences with members of the British ministry, hoping to gain their support for Burr's plan of creating a Western Confederacy in the Valley of the Ohio. No sooner was Burr out of office than he went to Merry with new communications, which Merry hastened to send to his Government in a despatch marked "Most secret" in triplicate.[1]

"Mr. Burr (with whom I know that the deputies became very intimate during their residence here) has mentioned to me that the inhabitants of Louisiana seem determined to render themselves independent of the United States, and that the execution of their design is only delayed by the difficulty of obtaining previously an assurance of protection and assistance from some foreign Power, and of concerting and connecting their independence with that of the inhab-itants of the western parts of the United States, who must always have a command over them by the rivers which communicate with the Mississippi. It is clear that Mr. Burr (although he has not as yet confided to me the exact nature and extent of his plan) means to endeavor to be the instru-ment of effecting such a connection."

For this purpose Burr asked the aid of the British govern-ment, and defined the nature of the assistance he should need,—a British squadron at the mouth of the Mississippi, and a loan of half a million dollars.

"I have only to add that if a strict confidence could be placed in him, he certainly possesses, perhaps in a much greater degree than any other individual in this country, all the talents, energy, intrepidity, and firmness which are re-quired for such an enterprise."

[1] Merry to Harrowby, (No. 15), most secret, March 29, 1805.

Pending an answer to this proposal, Burr was to visit New Orleans and make himself the head of creole disaffection.

Merry was launched into the full tide of conspiracy. At the close of Jefferson's first term he saw reason to hope that he might soon repay with interest the debt of personal and political annoyance which he owed. While Yrujo was actively engaged in bringing upon Madison the anger of Spain and France, Merry endeavored to draw his Government into a system of open and secret reprisals upon the President.

That the new French minister was little better disposed than Merry and Yrujo has been already shown; but his causes for ill-will were of a different and less personal nature. Before Turreau's arrival at Washington in November, 1804, Pichon in one of his last despatches declared that Jefferson had already alienated every foreign Power whose enmity could be dangerous to the United States.

"The state of foreign relations offers a perspective which must put Mr. Jefferson's character to proof," Pichon wrote to Talleyrand in September, 1804.[1] "The United States find themselves compromised and at odds with France, England, and Spain at the same time. This state of things is in great part due to the indecision of the President, and to the policy which leads him to sacrifice everything for the sake of his popularity."

The complaint was common to all French ministers in the United States, and meant little more than that all Presidents and policies displeased them by stopping short of war on England, which was the object of French diplomacy; but this letter also showed that in Pichon's eyes the President had no friends. When Turreau arrived, a few weeks afterward, he quickly intimated that the President need expect from him not even such sentimental sympathy as had been so kindly given by Pichon.

At the same moment it was noticed that Jefferson changed his style of dress. "He has improved much in the article of dress," wrote Senator Plumer in December, 1804;[2] "he has

[1] Pichon to Talleyrand, 16 Fructidor, An xii. (Sept 3, 1804); Archives des Aff. Étr., MSS.
[2] Life of Plumer, p. 326.

laid aside the old slippers, red waistcoat, and soiled corduroy small-clothes, and was dressed all in black, with clean linen and powdered hair." Apparently the President had profited by the criticisms of the British minister, and was willing to avoid similar comments from the new French envoy; but he supposed that the Frenchman would show equal civility, and assume an equally republican style. He was mistaken. November 23, undisturbed by Merry's experience, Turreau presented himself at his first audience in full regimentals, and with so much gold lace that Jefferson was half inclined to resent it as an impertinence.[1] Turreau next refused to meet Merry at dinner. He followed up these demonstrations by embracing the cause of Yrujo, and ridiculing Madison to his face. He began by warning his Government that "these people have been thoroughly spoiled; it is time to put them back into their place."[2]

Turreau became intimate with the deputies from Louisiana, and notified Talleyrand that a separation of the western country from the Union was universally expected. Already, within three months of his arrival, he put his finger on the men who were to accomplish it.[3] Destréhan, he said, was a man of high merit; "but being only moderately ambitious, and head of a numerous family,—having acquired, too, a great personal esteem,—he is not likely to become the principal mover in innovations which are always dangerous without a combination of evidently favorable chances. It is still less likely that he will ever be the instrument of strangers who should seek to excite troubles for their personal advantage." As for Sauvé, much inferior to his colleague in abilities, he would be guided by Destréhan's influence. Derbigny was different. "Young still, with wit, ready expression, and French manners, I believe him to be greedy of fortune and fame; I suspect that every *rôle* will suit him, in order to acquire the one or the other; but there are men of more importance whom circumstances are taking to Louisiana."

Then Turreau, for the information of Talleyrand, drew a portrait of the military commander of Upper Louisiana, who

[1] Diary of J. Q. Adams (Nov. 23, 1804), i. 316.
[2] Turreau to Talleyrand, 27 Janvier, 1805; Archives des Aff. Étr., MSS.
[3] Turreau to Talleyrand, 9 Mars, 1805; Archives des Aff. Étr., MSS.

had his headquarters at St. Louis, and whose influence on future events was to be watched.

"General Wilkinson is forty-eight years of age. He has an amiable exterior. Though said to be well informed in civil and political matters, his military capacity is small. Ambitious and easily dazzled, fond of show and appearances, he complains rather indiscreetly, and especially after dinner, of the form of his government, which leaves officers few chances of fortune, advancement, and glory, and which does not pay its military chiefs enough to support a proper style. He listened with pleasure, or rather with enthusiasm, to the details which I gave him in regard to the organization, the dress, and the force of the French army. My uniform, the order with which I am decorated, are objects of envy to him; and he seems to hold to the American service only because he can do no better. General Wilkinson is the most intimate friend, or rather the most devoted creature, of Colonel Burr."

Talleyrand had become acquainted with Burr in the United States, and needed no warnings against him; but Turreau showed himself well informed:

"Mr. Burr's career is generally looked upon as finished; but he is far from sharing that opinion, and I believe he would rather sacrifice the interests of his country than renounce celebrity and fortune. Although Louisiana is still only a Territory, it has obtained the right of sending a delegate to Congress. Louisiana is therefore to become the theatre of Mr. Burr's new intrigues; he is going there under the ægis of General Wilkinson."

Perhaps Turreau received this information from Derbigny, which might account for his estimate of the young man. Certainly Derbigny knew all that Turreau reported, for in an affidavit[1] two years afterward he admitted his knowledge.

"In the winter of 1804–1805," Derbigny made oath, "being then at Washington City in the capacity of a deputy

---

[1] Affidavit of Peter Derbigny, Aug. 27, 1807. Clark's Proofs against Wilkinson; Note 18. App. p. 38.

from the inhabitants of Louisiana to Congress, jointly with Messrs. Destréhan and Sauvé, he was introduced to Colonel Burr, then Vice-president of the United States, by General Wilkinson, who strongly recommended to this deponent, and as he believes to his colleagues, to cultivate the acquaintance of Colonel Burr,—whom he used to call 'the first gentleman in America,' telling them that he was a man of the most eminent talents both as a politician and as a military character; and . . . General Wilkinson told him several times that Colonel Burr, so soon as his Vice-presidency would be at an end, would go to Louisiana, where he had certain projects, adding that he was such a man as to succeed in anything he would undertake, and inviting this deponent to give him all the information in his power respecting that country; which mysterious hints appeared to this deponent very extraordinary, though he could not then understand them."

What Derbigny in 1807 professed not to have understood, seemed in 1804 clear to Turreau and Merry as well as to others. Turreau closed his catalogue by the significant remark: "I am not the only person who thinks that the assemblage of such men in a country already discontented is enough to give rise to serious troubles there." The treasonable plans of Burr and Wilkinson were a matter of common notoriety, and roused anxious comment even in the mind of John Randolph, who was nursing at home the mortification of Judge Chase's acquittal.[1] Randolph complained of "the easy credulity of Mr. Jefferson's temper," which made the President a fit material for intriguers to work upon. Certainly at the close of his first administration Jefferson seemed surrounded by enemies. The New England Federalists, the Louisiana creoles, Burr and his crew of adventurers in every part of the Union, joined hands with the ministers of England and Spain to make a hostile circle round the President; while the minister of France looked on without a wish to save the government whose friendship Bonaparte had sought to obtain at the cost of the most valuable province and the most splendid traditions of the French people.

[1] Adams's Randolph, p. 157.

Chapter XVIII

A FTER AIDING to negotiate the Louisiana treaty at Paris, in April and May, 1803, Monroe, as the story has already told, being forbidden by Bonaparte to pursue his journey to Madrid, followed his alternative instructions, to take the post which Rufus King was vacating in London. King left England in the middle of May, 1803; Monroe arrived in London July 18, when the war between England and France was already two months old.

The mild Addington ministry was still in power, and nothing had yet happened to excite Monroe's alarm in regard to British policy in the United States. On the contrary, the ministry aided the Louisiana purchase with readiness that might reasonably have surprised an American minister, while the friendliest spirit was shown by Lord Hawkesbury in all matters of detail. Except the standing dispute about impressments, every old point of collision had been successfully removed by King, whose two conventions,—the one for discharging British debts recognized by treaty, the other for settling the boundaries of New England and of the northwest territory,—seemed to free the countries for the first time from the annoying inheritance of disputes entailed by the definitive treaty which closed the Revolutionary War in 1783. The calm which seemed to prevail throughout England in regard to her relations with America contrasted sharply with the excitement shown by the English people in all their allusions to the Corsican demon, as they thought him, whose regiments, gathering at Boulogne, they might expect to see at any moment encamped at Hastings, where no hostile camp-fire had burned since the night, seven hundred years before, when the body of an English king, hedged about with the dead bodies of a whole English aristocracy, lay stiff and stark on the bloody hillside, victims of another French adventurer. England was intent on her own imminent dangers; and under the strain which the renewal of her painful efforts brought with it, she was glad to leave America alone.

Yet calm as the atmosphere appeared to be, signs of future storm were not wholly wanting. Had Monroe been naturally anxious, he might, without seeking far, have found cause for anxiety serious enough to take away all appetite for Spanish travel, and to hold him close to his post until some one should consent to relieve him from an ungrateful and unpromising duty. The American minister at London in 1804 could hope to gain nothing either for his country or for himself, and he stood always on the verge of disaster; but when he was required to take a "high tone" in the face of a nation almost insane with anxiety, he challenged more chances of mortification than any but a desperate politician would have cared to risk.

Monroe had at first nothing to do but to watch the course of public opinion in England. During the autumn of 1803, while President Jefferson and Secretary Madison at Washington received Merry with a changed policy, and all through the winter, while Washington was torn by "canons of etiquette" and by contests of strength between Jefferson, Madison, Casa Yrujo, and Merry, the United States minister in London was left at peace to study the political problems which bore on his own fortunes and on those of his friends at home, as well as on the interests of the Union.

Beneath the calm of general society mutterings of discontent from powerful interests could be heard,—occasional outbursts of jealousy, revivals of old and virulent passions, inveterate prejudices, which made as yet but little noise in the Press or in Parliament, but which rankled in the breasts of individuals. One of the earlier symptoms of trouble came in a familiar shape. For twenty years, whenever a question had arisen of hostility to American trade or of prejudice against American character, the first of Englishmen to stimulate it, and the loudest to proclaim the dangers of Great Britain, had been John Baker Holroyd, Earl of Sheffield, whose memory might have been lost under the weight of his pamphlets had it not been embalmed in the autobiography of Gibbon. Lord Sheffield felt such devotion to the British navigation laws as could be likened only to the idolatry which a savage felt toward his fetich; one might almost have supposed that to him the State, the Church, and the liberties of England, the privileges of her nobility, and even the person of her sovereign, were sacred chiefly because they guaranteed the safety of her maritime system. This fanaticism of an honest mind led to results so extravagant as to become at times ridiculous. The existence of the United States was a protest against Lord Sheffield's political religion; and therefore in his eyes the United States were no better than a nation of criminals, capable of betraying their God for pieces of silver. The independence of America had shattered the navigation system of England into fragments; but Lord Sheffield clung the more desperately to his broken idol. Among the portions which had been saved were the West Indian colonies. If at that day the navigation laws had one object more important than another, it was to foster the prosperity of these islands, in order that their sugar and molasses, coffee and rum, might give freight to British shippers and employment to British seamen; but to Lord Sheffield the islands were only a degree less obnoxious than the revolted United States, for they were American at heart, complaining because they were forbidden to trade freely with New York and Boston, and even asserting that when the navigation laws were strictly enforced their slaves died of starvation and disease. Lord Sheffield seriously thought them ungrateful to murmur, and held it their duty to perish in silence rather than ask a relaxation of the law.

The rupture of the Peace of Amiens, in May, 1803, set Lord Sheffield again at work; and unfortunately the material lay ready to his hand. The whole subject of his discourse related to a single fact; but this fact was full of alarm to the English people. The extraordinary decrease of British tonnage in the American trade, the corresponding increase of American shipping, and the loud exultation of the Yankees over the British shipmasters were proofs of the danger which menaced England, whose existence depended on maritime strength. In the month of February, 1804, Lord Sheffield published a pamphlet,[1] which dwelt on these calamities as due to the wanton relaxation of the navigation laws and the senseless clamor of the colonies. He was answered in a pamphlet[2] written by one of the colonial agents; and the answer was convincing, so far

[1] Strictures, etc., on the Navigation and Colonial System of Great Britain. London, 1804.

[2] Claims of the British West Indian Colonists. By G. W. Jordan. London, 1804.

as Lord Sheffield's argument was concerned, but his array of statistics remained to disturb the British mind.

Monroe might therefore count on having, some day, to meet whatever mischief the shipping interest of Great Britain could cause. No argument was needed to prove that the navy would support with zeal whatever demands should be made by the mercantile marine. There remained the immense influence of the West Indian colonies to consider; and if this should be brought into active sympathy with the shipowners and the royal marine against American trade, no minister in England—not even Pitt himself at the height of his power— would be strong enough to resist the combination.

The staple product of the West Indian islands was sugar, and owing to several causes the profits of the planters had until 1798 been large. The insurrection of the Haytian negroes in 1792 annihilated for the time the supply of sugar from St. Domingo; prices rose in consequence, and a great increase in the number of sugar plantations naturally followed. Several of the Dutch and French islands fell into the hands of England, and adventurers flocked to them, eager to invest British capital in new sugar-fields. Under this impulse the supply again increased. Cuba, Porto Rico, Guadeloupe, and at last St. Domingo itself under Toussaint's rule poured sugar into the market. American ships carried French and Spanish sugar to Europe until it became a drug. The high price lasted till 1798; in that year Pitt even imposed a heavy additional duty upon it as a sure source of revenue. In 1799 the effect of over-production first became apparent. During the next few years the price of sugar fell, until great suffering began to prevail in the islands, and the planters wrote piteous letters of distress to England. Their agents wrote back that the English market was flooded with colonial produce: "Send no more sugar home; give it away rather!" was their advice,—and the colonists, without the means of purchasing even the necessaries of life, supplicated government to let them send their sugar to the United States, to be exchanged for American produce.[1]

This the government dared not do, for the shipping interest must in such a case be sacrificed. Debarred from this

[1] Lowe's Enquiry, 4th edition, 1808.

outlet for their produce, the colonists looked about them for some other resource; and since they were not allowed to act independently of the shipmasters, they saw no other course than to join hands with the shipping interest, and to invoke the aid of the navigation laws. The glut of the European market was caused by American neutrals, who were allowed to carry French and Spanish sugars from the West Indies to Europe. If this neutral trade could be stopped, the supply of French and Spanish sugar would be left to rot in Cuba and Guadeloupe, while British colonial produce would enjoy a monopoly throughout Europe.

Even before the Peace of Amiens this policy gained many adherents, and the Peace tended to strengthen their influence. The Addington ministry was not only weak in character, but timid in policy; and by a natural reaction it threw restless and ambitious younger statesmen into an attitude of protest. A new departure was felt to be necessary, and the nervous energy of England, strained almost to insanity by the anxieties of ten years' desperate danger, exhausted itself in the cry for one great commanding spirit, who should meet Bonaparte with his own weapons on his own field.

This cry produced George Canning. Of him and his qualities much will be said hereafter, when his rise to power shall have made him a more prominent figure; here need be noticed only the forces which sought assertion through him, and the nature of the passions which he was peculiarly qualified to express. At all times nations have been most imperilled by the violence of disappointed or terrified interests; but the danger was never so great as when these interests joined to a greed for selfish gain the cry for an unscrupulous chief. Every American schoolboy once knew by heart the famous outburst of Canning, which began, "Away with the cant of 'measures, not men'!" but of the millions of persons who read or heard this favorite extract few understood its meaning to American interests and feelings. This celebrated speech, made Dec. 8, 1802, at a time when Addington's cautious ministry still held office, was intended to dwarf Addington and elevate Pitt,— to ridicule caution and extol violence. "Sir," cried Canning, "to meet, to check, to resist, to stand up against Bonaparte, we want arms of the same kind. I vote for the large military

establishments with all my heart; but for the purpose of cop-
ing with Bonaparte, one great, commanding spirit is worth
them all."

"Arms of the same kind" were, speaking generally, irresponsible violence and disregard of morality. The great, commanding spirit of the moment was Mr. Pitt; but between the
lines of this speech, by the light of its author's whole career,
the secret was easily read that in his opinion the man of the
future who could best meet Bonaparte on his own ground
with his own weapons was not William Pitt, but George
Canning.

After many months of warfare against Addington, Canning
was gratified. In May, 1804, Addington retired from office,
carrying into the House of Lords the new title of Lord Sidmouth, while Pitt returned to power. No one of note returned with him. His old colleague, Lord Grenville, refused
to join his Administration, and Charles James Fox was personally excluded by King George. To fill the Foreign Office
Pitt could find no better man than Lord Harrowby,—a personage of very second-rate importance in politics. With a
Cabinet so weak as to command little respect, and reactionary
as was required to suit the King's growing prejudices, Pitt
was obliged to disguise his feebleness by the vigor of his measures. While creating, by expenditure of money, a new coalition against Napoleon, he was unable to disregard the great
moneyed and social interests which were clamoring for a spirited policy against neutrals and especially against America. In
private he avowed his determination to re-establish the old
system, and his regret that he should ever have been, most
reluctantly, induced to relax the maritime rights of Britain.[1]

That Monroe should have been the last person in London
to know the secret thoughts of Pitt was not surprising. The
Board of Trade commonly exerted more influence than the
Foreign Office over the relations of England with the United
States; and George Rose, Vice-President of the Board of
Trade, Pitt's devoted friend and a Tory after Lord Sheffield's
heart, would never have chosen Monroe as a confidant of

[1] Anti-Jacobin Review, August, 1807, p. 368; Introduction to Reports, etc.,
on Navigation, p. 22; Atcheson's American Encroachments, London, 1808,
p. lxxvii; Baring's Inquiry, London, 1808, p. 73.

schemes under discussion in his department. Lord Harrowby was but the mouthpiece of other men. From him Monroe could expect to hear only what had already been decided. Nevertheless a little study of the mercantile interests of the city, and a careful inquiry into the private opinions of men like Rose and Canning, might have thrown some light on the future, and would naturally have roused anxiety in the mind of Monroe.

Pitt's return to power, with the intention of changing the American policy which had been pursued since the negotiation of Jay's treaty, happened very nearly to coincide with the arrival at the Foreign Office of Merry's most alarming despatches, announcing that Madison required the total abandonment of impressments, the restriction of blockades and the right of search, and complete freedom in the colonial trade, as the conditions on which the friendship of the United States could be preserved. The announcement of President Jefferson's high tone was accompanied by the British minister's account of his own social mortifications by the President and the Secretary of State; of the Senate's refusal to approve the fifth article of Rufus King's boundary convention, in order to attack the British right of navigating the Mississippi; and by drafts of bills pending in Congress, under which any British admiral, even though it were Nelson himself, who should ever have taken a seaman out of an American vessel, was to be arrested in the streets of the first American port where he might go ashore, and to suffer indefinite imprisonment among thieves and felons in the calaboose.

May 30, 1804, Monroe had his first interview with Lord Harrowby. In such cases the new secretary, about to receive a foreign minister, commonly sent for the late correspondence, in order to learn something about the subjects on which he was to have an opinion. Beyond a doubt Lord Harrowby had on his table the despatches of Merry, written between November and April, which he probably finished reading at about the moment when Monroe was announced at the door.

Under such circumstances, Monroe reported to his Government that Lord Harrowby's manners were designedly unfriendly; his reception was rough, his comments on the

Senate's habit of mutilating treaties were harsh, his conduct throughout the interview was calculated to wound and to irritate.[1] After this unpromising experience, two months were allowed to pass without further demonstration on either side. Then Lord Harrowby called Monroe's attention to the twelfth article of Jay's treaty, which regulated the commercial relations between the British West Indies and the United States, and which had expired by limitation. He suggested its renewal, according to its old terms, until two years after the next general peace. To this offer Monroe replied, with the utmost frankness, "that the President wished to postpone this matter until he could include impressment and neutral rights in the treaty; that we must begin *de novo*; that America was a young and thriving country; that in 1794 she had had little experience, since then she understood her interests better; and that a new treaty should omit certain things from that of 1794, and include others. The most urgent part was that which respected our seamen."[2]

An approaching contact of opposite forces always interests men's imagination. On one side, Pitt and Lord Harrowby stood meditating the details of measures, which they had decided in principle, for taking from the United States most of the commercial advantages hitherto enjoyed by them; on the other side stood Monroe and Jefferson, equally confident, telling the Englishmen that very much greater advantages must be conceded. That one or the other of these forces must very soon give way was evident; and if ever an American minister in London needed to be on the alert, with every faculty strained to its utmost, the autumn of 1804 was such a moment. Monroe, aware of his danger, gave full warning to the President. Even as early as June 3, after his first interview with Lord Harrowby, he wrote that a change of policy was imminent. "My most earnest advice is to look to the possibility of such a change."[3]

Lord Harrowby also gave every reasonable warning. His reply to Monroe's demands for further negotiation was simple,—nothing need be expected from him. He refused to do

[1] Monroe to Madison, June 3, 1804; State Papers, iii. 92.
[2] Monroe to Madison, Aug. 7, 1804; State Papers, iii. 94.
[3] Monroe to Madison, June 3, 1804; State Papers, iii. 92.

any business at all, on the plea of other occupations incident to the formation of a new ministry.[1] Monroe sent him the draft of the comprehensive treaty which Madison had forwarded, but Lord Harrowby declined for the present to discuss it. Then Monroe came to the conclusion that his presence in London was no longer necessary; and accordingly, Oct. 8, 1804, he started for Paris and Madrid. Until July 23, 1805, the legation at London was left in charge of a secretary.

A month after his departure, Lord Harrowby wrote a letter of instructions[2] to Merry in reply to the series of despatches received from Washington.

"His Majesty's government," he said, "have perceived with considerable concern, from some of your most recent despatches, the increasing acrimony which appears to pervade the representations that have been made to you by the American Secretary of State on the subject of the impressment of seamen from on board of American ships. The pretension advanced by Mr. Madison that the American flag should protect every individual sailing under it on board of a merchant-ship is too extravagant to require any serious refutation. In the exercise of the right, which has been asserted by his Majesty and his predecessors for ages, of reclaiming from a foreign service the subjects of Great Britain, whether they are found on the high seas or in the ports of his own dominions, irregularities must undoubtedly frequently occur; but the utmost solicitude has been uniformly manifested by his Majesty's government to prevent them as far as may be possible, and to redress them whenever they have actually taken place."

Intending to pursue the same course in the future, the Government would without delay give the strictest orders to its naval officers "to observe the utmost lenity in visiting ships on the high seas, and to abstain from impressments in the ports of the United States."

In regard to commercial questions, Lord Harrowby offered to consider the treaty of 1794 as in force until some new

[1] Monroe to Madison, Sept. 8, 1804; MSS. State Department Archives.
[2] Harrowby to Merry, Nov. 7, 1804; MSS. British Archives.

arrangement could be formed. Until the decision of the President should be known, it was "intended to propose to Parliament to lodge the power of regulating the commerce with America in the King in Council, in the same manner as before the treaty of 1794." The offer of considering the treaty as in force "must be regarded as a boon to America; and it was made merely under the persuasion that if accepted it would be accepted with a view to maintain a friendly relation between the two countries, and to avoid in the interval everything which could lead to interrupt it. If this system is followed in America, it will be followed here in every respect with an anxious desire for the continuance of harmony and cordiality."

The same conditional and semi-threatening disposition toward good-will ran through the rest of these instructions. In regard to the boundary convention, his Majesty's government would at all times be ready to reopen the whole subject; "but they can never acquiesce in the precedent which in this as well as in a former instance the American government has endeavored to establish, of agreeing to ratify such parts of a convention as they may select, and of rejecting other stipulations of it, formally agreed upon by a minister invested with full powers for the purpose."

Finally, Merry was to "avoid, as far as possible, any language which might be conceived to be of a menacing or hostile tendency, or which might be construed into an indication of a desire on the part of his Majesty's government to decline any discussion of the several points now pending between the two countries." Lord Harrowby clearly wished to encourage discussion to the utmost. He left the "canons of etiquette" unnoticed, and offered not even a hint at any change of policy meditated by his Government.

So matters remained in England during the last months of President Jefferson's first term. On both sides new movements were intended; but while those of the United States government were foreseen and announced in advance by Merry, those of the British ministry were hidden under a veil of secrecy, which might perhaps have been no more penetrable to Monroe had he remained in London to watch them than they were to him in his retreat at Aranjuez.

To the world at large nothing in the relations of the United States with England, France, or Spain seemed alarming. The world knew little of what was taking place. Only men who stood between these forces could understand their movements and predict the moment of collision; but if these men, like Merry, Turreau, and Yrujo, had been asked March 3, 1805, to point out the brightest part of Jefferson's political horizon, they would probably have agreed with one voice that everything in Europe threatened disaster, and that the only glimpse of blue sky was to be seen on the shores of Africa. The greatest triumph to be then hoped from Jefferson's peace policy was the brilliant close of his only war.

During the year 1804 the little American fleet in the Mediterranean made famous some names which within ten years were to become more famous still. With the "Constitution," the only heavy frigate on the station after the loss of the "Philadelphia," and with half-a-dozen small brigs and schooners, Preble worked manfully at his task of annoying the Pacha of Tripoli. Three years' experience showed that a mere blockade answered no other purpose than to protect in part American commerce. It had not shaken the Pacha in the demand of black-mail as his condition of peace. Bainbridge, still held a prisoner in the town, believed that Jefferson must choose between paying what the Pacha asked, or sending eight or ten thousand men to attack him in his castle. Black-mail was the life of the small pirate rulers, and they could not abandon it without making a precedent fatal to themselves, and inviting insurrection from their subjects. Preble could only strike the coast with fear; and during the summer of 1804 he began a series of dashing assaults with the "Constitution," helped by four new craft,—the "Argus" and "Syren," fine sixteen-gun brigs; the "Nautilus" and "Vixen," fourteen-gun schooners; the "Enterprise," of twelve guns, and a captured Tripolitan brig of sixteen guns, re-named the "Scourge,"—all supported by eight small gunboats borrowed from the King of Naples who was also at war with Tripoli. Thus commanding a force of about one hundred and fifty guns, and more than a thousand men, August 3, carrying his flag-ship into the harbor, Preble engaged the Tripolitan batteries at very short range for two hours. Fortunately, the Mussulmans could not or did not depress their guns enough to injure the frigate, and after throwing many broadsides into the batteries and town, Preble retired without losing a man. His gunboat flotilla was equally daring, but not so lucky. One division was commanded by Lieutenant Somers, the other by Stephen Decatur. They attacked the Tripolitan gunboats and captured three, besides sinking more; but James Decatur was killed. A few days afterward, August 7, the attack was repeated, and some five hundred 24-lb. shot were thrown into the batteries and town. August 24 a third bombardment took place within the month; and although Preble knew that Barron was near at hand with a strong reinforcement, August 29 he carried his flotilla a fourth time into the harbor, and again threw several hundred solid shot into the town. A fifth bombardment, the heaviest of all, took place early in September. In these affairs, so poor was the Tripolitan gunnery or courage that the Americans suffered almost no loss beyond that of a few spars. The only serious disaster, besides the death of James Decatur, was never explained. Preble, wishing to try the effect of a fire-ship, on the night of September 4 sent one of his best officers, Lieutenant Somers, into the harbor with the ketch "Intrepid" filled with powder, bombs, and shell. The "Argus," "Vixen," and "Nautilus" escorted Somers to shoal water, and waited for him to rejoin them in his boats. They saw the batteries fire upon him; then they heard a sudden and premature explosion. All night the three cruisers waited anxiously outside, but Somers never returned. He and his men vanished; no vestige or tidings of them could ever be found.

Considering Preble's narrow means, the economy of the Department, and the condition of his small vessels, nothing in American naval history was more creditable than the vigor of his blockade in the summer of 1804; but he could not confidently assert that any number of such attacks would force the Pacha to make peace. A week after the loss of Somers in the "Intrepid" Commodore Samuel Barron arrived, bringing with him nearly the whole available navy of the United States, and relieved Preble from the command. Preble returned home, and was rewarded for his services by a gold medal from Congress. Two years afterward he died of consumption.

Barron had with him such a force as the United States

never before or since sent in hostile array across the ocean,—two forty-fours, the "Constitution" and the "President;" two thirty-eight gun frigates, the "Constellation" and the "Congress;" the "Essex," of thirty-two guns; the new brigs, "Hornet" of eighteen, and the "Syren" and "Argus" of sixteen; the twelve-gun schooners "Vixen," "Nautilus," and "Enterprise;" ten new, well-built American gunboats; and two bomb-vessels. With the exception of the frigates "Chesapeake" and "United States," hardly a sea-going vessel was left at home. Commanded by young officers like John Rodgers and Stephen Decatur, Chauncey, Stewart, and Isaac Hull, such a squadron reflected credit on Robert Smith's administration of the navy.

Nevertheless the Pacha did not yield, and Barron was obliged by the season to abandon hope of making his strength immediately felt. Six months later the commodore, owing to ill-health, yielded the command to John Rodgers, while the Pacha was still uninjured by the squadron. As the summer of 1805 approached, fear of Rodgers's impending attack possibly helped to turn the Pacha's mind toward concession; but his pacific temper was also much affected by events on land, in which appeared so striking a combination of qualities,—enterprise and daring so romantic and even Quixotic that for at least half a century every boy in America listened to the story with the same delight with which he read the Arabian Nights.

A Connecticut Yankee, William Eaton, was the hero of the adventure. Born in 1764, Eaton had led a checkered career. At nineteen he was a sergeant in the Revolutionary army. After the peace he persisted, against harassing difficulties, in obtaining what was then thought a classical education; in his twenty-seventh year he took a degree at Dartmouth. He next opened a school in Windsor, Vermont, and was chosen clerk to the Vermont legislature. Senator Bradley, in 1792, procured for him a captain's commission in the United States army. His career in the service was varied by insubordination, disobedience to orders, charges, counter-charges, a court-martial, and a sentence of suspension not confirmed by the Secretary of War. In 1797 he was sent as consul to Tunis, where he remained until the outbreak of the war with Tripoli in 1801.

Tunis was the nearest neighbor to Tripoli, about four hundred miles away; and the consul held a position of much delicacy and importance. In the year 1801 an elder brother of the reigning Pacha of Tripoli resided in Tunis, and to him Eaton turned in the hope of using his services. This man, Hamet Caramelli, the rightful Pacha of Tripoli, had been driven into exile some eight or nine years before by a rebellion which placed his younger brother Yusuf on the throne. Eaton conceived the idea of restoring Hamet, and by this act of strength impressing all the Mahometan Powers with terror of the United States. In pursuit of this plan he spent more than twenty thousand dollars, embroiled himself with the Bey of Tunis, quarrelled with the naval commanders, and in 1803 returned to America to lay his case before the President and Congress.

Although no one could be surprised that the President and his Cabinet hesitated to put themselves without reserve in the hands of an adventurer, Eaton's anger was extreme at finding the Government earnest for peace rather than war. Himself a Connecticut Federalist, a close friend of Timothy Pickering, he expressed his feelings in his private letters with the bitterness as well as with the humor of his class.[1]

"I waited on the President and the Attorney-General. One of them was civil, and the other grave. . . . I endeavored to enforce conviction on the mind of Mr. Lincoln of the necessity of meeting the aggressions of Barbary by retaliation. He waived the subject, and amused me with predictions of a political millennium which was about to happen in the United States. The millennium was to usher in upon us as the irresistible consequence of the goodness of heart, integrity of mind, and correctness of disposition of Mr. Jefferson. All nations, even pirates and savages, were to be moved by the influence of his persuasive virtue and masterly skill in diplomacy."

Eaton's interviews probably took place at the moment when the Louisiana treaty confirmed the Cabinet in its peace policy and in reliance on diplomacy. In March, 1804, Eaton

[1] Life of General William Eaton, Brookfield, 1813, p. 262.

succeeded in returning to the Mediterranean as naval agent, but without special powers for the purpose he had in mind.

"The President becomes reserved; the Secretary of War 'believes we had better pay tribute,'— he said this to me in his own office. Gallatin, like a cowardly Jew, shrinks behind the counter. Mr. Madison 'leaves everything to the Secretary of the Navy Department.' And I am ordered on the expedition by Secretary Smith,—who, by the by, is as much of a gentleman and a soldier as his relation with the Administration will suffer,—without any special instructions to regulate my conduct."

With no other authority to act as a military officer than a vague recommendation from the President as a man who was likely to be extremely useful to Barron, Eaton returned with Barron's large squadron. He felt himself ill-treated, for he was irritable and self-asserting by nature, and was haunted by a fixed idea too unreasonable for the President to adopt; but he chose to act without authority rather than not act at all, for he was born an adventurer, and difficulties which seemed to cooler heads insurmountable were nothing in his eyes. Sept. 5, 1804, he arrived at Malta, and thence sailed to Alexandria, for in the meanwhile Hamet had been driven to take refuge in Egypt, and Eaton on reaching Cairo, Dec. 8, 1804, found that the object of his search was shut up in Minyeh on the Nile with some rebellious Mamelukes, besieged by the viceroy's troops. After infinite exertions and at no little personal danger, Eaton brought Hamet to Alexandria, where they collected some five hundred men, of whom one hundred were Christians recruited on the spot. Eaton made a convention with Hamet, arranged a plan of joint operations with Barron, and then at about the time when President Jefferson was delivering his second Inaugural Address, the navy agent led his little army into the desert with the courage of Alexander the Great, to conquer an African kingdom.

So motley a horde of Americans, Greeks, Tripolitans, and Arab camel-drivers had never before been seen on the soil of Egypt. Without discipline, cohesion, or sources of supply, even without water for days, their march of five hundred miles was a sort of miracle. Eaton's indomitable obstinacy

barely escaped ending in his massacre by the Arabs, or by
their desertion in a mass with Hamet at their head; yet in
about six weeks they succeeded, April 17, 1805, in reaching
Bomba, where to Eaton's consternation and despair he found
no American ships.[1]

"Nothing could prevail on our Arabs to believe that any
had been there. They abused us as imposters and infidels,
and said we had drawn them into that situation with
treacherous views. All began now to think of the means of
individual safety; and the Arabs came to a resolution to
separate from us the next morning. I recommended an attempt to get into Derne. This was thought impracticable. I
went off with my Christians, and kept up fires upon a high
mountain in our rear all night. At eight the next morning,
at the instant when our camp was about breaking up, the
Pacha's casnadar, Zaid, who had ascended the mountain for
a last look-out, discovered *a sail*! It was the 'Argus;' Captain Hull had seen our smokes, and stood in. Language is
too poor to paint the joy and exultation which this messenger of life excited in every breast."

Drawing supplies from the brig the little army rested a few
days; and then, April 25, moved against Derne, where they
found the town held by a garrison of eight hundred men who
had thrown up earthworks and loopholed the terraces and
houses for musketry. Eaton sent to the governor a flag of
truce, which was sent back with the Eastern message,—"My
head, or yours!" Three cruisers, the "Nautilus," "Argus," and
"Hornet," acted in concert with Eaton, and a vigorous combined attack, April 27, drove the governor and his garrison
from the town. Eaton received a ball through the left wrist,
but could not afford to be disabled, for on the news of his
arrival a large force was sent from Tripoli to dislodge him;
and he was obliged to fight another little battle, May 13,
which would have been a massacre had not the ships' guns
held the Tripolitans in awe. Skirmishing continued another
month without further results. Eaton had not the force to
advance upon Tripoli, which was nearly seven hundred miles

[1] Life of Eaton, p. 328.

to the westward, and Hamet found no such popular support at Derne as he had hoped.

What influence Eaton's success at Derne had on the Pacha at Tripoli was never perfectly understood; but the Pacha knew that Rodgers was making ready for an assault, beside which the hottest of Preble's bombardments would seem gentle; Eaton at Derne with Hamet was an incessant and indefinite threat; his own subjects were suffering, and might at any moment break into violence; a change of ruler was so common a matter, as Yusuf had reason to remember, that in the alternative of losing his throne and head in one way or the other, he decided that peace was less hazardous than war. Immediately upon hearing that his troops had failed to retake Derne, he entered into negotiations with Tobias Lear, the American Consul-General at Algiers, who had come to Tripoli for the purpose; and on this occasion the Pacha negotiated with all the rapidity that could be wished. June 3, 1805, he submitted to the disgrace of making peace without being expressly paid for it, and Lear on his side consented to ransom the crew of the "Philadelphia" for sixty thousand dollars.

When Eaton learned what Lear had done, his anger was great and not unreasonable. That Lear should have made a treaty which sacrificed Eaton's Mahometan allies, and paid sixty thousand dollars for the imprisoned seamen at a moment when Eaton held Derne, and could, as he thought, with two hundred marines on shore and an immense fleet at sea drive the Pacha out of his dominions within six weeks, was astonishing. Lear's only excuse was the fear of causing a massacre of the "Philadelphia's" crew,—a reason which Eaton thought unfounded and insufficient, and which was certainly, from a military point of view, inadmissible. The treaty left the Mahometan allies at Derne to be massacred, and threw Hamet on Eaton's hands. Deposited at Syracuse with a suite of thirty persons without means of support, Caramelli became a suppliant for alms to the United States Congress. Eaton declared the treaty disgraceful, and thenceforth his grievances against the government took an acute form. The settlement of his accounts was slow and difficult. He returned to America and received great attentions, which made him none the less loud in complaint, until at last he died in 1811 a victim to drink and to craving for excitement. Eaton was beyond question a man of extraordinary energies and genius; he had even the rare courage to displease his own Federalist friends in 1807, because of defending Jefferson who had done nothing for him, but who at a critical moment represented in his eyes the Union.

Meanwhile peace with Tripoli was obtained without tribute, but at the cost of sixty thousand dollars, and at the expense of Eaton and his desperate band of followers at Derne. Hamet Caramelli received at last a small sum of money from Congress, and through American influence was some years afterward made governor of Derne. Thus after four years of unceasing effort the episode of the Tripolitan war came to a triumphant end. Its chief result was to improve the navy and give it a firmer hold on popular sympathy. If the once famous battles of Truxton and the older seamen were ignored by the Republicans, Preble and Rodgers, Decatur and Hull, became brilliant names; the midnight death of Somers was told in every farmhouse; the hand-to-hand struggles of Decatur against thrice his numbers inflamed the imagination of school-boys who had never heard that Jefferson and his party once declaimed against a navy. Even the blindest could see that one more step would bring the people to the point so much dreaded by Jefferson, of wishing to match their forty-fours against some enemy better worthy of their powers than the pirates of Tripoli.

There was strong reason to think that this wish might soon be gratified; for on the same day when Lear, in the "Essex," appeared off Tripoli and began his negotiation for peace, Monroe's travelling-carriage rumbled through the gates of Madrid and began its dusty journey across the plains of Castile, bearing an angry and disappointed diplomatist from one humiliation to another.

HISTORY OF
THE UNITED STATES
OF AMERICA

DURING THE SECOND ADMINISTRATION OF

THOMAS JEFFERSON

1805–1809

Contents

Chapter I

A SECOND TIME President Jefferson appeared at the Capitol, escorted with due formalities by a procession of militia-men and other citizens; and once more he delivered an inaugural address, "in so low a voice that not half of it was heard by any part of the crowded auditory."[1] The second Inaugural roused neither the bitterness nor the applause which greeted the first, although in part it was intended as a cry of triumph over the principles and vanishing power of New England.

Among Jefferson's manuscripts he preserved a curious memorandum explaining the ideas of this address. As the first Inaugural declared the principles which were to guide the government in Republican hands, the second should report the success of these principles, and recall the results already reached. The task deserved all the eloquence and loftiness of thought that philosophy could command; for Jefferson had made a democratic polity victorious at home and respectable in the world's eyes, and the privilege of hearing him reaffirm his doctrines and pronounce their success was one that could never be renewed. The Moses of democracy, he had the glory of leading his followers into their promised and conquered Canaan.

Jefferson began by renewing the professions of his foreign policy: —

> "With nations, as with individuals, our interests, soundly calculated, will ever be found inseparable from our moral duties; and history bears witness to the fact that a just nation is taken on its word, when recourse is had to armaments and wars to bridle others."

The sentiments were excellent; but many of Jefferson's followers must have asked themselves in what history they could find the fact, which the President asserted, that a just nation was taken on its word; and they must have been still more

[1] Diary of J. Q. Adams (March 4, 1805), i. 373.

perplexed to name the nation, just or unjust, which was taken on its word by any other in the actual condition of the world. Without dwelling on this topic, which had already become one of interest in the councils of his Cabinet, Jefferson, passing to practical questions involved in redemption of debt, advanced a new idea.

"Redemption once effected," he said, "the revenue thereby liberated may, by a just repartition among the States and a corresponding amendment of the Constitution, be applied, *in time of peace*, to rivers, canals, roads, arts, manufactures, education, and other great objects within each State. *In time of war*,—if injustice, by ourselves or others, must sometimes produce war,—increased as the same revenue will be increased by population and consumption, and aided by other resources reserved for that crisis, it may meet within the year all the expenses of the year without encroaching on the rights of future generations by burdening them with the debts of the past. War will then be but a suspension of useful works, and a return to a state of peace a return to the progress of improvement."

Ten years earlier, in the mouth of President Washington, this sentiment would have been generally denounced as proof of monarchical designs. That Jefferson was willing not only to assume powers for the central government, but also to part from his States-rights associates and to gratify the Northern democrats by many concessions of principle, his first Administration had already proved; but John Randolph might wonder to see him stride so fast and far toward what had been ever denounced as Roman imperialism and corruption; to hear him advise a change of the Constitution in order to create an annual fund for public works, for the arts, for education, and even for such manufactures as the people might want,—a fund which was to be distributed to the States, thus putting in the hands of the central government an instrument of corruption, and making the States stipendiaries of Congress. Every principle of the Republican party, past or to come, was put to nought by a policy which contradicted the famous sentiment of Jefferson's first annual message: "Sound principles will not justify our taxing the industry of our fellow-citizens to accumulate treasure for wars to happen we know not when, and which might not perhaps happen but from the temptations offered by that treasure." Yet pregnant as this new principle might be in connection with the Constitution and the Union, its bearing on foreign affairs was more startling. Jefferson, the apostle of peace, asked for a war fund which should enable his government to wage indefinite hostilities without borrowing money!

Quitting this dangerous ground, the President spoke of the Louisiana purchase. Then followed a paragraph upon religion. Next he came to the subject of the Indians, and chose this unusual medium for enforcing favorite philosophical doctrines. The memorandum written to explain his address declared the reasons that led him to use the mask of Indian philanthropy to disguise an attack upon conservatism.[1]

"Every respecter of science," said this memorandum, "every friend to political reformation, must have observed with indignation the hue-and-cry raised against philosophy and the rights of man; and it really seems as if they would be overborne, and barbarism, bigotry, and despotism would recover the ground they have lost by the advance of the public understanding. I have thought the occasion justified some discountenance of these anti-social doctrines, some testimony against them; but not to commit myself in direct warfare on them, I have thought it best to say what is directly applied to the Indians only, but admits by inference a more general extension."

In truth, under the lead of Napoleon and Pitt, Europe seemed bent on turning back the march of time and renewing the bigotry and despotism of the Middle Ages; but this occasion hardly dignified Jefferson's method of bearing testimony against the danger, by not committing himself to direct warfare upon it, but by applying to Indians the homily which by inference included the churches of New England.

"The aboriginal inhabitants of these countries," said the President to his great audience, "I have regarded with the commiseration their history inspires. Endowed with the

[1] Jefferson's Writings (Ford), viii. 341.

faculties and the rights of men, breathing an ardent love of liberty and independence, and occupying a country which left them no desire but to be undisturbed, the stream of overflowing population from other regions directed itself on these shores."

If the Boston newspapers were not weary of ridiculing Jefferson's rhetoric, this sentence was fitted to rouse their jaded amusement; but in a few moments they had reason to feel other emotions. He said that he had done what humanity required, and had tried to teach the Indians agriculture and other industries in order to prepare them for new conditions of life,—a claim not only true, but also honorable to him. Unfortunately these attempts met with obstacles from the Indians themselves:—

"They are combated by the habits of their bodies, prejudice of their minds, ignorance, pride, and the influence of interested and crafty individuals among them, who feel themselves something in the present order of things, and fear to become nothing in any other. These persons inculcate a sanctimonious reverence for the customs of their ancestors; that whatsoever they did must be done through all time; that reason is a false guide, and to advance under its counsel, in their physical, moral, or political condition, is perilous innovation; that their duty is to remain as their Creator made them, ignorance being safety, and knowledge full of danger. In short, my friends, among them is seen the action and counter-action of good sense and bigotry; they too have their anti-philosophers, who find an interest in keeping things in their present state, who dread reformation, and exert all their faculties to maintain the ascendency of habit over the duty of improving our reason and obeying its mandates."

Gallatin remonstrated in vain against this allusion to New England habits;[1] the President could not resist the temptation to strike once more his old enemies. Gallatin, whose sense of humor was keener than that of Jefferson, must have been amused by the travesty of New England under the war-paint

[1] Gallatin's Writings, i. 227.

and blankets of the Choctaws and Kickapoos; but Jefferson was never more serious than in believing that the people of Massachusetts and Connecticut were held in darkness by a few interested "medicine-men," and that he could, without committing himself in direct warfare, insult the clergy, lawyers, and keen-witted squirarchy of New England, thus held up "by inference" to the world as the equivalent to so many savages.

The rest of the Inaugural was chiefly devoted to the press and its licentiousness. Jefferson expressed himself strongly in regard to the slanders he had received, and even hinted that he would be glad to see the State laws of libel applied to punish the offenders; but he pointed out that slander had no political success, and that it might safely be disregarded as a political weapon. He urged "doubting brethren" to give up their fears and prejudices, and to join with the mass of their fellow-citizens. "In the mean time let us cherish them with patient affection; let us do them justice, and more than justice, in all competitions of interest." Finally, as though to silence the New-England pulpit, he closed with a few words which the clergy might perhaps think misplaced in the mouth of so earnest a deist,—an invocation of "that Being in whose hands we are, who led our forefathers, as Israel of old," to the "country flowing with all the necessaries and comforts of life, . . . and to whose goodness I ask you to join with me in supplications."

The Second Inaugural strode far beyond the first in the path of democracy, away from the landmarks of Virginia republicanism, betraying what Jefferson's friends and enemies alike thought a craving for popularity. If this instinct sometimes led him to forget principles he had once asserted, and which he would some day again declare vital, the quality was so amiable as to cover many shortcomings; but its influence on national growth could not be disputed. Jefferson cherished but one last desire,—to reach the end of his next term without disaster. He frankly expressed this feeling in a letter written to General Heath soon after the autumn election of 1804, which gave him the electoral vote of Massachusetts:—

"I sincerely join you," said he, "in congratulations on the

return of Massachusetts into the fold of the Union. This is truly the case wherein we may say, 'This our brother was dead, and is alive again; and was lost, and is found.' It is but too true that our Union could not be pronounced entirely sound while so respectable a member as Massachusetts was under morbid affection. All will now come to rights. . . . The new century opened itself by committing us on a boisterous ocean; but all is now subsiding; peace is smoothing our path at home and abroad; and if we are not wanting in the practice of justice and moderation, our tranquillity and prosperity may be preserved until increasing numbers shall leave us nothing to fear from abroad. With England we are in cordial friendship; with France in the most perfect understanding; with Spain we shall always be bickering, but never at war till we seek it. Other nations view our course with respect and friendly anxiety. Should we be able to preserve this state of public happiness, and to see our citizens, whom we found so divided, rally to their genuine principles, I shall hope yet to enjoy the comfort of that general good-will which has been so unfeelingly wrested from me, and to sing at the close of my term the *Nunc dimittis, Domine*, with a satisfaction leaving nothing to desire but the last great audit."[1]

He could not forgive the New England clergy their want of feeling in wresting from him ever so small a share of the general good-will, and he looked forward with impatience to the moment when he should enjoy universal applause and respect. In December, 1804, when this letter was written, he felt confident that his splendid triumph would last unchecked to the end of his public career; but the prize of general good-will, which seemed then almost won, continually eluded his grasp. The election of November, 1804, was followed by the session of 1804–1805, which stirred bad blood even in Virginia, and betrayed a spirit of faction among his oldest friends. His Inaugural Address of March, 1805, with its mixture of bitter-sweet, was answered within a few weeks by Massachusetts. At the April election the Federalists reversed the result of November, and re-elected Caleb Strong as

[1] Jefferson to General Heath, Dec. 13, 1804; Jefferson MSS.

governor by a vote of about 35,200 against 33,800, with a Federalist majority in the Legislature. Even in Pennsylvania divisions among Jefferson's followers increased, until in the autumn of 1805 Duane and Leib set up a candidate of their own choice for governor, and forced McKean, Dallas, and Gallatin's friends to unite with the Federalists in order to re-elect McKean. Jefferson balanced anxiously between these warring factions, trying to offend neither Duane nor John Randolph, nor even Burr, while he still drew the mass of moderate Federalists to sympathize in his views.

Thus the new Presidential term began, bringing with it little sign of change. The old arrangements were continued, with but one exception. Madison, Gallatin, Robert Smith, and Dearborn remained in the Cabinet; but Attorney-General Lincoln resigned, and Robert Smith asked to be transferred from the Navy Department to the Attorney-General's office.[1] After some hesitation Jefferson yielded to Smith's request and consented to the transfer. As Smith's successor in the Navy Department Jefferson selected Jacob Crowninshield, a member of Congress from Massachusetts, who was then at Washington. Crowninshield, in consequence of his wife's objection to leaving her family, declined the offer, Jan. 29, 1805,[2] but the President nevertheless sent the nomination to the Senate, March 2, 1805, together with that of Robert Smith, "now Secretary of the Navy to be Attorney-General of the United States." The same day the Senate confirmed both appointments, and the commissions were regularly issued, March 3,—Robert Smith apparently ceasing thenceforward to possess any legal authority over the Navy Department.

Nevertheless Crowninshield persisted in declining the office, and Robert Smith continued to act as Secretary of the Navy, probably by the verbal request of the President. At length he consented to retain his old position permanently, and Jefferson sought for a new attorney-general. He offered the post, June 15, to John Julius Pringle of South Carolina, who declined. He then offered it, July 14, to John Thomson Mason, who also declined. August 7, Jefferson wrote to

[1] Jefferson to Robert Smith, Jan. 3, 1805; Jefferson MSS.
[2] Crowninshield to Jefferson, Jan. 29, 1805; Jefferson MSS. State Department Archives.

Senator Breckinridge of Kentucky, asking him to accept the office of attorney-general, and a temporary commission was the same day issued to him.

When Congress met, Dec. 2, 1805, Breckinridge was attorney-general under a temporary commission, and Robert Smith, who had ceased to be Secretary of the Navy on the confirmation of his successor, March 3, was acting as secretary under no apparent authority. Dec. 20, 1805, the President sent a message to the Senate making nominations for vacancies which had occurred during the recess, for which commissions had been granted "to the persons herein respectively named." One of these persons was John Breckinridge of Kentucky to be Attorney-General of the United States, and the nomination was duly confirmed. Breckinridge's permanent commission bore date Jan. 17, 1806.

These dates and facts were curious for the reason that Robert Smith, who had ceased to be Secretary of the Navy, March 3, 1805, ceased necessarily to be attorney-general on the confirmation of Breckinridge, and continued to act as Secretary of the Navy without authority of law. The President did not send his name to the Senate, or issue to him a new commission either permanent or temporary. On the official records of the Department of State, not Robert Smith but Jacob Crowninshield was Secretary of the Navy from March 3, 1805, till March 7, 1809, when his successor was appointed, although Jacob Crowninshield died April 15, 1808, and Robert Smith never ceased to act as Secretary of the Navy from his appointment in 1801 to his appointment as Secretary of State in 1809. During the whole period of Jefferson's second administration, his Secretary of the Navy acted by no known authority except the verbal request or permission of the President.

In perfect quiet, disturbed only by rumors of wars abroad, spring crept forward to summer, summer ripened to autumn. Peace was restored with Tripoli; commerce grew apace; the revenue rose to $14,000,000; the Treasury was near a surfeit; no sign appeared of check to the immense prosperity which diffused itself through every rivulet in the wilderness, and the President could see no limit to its future increase. In 1804 he had sent out an expedition under Captain Meriwether Lewis to explore the Louisiana purchase along the course of the Missouri River. May 14, 1804, Lewis and his party began their journey from St. Louis, and without serious difficulty reached the Mandan towns, sixteen hundred and nine miles from the starting point, where, Nov. 1, 1804, they went into winter quarters. April 8, 1805, Lewis resumed his journey to the westward, sending the report of his wanderings to Washington. This report told only of a vast region inhabited by Indian tribes and disturbed by the restless and murderous Sioux, but it served to prove the immensity of the new world which Jefferson's government had given to the American people. Other explorations had been begun along the line of the Red and Washita rivers. In such contributions to human knowledge Jefferson took keen interest, for he had no greater delight than in science and in whatever tended to widen the field of knowledge.

These explorations of the territory beyond the Mississippi had little immediate bearing on the interests of commerce or agriculture; but the government was actively engaged in measures of direct value. July 4, 1805, William Henry Harrison, Governor of the Indiana Territory, closed a bargain with the Wyandots, Ottawas, and other Indian tribes, by which the Indian title over another part of Ohio was extinguished. The Indians thenceforward held within the State of Ohio only the country west of Sandusky and north of the old line fixed by the treaty of Greenville. Within the year the Piankeshaw tribe sold for a small annuity a tract of land in southern Indiana, along the Ohio River, which made the United States government master of the whole north bank of the Ohio to its mouth. These concessions, of the utmost value, were obtained at a trifling cost. "The average price paid for the Indian lands within the last four years," wrote the Secretary of War,[1] "does not amount to one cent per acre." The Chickasaws and Cherokees sold a very large district between the Cumberland and Tennessee rivers in Tennessee, so that thenceforward the road from Knoxville to Nashville passed through no Indian land. In Georgia the Creeks were induced to sell an important territory between the Oconee and Ocmulgee rivers. In these

[1] Dearborn to Robertson, March 20, 1805; State Papers, vol. v.; Indian Affairs, i. 700.

treaties provision was also made for horse-roads through the Creek and Cherokee country, both from Knoxville and from central Georgia to the Mobile River.

Besides the many millions of acres thus gained for immediate improvement, these treaties had no little strategic value in case of war. No foreign country could fail to see that the outlying American settlements were defenceless in their isolation. Even the fort and village at Detroit were separated from the nearest white village by a wide Indian country impassable to wagons or artillery; and the helplessness of such posts was so evident as to impress every observer.

"The principles of our government," said Jefferson when danger at last arose,[1] "leading us to the employment of such moderate garrisons in time of peace as may merely take care of the post, and to a reliance on the neighboring militia for its support in the first moments of war, I have thought it would be important to obtain from the Indians such a cession in the neighborhood of these posts as might maintain a militia proportioned to this object."

This "principle of our government" that the settlers should protect the army, not the army the settlers, was so rigorously carried out that every new purchase of Indian lands was equivalent to providing a new army. The possession of Sandusky brought Detroit nearer its supports; possession of the banks of the Ohio strengthened Indiana. A bridle-path to New Orleans was the first step toward bringing that foreign dependence within reach; and although this path must necessarily pass through Spanish territory, it would enable the government in an emergency to hear from Louisiana within six weeks from the despatch of an order.

In spite of these immense gains, the military situation was still extremely weak. The Indians held in strong force the country west of Sandusky. The boundary between them and the whites was a mere line running from Lake Erie south and west across Ohio, Indiana, and Illinois to the neighborhood of St. Louis. Directly on this boundary line, near Greenville, lived the Shawanese, among whom a warrior named

[1] Message of Jan. 30, 1808; State Papers, vol. v.; Indian Affairs, i. 752.

Tecumthe, and his brother called the Prophet were acquiring an influence hostile to the white men. These Indians, jealous of the rapid American encroachments, maintained relations with the British officials in Canada, and in case of a war between the United States and England they were likely to enter into a British alliance. In this case unless the United States government could control Lake Erie, nothing was more certain than that Detroit and every other post on the Lakes beyond must fall into British hands, and with them the military possession of the whole Northwest. Whether Great Britain could afterward be forced to surrender her conquests remained to be seen.

Even in Kentucky the country between the Tennessee River and the Mississippi still belonged to the Chickasaws; and south of the Tennessee River as far as the Gulf of Mexico, and east to the Ocmulgee, all belonged to Cherokees, Creeks, and Choctaws, who could not boast, like the Chickasaws, that "they had never spilt the blood of a white man." These tribes maintained friendly relations with the Spanish authorities at Mobile and Pensacola, and, like the Shawanese and Northwestern Indians, dreaded the grasping Americans, who were driving them westward. In case of war with Spain, should New Orleans give trouble and invite a Spanish garrison, the Indians might be counted as Spaniards, and the United States government might be required to protect a frontier suddenly thrust back from the Floridas to the Duck River, within thirty miles of Nashville.

The President might well see with relief every new step that brought him within nearer reach of his remote military posts and his proconsular province at New Orleans. That he should dread war was natural, for he was responsible for the safety of the settlements on the Indian frontier, and he knew that in case of sudden war the capture of these posts was certain, and the massacre of their occupants more than probable. New Orleans was an immediate and incessant danger, and hardly a spot between New Orleans and Mackinaw was safe.

Anxiety caused by these perils had probably much to do with the bent of the President's mind toward internal improvements and democratic rather than Virginia principles. In 1803 the United States government became owner of a territory which dwarfed the States themselves, and which at its most important point contained a foreign population governed by military methods. Old political theories had been thrown aside both in the purchase and in the organization of this New World; their observance in its administration was impossible. The Louisiana purchase not only required a military system of government for itself, but also reacted on the other national territory, and through it on the States in their relations to Washington. New England was thrown to the verge of the political system; but New York and Pennsylvania, Georgia and Tennessee, Ohio and Kentucky found many new interests which they wanted the central government to assist, and Virginia, holding the power and patronage of the central government, had every inducement to satisfy these demands.

So it happened that Jefferson gave up his Virginia dogmas, and adopted Gallatin's ideas. They were both jealous of the army and navy; but they were willing to spend money with comparative liberality on internal improvements; and the wisdom of this course was evident. Even in a military point of view, roads and canals were more necessary than forts or ships.

The first evidence of change was the proposed fund for internal improvements and war purposes described in the second Inaugural Address. The suggestion was intended to prepare the public for a relaxation of Gallatin's economy. Although the entire debt could not be paid before 1817, only ten and a half millions of bonds remained to be immediately dealt with. By the year 1809 these ten and a half millions would be discharged; and thereafter Gallatin might reduce his annual payments of principal and interest from $8,000,000 to $4,500,000, freeing an annual sum of $3,500,000 for use in other directions. During the next three years Gallatin was anxious to maintain his old system, and especially to preserve peace with foreign nations; but after the year 1808 he promised to relax his severity, and to provide three or four millions for purposes of internal improvement and defence. The rapid increase of revenue helped to create confidence in this calculation, and to hasten decision as to the use of the promised surplus. The President had already decided to convert it into a permanent reserve fund. He looked forward to the moment when, as he expressed it, he could "begin upon canals, roads, colleges, etc."[1] He no longer talked of "a wise and frugal government which shall restrain men from injuring one another, which shall leave them otherwise free to regulate their own pursuits of industry and improvement, and shall not take from the mouth of labor the bread it has earned;" he rather proposed to devote a third of the national revenues to improvements and to regulation of industries.

This theory of statesmanship was broader than that which he had proclaimed four years earlier. Jefferson proved the liberality and elevation of his mind; and if he did this at some cost to his consistency, he did only what all men had done whose minds kept pace with the movement of their time. So far as he could see, at the threshold of his second term, he had every reason to hope that it would be more successful than his first. He promised to annihilate opposition; and no serious obstacle seemed in his path. No doubt his concessions to the spirit of nationality, in winning support from moderate Federalists and self-interested democrats, alienated a few States-rights Republicans, and might arouse uneasiness among old friends; but to this Jefferson resigned himself. He parted company with the "mere metaphysical subtleties" of John Randolph. Except in his aversion to military measures and to formal etiquette, he stood nearly where President Washington had stood ten years before.

The New England hierarchy might grumble, but at heart Massachusetts was already converted. Only with the utmost difficulty, and at the cost of avoiding every aggressive movement, could the Federalists keep control of their State governments. John Randolph flattered himself that if Jefferson's personal authority were removed from the scale, Virginia would again incline to her old principles; but he was mistaken. So long as Virginia held power, she was certain to use it. At no time since the Declaration of Independence had the prospects of nationality seemed so promising as in the spring of 1805. With the stride of the last four years as a standard for the future, no man could measure the possible effects of the coming four years in extending the powers of the government

---

[1] Jefferson to Gallatin, May 29, 1805; Gallatin's Writings, 232.

and developing the prosperity of the nation. Gallatin already meditated schemes of internal improvements, which included four great thoroughfares across the Alleghanies, while Fulton was nearly ready with the steamboat. The Floridas could not escape the government's grasp. Even New England must at last yield her prejudices to the spirit of democratic nationality.

No one could wonder if Jefferson's head was somewhat turned by the splendors of such a promise. Sanguine by nature, he felt that every day made more secure the grandeur of his destiny. He could scarcely be blamed for putting a high estimate on the value of his services, for in all modesty he might reasonably ask what name recorded in history would stand higher than his own for qualities of the noblest order in statesmanship. Had he not been first to conceive and to put in practice the theories of future democracy? Had he not succeeded in the experiment? Had he not doubled the national domain? Was not his government a model of republican virtues? With what offence against the highest canons of personal merit could he be charged? What ruler of ancient or modern times, what Trajan or Antonine, what Edward or Louis, was more unselfish or was truer to the interests intrusted to his care? Who had proposed to himself a loftier ideal? Among all the kings and statesmen who swayed the power of empire, where could one be found who had looked so far into the future, and had so boldly grappled with its hopes?

Chapter II

DURING THE ADMINISTRATIONS of Jefferson and Madison, the national government was in the main controlled by ideas and interests peculiar to the region south of the Potomac, and only to be understood from a Southern standpoint. Especially its foreign relations were guided by motives in which the Northern people felt little sympathy. The people of the Northern States seemed almost unwilling to know what the people of the Southern States were thinking or doing in certain directions, and their indifference was particularly marked in regard to Florida. Among the varied forms of Southern ambition, none was so constant in influence as the wish to acquire the Floridas, which at moments decided the action of the government in matters of the utmost interest; yet the Northern public, though complaining of Southern favoritism, neither understood nor cared to study the subject, but turned impatiently away whenever the Floridas were discussed, as though this were a local detail which in no way concerned the North. If Florida failed to interest the North, it exercised the more control over the South, and over a government Southern in character and purpose. Neither the politics of the Union nor the development of events could be understood without treating Florida as a subject of the first importance. During the summer and autumn of 1805,— a period which John Randolph justly regarded as the turning point of Republican administration,—Florida actually engrossed the attention of government.

On arriving at Madrid, Jan. 2, 1805, Monroe found Charles Pinckney waiting in no happy temper for a decision in regard to himself. Pinckney's recall was then determined upon, and his successor chosen. He was anxious only to escape the last humiliation of being excluded from the new negotiation by Monroe. From this fear he was soon relieved. Monroe shared his views; allowed him to take part in the conferences, and to put his name to the notes. The two ministers acted in harmony.

Nearly a month was consumed in the necessary preliminaries. Not until Jan. 28, 1805, were matters so far advanced that Monroe could present his first note.[1] Following his instructions, he put forward all the claims which had been so often discussed,—the Spanish and French spoliations; the losses resulting from suppression of the *entrepôt* at New Orleans in 1802; the claim of West Florida, and that to the Rio Bravo. With the note the two envoys enclosed the *projet* of a treaty,—to which could be made only the usual objection to one-sided schemes, that it required Spain to concede every point, and offered no equivalent worth mention. Spain was to cede both the Floridas, and also Texas as far as the Rio Colorado, leaving the district between the Colorado and the Rio Bravo as a border-land not to be further settled. She was to create a commission for arranging the spoliation and *entrepôt* claims; and this commission should also take cognizance of all claims that might be made by Spanish subjects against the United States government.

To this note and *projet* Don Pedro Cevallos quickly replied.[2] Availing himself of an inadvertent sentence in Monroe's opening paragraph, to the effect that it was necessary to examine impartially the several points at issue in each case, Cevallos informed the Americans that in accordance with their wish he would first examine each point separately, and then proceed to negotiation. He proposed to begin with the claims convention of August, 1802.

Commonly nothing gratified American diplomatists more than to discuss questions which they were ordered to take in charge. Yet the readiness shown by Cevallos to gratify this instinct struck Monroe as a bad sign; he saw danger of lowering the national tone, and even of becoming ridiculous, if he allowed the Spaniards to discuss indefinitely claims which the United States had again and again asserted to be too plain for discussion. He felt too the influence of Pinckney, who had never ceased to urge that nothing could be done with the Spanish government except through fear or force. He could not refuse discussion, but he entered into it with the intention of promptly cutting it short.[3]

To cut the discussion short was precisely what Cevallos

[1] Monroe and Pinckney to Cevallos, Jan. 28, 1805; State Papers, ii. 636.
[2] Cevallos to Monroe and Pinckney, Jan. 31, 1805; State Papers, ii. 636.
[3] Monroe and Pinckney to Madison, May 23, 1805; State Papers, ii. 667.

meant should not be done; and a contest began, in which the Spaniard had every advantage. Monroe replied to the Spanish note of January 31 by imposing an ultimatum at once.[1] "We consider it our duty to inform your Excellency that we cannot consent to any arrangement which does not provide for the whole subject" of the claims, including the French spoliations. "It is in his Majesty's power, by the answer which you give, to fix at once the relations which are to subsist in future between the two nations." Cevallos, leaving the ultimatum and the French spoliations unnoticed, rejoined by discussing the conditions which the King had placed on his consent to ratify the claims convention of 1802.[2] Taking up first the Mobile Act, he expressed in strong terms his opinion of it, and of the explanation given to it by the President. Nevertheless, he withdrew his demand that the Act should be annulled. The King's " well-founded motives of complaint in respect to that Act still exist," he said, "and his Majesty intends to keep them in mind, that satisfaction may be given by the United States; but as it relates to ratifying the convention of August, 1802, his Majesty agrees from this time to be satisfied in this respect." The question of French spoliations he reserved for separate discussion.

Monroe replied briefly by referring to his ultimatum, and by inviting discussion of the boundary question; but Cevallos, instead of taking up the matter of boundaries in his next note, discussed the French spoliation claims and the right of deposit at New Orleans.[3] To rebut the first, he produced a letter from Talleyrand dated July 27, 1804, in which Napoleon announced that neither Spain nor the United States must touch these claims, under penalty of incurring the Emperor's severe displeasure. In regard to the right of deposit, Cevallos took still stronger ground: —

"The edict of the Intendant of New Orleans, suspending the deposit of American produce in that city, did not interrupt, nor was it the intention to interrupt, the navigation of the Mississippi; consequently these pretended injuries

[1] Pinckney and Monroe to Cevallos, Feb. 5, 1805; State Papers, ii. 640
[2] Cevallos to Monroe and Pinckney, Feb. 10, 1805; State Papers, ii. 541.
[3] Cevallos to Monroe and Pinckney, Feb. 16, 1805; State Papers, ii. 643.

are reduced to this small point,—that for a short time the vessels loaded in the stream instead of taking in their cargoes at the wharves. . . . If the erroneous opinions which were formed in the United States, if the complaints published in the papers of your country,—as false as they were repeated,—that the navigation of the Mississippi was interrupted, if the virulent writings by which the public mind was heated, and which led to compromit the American government and tarnish the good name of that of Spain, were causes that the inhabitants of the western territory of the United States could not form a correct idea of what passed at New Orleans; and if, in this uncertainty, they were disappointed in the extraction of their produce, or suffered other inconveniences,—they ought to attribute the same to internal causes, such as the writings before mentioned, filled with inflammatory falsehoods, the violence of enthusiastic partisans, and other occurrences which on those occasions served to conceal the truth. The Government of Spain, so far from being responsible for the prejudices occasioned by these errors and erroneous ideas, ought in justice to complain of the irregular conduct pursued by various writers and other individuals in the United States, which was adapted to exasperate and mislead the public opinion, and went to divulge sentiments the most ignominious, and absurdities the most false, against the government of his Majesty and his accredited good faith."

Not satisfied with this rebuttal, Cevallos added that the persons who complained of this trifling inconvenience "had been enjoying the rights of deposit for four years more than was stipulated in the treaty, and this notwithstanding the great prejudice it occasioned to his Majesty's revenue, by making New Orleans the centre of a most scandalous contraband trade, the profits of which it is not improbable but that some of those individuals have in part received." Finally, he affirmed the Intendant's right to prohibit the deposit.

On receiving this paper, Monroe hesitated whether to break off the negotiation; but quickly came to the decision not to do so. His instructions expressly authorized him to abandon the *entrepôt* claims; while a rupture founded on the

French spoliations, in the face of Talleyrand's threats, was rupture with France as well as with Spain, and exceeded his authority. He concluded to go on, although he saw that every new step involved new dangers.

Before Monroe had prepared a reply to the sharp letter on the claims convention, Cevallos wrote again.[1] In this letter, dated February 24, he discussed the West Florida boundary, and contented himself with stating the Spanish case as it stood on the treaties and public evidence. His argument contained no new points, but was evidently intended to lure the Americans into endless discussion. Monroe was obliged to follow where Cevallos led. February 26 he replied to the Spanish note on the claims. Beginning with complaints that Cevallos had not met with directness the American proposals; branching into other complaints that he had renewed propositions which Monroe had already declared incompatible with the rights of the United States; that he had charged the American government with trying to obtain double payment for the same loss, and had branded the whole American people as being in league with smugglers; that he had attacked the freedom of the press, and had called the right of deposit a charity of King Charles,—after adding that "it was impossible for us to have received a note which could have been more unexpected," the two American envoys began to discuss the French spoliation claims, "on the presumption that no premeditated outrage was intended."[2]

After a long argument on the French spoliations, Monroe's note next reached the most delicate point in discussion,—the positive order of Napoleon forbidding recognition of the claims. Treating the order as though it were only an expression of opinions, Monroe said, "We have received them with the consideration which is due to the very respectable authority from which they emanate. On all treaties between independent Powers each party has a right to form its own opinion. Every nation is the guardian of its own honor and rights; and the Emperor is too sensible of what is due to his own glory, and entertains too high a respect for the United States, to wish them to abandon a just sense of what is due

[1] Cevallos to Monroe and Pinckney, Feb. 24, 1805; State Papers, ii. 644.
[2] Monroe and Pinckney to Cevallos, Feb. 26, 1805; State Papers, ii. 646.

to their own." Appealing finally to the positive orders of his own government, Monroe repeated that on these claims he must insist. Cevallos replied with a disavowal of "premeditated outrage;" and there, March 1, 1805, after Monroe had passed two months in Spain, he found himself at his starting-point, at a loss how to go forward or to recede.

Monroe received early in February Talleyrand's letter of Dec. 21, 1804, on the boundary of West Florida;[1] he next suffered the mortification of listening to Talleyrand's order of July 27, 1804, forbidding Spain to "condescend" to pay or even to discuss the French spoliation claims; and from these documents he saw that for nearly a year past the French and Spanish governments had combined to entrap and humiliate him. The fault was his own, for he had received plain, not to say rude, warning; but he was perhaps only the more angry on that account, and in his irritation he undertook to terrify Napoleon. March 1, 1805, under the full consciousness of his situation, he wrote to Armstrong at Paris;[2] —

"It cannot be doubted that if our Government could be prevailed on to give ground, that of France would be very glad of it, as it would be to take us and all our concerns, especially our funds, under its care. We are inclined to believe, with almost equal confidence, if we are firm, and show that we are not only able but resolved to take care of ourselves, that she will let us do so, and in regard to this question with Spain throw her weight into our scale to promote an adjustment between us on the fair principles insisted on by our Government. To bring her to this, she must clearly understand that the negotiation is about to break up without doing anything, and that the failure is entirely owing to the part she has taken against us. When she sees that this is the literal fact, I do not think that her government will expose itself to the consequences resulting from it. It is not prepared to quarrel with us for many reasons: first, as we are a republic, and that system of government too recently overset there, and the one established in its stead too feebly founded, to make it a desirable object

[1] Monroe's diary at Aranjuez, March 16, 1805; Monroe MSS.
[2] Monroe to Armstrong, March 1, 1805; MSS. State Department Archives.

with the Emperor; second, as she relies altogether for sup
plies on our flag, and on our merchants and people for
many other friendly offices in the way of trade, which none
others can render; third, as our government pursues, by
prohibiting our trade with St. Domingo, and in many
other respects, a system of the most friendly accommodation to the interests of France, she ought not to hazard
those advantages if there were no other objections to a rupture with us; fourth,—but there are other and much
stronger objections to it,—we should come to a good understanding with England. . . . These considerations incline us to think that a rupture with us is an event which
of all others she least seeks at the present time; and that it
is only necessary to let her see distinctly that one with
Spain is on the point of taking place, and will be owing
altogether to her support of her pretensions, to induce
France to change her policy and tone in the points depending here."

Pursuing this train of reasoning, Monroe tested its correctness by challenging a direct issue of courage. His letter, thus
inspired, reached Paris in due time, and its ideas were pressed
by Armstrong on members of the French government. Their
answer was prompt and final; it was instantly reported by
Armstrong to Monroe in a letter[1] so pregnant with meaning
that two of its sentences may be said to have decided the fate
of Jefferson's second administration: —

"On the subject of indemnity for the suspended right of
deposit (professing to know nothing of the ground on
which the interruption had been given) they would offer
no opinion. On that of reparation for spoliations committed on our commerce by Frenchmen within the territory of
his Catholic Majesty, they were equally prompt and decisive, declaring that our claim, having nothing of solidity in
it, must be abandoned.

"With regard to boundary, we have, they said, already
given an opinion, and see no cause to change it. To the
question, What would be the course of this government in

[1] Armstrong to Monroe, March 12 and 18, 1805; State Papers, ii. 636.

the event of a rupture between us and Spain? they answered, We can neither doubt nor hesitate,—we must take
part with Spain; and our note of the 30th Frimaire [Dec.
21, 1804] was intended to communicate and impress this
idea."

This stern message left Monroe helpless. To escape from
Madrid without suffering some personal mortification was his
best hope; and fortunately Godoy took no pleasure in personalities. The Spaniard was willing to let Monroe escape as soon
as his defeat should be fairly recorded. The month of March
had nearly passed before Monroe received Armstrong's letter;
meanwhile Cevallos consumed the time in discussing the West
Florida boundary. At the end of the month Monroe, fully
aware at last of his situation, attempted to force an issue.
March 30 he wrote to Cevallos that he was weary of delay:[1]

"It neither comports with the object of the present mission nor its duties to continue the negotiation longer than
it furnishes a well-founded expectation that the just and
friendly policy which produced it, on the part of the United
States, is cherished with the same views by his Catholic
Majesty."

Unfortunately he had no excuse for breaking abruptly a negotiation which he had himself invited; and Cevallos meant
to give him at that stage no such excuse, for the important
question of the Texan boundary remained to be discussed,
and Talleyrand's instructions on that point must be placed on
record by Spain.

Monroe wrote to Cevallos, April 9, that he considered "the
negotiation as essentially terminated by what has already occurred.[2] . . . Should his Majesty's government think proper
to invite another issue, on it will the responsibility rest for the
consequences. The United States are not unprepared for, or
unequal to, any crisis which may occur." Three days later he
repeated the wish to " withdraw from a situation which, while
it compromits the character of our government, cannot be
agreeable to ourselves."[3] Cevallos took no notice of the

---

[1] Pinckney and Monroe to Cevallos, March 30, 1805; State Papers, ii. 657.
[2] Monroe and Pinckney to Cevallos, April 9, 1805; State Papers, ii. 658.
[3] Monroe and Pinckney to Cevallos, April 12, 1805; State Papers, ii. 660.

threats, and contented himself with repelling the idea that the blame of breaking off the negotiation should rest upon him. Nevertheless he hastened to record the opinion of his Government in regard to the last claim of the United States,—the Texan boundary.

Here again Cevallos followed the guidance of Talleyrand. The dividing-line between Louisiana and Texas, he said, ought to be decided by the line between the French and Spanish settlements. The French post of Natchitoches, on the Red River, was distant seven leagues from the Spanish post of Nuestra Señora de los Adaes; and therefore the boundary of Louisiana should run between these two points southward, along the watershed, until it reached the Gulf of Mexico between the Marmentou and the Calcasieu,—a boundary which deprived the United States not only of Texas, but of an important territory afterward included in the State of Louisiana.[1]

Eager as Monroe was to close the negotiation, he could not leave this note without reply; and accordingly he consumed another week in preparing more complaints of Cevallos' dilatory conduct, and in proving that Texas was included in the grant made by Louis XIV. to Anthony Crozat in 1712. After disposing of that subject, he again begged for a conclusion. "As every point has been thus fully discussed, we flatter ourselves that we shall now be honored with your Excellency's propositions for the arrangement of the whole business."[2] He flattered himself in vain; ten days passed without an answer. May 1, at a private interview, he tried to obtain some promise of action, without better result than the usual obliging Spanish expressions; a week afterward he made another attempt, with the same reply, followed on Monroe's part by an offer to concede even the point of dignity. "Would Señor Cevallos listen to a new and more advantageous offer on the part of the United States?" Cevallos replied that such a step would be premature, as the discussion was not yet ended.[3] Monroe had no choice but to break through the diplomatic net in which he had wound himself; and at length, May 12, 1805, he

---

[1] Cevallos to Pinckney and Monroe, April 13, 1805; State Papers, ii. 660.
[2] Monroe and Pinckney to Cevallos, April 20, 1805; State Papers, ii. 662.
[3] Monroe and Pinckney to Madison, 23 May, 1805; State Papers, ii. 668.

sent a general ultimatum to the Spanish government: If Spain would cede the Floridas, ratify the claims convention of August, 1802, and accept the Colorado as the Texan boundary, the United States would establish a neutral territory a hundred miles wide on the eastern bank of the Colorado, from the Gulf to the northern boundary of Louisiana; would assume the French spoliation claims, abandon the *entrepôt* claims, and accept the cession of West Florida from the King, thereby abandoning the claim that it was a part of Louisiana.[1]

To this note Cevallos replied three days afterward by a courteous but decided letter, objecting in various respects to Monroe's offers, and summing up his objections in the comment that this scheme required Spain to concede everything and receive nothing; she must give up both the Floridas, half of Texas, and the claims convention, while she obtained as an equivalent for these concessions only an abandonment of claims which she did not acknowledge:[2] —

> "The justice of the American government will not permit it to insist on propositions so totally to the disadvantage of Spain; and however anxious his Majesty may be to please the United States, he cannot on his part assent to them, nor can he do less than consider them as little comfortable to the rights of his Crown."

Three days later Monroe demanded his passports. For once, Cevallos showed as much promptness as Monroe could have desired. Without expressing a regret, or showing so much as a complimentary wish to continue the negotiation, Cevallos sent the passports, appointed the very next day for Monroe's audience of leave, and bowed the American envoy out of Spain with an alacrity which contrasted strongly with the delays that had hitherto wasted five months of time most precious to the American minister at the Court of St. James. In truth, the Prince of Peace had no longer an object to gain by detaining Monroe; he had won every advantage which could be wrung from the situation, except that of proving the defeat of the United States by publishing it to the world. For this, he could trust Monroe.

[1] Pinckney and Monroe to Cevallos, May 12, 1805; State Papers, ii. 665.
[2] Cevallos to Monroe and Pinckney, May 15, 1805; State Papers, ii. 666.

After writing an angry letter to the French ambassador at Madrid, Monroe went his way, May 26, leaving Pinckney to maintain the forms of diplomatic relations with the Spanish government. Pinckney had still more to suffer before escaping from the scene of his diplomatic trials. The Spaniards began to plunder American commerce; the spoliations of 1798 were renewed; the garrisons in West Florida and Texas were reinforced; Cevallos paid no attention to complaints or threats. In October Pinckney took leave and returned to America, and George W. Erving was sent from London to take charge of the legation at Madrid. Erving made an excellent representative within the narrow field of action open to him as a mere *chargé d'affaires*; but he could do little to stem the current of Spanish desperation. The Prince of Peace, driven by France, England, and America nearer and nearer to the precipice that yawned for the destruction of Spain, was willing to see the world embroiled, in the hope of finding some last chance in his favor. When Erving in December, five months after Monroe's departure, went to remonstrate against seizures of American ships in flagrant violation of the treaty of 1795, Godoy received him with the good-natured courtesy which marked his manners. "How go our affairs?" he asked; "are we to have peace or war?" Erving called his attention to the late seizures. The Prince replied that it was impossible for Spain to allow American vessels to carry English property. "But we have a treaty which secures us that right," replied Erving. "Certainly, I know you have a treaty, for I made it with Mr. Pinckney," rejoined Godoy; and he went on with entire frankness to announce that the "free-goods" provision of that treaty would no longer be respected. Then he continued, with laughable coolness, —

"You may choose either peace or war. 'T is the same thing to me. I will tell you candidly, that if you will go to war this certainly is the moment, and you may take our possessions from us. I advise you to go to war now, if you think that is best for you; and then the peace which will be made in Europe will leave us two at war."[1]

Defiance could go no further. Elsewhere the Prince openly

[1] Erving to Madison, Dec. 7, 1805; MSS. State Department Archives.

said that the United States had brought things to such a point as to leave Spain indifferent to the consequences. In war the President could only seize Florida; and Florida was the price he asked for remaining at peace. Mexico and Cuba were beyond his reach. Meanwhile Spain not only saved the money due for the old claims, but plundered American commerce, and still preserved her title to the Floridas and Texas,—a title which, at least as concerned the Floridas, the Americans must sooner or later extinguish.

Such was the result of the President's diplomacy in respect to Spain. War was its only natural outcome,—war with Spain; war with Napoleon, who must make common cause with King Charles; coalition with England; general recurrence to the ideas and precedents of the last Administration. Jefferson had exasperated Spain and irritated France. He must next decide whether this policy should be pursued to its natural result.

Meanwhile Monroe returned to Paris, where he passed six weeks with Armstrong and with his French acquaintances in conference on the proper course to be pursued. Talleyrand was absent in Italy with the Emperor, who May 26 received at Milan the iron crown of the Lombard kings. That Napoleon was the real element of danger was clear to both envoys. A policy which should force France to interfere on behalf of the United States was their object; and on this, as on many points, Armstrong's ideas were more definite than those of Monroe, Madison, or Jefferson. Even before Monroe left Madrid, he received a letter from Armstrong in which the outline of a decisive plan was sketched:—

> "It is simply to take a strong and prompt possession of the northern bank of the Rio Bravo, leaving the eastern limit *in statu quo*. A stroke of this kind would at once bring Spain to reason, and France to her rescue, and without giving either room to quarrel. You might then negotiate, and shape the bargain pretty much as you pleased."[1]

Evidently the seizure of Texas, leaving West Florida untouched, was the only step which the President could prop-

[1] Armstrong to Monroe, May 4, 1805; MSS. State Department Archives.

erly take; for Texas had been bought and paid for, whereas West Florida beyond doubt had never been bought at all. Armstrong saw the weak point of Napoleon's position, and wished to attack it. He had no trouble in bringing Monroe to the same conclusion, although in yielding to his arguments Monroe tacitly abandoned the ground he had been persuaded by Livingston to take two years before, that West Florida belonged to Louisiana.

"There is no shade of difference in our opinions," wrote Armstrong to Madison after Monroe's arrival at Paris,[1] "and so little in the course to be pursued with regard to Spain that it is scarcely worth noticing. The whole may be reduced to this: that instead of assailing the Spanish posts in West Florida, or even indicating an intention to do so, I would (from motives growing more particularly out of the character of the Emperor) restrict the operations to such as may have been established in Louisiana. This, with some degree of demonstration that we meditate an embargo on our commercial intercourse with Spain and her colonies, would compel this government to interpose promptly and efficiently, and with dispositions to prevent the quarrel from going further."

Throughout these Spanish negotiations ran a mysterious note of corruption which probably came not from Cevallos, Godoy, or King Charles; for Spain was always the party to suffer, and France was always the party to profit by Spanish sacrifices. That the jobbery had its origin in Napoleon was improbable, for he too suffered from it. Neither Napoleon nor Godoy was open to bribery in such a sense; they were so high in power that small pecuniary motives had no influence on their acts. Yet the Treasuries both of France and Spain were in trouble, and were seeking resources. That Talleyrand had private motives for conniving in their expedients cannot be proved; but in 1805, as in 1798, every attempt to turn negotiation into a job came from Talleyrand's intimate circle, the subordinates of the French Foreign Office.[2] In June, Monroe found at Paris the same hints at the influence of

[1] Armstrong to Madison, July 3, 1805; MSS. State Department Archives.
[2] Cf. Correspondance de Napoleon, xxxii. 321.

money which had irritated him in the preceding autumn; and he wrote to Madison in a tone which showed that he gave them weight.

"I have conferred much," he said,[1] "with the gentleman alluded to in my letter from Bordeaux of December 16, and from what I can gather am led to believe that France has withheld her opinion on the western limits [Texas], to favor our pretensions when she thinks proper to take a part in it; that she does not think it proper so to do in the present stage, or until our Government acts so as to make Spain apply to her. He thinks she will then act; and settling the Spanish spoliation business as by the treaty of 1802, and getting all that can be got for Florida (he says eight millions of dollars are expected), promote an adjustment."

If Jefferson's administration cared to commit an error of colossal proportions, it had but to follow the hints of these irresponsible agents of Marbois and Talleyrand, who presumed to say in advance what motives would decide the mind of Napoleon. No man in France—neither Talleyrand nor Berthier, nor even Duroc—knew the scope of the Emperor's ambition, or could foretell the expedients he would use or reject. Monroe's friend was ill-informed, or deceived him. France had not withheld her opinion on the western limits; on the contrary, her opinion had been exactly followed by Spain. Not Talleyrand, much less Napoleon, but Cevallos himself had withheld that opinion from Monroe's knowledge, doubtless because he wished to keep a weapon in reserve for use at close quarters if his antagonist should come so near. Had Monroe not been discomfited before Cevallos exhausted his arsenal, this weapon would certainly have been used for a final blow. Cevallos still held it in reserve.

Leaving the Spanish affair embroiled beyond disentanglement, Monroe recrossed the Channel, and July 23 found himself again in London. During a century of American diplomatic history a minister of the United States has seldom if ever within six months suffered, at two great Courts, such

[1] Monroe to Madison, June 30, 1805; MSS. State Department Archives.

contemptuous treatment as had then fallen to Monroe's lot. That he should have been mortified and anxious for escape was natural. He returned to England, meaning to sail as quickly as possible for America. "It was very much my wish," he wrote.[1] Hoping to sail at latest by November 1, he selected his ship, and gave notice to the British Foreign Office. In his own interests no step could have been wiser, but it was taken too late; the time lost in Spain and at Paris had been fatal to his plan, and he could no longer avoid another defeat more serious, and even more public, than the two which had already disturbed his temper.

That the American minister in London at any time should for six months leave his post, even in obedience to instructions, was surprising; but that he should have done this in 1804, after Pitt's return to power, was matter of amazement. Monroe expected an unfriendly change of policy in the British government. As early as June, 1804, he wrote to Madison: "My most earnest advice is to look to the possibility of such a change."[2] Four months later, although the attitude of the British ministry had become more threatening, Monroe started for Madrid, leaving Pitt in peace, unwatched, to take his measures and to fix beyond recall his change of policy. July 23, 1805, when the American minister at last returned from his Spanish journey and arrived in London, after some weeks lost at Paris, he found a state of affairs such as might have alarmed the most phlegmatic of men.

Pitt had made good use of Monroe's absence. During the winter of 1804–1805 Parliament passed several Acts tending to draw all the West Indian commerce into British hands. Throughout the West Indies free ports were thrown open to the enemy's vessels, which were encouraged to bring there the produce of their colonies, receiving British merchandise in return, while the Act further provided for the importation of this enemy's produce into Great Britain in British ships. Other Acts and Orders extended the system of licenses, by which British subjects were allowed to trade with their enemies in neutral vessels, and concluded by requiring that all

[1] Monroe to Madison, Oct. 18, 1805; State Papers, iii. 106.
[2] Monroe to Madison, June 3, 1805; State Papers, iii. 93.

their trade with the French islands should be carried on through the free ports alone.[1]

These measures were intended to force the trade of the French and Spanish colonies into a British channel; but all were secondary to a direct attack on American commerce. While Parliament and Council devised the legislation and rules necessary for taking charge of the commerce of Cuba, Martinique, and the other hostile colonies, the Lords of Appeals were engaged in providing the law necessary for depriving America of the same trade. July 23, 1805, Sir William Scott pronounced judgment in the case of the "Essex." Setting aside his ruling in the case of the "Polly,"[2] he held that the neutral cargo which came from Martinique to Charleston, and thence to London, was good prize unless the neutral owner could prove, by something more than the evidence of a custom-house entry, that his original intention had been to terminate the voyage in an American port. In consequence of this decision, within a few weeks American ships by scores were seized without warning; neutral insurance was doubled; and the British merchantmen vied with the royal navy in applauding the energy of William Pitt.

Of the decision as a matter of morality something might be said. That Pitt should have planned such a scheme was not surprising, for his moral sense had been blunted by the desperation of his political struggle; but the same excuse did not apply to Sir William Scott. The quarrel between law and history is old, and its source lies deep. Perhaps no good historian was ever a good lawyer: whether any good lawyer could be a good historian might be equally doubted. The lawyer is required to give facts the mould of a theory; the historian need only state facts in their sequence. In law Sir William Scott was considered as one of the greatest judges that ever sat on the English bench, a man of the highest personal honor, sensitive to any imputation on his judicial independence,—a lawyer in whom the whole profession took pride. In history he made himself and his court a secret instrument for carrying out an act of piracy. The law defends him by throwing responsibility upon the political chiefs who were bound to make compen-

[1] Act of April 10, 1805; Instructions of June 29, 1805; Orders of Aug. 3, 1805.
[2] See First Administration, p. 524.

sation to the plundered merchants if compensation was due. The judge's duty began and ended by declaring what was law. Experience had proved that the evidence previously required to convince the court of a certain fact was insufficient. The judge said this, and no more. History replies that whatever may be the strictly professional aspect of this famous judgment, in its nature it was a political act, and was known by the judge to be such. As a political measure its character was equivalent to a declaration of war, and did not materially differ from the more violent seizure of the Spanish treasure-ships by Pitt's order in the previous October. The lawyers justified that seizure also; the King's Advocate defended it in the House of Commons by the simple explanation that England was not in the habit of declaring war, but usually began hostilities by some act of force.[1] Lord Grenville, whom Pitt had entreated, only a few months before, to join the new ministry, and who was certainly considered as, next to Pitt himself, the highest political authority in England, was not deterred by this reasoning from denouncing the seizure of the Spanish galleons as an atrocious act of barbarity, contrary to all the law of nations, which stamped indelible infamy on the English name. Lord Grey, another high authority, stigmatized it as combining violence, injustice, and bad faith. The seizure of the American ships was an act different in its nature only in so far as Sir William Scott condescended to throw over it in advance the ermine that he wore.

Monroe reached London on the very day when Sir William Scott pronounced his fatal decision in the case of the "Essex." Lord Harrowby no longer presided over the Foreign Office; he had taken another position, making way for Lord Mulgrave. The new Foreign Secretary was, like most of Pitt's ministers in 1805, a Tory gentleman of moderate abilities. Except as a friend of Pitt he was unknown. His character and opinions seemed wholly without importance. To Lord Mulgrave, Monroe addressed himself; and he found the Foreign Secretary as ready to discuss, and as slow to concede, as Don Pedro Cevallos had ever been.[2] "He assured me in the most

[1] Speech of Sir John Nicholl (Advocate-General), Feb. 11, 1805; Cobbett's Debates, iii. 407.

[2] Monroe to Madison, Aug. 16, 1805; State Papers, iii. 103.

explicit terms that nothing was more remote from the views of his Government than to take an unfriendly attitude toward the United States; he assured me also that no new orders had been issued, and that his Government was disposed to do everything in its power to arrange this and the other points to our satisfaction." Yet when Monroe called his attention to the seizure of a score of American vessels in the Channel, by British naval officers who declared themselves to be acting by order, Lord Mulgrave quietly replied that the Rule of 1756 was good law, and that his Government did not mean to relax in the slightest degree from the rigor of Sir William Scott's decision.[1]

Monroe had felt the indifference or contempt of Lord Harrowby, Talleyrand, and Cevallos: that of Lord Mulgrave was but one more variety of a wide experience. The rough treatment of Monroe by the Englishman was a repetition of that which he had accepted or challenged at the hands of the Frenchman and Spaniard. Lord Mulgrave showed no wish to trouble himself in any way about the United States. He would not discuss the questions of impressment and commerce; and his only sign of caring to explain or excuse the measures of his Government was in regard to Captain Bradley of the "Cambrian," who had been recalled from the American station for violations of neutrality. Monroe complained that Bradley had since been given a ship of the line. Mulgrave explained that the command of a line-of-battle ship was not necessarily a promotion, especially to an active officer accustomed to the independence and prize-money of the "Cambrian's" cruising ground.

With this result Monroe's diplomatic activity for the year 1804–1805 came to an end. The only conclusion he drew from it was one which Jefferson seemed little likely to adopt. He urged his Government to persevere in its course, and to threaten war upon France, Spain, and England at once.[2] "We probably shall never be able to settle our concerns with either Power without pushing our just claims on each with the greatest decision. . . . I am strong in the opinion that a pres-

[1] Monroe to Madison, Aug. 20, 1805; State Papers, iii. 105.
[2] Monroe to Madison, Oct. 18, 1805; State Papers, iii. 106. Monroe to Colonel Taylor, Sept. 10, 1810; Monroe MSS., State Department Archives.

sure on each at the same time would produce a good effect with the other."

Nevertheless, Monroe had not yet reached the bottom of his English disaster. Neither the Acts of Parliament, the Orders in Council, nor the Judgment of the Lords of Appeal satisfied the suffering interests of England, however harsh they might seem to the interests of America. The new rules, the extension of licenses, the opening of free ports, tended to please the navy and shipping interests, but left the British colonists in a worse position than before; for as matters stood the whole produce of the West Indian Islands, French, Spanish, and British, was to be collected in a single mass and thrown on the London market. The warehouses on the Thames were to be overfilled with sugar, on the chance that neutral ships might convey it to France. For five years the colonists had insisted that their distress was due to excess in production; but how could they check production when the French and Spanish islands were encouraged to produce? Forgetting in their despair the attachment they felt to America, the colonists attributed all their troubles to American competition. The East India Company, whose warehouses were also loaded with unsalable goods, could discover no better reason than the same neutral rivalry for the cessation of Continental demand. The shipowners, not yet satisfied by Sir William Scott's law, echoed the same cry. All the interested classes of England, except the manufacturers and merchants who were concerned in commerce with the United States, agreed in calling upon government to crush out the neutral trade. Sir William Scott had merely required an additional proof of its honesty; England with one voice demanded that, honest or not, it should be stopped.

This almost universal prayer found expression in a famous pamphlet that has rarely had an equal for ability and effect. In October, 1805, three months after the "Essex" decision, while Monroe was advising Madison to press harder than ever on all the great belligerent Powers, appeared in London a book of more than two hundred pages, with the title: "War in Disguise; or, the Frauds of the Neutral Flags." The author was James Stephen, a man not less remarkable for his own qualities than for those which two generations of descendants have inherited from him; but these abilities, though elevating him immensely above the herd of writers who in England bespattered America with abuse, and in America befouled England, were yet of a character so peculiar as to bar his path to the highest distinction. James Stephen was a high-minded fanatic, passionately convinced of the truths he proclaimed. Two years after writing "War in Disguise," he published another pamphlet, maintaining that the Napoleonic wars were a divine chastisement of England for her tolerance of the slave-trade; and this curious thesis he argued through twenty pages of close reasoning.[1] Through life a vehement enemy of slavery, at a time when England rang with abuse of America, which he had done much to stimulate, he had the honesty and courage to hold America up as an example before Europe, and to assert that in abolishing the slave-trade she had done an act for which it was impossible to refuse her the esteem of England, and in consequence of which he prayed that harmony between the two countries might be settled on the firmest foundation.

This insular and honest dogmatism, characteristic of many robust minds, Stephen carried into the question of neutral trade. He had himself begun his career in the West Indies, and in the prize-court at St. Kitt's had learned the secrets of neutral commerce. Deeply impressed with the injury which this trade caused to England, he believed himself bound to point out the evil and the remedy to the British public. Assuming at the outset that the Rule of 1756 was a settled principle of law, he next assumed that the greater part of the neutral trade was not neutral at all, but was a fraudulent business, in which French or Spanish property, carried in French or Spanish ships, was by means of systematic perjury protected by the prostituted American flag.

How much of this charge was true will never be certainly known. Stephen could not prove his assertions. The American merchants stoutly denied them. Alexander Baring, better informed than Stephen and far less prejudiced, affirmed that the charge was untrue, and that if the facts could be learned,

[1] New Reasons for abolishing the Slave-Trade, 1807.

more British than enemy's property would be found afloat under the American flag. Perhaps this assertion was the more annoying of the two; but to prove either the one or the other was needless, since from such premises Stephen was able to draw a number of startling conclusions which an English public stood ready to accept. The most serious of these was the certain ruin of England from the seduction of her seamen into this fraudulent service; another was the inevitable decay of her merchant marine; still another pointed to the loss of the Continental market; and he heightened the effect of all these evils by adding a picture of the British admiral in the decline of life raised to the peerage for his illustrious actions, and enjoying a pension from the national bounty, but still unable to spend so much money as became an English peer, because his Government had denied to him the "safe booty" of the neutral trade![1] Humor was not Stephen's strongest quality, or he never would have caricatured the British mind so coarsely; but coarse as the drawing might be, England was not conscious of the caricature. Cobbett alone could have done justice to the pecuniary sanctity of the British peerage; but on this point humor was lost to the world, for Cobbett and Stephen were in accord.

Thus a conviction was established in England that the American trade was a fraud which must soon bring Great Britain to ruin, and that the Americans who carried on this commerce were carrying on a " war in disguise" for the purpose of rescuing France and Spain from the pressure of the British navy. The conclusion was inevitable. "Enforce the Rule of 1756!" cried Stephen; "cut off the neutral trade altogether!" This policy, which went far beyond the measures of Pitt and the decision of Sir William Scott, was urged by Stephen with great force; while he begged the Americans, in temperate and reasonable language, not to make war for the protection of so gross a fraud. Other writers used no such self-restraint. The austere and almost religious conviction of Stephen could maintain itself at a height where no personal animosity toward America mingled its bitterness with his

[1] War in Disguise, pp. 131–133.

denunciations; but his followers, less accustomed than he to looking for motives in their Bibles, said simply that the moment for going to war with the United States had come, and that the opportunity should be seized.[1]

[1] Bosanquet, Causes of the Depreciation, etc. p. 42.

Chapter III

THE EIGHTH CONGRESS had hardly expired, March 3, 1805, amid the confusion and ill-temper which followed the failure of impeachment, when President Jefferson and Secretary Madison began to hear the first mutterings of European disaster. Talleyrand's letter to Armstrong, Dec. 21, 1804, arrived with its blunt announcement that Napoleon meant to oppose every step of Monroe's negotiation at Madrid, and with its declaration that West Florida had not been included in the retrocession of Louisiana to France, but had been refused to France by King Charles. Jefferson was then at Monticello, and thither the documents from Paris followed him. He wrote to Madison that Monroe's case was desperate.

"I consider," said the President,[1] "that we may anticipate the effect of his mission. On its failure as to the main object, I wish he may settle the right of navigating the Mobile, as everything else may await further peaceable proceedings; but even then we shall have a difficult question to decide,—to wit, whether we will let the present crisis in Europe pass away without a settlement."

This letter showed that as early as the month of March, 1805, the President foresaw Monroe's disasters, and began to speculate upon the next step to be taken. The attempt to obtain Florida through Spanish fears had failed; but his first impression was that everything might go on as before, if the Spaniards would consent to a free navigation of the Mobile. Madison was still more vague; his first impulse was to retrace his steps. He wrote to the President a singular letter of contradictions.

"I cannot entirely despair," said he, March 27,[2] "that Spain, notwithstanding the support given by France to her claim to West Florida, may yield to our proposed arrangement, partly from its intrinsic value to her, partly from an apprehension of the interference of Great Britain; and that

---

[1] Jefferson to Madison, March 23, 1805; Madison MSS.
[2] Madison to Jefferson, March 27, 1805; Jefferson MSS.

this latter consideration may, as soon as France despairs of her pecuniary object, transfer her weight into our scale. If she [France] should persist in disavowing her right to sell West Florida to the United States, and above all can prove it to have been the mutual understanding with Spain that West Florida was no part of Louisiana, it will place our claim on very different ground,—such probably as would not be approved by the world, and such certainly as would not with that approbation be maintained by force. If our right be good against Spain at all, it must be supported by those rigid maxims of technical law which have little weight in national questions generally, and none at all when opposed to the principles of universal equity. The world would decide that France having sold us the territory of a third party, which she had no right to sell, that party having even remonstrated against the whole transaction, the right of the United States was limited to a demand on France to procure and convey the territory, or to remit *pro tanto* the price, or to dissolve the bargain altogether."

For eighteen months every French and Spanish agent in Washington, Paris, and Madrid had assured Madison, in language varying between remonstrance and insult, that Spain had not ceded West Florida to France; the records of the State Department proved that France had asked for West Florida and had been refused; Jefferson had not ventured to record a claim to West Florida when he received possession of Louisiana, and had been obliged to explain, in language which Gallatin and Randolph thought unsatisfactory, the words of the Mobile Act. In spite of this, Madison committed himself and government to the claim that West Florida was a part of Louisiana; he pressed that claim, not against France, but against Spain; he brought Monroe to a rupture with the Spanish government on that issue,—yet with these recollections fresh in his mind, he suddenly told Jefferson that if France could prove a matter of common notoriety, the world would decide that the United States had acted without regard to law or equity, while in any case the claim to West Florida as against Spain was a mistake.

That Madison should have followed a train of reasoning so

singular, was less surprising than that he should have ad
vanced so far without showing a sign that he was prepared
for the next step. Knowing as early as March, 1805, that his
plans were defeated, and that he might expect a repulse from
Spain and France, he selected a new minister to succeed
Pinckney at Madrid. This diplomatist, whose career was to be
as futile if not as noisy as that of his predecessor from South
Carolina, was James Bowdoin of Massachusetts, son of a celebrated governor of that State. Jefferson wrote privately to
him, April 27, announcing the appointment; and the tone of
the letter implied that in the month's interval since the arrival
of Talleyrand's manifesto the President's pacific views had suffered a change.

"Our relations with that nation are vitally interesting,"
he wrote.[1] "That they should be of a peaceable and friendly
character has been our most earnest desire. Had Spain met
us with the same disposition, our idea was that her existence on this hemisphere and ours should have rested on
the same bottom, should have swum or sunk together. We
want nothing of hers, and we want no other nation to possess what is hers; but she has met our advances with jeal
ousy, secret malice, and ill-faith. Our patience under this
unworthy return of disposition is now on its last trial, and
the issue of what is now depending between us will decide
whether our relations with her are to be sincerely friendly
or permanently hostile. I still wish, and would cherish, the
former, but have ceased to expect it."

Jefferson had the faculty, peculiar to certain temperaments,
of seeing what he wished to see, and of believing what he
willed to believe. Few other Americans could have seriously
talked of the Spanish empire in America as swimming or sinking with that of the United States; but Jefferson, for the moment, thought that the earthen pot of Spanish dominion
could trust itself to float safely under charge of the iron energy of American democracy. He could gravely say in regard
to Spain, "we want nothing of hers," when for eighteen
months he had exhausted every resource, short of force, to

[1] Jefferson's Writings (Ford), viii. 350.

gain Baton Rouge, Mobile, and Pensacola, not to speak of East Florida and Texas. He charged that Spain met his advances with jealousy, secret malice, and ill-faith, after his ministers had intrigued with Napoleon for nearly two years, in the constant hope of depriving her of her property. Dec. 13, 1804, he wrote to General Heath: "With Spain we shall always be bickering, but never at war till we seek it;"[1] and six months later he wrote to Bowdoin that her secret malice and ill faith were leading to permanently hostile relations. He had not much further to go; for if he meant to maintain his authority among rulers, the war that would never come till he sought it must be sought.

As Monroe's overthrow became more and more evident, the President grew uneasy, and turned restlessly from one device to another. In the first days of August Monroe's despatches arrived, announcing that he had left Madrid, and that all his offers had been rejected by Spain. Madison was in Philadelphia, where his wife was detained by a long and troublesome lameness. The President was at Monticello. A brisk interchange of letters took place, marking from day to day the fluctuations of feeling peculiar to the characters of the two men. One question alone was to be decided,—should they seize this moment to break with Napoleon?

Madison's first reflections reached no result. He shrank from admitting that the government stood between war and humiliation more dangerous than war.

> "The business at Madrid," he said, August 2,[2] "has had an awkward termination, and if nothing, as may be expected, particularly in the absence of the Emperor, should alleviate it at Paris, involves some serious questions. After the parade of a mission extraordinary, a refusal of all our overtures in a haughty tone without any offer of other terms, and a perseverance in withdrawing a stipulated provision for claims admitted to be just, without *ex post facto* conditions manifestly unreasonable and inadmissible, form a strong appeal to the honor and sensibility of this country."

[1] See p. 608.
[2] Madison to Jefferson, Aug. 2, 1805; Jefferson MSS.

The conclusion drawn from this somewhat mild review was not such as Monroe, Armstrong, or Livingston had recommended.

"I find that, as was apprehended from the tenor of former communications," continued the secretary, "the military *status quo* in the controverted districts, the navigation of the rivers running through West Florida, and the spoliations subsequent to the convention of 1802 have never had a place in the discussions. Bowdoin may perhaps be instructed, consistently with what has passed, to propose a suspension of the territorial questions, the deposit, and the French spoliations, on condition that those points be yielded, with an incorporation of the convention of 1802 with a provision for subsequent claims. This is the utmost within the Executive purview. If this experiment should fail, the question with the Legislature must be whether or not resort is to be had to force, to what extent, and in what mode. Perhaps the instructions to Bowdoin would be improved by including the idea of transferring the sequel of business hither. This would have the appearance of an advance on the part of Spain, the more so as it would be attended with a new mission to this country, and would be most convenient for us also, if not made by Spain a pretext for delay."

Madison, after enduring one "refusal of all our overtures in a haughty tone," suggested that another be invited. The slightly patronizing air which characterized Jefferson's attitude toward Madison, but which he never betrayed toward Gallatin, was explained by this want of directness in Madison's nature, and by the habitual slowness of his decisions. The action suggested by Madison threw the control of events into the hands of France. This at least was the opinion of Jefferson, whose mind was wrought by the news from Pinckney to a state of steadily growing alarm.

"I think the *status quo*, if not already proposed, should be immediately offered through Bowdoin," wrote Jefferson, August 4, before receiving Madison's letter of August 2.[1] "Should it even be refused, the refusal to settle a limit is not of itself a sufficient cause of war, nor is the withholding a ratification worthy of such a redress. Yet these acts show a purpose, both in Spain and France, against which we ought to provide before the conclusion of a peace. I think, therefore, we should take into consideration whether we ought not immediately to propose to England an eventual treaty of alliance, to come into force whenever (within —— years) a war shall take place with Spain or France."

Three days later he wrote again, and his alarm had increased:[2] —

"The papers now enclosed to you confirm me in the opinion of the expediency of a treaty with England, but make the offer of the *status quo* [to Spain] more doubtful; the correspondence will probably throw light on that question. From the papers already received I infer a confident reliance on the part of Spain on the omnipotence of Bonaparte, but a desire of procrastination till peace in Europe shall leave us without an ally."

Ten days more passed; the whole mortification became evident; the President's anger and alarm rose to feverishness.[3] He wrote to Madison, August 17, —

"I am anxious to receive opinions respecting our procedure with Spain, as should negotiations with England be advisable they should not be postponed a day unnecessarily, that we may lay their result before Congress before they rise next spring. Were the question only about the bounds of Louisiana, I should be for delay. Were it only for spoliations, just as this is as a cause of war, we might consider if no other expedient were more eligible for us. But I do not view peace as within our choice. I consider the cavalier conduct of Spain as evidence that France is to settle with us for her, — and the language of France confirms it, — and

[1] Jefferson's Writings (Ford), viii. 374.
[2] Jefferson to Madison, Aug. 7, 1805; Works, iv. 583.
[3] Jefferson to Madison, Aug. 17, 1805; Jefferson MSS.

that if she can keep us insulated till peace, she means to enforce by arms her will, to which she foresees we will not truckle, and therefore does not venture on the mandate now. We should not permit ourselves to be found off our guard and friendless."

The President's plan presented difficulties which Madison could not fail to see. That Jefferson should wish Pitt to fight the battles of the United States was natural; but Pitt was little in the habit of doing gratuitous favors, and might reasonably ask what price he was to receive for conquering the Floridas and Texas for the United States. Madison's comments on the President's proposed British treaty pointed out this objection. Madison agreed that the Executive should take provisional measures, on which Congress might act.[1] "An eventual alliance with Great Britain, if attainable from her without inadmissible conditions, would be for us the best of all possible measures; but I do not see the least chance of laying her under obligations to be called into force at our will without correspondent obligations on our part." Objection to the President's plan was easy; but when the secretary came to a plan of his own, he could suggest nothing more vigorous than to renew a moderate degree of coquetry with Merry, which would have the side advantage of alarming France and Spain, "from whom the growing communication with Great Britain would not be concealed."

Such a weapon was no doubt as effective against Napoleon as heelless slippers against Pitt; but the President thought the situation to have passed beyond such tactics. Madison's proposed coquetry with Merry met with less favor in Jefferson's eyes than his own proposed one-sided alliance with England had met in the eyes of Madison. Upon a treaty of alliance with England the President was for the moment bent, and he met Madison's objections by arguments that showed lively traits of the writer's sanguine temper. He complained that Madison had misconceived the nature of the proposed British treaty. England should stipulate not to make peace without securing West Florida and the spoliation claims to America,

[1] Madison to Jefferson, Aug. 20, 1805; Jefferson MSS.

while American co-operation in the war would be sufficient inducement to her for making this contract.[1]

"Another motive much more powerful would indubitably induce England to go much further. Whatever ill humor may at times have been expressed against us by individuals of that country, the first wish of every Englishman's heart is to see us once more fighting by their sides against France; nor could the King or his ministers do an act so popular as to enter into an alliance with us. The nation would not weigh the consideration by grains and scruples; they would consider it as the price and pledge of an indissoluble friendship. I think it possible that for such a provisional treaty they would give us their general guaranty of Louisiana and the Floridas. At any rate we might try them; a failure would not make our situation worse. If such a one could be obtained, we might await our own convenience for calling up the *casus fœderis*. I think it important that England should receive an overture as early as possible, as it might prevent her listening to terms of peace."

If Jefferson was right in thinking that every Englishman's heart yearned toward America, he was unfortunate in delaying his offer of indissoluble friendship until the moment when Sir William Scott delivered his opinion in the case of the "Essex." Madison's scheme was equally unpromising, because he had made a personal enemy of Merry, on whom the success of Madison's tactics depended. Each of the two high authorities felt the weakness of the other, and the secretary even went so far as to hint, in courteous language, that the President's idea was unpractical:—

"The more I reflect on the papers from Madrid, the more I feel the value of some eventual security for the active friendship of Great Britain, but the more I see at the same time the difficulty of obtaining it without a like security to her of ours. If she is to be *bound*, we must be *so too*, either to the same thing,—that is to join her in the war,—or to do what she will accept as equivalent to such an obligation.

[1] Jefferson to Madison, Aug. 27, 1805; Works, iv. 585.

What can we offer to her? A mutual guaranty, unless so shaped as to involve us pretty certainly in her war, would not be satisfactory. To offer commercial regulations or concessions on points in the law of nations as a certain payment for aids which might never be received or required, would be a bargain liable to obvious objections of the most serious kind. Unless, therefore, some arrangement which has not occurred to me can be devised, I see no other course than such an one as is suggested in my last letter."[1]

In this state of things, the remaining members of the Cabinet were asked for their opinions; and in the course of a few days the President received written papers from Gallatin and Robert Smith. Gallatin was annoyed at the results of Jefferson's diplomacy. Emphatically a Northern man, he cared little for Florida; and a war with Spain would have been in his eyes a Southern war. He made no concealment of his opinion that the whole negotiation rested on a blunder; and he told Madison as much, with a bluntness which the secretary could scarcely have relished.

"The demands from Spain were too hard," said he,[2] "to have expected, even independent of French interference, any success from the negotiation. It could only be hoped that the tone assumed by our negotiators might not be such as to render a relinquishment or suspension of some of our claims productive of some loss of reputation. If we are safe on that ground, it may be eligible to wait for a better opportunity before we again run the risk of lowering the national importance by pretensions which our strength may not at this moment permit us to support. If from the manner in which the negotiation has been conducted that effect has already been produced, how to save character without endangering peace will be a serious and difficult question."

These words were written before he had seen Monroe's despatches. When the whole correspondence was put into his hands he read it, and in returning it to Madison made the dry

[1] Madison to Jefferson, Sept. 1, 1805; Jefferson MSS.
[2] Gallatin to Madison, Aug. 6, 1805; Gallatin's Writings, i. 237.

comment that the business had not ended quite so badly as he had previously supposed.[1] The phrase bore a double meaning, for even Madison must have admitted that the business could not have ended much worse.

Gallatin sent to the President a remarkable paper,[2] in substance an argument for peace, and in tenor a criticism of the grounds which Jefferson, Madison, Monroe, Livingston, and Pinckney had thought proper to take in their dispute with Spain. Gallatin held that, owing to the "unpardonable oversight or indifference" of Livingston and Monroe in failing to insist on a boundary to Louisiana, the United States government was debarred from holding Spain responsible for the inevitable consequences of its own fault. Neither Spain's qualified refusal to ratify the claims convention of 1802 nor her rejection of the French spoliation claims would justify war. As a matter of abstract justice, war was not to be defended; as a matter of policy, it could not be recommended. The expense and loss would exceed the value of Florida; the political result would entangle America in alliance with England; and, "in fine, a subversion of all our hopes must be the natural consequence." Renewal of negotiation was the proper step, with the Sabine and Perdido as boundaries and a temporary arrangement under the *status quo*, acceptance of the Spanish condition precedent to ratifying the claims convention, and insistence against the new spoliations which French and Spanish privateers were daily making on American commerce in the West Indies. Pending the result of this negotiation Congress might spend some money on the militia, and might appropriate a million dollars annually to build ships of the line.

In effect, Gallatin threw his influence on the side of Madison against the President's semi-warlike views. The opinion of Robert Smith did not weaken the force of Gallatin's reasoning. Already a perceptible division existed in the Cabinet between the Treasury and the Navy. Hardly three months before the Spanish embarrassment, Gallatin had spoken to the

[1] Madison to Jefferson, Sept. 1, 1805; Jefferson MSS.
[2] Gallatin to Jefferson, Sept. 12, 1805; Gallatin's Writings, i. 241.

President in strong terms of Robert Smith's administration, and had added,[1] —

> "On this subject,—the expense of the Navy greater than the object seemed to require, and a merely nominal accountability,—I have, for the sake of preserving perfect harmony in your councils, however grating to my feelings, been almost uniformly silent."

Smith's present views tended to confirm Gallatin in his irritation, and to reconcile Jefferson to abandoning his energetic schemes. The Secretary of the Navy said that throughout these negotiations Spain had presumed much on American predilection for peace, and on the want of means to annoy her either by land or by water. He urged the necessity of working on her fears, and advised that Congress be recommended to provide additional gunboats, to put all the frigates in commission, and to build twelve seventy fours. With these means he was disposed to take a commanding attitude; and if Spain were supported by France, to make an alliance with England.[2]

Gallatin and Robert Smith agreed only on one point,— that the affair had been mismanaged. Both secretaries held that America had made pretensions which she had not strength at the moment to support. Rather than "again run the risk of lowering national importance," Gallatin preferred to submit to the consequent loss of reputation, and return to a true peace-policy. Robert Smith wished to maintain a high tone, and to arm. All Jefferson's instincts were with Gallatin; but the path that Gallatin proposed was hard and mortifying, and although he made it as little abrupt as possible, he could not prevent it from seeming what it was,—a severe humiliation to the President. Not without some inward struggle could a President of the United States bow his neck to such a yoke as Spain and France imposed.

At that moment, the middle of September, arrived Armstrong's letter advising the military occupation of Texas and a cessation of intercourse with Spain. His plan was the first

[1] Gallatin to Jefferson, May 30, 1805; Gallatin's Writings, i. 233.
[2] Robert Smith to Jefferson, Sept. 10, 1805; Jefferson MSS.

well-considered suggestion yet made for carrying out the policy hitherto pursued; and although contrary to Gallatin's advice, it agreed so well with the President's views that he caught at it with the relief of a man unable to solve his own problem, who hears another explain what to himself is inexplicable. Jefferson seized Armstrong's idea, and uniting it with his own, announced the result to Madison as the true solution of the difficulty:[1] —

> "Supposing a previous alliance with England to guard us in the worst event, I should propose that Congress should pass acts (1) authorizing the Executive to suspend intercourse with Spain at discretion; (2) to dislodge the new establishments of Spain between the Mississippi and Bravo; (3) to appoint commissioners to examine and ascertain all claims for spoliation."

Here at length was a plan,—uncertain, indeed, because dependent on British help, but still a scheme of action which could be discussed. The President appointed October 4 as the day on which the Cabinet should reunite at Washington to consider his project, but Madison replied that he could not return so soon; and in order that the Cabinet should know his views, he explained at some length the course he advised, which differed widely from that of the President.

> "With respect to Great Britain," he said,[2] "I think we ought to go as far into an understanding on the subject of an eventual coalition in the war as will not preclude us from an intermediate adjustment, if attainable, with Spain. I see not, however, much chance that she will positively bind herself not to make peace, while we refuse to bind ourselves positively to make war,—unless, indeed, some positive advantage were yielded on our part in lieu of an engagement to enter into the war. No such advantage as yet occurs as would be admissible to us and satisfactory to her."

In regard to England, therefore, Madison had nothing to

[1] Jefferson to Madison, Sept. 16, 1805; Works, iv. 587.
[2] Madison to Jefferson, Sept. 30, 1805; Jefferson MSS.

propose except negotiation without end. Having settled this point, he went on:—

> "At Paris I think Armstrong ought to receive instructions to extinguish in the French government every hope of turning our controversy with Spain into a French job, public or private; to leave them under apprehensions of an eventual connection between the United States and Great Britain; and to take advantage of any change in the French Cabinet favorable to our objects with Spain."

To leave Bonaparte "under apprehensions" was to be the object of Madison's diplomacy at Paris,—a task which several European governments were then employing half a million armed men to accomplish, hitherto without success, but which Madison hoped to effect by civilities to Merry.

After this decision, nothing remained but to mark out a line of conduct in regard to Spain. In the course of the summer Bowdoin, the new minister, had sailed; but on arriving in Spain, and learning the failure of Monroe's negotiation, he went to Paris and London without visiting Madrid.

> "As to Spain herself," continued Madison, "one question is, whether Bowdoin ought to proceed or not to Madrid. My opinion is that his trip to Great Britain was fortunate, and that the effect of it will be aided by his keeping aloof until occurrences shall invite him to Spain. . . . The nicest question, however, is whether any, or what, steps should be taken for a communication with the Spanish government on the points not embraced by the late negotiation. On this question my reflections disapprove of any step whatever other than such as may fall within the path to be marked out for Armstrong, or as may be within the sphere of Claiborne's intercourse with the Marquis of Casa Calvo. Perhaps the last may be the best opportunity of all for conveying to Spain the impressions we wish, without committing the government in any respect more than may be advisable. In general it seems to me proper that Claiborne should hold a pretty strong language in all cases, and particularly that he should go every length the law will warrant against Morales and his project of selling lands. If Congress

should be not indisposed, proceedings may be authorized that will be perfectly effectual on that as well as other points; but before their meeting there will be time to consider more fully what ought to be suggested for their consideration."

Having brought the government face to face with the government of Spain, in the belief that Spain and France must yield to a peremptory demand,—finding that Spain not only refused every concession, but renewed depredations on American commerce and took an attitude of indifference to threats or entreaties,—Madison proposed no more vigorous measure than to "go every length the law will warrant" against certain Spanish land-grants.

Such a course pleased no one, and threatened to create new dangers. Monroe and Armstrong urged that a supposed devotion to peace on the part of the President weighed heavily against him with Spain and France. Jefferson approved their proposed aggressive policy, as he wrote to Madison, chiefly because it would "correct the dangerous error that we are a people whom no injuries can provoke to war."[1] He shrank from war, except under the shield of England, and yet he feared England for an ally even more than Spain for an enemy. His perplexity ended in helplessness. The Cabinet meeting was held October 4; but he reported to Madison that nothing came of it:[2]

"The only questions which press on the Executive for decision are whether we shall enter into a provisional alliance with England, to come into force only in the event that *during the present war* we become engaged in war *with France*, leaving the declaration of the *casus fœderis* ultimately with us; whether we shall send away Yrujo, Casa Calvo, Morales; whether we shall instruct Bowdoin not to go to Madrid till further orders. But we are all of the opinion that the first of these questions is too important and too difficult to be decided but on the fullest consideration, in which your aid and counsel should be waited for."

[1] Jefferson to Madison, Sept. 18, 1805; Jefferson MSS.
[2] Jefferson's Writings (Ford), viii. 380.

Again Madison wrote back his opinion. More than six months had elapsed since the President, March 23, despaired of Monroe's mission; every alternative had been repeatedly discussed; every advice had been taken. Congress would soon meet; something must be decided,—in reality delay was itself a decision; yet the President and Secretary of State seemed no nearer a result than they had been six months before. Meanwhile the European packets brought news that put a different face on the problem. Sir William Scott's decision in the case of the "Essex" arrived; seizures of American ships by England began; Pitt's great coalition with Russia and Austria against Napoleon took the field, and August 27 Napoleon broke up the camp at Boulogne and began his long-intended movement across the Rhine. Upon Madison's mind this European convulsion acted as an additional reason for doing nothing:[1] —

"Considering the probability of an extension of the war against France, and the influence that may have on her temper toward the United States, the uncertainty of effecting with England such a shape for an arrangement as alone would be admissible, and the possible effects elsewhere of abortive overtures to her, I think it very questionable whether a little delay may not be expedient, especially as in the mean time the English pulse will be somewhat felt by the discussions now on foot by Mr. Monroe."

Accordingly the Secretary advised that Morales, Casa Calvo, and Yrujo should be ordered out of the country, while Bowdoin should remain in England,—and so left it.

Madison's measures and conduct toward Europe showed the habit of avoiding the heart of every issue, in order to fret its extremities. This mark of Madison's character as a diplomatist led him into his chief difficulties at home and abroad; but the Spanish imbroglio of 1805 first brought the weakness into public notoriety, and he recovered from the subsequent revelation only after years of misfortune. The same habit of mind made him favor commercial restrictions as a means of coercion. So he disregarded Armstrong's idea of seizing

[1] Madison to Jefferson, Oct. 16, 1805; Jefferson MSS.

Texas, but warmly approved of his passing suggestion as to an embargo:[1] —

> "The efficacy of an embargo cannot be doubted. Indeed, if a commercial weapon can be properly shaped for the Executive hand, it is more and more apparent to me that it can force all the nations having colonies in this quarter of the globe to respect our rights."

This mental trait was closely connected with Madison's good qualities,—it sprang from the same source as his caution, his respect for law, his instinctive sense of the dangers that threatened the Union, his curious mixture of radical and conservative tastes; but whatever its merits or defects, it led to a strange delusion when it caused him to believe that a man like Napoleon could be forced by a mere pin-prick to do Jefferson's will.

Jefferson himself was weary of indecision. He had rested his wish for an English alliance on the belief that Napoleon meant to make peace in Europe in order to attack America; and this idea, never very reasonable, could have no weight after Napoleon had plunged into a general European war. No sooner did he receive Madison's letter of October 16, than he again changed his plan.

> "The probability of an extensive war on the continent of Europe, strengthening every day for some time past, is now almost certain," he wrote October 23 to Madison.[2] "This gives us our great desideratum, time. In truth it places us quite at our ease. We are certain of one year of campaigning at least, and one other year of negotiation for their peace arrangements. Should we be now forced into war, it is become much more questionable than it was whether we should not pursue it unembarrassed by any alliance, and free to retire from it whenever we can obtain our separate terms. It gives us time, too, to make another effort for peaceable settlement. Where should this be done? Not at Madrid, certainly. At Paris! through Armstrong, or Armstrong and Monroe as negotiators, France as the mediator,

[1] Madison to Jefferson, Sept. 14, 1805; Jefferson MSS.
[2] Jefferson's Writings (Ford), viii. 380.

the price of the Floridas as the means. We need not care who gets that, and an enlargement of the sum we had thought of may be the bait to France, while the Guadalupe as the western boundary may be the soother of Spain; providing for our spoliated citizens in some effectual way. We may announce to France that determined not to ask justice of Spain again, yet desirous of making one other effort to preserve peace, we are willing to see whether her interposition can obtain it on terms which we think just; that no delay, however, can be admitted; and that in the mean time should Spain attempt to change the *status quo*, we shall repel force by force, without undertaking other active hostilities till we see what may be the issue of her interference."

A similar letter was sent on the same day to Gallatin; and the next day Jefferson wrote to Robert Smith, suggesting the same idea, with some characteristic additions.[1]

Jefferson's idea that Napoleon would require two years of war seemed reasonable; for how could Jefferson know that Ulm had already surrendered, that Austerlitz would be fought within six weeks, and that peace would be restored before the new year, with the Emperor Napoleon more terrible than ever? In truth Jefferson only reverted to his policy of peace which he had seemed to abandon, but to which he really clung even when most earnest for a British alliance. His conduct in that sense was at least consistent. So much could hardly be said for Madison, even though the President apparently yielded to the secretary's advice. Of all the points on which Madison, and Monroe in obedience to his orders, had most strongly insisted, even to the extent of offending Talleyrand, the strongest was that under no circumstances should the Florida negotiation be turned into a bribe to France. As late as September 30, in writing the opinion intended to guide the Cabinet, Madison asked authority "to extinguish in the French government every hope of turning our controversy with Spain into a French job, public or private."[2] The President's suggestion of October 23 avowedly turned the

---

[1] Jefferson's Writings (Ford), viii. 381.
[2] Madison to Jefferson, Sept. 30, 1805; Jefferson MSS.

controversy with Spain into a French job, which must inevitably become private as well as public.

Madison made no protest. He soon returned to Washington, and there, Nov. 12, 1805, a Cabinet meeting was held, whose proceedings were recorded by the President in a memorandum, probably written at the moment. This memorandum closed a record, unusually complete, of an episode illustrating better than any other the peculiarities of Jefferson and Madison, and the traits of character most commonly alleged as their faults.[1]

"*1805, Nov. 12.* Present, the four secretaries; subject, Spanish affairs.—The extension of the war in Europe leaving us without danger of a sudden peace, depriving us of the chance of an ally, I proposed we should address ourselves to France, informing her it was a last effort at amicable settlement with Spain, and offer to her, or through her, (1) A sum of money for the rights of Spain east of Iberville, say the Floridas; (2) To cede the part of Louisiana from the Rio Bravo to the Guadalupe; (3) Spain to pay within a certain time spoliations under her own flag, agreed to by the convention (which we guess to be a hundred vessels, worth two millions), and those subsequent (worth as much more), and to hypothecate to us for those payments the country from Guadalupe to Rio Bravo. Armstrong to be employed. The first was to be the exciting motive with France, to whom Spain is in arrears for subsidies, and who will be glad also to secure us from going into the scale of England; the second, the soothing motive with Spain, which France would press *bonâ fide*, because she claimed to the Rio Bravo; the third, to quiet our merchants. It was agreed to unanimously, and the sum to be offered fixed not to exceed five million dollars. Mr. Gallatin did not like purchasing Florida under an apprehension of war, lest we should be thought in fact to purchase peace. We thought this overweighed by taking advantage of an opportunity which might not occur again of getting a country essential to our peace and to the security of the commerce of the Mississippi. It was agreed that Yrujo should be sounded

[1] Cabinet Memoranda; Jefferson's Writings (Ford), i. 308.

through Dallas whether he is not going away, and if not, he should be made to understand that his presence at Washington will not be agreeable, and that his departure is expected. Casa Calvo, Morales, and all the Spanish officers at New Orleans are to be desired to depart, with a discretion to Claiborne to let any friendly ones remain who will resign and become citizens, as also women receiving pensions to remain if they choose."

Chapter IV

PRESIDENT JEFFERSON's decision, in October, 1805, to retrace his steps and reverse a policy which had been publicly and repeatedly proclaimed, was the turning-point of his second Administration. No one can say what might have happened if in August, 1805, Jefferson had ordered his troops to cross the Sabine and occupy Texas to the Rio Bravo, as Armstrong and Monroe advised. Such an act would probably have been supported, as the purchase of Louisiana had been approved, by the whole country, without regard to Constitutional theories; and indeed if Jefferson succeeded to the rights of Napoleon in Louisiana, such a step required no defence. Spain might then have declared war; but had Godoy taken this extreme measure, he could have had no other motive than to embarrass Napoleon by dragging France into a war with the United States, and had this policy succeeded, President Jefferson's difficulties would have vanished in an instant. He might then have seized Florida; his controversies with England about neutral trade, blockade, and impressment would have fallen to the ground; and had war with France continued two years, until Spain threw off the yoke of Napoleon and once more raised in Europe the standard of popular liberty, Jefferson might perhaps have effected some agreement with the Spanish patriots, and would then have stood at the head of the coming popular movement throughout the world,— the movement which he and his party were destined to resist. Godoy, Napoleon, Pitt, Monroe, Armstrong, John Randolph, and even the New England Federalists seemed combined to drag or drive him into this path. Its advantages were so plain, even at that early moment, as to overmaster for a whole summer his instinctive repugnance to acts of force.

After long hesitation, Jefferson shrank from the step, and fell back upon his old policy of conquering by peace; but such vacillations were costly. To Gallatin the decision was easy, for he had ever held that on the whole the nation could better afford a loss of dignity than a war; but even he allowed that loss of dignity would cost something, and he could not foretell what equivalent he must pay for escape from a Franco-

Spanish war. Neither Jefferson nor Gallatin could expect to be wholly spared; but Madison's position was worse than theirs, for he had still to reckon with his personal enemies,— John Randolph, Yrujo, and Merry,—and to overawe a *quasi* friend more dangerous than an enemy,—the military diplomate, Turreau.

Turreau during this summer kept his eye fixed on the Secretary of State, and repeatedly hinted, in a manner extremely frank, that he meant to tolerate no evasions. He wrote to Talleyrand in a tone of cool confidence. July 9 he said that the Emperor's measures for the protection of Florida were sufficient:

> "The intervention of France in the negotiations with Spain has stopped everything. They have been affected by it here, but have not shown to me any discontent at it. 'Well,' said Mr. Jefferson to me lately, 'since the Emperor wishes it, the arrangement shall be adjourned to a more favorable time.' "

That Jefferson made this remark could be believed only by his enemies, for it contradicted the tenor of his letters to Madison; but although Turreau doubtless overstated the force of the words, he certainly gave to Talleyrand the impression that the President was reduced to obedience. The impression was enough; correct or not, it strengthened Napoleon's natural taste for command.

A few weeks afterward, Turreau wrote to Madison a note in regard to General Moreau's reception in the United States. In a tone excessively military he said:[1] —

> "General Moreau ought not (*ne doit point*) to be, in a foreign country, the object of honors which the consideration of his services would formerly have drawn upon him; and it is proper (*il convient*) that his arrival and his residence in the United States should be marked by no demonstration which passes the bounds of hospitality."

Madison was indignant at this interference, and proposed to resent it. The President encouraged him to do so, on the

[1] Turreau to Madison, 26 Thermidor, An xiii. (Aug. 14, 1805); MSS. State Department Archives.

express ground that they had not ventured to resent the conduct of France in regard to Monroe's negotiation:[1] —

> "The style of that government in the Spanish business
> was calculated to excite indignation; but it was a case in
> which that might have done injury. But the present is a case
> which would justify some notice in order to let them un-
> derstand we are not of those Powers who will receive and
> execute mandates."

Meanwhile General Smith, who had not resented the repudiation of his niece by the Emperor, and to whom Madison showed the offensive letter, undertook to soothe the
irritation. "He says," wrote Madison in his next letter to the
President,[2] "that Turreau speaks with the greatest respect, and
even affection, toward the Administration; and such are the
dispositions which it is certain he has uniformly manifested
to me." Upon these assurances Madison toned down the severity he had intended.

Turreau had resided hardly six months in the United States
before he announced to Talleyrand the conviction of all
American politicians that any war would end in driving from
office the party which made it:[3] —

> "To such an extent is the actual Administration con-
> vinced of this fact, that it allows itself to be outraged every
> day by the English, and accepts all the humiliations they
> care to impose; and notwithstanding the contempt gener-
> ally felt here for Spain, against whom a war was last year
> quite openly provoked, the members of the United States
> government have not dared to undertake it, although sure
> of beginning it with public opinion in their favor. And no
> one need think that this indisposition to war depends only
> on the personal character and the philanthropic principles
> of Mr. Jefferson, for it is shared by all the party leaders,
> even by those who have most pretensions and well-founded
> hopes to succeed the actual President,—such as Mr.
> Madison."

[1] Jefferson to Madison, Aug. 25, 1805; Works, iv. 584.
[2] Madison to Jefferson, Sept. 1, 1805; Jefferson MSS.
[3] Turreau to Talleyrand, 20 Messidor, An xiii. (July 9, 1805); Archives des
Aff. Étr., MSS.

Turreau's sketch of American character and ambition was long and interesting, and suggested the vulnerable point where France should throw her strength against this new people. Neither as a military nor as a naval power did he think the United States formidable. Their government made no concealment of its weakness: —

"They especially lack trained officers. The Americans are to-day the boldest and the most ignorant navigators in the universe. In brief, it seems to me that, considering the weakness of the military constitution, the Federal government, which makes no concealment of this weakness, will avoid every serious difference which might lead to aggression, and will constantly show itself an enemy to war. But does the system of encroachment which prevails here agree with a temper so pacific? Certainly not, at first sight; and yet unless circumstances change, the United States will succeed in reconciling the contradiction. To conquer without war is the first fact in their politics (*Conquérir sans guerre, voilà les premiers faits politiques.*)"

These reflections were written early in July, 1805, before the President and his Cabinet had begun to discuss Monroe's failure and the policy of a Spanish war, and more than three months before the President wholly abandoned the thought of warlike measures. Turreau's vision was keen, but he had no excuse for short-sightedness. Madison made little effort to disguise his objects or methods.

"I took occasion to express to Mr. Madison," wrote Turreau in the same despatch, "my astonishment that the schemes of aggrandizement which the United States government appeared to have, should be always directed toward the south, while there were still in the north important and convenient territories, such as Canada, Nova Scotia, etc. 'Doubtless!' replied the secretary, 'but the moment has not yet come! When the pear is ripe it will fall of itself.'"

Had Turreau asked why, then, Madison gave so violent a shaking to the Florida pear-tree, Madison must have answered, with the same candor, that he did so because he supposed the Florida pear to be ripe. The phrase was an admission and an invitation,—an admission that Florida would have been left alone if Spain had been as strong as England; and an invitation to Turreau to interpose with safety the sword of France. Turreau could not doubt the effect of his own blunt interference. So confident had the new French minister already become, in July, 1805, that he not only told Madison to stop these petty larcenies of Spanish property, but also urged Napoleon to take the Floridas and Cuba into his own hand solely to check American aggression. "I believe that France alone can arrest these American enterprises and baffle (*déjouer*) their plan."

Had Turreau's discipline stopped there, much might have been said in his favor; but in regard to still another matter he used expressions and made demands such as Madison never yet had heard from a diplomatic agent, although the secretary's experience was already considerable. Neither Yrujo nor Merry had succeeded in giving to their remonstrances or requests the abruptness of Napoleon's style.

The Federalist newspapers during Jefferson's first term had found so little reason for charging him with subservience to France, that this old and stale reproach had nearly lost its weight. Neither the New England merchants whom France had plundered, and whose claims Jefferson consented to withdraw, nor the British government or British newspapers had thought it worth their while to press the charge that Jefferson was led astray by love or fear of Napoleon or the Empire. Not until the winter of 1805–1806 did the doctrine of French influence recover a certain share of strength; but as John Randolph and his friends, who detested Madison, were outraged by the conduct of France in Spanish affairs, so Timothy Pickering and the whole body of Federalists, who hated the South and the power which rested on the dumb vote of slaves, were exasperated by the conduct of France in regard to their trade with St. Domingo. In both cases Madison was the victim.

St. Domingo was still in name and in international law a colony of France. Although Rochambeau surrendered himself and his few remaining troops as prisoners of war to the English in November, 1803; although the negroes in January, 1804, proclaimed their independence, and held undisputed control of the whole French colony, while their ports were open, and not an armed vessel bearing the flag of France pretended to maintain a blockade,—yet Napoleon claimed that the island belonged to him. General Ferrand still held points in the Spanish colony for France, and defeated an invasion attempted by Dessalines; nor did any government betray a disposition to recognize the black empire, or to establish relations with Dessalines or Christophe, or with a negro republic. On the other hand, the trade of Hayti, being profitable, was encouraged by every government in turn; but because it was, even more than other West Indian trade, unprotected by law, the vessels which carried it were usually armed, and sailed in company. In the winter of 1804–1805, soon after General Turreau's arrival at Washington, a flotilla armed with eighty cannon and carrying crews to the number of seven hundred men, set sail from New York with cargoes which included contraband of war of all kinds. Turreau remonstrated with Madison, who assured him that a law would soon be reported for correcting this abuse.

A Bill was accordingly reported; but it prohibited only the armed commerce and put the trade under heavy bonds for good behavior. To answer Turreau's object the trade must be prohibited altogether. Dr. Logan, one of the senators from Pennsylvania, who led the Northern democrats, with the "Aurora's" support, in hostility to the Haytian negroes, moved an amendment to the Bill when it came before the Senate. He proposed to prohibit every kind of commerce with St. Domingo; and the Senate was so closely divided as to require the casting vote of the Vice-President. Burr gave his voice against Dr. Logan's amendment, and the Bill accordingly passed, March 3, 1805, leaving the unarmed trade still open.

Turreau duly reported these matters to his Government.[1] The facts were public, and were given needless notoriety by the merchants themselves. On the return of the Haytian flotilla to New York, they celebrated the event in a public dinner, and the company drank a health to the government of Hayti. Another expedition was reported to be preparing. General Ferrand issued severe proclamations against the

[1] Turreau to Talleyrand, 30 Germinal, An xiii. (April 20, 1805); Archives des Aff. Étr., MSS.

trade,[1] and Madison remonstrated strongly against Ferrand. One armed American vessel, which had carried three cargoes of powder to the Haytians, was taken by a British cruiser, sent into Halifax, and there condemned by the British court as good prize for carrying on an unlawful trade.

Early in August, 1805, after Monroe's return to London, and while Jefferson and Madison were discussing the problem of protecting themselves from French designs, the Emperor Napoleon, who had returned from Italy and gone to the camp at Boulogne, received Turreau's despatch, and immediately wrote in his own emphatic style to Talleyrand:[2] —

"The despatch from Washington has fixed my attention. I request you to send a note to the American minister accredited to me. You will join to it a copy of the judgment [at Halifax]; and you will declare to him that it is time for this thing to stop (*que cela finisse*); that it is shameful (*indigne*) in the Americans to provide supplies for brigands and to take part in a commerce so scandalous; that I will declare good prize everything which shall enter or leave the ports of St. Domingo; and that I can no longer see with indifference the armaments evidently directed against France which the American government allows to be made in its ports."

In this outburst of temper Napoleon's ideas of law became confused. The American government did not dispute his right to seize American vessels trading with Hayti: the difficulty was that he did not or could not do so, and for this reason he made the demand that the American government should help him in doing what he was powerless to effect without its aid. Talleyrand immediately wrote to Armstrong a letter in which he tried to put the Emperor's commands into a shape more diplomatic, by treating the Haytians as enemies of the human race, against whom it was right that the United States should interpose with measures of hostility:[3] —

[1] State Papers, ii. 728.
[2] Napoleon to Talleyrand, 22 Thermidor, An xiii. (Aug. 10, 1805); Correspondance, xi. 73.
[3] Talleyrand to Armstrong, 29 Thermidor, An xiii. (Aug. 16, 1805); State Papers, ii. 726.

"As the seriousness of the facts which occasion this complaint obliges his Majesty to consider as good prize everything which shall enter into the part of St. Domingo
occupied by the rebels, and everything coming out, he per-
suades himself that the government of the United States
will take on its part, against this commerce at once illicit
and contrary to all the principles of the law of nations, all
the repressive and authoritative measures proper to put an
end to it. This system of impunity and tolerance must last
no longer (*ne pourrait durer davantage*)."

For the third time within six months Talleyrand used the
word "must" to the President of the United States. Once the
President had been told that he must abandon his Spanish
claims; then that he must show no public respect for Moreau;
finally he was told still more authoritatively that he must stop
a trade which France was unable to stop, and which would
continue in British hands if Congress should obey Napoleon's
order. Talleyrand directed Turreau to repeat at Washington
the Emperor's remonstrance, and Turreau accordingly echoed
in Madison's ear the identical words, "must last no longer."[1]
His letter, to his indignation, received no answer or notice.

Thus at the moment when Congress was to meet, Dec. 2,
1805, serious problems awaited it. The conduct of Spain was
hostile. At sea Spanish cruisers captured American property
without regard to treaty-rights; on land Spanish armed forces
made incursions from Florida and Texas at will.[2] The conduct
of France was equally menacing, for Napoleon not only sustained Spain, but also pressed abrupt demands of his own
such as Jefferson could not hear without indignation. As
though Congress had not enough difficulty in dealing with
these two Powers, Great Britain also took an attitude which
could be properly met by no resistance short of a declaration
of war.

During the whole year the conduct of England changed
steadily for the worse. The blockade of New York by the two
frigates "Cambrian" and "Leander" became intolerable, exasperating even the mercantile class, who were naturally friendly

[1] Turreau to Madison, Jan. 3, 1806; State Papers, ii. 726.
[2] State Papers, ii. 682–695.

to England, and who had most to dread from a quarrel. On board the "Leander" was a young midshipman named Basil Hall, who in later years described the mode of life he led in this service, and whose account of the blockade, coming from a British source, was less liable than any American authority to the charge of exaggeration.

"Every morning at daybreak," according to his story,[1] " we set about arresting the progress of all the vessels we saw, firing off guns to the right and left to make every ship that was running in heave to, or wait until we had leisure to send a boat on board 'to see,' in our lingo, ' what she was made of.' I have frequently known a dozen, and sometimes a couple of dozen, ships lying a league or two off the port, losing their fair wind, their tide, and worse than all their market, for many hours, sometimes the whole day, before our search was completed."

An informality in papers, a suspicion of French ownership, a chance expression in some private letter found and opened in the search, insured seizure, a voyage to Halifax, detention for months, heavy costs, indefinite damage to vessel and cargo, and at best release, with no small chance of re-seizure and condemnation under some new rule before the ship could reach port.

Such vexations were incident to a state of war. If the merchants of New York disliked them, the merchants might always ask Government to resent them; but in truth commerce found its interest in submission. These vexations secured neutral profits; and on the whole the British frigates and admiralty courts created comparatively little scandal by injustice, while they served as a protection from the piratical privateers of Spain and France. Madison, Gallatin, and the newspapers grumbled and complained; but the profits of neutrality soothed the offended merchant, and the blockade of New York was already a fixed practice. Had the British commanders been satisfied with a moderate exercise of their power, the United States would probably have allowed the habit of neu-

[1] Fragments of Voyages and Travels, by Captain Basil Hall, R. N., F. R. S., London, 1856.

tral blockade to grow into a belligerent right by prescription. Neither the mercantile class nor the government would have risked profit or popularity on such a stake; but fortunately the British officers steadily became more severe, and meanwhile in their practice of impressment roused extreme bitterness among the seafaring classes, who had nothing to gain by sub mission. In Basil Hall's words, the British officers took out of American vessels every seaman " whom they had reason, or supposed or said they had reason, to consider" a British sub ject, "or whose country they guessed from dialect or appearance." By these impressments American vessels were often left short-handed, and were sometimes cast away or foundered. In such cases the owners were greatly irritated; but commonly the exasperation was most deeply felt by the laboring class and among the families of seafaring men. The severity with which impressment was enforced in 1805 excited hatred toward England among people who had at best no reason to love her. More than twenty years afterward, when Basil Hall revisited New York, he was not surprised to find the name of his old ship, the "Leander," still held in detestation. Not only were the duties harsh, but, as he frankly admitted, they were harshly performed.

After Pitt's return to power impressments increased until they averaged about a thousand a year. Among them were cases of intolerable outrage; but neither President, Congress, nor people, nor even the victims themselves, cared as a body to fight in defence of their rights and liberties. Where an American-born citizen had been seized who could prove his birth, Madison on receiving the documents sent them to Monroe, who transmitted them to the British Admiralty, which ordered an inquiry; and if the man had not been killed in action or died of disease and hard usage, he was likely, after a year or two of service, to obtain a release. The American-born citizen was admitted to be no subject for impressment, and the number of such persons actually taken was never so large as the number of British-born sailors who were daily impressed; but both the mercantile and the national marine of the United States were largely manned by British seamen, and could not dispense with them. According to Gallatin's calculation,[1] American tonnage increased after 1803 at the rate of about seventy thousand tons a year; and of the four thousand two hundred men required to supply this annual increase, about two thousand five hundred were British. If the British marine lost two thousand five hundred men annually by desertion or engagement in the American service, even after recovering one thousand seamen a year by impressment, the British navy made good only a fraction of the loss. On the other hand, if the United States government went to war to protect British seamen, America would lose all her mercantile marine; and these same seamen for whom she was fighting must for the most part necessarily return to their old flag, because they would then have no other employer. The immediate result of war must strengthen the British marine by sending back to it ten thousand seamen whom America could no longer employ.

Nations rarely submit to injury without a motive. If Jefferson and the Republican party, if Timothy Pickering and George Cabot, the merchants of Boston and New York, and even the seamen themselves, rejected the idea of war, it was because they found a greater interest in maintaining peace. This interest consisted, as regarded England, in the large profits realized in neutral freights. So long as the British navy protected this source of American wealth, Americans said but little about impressments; but in the summer of 1805 Pitt thought proper to obstruct this source, and suddenly the whole American seaboard, from Machias to Norfolk, burst into excitement, and demanded that the President should do something,—they knew not what, but at moments they seemed to ask for war.

The news of Sir William Scott's decision in the case of the "Essex" reached America in the month of September, while the President and Madison were discussing an alliance with England to protect themselves against France and Spain. The announcement that Great Britain had suddenly begun to seize American ships by scores at the moment when Jefferson counted most confidently on her willingness to oblige, was a blow to the Administration so severe that a long time elapsed

[1] Gallatin to Jefferson, April 16, 1807; Works, i. 335.

before either Jefferson or Madison realized its violence. Their minds were intent on the Spanish problem; and with the question of war pressing upon them from the south, they did not at once perceive that another war was actually declared against their commerce from the north. Jefferson disliked commercial disputes, and gladly shut his eyes to their meaning; Madison felt their importance, but was never quick to meet an emergency.

Merry was near Philadelphia during the autumn, when Mrs. Madison's illness obliged the secretary to remain in that city. Early in September Merry wrote to his Government that the complete failure of Monroe's Spanish mission was no secret, and that Madison expected some collision with Spain in West Florida, but would wait for the meeting of Congress before taking action. "Such a determination on the part of the President," continued Merry,[1] "is so consonant with his usual caution and temporizing system (to which the opposition here give the character of timidity and irresolution), that I cannot but be disposed to give entire credit to the information." Shortly after the date of this despatch, news arrived that the British government had altered its rules in regard to the neutral carrying-trade, and that British cruisers were everywhere seizing American ships. Merry, who had not been forewarned by Lord Mulgrave, and who had no wish to see his own position made more uncomfortable than it already was, became uneasy. "The sensation and clamor," he wrote,[2] "excited by this news from England (which has already caused the insurance on such cargoes to be raised to four times the usual premium) is rendered the greater by such events having been totally unexpected, and by the merchants here having, on the contrary, considered themselves as perfectly secured against them." Merry saw that his Government had in the midst of peace taken a measure which Madison could hardly fail to denounce as an act of war. Dreading a violent explosion, the British minister waited anxiously; but, to his surprise, nothing happened. "Although I have seen Mr. Madison twice since the attention of the public has been so much engaged with this object, he has not thought proper to mention

[1] Merry to Mulgrave, Sept. 2, 1805; MSS. British Archives.
[2] Merry to Mulgrave, Sept. 30, 1805; MSS. British Archives.

it to me."[1] At first Merry could not account for this silence; only by degrees was he taught to connect it with the Spanish quarrel, and to understand that Madison hoped to conciliate England in order to overawe France. In this play of cross-purposes Merry's account of Madison's conversation was not calculated to alarm the British government:[2] —

"Before I quitted the vicinity of Philadelphia to return to this place [Washington], I had an interview with Mr. Madison, who having then received accounts from Mr. Monroe respecting the detention by his Majesty's ships of several American vessels in consequence of their being loaded with the produce of the enemy's colonies, brought forward that subject to me,—speaking upon it, however, with much more moderation than from his natural irritability, and the sensation which it had produced throughout this country, I could have expected on his part. It is unnecessary for me to trouble your Lordship by detailing to you the several observations which he made to me to endeavor to prove the impropriety of the principle upon which the detention of those vessels has taken place. . . . As I had the honor to observe in the former part of this letter, the American Secretary of State delivered his sentiments on this subject with great temper, and concluded by expressing only a wish that Mr. Monroe's remonstrances upon it might prove so far efficacious as at least to procure the liberation of the vessels and cargoes which were already detained, as well as of those which might be stopped before the new system adopted by his Majesty's government in regard to the trade in question should be generally known. Our conversation afterward turned upon some circumstances, the accounts of which had just been received, of the recent conduct of Spain toward this country, when Mr. Madison was much less reserved in expressing his sentiments than on former occasions, and gave me the detail of the perfidious and insolent proceedings of some of the Spanish officers who still remain at New Orleans, and of others who command in the disputed territory,—which, combined with informa-

[1] Merry to Mulgrave, Sept. 30, 1805; MSS. British Archives.
[2] Merry to Mulgrave, Nov. 3, 1805; MSS. British Archives.

tion he had received of the departure of four hundred troops with a quantity of military stores from the Havana, supposed to be destined to reinforce the garrisons in East and West Florida, and with a report which prevailed at New Orleans of a considerable force advancing from Mexico toward Louisiana, could not, he observed, fail to render the differences subsisting between the two governments still more difficult of accommodation."

This conversation took place about the middle of October, before the President had decided to acquiesce in the acts of Spain and France. As a result of the high tone taken toward England in the winter of 1803–1804, the secretary's mildness might well surprise a British minister, who was not quick of comprehension, and required to be told in plain language the meaning of Madison's manœuvres. No sooner had Merry returned to Washington than "a confidential person" was sent to him to explain the mystery:[1] —

> "On this subject it has been remarked to me by a person in a confidential situation here that the detention of the American vessels by his Majesty's ships has happened very unseasonably to divert the attention of the people of the United States and of the Government from a proper consideration of the grievances and injuries which they have experienced from Spain, and which the Government were disposed and had actually taken the measures to resent; and he conceived that when the state of the relations between the United States and other Powers should be laid by the President before Congress at their approaching meeting, the circumstance above-mentioned, of what is considered to be so unfriendly a proceeding on the part of Great Britain, will have the same effect upon the resolutions of that body by blunting the feelings which would otherwise have been excited by the conduct of Spain, supported by France, against this country."

The "confidential person" usually employed by Jefferson and Madison on such errands was either Robert or Samuel Smith; partly because both these gentlemen were a little in-

[1] Merry to Mulgrave, Nov. 3, 1805; MSS. British Archives.

clined to officiousness, partly because they were men of the world, or what Pichon called *"hommes fort polis."* In this instance the agent was probably the Secretary of the Navy. In telling the British minister that the President had already taken measures to resent the conduct of Spain, this agent was unwise, not so much because the assertion was incorrect, as because Merry knew better. In the same despatch, written Nov. 3, 1805, Merry informed his Government of the President's hopes of an agreement with Spain, founded on the war in Europe,—hopes which had been entertained only ten days, since October 23. He had the best reason to be well informed on this subject, for he drew his information directly from Jefferson himself.

That Merry should have been exceedingly perplexed was no wonder. Two years had elapsed since his first arrival in Washington, when he had been harshly treated without sufficient reason, by President, Cabinet, and Congress; and on returning to the same place in this autumn of 1805, immediately after his Government had made war on United States commerce, he found himself received with surprising cordiality. Immediately on his return, about October 20, he called at the White House. Instead of finding the President in a passion, denouncing Pitt and the British nation, as he might reasonably have expected, Merry was delighted to find Jefferson in his most genial humor. Not a word was said about British outrages; his conversation assumed the existence of a close concert and alliance between England and the United States:[1] —

"Upon my seeing the President on my return to this place a fortnight ago, he spoke to me with great frankness respecting the state of affairs between this country and Spain; saying that it was possible that the accumulation of the injuries which they had sustained might produce a resolution on the part of the Congress to resent them. With a view to the hostile situation of affairs, he lamented that unfortunately [notwithstanding] the superiority of his Majesty's naval force and the vigilance of his officers, it had not been possible to prevent the enemy's fleet from crossing

[1] Merry to Mulgrave, Nov. 3, 1805; MSS. British Archives.

the Atlantic. He said that this experience would render it necessary for the United States to proceed with great caution and to gain time, in order to put their principal seaports in a state of defence, for which he had already given directions. In the event of hostilities he considered that East and West Florida, and successively the Island of Cuba, the possession of which was necessary for the defence of Louisiana and Florida, as being the key to the Gulf of Mexico, would, in the manner in which that island might and would be attacked, be an easy conquest to them. He, however, expressed that his individual voice would constantly be for the preservation of peace with every Power, till it could no longer be kept without absolute dishonor."

Such speculations were not so practical as to affect Merry's antipathy to the American government, but he reported them to Lord Mulgrave without comment, as intended to express the President's plan in case of a Spanish war. Meanwhile the Secretary of State was engaged in composing a pamphlet, or book, to prove that the new rule adopted by Great Britain was an act of bad faith, in violation of international law. The task was not difficult.

Such was the diplomatic situation at Washington, Nov. 12, 1805, when the Cabinet adopted Jefferson's plan of reopening negotiations for the purchase of Florida on the line so persistently recommended by the irresponsible creatures of Talleyrand, and so steadily rejected to that moment by Madison and Monroe. Congress was to meet in three weeks, and within that time the diplomatic chaos must be reduced to order.

Chapter V

AUGUST 27, 1805, President Jefferson, writing to Madison from Monticello, said:[1] "Considering the character of Bonaparte, I think it material at once to let him see that we are not of the Powers who will receive his orders." In Europe, on the same day, the Emperor broke up the camp at Boulogne and set his army in motion toward Ulm and Austerlitz. September 4 he was at Paris, busy with the thousand details of imminent war: his armies were in motion, his vast diplomatic and military plans were taking shape.

The United States minister at Paris had little to do except to watch the course of events, when during the Emperor's absence at Boulogne he received a visit from a gentleman who had no official position, but who brought with him a memorandum, written in Talleyrand's hand, sketching the outlines of an arrangement between the United States and Spain. The United States, said this paper, should send another note to the Government at Madrid, written in a tone and manner that would awaken Spain from her indifference. In this note the Prince of Peace should be warned of the consequences that would follow a persistence in his course, and should be encouraged to join with the United States in referring to Napoleon the matters in dispute. In case Spain would not unite in asking the good offices of France, a copy of the note must be sent by Armstrong to Talleyrand, with a request for the good offices of Napoleon. "The more you refer to the decision of the Emperor, the more sure and easy will be the settlement." If Spain, on the Emperor's representations, should consent to part with the Floridas, as she no doubt would do, France would propose the following terms: Commercial privileges in Florida as in Louisiana; the Rio Colorado and a line northwestwardly, including the headwaters of all those rivers which fall into the Mississippi, as the western boundary of Louisiana, with thirty leagues on each side to remain unoccupied forever; the claims against Spain, excluding the French spoliations, to be paid by bills on the Spanish colonies; and,

---

[1] Jefferson to Madison, Aug. 27, 1805; Writings, iv. 585.

finally, ten million dollars to be paid by the United States to Spain.

Armstrong rejected the conditions on the spot. They sacrificed, he said, the whole country between the Colorado and the Rio Bravo; abandoned the claim to West Florida, the claim to damages from the violation of *entrepôt* at New Orleans, and the claim, estimated at six millions, for French spoliations. They gave to Spain an accommodation for her payments beyond what she herself required; and they exacted the enormous sum of ten million dollars for a barren and expensive province.

September 4, the day of Napoleon's return to Paris, a long conversation followed. On both sides vigorous argument was pressed; but the Frenchman closed by saying: "I see where the shoe pinches. It is 'the enormous sum of ten million dollars;' but say seven! Your undisputed claims on Spain amount to two and a half or three millions. The arrangement as thus altered would leave four for Spain. Is not this sum within the limits of moderation?" Armstrong replied that he had nothing to say on the money transaction, but would immediately transmit Talleyrand's memorandum to the President. His despatch on the subject was accordingly sent, Sept. 10, 1805.[1]

Armstrong had little acquaintance with the person who brought the memorandum for his sole credential, and knew him only as a political agent of the government, who rested his claim to credit not on any authority from the Emperor, but on an unsigned document in Talleyrand's handwriting. "This form of communication he said had been preferred on account of greater security; it was a proof of the minister's habitual circumspection, and of nothing else." To most Frenchmen it might have seemed rather an example of Talleyrand's supposed taste for jobbery, and the United States government had reason to know what was likely to be the outcome of such overtures; but Armstrong was not unused to intrigue, and did not affect virtue above the comprehension of the society in which he lived.

A fortnight afterward the Emperor left Paris for his campaign in Germany. While Armstrong's despatch was still on

---

[1] Armstrong to Madison, Sept. 10, 1805, MSS. State Department Archives.

its way to Washington, Napoleon captured Ulm, and November 13 entered Vienna. On the same day the despatch reached the United States.

Jefferson's Cabinet council of November 12 had barely come to its long-disputed conclusion, and decided to reopen the Florida negotiation as a French bargain, when Talleyrand's memorandum arrived, fixing definitely his terms. Naturally, the President supposed that Florida might thenceforward be looked upon as his own. At the next Cabinet he laid Armstrong's letter before the four secretaries; and the result of their deliberation was recorded in his own hand:[1] —

"November 19. Present the same.— Since our last meeting we have received a letter from General Armstrong containing Talleyrand's propositions, which are equivalent to ours nearly, except as to the sum, he requiring seven million dollars. He advises that we alarm the fears of Spain by a vigorous language and conduct, in order to induce her to join us in appealing to the interference of the Emperor. We now agree to modify our propositions, so as to accommodate them to his as much as possible. We agree to pay five million dollars for the Floridas as soon as the treaty is ratified by Spain, a vote of credit obtained from Congress, and orders delivered us for the surrender of the country. We agree to his proposition that the Colorado shall be our western boundary, and a belt of thirty leagues on each side of it to be kept unsettled. We agree that joint commissioners shall settle all spoliations, and to take payment from Spain by bills on her colonies. We agree to say nothing about the French spoliations in Spanish ports which broke off the former convention. We propose to pay the five millions after a simple vote of credit, by stock redeemable in three years, within which time we can pay it. We agree to order to the commanding officer at Natchitoches to patrol the country on this side the Sabine and all the Red River as being in our possession, except the settlement of Bayou Pierre, which he is not to disturb unless they aggress; he is to protect our citizens and repel all invasions of the pre-

[1] Cabinet Memoranda; Jefferson's Writings (Ford), i. 309.

ceding country by Spanish soldiers; to take all offenders without shedding blood, unless his orders cannot otherwise be executed."

At last, after more than six months of hesitation, a Spanish policy was fixed; and since it conceded every point which had been required by France, the President might reasonably hope that his difficulties were at an end. He did not venture to send instructions to Armstrong at once, because the authority of Congress was needed before pledging the government to pay so large a sum of money; but Congress was to meet within a few weeks, and Jefferson could safely assume that the instructions would not be delayed beyond the New Year.

The President was greatly relieved to see the end of this annoying imbroglio; the more, because he could no longer shut his eyes to the conduct of Great Britain. The merchants of Boston, New York, Philadelphia, and Baltimore were frantic with rage and despair, hearing every day of new seizures, which swelled their losses to a sum then quite appalling, and carried ruin to their fairest fortunes. The carrying-trade was not a matter about which Jefferson cared to quarrel, for he held that Americans should not meddle with a commerce which did not belong to them; yet the public anger was far stronger against England than against Spain, and although the newspapers talked incessantly of a Spanish war, Jefferson soon felt that he should find great difficulty in preserving a British peace. That he should incline to a war with Spain in alliance with England was natural; but under no circumstances, and for no object, did Jefferson wish for war with Great Britain. From the first he had relied upon his power to coerce her by peaceable means; and the time had come when some coercion must be applied. No one could longer doubt that Pitt meant to keep what he had taken, and that the British policy was preconcerted with deliberate purpose.

When Merry next called at the State Department he heard nothing more about the misconduct of Spain or the advantages of a powerful British navy.

"The lively sensation" produced by the seizures, wrote Merry to Mulgrave,[1] December 2, "appears to have in-

[1] Merry to Mulgrave, Dec. 2, 1805; MSS. British Archives.

creased considerably since I had the honor of writing to your Lordship by the last mail. The commercial bodies at Philadelphia, Baltimore, and Norfolk have held public meetings on this subject, and come to resolutions to transmit to the Government of the United States particular statements of the injuries they allege to be sustaining daily in their trade. I am sorry to add that those public prints which are considered as the organs of the Government . . . have of late lost sight in a great measure of their complaints against Spain, with a view, as may be suspected, to excite and direct the whole national indignation against Great Britain. . . .

"In addition, my Lord, to these circumstances, I have been sorry to find in my recent conversations with Mr. Madison that he has treated this subject in a much more serious light than he had at first represented it to me. At my last interview with him, two days ago, he said that he had flattered himself that Mr. Monroe's remonstrances to your Lordship would not only have produced the liberation of all the vessels which should have been detained previously to the 1st November, but that, as that minister had been promised an answer in writing to his representations, the reconsideration of the matter which would probably have taken place before a written answer was given might have induced his Majesty's government, if not to give up entirely, at least to modify to a tolerable degree, the principle upon which they acted. It was true that the answer in question had not as yet reached him, nor had he heard lately from Mr. Monroe; but he had recently received information from an authentic though not an official quarter, which gave him the strongest reason to apprehend that if any reply at all in writing should be made on the subject, it would contain nothing satisfactory."

Madison raised his tone awkwardly. Mysterious "information from an authentic quarter" was scarcely sufficient ground for so abrupt a change, but Merry failed to press him on this point. The secretary told the British minister that the government of England had committed "an act of commercial hostility on this country, and that the citizens of the United

States would have a just claim of indemnity for whatever effective losses they might sustain in consequence of it; and he feared that these would be very considerable." He hinted that measures would be taken to seek redress; and although he did not then foreshadow these measures, Merry read two days afterward in the "National Intelligencer" the Resolutions and speech in which Madison, in the year 1794, had urged commercial restrictions as the true policy of the United States against the same British outrages. The motive of republication was plain.

At about the same time Madison finished his pamphlet called "Examination of the British Doctrine," which in the course of the coming session was laid on the desk of every senator and member. The book was creditable to his literary and scholarly qualities. Clear, calm, convincing, it left the British government no excuse for its conduct; but, not without reason, John Randolph objected that as an argument it was but a shilling pamphlet against eight hundred British ships of war. That Pitt could occasionally be convinced of his mistakes was certain; but no reasoners except Napoleon and Moreau had ever effectually convinced him.

Meanwhile the President prepared his Message. Of all Jefferson's writings none had a livelier interest than the Annual Message at the meeting of the Ninth Congress. The Second Inaugural, nine months before, prepared the public for new political opinions; but the Message surprised even those who looked for surprises. The Second Inaugural seemed to sweep old Republican principles to the common rubbish-heap of out-worn political toys. The Message went even further, and seemed to announce that the theory of foreign affairs on which the Republican Administration began its career must be abandoned. Jefferson intended it to carry such a meaning.

"The love of peace," he wrote to one of his old friends,[1] "which we sincerely feel and profess, has begun to produce an opinion in Europe that our government is entirely in Quaker principles, and will turn the left cheek when the right has been smitten. This opinion must be corrected when just occasion arises, or we shall become the plunder

[1] Jefferson to Judge Cooper, Feb. 18, 1806; Jefferson MSS.

of all nations. The moral duties make no part of the political system of those governments of Europe which are habitually belligerent."

The Message began by an allusion to the yellow fever; from which it quickly turned to discuss the greater scourge of war:—

"Since our last meeting the aspect of our foreign relations has considerably changed. Our coasts have been infested and our harbors watched by private armed vessels; some of them without commissions, some with illegal commissions, others with those of legal form, but committing piratical acts beyond the authority of their commissions. . . . The same system of hovering on our coasts and harbors, under color of seeking enemies, has been also carried on by public armed ships, to the great annoyance and oppression of our commerce. New principles, too, have been interpolated into the law of nations, founded neither in justice nor the usage or acknowledgment of nations. . . . With Spain our negotiations for a settlement of differences have not had a satisfactory issue. . . . Propositions for adjusting amicably the boundaries of Louisiana have not been acceded to. . . . Inroads have recently been made into the territories of Orleans and the Mississippi; our citizens have been seized and their property plundered in the very parts of the former which had actually been delivered up by Spain, and this by the regular officers and soldiers of that government. I have therefore found it necessary at length to give orders to our troops on that frontier to be in readiness to protect our citizens and to repel by arms any similar aggressions in future. Other details necessary for your full information of the state of things between this country and that shall be the subject of another communication. In reviewing these injuries from some of the belligerent Powers, the moderation, the firmness, and the wisdom of the Legislature will all be called into action. We ought still to hope that time, and a more correct estimate of interest as well as of character, will produce the justice we are bound to expect; but should any nation deceive itself by false calculations, and disappoint that expectation, we must join in the unprofitable contest of trying which party can do the other the most harm. Some of these injuries may perhaps admit a peaceable remedy. Where that is competent it is always the most desirable. But some of them are of a nature to be met by force only, and all of them may lead to it."

From this preamble the public would naturally infer that measures of force were to be the object of the special message promised in regard to Spanish aggressions. As though to leave no doubt on the subject, the President urged the fortification of sea-ports, the building of gun-boats, the organization of militia, the prohibition of the export of arms and ammunition; and added that the materials for building ships of the line were on hand.

All this formality of belligerent language was little better than comedy. Jefferson could hardly be charged with a wish to deceive, since he could not wear the mask of deception. Both friends and enemies were amused to see how naturally he betrayed objects which his plan required should be concealed. In the first draft of the Message, sent for correction to Gallatin, the financial prospect was as pacific as the diplomatic was warlike; the Message not only announced a surplus for the coming year, but suggested the reduction of taxes. Gallatin pointed out that the English seizures alone would affect the revenue, and any measure of retaliation would still further diminish it; while the navy had increased its estimates from six hundred and fifty thousand dollars to one million and seventy thousand dollars. As for the hint at a reduction of taxes, Gallatin at once struck it out.[1] "As it relates to foreign nations, it will certainly destroy the effect intended by other parts of the Message. They never can think us serious in any intentions to resist, if we recommend at the same time a diminution of our resources." The President made these corrections, and returned the draft for revisal, with a note:[2] —

"On reviewing what had been prepared as to Great Britain and Spain, I found it too soft toward the former compared with the latter, and that so temperate a notice of the

[1] Gallatin to Jefferson, Nov. 21, 1805; Gallatin's Writings, i. 261.
[2] Jefferson to Gallatin, Nov. 24, 1805; Gallatin's Writings, i. 264.

greater enormity of British invasions of right might lessen the effect which the strong language toward Spain was meant to produce at the Tuileries. I have therefore given more force to the strictures on Britain."

In studying "the effect which the strong language toward Spain was meant to produce at the Tuileries," Jefferson had in mind the effect which his strong language produced at the Tuileries in 1803. He played a game of finesse hardly safe in the face of men like Godoy, Talleyrand, and Napoleon, whose finesse was chiefly used to cover force, and was not betrayed or derided by factious opposition in the press. Besides being unsafe, it was unfair to himself. Jefferson was an honest man, and in putting on the outward appearance of a Talleyrand, he resembled an amateur imitating Talma and Garrick. Gestures and tones alike were unnatural, awkward, and false; they exposed him to ridicule. If President Jefferson had taken the public into his confidence, he would have told the people that under no circumstances would he consent to war; but that if the great Powers of Europe combined to injure America, she would close her ports, abandon her commerce, shut herself within her own continent, and let the world outside murder and rob elsewhere. Such an avowal implied no disgrace; the policy it proclaimed was the alternative to war; and as the radical doctrine of the Republican party, the course was not only that which Jefferson meant to take, but it was that which he took. The avowal might have invited aggression, and have been followed by failure; but he would have done better to fail on a direct issue of principle, than to fail after evading the issue until the issue itself was lost.

To carry out his scheme, the President put forward two policies,—a public and a secret; or, as he called it, an ostensible and a real one. The warlike recommendations of the Annual Message were the public and ostensible policy; the real one was to be expressed in a secret message, announced in advance. To this coming message the President next turned his attention; but he found himself quickly involved in complications of his own creating. He had not only to recommend a double series of measures to Congress, but he had to frame a double series of replies which Congress was to return to him. He tried at first to combine the two answers in one. After writing a secret message asking for money to buy Florida, he drafted a series of Resolutions[1] which Congress was to adopt in reply to both messages at once, and in which "the citizens of the United States, by their Senate and Representatives in Congress assembled, do pledge their lives and fortunes" to maintain the line of the Sabine and the free navigation of the Mobile, pending negotiations, while the President should be authorized to take whatever unappropriated moneys might lie in the Treasury in order to carry these Resolutions into effect.

Clearly this would not do; and Gallatin undertook to set the matter right.

"The apparent difficulty in framing the Resolutions," he wrote to the President,[2] "arises from the attempt to blend the three objects together. The same reasons which have induced the President to send two distinct messages render it necessary that the public Resolutions of Congress should be distinct from the private ones; that those which relate to the war posture of the Spanish affairs, which are intended to express the national sense on that subject, and to enable the President to take the steps which appear immediately necessary on the frontier, should not be mixed with those proceedings calculated only to effect an accommodation."

The Secretary of the Treasury frequently corrected his chief, and still more frequently hinted a correction. Only a few days had passed since Jefferson had spoken to Gallatin of the "strong language toward Spain" as "meant to produce an effect at the Tuileries." Gallatin ignored this object, and spoke of the strong language toward Spain as intended to express the national sense, and as restricted in its bearing to the steps immediately necessary for protecting the frontier. The difference was worth noting. Evidently Gallatin felt no great confidence in producing an effect on the Tuileries.

"The course now recommended," he continued, "is precisely that which was followed in the Louisiana business

[1] Jefferson to Gallatin: Spanish Resolutions, 1805; Gallatin's Writings, i. 277.
[2] Gallatin to Jefferson, Dec. 3, 1805; Gallatin's Writings, i. 278.

when the deposit was withdrawn. A public Resolution
. . . was moved by Randolph, and adopted by the House.
A committee in the mean while brought in a confidential
report sufficient to support and justify the President in the
purchase he was going to attempt, and to this an appropriation law in very general terms was added. To follow a similar course appears not only best, but will also, as founded
on precedent, be the smoothest mode of doing the business
in Congress."

The President adopted Gallatin's suggestions.[1] The double
messages breathing war and peace were prepared. The double
answers were sketched out. Congress had only to act with the
same quickness and secrecy which it had shown in the Louisiana business; and of its readiness to do so, no one in the
Cabinet seemed to doubt.

Yet nations could not so readily as individuals swing about
on a course opposite to that which they had been led to expect. The American public had been wrought to anger against
Spain. Of the negotiations little was publicly known. Monroe
had come, and gone; the Marquis Yrujo had remonstrated,
and had written in newspapers; but the rights and wrongs of
the Spanish dispute remained a mystery to the public at large,
which knew only that Spain had rejected all the offers made
by the United States, had resumed her depredations on American commerce, and had taken a menacing attitude at Mobile
and on the Sabine. Throughout the year the Republican press
had followed hints from the Government at Washington, all
looking toward a rupture with Spain. The same newspapers
had shown at first a wish to make light of the late British
seizures, — a course which misled the Federalist press into denunciations of England such as would never have been risked
had the party in power not seemed disposed to apologize for
England's conduct. The country at large was prepared to hear
the President advise a rupture with Spain, and upon that rupture to found his hope of success in negotiating with Pitt.
The warlike tone of the Annual Message was certain to give
additional strength to this expectation; and Jefferson might
have foreseen that the sudden secret change of tone to be

[1] Jefferson to Gallatin, Dec. 4, 1805; Gallatin's Writings, i. 281.

taken immediately afterward in the special message on Spanish affairs would produce bewilderment among his followers.

No one could doubt where the confusion would first appear. The last session had ended in a series of quarrels, in which party distinctions had been almost forgotten. The summer had done nothing to reunite the factions; on the contrary, it had done much to widen the breach. Already the "Aurora" announced that the Yazoo question was to determine "the relations, the principles, the characters, and the strength of parties in the next session of Congress;" and the public knew that the Yazoo question had passed beyond the stage of rational argument, and had become the test of personal devotion, the stepping-stone to favor or proscription with the next President. Three years before the election of 1808 Congress was already torn by a Virginia feud,—a struggle for power between John Randolph and James Madison.

As though to hurry and prolong this struggle, Jefferson announced, after his second inauguration, that he should retire at the close of his term, March 4, 1809. Without expressly recommending Madison as his successor, his strong personal attachment insured to the Secretary of State the whole weight of Executive influence. The whole weight was needed. The secretary, with all his amiable qualities, was very far from controlling the voice of Virginia. His strength lay rather among the Northern democrats, semi-Federalists, or "Yazoo men," as they were called, who leaned toward him because he, of all the prominent Virginians, was least Virginian. His diplomatic triumph in buying Louisiana had given him an easy advantage over his rivals; but even his reputation might sink with the failure of the Spanish treaty and the aggression of England.

No one who knew the men, or who had followed the course of President Jefferson's first Administration, could feel surprise that Madison's character should act on John Randolph as an irritant. Madison was cautious, if not timid; Randolph was always in extremes. Madison was apt to be on both sides of the same question, as when he wrote the "Federalist" and the Virginia Resolutions of 1798; Randolph pardoned dalliance with Federalism in no one but himself. Madison was in person small, retiring, modest, with quiet malice in his humor, and with marked taste for closet politics and delicate management; Randolph was tall in stature, abrupt in manner, self-asserting in temper, sarcastic, with a pronounced taste for publicity, and a vehement contempt for those silent influences which more practical politicians called legitimate and necessary, but which Randolph, when he could not control them, called corrupt. Jefferson soon remarked, in regard to what Randolph denounced as back-stairs influence, "We never heard this while the declaimer was himself a back-stairs man."[1] Just as the criticism was, no one could deny that Randolph seemed much out of place on the back-stairs of the White House, whereas Madison seemed to him in place nowhere else. The Spanish papers, which Randolph must read, were not likely to increase his respect for the Secretary of State; while Madison's candidacy made a counter-movement necessary for those Virginians who would not be dragged at the heels of the Northern democracy.

Long before the month of December Randolph foresaw the coming trouble. The Yazoo men in the Ninth Congress were more numerous than ever; and they were credited with the wish to eject Speaker Macon from the chair, and to put some Northern democrat in Randolph's place at the head of the Committee of Ways and Means. Oct. 25, 1805, Randolph wrote to Gallatin from Bizarre: —

"I look forward to the ensuing session of Congress with no very pleasant feelings. To say nothing of the disadvantages of the place, natural as well as acquired, I anticipate a plentiful harvest of bickering and blunders; of which, however, I hope to be a quiet, if not an unconcerned, spectator. . . . I regret exceedingly Mr. Jefferson's resolution to retire, and almost as much the premature annunciation of that determination. It almost precludes a revision of his purpose, to say nothing of the intrigues which it will set on foot. If I were sure that Monroe would succeed him, my regret would be very much diminished."[2]

Intrigue and dissension could not be confined to the House, but must spread to the Senate, and could hardly fail

[1] Jefferson to Bidwell, July 5, 1806; Writings, v. 14.
[2] Adams's Randolph, p. 161.

to affect even the Cabinet. While Gallatin's personal sympathies were with Madison, his political bias was on the opposite side. The old Republicans, with John Randolph at their
head, had steadily protected the Treasury from jobs and extravagance; without their help Gallatin would lie at the mercy
of the Northern democrats, who were not behind the Federalists in their willingness to spend money. He might expect
an alliance between the Northern democrats and the Smith
faction which controlled the Navy Department. To such a
combination he must have foreseen that Madison would
yield.

In the face of such latent feuds nothing could be more hazardous than to spring upon Congress, in Madison's interests,
a new, tortuous, complicated Spanish policy, turning on the
secret assurance that France could be bribed with five million
dollars, at the moment when Congress would be required to
begin a commercial war upon England. Whether Madison
was responsible for these measures or not, his enemies would
charge him with the responsibility; and even without such
attacks from his own party, he was struggling with enemies
enough to have crushed Jefferson himself.

Early in December, all the actors in the drama assembled,
to play another act in a tragi-comedy of increasing interest.
With his old sanguine hopes, but not with all his old self-
confidence, the President watched them slowly arrive,—
Democrats, Federalists, Southern Republicans, all equally ignorant of what had been done, and what they were expected
to do; but more curious, better-informed, and more sharp-
sighted than these, the three diplomatists, Turreau, Merry,
and Yrujo, waiting with undisguised contempt to see what
species of coercion was to be employed against England,
France, and Spain.

To impose on hostile forces and interests the compulsion
of a single will was the task and triumph of the true politician,
which had been accomplished, under difficult conditions, by
men of opposite characters. A political leader might be com-
bative and despotic, or pliant and conciliatory. The method
mattered little, provided it obtained success,—but success depended more on character than on manœuvres. In the winter
of 1805–1806 President Jefferson dealt with a problem such as

few Americans have been required to solve. Other Presidents have met with violent opposition both within and without the ranks of their party; but no other President has been obliged to face a hostile minority, together with violent factiousness in the majority, and at the same time a spirit of aggression showing itself in acts of war from three of the greatest Powers of Europe. By what resources of skill or character President Jefferson was to restrain this disorder from becoming chaos, only a prophet could foretell. If ever the Federalist "crisis" seemed close at hand, it was in December, 1805. Some energetic impulse could alone save the country from drifting into faction at home and violence abroad.

All might go well if England, France, and Spain could be obliged to respect law. To restrain these three governments was Jefferson's most urgent need. The three envoys waited to see what act of energy he would devise to break through the net which had been drawn about him. Turreau enjoyed most of his confidence; and soon after the meeting of Congress, at the time when Jefferson was publicly using "strong language toward Spain," meant to produce an effect at the Tuileries, Turreau wrote interesting accounts of his private conversation for the guidance of Talleyrand and Napoleon:[1] —

"One may perhaps draw some inferences in regard to the true sense of the Message from some words which escaped the President in a private conversation with me. 'I see with pain,' he said, 'that our people have a tendency toward commerce which no other kind of interest will be able to balance; we should be essentially agricultural, and yet agriculture will never be more than a secondary interest here.' . . . In a preceding interview the President invited me to a discussion of Spanish affairs. . . . After some complaints about Spanish privateers, and the protection which Spain granted to ours in particular, Mr. Jefferson expanded on the griefs of the Americans in regard to some excursions of Spanish patrols beyond the limits provisionally established, and, in consequence, within the territory of Louisiana. I replied that doubtless the Spanish government had not authorized these steps, and that the mistakes of a few sub-

[1] Turreau to Talleyrand, Jan. 20, 1806; Archives des Aff. Étr., MSS.

alterns could not produce serious differences between the two Powers. 'That is true; but,' he added, 'these Spaniards are so stupid (*bêtes*), their government so detested,' etc. It was not easy to contradict him on this point. As for the English, his complaints and reproaches have been much more serious. He has assured me that they have taken five hundred American ships; that they could not have done more harm had they been at war with America; yet that England would in vain try, as against the Americans, to destroy neutral rights. 'In that respect,' added Mr. Jefferson, ' we have *principles* from which we shall never depart; our people have commerce everywhere, and everywhere our neutrality should be respected. On the other hand, we do not want war,—and all this is very embarrassing.' "

Turreau's comment on these words may have affected the policy of Napoleon, as it must certainly have had weight with Talleyrand:—

"If your Excellency was not already acquainted with the man and his government, this last phrase would be enough to enable you to judge the one and the other."

Chapter VI

THE NINTH CONGRESS met Dec. 2, 1805. During no period of eight years did Congress contain a smaller number of remarkable members than during the two administrations of Jefferson, from 1801 to 1809; and if the few Federalists in opposition were left out of view, the American people had in the Ninth Congress hardly a single representative, except John Randolph, capable of controlling any vote but his own. In the Senate, when George Clinton took his seat as Vice-President, he saw before him, among the thirty-four senators, not less than twenty-seven who belonged to his own party; yet among these twenty-seven Republican members of the Senate was not one whose name lived. Senator Bradley of Vermont exercised a certain influence in his day, like Dr. Mitchill of New York, or Samuel Smith of Maryland, or William B. Giles of Virginia, or Abraham Baldwin and James Jackson of Georgia. These were the leaders of the Senate, but they were men whose influence was due more to their office than to their genius; the Government gave them more weight than they could give back to it. Breckinridge of Kentucky had become attorney-general, and his seat was filled by John Adair. In the whole Senate not a Republican member could be found competent to defend a difficult financial or diplomatic measure as Gallatin or Madison could have done it, or would have wished it to be done.

In the House the Administration could count upon equally little aid. Setting aside John Randolph and Joseph Nicholson, who were more dangerous than any Federalist of New England to Government, the huge Republican majority contained no man of note. Its poverty was startling. Gallatin clung to Randolph as the only member of the House competent to conduct the public business; and no small part of Randolph's arrogance toward his own followers was due to his sense of intellectual superiority, and to the constant proof that they could do no business without his aid. Randolph was rarely arrogant in the face of men whose abilities were superior to his own, or whose will was stronger; he domineered over those whom he thought his inferiors, but he liked no contest in which he saw an uncertain hope of victory. In the Ninth Congress he met no rival in his own party. Massachusetts sent a new member, from whose oratory much was expected,—a certain Barnabas Bidwell; "but as a popular speaker he never can stand as the rival of John Randolph," was the comment of a Massachusetts senator on listening to him in the House.[1] New York, New Jersey, and Pennsylvania were represented by an almost solid mass of Democrats, without a single leader. Virginia and the other Southern States sent many men of excellent character and of the best social position to Washington, but not one who made a national name or who tried to master the details of public business. Perhaps the ablest new member was Josiah Quincy of Boston, whose positive temper, marked abilities, and vehement Federalism made him troublesome to the majority rather than useful in legislation.

When the House met, it proceeded at once to the election of a Speaker; and the old feuds of the last session broke out again. Fifty-four votes were required to elect; and on the first ballot Macon had but fifty-one. Twenty-seven Republicans voted for Joseph B. Varnum of Massachusetts, besides others who threw away their votes on candidates from Virginia and Pennsylvania. Only at the third ballot did Macon get a majority, and even then he received but fifty-eight votes, while the full strength of his party was more than one hundred. His first act was to reappoint Randolph and Nicholson on the Ways and Means Committee, where a place was also given to Josiah Quincy.

The President's Message was read December 3, and produced the effect to be expected. The country received it with applause as a proof of vigor. In Baltimore, and along the seaboard, it was regarded as equivalent to a declaration of war against Spain; it stopped trade, raised insurance, and encouraged piracy. The Federalist press throughout the country, except the "Evening Post," affected to admire and praise it. "Federalism revived!" said the bitter "Washington Federalist;" "dignified, firm, and spirited." "This day we have been astonished," wrote a correspondent to the "Boston Centinel;"[2]

[1] Diary of J. Q. Adams (March 8, 1806), i. 419.
[2] Columbian Centinel, Dec. 21, 1805.

"the President's speech is, in principle, almost wholly on the Washington and Adams system. It has puzzled the Federalists and offended many of the Democrats. It is in perfect nonconformity to all the former professions of the party." The Federalists exaggerated their applause in order to irritate John Randolph and his friends, who could not fail to see that the Message strengthened Madison at the expense of the old Republicans. Jefferson's private language was not less energetic than his public message. Among the favorite ideas which the President urged was that of claiming for America the ocean as far as the Gulf Stream, and forbidding hostilities within the line of deep-sea soundings.[1] One of the Massachusetts senators to whom he argued this doctrine inquired whether it might not be well, before assuming a claim so broad, to wait for a time when the Government should have a force to maintain it. The President replied by insisting that the Government, "should squint at it;"[2] and he lost no chance of doing so. He assured his friends that no privateer would ever again be permitted to cruise within the Gulf Stream.[3]

Such an attitude, public and private, roused much interest. Congress waited anxiously for the promised special message on Spanish affairs, and did not wait long. December 6, only three days after the Annual Message was sent in, the special and secret message followed; the House closed its doors, and the members listened eagerly to a communication which they expected to be, what it actually was, a turning-point in their politics.

The Message[4] very briefly narrated the story of the unratified claims convention, ending in Monroe's diplomatic misfortunes, and announced that the Spaniards showed every intention of advancing from Texas, until they should be repressed by force.

"Considering that Congress alone is constitutionally invested with the power of changing our condition from peace to war, I have thought it my duty to await their

[1] Cabinet Memoranda; Jefferson's Writings (Ford), i. 308.
[2] Diary of J. Q. Adams (Nov. 30, 1805), i. 376.
[3] Jefferson to Monroe, May 4, 1806; Writings (Ford), viii. 447.
[4] State Papers, ii. 613.

authority for using force in any degree which could be avoided. I have barely instructed the officers stationed in the neighborhood of the aggressions to protect our citizens from violence, to patrol within the borders actually delivered to us, and not to go out of them but when necessary to repel an inroad or to rescue a citizen or his property."

Passing next to the conduct of Napoleon, the Message mentioned the decided part taken by France against the United States on every point of the Spanish dispute,—

"her silence as to the Western boundary leaving us to infer her opinion might be against Spain in that quarter. Whatever direction she might mean to give to these differences, it does not appear that she has contemplated their proceeding to actual rupture, or that at the date of our last advices from Paris her Government had any suspicion of the hostile attitude Spain had taken here. On the contrary, we have reason to believe that she was disposed to effect a settlement on a plan analogous to what our ministers had proposed, and so comprehensive as to remove as far as possible the grounds of future collision and controversy on the eastern as well as western side of the Mississippi. The present crisis in Europe is favorable for pressing such a settlement, and not a moment should be lost in availing ourselves of it. Should it pass unimproved, our situation would become much more difficult. Formal war is not necessary, it is not probable it will follow; but the protection of our citizens, the spirit and honor of our country, require that force should be interposed to a certain degree. It will probably contribute to advance the object of peace. But the course to be pursued will require the command of means which it belongs to Congress exclusively to yield or to deny. To them I communicate every fact material for their information, and the documents necessary to enable them to judge for themselves. To their wisdom, then, I look for the course I am to pursue, and will pursue with sincere zeal that which they shall approve."

After the reading of this Message the House was more perplexed than ever. The few Federalists sneered. The warlike tone of the Annual Message, contradicting their theory of Jefferson's character, had already ended, as they believed, in surrender. John Randolph was angry. He felt that the President had assumed, for Madison's political profit, the tone of public bravado toward England and Spain, while Congress was required to overrule Madison's bold policy and to impose on the country what would seem a crouching cowardice of its own. The Message was at once referred to a special committee of seven members, with Randolph at its head, his friend Nicholson second in the number, John Cotton Smith, a vigorous Federalist, coming third; while, whether the Speaker intended it or not, the only person in the committee on whom the President could depend for useful service was Barnabas Bidwell, the new member from Massachusetts. Bidwell's conversion from Federalism was but recent, and neither his Federalism nor his democracy was of a kind that Randolph loved.

To this point the Louisiana precedent was closely followed, and Randolph seemed to have no excuse for refusing to do in 1805 what he had done in 1802; yet nothing could be surer than that the Randolph of 1805 was a very different man from the Randolph of three years before, as the Republican party of 1805 widely differed from the party which first elected Jefferson to the Presidency. No double-dealing, hesitation, or concealment was charged against Randolph. According to his own story, he called upon the President immediately, and learned, not without some surprise, that an appropriation of two millions was wanted to purchase Florida. He told the President without reserve "that he would never agree to such a measure, because the money had not been asked for in the Message; that he could not consent to shift upon his own shoulders or those of the House the proper responsibility of the Executive; but that even if the money had been explicitly demanded, he should have been averse to granting it, because, after the total failure of every attempt at negotiation, such a step would disgrace us forever,"—with much more to the same effect, which was mildly combated by Jefferson.[1]

The next day, December 7, the committee met, and Ran-

---

[1] First Letter of Decius, in the "Richmond Enquirer," August, 1806.

dolph, as he probably expected, found that Bidwell alone intended to support the Administration. Bidwell did not venture to act as the direct mouthpiece of the President, but undertook on his own authority to construe the Message as a demand for money, and proposed a grant to that effect. The rest of the committee gravely followed Randolph in professing to find no such meaning in the Message; Bidwell's motion had no supporter, and was promptly overruled. Jefferson's labored Resolutions, which Nicholson carried in his pocket for the committee to adopt, were suppressed; Nicholson returned them the next day to Gallatin, with a brief expression of his own decided disapproval.[1]

The committee separated, not to meet again for a fortnight; but during the following week Randolph had several interviews with the President and Secretary of State. Madison told him "that France would not permit Spain to adjust her differences with us; that France wanted money, and that we must give it to her, or have a Spanish and French war."[2] If Madison said this he told the truth. Randolph made an unfair use of the confidential words; for he proclaimed them as his excuse for declaring a public and personal war on the Secretary of State, which he waged thenceforward in a temper and by means so revolting as in the end to throw the sympathies of every unprejudiced man on the side of his victim.

"From the moment I heard that declaration," said Randolph afterward, "all the objections I originally had to the procedure were aggravated to the highest possible degree. I considered it a base prostration of the national character to excite one nation by money to bully another nation out of its property; and from that moment, and to the last moment of my life, my confidence in the principles of the man entertaining those sentiments died, never to live again."

These words would have carried more conviction had Randolph's quarrel with Madison not been of much older date. In truth he wanted a means to break down the secretary's chance of election as President, and he thought to find it here.

[1] Nicholson to Gallatin, Dec. 8, 1805; Gallatin MSS.
[2] Decius, No. 1; Randolph's speech of April 5, 1806; Annals of Congress, 1805–1806, pp. 984–985.

As he said openly in Congress and in the press, "his confidence in the Secretary of State had never been very high, but now it was gone forever."[1]

The serious charge against Madison was one which Madison alone could reveal. Down to October 23 he had held Randolph's view and had protested against turning the Spanish negotiation into a French job. He could hardly blame Randolph for adhering to an opinion which had been held by President and Cabinet until within a few weeks, when they had abandoned it without explanation or excuse.

Stubbornly refusing to act, Randolph, December 14, mounted his horse and rode to Baltimore, leaving the President for the moment helpless. Every hour's delay shook party discipline, and imperilled Armstrong's success. The President appealed to Nicholson; but Nicholson also disliked the intended policy, and could be persuaded to use his influence only so far as would enable the committee to act, with the understanding that its action would be adverse to the President's wishes. Although the situation was still secret, it threatened to become scandalous, and soon became so altogether.

December 21 Randolph returned. As he dismounted at the Capitol, he was received by Nicholson, who told him of the irritation which his delay had caused. The committee was instantly called together. As Randolph went to the committee-room he was met by Gallatin, who put into his hands a paper headed, "Provision for the purchase of Florida." Although Gallatin's relations with Randolph were friendly, they did not save the Secretary of the Treasury from a sharp rebuff. Randolph broke out roughly: he would not vote a shilling for the purchase of Florida; the President should not be allowed to throw upon Congress the odium "of delivering the public purse to the first cut-throat that demanded it;" on the record the Executive would appear as recommending manly and vigorous measures, while Congress would appear as having forced him to abandon them, when in fact it was acting all the while at Executive instigation; "I do not understand this double set of opinions and principles,—the one ostensible,

[1] Decius, No. 1.

the other real: I hold true wisdom and cunning to be utterly incompatible." With this sweeping censure of President, Cabinet, and party, Randolph turned his back on Gallatin and walked to the committee-room. There he had no trouble in carrying matters with a high hand. Instead of recommending an appropriation, the committee instructed Randolph to write to the Secretary of War asking his opinion what force was needed to protect the Southern frontier.

Christmas was then at hand, and not a step had yet been taken. Unless the spirit of faction could be crushed, not only was the fate of Madison sealed, but the career of Jefferson himself must end in failure. Nothing could be done with Randolph, who in a final interview at the White House, flatly declared "that he too had a character to support and principles to maintain," and avowed his determined opposition to the whole scheme of buying Florida of France. Jefferson, little as he liked to quarrel, accepted the challenge. Negotiations then ceased, and a party schism began.

If Randolph could not be overcome in debate, he might at least be overborne by numbers; if the best part of the old Republican party went with him, the rank and file of Northern and Western democrats would remain to support the Administration. Once more the committee was called together. Bidwell moved to appropriate two millions for foreign relations; the majority rejected his motion and adopted a report echoing the warlike tone of the President's public message, and closing with a Resolution to raise troops for the defence of the Southern frontier "from Spanish inroad and insult, and to chastise the same." This report was laid before the House by Randolph Jan. 3, 1806, when two additional Resolutions were immediately moved,—one appropriating money for extraordinary expenses in foreign intercourse, the other continuing the Mediterranean Fund for a new term of years; and the three Resolutions were referred to the House in Committee of the Whole, with closed doors.

Monday, Jan. 6, 1806, the debate began; and throughout the following week the House sat in secret session, while Randolph strained every nerve to break the phalanx of democrats which threatened to overwhelm him. Perpetually on the floor, he declaimed against the proposed negotiation at

Paris; while Nicholson, unwillingly consenting to vote for the two millions, said openly that he hoped in God the negotiation would fail. When at length a vote could be reached, the Administration carried its point,—seventy-two members supporting the President, against a minority of fifty-eight; but in this minority was included no small number of the most respectable Republicans. Twelve of the twenty-two Virginia members broke away from the President; and for the first time in a struggle vital to Jefferson's credit, more than half the majority consisted of Northern men.

The House having recovered control of the matter, thrust Randolph aside, rapidly passed a Bill appropriating two million dollars for extraordinary expenses in foreign relations, and Jan. 16, 1806, sent it to the Senate by a vote of seventy-six to fifty-four. It was accompanied by a secret message explaining that the money was intended for the purchase of Spanish territory east of the Mississippi. The Senate closed its doors, and with the least possible debate, Feb. 7, 1806, passed the bill, which, February 13, received the President's approval. Not until March 13,[1] six months after Armstrong's despatch had been written, did Madison at length send to Paris a public authority for Armstrong to offer France five million dollars for Florida and Texas to the Colorado,—an authority which should have been secret and prompt, to be worth sending at all.

Jefferson carried his point; he won a victory over Randolph, and silenced open resistance within the party; but his success was gained at a cost hitherto unknown in his experience. The men who were most obedient in public to his will growled in private almost as fiercely as Randolph himself. Senator Bradley made no secret of his disgust. Senator Anderson of Tennessee frankly said that he wished the Devil had the Bill; that the opposition did not half know how bad it was; that it was the most pernicious measure Jefferson had ever taken; "but so it was, so he would have it, and so it must be!"[2] Three Republican Senators—Bradley, Logan, and Mitchill—absented themselves at the final vote; four more—

[1] Madison to Armstrong and Bowdoin, March 13, 1806; State Papers, iii. 539.

[2] Diary of J. Q. Adams (Feb. 8, 1806), i. 405.

Adair, Gilman, Stone, and Sumter—voted against the Bill, which on its third reading obtained only seventeen voices in its favor against eleven in opposition. Worse than this, the malcontents felt that for the first time in the history of their party the whip of Executive power had been snapped over their heads; and, worst of all, the New England Federalists took for granted that Jefferson had become a creature of Napoleon. Of all political ideas that could gain a lodgment in the public mind, this last was the most fatal!

That either Jefferson or Madison was led by French sympathies has been shown to be untrue. Both of them submitted to the violence of all the belligerents alike, and their eagerness for Florida caused them by turns to flatter and to threaten Spain, France, and England; but not even for the sake of Florida would they have taken either a direct or an indirect part with France. Their unwillingness to offend Napoleon rose not from sympathy with him, but from the conviction that he alone could give Florida to the United States without the expense and losses inevitable in a war. Unhappily the public knew little of what President Jefferson had done or was doing; and another piece of legislation, carried through Congress at the same moment with the "Two-million Act," went far to fix the Federalists in their belief that the Administration obeyed the beck and call of the French Emperor.

The Annual Message made no allusion to St. Domingo; no public announcement had been given that the Executive wished for further legislation in regard to its trade, when, Dec. 18, 1805, Senator Logan of Pennsylvania brought forward a Bill to prohibit the trade altogether. That he acted without concert with Madison was not to be conceived. Logan privately admitted as his only object the wish of enabling Madison to tell the French government that the trade was forbidden, and that the merchants who carried it on did so at their own peril.[1] The Federalist senators opposed the Bill, and were joined by several Republicans. General Smith and Dr. Mitchill spoke against it. The opposition showed that the measure would sacrifice several hundred thousand dollars of revenue; that it would close the last opening

[1] Diary of J. Q. Adams (Jan. 15, 1806), i. 383.

which the new British policy left for American commerce with the West Indies; that it would throw the commerce with St. Domingo wholly into British hands; that it was an attempt to carry out French objects by American legislation, which would endanger the property and lives of American citizens in the island; and finally, that it was done in obedience to Napoleon's orders. December 27 the Senate called for the diplomatic correspondence on the subject, and the President communicated the extraordinary notes in which Talleyrand and Turreau declared that the commerce "must" not continue. The Senate received this mandate without protest or remonstrance; and after a long debate passed the Bill, Feb. 20, 1806, by a party vote of twenty-one to eight. Of the twenty-seven Republican senators, Stone of North Carolina alone voted against it. Amid execrations against the Haytian negroes, the Bill was next forced through the House almost without debate, and Feb. 28, 1806, received the President's signature.

This law,[1] limited to one year, declared that any American vessel " which shall be voluntarily carried, or shall be destined to proceed" to St. Domingo should be wholly forfeited, ship and cargo. Passed in consequence of Napoleon's positive order, communicated by the President to Congress as though to overawe objection, the Act violated the principles of international law, sacrificed the interests of Northern commerce, strained the powers of the Constitution as formerly construed by the party of States-rights, and, taken in all its relations, might claim distinction among the most disgraceful statutes ever enacted by the United States government. Nevertheless, this measure, which bore on its face the birth-mark of Napoleonic features, did in fact owe its existence chiefly to a different parentage. In truth, the Southern States dreaded the rebel negroes of Hayti more than they feared Napoleon. Fear often made them blind to their own attitudes; in this instance it made them indifferent to the charge of servility to France. The opportunity to declare the negroes of Hayti enemies of the human race was too tempting to be rejected; and not only did the Southern Republicans eagerly seize it, but they per-

---

[1] Act of Feb. 28, 1806; Annals of Congress, 1805–1806, p. 1228.

suaded their Northern allies to support them. John Randolph himself, though then wearying the House day after day with cries that Madison had sold the honor of the United States to France, never alluded to this act of subservience, which would have made any other Administration infamous, and quietly absented himself at the vote, that he might seem neither to obey Bonaparte's mandate nor to oppose the Bill. Of the twenty-six voices against it, nearly all were Federalists; yet in this curious list, side by side with Josiah Quincy, Samuel Dana, and John Cotton Smith, stood the names of Jacob Crowninshield and Matthew Lyon, democrats of the deepest dye and objects of John Randolph's bitterest sneers.

The "Two-million Act" and the Act forbidding commerce with St. Domingo were measures equally necessary for the success of the Florida purchase. Without conciliating Napoleon at St. Domingo, Jefferson could not expect his help at Paris. These measures, together with some appearance of military activity, completed the Executive scheme of foreign policy in regard to France and Spain; the more difficult task remained of dealing with England.

When the first news of Sir William Scott's decision in the case of the "Essex" arrived in America, the merchants were indignant; and their anger steadily rose as the confiscation of American ships became more general, until at length, in December, 1805, Stephen's pamphlet, "War in Disguise," arrived, and was reprinted in the newspapers. By the close of the year 1805 no one could longer doubt that Great Britain had, so far as suited her purposes, declared war against the United States.

The issue was simple. The United States might make war in return, or submit. Any measure short of open hostilities had unquestionably been taken into Pitt's account, and would produce no effect on his policy. War alone could move him from his purpose; but war would destroy American commerce and ruin Federalist resources, while any retaliation short of war would not only prove ineffective, but would injure the American merchants alone. Their dilemma was so unavoidable that they could not fail to be caught in it. George Cabot saw their danger from the first. Much against his will the merchants of Boston placed him upon a committee to draw a remonstrance to Congress against the British doctrine of neutral trade. "Our friend Cabot," wrote Fisher Ames,[1] "is much, too much, mortified that he is one of them. He hates hypocrisy, and respects principles; and he dreads lest the popular feeling should impel the committee to deny what he believes to be true, or to ask for what he knows to be mischievous." The Boston "Memorial,"[2] drawn by James Lloyd, was as cautious as popular feeling would tolerate, and asked no action from Government except the appointment of a special mission to strengthen the hands of Monroe at London; but Cabot signed it with extreme reluctance, and only with the understanding that it did not represent his personal views. The Philadelphia "Memorial" closed with stronger language, suggesting that war must be the result if Great Britain refused redress. The Baltimore "Memorial," drawn by William Pinkney, spoke in strong tones, but offered no advice. Toward the middle of January, 1806, these memorials, together with others, were sent to Congress by the President, with a Message inviting the Legislature to take the matter in hand, but offering no opinion as to the proper course to pursue.[3]

The fears of George Cabot were quickly justified. He chiefly dreaded the theories of the Republican party, which in his opinion were more destructive to American commerce than the British doctrines themselves or the demands of James Stephen. Jefferson and Madison were bent on testing the theory of the first Inaugural Address,—that commerce was the handmaid of agriculture; but in the harshest application of the slave-code of South Carolina or Georgia such treatment as agriculture proposed to her handmaid would have been rejected as inhuman, for it was a slow torture.

The theory of peaceable coercion, on which Jefferson relied, had often been explained as a duel in which either side counted upon exhausting its opponent by injuring itself. As Madison once said of the British manufacturers: "There are three hundred thousand souls who live by our custom: let them be driven to poverty and despair, and what will be the consequence?" The question was more easily asked than an-

[1] Ames to Pickering; Ames's Works, i. 342. Cf. Lodge's Cabot, p. 315.
[2] Boston Memorial; Annals of Congress, 1806–1809, Appendix, p. 890.
[3] Message of Jan. 17, 1806; State Papers, ii. 727.

swered, for in the actual condition of Europe economical laws were so violently disturbed that no man could venture to guess what fresh extravagance might result from new delirium; but while the three hundred thousand Englishmen were starving, three hundred thousand Americans would lose the profit on their crops, and would idly look at empty warehouses and rotting ships. English laborers had for many generations been obliged to submit to occasional suffering; Americans were untrained to submission. Granting that the Boston merchant, like the injured Brahmin, should seat himself at the door of the British offender, and slowly fast to death in order that his blood might stain the conscience of Pitt, he could not be certain that Pitt's conscience would be stimulated by the sacrifice, for the conscience of British Tories as regarded the United States had been ever languid. Cabot saw no real alternative between submission to Great Britain and the entire sacrifice of American commerce. He preferred submission.

The subject in all its bearings quickly came before Congress. Jan. 15, 1806, the Senate referred to a special committee that part of the President's Message which related to the British seizures. February 5, General Smith reported on behalf of the committee a series of Resolutions denouncing these seizures as an encroachment on national independence, and recommending the prohibition of British woollens, linens, silks, glass-wares, and a long list of other articles. On this Resolution the debate began, and soon waxed hot.

Chapter VII

NOTHING IN JEFFERSON'S life was stranger to modern ideas of politics than the secrecy which as President he succeeded in preserving. For two months the people of the United States saw their representatives go day after day into secret session, but heard not a whisper of what passed in conclave. Angry as Randolph was, and eager as the Federalists were to make mischief, they revealed not even to the senators or the foreign ministers what was passing in the House; and the public at large, under their democratic government, knew no more than Frenchmen of their destinies of war and peace. Such a state of things was contrary to the best traditions of the Republican party: it could not last, but it could end only in explosion.

When the debate on Smith's non-importation Resolutions began in the Senate February 12, the previous struggle which had taken place over the Spanish policy and the "Two-million Act" was still a secret; Randolph's schism was unknown beyond the walls of the Capitol; the President's scheme of buying West Florida from France after having, as he maintained, bought it once already, was kept, as he wished, untold. The world knew only that some mysterious business was afoot; and when Senator Samuel Smith's attack on trade began, the public naturally supposed it to be in some way connected with the measures so long discussed in secret session.

The President's attitude became more and more uneasy. Jefferson disliked and dreaded the point in dispute with England. The Spanish policy was his own creation, and he looked upon it with such regard as men commonly bestow upon unappreciated inventions,—he depended on its success to retrieve defeats elsewhere; but for the very reason that he exhausted his personal influence to carry the Spanish policy against opposition, he left British questions to Congress and his party. Where England was to be dealt with, Madison took the lead which Jefferson declined. For many years past Madison had been regarded as the representative of a policy of commercial restriction against Great Britain. To revive his influence, his speeches and resolutions of 1794[1] were reprinted in the "National Intelligencer" as a guide for Congress; his pamphlet against the British doctrines of neutral trade was made a political text-book; while his friends took the lead in denouncing England and in calling for retaliation. He himself lost no chance of pressing his views, even upon political opponents. "I had considerable conversation with Mr. Madison," wrote one of them February 13, "on the subjects now most important to the public. His system of proceeding toward Great Britain is to establish permanent commercial distinctions between her and other nations,—a retaliating navigation act, and aggravated duties on articles imported from her."[2] By his own choice, and in a manner almost defiant of failure, Madison's political fortunes were united with the policy of coercing England through restrictions of trade.

At first much was said of an embargo. Senator Jackson of Georgia, Dec. 20, 1805, declared with his usual vehemence in favor of this measure. "Not a nation," said he, "exists which has West Indian colonies but is more or less dependent on us, and cannot do without us; they must come to our terms, or starve. On with your embargo, and in nine months they must lie at your feet!" John Randolph, sure to oppose whatever Madison wished, also looked with favor on this course. "I would (if anything) have laid an embargo," he said.[3] The embargo party at best was small, and became smaller when toward the close of December, 1805, news arrived that Admiral Nelson had fought a great naval battle, October 21, against the combined French and Spanish fleets, off Cape Trafalgar, ending in a victory so complete as to leave England supreme upon the ocean. The moral effect of Nelson's triumph was great. Embargo was the last step before war, and few Americans cared to risk war with England under any circumstances; with harbors undefended and without an ally on the ocean, war was rashness which no one would face. Madison's more gentle plan of partial restrictions in trade became the Republican policy.

[1] Annals of Congress, 1793–1795, p. 155.
[2] Diary of J. Q. Adams (Feb. 13, 1806), i 408.
[3] Randolph's Speech of March 5, 1806; Annals of Congress, 1805–1806, p. 571.

Even before Senator Samuel Smith reported his Resolutions, February 5, to the Senate, the British minister Merry wrote to his Government that the members most opposed to commercial restrictions, despairing of effectual resistance, would endeavor only to limit the number of articles to be prohibited, and to postpone the date on which the law should take effect, in order to send a special mission to England and negotiate an amicable arrangement. Merry added that a special mission had been under discussion from the first: —

"But I now learn that it has been, and continues to be, opposed by the President, who wishes that Mr. Monroe . . . should continue to carry on the negotiation alone. Matters, however, being now brought to a disagreeable crisis by the clamor of the nation and the instigation of the Administration, some of the members of the Senate are, I find, endeavoring to engage the rest of their body to join them in exercising their constitutional privilege of advising the President on the occasion; and that their advice to him will be to suspend any step that can have a hostile tendency until the experiment has been tried of an extraordinary mission."[1]

Merry was exactly informed as to the fate of General Smith's Resolutions even before they had been reported to the Senate. They were three in number; but only the third, which recommended non-importation, was drawn by Smith. The first and second, the work of Senator Adams of Massachusetts, were not wholly welcome either to the Administration or to the minority. The first declared the British seizures "an unprovoked aggression," a "violation of neutral rights," and an "encroachment upon national independence." The second requested the President to "demand and insist upon" indemnity, and to make some arrangement about impressments. The first Resolution, although fatal to future Federalist consistency, was unanimously adopted by the Senate, February 12, almost without debate, — even Timothy Pickering recording his opinion that the British government had encroached upon national independence. The second Resolution was

[1] Merry to Mulgrave, Feb. 2, 1806; MSS. British Archives.

criticised as an attempt at dictation to the Executive, which would give just cause of offence to the President. By this argument the Senate was induced to strike out the words "and insist;" but although the Resolution, thus altered, was weak, seven Republican senators voted against it as too strong.

The reason of this halting movement had been explained by Merry to Lord Mulgrave nearly two weeks before. The Senate stumbled over the important personality of James Monroe. The next Presidential election, some three years distant, warped the national policy in regard to a foreign encroachment. Senator Samuel Smith, ambitious to distinguish himself in diplomacy, having failed to obtain the mission to Paris, wished the dignity of a special envoy to London, and was supported by Wilson Cary Nicholas. The friends of Madison were willing to depress Monroe, whom John Randolph was trying to elevate. Even Mrs. Madison, in the excitement of electioneering, allowed herself to talk in general society very slightingly of Monroe;[1] and there were reasons which made interference from Mrs. Madison peculiarly irritating to Monroe's friends.[2] Dr. Logan, the senator from Pennsylvania, while helping Madison to satisfy Napoleon in regard to St. Domingo, was prominent in suggesting that it would be well to set Monroe gently aside.[3] This coalition of Madison, Smith, Logan, and Wilson Cary Nicholas was so strong as to control the Senate.

The second Resolution was adopted Feb. 14, 1806; and a week afterward, General Smith and Dr. Mitchill were appointed a committee to carry the two Resolutions to the White House. Two years later, in response to Monroe's complaints, President Jefferson explained how these senators managed to impose on the Executive a policy of their own.

"After delivering the Resolutions," said Jefferson[4] in an aggrieved tone, "the committee entered into free conversation, and observed that although the Senate could not in form recommend any extraordinary mission, yet that as in-

[1] Diary of J. Q. Adams (March 13, 1806), i. 420.
[2] Adams's Randolph, p. 203.
[3] Diary of J. Q. Adams (Feb. 1, 1806), i. 395.
[4] Jefferson to Monroe, March 10, 1808; Works, v. 253.

dividuals there was but one sentiment among them on the measure, and they pressed it. I was so much averse to it, and gave them so hard an answer, that they felt it and spoke of it. But it did not end here. The members of the other House took up the subject and set upon me individually, and these the best friends to you as well as myself, and represented the responsibility which a failure to obtain redress would throw on us both, pursuing a conduct in opposition to the opinion of nearly every member of the Legislature. I found it necessary at length to yield my own opinion to the general sense of the national council, and it really seemed to produce a jubilee among them."

Jefferson saw his most devoted followers waver in their allegiance, and was reduced to temporize in order to avoid worse evils. General Smith in the Senate seemed interested in embarrassing him. If Smith could not be minister to England, he was bent upon becoming minister to France. Armstrong had challenged attack by his management of American claims before the French commission, and had written to the French government an indiscreet letter against a certain claim made by a firm of Nicklin & Griffith, of Philadelphia. When the President nominated him as special minister, with Bowdoin, to conduct the new Florida negotiation, a strong opposition appeared in the Senate, at the head of which was General Smith. March 17 the vote was taken; the Senate was equally divided, fifteen to fifteen, and Vice-President Clinton's voice alone saved Armstrong from rejection. Had the Senate been left to follow out its own aims, the President's authority might perhaps have been shaken, and a period of faction might have followed; but fortunately for the President and for the Secretary of State, among the enemies with whom they had to deal was one whose temper passed the bounds of common-sense.

Until the month of March, 1806, Randolph's opposition was confined to Spanish affairs in secret session. The House was even slower than the Senate to take up the matter of British relations. Dec. 4, 1805, the subject was referred to the Committee of Ways and Means. Jan. 17, 1806, another message was sent to the same committee; but day after day passed without bringing a report from Randolph, until Smilie of Pennsylvania moved to discharge the Committee of Ways and Means in order to bring the subject before the House in Committee of the Whole. Randolph was ill and absent when the House, Jan. 29, 1806, decided to take the matter from his hands.

On the same day Andrew Gregg, a member from Pennsylvania, moved a Resolution forbidding the importation of all goods the growth or product or manufacture of Great Britain. Still the House left the subject without decision or discussion. February 10 Joseph Nicholson introduced another Resolution, which came probably from Gallatin. Gregg's nonimportation measure would cost the Treasury five million dollars a year, and Gallatin preferred a less sweeping prohibition. Even Senator Smith's scheme was too strong for Nicholson, who pointed out that coarse woollens, Jamaica rum, Birmingham hardware, and salt were necessities with which America could not supply herself, nor could any nation except England supply her. Nicholson's Resolution prohibited only such British goods as might be replaced by other nations than England, or might be produced at home,—manufactures of leather, tin, brass, hemp, flax, silk; high priced woollens; woollen hosiery, glass, silver, and plated ware, paper, pictures, prints,—a formidable list of articles, which if not, like Jamaica rum, necessary to America, were essentials to civilized existence.

Other Resolutions were introduced, but those of Gregg and Nicholson by common consent maintained pre-eminence; and between the policies marked by them as complete or partial non-importation Congress had to decide. Although the subject was before the House, the month of February passed without debate. Not until March 5, 1806, did Gregg call up his Resolution. In doing so, he made a speech studiously moderate. He seemed disinclined to defend the carrying-trade, and abstained from treating the British seizures as cause for war, but rather threw the weight of his argument on the manifest outrage of impressments; yet even this he treated as though it were a question of unfriendly fiscal regulation.

"I have no apprehension whatever of a war," he said,

"Great Britain is too well versed in the business of calculation, and too well acquainted with her own interest, to persevere in this lawless system at the hazard of losing customers whose annual purchases of her manufactures and other merchandise exceeds, I believe, thirty millions of dollars."

Gregg would not endanger peace, but he would say to Great Britain,—

"in this mild and moderate, though manly and firm, language: 'You have insulted the dignity of our country by impressing our seamen and compelling them to fight your battles against a Power with whom we are at peace; you have plundered us of much property by that predatory war which you authorize to be carried on against our commerce. To these injuries, insults, and oppression we will submit no longer. . . . If you persist in your hostile measures, if you absolutely refuse acceding to any propositions of compromise, we must slacken those bonds of friendship by which we have been connected. You must not expect hereafter to find us in your market purchasing your manufactures to so large an amount.' This is their vulnerable part; by attacking them in their warehouses and workshops, we can reach their vitals."

If Pitt should retaliate, Gregg would go further; he would confiscate all the private property belonging to British subjects on which he could lay his hands, treaty stipulations to the contrary notwithstanding.

The Pennsylvanian contented himself with pacific measures, and his oratory had the merit of consistency with his party doctrines and principles; but the democracy of Massachusetts, which would never understand or obey the theories of Virginia and Pennsylvania, could not rest content with Gregg's Quaker ideas.

"After the course we are now taking," said Crowninshield, "should Britain persist in her captures and in her oppressive treatment of our seamen, and refuse to give them up, I would not hesitate to meet her in war. But, as I observed before, I do not believe Great Britain will go to war. Our trade is too valuable to her. She knows, too, that in such an event she will lose her eastern provinces; the States of Vermont and Massachusetts will ask no other assistance than their own militia to take Canada and Nova Scotia. Some of her West Indian islands will also fall. She knows also other things. Her subjects own sixteen millions of the old public debt of the United States, eight millions of the Louisiana stock, and three or four millions bank stock, and have private debts to the amount of ten or twelve millions,—amounting in the whole to nearly forty millions of dollars. Will Great Britain, by going to war, risk her provinces and this large amount of property? I think she will not put so much to hazard."

When Crowninshield sat down, John Randolph took the floor. In Randolph's long career of oratorical triumphs, no such moment had offered itself before, or was to occur again. Still in Virginian eyes the truest and ablest Republican in Congress, the representative of power and principle, the man of the future, Randolph stood with the halo of youth, courage, and genius round his head,—a sort of Virginian Saint Michael, almost terrible in his contempt for whatever seemed to him base or untrue. He began by saying that he entered on the subject "manacled, handcuffed, and tongue-tied;" his lips were sealed; he could but "hobble over the subject as well as his fettered limbs and palsied tongue would enable him to do it;" and with this preamble he fell upon Gregg and Crowninshield:[1] —

"It is mere waste of time to reason with such persons; they do not deserve anything like serious refutation. The proper arguments for such statesmen are a strait-waistcoat, a dark room, water-gruel, and depletion."

The proposed confiscation of British property called out a sneer at Crowninshield: —

"God help you if these are your ways and means for carrying on war! if your finances are in the hands of such a chancellor of the exchequer! Because a man can take an

[1] Annals of Congress, 1805–1806, p. 555.

observation and keep a log-book and a reckoning, can navigate a cock-boat to the West Indies or the East, shall he aspire to navigate the great vessel of State, to stand at the helm of public councils? *Ne sutor ultra crepidam!*"

Again and again he turned aside to express contempt for the Northern democrats:—

"Shall this great mammoth of the American forest leave his native element and plunge into the water in a mad contest with the shark? Let him stay on shore, and not be excited by the muscles and periwinkles on the strand!"

On the point of policy Randolph took ground which, if not warlike, was at least consistent,—the ground which all Southern Republicans of the Jefferson school would have taken, if shame had not withheld them. Even if determined in the end to submit, the President and Secretary wished to keep up the form of resistance. Randolph declared that the form was absurd; he would do nothing to protect "this mushroom, this fungus of war,"—a carrying-trade which at the first moment of peace would no longer exist:—

"I will never consent to go to war for that which I cannot protect. I deem it no sacrifice of dignity to say to the Leviathan of the deep: We are unable to contend with you in your own element; but if you come within our actual limits, we will shed our last drop of blood in their defence."

Had Randolph contented himself with taking this position, he could not have been overthrown, for he carried with him the secret sympathy of the Southern Republicans; but he had not the self-control that was needed in the face of an opponent so pliant and conciliatory as Jefferson. Randolph took rare pleasure in making enemies, while Jefferson never made one enemy except to gain two friends. Not satisfied with attacking Crowninshield and Gregg, Randolph gave full play to his anger against the whole House, and even assailed the Executive:—

"I have before protested, and I again protest, against secret, irresponsible, overruling influence. The first question I asked when I saw the gentleman's Resolution was, Is this a measure of the Cabinet? Not of an open declared Cabinet, but of an invisible, inscrutable, unconstitutional Cabinet, without responsibility, unknown to the Constitution. I speak of back-stairs influence,—of men who bring messages to this House, which, although they do not appear on the Journals, govern its decisions. Sir, the first question that I asked on the subject of British relations was, What is the opinion of the Cabinet; what measures will they recommend to Congress?—well knowing that whatever measures we might take they must execute them, and therefore that we should have their opinion on the subject. My answer was (and from a Cabinet minister too), *There is no longer any Cabinet!*"

Though forbidden to mention what had occurred in secret session, "manacled, handcuffed, and tongue-tied" as he was, Randolph dragged the Spanish secret to light:—

"Like true political quacks, you deal only in handbills and nostrums. Sir, I blush to see the record of our proceedings; they resemble nothing but the advertisements of patent medicines. Here you have 'the worm-destroying lozenges;' there 'Church's cough-drops;' and to crown the whole, 'Sloan's vegetable specific,'—an infallible remedy for all nervous disorders and vertigoes of brainsick politicians. . . . And where are you going to send your political panacea, resolutions and handbills excepted; your sole arcanum of government, your King Cure-all? To Madrid? No! you are not such quacks as not to know where the shoe pinches. To Paris! You know at least where the disease lies, and there you apply your remedy. When the nation anxiously demands the result of your deliberations, you hang your head and blush to tell. You are afraid to tell!"

Randolph next attacked Madison. He took up the secretary's late pamphlet and overwhelmed its argument with contempt. He declared that France was the real enemy of America; that England was acting under the dictates of necessity; that the situation of Europe had completely changed since 1793, and that England occupied the place which France then held: "she is the sole bulwark of the human race against

universal dominion,—no thanks to her for it!" As for a policy, he proposed to abandon commerce and to amputate mercantile interests:—

"I can readily tell gentlemen what I will not do. I will
not propitiate any foreign nation with money. I will not
launch into a naval war with Great Britain. . . . I will send
her money on no pretext whatever; much less on pretence
of buying Labrador or Botany Bay, when my real object
was to secure limits which she formally acknowledged at
the Peace of 1783. I go further: I would, if anything, have
laid an embargo; this would have got our own property
home, and our adversary's into our power. If there is any
wisdom left among us, the first step toward hostility will
always be an embargo. In six months all your mercantile
megrims would vanish. As to us, although it would cut
deep, we can stand it."

Before closing this desultory harangue, the orator once
more turned to taunt the President:—

"Until I came into the House this morning, I had been
stretched on a sick bed; but when I behold the affairs of
this nation—instead of being where I hoped, and the people believed they were, in the hands of responsible men—
committed to Tom, Dick, and Harry, to the refuse of the
retail trade of politics, I do feel, I cannot help feeling, the
most deep and serious concern. . . . I know, sir, that we
may say, and do say, that we are independent (would it
were true!), as free to give a direction to the Executive as
to receive it from him; but do what you will, foreign relations, every measure short of war, and even the course of
hostilities, depends upon him. He stands at the helm, and
must guide the vessel of State. You give him money to buy
Florida, and he purchases Louisiana. You may furnish
means; the application of those means rests with him. Let
not the master and mate go below when the ship is in distress, and throw the responsibility upon the cook and the
cabin-boy! I said so when your doors were shut; I scorn to
say less now they are open. Gentlemen may say what they
please; they may put an insignificant individual to the ban
of the republic: I shall not alter my course."

That such a speech from a man so necessary to the Government should throw consternation among the majority, was a matter of course. No such event had ever happened in Congress as the public rebellion of a great party leader. The Federalists had quarrelled as bitterly, but had made no such scandal. Yet serious as Randolph's defection might be, it would have done little harm had it not been that in denouncing the course taken by Jefferson and Madison he had much secret sympathy. Nay, as regarded Gregg's Resolution, he expressed the feelings of the President himself and of the Cabinet. The so-called resistance to England, like the resistance to Spain, was a sham, and all parties agreed with Randolph in opposing serious retaliation.

Nothing was needed but that Randolph should keep his temper in order to win a triumph. Napoleon could be trusted to give Jefferson no more provinces at any price, for within a few days after Randolph's outbreak news arrived that the battle of Austerlitz had been fought, and the Treaty of Pressburg signed. Jefferson himself could be trusted to prevent Gregg's Resolution from passing, for the news that Pitt was dead and Fox in power arrived almost at the same moment with that of Austerlitz. The entire situation had changed; an entirely new policy must be invented, and this could hardly fail to follow Randolph's ideas. He had only to wait; but meanwhile he was consumed by a fever of rage and arrogance. Thinking that the time had come to destroy the Secretary of State, he set himself vigorously to the task. Day after day he occupied the floor, attacking Madison with more and more virulence. He insisted that "the business from first to last had been managed in the most imbecile manner."

"I do not speak of the negotiator [Monroe]—God forbid!—but of those who drew the instruction of the man who negotiated. We bought Louisiana from France under the terms of the Treaty of San Ildefonso. According to the Executive understanding, that country extended to the Perdido and the River Bravo. We immediately legislated on our first claim and passed a law erecting the bay and shores of the Mobile into a revenue district. What was the fact? That we were legislating without information. We had never been told that Laussat had been directed to receive the country only to the Iberville and the Lakes. We consequently legislated in error, for want of Executive information. This was the beginning."[1]

At length, April 7, Randolph committed his last and fatal blunder by going formally into opposition.

"I came here," he said, "prepared to co-operate with the Government in all its measures. I told them so. But I soon found there was no choice left, and that to co-operate in them would be to destroy the national character. I found I might co-operate, or be an honest man. I have therefore opposed, and will oppose them."

Such tactics, in the face of a man so supple as President Jefferson, invited failure. With every weapon of offence in his hand, and with the assurance of triumph, Randolph threw his chances away and found himself within a few weeks delivered to the mercy of Secretary Madison and the Northern democrats. Jefferson's strong qualities were called into play by Randolph's method of attack. Jefferson was not apt to be violent, nor was he despotic in temper; but he was, within certain limits, very tenacious of his purpose, and he had to a certain degree the habits of a paternal despot. Randolph's sudden assault, carrying with it some twenty-five or thirty of the ablest and best Republicans in Congress, greatly alarmed the President, who set himself quietly and earnestly to the task of restoring order to his shattered columns. The Northern democrats were easily held firm, for they hated Randolph and had little love for Virginia. As for the rebellious cohort of "old Republicans," Jefferson exhausted his resources in coaxing them to desert their leader.

March 13 the House laid Gregg's Resolution aside; Nicholson's was then taken up, adopted March 17, and sent to a special committee to be framed as a Bill. Meanwhile the President busily conciliated opposition; and his first thought was of Monroe in London, certain to become the centre of intrigue. March 16 Jefferson wrote to warn his old friend against the danger of making common cause with Randolph.

[1] Annals of Congress, 1805–1806, p. 961.

The task was difficult, because it was necessary at the same time to break the news that Monroe must submit to the implied censure of a special mission.

"Some of your new friends," wrote Jefferson,[1] "are attacking your old ones, out of friendship for you, but in a way to render you great injury. . . . Mr. Nicholson's Resolutions will be passed this week, probably by a majority of one hundred Republicans against fifteen Republicans and twenty-seven Federalists. When passed, I shall join Mr. Pinkney of Maryland as your associate for settling our differences with Great Britain. He will depart on a fortnight's notice, and will be authorized to take your place whenever you think yourself obliged to return."

Two days later he wrote again.[2] In the interval Nicholson's Resolution had been adopted by a vote of eighty-seven to thirty-five, and Randolph's minority of Republican members had been reduced, beyond the President's hope, to a mere half-dozen grumblers.

"Mr. R. withdrew before the question was put," wrote Jefferson. "I have never seen a House of Representatives more solidly united in doing what they believe to be the best for the public interest. There can be no better proof than the fact that so eminent a leader should at once, and almost unanimously, be abandoned."

At the same moment Randolph wrote to Monroe that the Republican party was broken in pieces, and that the "old Republicans" were united in the support of Monroe against Madison for the Presidency.[3] Randolph complained bitterly of the atmosphere of intrigue which surrounded the Administration; but as regarded him at least, Jefferson's retort was plausible that he had never found fault with intrigue so long as he had a share in it. After challenging the contest with Madison, he had only himself to blame if the President, who was a master of intrigue, used the weapon freely to defend his favorite and himself.

[1] Jefferson to Monroe, March 16, 1806; Jefferson MSS.
[2] Jefferson to Monroe, March 18, 1806; Jefferson MSS.
[3] Adams's Randolph, p. 199–202.

To detach Randolph's friends from their leader was an object which the President pursued with zeal and success. He was a little disposed to overawe Monroe; but he was glad to conciliate Joseph Nicholson, next to Randolph the most formidable "old Republican" in public life. Nicholson was torn by conflicting sympathies; he loved Randolph, and he did not love Madison. On the other hand he was attached to Gallatin by marriage and respect. A poor man, with a large family, Nicholson found the life of a Congressman unprofitable; and when he was offered a seat on the Bench as Judge of the Sixth Maryland Circuit, he accepted the appointment. April 9, 1806, his letter of resignation was read to the House, and the democrats knew that Randolph had lost his strongest friend.

The Speaker remained to be dealt with. To overawe Macon was impossible; to buy him was out of the question; to crush him was only a last resort; no other resource was left than to coax him.

"Some enemy, whom we know not, is sowing tares between us," wrote the President to the Speaker, at the moment when he was warning Monroe and Nicholson escaped to the bench.[1] "Between you and myself nothing but opportunities of explanation can be necessary to defeat these endeavors. At least, on my part, my confidence in you is so unqualified that nothing further is necessary for my satisfaction."

Jefferson never was more sincere than in making this advance to a friend from whom the course of events threatened to part him: but unfortunately the point of doubt was not so much Jefferson's confidence in Macon as it was Macon's confidence in Jefferson. At bottom remained the unpleasant thought that Jefferson had ceased to be either a Virginian or a Republican; had chosen other friends and advisers than Macon, other objects and ambitions than Macon pursued.

Even Randolph was treated with delicacy. Jefferson would gladly have won him back, had Randolph admitted a hope that he would accept Madison's candidacy; but on that point no compromise could be conceived. Madison's fate was trem-

---

[1] Jefferson's Writings (Ford), viii. 439.

bling in the balance. Sacrifice of Madison was impossible to the President, and nothing short of sacrifice would satisfy Randolph. The "old Republican" schism must therefore be left to itself; the schismatics were too honest and respectable to be dealt with. The President exhausted his power when he won back the wavering, fixed Gallatin in allegiance to Madison, and carried Nicholson out of the arena; but although gentle and forbearing in regard to these honest, and as he thought, misguided men, Jefferson did not think it necessary to show equal deference to the merely selfish interests which had made use of this moment of confusion in order to exact terms from the Government. He showed that he could punish, by making an example of General and Senator Samuel Smith.

Robert Smith in the Cabinet was so near to his brother Samuel in the Senate that Jefferson could no longer trust his secrets to the Cabinet itself. After crushing in the House Randolph's opposition to the Spanish policy, and after yielding to Smith and the Senate in regard to a special English mission, the President was required to make certain appointments, one of which was that of a new minister to aid and succeed Monroe in London, whence it was supposed that Monroe wished to return. General Smith's wider plan assumed that Monroe was on his way home, and would be succeeded by a regular minister, assisted, for commercial negotiations, by a special envoy. The special envoy was to be himself; the permanent minister was to be his brother-in-law Wilson Cary Nicholas. He had even written to assure Nicholas of the appointment, when his project was defeated by the secret and unexpected interference of the President.

April 1, 1806, Samuel Smith wrote to his brother-in-law an account of his hopes and disappointment:[1]

"Monroe had written that he would leave Great Britain in November; therefore a mission of two,—one to remain as minister, the other a merchant of some distinction and of general information to go as envoy extraordinary, —was desired by all; and here, this proposal generally—I may say universally—meant S. S. Two only exceptions: As Monroe

[1] Samuel Smith to W. C. Nicholas, April 1, 1806; Nicholas MSS.

will remain until the whole business shall be settled, many wish now an able merchant to join him; in either case to make a commercial treaty with Great Britain. To such a treaty there is a rooted aversion in the mind of the President and Mr. Madison. I ought to apologize for leading you into error. I still do believe that you were originally intended for London. A good Federalist is to succeed Monroe, and has been privately written to by the President without the knowledge of any of his Cabinet; they appeared astonished when he mentioned what he had done."

The good Federalist thus put over Smith's head was William Pinkney, a prominent lawyer of Smith's city of Baltimore. Such a step without consulting the Smiths, and against their personal interests, was a strong measure on the part of Jefferson, quite out of keeping with his ordinary practice. Offence of tried friends in order to conciliate Federalists was little to his taste; but General Smith's conduct had become so factious as to warrant reproof. Smith was reduced to submission. He had not shared in Randolph's bitterness against the Spanish policy, but he had attempted to make use of the old Republican schism for his personal objects; and after Randolph's overthrow, Smith could no longer venture upon open opposition. Though beaten by only one vote in his attack on Armstrong's nomination, Smith felt that his defeat was made final by the collapse of Randolph's rebellion. He admitted to Nicholas that no effective resistance could be made to the Florida purchase, and that nothing remained but obedience to the President's will: —

"The question was simply, Buy or fight! Both Houses by great majorities said, Buy! The manner of buying appears a little disagreeable. Politicians will believe it perfectly honest to induce France 'by money' to coerce Spain to sell that which she has absolutely declared was her own property, and from which she would not part. Mr. Randolph expects that this public explosion of our views and plans will render abortive this negotiation, and make the Executive and poor little Madison unpopular. Against this last he vents his spleen. However, he spares nobody, and by this conduct has compelled *all* to rally round the Executive for *their own preservation*. From the Potomac north and east, the members adhere to the President; south they fall daily from their allegiance."

Thus, after four months of confusion, victory declared itself on the President's side.[1] Randolph's violence, even more than Jefferson's dexterity, was fatal to the old Republican uprising. As early as April 1 discipline was restored, with Madison stronger than ever before. The few remaining days of the session only confirmed the result.

[1] Cf. Jefferson to W. C. Nicholas, March 24 and April 13, 1806. Writings (Ford), viii. 434.

Chapter VIII

THE PRESIDENT'S TRIUMPH was decided as early as March 17, for on that day General Smith's assault upon Armstrong was defeated in the Senate by Vice-President Clinton's casting vote; and in the House, Randolph's resistance to the non-importation policy against England ended in his discomfiture and withdrawal; but although even at that early moment no one could doubt Jefferson's irresistible strength, yet no one who knew John Randolph could suppose that either the President or his Secretary of State was in future to sleep on roses.

The session ended April 21; and during the few weeks that intervened between Randolph's defeat, March 17, and the adjournment, the exasperated Virginian developed a strange and unequalled genius. His position was new. The alternation of threat and entreaty, of lofty menace and reluctant obedience, which marked the conduct of the State Department in its dealings with France and England, had no real admirer in the United States. When Randolph denounced the change in Spanish policy, not a voice was raised in its defence, and the public wondered that so powerful a President should be left an unprotected victim to assaults so furious. In truth Madison himself must have been tongue-tied; no resource of logic could excuse his sudden abandonment of the determination "to extinguish in the French government every hope of turning our controversy with Spain into a French job, public or private." Even had he succeeded in excusing himself, his success must have proved that Randolph's crime consisted in maintaining the ground which had been taken and held by President, secretary, and plenipotentiaries down to the moment, Oct. 23, 1805, when without explanation the ground was abandoned. Silence and numbers were the only arguments in defence of such a change, and to these forms of logic the followers of the Administration at first resorted. "It is a matter of great astonishment to me," wrote Wilson Cary Nicholas to Jefferson April 2, "that such a philippic as we have seen could have been uttered in Congress, and not one word said in justification of the Administration."[1] Toward the end of the session this silence ceased, the majority made great efforts to answer Randolph; but the answers were weaker than the silence.

Besides this difficulty in the nature of the case, the majority felt more than ever the advantage enjoyed by Randolph in his vigor and quickness of mind. For two months he controlled the House by audacity and energy of will. The Crowninshields, Varnums, and Bidwells of New England, the Sloans, Smilies, and Findleys of the Middle States, could do nothing with him; but by the time he had done with them they were bruised and sore, mortified, angry, and ridiculous. The consciousness of this superiority, heightened to extreme arrogance by the need of brushing away every moment a swarm of flies which seemed never to know they were crushed, excited Randolph to madness. He set no bounds to the expression of his scorn not only for the Northern democrats, but for the House itself and for the whole government. At one member he shook his fist, and imperiously bade him sit down or to go down the back-stairs; another member he called an old toothless driveller, superannuated, and mumbling in second dotage.[2] He flung Madison's pamphlet with violent contempt on the floor of the House; and he told the House itself that it could not maintain a decision two hours together against the Yazoo lobby.

Sloan of New Jersey, a sort of butt in the party, who could not forgive Randolph's allusion to the "vegetable specific," retorted that Randolph behaved like "a maniac in a strait-jacket accidentally broke out of his cell." No doubt his conduct was open to the charge; but none the less the maniac gave great trouble and caused extreme confusion. Even after three fourths of the House came to share Sloan's opinion, and began the attempt to control Randolph by every means in their power, they found the task beyond them.

The Non-importation Bill, framed on Nicholson's Resolution, was quickly reported, and March 25 the House agreed to fix November 15 as the date on which the Act should go into operation. Randolph could not prevent its passage, but

[1] W. C. Nicholas to Jefferson, April 2, 1806; Jefferson MSS.
[2] Annals of Congress, 1805–1806, p. 1107.

he could make it contemptible, if it was not so already; and he could encourage the Government and people of England to treat it with derision.

"Never in the course of my life," he cried,[1] "have I witnessed such a scene of indignity and inefficiency as this measure holds forth to the world. What is it? A milk-and-water Bill! A dose of chicken-broth to be taken nine months hence! . . . It is too contemptible to be the object of consideration, or to excite the feelings of the pettiest State in Europe."

The Bill immediately passed by a vote of ninety-three to thirty-two; but every man on the floor felt that Randolph was right, and every foreign minister at Washington adopted his tone.

Two days afterward he called up certain Resolutions denouncing as unconstitutional the union of civil and military authority in the same person, and declaring that a contractor under Government was a civil officer, and as such incapable of holding a seat in the House. These Resolutions struck in every direction; they were a reproof to the House, to the President, and to individual members like Matthew Lyon, who had taken mail contracts, or John Smith, the senator from Ohio, who was a large contractor for army supplies. General Wilkinson at St. Louis held civil and military powers; the new territory about to be organized under the name of Michigan was to have a governor of the same sort. A vote against Randolph's Resolutions contravened one of the cardinal principles of the Republican party; a vote for them censured the party itself and embarrassed Government. Beaten by very large majorities on these two declaratory points, Randolph succeeded in carrying through the House a Bill that rendered military and naval officers incapable of holding also any civil office. This measure slept quietly on the table of the Senate.

Hardly a day passed without bringing the House into some similar dilemma. March 29 the Senate sent down a Bill for settling the Yazoo claims; it had passed the Senate by a vote

[1] Annals of Congress, March 26, 1806, p. 851.

of nineteen to eleven soon after the death of its hottest opponent, Senator James Jackson of Georgia. Randolph exultingly seized upon the Bill in order to plaster it, like the hue-and-cry after a runaway thief, against the very doors of the White House:—

"This Bill may be called the Omega, the last letter of the political alphabet; but with me it is the Alpha. It is the head of the divisions among the Republican party; it is the secret and covert cause of the whole. . . . The whole weight of the Executive government presses it on. We cannot bear up against it. The whole Executive government has had a bias to the Yazoo interest ever since I had a seat here. This is the original sin which has created all the mischiefs which gentlemen pretend to throw on the impressment of our seamen, and God knows what. This is the cause of those mischiefs which existed years ago."

The Yazoo sin, he said, had been one principal cause of his failure in the impeachment of Justice Chase; the secret mechanism of Government would be so powerfully brought to bear on members that if the Bill were postponed over Sunday he would not give a farthing for the issue; gentlemen would come in with speeches ready cut-and-dried until a majority dwindled to nothing. Exasperating and insulting as this language was, the House did not resent it; and a motion that the Bill be rejected passed by a vote of sixty-two to fifty-four, while Randolph exulted over its fate.

March 31 Randolph, aided by the Federalists and some thirty Republicans, succeeded in removing the injunction of secrecy from the Spanish proceedings. No sooner was the Journal published, and he found that it did not contain the President's secret message of Dec. 6, 1805, than he seized this chance to make public all that had occurred in secret session. April 5, after moving that the injunction of secrecy should be taken from the Message, he entered into the history of his own relations with the President and Secretary of State in the tangled threat of Spanish negotiations. His remarks that day, though severe, were comparatively temperate; but when the debate was renewed April 7, he announced that he meant to oppose the Government, because he had to choose between opposition and dishonesty. He charged that Madison had tried to get money from the Treasury for this negotiation without waiting for a vote of Congress; and he declared that the documents, "if published, would fix a stain upon some men in the government and high in office which all the waters in the ocean would not wash out." His denunciations began to rouse passion; if his opponents could not equal him in debate, they could in violence of temper. Madison's brother-in-law, John G. Jackson of Virginia, took up his charges in a high tone, and several expressions passed which foreshadowed a duel. On the vote Randolph was beaten by a majority of seventy-four to forty-four; but he had published the secrets of Madison's friends, and their refusal to print the Message showed the want of courage with which they were chiefly charged.

On every point of real importance Randolph's authority overawed the House. The President in his Annual Message had talked much of defences, and had even hinted his readiness to build seventy-fours. A committee of the House reported Resolutions advising that the sum of one hundred and fifty thousand dollars should be spent in fortifying harbors; that two hundred and fifty thousand dollars should be appropriated to build fifty gunboats; and that six hundred and sixty thousand dollars should be voted toward building six line-of-battle ships. When these Resolutions were brought up March 25, only thirty members could be found to vote for the seventy-fours. April 15 the subject came up again in connection with the Bill for fortifying harbors and building gunboats. Josiah Quincy made a strong argument, warning Congress that in the sacrifice of commercial interests which lay at the bottom of its policy, there was danger not only to the prosperity but to the permanence of the Union. He remarked that while seventeen millions had been voted to buy Louisiana and Florida for the sake of securing the South and West; while in this single session four hundred and fifty thousand dollars must be voted for Indian lands,—yet the entire sum expended since the foundation of the government in fortifications for the nine capital harbors of the Union was only seven hundred and twenty-four thousand dollars. The city of New York, with at least one hundred million dollars of capital in deposit, might at any moment be laid under contribution by two line-of-battle ships. Quincy begged the House to bear in mind that the ocean could not be abandoned for the land by the people of New England, of whom thousands would rather see a boat-hook than all the sheep-crooks in the world:—

> "Concerning the land of which the gentleman from Virginia [Randolph] and the one from North Carolina [Macon] think so much, they think very little. It is in fact to them only a shelter from the storm, a perch on which they build their eyrie and hide their mate and their young while they skim the surface or hunt in the deep."

Quincy's speech was far superior to the ordinary level of Congressional harangues, and its argument was warmly supported by a democrat as extreme as Matthew Lyon; but barely thirty votes could be mustered against Randolph's economy; and although the New England democrats joined hands with the New England Federalists in supporting an appropriation for building two new frigates in place of others which had been lost or condemned, they could muster only forty-three votes against Randolph's phalanx.

Probably no small part of Randolph's hostility to the navy was due to his personal dislike for Robert Smith the secretary, and for his brother Samuel the senator. This enmity already showed signs of serious trouble in store. Gallatin struggled in vain with Robert Smith's loose habit of accounts. Joseph Nicholson, closely allied to Gallatin, naturally drew away from the Smiths, whose authority in Maryland roused ill-feeling. Randolph took sides with Gallatin and Nicholson, the more because Samuel Smith had undertaken to act an independent part in the politics of the session, and had too plainly betrayed selfish motives. When Randolph, after delaying the navy estimates as long as he could, moved the appropriations April 10, he took the opportunity to be more than usually offensive. He said that an Appropriation Bill was a mere matter of form; that the items might as well be lumped together; that the secretary would spend twice the amount if he chose, as he had done the year before, and that the House would have to make up the deficiency. "A spendthrift," said he, "can never be supplied with money fast enough to anticipate his wants."

The Bill passed, of course; but the navy was reduced to the lowest possible point, and fifty gunboats were alone provided in response to the President's strong recommendations. Randolph and his friends believed only in defence on land, and their theory was no doubt as sound as such theories could ever be; but it was the curse of "old Republican" principles that they could never be relaxed without suicide, and never enforced without factiousness. For defence on land nothing was so vital as good roads. A million dollars appropriated for roads to Sackett's Harbor, Erie, Detroit, St. Louis, and New Orleans would have been, as a measure of land defence, worth more than all the gunboats and forts that could be crowded along the Atlantic; but when the Senate sent down a Bill creating commissioners to lay out the Cumberland road to the State of Ohio, although this road was the result of a contract to which Congress had pledged its faith, so many Republicans opposed it under one pretext or another, with John Randolph among them, that a change of four votes would have defeated the Bill. No more was done for national defence by land than by water, although the echo of Nelson's guns at Trafalgar was as loud as the complaints of plundered American merchants, and of native American seamen condemned to the tyranny and the lash of British boatswains.

The drift of Randolph's opposition was easily seen; he wanted to cover the Administration with shame for having taken a warlike tone which it never meant to support. His tactics were calculated to make Madison contemptible at home and abroad by inviting upon him the worst outrages of foreign governments. That he succeeded so far as foreign governments were concerned was almost a matter of course, since even without his aid Spain, France, and England could hardly invent an outrage which they had not already inflicted; but at home Randolph's scheme failed, because Madison could be degraded only by making the American people share in his humiliation. The old Republicans relieved Madison of responsibility for national disgrace, and made Congress itself answerable for whatever disasters might follow,—a result made clear by Randolph's last and most mischievous assault. To meet the five millions required for the purchase of Florida, at a moment when the Non-importation Act threatened to cut down the revenue, Gallatin needed all the existing taxes, including the Mediterranean Fund, which ceased by law after the peace with Tripoli. April 14 Randolph suddenly, without the knowledge or consent of Gallatin, moved to repeal the duty on salt. This heavy and unpopular tax produced about half a million dollars, and its repeal was so popular that no one dared oppose it. The next day Randolph brought in a Bill repealing the salt tax and continuing the Mediterranean Fund. By that time members had become aware of his factious motives, and denounced them; but so far from disavowing his purpose, the chairman of the Committee of Ways and Means proclaimed that since he could not force the Government to keep within the limit of specific appropriations he meant to sequester the revenue so as to leave but a scanty surplus. After his speech the Bill was engrossed without opposition, the Federalists being pleased to embarrass Government, and the Republicans afraid of sacrificing popularity. April 17 the Bill passed by a vote of eighty-four to eleven and was sent to the Senate. The part which related to the salt tax was there struck out; but when, April 21, the last day of the session, the Bill so mutilated came again before the House, Randolph exerted to the utmost his powers of mischief, not so much in order to repeal the salt tax as to destroy the Senate Bill, and so deprive Government of its still greater resource, the Mediterranean Fund, which produced nearly a million. He induced the House to insist upon its own Bill. A committee of conference was appointed; the Senate would not recede; Randolph moved that the House adhere. Angry words passed; ill-temper began to prevail; and when at last Randolph was beaten by the narrow vote of forty-seven to forty, his relative Thomas Mann Randolph, the President's son-in-law, suddenly rose and spoke of his namesake in terms intended for a challenge; while Sloan of New Jersey occupied part of the night with a long diatribe against the chairman of the Ways and Means Committee.

Never had worse temper been seen at Washington than in the last weeks of this session. Madison's friends, conscious that their attitude was undignified, became irritable, and longed for a chance to prove their courage. Randolph was not the only enemy who devoted the energy of personal hatred to the task of ruining the Secretary of State. In the case of Randolph Madison was not to blame, and neither challenged nor wished a contest. Even the policy which Randolph so violently assailed was less the policy of the secretary than of the President. Madison did nothing to invite the storm, and could have done nothing to escape it; but another tempest raged, to which he voluntarily exposed himself.

The Marquis of Casa Yrujo passed the autumn of 1805 in Philadelphia, and in obedience to instructions tried to renew friendly relations with the Secretary of State. During Madison's stay in the city Yrujo induced the secretary to accept an invitation to dinner to meet Governor McKean, Yrujo's father-in-law. The marquis paid no attention to the hints sent him from the President that he would confer a favor on the United States government by returning to Spain without delay. He was well aware that he had nothing to gain by conferring more favors on Jefferson; and the conduct of Turreau and Merry was not such as to deter a Spanish minister from defying to his heart's content the authority of the President.

On the appearance of the Annual Message, which contained a general and loose statement of grievances against Spain, Yrujo wrote Dec. 6, 1805, a keen note to the Secretary of State, criticising, not without justice, the assertions made by the President. To Yrujo's note, as to the St. Domingo note of Turreau, the secretary made no reply. He held that the contents of an Executive communication to Congress were not open to diplomatic discussion, — a doctrine doubtless correct in theory and convenient to the Executive, but offering the disadvantage that if foreign governments or their envoys chose to disregard it, the Secretary of State must either enforce discipline or submit to mortification. Madison accepted the challenge; he meant to enforce discipline, and aimed at expelling Yrujo from the country. The Cabinet decided that Yrujo, pending the request for his recall, should receive no answer to his letters, and should not be permitted to remain in Washington.

Backed by the President's authority and by the power of the government, Madison might reasonably expect an easy victory over the Spaniard, and he acted as though it were a matter of course that Yrujo should accept his fate; but Yrujo seemed unconscious of peril. Although the Spanish minister's presence at the capital was well known not to be desired by the President, the society of Washington was startled Jan. 15, 1806, by learning that the marquis had arrived. The same evening Yrujo, dining with General Turreau, received a formal note which roused him to passion only equalled by the temper of John Randolph. The exasperating letter, signed by Madison, said that as the President had requested Yrujo's recall, and as Cevallos had intimated that the marquis wished to return to Spain on leave, it had been supposed that the departure would have taken place at once, and therefore his appearance at Washington was a matter of surprise:—

"Under these circumstances the President has charged me to signify to you that your remaining at this place is dissatisfactory to him; and that although he cannot permit himself to insist on your departure from the United States during an inclement season, he expects it will not be unnecessarily postponed after this obstacle has ceased."

A routine diplomatist would have protested and obeyed; but Yrujo was not a routine diplomatist. Not in order to learn correct deportment had he read the "Aurora" or studied the etiquette of Jefferson's *pêle-mêle*. Minister and marquis as he was, he had that democratic instinct which always marked the Spanish race and made even the beggars proud; while his love of a fray shocked Turreau and caused Merry to look upon his Spanish colleague as a madman. At that moment Madison was little esteemed or feared by any one; the recoil of his foreign policy had prostrated him, and Randolph was every day, in secret session, overwhelming him with contempt. Yrujo had no reason to fear the result of a contest; but even had there been cause for fear, he was not a man to regard it.

Turreau in vain attempted to restrain him; nothing would satisfy Yrujo but defiance. January 16, the day after receiving Madison's letter, the Spanish minister answered it.

"As the object of my journey is not with a view to hatch plots," said he, with a side-blow at Madison which the secretary soon understood, "my arrival here is an innocent and legal act, which leaves me in the full enjoyment of all my rights and privileges, both as a public character or a private individual. Making use therefore of these rights and privileges, I intend remaining in the city, four miles square, in which the Government resides, as long as it may suit the interest of the King my master or my own personal convenience. I must at the same time add that I shall not lose sight of these two circumstances as respects the period and season in which our mutual desires for my departure from the United States are to be accomplished."

Having thus retaliated Madison's insult, Yrujo next made his revenge public. January 19 he sent to the Department a formal protest, couched in language still more offensive than that of his letter: —

"Having gone through the personal explanations which for just motives I was compelled to enter into in my first answer to your letter of the 15th inst., I must now inform you, sir, what otherwise would then have constituted my sole reply; namely, that the envoy extraordinary and minister plenipotentiary of his Catholic Majesty near the United States receives no orders except from his sovereign. I must also declare to you, sir, that I consider both the style and tenor of your letter as indecorous, and its object an infraction of the privileges attached to my public character."

Finally he sent to his colleagues copies of this correspondence, which soon afterward was printed in every Federalist newspaper, together with the note criticising the Annual Message, the reception of which had never been acknowledged by the Secretary of State.

Thus far Madison gained no credit in the scuffle, but merely called upon his own head one more intolerable insult. Perhaps in Yrujo's apparent madness some share of method might be detected; for he knew the character of Madison, — his willingness to irritate and his reluctance to strike. At all

events, the Spaniard remained at Washington and defied the
Government to do its worst. The Cabinet consulted, examined into the law, inquired for precedents, and at last decided
that the Government could not expel him. Merry took Yrujo's
part, and Turreau had much to do with moderating the President's measures and with checking interference from Congress.[1] The Government in all its branches was overawed, and
even the senators were alarmed. "The marquis's letters last
published seem to have frightened many of them so that
probably nothing will be done."[2] So wrote a member of the
Senate who alone exerted himself to strengthen the President's hands. Yrujo remained a fortnight or more at Washington, and after carrying his point returned at his leisure to
Philadelphia. The only measure which Madison ventured to
take was that of refusing to hold any communication with
him or to receive his letters; but even this defence was turned
by Yrujo into a vantage-ground of attack.

Among other adventurers then floating about the world
was one Francesco de Miranda, a native of Caraccas, who for
twenty years had been possessed by a passion for revolutionizing his native province, and for becoming the Washington
of Spanish America. Failing to obtain in England the aid he
needed, he came to New York in November, 1805, with excellent letters of introduction. Miranda had a high reputation;
he was plausible and enthusiastic; above all, he was supposed
to represent a strong patriot party in Spanish America. War
with Spain was imminent; the President's Annual Message
seemed almost to declare its existence. In New York Miranda
instantly became a hero, and attracted about him every ruined
adventurer in society, among the rest a number of Aaron
Burr's friends. Burr himself was jealous, and spoke with contempt of him; but Burr's chief ally Dayton, the late Federalist
senator from New Jersey, was in Miranda's confidence. So
was John Swartwout the marshal, Burr's devoted follower; so
was William Steuben Smith, surveyor of the port, one of the
few Federalists still left in office. These, as well as a swarm of
smaller men, clustered round the Spanish American patriot,
either to help his plans or to further their own. By Smith's

[1] Diary of J. Q. Adams (Feb. 15, 1806), i. 410.
[2] Diary of J. Q. Adams (Feb. 20, 1806), i. 414.

advice Miranda hired the ship "Leander," owned by one Ogden and commanded by a Captain Lewis; with Smith's active
aid Miranda next bought arms and supplies, and enlisted
men.

Meanwhile Miranda went to Washington. Arriving there
in the first days of the session, before the pacific secret message and its sudden change of policy toward Spain were
publicly known, he called upon the Secretary of State. December 11 he was received by the secretary at the Department; then invited to dine; then he put off his departure in
order to dine with the President at the White House,—at a
time when he was engaged, in conjunction with the surveyor
of the port of New York, in fitting out a warlike expedition
against Spanish territory. What passed between him and
Madison became matter of dispute. The secretary afterward
admitted that Miranda told of his negotiations with the British government, and made no secret of his hopes to revolutionize Colombia; to which Madison had replied that the
government of the United States could not aid or countenance any secret enterprise, and was determined to interfere
in case of any infraction of the law. Miranda's account of the
secretary's conversation was very different; he wrote to
Smith, from Washington, letters representing Madison to be
fully aware of the expedition then fitting out, and to be willing that Smith should join it. He made a parade of social relations with the President and secretary, and on returning to
New York was open in his allusions to the complicity of
Government. Doubtless his statements were false, and those
of Madison were alone worthy of belief; but the Secretary of
State was not the less compromised in the opinion of his
enemies.

Miranda quickly returned to New York; and when about a
month later the "Leander" was ready to sail, he wrote a letter
to Madison announcing his intended departure, and taking a
sort of formal and official leave, as though he were a confidential emissary of the President. He had the assurance to add
that "the important matters" which he had communicated
" will remain, I doubt not, in the deepest secret until the final
result of this delicate affair. I have acted here on that supposition, conforming myself in everything to the intentions of

the Government, which I hope I have seized and observed with exactitude and discretion."[1]

Ten days afterward the "Leander" sailed with a party of filibusters for the Spanish main, and the Secretary of State awoke to the consciousness that he had been deceived and betrayed. Fortunately for Madison, Miranda had not left behind him a copy of this letter, but had merely told his friends its purport. The letter itself remained unseen; but the original still exists among the Archives of the State Department, bearing an explanatory note in Madison's handwriting, that Miranda's "important" communications related to " what passed with the British government," and that in saying he had conformed in New York to the President's intentions, Miranda said what was not true.

Then Madison, after receiving and entertaining Miranda at Washington while a high government official was openly enlisting troops for him at New York, ordered the Spanish minister to leave the Federal city, and refused to receive the minister's communications on any subject whatever. He had driven Casa Calvo and Morales from Louisiana, and at the same time allowed a notorious Spanish rebel to organize in New York a warlike expedition against Spanish territory.

Madison could hardly suppose that Yrujo would fail to make him pay the uttermost penalty for a mistake so glaring. Never before had the Spaniard enjoyed such an opportunity. After defying the secretary at Washington, Yrujo returned to Philadelphia, where he arrived on the evening of February 4. As he stepped from his carriage letters were put into his hand. Three of these letters were from the Spanish consul at New York, and contained only the notice that the "Leander" was about to sail.[2] Serious as this news was, it did not compare in importance with information furnished by Jonathan Dayton. For reasons of his own Dayton kept Yrujo informed of events unknown even to Merry and Turreau, and unsuspected by the President or his Cabinet. In some cases he probably tried to work on Yrujo's credulity.

"The Secretary of State," according to Dayton's story,

[1] Miranda to Madison, Jan. 22, 1806; Madison MSS.
[2] Yrujo to Cevallos, Feb. 12, 1806; MSS. Spanish Archives.

" with whom Miranda had two conferences, doubtless suspecting the origin of this mission, had at first treated him
with reserve; but at last had opened himself so far as to say
that he did not know whether the United States would or
would not declare war against Spain, because this step must
depend on Congress; that in this uncertainty he could not
permit himself to offer Miranda the aid asked; but that if
private citizens in the United States chose to advance their
funds for the undertaking, as Miranda had suggested, the
Government would shut its eyes to their conduct, provided
that Miranda took his measures in such a way as not to
compromise the Government. At the same time the secretary coincided in Miranda's idea that in case the United
States should determine upon war with Spain, this undertaking would prove to be a diversion favorable to the views
of the American government."

This had been told to Yrujo, and reported by him to his
Government before the visit to the capital. In the excitement
caused by Madison's order to leave Washington, Yrujo confided in General Turreau, and went so far as to hint to Madison himself his knowledge that Madison was engaged in
"hatching plots" against Spain. Dayton's latest information
was still more serious. Besides exact details in regard to the
force and destination of Miranda, Dayton said it had been
agreed between Madison and Miranda that the Government
should use the pretext of asking Yrujo's recall in order to
refuse to receive communications from him, and thus prevent him from claiming official interference against the
"Leander."

No sooner did the idea of a profound intrigue effect a lodgment in the Spaniard's mind, than he turned it into a means
of wounding the Secretary of State. After writing letters the
whole night, and sending off swift-sailing pilot-boats to warn
the Spanish authorities of Miranda's plans, the marquis
turned his attention to the secretary. He sent a letter to the
Department, complaining that the "Leander" had been allowed to sail; but knowing that the Department would decline to receive his letter, he took another measure which

secured with certainty a hearing. He wrote a similar letter to Turreau, begging his interference.[1]

Turreau could not refuse. No sooner did he receive Yrujo's letter, February 7, than he went to the Department and had an interview with the secretary, which he reported to Yrujo on the same day:[2] —

"I was this morning with Madison. I imparted to him my suspicions and yours. I sought his eyes, and, what is rather rare, I met them. He was in a state of extraordinary prostration while I was demanding from him a positive explanation on the proceedings in question. It was with an effort that he broke silence, and at length answered me that the President had already anticipated my representations by ordering measures to be taken against the accomplices who remained in the country and against the culprits who should return. I leave you to judge whether I was satisfied by this answer, and I quitted him somewhat abruptly in order to address him in writing. I am occupied in doing so."

Madison might well show disturbance. To conciliate Turreau and Napoleon had been the chief object of his policy since the preceding October. For this he had endured arrogance such as no other American secretary ever tolerated. The Florida negotiation had not yet begun; John Randolph had delayed it and declaimed against it until Madison's reputation was involved in its success. Turreau held its fate in his hand; and suddenly Turreau appeared, demanding that Madison should prove himself innocent of charges that involved a quarrel with France as the ally and protector of Spain, while Madison had in his desk the parting letter from Miranda which if published would have proved the truth of these charges to the mind of every diplomatist and political authority in Europe.

Before many days had passed, Yrujo set the Federalist press at work. The President removed Smith from his office of surveyor, and caused both Smith and Ogden to be indicted.

[1] Yrujo to Turreau, Feb. 4, 1806, MSS. Spanish Archives.
[2] Turreau to Yrujo, Feb. 7, 1806; MSS. Spanish Archives.

Indignant at being, as they believed, sacrificed to save Madison, Smith and Ogden sent memorials to Congress, which were presented by Josiah Quincy, April 21, the last day of the session, when the House was already irritable and the endurance of Madison's friends was exhausted by the vexatious attacks to which they had been for so many months exposed without capacity to reply or power to prevent them. John G. Jackson of Virginia, who had already invited a duel with Randolph, broke into a furious tirade against Quincy. "I say it is a base calumny of which the gentleman has made himself the organ; and in saying so I hold myself responsible in any place the gentleman pleases." The House voted by an immense majority to return the memorials to the men from whom they came. The charges against the secretary were hustled aside, and Congress adjourned with what little dignity was left it; but Yrujo won his victory, and gave to the Secretary of State the fullest equivalent for the secretary's assault. For another year he defied his enemy by remaining as Spanish minister in America; but he held no more relations with Government, and at his own request was then sent to represent Don Carlos IV. at the Court of Eugène Beauharnais at Milan.

Thus the first session of the Ninth Congress closed, April 21, 1806, leaving the Administration master of the field, but strong in numbers alone. How long a government could maintain its authority by mere momentum of inert mass had become a serious question to Jefferson and his successor.

Chapter LX

As THE MEMBERS of Congress, after their wrangles, at last, April 22, wandered homeward, and John Randolph's long, lean figure disappeared on horseback beyond the Potomac, both the President and the Secretary of State drew a sigh of relief; for never before in the history of the Government had a President been obliged to endure such public insults and outrages at the hands of friend and enemy alike. The Federalists had quarrelled with each other as bitterly as the Republicans were quarrelling, but in Congress at least they had held their peace. Under their sway neither Spain, France, nor England insulted them or their Presidents with impunity. Sanguine as Jefferson was, he could not but feel that during two sessions he had been treated with growing disrespect both in Congress and abroad; and that should the contempt for his authority increase, his retirement would offer melancholy proof that the world no longer valued his services. So clearly did he see the danger that, as has been shown, he would gladly have changed the external appearance of his policy. February 18, 1806, he wrote his letter declaring himself convinced that Europe must be taught to know her error in supposing his Government to be "entirely in Quaker principles;"[1] and that unless this idea could be corrected, the United States would become the plunder of all nations. The attempt to teach Europe her error made his position worse. A month later, after the President had done all that he dared to do toward alarming the fears of Europe, the British minister at Washington wrote that both the American government and the American people, so far from meaning to use force, were trembling lest Great Britain should declare war:[2]

"The fear and apprehension of such a crisis is manifestly so great that I think I may venture to say that should his Majesty's government, in consequence of the menace insinuated in the President's Message, have thought proper to make any demonstration of their determination to resist

[1] See p. 679.
[2] Merry to Lord Mulgrave, March 19, 1806; MSS. British Archives.

whatever measures might be adopted here, by sending a reinforcement to the British squadron on the American station sufficiently great to be noticed, such a measure on their part would have the salutary effect of putting a stop at once to all the hostile proceedings of this Government."

In view of speeches like those of Gregg, Crowninshield, and Randolph, with their running commentary on the President's policy, such a conclusion as that which Merry had reached could not be called unjust. A few weeks afterward the British minister found his theory put to a severe test. April 25, 1806, soon after the adjournment of Congress, an event occurred which seemed calculated to bring the two nations into collision. The "Leander," the "Cambrian," and the "Driver," blockading the port of New York, were in the habit of firing shot across the bows of merchant vessels in order to bring them to. According to the British account,—which was of course as favorable to the frigate as possible,—a shot fired by the "Leander" to stop a passing vessel happened by an unlucky chance to be in line with a coasting sloop far beyond, and killed one John Pierce, brother of the coaster's captain. Making his way to the city with the mangled body of his brother, the captain roused New York to excitement over the outrage. A meeting of citizens was held at the Tontine Coffee-house; but the Republicans allowed the Federalist leaders to conduct it. Rufus King, Oliver Wolcott, and other well-known enemies of President Jefferson reported a series of resolutions censuring the Government for permitting the seizures, impressments, and murders which were a consequence of the blockade, recommending that all intercourse with the blockading squadron should be stopped, and advising that John Pierce should be buried with a public funeral. Meanwhile the people took the law into their own hands, intercepting supplies for the squadron, and compelling the few British officers on shore to hide themselves. Pierce's funeral was turned into a popular demonstration. Captain Whitby of the "Leander" was indicted for murder by the grand jury; and the mayor despatched to Washington the necessary affidavits, on which the President might rest such further action as should seem fit.

Jefferson was greatly annoyed at this new misfortune, which allowed his Federalist enemies to charge upon him responsibility for British aggressions. In truth the Federalist merchants were the chief opponents of war with England; and their patriotic feeling was for the most part a sham. Yet the matter could not be ignored; and accordingly, May 3, the President issued a proclamation closing the ports and harbors of America forever to the three British frigates and to their commanders, and ordering all officers of the United States to arrest Captain Whitby wherever he might be found within American jurisdiction. This manner of redressing his own wrongs placed Jefferson at a disadvantage in asking for redress from Fox, who might naturally reply that if the United States government chose to make its appeal to municipal law, it could not expect the Government of Great Britain to offer further satisfaction; but popular excitement was for the moment more important than diplomatic forms.

Jacob Crowninshield, returning from Washington to Massachusetts after the adjournment of Congress, happened to be in New York at the time of Pierce's funeral, and wrote to the President on the subject. The President, May 13, answered his letter at some length.

"Although the scenes which were acted on shore," he said,[1] "were overdone with electioneering views, yet the act of the British officer was an atrocious violation of our territorial rights. The question what should be done was a difficult one. The sending three frigates was one suggestion. . . . While we were thus unable to present a force of that kind at New York, we received from Mr. Merry the most solemn assurances that the meeting of the three British vessels at New York was entirely accidental, from different quarters, and that they were not to remain. We concluded, therefore, that it was best to do what you have seen in the proclamation, and to make a proper use of the outrage and of our forbearance at St. James's to obtain better provisions for the future."

This was not all. Jefferson avowed himself in favor of a

[1] Jefferson's Writings (Ford), viii. 451.

navy. His fifty new gunboats would, he thought, put New Orleans and New York in safety:

> "But the building some ships of the line, instead of our most indifferent frigates, is not to be lost sight of. That we should have a squadron properly composed to prevent the blockading our ports is indispensable. The Atlantic frontier, from numbers, wealth, and exposure to potent enemies, has a proportionate right to be defended with the western frontier, for whom we keep up three thousand men. Bringing forward the measure, therefore, in a moderate form, placing it on the ground of comparative right, our nation, which is a just one, will come into it, notwithstanding the repugnance of some on the subject when first presented."

That Jefferson should repeat the opinions and echo the arguments of the Federalist Presidents was an experience worth noting; but as a matter of statesmanship, there was reason to fear that the change came too late. The theory of peaceable coercion had been made the base of Jefferson's foreign policy; and upon it his fortunes must stand or fall. Merry, though willing to quiet President Jefferson's fears so far as concerned the accident of Pierce's death, was little affected by the outcry of New York, for he saw that the United States government could not change its pacific system. He wrote to Fox an urgent remonstrance against concession to American demands:[1]

> "I consider it my duty to accompany this statement with a conviction on my part, from what is evident of the division of parties throughout the United States, from the weakness of the Government, from the prominent passion of avarice which prevails among every class of the community, and their intolerance under internal taxes, which must be imposed in the event of a war with any Power, that should his Majesty's government consider the pretensions that are asserted from hence as unjust, and be therefore disposed to resist them, such a resistance would only be attended with the salutary effect of commanding from this Government that respect which they have recently lost toward Great Britain."

[1] Merry to C. J. Fox, May 4, 1806; MSS. British Archives.

Within the last year England had seized a large portion of American shipping and commerce; hundreds of American citizens had been taken by force from under the American flag, some of whom were already lying beneath the waters off Cape Trafalgar; the port of New York had been blockaded by a British squadron, which drew its supplies from the city, and lay habitually within its waters, except when engaged in stopping and searching vessels beyond the three-mile line; and at last an American citizen was killed within American jurisdiction by the guns of the blockading squadron. In return the United States government had threatened to buy no more fine woollens and silks from England; and had stopped the fresh meat and vegetables which the officers of the "Cambrian" and "Leander" were in the habit of procuring in the New York market. That Merry should still complain, that he should wish to stifle even this whisper of protest, and should talk of the American government in the same breath as trembling with fear and as having lost respect toward England, showed that he had a memory better than his powers of observation. He was still brooding over Jefferson's *pêle-mêle* and his heelless slippers.

For that offence, committed in the heyday of diplomatic triumph, the President had bitterly atoned. As Jefferson twisted and twined along a course daily becoming more tortuous, he found that public disaster was followed by social trials; on all sides he felt the reaction of his diplomatic failures. This kind of annoyance left little trace in history, and was commonly forgotten or ignored by the people; but Jefferson was more than commonly sensitive to social influences, and if it annoyed him to be slandered, it annoyed him still more to be laughed at. He could not retaliate, and the more he exerted himself to appear above his vexations, the more he exposed himself to ridicule.

General Turreau, with grim amusement, reported faithfully what he saw and heard. At one moment Jefferson, trying to discover some plan for checking British authority, broached to the minister of Napoleon a scheme for uniting all Christian Powers in a novel alliance against each other's aggressions.

"Your Excellency will of course understand," wrote the

sardonic Turreau to the saturnine Talleyrand,[1] "that it is not a system of armed neutrality which Mr. Jefferson would like to see established. Everything which tends to war is too far removed from his philanthropic principles, as it is from the interests of his country and the predominant opinion. The guaranty of neutrals would repose on the inert force of all the Powers against the one that should violate the neutral compact, and whose vessels would then find all foreign ports shut to them."

Turreau was amused by the incongruity of inviting Napoleon Bonaparte not only to protect neutral rights, but to do so by peaceful methods, and to join with Great Britain in a Christian confederation which should have for its main object the protection of American commerce, in order to save President Jefferson the expense of protecting it himself; but the humor of the scheme was not to be compared with its rashness. Had Jefferson foreseen the future, he would have abstained from suggesting ideas to a despot of Napoleon's genius.

Turreau entertained at heart a liking for Jefferson; and indeed no one could come within the President's kindly influence without admitting its charm. "There is something voluptuous in meaning well." There was something voluptuous in Jefferson's way of meaning well; and if the quality increased the anger of the New England Puritans, who saw in it only hypocrisy, or if it drove John Randolph nearly to frenzy, it softened the hearts of bystanders like Turreau, who atoned for their weakness toward the President by contempt for his favorite the Secretary of State. May 10 Turreau wrote to Talleyrand:

"This infatuation of Mr. Jefferson for a commonplace man, whose political opinions are becoming every day more and more an object of suspicion to the leaders of the dominant party, will not surprise those who know the actual chief of the Federal government. Mr. Jefferson as a private man joins to estimable qualities an uncommon degree of instruction; he cultivates successfully philosophy, the sci-

---

[1] Turreau to Talleyrand, Jan. 15, 1806; Archives des Aff. Étr., MSS.

ences, and the arts; he knows well the true interests of his country; and if he seems sometimes to sacrifice them, or at least to offend them, when they do not accord with his extreme popularity, this is not with him the result of matured reflection, but only of a kindly sentiment, the impulse of which he blindly follows. But in my opinion Mr. Jefferson lacks the first of the qualities which make a statesman; he has little energy, and still less of that audacity which is indispensable in a place so eminent, whatever may be the form of government. The slightest event makes him lose his balance, and he does not even know how to disguise the impression he receives. Although the last session was quite stormy, it was easy to foresee that everything would end in propositions of agreement, because no one wished war; and yet Mr. Jefferson has worried himself so much with the movements of Congress that he has made himself ill, and has grown ten years older. Not that he has yet reached the point of repenting having begun a second term. What has further contributed to render his position disagreeable is the drawing off of a part of his friends, and even of the diplomatic corps, who, with the exception of the French minister, no longer visit the President. This isolation renders him the more sensible to the reiterated outrages he receives in Congress even in open session. I have certain information that he has been extremely affected by it."[1]

Neither these annoyances nor the unlucky accident of Pierce's death, following so long a series of political misfortunes, could prevent the skies from clearing with the coming spring. If the Southern Republicans for a time seemed, as General Smith said, to be falling away daily from the Administration, the President could still congratulate himself on the steadiness of the Northern democrats, who asked for no better fortune than to be rid forever of John Randolph's tyranny. On the whole, Jefferson was well pleased with the behavior of his majority. His chief care was to find a parliamentary leader who could take Randolph's place; and he was willing that this leadership should pass out of Virginia hands, even though it should fall into the hands of Massachusetts. He

[1] Turreau to Talleyrand, May 10, 1806; Archives des Aff. Étr., MSS.

wrote to Barnabas Bidwell, urging him to take the vacant position:[1] —

> "The last session of Congress was indeed an uneasy one for a time; but as soon as the members penetrated into the views of those who were taking a new course, they rallied in as solid a phalanx as I have ever seen act together. They want only a man of business and in whom they can confide to conduct things in the House, and they are as much disposed to support him as can be wished. It is only speaking a truth to say that all eyes look to you."

Jefferson's great hope seemed likely soon to be realized beyond his own anticipations, when New England should not only accept democratic principles, but should also control the party which Virginia had brought into power. In the April election of 1806 Massachusetts chose a democratic legislature; the Federalist Governor Strong was re-elected by only a few hundred votes, while a democrat was actually elected for lieutenant-governor. The conduct of England, which caused Jefferson his most serious difficulties abroad, worked in his favor among the people of America, who were more patriotic than their leaders, and felt by instinct that whatever mistakes in policy their Government might commit, support was the alternative to anarchy.

The factions in New York and Pennsylvania fought their tedious and meaningless battles, which had no longer a national interest. The newspapers continued to find in personal abuse the most lively amusement they could furnish to their readers. The acts of Jefferson and Madison were extolled or vilified according to the partisan division of the press; and material for attack and defence was never lacking. During the summer of 1806 Miranda's expedition and the trial of Smith and Ogden, which resulted from it, filled many columns of the papers. Conviction of these two men for violating the neutrality laws seemed to be the President's earnest wish; yet when members of the Administration were subpœnaed for the defence, Jefferson ordered them to disobey the summons, alleging that their attendance in court would interfere with

[1] Jefferson to Bidwell, July 5, 1806; Works, v. 14; Jefferson MSS.

their performance of official duties. The question whether this rule was proper in practice or correct in law came soon afterward before the Supreme Court, and received elaborate discussion; but in the case of Smith and Ogden, the refusal of Madison to obey the subpœna was a political necessity. Had he been forced into the witness-box, he must have produced Miranda's letter; and in the face of evidence so compromising to the superior officers of government, no jury would have convicted a subordinate.

Before the trial began, the President removed Smith from his office of surveyor of the port of New York; and after its close he removed Swartwout from the post of marshal. The reasons for punishing Swartwout were given in a Cabinet memorandum written by Jefferson: —

"Swartwout the marshal, to whom in his duel with Clinton Smith was second, summoned a panel of jurors the greater part of which were of the bitterest Federalists. His letter, too, covering to a friend a copy of 'Aristides,' and affirming that every fact in it was true as Holy Writ. Determined unanimously that he be removed."

Thanks to Swartwout's jury and to Madison's share in Miranda's confidence, Smith was acquitted. As in many other government cases, the prosecution ended in a failure of justice.

The Spaniards easily defeated Miranda, and captured or drove away his forces. Events followed with such rapidity that this episode was soon forgotten. Yrujo did his utmost to keep it alive. The Federalist newspapers printed more than one attack on Madison evidently from Yrujo's pen, which annoyed the secretary and his friends; while Yrujo remained in the country only by way of bravado, to prove the indifference of his Government to the good-will of the United States. On the Texan frontier the Spaniards showed themselves in increasing numbers, until a collision seemed imminent. Wilkinson, on his side, could collect at Natchitoches no force capable of holding the Red River against a serious attack. Whether Wilkinson himself were not more dangerous than the Spaniards to the government of the United States was a question which disturbed men like John Randolph more than it seemed to interest Jefferson.

Fortunately the Treasury was as strong as the Army and the Foreign Department were weak. Gallatin made no mistakes; from the first he had carried the Administration on his shoulders, and had defied attack. Duane hated him, for Gallatin's influence held Duane in check, and seemed the chief support of Governor McKean in Pennsylvania; but Duane's malignity could find no weak point in the Treasury. The revenue reached $14,500,000 for 1806, and after providing the two millions appropriated for the Florida purchase, left a balance for the year of four hundred thousand dollars beyond all current demands. The Treasury held a surplus of at least four millions. The national debt was reduced to less than $57,500,000; and this sum included the Louisiana stock of $11,250,000, which could not be paid before the year 1818. After the year 1808, Gallatin promised an annual surplus of five or six millions, ready for any purpose to which Congress might choose to apply it. Even the Federalists gave up the attempt to attack the management of the Treasury; and if they sometimes seemed to wish for a foreign war, it was chiefly because they felt that only a war could shake the authority and success of Gallatin. "For many years past," wrote Timothy Pickering in 1814,[1] "I have said, 'Let the ship run aground! The shock will throw the present pilots overboard; and then competent navigators will get her once more afloat, and conduct her safely into port.'" Only war with England, by breaking down the Treasury, could effect Pickering's purpose.

Of such a war, in spite of the Rule of 1756, the blockade of New York, the impressment of seamen, and the slaughter of Pierce, there was no immediate prospect. The death of William Pitt and the accession of Charles James Fox to power quieted fear. The American people were deliberately resolved not to join in the outburst of passion which Pierce's death caused in New York. Little sense was felt of a common interest between agriculture and shipping; so that even the outrage of Pierce passed without stirring men who followed the

[1] Pickering to Gouverneur Morris, Oct. 21, 1814; Lodge's Cabot, p. 535.

plough and swung the scythe.. New York was but a sea-port,
half foreign in population and interests, an object of jealousy
to good citizens, who looked askance at manufactures and
middlemen. The accidental death of a seaman was no matter
of alarm. Every patriotic American wanted peace with England, and was glad to be told that Fox had promised pleasant things to Monroe.

Although the merchants had been robbed, the people at
large were more prosperous and contented than ever. The
summer of 1806 was one of quiet and rapid progress. While
Europe tossed on her bed of pain, and while Russia built up
the fourth coalition against Napoleon, only to drench with
blood the battle-fields of Jena, Eylau, and Friedland, the
United States moved steadily toward their separate objects,
caring little for any politics except their own. In foreign affairs their government, after threatening to break through the
bounds it had set to its own action and to punish the offenders of its dignity, ended by returning to its old ground and
by avowing, as in 1801, that war was not one of its weapons.
In domestic matters no serious division of opinion existed.
The American people went to their daily tasks without much
competition or mental effort, and had no more wish to wran-
gle about problems of the future than to turn back on their
path and face Old-World issues. Every day a million men
went to their work, every evening they came home with some
work accomplished; but the result was matter for a census
rather than for history. The acres brought into cultivation, the
cattle bred, the houses built, proved no doubt that human
beings, like ants and bees, could indefinitely multiply their
numbers, and could lay up stores of food; but these statistics
offered no evidence that the human being, any more than the
ant and bee, was conscious of a higher destiny, or was even
mechanically developing into a more efficient animal. As far
as politics proved anything, the evidence seemed to show that
the American tended already to become narrow in his views
and timid in his methods. The great issues of 1776 and of 1787
had dwindled into disputes whether robbery and violence
should be punished by refusing to buy millinery and hardware from the robbers, and whether an unsuccessful attempt
to purloin foreign territory should be redeemed by bribing a

more powerful nation to purloin it at second hand. The great issues of democracy and republicanism were still alive, but their very success removed these subjects for the moment from the field of politics. That a democracy could for so long a time maintain itself above Old-World miseries was a triumph; but thus far the democracy had been favored by constant good fortune, and even in these five years conservatives thought they felt a steady decline of moral tone. What would happen when society should be put to some violent test?

In politics nothing that proved progress could be seen. In other directions little positive result had been reached.

Far in the wilderness a few men, in the pay of the United States government, were toiling for the advancement of knowledge. In the summer of 1805 General Wilkinson ordered Lieutenant Pike, a young officer in the first infantry, to take a sergeant, a corporal, and seventeen privates, and ascertain the true sources of the Mississippi. For scientific purposes such a party of explorers could do little of permanent value, but as a military reconnoissance it might have uses. Lieutenant Pike worked his way up the stream from St. Louis. October 16, 1805, he reached a point two hundred and thirty-three miles above the Falls of St. Anthony, and there stopped to establish a winter station. December 10 he started again with a part of his men and went northward with sleds until, Jan. 8, 1806, he reached a British trading-station on Sandy Lake, from which he struggled to Leech Lake, where another British establishment existed. His visit was rather an act of formal authority than a voyage of exploration; but he notified both the British and the Indian occupants of the territory that they were under the rule of the United States government. After accomplishing this object he began his return march February 18, and reached St. Louis April 30, 1806, having shown such energy and perseverance in this winter journey as few men could have surpassed.

General Wilkinson was so well pleased with the success of the expedition that he immediately ordered Pike upon another. This time the headwaters of the Arkansas and Red rivers were to be explored as far as the Spanish settlements of New Mexico. July 15, 1806, with about the same number of

men as before, Pike left St. Louis, and September 1 reached
the Osage towns on the Missouri River. Striking across the
prairie, he marched through a country filled with jealous Paw-
nee Indians, till he reached the Arkansas River, and ascending
its branches, left a permanent monument to his visit by giving
his name to Pike's Peak in Colorado. Turning toward the
southwest, he entangled himself in the mountains; and after
suffering terribly in snow and ice, at last, Feb. 26, 1807, was
stopped by the Spanish authorities at Santa Fé, who sent him
to Chihuahua, and thence allowed him to return through
Texas to the United States.

Both these expeditions were subordinate to the larger exploration of Lewis and Clark, which President Jefferson himself organized, and in which he took deep interest. After
passing the winter at the Mandan village, as has been already
told, Lewis with thirty-two men set out April 7 in boats and
canoes for the headwaters of the Missouri. The journey
proved to be full of labor, but remarkably free from danger;
the worst perils encountered were from rattlesnakes and
bears. The murderous Sioux were not seen; and when, August 11, Lewis reached the end of river navigation, and found
himself at the base of the mountains that divided the waters
of the Missouri from those of the Columbia, his greatest anxiety was to meet the Indians who occupied the line of passage. His troubles rose from the poverty, rather than from the
hostility, of these tribes. They supplied him with horses and
with such provisions as they had, and he made his way peacefully down the western slope until he could again take canoes.
November 7 the explorers reached the mouth of the Columbia River, and saw at last the ocean which bounded American
ambition. There they were forced to pass the winter in extreme discomfort, among thievish and flea-bitten Indians, until March 26, 1807, they could retrace their steps.

Creditable as these expeditions were to American energy
and enterprise, they added little to the stock of science or
wealth. Many years must elapse before the vast region west of
the Mississippi could be brought within reach of civilization.
The crossing of the continent was a great feat, but was nothing more. The French explorers had performed feats almost
as remarkable long before; but, in 1805, the country they ex-

plored was still a wilderness. Great gains to civilization could be made only on the Atlantic coast under the protection of civilized life. For many years to come progress must still centre in the old thirteen States of the Union. The expeditions of Lewis and Pike returned no immediate profits; but in the city of New York men were actively engaged in doing what Lewis could not do,—bringing the headwaters of the western rivers within reach of private enterprise and industry. While Lewis slowly toiled up the Missouri River, thinking himself fortunate if he gained twenty miles a day against the stream, the engine which Robert Fulton had ordered from the works of Watt and Bolton in England had been made, and Fulton returned to New York to superintend its use. With the money of Chancellor Livingston he began to construct the hull of his new steamboat and adjust it to the engine.

The greatest steps in progress were often unconsciously taken, and Fulton's steamboat was an example of this rule. Neither in private talk nor in the newspapers did his coming experiment rouse much notice. To the public, Fulton's idea, though visionary, was not new. Indeed Fulton stood in imminent danger of being forestalled by rivals. In 1804 Oliver Evans experimented with a stern-wheel steamboat on the Delaware River, while at the same time John C. Stevens was experimenting with a screw-propeller on the Hudson. Nothing practical had as yet come from these attempts. The public seemed to regard them as matters which did not concern it, and the few thousand dollars needed to pay for a proper engine and hull could with difficulty be wrung from capitalists, who were derided for their folly. Fulton worked with better support than his predecessors had enjoyed, but with little encouragement or show of interest from the press or the public.

So far as concerned activity of mind, politics still engrossed public attention. The summer of 1806, quiet and prosperous as it seemed, betrayed uneasiness,—a mysterious political activity, connected with no legitimate purpose of party. Except in Connecticut and Massachusetts, the Federalists, as an organized body, could hardly be said to exist. Democrats, Republicans, and Federalists were divided for the moment rather by social distinctions than by principle; but the division was not the less real. Every year added strength to the national instinct; but every year brought also a nearer certainty that the denationalizing forces, whether in New England under Timothy Pickering, or in Virginia under John Randolph, or in Louisiana under some adventurer, would make an effort to break the chain that hampered local interests and fettered private ambition. Under a Virginia President and a slave-owning majority of Congress, the old anti-national instinct of Virginia was paralyzed, and the dangers to rise from it were postponed; but the freer play was given to the passions of Boston and New Orleans,—to the respectable seditiousness of Timothy Pickering and the veneered profligacy of Aaron Burr. The time had come when Burr was to bring his conspiracy to the test of action, and to try the strength of a true democracy. During the autumn of 1806 Burr's projects and movements roused a sudden panic, less surprising than the tolerance with which his conspiracy had been so long treated by the President and the press.

Chapter X

WHEN BURR ceased to be Vice-President of the United States, March 4, 1805, he had already made himself intimate with every element of conspiracy that could be drawn within his reach. The list of his connections might have startled Jefferson, if the President's easy optimism had not been proof to fears. In London, Burr's friend Colonel Williamson confided his plans to Pitt and Lord Melville. At Washington the British minister, Merry, wrote to Lord Mulgrave in support of Williamson's negotiation. The creole deputies from New Orleans were Burr's friends, and Derbigny was acquainted with "certain projects" he entertained. General Wilkinson, governor of the Louisiana Territory, whose headquarters were at St. Louis, closely attached to Burr almost from childhood, stood ready for any scheme that promised to gratify inordinate ambition. James Brown, Secretary of the Territory, was Burr's creature. Judge Prevost, of the Superior Court at New Orleans, was Burr's stepson. Jonathan Dayton, whose term as senator ended the same day with Burr's vice-presidency, shared and perhaps suggested the "projects." John Smith, the senator from Ohio, was under the influence of Burr and Dayton. John Adair of Kentucky was in Wilkinson's confidence. The Swartwouts in New York, with the "little band" who made Burr their idol, stood ready to follow him wherever he might lead. In South Carolina Joseph Allston, the husband of Theodosia Burr, might be induced to aid his father-in-law; and Allston was supposed to be the richest planter in the South, worth a million of dollars in slaves and plantations. The task of uniting these influences and at a given moment raising the standard of a new empire in the Mississippi Valley seemed to an intriguer of Burr's metal not only feasible, but certain of success.

After the parting interview with Merry in March, 1805, when they arranged terms to be asked of the British government, Burr went to Philadelphia, and in April crossed the mountains to Pittsburg, on his way to New Orleans. Wilkinson was to have joined him; but finding that Wilkinson had been delayed, Burr went on alone. Floating down the Ohio, his ark lashed to that of Matthew Lyon, he first stopped a few hours at an island about two miles below Parkersburg, where an Irish gentleman named Blennerhassett lived, and where he had spent a sum, for that day considerable, in buildings and improvements. The owner was absent; but Mrs. Blennerhassett was at home, and invited Burr to dinner. The acquaintance thus begun proved useful to him. Passing to Cincinnati, he became, May 11, 1805, a guest in the house of Senator Smith. Dayton was already there; but Wilkinson arrived a few days later, after Burr had gone on by land to Nashville. Wilkinson publicly talked much of a canal around the Falls of the Ohio River, to explain the community of interest which seemed to unite himself with Burr, Dayton, and Senator Smith; but privately he wrote, May 28, to John Adair, soon to be Breckinridge's successor as senator from Kentucky: "I was to have introduced my friend Burr to you; but in this I failed by accident. He understands your merits, and reckons on you. Prepare to visit me, and I will tell you all. We must have a peep at the unknown world beyond me."

Meanwhile Burr reached Nashville in Tennessee, where he was received with enthusiastic hospitality. Every one at or near the town seemed to contend for the honor of best treating or serving him.[1] Dinners were given, toasts were drunk; the newspapers were filled with his doings. No one equalled Andrew Jackson in warmth of devotion to Colonel Burr. At all times of his life Jackson felt sympathy with a duellist who had killed his man; but if his support was enlisted for the duellist who had killed Hamilton, his passions were excited in favor of the man who should drive the Spaniards from America; and Burr announced that this was to be the mission of his life. As major-general of the Tennessee militia, Jackson looked forward to sharing this exploit.

After spending a week or more at Nashville, Burr descended in one of General Jackson's boats to the mouth of the Cumberland, where his ark was waiting; and June 6 he joined General Wilkinson at Fort Massac, — a military post on the north shore of the Ohio River, a few miles above its junction with the Mississippi. The two men remained together at

[1] Deposition of Matthew Lyon; Wilkinson's Memoirs, ii. Appendix, lxviii.

Massac four days, and Burr wrote to his daughter, Mrs. Allston: "The General and his officers fitted me out with an elegant barge,—sails, colors, and ten oars,—with a sergeant and
ten able, faithful hands. Thus equipped, I left Massac on the
10th June." Wilkinson supplied him also with a letter of introduction to Daniel Clark, the richest and most prominent
American in New Orleans. Dated June 9, 1805, it announced
that the bearer would carry secrets. "To him I refer you for
many things improper to letter, and which he will not say to
any other."

While Burr went down the river to New Orleans, Wilkinson turned northward to St. Louis, where he arrived July 2.
He was in high spirits and indiscreet. Two of his subordinate
officers, Major Hunt and Major Bruff, afterward told how he
sounded them,—and Major Bruff's evidence left no doubt
that Wilkinson shared in the ideas of Burr and Dayton; that
he looked forward to a period of anarchy and confusion in
the Eastern States, as the result of democracy; and that he
intended to set up a military empire in Louisiana. Already,
June 24, he signed Lieutenant Pike's instructions to explore
the headwaters of the Arkansas River. Adair, certainly in the
secret, believed the object of this expedition to be the opening
of a road to Santa Fé and to the mines of Mexico.[1] Every
recorded letter or expression of Wilkinson during the spring
and summer of 1805 showed that he was in the confidence of
Burr and Dayton; that he gave them active aid in their
scheme for severing the Union; and that they in their turn
embraced his project of Mexican conquest.

Burr reached New Orleans June 25, 1805, and remained a
fortnight, entertained by the enemies of Governor Claiborne
and of the Spaniards. Conspiracies were commonly most active and most dangerous when most secret; and the mark of
secrecy, almost wholly wanting to this conspiracy in the
Northern States, was never removed, by any public inquiry or
admission, from its doings at New Orleans. According to the
story afterward told by Wilkinson on the evidence of Lieutenant Spence, Burr on his arrival in Louisiana became acquainted with the so-called Mexican Association,—a body of

[1] Adair to Wilkinson, Jan. 27, 1806; Wilkinson's Memoirs, ii. Appendix,
lxxvii.

some three hundred men, leagued together for the emancipation of Mexico from Spanish rule.[1] Of this league Daniel Clark afterward declared that he was not a member; but if his safety as a merchant required him to keep aloof, his sympathies were wholly with the Association. After Burr's arrival, and under his influence, the scheme of disunion was made a part of the Mexican plan; and these projects soon became so well known in New Orleans as to reach the ears of the Spanish agents and excite their suspicions, until Clark two months later complained to Wilkinson that Burr's indiscretion was bringing them all into danger.[2] Clark's letter was written as though he were an innocent bystander annoyed at finding himself included in an imaginary conspiracy against the Spanish government. In truth it seemed also to be written as a warning to Burr against trusting a certain "Minor of Natchez":—

"Were I sufficiently intimate with Mr. Burr, and knew where to direct a line to him, I should take the liberty of writing to him. Perhaps, finding Minor in his way, he was endeavoring to extract something from him,—he has amused himself at the blockhead's expense,—and then Minor has retailed the news to his employers. Inquire of Mr. Burr about this and let me know on my return [from Vera Cruz], which will be in three or four months. The tale is a horrid one if well told. Kentucky, Tennessee, the State of Ohio, the four territories on the Mississippi and Ohio, with part of Georgia and Carolina, are to be bribed with the plunder of the Spanish countries west of us to separate from the Union."

This letter, written by Clark, Sept. 7, 1805, showed that Burr's plans were notorious at New Orleans, and that his indiscretion greatly annoyed his friends. Two years afterward, Wilkinson reminded Clark of the letter.[3]

"You will recollect," wrote Wilkinson, "you desired me

[1] Wilkinson's Memoirs, ii. 283
[2] Daniel Clark to Wilkinson, Sept. 7, 1805; Wilkinson's Memoirs, ii. Appendix, xxxiii.
[3] Wilkinson to Clark, Oct. 12, 1807; Clark's Proofs, p. 154.

to write Burr on the subject, which I did, and also gave his brother-in-law, Dr. Brown, an extract of your letter to transmit him."

Burr's reply has been preserved: —

"Your letter of November," he wrote to Wilkinson,[1] Jan. 6, 1806, " which came, I believe, through J. Smith, has been received and answered. Your friend [Clark] suspects without reason the person [Minor] named in his letter to you. I love the society of that person; but surely I could never be guilty of the folly of confiding to one of his levity anything which I wished not to be repeated. Pray do not disturb yourself with such nonsense."

Daniel Clark and Wilkinson were therefore assured, not that the tale was untrue, but that Burr had not confided to Minor, or "to one of his levity" anything which Burr " wished not to be repeated." Nevertheless Clark, whose abilities were far greater than those of Burr, and whose motives for secrecy were stronger, knew that Burr must have talked with extreme indiscretion, for his plans had already come to the ears of the Spanish agents in Louisiana. Many residents of New Orleans knew of the scheme, — "many absurd and wild reports are circulated here," wrote Clark; and whether they shared it or not, they certainly did not denounce it.

No plea of ignorance could avail any of Burr's friends. His schemes were no secret. As early as Aug. 4, 1805, more than a month before Daniel Clark sent his warning to General Wilkinson, the British minister was so much alarmed at the publicity already given to the plot that he wrote to Lord Mulgrave a panic-stricken letter, evidently supposing that the scheme was ruined by Burr's indiscretion:[2] —

"He or some of his agents have either been indiscreet in their communications, or have been betrayed by some person in whom they considered that they had reason to confide; for the object of his journey has now begun to be noticed in the public prints, where it is said that a convention is to be called immediately from the States bordering

[1] Wilkinson's Memoirs, ii. Appendix, lxxxvi.
[2] Merry to Mulgrave, Aug. 4, 1805; MSS. British Archives.

on the Ohio and Mississippi for the purpose of forming a separate government. It is, however, possible that the business may be so far advanced as, from the nature of it, to render any further secrecy impossible."

The French minister was hardly less well informed. Feb. 13, 1806, Turreau wrote to his government,[1] mentioning Miranda's departure, and adding,—

"The project of effecting a separation between the Western and Atlantic States marches abreast with this one. Burr, though displeased at first by the arrival of Miranda, who might reduce him to a secondary *rôle*, has set off again for the South, after having had several conferences with the British minister. It seems to me that the Government does not penetrate Burr's views, and that the difficult circumstances in which it finds itself, and where it has placed itself, force it to dissimulate. This division of the confederated States appears to me inevitable, and perhaps less remote than is commonly supposed; but would this event, which England seems to favor, be really contrary to the interests of France? And, assuming it to take place, should we not have a better chance to withdraw, if not both confederations, at least one of them, from the yoke of England?"

That Burr should have concealed from his principal allies— the creoles of New Orleans—plans which he communicated so freely elsewhere, was not to be imagined. Burr remained only about a fortnight at New Orleans; then returned on horseback through Natchez to Nashville, where he became again the guest of Andrew Jackson. He passed the month of August in Tennessee and Kentucky; then struck into the wilderness across the Indiana Territory to St. Louis in order to pass a week more with General Wilkinson and Secretary Brown. He found Wilkinson discouraged by the rebuffs he had met in attempting to seduce his subordinate officers and the people of the territory into the scheme. Although Wilkinson afterward swore solemnly that he had no part or parcel in Burr's disunion project, his own evidence proved that the subject had been discussed between them, and that his fears

[1] Turreau to Talleyrand, Feb. 13, 1806; Archives des Aff. Étr., MSS.

760 SECOND ADMINISTRATION OF JEFFERSON

of failure had at the time of their meeting at St. Louis checked his enthusiasm:[1] —

> "Mr. Burr, speaking of the imbecility of the government, said it would moulder to pieces, die a natural death, — or words to that effect; adding that the people of the Western country were ready to revolt. To this I recollect replying that if he had not profited more by his journey in other respects, he had better have remained at Washington or Philadelphia; for 'surely,' said I, 'my friend, no person was ever more mistaken. The Western people disaffected to the government! They are bigoted to Jefferson and democracy.'"

Wilkinson afterward claimed to have written at that time a letter to the Secretary of the Navy warning him against Burr; but the letter never reached its supposed address. He certainly gave to Burr a letter of introduction to Governor Harrison, of the Indiana Territory, which suggested decline of sympathy with the conspiracy; for it urged Harrison to return the bearer as the Territorial delegate to Congress, — a boon on which the Union "may much depend."[2]

Burr reached St. Louis Sept. 11, 1805; he left it September 19, for Vincennes and the East. Two months afterward he arrived at Washington and hurried to the British legation. His friend Dayton, who had been detained by a long illness in the West, arrived and made his report to Merry only two days before.

The conspiracy counted on the aid of Great Britain, which was to be the pivot of the scheme; but Burr's hopes were blasted by learning from Merry that no answer had been received from the British government in reply to the request for money and ships. Merry explained that an accident had happened to the packet-boat, but both had reason to know that hope of aid from the British government had vanished.

> "These disappointments gave him, he [Burr] said,[3] the deepest concern, because his journey through the Western

[1] Wilkinson's Evidence, Burr's Trial; Annals of Congress, 1807–1808, p. 611.
[2] Wilkinson's Memoirs, ii. 303.
[3] Merry to Lord Mulgrave, Nov. 25, 1805; MSS. British Archives.

country and Louisiana as far as New Orleans, as well as through a part of West Florida, had been attended with so much more success than he had even looked for, that everything was in fact completely prepared in every quarter for the execution of his plan; and because he had therefore been induced to enter into an engagement with his associates and friends to return to them in the month of March next, in order to commence the operations. He had been encouraged, he said, to go such lengths by the communications he had received from Colonel Williamson, which gave him some room to hope and expect that his Majesty's government were disposed to afford him their assistance. . . . He was sensible that no complete understanding on the subject could well take place without verbal communication; but he flattered himself that enough might be explained in this way to give a commencement to the business, and that any ulterior arrangements might safely be left till the personal interviews he should have with the persons properly authorized for the purpose, whom he recommended to be sent with the ships of war, which it was necessary should cruise off the mouth of the Mississippi at the latest by the 10th of April next, and to continue there until the commanding officer should receive information from him or from Mr. Daniel Clark of the country having declared itself independent. He wished the naval force in question to consist of two or three ships of the line, the same number of frigates, and a proportionable number of smaller vessels."

The British minister was curious to know precisely the result of the Western tour; but on this subject Burr talked vaguely, and, contrary to his usual custom, mentioned few names.

"Throughout the Western country persons of the greatest property and influence had engaged themselves to contribute very largely toward the expense of the enterprise; at New Orleans he represented the inhabitants to be so firmly resolved upon separating themselves from their union with the United States, and every way to be so completely prepared, that he was sure the revolution there would be accomplished without a drop of blood being shed, the American force in that country (should it not, as he had good reason to believe, enlist with him) not being sufficiently strong to make any opposition. It was accordingly there that the revolution would commence, at the end of April or the beginning of May, provided his Majesty's government should consent to lend their assistance toward it, and the answer, together with the pecuniary aid which would be wanted, arrived in time to enable him to set out the beginning of March."

From Pitt, besides the naval force, Burr wanted a credit for one hundred and ten thousand pounds, to be given in the names of John Barclay of Philadelphia, and Daniel Clark of New Orleans. In his report to Merry on the results of the Western tour he said no more than he had a right to say, without violent exaggeration. He barely hinted at complicity on the part of Wilkinson, Smith, Adair, and Andrew Jackson. He gave Merry clearly to understand that the heart of his plot was not in the Ohio Valley, but at New Orleans. He laid little weight on the action of Kentucky or Tennessee; with him, the point of control was among the creoles.

"Mr. Burr stated to me—what I have reason to believe to be true from the information I have received from other quarters—that when he reached Louisiana he found the inhabitants so impatient under the American government that they had actually prepared a representation of their grievances, and that it was in agitation to send deputies with it to Paris. The hope, however, of becoming completely independent, and of forming a much more beneficial connection with Great Britain, having been pointed out to them, and this having already prevailed among many of the principal people who are become his associates, they had found means to obtain a suspension of the plan of having recourse to France."

Burr impressed Merry with the idea that West Florida was also to be taken within the scope of his scheme. "The overture which had been made to him at New Orleans from a person of the greatest influence in East and West Florida, and the information he had otherwise acquired respecting the state of those countries," were among the reasons which he pressed upon the British government as motives for aiding the conspiracy with a naval force. England was then at war with Spain.

One more argument was pressed by Burr, for no one knew better than he the use to which New England might be put.

"He observed—what I readily conceive may happen that when once Louisiana and the Western country became independent, the Eastern States will separate themselves immediately from the Southern; and that thus the immense power which is now risen up with so much rapidity in the western hemisphere will, by such a division, be rendered at once informidable."

Whatever may have been Merry's sympathies or wishes, he could do no more than report Burr's conversation to Lord Mulgrave with as much approval as he dared give it. Meanwhile Burr was thrown into extreme embarrassment by the silence of Mulgrave. Burr's report showed that the creoles in New Orleans, with Daniel Clark as their financial ally, were induced to countenance the conspiracy only because they believed it to be supported by England. Without that support, Burr could not depend on creole assistance. Had he been wise, he would have waited; and perhaps he might in the end have brought the British government to accept his terms. If Pitt intended to plunder American commerce and to kidnap American citizens, he must be prepared to do more; and Burr might calculate on seeing the British Tories placed by their own acts in a position where they could not afford to neglect his offers.

Burr stayed a week in Washington; and although the object of his Western journey was so notorious that even the newspapers talked about it, his reception at the White House and at the departments was as cordial as usual. About Dec. 1, 1805, he returned to Philadelphia, where he began the effort to raise from new sources the money which till then he hoped to provide by drafts on the British treasury. The conspirators were driven to extraordinary shifts. Burr undertook the task of drawing men like Blennerhassett into his toils, and induced

Dayton to try an experiment, resembling the plot of a comic opera rather than the seriousness of historical drama.

Dec. 5, 1805, as Miranda was leaving New York to entrap Madison, three days after Burr had returned to Philadelphia from his unsatisfactory interview with Merry, the Marquis of Casa Yrujo, as yet innocent of conspiracy, and even flattering himself upon having restored friendly relations with the Government, received a secret visit at his house in Philadelphia from Jonathan Dayton, whom he had known at Washington as the Federalist senator from New Jersey. Dayton, in a mysterious manner, gave him to understand that the Spanish government would do well to pay thirty or forty thousand dollars for certain secrets; and finding the marquis disposed to listen, Dayton recited a curious tale.

"This secret," said he,[1] "is known at the present moment to only three persons in this country. I am one of them; and I will tell you that toward the end of the last session and near the end of last March Colonel Burr had various very secret conferences with the British minister, to whom he proposed a plan not only for taking the Floridas, but also for effecting the separation and independence of the Western States,—a part of this plan being that the Floridas should be associated in this new federative republic; England to receive as the price of her services a decisive preference in matters of commerce and navigation, and to secure these advantages by means of a treaty to be made as soon as she should recognize this new republic. This plan obtained the approval of the British minister, who sent it and recommended it to his Court. Meanwhile Colonel Burr has been in New Orleans, in the Mississippi Territory, in the States of Tennessee, Kentucky, and Ohio, to sound and prepare their minds for this revolution. In all these States he has found the most favorable disposition, not only for this emancipation, which the Western States evidently desire, but also for making an expedition against the kingdom of Mexico. This is an idea that occurred to us after sending the first plan to London; and having given greater extension to the project, Colonel Burr sent to London a

[1] Yrujo to Cevallos, Dec. 5, 1805; MSS. Spanish Archives.

despatch with his new ideas to Colonel Williamson,—an English officer who has been many years in this country, and whose return he expects within a month or six weeks. The first project was very well received by the English Cabinet, and more particularly by Mr. Dundas, or Lord Melville, who was the person charged with this correspondence; but as he had reason to fear dismission from office for causes well known through the debates of Parliament, this plan has suffered some delay; but Mr. Pitt has again turned his attention to it."

On the strength of this information Dayton seriously proposed to terrify Yrujo and Don Carlos IV. into paying the expenses of Burr's expedition. An idea so fantastic could have sprung from no mind except Burr's; but, fantastic as it was, he pursued it obstinately, although by doing so he betrayed to Spain the followers whom he was striving to inveigle into an imaginary assault on Spanish empire. Dayton asserted that the revolution would begin on the appearance of the British squadron off the coast of West Florida in February or March, 1806; that to make this revolution more popular, after the Floridas were taken, the expedition against Mexico would be attempted; that they feared no opposition from a government so weak as the Federal; that the United States troops were all in the West, and that Colonel Burr had caused them to be sounded in regard to the expedition against Mexico; that they were all ready to follow him, and he did not doubt that there existed in them the same disposition to sustain the rights of the Western States, in which they lived, against the impotent forces of the Federal government; that Mexico was to be assailed, in co-operation with the English fleet, by troops to be disembarked at Tampico or thereabout; and that the revolutionized Spanish possessions would be made republics.

To reveal such a plan was to destroy its chance of success; and in thus presenting himself before the Spanish minister Dayton appeared as a traitor not only to the Union, but also to the conspirators with whom he was engaged. Such a character was not likely to create confidence. Yrujo instantly saw that Burr stood behind Dayton; that England could not have encouraged the conspiracy, for, had she done so, the conspirators would never come to beg a few thousand dollars from Spain; and that the Mexican scheme, if it ever existed, must have been already abandoned, or it would not have been revealed. Dismissing the ex-senator with civility and a promise to talk with him further, Yrujo wrote to his Government a long account of the interview. He pointed at once to Clark as the person through whom Burr drew his information about Mexico. Yrujo was perplexed only by Jefferson's apparent blindness to the doings in the West. The marquis was a Spaniard; and for twenty years the people of the United States had talked of Spaniards with contempt. Even Jefferson freely assumed their faithlessness and paltriness; but surely if Yrujo had cared to concentrate in a few words his opinion of American political character, no American could have wondered if these few words, like a flash of lightning, left no living thing where they struck.

> "I am sure," he wrote to Cevallos, "that the Administration will not let itself be deceived by Colonel Burr's wiles; but I know that the President, although penetrating and detesting as well as fearing him, and for this reason, not only invites him to his table, but only about five days ago had a secret conference with him which lasted more than two hours, and in which I am confident there was as little good faith on the one side as there was on the other."

The assertion could not be denied. The White House rarely saw, within a few days' interval, two less creditable guests than Aaron Burr, fresh from confiding his plans to Anthony Merry, and Francesco de Miranda, openly engaged in a military attack from the port of New York upon the dominions of Spain.

Yrujo was at first inclined to distrust Dayton; but Miranda's undertaking, which crossed Burr's plans, gave to the ex-senator the means of proving his good faith. Indeed, in a few days more, Dayton made a clean breast, admitting that England had disappointed Burr's expectations, and that Burr had authorized the offer to sell his services to Spain.

> "I have had with him two very long conferences," wrote

Yrujo three weeks later,[1] "in which he has told me that
Colonel Burr will not treat with Miranda, whom he considers imprudent, and wanting in many qualities necessary for
an undertaking of such magnitude as he has on hand. Miranda has returned to New York, much piqued at finding
that Colonel Burr was very determined to have nothing to
do with him. He also told me that Colonel Williamson,
who was sent to London with the plan for the British ministry, not finding Mr. Pitt so warm as Lord Melville for the
project of raising the Western States, had turned to plans
in that capital, and showed, by the want of exactness in his
correspondence, that he was not following up the object
with the same zeal as at first he undertook it; that in consequence they were disposed to despatch to London a New
York gentleman named Warton, well known for his intimacy with Burr, but that on the verge of his departure another plan suggested itself to Burr, which he seems rather
inclined to execute. This plan, excepting the attack on the
Floridas, has the same object, which he, as well as his chief
friends, hope may be put in execution even without foreign
aid. For one who does not know the country, its constitution, and, above all, certain localities, this plan would appear almost insane; but I confess, for my part, that in view
of all the circumstances it seems to me easy to execute, although it will irritate the Atlantic States, especially those
called central,—that is, Virginia, Maryland, Delaware,
Pennsylvania, New Jersey, and New York. It is beyond
question that there exists in this country an infinite number
of adventurers, without property, full of ambition, and
ready to unite at once under the standard of a revolution
which promises to better their lot. Equally certain is it that
Burr and his friends, without discovering their true object,
have succeeded in getting the good-will of these men, and
inspiring the greatest confidence among them in favor of
Burr."

The "almost insane" plan which Dayton unfolded to the
Spanish minister was nothing less than to introduce by degrees into the city of Washington a certain number of men in

[1] Yrujo to Cevallos, Jan. 1, 1806; MSS. Spanish Archives.

disguise, well armed, who, at a signal from Burr, were to seize the President, Vice-President, and the President of the Senate,—the substitute always named at the beginning of each session, in case of the death, illness, or absence of the two first. Having thus secured the heads of government, the conspirators were to seize the public money deposited in the Washington and Georgetown banks, and to take possession of the arsenal on the Eastern Branch. Burr hoped by this blow to delay or paralyze opposition, and perhaps to negotiate with the individual States an arrangement favorable to himself; but in the more probable case that he could not maintain himself at Washington, he would burn all the national vessels at the Navy Yard, except the two or three which were ready for service, and embarking on these with his followers and the treasure, he would sail for New Orleans and proclaim the emancipation of Louisiana and the Western States.

Wild as this scheme was, it occupied Burr's mind for the rest of the winter, and he made many efforts to draw discontented officers of the government into it. He sounded Commodore Truxton, without revealing his whole object; but to William Eaton, the hero of Derne, he opened himself with as much confidence as to Merry and Yrujo. Eaton was at Washington in January and February, 1806, sore at the manner in which his claims were treated by Congress, and extravagant in ideas of his own importance. To him Burr laid open the whole secret, even in regard to the plan for attacking Washington. The story was the same which had been told to Merry and Yrujo.[1] He spoke of Wilkinson as his second in command; of his son-in-law, Allston, as engaged in the enterprise; and of New Orleans as the capital of his Western empire, whence an expedition would be sent for the conquest of Mexico. The line of demarcation was to be the Alleghany Mountains; and although he expressed some doubts about Ohio, he declared himself certain of Kentucky and Tennessee.

"If he could gain over the marine corps and secure to his interests the naval commanders Truxton, Preble, Decatur, and others, he would turn Congress neck and heels out of

[1] Deposition of General Eaton; Life of William Eaton, p. 396.

doors, assassinate the President (or what amounted to that), and declare himself the protector of an energetic government."

The scheme of attacking Washington was merely an episode due to Burr's despair of British or Spanish aid. Burr was reduced to many devices in order to keep his conspiracy alive. December 12, immediately after the disappointing interview with Merry, and Dayton's first advance to Casa Yrujo, Burr wrote to Wilkinson a letter evidently intended to conceal his diplomatic disaster and to deceive his friend. He said that there would be no war with Spain, and foretold the peaceful course of Government.[1] "In case of such warfare, Lee would have been commander-in-chief. Truth, I assure you. He must you know come from Virginia." As to the conspiracy, he reserved it for a few short lines, intelligible enough to those who knew that New Orleans was to declare its independence on the arrival of a British squadron in February, and that the revolutionary government would at once send a delegation to Natchez or St. Louis to make a formal tender of military command to General Wilkinson.

"On the subject of a certain speculation it is not deemed material to write till the whole can be communicated. The circumstance referred to in a letter from Ohio remains in suspense. The auspices, however, are favorable, and it is believed that Wilkinson will give audience to a delegation, composed of Adair and Dayton, in February."

Meanwhile the Government asked no questions. Denunciation of Burr and Wilkinson was dangerous; it was tried again and again with disastrous results. Major Bruff, at St. Louis, who suspected the truth, dared not bring such a charge against his superior officer:[2] but a certain Judge Easton, to whom Burr confided at St. Louis, ventured to write a letter to a senator of the United States charging Wilkinson with being concerned in Miranda's expedition; and was told

[1] Burr to Wilkinson, Dec. 12, 1806; Wilkinson's Memoirs, ii. Appendix, lxxxiv.
[2] Evidence of Major Bruff, Burr's Trial; Annals of Congress, 1807–1808, p. 597.

in reply that the letter was burned, and that the writer should mind his own business, and take care how he meddled with men high in power and office. So thick an atmosphere of intrigue, especially in Spanish matters, was supposed to pervade the White House; men's minds were so befogged with public messages about a Spanish war and secret messages about peace, with private encouragement to Miranda and public punishment of Miranda's friends, with John Randolph's furious charges of duplicity and Madison's helpless silence under these charges,—that until the President himself should say the word, Burr, Wilkinson, Dayton, and their associates were safe, and might hatch treason in the face of all the world.

President Jefferson had already too many feuds on his hands, and Burr had still too many friends, to warrant rousing fresh reprisals at a time when the difficulties of the Administration were extreme. The President continued to countenance Burr in public, alleging in private that the people could be trusted to defeat his schemes. Doubtless the people could be trusted for that purpose, but they had instituted a government in order to provide themselves with proper machinery for such emergencies, and the President alone could set it in action. General Eaton made an attempt to put the President on his guard. He first consulted two leading Federalist Congressmen,—John Cotton Smith and Samuel Dana,—who advised him to hold his tongue, for his solitary word would not avail against the weight of Burr's character.[1] Nevertheless, in March, 1806, he called at the White House and saw the President.

"After a desultory conversation, in which I aimed to draw his attention to the West, I took the liberty of suggesting to the President that I thought Colonel Burr ought to be removed from the country, because I considered him dangerous in it. The President asked where he should send him. I said to England or Madrid. . . . The President, without any positive expression, in such a matter of delicacy, seemed to think the trust too important, and ex-

[1] Evidence of William Eaton, Burr's Trial; Annals of Congress, 1807–1808, pp. 511, 512.

pressed something like a doubt about the integrity of Mr. Burr. I frankly told the President that perhaps no person had stronger grounds to suspect that integrity than I had; but that I believed his pride of ambition had so predominated over his other passions that when placed on an eminence and put on his honor, a respect to himself would secure his fidelity. I perceived that the subject was disagreeable to the President; and to bring him to my point in the shortest mode, and in a manner which would point to the danger, I said to him, if Colonel Burr was not disposed of, we should in eighteen months have an insurrection, if not a revolution, on the waters of the Mississippi. The President said he had too much confidence in the information, the integrity, and attachment of the people of that country to the Union, to admit any apprehensions of that kind."

If the President had confidence in the people of New Orleans, he had not shown it in framing a form of government for them; and if he admitted no apprehensions in March, 1806, he admitted many before the year closed. In truth, he deceived himself. That he was afraid of Burr and of the sympathy which Burr's career had excited, was the belief of Burr himself, who responded to Jefferson's caution by a contempt so impudent as to seem even then almost incredible. Believing that the President dared not touch him, Burr never cared to throw even a veil over his treason. He used the President's name and the names of his Cabinet officers as freely as though he were President himself; and no one contradicted or disavowed him. So matters remained at Washington down to the close of the session.

"I detailed," said Eaton,[1] "the whole project of Mr. Burr to certain members of Congress. They believed Colonel Burr capable of anything, and agreed that the fellow ought to be hanged, but thought his projects too chimerical, and his circumstances too desperate, to give the subject the merit of serious consideration."

[1] Deposition of Jan. 26, 1807; Life of Eaton, p. 401.

Chapter XI

THE DEATH of Pitt destroyed all immediate possibility of drawing England into conspiracy with Burr,—if indeed a possibility had ever existed. The attempt to obtain money from Spain was equally hopeless. Except for Madison's conduct in receiving Miranda and refusing to receive Yrujo, Dayton would probably have obtained nothing from Spain; but the information he was able to give Yrujo in regard to Miranda's plans and proceedings deserved reward, and Dayton received at different times sums of money, amounting in all to about three thousand dollars, from the Spanish treasury. Dayton's private necessities required much larger sums.

Burr was also ruined. He could not return to New York, where an indictment hung over his head. Conspiracy was easier than poverty; but conspiracy without foreign aid was too wild a scheme for other men to join. Jefferson might at that moment have stopped Burr's activity by sending word privately to him and his friends that their projects must be dropped; but Jefferson, while closing every other path, left that of conspiracy open to Burr, who followed it only with much difficulty. In order to retain any friends or followers he was obliged to deceive them all, and entangle himself and them in an elaborate network of falsehood. Dayton alone knew the truth, and helped him to deceive.

April 16, 1806, a few days before the adjournment of Congress, Burr wrote to Wilkinson a letter implying that Wilkinson had required certain conditions and an enlargement of the scheme; Burr assured him that his requirements, which probably concerned aid from Truxton, Preble, Eaton, and Decatur, had been fully satisfied:—

> "The execution of our project is postponed till December. Want of water in Ohio rendered movement impracticable; other reasons rendered delay expedient. The association is enlarged, and comprises all that Wilkinson could wish. Confidence limited to a few. Though this delay is irksome, it will enable us to move with more certainty and dignity. Burr will be throughout the United States this

summer. Administration is damned which Randolph aids. Burr wrote you a long letter last December, replying to a short one deemed very silly. Nothing has been heard from the Brigadier since October. Is Cushing and Porter right? Address Burr at Washington."[1]

Burr's letters to Wilkinson were always in cipher, and mysteriously worded; but in this despatch nothing was unintelligible. Wilkinson afterward explained that he was himself the "Brigadier," and the two names were those of officers under his command.

The same western mail which carried this letter to Wilkinson carried another to Blennerhassett, inviting him to join in a "speculation," which would "not be commenced before December, if ever." Probably Burr made many other efforts to obtain money from petty sources; he certainly exerted himself to delude the Spanish government into lending him assistance. Hitherto he had left this task to Dayton, his secretary of state, but May 14, 1806, the Spanish minister wrote to Don Pedro Cevallos,[2] —

"The principal [Burr] has opened himself to me; and the communications I have had with him confirm me in the idea, not only of the probability, but even of the facility, of his success, under certain circumstances. To insure it, some pecuniary aid on our part and on that of France is wanted. I have been careful to be very circumspect in my answers, and have not compromised myself in any manner; but when I return to Spain next spring I shall be bearer of the whole plan, with the details that may be wanted. There will also arrive in Spain before long, more or less simultaneously with me though by different ways, two or three very respectable persons, both from Louisiana and from Kentucky and Tennessee, with the same object. They all consider the interests of these countries as united and in conformity with those of Spain and France; but the principal, or more correctly the principals, here do not wish to open themselves to the Emperor Napoleon's minister [Turreau], as they lack confidence in him. Consequently, it will

[1] Wilkinson's Memoirs, ii. Appendix, lxxxiii.
[2] Yrujo to Cevallos, May 14, 1806; MSS. Spanish Archives.

be proper either not to communicate the matter at all to that government, or to do it with the intimation that its representative here shall not have the least notice of it; for, I repeat, they have no confidence in him, and this has been a condition imposed on me in the communications I have received."

Finding Yrujo obstinate in refusing to advance money, Burr tried to alarm him by pretending to take up again the scheme of attacking Florida and Mexico. June 9, 1806, Yrujo wrote another long despatch on the subject. Burr, he said, had suddenly ceased to visit him as frequently as usual, and Dayton had explained the coldness as due to Burr's belief that the new Administration in England would be more liberal and zealous than that of Pitt. Dayton added that Burr was drawing up new instructions for Williamson; that he had even decided to send Bollman to London to invite co-operation from the British government in an attack on the Spanish possessions. Dayton professed to have acted as the protector of Spain from Burr's unprincipled ambition.

"Dayton told me[1] he had observed to Burr that although he (Burr) was assuredly the principal, yet a plan of this nature ought to be put in deliberation in the cabinet council which certain chiefs are to hold in New Orleans in the month of December next, and that for his own part he thought this idea unjust and impolitic; to which Burr answered that they would always be able to alter the plan as circumstances should require, and that in fact this point, or at least the direction to be given to it, would be determined in New Orleans. Dayton told me that he would oppose with all his strength measures of this nature, and that he knew General Wilkinson, who was to be a member of the Congress, would make the same opposition; and that in order to drive the idea of such a temptation out of Burr's head, and of other people's also, it would be well for us to reinforce our garrisons at Pensacola and Mobile, and that then the circumstance of our respectable condition of defence might be used as a weighty argument for abandoning

[1] Yrujo to Cevallos, June 9, 1806; MSS. Spanish Archives.

such a project. After holding this conference with me, Day ton returned to his residence; and before starting, wrote me a note to say that the night before Burr had read him the instructions to be given to Bollman, and that they were of the tenor indicated to me."

Godoy and Cevallos were hardly so imbecile as to pay for creating at New Orleans a new American empire more dangerous to Spanish possessions than the peaceful republic over which Jefferson presided at Washington. Don Pedro Cevallos read Yrujo's despatches with great interest. At first he even hinted that if the United States were bent on forcing a war with Spain, these adventurers, in case of actual hostilities, might be made useful;[1] but this suggestion was accompanied by many warnings to Yrujo not to commit himself or to contribute money, and at last by a flat announcement that the King would not in any way encourage Burr's designs.[2]

The conspirators were in a worse position as regarded England. By a fatal stroke of ill-luck, Merry's despatch of Nov. 25, 1805, written to be read in secrecy by the Tory Lord Mulgrave, was received at the Foreign Office Feb. 2, 1806, ten days after Pitt's death, and was probably opened by Charles James Fox,—almost the last man in England to whom Merry would have willingly shown it. The only answer received by Merry reached Washington about June 1, 1806, and consisted in the dry announcement that his Majesty had been pleased to listen favorably to Mr. Merry's request for a recall, and had appointed the Hon. David Montague Erskine as his successor.

Merry complained piteously that he had never suggested a wish to be recalled, that he had indeed the strongest desire to remain, and felt himself greatly aggrieved at his treatment; but Fox was remorseless, and Merry could only prepare for Erskine's arrival. Smarting under this sudden reproof, Merry held his parting interview with Burr. Doubtless it was as little cheerful on one side as on the other; but Merry did not think himself required to give an immediate or a minute account of it to Fox. He waited until Erskine's arrival, and then, in one

[1] Cevallos to Casa Yrujo, March 28, 1806; MSS. Spanish Archives.
[2] Cevallos to Casa Yrujo, July 12, 1806; MSS. Spanish Archives.

of his last despatches, Nov. 2, 1806, after Burr had begun his operations in the West, Merry wrote,[1] —

"I saw this gentleman [Burr] for the last time at this place [Washington] in the month of June last, when he made particular inquiry whether I had received any answer from my Government to the propositions he had requested me to transmit to them, and lamented exceedingly that I had not, because he, and the persons connected with him at New Orleans, would now, though very reluctantly, be under the necessity of addressing themselves to the French and Spanish governments. He added, however, that the disposition of the inhabitants of the Western country, and particularly Louisiana, to separate themselves from the American Union was so strong that the attempt might be made with every prospect of success without any foreign assistance whatever; and his last words to me were that, with or without such support, it certainly would be made very shortly."

After receiving this rebuff from England, Burr and Dayton needed singular impudence to threaten Yrujo with the terror of Charles James Fox; but impudence had become their only resource. Every step taken thenceforward by the conspirators was taken by means of a new imposture; until at last they became petty swindlers who lived from day to day by cheating each other. How flagrant their imposture was, has been partly shown in their attempt to deceive Yrujo; but their treatment of Wilkinson was far more dishonest.

Toward the end of July, 1806, Burr had accomplished all that could be done in the East, and prepared to begin his campaign to New Orleans. By strenuous efforts money had been raised to set the subordinate adventurers in motion. Among these were Erick Bollman, famous for an attempt to rescue Lafayette from confinement at Olmütz; a French officer named De Pestre, or Dupiester; Samuel Swartwout, a younger brother of Robert; and finally young Peter V. Ogden, a nephew of Dayton. The time had come when each actor must take his place, and must receive orders as to the *rôle* he was to play.

[1] Merry to C. J. Fox, June 1, 1806; MSS. British Archives.

Of all Burr's intimates, Wilkinson was not only the most important, but also the most doubtful. He had hung back and had made conditions. Since October, 1805, nothing had been heard from him, and his last letter had contained objections "deemed very silly." At last a letter, dated May 13, arrived. This letter never saw the light; afterward, at the trial, Wilkinson challenged its production, and accused Burr of falsehood in asserting that it had been destroyed at Wilkinson's request or with his knowledge. Only one conclusion might be taken as certain in regard to its contents,—they did not suit the situation of Dayton and Burr.

Dayton's reply was dated July 24, 1806, and was sent by his nephew, Peter V. Ogden, to Wilkinson.

"It is now well ascertained that you are to be displaced in next session," wrote Dayton, working on his old friend's pride and fears. "Jefferson will affect to yield reluctantly to the public sentiment, but yield he will. Prepare yourself, therefore, for it. You know the rest. You are not a man to despair, or even despond, especially when such prospects offer in another quarter. Are you ready? Are your numerous associates ready? Wealth and glory! Louisiana and Mexico!"

Together with this exhortation from Dayton, Burr sent a cipher despatch, afterward famous as the key to the whole conspiracy. Published at different times with varying versions, as suited Wilkinson's momentary objects, the correct reading probably ran very nearly as follows:—

"July 29, 1806. Your letter, postmarked 13th May, is received. At length I have obtained funds, and have actually commenced. The Eastern detachments, from different points and under different pretences, will rendezvous on the Ohio 1st of November. Everything internal and external favors our views. Naval protection of England is secured. Truxton is going to Jamaica to arrange with the admiral on that station. It will meet us at the Mississippi. England, a navy of the United States, are ready to join, and final orders are given to my friends and followers. It will be a host of choice spirits. Wilkinson shall be second to Burr only; Wilkinson shall dictate the rank and promotion of his officers.

Burr will proceed westward 1st August, never to return. With him goes his daughter; the husband will follow in October, with a corps of worthies. Send forthwith an intelligent and confidential friend with whom Burr may confer; he shall return immediately with further interesting details; this is essential to concert and harmony of movement. Send a list of all persons known to Wilkinson west of the mountains who could be useful, with a note delineating their characters. By your messenger send me four or five commissions of your officers, which you can borrow under any pretence you please; they shall be returned faithfully. Already are orders given to the contractor to forward six months' provisions to points Wilkinson may name; this shall not be used until the last moment, and then under proper injunctions. Our object, my dear friend, is brought to a point so long desired. Burr guarantees the result with his life and honor, with the lives and honor and the fortunes of hundreds, the best blood of our country. Burr's plan of operation is to move down rapidly from the Falls, on the 15th of November, with the first five hundred or a thousand men, in light boats now constructing for that purpose; to be at Natchez between the 5th and 15th of December, there to meet you; there to determine whether it will be expedient in the first instance to seize on or pass by Baton Rouge. On receipt of this, send Burr an answer. Draw on Burr for all expenses, etc. The people of the country to which we are going are prepared to receive us; their agents, now with Burr, say that if we will protect their religion, and will not subject them to a foreign Power, that in three weeks all will be settled. The gods invite us to glory and fortune; it remains to be seen whether we deserve the boon. The bearer of this goes express to you. He is a man of inviolable honor and perfect discretion, formed to execute rather than project, capable of relating facts with fidelity, and incapable of relating them otherwise; he is thoroughly informed of the plans and intentions of Burr, and will disclose to you as far as you require, and no further. He has imbibed a reverence for your character, and may be embarrassed in your presence; put him at ease, and he will satisfy you."

Had Burr and Dayton not felt strong reason to doubt Wilkinson's course, they would not have invented a tissue of falsehoods such as these letters contained. So far as concerned Wilkinson's future conduct, no one could deny that this gross deception set him free from any ties that might have previously bound him to Dayton or Burr.

Furnished with these and other letters almost equally compromising, Ogden and Swartwout, at the end of July, started on their way. Swartwout was directed to see Adair in Kentucky, and to deliver to him despatches, the contents of which have never been made known, but were doubtless identical with the letters to Wilkinson. At the same time Erick Bollman started by sea with similar despatches for New Orleans.

Early in August Burr followed, taking with him his daughter Mrs. Allston, and his chief of staff Colonel De Pestre. After crossing the mountains he threw aside ordinary caution. At Canonsburg, about fifteen miles beyond Pittsburg, he stopped at the house of an old friend, Colonel Morgan, and there so freely asserted the imbecility of the Federal government and the certainty of a speedy separation of the Western States from the Eastern, that Morgan thought himself bound to give President Jefferson a warning.

The conversation at Canonsburg took place in the afternoon and evening of August 22. A few days afterward Burr arrived at Blennerhassett's island, where he found the owner waiting with enthusiasm to receive him. Of all the eager dupes with whom Burr had to deal, this intelligent and accomplished Irish gentleman was the most simple. After wasting half his property on his island, he discovered that he had left himself not more than thirty or forty thousand dollars to live upon; and this small property was invested in funds which produced so little as to leave him always embarrassed. He wished ardently to make his fortune by some bold speculation; and Burr had no more pressing necessity than to obtain the funds which Blennerhassett burned to invest. Burr said to Blennerhassett in effect what he said to Wilkinson; but Blennerhassett was less able than Wilkinson to detect falsehood. The actual speculation which was to make Blennerhassett's fortune seemed certain of success. Burr had invented more than one way of getting money; and among his various expedients none was more ingenious than that of buying a certain Spanish claim, known as the Bastrop grant, covering an immense district on the Red River, and supposed to be owned in part by one Lynch in Kentucky. Burr had undertaken to buy Lynch's interest for forty thousand dollars, of which only four thousand or five thousand dollars need be paid in money; and he persuaded Blennerhassett that on the most moderate estimate, they could reap from it the profit of a million. Blennerhassett was assured that before the end of the year Louisiana would be independent, with Burr for its ruler, under the protection of England. Wilkinson and the United States army were pledged to accept the revolution and to support Burr. Tennessee was secured; and though Kentucky and Ohio were doubtful, they would end by following Tennessee. The government at Washington would fall to pieces, and the new empire under a stronger government, would rise at once to power. Then Bastrop's grant would take character; its actual cheapness was due to doubts as to its validity: but the moment its validity was decided by the new government, all whose members would be interested in it, the value of the grant would become enormous; emigration would be directed to the spot, and Blennerhassett's fortune would be vast. He would, meanwhile, go at once as minister to England, with Erick Bollman for secretary of legation.[1]

In an incredibly short time Blennerhasset's head was turned. Unluckily for him, his wife's head was turned even more easily than his own; and the charms of Theodosia Allston, who became a guest at the island, dazzled the eyes of both. Before Burr had been two days in the house, Blennerhassett was so enthusiastic a supporter of the scheme that he set himself to work, under Burr's eye, to publish a series of essays in order to show the State of Ohio that disunion was an infallible cure for all its natural or acquired ills. The first of these essays was quickly finished, taken to Marietta, and printed in the "Ohio Gazette" of September 4 under the signature "Querist."

September 2, before the "Querist" appeared, Burr continued his journey down the river to Cincinnati, where he ar-

[1] Blennerhassett Papers, p. 351.

rived September 4, and remained a few days with Senator
Smith, talking freely about the impotence of the government,
the rights and wrongs of the Western people, and their inducements to set up a separate empire. September 10 he
crossed the river to Lexington in Kentucky, and shortly after
ward went to Nashville in Tennessee.

Owing chiefly to the friendship of Andrew Jackson, the
town of Nashville was strongly attached to Burr, and was
supposed to favor the disunion scheme. Tennessee was the
only State which Burr always claimed positively as his own.
Whether he had better grounds for his confidence in Jackson
than for his faith in Wilkinson and Daniel Clark might be
doubted; but Tennessee was at least vehement in hatred of
the Spaniards. The Spaniards were pressing close against Wilkinson's little force at Natchitoches, and Burr made use of the
threatened war in order to cover his own scheme. September
27 a public dinner was given to him at Nashville, and Jackson
offered as a toast the old sentiment of 1798: "Millions for defence; not a cent for tribute." A few days later Burr returned
to Kentucky; and within a week suddenly appeared in the
newspaper at Nashville a strange proclamation signed "Andrew Jackson, Major-General Second Division," and dated
Oct. 4, 1806, in which the brigade commanders were ordered
to place their brigades at once on such a footing as would
enable them on the shortest notice to supply their quotas
"when the government and constituted authorities of our
country" should require them to march. This unauthorized
step was commonly supposed to be taken in the interest of
Burr's conspiracy, and compromised Jackson gravely in the
eyes of the Government at Washington.

Meanwhile Theodosia Allston and her husband had been
left in charge of the Blennerhassetts, while Blennerhassett
himself behaved as though he were a village school-boy playing the part of chieftain in an imaginary feudal castle. He
went about the country raising recruits and buying supplies,
chattering to every young and active man he met about the
expedition which was to make their fortunes. He confided in
his gardener, a simple, straightforward fellow named Peter
Taylor, "that Colonel Burr would be king of Mexico, and that
Mrs. Allston would be queen of Mexico whenever Colonel

Burr died." He added that Burr "had a great many friends in the Spanish territory; two thousand Roman Catholic priests were enlisted in his corps; that those priests and the societies which belonged to them were a strong party; that the Spaniards, like the French, had got tired of their government and wanted to swap it; that the British were also friends to this expedition; and that he was the very man who was to go to England on this piece of business for Colonel Burr." When at the subsequent trial Taylor told this tale, the world was incredulous, and insisted upon disbelieving his story; but Blennerhassett's papers proved the extent of his delusion. By common consent the Blennerhassetts and Allstons agreed that Theodosia was to inherit the empire from her father; but doubts existed whether Allston could take the crown as Theodosia's husband. "I will win it by a better title," he cried,— "by my deeds in council and in field!"[1] Mrs. Blennerhassett was impatient to exchange her solitary island for the court of her young empress; and Blennerhassett longed to set sail as minister for England with Erick Bollman for secretary of legation. Under the influence of this intoxication, Blennerhassett offered to advance money to the extent of all his property for Burr's use if Allston would give him a written and sealed guaranty to a certain amount; which Allston did.[2]

Leaving his wife at the island, while fifteen boats were building at Marietta and kilns for baking bread were constructed on the island itself, Blennerhassett went with the Allstons down the river to Lexington, and there rejoined Burr on his return from Nashville, about October 1. No time had been lost. The boats building at Marietta would carry about five hundred men; others to be built elsewhere would carry five hundred more. Recruiting went rapidly forward. Finally, the purchase-money for Lynch's interest in Bastrop's grant, about four or five thousand dollars, was paid; and Blennerhassett congratulated himself on owning a share in four hundred thousand acres of land in the heart of Louisiana.

To communicate with his friends in New York and Philadelphia, Burr sent De Pestre October 25, with directions to report the movements of the Western conspirators to the

[1] Blennerhassett Papers, p. 333; Blennerhassett to Allston, March 2, 1811.
[2] Blennerhassett Papers, pp. 397, 535.

Marquis of Casa Yrujo, as well as to Swartwout and Dayton. Burr gave De Pestre to understand that one object of his mission was to blind the Spanish minister in regard to the schemes against Mexico and Florida; in reality De Pestre's mission was probably for the purpose of raising money. Yrujo was already well informed from other sources. November 10, before De Pestre's arrival, the Marquis wrote to his Government that some five hundred men were collecting on the upper Ohio to move down the river in squads:[1] —

"Colonel Burr will go down with them under pretext of establishing them on a great land-purchase he is supposed to have made. In passing Cincinnati they expect to get possession of five thousand stand of arms which the government deposited there at the time of its differences with us about the navigation of the Mississippi. After thus dropping the mask, this armed troop will follow down the course of the Mississippi. Colonel Burr will stop at Natchez, where he will wait until the Assembly of New Orleans has met, which will happen at once; and in this meeting (*junta*) they will declare the independence of the Western States, and will invite Burr meanwhile to place himself at the head of their government. He will accept the offer, will descend to New Orleans, and will set to work, clothed in a character which the people will have given him I understand that Colonel Burr has already written the declaration of independence, and that it is couched in the same terms that the States adopted in theirs against Great Britain. This circumstance is the more notable inasmuch as the actual President was the person who drew it up in 1776. When Burr made the project of acting in agreement with England and seizing the Floridas, he expected to master them with troops that should accompany him from Baton Rouge. Although I am assured that this project is abandoned, and that on the contrary he wishes to live on good terms with Spain, I have written to Governor Folch of West Florida to be on his guard; and although I am persuaded that by means of Governor Folch's connection with General Wilkinson, he must be perfectly informed of the

[1] Yrujo to Cevallos, Nov. 10, 1806; MSS. Spanish Archives.

state of things and of Burr's intentions, I shall write to-day or to-morrow another letter to the Governor of Baton Rouge to be on the alert."

Yrujo believed that Wilkinson, the General in command of the American army, then supposed to be on the point of attacking the Spanish force in his front, was secretly and regularly communicating with the Spanish Governor of West Florida.

Burr was engaged in deceiving every one; but his attempt to deceive Yrujo, if seriously meant, was the least comprehensible of all his manœuvres. December 4 the Spanish minister wrote to his Government another despatch which betrayed his perplexity at Burr's conduct: —

"I am positively assured," he said, "that from one day to another will embark from New York for New Orleans, to join Colonel Burr in Louisiana, three of his intimate friends, depositaries of his whole confidence; namely, Mr. Swartwout, lately marshal of the district of New York, a certain Dr. Erwin, and the famous Colonel Smith, the same who was implicated in the business of Miranda, and whose son went out as an aide-de-camp of that adventurer. Accordingly I wrote to the governors of both Floridas and to the Viceroy of Mexico, giving them a general idea of this affair, and recommending them to watch the movements of Colonel Burr and of his adventurers. This is an excess of precaution, since by this time they must not only know through the New Orleans and Natchez newspapers of the projects attributed to Colonel Burr, but also through the confidential channel of the No. 13 of the Marquis of Casa Calvo's cipher with the Prince of Peace, who is one of the conspirators, and who is to contribute very efficaciously to the execution of the scheme in case it shall be carried into effect."

The person designated as No. 13 in the cipher used between Casa Calvo and Godoy was the general-in-chief of the American forces, Wilkinson. The Marquis's despatch next mentioned the arrival of De Pestre, who appeared about November 27 at Yrujo's house: —

"About a week ago a former French officer came to see me, one of Burr's partisans, who came from Kentucky in search of various articles for the execution of his undertaking. . . . This officer handed me a letter from Colonel Burr, in which, after recommending him to me, the writer said simply that as this person had lately visited those States, he could give me information about them worthy of my curiosity. The date of this letter was Lexington, October 25."

De Pestre gave to Yrujo the assurance that all was going well with the undertaking; but the special message he was charged to deliver seemed to be the following: —

"He also told me, on the part of the Colonel, that I should soon hear that he meant to attack Mexico, but that I was not to believe such rumors; that on the contrary his plans were limited to the emancipation of the Western States, and that it was necessary to circulate this rumor in order to hide the true design of his armaments and of the assemblages of men which could no longer be kept secret; that Upper and Lower Louisiana, the States of Tennessee and Ohio, stood ready and ripe for his plans, but that the State of Kentucky was much divided; and as this is the most important in numbers and population, an armed force must be procured strong enough to control the party there which should be disposed to offer resistance. He added, on Burr's part, that as soon as the revolution should be complete, he should treat with Spain in regard to boundaries, and would conclude this affair to the entire satisfaction of Spain; meanwhile he wished me to write to the Governor of West Florida to diminish the burdens on Americans who navigate the Mobile River, and ask him, when the explosion should take place, to stop the courier or couriers who might be despatched by the friends of Government from New Orleans."

Burr's message caused Yrujo to warn all the Spanish officials in Florida, Texas, and Mexico that "although No. 13 seems to have acted in good faith hitherto, his fidelity could not be depended upon if he had a greater interest in violating it, and that therefore they must be cautious in listening to him and be very vigilant in regard to events that would probably happen in their neighborhood." De Pestre's mission made Yrujo more suspicious than ever, and he spared no precaution to render impossible the success of any attack on Florida or Mexico.

After De Pestre had visited New York, he returned to Philadelphia, and December 13 again called upon Yrujo.

"He told me," reported Yrujo,[1] "that he had seen Mr. Swartwout in New York, whom he had informed of Burr's wish that he, as well as Dr. Erwin, Colonel Smith, and Captain Lewis, who was captain of the merchant ship 'Emperor' and brother of the captain of Miranda's vessel the 'Leander,' should set out as soon as possible for New Orleans. Likewise he instructed him, on the part of the colonel, that the youths enlisted to serve as officers should set out as soon as possible for their posts. These, my informant told me, are different. Some two or three of them, the quickest and keenest, go to Washington to observe the movements of Government, to keep their friends in good disposition, and to despatch expresses with news of any important disposition or occurrence. Three go to Norfolk to make some despatch of provisions. A good number of them will go direct to Charleston to take command as officers, and see to the embarkation of the numerous recruits whom Colonel Burr's son-in-law has raised in South Carolina. He himself will then have returned there from Kentucky, and will embark with them for New Orleans. The rest will embark directly for that city from New York."

Yrujo could not see the feebleness of the conspiracy. So far as he knew, the story might be true; and although he had been both forewarned and forearmed, he could not but feel uneasy lest Burr should make a sudden attack on West Florida or Texas. The Spanish minister was able to protect Spanish interests if they were attacked; but he would have preferred to prevent an attack, and this could be done by the United States government alone. The indifference of President Jeffer-

---

[1] Yrujo to Cevallos, Dec. 16, 1806; MSS. Spanish Archives.

son to Burr's movements astounded many persons besides Yrujo. "It is astonishing," wrote Merry in November,[1] "that the Government here should have remained so long in ignorance of the intended design as even not to know with certainty at this moment the object of the preparations which they have learned are now making." Merry would have been still more astonished had he been told that the President was by no means ignorant of Burr's object; and Yrujo might well be perplexed to see that ignorant or not, the President had taken no measure for the defence of New Orleans, and that the time had passed when any measure could be taken. The city was in Wilkinson's hands. Even of the five small gunboats which were meant to be stationed at the mouth of the Mississippi, only one was actually there. That Burr and Wilkinson should meet resistance at New Orleans was not to be imagined. Yrujo saw no chance of checking them except in Ohio and Kentucky.

[1] Merry to C. J. Fox, Nov. 7, 1806; MSS. British Archives.

Chapter XII

HAD BURR succeeded in carrying out his original plan of passing the Falls of the Ohio as early as November 15, he might have reached New Orleans with all his force; but he made too many delays, and tried too far the patience of Ohio. October 1 he returned from Nashville to Lexington, where he was joined by Blennerhassett and Allston. From that moment he was beset by difficulties and growing opposition.

As yet the Government at Washington had not moved, and Burr freely said that his military preparations were made with its knowledge and for the probable event of war with Spain; but he had not foreseen that these tactics might rouse against him the class of men from whom he had least reason to expect opposition. In Kentucky a respectable body of old Federalists still existed, with Humphrey Marshall at their head. The United States District Attorney, Joseph H. Daveiss, was also a Federalist, left in office by Jefferson. Burr's admirers were Republicans, so numerous that the President shrank from alienating them by denouncing Burr, while they in their turn would not desert Burr until the President denounced him. The Federalists saw here a chance to injure their opponents, and used it.

As early as the year 1787 Governor Miró, the Spanish ruler of Louisiana, tried to organize a party in Kentucky for establishing an independent empire west of the Alleghanies under the protection of Spain. His chief agent for that purpose was James Wilkinson.[1] The movement received no popular support, and failed; but during the next ten years the Spanish governors who succeeded Miró maintained relations with Wilkinson and his friends, always hoping that some change in American politics would bring their project into favor. Godoy's policy of conciliation with America crossed these intrigues. His treaty of 1795 did much to neutralize them, but his delivery of Natchez in 1798 did more. The settlement of boundary came at a moment when Kentucky, under the lead of Jefferson and Breckinridge, seemed about to defy the

[1] Gayarré's Louisiana; Spanish Domination, pp. 192–199.

United States government, and when the celebrated Kentucky Resolutions promised to draw the Western people into the arms of Spain. Talleyrand's indignation at Godoy's conduct[1] was not more acute than the disgust felt by the Spanish officials at New Orleans.

The Spanish intrigues among the Republicans of Kentucky were not wholly unknown to the Federalists in that State; and as time went on, Humphrey Marshall and Daveiss obtained evidence warranting an assault on the Republicans most deeply implicated.[2] The attempt was a matter of life and death to the Spanish pensioners; and in a society so clannish as that of Kentucky, violence was not only to be feared, but to be counted upon. Daveiss took the risks of personal revenge, and laid his plans accordingly.

Burr's appearance on the Ohio and at St. Louis in Wilkinson's company during the summer of 1805 called attention to the old Spanish conspiracy, and gave Daveiss the opportunity he wanted. As early as Jan. 10, 1806, while Burr was still struggling at Washington to save his plot from collapse for want of foreign aid, and while John Randolph was beginning his invectives in Congress, the district-attorney wrote to the President a private letter denouncing the old Spanish plot, and declaring that it was still alive.[3] "A separation of the Union in favor of Spain is the object *finally*. I know not what are the means." Assuming that Jefferson was ignorant of the facts, because he had "appointed General Wilkinson as Governor of St. Louis, who, I am convinced, has been for years, and now is, a pensioner of Spain," Daveiss asserted his own knowledge, and contented himself with a general warning; —

"This plot is laid wider than you imagine. Mention the subject to no man from the Western country, however high in office he may be. Some of them are deeply tainted with this treason. I hate duplicity of expression; but on this subject I am not authorized to be explicit, nor is it necessary. You will despatch some fit person into the Orleans country to inquire."

[1] See History of First Administration, p. 489.
[2] Marshall's History of Kentucky, ii. 376–384.
[3] Daveiss to Jefferson, Jan. 10, 1806, View of the President's Conduct, by J. H. Daveiss, 1807. Clark's Proofs, pp. 177–179.

February 10 Daveiss wrote again calling attention to Burr's movements during the previous summer, and charging both him and Wilkinson with conspiracy.[1] At about the time when these letters arrived, the President received another warning from Eaton. The air was full of denunciations, waiting only for the President's leave to annihilate the conspirators under popular contempt. A word quietly written by Jefferson to one or two persons in the Western country would have stopped Burr short in his path, and would have brought Wilkinson abjectly on his knees. A slight change in the military and naval arrangements at New Orleans would have terrified the creoles into good behavior, and would have made Daniel Clark denounce the conspiracy.

The President showed Daveiss's letter to Gallatin, Madison, and Dearborn; but he did not take its advice, and did not, in his Cabinet memoranda of October 22,[2] mention it among his many sources of information. February 15 he wrote to Daveiss[3] a request to communicate all he knew on the subject. No other acts followed, nor was either Wilkinson or Burr put under surveillance.

Perhaps this was what Daveiss wished; for if Jefferson pursued his course much further, he was certain to compromise himself in appearing to protect Burr and Wilkinson. Daveiss not only continued to write letter after letter denouncing Wilkinson to the President, without receiving answer or acknowledgment; he not only made a journey to St. Louis in order to collect evidence, and on his return to Kentucky wrote in July to the President that Burr's object was "to cause a revolt of the Spanish provinces, and a severance of all the Western States and Territories from the Union, to coalesce and form one government,"—but he also took a new step, of which he did not think himself obliged to inform the President in advance. He established at Frankfort a weekly newspaper, edited by a man so poor in character and means that for some slight gain in notoriety he could afford to risk a worthless life. John Wood was a newspaper hack, not quite so successful as

[1] Daveiss to Jefferson, Feb. 10, 1806; View, etc. Cf. Marshall's History of Kentucky, ii. 401.
[2] See p. 795.
[3] Jefferson to Daveiss, Feb. 15, 1806; View, etc. Clark's Proofs, p. 179.

Cheetham and Duane, or so vile as Callender. Having in 1801 written a "History of the last Administration," after getting from Colonel Burr, by working upon his vanity, an offer to buy and suppress the book, it was probably Wood who furnished Cheetham with the details of the transaction, and connived at Cheetham's "Narrative of the Suppression," in order to give notoriety to himself. Cheetham's "Narrative" called for a reply, and Wood in 1802 printed a "Correct Statement." Both pamphlets were contemptible; but Cheetham was supported by the Clintons, while Wood could find no one to pay for his literary wares. He drifted to Richmond, and thence across the mountains; until, in the winter of 1805–1806, he dropped quietly, unnoticed, into the village of Frankfort, in Kentucky. Humphrey Marshall and District Attorney Daveiss needed such a man.

July 4, 1806, appeared at Frankfort the first number of the "Western World,"— a weekly newspaper edited by John Wood. The society of Kentucky was alarmed and irritated to find that the "Western World" seemed to have no other object for its existence than to drag the old Spanish conspiracy to light. Passions were soon deeply stirred by the persistency and vehemence with which this pretended Republican newspaper clung to the subject and cried for an investigation. Wood had no fancy for being made the object of assassination, but he was given a fighting colleague named Street; and while Wood hid himself, Street defended the office. In spite of several attempts to drive Street away or to kill him, the "Western World" persevered in its work, until October 15 it published an appeal to the people, founded on Blennerhassett's "Querist" and on the existence of a Spanish Association. Meanwhile two men in high position dreaded exposure, —Judge Sebastian, of the Court of Appeals of Kentucky, and Judge Innis, of the United States District Court.

Daveiss was right in thinking the Spanish conspiracy of 1787–1798 closely allied with Burr's conspiracy of 1805. In striking at Sebastian and Innis, he threw consternation into the ranks of Burr's friends, all of whom were more or less familiar with the Spanish intrigue. Senator Adair, bolder than the rest, stood by Wilkinson and defied exposure; but the greater number of Wilkinson's accomplices were paralyzed.

Daveiss gave them no respite. In October Burr's appearance in Kentucky offered a chance to press his advantage. Jefferson's persistent silence and inaction left the energetic district-attorney free to do what he liked; and nothing short of compromising the Administration satisfied his ambition.

Burr passed the month of October in Kentucky; but his preparations were far from complete. The delay was probably due to the time consumed in getting Blennerhassett's money. At last Burr paid to Lynch the purchase-money of four or five thousand dollars for Bastrop's grant. He had already ordered the construction of boats and enlistment of men at various points on the Ohio, and especially at Marietta, near Blennerhassett's island; but he waited too long before beginning operations on the Cumberland, for not till November 3 did Andrew Jackson at Nashville receive a letter from Burr, inclosing three thousand dollars in Kentucky bank-notes, with orders for the building of five large boats, the purchase of supplies, and the enlistment of recruits,—all of which was promptly undertaken by Jackson, but required more time than could be spared by Burr.

Meanwhile Burr's affairs were going ill in the State of Ohio. Blennerhassett's foolish "Querist," and the more foolish conversation of both Blennerhassett and Burr, combined with the assaults of the "Western World," drew so much attention to the armaments at the island that Mrs. Blennerhassett, left alone while her husband was with Allston and Burr in Kentucky, became alarmed, and thought it necessary to send them a warning. October 20 she wrote to Burr that he could not return with safety. Thinking the note too important to be trusted to the post, and ignorant of Burr's address, she sent her gardener, Peter Taylor, on horseback, through Chillicothe, to Cincinnati, with orders to ask Senator Smith for the address. Taylor reached Cincinnati October 23, after three days of travel, and went, according to his mistress's orders, directly to Senator Smith's house, which was in the same building with his store,—for Smith was a store-keeper and army contractor. The senator was already too deeply compromised with Burr, and his courage had begun to fail. At first he denied knowledge of Burr or Blennerhassett. In Taylor's words, "He allowed he knew nothing of either of them; that

I must be mistaken; this was not the place. I said, 'No; this was the right place,—Mr. John Smith, storekeeper, Cincinnati.'" In the end, Smith took him upstairs, and gave him, with every injunction of secrecy, a letter to be delivered to Burr at Lexington. Taylor reached Lexington October 25, found Burr, delivered his letters, and candidly added: "If you come up our way the people will shoot you." The following Monday, October 27, the gardener started on his return, taking Blennerhassett with him, and leaving Burr at Lexington to face the storms that threatened from many quarters at once.

The impossibility of returning to the island was but one warning; another came from Senator Smith, who dreaded exposure. The letter he sent by Peter Taylor, dated October 23, affected ignorance of Burr's schemes, and demanded an explanation of them. October 26 Burr sent the required disavowal:—

"I was greatly surprised and really hurt," said Burr,[1] "by the unusual tenor of your letter of the 23d, and I hasten to reply to it, as well for your satisfaction as my own. If there exists any design to separate the Western from the Eastern States, I am totally ignorant of it. I never harbored or expressed any such intention to any one, nor did any person ever intimate such design to me."

From that moment to the last day of his life Burr persisted in this assertion, coupling it always in his own mind with a peculiar reservation. What he so solemnly denied was the intention to separate the Western States "by force" from the Eastern; what he never denied was the plan of establishing a Western empire by consent.

Of disunion Burr never again dared to speak. On that subject he was conscious of having already said so much as to make his stay in Kentucky a matter of some risk. The leading Republicans would have rejoiced at his departure; but to desert him was more than their tempers would allow. Daveiss saw another opportunity to compromise his enemies, and used it. A week after Blennerhassett and Peter Taylor left

[1] Burr to John Smith, Oct. 26, 1806; Senate Report, p. 33.

Lexington, carrying with them Burr's letter in reply to Senator Smith, on the same day when Andrew Jackson at Nashville received Burr's order, with Kentucky bank-notes for the sum of three thousand dollars, the United States District Court opened its session at Frankfort. Within eight and forty hours, November 5, District-Attorney Daveiss rose in court and made complaint against Burr for violating the laws of the United States by setting on foot a military expedition against Mexico. Besides an affidavit to this effect, the district-attorney asserted in court that Burr's scheme extended to a revolution of all the Western States and Territories.

In the nervous condition of Kentucky society, this attack on Burr roused great attention and hot criticism. The judge who presided over the court was the same Harry Innis who had been privy to the Spanish conspiracy, and was harassed by the charges of the "Western World." Daveiss could count with certainty upon the course which a man so placed would follow. The judge took three days to reflect, and then denied the motion; but Burr could not afford to rest silent. November 8, when Judge Innis overruled the motion and denied the process, Burr appeared in court and challenged inquiry. The following Wednesday, November 12, was fixed for the investigation. A grand-jury was summoned. Burr appeared, surrounded by friends, with Henry Clay for counsel, and with strong popular sympathy in his favor. Daveiss too appeared, with a list of witnesses summoned; but the chief witness was absent in Indiana, and Daveiss asked a postponement. The jury was discharged; and after a dignified and grave harangue from the accused, Burr left the court in triumph.[1] On the strength of this acquittal he ventured again to appear in Cincinnati, November 23, in confidential relations with Senator Smith; but the term of his long impunity was soon to end.

October 22, while Burr was at Lexington, President Jefferson held a Cabinet council at Washington. The Spaniards were then threatening an attack upon Louisiana, while Wilkinson's force in the Mississippi and Orleans Territories amounted only to ten hundred and eighty-one men, with

---

[1] Marshall's History of Kentucky, ii. 396.

two gunboats. Memoranda, written at the time by Jefferson, detailed the situation as it was understood by the Government:[1] —

"During the last session of Congress, Colonel Burr who was here, finding no hope of being employed in any department of the government, opened himself confidentially to some persons on whom he thought he could rely, on a scheme of separating the Western from the Atlantic States, and erecting the former into an independent confederacy. He had before made a tour of those States, which had excited suspicions, as every motion does of such a Catilinarian character. Of his having made this proposition here we have information from General Eaton through Mr. Ely and Mr. Granger. He went off this spring to the Western country. Of his movements on his way, information has come to the Secretary of State and myself from John Nicholson and Mr. Williams of the State of New York, respecting a Mr. Tyler; Colonel Morgan, Nevill, and Roberts, near Pittsburg; and to other citizens through other channels and the newspapers. We are of opinion unanimously that confidential letters be written to the Governors of Ohio, Indiana, Mississippi, and New Orleans; to the district-attorney of Kentucky, of Tennessee, of Louisiana, to have him strictly watched, and on his committing any overt act, to have him arrested and tried for treason, misdemeanor, or whatever other offence the act may amount to; and in like manner to arrest and try any of his followers committing acts against the laws. We think it proper also to order some of the gunboats up to Fort Adams to stop by force any passage of suspicious persons going down in force. General Wilkinson being expressly declared by Burr to Eaton to be engaged with him in this design as his lieutenant, or first in command, and suspicions of infidelity in Wilkinson being now become very general, a question is proposed what is proper to be done as to him on this account, as well as for his disobedience of orders received by him June 11 at St. Louis to descend with all practical despatch to New Orleans to mark out the site of certain defensive works

[1] Cabinet Memoranda; Writings (Ford), i. 318.

there, and then repair to take command at Natchitoches, on which business he did not leave St. Louis till September. Consideration adjourned.

"October 24. It is agreed unanimously to call for Captain Preble and Decatur to repair to New Orleans, by land or by sea as they please, there to take command of the force on the water, and that the 'Argus' and two gunboats from New York, three from Norfolk, and two from Charleston shall be ordered there, if on a consultation between Mr. Gallatin and Mr. Smith the appropriations shall be found to enable us; that Preble shall, on consultation with Governor Claiborne, have great discretionary powers; that Graham shall be sent through Kentucky on Burr's trail, with discretionary powers to consult confidentially with the Governors to arrest Burr if he has made himself liable. He is to have a commission of Governor of [Upper] Louisiana, and Dr. Browne is to be removed. Letters are to be written by post to Governor Claiborne, the Governor of Mississippi, and Colonel Freeman to be on their guard against any surprise of our posts or vessels by him. The question as to General Wilkinson postponed till Preble's departure, for future information."

Although these measures provided no protection against the chance of Wilkinson's misconduct, they could not fail to put an instant stop to Burr's activity. All that remained was to carry them out. Unfortunately Gallatin found that his hands and those of Robert Smith were tied by Acts of Congress. The next day the Cabinet met again.

"October 25. A mail arrived yesterday from the westward, and not one word is heard from that quarter of any movements by Colonel Burr. This total silence of the officers of the government, of the members of Congress, of the newspapers, proves he is committing no overt act against law. We therefore rescind the determination to send Preble, Decatur, the 'Argus,' or the gunboats, and instead of them to send off the marines which are here to reinforce, or take place of, the garrison at New Orleans, with a view to Spanish operations; and instead of writing to the Governors, etc., we send Graham on that route, with confidential authority to inquire into Burr's movements, put the Governors, etc., on their guard, to provide for his arrest if necessary, and to take on himself the government of [Upper] Louisiana. Letters are still to be written to Claiborne, Freeman, and the Governor of Mississippi to be on their guard."

The result of this Cabinet discussion, extending from October 22 to October 25, was merely an order to John Graham, Secretary of the Orleans Territory, to stop in Ohio and Kentucky on his way westward and inquire into Burr's movements.

Graham, following orders received from Madison, reached Marietta about the middle of November, when Burr should have already begun his movement, according to the original plan. Blennerhassett, who had been told by Burr that Graham was concerned in the plot, welcomed him with great cordiality, and talked much more freely than wisely. The information which crowded on Graham at Marietta led him to go at the end of November to Chillicothe, where the Legislature was in session, and where he caused a law to be passed, December 2, empowering the governor to use the militia against the conspirators. Had this measure, or one equally energetic, been taken by the President three months earlier, it would have put an end to Burr's projects before they were under way, would have saved many deluded men from ruin, and would have prevented much trouble at New Orleans; but Graham's progress was not quite so rapid, even though late, as it should have been.

Burr had ample warning. November 25 District-Attorney Daveiss renewed his motion in court at Frankfort, and the court appointed December 2 as the day for hearing evidence. Henry Clay became uneasy, and exacted from Burr a written denial of the projects imputed to him. Fortified with this evidence to his own credulity, Clay again went into court with Burr, "for whose honor and innocence," he said, "he could pledge his own," and assailed the district-attorney. A second time the scene of outraged virtue was acted. Once more the witnesses vanished. Senator Smith saddled his horse and fled; Adair would not appear; and the judge lent his weight to the criminal. To crown all, December 5 the grand-jury of twenty-two persons signed a paper declaring that they could discover nothing improper or injurious to the interests of the United States government in the conduct of Burr and Adair. Burr was discharged, with enthusiastic applause, without a stain on his character; and to prove its devotion, the society of Frankfort gave a ball in his honor.[1]

Nov. 25, 1806, was a date to be remembered in the story of Burr's adventures. On that day Daveiss made his second motion in court at Frankfort, while at Washington the Government at length woke to action. An officer, bringing despatches from General Wilkinson at Natchitoches, presented himself at the White House with news so startling that Jefferson immediately called his Cabinet together. Another memorandum in the President's handwriting recorded the action taken: —

"November 25. Present at first the four heads of department; but after a while General Dearborn withdrew, unwell. Despatches from General Wilkinson to myself of October 21, by a confidential officer (Lieutenant Smith), show that overtures have been made to him which decide that the present object of the combination is an expedition by sea against Vera Cruz; and by comparing the contents of a letter from Cowles Meade to the Secretary of State, with the information from Lieutenant Smith that a Mr. Swartwout from New York, brother of the late marshal, had been at General Wilkinson's camp, we are satisfied that Swartwout has been the agent through whom overtures have been made to Wilkinson. We came to the following determinations, — that a proclamation be issued (see it), and that orders go as follows: To Pittsburg, if we have a military officer there; . . . Marietta, Mr. Gallatin is to write to the collector; . . . General Dearborn to write to Governor Tiffin, . . . and to write to General Jackson, supposed to be the general of the brigade on the Virginia side of the river; . . . Louisville, General Dearborn to write to the Governor of Kentucky; . . . Massac, General Dearborn to give orders to Captain Bissell of the same tenor, and

[1] National Intelligencer, Jan. 12, 1807.

particularly to stop armed vessels suspected on good grounds to be proceeding on this enterprise, and for this purpose to have in readiness any boats he can procure fitted for enabling him to arrest their passage; Chickasaw Bluffs, give same orders as to Bissell; New Orleans, General Wilkinson to direct the station of the armed vessels; and if the arrangements with the Spaniards will permit him to withdraw, let him dispose of his force as he thinks best to prevent any such expedition or any attempt on New Orleans, or any of the posts or military stores of the United States. (He is also to arrest persons coming to his camp and proposing a concurrence in any such enterprise, and suspected of being in camp with a view to propagate such propositions. This addition is made by General Dearborn with my approbation.)"

The orders to Wilkinson were instantly sent. "You will use every exertion in your power," Dearborn said,[1] "to frustrate and effectually prevent any enterprise which has for its object, directly or indirectly, any hostile act on any part of the territories of the United States, or on any of the territories of the King of Spain." Persons found in or about the military camps or posts, with evident intention of sounding officers or soldiers, were to be arrested, and if not amenable to martial law, were to be delivered over to the civil authorities.

The orders were remarkable chiefly for the power they trusted in the hands of Wilkinson, and the confidence they showed in his good faith. Yet nothing could on its face be more suspicious than his report. The idea that Burr's expedition could be directed against Vera Cruz was unreasonable, and contrary to the tenor of the President's information from all other sources.[2] A moment's thought should have satisfied the President that Wilkinson was deceiving him, and that the city of New Orleans must be the real point of danger. In truth, Wilkinson's letters suppressed more than they told, and were more alarming than the warnings of Eaton or of Daveiss; for they proved that Wilkinson was playing a double

[1] Dearborn to Wilkinson, Nov. 27, 1806; Report of Committee, Feb. 26, 1811; 3 Sess. 11 Cong. p. 408.
[2] See Cabinet Memoranda of October 22, p. 795.

part. No measure that promised safety could be taken which would not require an instant removal of Wilkinson and a vigorous support of Claiborne at New Orleans.

Nov. 27, 1806, the same day with Dearborn's letter, the proclamation was issued.[1] Without mentioning Burr's name, it announced that sundry persons were conspiring against Spain, contrary to the laws; it warned all persons whatsoever to withdraw from such conspiracy; and it directed all officers, civil and military, of the United States to seize and detain all persons and property concerned in the enterprise.

The last chance of stopping the conspirators before they could enter the Mississippi was at Fort Massac. Beyond that point they could not easily be molested until they should reach a country more friendly than Ohio or Kentucky to their purposes; but the President had reason to suppose that his proclamation came in ample time to stop the conspirators while they were still on the Ohio River.

The Governor of Ohio, without waiting for the proclamation, acted promptly. On Graham's request, the necessary law was passed, and measures were taken to seize Burr's boats at Marietta. The boats and supplies were brought by Burr's men to Blennerhassett's island; but finding that militia were about to take possession of the island itself, the conspirators, with Blennerhassett in their company, at midnight of December 10–11, fled down the river,—a half-dozen ill-fitted boats, with thirty or forty men,—and passed the Falls of the Ohio at about the time when Burr and Adair entered Nashville.

Graham, leaving Ohio, reached Kentucky December 22, and induced the Governor and Legislature, December 24, to follow the example of Ohio; but he lost much time between Chillicothe and Frankfort, so that even after driving Burr from Ohio to Kentucky, and from Kentucky to Tennessee, the quickest pursuit could not prevent the conspirators from taking their path down the Cumberland. Graham in Ohio heard nothing of Burr's doings in Tennessee, although since November 3 Jackson's close friend Patton Anderson was scouring the country round Nashville for recruits, and had raised a company of seventy-five men. As Burr went farther

[1] Proclamation of Nov. 27, 1806; Wilkinson's Memoirs, ii. Appendix, xcvii.

South, the secrecy of his intimates became more closely guarded, and their movements more obscure.

Burr and Adair reached Nashville December 14, and went directly to the river, where their boats were building. By that time Burr was well trained in the comedy he had within the last month so often played. Senator Smith of Ohio began it October 23, by writing the request that Burr's design should be "candidly disclosed," because Smith had fears that it might interrupt the tranquillity of the country. A month later Henry Clay made the same request. No sooner did Burr reach Clover Bottom, where his boats were building under Andrew Jackson's charge, than he found himself required to repeat the familiar formula. Jackson, in company with General Overton as his witness, soon appeared at Clover Bottom, and intimated as plainly as had been done by John Smith and Henry Clay that his own credit required a disavowal of designs against the Union. Burr, with his usual dignified courtesy, instantly complied; and his denials were accepted as satisfactory by Jackson.

On Jackson's part this conduct was peculiarly surprising, because more than a month before he had written to Governor Claiborne[1] at New Orleans a secret denunciation of Burr and Wilkinson, couched in language which showed such intimate knowledge of Burr's plans as could have come only from Burr himself or Adair. In accepting Burr's disavowals, December 14, Jackson did not mention to Burr his denunciatory letter written to Claiborne, November 12, in which he had said, "I fear treachery has become the order of the day." Like Senator Smith, he was satisfied to secure his own safety; and upon Burr's denial of treasonable schemes, Jackson, although he did not write to Claiborne to withdraw the secret charges, went on building boats, providing supplies, and enlisting men for Colonel Burr's expedition. His motives for this conduct remained his own secret. Many of the best-informed persons in Tennessee and Kentucky, including Burr's avowed partisans, held but a low opinion of Jackson's character or veracity. Eight years afterward Jackson and John Adair once more appeared on the stage of New Orleans

[1] Jackson to Claiborne, Nov. 12, 1806; Burr's Trial. Annals of Congress, 1807–1808, p. 571.

history, and quarrelled, with charges and countercharges of falsehood and insinuations of treason.

"Whatever were the intentions of Colonel Burr," wrote Adair in a published letter,[1] "I neither organized troops at that time, nor did I superintend the building of boats for him; nor did I write confidential letters recommending him to my friends; nor did I think it necessary, after his failure was universally known, to save myself by turning informer or State witness."

By that time the people of Nashville had heard what was doing in Ohio and Kentucky. The public impeachment of the conspirators checked enlistments and retarded purchases; but Burr seemed to fear no such personal danger as had prevented his return to Blennerhassett's island. The Governor and Legislature of Ohio had taken public measures to seize boats and supplies as early as December 2; Burr had been driven from Kentucky, and Blennerhassett had fled from his island, by December 11; but ten days later Burr was still fitting out his boats at Nashville, undisturbed by the people of Tennessee. December 19 the President's proclamation reached Nashville,[2] but still nothing was done.

At last some unmentioned friend brought to Burr a secret warning that the State authorities must soon take notice of his armaments. The authorities at Nashville could no longer delay interference, and Burr was made to understand that his boats would be seized, and that he was himself in danger unless he should immediately escape; but between December 19 and 22 he was undisturbed. The announcement that Graham was expected to arrive December 23 probably decided his movements; for on the 22d he hastily abandoned all except two of his boats, receiving back from Jackson seventeen hundred and twenty-five dollars and taking the two boats and other articles for his voyage.[3] Jackson afterward declared that he suffered in the end a loss of five hundred dollars by a note which Burr had induced him to indorse, and which was returned from New York protested. Without further hindrance

[1] Letters of General Adair and General Jackson, 1817.
[2] Parton's Burr, ii. 87.
[3] Parton's Jackson, i. 322.

Burr then floated down the Cumberland River, taking with him a nephew of Mrs. Jackson, furnished by his uncle with a letter of introduction to Governor Claiborne,—a confidence the more singular because Governor Claiborne could hardly fail, under the warnings of General Jackson's previous secret letter, to seize and imprison Burr and every one who should be found in his company.

Thus, by connivance, Burr escaped from Nashville three days after news of the President's proclamation had arrived. The Government had two more chances to stop him before reaching Natchez. He must join Blennerhassett and Comfort Tyler at the mouth of the Cumberland, and then move down the Ohio River past Fort Massac, garrisoned by a company of the First Infantry, commanded by a Captain Bissell. Having passed Massac, he must still run the gauntlet at Chickasaw Bluff, afterward called Memphis, where another military post was stationed. The War Department sent orders, November 27, to the officers commanding at Massac and Chickasaw Bluff to be on their guard.

December 22 Burr left Nashville, while Adair at about the same time started for New Orleans on horseback through the Indian country. At the mouth of the Cumberland, Burr joined Blennerhassett, who had with him the boats which had succeeded in escaping the Ohio militia. The combined flotilla contained thirteen boats, which carried some sixty men and as many stand of arms, the arms being stowed in cases as cargo. December 25 Burr sent a note to Captain Bissell announcing that he should soon reach Fort Massac on his way South, and should stop to pay his respects. Bissell had received neither the President's proclamation nor the orders from the Secretary of War. As an old friend of Burr, he sent a cordial welcome to the party. In the night of December 29 the boats passed the fort, and landed about a mile below. The next morning Captain Bissell went in his own boat to pay his respects to Colonel Burr, who declined invitations to breakfast and dinner, but asked a furlough of twenty days for a Sergeant Dunbaugh, who had been persuaded to join the expedition. Bissell gave the furlough December 31, and Burr's party at once started for the Mississippi. Five days afterward, January 5, Bissell received a letter, dated January 2, from

Andrew Jackson, as Major-General of Tennessee militia, warning him to stop any body of men who might attempt to pass, if they should appear to have illegal enterprises in view. The President's proclamation had not yet reached Fort Massac, nor had Captain Bissell received any instructions from Washington.[1]

The proclamation, dated November 27, and sent immediately to the West, reached Pittsburg December 2,[2] and should, with ordinary haste, have reached Fort Massac—the most important point between Pittsburg and Natchez—before December 15. The orders which accompanied it ought to have prevented any failure of understanding on the part of Captain Bissell. Bissell's reply to Jackson, dated January 5, reached Nashville January 8, and was forwarded by Jackson to Jefferson, who sent it to Congress with a message dated January 28. Twenty-three days were sufficient for the unimportant reply; forty days or more had been taken for the orders to reach Massac, although they had only to float down the river. That some gross negligence or connivance could alone explain this shortcoming was evident; but the subject was never thought to need investigation by President or Congress. The responsibility for Burr's escape was so equally distributed between the President himself, the War Department, and the many accomplices or dupes of Burr in Kentucky and Tennessee, that any investigation must have led to unpleasant results.

Burr for the moment escaped, and everything depended on the action of Wilkinson. Dayton and the other conspirators who remained in the Eastern States thought it a matter of small consequence whether Burr carried with him a party of sixty men or of six hundred. Doubtless the unexpected energy shown by the people and the legislatures of Ohio and Kentucky proved the futility of attempting to revolutionize those States; but if Wilkinson were true to Burr, and if the city of New Orleans should welcome him, it remained to be seen whether the Government at Washington could crush the rebellion. A blockade of the Mississippi was no easy affair, and

[1] Bissell to Andrew Jackson, Jan. 5, 1807; Annals of Congress, 1806–1807, p. 1017.
[2] Jefferson to Wilkinson, Jan. 3, 1807; Burr's Trial. Annals of Congress, 1807–1808, p. 580.

slow in its results; England, France, and Spain might have much to say.

Meanwhile Humphrey Marshall and his friend Daveiss enjoyed the triumph they had won. In spite of silent opposition from the Republican leaders, Marshall drove the Kentucky Legislature into an inquiry as to the truth of the charge that Judge Sebastian was a Spanish pensioner. Sebastian instantly resigned. The committee took no notice of this admission of guilt, but summoned Judge Innis to testify. Very reluctantly Innis appeared before the committee and began his evidence, but broke down in the attempt, and admitted the truth of what had been alleged.[1] Before the close of the year Daveiss and Marshall drove Burr and Adair out of the State, forced Sebastian from the bench, humiliated Innis, and threw ridicule upon young Henry Clay and the other aggressive partisans of Jefferson, besides placing Jefferson himself and his Secretary of State in an attitude neither dignified nor creditable. Of all the persons connected with the story of Burr's expedition, Daveiss and Marshall alone showed the capacity to conceive a plan of action and the courage to execute the plan they conceived; but Jefferson could not be expected to feel satisfaction with services of such a nature. A few months later he appointed another person to succeed Daveiss in the office of district-attorney.

[1] Report of the Select Committee to the Kentucky Legislature, Dec. 2, 1806; National Intelligencer, Jan. 7, 1807.

Chapter XIII

S AMUEL SWARTWOUT and Peter V. Ogden, the young men whom Burr and Dayton charged with the duty of carrying despatches to Louisiana, crossed the Alleghanies in August and floated down the Ohio River to Louisville.[1] There they stopped to find Adair, for whom they brought letters from Burr. After some search Swartwout delivered the letters, and continued his journey. Adair never made known the contents of these papers; but they probably contained the same information as was conveyed in the despatches to Wilkinson which came in their company.

Supposing Wilkinson to be at St. Louis, the two young men bought horses and rode across the Indiana Territory to Kaskaskias; but finding that the General had gone down the Mississippi, they took boat and followed. At Natchez they learned that the object of their search had gone up the Red River. Swartwout was obliged to follow him; but Ogden went to New Orleans with despatches from Burr to his friends in that city.

Among the mysteries that still surround the conspiracy, the deepest covers Burr's relations in New Orleans. That he had confederates in the city was proved not only by Ogden's carrying letters, but also by Erick Bollman's arrival by sea, as early as September 27, with a duplicate of Burr's letter of July 29 to Wilkinson; and above all, by the significant disappearance of Burr's letters carried by Ogden and Bollman to persons in New Orleans. The persons implicated proved their complicity by keeping Burr's letters and his secret.

One of these correspondents was almost certainly Judge Prevost, Burr's stepson, whom Jefferson had appointed District Judge for the Territory of Orleans. That Daniel Clark was another hardly admits of doubt. Swartwout assured Wilkinson of the fact;[2] but apart from this evidence, the same reasons which obliged Burr to confide in Wilkinson required him to confide in Clark. The receivers of the letters, whoever they were, hastened to make their contents known to every

[1] Wilkinson's Evidence, Burr's Trial; Annals of Congress, 1807–1808, p. 515.
[2] Wilkinson to Daniel Clark, Oct. 5, 1807; Clark's Proofs, p. 154.

one whom they could trust. Immediately after the arrival of Bollman and Dayton about October 1, before any serious alarm had risen in Ohio, the town of New Orleans rang with rumors of Burr's projects. The news excited more consternation than hope; for although the creoles had been bitter in complaints of Claiborne's administration and of the despotism imposed upon them by Congress, they remembered their attempt to revolt in 1768, and were far from eager to risk their safety again. Nevertheless, the temper of the people was bad; and no one felt deeper anxiety as to the number of Burr's adherents than Governor Claiborne himself.

Nearly three years had elapsed since Dec. 20, 1803, when the Spanish governor surrendered Louisiana to the United States, and the history of the Territory during that time presented an uninterrupted succession of bickerings. The government at Washington was largely responsible for its own unpopularity in the new Territory, its foreign and domestic policy seeming calculated to create ill-feeling, and after creating it, to keep it alive. The President began by appointing as Governor of Louisiana a man who had no peculiar fitness for the place. Claiborne, in contrast with men like Wilkinson, Burr, and Daniel Clark, rose to the level of a hero. He was honest, well-meaning, straightforward, and thoroughly patriotic; but these virtues were not enough to make him either feared or respected by the people over whom he was to exercise despotic powers; while Claiborne's military colleague, Wilkinson, possessed fewer virtues and a feebler character. The French Prefect, Laussat, who remained for a time in New Orleans to protect French interests, wrote his Government April 8, 1804, an interesting account of the situation as seen by French eyes:[1]

"It was hardly possible that the government of the United States should have made a worse beginning, and that it should have sent two men (Messrs. Claiborne, governor, and Wilkinson, general) less fit to attract affection. The first, with estimable private qualities, has little capacity and much awkwardness, and is extremely beneath his place;

[1] Laussat to Decrès, 18 Germinal, An xii. (April 8, 1804); Archives de la Marine, MSS. Gayarré's Louisiana, iii. 10.

the second, already long known here in a bad way, is a flighty, rattle-headed fellow, often drunk, who has committed a hundred impertinent follies. Neither the one nor the other understands a word of French or Spanish. They have on all occasions, and without delicacy, shocked the habits, the prejudices, the character of the population."

Claiborne began his sway, assuming that the creoles were a kindly but ignorant and degraded people, who must be taught the blessings of American society. The creoles, who considered themselves to be more refined and civilized than the Americans who descended upon them from Kentucky and Tennessee, were not pleased that their language, blood, and customs should be systematically degraded, in defiance of the spirit in which the treaty of cession had been made. Their anger was not without an element of danger. England and France could safely defy public opinion and trample on prostrate races. Their empire rested on force, but that of Jefferson rested on consent; and if the people of New Orleans should rebel, they could not be conquered without trouble and expense, or without violating the free principles which Jefferson was supposed to represent.

The colonists in Louisiana had been for a century the spoiled children of France and Spain. Petted, protected, fed, paid, flattered, and given every liberty except the rights of self-government, they liked Spain[1] and loved France, but they did not love the English or the Americans; and their irritation was extreme when they saw Claiborne, who knew nothing of their society and law, abolish their language, establish American judges who knew only American law, while he himself sat as a court of last resort, without even an attorney to advise him as to the meaning of the Spanish law he administered. At the same time that as judge he could hang his subjects, as intendant he could tax them, and as governor he could shoot the disobedient. Even under the Spanish despotism, appeal might be made to Havana or Madrid; but no appeal lay from Claiborne's judgment-seat.

Before this temporary system was superseded, the creoles already yearned for a return to French or Spanish rule. They

[1] Gayarré, Spanish Domination, p. 627.

had but one hope from the United States,—that, in the terms of the treaty, Louisiana might be quickly admitted into the Union. This hope was rudely dispelled. Not only did Congress treat their claims to self-government with indifference, but the Territory was divided in halves, so that it must be slower to acquire the necessary population for a State; while as though to delay still longer this act of justice, the growth of population was checked by prohibiting the slave-trade. Years must pass before Louisiana could gain admission into the Union; and even when this should happen, it must be the result of American expansion at creole expense.

Jefferson's Spanish policy, which kept the country always on the verge of a war with Spain, prevented the French and Spanish population from feeling that their submission was final. In case of war between the United States and Spain, nothing would be easier than to drive Claiborne away and replace Casa Calvo in the government. Claiborne soon found himself confronted by an opposition which he could neither control nor understand. Even the leading Americans joined it. Daniel Clark, rich, eccentric, wild in his talk and restless in his movements, distinguished himself by the personal hatred which he showed for Claiborne; Evan Jones, another wealthy resident, rivalled Clark; Edward Livingston, who had come to New Orleans angry with Jefferson for removing him as a defaulter from office, joined the old residents in harassing the Governor; while the former Spanish officials, Casa Calvo and Morales, remained at New Orleans under one or another pretext, keeping the Spanish influence alive, and maintaining communications with Governor Folch of West Florida, who controlled the Mississippi at Baton Rouge, and with General Herrera, who commanded the Spanish force in Texas. So bad was the state of feeling that when Oct. 1, 1804, the new territorial system was organized, Messrs. Boré, Bellechasse, Cantrelle, Jones, and Daniel Clark, whom the President had named as members of the legislative council, refused to accept the office; while Messrs. Sauvé, Destréhan, and Derbigny were deputed by a popular assembly to present their grievances at Washington. Two months elapsed before Governor Claiborne could form any council at all; not until Dec. 4, 1804, was a quorum obtained.

No pretence of disguising their feelings was made by the Spanish population. In French minds the power of Bonaparte was a stronger reliance than the power of Spain; no Frenchman willingly admitted that Napoleon meant to sacrifice Louisiana forever.[1]

"The President's Message," wrote Governor Claiborne to Madison, Dec. 11, 1804,[2] "has been translated into the French language, and I will take care to have it circulated among the people. It will tend to remove an impression which has heretofore contributed greatly to embarrass the local administration; to wit, that the country west of the Mississippi would certainly be re-ceded to Spain, and perhaps the whole of Louisiana. So general has been this impression, particularly as relates to the country west of the Mississippi, that many citizens have been fearful of accepting any employment under the American government, or even manifesting a respect therefor, lest at a future time it might lessen them in the esteem of Spanish officers."

Under the remonstrances of Sauvé, Destréhan, and Derbigny, and at the intercession of John Randolph, Congress was induced to yield a single point. The Act of March 2, 1805, gave Louisiana ordinary Territorial rights, an elected legislature, and a delegate to Congress. After its passage, Claiborne wrote to Madison that the people were disappointed; and in fact the concessions were so trivial as to irritate rather than soothe. Claiborne, whom the people obstinately disliked, was re-appointed governor under the Act, and nothing in reality was changed.

Burr visited New Orleans in June and July, 1805. The new Legislature assembled, Nov. 4, 1805, when Claiborne found himself surrounded by a council partly elected by the Legislature, and a Legislature wholly elected by the people. He was soon at odds with both. The leader of opposition was Daniel Clark; and for a moment in May, 1806, the quarrel went so far that the two legislative bodies were on the point of voluntary disbandment, and a majority of the council actually

[1] Laussat to Decrès, 18 Germinal, An xii. (April 8, 1804); Archives de la Marine, MSS.
[2] Gayarré's Louisiana, iii. 35.

resigned. The Legislature chose Daniel Clark as their delegate to Congress. Claiborne thought that the choice was made merely out of personal spite; but no sooner did he hear of Burr's disunion scheme than he wrote to Madison,[1] —

> "If this be the object of the conspirators, the delegate to Congress from this Territory, Daniel Clark, is one of the leaders. He has often said that the Union could not last, and that had he children he would impress early on their minds the expediency of a separation between the Atlantic and Western States."

In the same month of May Lieutenant Murray of the artillery, an intimate friend of Daniel Clark, came with a Lieutenant Taylor from Fort Adams to New Orleans, and heard the ordinary conversation of society.

> "Lieutenant Taylor and myself," he afterward testified,[2] " were invited to dine with a gentleman there whose name was on the list before mentioned [of persons engaged in an expedition against Mexico]; it was Judge Workman. We three dined together. After the cloth was removed, Mr. Lewis Kerr came in. . . . After a number of inquiries about Baton Rouge and the Red River country, they proceeded to lay open their plan of seizing upon the money in the banks at New Orleans, impressing the shipping, taking Baton Rouge, and joining Miranda by way of Mexico. . . . When I told Mr. Clark that I was calculated on as the officer to attack Baton Rouge, he advised me by all means to do it. He urged as an inducement that he was coming on to Congress, and would do all he could in my favor; that he would represent to the Government that it would require a large force to retake it; and he further observed that, at any rate, if the Government should be disposed to trouble me, before they could send off a sufficient force I should be in a situation to take care of myself."

This attempt to seduce officers of the United States army into Burr's conspiracy was flagrant; for although Burr's name

[1] Gayarré's Louisiana, iii. 161.
[2] Report of the Committee to inquire into the Conduct of General Wilkinson, Feb. 26, 1811; 3 Sess. 11 Cong. p. 320.

was not mentioned, no one could fail to see that the seizure of government money in the banks at New Orleans was an act of treason, and that the attack on West Florida implied a permanent military establishment on the Gulf.

June 7, 1806, the first Louisiana legislature adjourned, and Governor Claiborne felt relief as deep as was felt by Jefferson at escaping the stings of John Randolph; but although for a time Claiborne flattered himself that his difficulties were lessening, he soon became aware that some mystery surrounded him which he could not penetrate. General Herrera began to press upon the Red River from Nacogdoches in Texas with a force considerably stronger than any which Claiborne could oppose to him. The militia showed indifference. August 28 the Governor wrote to the Secretary of War that the French population would not support the government in case of hostilities.[1] September 9 he wrote to Cowles Meade, then acting-governor of the Mississippi Territory, a letter of uneasiness at the behavior of Wilkinson's troops: "My present impression is that *all is not right*. I know not whom to censure, but it seems to me that there is wrong somewhere." The militia could not be stimulated to action against Herrera, and the feeling of hostility between Americans and creoles was so bitter that Claiborne intervened for fear of violence.[2]

October 6, 1806, the Governor returned to New Orleans after a tour of inspection. Erick Bollman had been then ten days in the city, and young Ogden had arrived about October 1, bringing Burr's despatches. According to Bellechasse and Derbigny the creole society was already much excited; but this excitement showed itself to Claiborne in a display of assumed stolidity.

"There is in this city," wrote Claiborne to the Secretary of War October 8,[3] "a degree of apathy at the present time which mortifies and astonishes me; and some of the native Americans act and discourse as if perfect security everywhere prevailed. . . . I fear the ancient Louisianians of New Orleans are not disposed to support with firmness the

[1] Gayarré's Louisiana, iii. 151.
[2] Gayarré's Louisiana, iii. 153.
[3] Gayarré's Louisiana, iii. 154.

American cause. I do not believe they would fight against us; but my present impression is that they are not inclined to rally under the American standard."

Claiborne's spirits fluctuated from day to day as he felt the changes in a situation which he could not fathom. October 17 he was elated because the militia of New Orleans unexpectedly, and contrary to the tenor of all its previous conduct, made a voluntary tender of services. November 7 he was again discouraged; and November 15, and even as late as November 25, he fell back into despondency. During all that time the enemies whom he feared were Spaniards in Texas and West Florida; the thought of conspiracy among the apathetic creoles had not yet entered his mind.

Yet around him the city was trembling with excitement; and of all persons in the city Daniel Clark was the one whose conduct showed most signs of guilty knowledge. A few months later, he collected affidavits from four or five of the most important gentlemen in New Orleans to show what his conduct had been. At the moment when Bollman and Ogden arrived, Clark was preparing for his journey to Washington, where he meant to take his seat in Congress as the Territorial delegate. The news brought by Bollman and Ogden that Burr was on his way to New Orleans placed him in a dilemma. Like Senator Smith and Andrew Jackson, his chief anxiety regarded his own safety; and he adopted an expedient which showed his usual intelligence. An affidavit of Bellechasse,[1] on whose character he mainly depended, narrated that—

"in the month of October, a very few days before Mr. Clark left this city to go to Congress, he called together a number of his friends, and informed them of the views and intentions imputed to Colonel Burr, which were then almost the sole topic of conversation, and which, from the reports daily arriving from Kentucky, had caused a serious alarm; and he advised them all to exert their influence with the inhabitants of the country to support the Government of the United States and to rally round the Governor, although he thought him incapable of rendering much

[1] Clark's Proofs, p. 145.

service as a military man,—assuring them that such conduct only would save the country if any hostile projects were entertained against it, and that this would be the best method of convincing the Government of the United States of the attachment of the inhabitants of Louisiana, and of the falsity of all the reports circulated to their prejudice. And Mr. Clark strongly recommended to such members of the Legislature as were then present not to attend any call or meeting of either House in case Colonel Burr should gain possession of the city, stating that such a measure would deservedly expose every individual concerned to punishment, and would occasion the ruin of the country."

According to Bellechasse, the society of New Orleans between Oct. 1 and Oct. 15, 1806, was in serious alarm. Burr's intentions formed "almost the sole topic of conversation;" daily reports were arriving from Kentucky, although in Kentucky, down to October 1, no alarm existed, and Burr's intentions were not even developed. Each of the four affidavits which Clark obtained, one of them signed by Peter Derbigny, affirmed that about the middle of October, 1806, Burr's projects were the general theme of conversation in the city; but nothing was more certain than that this knowledge of Burr's projects must have come not from Kentucky, but from Burr's own letters and from the messages brought by Ogden and Bollman.

Clark, having thus secured himself from the charge of abetting Burr, sailed for the Atlantic coast, and in due time made his appearance at Washington; but neither he nor Bellechasse nor Derbigny nor Bouligny, although officers of the government, giving each other excellent advice, communicated to Governor Claiborne what they knew about Burr's plans. From October 1 to November 25, the projects of Burr were "the exclusive subject of every conversation" in the city, yet the single official who ought to have been first informed, and who bore all responsibility, had not a suspicion that any conspiracy existed. Claiborne's isolation was complete. This isolation was natural, since all the gentlemen of New Orleans quarrelled with the Governor; but the same silence was preserved where their social relations were friendly. Neither

Clark nor any of the persons who talked so much with each other about Burr's projects communicated with General Wilkinson, who was in full sympathy with their hatred of Claiborne. Wilkinson stood in relations of close confidence with Clark; intimate letters passed between them as late as October 2.[1] Clark knew that Wilkinson was Burr's most intimate friend; yet he neither warned Claiborne nor Wilkinson nor President Jefferson, although as early as October 15 he warned a number of other gentlemen who needed no warning, and although October 17 the militia of New Orleans, evidently in consequence of his advice, tendered their services to the Governor.

For two months, between September 27 and November 25, Burr's emissaries were busy in New Orleans, without suspicion or hindrance from the United States authorities; while every prominent Frenchman in the Territory knew the contents of Burr's letter to Wilkinson as soon as Wilkinson could have known them. That Burr had few active adherents might be true; but nothing showed that Bollman regarded the result of his mission as unfavorable. Toward the end of October Bollman sent letters by a certain Lieutenant Spence, who reached Lexington in due course, and November 2 delivered his despatches to Burr;[2] but whatever their contents may have been, they were not so decisive against Burr's hopes as to stop his movement. The people of New Orleans were careful not to commit themselves, but they guarded Burr's secret with jealousy. They warned no United States official of the danger in which the city stood; they wrote no letters to the President; they sent no message to Burr forbidding his approach.

This was the situation in New Orleans Nov. 25, 1806, the day when District-Attorney Daveiss at Frankfort made his second attempt to procure an indictment against Burr, and when President Jefferson at Washington was startled into energy by receiving a letter, almost equivalent to a confession, from General Wilkinson. From the Ohio River to the Gulf of

[1] Clark to Wilkinson, Oct. 2, 1806; Clark's Proofs, p. 157.
[2] Wilkinson's Evidence, Burr's Trial; Annals of Congress, 1807–1808, p. 518. Evidence of Lieutenant Spence, Report of House Committee, Feb. 26, 1811; 3 Sess. 11 Cong., p. 312.

Mexico the conspiracy had numerous friends; and in New Orleans it had the most alarming of all qualities,—silence.

Meanwhile young Samuel Swartwout, after parting from his friend Ogden, had slowly ascended the Red River, pursuing General Wilkinson, as Evangeline pursued Gabriel, even as far as "the little inn of the Spanish town of Adayes." The military point for Wilkinson to decide was whether he should make an effort to drive the Spaniards back to their town of Adayes, or whether he should allow them to fix themselves on the Red River. The movements of the Spanish General Herrera, who had brought a considerable mounted force to Nacogdoches, were supposed at the moment by many persons to have been made in concert with Burr; but in reality they were doubtless intended only to derange the plan, recommended by Armstrong and Monroe to Jefferson, by which Texas should be seized for the United States, while West Florida for the moment should be left aside. The Spanish government saw the danger, and sent a little army of some fifteen hundred men to the Red River, where they posted a strong garrison at Bayou Pierre, and pressed close upon Natchitoches. The Americans, instead of taking the offensive and advancing with five thousand men, as Wilkinson wished, to the Rio Grande, were thrown upon the defensive, and trembled for New Orleans, protected only by a French militia which neither Claiborne nor Wilkinson could trust.

Under orders from Washington, General Wilkinson reached Natchitoches September 22, and found the Spaniards in force between his own post and the Sabine. For a few days Wilkinson talked loudly, after his peculiar manner. War seemed imminent. September 28 he wrote from Natchitoches a letter to Senator Smith of Ohio, the contractor for his supplies:[1] —

> "I have made the last effort at conciliation in a solemn appeal to Governor Cordero at Nacogdoches, who is chief in command on this frontier. Colonel Cushing bore my letter, and is now with the Don. I expect his return in four days; and then,—I believe, my friend, I shall be obliged to fight and flog them."

Governor Cordero, whose object was probably no more

than to restrict American possession within the narrowest possible limits, withdrew his troops from Bayou Pierre, September 27, to the west bank of the Sabine, and left open to Wilkinson the road to the eastern bank. The Spanish forces recrossed the Sabine before September 30, but a week later, October 8, General Wilkinson had not begun his ostentatious march, of some fifty miles, to retake possession of the east bank of the river.

On the evening of October 8, General Wilkinson was sitting with Colonel Cushing, of the Second Infantry, alone in the Colonel's quarters at Natchitoches, discussing the military problem before them, when a young man was introduced who said that his name was Swartwout, and that he brought a letter of introduction from General Dayton. After some little ordinary talk, Colonel Cushing having for a moment been called out of the room, Swartwout slipped into General Wilkinson's hands a packet which he said contained a letter from Colonel Burr. Wilkinson received the letter, and soon afterward retired to his chamber, where he passed the rest of the evening in the labor of deciphering Burr's long despatch of July 29.[1]

If the falsehoods contained in the letters of Burr and Dayton found any credit in Wilkinson's mind, they should have decided him to follow his old bent toward revolution. Everything beckoned him on. His secret relations, nearly twenty years old, with the Spanish officials guaranteed to him the connivance of the Spanish force. The French militia of Louisiana, deaf to Governor Claiborne's entreaties, would have seen with pleasure Claiborne deposed. About five hundred United States troops were under Wilkinson's command on the Red River, of whom few were native Americans, or cared for the Government except to obtain their pay. In New Orleans a breath would blow away the national authority; and what power would restore it? If it were true, as Burr wrote, that a British fleet stood ready to prevent a blockade of the Mississippi, the success of the Western empire seemed assured.

Severance of the ties that bound him to Dayton and Burr

[1] See p. 777.

was not a simple matter for Wilkinson. That they were old friends was something; and that all three had fought side by side under the walls of Quebec in the winter of 1776, with the father of young Peter Ogden for a friend, and with Benedict Arnold for their commander, was still more; but the most serious difficulty was that Wilkinson stood in the power of these men, who knew his thoughts and could produce his letters, and who, in case of his deserting them, would certainly do their utmost to destroy what character he possessed.

Whatever may have been his reflections, Wilkinson took at once measures to protect his own interests. Like Senator Smith, Andrew Jackson, and Daniel Clark, his first step was to provide against the danger of being charged with misprision of treason. The morning after Swartwout's arrival, Wilkinson took Colonel Cushing aside, and after telling him the contents of Burr's letter, announced that he meant to notify the President of the plot, and that after making some temporary arrangement with the Spaniards, he should move his whole force to New Orleans. In one sense this avowal was an act of patriotism; in another light it might have been regarded as an attempt to sound Colonel Cushing, whose assistance was necessary to the success of the plot.

In any case the deliberation of his conduct proved no eagerness to act. A week passed. Although time pressed, and Burr was to move down the Ohio River November 15, Wilkinson did not yet warn the President or the authorities in Mississippi and Tennessee, or the commanding officers at Fort Adams or Chickasaw Bluffs. About October 15 a troop of militia reached Natchitoches; and Wilkinson confided his plans to Colonel Burling, who accompanied it. One might almost have suspected that he was systematically sounding his officers. Not until October 21 did he send the promised letter to President Jefferson, and in that letter he did not so much as mention Burr's name.[1] He spoke of the expedition as destined for Vera Cruz. "It is unknown under what authority this enterprise has been projected, from whence the means of its support are derived, or what may be the intentions of its leaders in relation to the Territory of Orleans." The communi-

---

[1] Wilkinson to Jefferson, Oct. 20 and 21, 1806; Wilkinson's Memoirs, ii. Appendix, xcv.

cation was so timed as to reach Washington after Burr should have passed down the Ohio; and it was so worded as to protect Wilkinson in case of Burr's failure, but in no event to injure Burr.

After sending this despatch to Washington by a special messenger, Wilkinson wrote October 23 a letter of mysterious warning to Lieutenant-Colonel Freeman, who commanded at New Orleans.[1] He wrote also a letter to Burr, which he afterward recovered at Natchez and destroyed.[2] He sent his force forward to the Sabine, and passed ten days in making an arrangement with the Spanish officers for maintaining the relative positions of the outposts. Not until November 5 did he return to Natchitoches. Then, at last, his movements became as rapid as they had hitherto been dilatory.

November 7 he wrote to Colonel Cushing from Natchitoches:[3] "On the 15th of this month Burr's declaration is to be made in Tennessee and Kentucky. Hurry, hurry after me; and if necessary, let us be buried together in the ruins of the place we shall defend!" He had at last chosen his part; and having decided to act as the savior of the country, he began to exaggerate the danger. "If I mistake not, we shall have an insurrection of blacks as well as whites to combat."[4] "I shall be with you by the 20th instant," he wrote to Freeman the same day;[5] "in the mean time be you as silent as the grave!" He left Natchitoches November 7, and reached Natchez on the 11th, whence he wrote "from the seat of Major Minor" a letter of alarm to the President, confiding to the messenger an oral account of Burr's letter, for Jefferson's benefit:[6] - -

"This is indeed a deep, dark, and widespread conspiracy, embracing the young and the old, the Democrat and the Federalist, the native and the foreigner, the patriot of '76 and the exotic of yesterday, the opulent and the needy, the 'ins' and the 'outs;' and I fear it will receive strong support

[1] Wilkinson to Freeman, Oct. 23, 1806; Wilkinson's Memoirs, ii. Appendix, ci.
[2] Wilkinson's Evidence, Burr's Trial; Annals of Congress, 1807–1808, p. 541.
[3] Wilkinson to Cushing, Nov. 7, 1806; Memoirs, ii. Appendix, xcix.
[4] Ibid.
[5] Ibid.
[6] Wilkinson to Jefferson, Nov. 12, 1806; Memoirs, ii. Appendix, c.

in New Orleans from a quarter little suspected. . . . I gasconade not when I tell you that in such a cause I shall glory to give my life in the service of my country; for I verily believe such an event to be probable, because, should seven thousand men descend from the Ohio,—and this is the calculation,—they will bring with them the sympathies and good wishes of that country, and none but friends can be afterward prevailed on to follow them. With my handful of veterans, however gallant, it is improbable I shall be able to withstand such a disparity of numbers."

If this was not gasconade, it sounded much like intoxication; but on the same day the writer indulged in another cry of panic. He should have written to Governor Claiborne a month before; but having made up his mind to speak, he was determined to terrify:[1] —

"You are surrounded by dangers of which you dream not, and the destruction of the American government is seriously menaced. The storm will probably burst in New Orleans, where I shall meet it, and triumph or perish!"

If the courage of Claiborne did not, on the arrival of this letter, wholly desert him, his heart was stout; but he had yet another shock to meet, for on the same day that Wilkinson at Natchez was summoning this shadowy terror before his eyes, Andrew Jackson at Nashville was writing to him in language even more bewildering than that of Wilkinson:[2] —

"I fear treachery has become the order of the day. This induces me to write you. Put your town in a state of defence; organize your militia, and defend your city as well against internal enemies as external. My knowledge does not extend so far as to authorize me to go into details, but I fear you will meet with an attack from quarters you do not at present expect. Be upon the alert! Keep a watchful eye on our General [Wilkinson], and beware of an attack as well from your own country as Spain! I fear there is something rotten in the state of Denmark. . . . Beware of

[1] Wilkinson to Claiborne, Nov. 12, 1806; Memoirs, ii. 328.
[2] Jackson to Claiborne, Nov. 12, 1806; Burr's Trial. Annals of Congress, 1807–1808, p. 571.

the month of December! . . . This I will write for your own eye and for your own safety. Profit by it, and the ides of March remember!"

A storm of denunciations began to hail upon Claiborne's head; but buffeted as he was, he could only bear in silence whatever fate might be in store, for General Wilkinson, who was little more trustworthy or trusted than Burr himself, arrived in New Orleans November 25, and took the reins of power.

Chapter XIV

FOR SEVERAL DAYS after Wilkinson's arrival at New Orleans he left the conspirators in doubt of his intentions. No public alarm had yet been given; and while Colonel Cushing hurried the little army forward, Wilkinson, November 30, called on Erick Bollman, and had with him a confidential interview. Not until December 5 did he tell Bollman that he meant to oppose Burr's scheme; and even then Bollman felt some uncertainty. December 6 the General at length confided to the Governor his plan of defence, which was nothing less than that Claiborne should consent to abdicate his office and invest Wilkinson with absolute power by proclaiming martial law.

Considering that this extraordinary man knew himself to be an object of extreme and just suspicion on Claiborne's part, such a demand carried effrontery to the verge of insolence; and the tone in which it was made sounded rather like an order than like advice.

"The dangers," said he,[1] "which impend over this city and menace the laws and government of the United States from an unauthorized and formidable association must be successfully opposed at this point, or the fair fabric of our independence, purchased by the best blood of our country, will be prostrated, and the Goddess of Liberty will take her flight from this globe forever. Under circumstances so imperious, extraordinary measures must be resorted to, and the ordinary forms of our civil institutions must for a short period yield to the strong arm of military law."

Claiborne mildly resisted the pressure, with much good temper refusing to sanction either the impressment of seamen, the suspension of the writ of habeas corpus, the declaration of martial law, or the illegal arrest of suspected persons, while he insisted on meeting the emergency with the ordinary legal means at his disposal. Wilkinson was obliged to act in defiance of his advice.

Sunday, December 14, arrests at New Orleans began. Boll-

[1] Gayarré's Louisiana, iii. 163.

man was first to be seized. Swartwout and Ogden had been arrested at Fort Adams. These seizures, together with that of Bollman's companion, Alexander, and Wilkinson's wild talk, spread panic through the city. The courts tried to interpose, and applied for support to Governor Claiborne. The Governor advised Wilkinson to yield to the civil authorities; but Wilkinson refused, thus establishing in the city something equivalent to martial law. He knew, or believed, that both Judge Workman and Judge Prevost were engaged in the conspiracy with Burr, and he was obliged to defy them, or to risk his own success. The only effect of the attempt to enforce the writ of habeas corpus in favor of the prisoners was to draw out what had been hitherto concealed,—Burr's letter of July 29. Not until December 18 did Wilkinson send a written version of that letter to the President.[1] In order to warrant the arrests of Swartwout and Ogden, Wilkinson, December 26, swore to an affidavit which embodied Burr's letter.

This step brought the panic in New Orleans to a climax. Wilkinson's military measures were evidently directed rather against the city than against Burr. His previous complicity in the projects of Burr was evident. His power of life and death was undisputed. Every important man in New Orleans was a silent accomplice of Burr, afraid of denunciation, and at Wilkinson's mercy. He avowed publicly that he would act with the same energy, without regard to standing or station, against all individuals who might be participants in Burr's combination; and it would have been difficult for the best people in New Orleans to prove that they had no knowledge of the plot, or had given it no encouragement. The creole gentlemen began to regret the mild sway of Claiborne when they saw that their own factiousness had brought them face to face with the chances of a drumhead court-martial.

Wilkinson's violence might have provoked an outbreak from the mere terror it caused, had he not taken care to show that he meant in reality to protect and not to punish the chief men of the city. After the first shock, his arrests were in truth reassuring. The people could afford to look on while he

[1] President's Message of Jan. 22, 1807. Annals of Congress, 1806—1807, p. 43.

seized only strangers, like Bollman and Alexander; even in Swartwout and Ogden few citizens of New Orleans took much personal interest. Only in case the General had arrested men like Derbigny or Edward Livingston or Bellechasse would the people be likely to resist; and Wilkinson showed that he meant to make no arrests among the residents, and to close his eyes against evidence that could compromise any citizen of the place. "Thank God!" he wrote to Daniel Clark, December 10,[1] "your advice to Bellechasse, if your character was not a sufficient guaranty, would vindicate you against any foul imputation." In another letter, written early in January, he added,[2] —

> "It is a fact that our fool [Claiborne] has written to his contemptible fabricator [Jefferson], that you had declared if you had children you would teach them to curse the United States as soon as they were able to lisp."

Claiborne had brought such a charge only a few weeks before, and Wilkinson must have heard it from Claiborne himself, who had already written to withdraw it on learning Clark's advice to Bellechasse. Nevertheless Wilkinson continued, —

> "*Cet bête* [Claiborne] is at present up to the chin in folly and vanity. He cannot be supported much longer, for Burr or no Burr we shall have a revolt if he is not removed speedily. The moment Bonaparte compromises with Great Britain will be the signal for a general rising of French and Spaniards; and if the Americans do not join, they will not oppose. Take care! Suspicion is abroad; but you have a friend worth having."

Clark's business correspondents in New Orleans delivered to Wilkinson a letter which came to them from Burr without address, but which was intended for Bollman.[3] "For your own sake," said the General, "take that letter away! Destroy, and say nothing of it!" A year later, when the frightened crew of conspirators recovered from their panic and began to turn

---

[1] Wilkinson to Daniel Clark, Dec. 10, 1806; Clark's Proofs, p. 150.
[2] Clark's Proofs, p. 151.
[3] Wilkinson to Daniel Clark, March 20, 1807; Clark's Proofs, p. 151.

upon him with ferocity on account of his treason to them and to Burr, Wilkinson wrote to Daniel Clark a last letter, mentioning in semi-threatening language the written evidence in his possession against Clark himself, and adding,[1] —

"Much pains were taken by Bollman to induce me to believe you were concerned. Swartwout assured me Ogden had gone to New Orleans with despatches for you from Burr, and that you were to furnish provisions, etc. Many other names were mentioned to me which I have not exposed, nor will I ever expose them unless compelled by self-defence. . . ."

Wilkinson never did expose them, nor did he molest in any serious degree the society of New Orleans.

Had Wilkinson been satisfied to secure the city without magnifying himself, he might perhaps have won its regard and gratitude; but he could do nothing without noise and display Before many days had passed he put an embargo on the shipping and set the whole city at work on defences. He spread panic-stricken stories of Burr's force and of negro insurrection. He exasperated the judges and the bar, alienated Claiborne, and disgusted the creoles. Nothing but a bloody convulsion or an assault upon the city from Burr's armed thousands could save Wilkinson from becoming ridiculous.

Jan. 12, 1807, the Legislature met. Probably at no time had Burr's project received much avowed support, even among those persons to whom it had been confided. Men of wealth and character had no fancy for so wild a scheme. The conduct of Daniel Clark was an example of what Burr had to expect from every man of property and standing. The Legislature was under the influence of conservative and somewhat timid men, from whom no serious danger was to be expected, and whose fears were calculated to strengthen rather than to weaken the government; yet it was true that Burr had counted upon this meeting of the Legislature to declare Louisiana independent, and to offer him the government. He was to have waited at Natchez for a delegation to bring him the offer; and he was supposed to be already at Natchez. The city

[1] Wilkinson to Daniel Clark, Oct. 5, 1807; Clark's Proofs, p. 154.

had been kept for a month in a state of continual alarm, distracted by rumors, and expecting some outbreak from day to day, assured by Wilkinson that Burr with seven thousand men might appear at any moment, with a negro insurrection behind him and British ships in the river, when suddenly John Adair rode into town, and descended at the door of Madame Nourage's boarding-house. Judge Prevost, Burr's stepson, was so indiscreet as to announce publicly that General Adair, second in command to Burr, had arrived in town with news that Burr would follow in three days, and that it would soon be seen whether Wilkinson's tyranny would prevail.[1] The same afternoon Lieutenant-Colonel Kingsbury of the First Infantry, at the head of a hundred and twenty men, appeared at the door of the hotel and marched Burr's second in command to prison. Adair afterward claimed that if he had been allowed forty-eight hours no one could have arrested him, for he had more friends in New Orleans than the General had; but even he must have seen that the conspiracy was dead. For a moment his arrest, and a few others made at the same time, caused excitement, and Wilkinson ordered detachments of troops to patrol the city; but thenceforward confidence began to return and soon the crisis passed away, carrying with it forever most of the discontent and danger which had marked the annexation of Louisiana. If New Orleans never became thoroughly American, at least it was never again thoroughly French.

Unfortunately for Wilkinson's hopes of figuring in the character of savior to his country, Burr's expedition met with an inglorious and somewhat ridiculous end before it came within sight of Wilkinson or his command. After leaving Fort Massac, the little flotilla entered the Mississippi, and in a few days reached Chickasaw Bluffs, where a small military post of nineteen men was stationed, commanded by a second lieutenant of artillery, who had received no more instructions than had been received by Captain Bissell. So far from stopping the flotilla, Lieutenant Jackson was nearly persuaded to join it, and actually accepted money from Burr to raise a company

---

[1] Deposition of John Shaw, Burr's Trial; Annals of Congress, 1807–1808, p. 573.

in his service.[1] January 6, leaving Chickasaw Bluffs, the flotilla again descended the river until, January 10, it reached the mouth of Bayou Pierre, about thirty miles above Natchez. There Burr went ashore, and at the house of a certain Judge Bruin he saw a newspaper containing the letter which he had himself written in cipher to Wilkinson July 29, and which Wilkinson had published December 26.

From the moment Burr saw himself denounced by Wilkinson, his only hope was to escape. The President's proclamation had reached the Mississippi Territory; Cowles Meade, the acting-governor, had called out the militia. If Burr went on he would fall into the hands of Wilkinson, who had every motive to order him to be court-martialled and shot; if he stayed where he was, Cowles Meade would arrest and send him to Washington. Moving his flotilla across the river, Burr gave way to despair. Some ideas of resistance were entertained by Blennerhassett and the other leaders of the party; but they were surprised to find their "emperor" glad to abdicate and submit. January 17 Burr met Acting-Governor Cowles Meade and surrendered at discretion. His conversation at that moment was such that Meade thought him insane.[2] January 21 he caused his cases of muskets, which had been at first secreted in the brush, to be sunk in the river. After his surrender he was taken to Washington, the capital of the Territory, about seven miles from Natchez. A grand-jury was summoned, and the attorney-general, Poindexter, attempted to obtain an indictment. The grand-jury not only threw out the bill, but presented the seizure of Burr and his accomplices as a grievance. The very militia who stopped him were half inclined to join his expedition. Except for a score of United States officials, civil and military, he might have reached New Orleans without a check.

Fortunately neither the civil nor the military authorities of the national government were disposed to be made a jest. The grand-jury could grant but a respite, and Burr had still to decide between evils. If he fell into Wilkinson's hands he risked a fate of which he openly expressed fear. During the

[1] Evidence of Lieutenant Jacob Jackson, Burr's Trial; Annals of Congress, 1807—1808, p. 683.
[2] Blennerhassett Papers, p. 426.

delay his men on the flotilla had become disorganized and insubordinate; his drafts on New York had been returned protested; he knew that the military authorities at Fort Adams were determined to do what the civil authorities had failed in doing; and his courage failed him when he realized that he must either be delivered to President Jefferson, whom he had defied, or to General Wilkinson, whom he had tried to deceive.

Feb. 1, 1807, after sending to his friends on the flotilla a note to assure them of his immediate return,[1] Burr turned his back on them, and left them to the ruin for which he alone was responsible. Disguised in the coarse suit of a Mississippi boatman, with a soiled white-felt hat, he disappeared into the woods, and for nearly a month was lost from sight. Toward the end of February he was recognized in a cabin near the Spanish frontier, about fifty miles above Mobile; and his presence was announced to Lieutenant Gaines, commanding at Fort Stoddert, near by. Gaines arrested him. After about three weeks of confinement at Fort Stoddert he was sent to Richmond in Virginia. In passing through the town of Chester, in South Carolina, he flung himself from his horse and cried for a rescue; but the officer commanding the escort seized him, threw him back like a child into the saddle, and marched on. Like many another man in American history, Burr felt at last the physical strength of the patient and long-suffering government which he had so persistently insulted, outrayed, and betrayed.

Not until the end of March, 1807, did Burr reach Richmond; and in the mean while a whole session of Congress had passed, revolution after revolution had taken place in Europe, and a new series of political trials had begun for President Jefferson's troubled Administration. The conspiracy of Burr was a mere episode, which had little direct connection with foreign or domestic politics, and no active popular support in any quarter. The affairs of the country at large felt hardly a perceptible tremor in the midst of the excitement which convulsed New Orleans; and the general public obstinately refused to care what Burr was doing, or to believe that

[1] Blennerhassett Papers, p. 206.

he was so insane as to expect a dissolution of the Union. In spite of the President's proclamation of Nov. 27, 1806, no special interest was roused, and even the Congress which met a few days later, Dec. 1, 1806, at first showed indifference to Burr and his affairs.

If this was a matter for blame, the fault certainly lay with the President, who had hitherto refused to whisper a suspicion either of Burr's loyalty or of the patriotism which Jefferson believed to characterize Louisiana, the Mississippi Territory, and Tennessee. Even the proclamation had treated Burr's enterprise as one directed wholly against Spain. The Annual Message, read December 2, showed still more strongly a wish to ignore Burr's true objects. Not only did it allude to the proclamation with an air of apology, as rendered necessary by "the criminal attempts of private individuals to decide for their country the question of peace or war," but it praised in defiance of evidence the conduct of the militia of Louisiana and Mississippi in supporting Claiborne and Wilkinson against the Spaniards:—

> "I inform you with great pleasure of the promptitude with which the inhabitants of those Territories have tendered their services in defence of their country. It has done honor to themselves, entitled them to the confidence of their fellow-citizens in every part of the Union, and must strengthen the general determination to protect them efficaciously under all circumstances which may occur."

On some subjects Jefferson was determined to shut his eyes. He officially asserted that the Orleans militia had done honor to themselves and won the confidence of their fellow-citizens at a moment when he was receiving from Governor Claiborne almost daily warnings that the Orleans militia could not be trusted, and would certainly not fight against Spain.

By this course of conduct Jefferson entangled himself in a new labyrinth of contradictions and inconsistencies. Until that moment, his apparent interests and wishes led him to ignore or to belittle Burr's conspiracy; but after the moment had passed, his interests and convictions obliged him to take the views and share the responsibilities of General Wilkinson.

Thus John Randolph found fresh opportunities to annoy the President, while the President lost his temper, and challenged another contest with Luther Martin and Chief-Justice Marshall.

After shutting his ears to the reiterated warnings of Eaton, Truxton, Morgan, Daveiss, and even to the hints of Wilkinson himself; after neglecting to take precautions against Burr, Wilkinson, or the city of New Orleans, and after throwing upon the Western people the responsibility for doing what the government had been instituted to do; after issuing a proclamation which treated Burr's armament as a filibustering venture like that of Miranda; and after sending to Congress an Annual Message which excused the proclamation on the ground that it was an act of good faith toward Spain, although Spain took no such view of it,—Jefferson could not reasonably expect the opposition in Congress to accept without a protest sudden legislation resting on the theory that the Constitution and the Union were in danger.

The month of December, 1806, passed at Washington without producing a public display of uneasiness on the President's part; the Government was waiting to hear from Kentucky and Ohio. Outwardly Jefferson continued to rely on the patriotism of the people of Louisiana, but inwardly he was troubled with fears. December 22 Robert Smith, anxious to save himself from possible calamity, wrote to him a letter of remonstrance.

"In the course of our various communications," said Smith,[1] "in relation to the movements of Colonel Burr in the Western country, I have from time to time expressed the opinions which, as they were not at all countenanced by any of the other gentlemen, I did not deem it expedient to press upon your attention. . . . If, as was proposed on the 24th of October, the sloops-of-war and the gunboats stationed at Washington, New York, Norfolk, and Charleston had been sent to New Orleans under the command of Commodore Preble, with Captain Decatur second in command, we would at this time have nothing to apprehend from the military expedition of Colonel Burr. Such a naval

[1] Robert Smith to Jefferson, Dec. 22, 1806; Jefferson MSS.

force joined to the ketches and gunboats now on the Mississippi, would beyond a doubt have been sufficient to suppress such an enterprise. But this step, momentous as it was, the Executive could not take consistently with the limitations of existing statutes and with the spirit manifested by the House of Representatives at their last session. The approaching crisis will, I fear, be a melancholy proof of the want of forecast in so circumscribing the Executive within such narrow limits."

Robert Smith, conscious of being the person whom Congress most distrusted, grasped at the idea of freeing himself from restraint, and did not stop to ask whether Burr's impunity were due to want of forecast in Congress or in the Executive. He was alarmed; and the President's reply to his letter showed that Jefferson was equally uncomfortable.[1]

"What I had myself in contemplation," the President answered, "was to wait till we get news from Louisville of December 15, the day of Burr's proposed general rendezvous. The post comes from thence in twelve days. The mail next expected will be of that date. If we then find that his force has had no effectual opposition at either Marietta or Cincinnati, and will not be stopped at Louisville, then, without depending on the opposition at Fort Adams (though I have more dependence on that than any other), I should propose to lay the whole matter before Congress, ask an immediate appropriation for a naval equipment, and at the same time order twenty thousand militia, or volunteers, from the Western States to proceed down the river to retake New Orleans, presuming our naval equipment would be there before them. In the mean time I would recommend to you to be getting ready and giving orders of preparation to the officers and vessels which we can get speedily ready."

Not a trace of confidence in the people of Louisiana was to be detected in this plan of operations. The duty of the government not only to act, but to act with extreme quickness and vigor, before Burr should come within a long distance of

[1] Jefferson's Writings (Ford), viii. 504.

New Orleans, was avowed. The idea of calling out twenty thousand men to retake New Orleans showed a degree of alarm contrasting strongly with the equanimity that preceded it, and with the inertness which had allowed such an emergency to arise. The difference of tone between this letter and the President's public language was extreme. Nevertheless, the Western mail arrived, bringing news that the State of Ohio had seized the greater part of Burr's boats, that six or eight had escaped, and that Burr had gone to Nashville; and in this partly satisfactory report the President saw reason for further silence. Next came, Jan. 2, 1807, Wilkinson's letter of November 12 from Natchez, with its pledge to perish in New Orleans, and with messages, not trusted to writing, but orally imparted to the messenger, about Burr's cipher letters and their contents. Still the President made no sign. For want of some clew his followers were greatly perplexed; and men like John Randolph, who hated the President, and Samuel Smith, who did not love him, began to suspect that at last the Administration was fairly at a standstill. Randolph, with his usual instability, swayed between extremes of scepticism. At one moment he believed that the situation was most serious; at another, that the conspiracy was only a Spanish intrigue. January 2 he wrote to Monroe, in London, a letter full of the conviction that Spain was behind Burr:[1] "I am informed also, through a very direct and respectable channel, that there is a considerable party about Lexington and Frankfort highly propitious to his views, and with strong Spanish prepossessions. Some names which have been mentioned as of the number would astonish you." Jefferson's conduct irritated him more than that of Burr or Yrujo: —

"The state of things here is indeed unexampled. Although the newspapers teem with rumors dangerous to the peace and safety of the Union, and notwithstanding Government give full faith and credit to the existence of a formidable conspiracy, and have given information and instructions to the several State authorities how to act (under which Ohio has done herself much honor), yet not one syllable has been communicated to Congress on the subject.

[1] Randolph to Monroe, Jan. 2, 1807; Monroe MSS.

There are some other curious circumstances which I must reserve for oral communication, not caring to trust them by letter. One fact, however, ought not to be omitted. The army (as it is called) is in the most contemptible state, unprovided with everything, and men and officers unacquainted with their duties."

In what state Randolph expected the army to be, after six years of such legislation as his, could not be guessed. Officers and soldiers, distributed by companies, in forts hundreds of miles distant from each other, could hardly become acquainted with any other duties than those of a frontier garrison. General Smith did not, like Randolph, complain of others for the consequences of his own acts. He too wrote at that moment a confidential letter, describing the situation, to his brother-in-law, Wilson Cary Nicholas:[1] —

"I fear that Burr will go down the river and give us trouble. The proclamation, it seems, in the Western country is very little attended to. They, no doubt, seeing no exertion making, consider that it has originated from false information. The President has not yet given any kind of information to Congress, and gentlemen (Giles among the number) will not believe that there is any kind of danger. . . . Burr's letter to Wilkinson is explicit. (This is secret.) He had passed the Alleghany *never*, *never* to return; his object, New Orleans,—open and avowed. And yet not one step taken, except the proclamation! Duane calls on Congress to act. How can Congress act? Would you force from the Executive the information they are unwilling to give? This would be imprudent. I have (with consent of the President) introduced a Resolution proposing an addition to our military establishment. Will it pass? That I can't tell. . . . It is curious that the nation should depend on the unauthorized exertions of a man whose honor and fidelity were doubted by all except a very, very few, not five in the United States, for its preservation and character. Had he not disclosed the conspiracy, the President would have folded his arms and let the storm collect its whole strength.

[1] Samuel Smith to W. C. Nicholas, Jan. 9, 1807; Nicholas MSS.

Even now, not an energetic measure has been taken except by him [Wilkinson] and Tiffin."

Another week passed. Then at last, January 16, John Randolph rose in the House and moved a Resolution asking the President what he knew about Burr's affairs, and what he had done or meant to do in the matter. "The United States are not only threatened with external war," Randolph said, "but with conspiracies and treasons, the more alarming from their not being defined; and yet we sit and adjourn, adjourn and sit, take things as schoolboys, do as we are bid, and ask no questions!" His Resolution annoyed the democrats; but his sneers were more convincing than his arguments, and after some contradictory and unorganized resistance, a majority supported him. The Resolution was adopted and sent to the President.

Two days afterward, January 18, Wilkinson's despatches from New Orleans to December 18, embracing his first written version of Burr's cipher despatch reached Washington. The country learned that Wilkinson had arrested Bollman and other accomplices of Burr, and in defiance of their legal rights had shipped them to Washington for trial. Jefferson was obliged to decide whether he should sustain or repudiate Wilkinson; and in the light of Burr's revelations and Wilkinson's *quasi* confession, he could not deny that a serious conspiracy existed, or affirm that the General had gone beyond the line of duty, even though he had violated the laws. Dearborn's instructions, indeed, had to some extent authorized the arrests. At that moment if the President had repudiated Wilkinson, he would have only diverted public indignation from Burr, and would have condemned the Executive itself, which after so many warnings had left such power in the hands of a man universally distrusted.

Thus at last Jefferson was obliged to raise his voice against Burr's crimes. Thenceforward a sense of having been made almost a party to the conspiracy gave a sting of personal bitterness to the zeal with which he strove to defend Wilkinson and to punish Burr. Anxiety to excuse himself was evident in the Message which he sent to Congress January 22, in response to Randolph's Resolution of January 16.

"Some time in the latter part of September," he said, "I received intimations that designs were in agitation in the Western country, unlawful and unfriendly to the peace of the Union, and that the prime mover in these was Aaron Burr."

He had received such intimations many times, and long before the month of September.

"It was not till the latter part of October that the objects of the conspiracy began to be perceived."

Absolute truth would have required the President to say rather that it was not till the latter part of October that inquiry on his part began to be made.

"In Kentucky a premature attempt to bring Burr to justice, without a sufficient evidence for his conviction, had produced a popular impression in his favor and a general disbelief of his guilt. This gave him an unfortunate opportunity of hastening his equipments."

Complaint of District-Attorney Daveiss was natural; but the reproof was inexact in every particular. The attempt to indict Burr, if any attempt were to be made, was not premature. The impression in his favor did not give Burr an opportunity to hasten his equipments, since Graham appeared at Marietta the same day with the news of Burr's first discharge at Frankfort. Finally, if Daveiss's attempt failed, the fault was chiefly with the Government at Washington, which had taken no measures to direct or to support it, and which was represented on the bench by a judge himself implicated in the charge.

"On the whole," said the Message, "the fugitives from the Ohio, with their associates from Cumberland, or any other place in that quarter, cannot threaten serious danger to the city of New Orleans."

Yet a conspiracy against the Union existed; the President communicated Burr's cipher letters; he proclaimed Burr's expectation of seizing upon New Orleans, as well as the panic prevailing there; and he approved Wilkinson's arrest of Bollman and Swartwout. Finally, the Message spoke of the people in New Orleans in a tone of confidence quite different from that of Wilkinson's despatches, communicated with the Message itself.[1]

The Senate interpreted the Message in the sense it was doubtless meant to bear,—as a request from the President for support. Bollman and Swartwout, who would arrive in Washington within a few days or hours, had been illegally arrested, and they, as well as the other conspirators, could not without special legislation be held longer in custody. Giles at once introduced a Bill suspending for three months the writ of habeas corpus with respect to such persons; and the necessity of this measure seemed so obvious to the Senate that the Rules were suspended by unanimous consent, and the Bill was passed on the same day through all its stages. Bayard alone voted against it.[2]

Monday, January 26, the Bill was brought before the House, and Eppes of Virginia, the President's son-in-law, immediately moved its rejection. The debate that followed was curious, not only on account of the constitutional points discussed, but also on account of the division of sentiment among the President's friends, who quoted the Message to prove that there was no danger to public safety such as called for a suspension of habeas corpus, and appealed to the same Message to prove the existence of a more wanton and malignant insurrection than any that had ever before been raised against the Government. John Randolph intimated that the President was again attempting to evade responsibility.

> "It appears to my mind," said he, "like an oblique attempt to cover a certain departure from an established law of the land, and a certain violation of the Constitution of the United States, which we are told have been committed in this country. Sir, recollect that Congress met on the first of December; that the President had information of the incipient stage of this conspiracy about the last of September; that the proclamation issued before Congress met; and yet

[1] Wilkinson to Jefferson, Dec. 14, 1806; Annals of Congress, 1806–1807, p. 1009.
[2] Diary of J. Q. Adams (Jan. 23, 1807), i. 445.

that no suggestion, either from the Executive or from either branch of the Legislature, has transpired touching the propriety of suspending the writ of habeas corpus until this violation has taken place. I will never agree in this side way to cover up such a violation by a proceeding highly dangerous to the liberty of the country, or to agree that this invaluable privilege shall be suspended because it has been already violated,—and suspended, too, after the cause, if any there was for it, has ceased to exist. . . . With whatever epithets gentlemen may dignify this conspiracy, . . . I think it nothing more nor less than an intrigue!"

The Bill was accordingly rejected by the great majority of one hundred and thirteen to nineteen. On the same day the attorney-general applied to Judge Cranch of the District Court for a warrant against Bollman and Swartwout on the charge of treason, filing Wilkinson's affidavit and a statement given under oath by William Eaton in support of the charge. The warrant was issued; Bollman and Swartwout at once applied to the Supreme Court, then in session, for a writ of habeas corpus. February 13 Chief-Justice Marshall granted the writ; February 16 their counsel moved for their discharge, and February 21 the chief-justice decided that sufficient evidence of levying war against the United States had not been produced to justify the commitment of Swartwout, and still less that of Bollman, and therefore that they must be discharged. Adair and Ogden, who had been sent to Baltimore, were liberated by Judge Nicholson.

The friends of the Administration, exasperated at this failure of justice, again talked of impeaching the judges.[1] Giles threatened to move an amendment of the Constitution taking all criminal jurisdiction from the Supreme Court. Meanwhile Randolph and the Federalists assailed Wilkinson, and by implication the President. They brought forward a Resolution declaring the expediency of making further provision by law for securing the privilege of habeas corpus; and in the warm debate raised by this manœuvre John Randolph made himself conspicuous by slurs upon Wilkinson, whom he did not scruple to charge with double treason,—to the Constitution and

[1] Diary of J. Q. Adams (Feb. 21, 1807), i. 459.

to Burr. By a close vote of sixty to fifty-eight this Resolution was indefinitely postponed; but the debate showed the settled drift of Randolph's tactics. He meant to attack the President by attacking Wilkinson; and the President could no longer evade responsibility for Wilkinson's acts. To be thwarted by Chief-Justice Marshall and baited by John Randolph; to be made at once the scapegoat of Burr's crimes and of Wilkinson's extravagances,—was a fate peculiarly hard to bear, but was one which Jefferson could not escape.

Thenceforward the situation changed. What seemed to be the indictment and trial of Burr became, in a political point of view, the trial of Wilkinson, with John Randolph acting as accuser and President Jefferson as counsel for the defence, while Chief-Justice Marshall presided in judgment. No more unpleasant attitude could be readily imagined for a man of Jefferson's high position and pure character than to plead before his two most formidable and unforgiving enemies as the patron and protector of a client so far beneath respect. Driven by forces which allowed no choice of paths, he stood by the man who had saved him; but in order to understand precisely what he effected in sustaining Wilkinson, Americans must look in the archives of the King of Spain for knowledge of facts disbelieved by the President of the United States.

"According to appearances," wrote Yrujo Jan. 28, 1807,[1] "Spain has saved the United States from the separation of the Union which menaced them. This would have taken place if Wilkinson had entered cordially into the views of Burr,—which was to be expected, because Wilkinson detests this government, and the separation of the Western States has been his favorite plan. The evil has come from the foolish and pertinacious perseverance with which Burr has persisted in carrying out a wild project against Mexico. Wilkinson is entirely devoted to us. He enjoys a considerable pension from the King. With his natural capacity and his local and military knowledge, he anticipated with moral certainty the failure of an expedition of this nature. Doubtless he foresaw from the first that the improbability of success in case of making the attempt would leave him like the

[1] Yrujo to Cevallos, Jan. 28, 1807; MSS. Spanish Archives.

dog in the fable with the piece of meat in his mouth; that is, that he would lose the honorable employment he holds and the generous pension he enjoys from the King. These considerations, secret in their nature, he could not explain to Burr; and when the latter persisted in an idea so fatal to Wilkinson's interests, nothing remained but to take the course adopted. By this means he assures his pension; and will allege his conduct on this occasion as an extraordinary service, either for getting it increased, or for some generous compensation. On the other hand this proceeding secures his distinguished rank in the military service of the United States, and covers him with a popularity which may perhaps result in pecuniary advantages, and in any case will flatter his vanity. In such an alternative he has acted as was to be expected; that is, he has sacrificed Burr in order to obtain, on the ruins of Burr's reputation, the advantages I have pointed out."

Whether Yrujo was right in his theory of Wilkinson's motives might be doubted, but on one point he could not be mistaken. The general-in-chief of the United States Army was in the employment of Don Carlos IV.; he enjoyed a pension of two thousand dollars a year in consideration of secret services, and for twenty years the services had been rendered and the pension had been paid.[1]

[1] Clark's Proofs against Wilkinson, 1809.

Chapter XV

J EFFERSON'S EFFORT to suppress the scandal of Burr's disunion scheme had its source in motives both pure and generous. Distressed by the factiousness of the last session, he
could feel no wish more ardent than to restore harmony to
his party. The struggle for the succession threatened to tear
from his brows the hard-won laurels which were his only
pleasure, and the reward for infinite labors and mortifications.
So far as he could, he stifled discussion in regard to the coming change.

> "The question," he wrote to Leiper of Pennsylvania,[1]
> "cannot be touched without endangering the harmony of
> the present session of Congress, and disturbing the tran-
> quillity of the nation itself prematurely and injuriously.
> . . . The present session is important as having new and
> great questions to decide, in the decision of which no schis-
> matic views should take any part."

In this spirit the President shaped his acts. Reunion in a
common policy, a controlling impulse, was the motive of his
gentleness toward Randolph and the Virginia schismatics, as
it was that of his blindness to the doings of Burr.

The Annual Message of December, 1806, was intended to
unite the party on a new plane of action, and to prepare the
way for Madison's gentle rule. Foreign affairs were to be allowed to drop from sight; France, England, and Spain were
to be forgotten; Florida was to be ignored; political energy
was to be concentrated upon the harvesting of fruits already
ripe. For six years, carrying out the policy of discharging public debt, Gallatin had pursued his economies, in the opinion
of many good men pressing them so far as to paralyze Government. The time had come when he could do no more.
Twenty-four millions of debt had been paid. Of the remainder about ten millions only could be dealt with; and arrangements were made for discharging these ten millions before
Jefferson's term should end. Meanwhile the revenue was
growing; the surplus must be disposed of, and the period of

[1] Jefferson's Writings (Ford), viii. 502.

pinching economies might cease. Henceforward Republicans, Democrats, and Federalists might agree on some common system of expenditure.

"The question now comes forward," said the Annual Message, "to what other objects shall these surpluses be appropriated, and the whole surplus of impost, after the entire discharge of the public debt, and during those intervals when the purposes of war shall not call for them? Shall we suppress the impost, and give that advantage to foreign over domestic manufactures? On a few articles of more general and necessary use the suppression in due season will doubtless be right; but the great mass of the articles on which impost is paid are foreign luxuries, purchased by those only who are rich enough to afford themselves the use of them. Their patriotism would certainly prefer its continuance and application to the great purposes of the public education, roads, rivers, canals, and such other objects of public improvement as it may be thought proper to add to the constitutional enumeration of federal powers. By these operations new channels of communication will be opened between the States, the lines of separation will disappear, their interests will be identified, and their union cemented by new and indissoluble ties. Education is here placed among the articles of public care, not that it would be proposed to take its ordinary branches out of the hands of private enterprise, which manages so much better all the concerns to which it is equal; but a public institution can alone supply those sciences which, though rarely called for, are yet necessary to complete the circle, all the parts of which contribute to the improvement of the country, and some of them to its preservation."

With an air of apology, as though his old opinions were no longer of practical interest, the President added that an amendment to the Constitution would be necessary in order to bring these new functions within the enumerated objects of government; but to such an amendment he saw no objection, nor did he apprehend difficulty in obtaining it. A broad system of internal improvements; a national university; "a steady, perhaps a quickened, pace in preparations for the defence of our seaport towns and waters; an early settlement of the most exposed and vulnerable parts of our country; a militia so organized that its effective portions can be called to any point in the Union, or volunteers instead of them, to serve a sufficient time,"—these were the objects to which Congress should devote its energies, in order that when the two remaining years of Jefferson's power should come to an end, the fabric of Republican government might be complete.

That Federalist and Democrat could join in accepting such a scheme of action, and could lay aside forever their old, unprofitable disputes, seemed no wild dream. The hope was strengthened by a paragraph of the Message which held out the prospect of removing another serious barrier to perfect harmony:—

> "I congratulate you, fellow-citizens, on the approach of the period at which you may interpose your authority constitutionally to withdraw the citizens of the United States from all further participation in those violations of human rights which have been so long continued on the unoffending inhabitants of Africa, and which the morality, the reputation, and the best interests of our country have long been eager to proscribe."

Almost ignoring foreign politics, Jefferson recommended Congress to abolish the slave-trade, begin a system of national roads and canals, found a national university, fortify the coasts, and organize the national militia; and had Congress been able or willing to follow promptly his advice, many difficulties would have been overcome before the year 1810 which seemed even twenty years later to bar the path of national progress. Congress, indeed, never succeeded in rising to the level of Jefferson's hopes and wishes; it realized but a small part of the plan which he traced, and what it did was done with little system. The slowness with which political movement lagged behind industrial and social progress could be measured by the fate of President Jefferson's scheme of 1806 for crowning the fabric of Republican government. Not by means of the government, or by virture of wisdom in the persons trusted with the government, were Jefferson's objects destined at last to be partially attained.

Notwithstanding the favor shown to internal improvements, John Randolph exulted in the President's Message, which he regarded as expressing his own views. He scoffed at the Smiths, Crowninshields, and other orators who in the last session had talked loudly of war.[1]

"The Message," he wrote to Nicholson, "was, as you supposed, wormwood to certain gentry. They made wry faces, but in fear of the rod and in hopes of sugar-plums swallowed it with less apparent repugnance than I had predicted."

General Smith and the politicians who wanted armaments were annoyed.

"We have established theories," wrote Smith,[2] "that would stare down any possible measures of offence or defence. Should a man take a patriotic stand against those destructive and seductive fine-spun follies, he will be written down very soon. Look at the last Message! It is such that the President cannot recommend (although he now sees the necessity) any augmentation of the army. Nay I, even I, did not dare to bring forward the measure until I had first obtained his approbation. Never was there a time when Executive influence so completely governed the nation!"

No man of ordinary sense could fail to feel some shame at the recollection of what had taken place in regard to Florida, or to wish that it might be forgotten; and the friends of Madison had every reason for ignoring it and for welcoming Randolph's followers back into the party, if they would consent to come. The session took character from this spirit of reconciliation. The first Bill adopted by Congress suspended, at the President's judgment, the operation of the Non-importation Act passed in April; and Randolph did not fail to suggest that his sarcasms against those who had urged this law were justified by its instant suspension. The next important measure, brought forward under the President's patronage, was the abolition of the duty on salt; and Randolph reminded the

[1] Adams's Randolph, p. 206.
[2] Adams's Randolph, p. 208.

House that this relief from taxation followed close upon his own strenuous efforts of the year before. Throughout the session Randolph took the tone of a dictator; and on most questions a majority of the House tried only to vie with him in the race for popularity. Old subjects of dispute were laid aside; the Yazoo claims were forgotten. In regard to the army and navy, Randolph was allowed to have his way; in the case of Bollman and Swartwout, he stopped the attempt to suspend the writ of habeas corpus; in sympathy with his opinions the House cut down appropriations, refused to fortify New York, declined to increase the army, and reverted to the first principles of the Republican party. The session of 1806–1807 was a perpetual effort to win back the confidence and support of Virginia for Madison, and leave no excuse for defection to Monroe.

General Smith thought Executive influence more powerful than ever, but the President seemed to influence only by disguising his weakness. Little or no attention was paid to his wishes. He would gladly have built ships of the line, he would willingly have fortified New York, he would have liked two more regiments to garrison the military posts; but he could do nothing in face of the reaction which, at Randolph's bidding, swept the Southern Republicans back to their practices of 1801 and their professions of 1798. The force of reactionary feeling was shown in speeches which revealed a dangerous chasm between North and South. On the question of fortifying New York, Southern Republicans took ground which caused New York Democrats to feel toward Virginia a disgust as deep as ever had been felt by Burr. Nelson of Maryland favored abandoning the cities altogether in case of attack:[1] "When the enemy comes, let them take our towns, and let us retire into the country." Holland of North Carolina regarded the seaboard cities as so many enemies:[2]

> "If New York and our other cities were only tolerably fortified, Mr. Holland was confident that we should go to war. He lamented the consequences of that disposition that is for novelty in this country,—a disposition that cannot

[1] Annals of Congress, 1806–1807, p. 389.
[2] Annals of Congress, 1806–1807, p. 598.

be quelled. Our commercial towns are defenceless, and that is our only safety at present. I want to see not a single ship, or any preparation for war."

Eppes of Virginia, the President's son-in-law, spoke hotly against the doctrine of defence:—

"If there is any principle which ought to be hooted at in a Republican government, it is the very principle laid down by the gentleman from New York as the basis of his reasoning,—that to preserve peace we ought to be prepared for war. Sir, it is this very principle which is the source of all the miseries of Europe."

John Randolph also favored abandoning New York in case of attack:[1] —

"Suppose New York ever so well fortified, an army may land above the city and cut off its intercourse with the country. A fortification there would be made for the enemy. Not a man of our army would have escaped in the last war from Long Island, if the enemy's general had not been treacherous to his duty; and all the calamities of that campaign might have been avoided if our army had retreated into the country "

Answer to arguments like these was of course impossible. The only final answer was to take the Southern people at their word, and to assert as a principle the rule that seaboard cities, being entitled to no protection from government in case of attack, should have the right to protect themselves by inviting the enemy to occupy them. Boston and New York had no reason to fear the operation of such a rule, if it suited the interests of Virginia; but as an argument even this logic would have availed nothing, because so deep was Virginian antipathy to cities that Randolph and all his friends would have answered with one voice, "We expect no better!"

The unwillingness of the Southern Republicans to fortify extended only to forts and ships, not to gunboats. Randolph had not much faith in gunboats; but his friends were willing to spend comparatively large sums on these cheap defences

[1] Annals of Congress, 1806–1807, p. 610.

Their theory was reasonable. A coast like that of America could not be protected by fixed fortifications alone,—only some system of movable batteries could answer the whole purpose; but in such a system everything depended on the effectiveness of the battery to be selected, and no one could say that the gunboat would prove to be effective. Most sea-going people pronounced it a failure; and in the navy, gunboat service was never popular. The real argument for gunboats was their assumed cheapness; but Gallatin and the Northern Democrats, as well as the Federalists, foresaw that the supposed economy was a delusion. A gunboat cost some ten thousand dollars or less, and a whole flotilla of gunboats could be built for the price of a frigate; but no one could say how much this flotilla would cost in annual repairs or in actual service. The life of a gunboat was short.

These doubts had no effect on the majority of the House. "Fortifications will be of no possible service unless they are manned," argued Nelson,[1] "and to man them we must have a large standing army." He wanted to know whether the House was prepared to adopt a system that would require the raising of above one hundred thousand men. If forts were of no possible service unless they were always manned,—new as the assertion was,—surely gunboats were open to the same objection; yet Nelson wanted to spend three hundred thousand dollars in building gunboats, and he was willing to build any number of gunboats the navy might ask for.[2]

The Northern seaboard representatives rejected the offer of gunboats, and allowed the Southern States to dispose of them. No appropriation for fortifying New York could be obtained. The theory that seaboard cities could not be defended received general assent; but many of the members went further, and declared that no danger to those cities existed. A policy of neglecting defence might be safe in peace, when foreign nations had every interest to avoid a war; but nothing could warrant the common assertion that danger of war existed only from America herself, at a moment when France was attacking American commerce by measures of actual warfare, when England was hesitating whether to permit America

[1] Annals of Congress, 1806–1807, p. 398.
[2] Annals of Congress, 1806–1807, p. 400.

to trade at all except with the British Islands, and when diplomatic relations with Spain had ceased, the ministers at Madrid and Washington had been withdrawn, and a Spanish army was threatening New Orleans.

Willis Alston of North Carolina, chiefly known as an object of Randolph's peculiar contempt and personal violence, took as strong ground as Randolph himself on these questions. On the other hand Josiah Quincy showed in a high degree the art of irritating opponents by his manner of expressing a low opinion of their sense and motives; and the Southern members resented this treatment the more because Quincy was a man well born and well educated, whose social standing could not be questioned. In reply to his taunts Alston resorted to the well-worn commonplaces of the Republican party. "The present Administration," said he, "has taken up a new system of defence,—it is that of saving the public money. This system is new, and not known in Federal times. We have not gone on increasing taxes, like our predecessors." The assertion could not be denied; but Quincy's retort was not the less pungent. "The Federal Administration," he replied, "saved the country from danger and disgrace: I wish I could say as much of their successors."

The whole issue lay in these short charges and counter-charges. To some extent the President, his Cabinet, and the Senate had become converted to Federalist views; but the influence of Randolph and of popular prejudices peculiar to Southern society held the House stiffly to an impracticable creed. Whatever the North and East wanted the South and West refused. Jefferson's wishes fared no better than the requests of the State and city of New York; the House showed no alacrity in taking up the subject of roads, canals, or universities. The only innovation which made its way through Congress was the Act of Feb. 10, 1807, appropriating fifty thousand dollars for the establishment of a coast survey, for this was an object in which the Southern States were interested as deeply as the Northern. Even the Senate's appropriation for beginning the Cumberland Road was indefinitely postponed by the House.

This jealousy of government could not without ill-temper be so severely enforced. Randolph's manners were unconsciously imitated by the men who imitated his statesmanship, and the Southern Republicans treated their Northern allies with autocratic harshness as offensive as that of Randolph. The Federalist members, for the most part able to hold their own and even to return such treatment with manners still more arrogant, enjoyed the irritation of Democrats like Sloan and Smilie, Bidwell and Varnum. If the Southern planters refused to aid in fortifying New York, the Federalists were the stronger for the refusal; and if Virginia was anxious not to risk her tobacco and corn for the sake of Boston, New York, and Philadelphia, the Federalists for the most part hoped that the Northern cities might be induced to take care of themselves. Yet although the Federalists were not sorry to see the Pennsylvania Democrats ground under the heel of Virginia, they were surprised to find how rapidly the sectional spirit increased in the Southern States when slavery was in question. The debate on the abolition of the slave-trade startled Democrats and Federalists alike.

The paragraph in the President's Message which related to the slave-trade was regularly referred to a special committee. Peter Early of Georgia was chairman, while Thomas Mann Randolph of Virginia, John Campbell of Maryland, Thomas Keenan of North Carolina, and three Northern representatives completed the number. Early took the subject promptly in hand, and Dec. 15, 1806, reported a Bill, which was referred to the House in committee, and came up two days afterward for debate. The Bill declared the importation of negroes as slaves unlawful; imposed a fine on the importer, with forfeiture of ship and cargo; and authorized the President to employ the armed vessels of the United States in enforcing the law.

Under the Act which prescribed rules for forfeiture, the cargo of a forfeited vessel was to be sold on behalf of the United States government. The cargo of a slave-ship consisted in negroes. Under Early's Bill, every negro imported thenceforth into the country became forfeit to the United States, and must be sold by the United States government to the highest bidder.

The Pennsylvania Democrats, imbued with Quaker principles in regard to slavery, could scarcely be expected to approve of a policy which made the government an owner and trader in slaves. The New Englanders, though the slave-trade had been to a great extent a Rhode Island interest, were little inclined to adopt a law under which any cargo of negroes that might be driven on their coast must be sold at public auction in the streets of Newport or Boston; and perhaps even some of the Southern members might have admitted that the chance of collusion between importers and buyers was a serious objection to the Bill. No one could suppose that such a measure would pass without strenuous opposition, and no one could have felt surprise at seeing Sloan of New Jersey immediately rise to offer an amendment providing that every forfeited negro should be entitled to freedom.[1]

Upon this amendment a debate began which soon became hot. Early took the ground that without his provision for forfeiture and sale, the law would be ineffectual; that no man in the South would inform against the slave-dealer if his act were to turn loose a quantity of savage negroes on the public at large.

> "We must either get rid of them or they of us; there is no alternative; and I leave it to gentlemen to be determined which course would be pursued. There can be no doubt on this head. I will speak out; it is not my practice to be mealy-mouthed on a subject of importance. Not one of them would be left alive in a year."

The Southern members supported Early, and the Northern members knew not what to propose. The negroes could not be returned to Africa, because they were all brought from the interior, and the coast tribes would re-enslave or massacre them. Pennsylvania and Ohio were little more anxious than Virginia to receive such citizens. Binding them to masters for a term of years was suggested, but objections were made on both sides.

The debate was adjourned, resumed, adjourned again; and although the Northern speakers were forbearing, the Southern members more and more lost their temper.

> "You have got into a great difficulty," said David R.

[1] Annals of Congress, 1806–1807, p. 168.

Williams of South Carolina;[1] "you are completely hobbled. It is so bad that you cannot go on, and you must stick where you are. Let me ask what is the usual conduct of legislatures on local subjects. Do they not inquire of those who are informed? Are they not guided by those who are competent to judge? The gentlemen from the South, who understand this subject, tell you how this business must be done; but the gentlemen over the way seem anxious now, as on a former occasion, to draw a revenue from the blood and sweat of the miserable Africans. I will not say that this is their motive, but their conduct certainly justifies a suspicion that their object is to pass such a law as will connive at the continuance of the trade for the emoluments of their constituents."

The discussion was further embittered by a motion made by Smilie of Pennsylvania to make the importation of negroes a felony to be punished by death. This proposition called out another display of Early's frankness.

"We have been asked," said he,[2] "what punishment can be considered too severe for so atrocious a crime. Without answering the question in the abstract, it will be sufficient to answer it by a practical view of the subject. How do people consider the transaction? Do they consider it such an atrocious crime? They do not."

The Pennsylvania philanthropists had assumed that they could at least follow Jefferson in holding slavery to be an evil and the slave-trade to be a violation of human rights; but even these points were no longer conceded.

"All the people in the Southern States," continued Early, "are concerned in slavery. It is not, then, considered as criminal. . . . I will tell the truth,—a large majority of people in the Southern States do not consider slavery as even an evil."

The death-penalty was rejected by a vote of sixty-three to fifty-three, almost the whole Pennsylvania delegation voting

[1] Annals of Congress, 1806–1807, p. 183.
[2] Annals of Congress, 1806–1807, p. 238.

in its favor. Bidwell of Massachusetts then moved an amendment, "that no person shall be sold as a slave by virtue of this Act;" and the House divided, sixty against sixty,[1] nearly all the Pennsylvanians supporting Bidwell, while ten of the seventeen New York members showed the influence of slavery in their State by voting with the Southern slave-owners. Six Southern men, including the member for Delaware, joined the Pennsylvanians and New Englanders in this protest against turning the government into a slave-trading agency, while but two Northern men besides the members from New York voted with the South. Macon, the Speaker, by his casting vote threw out the amendment.

Even after this point was carried, notwithstanding the time wasted in going over and over again the same arguments on either side, the Bill made no progress. Men like Sloan and Smilie were not gifted with great genius, but found infinite resources in their patient obstinacy; and no one could fail to see that the true sympathies of the House were with them. Their first object was to prevent the forfeiture of the negroes, because forfeiture implied title, and the United States government could have no title in these human beings, mere captives in war of barbarous tribes; but on that point the House was decidedly against them, and even Josiah Quincy insisted that they were wrong. Forced to yield on the issue of forfeiture, they resisted with the greater obstinacy the sale of the forfeited negroes; and their objections were so obviously sound that in spite of adverse votes they held the Bill in suspense, and even secured its recommittal to a select committee of their own choice.

The Southerners, who insisted that their knowledge and experience should guide the House on a matter which they then preferred to consider local, chafed under the patient stolidity of Quaker conscientiousness, but submitted, rather in defiance than in conciliation, to throw the Bill into Northern hands. The recommittal was ordered Jan. 8, 1807, by a vote of 76 to 46; January 20 the new Bill was reported, and the struggle began again as at first. January 28 the Senate sent down a Bill of its own for the same purpose. The Senate debates

[1] Annals of Congress, 1806–1807, p. 267.

during the session were not reported, and those of the House were reported only in part, and briefly; but by some means the Senate was persuaded to introduce one rigorous provision into its Bill, prohibiting the coastwise domestic slave-trade in vessels of less burden than forty tons, so that small craft found at sea with cargoes of slaves could not escape under pretence of being engaged in the domestic slave-trade. At best, the Bill could not be effective. The Southern members frankly said that they could frame no Bill likely to be executed, which would prevent slave-traders from smuggling negroes across the Florida boundary or from the West Indian Islands; but the prohibition of the coastwise transport of negroes in small vessels seemed necessary in order to maintain even a pretence of stopping the trade, and the Senate saw no objection to it.

The House hesitated painfully between Pennsylvanian and Virginian influence. Very rarely did the Pennsylvanians assert themselves, and they did so with great moderation; but they were conscientious men, and they had behind them not only the moral support of Jefferson, but also the steady influence of Secretary Gallatin, whose determined hostility to slavery and the slave-trade was proved at every moment of his public life. When, Feb. 9, 1807, the debate was resumed in Committee of the Whole, a majority began by voting in favor of the death-penalty. The next question rose on a new section in regard to forfeitures. The Pennsylvania Bill provided that the forfeited negroes should be indentured for a term of years in some free State or Territory. The proposition seemed reasonable in itself, and calculated to give no offence to the South; but Early declared that the inhabitants of the Southern States would resist this provision with their lives.[1] "We want no civil wars, no rebellions, no insurrections, no resistance to the authority of the government. Give effect, then, to this wish, and do not pass this Bill as it now stands."

Even Pennsylvania patience was disturbed by an outbreak so extravagant. Smilie, who was Irish by birth, obliged Early to take back and explain away his words; but the flash of temper answered its purpose,—Early carried his point. Throughout the struggle the Southern representatives took

[1] Annals of Congress, 1806–1807, p. 477.

the ground that the subject belonged to them; that they were well aware of the defects in the Bill; that they did not expect wholly to stop the trade, although they wished to do so; but that any stronger measure would revolt public opinion in the South, and would leave the trade open, because no one would venture to enforce the Act. Under such circumstances, seeing that in any case the trade would continue, the Pennsylvanians naturally argued that if only in order to assert a principle, the law should be made severe; but they were abandoned by the New Englanders, and beaten. Eleven of the Pennsylvanians clung to the death-penalty in spite of Quaker principles; while not only Barnabas Bidwell, but even Josiah Quincy deserted them. The House ended by leaving to each State the decision as to the fate of the forfeited negroes; and at length, February 13, weary of the interminable dispute, the House adopted the Senate Bill with some amendments.

Hitherto John Randolph had taken little part in the debate; he voted steadily with the Southern representatives, but his well-known antislavery theories kept him quiet. His silence did not last. The Senate disagreed to one of the amendments which had passed the House; a committee of conference reported, and the Bill came up again on their report. In a final debate the Southern members attacked the prohibition of the coastwise trade, the whole measure being thus in their eyes vitiated. Early declared that the Act would not prevent the introduction of a single slave; Randolph asserted that the coastwise prohibition touched the right of private property:[1] "He feared lest, at a future period, it might be made the pretext of universal emancipation; he had rather lose the Bill, he had rather lose all the Bills of the session, he had rather lose every Bill passed since the establishment of the government, than agree to the provision contained in this slave-bill. It went to blow up the Constitution in ruins." He prophesied that if ever the time of disunion between the States should arrive, the line of severance would not be between Eastern and Western, but between slaveholding and non-slaveholding States. He said that if ever the time should come when the South should have to depend on the North for assistance

[1] Annals of Congress, 1806–1807, p. 626.

854 SECOND ADMINISTRATION OF JEFFERSON

against the slaves, he should despair. "All he asked was that the North should remain neutral; that it should not erect itself into an abolition society." The vehemence of the Southern orators was in this instance natural, for the coastwise prohibition cut far more deeply into the constitutional rights of slave-owners than all the other provisions of the Bill which they had so obstinately and successfully resisted; yet on the division they were beaten by the large majority of sixty-three to forty-nine. New York, which cared little for the slaves, cared less for the Constitution, and reversed its former vote. The Senate Bill, Feb. 26, 1807, was sent to the President.[1]

That Randolph and other States-rights Republicans should be deeply irritated was a matter of course. In their effort to tone the Bill to make it suit the opinions of slaveholding communities, they exhausted their strength and the public patience; and they found a precedent slipped upon them, which would warrant almost any legislative interference with slavery. Randolph, alive to the bearings of all legislation which touched his class interests, at once introduced a Bill to explain and amend the Act. Josiah Quincy promptly moved its reference. The day was February 27, and in another week the Ninth Congress would expire. Randolph opposed the reference, and urged the immediate passage of his Bill, but was defeated by a vote of sixty to forty-nine. His Bill was referred to the House in committee; it was even made an order for the next day, but it was never taken up.

Randolph declared the hope that should his Bill fail, the Virginia delegation would wait on the President and remonstrate against his signing the Act for Prohibiting the Slave Trade; but no such step was taken, and March 2, 1807, President Jefferson approved this alarming measure. He at least had no constitutional scruples, and paid no attention to the scruples of others. The only result of the long sectional struggle was to disgust the Southern Republicans and their Pennsylvanian allies alike; while, so far from obtaining a law which should suit Southern views of the slave-trade, their Act shocked the pride and threatened the property of every slave-owner in the South.

[1] Annals of Congress, 1806–1807, p. 635.

The disasters of the Southern, or what was afterward known as the States-rights, party were largely due to temper. The habit of command, giving self-confidence and vigor of will, opened a boundless field for extravagances. The strength of men like Randolph and Early was their chief weakness; they had every sense except the sense of proportion. The mole-hill which tripped them seemed as serious an obstacle as the distant mountain range, where a false step would dash them to fragments; and when at last they reached the mountain range, with its impassable chasms, where temper was helpless, they saw in it only a mole-hill. That men like Sloan, the butt of the house, and like Smilie and Findley, the ordinary representatives of an intellectual mediocrity somewhat beneath the Pennsylvanian average, should habitually end in carrying their points, in singular and unexpected ways, against the ablest leaders of New England Federalism and the most gifted masters of Virginian oratory; that they should root up everything in their path, and end by giving to the whole country the characteristics of their own common-place existence,—was partly due, not to their energy or their talents, but to the contempt which their want of genius inspired. Not their own wisdom, but their antagonists' errors decided the result, and overthrew successively Church and State in New England and a slave-owning oligarchy throughout half the continent. The Southern gentry could not learn patience. John Randolph, in many respects the most gifted man produced by the South in his generation, and certainly the one who most exaggerated the peculiar qualities and faults of his class, flung away the advantages of every success by attempting to punish his opponents,—as though the hare had stopped in his race to beat the tortoise with a whip. Punishment of Pennsylvania Democrats was waste of time and strength; sarcasm did not affect them; social contempt did not annihilate them; defeats made no impression upon them. They had no leaders and no well-defined policy, but they gravitated like inert weights to an equilibrium. What they wanted they were sure in the end to get.

Randolph's disappointment in regard to the slave-bill was but a single example of a law. After domineering over the House during the whole session, and impressing his own character upon its acts, he attempted at the end to coerce it into a quarrel with the Senate. A Bill for repealing the salt-tax and continuing the Mediterranean Fund was sent to the Senate, and the Senate sent it back with an amendment which reduced the duty on salt from twenty cents a bushel to twelve cents, without wholly abolishing it. Usage and courtesy required that a committee of conference should be appointed; but Randolph insisted that the House should abruptly adhere to its original Bill, and he carried his point by the large majority of ninety-three to twenty.[1] The Senate accepted the challenge, and in its turn voted to adhere. The Bill was lost; and while the salt-tax continued in force, producing some five hundred thousand dollars, the Mediterranean Fund, producing one million two hundred thousand dollars, must expire by limitation. Congress reached this point February 26, the same day when the slave-bill was passed against Randolph's protest.

The Pennsylvania members allowed themselves to be drawn into this step; but they had hardly given their votes before waking to their mistake. The next day a committee was moved to reconsider the subject; and in spite of Randolph's remonstrances, the motion was carried by sixty to forty, every Pennsylvanian changing his vote. Randolph, exasperated to the last degree, attempted to block the measure by obstinacy. When the new Bill was taken up in committee of the whole House February 28, he consumed the day in dilatory motions, calling the yeas and nays until he could no longer induce one fifth of the members to support him in asking for them. The House sat until half-past one in the morning; and when at last the Bill came to a vote, Randolph and his friends left the House without a quorum.[2] After several counts, a quorum was reported, and the Bill was passed; but the yeas and nays were not taken, and many suspicions were expressed that a quorum was not actually present. Nevertheless the Pennsylvanians won their victory; the Bill became law at the last moment of the session. Randolph's conduct ended in destroying his own influence; and the Pennsylvanians felt that the time had come when an alliance with the Democrats of New

[1] Annals of Congress, 1806–1807, p. 635.
[2] Diary of J. Q. Adams, i. 464.

England against the oligarchy of Virginia could no longer be postponed.

This was the situation at Washington when, on the last day of the Ninth Congress, a messenger arrived from England bringing from Monroe and Pinkney a treaty of commerce. The President's attempt to unite his party on a liberal domestic policy had not succeeded; and many years were to pass before Congress should see another session devoted to domestic affairs.

Chapter XVI

WHILE THE SUMMER OF 1806 was passing in America, carrying Burr and his insane projects to failure, General Armstrong in Paris was watching the progress of another adventurer, whose plans were as dark as those of Burr, but whose genius was of a very different order. Talleyrand's mysterious instructions regarding Florida were given to Armstrong early in September, 1805. Ulm capitulated October 17; the battle of Trafalgar was fought October 21. Napoleon was thenceforward master of the Continent, and England of the ocean. December 2 Napoleon won the decisive battle of Austerlitz, and December 26 he signed the treaty of Pressburg which humbled Austria.

The wit of man often lagged behind the active movement of the world; but never had diplomatists a harder task than to keep abreast of Napoleon. Other men had moments of repose; but Napoleon's mind seemed never to rest. His schemes were developed, and swept over Europe like so many storm-centres. His plans sometimes succeeded and sometimes failed, but the success or the failure equally implied a greater effort behind; and while Armstrong and his brother diplomatists speculated about the Emperor's motives in pursuing one object, the Emperor was already devising and using new machinery for gaining another. At the close of the war with Austria, Armstrong needed to learn whether Napoleon still wanted money, whether Talleyrand favored the sale of Florida, whether the treaty of Pressburg had or had not left American affairs where they were; and none of these questions could be answered except by Napoleon himself, who was already far advanced in schemes which no one could fathom, and which largely depended for their success on the skill with which he could conceal them from Jefferson.

Armstrong could only wait. Through the winter of 1805–1806, while John Randolph's opposition delayed Madison's instructions to the minister at Paris, Armstrong had nothing to do. The Emperor and Talleyrand returned to Paris at midnight Jan. 26, 1806. More powerful than ever and more absolute, Napoleon came back from Vienna rich with the contributions he had levied in Germany, but angry at the condition into which Marbois had brought the Treasury of France. Within twelve hours after arriving at the Tuileries he called a council of his ministers, disgraced Marbois, and appointed Mollien in his place.

That this revolution in the Cabinet had some bearing upon American interests was more than likely; for not only was Marbois an honest man and a warm friend of the United States, but the weight that dragged him down was nothing less than the weight of Spanish finances. The story may be shortly told.[1] Napoleon's wars and repudiation of every inconvenient debt threw the French mercantile class into general bankruptcy. In the want of coin to supply the demands of the Emperor and of the merchants, the Bank of France issued dangerous amounts of paper money. To support these issues specie had to be obtained; and the empire which produced specie was Spain. Spain might be forced to give up her treasures; her arrears of subsidy alone would if paid add greatly to Marbois's resources. Yet the treasures of Spain were shut in Mexico and Peru; they could be brought to Europe only under danger of capture; and a means by which ten or twenty million Mexican dollars could run the gauntlet of British cruisers and reach in safety the Bank of France was a matter of necessity to Marbois.

The ordinary business of the Treasury in discounts and contracts was conducted through a firm called the "Négociants réunis," consisting of three capitalists,—Messrs. Ouvrard, Desprez, and Vanlerberghe. Ouvrard, the most active of the three, went to Madrid; and by lending assistance to the sorely pressed Treasury and trade of Spain induced the Spanish government to give him the privilege of importing bullion from Mexico at the rate of seventy-five cents on the dollar. The risk of importation was worth twenty-five per cent on any cargo; but Ouvrard meant to escape all risk. He had plans of his own, involving partnership with the British government itself through the Hopes and Barings of Amsterdam and London; he proposed to draw some five million dollars from Mexico by giving to the United States government drafts on South

[1] Thiers, Consulat et Empire, vi. 30.

America in settlement of the Spanish spoliations, besides getting no less than ten million dollars from the United States government for the Floridas.

The unnamed negotiator who came to Armstrong in September, 1805, with Talleyrand's autograph instructions was an agent of Marbois and Ouvrard, whose errand was doubtless known to the Emperor. Meanwhile the Treasury, the Bank, and the "Négociants réunis" supported each other by loans, discounts, and indorsements, largely resting on Spanish bonds, and made face as well as they could against commercial embarrassments and Napoleon's arbitrary calls for great sums of coin; but the Treasury, being in truth the only solvent member of the partnership, must ultimately be responsible for the entire loss whenever matters should come to liquidation.

This was the state of the finances when, Jan. 27, 1806, Napoleon called Marbois and Ouvrard before him. No one charged criminality on any of the parties to the affair. In truth one person alone was to blame, and that person was the Emperor himself; but men who served such masters were always in the wrong,—and in fact Marbois, Ouvrard, Desprez, and Vanlerberghe accepted their fate. Marbois was disgraced; while the three others were obliged to surrender all their property under the alternative of going to Vincennes, with its memories of the Duc d'Enghien.

The dismissal of Marbois and the ruin of Ouvrard had no immediate effect on the Florida negotiation. So far from discouraging Armstrong's hopes, they seemed at first likely to bring about some arbitrary decision, after the Emperor's well-known style of settling questions in which he had an interest. In the middle of February Armstrong wrote in some alarm to Madison:[1] —

"All the points in controversy between his Catholic Majesty and the United States were submitted on the 14th instant to this Government by the Spanish ambassador, with an order from his Court to solicit the immediate interposition of the Emperor and King. That his Majesty will take upon himself the mediation is not to be questioned; but

[1] Armstrong to Madison, Feb. 17, 1806; MSS. State Department Archives.

the form he may think proper to give to it is a point equally doubtful and important. Should this movement on the part of Spain have been spontaneous, growing merely out of her own policy and feelings, there is reason to believe that I may be able to prevent any sudden and unfavorable determination from being taken; but if, on the other hand, it should have been either dictated or invited by this Cabinet, the presumption is strong that the decision is already taken, and will present only the alternative,—submission or hostility. Of the two conjectures, the latter is the more probable."

For the moment, while Napoleon was struggling with the confusion of his finances, he held Florida in reserve as a resource for extremity. Armstrong was officially or semi-officially told that the Emperor supposed the whole matter of the Spanish-American dispute to be regularly before him by consent of both parties.[1] He had another long interview with his unnamed negotiator, who pressed him to accept Spanish drafts on South America in payment of the claims for Spanish spoliations, and who argued with much obstinacy that Florida was well worth ten million dollars to the United States.

During all this time Armstrong had heard not a word from his Government. While the minister was listening to these whispers of imperial policy at Paris, Madison had but begun to write the long-delayed instructions which were in effect an acceptance of Talleyrand's proffered terms. The long-delayed "Two-Million Act" received the President's signature Feb. 13, 1806; but not until March 13 did Madison sign the instructions which contained the project of a convention.[2] This despatch was accompanied by another of March 15, which contained an explanation of the Miranda affair and long complaints of Yrujo's conduct. The law prohibiting trade with St. Domingo, "although it must be understood to have proceeded . . . not from any rightful requisition on the part of France, and still less from a manner of pressing it which might have justly had a contrary tendency," was enclosed in

[1] Armstrong to Madison, March 9, 1806; MSS. State Department Archives.
[2] Madison to Armstrong and Bowdoin, March 13, 1806; MSS. State Department Archives.

the despatch, with instructions to sound the French government in the hope of inducing Napoleon to lay aside his objections to the traffic.

The packet sailed at once; and after a voyage of the usual length arrived in France in time to bring the despatches, May 1, to Armstrong's hands. No apparent change had then taken place in the Emperor's plans; but during the three months of labor since his return from Austria he had succeeded in restoring order to his finances and was richer than ever before. The Spanish government sent to Paris a certain Señor Izquierdo as special agent to make a financial arrangement with Napoleon; and through him much business was done unknown to the department over which Talleyrand presided. In short the situation had changed, although no one, even among the Emperor's immediate household, knew what had taken place.

In pursuance of the secret memorandum in Talleyrand's handwriting, Armstrong, May 1, sent a note to the Foreign Office in the language of his instructions. Talleyrand acted promptly; May 2 he carried Armstrong's note to Napoleon's closet.[1] Without discussing the matter the Emperor said: "I have some papers in relation to that business which you have not seen." The next day these papers were given to him. They consisted in maps and charts of the Floridas, with many arguments to prove their military and naval importance to Spain, and a formal declaration from Don Carlos IV. that on no account would he consent to alienate them either by sale or otherwise.

Talleyrand immediately sent for the American minister and told him what had occurred. Only a few weeks before, with equal appearance of seriousness, Armstrong had been assured that the whole matter was in the Emperor's hands by the request of the Spanish government. May 3 he was suddenly told that King Charles would on no account consent to alienate Florida. If the first story were true the second must be false. Armstrong hinted as much. "Though I have not seen the overture on paper," said he, "yet I am not the less assured that it had existence; and if I have not been much deceived,

[1] Armstrong to Madison (private), May 4, 1806; MSS. State Department Archives.

it may at this moment be found in the portfolio of M. Ouvrard."

"That may be," replied Talleyrand; "but it is not the less true that circumstances have produced an entire change in the dispositions of Spain." Then, as though to protect himself from the charge of deception by making a counter-charge against Armstrong, he suddenly hinted that Armstrong's own conduct had much to do with alarming the pride of Spain.

"Do you know," said he, "that Mr. Erving has communicated to the Prince of Peace the confidential propositions of which you were made the depositary last summer, and that they were derived from Mr. Bowdoin, as it would appear for the express purpose of being so communicated?"

At this unexpected shock, coming instantly after the other, Armstrong was thunderstruck.

"You may readily imagine my confusion and astonishment at this discovery," he continued in his narrative to Madison. "I had confided the propositions to Mr. Bowdoin under the most solemn injunctions of secrecy. . . . Could I believe that a man to whom his country has committed so high an office could so flagrantly violate a trust so sacred?"

His anger was diverted from Talleyrand to his colleague; but in spite of this successful diversion, one might suppose Armstrong capable, even in anger, of seeing that Talleyrand's story was not altogether clear,—that he was trying to distract attention from his own failures.

The more closely Ouvrard's scheme was brought to light, the more clearly it seemed to take the form of an intrigue or a job. The notorious corruption that surrounded Talleyrand explained the favor shown it by the French Foreign Office; but neither the Emperor of France nor the King of Spain was ruled in such matters by subordinates, and Armstrong began to feel the error of making his own Government the instrument of Ouvrard's speculations. Too deeply involved to draw back he took refuge in caution, and said even to the Secretary of State as little as he could. Above all, he avoided reference to possible corruption involved in the bargain. His colleague Bowdoin, whose garrulity had already annoyed him, did not imitate Armstrong's reticence, but wrote to the President the facts which Jefferson least cared to know. The profits on the Louisiana stock, he said,[1] had stimulated jobbery; fifteen per cent discount on one million seven hundred and ten thousand dollars had been divided among the individuals concerned. The two Floridas were offered by Daniel Parker, agent of the Hopes in Amsterdam, who came with a letter of recommendation from Labouchere, Sir Francis Baring's son-in-law, and who held or pretended to hold powers of transfer from the Prince of Peace. The highest point to which the propositions could be traced was to one Cazeneau, Parker's friend, who lived in Talleyrand's house. Some time afterward Bowdoin added[2] that a new negotiator had appeared,—a former private secretary to Talleyrand,—a M. Dautremont, who came to Skipwith, the American consul at Paris, and after explaining that the X. Y. Z. business and the jealousy of the American government had caused much uneasiness in matters of this delicate nature, suggested that other means less exposed than money to observation might be devised. He thought well of land-grants to Talleyrand's brother, in which Skipwith might take a share.

With so many different persons and interests involved in the Floridas and the claims, Armstrong might feel confident that a single rebuff from the Emperor would not end the matter. After a few weeks Talleyrand quietly instigated the American minister to renew his request, which was done by a note of May 25;[3] and May 28 Armstrong received in reply an official assurance of "his Majesty's wishes to see the controversy amicably terminated, and his readiness to lend himself to that object." Talleyrand was not only in earnest but in haste; for on the same day, May 28, he wrote to M. de Vandeul, who was in charge of the French embassy at Madrid, a cautious letter of instructions. The United States government, he said,[4] seemed disposed to renew negotiations with

---

[1] Bowdoin to Jefferson, May 20, 1806; Jefferson MSS.
[2] Bowdoin to Jefferson, Oct. 20, 1806; Jefferson MSS.
[3] Armstrong to Madison, Oct. 10, 1806; MSS. State Department Archives.
[4] Talleyrand to Vandeul, May 21, 1806; Archives des Aff. Étr., MSS.

Spain. He ran over the points in dispute, and sketched the outlines of an arrangement, including the cession of West Florida.

"You will have, sir, to express no official opinion on this point," he said. "I need only tell you, in order that you may make use of it in your conversations, that this part of the Floridas must be warmly desired by the Americans, because it closes the mouths of several rivers which have a great part of their course within the United States. Under another Power Florida, so situated, can intercept American commerce; and since the Province is thinly populated and very accessible by land, it is to be presumed that the United States would seize the first pretext for invasion. If Spain is not bent on preserving this colony, she may listen to the American propositions; and all that she would have to remark in making this arrangement is that West Florida, which brings very little revenue to her, would be a much more valuable possession for the United States."

Vandeul was intimate with G. W. Erving, the American *chargé* at Madrid; and with friendly zeal he entered into the negotiation. Taking Talleyrand's despatch and Armstrong's note, a copy of which was inclosed for his guidance, he went to the Prince of Peace, with whom he had a long conversation June 18, 1806.

"To tell your Excellency the truth," he wrote the next day to Talleyrand,[1] "I ought to inform you that the Prince of Peace appears to me to hold pronounced opinions excessively opposed to the conciliatory views which I should have wished to find in him. Nevertheless I did my best to bring him to less passionate ideas, and asked him whether he did not think it a matter of general interest that the old relations should be restored between Spain and the United States, even admitting (for this is one of the Prince's allegations) that they were only suspended for the moment as to official forms. He answered me that this state of things was in no way prejudicial to the interests of the two countries; that commerce continued between them under the

[1] Vandeul to Talleyrand, June 19, 1806; Archives des Aff. Étr., MSS.

safeguard of reciprocal good faith; and that this mode of existence might last a long time without disquieting Spain."

Vandeul was obliged to urge the Emperor's wish for a reconciliation and the advance made by Armstrong at Paris. Thereupon Godoy suddenly changed his tone. "At bottom," said he, "we are quite ready to see where they want to come out; you may assure your Court of that." Vandeul thanked him, and added that he hoped the Prince would be pleased to have the matter negotiated at Paris. "Well, granted again!" answered Godoy; "I see no inconvenience in consenting to that." "Your Excellency authorizes me to inform M. de Talleyrand by my first despatch?" "By your first despatch."

Greatly pleased at his success, Vandeul immediately wrote to Talleyrand. A few days afterward he returned to the Prince of Peace, and in a long interview undertook to dispose of the whole subject.[1] Godoy objected chiefly that as yet no official representation had been made on which the Government of Spain could act. Vandeul urged that Armstrong's note and Talleyrand's instructions were sufficient proof that the Americans had changed their tone and system. In his earnestness he insisted upon expressing his opinion on all the points in dispute, including the cession of West Florida.

"Then the Prince gave way entirely to the accession that I asked; and in a manner that I found not only open, but even friendly, told me to renew to you what he had previously authorized me to write to you, and to add that ministerial measures should decidedly be taken for a suitable expression of the intentions of the Spanish Court both to your Highness and to the American ministers, with views of conciliation and definite arrangement, in the dispute with the United States."

Vandeul was convinced that the Prince spoke the truth, and he hurried to tell Erving. The American *chargé*, though far from friendly to Spain, believed that Godoy was honest; and he hastened to notify Armstrong. Armstrong had no doubt that all was well, and lost no time in consulting Talleyrand,

[1] Vandeul to Talleyrand, June 23, 1806; Archives des Aff. Étr., MSS.

who had every motive to feel sure of success. The Spanish imbroglio seemed on the verge of a friendly settlement.

Suddenly occurred one of the scenes of melodrama to which the Emperor's servants were accustomed. When Talleyrand brought Vandeul's despatch to his master, Napoleon broke into a passion. Rebuking Talleyrand sharply for having pressed the matter in its first stages, he threatened to degrade and punish Vandeul; and he ordered Talleyrand not only to reprimand his subordinate in the severest manner, but himself to meddle no more with the subject.[1] His orders were instantly followed with the blind obedience which marked the Emperor's service. Vandeul was still congratulating himself on his success, and waiting for a letter of approval from Paris, when a despatch arrived which shivered his diplomatic triumph. Without a word of explanation, Talleyrand administered the reproof he had been ordered to give. Vandeul was told that he had gone altogether beyond his instructions:[2] —

"To cause the negotiations of these two Governments to be opened under his Majesty's eyes would be to associate him in all their quarrels and to render him more or less responsible for the results. He will see with pleasure the return of a good understanding between the two countries; but they alone can judge what means of reconciliation suit their respective interests."

A few days afterward came another and sharper reprimand:[3] —

"In demanding that the negotiation should take place at Paris, in making overtures to the United States minister while he has not even received instructions from his Government, in leading the Prince of Peace to believe that everything would be done under the mediation of France,—you exceed the instructions marked out for you; and such is the effect of one false step, that it inevitably draws others after it before the system which has been forsaken can be resumed. That Spain and the United States

[1] Armstrong to Madison, Oct. 10, 1806; MSS. State Department Archives.
[2] Talleyrand to Vandeul, July 3, 1806; Archives des Aff. Étr., MSS.
[3] Talleyrand to Vandeul, July 12, 1806; Archives des Aff. Étr., MSS.

should seek a reconciliation is to be desired; but leave to them the opening of negotiation, and take only such steps as are marked out for you,—such are his Majesty's orders. The United States and Spain will communicate their intentions to each other. You cannot charge yourself with the always embarrassing functions of an intermediary without being formally authorized to do it; for the Government alone can know whether this step is consistent with its interests of the moment and with the general plan it has formed for itself."

That the words of this despatch were taken from the Emperor's lips is more than likely. Talleyrand's notes always repeated as nearly as possible the exact expressions of his master; and the expressions of this note were Napoleonic even in their confusion of facts and ideas. Above all, the concluding sentence, which was probably as mysterious to Talleyrand as to the Americans, marked the proceeding with the peculiar stamp of Napoleon's mind. No one but himself should judge whether the cession of Florida was "consistent with his interests of the moment and with the general plan he had formed for himself." Probably for the first time, July 12, 1806, Talleyrand learned that Napoleon had a general plan which was inconsistent with complete reconciliation between Spain and the United States; yet he could no longer doubt that the same general plan had controlled the Emperor's conduct at least as far back as May 1. From this reticence he might infer that his own fall approached. Another proof that his credit waned came in a form more gracious, but not less convincing. Napoleon conferred on him an Italian principality. The Ex-Bishop of Autun became Prince of Benevento.

Had Armstrong been allowed to know every detail of this transaction, he could not have penetrated Napoleon's secret; but for weeks he was kept in dense ignorance. Aware that the Prince of Peace had consented to negotiate, informed that Izquierdo had received powers and was authorized to proceed, Armstrong still found an invisible barrier across his path,— frivolous difficulties of form and unmeaning references to Madrid,—which no effort of his could remove. At a hint from Talleyrand he went to Marshal Duroc, a man of high character and abilities, who stood as near as the nearest to the Emperor, and who was conducting with Izquierdo the Spanish negotiations which Napoleon had taken from Talleyrand. Duroc seemed well disposed toward America; and through him Armstrong succeeded in putting into Napoleon's hands the project of a treaty between the United States and Spain. After reading it attentively, the Emperor quietly returned it, without a word.

Foiled again by this impenetrable mystery, Armstrong dreamed of forcing the Emperor's hand. He could at least, by an official note, compel Talleyrand and Izquierdo either to act or to explain their inaction; but from this step he was dissuaded by Talleyrand and Duroc, who reasoned that precipitancy might do harm, but could do no good.

Meanwhile Talleyrand wrote a despatch[1] to Turreau at Washington; and if Turreau understood its meaning, his insight was clearer than that of the Prince of Benevento himself. The tone of this instruction varied between a caress and a threat; but the threat came last, and was most significant:—

"His Majesty would be pained to remark that the United States, to whose prosperity France has at all times contributed,—that Spain, in whom she takes a like interest,—should revive in America quarrels that are beginning to slumber in Europe. The United States, which owe their fortune to commerce, are interested in peace; they have reason to wish it with their neighbors; and if, comparing their force with that of a colony, they can promise themselves success at first, they can also bear in mind (reconnaître) that the colonies are not alone, and that Europe has always gone to their aid. Take care, sir, to maintain the United States in the views of conciliation with which the news of the events of the last campaign may have inspired them. A sense of their true interests would suffice to make them true to this disposition, even though they had not bound themselves to it by the demand they have made on his Majesty the Emperor to intervene in their discussions with Spain, and to employ his good offices for the re-establishment of a perfect harmony between the two Powers. His Majesty, without

[1] Talleyrand to Turreau, July 31, 1806; Archives des Aff. Étr., MSS.

putting himself forward as mediator in circumstances where other interests, which directly concern his empire, ought to fix his whole attention, will regard whatever the United States and Spain may do toward a reconciliation as an evidence of friendship toward himself."

Sept. 25, 1806, the Emperor returned to Germany to begin a war with Prussia which was to lead him far. His departure put an end to whatever hopes Armstrong still cherished, while it left the United States in a mortifying attitude. After having been defied by Spain, Jefferson found himself deluded by France. No imagination could conceive the purpose for which Napoleon meant to use the United States government; but that he had some scheme, to which President Jefferson must be made subservient, was clear. Armstrong tried in vain to penetrate the mystery. Whatever it might be, it was as yet hidden in the recesses of Napoleon's mind.

No sooner had the Emperor left Paris than the American minister, September 30, wrote a note of inquiry to Izquierdo, who replied in substance that his powers had been suspended or recalled. Nothing remained but for Armstrong to inform the President of all the facts connected with the failure of his negotiation, and then to wait at Paris, with what patience he could command, for the moment when Napoleon should consent to reveal the meaning of these mysterious manœuvres. Yet in diplomacy as in war, nations were commonly lost when they allowed Napoleon to take the initiative, and to choose his own time and place for attack. The United States government had every reason to be on its guard.

Napoleon reached the battle-field of Jena Oct. 14, 1806, and crushed the Prussian army. October 27 the conquering French battalions made a triumphal entry into Berlin. November 25,—the day so frequently occurring in the story of Burr's conspiracy, when Jefferson received General Wilkinson's despatch, and when Wilkinson himself reached New Orleans,—the Emperor Napoleon left Berlin for Poland and Russia. Before leaving Berlin he signed a paper destined to become famous throughout the world under the name of the Berlin Decree. This extraordinary mandate, bearing the date of Nov. 21, 1806, began by charging that England disregarded the law of nations. She made non-combatants prisoners of war; confiscated private property; blockaded unfortified harbors and mouths of rivers, and considered places as blockaded though she had not a single ship before them,—even whole coasts and empires. This monstrous abuse of the right of blockade had no other object than to raise the commerce and industry of England on the ruin of the commerce and industry of the Continent, and gave a natural right to use against her the same weapons and methods of warfare. Therefore, until England should recognize and correct these violations of law, it was decreed—(1) That the British Isles were in a state of blockade; (2) That all intercourse with them was prohibited; (3) That every Englishman found within French authority was a prisoner of war; (4) That all British property, private as well as public, was prize of war; (5) That all merchandise coming from England was prize of war; (6) That half the product of such confiscations should be employed to indemnify merchants whose property had been captured by British cruisers; (7) That no ship coming from England or her colonies should be admitted into any port; (8) That every vessel trying to elude this rule by means of false papers should be confiscated.

This decree, which cut the roots of neutral rights and of American commerce with Europe, was published at Paris in the "Moniteur" of Dec. 5, 1806. At the same time news arrived that Hamburg, and nearly all the north coast of Germany along the German Ocean and the Baltic, had fallen into Napoleon's hands, or was certain soon to become his prey. When Armstrong, watching with keen interest the rapid progress of French arms, took up the "Moniteur" which contained the Berlin Decree, he might well have started to his feet with the cry that at last he understood what the Emperor would be at. A part of the enigma which had perplexed diplomacy was explained, and what was not yet revealed might vaguely be divined.

December 10 Armstrong wrote to Decrès, the Minister of Marine, to ask of him, in Talleyrand's absence, an explanation of the decree. For some days no answer was received. "Much is said here," he wrote to Madison, "of qualifications which are to be given to the *arrêté* of November 20 [21], and which would indeed make it very harmless; but these are rather to be hoped for than believed in." When Decrès' reply arrived, dated December 24, it went far to confirm Armstrong's fears, by avoiding decisive and official explanation.[1]

"I consider the imperial decree of the 21st of November last," wrote Decrès, "as thus far conveying no modification of the regulations at present observed in France with regard to neutral navigators, nor consequently of the convention of Sept. 30, 1800, with the United States of America; . . . but it will be proper that your Excellency should communicate with the Minister of Exterior Relations as to what concerns the correspondence of citizens of the United States with England. . . . It will not escape General Armstrong that my answers cannot have the development which they would receive from the Minister of Exterior Relations, and that it is naturally to him that he ought to address himself for these explanations, which I am very happy to give him, because he wishes them, but upon which I have much less positive information than the Prince of Benevento."

With this explanation, such as it was, Armstrong was obliged to content himself; and the year 1806 closed, leaving President Jefferson at the mercy of battles soon to be fought in the most distant corner of Germany, where the Emperor Alexander of Russia was gathering his forces for a conflict more terrible than Europe had yet seen.

[1] Armstrong to Madison, Dec. 24, 1806; State Papers, ii. 805.

Chapter XVII

WHILE ARMSTRONG coped with Napoleon in Paris, Monroe enjoyed a brief moment of sunshine on the other side of the Channel. After his diplomatic disasters he might think himself happy, though he only threw from his own shoulders upon those of Armstrong and Bowdoin the Florida negotiation which had thus far injured the reputation of every man connected with it; but he had double cause of rejoicing. He not only escaped from Talleyrand and Godoy, but also from William Pitt, whose body he saw carried amidst the pompous mournings of London in funeral state to Westminster Abbey, and left in solemn grandeur by the side of his great father. Pitt died Jan. 23, 1806, exhausted by the anxieties of office.

At last Fortune smiled upon Monroe with caresses more winning than any she had shown since her last sudden appearance before his eyes under the outward semblance of Barbé Marbois in Livingston's garden on the Boulevard Montmartre. Old King George, knowing no Tory competent to succeed Pitt or capable of controlling Parliament, summoned Lord Grenville and submitted to Charles James Fox. Grenville became First Lord of the Treasury; Fox took charge of the Foreign Office; Erskine became Lord Chancellor; Sidmouth, Lord Privy Seal. The union of different party chiefs was so general as to give the Ministry the nickname of All the Talents. By February 7 the revolution was completed.

Monroe was greatly pleased, as well he might be, for his position in England had been hitherto far from comfortable. To soothe the Tories,—who were prejudiced against him not only as American minister, but also as having when minister to France actively sympathized with the French Directory in hostility to England,—Monroe had thought himself obliged to shun the society of the Whigs, and had been restricted to such social relations as Pitt's friends would supply, which under the best of circumstances were neither extensive nor amusing. Fox made amends for this self-denial. His statesmanship was broad and liberal, his manners charming, and he had the quality, most rare in politics, of entire frankness and truthfulness. In a few days Monroe wrote home that he had enjoyed his first interview with the new secretary, "who in half an hour put me more at my ease than I have ever felt with any person in office since I have been in England."[1] Fox said little, but held out hopes; and Monroe had so long been left without even hope to nourish him that he gladly fed upon the unaccustomed diet. Nevertheless, more than a month passed before he ventured to make formal application[2] for an order to suspend the seizure and condemnation of American vessels under the rule established by Pitt and Sir William Scott. At length, April 17, at the Queen's drawing-room Fox took the American minister aside and announced himself ready to begin negotiation, and to pursue it without delay till it should be concluded.[3] He said that no trouble need be feared about the colonial trade, but that there would be objections to making payments for property already taken; meanwhile the seizures and condemnations were to be stopped.

The 1st of May arrived. Three months had passed since the new Ministry took office, yet nothing had been publicly done to satisfy the United States. The reason was well known. Fox was obliged to overcome many kinds of opposition both in and out of the Cabinet. The West Indian colonies, the royal navy, the mercantile shipping interest, the Tory country gentlemen, and the Court were all opposed to concessions, and only the Treasury favored them. To increase Fox's difficulties, news began to arrive from the United States of the debate in Congress on the Non-importation Act, of the loose talk of Congressmen and the vaporings of the press; and to crown all came the story that the mob of New York had taken the punishment of Pierce's manslaughter into its own hands. The English people honestly believed the Americans to be cheating them in the matter of the colonial trade; they suspected that their Yankee cousins were shrewd, and they could plainly see that Jefferson and Congress were trying to hide behind the shadow of Napoleon. Non-importation and commercial

---

[1] Monroe to Madison, Feb. 12, 1806; MSS. State Department Archives.
[2] Monroe to Madison, April 3, 1806; State Papers, iii. 115.
[3] Monroe to Madison, April 18, 1806; State Papers, iii. 116.

restriction had no other object than to give England the alternative of surrendering either to France or to America what she believed to be the price of her existence without the chance of fighting for it. Two thirds of the British people understood the Non-importation Act as a threat,—as though the Americans said, "Surrender to us your commerce and your shipping, or surrender your liberties to France."

Whatever were the faults or sins of England, they were at least such as Americans could understand. Her Government was guided, as a rule, by interests which were public, permanent, and easily measured. The weight of interests which had driven Pitt into his assault on American commerce was not lessened by the death of Pitt or by the return of Lord Grenville to power. On every side Fox found these interests active in opposition and earnest in pressing arguments against concession. Englishmen were used to giving and receiving hard blows. Seldom long at peace, they had won whatever was theirs by creating a national character in which personal courage was as marked a quality as selfishness; for in their situation no other than a somewhat brutal energy could have secured success. They knew what to think of war, and could measure with some approach to exactness its probable costs and returns, but they were quite unused to being conquered by peace; and they listened with as much contempt as anger to the American theory that England must surrender at discretion if Americans should refuse any longer to buy woollen shirts and tin kettles. Englishmen asked only whether America would fight, and they took some pains to make inquiries on that point; but it happened that of all the points in question this, which to Englishmen was alone decisive, could be answered in a syllable: No! America would not fight. The President, Congress, the press of both parties in the United States agreed only in this particular. John Randolph's speech on Gregg's Resolution was reprinted in London with a long preface by James Stephen, and proved conclusively that America would submit. Merry came as near to a laugh as his gravity would permit in expressing his contempt for the idea of war, and in urging his Government to resent the Non-importation Act; and although Fox probably thought poorly of Merry's judgment, he could not but show his despatches to the Cabinet if the Cabinet wished to read them. After the slaughter of Pierce, when the Federalist newspapers in New York and the irresponsible mob of seamen clamored for warlike measures, the only effect of the outcry upon England was to stimulate the anti-American prejudice and to embarrass the well-meant efforts of Fox, until his chief newspaper, the "Morning Chronicle," in a moment of irritation plainly told the Americans that they were much mistaken if they thought a war would be so very unpopular in England; and if they knew this, they would not hector or bully so much. Even the powerful interests directly engaged in trade with the United States made no attempt to protect themselves; they did not see that the British nation was ready and eager to cut its own throat in its desperate anxiety to save its own life. The contest with France had made all Europe violent and brutal; but England could boast that at the sound of British cannon the chaos had become order, that the ocean had been divided from the land, and as far as the ocean went, that her fleets made law. Two Powers only remained to be considered by Great Britain,— Russia and the United States. Napoleon showed an evident intention to take charge of the one; England thought herself well able to give law to the other.

Against such public inclination toward measures of force Fox struggled as he could, without united support even in the Cabinet. Men like Lord Sidmouth were little inclined to risk the fate of the new Administration by concessions to America; and the Tories, led by Canning and Spencer Perceval, profited by every English prejudice in order to recover their control of the government. Fox could carry his point only by adopting half-measures. Instead of procuring a new judicial decision or issuing an Order in Council, as had been done in previous times, for replacing American commerce in its old privileges, he caused Government to adopt a measure intended to produce the same effect, but resting on a principle quite as objectionable to Americans as the Rule of 1756 itself had ever been. May 16, 1806, the ministers of neutral Powers were notified that the King had ordered a blockade of the whole French and German coast from Brest to the river Elbe, but that this blockade was to be strict and rigorous only between Ostend and the Seine; while elsewhere neutral ships should not be liable to seizure in entering or leaving the blockaded ports except under the usual conditions which made them seizable in any case. Under this blockade an American ship laden in New York with sugar, the product of French or Spanish colonies, might sail in safety for Amsterdam or Hamburg. Monroe wrote:[1] "It seems clearly to put an end to further seizures on the principle which has been heretofore in contestation."

English statutes, like English law, often showed peculiar ingenuity in inventing *a posteriori* methods of reaching their ends; but no such device could be less satisfactory than that of inventing a fictitious blockade in order to get rid of a commercial prohibition. Interminable disputes arose in the course of the next few years in regard to the objects and legality of this measure, which came to be known as Fox's blockade, and as such became a point of honor with England; but its chief interest was its reflection of the English mind. To correct a dangerous principle by setting an equally dangerous precedent; to concede one point by implication, and in doing so to assert another not less disputed; to admit a right by appearing to deny it; and to encourage commerce under the pretence of forbidding it,—was but admitting that the British government aimed at illegitimate objects. America had always contested the legality of paper blockades as emphatically as she had contested the Rule of 1756, and could no more submit to the one than to the other, although in this case the paper blockade was invented in order to conciliate and satisfy her. The measure was intended for a temporary expedient pending negotiation; yet such was the condition of England that Fox's blockade became six years afterward one of the chief pretexts under which the two countries entered upon a war.

Another fortnight elapsed, but Monroe made no further progress. Whenever he saw Fox the subjects in dispute were discussed; but news arrived that the Non-importation Act had passed both Houses of Congress, and the difficulty of obtaining favors was increased by the attempt at compulsion. Fox showed less and less willingness to concede principles, although he did not, as Monroe feared, declare that the Act

[1] Monroe to Madison, May 17, 1806; State Papers, iii. 124.

relieved him from any promises he might have made or from the fulfilment of any hopes he might have held out. Thus the matter stood, balanced almost equally between opposite chances, when, May 31, 1806, news arrived from America that Monroe's powers were superseded by the appointment of a special mission, in which he was to be associated with William Pinkney of Maryland.

The blow to Monroe's pride was great, and shook his faith in the friendship of Jefferson and Madison. Three years had elapsed since he had himself been sent abroad to share Livingston's negotiations, and he had the best reason to know how easily the last comer could carry away the prizes of popularity. The nomination of a colleague warned him that he had lost influence at home, and that Jefferson, however well disposed, no longer depended on him. This was in substance the truth; but other and graver troubles were revealed in part to Monroe's eyes when William Pinkney arrived in London June 24, bringing with him the new instructions which were to become the foundation of the treaty.

These instructions[1] began by treating the Non-importation Act as at once a domestic and a foreign regulation, a pacific and a hostile act, a measure with which England had no right to be angry, and one which was calculated to anger her,— strictly amicable and at the same time sharply coercive. After this preamble, in which the threat was clearer than the explanation, followed an order precluding the possibility of successful negotiation. Monroe was to begin by imposing an ultimatum. The British government must expressly repudiate the right and forbid the practice of impressment, or not only could no treaty be made, but the Non-importation Act should be enforced. "So indispensable is some adequate provision for the case that the President makes it a necessary preliminary to any stipulation requiring a repeal of the Act shutting the market of the United States against certain British manufactures."

Besides this condition precedent, the instructions prescribed as another ultimatum the restoration of the trade with enemies' colonies on its old foundation and indemnity

---

[1] Madison to Monroe and Pinkney, May 17, 1806; State Papers, iii. 119.

for the captures made under Sir William Scott's late decisions. Three ultimata, therefore, were fixed as conditions without which no treaty could receive the President's assent or procure a repeal of the Non-importation Act. The numerous requests to be further made upon Fox concerned many different points in dispute,—contraband, blockade, discriminating duties, immunity of neutral waters, East and West Indian trade, and trade with Nova Scotia; but these were matters of bargain, and the two negotiators might to some extent use discretion in dealing with them. Yet every demand made by the United States required a corresponding concession from England, for which no equivalent could be offered by the American negotiators except the repeal of the Non-importation Act.

Monroe knew that Jefferson had ever strongly opposed any commercial treaty with Great Britain, and that he never spoke of Jay's treaty except with disgust and something like abhorrence. Again and again Jefferson had said and written that he wished for no treaty; that he preferred to rely on municipal legislation as his safeguard against attack; and that he would not part with this weapon in order to obtain the doubtful protection of an agreement which England could always interpret to suit herself. Pinkney could add that Jefferson, as every one in Washington was aware, had been unwillingly driven into the present negotiation by the Senate, and that as the measure was not his its success would hardly be within his expectation; that it would embarrass his relations with Napoleon, endanger if not ruin the simultaneous negotiation for Florida, and exalt Monroe, the candidate of Randolph, at the expense of Madison, who was already staggering under the attacks of his enemies.

Monroe was well informed of the efforts made to raise or to depress his own fortunes at Washington, and could see how easily his rival, the Secretary of State, might play a double part. Nothing could be simpler than such tactics. Madison had only to impose on Monroe the task of negotiating a treaty under impossible conditions. If the treaty should fail, the blame would fall upon Monroe; if it should succeed, the credit would be divided with Pinkney. No one could suppose that Madison would make any great effort to secure the success of a negotiation when success might make the negotiator the next President of the United States.

Monroe could not doubt the President's coldness toward the treaty; he could not fail to see that the secretary's personal wishes were rather against than for it; and when he studied the instructions he could not but admit that they were framed, if not with the intention, at all events with the effect, of making a treaty impossible. No harder task could well have been imposed than was laid upon Monroe. Not even when he had been sent to Madrid in defiance of Talleyrand and Godoy, to impose his own terms on two of the greatest Powers in the world, had his chance of success been smaller than when his Government required him to obtain from England, after the battle of Trafalgar, concessions which England had steadily refused when she was supposed to be drawing almost her last gasp. For a British ministry to abandon the Rule of 1756 was to challenge opposition; to throw open the colonial trade was to invite defeat; but to surrender the so-called right of impressment was to rush upon destruction. No minister that had ever ruled over the House of Commons could at such a moment have made such a treaty without losing his place or his head.

If America wanted such concessions she must fight for them, as other nations had done ever since mankind existed. England, France, and Spain had for centuries paid for their power with their blood, and could see no sufficient reason why America should take their hard-won privileges without a challenge. Jefferson thought otherwise. In his opinion, all the three Powers would end by conceding American demands, not as a matter of abstract right but for fear of throwing the United States into the arms of an enemy. The instructions to Monroe rested on this idea; and that no doubt might remain, Jefferson wrote to Monroe a private letter which expressed the doctrine in set terms.

"No two countries upon earth," said the President,[1] "have so many points of common interest and friendship; and their rulers must be great bunglers indeed if with such dispositions they break them asunder. The only rivalry that

[1] Jefferson to Monroe, May 4, 1806; Works, v. 12.

can arise is on the ocean. England may by petty-larceny thwartings check us on that element a little; but nothing she can do will retard us there one year's growth. We shall be supported there by other nations, and thrown into their scale to make a part of the great counterpoise to her navy. If, on the other hand, she is just to us, conciliatory, and encourages the sentiment of family feelings and conduct, it cannot fail to befriend the security of both. We have the seamen and materials for fifty ships of the line and half that number of frigates; and were France to give us the money and England the dispositions to equip them, they would give to England serious proofs of the stock from which they are sprung and the school in which they have been taught, and added to the efforts of the immensity of sea-coast lately united under one Power would leave the state of the ocean no longer problematical. Were, on the other hand, England to give the money and France the dispositions to place us on the sea in all our force, the whole world, out of the continent of Europe, might be our joint monopoly. We wish for neither of these scenes. We ask for peace and justice from all nations, and we will remain uprightly neutral in fact."

This was masterful not to say dictatorial language; for it came in support of categorical claims which, however just, were vehemently opposed by every conservative interest in England. The claims which Monroe was to make as ultimata could not be conceded by England without opening the door to claims more sweeping still. In the same breath with which the President threatened England with fifty ships of the line in case she would not abjure the right of impressment and the Rule of 1756, he added:—

"We begin to broach the idea that we consider the whole Gulf Stream as of our waters, in which hostilities and cruising are to be frowned on for the present, and prohibited as soon as either consent or force will permit us. We shall never permit another privateer to cruise within it, and shall forbid our harbors to national cruisers. This is essential for our tranquillity and commerce."

These were bold words, but not well suited to Monroe's

task or likely to encourage his hopes. President Jefferson was not only bent upon forcing England to abandon by treaty the right of impressment and the control of the colonial trade; he not only asked for liberal favors in many different directions, which required the whole fabric of British legislation to be reconstructed, without equivalent on the part of the United States,—but he had also "begun to broach the idea" that he should dictate where England's line-of-battle ships might sail upon the ocean. Monroe knew how such language would sound to English ears strained to hear the distant thunders from Trafalgar, and how such words would look to English eyes, dim with tears, as they watched their hero borne through the shrouded streets of London to rest in his glory beneath the dome of St. Paul's. That England was inflated with her triumphs, mad in her pretensions, intolerable in her arrogance, was true. A people that had swept the ocean of enemies and held the winds and waves for subjects could hardly fail to go mad with the drunkenness of such stormy grandeur. The meanest beggar in England was glorified with the faith that his march was o'er the mountain waves and his home upon the deep; and his face would have purpled with rage at the idea that Jefferson should dare to say that the squadrons of England must back their topsails and silence their broadsides when they reached the edge of the Gulf Stream.

With this picture before his eyes, Monroe could feel no great confidence either in his own success or in the good faith of the President's instructions, which tied him to impossible conditions. Nevertheless he accepted the task; and as he had gone to Spain with the certainty of defeat and mortification, he remained in London to challenge a hopeless contest. As though to destroy his only chance of success, on the very day of Pinkney's arrival Fox fell ill. His complaint was soon known to be dropsical, and his recovery hopeless. Two months passed, while the American envoys waited the result. Aug. 20, 1806, Fox, being still unable to do business, appointed Lord Holland and Lord Auckland to carry on the negotiation in his place. No better men could have been selected. Lord Holland especially, Fox's favorite nephew and the most liberal of all Whig noblemen, was warmly disposed

to make the negotiation a success; but much invaluable time
had been lost, and Napoleon was on the eve of Jena.

The negotiation began in earnest August 27, but proved to
be long and arduous. The two British commissioners, though
courteous and friendly, stood in constant fear of the charge
that they had surrendered vital English interests under American threats. They were especially hampered by the Admiralty,
the atmosphere of which, as Lord Holland complained,[1]
made those who breathed it shudder at anything like concessions to the Americans; while the Treasury, though naturally
still less yielding, listened willingly to every expedient that offered hope for the revenue. September 1 began the struggle
over impressments; and from the outset Monroe saw that the
American claim had no chance of success, while the case of
the West Indian trade was almost equally desperate. Only one
serious discussion had taken place when the death of Fox,
September 13, produced a new delay of several weeks; and on
resuming the negotiation, Monroe and Pinkney were required
to deal with a new Foreign Secretary,—Charles Grey, Lord
Howick,—to be better known in English history as Earl
Grey. Such a change boded no good to the Americans. All
Fox's influence could not counteract the Tory instincts of Parliament; and what Fox could not do when the Whigs were
strong could much less be done by Lord Howick when the
Ministry was every day tottering to its fall.

November 11 the American negotiators wrote home that
they had decided to disregard their instructions and to abandon impressments,—accepting, instead of a formal article
on the subject, a note in which the British commissioners
pledged their government to exercise the strictest care not to
impress American citizens, and to afford prompt redress
should injury be inflicted while impressing British seamen.
Having thus made up his mind to violate instructions on the
chief point of negotiation, Monroe found nothing to prevent
his doing so in other respects. His progress under William
Pinkney's influence was rapid; his good nature, in the face of
Lord Holland's difficult position, was extreme; and at the end
of a few weeks, Dec. 31, 1806, Jefferson's favorite diplomatic

[1] Memoirs of Lord Holland, ii. 98–103.

agent set his name to a treaty which, taking its omissions and admissions together, surpassed Jay's treaty in outraging Jefferson's prejudices and express desires.

That a people, like an individual, should for a time choose to accept a wrong, like impressment or robbery, without forcible resistance implied no necessary discredit. Every nation at one time or another had submitted to treatment it disliked and to theories of international law which it rejected. The United States might go on indefinitely protesting against belligerent aggressions while submitting to them, and no permanent evil need result. Yet a treaty was a compromise which made precedent; it recorded rules of law which could not be again discarded; and above all, it abandoned protest against wrong. This was doubtless the reason why Jefferson wished for no treaties in the actual state of the world; he was not ready to enforce his rights, and he was not willing to compromise them.

The treaty signed by Monroe and Pinkney Dec. 1, 1806, was remarkable for combining in one instrument every quality to which Jefferson held most strenuous objections. The three ultimata were all abandoned; impressments were set aside under a diplomatic memorandum which rather recorded the right than restrained its exercise; no indemnity was obtained for the ravages made on American commerce in 1805; and in regard to the colonial trade, a compromise was invented which no self-respecting government could admit. Article XI. of the treaty imposed the condition that West Indian produce, coming from French or Spanish colonies, and *bonâ fide* the property of United States citizens, might be exported from American ports to Europe on condition that it should have paid to the United States custom-house a duty of not less than two per cent *ad valorem*, which could not be returned in drawback; while European merchandise might in the same way be re-exported from the United States to the West Indies, provided it paid not less than one per cent *ad valorem* in duties to the American Treasury. This provision was only to be compared with Article XII. of Jay's treaty, in which Lord Grenville insisted and Jay agreed that the United States should export no cotton. Even Pitt had never proposed anything so offensive as the new restriction. He had indeed required that the American merchant whose ship arrived at Baltimore or Boston with a cargo of sugar or coffee from Cuba should unload her, carry the hogsheads and cases into a warehouse, and pass them through all the forms of the American custom-house; after which he must turn about and stow them again on shipboard,—an operation which was usually reckoned as equivalent, in breakage, pilfering, and wages, to a charge of about ten per cent on the value of the cargo; but he had not ventured to levy a duty upon them to be paid to the United States government. One step more, and—as a clever London pamphleteer suggested—the British government would require the American stevedores to wear the King's livery.[1] Had it been stipulated that the custom-house payments should be taken as full proof of neutrality and complete protection from seizure, the American merchant might have found a motive for submitting to the tax; but the treaty further insisted that both goods and vessel must be in good faith American property,—a condition which left the door open as widely as ever to the arbitrary seizures of British cruisers and to the equally arbitrary decisions of admiralty courts.

"We flatter ourselves," wrote Monroe and Pinkney to Madison,[2] "that the sum agreed to be paid will not be felt as a heavy one by our merchants, whose patriotism will be gratified by the recollection that the duty which they pay will redound to the advantage of their country."

Mercantile patriotism was proverbially elastic; yet in the present instance not so much the merchants' gratification as that of the President was to be considered,—and Jefferson's patriotism could hardly approve this tax for the protection of British shipping and produce, which would on the one hand excite the anger of Napoleon, while on the other it conferred advantages merely during the period of war. Another objection existed which in Jefferson's eyes was fatal. He believed implicitly in the efficacy of commercial restrictions; he thought the Non-importation Act a better guaranty of good treatment than the best treaty ever made, and was quite ready

[1] Oil without Vinegar, Medford, London, 1807.
[2] Monroe and Pinkney to Madison, Jan. 3, 1807; State Papers, iii. 145.

to try the experiment of such a measure against England. Yet Article V. of Monroe's treaty pledged him for ten years to abstain from every attempt to discriminate against British commerce.

The smaller points conceded by Monroe and Pinkney were not less likely than the greater ones to disturb Jefferson's temper. The British commissioners refused to remove the export duty of two and a half per cent on British manufactures which Americans paid in excess of what was paid by European consumers. Trade with the British East Indies was restricted to ships which should sail directly from America and return directly thither,—a provision less favorable than Jay had secured. The trade with the British West Indies was a subject so delicate in Parliament that the two Englishmen refused to touch it, saying that any sanction of this trade, coupled with their sanction of the neutral trade with French and Spanish colonies, would endanger the treaty. They would enter into no arrangement of the trade with Nova Scotia, New Brunswick, and Canada. They also refused to accept Madison's ideas in regard to blockades.

Bad as all this was, and contrary to Madison's instructions and Jefferson's private letters, it was not yet the worst. After Monroe had violated his orders,—had abandoned the ultimata and accepted the commercial restrictions which the President disliked,—when the four commissioners were about to sign the treaty, Monroe and Pinkney were startled to hear that the two Englishmen meant to append an explanatory note to their signatures. News of the Berlin Decree had reached England, and its gravity was at once recognized. The British negotiators formally notified Monroe and Pinkney that unless the American government, before ratification, should give security that it would not recognize the decree, his Majesty George III. would not consider himself bound by the signatures of his commissioners.[1] Signature under such a condition seemed rather the act of a suppliant people than of one which had not yet so much as bought the sword it should have used. Nevertheless Monroe signed.

Monroe was often called a very dull man. He was said to

[1] American State Papers, iii. 151.

follow the influence of those who stood near him, and was charged by different and opposed politicians with having a genius for blunders; but either Jefferson or Madison might be excused for suspecting that no man on whom they implicitly relied could violate instructions, sacrifice the principles of a lifetime, and throw infinite embarrassments on his Government without some ulterior motive. They could not be blamed for suspecting that Monroe, in signing his treaty, thought more of the Federalist vote than he did of Madison's political promotion.

Monroe afterward defended his treaty in writings more or less elaborate, but his most candid account of his diplomacy in these years was given in a letter to Colonel Taylor of Caroline, written in the year 1810. Of the British treaty, he said:[1] —

"The failure of our business with Spain and the knowledge of the renewal of the negotiation and the manner of it, which were known to every one, were sensibly felt in our concerns with England. She was not willing to yield any portion of what she called her maritime rights, under the light pressure of the non-importation law, to a Power which had no maritime force, not even sufficient to protect any one of its ports against a small squadron, and which had so recently submitted to great injuries and indignities from Powers that had not a single ship at sea. Under such circumstances, it seemed to me to be highly for the interest of our country and to the credit of our government to get out of the general scrape on the best terms we could, and with that view to accommodate our differences with the great maritime Power on what might be called fair and reasonable conditions, if such could be obtained. I had been slighted, as I thought, by the Administration in getting no answers to my letters for an unusual term, and in being subjected to a special mission, notwithstanding my remonstrance against it on a thorough conviction of its inutility, and by other acts which I could not but feel; yet believing that my service in England would be useful there,

[1] Monroe to Colonel Taylor, 10 Sept., 1810; Monroe MSS., State Department Archives.

and by means thereof give aid to the Administration and to the Republican cause at home, I resolved to stay, and did stay for those purposes. The treaty was an honorable and advantageous adjustment with England. I adopted it in the firm belief that it was so, and nothing has since occurred to change that opinion."

Chapter XVIII

MONROE WAS singularly unfortunate in diplomacy. His disasters came not in any ordinary form of occasional defeat or disappointment, but in waves and torrents of ill-luck. No diplomatist in American history, except Monroe and Pinkney, ever signed a treaty in flagrant contradiction to orders, and at the same time submitted to be told that the opposite party to the contract reserved a right to break it; but if any other man had taken such a step it would have answered for a lifetime, and his mortifications would have ended there. No one could assume that the British ministry would care to do more, pending the ratification of its own treaty. Fox's successor, one of the most liberal Whig noblemen, having imposed on the United States terms which would have been hard as the result of war, with the addition that even these terms were conditional on a declaration of hostilities between the United States and France, the liberal Whigs might be supposed willing to wait for some new pretext before publicly tearing their own treaty to pieces.

If Monroe flattered himself that he had for the moment checked British aggression, he quickly learned his error. The treaty had been signed barely a week when a new Order in Council appeared, which surpassed any belligerent measure of the Tories.[1] Beginning with the premise that Napoleon's Berlin Decree "would give to his Majesty an unquestionable right of retaliation, and would warrant his Majesty in enforcing the same prohibition of all commerce with France which that Power vainly hopes to effect against the commerce of his Majesty's subjects," the order added that King George felt himself bound "to retort upon them the evils of their own injustice," and therefore "ordered that no vessel shall be permitted to trade from one port to another, both which ports shall belong to, or be in the possession of, France or her allies." In other words the Whig ministers, ignoring their fresh treaty with the United States and even the note appended to it, declared that they would not wait for America to resent the Berlin Decree, but that United States vessels

---

[1] Order in Council, of Jan. 7, 1807; American State Papers, iii. 267.

must in future, as a retort for that decree, be deprived of the right to sail from one European port to another. The custom had hitherto prevailed among American shippers of seeking a market according to ruling prices, partly perhaps at Bilbao or Bordeaux, partly at some other French or Mediterranean port. Lord Howick's order of Jan. 7, 1807, which cut short this coasting privilege, was a blow to American commerce sharper than the famous decision of Sir William Scott in the case of the "Essex." Its apparent effect was to double the cost and risk of neutral commerce, while incidentally it asserted a right to prohibit such trade altogether.

Unfortunately more remained behind. The new order was not only an act of violence; it was, according to the Tories, also one of meanness. On its face it purported to be a measure of retaliation, taken in order to retort upon France the evils of Napoleon's injustice. In the Parliamentary debate four weeks afterward, when the order was attacked, all parties argued it as a matter of retaliation. The King's advocate, Sir John Nicholls, who defended it, took the ground that for the moment no severer retaliation was needed; while Spencer Perceval and Lord Castlereagh held that Napoleon's decree should have been retaliated in full.

> "You might turn the provisions of the French decree against themselves," said Perceval;[1] "and as they have said that no British goods should sail freely on the seas, you might say that no goods should be carried to France except they first touched at an English port. They might be forced to be entered at the custom-house, and a certain entry imposed, which would contribute to advance the price and give a better sale in the foreign market to your own commodities."

Sir John Nicholls replied:[2]

> "It was not denied that some steps in retaliation were necessary; and the question was how far the steps that had been taken were adequate. . . . It was necessary to allow a fair trial to what ministers had adopted."

[1] Cobbett's Debates, viii. 632.
[2] Cobbett's Debates, viii. 635.

All this seemed clear and frank; it was equivalent to saying that the rules of international law were henceforth to be laid aside, and that the doctrine of retaliation was to be the measure of England's rights. Yet this was not the form in which Lord Howick addressed President Jefferson.

"His Majesty," wrote Lord Howick to Erskine,[1] " with that forbearance and moderation which have at all times distinguished his conduct, has determined for the present to confine himself to the exercise of the power given him by his decided naval superiority in such a manner only as is authorized by the acknowledged principles of the law of nations."

In Parliament the measure was represented as an extra-legal act, justified by the illegality of the Berlin Decree. In diplomacy it was represented as an act "authorized by the acknowledged principles of the law of nations." The reason of the self-contradiction was evident. Only a week before this letter was written, the ministers had concluded a treaty with the United States involving the rights of neutrals, and had attached to it a note to the effect that if the United States failed to resist the Berlin Decree England would acquire the right to retaliate, but had not hinted that retaliation was intended until the case of acquiescence should happen. As the matter stood, the British government had no right to retaliate, but was bound to wait for America to act; and Lord Howick's order, from that point of view, could not be defended.

From every other point of view the Order was equally indefensible; and within a year the Whigs were obliged to take the ground that it was not an act of retaliation at all, but an application of the Rule of 1756. Strange to say, this assertion was probably true. Unlikely as it seemed that Earl Grey, Lord Holland, and Lord Grenville could be parties to a transaction so evasive, their own admissions left no doubt that Napoleon's Berlin Decree was the pretext, not the cause, of Lord Howick's order; that Lord Howick's true intention was to go one step further than Pitt in applying the Rule of 1756 against United States commerce; that he aimed only at cutting off the

[1] Howick to Erskine, Jan. 8, 1807; Cobbett's Debates, x. 558. Erskine to Madison, March 12, 1807; American State Papers, iii. 158.

neutral trade at one end of the voyage, as Pitt had cut it off at the other.

This criticism of the Whig ministry was made not so much in America as in England. The Whigs never offered an intelligible defence. Lord Grenville and Lord Howick argued at much length in Parliament, but convinced no one that their argument was sound; even the "Edinburgh Review" was ashamed of the task, and became unintelligible when it touched upon this party measure.[1] Whether the conduct of Lord Grenville's administration was, as a vigorous Tory pamphleteer said,[2] a piece of chicanery of which an attorney's clerk would have been ashamed, was a matter for English historians to decide. In England at that day none but a few merchants or Republicans believed in the honor or honesty of the United States government or people; but in this instance it was not the honor or honesty of Americans that the English critics denied: it was, on the contrary, the good faith of their own most distinguished and most trusted noblemen,—Lord Grenville and Lord Sidmouth, Earl Grey and Lord Holland, Lord Erskine and Lord Lansdowne, Lord Ellenborough and Earl Fitzwilliam; and in the light of such conduct and criticism, Americans could not be greatly blamed if they refused to admit the ground on which these English gentlemen claimed a better reputation for truth or honesty than they were willing to allow Napoleon. Robbery against robbery, the English mode of pillage seemed on the whole less respectable than the French.

The Whigs were liberal by tradition and instinct; well disposed toward peace and commerce with all nations, they knew that neutral ships alone could carry British manufactures to a European market. Every impediment put in the way of neutral commerce was an additional burden on British produce; every market closed to neutrals was a market closed to England. From a Whig point of view Lord Howick's order violated the rules of political economy and common-sense; not to be defended or excused, it equalled in violence the aggressions of Pitt, and in bad faith rivalled the deceptions of

[1] Edinburgh Review, xxii. 485.
[2] T. P. Courtney's Additional Observations on the American Treaty, London, 1808, p. 89.

Napoleon. Yet this measure was the last act of a Ministry more liberal than England was destined to see again for twenty years. Hardly had Lord Grenville made this concession to Tory prejudice when the old King, nearly blind and on the verge of insanity, clinging to his prejudices with the persistence of age, seized the pretext of some small concession to the Roman Catholics and turned the Whigs out of his councils. March 26, 1807, Lord Grenville and Lord Howick announced to the two Houses of Parliament their dismissal from office.

If the friendly Whigs, after imposing on the United States such a treaty, had thought themselves still obliged to lop off another main limb of American commerce, which Pitt had spared, the Tories were not likely to rest until they had put an end to American neutral commerce altogether. This result was foreshadowed by Spencer Perceval and Lord Castlereagh in their speeches on Lord Howick's order, and was the end to which the legislation and public opinion of England had pointed for years. The time for negotiation had gone by, and nothing remained for the United States but a trial of strength.

For this final test Jefferson was ready. Congress had placed in his hands powers which in his opinion were ample to protect American interests abroad and at home. On sufficient provocation he could exclude British ships-of-war from American waters, and if they should refuse to depart he might enforce the Non-importation Act against British commerce. His conduct proved that he felt neither fear nor hesitation. He had never expected a satisfactory treaty from England, and he had good reason to know that Monroe's treaty, if Monroe should succeed in making one, must be worse than none. Early in February, 1807, arrived the despatch from Monroe and Pinkney announcing that the two envoys had decided to depart from their instructions and to abandon the impressment ultimatum. Madison replied,[1] February 3, that no such treaty would be ratified, and that it would be better to let the negotiation quietly terminate, leaving each party to follow an informal understanding; but that if such a treaty should have been signed, the British commissioners should be

[1] Madison to Monroe and Pinkney, Feb. 3, 1807; State Papers, iii. 153.

candidly apprised of the reasons for not expecting its ratification. That Monroe's treaty, if he made one, would be rejected and returned without ratification to the British government was certain long before it reached America.

On that point, as on the inflexibility of England, no doubt could exist. President Jefferson and Secretary Madison were as determined, in case of necessity, to attack British manufactures as Spencer Perceval and George Rose were bent upon cutting off American trade; but although the Americans fully meant to use commercial weapons against British aggression, they earnestly wished for a good working arrangement under which, without a treaty, peace and commerce could be secure. So far from challenging a rupture, they were anxious only to encourage cordial relations. Throughout the winter of 1806–1807 Jefferson made of his attachment to England a foundation for all his policy at home and abroad. Congress, under the security of Fox's friendship, left foreign affairs alone, and quarrelled only about domestic matters; while General Turreau's temper was made more irritable by the attentions lavished upon David Montague Erskine, the new British minister, who, Nov. 4, 1806, put an end to the adventures of Merry at Washington, and began the easy task of winning popularity.

The winter of 1805–1806 had been favorable to Turreau, who saw France control American policy toward Spain and St. Domingo; while a stringent Act of Congress prohibiting the importation of British manufactures brought within his sight the chief object of French diplomacy in America,—a war between the United States and England. The winter of 1806–1807 promised to undo this good work, and even to bring the United States to the verge of war with France. The first measure recommended by the President and adopted by Congress—the suspension of the Non-importation Act—annoyed Turreau. Monroe's treaty was signed in London December 1; at Washington Turreau wrote, December 12,[1] soon after Congress met,—

> "If I am to judge by the talk and countenances of the great people, this Congress will be more favorable to

[1] Turreau to Talleyrand, Dec. 12, 1806; Archives des Aff. Étr., MSS.

England than the last was; and already its leader, under the President's own invitation, shows a benevolent disposition toward the British government. I had the honor to see Mr. Jefferson the evening before Congress met, and to say to him, on the subject of Spanish differences, that probably all the negotiations entered into by the Government with that Power, as well as with England, would succeed. 'Really,' replied the President, 'I have reason to think that the English are going to make an arrangement with us, and that it would be already done if Mr. Fox's death had not interrupted negotiation. Perhaps we shall even obtain,' he added, 'the right to extend our maritime jurisdiction, and to carry it as far as the effect of the Gulf Stream makes itself felt,—which would be very advantageous both to belligerents and to neutrals.' "

To persons who knew that Jefferson was then angry with Napoleon for his faithless conduct in preventing the new Florida negotiation, this assurance of English friendship gave a measure of the President's diplomacy. He was willing to irritate and alarm the French minister, and he succeeded. Turreau took refuge in speculations and sharp criticisms:—

"I know not whether to attribute this first effect of pronounced favor in regard to England to the last despatches of the two envoys negotiating at London, or to the first overtures of Mr. Erskine, who arrived here a few days ago, and with whom they seem already infatuated (*très engoué*); . . . or, finally, whether it may not be the result of some hints from Alexander,—for whom the Federal government, and particularly Mr. Jefferson, have an admiration which borders on delirium. And your Excellency may recall that last spring the President talked of making overtures to the Russian sovereign relative to a plan of unarmed maritime confederation, which was then his great object, and which, as he assured me in our last interview, he has not given up,—making, as his custom is, a grand eulogium of Alexander and his savages."

Madison, even in prosperous times never a favorite with General Turreau, managed as usual to draw upon himself the chief weight of diplomatic suspicion and wrath.

"The unexpected change in the views of the Federal government," continued Turreau, "is such that the secretary's bearing toward me is deranged by it. Not that he has renounced his system of attentions (*prévenances*) toward the minister of France, whom he does not love, and whom, as I have unfortunately good reason to know, he distrusts; not that he has weakened his protestations, reiterated to satiety, of personal attachment to the interests of France, and of the Government's constant wish to maintain and strengthen the friendly relations which unite it with that Power,—but the Secretary of State has forgotten that at the beginning of this year [1806], and particularly after the event of Austerlitz, the only subject of our private conversations was complaint of England, and the fixed resolution of the Federal government to stop the course of her wrongs either by repression or reprisals. He has forgotten that the steps taken by the Executive to obtain from Congress the famous Non-importation Bill, now suspended, were so marked and ill-concealed that John Randolph called attention to them, and flung severe, or rather humiliating, taunts at the agents of ministerial influence. Now Mr. Madison no longer talks to me about England; he tries to keep out of our conversations whatever relates to that Power, and far from making complaints of her, the Federal government 'has to congratulate itself that the ministry of Mr. Fox, though unfortunately too short, has nevertheless sufficed to bring the Cabinet of St. James to moderate sentiments.' "

Neither Jefferson nor Madison took direct notice of Napoleon's conduct in regard to Florida, but they led Turreau to think that England was their favorite; and Turreau's dislike of America and Americans became in consequence more decided. He hoped for Burr's success in order to relieve the pressure upon him:[1] —

"It seems to me that Burr's success cannot be contrary to the interests of France, although I am convinced that England will favor him,—doubtless with other hopes; but if we had to-day the Floridas, the importance of which I have

[1] Turreau to Talleyrand, Jan. 12, 1807; Archives des Aff. Étr., MSS.

felt it my duty to recall to you, I think I can guarantee that New Orleans would be ours if we only showed a wish for it. All reports, and I have had such, both official and positive, agree as to the regrets expressed by the great majority of inhabitants at not living under French rule."

In the middle of February, at a moment when Americans expected daily the arrival of a British treaty marked by generous concessions, Napoleon's Berlin Decree reached the United States. Commerce was instantly paralyzed, and merchants, Congressmen, Cabinet, and President turned to Turreau anxiously inquiring what was meant by this blockade of the British Islands by a Power which could not keep so much as a frigate at sea. Turreau could give them no answer. "Your Excellency will readily believe," he wrote home,[1] "that this circumstance does not put us in a better position here." The influence of France in the United States was never lower than at the moment when England turned Lord Grenville and Lord Erskine out of power, in order to install Spencer Perceval and Lord Eldon at the head of a Tory reaction. Jefferson's objections to a British treaty would have had no weight with the Senate if the treaty had been tolerable; the Berlin Decree and the Emperor's conduct in regard to Florida would have reconciled Madison to almost any British alliance. Turreau was so well aware of the danger that he exerted himself in remonstrances and semi-threats, and told[2] one member of the Cabinet after another that "at a moment when Europe, leagued together against the maritime tyranny of England, was laboring to throw off the yoke of that Power and to secure for all navigating nations freedom of commerce and the seas," it was particularly improper for the United States to accept any treaty which did not expressly secure all disputed points, and that no treaty would be observed by England unless made under the auspices and by the guaranty of Napoleon.

In view of the recent fate that had overtaken Powers like Switzerland and Venice, which had put themselves under the auspices of Napoleon, this argument produced no conviction.

[1] Turreau to Talleyrand, Feb. 23, 1807; Archives des Aff. Étr., MSS.
[2] Turreau to Talleyrand, April 1, 1807; Archives des Aff. Étr., MSS.

Turreau might better have left to the English the task of repairing Napoleon's mistakes; but these mistakes had accumulated until it depended upon England alone whether the
United States should join her in the war. Not only had the
Emperor offended Jefferson and Madison by his peremptory
stoppage of the Florida purchase,—he had also declared war
upon American commerce in a decree which Jefferson and
Madison could not but suspect to be in some mysterious way
connected with his sudden change of front toward Spain and
Florida; while in the face of these difficulties he left his own
minister at Washington in such discredit that Turreau was reduced to beg sixty thousand dollars from the American Treasury to meet consular expenditures at a moment when he
should have been pressing complaints about the frigate "Im-
pétueux," destroyed by the English within American jurisdiction, and when he should have been threatening the most
fatal consequences if President Jefferson should sign any
treaty whatever with England.[1]

In this temper all parties waited for the news from England, which could not long be delayed; until March 3, 1807,
the last day of the session, a rumor reached the Capitol that a
messenger had arrived at the British legation with a copy of
the treaty negotiated by Pinkney and Monroe. The news was
true. No sooner did Erskine receive the treaty than he hurried
with it to Madison, "in hopes that he would be induced to
persuade the President either to detain the Senate, which he
has the power by the Constitution to do, or to give them
notice that he should convene them again." Unlike Merry,
Erskine was anxious for a reconciliation between England and
America; he tried honestly and over-zealously to bring the
two governments into accord, but he found Madison not
nearly so earnest as himself:

> "The first question he asked was, what had been deter-
> mined on the point of impressment of seamen, claimed as
> British, out of American ships; and when I informed him
> that I had not perceived anything that directly referred to
> that question in any of the Articles of the copy of the treaty
> which I had received, he expressed the greatest astonish-

[1] Turreau to Talleyrand, May 15, 1807; Archives des Aff. Étr., MSS.

ment and disappointment. . . . The note which was delivered in to the American commissioners, previous to the signature of the treaty, by Lords Holland and Auckland, relative to Bonaparte's decree of November 21, particularly attracted his attention; and he observed that the note itself would have prevented, he was convinced, the ratification of the treaty, even if all the Articles of it had been satisfactory, and all the points settled upon the terms that had been required by their commissioners."[1]

At ten o'clock the same night the two Houses of Congress, when ready to adjourn, sent a joint committee to wait upon the President, who was unwell, and unable to go as usual to the Capitol. Dr. Mitchill, the senator from New York, a member of this committee, asked the President whether there would be a call of the Senate to consider the treaty.[2] "Certainly not," replied Jefferson; and he added that "the only way he could account for our ministers having signed such a treaty under such circumstances was by supposing that in the first panic of the French imperial decree they had supposed a war to be inevitable, and that America must make common cause with England. He should, however, continue amicable relations with England, and continue the suspension of the Non-importation Act."

The senators received this rebuff with ill-concealed annoyance. Jefferson's act in refusing to consult them about a matter so important as a British treaty—and one which from the first had been their own rather than the President's scheme—was another instance of the boldness which sometimes contradicted the theory that Jefferson was a timid man. To ordinary minds it seemed clear that the President needed support; that he could not afford single-handed to defy England and France; that the circle of foreign enemies was narrowing about him; and that to suppress of his own will a treaty on which peace and war might depend, exposed him to responsibilities under which he might be crushed. Although the treaty was not yet published, enough had been said to make senators extremely curious about its contents; and they were

[1] Erskine to Howick, March 6, 1807, MSS. British Archives.
[2] Diary of J. Q. Adams, i. 495.

not pleased to learn that the President meant to tell them nothing, and cared too little for their opinion to ask it. Of all the senators the most formidable intriguer was Samuel Smith of Maryland, who wrote the next day confidentially to Wilson Cary Nicholas a letter full of the fresh impressions which gave life to Smith's private language:[1]

"A copy of the treaty arrived last evening. The President is angry with it, and to Dr. Mitchill and Mr. Adams (who carried the last message) expressed his anger in strong, very strong terms, telling in broad language the cause of his wrath. He requested the doctor to tell the senators his objections. If the doctor repeated correctly, then I must be permitted to think there was not a little of the heightening. He said the President was at present determined to send the original back the moment it shall be received, without submitting it to the Senate. He was sick, it is true,—vexed and worried; he may think better of it, for Madison (expecting less than he had) differs with him as to calling the Senate, and R[obert] S[mith] concurs in opinion with M[adison]. . . . I stopped here, and I have seen the President and Mr. M[adison]. It seems the impressment of seamen was a *sine qua non* in the instructions. The P[resident] speaks positively that, without full and formal satisfaction shall be made thereupon, he will return the treaty without consulting the Senate; and yet he admits the treaty, so far as to all the other points, might be acceptable,—nay, that there are but few exceptions to it in his mind. I fancy the merchants would be perfectly pleased therewith. If then in all other points it would please, will the responsibility not be very great on him should he send it back without consulting the Senate? M[adison] in answer to this query said, 'But if he is determined not to accept, even should the Senate advise, why call the Senate together?' I could give no answer to this question. If by his unusual conduct the British continue or increase their depredations (which he cannot prevent), what will be the outcry? *You* may advise him. He stumped us by his positive manner. . . . Will not M[onroe] and P[inkney] both conceive themselves in-

[1] S. Smith to W. C. Nicholas, March 4, 1807; Nicholas MSS.

sulted, and return to make war on the Administration? The whole subject ought, I conceive, to have been treated as one of great delicacy."

In another letter, written the same day, General Smith rehearsed the story in a few words, which proved that Smith had a full share of the shrewdness that was lacking in Jefferson. He saw the future as clearly as politicians often saw what philosophers overlooked; but his jealousy of Jefferson appeared in every word:[1] —

"The Senate, agreeably to the first construction (given by General Washington and his Administration, of which Jefferson was one,—given, too, immediately after the knowledge of what was the intention of the convention that framed it), did *unanimously* advise the President to negotiate a treaty with Great Britain. The Senate agreed to his nomination of the negotiators. A treaty was effected. It arrives. It is well known that he was *coerced* by the Senate to the measure; and he refuses to submit it to their approbation. What a responsibility he takes! By sending it back he disgraces his ministers, *and Monroe is one*. Monroe and Pinkney come home, and in justification publish the treaty. It may appear good to the eyes of all unprejudiced men,— I suspect it will. By a refusal to accede to it the British continue their depredations, to the amount perhaps of their whole system of 'You shall not trade in time of war where you are refused in time of peace;' the impressment is carried to an excess bounded only by their power; immense losses are sustained; a general outcry will ensue; all will say, 'If Monroe's treaty had succeeded, those losses would not have happened; why was it refused?' Jealousy of Monroe, and unreasonable antipathy by Jefferson and Madison to Great Britain!—this will be said, this will be believed. And Monroe will be brought forward; new parties will arise, and those adverse politically will be brought together by interest. . . . Shall we put all to jeopardy because we have not got all we ask? Will we go to war? No! What will we do to coerce? More non-importation. Will Congress under

[1] S. Smith to W. C. Nicholas, March 4, 1807; Nicholas MSS.

such circumstances consent to continue their non-importation? I suspect not; I cannot believe they will. Then where
shall we be? J. Randolph will take his stand and ask, 'Shall
we hazard everything for a set of men who, etc.? What, put
the landed interest to such inconvenience! The fair merchant is satisfied; the country is flourishing,' etc. But I have
not time to make a speech. Monroe will be called a martyr,
and the martyr will be the President. And why? Because he
has done right, and his opponent has advised wrong. The
people care little or nothing about the seamen."

The more closely the subject was studied the more clearly
it appeared that Monroe had to all appearance knowingly
embarrassed the Administration by signing a treaty in contravention of the President's orders; but Jefferson added
unnecessarily to his embarrassment by refusing the treaty before he read it. Tacit abandonment of impressments was the
utmost concession that the President could hope from England, and even this he must probably fight for; yet he refused to consult the Senate on the merits of Monroe's treaty
for a reason which would have caused the withholding of
every treaty ever made with England. That the public should
be satisfied with this imperious treatment was an extravagant
demand. No act of Jefferson's administration exposed him to
more misinterpretation, or more stimulated a belief in his
hatred of England and of commerce, than his refusal to lay
Monroe's treaty before the Senate.

Perhaps the President would have been less decided had he
known at first how faulty the treaty was. Not until it had been
studied for weeks did all its faults become evident; and not
until it was read in the light of Lord Howick's Order in
Council did its character admit of no more doubt. When
news of this order reached Washington, about ten days after
the treaty, Madison wrote to Erskine a letter[1] which showed
an effort to treat the new restriction of neutral trade as
though it might have some shadow of legality in the background, and as though it were not directed solely against
America; but the truth soon became too evident for such mild
treatment, and Madison was obliged ten days afterward to

[1] Madison to Erskine, March 20, 1807; State Papers, iii. 158.

interrupt his study of Monroe's treaty in order to tell Erskine that the operation of the new order "would be a proceeding as ruinous to our commerce as contrary to our essential rights."[1]

To Monroe the President wrote with the utmost forbearance and kindness.[2] Instead of reproaching, Jefferson soothed the irritation of his old friend, contradicted newspaper reports which were calculated to wound Monroe's feelings, and pressed upon him the government of New Orleans Territory: "It is the second office in the United States in importance, and I am still in hopes you will accept it; it is impossible to let you stay at home while the public has so much need of talents." In regard to the treaty he said little; but what he did say was more severe than any criticism yet made to others. "Depend on it, my dear Sir, that it will be considered as a hard treaty when it is known. The British commissioners appear to have screwed every Article as far as it would bear, — to have taken everything and yielded nothing." He urged Monroe, if nothing better could be got, "to back out of the negotiation" as well as he could, letting it die insensibly, and substituting some informal agreement until a more yielding temper should rise. Next the President wrote privately to Bowdoin, his wandering minister to Spain, to whom Armstrong had shut the doors of the legation at Paris for betraying its secrets, and who in return was abusing Armstrong with recriminations. If a quarrel should arise with England, it might at least be made to bring Florida again within reach.

"I have but little expectation," wrote the President to Bowdoin,[3] "that the British government will retire from their habitual wrongs in the impressment of our seamen, and am certain that without that we will never tie up our hands by treaty from the right of passing a non-importation or non-intercourse Act to make it her interest to become just. This may bring on a war of commercial restrictions. To show, however, the sincerity of our desire for conciliation, I have suspended the Non-importation

---

[1] Madison to Erskine, March 29, 1807; State Papers, iii, 159.
[2] Jefferson to Monroe, March 21, 1807; Works, v. 52.
[3] Jefferson to Bowdoin, April 2, 1807; Works, v. 63.

Act. This state of things should be understood at Paris, and every effort used on your part to accommodate our differences with Spain under the auspices of France, with whom it is all important that we should stand in terms of the strictest cordiality. In fact we are to depend on her and Russia for the establishment of neutral rights by the treaty of peace, among which should be that of taking no persons by a belligerent out of a neutral ship, unless they be the soldiers of an enemy. Never did a nation act toward another with more perfidy and injustice than Spain has constantly practised against us; and if we have kept our hands off of her till now, it has been purely out of respect to France, and from the value we set on the friendship of France. We expect, therefore, from the friendship of the Emperor that he will either compel Spain to do us justice or abandon her to us. We ask but one month to be in possession of the city of Mexico."

In reality Jefferson needed somewhat more than a month to be in possession of Mexico, although the Spaniards might without much difficulty have reached New Orleans in less time. Had the Federalist press been able to print the letter to Bowdoin, with its semi-admissions of intent to wage a commercial war against England in dependence upon Napoleon in order to gain the Floridas, the scandal would have been as great as that caused by the famous letters to Mazzei and Paine; but in truth this flighty talk had no influence or importance, and the time was close at hand when Jefferson was to become helpless. Between the will of England and France on one side and the fixed theories of Virginia and Pennsylvania on the other, Jefferson's freedom of action disappeared.

Madison, who rarely accepted either horn of a dilemma with much rapidity, labored over new instructions to Monroe which were to make the treaty tolerable, and called Gallatin and General Smith to his aid, with no other result than to uncover new and insuperable difficulties. April 20 he wrote to Jefferson at Monticello:[1] —

"The shape to be given to the instructions to our com-

[1] Madison to Jefferson, April 20, 1807; Jefferson MSS.

missioners becomes more and more perplexing. I begin to suspect that it may eventually be necessary to limit the treaty to the subject of impressments, leaving the colonial trade, with other objects, to their own course and to the influence which our reserved power over our imports may have on that course. In practice the colonial trade and everything else would probably be more favored than they are by the Articles forwarded, or would be by any remodifications to be expected. The case of impressments is more urgent. Something seems essential to be done, nor is anything likely to be done without carrying fresh matter in the negotiation. I am preparing an overture to disuse British seamen, in the form of an ultimatum, graduated from an exception of those who have been two years in our navigation to no exception at all other than such as have been naturalized."

A few days later news arrived that the Whigs had been driven from office, and a high Tory ministry had come into power. Madison was more than ever perplexed, but did not throw aside his treaty.

"A late arrival from London," he wrote again,[1] April 24, "presents a very unexpected scene at St. James's. Should the revolution stated actually take place in the Cabinet, it will subject our affairs there to new calculations. On one hand the principles and dispositions of the new Ministry portend the most unfriendly course. On the other hand, their feeble and tottering situation and the force of their ousted rivals, who will probably be more explicit in maintaining the value of a good understanding with this country, cannot fail to inspire caution. It may happen also that the new Cabinet will be less averse to a *tabula rasa* for a new adjustment than those who formed the instrument to be superseded."

Jefferson's reply to these suggestions showed no anxiety except the haunting fear of a treaty,—a fear which to Monroe's eyes could have no foundation. "I am more and more convinced," the President wrote April 21,[2] "that our best course

---

[1] Madison to Jefferson, April 24, 1807; Jefferson MSS.
[2] Jefferson to Madison, April 21, 1807; Works, v. 69.

is to let the negotiation take a friendly nap;" and May 1 he added:[1] "I know few of the characters of the new British Administration. The few I know are true Pittites and anti-American. From them we have nothing to hope but that they will readily let us back out." In view of George Canning's character and antecedents and of Spencer Perceval's speeches, Jefferson's desire to be allowed to back out of his treaty was superfluous. That Canning and Perceval would make any effort to hold him to his bargain was quite unlikely, but that they would let him back out was still more so. They had in view more expeditious ways of ejecting him.

Nevertheless Madison was allowed to perfect his new instructions to Monroe and Pinkney. May 20 they were signed and sent. Before they reached London a British frigate had answered them in tones which left little chance for discussion.

[1] Jefferson to Madison, April 21, 1807; Works, v. 74.

Chapter XIX

ARCH 30, 1807, in a room at the Eagle Tavern in Richmond, Aaron Burr was brought before Chief-Justice Marshall for examination and commitment. Although Burr had been but a few days in the town, he was already treated by many persons as though he had conferred honor upon his country. Throughout the United States the Federalists, who formed almost the whole of fashionable society, affected to disbelieve in the conspiracy, and ridiculed Jefferson's sudden fears. The Democrats had never been able to persuade themselves that the Union was really in danger, or that Burr's projects, whatever they were, had a chance of success; and in truth Burr's conspiracy, like that of Pickering and Griswold, had no deep roots in society, but was mostly confined to a circle of well-born, well-bred, and well-educated individuals, whose want of moral sense was one more proof that the moral instinct had little to do with social distinctions. In the case of Burr, Jefferson himself had persistently ignored danger; and no one denied that if danger ever existed, it had passed. Burr was fighting for his life against the power of an encroaching government; and human nature was too simply organized to think of abstract justice or remote principles when watching the weak fight for life against the strong. Even the Democrats were more curious to see Burr than to hang him; and had he gone to the gallows, he would have gone as a hero, like Captain Macheath amidst the admiring crowds of London.

Between Captain Macheath and Colonel Burr was more than one point of resemblance, and the "Beggar's Opera" could have been easily paralleled within the prison at Richmond; but no part of Burr's career was more humorous than the gravity with which he took an injured tone, and maintained with success that Jefferson, being a trivial person, had been deceived by the stories of Eaton and Wilkinson, until, under the influence of causeless alarm, he had permitted a wanton violation of right. From the first step toward commitment, March 30, to the last day of the tedious trials, October 20, Burr and his counsel never ceased their effort to convict Jefferson; until the acquittal of Burr began to seem a matter of secondary importance compared with the President's discomfiture.

Over this tournament the chief-justice presided as arbiter. Blennerhassett's island, where the overt act of treason was charged to have taken place, lay within the chief-justice's circuit. According as he might lean toward the accused or toward the government, he would decide the result; and therefore his leanings were a matter of deep interest. That he held Federalist prejudices and nourished a personal dislike to Jefferson was notorious; but apart from political feelings he had given no clew to his probable legal bias except in his recent decision upon the case of Bollman and Swartwout. In discharging these two agents of Burr on the ground that no overt act of levying war was alleged against them, Marshall had taken occasion to define the law of treason as a guide to the attorney-general in the coming indictment of Burr:—

> "It is not the intention of the Court to say that no individual can be guilty of this crime who has not appeared in arms against his country. On the contrary, if war be actually levied,—that is, if a body of men be actually assembled for the purpose of effecting by force a treasonable purpose,—all those who perform any part, however minute, or however remote from the scene of action, and who are actually leagued in the general conspiracy, are to be considered as traitors. But there must be an actual assembling of men for the treasonable purpose, to constitute a levying of war."

On the strength of this opinion, the attorney-general undertook to convict Burr of treason for the acts committed under his direction at Blennerhassett's island, although at the time when these acts were committed Burr himself was in Kentucky, two hundred miles away.

The task was difficult, and Burr's experience as a lawyer enabled him to make it more difficult still. He retained the ablest counsel at the bar. First of these was Edmund Randolph, prominent among the older Virginia lawyers, who had been attorney-general and Secretary of State in President Washington's Cabinet. Edmund Randolph's style of address was ponderous, and not always happy; to balance its defects Burr employed the services of John Wickham, another Virginian, whose versatility and wit were remarkable. A third Virginian, Benjamin Botts, was brought into the case, and proved a valuable ally. Finally Luther Martin was summoned from Baltimore; and Martin's whole heart was with his client. In defending Justice Chase, Luther Martin had made a great name; but hatred for the Democrats and their President became a secondary passion in his breast. His zeal for Burr was doubled by a sudden idolatry which the sexagenarian conceived for Burr's daughter Theodosia, who came to her father's side at Richmond.

The government was represented by no one of equal force with these opponents. John Breckinridge, the Attorney-General of the United States, died in December, 1806. Jan. 20, 1807, President Jefferson appointed Cæsar A. Rodney to the post. Although Rodney's abilities were respectable, he could hardly have wished to be confronted at once by the most important and difficult State prosecution ever tried under Executive authority. Rodney's duties or his health prevented him from attendance. He barely appeared at Richmond in the preliminaries, and then left the case in the hands of the district-attorney, George Hay, who took his orders directly from Jefferson, with whom he was in active correspondence. To assist Hay the President engaged the services of William Wirt, then thirty-five years old, and promising to become an ornament to the bar; but in the profession of the law age gave weight, and Wirt, though popular, conscientious, admired, and brilliant in a florid style of oratory, suffered as a lawyer from his youth and his reputation as an orator. He was hardly more capable than Hay of conducting a case which drew upon every resource of personal authority. The third counsel, Alexander McRae, Lieutenant-Governor of Virginia, was inferior both in ability and in tact to either of his associates. His temper irritated Hay and offended the Court, while his arguments added little strength to the prosecution.

The first object of the government was to commit Burr for trial on the charge of treason as well as of misdemeanor; but Marshall promptly checked all hopes of obtaining aid from the court. April 1 the chief-justice delivered an opinion on the question of commitment, and took that opportunity to give the district-attorney a warning. Declining to commit Burr for treason without evidence stronger than the affidavits of Eaton and Wilkinson, Marshall blamed the Executive with asperity for neglect of duty in providing proof of treason:—

"Several months have elapsed since this fact did occur, if it ever occurred. More than five weeks have elapsed since the opinion of the Supreme Court has declared the necessity of proving the fact if it exists. Why is it not proved? To the Executive government is intrusted the important power of prosecuting those whose crimes may disturb the public repose or endanger its safety. It would be easy in much less time than has intervened since Colonel Burr has been alleged to have assembled his troops, to procure affidavits establishing the fact."

Accordingly Burr was committed only for misdemeanor, and five securities immediately offered themselves on his behalf. At three o'clock on the afternoon of April 1 he was again at liberty, under bonds for ten thousand dollars to appear at the next circuit court, May 22, at Richmond.

Marshall's reproof of Executive slowness was not altogether respectful to the co-ordinate branch of government. No doubt treasonable assemblages had taken place in December, and affidavits could have been brought from Marietta or Nashville within six or eight weeks had the government known precisely what would be needed, or where the evidence was to go; but no judge could reasonably require that the Executive should within five weeks obey a hint from the Supreme Court which implied a long correspondence and inquiry at spots so remote as Blennerhassett's island, Lexington, Nashville, Fort Massac, and Chickasaw Bluffs. Jefferson was naturally indignant at being treated with so little courtesy. He wrote with extreme bitterness about Marshall's "tricks to force trials before it is possible to collect the evidence."[1] He returned threat for threat, with something in addition:—

"In what terms of decency can we speak of this? As if an express could go to Natchez or the mouth of the Cumber-

[1] Jefferson to W. B. Giles, April 20, 1807; Works, v. 65.

land and return in five weeks, to do which has never taken less than twelve! . . . But all the principles of law are to be perverted which would bear on the favorite offenders who endeavor to overturn this odious republic! . . . All this, however, will work well. The nation will judge both the offender and judges for themselves. If a member of the Executive or Legislature does wrong, the day is never far distant when the people will remove him. They will see then and amend the error in our Constitution which makes any branch independent of the nation. They will see that one of the great co-ordinate branches of the government, setting itself in opposition to the other two and to the common-sense of the nation, proclaims impunity to that class of offenders which endeavors to overturn the Constitution, and are protected in it by the Constitution itself; for impeachment is a farce which will not be tried again. If their protection of Burr produces this amendment, it will do more good than his condemnation would have done; . . . and if his punishment can be commuted now for a useful amendment of the Constitution, I shall rejoice in it."

In substance Jefferson said that if Marshall should suffer Burr to escape, Marshall himself should be removed from office. No secret was made of this intention. The letter in which Jefferson announced the threat was written to the Virginia senator William B. Giles, who had been foremost in every attack upon the Judiciary, and would certainly lead the new one; but Giles was not the confidant of a secret,—the idea was common, as Marshall knew. The little society that swarmed in the court-room and in the streets of Richmond could see without an effort that the President courted a challenge from Marshall, and that the chief-justice on his side, for a second or third time, welcomed a trial of skill and address with the President. If Marshall was in truth the gloomy and malignant conspirator that Jefferson imagined him to be, he might easily excuse or justify the President's intended course.

Punctually, May 22, the next act began. The question of commitment had been a matter of no great consequence; that of indictment was vital. Burr must be indicted, not merely for misdemeanor, but for treason; and to leave no doubt of success, the government summoned a cloud of witnesses to appear before the grand jury. The town swarmed with conspirators and government agents. The grand jury—containing some of the most respected citizens of Virginia—was sworn, and the court instructed the clerk to place John Randolph as foreman. A long delay ensued. General Wilkinson, the most important witness for government, was on his way from New Orleans; and while waiting his arrival from day to day, the grand jury took evidence and the court listened to the disputes of counsel. The district-attorney moved to commit Burr on the charge of treason, while Burr on his side moved for a subpœna *duces tecum* to be directed to the President, requiring him to produce certain papers in evidence. This motion was evidently part of a system adopted by the defence for annoying and throwing odium on the Executive,—a system which Burr's counsel rather avowed than concealed, by declaiming against the despotism of government and the persecution of which Burr was a victim. Luther Martin, at the first moment of his appearance in court, launched into an invective against Jefferson:—

"The President has undertaken to prejudge my client by declaring that 'of his guilt there can be no doubt.' He has assumed the knowledge of the Supreme Being himself, and pretended to search the heart of my highly respected friend. He has proclaimed him a traitor in the face of that country which has rewarded him. He has let slip the dogs of war, the hell-hounds of persecution, to hunt down my friend. And would this President of the United States, who has raised all this absurd clamor, pretend to keep back the papers which are wanted for this trial, where life itself is at stake?"

A long argument followed. Hay, while admitting that the President might be generally subpœnaed as a witness, held that no need of a subpœna had been shown, and that in any case a subpœna *duces tecum* ought not to be issued. The chief-justice, after hearing counsel on both sides, read June 13 an elaborate decision, which settled the point in Burr's favor.

"If upon any principle," said he, "the President could be construed to stand exempt from the general provisions of the Constitution, it would be because his duties as chief magistrate demand his whole time for national objects. But it is apparent that this demand is not unremitting; and if it should exist at the time when his attendance on a court is required, it would be sworn on the return of the subpœna, and would rather constitute a reason for not obeying the process of the court than a reason against its being issued. . . . It cannot be denied that to issue a subpœna to a person filling the exalted station of the chief magistrate is a duty which would be dispensed with much more cheerfully than it would be performed; but if it be a duty, the court can have no choice in the case."

Nothing could irritate Jefferson more sensibly than this decision. Only a few months before, in the trial of Smith and Ogden for complicity with Miranda, he had ordered his Cabinet to disregard the summons of the court. Luther Martin did not fail to fling reproach on him for this act. "In New York, on the farcical trial of Ogden and Smith, the officers of the government screened themselves from attending, under the sanction of the President's name. Perhaps the same farce may be repeated here." To be insulted by Martin and to be ordered about the country by Marshall, exasperated Jefferson beyond reason. He wrote letter after letter to Hay, filled with resentment:—

"The leading feature of our Constitution is the independence of the Legislature, Executive, and Judiciary of each other; and none are more jealous of this than the Judiciary. But would the Executive be independent of the Judiciary if he were subject to the *commands* of the latter, and to imprisonment for disobedience; if the smaller courts could bandy him from pillar to post, keep him constantly trudging from north to south and east to west, and withdraw him entirely from his executive duties?"[1]

The Judiciary never admitted the propriety of this reasoning,[2] which was indeed no answer to Marshall's argument. Unless the President of the United States were raised above

[1] Jefferson to Hay, June 20, 1807; Works, v. 102.
[2] U.S. *vs.* Kendall, Cranch's Circuit Court Reports, v. 385.

the rank of a citizen, and endowed with more than royal prerogatives, no duty could be more imperative upon him than
that of lending every aid in his power to the Judiciary in a
case which involved the foundations of civil society and government. No Judiciary could assume at the outset that Executive duties would necessarily be interrupted by breaking
Jefferson's long visits to Monticello in order to bring him for
a day to Richmond. Consciousness of this possible rejoinder
disturbed the President's mind so much that he undertook to
meet it in advance:—

> "The Judge says '*it is apparent* that the President's duties
> as chief magistrate do not demand his whole time, and are
> not unremitting.' If he alludes to our annual retirement
> from the seat of government during the sickly season, he
> should be told that such arrangements are made for carry-
> ing on the public business, at and between the several sta-
> tions we take, that it goes on as unremittingly there as if
> we were at the seat of government."

The district-attorney would hardly have dared tell this to
the chief-justice, for he must have felt that Marshall would
treat it as an admission. If arrangements could be made for
carrying on the public business at Monticello, why could they
not be made for carrying it on at Richmond?

Perhaps temper had more to do with Jefferson's reasoning
than he imagined. Nothing could be better calculated to net-
tle a philosophic President who believed the world, except
within his own domain, to be too much governed, than the
charge that he himself had played the despot and had trampled upon private rights; but that such charges should be
pressed with the coarseness of Luther Martin, and should depend on the rulings of John Marshall, seemed an intolerable
outrage on the purity of Jefferson's intentions. In such cases
an explosion of anger was a common form of relief. Even
President Washington was said to have sometimes dashed his
hat upon the ground, and the second President was famous
for gusts of temper.

"I have heard, indeed," wrote Jefferson,[1] "that my pre-

[1] Jefferson to William Short, June 12, 1807; Works, v. 93. Cf. Jefferson MSS.

decessor sometimes decided things against his Council by dashing and trampling his wig on the floor. This only proves, what you and I knew, that he had a better heart than head."

Wigs were Federalist symbols of dignity and power. Republicans wore no wigs, and could use no such resource in moments of rage; but had President Jefferson worn the full paraphernalia of Federalism, — wig and powder, cocked hat and small sword, — he would never have shown his passion in acts of violence or in physical excitement. His sensitiveness relieved itself in irritability and complaints, in threats forgotten as soon as uttered, or in reflections tinged with a color of philosophic thought. His first impulse was to retaliate upon Martin and thrust him into the criminal dock. He wrote to Hay,[1] —

"Shall we move to commit Luther Martin as *particeps criminis* with Burr? Graybell will fix upon him misprision of treason at least. And at any rate his evidence will put down this unprincipled and impudent Federal bulldog, and add another proof that the most clamorous defenders of Burr are all his accomplices."

To the attorney-general he wrote in the same words:[2] "I think it material to break down this bulldog of Federalism." Jefferson's irritation rarely lasted long, and it evaporated with these words. Martin railed unmolested.

No one fretted by personal feeling could cope with the Rhadamanthine calm of John Marshall. The President could not successfully strike back; he was fortunate if he should succeed in warding off his enemies' blows. In the midst of these controversies and irritations, June 15, General Wilkinson arrived. The audiences which in those days still crowded to the theatre and laughed at the extraordinary wit and morality of the "Beggar's Opera," found none of its possible allusions more amusing than the often-quoted line which seemed meant to point at James Wilkinson. "That Jemmy Twitcher should peach me, I own surprised me. 'T is a plain proof that

[1] Jefferson to Hay, June 19, 1807; Works, v. 98.
[2] Jefferson to Rodney, June 19, 1807; Jefferson MSS.

the world is all alike, and that even our gang can no more trust one another than other people." Wilkinson had not a friend; even Daniel Clark turned against him. To break him down, to prove by his own confession that he was a pensioner of Spain and an accomplice with Burr, was the known object of the defence; but the disgrace of Wilkinson would also discredit the President and shake the Administration which Wilkinson had saved. Whatever the consequences might be, Jefferson could not allow Wilkinson to suffer.

When Major Bruff, of the artillery, came from St. Louis to Washington early in March, 1807, three months before Burr's indictment, he made bitter complaints to the Secretary of War, accusing the general, under whose orders he served, of being a spy of Spain and a traitor with Burr.[1] General Dearborn listened without contradiction, and replied that there had been a time when General Wilkinson did not stand well with the Executive, but his energetic measures at New Orleans had regained him Executive confidence, and the President would sustain him; that after the actual bustle was over there might perhaps be an inquiry, but meanwhile Wilkinson must and would be supported. Attorney-General Rodney went even further.

"What would be the result," he asked Bruff, "if all your charges against General Wilkinson should be proven? Why, just what the Federalists and the enemies of the present Administration wish,—it would turn the indignation of the people from Burr on Wilkinson. Burr would escape, and Wilkinson take his place."

Rodney did not add, what was patent to all the world, that if Wilkinson were to be convicted, President Jefferson himself, whose negligence had left the Western country, in spite of a thousand warnings, at the General's mercy, could not be saved from the roughest handling. The President and his Cabinet shrank from Marshall's subpœnas because under the examination of Wickham, Botts, and Luther Martin they would be forced either to make common cause with the General, or to admit their own negligence. The whole case hung to-

[1] Major Bruff's Testimony, Burr's Trial; Annals of Congress, 1807–1808, pp. 598–600.

gether. Disobedience of the subpœna was necessary for the support of Wilkinson; support of Wilkinson was more than ever necessary after refusing to obey the subpœna. The President accepted his full share in the labor. No sooner did he hear of Wilkinson's arrival, at the moment when his own subpœna was issued and defied, than he wrote a letter calculated to give the General all the confidence he needed:[1] —

"Your enemies have filled the public ear with slanders and your mind with trouble on that account. The establishment of their guilt will let the world see what they ought to think of their clamors; it will dissipate the doubts of those who doubted for want of knowledge, and will place you on higher ground in the public estimate and public confidence. No one is more sensible than myself of the injustice which has been aimed at you. Accept, I pray you, my salutations and assurances of respect and esteem."

As an American citizen Jefferson had the right to respect and esteem whom he pleased, and need not even excuse his friendships. The world often loved and cherished its worst rogues,—its Falstaffs, Macheaths, and Burrs,—and Jefferson was not exempt from such weakness; but that his respect and esteem for Wilkinson should require him to retain a pensioned Spanish spy and a confederate with Burr and Dayton at the head of the United States army during several years of extreme public danger, was a costly consequence to the people whose confidence Jefferson claimed and held. John Randolph saw this point clearly, and his bloodhound instinct detected and followed, without hesitation, the trail that led to the White House. Whether the chief-justice intended it or not, he never struck Jefferson a blow so mischievous as when he directed the clerk to place John Randolph as foreman of the grand jury.[2] Randolph's nature revolted from Wilkinson; and if the President and the General could be gibbeted together, Randolph was the man to do it.

Such was the situation when the General was sworn and sent before the grand jury June 15, where his appearance, if his enemy could be believed, was abject.

[1] Jefferson to Wilkinson, June 21, 1807; Works, v. 109.
[2] Wilkinson's Memoirs, ii. 6.

"Under examination all was confusion of language and of looks," wrote Randolph to Nicholson.[1] "Such a countenance never did I behold; there was scarcely a variance of opinion among us as to his guilt. Yet this miscreant is hugged to the bosom of Government while Monroe is denounced."

Randolph ardently wished to indict the General at the same time with Burr; and while he strained every nerve to effect this purpose in the grand-jury room, Burr and his counsel in the court-room moved for an attachment against Wilkinson for attempting to obstruct the free course of justice by oppression of witnesses. The district-attorney resisted both attempts with all his authority; and June 24, to the disappointment of his enemies, Wilkinson escaped.

"Yesterday," wrote Randolph, June 25,[2] "the grand jury found bills for treason and misdemeanor against Burr and Blennerhassett *una voce*, and this day presented Jonathan Dayton, ex-senator, John Smith of Ohio, Comfort Tyler, Israel Smith of New York, and Davis Floyd of Indiana, for treason; but the mammoth of iniquity escaped,—not that any man pretended to think him innocent, but upon certain wire-drawn distinctions that I will not pester you with. Wilkinson is the only man that I ever saw who was from the bark to the very core a villain. The proof is unquestionable; but, my good friend, I cannot enter upon it here. Suffice it to say that I have seen it, and that it is not susceptible of misconstruction. Burr supported himself with great fortitude. He was last night lodged in the common town jail (we have no State prison except for convicts), where I daresay he slept sounder than I did. Perhaps you never saw human nature in so degraded a situation as in the person of Wilkinson before the grand jury; and yet this man stands on the very summit and pinnacle of Executive favor, while James Monroe is denounced."

In the debates of the next session, when Randolph followed up his attacks on Jefferson by trying to identify him

[1] Randolph to Nicholson, June 28, 1807; Nicholson MSS.
[2] Randolph to Nicholson, June 25, 1807; Nicholson MSS.

with Wilkinson's misdeeds, a fuller account was given of the plea which saved Wilkinson from presentment.

"There was before the grand jury," said Randolph,[1] "a motion to present General Wilkinson for misprision of treason. This motion was overruled upon this ground,— that the treasonable (overt) act having been alleged to be committed in the State of Ohio, and General Wilkinson's letter to the President of the United States having been dated, though but a short time, prior to that act, this person had the benefit of what lawyers would call a legal exception, or a fraud; but I will inform the gentleman that I did not hear a single member of the grand jury express any other opinion than that which I myself expressed, of the moral, not of the legal, guilt of the party."

In the evidence taken by a Congressional committee in 1811 regarding Wilkinson,[2] several members of the grand jury were called to testify; and their accounts showed that the motion to present General Wilkinson for misprision of treason was made by Littleton W. Tazewell, and supported by Randolph and three or four other members of the grand jury. One witness thought that the vote stood 9 to 7.

Narrow though the loophole might be, Wilkinson squeezed through it. The indictment of Burr was at length obtained. The conspirators, who had at first vehemently averred that Wilkinson would never dare to appear, and who if he should appear intended to break him down before the grand jury, were reduced to hoping for revenge when he should come on the witness-stand. Meanwhile, June 26, Burr pleaded not guilty, and the court adjourned until August 3, when the trial was to begin.

Thus far the President had carried everything before him. He had produced his witnesses, had sustained Wilkinson, indicted Burr, and defied Marshall's subpœnas. This success could not be won without rousing passion. Richmond was in the hands of the conspirators, and they denounced Jefferson

[1] Annals of Congress, Jan. 11, 1808; Session of 1807–1808, p. 1397.
[2] Report of the Committee appointed to inquire into the Conduct of General Wilkinson, Feb. 26, 1811, pp. 281, 298. Cf. National Intelligencer, Aug. 3, 1807.

publicly and without mercy, as they denounced Wilkinson and every other government officer.

"As I was crossing the court-house green," said an eye-witness,[1] "I heard a great noise of haranguing some distance off. Inquiring what it was, I was told it was a great blackguard from Tennessee, one Andrew Jackson, making a speech for Burr and damning Jefferson as a persecutor."

Hay wrote to the President, June 14:[2] —

"General Jackson, of Tennessee, has been here ever since the 22d, denouncing Wilkinson in the coarsest terms in every company. The latter showed me a paper which at once explained the motive of this incessant hostility. His own character depends on the prostration of Wilkinson's."

This paper was no doubt Jackson's secret denunciation to Claiborne. Young Samuel Swartwout, who had some reason to complain of the ridiculous figure he had been made to cut, jostled Wilkinson in the street, and ended by posting him for a coward. John Randolph echoed Luther Martin's tirades against the President. Randolph was in despair at Jefferson's success.

"My friend," he wrote to Nicholson,[3] "I am standing on the soil of my native country divested of every right for which our fathers bled. Politics have usurped the place of law, and the scenes of 1798 are again revived. Men now see and hear, and feel and think, *politically*. Maxims are now advanced and advocated which would almost have staggered the effrontery of Bayard or the cooler impudence of Chauncey Goodrich when we were first acquainted."

All this work was but skirmishing. The true struggle had still to come. So long as the President dealt only with grand jurors and indictments, he could hardly fail to succeed; but the case was different when he dealt directly with Chief-Justice Marshall and with the stubborn words of the Constitution, that "no person shall be convicted of treason unless

[1] Parton's Life of Burr, ii. 107.
[2] Hay to Jefferson, June 14, 1807; Jefferson MSS.
[3] Randolph to Nicholson, June 25, 1807; Adams's Randolph, p. 221.

on the testimony of two witnesses to the same overt act, or on confession in open court." The district-attorney was ready with a mass of evidence, but the chief-justice alone could say whether a syllable of this evidence should be admitted; and hitherto the chief-justice had by no means shown a bias toward the government. Hay was convinced that Marshall meant to protect Burr, and he wrote to the President on the subject:[1] —

"The bias of Judge Marshall is as obvious as if it was stamped upon his forehead. I may do him injustice, but I do not believe that I am, when I say that he is endeavoring to work himself up to a state of f[irmness?] which will enable [him] to aid Burr throughout the trial without appearing to be conscious of doing wrong. He seems to think that his reputation is irretrievably gone, and that he has now nothing to lose by doing as he pleases. His concern for Mr. Burr is wonderful. He told me many years ago, when Burr was rising in the estimation of the Republican party, that he was as profligate in principle as he was desperate in fortune. I remember his words; they astonished me. Yet when the grand jury brought in their bill, the chief-justice gazed at him for a long time, without appearing conscious that he was doing so, with an expression of sympathy and sorrow as strong as the human countenance can exhibit without palpable emotion."

August 3 the court opened its session and the trial began. Not until August 17 was the jury impanelled; and meanwhile a new figure appeared at Burr's side. Blennerhassett arrived in Richmond August 4, and was brought before the court August 10. He began at once a private journal of the trial, which remained the only record of what passed among the conspirators. As each witness appeared, Blennerhassett told the gossip regarding him.

"The once redoubted Eaton,"[2] who was put first upon the stand, "has dwindled down in the eyes of this sarcastic town into a ridiculous mountebank, strutting about the

[1] Hay to Jefferson, Aug. 11, 1807; Jefferson MSS.
[2] Blennerhassett Papers, p. 315.

streets under a tremendous hat, with a Turkish sash over colored clothes, when he is not tippling in the taverns, where he offers up with his libations the bitter effusions of his sorrows."

"Old sly-boots" Dayton,[1] he said, was lurking about corners.

Wilkinson[2] "exhibited the manner of a sergeant under a court-martial rather than the demeanor of an accusing officer confronted with his culprit. His perplexity and derangement, even upon his direct examination, has placed beyond all doubt 'his honor as a soldier and his fidelity as a citizen.' "

These comments were sharp, yet the pages of Blennerhassett's diary were not so severe upon any of the witnesses for the government as they were upon Burr himself. Blennerhassett had wakened to the discovery that Burr was, after all, but a vulgar swindler. The collapse of Burr's courage when confronted by Cowles Meade and the Mississippi militia at Cole's Creek January 17; his desertion of Blennerhassett and his flight toward Spanish territory; the protest of the bills which he had drawn on pretended funds in New York, and which Blennerhassett had indorsed under Allston's guaranty; the evident wish of Allston to repudiate this guaranty as he had repudiated Burr; and the ruin which had fallen on Blennerhassett's property at the island,—taught the Irishman how thoroughly he had been duped:[3] —

"The present trial cannot fail to furnish ample testimony, if not to the guilt, at least to the defect of every talent under the assumption of which this giddy adventurer has seduced so many followers of riper experience and better judgment than myself."

Yet Burr's mastership in deportment, his superficial dignity, his cheerfulness and sanguine temperament, and the skill with which he managed legal tactics, made an impression on Blennerhassett's mind: —

[1] Blennerhassett Papers, p. 397.
[2] Blennerhassett Papers, p. 422.
[3] Blennerhassett Papers, p. 373.

"As a jockey might restore his fame in the course after he had injured it on the tight-rope, so, perhaps, the little 'Emperor' at Cole's Creek may be forgotten in the attorney at Richmond."[1]

For a few days the trial went on undisturbed, while the government put Eaton, Truxton, Peter Taylor, the Morgans, and a number of other witnesses on the stand to prove an overt act of treason at Blennerhassett's island; but nothing short of Blennerhassett's own confession could place the matter in a clear light, and Burr's chief fear was evidently that Blennerhassett should turn State's evidence. To prevent this, Allston was persuaded to pay the more pressing demands against Blennerhassett, and Burr exerted himself to conciliate him. On the other hand, Jefferson seemed to hope that he could be won over.[2] Duane, of the "Aurora," visited him in prison August 23, and offered to serve as an intermediary with the government.[3] Had matters gone as the President hoped, something might have come of this manœuvre; but before further pressure could be employed, the chief-justice struck the prosecution dead.

August 19 Burr's counsel suddenly moved to arrest the evidence. The government, they said, had gone through all its testimony relating to the overt act charged in the indictment; it admitted that Burr was hundreds of miles distant from the scene; and as the district-attorney was about to introduce collateral testimony of acts done beyond the jurisdiction of the court, it became the duty of the defence to object.

For ten days this vital point was argued. All the counsel on either side exerted themselves to the utmost. Wickham's opening speech on the nature of treason was declared by as good a judge as Littleton Tazewell to be "the greatest forensic effort of the American bar."[4] Luther Martin spoke fourteen hours, beginning with an almost passionate allusion to his idol Theodosia. William Wirt exhausted his powers of argument and oratory, and in the course of his address made the rhetorical display which became familiar to every American,

[1] Blennerhassett Papers, p. 343.
[2] Jefferson to Hay, Aug. 20, 1807; Works, v. 174.
[3] Blennerhassett Papers, p. 356.
[4] Grigsby's Tazewell, p. 73.

and which introduced a sort of appeal to Blennerhassett to turn against the more guilty crew who were trying to sacrifice him to save themselves:—

"Who is Blennerhassett? A native of Ireland, a man of letters, who fled from the storms of his own country to find quiet in ours."

George Hay was neither so efficient nor so dexterous as Wirt, and either intentionally or by awkwardness succeeded in giving the impression of threatening the court:[1]—

"Mr. Bott says that we are now advocating opinions which on Fries' trial we condemned. . . . I beg leave to assure the gentleman that the censure which the judge drew on himself was not on account of his opinions, however incorrect they might be, but for his arbitrary and irregular conduct at the trial, which was one of the principal causes for which he was afterward impeached. He attempted to wrest the decision from the jury, and prejudge the case before hearing all the evidence in it,—the identical thing which this court is now called on by these gentlemen to do."

That Hay, knowing well Jefferson's thoughts and the magic that hung about the word "impeachment," should have used these words inadvertently seemed hardly credible. If he did so, his clumsiness was as offensive as the threat could have been, for the idea of impeachment was in the air of the court-house. Burr's counsel at once retaliated.[2] "It was very kind of the gentleman to remind the court of the danger of a decision of the motion in favor of the prisoner." Hay protested that he had spoken innocently, and the chief-justice said that the allusion had not been taken as personal; but the unpleasant impression remained. "The gentleman plainly insinuated the possibility of danger to the court," persisted the defence; and Luther Martin added,[3]—

"I do not know whether it were intended by this observation that your honors should be apprehensive of an im-

[1] Burr's Trial, ii. 193.
[2] Burr's Trial, ii. 238.
[3] Burr's Trial, ii. 369.

peachment in case you should decide against the wishes of the government. I will not presume that it was used with that view, but it is susceptible of being so misunderstood, however innocently or inadvertently it may have been made."

August 31 the chief-justice read his decision. Much the longest of Marshall's judicial opinions; elaborately argued, with many citations, and with less simple adherence to one leading thought than was usual in his logic,—this paper seemed, in the imagination of Marshall's enemies, to betray a painful effort to reconcile his dictum in Bollman's case with the exclusion of further evidence in the case of Burr. To laymen, who knew only the uncertainties of law; who thought that the assemblage on Blennerhassett's island was such an overt act as might, without violent impropriety, be held by a jury to be an act of levying war; and who conceived that Burr, although absent from the spot, was as principal present in a legal sense such as would excuse a jury in finding him guilty,—an uneasy doubt could not fail to suggest itself that the chief-justice, with an equal effort of ingenuity, might have produced equal conviction in a directly opposite result. On the other hand, the intent of the Constitution was clear. The men who framed that instrument remembered the crimes that had been perpetrated under the pretence of justice; for the most part they had been traitors themselves, and having risked their necks under the law they feared despotism and arbitrary power more than they feared treason. No one could doubt that their sympathies, at least in 1788, when the Constitution was framed, would have been on the side of Marshall's decision. If Jefferson, since 1788, had changed his point of view, the chief-justice was not under obligations to imitate him.

"If it be said that the advising or procurement of treason is a secret transaction which can scarcely ever be proved in the manner required by this opinion, the answer which will readily suggest itself is that the difficulty of proving a fact will not justify conviction without proof."

At the close of his decision the chief-justice, with simple

dignity which still compels respectful admiration, took up the gauntlet which the district-attorney had flung at his feet. As though turning from the crowd in the court-room to look for a moment directly into the eyes of the President, the threatened chief-justice uttered a few words that were at once answer and defiance:—

"Much has been said in the course of the argument on points on which the Court feels no inclination to comment particularly, but which may perhaps not improperly receive some notice.

"That this Court dares not usurp power is most true; that this Court dares not shrink from its duty is not less true. No man is desirous of placing himself in a disagreeable situation; no man is desirous of becoming the peculiar subject of calumny; no man, might he let the bitter cup pass from him without self-reproach, would drain it to the bottom; but if he has no choice in the case,—if there is no alternative presented to him but a dereliction of duty or the opprobrium of those who are denominated the world,—he merits the contempt as well as the indignation of his country who can hesitate which to embrace. . . .

"No testimony relative to the conduct or declarations of the prisoner elsewhere and subsequent to the transactions on Blennerhassett's island can be admitted; because such testimony, being in its nature merely corroborative, and incompetent to prove the overt act in itself, is irrelevant until there be proof of the overt act by two witnesses."

On the following day, September 1, District-Attorney Hay abandoned the case, and the jury entered a verdict of "Not guilty." Hay instantly reported to Monticello the result of his efforts, and added criticisms upon Marshall:[1]—

"Wirt, who has hitherto advocated the *integrity* of the chief-justice, now abandons him. This last opinion has opened his eyes, and he speaks in the strongest terms of reprobation."

[1] Hay to Jefferson, Sept. 1, 1807; Jefferson MSS.

September 4 Jefferson replied in the tone which always accompanied his vexation:[1] —

"Yours of the 1st came to hand yesterday. The event has been what was evidently intended from the beginning of the trial; that is to say, not only to clear Burr, but to prevent the evidence from ever going before the world. But this latter case must not take place. It is now, therefore, more than ever indispensable that not a single witness be paid or permitted to depart until his testimony has been committed to writing. . . . These whole proceedings will be laid before Congress, that they may decide whether the defect has been in the evidence of guilt, or in the law, or in the application of the law, and that they may provide the proper remedy for the past and the future."

Accordingly, although the trial for treason was at an end, the district-attorney pressed the indictment for misdemeanor; and until October 19 the chief-justice was occupied in hearing testimony intended for use not against Burr, but against himself. Then at last the conspirators were suffered to go their way, subject to legal proceedings in Ohio which the government had no idea of prosecuting; while the President, mortified and angry, prepared to pursue Marshall instead of Burr. The Federalists, who always over-rated the strength of party passions, trembled again for the Judiciary; but in truth nothing was to be feared. The days of Jefferson's power and glory had passed forever, while those of Marshall had barely begun. Even on the testimony, the President's case was far from being so clear as he had hoped and expected. His chief witness, Wilkinson, could only with difficulty be sustained; and the district-attorney, who began by pledging himself before the court to show the falsity of the charges which had been brought against the General, ended by admitting their truth.

"The declaration which I made in court in his favor some time ago," wrote Hay to the President at the close,[2] " was precipitate; and though I have not retracted it, everybody sees that I have not attempted the task which I in fact promised to perform. My confidence in him is shaken, if

[1] Jefferson to Hay, Sept. 4, 1807; Works, v. 187. Cf. Jefferson MSS.
[2] Hay to Jefferson, Oct. 15, 1807; Jefferson MSS.

not destroyed. I am sorry for it, on his own account, on the public account, and because you have expressed opinions in his favor; but you did not know then what you will soon know, and what I did not learn until after—long after—my declaration above mentioned."

The hint was strong. If Wilkinson were discredited, Jefferson himself was in danger. To attack the Supreme Court on such evidence was to invite a worse defeat than in the impeachment of Chase. Meanwhile the country had graver dangers to think about, and enemies at its doors who were not to be curbed by proclamations or impeachments.

Chapter I

JUNE 22, 1807, while Jefferson at Washington was fuming over Chief-Justice Marshall's subpœna, and while the grand jury at Richmond were on the point of finding their indictment against Burr, an event occurred at sea, off the entrance to Chesapeake Bay, which threw the country into violent excitement, distracting attention from Burr, and putting to a supreme test the theories of Jefferson's statesmanship.

That the accident which then happened should not have happened long before was matter for wonder, considering the arbitrary character of British naval officers and their small regard for neutral rights. For many years the open encouragement offered to the desertion of British seamen in American ports had caused extreme annoyance to the royal navy; and nowhere had this trouble been more serious than at Norfolk. Early in 1807 a British squadron happened to be lying within the Capes watching for some French frigates which had taken refuge at Annapolis. One or more of these British ships lay occasionally in Hampton Roads, or came to the navy-yard at Gosport for necessary repairs. Desertions were of course numerous; even the American ships-of-war had much difficulty from loss of men,—and March 7 a whole boat's crew of the British sixteen-gun sloop "Halifax" made off with the jolly-boat and escaped to Norfolk. The commander of the "Halifax" was informed that these men had enlisted in the American frigate "Chesapeake," then under orders for the Mediterranean. He complained to the British consul and to Captain Decatur, but could get no redress. He met two of the deserters in the streets of Norfolk, and asked them why they did not return. One of them, Jenkin Ratford by name, replied, with abuse and oaths, that he was in the land of liberty and would do as he liked. The British minister at Washington also made complaint that three deserters from the "Melampus" frigate had enlisted on the "Chesapeake." The Secretary of the Navy ordered an inquiry, which proved that the three men in question, one of whom was a negro, were in fact on board the "Chesapeake," but that they were native Americans who had been improperly impressed by the "Melampus," and therefore were not subjects for reclamation by the British government. The nationality was admitted, and so far as these men were concerned the answer was final; but the presence of Jenkin Ratford, an Englishman, on board the "Chesapeake" under the name of Wilson escaped notice.

The admiral in command of the British ships on the North American station was George Cranfield Berkeley, a brother of the Earl of Berkeley. To him, at Halifax, the British officers in Chesapeake Bay reported their grievances; and Admiral Berkeley, without waiting for authority from England, issued the following orders, addressed to all the ships under his command: —

"Whereas many seamen, subjects of his Britannic Majesty, and serving in his ships and vessels as per margin ["Bellona," "Belleisle," "Triumph," "Chichester," "Halifax," "Zenobia"], while at anchor in the Chesapeake, deserted and entered on board the United States frigate called the 'Chesapeake,' and openly paraded the streets of Norfolk, in sight of their officers, under the American flag, protected by the magistrates of the town and the recruiting officer belonging to the above-mentioned American frigate, which magistrates and naval officer refused giving them up, although demanded by his Britannic Majesty's consul, as well as the captains of the ships from which the said men had deserted:

"The captains and commanders of his Majesty's ships and vessels under my command are therefore hereby required and directed, in case of meeting with the American frigate 'Chesapeake' at sea, and without the limits of the United States, to show to the captain of her this order, and to require to search his ship for the deserters from the before-mentioned ships, and to proceed and search for the same; and if a similar demand should be made by the American, he is to be permitted to search for any deserters from their service, according to the customs and usage of civilized nations on terms of peace and amity with each other."

The admiral's conception of the "customs and usage of civilized nations" did not expressly require the use of force; and any captain or commander who received this circular must at once have asked whether, in case the American captain should refuse to allow a search,—as was certain,—force should be employed. The order, dated June 1, 1807, was sent to Chesapeake Bay by the frigate "Leopard," commanded by Captain S. P. Humphreys; and since the "Leopard" was the admiral's flagship, Captain Humphreys was probably acquainted with the meaning of his instructions. The "Leopard" arrived at Lynnhaven on the morning of June 21; and Captain Humphreys reported his arrival and orders to Captain John Erskine Douglas of the "Bellona," a line-of-battle ship, then lying with the "Melampus" frigate in Lynnhaven Bay, enjoying the hospitality of the American government. Apparently Captain Douglas carried verbal explanations of the order from Captain Humphreys, for he made no attempt to qualify its extremest meaning. The "Leopard" remained twenty-four hours with the "Bellona," while the two commanders were in consultation. The next morning, June 22, at 4 A. M., the "Leopard" made sail,[1] and two hours later re-anchored a few miles to the eastward, and about three miles north of Cape Henry Lighthouse.

The "Chesapeake," during the difficulties at Norfolk and afterward, lay in the Eastern Branch at Washington. The inefficiency of the Government in doing those duties which governments had hitherto been created to perform, was shown even more strikingly in the story of the "Chesapeake" than in the conspiracy of Burr. The frigate "Constitution" had sailed for the Mediterranean in August, 1803. The Government knew that her crew were entitled to their discharge, and that the President had no right to withhold it. The country was at peace; no emergency of any kind existed. A single ship of about one thousand tons burden needed to be fitted for sea at a date fixed three years beforehand; yet when the time came and the "Constitution" ought to have reached home, the "Chesapeake" had not so much as begun preparation. Captain James Barron was selected to command her as commodore of

---

[1] James's Naval History, iv. 329.

the Mediterranean squadron; Captain Charles Gordon—a native of the eastern shore of Maryland, the youngest master-commandant on the list—was appointed as her captain. Both were good officers and seamen; but Gordon received his orders only February 22, and could not take command until May 1,—long after he should have reached Gibraltar. Such was the inefficiency of the navy-yard at Washington that although the Secretary of the Navy had the "Chesapeake" under his eye and was most anxious to fit her out, and although Gordon fretted incessantly, making bitter complaints of delay, the frigate still remained in the mechanics' hands until the month of May. According to Commodore Barron the Washington navy-yard was more than incompetent.[1] "I have long known," he claimed to have written, "the perverse disposition of the rulers of that establishment." Yet he urged Gordon to complete his outfit at Washington, because the Norfolk yard was worse.[2] "I would by no means advise your leaving the navy-yard with any unfinished work and depend on Norfolk. You will experience more difficulty and trouble than you can imagine." As Burr's trial showed that the army was honeycombed by incompetence and conspiracy, so Barron's court-martial proved that nothing in naval administration could be depended upon.

For much of this, Congress and the people were responsible, and they accepted their own feebleness as the necessary consequence of a system which acted through other agencies than force; but much was also due to the Administration and to the President's instincts, which held him aloof from direct contact with both services. Jefferson did not love the deck of a man-of-war or enjoy the sound of a boatswain's whistle. The ocean was not his element; and his appetite for knowledge never led him to criticise the management of his frigates or his regiments so long as he could shut his eyes to their shortcomings. Thus while Wilkinson was left at his own pleasure to create or to stifle a rebellion at New Orleans, the crew of the "Constitution" were in a state of mutiny in the Mediterranean, and the officers of the "Chesapeake" were helpless under the control of the navy-yard at Washington.

[1] Barron's Court-martial, p. 241.
[2] Barron to Gordon, May 1, 1807; Court-martial, p. 239.

At length, in the earliest days of June, Gordon dropped down the Potomac. The "Chesapeake" was to carry on this cruise an armament of forty guns,—twenty-eight 18-pounders and twelve 32-pound carronades; but owing to the shoals in the river she took but twelve guns on board at Washington, the rest waiting her arrival at Norfolk. With these twelve guns Gordon tried to fire the customary salute in passing Mount Vernon; and he wrote to the secretary in exasperation at the result of this first experience:[1] —

> "Had we been engaged in an active war I should suspect the officers of the yard with having a design on my character; but fortunately Mount Vernon drew our attention to the guns before we could apprehend any danger from an enemy. In the act of saluting that place I was struck with astonishment when the first lieutenant reported to me that neither the sponges nor cartridges would go in the guns. I immediately arrested my gunner; but on his satisfying me that he had received them from the gunner of the yard I released him, and hold Mr. Stevenson responsible."

The mistakes were easily corrected, and the ship arrived in Hampton Roads without further incident. Commodore Barron, who first came aboard June 6, wrote[2] at once to the secretary, "that from the extreme cleanliness and order in which I found her I am convinced that Captain Gordon and his officers must have used great exertions. Captain Gordon speaks in high terms of his lieutenants. The state of the ship proves the justice of his encomiums."

Nevertheless much remained to be done, and in spite of the secretary's urgency the ship was still delayed in Hampton Roads. From June 6 to June 19, notwithstanding bad weather, the whole ship's company were hard worked. The guns were taken on board and fitted; water was got in; spars and rigging had to be overhauled, and stores for four hundred men on a three-years cruise were shipped. June 19 the guns were all fitted, and the crew could for the first time be assigned to their stations at quarters. According to the custom of the service,

[1] Captain Gordon to the Secretary of the Navy, June 22, 1807; Court martial, p 259.

[2] Barron to the Secretary of the Navy, June 6, 1807; Court-martial, p. 371.

the guns were charged with powder and shot. They had no locks, and were fired by the old-fashioned slow-match, or by loggerheads kept in the magazine and heated red-hot in the galley fire whenever need for them arose.

June 19 Captain Gordon considered the ship ready for sea, and wrote to the commodore on shore,[1] "We are unmoored and ready for weighing the first fair wind." Both Captain Gordon and Commodore Barron were aware that the decks were more or less encumbered, and that the crew had not been exercised at the guns; but they were not warranted in detaining her on that account, especially since the guns could be better exercised at sea, and the ship was already four months behind time. Accordingly, June 21, Commodore Barron came on board, and at four o'clock in the afternoon the "Chesapeake" weighed anchor and stood down the Roads; at six o'clock she came to, dropped anchor, called all hands to quarters, and prepared to start for sea the next morning. From Lynnhaven Bay the "Leopard," which had arrived from Halifax only a few hours before, could watch every movement of the American frigate.

At a quarter-past seven o'clock on the morning of June 22 the "Chesapeake" got under way with a fair breeze. Her ship's company numbered three hundred and seventy-five men and boys, all told, but, as was not uncommon in leaving port, much sickness prevailed among the crew, and by the doctor's order the sick seamen were allowed to lie in the sun and air on the upper deck. The gun-deck between the guns was encumbered with lumber of one sort or another; the cables were not yet stowed away; four of the guns did not fit quite perfectly to their carriages, and needed a few blows with a maul to drive the trunnions home, but this defect escaped the eye; in the magazine the gunner had reported the powder-horns, used in priming the guns, as filled, whereas only five were in fact filled. Otherwise the ship, except for the freshness of her crew, was in fair condition.

At nine o'clock, passing Lynnhaven Bay, the officers on deck noticed the "Bellona" and "Melampus" at anchor. The "Leopard" lay farther out, and the "Bellona" was observed to

[1] Gordon to Barron, June 19, 1807, p. 367.

be signalling. A story had been circulated at Norfolk that the captain of the "Melampus" threatened to take his deserters out of the "Chesapeake;" but rumors of this sort roused so little attention that no one on board the American frigate gave special notice to the British squadron. The "Melampus" lay quietly at anchor. Had Barron been able to read the "Bellona's" signals he would have suspected nothing, for they contained merely an order to the "Leopard" to weigh and reconnoitre in the southeast by east.[1] The British squadron was in the habit of keeping a cruiser outside to overhaul merchant-vessels; and when the "Leopard" stood out to sea, the officers of the "Chesapeake" naturally supposed that this was her errand.

At noon Cape Henry bore southwest by south, distant one or two miles. The day was fine; but the breeze then shifted to the south-southeast, and began to blow fresh. The change of wind brought the "Leopard" to windward. At about a quarter-past two the "Chesapeake" tacked in shore to wait for the pilot-boat which was to take off the pilot. The "Leopard" tacked also, about a mile distant. At the same time dinner was served at the commodore's table, and Barron, Gordon, Captain Hall of the marines, Dr. Bullus and his wife sat down to it. Captain Gordon afterward testified that as they were dining Commodore Barron noticed the British frigate through the larboard forward port of the cabin, and made the remark "that her movements appeared suspicious, but she could have nothing to do with us."[2] Barron positively denied ever having made the remark; but whether he said it or not, nothing more than a passing doubt occurred to him or to any other person on board. Gordon returned to his work; the crew began to stow away the cable; and at a quarter before three o'clock, the pilot-boat nearing, the "Chesapeake" again stood out to sea, the "Leopard" immediately following her tack.

At about half-past three o'clock, both ships being eight or ten miles southeast by east of Cape Henry, the "Leopard" came down before the wind, and rounding to, about half a cable's length to windward, hailed, and said she had despatches for the commodore. Barron returned the hail and

[1] James's Naval History, iv. 329.
[2] Court-martial, p. 101.

replied, "We will heave to and you can send your boat on board of us." British ships-of-war on distant stations not infrequently sent despatches by the courtesy of American officers, and such a request implied no hostile purpose. British ships also arrogated a sort of right to the windward; and the "Leopard's" manœuvre, although one which no commander except an Englishman would naturally have made, roused no peculiar attention. The "Leopard's" ports were seen to be triced up; but the season was midsummer, the weather was fine and warm, and the frigate was in sight of her anchorage. Doubtless Barron ought not to have allowed a foreign ship-of-war to come alongside without calling his crew to quarters,—such was the general rule of the service; but the condition of the ship made it inconvenient to clear the guns, and the idea of an attack was so extravagant that, as Barron afterward said, he might as well have expected one when at anchor in Hampton Roads. After the event several officers, including Captain Gordon, affirmed that they felt suspicions; but they showed none at the time, and neither Gordon nor any one else suggested, either to the commodore or to each other, that it would be well to order the crew to quarters.

Barron went to his cabin to receive the British officer, whose boat came alongside. At a quarter before four o'clock Lieutenant Meade from the "Leopard" arrived on board, and was shown by Captain Gordon to the commodore's cabin. He delivered the following note:—

"The captain of his Britannic Majesty's ship 'Leopard' has the honor to enclose the captain of the United States ship 'Chesapeake' an order from the Honorable Vice-Admiral Berkeley, commander-in-chief of his Majesty's ships on the North American station, respecting some deserters from the ships (therein mentioned) under his command, and supposed to be now serving as part of the crew of the 'Chesapeake.'

"The captain of the 'Leopard' will not presume to say anything in addition to what the commander-in-chief has stated, more than to express a hope that every circumstance respecting them may be adjusted in a manner that the harmony subsisting between the two countries may remain undisturbed."

Having read Captain Humphrey's note, Commodore Barron took up the enclosed order signed by Admiral Berkeley. This order, as the note mentioned, designated deserters from certain ships. Barron knew that he had on board three deserters from the "Melampus," and that these three men had been the only deserters officially and regularly demanded by the British minister. His first thought was to look for the "Melampus" in the admiral's list; and on seeing that Berkeley had omitted it, Barron inferred that his own assurance would satisfy Captain Humphreys, and that the demand of search, being meant as a mere formality, would not be pressed. He explained to the British lieutenant the circumstances relating to the three men from the "Melampus," and after some consultation with Dr. Bullus, who was going out as consul to the Mediterranean, he wrote to Captain Humphreys the following reply: —

"I know of no such men as you describe. The officers that were on the recruiting service for this ship were particularly instructed by the Government, through me, not to enter any deserters from his Britannic Majesty's ships, nor do I know of any being here. I am also instructed never to permit the crew of any ship that I command to be mustered by any other but their own officers. It is my disposition to preserve harmony, and I hope this answer to your despatch will prove satisfactory."

Such an answer to such a demand was little suited to check the energy of a British officer in carrying out his positive orders. If Barron had wished to invite an attack, he could have done nothing more to the purpose than by receiving Berkeley's orders without a movement of self-defence.

Meanwhile, at a quarter-past four the officer of the deck sent down word that the British frigate had a signal flying. The lieutenant understood it for a signal of recall, as he had been half an hour away, and as soon as the letter could be written he hurried with it to his boat. No sooner had he left the cabin than Barron sent for Gordon and showed him the letters which had passed. Although the commodore hoped that the matter was disposed of, and assumed that Captain Humphreys would give some notice in case of further action, he could not but feel a show of energy to be proper, and he directed Gordon to order the gun-deck to be cleared. Instantly the officers began to prepare the ship for action.

Had the British admiral sent the "Bellona" or some other seventy-four on this ugly errand, Barron's error would have been less serious; for the captain of a seventy-four would have felt himself strong enough to allow delay. Sending the "Leopard" was arrogance of a kind that the British navy at that time frequently displayed. In 1804, when the Spanish treasure-ships were seized, the bitterest complaint of Spain was not that she had been made the unsuspecting victim of piracy, but that her squadron had been waylaid by one of only equal force, and could not in honor yield without a massacre which cost four ships and three hundred lives, besides the disgrace of submission to an enemy of not superior strength. The "Leopard" did indeed carry fifty-two guns, while the "Chesapeake" on this cruise carried only forty; but the "Chesapeake's" twelve carronades threw heavier shot than the "Leopard's" heaviest, and her broadside weighed 444 pounds, while that of the "Leopard" weighed 447. In tonnage the "Chesapeake" was a stronger ship and carried a larger crew than the "Leopard;" and a battle on fair terms would have been no certain victory. That Captain Humphreys felt it necessary to gain and retain every possible advantage was evident from his conduct. He could not afford to run the risk of defeat in such an undertaking; and knowing that the "Chesapeake" needed time to prepare for battle, he felt not strong enough to disregard her power of resistance, as he might have done had he commanded a ship of the line. To carry out his orders with as little loss as possible was his duty; for the consequences, not he but his admiral was to blame. Without a moment of delay, edging nearer, he hailed and cried: "Commodore Barron, you must be aware of the necessity I am under of complying with the orders of my commander-in-chief."

Hardly more than five minutes passed between the moment when the British officer left Commodore Barron's cabin and the time when Barron was hailed. To get the ship ready for action required fully half an hour. Barron, after giving the order to clear the guns, had come on deck and was standing in the gangway watching the "Leopard" with rapidly increasing anxiety, as he saw that the tompions were out of her guns and that her crew were evidently at quarters. He instantly repeated the order to prepare for battle, and told Gordon to hurry the men to their stations quietly without drum-beat. Gordon hastened down to the gun-deck with the keys of the magazine; the crew sprang to their quarters as soon as they understood the order. Barron, aware that his only chance was to gain time, remained at the gangway and replied through his trumpet: "I do not hear what you say." Captain Humphreys repeated his hail, and Barron again replied that he did not understand. The "Leopard" immediately fired a shot across the "Chesapeake's" bow;[1] a minute later another shot followed; and in two minutes more, at half-past four o'clock, the "Leopard" poured her whole broadside of solid shot and canister, at the distance of one hundred and fifty or two hundred feet, point-blank into the helpless American frigate. Before the gunner of the "Chesapeake" got to his magazine he heard the first gun from the "Leopard;" just as he opened and entered the magazine the "Leopard's" broadside was fired.

No situation could be more trying to officers and crew than to be thus stationed at their guns without a chance to return a fire. The guns of the "Chesapeake" were loaded, but could not be discharged for want of lighted matches or heated loggerheads; and even if discharged, they could not be reloaded until ammunition should be handed from the magazine. Time was required both to clear the guns and to fire them; but the "Leopard's" first broadside was thrown just as the crew were beginning to clear the deck. The crew were fresh and untrained; but no complaint was made on this account,—all were willing enough to fight. The confusion was little greater than might have occurred under the same circumstances in the best-drilled crew afloat; and the harshest subsequent scrutiny discovered no want of discipline, except that toward the

[1] James's Naval History, iv. 330.

end a few men left their guns, declaring that they were ready to fight but not to be shot down like sheep. About the magazine the confusion was greatest, for a crowd of men and boys were clamoring for matches, powder-flasks, and loggerheads, while the gunner and his mates were doing their utmost to pass up what was needed; but in reasonable time all wants could have been supplied. On the upper deck both officers and men behaved well. Barron, though naturally much excited, showed both sense and courage. Standing in the open gangway fully exposed to the "Leopard's" guns, he was wounded by the first broadside, but remained either there or on the quarter-deck without noticing his wound, while he repeatedly hailed the "Leopard" in the hope of gaining a moment's time, and sent officer after officer below to hurry the men at the guns. Neither among the officers nor among the crew was courage the resource that failed them. Many of the men on the upper deck exposed themselves unnecessarily to the flying grapeshot by standing on the guns and looking over the hammocks, till Barron ordered them down. Careful subsequent inquiry could detect no lack of gallantry except in the pilot, who when questioned as to the commodore's behavior had the manliness to confess his alarm,—"I was too bad scared myself to observe him very particularly."

The British account, which was very exact, said that the "Leopard's" fire lasted fifteen minutes,—from 4.30 to 4.45 P. M.,—during which time three full broadsides were discharged without return. No one could demand that Commodore Barron should subject his crew and ship to a longer trial when he had no hope of success. The time in which the "Leopard" could have sunk the "Chesapeake" might be a matter of doubt; but in the next battle between similar ships, five years afterward, the "Constitution," with about the "Leopard's" armament, totally disabled the "Guerriere" in less than thirty minutes, so that she sank within twenty-four hours,— though at the time of the action a heavy sea was running, and the "Guerriere" fought desperately with her whole broadside of twenty-five guns. June 22, 1807, the sea was calm; the "Leopard" lay quietly within pistol-shot; the "Chesapeake" could not injure her; and if the "Leopard" was as well fought as the "Constitution" she should have done at least equal damage. If she did not succeed, it was not for want of trying. The official survey, taken the next day, showed twenty-two round-shot in the "Chesapeake's" hull, ten shot-holes in the sails, all three masts badly injured, the rigging much cut by grape, three men killed, eight severely and ten slightly wounded, including Commodore Barron,—which proved that of the seventy or eighty discharges from the "Leopard's" guns a large proportion took effect.

After enduring this massacre for fifteen minutes, while trying to fire back at least one gun for the honor of the ship, Commodore Barron ordered the flag to be struck. It was hauled down; and as it touched the taffrail one gun was discharged from the gun-deck sending a shot into the "Leopard." This single gun was fired by the third lieutenant, Allen, by means of a live coal which he brought in his fingers from the galley.

The boats of the "Leopard" then came on board, bringing several British officers, who mustered the ship's company. They selected the three Americans who had deserted from the "Melampus," and were therefore not included in Berkeley's order. Twelve or fifteen others were pointed out as English deserters, but these men were not taken. After a search of the ship, Jenkin Ratford was dragged out of the coal-hole; and this discovery alone saved Captain Humphreys from the blame of committing an outrage not only lawless but purposeless. At about seven o'clock the British officers left the ship, taking with them the three Americans and Jenkin Ratford. Immediately afterward Commodore Barron sent Lieutenant Allen on board the "Leopard" with a brief letter to Captain Humphreys:—

"I consider the frigate 'Chesapeake' your prize, and am ready to deliver her to any officer authorized to receive her. By the return of the boat I shall expect your answer."

The British captain immediately replied as follows:

"Having to the utmost of my power fulfilled the instructions of my commander-in-chief, I have nothing more to desire, and must in consequence proceed to join the remainder of the squadron,—repeating that I am ready to give you every assistance in my power, and do most sincerely deplore that any lives should have been lost in the execution of a service which might have been adjusted more amicably, not only with respect to ourselves but the nations to which we respectively belong."

At eight o'clock Barron called a council of officers to consider what was best to be done with the ship, and it was unanimously decided to return to the Roads and wait orders. Disgraced, degraded, with officers and crew smarting under a humiliation that was never forgotten or forgiven, the unlucky "Chesapeake" dragged her way back to Norfolk.

There she lay for many months. Barron's wrong was in the nature of a crime. His brother officers made severe comments on his conduct; and Captain Gordon and some of his fellow-sufferers joined in the cry. One of his harshest critics was Stephen Decatur. Public sentiment required a victim. A court of inquiry which sat at Norfolk in October reported strongly against the commodore. He was charged with neglect of duty, with having failed to prepare his ship for action, with having surrendered prematurely, with having discouraged his men; but beneath all these charges lay an unjust belief in his want of courage. After six months delay, Barron was brought before a court-martial Jan. 4, 1808, and allowed to make his defence.

The court-martial took place at Norfolk, on board the "Chesapeake,"—his own ship, which recalled at every moment his disgrace. The judges were his juniors, with the single exception of Captain John Rodgers, who was president of the court. Among them sat Stephen Decatur,—a brilliant officer, but one who had still to undergo the experience of striking his flag and of hearing the world suspect his surrender to be premature. Decatur held strong opinions against Barron, and not only expressed them strongly, but also notified Barron of them in order that he might, if he pleased, exercise the privilege of challenging. Barron made no objection, and Decatur unwillingly kept his place. In other respects Barron was still more hardly treated by fortune; the first lieutenant of the "Chesapeake" had died in the interval; Dr. Bullus, whose evidence was of the utmost importance, could not appear;

Captain Gordon turned against him, and expressed the free opinion that Barron had never meant to resist; Captains Murray, Hull, and Chauncey, on the court of inquiry, had already made a hostile report; and the government prosecutor pressed every charge with a persistency that, as coming from the Department, seemed almost vindictive.

From January 4 to February 8 the court-martial tried charges against Barron, after which it continued until February 22 trying Captain Gordon, Captain Hall of the marines, and William Hook the gunner. The result of this long, searching, and severe investigation was remarkable, for it ended in a very elaborate decision[1] that Barron was blameless in every particular except one. He had not been negligent of his duty; he was not to blame for omitting to call the crew to quarters before he received Captain Humphreys' letter; he did well in getting the men to quarters secretly without drum-beat; he did not discourage his men; he had shown coolness, reflection, and personal courage under the most trying circumstances; he was right in striking his flag when he did, — but he was wrong in failing to prepare for action instantly on reading Admiral Berkeley's order; and for this mistake he was condemned to suspension for five years from the service, without pay or emoluments.

Barron had argued that although his judgment on this point proved to be mistaken, it was reasonable, and in accord with his instructions. He produced the orders of the Secretary of the Navy, dated May 15, 1807, written with full knowledge that the deserters from the "Melampus" had been claimed by the British minister, and that a British squadron was lying in Chesapeake Bay. "Our interest as well as good faith requires," said the secretary, ". . . that we should cautiously avoid whatever may have a tendency to bring us into collision with any other Power." Barron urged that if he had given the order to prepare for battle as required by the court-martial, he must have detained by force the British lieutenant and his boat's crew, which would have had a direct "tendency to bring us into collision," or he must have let them go, which would have hurried the collision. He said that he had tried to gain

[1] Court-martial, pp. 337–350.

time by keeping the appearances of confidence and good-will. He admitted that he had failed, but claimed that the failure was due to no fault which could have been corrected at that moment by those means.

The defence was open to criticism, especially because Barron himself could claim to have made no use of the time he gained. Yet perhaps, on the whole, the court-martial might have done better to punish Barron for his want of caution in permitting the British frigate to approach. This was his first error, which could not be retrieved; and Barron could hardly have complained of his punishment, even though every officer in the service knew that the rule of going to quarters in such cases was seldom strictly observed. The President and the Secretary of the Navy could alone say whether Barron had understood their orders correctly, and whether his plea, founded on the secretary's instructions, was sound. In the light of Jefferson's diplomacy, Barron's course accorded with his instructions; and perhaps, had the President claimed his own share in the "Chesapeake's" disaster, he would have refused to degrade a faithful, able, and gallant seaman for obeying the spirit and letter of his orders. Unfortunately such an interference would have ruined the navy; and so it happened that what Jefferson had so long foreseen took place. He had maintained that the frigates were a mere invitation to attack; that they created the dangers they were built to resist, and tempted the aggressions of Great Britain, which would, but for these ships, find no object to covet; and when the prediction turned true, he was still obliged to maintain the character of the service. He approved the sentence of the court-martial.

So far as the service was concerned, Barron's punishment was not likely to stimulate its caution, for no American captain, unless he wished to be hung by his own crew at his own yard-arm, was likely ever again to let a British frigate come within gunshot without taking such precautions as he would have taken against a pirate; but though the degradation could do little for the service, it cost Barron his honor, and ended by costing Decatur his life.

Meanwhile, Captain Humphreys reported to Captain Douglas on the "Bellona," and Captain Douglas reported the whole affair to Admiral Berkeley at Halifax, who received at the same time accounts from American sources. The admiral immediately wrote to approve the manner in which his orders had been carried out. "As far as I am enabled to judge," he said[1] in a letter to Captain Humphreys, dated July 4, "you have conducted yourself most properly." The inevitable touch of unconscious comedy was not wanting in the British admiral, whose character recalled Smollett's novels and memories of Commodore Hawser Trunnion. "I hope you mind the public accounts which have been published of this affair as little as I do," he continued; "we must make allowances for the heated state of the populace in a country where law and every tie, both civil and religious, is treated so lightly." No broader humor could be found in "Peregrine Pickle" than in one breath to approve an act so lawless that no man of common-sense even in England ventured to defend it as lawful, and in the next to read the Americans a moral lecture on their want of law and religion; yet grotesque as this old-fashioned naval morality might be, no man in England noticed either its humor or its absurdity.

As though to show that he meant no humor by it, the admiral, August 25, called a court-martial, which the next day sentenced Jenkin Ratford to be hanged, and the three American deserters from the "Melampus" to receive five hundred lashes each. The last part of the sentence was not carried out, and the three Americans remained quietly in prison; but August 31, Jenkin Ratford was duly hanged from the foreyard arm of his own ship, the "Halifax."

[1] Marshall's Naval Biography, iv. 895.

Chapter II

FOR THE FIRST TIME in their history the people of the United States learned, in June, 1807, the feeling of a true national emotion. Hitherto every public passion had been more or less partial and one-sided; even the death of Washington had been ostentatiously mourned in the interests and to the profit of party: but the outrage committed on the "Chesapeake" stung through hide-bound prejudices, and made democrat and aristocrat writhe alike. The brand seethed and hissed like the glowing olive-stake of Ulysses in the Cyclops' eye, until the whole American people, like Cyclops, roared with pain and stood frantic on the shore, hurling abuse at their enemy, who taunted them from his safe ships. The mob at Norfolk, furious at the sight of their dead and wounded comrades from the "Chesapeake," ran riot, and in the want of a better object of attack destroyed the water-casks of the British squadron. July 29 the town forbade communication with the ships in Lynnhaven Bay, which caused Captain Douglas to write to the Mayor of Norfolk a letter much in the tone of Admiral Berkeley.

"You must be perfectly aware," said he, "that the British flag never has been, nor will be, insulted with impunity. You must also be aware that it has been, and still is, in my power to obstruct the whole trade of the Chesapeake since the late circumstance; which I desisted from, trusting that general unanimity would be restored. . . . Agreeably to my intentions, I have proceeded to Hampton Roads, with the squadron under my command, to await your answer, which I trust you will favor me with without delay."

He demanded that the prohibition of intercourse should be "immediately annulled." The Mayor sent Littleton Tazewell to carry an answer to this warlike demand from the "Bellona," and Tazewell was somewhat surprised to find Captain Douglas highly conciliatory, and unable to see what the people of Norfolk could have found in his letter which could be regarded as "menacing;" but meanwhile all Virginia was aroused, an attack on Norfolk was generally expected, the coast was patrolled by an armed force, and the British men-of-war were threatened by mounted militia.

In the Northern States the feeling was little less violent. Public meetings were everywhere held. At New York, July 2, the citizens, at a meeting over which De Witt Clinton presided, denounced "the dastardly and unprovoked attack" on the "Chesapeake," and pledged themselves to support the government "in whatever measures it may deem necessary to adopt in the present crisis of affairs." At Boston, where the town government was wholly Federalist, a moment of hesitation occurred.[1] The principal Federalists consulted with each other, and decided not to call a town-meeting. July 10 an informal meeting was called by the Republicans, over which Elbridge Gerry presided, and which Senator J. Q. Adams alone among the prominent Federalists attended. There also a resolution was adopted, pledging cheerful co-operation "in any measures, however serious," which the Administration might deem necessary for the safety and honor of the country. In a few days public opinion compelled the Federalists to change their tone. A town-meeting was held at Faneuil Hall July 16, and Senator Adams again reported resolutions, which were unanimously adopted, pledging effectual support to the government. Yet the Essex Junto held aloof; neither George Cabot, Theophilus Parsons, nor Timothy Pickering would take part in such proceedings, and the Federalist newspaper which was supposed to represent their opinions went so far as to assert that Admiral Berkeley's doctrine was correct, and that British men-of-war had a right to take deserters from the national vessels of the United States. In private, this opinion was hotly maintained; in public, its expression was generally thought unwise in face of popular excitement.

President Jefferson was at Washington June 25, the day when news of the outrage arrived; but his Cabinet was widely scattered, and some time passed before its members could be reassembled. Gallatin was last to arrive; but July 2, at a full meeting, the President read the draft of a proclamation, which was approved, and the proclamation issued on the

[1] New England Federalism, p. 182.

same day. It rehearsed the story of American injuries and for-bearance, and of British aggressions upon neutral rights; and so moderate was its tone as to convey rather the idea of dep-recation than of anger:—

> "Hospitality under such circumstances ceases to be a duty; and a continuance of it, with such uncontrolled abuses, would tend only, by multiplying injuries and irri-tations, to bring on a rupture between the two nations. This extreme resort is equally opposed to the interests of both, as it is to assurances of the most friendly dispositions on the part of the British government, in the midst of which this outrage has been committed. In this light the subject cannot but present itself to that government, and strengthen the motives to an honorable reparation of the wrong which has been done, and to that effectual control of its naval commanders which alone can justify the govern-ment of the United States in the exercise of those hospital-ities it is now constrained to discontinue."

With this preamble the proclamation required all armed vessels of Great Britain to depart from American waters; and in case of their failing to do so, the President forbade inter-course with them, and prohibited supplies to be furnished them.

At the same Cabinet meeting, according to Jefferson's memoranda,[1] other measures were taken. The gunboats were ordered to points where attack might be feared. The Presi-dent was to "recall all our vessels from the Mediterranean, by a vessel to be sent express, and send the 'Revenge' to England with despatches to our minister demanding satisfaction for the attack on the 'Chesapeake;' in which must be included—(1) a disavowal of the act and of the principle of searching a public armed vessel; (2) a restoration of the men taken; (3) a recall of Admiral Berkeley. Communicate the incident which has happened to Russia." Two days afterward, at another Cabinet meeting, it was "agreed that a call of Congress shall issue the fourth Monday of August (24), to meet the fourth Monday in October (26), unless new occurrences should

---

[1] Cabinet Memoranda; Writings (Ford), i. 324.

render an earlier call necessary. Robert Smith wished an earlier call." He was not alone in this wish. Gallatin wrote privately to his wife that he wanted an immediate call, and that the chief objection to it, which would not be openly avowed, was the unhealthiness of Washington city.[1]

The news of Captain Douglas's threatening conduct and language at Norfolk produced further measures. July 5 "it was agreed to call on the governors of the States to have their quotas of one hundred thousand militia in readiness. The object is to have the portions on the sea-coast ready for any emergency; and for those in the North we may look to a winter expedition against Canada." July 7 it was "agreed to desire the Governor of Virginia to order such portion of militia into actual service as may be necessary for defence of Norfolk and of the gunboats at Hampton and in Matthews County." Little by little Jefferson was drawn into preparations for actual war.

Even among earnest Republicans the tone of Jefferson's proclamation and the character of his measures were at first denounced as tame. John Randolph called the proclamation an "apology;" Joseph Nicholson wrote to Gallatin a remonstrance.

> "But one feeling pervades the nation," said he;[2] "all distinctions of Federalism and Democracy are vanished. The people are ready to submit to any deprivation; and if we withdraw ourselves within our own shell, and turn loose some thousands of privateers, we shall obtain in a little time an absolute renunciation of the right of search for the purposes of impressment. A parley will prove fatal; for the merchants will begin to calculate. They rule us, and we should take them before their resentment is superseded by considerations of profit and loss. I trust in God the 'Revenge' is going out to bring Monroe and Pinkney home."

Gallatin, who had hitherto thrown all his influence on the side of peace, was then devoting all his energies to provision for war. He answered Nicholson that the tone of Government, though he thought it correct, was of little consequence,

[1] Adams's Gallatin, p. 358.
[2] Nicholson to Gallatin, July 14, 1807; Adams's Gallatin, p. 360.

for in any case the result would be the same; he was confident that England would give neither satisfaction nor security.[1]

"I will, however, acknowledge that on that particular point I have not bestowed much thought; for having considered from the first moment war was a necessary result, and the preliminaries appearing to me but matters of form, my faculties have been exclusively applied to the preparations necessary to meet the times. And although I am not very sanguine as to the brilliancy of our exploits, the field where we can act without a navy being very limited, and perfectly aware that a war, in a great degree passive, and consisting of privations, will become very irksome to the people, I feel no apprehension of the immediate result. We will be poorer both as a nation and as a government, our debt and taxes will increase, and our progress in every respect be interrupted; but all those evils are not only not to be put in competition with the independence and honor of the nation, they are moreover temporary, and a very few years of peace will obliterate their effects. Nor do I know whether the awakening of nobler feelings and habits than avarice and luxury might not be necessary to prevent our degenerating, like the Hollanders, into a nation of mere calculators."

Jefferson followed without protest the impulse toward war; but his leading thought was to avoid it. Peace was still his passion, and his scheme of peaceful coercion had not yet been tried. Even while the nation was aflame with warlike enthusiasm, his own mind always reverted to another thought. The tone of the proclamation showed it; his unwillingness to call Congress proved it; his letters dwelt upon it.

"We have acted on these principles," he wrote in regard to England,[2] — "(1) to give that Government an opportunity to disavow and make reparation; (2) to give ourselves time to get in the vessels, property, and seamen now spread over the ocean; (3) to do no act which might compromit

[1] Gallatin to Nicholson, July 17, 1807; Adams's Gallatin, p. 361.
[2] Jefferson to Bidwell, July 11, 1807; Works, v. 125.

Congress in their choice between war, non-intercourse, or any other measure."

To Vice-President Clinton he wrote,[1] that since the power of declaring war was with the Legislature, the Executive should do nothing necessarily committing them to decide for war in preference to non-intercourse, "which will be preferred by a great many." Every letter[2] written by the President during the crisis contained some allusion to non-intercourse, which he still called the "peaceable means of repressing injustice, by making it the interest of the aggressor to do what is just, and abstain from future wrong." As the war fever grew stronger he talked more boldly about hostilities, and became silent about non-intercourse;[3] but the delay in calling Congress was certain to work as he wished, and to prevent a committal to the policy of war.

To no one was this working of Jefferson's mind more evident than to General Turreau, whose keen eyes made the President uneasy under the sense of being watched and criticised. Turreau, who had left Washington for the summer, hurried back on hearing of the "Chesapeake" disaster. On arriving, he went the same evening to the White House, "where there had been a dinner of twenty covers, composed, they say, of new friends of the Government, to whom Mr. Madison had given a first representation two days before. Indeed, I knew none of the guests except the Ambassador of England and his secretary of legation. The President received me even better than usual, but left me, presently, to follow with the British minister a conversation that my entrance had interrupted."[4]

Then came a touch of nature which Turreau thought strikingly characteristic. No strong power of imagination is needed to see the White House parlor, on the warm summer night, with Jefferson, as Senator Maclay described him, sitting in a lounging manner on one hip, with his loose, long figure,

[1] Jefferson to the Vice-President, July 6, 1807; Works, v. 115.
[2] Jefferson to Governor Cabell, June 29, 1807, Works, v. 114; to Mr. Bowdoin, July 10, 1807, Works, v. 123; to M. Dupont, July 14, 1807, Works, v. 127; to Lafayette, July 14, 1807, Works, v. 129.
[3] Jefferson to Colonel Taylor, Aug. 1, 1807; Works, v. 148.
[4] Turreau to Talleyrand, July 18, 1808; Archives des Aff. Étr. MSS.

and his clothes that seemed too small for him, talking, without a break, in his rambling, disjointed way, showing deep excitement under an affectation of coolness, and at every word and look betraying himself to the prying eyes of Talleyrand's suspicious agent. What Jefferson said, and how he said it, can be told only in Turreau's version; but perhaps the few words used by the prejudiced Frenchman gave a clearer idea of American politics than could be got from all other sources together: —

"This conversation with the British minister having been brought to an end, Mr. Jefferson came and sat down by my side; and after all the American guests had successively retired, Mr. Erskine, who had held out longest, — in the hope, perhaps, that I should quit the ground, — went away also. The President spoke to me about the 'Chesapeake' affair, and said: 'If the English do not give us the satisfaction we demand, we will take Canada, which wants to enter the Union; and when, together with Canada, we shall have the Floridas, we shall no longer have any difficulties with our neighbors; and it is the only way of preventing them. I expected that the Emperor would return sooner to Paris, — and then this affair of the Floridas would be ended.' Then, changing the subject, he asked me what were the means to employ in order to be able to defend the American harbors and coasts. I answered that the choice of means depended on local conditions, and that his officers, after an exact reconnoissance, ought to pronounce on the application of suitable means of defence. — 'We have no officers!' — He treated twenty-seven different subjects in a conversation of half an hour; and as he showed, as usual, no sort of distrust, this conversation of fits and starts (*à bâtons rompus*) makes me infer that the event would embarrass him much, — and Mr. Madison seemed to me to share this embarrassment. . . . Once for all, whatever may be the disposition of mind here, though every one is lashing himself (*se batte les flancs*) to take a warlike attitude, I can assure your Highness that the President does not want war, and that Mr. Madison dreads it still more. I am convinced that these two personages will do everything that is possible to avoid it, and that if Congress, which will be called together only when an answer shall have arrived from England, should think itself bound, as organ of public opinion, to determine on war, its intention will be crossed by powerful intrigues, because the actual Administration has nothing to gain and everything to lose by war."

Turreau was not the only observer who saw beneath the surface of American politics. The young British minister, Erskine, who enlivened his despatches by no such lightness of touch as was usual with his French colleague, wrote to the new Foreign Secretary of England, George Canning, only brief and dry accounts of the situation at Washington, but showed almost a flash of genius in the far-reaching policy he struck out.

"The ferment in the public mind," he wrote July 21,[1] "has not yet subsided, and I am confirmed in the opinion . . . that this country will engage in war rather than submit to their national armed ships being forcibly searched on the high seas. . . . Should his Majesty think fit to cause an apology to be offered to these States on account of the attack of his Majesty's ship 'Leopard' on the United States frigate 'Chesapeake,' it would have the most powerful effect not only on the minds of the people of this country, but would render it impossible for the Congress to bring on a war upon the other points of difference between his Majesty and the United States at present under discussion."

A single blow, however violent, could not weld a nation. Every one saw that the very violence of temper which made the month of July, 1807, a moment without a parallel in American history since the battle of Lexington, would be followed by a long reaction of doubt and discord. If the President, the Secretary of State, and great numbers of their stanchest friends hesitated to fight when a foreign nation, after robbing their commerce, fired into their ships of war, and slaughtered or carried off their fellow-citizens,—if they preferred "peaceable means of repressing injustice" at the moment when every nerve would naturally have been strung to

[1] Erskine to Canning, July 21, 1807; MSS. British Archives.

recklessness with the impulse to strike back,—it was in the highest degree unlikely that they would be more earnest for war when time had deadened the sense of wrong. Neither England, France, nor Spain could fail to see that the moment when aggression ceased to be safe had not yet arrived.

The people were deeply excited, commerce for the moment was paralyzed, no merchant dared send out a ship, and the country resounded with cries of war when the "Revenge" sailed, bearing instructions to Monroe to demand reparation from the British government. These instructions, dated July 6, 1807, were framed in the spirit which seemed to characterize Madison's diplomatic acts. Specific redress for a specific wrong appeared an easy demand. That the attack on the "Chesapeake" should be disavowed; that the men who had been seized should be restored; that punctilious exactness of form should mark the apology and retribution,—was matter of course; but that this special outrage, which stood on special ground, should be kept apart, and that its atonement should precede the consideration of every other disputed point, was the natural method of dealing with it if either party was serious in wishing for peace. Such a wound, left open to fester and smart, was certain to make war in the end inevitable. Both the President and Madison wanted peace; yet their instructions to Monroe made a settlement of the "Chesapeake" outrage impracticable by binding it to a settlement of the wider dispute as to impressments from merchant vessels.

"As a security for the future," wrote Madison,[1] "an entire abolition of impressments from vessels under the flag of the United States, if not already arranged, is also to make an indispensable part of the satisfaction."

Among the many impossibilities which had been required of Monroe during the last four years, this was one of the plainest. The demand was preliminary, in ordinary diplomatic usage, to a declaration of war; and nothing in Jefferson's Presidency was more surprising than that he should have thought such a policy of accumulating unsettled causes for war consistent with his policy of peace.

[1] Madison to Monroe, July 6, 1807; State Papers, iii. 183.

While the "Revenge" was slowly working across the Atlantic, Monroe in London was exposed to the full rigor of the fresh storm. News of the "Chesapeake" affair reached London July 25; and before it could become public Canning wrote to Monroe a private note,[1] cautiously worded, announcing that a "transaction" had taken place "off the coast of America," the particulars of which he was not at present enabled to communicate, and was anxious to receive from Monroe:—

> "But whatever the real merits and character of the transaction may turn out to be, Mr. Canning could not forbear expressing without delay the sincere concern and sorrow which he feels at its unfortunate result, and assuring the American minister, both from himself and on the behalf of his Majesty's government, that if the British officers should prove to have been culpable, the most prompt and effectual reparation shall be afforded to the government of the United States."

When on Monday morning, July 27, Monroe read in the newspapers the account of what had taken place, and realized that Canning, while giving out that he knew not the particulars, must have had Admiral Berkeley's official report within his reach if not on his table, the American minister could not but feel that the British secretary might have spoken with more frankness. In truth ministers were waiting to consult the law, and to learn whether Berkeley could be sustained. The extreme Tories, who wanted a quarrel with the United States; the reckless, who were delighted with every act of violence, which they called energy; the mountebanks, represented by Cobbett, who talked at random according to personal prejudices,—all approved Berkeley's conduct. The Ministry, not yet accustomed to office, and disposed to assert the power they held, could not easily reconcile themselves to disavowing a British admiral whose popular support came from the ranks of their own party. Seeing this, Monroe became more and more alarmed.

The tone of the press was extravagant enough to warrant despair. July 27 the "Morning Post," which was apt to draw

---

[1] Canning to Monroe, July 25, 1807; State Papers, iii. 187.

its inspiration from the Foreign Office, contained a diatribe on the "Chesapeake" affair.

> "America," it said, "is not contented with striking at the very vitals of our commercial existence; she must also, by humbling our naval greatness and disputing our supremacy, not only lessen us in our own estimation, but degrade us in the eyes of Europe and of the world. . . . It will never be permitted to be said that the 'Royal Sovereign' has struck her flag to a Yankee cockboat."

In the whole press of England, the "Morning Chronicle" alone deprecated an American war or blamed Berkeley's act; and the "Morning Chronicle" was the organ of opposition.

Monroe waited two days, and heard no more from Canning. July 29, by a previous appointment, he went to the Foreign Office on other business.[1] He found the Foreign Secretary still reticent, admitting or yielding nothing, but willing to satisfy the American government that Berkeley's order had not been the result of instructions from the Tory ministry. Monroe said he would send a note on the subject, and Canning acquiesced. Monroe on the same day sent his letter, which called attention to the outrage that had been committed and to its unjustifiable nature, expressing at the same time full confidence that the British government would at once disavow and punish the offending officer. The tone of the note, though strong, was excellent, but on one point did not quite accord with the instructions on their way from Washington.

> "I might state," said Monroe, "other examples of great indignity and outrage, many of which are of recent date; . . . but it is improper to mingle them with the present more serious cause of complaint."

Monday, August 3, Canning sent a brief reply. Since Monroe's complaint was not founded on official knowledge, said Canning, the King's government was not bound to do more than to express readiness to make reparation if such reparation should prove to be due:[2] —

[1] Monroe to Madison, Aug. 4, 1807; State Papers, iii. 186.
[2] Canning to Monroe, Aug. 3, 1807; American State Papers, iii. 188.

"Of the existence of such a disposition on the part of the British government you, sir, cannot be ignorant. I have already assured you of it, though in an unofficial form, by the letter which I addressed to you on the first receipt of the intelligence of this unfortunate transaction; and I may perhaps be permitted to express my surprise, after such an assurance, at the tone of that representation which I have just had the honor to receive from you. But the earnest desire of his Majesty to evince in the most satisfactory manner the principles of justice and moderation by which he is uniformly actuated, has not permitted him to hesitate in commanding me to assure you that his Majesty neither does nor has at any time maintained the pretension of a right to search ships of war in the national service of any State for deserters."

If it should prove that Berkeley's order rested on no other ground than the simple and unqualified pretension to such a right, the King had no difficulty in disavowing it, and would have none in showing his displeasure at it.

Although Monroe thought this reply to be "addressed in rather a harsh tone," as was certainly the case, he considered it intended to concede the essential point, and he decided to say no more without instructions. He might well be satisfied, for Canning's "surprise" was a mild expression of public feeling. Hitherto the British press had shown no marked signs of the insanity which sometimes seized a people under the strain of great excitement, but the "Chesapeake" affair revealed the whole madness of the time. August 6, three days after Canning had disavowed pretension to search national vessels, the "Morning Post" published an article strongly in favor of Berkeley and war. "Three weeks blockade of the Delaware, the Chesapeake, and Boston Harbor would make our presumptuous rivals repent of their puerile conduct." August 5 the "Times" declared itself for Berkeley, and approved not only his order, but also its mode of execution. The "Courier" from the first defended Berkeley. Cobbett's peculiar powers of mischief were never more skilfully exerted:——

"I do not pretend to say that we may not in this instance have been in the wrong, because there is nothing authentic upon the subject; nor am I prepared to say that our right of search, *in all cases*, extends to ships of war. But of this I am certain, that if the laws of nations do not allow you to search for deserters in a friend's territory, neither do they allow that friend to inveigle away your troops or your seamen, to do which is an act of hostility; and I ask for no better proof of inveigling than the enlisting and refusing to give up such troops or seamen."

Owing to his long residence in the United States, Cobbett was considered a high authority on American affairs; and he boldly averred that America could not go to war without destroying herself as a political body. More than half the people of America, he said, were already disgusted with the French bias of their government.

In the face of a popular frenzy so general, Monroe might feel happy to have already secured from Canning an express disavowal of the pretension to search ships of war. He was satisfied to let the newspapers say what they would while he waited his instructions. A month passed before these arrived. September 3 Monroe had his next interview, and explained the President's expectations,—that the men taken from the "Chesapeake" should be restored, the offenders punished, a special mission sent to America to announce the reparation, and the practice of impressment from merchant-vessels suppressed.[1] Canning listened with civility, for he took pride in tempering the sternness of his policy by the courtesy of his manner. He made no serious objection to the President's demands so far as they concerned the "Chesapeake;" but when Monroe came to the abandonment of impressment from merchant-vessels, he civilly declined to admit it into the discussion.

Monroe wrote the next day a note,[2] founded on his instructions, in which he insisted on the proposition which he had expressly discarded in his note of July 29, that the outrages rising from impressment in general ought to be considered as a part of the "Chesapeake" affair; and he concluded his argument by saying that his Government looked on this

[1] Monroe to Madison, Oct. 10, 1807; State Papers, iii. 191.
[2] Monroe to Canning, Sept. 7, 1807; State Papers, iii. 189.

complete adjustment as indispensably necessary to heal the deep wound which had been inflicted on the national honor of the United States. After the severity with which Monroe had been rebuked for disregarding his instructions on this point barely a few months before, he had no choice but to obey his orders without the change of a letter; but he doubtless knew in advance that this course left Canning master of the situation. The British government was too well acquainted with the affairs of America to be deceived by words. That the United States would fight to protect their national vessels was possible; but every one knew that no party in Congress could be induced to make war for the protection of merchant seamen. In rejecting such a demand, not only was Canning safe, but he was also sure of placing the President at odds with his own followers and friends.

A fortnight was allowed to pass before the British government replied. Then, September 23, Canning sent to the American legation an answer.[1] He began by requesting to know whether the President's proclamation was authentic, and whether it would be withdrawn on a disavowal of the act which led to it; because, as an act of retaliation, it must be taken into account in adjusting the reparation due. He insisted that the nationality of the men seized must also be taken into account, not as warranting their unauthorized seizure, but as a question of redress between government and government. In respect to the general question of impressment in connection with the specific grievance of the "Chesapeake," he explained at some length the different ground on which the two disputes rested; and while professing his willingness to discuss the regulation of the practice, he affirmed the rights of England, which, he said, —

"existed in their fullest force for ages previous to the establishment of the United States of America as an independent government; and it would be difficult to contend that the recognition of that independence can have operated any change in this respect, unless it can be shown that in acknowledging the government of the United States, Great Britain virtually abdicated her own rights as a naval Power,

[1] Canning to Monroe, Sept. 23, 1807; State Papers, iii. 199.

or unless there were any express stipulations by which the ancient and prescriptive usages of Great Britain, founded in the soundest principles of natural law, though still enforced against other independent nations of the world, were to be suspended whenever they might come in contact with the interests or the feelings of the American people."

After disposing of the matter with this sneer, Canning closed by earnestly recommending Monroe to consider whether his instructions might not leave him at liberty to adjust the case of the "Chesapeake" by itself:—

"If your instructions leave you no discretion, I cannot press you to act in contradiction to them. In that case there can be no advantage in pursuing a discussion which you are not authorized to conclude; and I shall have only to regret that the disposition of his Majesty to terminate that difference amicably and satisfactorily is for the present rendered unavailing.

"In that case his Majesty, in pursuance of the disposition of which he has given such signal proofs, will lose no time in sending a minister to America, furnished with the necessary instructions and powers for bringing this unfortunate dispute to a conclusion consistent with the harmony subsisting between Great Britain and the United States; but in order to avoid the inconvenience which has arisen from the mixed nature of your instructions, that minister will not be empowered to entertain, as connected with this subject, any proposition respecting the search of merchant-vessels."

Monroe replied,[1] September 29, that his instructions were explicit, and that he could not separate the two questions. He closed by saying that Canning's disposition and sentiments had been such as inspired him with great confidence that they should soon have been able to bring the dispute to an honorable and satisfactory conclusion. With this letter so far as concerned Monroe, the "Chesapeake" incident came to its end in failure of redress.

One more subject remained for Monroe to finish. His unfortunate treaty returned by Madison with a long list of

[1] Monroe to Canning, Sept. 29, 1807; State Papers, iii. 201.

changes and omissions, had been made by Monroe and Pinkney the subject of a letter to Canning as early as July 24;[1] but
the affair of the "Chesapeake" intervened, and Canning declined to touch any other subject until this was adjusted. No
sooner did he succeed in referring the "Chesapeake" negotiation to Washington than he turned to the treaty. That a measure
sure which had been the most unpopular act of an unpopular
Whig ministry could expect no mercy at Canning's hands,
was to be expected; but some interest attached to the manner
of rejection which he might prefer. In a formal note, dated
October 22, Canning addressed the American government in
a tone which no one but himself could so happily use,—a
tone of mingled condescension and derision.[2] He began by
saying that his Majesty could not profess to be satisfied that
the American government had taken effectual steps in regard
to the Berlin Decree; but the King had nevertheless decided,
in case the President should ratify Monroe's treaty, to ratify it
in his turn, "reserving to himself the right of taking, in consequence of that decree, and of the omission of any effectual
interposition on the part of neutral nations to obtain its revocation, such measures of retaliation as his Majesty might
judge expedient." Without stopping to explain what value a
ratification under such conditions would have, Canning continued that the President had thought proper to propose alterations in the body of the treaty:—

> "The undersigned is commanded distinctly to protest
> against a practice altogether unusual in the political trans-
> actions of States, by which the American government
> assumes to itself the privilege of revising and altering
> agreements concluded and signed on its behalf by its agents
> duly authorized for that purpose, of retaining so much of
> those agreements as may be favorable to its own views,
> and of rejecting such stipulations, or such parts of stipula-
> tions, as are conceived to be not sufficiently beneficial to
> America."

Without discussing the correctness of Canning's assertion
that the practice was "altogether unusual in the political trans-

---

[1] Monroe and Pinkney to Canning, July 24, 1807; State Papers, iii. 194.
[2] Canning to Monroe and Pinkney, Oct. 22, 1807; State Papers, iii. 198.

actions of States," Monroe and Pinkney might have replied that every European treaty was negotiated, step by step, under the eye of the respective governments, and that probably no extant treaty had been signed by a British agent in Europe without first receiving at every stage the approval of the King. No American agent could consult his government. Canning was officially aware that Monroe and Pinkney, in signing their treaty, had done so at their own risk, in violation of the President's orders. The requirement that the President of the United States should follow European rules was unreasonable; but in the actual instance Canning's tone was something more than unreasonable. His own note assumed for the British government "the privilege of revising and altering" whatever provisions of the treaty it pleased; and after a condition so absolute, he violated reciprocity in rejecting conditions made by the President because they were "unusual in the political transactions of States:"—

> "The undersigned is therefore commanded to apprise the American commissioners that, although his Majesty will be at all times ready to listen to any suggestions for arranging, in an amicable and advantageous manner, the respective interests of the two countries, the proposal of the President of the United States for proceeding to negotiate anew upon the basis of a treaty already solemnly concluded and signed, is a proposal wholly inadmissible."

With this denial of the right of others to exercise arbitrary methods, Canning declared the field open for the British government to give full range to its arbitrary will. A week afterward Monroe left London forever. He had taken his audience of leave October 7, and resigned the legation to Pinkney. October 29 he started for Portsmouth to take ship for Virginia. His diplomatic career in Europe was at an end; but these last failures left him in a state of mind easy to imagine, in which his irritation with Jefferson and Madison, the authors of his incessant misfortunes, outran his suspicions of Canning, whose pretence of friendship had been dignified and smooth.

For reasons to be given hereafter, the Ministry decided to disavow Admiral Berkeley's attack on the "Chesapeake;" but in order to provide against the reproach of surrendering

British rights, a proclamation[1] almost as offensive to the United States as Admiral Berkeley's order was issued, October 16. Beginning with the assertion that great numbers of British seamen "have been enticed to enter the service of foreign States, and are now actually serving as well on board the ships of war belonging to the said foreign States as on board the merchant-vessels belonging to their subjects," the proclamation ordered such seamen to return home, and commanded all naval officers to seize them, without unnecessary violence, in any foreign merchant-vessels where they might be found, and to demand them from the captains of foreign ships of war, in order to furnish government with the necessary evidence for claiming redress from the government which had detained the British seamen. Further, the proclamation gave warning that naturalization would not be regarded as relieving British subjects of their duties, but that, while such naturalized persons would be pardoned if they returned immediately to their allegiance, all such as should serve on ships-of-war belonging to any State at enmity with England would be guilty of high treason, and would be punished with the utmost severity of the law.

That the British public, even after the battle of Trafalgar and the firing upon the "Chesapeake," might have felt its pride sufficiently flattered by such a proclamation seemed only reasonable; for in truth this proclamation forced war upon a government which wished only to escape it, and which cowered for years in submission rather than fight for what it claimed as its due; but although to American ears the proclamation sounded like a sentence of slavery, the British public denounced it as a surrender of British rights. The "Morning Post," October 20 and 22, gave way to a paroxysm of wrath against ministers for disavowing and recalling Berkeley. "With feelings most poignantly afflicting," it broke into a rhapsody of unrestrained self-will. The next day, October 23, the same newspaper—then the most influential in the kingdom—pursued the subject more mildly:—

"Though the British government, from perhaps too rigid an adherence to the law of nations, outraged as they are by

[1] American State Papers, iii. 25.

964 SECOND ADMINISTRATION OF JEFFERSON

the common enemy, may, however irritated by her conduct, display a magnanimous forbearance toward so insignificant a Power as America, they will not, we are persuaded, suffer our proud sovereignty of the ocean to be mutilated by any invasion of its just rights and prerogatives. Though the right, tacitly abandoned for the last century, may be suffered to continue dormant, the Americans must not flatter themselves that the principle will be permitted to have any further extent. In the mildness of our sway we must not suffer our sovereignty to be rebelled against or insulted with impunity. . . . The sovereignty of the seas in the hands of Great Britain is an established, legitimate sovereignty,—a sovereignty which has been exercised on principles so equitable, and swayed with a spirit so mild, that the most humble of the maritime Powers have been treated as if they were on a perfect equality with us."

The same lofty note ran through all the "Morning Post's" allusions to American affairs:—

"A few short months of war," said a leading article, October 24, "would convince these desperate politicians of the folly of measuring the strength of a rising, but still infant and puny, nation with the colossal power of the British empire."

The "Times" declared that the Americans could not even send an ambassador to France,—could hardly pass to Staten Island,—without British permission.[1] "Right is power sanctioned by custom," said the "Times;" and October 20 and 22 it joined the "Morning Post" in denouncing the disavowal of Berkeley. The "Morning Chronicle" alone resisted the torrent which was sweeping away the traditions of English honor.

"Our Government," it said,[2] in support of its enemy, Canning, "in acting with prudence and wisdom, have to resist the pressure of a spirit not popular, like that in America, but as violent and as ignorant, with the addition of being in the highest degree selfish and sordid."

[1] The Times, Aug. 26, 1807.
[2] The Morning Chronicle, Aug. 6, 1807.

In the case of the "Chesapeake" the Ministry resisted that "selfish and sordid" interest; but Americans soon learned that the favor, such as it was, had been purchased at a price beyond its value. Canning's most brilliant stroke was for the moment only half revealed.

Chapter III

THE NEW MINISTRY which succeeded "All the Talents"
and took seat in Parliament April 8, 1807, represented
everything in English society that was most impervious to
reason. In its origin a creature of royal bigotry trembling on
the verge of insanity, before it had been a few short weeks in
office every liberal or tolerant Englishman was shocked to
find that this band of Tories, whose prejudices were such as
modern society could scarcely understand, and who had been
forced into office by the personal will of an almost imbecile
King, did in reality represent a great reaction of the English
people against tolerant principles, and reflected the true sense
of the nation as it had never been reflected by Grenville or
Fox. Parliament was dissolved April 27, though only four
months old; and June 22, when the "Leopard" was firing into
the "Chesapeake," the new Parliament met at Westminster
Hall, with a ministerial majority of more than two hundred
country squires, elected on the cry that the Church was in
danger.

From its nominal head, this Ministry was called the Portland administration; but its leader was Spencer Perceval, the
Chancellor of the Exchequer, and its mouthpiece was George
Canning, the Foreign Secretary. These two commoners—
men of no special family connection, of no estates, and little
so-called "stake in the country"—guided the aristocratic and
conservative society of England, and exaggerated its tendencies. In modern days little is remembered of Spencer Perceval
except that he became at last one of the long list of victims to
lunatic assassins; but for a whole generation no English Liberal mentioned the name of the murdered prime minister
without recalling the portrait drawn by Sydney Smith in the
wittiest and keenest of his writings,[1] in which Perceval was
figured as living at Hampstead upon stewed meats and claret,
and walking to church every Sunday before eleven young
gentlemen of his own begetting, with their faces washed and
their hair pleasingly combed.

In Sydney Smith's caricature there was little exaggeration.

[1] Peter Plymley's Letters, ix.

Spencer Perceval was forty-five years old, a lawyer of the best character, devoted to his family, his church, and sovereign; a man after Lord Eldon's heart, who brought to the Treasury Bench the legal knowledge and mental habits of a leader at the Chancery Bar and the political morality of a lawyer's brief. The criticism was not less revolting than remarkable, that many of the men whose want of political morality was most conspicuous in this story were, both in England and in America, models of private respectability and fanatical haters of vice. That Timothy Pickering and Roger Griswold should join hands with Aaron Burr was less wonderful than that Spencer Perceval and his friend James Stephen, the author of "War in Disguise," should adopt the violence of Napoleon as the measure of their own morals, and avow that they meant to respect no other standard. With the same voice Spencer Perceval expressed fear lest calling Parliament on a Monday should lead members into Sunday travel, and justified the bombardment of Copenhagen and the robbery of American commerce.

The Whigs thought little of his abilities. Sydney Smith, who delighted to ridicule him, said that he had the head of a country parson and the tongue of an Old Bailey lawyer.[1] The Tories admired and followed him as readily as they had once followed Pitt; but to an American, necessarily prejudiced, Sydney Smith's estimate seemed just. Every American critic placed Perceval in an order of intelligence not only below the Whigs, but below Lord Sidmouth. When confronted with the dulness of Spencer Perceval, Americans could even feel relief in the sarcasm of George Canning, which, unlike Perceval's speeches, had at least the merit of rhetoric.

Of George Canning, who passed so rapidly across the scene, and yet left so sharp an impression on the memory of America, something must be said, if only to explain how a man so gifted, and in later life so different in influence, should have thought it worth his while to challenge the hatred of a people whose future he, unlike his colleague Perceval, had imagination enough to foresee. George Canning was thirty-seven years old when he took charge of the

[1] Peter Plymley's Letters, i.

Foreign office. His father, who came from a very respectable but in no way eminent family, died in 1771; his mother having no means of support became a provincial actress, and the boy was adopted by an uncle, who sent him to Eton and Oxford. He left Oxford at the time when the French Revolution promised a new birth to Europe, and Canning was then a warm Republican from sympathy and conviction. The political reaction which followed swept the young man to the opposite extreme; and his vehemence for monarchy and the Tories gave point to a Whig sarcasm,—that men had often been known to turn their coats, but this was the first time that a boy had turned his jacket. In consequence of his conversion Pitt brought him into Parliament in 1793, and placed him in office in 1796. In the hotbed of Pitt's personal favor[1] Canning's natural faults were stimulated, until the irritation caused by his sarcastic wit and by what the stolid gentry thought his flippancy roused a sort of insurrection against him. Few men were more admired, and none was more feared or hated; for it was impossible to say what time-honored monument he might overthrow in defending.

No man in England flung himself more violently into the reaction against Republican ideas than this young Republican of 1789. Canning's contempt was unbounded for everything that savored of liberal principles; and in following the impulses of his passion he lost whatever political morality he had possessed. If one act in Bonaparte's career concentrated more than another the treason and violence of a lifetime, it was the *coup d'état* of the 18th Brumaire, in 1799, when he drove the Legislature at the point of the bayonet from the hall at St. Cloud, and annihilated French liberty, as he hoped, forever; yet this act, which might have been applauded by some English statesmen whose heads paid on Tower Hill the penalty for such treason to the liberties of their own country, threw Canning into paroxysms of delight.

"Huzza! huzza! huzza!" he wrote[2] on hearing the news; "for no language but that of violent and tumultuous and triumphant exclamation can sufficiently describe the joy

[1] Malmesbury's Diary, iv. 376.
[2] Canning to Boringdon, Nov. 19, 1799; Stapleton's Canning, p. 43.

and satisfaction which I feel at this complete overthrow and extinction of all the hopes of the proselytes to new princi- ples. . . . It is the lasting ridicule thrown upon all systems of democratic equality,—it is the galling conviction carried home to the minds of all the brawlers for freedom in this and every other country,—that there never was, nor will be, nor can be, a leader of a mob faction who does not mean to be the lord and not the servant of the people. It is this that makes the name of Bonaparte dear to me . . . Henceforth, with regard to France and the principles of France, or to any country similarly circumstanced as to extent, population, manners, etc., *Republican* and *fool* are synonymous terms."

Canning had several qualities in common with Bonaparte, and one of them was the habit of classifying under the head of fools persons whose opinions he did not fancy,—from the man who believed in a republic to the man who liked dry champagne. In his mouth such persons were either fools or liars; and Americans, with few exceptions, came under one or the other of these heads. After the 18th Brumaire the world contained but one leader of a mob faction, brawling for lib- erty; but he was President of the United States. No miracu- lous sagacity was needed to foretell what treatment he was likely to receive at the hands of two men like Canning and Bonaparte, should the empire of the world ever be divided between them. To throw lasting ridicule upon all systems of democratic equality was Canning's most passionate wish, and his success was marvellous. Even his squibs exploded like rockets. In literature, his "Needy Knife-grinder" was a harm- less piece of clever satire, but in the "Anti-Jacobin" it was a political event.

In Parliament Canning's influence was not yet very great. He relied too much on wit, and what was then called quiz- zing, or he imitated Pitt's oratory too closely; but even in the House of Commons he steadily won ground, and while Burke, Pitt, Fox, Windham, and Sheridan, one after another, disappeared or were thrown into the shade, Canning's figure became more prominent on the Treasury Bench between two such foils as Spencer Perceval and Lord Castlereagh. Although his mind ripened slowly, and was still far from maturity, he was already a master in choice of language; he always excelled in clearness of statement and skill of illustration; and if his taste had been as pure as his English, he would have taken rank with the greatest English orators. Some of his metaphors survived, with those of Burke and Sheridan. When Napoleon was forced back to the Elbe, "the mighty deluge, by which the Continent had been overwhelmed, began to subside; the limits of nations were again visible; and the spires and turrets of ancient establishments began to reappear above the subsiding wave." In addressing the people at Plymouth, he likened England to a line-of-battle ship; "one of those stupendous masses now reposing on their shadows in perfect stillness," but ready at a sign to ruffle, as it were, its swelling plumage, to awaken its dormant thunder. Such eloquence recalled Burke at his less philosophical moments. It contained more rhetoric than thought; but Canning was there at his best. At his worst, as Americans commonly saw him, his natural tones seemed artificial, and only his limitations seemed natural. To Americans Canning never showed himself except as an actor. As an instance of his taste, Americans could best appreciate the climax with which he once electrified the House of Commons in speaking of the Spanish American Republics: "I called the new world into existence to redress the balance of the old." The House cheered to the echo, while America stood open-mouthed in astonishment at the success of such extravagant egoism.

In the new Ministry of 1807, the lead was to the strongest; and Canning, who treated with almost open contempt his rival Lord Castlereagh, a man intellectually his inferior, could count upon a great destiny. Less scrupulous or less broad than Pitt, he held that Napoleon's course had absolved England from ordinary rules of morals. To fight Bonaparte with his own weapons had become the duty of Englishmen; and the first act of the new Administration showed what meaning was to be put on this favorite phrase.

February 8, Napoleon fought the desperate battle of Eylau, which closely resembled a defeat. His position was critical; but before Canning could fairly get control of events, Napoleon, June 14, again attacked the Russians at Friedland and won a decisive victory. June 25 Napoleon and Alexander held an interview on an island in the Niemen. The chief point in question was whether Alexander would abandon England; and this he was almost glad to do, for England had abandoned him. Alexander yielded to the force and flattery of Napoleon, and signed July 7 the treaty of Tilsit. By a private understanding the remaining neutrals were left to Napoleon to be dealt with as he pleased. Denmark was the only neutral power the control of which was necessary for the success of Napoleon's system, and August 2 he sent orders to Bernadotte, who was to command at Hamburg: "If England does not accept the mediation of Russia, Denmark must declare war upon her, or I will declare war on Denmark."[1] Finding that the Prince Royal hesitated, Napoleon, August 17, sent orders[2] to Bernadotte to hold himself ready with all his troops to march into Denmark either as ally or enemy, according to the issue of the pending negotiation. Threatened by this overwhelming danger, the Prince Royal of Denmark alternately promised and evaded the declaration of war; when suddenly his doubts were brought to an end by the diplomacy of Canning.

The British ministry had been secretly informed of what took place at Tilsit, and even without secret information could not have doubted the fate of Denmark. Vigor was necessary; and as early as July 19, before news had arrived of the formal signature of the Tilsit treaty, the Cabinet decided on sending to Copenhagen a large naval expedition which had been collected for a different purpose. July 26 the expedition, commanded by Lord Gambier, sailed from the Downs. It consisted of some twenty ships of the line, forty frigates, and transports containing twenty-seven thousand troops commanded by Lord Cathcart; and it carried a diplomatic agent with instructions to require from the Prince Royal of Denmark the delivery of the Danish fleet, as a temporary security for the safety of England.

The man whom Canning charged with this unpleasant duty was the same Jackson whose appointment as Minister to the United States had been opposed by Rufus King, and who had

[1] Correspondance, xv. 467.
[2] Napoleon to Berthier, Aug. 17, 1807; Correspondance, xv. 504.

subsequently gone as British minister to Berlin. Jackson's dogmatic temper and overbearing manners made him obnoxious even to the clerks of the Foreign Office;[1] but he was a favorite with Lord Malmesbury, who since Pitt's death had become Canning's political mentor, and Lord Malmesbury's influence was freely used in Jackson's behalf. Obeying his instructions, the British envoy went to Kiel and had an interview with the Prince Royal early in August, at about the time when Napoleon issued his first orders to Bernadotte. The Prince could only refuse with indignation Jackson's demand, and sent orders to Copenhagen to prepare for attack. He was in the situation of Barron on the "Chesapeake." Copenhagen had hardly a gun in position, and no troops to use in defence.

The British demand was in itself insulting enough, but Jackson's way of presenting it was said to have been peculiarly offensive, and London soon rang with stories of his behavior to the unfortunate Prince Royal.[2] Even the King of England seemed to think that his agent needed rebuke. Lord Eldon, who was one of the advisers and most strenuous supporters of the attack on Copenhagen,—although he said in private that the story made his heart ache and his blood run cold,—used to relate,[3] on the authority of old King George himself, that when Jackson was presented at Court on his return from Copenhagen the King abruptly asked him, "Was the Prince Royal upstairs or down, when he received you?" "He was on the ground floor," replied Jackson. "I am glad of it! I am glad of it!" rejoined the old King; "for if he had half the spirit of his uncle George III., he would infallibly have kicked you downstairs." The Prince did not kick Mr. Jackson, though the world believed he had reason to do so, but he declined to accept the British envoy's remark that in war the weak must submit to the strong; and Lord Gambier landed twenty thousand men, established batteries, and for three days and nights, from September 1 to September 5, bombarded Copenhagen. The city was neither invested nor assaulted nor intended to be occupied; it was merely destroyed, little by little,—as a

[1] Malmesbury's Diary, iv. 392.
[2] Morning Chronicle, Oct. 7, 1807.
[3] Campbell's Lord Chancellors, ix. 288, *n.*

bandit would cut off first an ear, then the nose, then a finger of his victim, to hasten payment of a ransom. At the end of the third day's bombardment, when at last the Danish ships were delivered, the bodies of near two thousand non-combatants lay buried in the smoking ruins of about one half the city. At the same time all the Danish merchant-vessels in English waters, with their cargoes, to the value of ten million dollars, were seized and confiscated; while the Danish factory in Bengal was, without warning, swept into England's pouch.

At the news of the awful tragedy at Copenhagen, Europe, gorged as for fifteen years she had been with varied horrors, shuddered from St. Petersburg to Cadiz. A long wail of pity and despair rose on the Continent, was echoed back from America, and found noble expression in the British Parliament. The attack upon the "Chesapeake" was a caress of affection compared with this bloody and brutal deed. As in 1804 Bonaparte—then only First Consul, but about to make himself a bastard Emperor—flung before the feet of Europe the bloody corpse of the Duc d'Enghien, so George Canning in 1807, about to meet Bonaparte on his own field with his own weapons, called the world to gaze at his handiwork in Copenhagen; and the world then contained but a single nation to which the fate of Copenhagen spoke in accents of direct and instant menace. The annihilation of Denmark left America almost the only neutral, as she had long been the only Republican State. In both characters her offences against Canning and Perceval, Castlereagh and Eldon, had been more serious than those of Denmark, and had roused to exasperation the temper of England. A single ship of the line, supported by one or two frigates, could without a moment's notice repeat at New York the tragedy which had required a vast armament at Copenhagen; and the assault on the "Chesapeake" had given warning of what the British navy stood ready to do. Other emphatic omens were not wanting.

About July 27—the day after Lord Gambier's fleet sailed from the Downs, and the day when Monroe first saw in the newspapers an account of the "Leopard's" attack on the "Chesapeake"—the American minister might have read a report made by a committee of the House of Commons on the commercial state of the West Indian Islands. The main evil, said the committee,[1] was the very unfavorable state of the foreign market, in which the British merchant formerly enjoyed nearly a monopoly. "The result of all their inquiries on this most important part of the subject has brought before their eyes one grand and primary evil from which all the others are easily to be deduced; namely, the facility of intercourse between the hostile colonies and Europe under the American neutral flag, by means of which not only the whole of their produce is carried to a market, but at charges little exceeding those of peace, while the British planter is burdened with all the inconvenience, risk, and expense resulting from a state of war." To correct this evil, a blockade of the enemies' colonies had been suggested; "and such a measure, if it could be strictly enforced, would undoubtedly afford relief to our export trade. But a measure of more permanent and certain advantage would be the enforcement of those restrictions on the trade between neutrals and the enemies' colonies which were formerly maintained by Great Britain, and from the relaxation of which the enemies' colonies obtain indirectly, during war, all the advantages of peace."

In its way this West Indian Report was stamped with the same Napoleonic character as the bombardment of Copenhagen or the assault on the "Chesapeake;" in a parliamentary manner it admitted that England, with all her navy, could not enforce a blockade by lawful means, and therefore it had become "a matter of evident and imperious necessity" that she should turn pirate. The true sense of the recommendation was neither doubted nor disputed in England, except as matter of parliamentary form. That the attempt to cut off the supply of French and Spanish sugar from Europe, either by proclaiming a paper blockade or the Rule of 1756, might result in war with the United States was conceded, and no one in private denied that America in such a case had just cause for war. The evidence upon which the Report founded its conclusion largely dealt with the probable effect on the colonies of a war with the United States; and the Report itself, in language only so far veiled as to be decent, intimated that although war would be essentially detrimental to the islands it would not be fatal,

[1] Cobbett's Debates, ix., Appendix lxxx.; Atcheson's American Encroachments, Appendix No. viii. 114.

and would be better than their actual condition. The excuse for what every reasonable Englishman frankly avowed to be "a system of piracy,"[1] was that the West Indian colonies must perish without it, and England must share their fate. In vain did less terrified men, like Alexander Baring or William Spence, preach patience, explaining that the true difficulty with the West Indies was an over-production of sugar, with which the Americans had nothing to do.

> "To charge the distresses of the West Indian planters upon the American carriers," said Spence,[2] "is almost as absurd as it would be for the assassin to lay the blame of murder upon the arsenic which he had purposely placed in the sugar-dish of his friend."

Thus Parliament, Ministry, navy, colonies, the shipping and the landed interest of England had wrought public opinion to the point of war with the United States at the moment when Lord Gambier bombarded Copenhagen and the "Leopard" fired into the "Chesapeake." The tornado of prejudice and purposeless rage which broke into expression on the announcement that a British frigate had fired into an American, surpassed all experience. The English newspapers for the year that followed the "Chesapeake" affair seemed irrational, the drunkenness of power incredible. The Americans, according to the "Morning Post" of Jan. 14, 1808, "possess all the vices of their Indian neighbors without their virtues;" and two days afterward the same newspaper—which gave tone to the country press—declared that England was irresistible: "Our vigor and energy have just reached that sublime pitch from which their weight must crush all opposition."

No one could say for how much of this extravagance Canning was directly responsible; but the tone of the press was certainly an echo of the tone he had so long taken, and which he stimulated. That he was really so reckless as he seemed need not be imagined; although eighteen months afterward, Lord Grenville with the utmost emphasis said in the House of Lords,[3] "I do firmly believe that it is the object of his

---

[1] The Radical Cause, etc., by William Spence, 1808, p. 43.
[2] The Radical Cause, etc., by William Spence, 1808, p. 19.
[3] Cobbett's Debates (Feb. 17, 1809), xii. 776.

Majesty's ministers to do everything in their power to force America into hostility with this country." Lord Grenville occasionally exaggerated, and he was probably mistaken in this instance; but he found it possible to believe ministers capable of acting with the motive he charged on them. In truth he had strong ground for the opinion he held, which was by no means peculiar to him. As early as July 27, 1807, the "Morning Chronicle," in announcing the first news of the "Chesapeake" affair, added: —

> "We trust it is of a nature to be adjusted without that most ruinous of all follies yet left us to be guilty of, — an American war. We have rather more fear than hope however on the subject, when we reflect that the present ministers are of those who consider an American war as rather desirable."

Within a short time the "Morning Post" avowed and proclaimed, in articles evidently inspired by Government, the wish for war with America:[1] —

> "A war of a very few months, without creating to us the expense of a single additional ship, would be sufficient to convince her of her folly by a necessary chastisement of her insolence and audacity."

In January, 1808, the same newspaper spoke even more plainly:[2] —

> "For us, we have always been of the opinion that in the present temper of the American government no relations of amity can be maintained with that nation unless at the expense of our dearest rights and most essential interests."

Perhaps this tone was taken partly with the idea of terrifying the Americans into obedience; but beyond question a strong party leaned to violence. Monroe, who had the best means of knowing, felt no doubts on this point, and warned the President of the danger to the United States.

"There has been," he wrote Aug. 4, 1807,[3] "at all times

[1] The Morning Post, Nov. 12, 1807.
[2] The Morning Post, Jan. 13, 1808.
[3] Monroe to Madison, Aug. 4, 1807; State Papers, iii. 186.

since the commencement of the present war, a strong party here for extending its ravages to them. This party is composed of the shipowners, the navy, the East and West India merchants, and certain political characters of great consideration in the State. So powerful is this combination that it is most certain that nothing can be obtained of the government on any point but what may be extorted by necessity."

Insane as such a policy might seem, Lord Grenville's charge against ministers had solid ground.

Special interests were commonly blind to the general good. That the navy, the mercantile marine, and the colonies should have favored war with America was not surprising; but that the mania should have seized upon the English nation at large was a phenomenon to be explained only by general causes. The true explanation was not far to seek; the secret, if secret it could be called, was the inevitable result of Jefferson's passion for peace,—social and political contempt. This feeling was unbounded, pervading all parties and all classes, and finding expression in the most gross as in the simplest and least intentional forms.

"Hatred of America," said one of the numerous British pamphleteers of the time,[1] "seems a prevailing sentiment in this country. Whether it be that they have no crown and nobility, and are on this account not quite a *genteel* Power; or that their manners are less polished than our own; or that we grudge their independence, and hanker after our old monopoly of their trade; or that they closely resemble us in language, character, and laws; or finally, that it is more our interest to live well with them than with any other nation in the world,—the fact is undeniable that the bulk of the people would fain be at war with them."

The Somersetshire squire and the chancery barrister in Westminster Hall—the extremes of national obtuseness and professional keenness—agreed in despising America. The pompous Lord Sidmouth, the tedious Lord Sheffield, the vivacious Canning, the religious Perceval, and the merry-

---

[1] Orders in Council; or, An Examination of the Justice, Legality, and Policy of the New System, etc. (London, 1808), p. 61.

andrew Cobbett—whose genius was peculiar in thinking itself popular—joined hands in spreading libels against a people three thousand miles away, who according to their own theory were too contemptible to be dangerous. Except a few Whig noblemen, a number of Yorkshire and Lancashire manufacturers and a great mass of the laboring people, or American merchants like the Barings, and one or two Scotch Liberals who wrote in the "Edinburgh Review," the English public had but one voice against Americans. Young Henry Brougham, not yet thirty years old, whose restless mind persistently asked questions which parsons and squires thought absurd or impious, speculated much upon the causes of this prejudice. Was it because the New York dinners were less elegant than those of London, or because the Yankees talked with an accent, or because their manners were vulgar? No doubt a prejudice might seize on any justification, however small; but a prejudice so general and so deep became respectable, and needed a correct explanation. The British nation was sometimes slow-witted, and often narrow-minded, but was not insane.

For a thousand years every step in the progress of England had been gained by sheer force of hand and will. In the struggle for existence the English people, favored by situation, had grown into a new human type,—which might be brutal, but was not weak; which had little regard for theory, but an immense and just respect for facts. America considered herself to be a serious fact, and expected England to take her at her own estimate of her own value; but this was more than could reasonably be asked. England required America to prove by acts what virtue existed in her conduct or character which should exempt her from the common lot of humanity, or should entitle her to escape the tests of manhood,—the trials, miseries, and martyrdoms through which the character of mankind had thus far in human history taken, for good or bad, its vigorous development. England had never learned to strike soft in battle. She expected her antagonists to fight; and if they would not fight, she took them to be cowardly or mean. Jefferson and his government had shown over and over again that no provocation would make them fight; and from the moment that this attitude was understood, America became fair prey. Jefferson had chosen his own methods of attack and defence, but he could not require England or France to respect them before they had been tried.

Contempt for America was founded on belief in American cowardice; but beneath the disdain lurked an uneasy doubt which gave to contempt the virulence of fear. The English nation, and especially the aristocracy, believed that America was biding her time; that she expected to become a giant; and that if she succeeded, she would use her strength as every other giant in the world's history had done before her. The navy foresaw a day when American fleets might cover the ocean. The merchant dreaded competition with Yankee shrewdness, for he well knew the antiquated processes, the time-honored percentages, the gross absurdities of English trade, the abuses of the custom-house, the clumsiness and extravagance of government. The shipowners had even more cause for alarm. Already the American ship was far in advance of the British model,—a swifter and more economical sailer, more heavily sparred and more daringly handled. In peace competition had become difficult, until the British shipowner cried for war; yet he already felt, without acknowledging it even to himself, that in war he was likely to enjoy little profit or pleasure on the day when the long, low, black hull of the Yankee privateer, with her tapering, bending spars, her long-range gun, and her sharp-faced captain, should appear on the western horizon, and suddenly, at sight of the heavy lumbering British merchantman, should fling out her white wings of canvas and fly down on her prey.

Contempt, mingled with vague alarm, was at the bottom of England's conduct toward America; and whatever the swarm of newspaper statesmen might say or think, the element of alarm was so great that the Tory ministers, although they might expect war, did not want it, and hoped to prevent it by the very boldness of their policy. Even Canning was cautious enough to prefer not to give America occasion for learning her strength. He meant to clip her wings only so far as she would submit to have her wings clipped; and he not only astonished but disgusted the over-zealous politicians who applauded Admiral Berkeley, by disavowing the admiral's doctrines of international law and recalling the admiral himself. The war faction broke into a paroxysm of rage[1] when this decision became known, and for a time Canning seemed likely to be devoured by his own hounds, so vociferous was their outcry. Monroe and Pinkney were loud in praise of Canning's and Perceval's temperate and candid behavior.[2]

Canning was obliged to defend himself, and under his promptings a long reply to his critics was written for the "Morning Post,"[3]—a newspaper version of the instructions carried by his special minister to Washington. He excused his treatment of Admiral Berkeley on the ground that lawyers recognized no right of search in national ships. The excuse was evidently feeble. The law, or at least the lawyers, of England had hitherto justified every act which the government had chosen to commit,—the seizure of the Spanish treasure-ships in 1804, accompanied by the unnecessary destruction of hundreds of lives; the secret seizure of the larger part of American commerce in 1805, by collusion with the Admiralty judges; the paper blockade of Charles James Fox in 1806; the Order in Council of January, 1807, by which Lord Howick cut off another main branch of neutral commerce with which England had no legal right to interfere; finally, the lawyers justified the bombardment of Copenhagen as an act of necessary defence, and were about to justify a general control of all neutral commerce as an act of retaliation. To suppose that law so elastic, or lawyers with minds so fertile, could discover no warrant for Berkeley's act was preposterous. To neutral commerce England had no legal right; yet she took it, and her lawyers invented a title. To her citizens and seamen she actually had a legal right, recognized by every court in Christendom; and if after a fair demand on the neutral government she found that her right could be satisfied only by violating neutral jurisdiction, the lawyers, in view of all their other decisions, must hold that such violation was a matter of expediency and not of law. Canning's critics in reply to his assertion that the lawyers would recognize no right of search in national ships, could fairly say that he was alone to blame,—he should have ordered them to find it. George

[1] Brougham to Lord Howick, Nov. 7, 1807; Brougham's Memoirs, i. 386.
[2] Brougham to Lord Howick, Nov. 7, 1807; Brougham's Memoirs, i. 383.
[3] The Morning Post, Oct. 23, 1807.

Canning could not seriously propose to sacrifice a vital English interest in obedience to the scrupulous legal morality of Spencer Perceval, Lord Eldon, Sir William Scott, and Sir Vicary Gibbs.

In truth, Canning had reasons more forcible. With a character not unlike that which Dryden ascribed to Lord Shaftesbury, he was pleased with the danger when the waves ran high; and if he steered too near the shoals in order to prove his wit, he did not wish to run the vessel ashore. He disavowed Admiral Berkeley, not because the lawyers were unable to prove whatever the government required, but because the right of searching foreign ships-of-war was not worth asserting, and would cost more than it could ever bring in return. Besides this obvious reason, he was guided by another motive which would alone have turned the scale. Perceval had invented a scheme for regulating neutral commerce. This measure had begun to take a character so stern that even its author expected it to produce war with the United States; and if war could be avoided at all, it could be avoided only by following Erskine's advice, and by sending to America, before the new Orders in Council, an apology for the attack on the "Chesapeake."

Chapter IV

THE ORDERS IN COUNCIL of Nov. 11, 1807, gave an impulse so energetic to the history of the United States; they worked so effectually to drive America into a new path, and to break the power and blot out the memory of Virginia and Massachusetts principles,—that every detail of their history was important. Englishmen were little likely to dwell on acts of which even at the time England was at heart ashamed, and which she afterward remembered with astonishment. To Americans alone the statesmanship of Spencer Perceval and George Canning was a matter of so much interest as to deserve study.

At the close of the year 1806 American merchants might, as always before, send cargoes of West Indian produce to any port on the continent not blockaded, provided they could satisfy British cruisers and courts that the cargo was in good faith neutral,—not French or Spanish property disguised. Jan. 7, 1807, Lord Howick issued the Order in Council which, under pretence of retaliation for Napoleon's Berlin Decree, cut off the coasting rights of neutrals. After that time the American merchant might still send a ship to Bordeaux; but if the ship, finding no market at Bordeaux, should resume her voyage, and make for Amsterdam or the Mediterranean, she became fair prize. Something has been already said[1] upon the character of Lord Howick's order, and on the subsequent debate in Parliament, when, February 4, Spencer Perceval attacked the Whig ministry for not carrying the principle of retaliation far enough. Two objects were to be gained, said Perceval[2] from the opposition bench: the first and greatest was to counteract the enemy's measures and protect English trade; the second was to distress France. Howick's order neither did nor could effect either object; and Perceval called for a measure which should shut out colonial produce from France and Spain altogether, unless it came from England and had paid a duty at a British custom-house to enhance the

[1]See p. 890.
[2]Cobbett's Debates, Feb. 4, 1807, viii. 620–656.

price. If Lord Howick's principle of retaliation was good for anything, Perceval contended it was good to this extent; and as for neutrals, there was no necessity for consulting them,— all they could reasonably expect was a notice.

The Whigs naturally replied to Perceval that before further punishing America for the acts of France, America should be allowed time to assert her own rights. This suggestion called out Lord Castlereagh, who frequently spoke the truth in ways inconvenient to his colleagues and amusing to his enemies. In this instance he admitted and even accented a point which became afterward the strongest part of the American argument. He ridiculed the idea of waiting for America to act, because notoriously the Berlin Decree had not been enforced against American commerce:—

> "This is one ground why we should look upon America with jealousy. It is an aggravation that she has, by a secret understanding with the French government, contrived to take her shipping out of the operation of the decree, that was at first general, and placed herself in a situation of connivance with the French government."

A few weeks afterward Perceval and Castlereagh took office. One of their first acts set on foot a parliamentary inquiry into the state of West Indian commerce. The report of this committee, presented to the House July 27, was ordered to be printed August 8. August 10 the House voted to take it into consideration early in the next session; and four days afterward Parliament was prorogued, leaving ministers to deal at their leisure with the "Chesapeake" affair, the Danish fleet, and Napoleon's attempts to exclude English manufactures and commerce from Europe.

Napoleon's Berlin Decree of Nov. 21, 1806, had remained till then almost a dead letter. The underwriters at Lloyds, alarmed at first by the seizures made under that decree, recovered courage between April and August, 1807, so far as to insure at low rates neutral vessels bound to Holland and Hamburg. This commerce attracted Napoleon's notice. August 19 he threatened his brother Louis, King of Holland, to send thirty thousand troops into his kingdom if the ports were not shut;[1] August 24 he sent positive orders[2] that his decree of Berlin should be executed in Holland; and in the last days of August news reached London that a general seizure of neutral vessels had taken place at Amsterdam.[3] From that moment no ship could obtain insurance, and trade with the Continent ceased. Soon afterward the American ship "Horizon" was condemned by the French courts under the Berlin Decree, and no one could longer doubt that the favor hitherto extended to American commerce had also ceased.

These dates were important, because upon them hung the popular defence of Perceval's subsequent Orders in Council. No argument in favor of these orders carried so much weight in England as the assertion that America had acquiesced in Napoleon's Berlin Decree. The President had in fact submitted to the announcement of Napoleon's blockade, as he had submitted to Sir William Scott's decisions, Lord Howick's Order in Council, the blockade of New York, and the custom of impressment, without effectual protest; but the Berlin Decree was not enforced against American commerce until about Sept. 1, 1807, and no one in America knew of the enforcement, or could have acted upon it, before the British government took the law into its own hands.

The month of September passed, and the British ministry was sufficiently busy with the bombardment of Copenhagen and the assault on the "Chesapeake," without touching neutral trade; but October 1 Lord Castlereagh wrote a letter[4] to Perceval, urging retaliation upon France in order to make her feel that Napoleon's anti-commercial system was useless, and in order to assert for future guidance the general principle that England would reject any peace which did not bring commerce with it. The idea presented by Castlereagh was clear and straightforward, — the double-or-quits of a gambler; and however open to the charge of ignorance or violence, it was not mean or dishonest.

[1]Napoleon to Champagny, Aug. 19, 1807; Correspondance, xv. 509.
[2]Same to Same, Aug. 24, 1807; Ibid., p. 542.
[3]Parliamentary Inquiry, 1808; Evidence of Robert Shedden and Mr. Hadley.
[4]Castlereagh to Perceval, Oct. 1, 1807; Castlereagh Correspondence, viii. 87.

In reply Perceval drew up a paper of suggestions[1] for the use of the Cabinet, dealing first with the justice, next with the policy of retaliation. Of its justice as against France he thought there could be no doubt, while Lord Howick's order had already asserted the principle as against neutrals, even before it could be known whether neutrals would retaliate on their own account; but apart from this precedent, "the injury which neutrals sustain is consequential; the measure is not adopted with a view to injure the neutrals, but to injure the enemy." Perhaps Perceval felt that this argument might lead too far, and that on such a doctrine England might appropriate the world on every declaration of war; for in the next paragraph he pleaded the particular war in which England was actually engaged as his warranty:—

> "When an enemy arises who declares to all the world that he will trample upon the law of nations, and hold at nought all the privileges of neutral nations when they do not suit his belligerent interests; and when by the great extent of his power he is enabled in great measure to act up to his declaration,—it is evident that if those Powers with which he is at war should continue to hold themselves bound to rules and obligations of which he will not acknowledge the force, they cannot carry on the contest on equal terms. And the neutral who would control their hostility by those rules and laws which their enemy refuses to recognize, and which such neutral does not compel that enemy to observe, ceases to be a neutral by ceasing to observe that impartiality which is the very life and soul of neutrality."

This allegation differed from the first. Perceval began by maintaining that England possessed a right, if she chose, to suppress the existence of America or of any other neutral, provided the suppression were consequential on an intent to injure France. He next argued that the existence of America might be equally suppressed because she had not yet succeeded in compelling France to observe neutral privileges,

---

[1] Original Suggestions to the Cabinet, Oct. 12, 1807; Perceval MSS.

which so far as she was concerned had not been violated. If these two propositions were worth making, they should have settled the question. Yet Perceval was not satisfied; he took a third ground:—

"This question, however, need not now be argued to the extent which was necessary to justify the assertion of the late Government; because whatever might be the doubts upon it when the decree of France first issued, and before it was known to what extent neutrals would resist or acquiesce in it, since those neutrals have acquiesced in it, or at least have not resisted or resented it to the extent of obtaining a formal recall of the decree and an open renunciation of the principle which dictated it, nor the abandonment of the practices which flow from it,—they by their acquiescence and submission have given to Great Britain a right to expect from them (when her interests require the exertion of measures of correspondent efficacy) a forbearance similar to that which they have shown toward her enemy."

If Perceval's two opening premises gave a strange idea of English statesmanship, his third was little creditable to the English bar. He took the ground that England might do what she would with American commerce, because America, whatever effort she might have made, had not already forced Napoleon to recall a decree from the application of which the United States notoriously had till within six weeks been exempted. Lord Castlereagh's doctrine that America's exemption aggravated her offence was a wide-minded argument by the side of Perceval's assertion that America's acquiescence was proved by the French decree itself. Considering that America had in this sense acquiesced in Sir William Scott's decisions and the wholesale confiscation of her commerce, in the impressment of her native citizens and their compulsory service in the British navy, in the blockade of New York, in Fox's paper blockade of the German coast, in Lord Howick's Order in Council, and perhaps even in the "Chesapeake" outrage,—Perceval's argument must have seemed convincing to Napoleon, if not to President Jefferson. If the law of nations thus laid down was sound, the continued presence of American citizens in British ships of war was alone sufficient proof of American acquiescence in impressment to warrant Napoleon in acting without regard to neutral rights. From a neutral or French point of view Perceval's reasoning not only conceded the legality of the Berlin Decree, but barred his own right of retaliation, since England, as the first and worst offender, could not properly profit by her own misdeeds.

There Perceval rested his case, so far as concerned the law. His three grounds were—(1) That as a neutral the United States could complain of no retaliation between belligerents, unless this retaliation was avowedly adopted with a view to injure neutrals; (2) That America ceased to be a neutral from the moment that she wished England to observe rules which France refused to recognize, and which America did not at once compel France to recognize; and (3) That the continued existence and recent enforcement of the Berlin Decree were sufficient proof of the neutral's acquiescence.

Thus a measure of vital consequence to England was proposed to the Cabinet on grounds which would hardly have been sufficient to warrant an injunction to restrain a private nuisance. So far as argument was concerned, Perceval had no more to say. Having in his opinion established his legal right to do what he pleased with American commerce, he next discussed the policy and extent of the proposed interference. His first idea was comparatively moderate.

"If we actually prohibit all intercourse between neutrals and the enemies' colonies," he continued, "or between neutrals and the enemies' continental possessions, it would be such a severe blow upon the trade of America as might make it no unreasonable choice on her part to prefer the dangers and chances of war to such a restriction upon her trade. I should therefore wish to leave such advantages still to neutral trade as to make it quite clear to be the policy of America, if she is wise, to prefer the neutral trade that will be left to her to the total stoppage of her trade with the enemy and with ourselves which a war might occasion. . . . With this view, therefore, I would recommend to relax thus far in the rigor of our retaliatory prohibitions as to leave to neutral nations the right of trading *directly* in articles of their own growth, produce, and manufacture exported in their own vessels to enemies' countries, and of importing from the enemies' countries for their own use articles the growth, produce, and manufacture of such enemies' countries; that is, leaving to them free the *direct* trade between the enemy and themselves in articles of their respective growth, etc., but to prohibit the re-exportation of any articles the growth, etc., of the enemies' countries or their colonies, or the carriage of them to any other country but their own."

Perceval's first suggestion was far from being so radical as the measure at last adopted. He proposed to cut off France from her colonies and force all trade between those colonies and Europe to pass through British hands; but an American ship laden with American cotton or wheat might still sail from the United States direct to France and return to the United States, or might carry provisions and lumber to Martinique and Cuba, carrying French or Spanish sugar back to New York. This so-called "direct" trade was to be untouched; the "indirect" or carrying trade between the West Indies and the continent of Europe was to be permitted only under special licenses to be issued by British authorities.

In this shape Perceval sent his suggestions to the Prime Minister, the Duke of Portland, who gave his entire approval to the principle of retaliation as against France, but wished to retaliate against France alone:[1] "Considering the unpopularity which, it cannot be denied, we are held in throughout the Continent, I very much doubt whether we should limit this intercourse beyond the actual dominions of France. I am well aware that by admitting the intercourse with Holland and Spain, France will obtain circuitously those supplies which she will stand in want of."

This disadvantage, the Duke thought, could be largely compensated by a rigid observance of the navigation laws. The Duke's opinion was very short, and barely hinted at the American question.

John Fane, Earl of Westmoreland, Lord Privy Seal,— *Sot Privé*, or Privy Fool, as Canning afterward nicknamed him by

[1] Opinion of the Duke of Portland; Perceval MSS.

a pun on the French word *sceau*,[1]—gave next his written opinion on the subject.[2] Going beyond either Perceval or Portland, he urged the expediency of stopping all trade with the enemy except through the medium of England,—"the effect of which must be either to distress them to such a degree as to induce a relaxation of their decrees, or to cause a great trade from this country. Its effect in case of an extension of hostility can certainly not be ascertained; but I am disposed to think that we cannot carry on war allowing our enemy advantages of commerce as in peace, and that if we only do what is right we must take our chance for the consequences."

The next opinion was apparently that of Lord Hawkesbury, the Home Secretary, who was also clear that Perceval's plan wanted energy. While supporting the Duke of Portland in narrowing its scope to France, or at the utmost to Holland, he favored harsher treatment of America:[3]

> "I incline strongly to the opinion that it is expedient to put an end, as far as in us lies, to all intercourse by sea between neutrals and the continental dominions of France, and possibly of Holland. I am satisfied that the measure of retaliation as proposed in the enclosed paper would have no other effect than to raise the price of colonial produce in France to a small degree. It would offend neutrals, particularly the Americans, and inflict no adequate injury upon the enemy. But if we should determine to prevent all intercourse whatever with the ports of France except by British license, we should have it in our power to destroy at once all the remaining commerce of France, which by means of neutrals is not inconsiderable, and to strike a most important blow against her agriculture by preventing the exportation of her wines."

Lord Hawkesbury kept in view the retaliatory character of the measure as a punishment of France. Lord Castlereagh, the Secretary for War, was not quite so careful.[4] He acquiesced in Perceval's scheme, provided it should reserve the right to

---

[1] Stapleton's Canning, p. 411.
[2] Opinion of the Earl of Westmoreland; Perceval MSS.
[3] Opinion of Lord Hawkesbury; Perceval MSS.
[4] Opinion of Lord Castlereagh; Perceval MSS.

extend its own application whenever the balance of advantage should favor the extension; but he added,—

> "I am of opinion that some decisive measure, in vindication of our own commerce and in counteraction of the unsocial system of France,—the principle of which is not the growth of this war, but was acted upon by her throughout the late short peace,—is become indispensable, not merely as a measure of commercial policy, but in order to put the contest in which we are engaged upon its true grounds in the view of our own people and of the world. It is no longer a struggle for territory or for a point of honor, but whether the existence of England as a naval power is compatible with that of France."

Avowing that a commercial transaction was his object, and that the punishment of France was secondary to a "vindication of our own commerce," Castlereagh assumed that punishment of France and "vindication" of English commerce were both belligerent rights, as though the right to kill an adversary in a duel implied the right to pick a bystander's pocket. His colleague and rival Canning was not so confused, for Canning's duties obliged him to defend the new policy against neutral objections. Carefully as the other ministers mingled the ideas of retaliation and of commerce, the double motive of Perceval's measure had never been concealed; the intention to permit a licensed trade with France was avowed. Perceval and Castlereagh wanted, not to take commerce from France, but to force commerce upon her; and none of their colleagues could detect this inconsistency so readily as Canning, whose duties would oblige him to assert before the world that retaliation alone was the object of a measure which he privately knew to have no motive but that of commercial rivalry. Canning's written opinion, beginning by affirming in strong terms the right and justice of retaliation, continued as follows:[1]—

> "The question of policy is all that remains; and in this view I should think all such modifications as go to lighten the burden imposed upon neutrals, and as are obviously

[1]Opinion of Mr. Canning; Perceval MSS.

intended for that purpose, more advisable than any direct reservations for our own interest and advantage. For this reason I would rather confine the measure to a part of the countries in the occupation of the enemy (a large part to be sure,—France and Holland, for instance), and apply it in all its rigor to that part, than extend it to the whole and relax it generally by complicated exceptions and regulations. And I would keep out of sight the exceptions in favor of ships going from this country, the benefit of which might be equally obtained by licenses; but the *publication* of that exception would give to the measure the air of a commercial rather than a political transaction."

By the end of October all the Cabinet opinions were in Perceval's hands, and he began the task of drafting the proposed orders. His original draft[1] contained an elaborate preamble, asserting that Napoleon's decrees violated the laws of nations, which Perceval broadly maintained were binding on one belligerent only when the obligation was reciprocally acknowledged by the other; that neutrals had not resented and resisted the outrage, "nor interposed with effect for obtaining the revocation of those orders, but on the contrary the same have been recently reinforced;" that Lord Howick's retaliatory order had served only to encourage Napoleon's attempts; that his Majesty had a right to declare all the dominions of France and her allies in a state of blockade; but "not forgetting the interests of neutral nations, and still desirous of retaliating upon the commerce of his enemies with as little prejudice to those interests" as was consistent with his purpose, he would for the present prohibit only trade which neutrals might be disposed to pursue in submission to the French decrees, and require that such trade should pass to or from some British port.

Then followed the order, which prohibited all neutral trade with the whole European sea-coast from Copenhagen to Trieste, leaving only the Baltic open. No American vessel should be allowed to enter any port in Europe from which British vessels were excluded, unless the American should clear from

[1] First Draft of Orders in Council, with remarks by Earl Bathurst; Perceval MSS.

some British port under regulations to be prescribed at a future time.

This draft was completed in the first days of November, and was sent to Lord Bathurst, President of the Board of Trade, who mercilessly criticised the preamble, and treated his colleague's law with as little respect as though Bathurst were an American.

"I wish the principle of retaliation," wrote Lord Bathurst, "not to be unqualifiedly advanced, for which I think there is no necessity. May it not be said that in a contest with an unprincipled enemy the doctrine of retaliation is one dangerous to admit without qualifications? I own I do not like the word. If my enemy commits an act of injustice, I am not therefore justified in committing the same, except so far as may be necessary, in consequence of his act, either to protect myself from injury, or prevent a recurrence to, or continuance in, such acts of injustice. All operations of war are justified only on the principle of defence. Retaliation seems to admit something of a vindictive spirit."

The Board of Trade was not usually scrupulous in dealing with American commerce; but in this instance Earl Bathurst let it be plainly seen that he wished to have no share of responsibility for Perceval's casuistry. The longer he studied the proposed order the less he liked it; and in the end he wrote an opinion contrary to his first. He withdrew his assent to the order altogether, and hinted some unpleasant truths in regard to it.

"Our ability to continue the war," he said,[1] "depends on our commerce; for if our revenues fail from a diminution of our commerce, additional imports will only add to the evil. The enemy forms one great military empire. The extent of country he covers does not render him so dependent on an export and import trade. The whole of that trade might perish and he could still continue the war. If one third of ours were to fail we should be soon reduced to peace."

[1] Opinion of Lord Bathurst in dissent to the Principle of Mr. Perceval's proposed Order; Perceval MSS.

The proposed order, Bathurst argued, not only restricted the neutral trade still further than had been done by Napoleon, but risked war with Russia and America, without materially hurting France; he added an argument which struck at the foundation of Perceval's policy:—

"The object of the proposed order, though general, is in fact nothing but the colonial trade carried on through America; and by making it general we unite Russia in defence of a trade with which she has no concern or any interest to defend. As far as America is concerned, it must be expected she will resist it; and an American war would be severely felt by our manufacturers, and even by the very class of merchants now so eager for some measure of relief. We might therefore have to fight for a rule of war, new, the policy of which would be questionable, to support an interest which would be the first to suffer by the war,— against two countries, one of which the order unnecessarily mixes in the question, and with both of which we have great commercial relations."

Bathurst closed by expressing a preference for the Rule of 1756, or for a blockade of the West Indian Islands,—which, if the Admiralty thought it practicable, Bathurst considered as the best of all the measures proposed; but besides this radical change, he demanded certain alarming reforms. He complained to Perceval that already, even under the existing orders, such abuses prevailed that in order to prevent a public parliamentary inquiry he had been obliged by the general clamor of merchants to investigate their grievances:[1]—

"The result of the examination established the truth of the vexations to which the trade is now subject by privateers, who are enabled to persevere in them in consequence of the commercial restrictions and the proceedings of the Court of Admiralty. In a communication I had with Sir William Scott, who had been very angry with the inquiry, I proposed some regulations which, indeed, I knew would be unsatisfactory unless there were some alterations in the

[1] Lord Bathurst to Spencer Perceval, Nov. 5, 1807; Perceval MSS.

proceedings of his Court,—a subject which I did not venture to touch."

Lord Bathurst's well-meant efforts for reform, gentle as they were, showed him the fortresses in which corruption was already entrenched. Sir William Scott, like his brother Lord Eldon, never relaxed his grasp on a profitable abuse. He gave cogent reasons for rejecting Lord Bathurst's suggestions, and could afford to disregard the danger of interference, for Spencer Perceval was completely under the influence of Lord Eldon. Bathurst urged Perceval to reform the license-system, so that at least the license should give complete protection to the cargo, no matter to whom the cargo might belong; and he hoped that this reform would put an end to the abuses of the Admiralty Court. "But," he added, "I did not venture to give this as my reason before Sir John Nichol [advocate-general], for you must be aware that both his profits and those of Sir William Scott depend much on privateers and the litigations which, it is my hope, will by this alteration be considerably diminished."

Many members of the British government and nearly the whole British navy were growing rich on the plunder of American commerce. From King George downward, mighty influences were involved in maintaining a system which corrupted law officers, judges, admirals, and even the King himself. Spencer Perceval's proposed Order in Council extended these abuses over whatever branches of commerce had hitherto been exempt; turned a new torrent of corruption into the government; and polluted the sources of British honor. In the light of Lord Bathurst's protest, and his significant avowal that the object of the proposed order, though general in form, was in fact nothing but the colonial trade carried on through America, Canning might well wish to *publish* nothing that would draw attention to what he called the "commercial" side of the affair. Jefferson's measures of peaceful coercion bore unexpected results, reacting upon foreign nations by stimulating every mean and sordid motive. No possible war could have so degraded England.

As the Cabinet came closer to the point, the political, or retaliatory, object of the new order disappeared, and its commercial character was exclusively set forth. In a letter written about November 30, by Spencer Perceval to Charles Abbot, Speaker of the House of Commons, not a word was said of retaliation, or of any political motive in this process of "re-casting the law of trade and navigation, as far as belligerent principles are concerned, for the whole world."

"The short principle is," said Perceval,[1] "that trade in British produce and manufactures, and trade either from a British port or with a British destination, is to be protected as much as possible. For this purpose all the countries where French influence prevails to exclude the British flag shall have no trade but to or from this country, or from its allies. All other countries, the few that remain strictly neu-tral (with the exception of the colonial trade, which back-ward and forward direct they may carry on), cannot trade but through this being done as an ally with any of the countries connected with France. If therefore we can ac-complish our purpose, it will come to this,—that either those countries will have no trade, or they must be content to accept it through us. This is a formidable and tremen-dous state of the world; but all the part of it which is par-ticularly harassing to English interests was existing through the new severity with which Bonaparte's decrees of exclu-sion against our trade were called into action. Our proceed-ing does not aggravate our distress from it. If he can keep out our trade he will; and he would do so if he could, independent of our orders. Our orders only add this cir-cumstance: they say to the enemy, 'If you will not have *our* trade, as far as we can help it you shall have *none*; and as to so much of any trade as you can carry on yourselves, or others carry on with you through us, if you admit it you shall pay for it. The only trade, cheap and untaxed, which you shall have shall be either direct from us, in our own produce and manufactures, or from our allies, whose in-creased prosperity will be an advantage to us.' "

These private expressions implied that retaliation upon France for her offence against international law was a pre-

[1] Spencer Perceval to Speaker Abbot, Diary and Correspondence of Lord Colchester, ii. 134.

tence on the part of Perceval and Canning, under the cover of which they intended to force British commerce upon France contrary to French wishes. The act of Napoleon in excluding British produce from French dominions violated no rule of international law, and warranted no retaliation except an exclusion of French produce from British dominions. The rejoinder, "If you will not have *our* trade you shall have *none*," was not good law, if law could be disputed when affirmed by men like Lord Eldon and Lord Stowell, echoed by courts, parliaments, and press,—not only in private, but in public; not only in 1807, but for long years afterward; and not only at moments, but without interruption.

Thus Canning, although he warned Perceval against betraying the commercial object of his orders, instructed[1] Erskine at Washington to point out that American ships might still bring colonial produce to England, under certain regulations, for re-export to France. "The object of these regulations will be the establishment of such a protecting duty as shall prevent the enemy from obtaining the produce of his own colonies at a cheaper rate than that of the colonies of Great Britain." Not to distress France, but to encourage British trade, was, according to Canning, the object of this "political" weapon.

Thus Perceval, in the debate of Feb. 5, 1808, in discussing the policy of his order, affirmed that the British navy had been "rendered useless by neutral ships carrying to France all that it was important for France to obtain."[2] The Rule of 1756, he said, would not have counteracted this result,—a much stronger measure was necessary; and it was sound policy "to endeavor to force a market." Lord Bathurst, a few days afterward, very frankly told[3] the House that "the object of these orders was to regulate that which could not be prohibited,—the circuitous trade through this country,"—in order that the produce of enemies' colonies might "be subjected to a duty sufficiently high to prevent its having the advantage over our own colonial produce;" and Lord Hawkesbury, in the same debate, complained[4] that neutrals supplied colonial produce

[1] Erskine to Madison, Feb. 23, 1808; State Papers, iii. 209.
[2] Cobbett's Debates, x. 328.
[3] Debate of Feb. 15, 1808; Cobbett's Debates, x. 471.
[4] Debate of Feb. 15, 1808; Cobbett's Debates, x. 485.

to France at a much less rate than the English paid for it. "To prevent this," he said, " was the great object of the Orders in Council." James Stephen's frequent arguments[1] in favor of the orders turned upon the commercial value of the policy as against neutrals; while George Rose, Vice-President of the Board of Trade, went still further, and not only avowed, in the face of Parliament, the hope that these Orders in Council would make England the emporium of all trade in the world, but even asserted, in an unguarded moment of candor, that it was a mistake to call the orders retaliatory,—they were a system of self-defence, a plan to protect British commerce.[2]

Thus, too, the orders themselves, while licensing the export through England to France of all other American produce, imposed a prohibitive duty on the export of cotton, on the ground—as Canning officially informed[3] the American government—that France had pushed her cotton manufactures to such an extent as to make it expedient for England to embarrass them.

According to the public and private avowals of all the Ministry, the true object of Perceval's orders was, not to force a withdrawal of the Berlin Decree so far as it violated international law, but to protect British trade from competition. Perceval did not wish to famish France, but to feed her. His object was commercial, not political; his policy aimed at checking the commerce of America in order to stimulate the commerce of England. The pretense that this measure had retaliation for its object and the vindication of international law for its end was a legal fiction, made to meet the objections of America and to help Canning in maintaining a position which he knew to be weak.

After this long discussion, and after conferences not only with his colleagues in the Cabinet, but also with George Rose, Vice-President of the Board of Trade, with James Stephen, who was in truth the author of the war on neutrals, and with a body of merchants from the city,—at last,

[1] Speech of James Stephen, March 6, 1809; Cobbett's Debates, xiii., Appendix lxxvi.

[2] Debate of March 3, 1812; report in Times and Morning Chronicle of March 4, 1812.

[3] Erskine to Madison, Feb. 23, 1808; State Papers, iii. 209.

Nov. 11, 1807, Spencer Perceval succeeded in getting his General Order approved in Council. In its final shape this famous document differed greatly from the original draft. In deference to Lord Bathurst's objections, the sweeping doctrine of retaliation was omitted, so that hardly an allusion to it was left in the text; the assertion that neutrals had acquiesced in the Berlin Decree was struck out; the preamble was reduced, by Lord Eldon's advice, to a mere mention of the French pretended blockade, and of Napoleon's real prohibition of British commerce, followed by a few short paragraphs reciting that Lord Howick's order of Jan. 7, 1807, had "not answered the desired purpose either of compelling the enemy to recall those orders or of inducing neutral nations to interpose with effect to obtain their revocation, but on the contrary the same have been recently enforced with increased rigor;" and then, with the blunt assertion that "his Majesty, under these circumstances, finds himself compelled to take further measures for asserting and vindicating his just rights," Perceval, without more apology, ordered in effect that all American commerce, except that to Sweden and the West Indies, should pass through some British port and take out a British license.

The exceptions, the qualifications, and the verbiage of the British Orders need no notice. The ablest British merchants gave up in despair the attempt to understand them; and as one order followed rapidly upon another, explaining, correcting, and developing Perceval's not too lucid style, the angry Liberals declared their belief that he intended no man to understand them without paying two guineas for a legal opinion, with the benefit of a chance to get a directly contrary opinion for the sum of two guineas more.[1] Besides the express provisions contained in the Order of November 11, it was understood that American commerce with the enemies of England must not only pass through British ports with British license, but that colonial produce would be made to pay a tax to the British Treasury to enhance its price, while cotton would not be allowed to enter France.

The general intention, however confused, was simple. After November 11, 1807, any American vessel carrying any cargo

[1] Baring's Inquiry, pp. 14, 15.

was liable to capture if it sailed for any port in Europe from which the British flag was excluded In other words, American commerce was made English.

This measure completed, diplomacy was to resume its work. Even Canning's audacity might be staggered to explain how the government of the United States could evade war after it should fairly understand the impressment Proclamation of October 17, the Order in Council of November 11, and the Instructions of George Henry Rose,—who was selected by Canning as his special envoy for the adjustment of the "Leopard's" attack on the "Chesapeake," and who carried orders which made adjustment impossible. Such outrages could be perpetrated only upon a helpless people. Even in England, where Jefferson's pacific policy was well understood, few men believed that peace could be longer preserved.

Chapter V

THE CURTAIN was about to rise upon a new tragedy,—the martyrdom of Spain. At this dramatic spectacle the United States government and people might have looked with composure and without regret, for they hardly felt so deep an interest in history, literature, or art as to care greatly what was to become of the land which had once produced Cortes, Cervantes, and Murillo; but in the actual condition of European politics their own interests were closely entwined with those of Spain, and as the vast designs of Napoleon were developed, the fortunes of the Spanish empire more and more deeply affected those of the American Union.

General Armstrong waited impatiently at Paris while Napoleon carried on his desperate struggle with the Emperor Alexander amid the ice and snows of Prussia. After the battle of Eylau the American minister became so restless that in May, 1807, he demanded passports for Napoleon's headquarters, but was refused. Had he gone as he wished, he might have seen the great battle of Friedland, June 14, and witnessed the peace of Tilsit, signed July 7, which swept away the last obstacle to Napoleon's schemes against Spain and America. After the peace of Tilsit, Armstrong could foresee that he should have to wait but a short time for the explanations so mysteriously delayed.

Except Denmark and Portugal, every State on the coast of Europe from St. Petersburg to Trieste acknowledged Napoleon's domination. England held out; and experience proved that England could not be reached by arms. The next step in the Emperor's system was to effect her ruin by closing the whole world to her trade. He began with Portugal. From Dresden, July 19, he issued orders[1] that the Portuguese ports should be closed by September 1 against English commerce, or the kingdom of Portugal would be occupied by a combined French and Spanish army. July 29 he was again in Paris. July 31 he ordered Talleyrand to warn the Prince Royal of Denmark that he must choose between war with England and war with France. That the turn would next come to the

[1] Napoleon to Talleyrand, July 19, 1807; Correspondance, xv. 433.

United States was evident; and Armstrong was warned by many signs of the impending storm. August 2, at the diplomatic audience, the brunt of Napoleon's displeasure fell on Dreyer, the Danish minister, and on his colleague from Portugal; but Armstrong could see that he was himself expected to profit by the lesson. He wrote instantly to the Secretary of State.[1]

"We had yesterday our first audience of the Emperor since his return to Paris. Happening to stand near the minister of Denmark, I overheard his Majesty say to that minister: 'So, M. Baron, the Baltic has been violated!' The minister's answer was not audible to me; nor did it appear to be satisfactory to the Emperor, who repeated, in a tone of voice somewhat raised and peremptory, 'But, sir, the Baltic has been violated!' From M. Dreyer he passed to myself and others, and lastly to the ambassador of Portugal, to whom, it is said, he read a very severe lecture on the conduct of his Court. These circumstances go far to justify the whispers that begin to circulate, that an army is organizing to the south for the purpose of taking possession of Portugal, and another to the north for a similar purpose with regard to Denmark; and generally, that, having settled the business of belligerents, with the exception of England, very much to his own liking, he is now on the point of settling that of neutrals in the same way. It was perhaps under the influence of this suggestion that M. Dreyer, taking me aside, inquired whether any application had been made to me with regard to a projected union of all commercial States against Great Britain, and on my answering in the negative, he replied: 'You are much favored, but it will not last!' "

A few days afterward another rumor ran through Paris. The Prince of Benevento was no longer Minister of Foreign Affairs, and his successor was to be M. de Champagny, hitherto Minister of the Interior. At first Armstrong would not believe in Talleyrand's disgrace. "It is not probable that this is very serious, or that it will be very durable," he wrote.[2] "A trifling

[1] Armstrong to Madison, Aug. 3, 1807; State Papers, iii. 243.
[2] Armstrong to Madison, Aug. 11, 1807; MSS. State Department Archives.

cause cannot alienate such a master from such a minister; and
a grave one could not fail to break up all connections between
them." Reasonable as this theory seemed, it was superficial.
The master and the minister had not only separated, but had
agreed to differ and to remain outwardly friends. Their paths
could no longer lie together; and the overwhelming power of
Bonaparte—who controlled a million soldiers with no enemy
to fight—made cabals and Cabinet opposition not only useless but ridiculous. Yet with all this, Talleyrand stood in silent
and cold disapproval of the Emperor's course; and since Talleyrand represented intelligent conservatism, it was natural to
suppose that the Emperor meant to be even more violent in
the future than in the past. The new minister, Champagny,
neither suggested a policy of his own, nor presumed, as Talleyrand sometimes dared, to argue or remonstrate with his
master.

Toward the end of August Dreyer's prophecy became true.
Napoleon's orders forced the King of Denmark and King
Louis of Holland to seize neutral commerce and close the
Danish and Dutch ports. The question immediately rose
whether United States ships and property were still to be
treated as exempt from the operation of the Berlin Decree by
virtue of the treaty of 1800; and the Emperor promptly decided against them.

"In actual circumstances," he wrote to Decrès,[1] "navigation offers all sorts of difficulties. France cannot regard as
neutral flags which enjoy no consideration. That of America, however exposed it may be to the insults of the English, has a sort of existence, since the English still keep
some measure in regard to it, and it imposes on them. That
of Portugal and that of Denmark exist no longer."

This opinion was written before the British ministry
touched the Orders in Council; and the "sort of existence"
which Napoleon conceded to the United States was already
so vague as to be not easily known from the extinction which
had fallen upon Portugal and Denmark. A few days afterward
General Armstrong received officially an order[2] from the

---

[1] Napoleon to Decrès, Sept. 9, 1807; Correspondance, xvi. 20.
[2] M. Regnier to the Procureur Général, Sept. 18, 1807; State Papers, iii. 244.

Emperor which expressly declared that the Berlin Decree admitted of no exception in favor of American vessels; and this step was followed by a letter[1] from Champagny, dated October 7, to the same effect. At the same time the Council of Prizes pronounced judgment in the case of the American ship "Horizon," wrecked some six months before near Morlaix. The Court decreed that such part of the cargo as was not of English origin should be restored to its owners; but that the merchandise which was acknowledged to be of English manufacture or to come from English territory should be confiscated under the Berlin Decree. To this decision Armstrong immediately responded in a strong note[2] of protest to Champagny, which called out an answer from the Emperor himself.

"Reply to the American minister," wrote Napoleon[3] to Champagny November 15, "that since America suffers her vessels to be searched, she adopts the principle that the flag does not cover the goods. Since she recognizes the absurd blockades laid by England, consents to having her vessels incessantly stopped, sent to England, and so turned aside from their course, why should the Americans not suffer the blockade laid by France? Certainly France is no more blockaded by England than England by France. Why should Americans not equally suffer their vessels to be searched by French ships? Certainly France recognizes that these measures are unjust, illegal, and subversive of national sovereignty; but it is the duty of nations to resort to force, and to declare themselves against things which dishonor them and disgrace their independence."

Champagny wrote this message to Armstrong November 24, taking the ground that America must submit to the Berlin Decree because she submitted to impressments and search.[4]

As a matter of relative wrong, Napoleon's argument was more respectable than that of Spencer Perceval and George Canning. He could say with truth that the injury he did to

[1] Champagny to Armstrong, Oct. 7, 1807; State Papers, iii. 245.
[2] Armstrong to Champagny, Nov. 12, 1807; State Papers, iii. 245.
[3] Napoleon to Champagny, Nov. 15, 1807; Correspondance, xvi. 165.
[4] Champagny to Armstrong, Nov. 24, 1807; State Papers, iii. 247.

America was wholly consequential on the injury he meant to inflict on England. He had no hidden plan of suppressing American commerce in order to develop the commerce of France; as yet he was not trying to make money by theft. His Berlin Decree interfered in no way with the introduction of American products directly into France; it merely forbade the introduction of English produce or the reception of ships which came from England. Outrageous as its provisions were, "unjust, illegal, and subversive of national sovereignty," as Napoleon himself admitted and avowed, they bore their character and purpose upon their face, and in that sense were legitimate. He had no secrets on this point. In a famous diplomatic audience at Fontainebleau October 14, Armstrong witnessed a melodramatic scene, in which the Emperor proclaimed to the world that his will was to be law.[1] "The House of Braganza shall reign no more," said he to the Portuguese minister; then turning to the representative of the Queen of Etruria,—the same Spanish princess on whose head he had five years before placed the shadowy crown of Tuscany,—

"Your mistress," he said, "has her secret attachments to Great Britain,—as you, Messieurs Deputies of the Hanse Towns are also said to have; but I will put an end to this. Great Britain shall be destroyed. I have the means of doing it, and they shall be employed. I have three hundred thousand men devoted to this object, and an ally who has three hundred thousand to support them. I will permit no nation to receive a minister from Great Britain until she shall have renounced her maritime usages and tyranny; and I desire you, gentlemen, to convey this determination to your respective sovereigns."

Armstrong obeyed the order; and in doing so he might easily have pointed out the machinery by which Napoleon expected to insure the co-operation of America in securing the destruction of England. He could combine the Berlin Decree with the baffled negotiations for Florida, and could understand why the Emperor at one moment dangled the tempting bait before Jefferson's eyes, and the next snatched it

[1] Armstrong to Madison, Oct. 15, 1807; MSS. State Department Archives.

away. This diplomatic game was one which Napoleon played with every victim he wished to ensnare, and the victim never showed enough force of character to resist temptation. German, Italian, Russian, Spaniard, American, had all been lured by this decoy; one after another had been caught and devoured, but the next victim never saw the trap, or profited by the cries of the last unfortunate. Armstrong knew that whenever Napoleon felt the United States slipping through his fingers, Florida would again be offered to keep Jefferson quiet; yet even Armstrong, man of the world as he was, tried to persuade himself that Napoleon did not know his own mind. One of his despatches at this crisis related a curious story, which he evidently believed to be true, and to prove the vacillating temper of Napoleon's Florida negotiation.

November 15 Armstrong wrote that the Emperor had left Fontainebleau for Italy; that great changes were predicted, among which it was rumored "that Portugal, taken from the Braganzas, may be lent to the children of the Toscan House, and that the Bourbons of Spain are at last to make way for Lucien Bonaparte, who, in atonement or from policy, is to marry the Queen Regent of Etruria." That the American minister should at that early day have been so well informed about projects as yet carefully concealed, was creditable to his diplomacy. Not till nearly a month later did Lucien himself, in his Italian banishment, receive notice of the splendid bribe intended for him.

In the same despatch of November 15 Armstrong discussed the Emperor's plans in their bearing on Florida. "We are, it seems, to be invited to make common cause against England, and to take the guaranty of the Continent for a maritime peace which shall establish the principle of 'free ships, free goods.'" Armstrong argued that it was wiser to act alone, even in case of war with England; in regard to Florida, France had done all that was to be expected from her, and had latterly become sparing even of promises. Finally, he told the anecdote already alluded to:—

"The fact appears to be, which I communicate with the most intimate conviction of its truth, that some sycophant, entering into the weakness of the Emperor, and perceiving

that he was only happy in giving a little more circumference to the bubble, seized the moment of Izquierdo's nomination, and pointing to the United States, said: 'These are
destined to form the last labor of the modern Hercules.
The triumph over England cannot be complete so long as
the commerce and republicanism of this country be permitted to exist. Will it then be wise to insulate it,—to divest
yourselves or your allies of those points which would place
you at once in the midst of it? With what view was it that
after selling Louisiana, attempts were made by France to
buy the Floridas from Spain? Was it not in the anticipation
of events which may make necessary to you a place in the
neighborhood of these States,—a point on which to rest
your political lever? Remember that Archimedes could not
move the world without previously finding a resting-place
for his screw. Instead, therefore, of parting with the Floridas, I would suggest whether we should not make the re-
possession of Canada a condition of a peace with England.'
The conception itself, and the manner in which it was presented, struck the Emperor forcibly. He mused a moment
upon it, and then in the most peremptory manner ordered
that the negotiation should not go on."

Armstrong regarded this anecdote as important. Perhaps he
had it, directly or indirectly, from Talleyrand, who used more
freedom of speech than was permitted to any other man in
France; but the task of penetrating the depths of Napoleon's
mind was one which even Talleyrand attempted in vain. From
the first, Florida had been used by Napoleon as a means of
controlling President Jefferson. "To enlarge the circumference
of his bubble" was a phrase keen and terse enough to have
come from Talleyrand himself; but this was not the purpose
for which Florida had hitherto been used in Napoleon's diplomacy, and in ordering that the negotiation should be
stopped, the Emperor might well have other motives, which
he preferred keeping to himself.

An observer far less intelligent than Armstrong might have
seen that in face of the great changes which his despatch announced for Italy, Portugal, and Spain, the time when Napoleon would need support from the United States had not

yet come. The critical moment was still in the future. Perhaps America might be forced into war by the "Chesapeake" outrage; at all events, she was further than ever from alliance with England, and the Emperor could safely wait for her adhesion to the continental system until his plans for consolidating his empire were more mature. For the present, Don Carlos IV. and the Prince of Peace were the chief objects of French diplomacy.

The story of Toussaint and St. Domingo was about to be repeated in Spain. Even while Armstrong wrote these despatches, the throne of Don Carlos IV. crumbled, almost without need of a touch from without. France had drawn from Spain everything she once possessed,—her navy, sacrificed at Trafalgar to Napoleon's orders; her army, nearly half of which was in Denmark; her treasures, which, so far as they had not been paid in subsidies to Napoleon, were shut up in Mexico. Nothing but the shell was left of all that had made Spain great. This long depletion had not been effected without extreme anxiety on the part of the Spanish government. At any time after the Prince of Peace returned to power in 1801, he would gladly have broken with France, as he proved in 1806; but he stood in much the same position as Jefferson, between the selfishness of England and the immediate interests of Spain. King Charles, anxious beyond measure for his own repose and for the safety of his daughter the Queen of Etruria, shrank from every strong measure of resistance to Napoleon's will, yet was so helpless that only a traitor or a coward could have deserted him; and Godoy, with all his faults, was not so base as to secure his own interests by leaving the King to Napoleon's mercy. For a single moment the King yielded to Godoy's entreaties. When the fourth European coalition was formed against Napoleon, and Prussia declared war, the Prince of Peace was allowed to issue, Oct. 6, 1806, a proclamation calling the Spanish people to arms. October 14 the battle of Jena was fought, and the news reaching Madrid threw the King and court into consternation; Godoy's influence was broken by the shock; the proclamation was recalled, and the old King bowed his head to his fate. Had he held firm, and thrown in his fortunes with those of England, Russia, and Prussia, the battle of Eylau might have stopped

Napoleon's career; and in any case the fate of Spain could not have been more terrible than it was.

The Prince of Peace begged in vain that King Charles would dismiss him and form a new ministry; the King could not endure a change. Napoleon laughed at the proclamation, but he knew Godoy to be his only serious enemy at Madrid. He took infinite pains, and exhausted the extraordinary resources of his cunning, in order to get possession of Spain without a blow. To do this, he forced Portugal into what he called a war. Without noticing Godoy's offence, immediately after the peace of Tilsit, as has been already told, the Emperor ordered the King of Portugal to execute the Berlin Decree. Unable to resist, Portugal consented to shut her ports to English commerce, but objected to confiscating British property. Without a moment's delay, Napoleon, October 12,[1] ordered General Junot, with an army of twenty thousand men, to enter Spain within twenty-four hours, and march direct to Lisbon; simultaneously he notified[2] the Spanish government that his troops would be at Burgos, November 1; and that this time "it was not intended to do as was done in the last war,— he must march straight to Lisbon."

After the peace of Tilsit, no Power in Europe pretended to question Napoleon's will, and for Spain to do so would have been absurd. King Charles had to submit, and he sent an army to co-operate with Junot against Portugal. The Emperor, who might at a single word have driven King Charles as well as the King of Portugal from the throne, did not say the word. Godoy's proclamation had given France cause for war; but Napoleon took no notice of the proclamation. He did not ask for the punishment of Godoy; he not only left the old King in peace, but took extraordinary care to soothe his fears. On the same day when he ordered Junot to march, he wrote personally to reassure the King:[3] "I will concert with your Majesty as to what shall be done with Portugal; in any case the suzerainty shall belong to you, as you have seemed to wish." Yet four days later he ordered[4] another

[1] Napoleon to General Clarke, Oct. 12, 1807; Correspondance, xvi. 80.
[2] Napoleon to Champagny, Oct. 12, 1807; Correspondance, xvi. 79.
[3] Napoleon to Charles IV., Oct. 12, 1807; Correspondance, xvi. 83.
[4] Napoleon to General Clarke, Oct. 16, 1807; Correspondance, xvi. 91.

army of thirty thousand men to be collected at Bayonne, to support Junot, who had no enemy to fear. That his true campaign was against Spain, not against Portugal, never admitted of a doubt; his orders to Junot hardly concealed his object:[1] —

"Cause descriptions to be made for me of all the provinces through which you pass,—the roads, the nature of the ground; send me sketches. Charge engineer officers with this work, which it is important to have; so that I can see the distance of the villages, the nature of the country, the resources it offers. . . . I learn this moment that Portugal has declared war on England and sent away the English ambassador: this does not satisfy me; continue your march; I have reason to believe that it is agreed upon with England in order to give time for the English troops to come from Copenhagen. You must be at Lisbon by December 1, as friend or as enemy. Maintain the utmost harmony with the Prince of Peace."

Junot entered Spain October 17, the same day that these orders were written, while Napoleon at Fontainebleau forced on the Spanish agent Izquierdo a treaty which might keep King Charles and Godoy quiet a little longer. This document, drafted by Napoleon himself, resembled the letter to Toussaint and the proclamation to the negroes of St. Domingo, with which Leclerc had been charged;[2] its motive was too obvious, and its appeal to selfishness too gross to deceive. It declared[3] that Portugal should be divided into three parts. The most northerly, with Oporto for a capital and a population of eight hundred thousand souls, should be given to the Queen of Etruria in place of Tuscany, which was to be swallowed up in the kingdom of Italy. The next provision was even more curious. The southern part of Portugal, with a population of four hundred thousand souls, should be given to the Prince of Peace as an independent sovereignty. The central part, with a population of two millions, and Lisbon

[1] Napoleon to Junot, Oct. 17, 1807; Correspondance, xvi. 98.
[2] See History of First Administration, p. 265.
[3] Correspondance de Napoleon I.; Projet de Convention, Oct. 23, 1807, xvi. 111.

for a capital, should be held by France subject to further agreement. By a final touch of dissimulation worthy of Shakespeare's tragic invention, Napoleon, in the last article of this treaty, promised to recognize Don Carlos IV. as Emperor of the two Americas.

The so-called treaty of Fontainebleau was signed Oct. 27, 1807. That it deceived Godoy or King Charles could hardly be imagined, but the internal and external difficulties of Spain had reached a point where nothing but ruin remained. In the whole of Spain hardly twenty thousand troops could be assembled; barely half-a-dozen frigates were fit for sea; the treasury was empty; industry was destroyed. Napoleon himself had no idea how complete was the process by which he had sucked the life-blood of this miserable land. Even in the court at Madrid and among the people signs of an immediate catastrophe were so evident that Napoleon could afford to wait until chaos should call for his control.

Meanwhile Junot marched steadily forward. He was at Burgos on the day fixed by Napoleon; he established permanent French depots at Valladolid and at Salamanca. Leaving Salamanca November 12, he advanced to Ciudad Rodrigo, and after establishing another depot there, he made a rapid dash at Lisbon. The march was difficult, but Junot was ready to destroy his army rather than fail to carry out his orders; and on the morning of November 30 he led a ragged remnant of fifteen hundred men into the city of Lisbon. He found it without a government. The Prince Regent of Portugal, powerless to resist Napoleon, had gone on board his ships with the whole royal family and court, and was already on his way to found a new empire at Rio Janeiro. Of all the royal houses of Europe, that of Portugal was the first to carry out a desperate resolution.

Napoleon's object was thus gained. Dec. 1, 1807, Junot was in peaceable possession of Lisbon, and French garrisons held every strategical point between Lisbon and Bayonne. In regard to Portugal Junot's orders were precise:[1] —

"So soon as you have the different fortified places in your hands, you will put French commandants in them, and will

[1] Napoleon to Junot, October 31, 1807; Correspondance, xvi. 128.

make yourself sure of these places. I need not tell you that you must not put any fortress in the power of the Spaniards, especially in the region which is to remain in my hands."

November 3, without the knowledge of Spain, the Emperor gave orders[1] that the army of reserve at Bayonne, under General Dupont, shall be ready to march by December 1; and November 11 he ordered[2] that the frontier fortresses on the Spanish border should be armed and supplied with provisions: —

"All this is to be done with the utmost possible secrecy, especially the armament of the places on the Spanish frontier on the side of the eastern Pyrenees. Give secret instructions, and let the corps march in such a manner that the first ostensible operations be not seen in that country before November 25."

At the same time a new army of some twenty thousand men was hurried across France to take the place, at Bayonne, of Dupont's army, which was to enter Spain. November 13, the Emperor ordered Dupont to move his first division across the frontier to Vittoria; and on the same day he despatched M. de Tournon, his chamberlain, with a letter to King Charles at Madrid, and with secret instructions[3] that revealed the reasons for these movements so carefully concealed from Spanish eyes: —

"You will also inform yourself, without seeming to do so, of the situation of the places of Pampeluna and of Fontarabia; and if you perceive armaments making anywhere, you will inform me by courier. You will be on the watch at Madrid to see well the spirit which animates that city."

Napoleon's orders were in all respects exactly carried out. Dec. 1, 1807, Junot was in possession of Portugal; Dupont was at Vittoria; twenty-five thousand French troops would, by December 20, hold the great route from Vittoria to Burgos,

[1] Napoleon to General Clarke, Nov. 3, 1807; Correspondance, xvi. 136.
[2] Napoleon to General Clarke, Nov. 11, 1807; Correspondance, xvi. 149.
[3] Napoleon to M. de Tournon, Nov. 13, 1807; Correspondance, xvi. 159.

and in two days could occupy Madrid.[1] The Spanish army was partly in Denmark, partly in Portugal. The Prince of Peace heard what was going on, and asked for explanations; but the moment for resistance had long passed. He had no choice but submission or flight, and Don Carlos was too weak to fly.

In Armstrong's despatch of November 15, already quoted, one more paragraph was worth noting. At the moment he wrote, Napoleon had just given his last orders; General Dupont had not yet received them, and neither Don Carlos IV. nor Lucien Bonaparte knew the change of plan that was intended. Only men like Talleyrand and Duroc could see that from the moment of the peace at Tilsit, Napoleon's movements had been rapidly and irresistibly converging upon Madrid,—until, by the middle of November, every order had been given, and the Spanish Peninsula lay, as the Emperor told Lucien, "in the hollow of his hand." Armstrong, writing a fortnight before the royal family of Portugal had turned their vessels' prows toward Brazil, asked a question which Napoleon himself would hardly have dared to answer:

"What will become of the royal houses of Portugal and Spain? I know not. By the way, I consider this question as of no small interest to the United States. If they were sent to America, or are even permitted to withdraw thither, we may conclude that the colonies which excite the imperial longing, and which are in its opinion necessary to France, are not on our side of the Atlantic. If on the other hand they are retained in Europe, it will only be as hostages for the eventual delivery of their colonies; and then, at the distance of three centuries, may be acted over again the tragedy of the Incas, with some few alterations of scenery and names."

All these measures being completed by November 15, the day when Armstrong wrote his despatch, the Emperor left Fontainebleau and went to Italy. He passed through Milan and Verona to Venice; and on his return, stopped a few hours

[1] Napoleon to General Clarke, Dec. 6, 1807; Correspondance, xvi. 183.

at Mantua,[1] on the night of December 13, to offer Lucien the throne of Spain.

Lucien's story[2] was that being summoned from Rome to an interview, he found his brother alone, at midnight of December 13, seated in a vast room in the palace at Mantua, before a great round table, almost entirely covered by a very large map of Spain, on which he was marking strategical points with black, red, and yellow pins. After a long interview, in which the Emperor made many concessions to his brother's resistance, Napoleon opened his last and most audacious offer:—

" 'As for you, choose!' As he pronounced these words," continued Lucien, "his eyes sparkled with a flash of pride which seemed to me Satanic; he struck a great blow with his hand, spread out broadly in the middle of the immense map of Europe which was extended on the table by the side of which we were standing. 'Yes, choose!' he said; 'you see I am not talking in the air. All this is mine, or will soon belong to me; I can dispose of it already. Do you want Naples? I will take it from Joseph, who, by the bye, does not care for it; he prefers Morfontaine. Italy,—the most beautiful jewel in my imperial crown? Eugene is but viceroy, and far from despising it he hopes only that I shall give it to him, or at least leave it to him if he survives me: he is likely to be disappointed in waiting, for I shall live ninety years; I must, for the perfect consolidation of my empire. Besides, Eugene will not suit me in Italy after his mother is repudiated. Spain? Do you not see it falling into the hollow of my hand, thanks to the blunders of your dear Bourbons, and to the follies of your friend the Prince of Peace? Would you not be well pleased to reign there where you have been only ambassador? Once for all, what do you want? Speak! Whatever you wish, or can wish, is yours, if your divorce precedes mine.' "

Lucien refused a kingdom on such terms, and Napoleon continued his journey, reaching Milan December 15. At that time his mind was intent on Spain and the Spanish colonies,

[1] Napoleon to Joseph, Dec. 17, 1807; Correspondance, xvi. 198.
[2] Lucien Bonaparte, Th. Jung. iii. 83, 113.

with which the questions of English and American trade were closely connected. Spencer Perceval's Orders in Council had appeared in the "London Gazette" of November 14, and had followed the Emperor to Italy. Some weeks afterward war was declared between England and Russia. No neutral remained except Sweden, which was to be crushed by Russia, and the United States of America, which Napoleon meant to take in hand. December 17, from the royal palace at Milan, in retaliation for the Orders in Council, and without waiting to consult President Jefferson, Napoleon issued a new proclamation, compared with which the Berlin Decree of the year before was a model of legality.

"Considering," began the preamble,[1] "that by these acts the English government has denationalized the ships of all the nations of Europe; that it is in the power of no government to compound its own independence and its rights,— all the sovereigns in Europe being jointly interested in the sovereignty and independence of their flag; that if by an inexcusable weakness, which would be an ineffaceable stain in the eyes of posterity, we should allow such a tyranny to pass into a principle and to become consecrated by usage, the English would take advantage of it to establish it as a right, as they have profited by the tolerance of governments to establish the infamous principle that the flag does not cover the goods, and to give to their right of blockade an arbitrary extension, contrary to the sovereignty of all States,"—

Considering all these matters, so important to States like Denmark, Portugal, and Spain, whose flags had ceased to exist, and of whose honor and interests this mighty conqueror made himself champion, Napoleon decreed that every ship which should have been searched by an English vessel, or should have paid any duty to the British government, or should come from or be destined for any port in British possession in any part of the world, should be good prize; and that this rule should continue in force until England should have "returned to the principles of international law, which are also those of justice and honor."

[1] Correspondance de Napoleon, xvi. 192; American State Papers, iii. 90.

Chapter VI

OCT. 29, 1807, Monroe left London, and November 14, the day when the Orders in Council were first published in the official "Gazette," he sailed from Plymouth for home.

Nearly five years had passed since Monroe received the summons from Jefferson which drew him from his retirement in Virginia to stand forward as the diplomatic champion of the United States in contest with the diplomatists of Europe; and these five years had been full of unpleasant experience. Since signing the Louisiana treaty, in May, 1803, he had met only with defeat and disaster. Insulted by every successive Foreign Secretary in France, Spain, and England; driven from Madrid to Paris and from Paris to London; set impossible tasks, often contrary to his own judgment,—he had ended by yielding to the policy of the British government, and by meeting with disapproval and disavowal from his own. As he looked back on the receding shores of England, he could hardly fail to recall the circumstances of his return from France ten years before. In many respects Monroe's career was unparalleled, but he was singular above all in the experience of being disowned by two Presidents as strongly opposed to each other as Washington and Jefferson, and of being sacrificed by two secretaries as widely different as Timothy Pickering and James Madison.

In America only two men of much note were prepared to uphold his course, and of these the President was not one; yet Jefferson exerted himself to disguise and soften Monroe's discredit. He kept the treaty a secret when its publication would have destroyed Monroe's popularity and strengthened Madison. When at length, after eight months' delay, the British note appended to the treaty was revealed, Monroe's friend Macon, though anxious to make him President, privately admitted that "the extract of the treaty which has been published has injured Monroe more than the return of it by the President."[1] John Randolph alone held up Monroe and his treaty as models of statesmanship; and although Randolph

[1] Macon to Nicholson, Dec. 2, 1807; Nicholson MSS.

was the only Republican who cared to go this length, Monroe found one other friend and apologist in a person who rivalled Randolph in his usual economy of praise. Timothy Pickering held that Merry and Erskine were no good Englishmen, but he was satisfied with Monroe.

"I sincerely wish an English minister here to be a very able man," he wrote[1] privately from Washington to a friend in Philadelphia,—"one who will feel and justly estimate the dignity of his country, and bring down the supercilious looks of our strutting Administration. The feebleness of Merry and Erskine have encouraged them to assume a vain importance and haughtiness as remote from the genuine spirit and as injurious to the solid interests of our country as they are irritating to Great Britain. The ridiculous gasconade of our rulers has indeed disgraced our nation. The sentiment above expressed is excited by the consideration that Great Britain is our only shield against the overwhelming power of Bonaparte; and therefore I view the maintenance of her just rights as essential to the preservation of our own. I have regretted to see our newspapers continue to reproach Monroe. His abilities you know how to estimate, but I never considered him as wanting in probity. An *enragé* relative to the French, and implicitly relying on the advice of Jefferson, his deportment did not permit his remaining the minister of the United States at Paris [in 1797]; but I have certain information that at London no one could conduct with more propriety than he does; and, such is his sense of the proceedings of our rulers, he lately said he did not know how long the British government would bear with our petulance."

This letter, written while Monroe was at sea, betrayed a hope that the notorious quarrel between him and Jefferson would prove to be permanent; but Pickering could never learn to appreciate Jefferson's genius for peace. Doubtless only personal friendship and the fear of strengthening Federalist influence prevented President Jefferson from denouncing Monroe's conduct as forcibly as President Washington had

[1] Pickering to Thomas Fitzsimons, Dec. 4, 1807; Pickering MSS.

denounced it ten years before; and Jefferson's grounds of complaint were more serious than Washington's. Monroe expected and even courted martyrdom, and never quite forgot the treatment he received. In private, George Hay, Monroe's son-in-law, who knew all the secrets of his career, spoke afterward of Jefferson as "one of the most insincere men in the world; . . . his enmity to Mr. Monroe was inveterate, though disguised, and he was at the bottom of all the opposition to Mr. Monroe in Virginia."[1] Peacemakers must submit to the charges which their virtues entail, but Jefferson's silence and conciliation deserved a better return than to be called insincere.

Monroe returned to Virginia, praised by George Canning and Timothy Pickering, to be John Randolph's candidate for the Presidency, while Jefferson could regard him in no other light than as a dupe of England, and Madison was obliged to think him a personal enemy. As a result of five years' honest, patient, and painstaking labor, this division from old friends was sad enough; but had Monroe been a nervous man, so organized as to feel the arrows of his outrageous fortune, his bitterest annoyance on bidding final farewell to Europe would have been, not the thought of his reception in America, not even the memory of Talleyrand's reproofs, or of the laurels won by Don Pedro Cevallos, or of Lord Harrowby's roughness, or Lord Mulgrave's indifference, or Lord Howick's friendly larcenies, or Canning's smooth impertinences,—as a diplomatist he would rather have felt most hurt that the British ministry had contrived a new measure of vital interest to America, and should have allowed him to depart without a word of confidence, explanation, or enlightenment as to the nature of the fresh aggression which was to close a long list of disasters with one which left to America only the title of an independent nation.

As early as October 3 the "Morning Post" announced at great length that his Majesty's government had adopted the principle of retaliation. November 10, while Monroe was still waiting at Portsmouth for a fair wind, the "Times" made known that a proclamation was in readiness for the King's

---

[1] Diary of J. Q. Adams, May 23, 1824, vi. 348.

signature, declaring France and all her vassal kingdoms in a state of siege: "The sum of all reasoning on the subject is included in this, that the Continent must and will have colonial productions in spite of the orders and decrees of its master, and we are to take care that she have no other colonial produce than our own." The fact that American commerce with the Continent was to be forbidden became a matter of public notoriety in London before November 13, and on Saturday, November 14, the day when Monroe's ship sailed from Portsmouth, the order appeared in the "Gazette;" yet Monroe himself would be obliged to appear before the President in official ignorance of a measure discussed and adopted under his eyes.

George Henry Rose, whom Canning selected as special envoy to settle the "Chesapeake" affair, and who sailed in the "Statira" frigate two days before Monroe, knew officially as little as Monroe himself of the coming order; but this ignorance was due to Canning's settled plan of keeping the "Chesapeake" affair independent of every other dispute. Canning could have had no deep motive in withholding official knowledge of the order from Monroe, Pinkney, and Rose; he could not have foreseen when or how the winds would blow; yet, by mere accident, one day's delay added greatly to the coming embarrassments of the American government. The departure of vessels depended on a favorable wind, and for some weeks before November 14 westerly winds prevailed. About that day the weather changed, and all the ships bound to America sailed nearly together. The "Statira" and "Augustus," carrying Rose and Monroe, started from Portsmouth for Norfolk; the "Revenge" set sail from Cherbourg, with despatches from Armstrong; the "Brutus," with London newspapers of November 12, departed from Liverpool for New York; and the "Edward," with London newspapers and letters to November 10, left Liverpool for Boston. All were clear of land by November 14, when the "Gazette" published the Order in Council; but for weeks afterward no other vessels crossed the Atlantic.

After the "Revenge" sailed for Europe in July, on her errand of redress for the "Chesapeake" outrage, the Americans waited more and more patiently for her return. The excitement which blazed in mid-summer from one end of the country to the other began to subside when men learned that Admiral Berkeley's orders had been issued without the authority or knowledge of his government, and would probably be disavowed. The news that came from Europe tended to chill the fever for war. The Peace of Tilsit, the Tory reaction in England, the bombardment of Copenhagen, the execution of the Berlin Decree in Holland, the threatened retaliation by Great Britain were events calculated to raise more than a doubt of the benefits which war could bring. In any case, the risks of commerce had become too great for legitimate trade; and every one felt that the further pursuit of neutral profits could end only in bringing America into the arms of one or the other of the Powers which were avowedly disputing pre-eminence in wrong.

The attack on the "Chesapeake," the trial of Aaron Burr, and the news from Copenhagen, Holland, and London made the summer and autumn of 1807 anxious and restless; but another event, under the eyes of the American people, made up a thousand fold, had they but known it, for all the losses or risks incurred through Burr, Bonaparte, or Canning. That the destinies of America must be decided in America was a maxim of true Democrats, but one which they showed little energy in reducing to practice. A few whose names could be mentioned in one or two lines,—men like Chancellor Livingston, Dr. Mitchill, Joel Barlow,—hailed the 17th of August, 1807, as the beginning of a new era in America,—a date which separated the colonial from the independent stage of growth; for on that day, at one o'clock in the afternoon, the steamboat "Clermont," with Robert Fulton in command, started on her first voyage. A crowd of bystanders, partly sceptical, partly hostile, stood about and watched the clumsy craft slowly forge its way at the rate of four miles an hour up the river; but Fulton's success left room for little doubt or dispute, except in minds impervious to proof. The problem of steam navigation, so far as it applied to rivers and harbors was settled, and for the first time America could consider herself mistress of her vast resources. Compared with such a step in her progress, the mediæval barbarisms of Napoleon and Spencer Perceval signified little more to her than the doings of Achilles and Agamemnon. Few moments in her history were more dramatic than the weeks of 1807 which saw the shattered "Chesapeake" creep back to her anchorage at Hampton Roads, and the "Clermont" push laboriously up the waters of the Hudson; but the intellectual effort of bringing these two events together, and of settling the political and economical problems of America at once, passed the genius of the people. Government took no notice of Fulton's achievement, and the public for some years continued, as a rule, to travel in sailing packets and on flat-boats. The reign of politics showed no sign of ending. Fulton's steamer went its way, waiting until men's time should become so valuable as to be worth saving.

The unfailing mark of a primitive society was to regard war as the most natural pursuit of man; and history with reason began as a record of war, because, in fact, all other human occupations were secondary to this. The chief sign that Americans had other qualities than the races from which they sprang, was shown by their dislike for war as a profession, and their obstinate attempts to invent other methods for obtaining their ends; but in the actual state of mankind, safety and civilization could still be secured only through the power of self-defence. Desperate physical courage was the common quality on which all great races had founded their greatness; and the people of the United States, in discarding military qualities, without devoting themselves to science, were trying an experiment which could succeed only in a world of their own.

In charging America with having lost her national character, Napoleon said no more than the truth. As a force in the affairs of Europe, the United States had become an appendage to England. The Americans consumed little but English manufactures, allowed British ships to blockade New York and Chesapeake Bay, permitted the British government to keep by force in its naval service numbers of persons who were claimed as American subjects, and to take from American merchant-vessels, at its free will, any man who seemed likely to be useful; they suffered their commerce with France and Spain to be plundered by Great Britain without resistance, or to be regulated in defiance of American rights. Nothing could exceed England's disregard of American dignity. When the "Bellona" and her consorts were ordered to

depart from Chesapeake Bay, her captain not only disregarded the order, but threatened to take by force whatever he
wanted on shore, and laughed at the idea of compulsion. On
land still less respect was shown to American jurisdiction.
When after the "Chesapeake" outrage the people talked of
war, the first act of Sir James Craig, governor-general of Canada, was to send messages[1] to the Indian tribes in the Indiana
Territory, calling for their assistance in case of hostilities; and
the effect of this appeal was instantly felt at Vincennes and
Greenville, where it gave to the intrigues of the Shawanese
prophet an impulse that alarmed every settler on the frontier.
Every subordinate officer of the British government thought
himself at liberty to trample on American rights; and while
the English navy controlled the coast, and the English army
from Canada gave orders to the northwestern Indians, the
British minister at Washington encouraged and concealed the
conspiracy of Burr.

The evil had reached a point where some corrective must
be found; but four years of submission had broken the national spirit. In 1805 the people were almost ready for war
with England on the question of the indirect, or carrying,
trade of the French and Spanish West Indies. After submitting on that point, in July, 1807, they were again ready to
fight for the immunity of their frigates from impressment; but
by the close of the year their courage had once more fallen,
and they hoped to escape the necessity of fighting under any
circumstances whatever, anxiously looking for some expedient, or compromise, which would reconcile a policy of resistance with a policy of peace. This expedient Jefferson and
Madison had for fifteen years been ready to offer them.

So confident was Jefferson in his theory of peaceable coercion that he would hardly have thought his administrative
career complete, had he quitted office without being allowed
to prove the value of his plan. The fascination which it exercised over his mind was quite as much due to temperament
as to logic; for if reason told him that Europe could be
starved into concession, temperament added another motive
still more alluring. If Europe persisted in her conduct America

[1] Sir James Craig to Lieutenant-Governor Gore, Dec. 6, 1807; Colonial
Correspondence, Canada, 1807, 1808, vol. i., MSS. British Archives.

would still be safe, and all the happier for cutting off connection with countries where violence and profligacy ruled supreme. The idea of ceasing intercourse with obnoxious nations reflected his own personality in the mirror of statesmanship. In the course of the following year he wrote to a young grandson, Thomas Jefferson Randolph, a letter[1] of parental advice in regard to the conduct of life.

"Be a listener only," he said; "keep within yourself, and endeavor to establish with yourself the habit of silence, especially on politics. In the fevered state of our country no good can ever result from any attempt to set one of these fiery zealots to rights, either in fact or principle. They are determined as to the facts they will believe, and the opinions on which they will act. Get by them, therefore, as you would by an angry bull; it is not for a man of sense to dispute the road with such an animal."

The advice was good, and did honor to the gentleness of Jefferson's nature; but a course of conduct excellent in social life could not be made to suit the arena of politics. As President of the United States, Jefferson was bent upon carrying out the plan of keeping within himself; but the bull of which he spoke as unfit for a man of sense to dispute with, and which he saw filling the whole path before him, was not only angry, but mad with pain and blind with rage; his throat and flanks were torn and raw where the Corsican wolf had set his teeth; a pack of mastiffs and curs were baiting him and yelling at his heels, and his blood-shot eyes no longer knew friend from foe, as he rushed with a roar of stupid rage directly upon the President. To get by him was impossible. To fly was the only resource, if the President would not stand his ground and stop the animal by skill or force.

Few rulers ever succeeded in running from danger with dignity. Even the absolute Emperor of Russia had not wholly preserved the respect of his subjects after the sudden somersault performed at Tilsit; and the Prince Regent of Portugal had been forced to desert his people when he banished himself to Brazil. President Jefferson had not their excuse for

[1] Jefferson to T. J. Randolph, Nov. 24, 1808; Works, v. 388.

flight; but resistance by force was already impossible. For more than six years he had conducted government on the theory of peaceable coercion, and his own friends required that the experiment should be tried. He was more than willing, he was anxious, to gratify them; and he believed himself to have solved the difficult problem of stopping his enemy, while running away from him without loss of dignity and without the appearance of flight.

General Turreau, after hoping for a time that the government would accept the necessity of war with England, became more and more bitter as he watched the decline of the war spirit; and September 4, barely two months after the assault on the "Chesapeake," and long before the disavowal of Berkeley was known, he wrote to Talleyrand a diatribe against the Americans:[1] —

"If the sentiments of fear and of servile deference for England with which the inhabitants of the American Union are penetrated, were not as well known as their indifference for everything which bears the name of French, what has passed since the attack on the frigate 'Chesapeake' would prove to the most vulgar observer not only that the Anglo-Americans have remained in reality dependent on Great Britain, but even that this state of subjection conforms with their affections as well as with their habits. He will also be convinced that France has, and will ever have, nothing to hope from the dispositions of a people that conceives no idea of glory, of grandeur, of justice; that shows itself the constant enemy of liberal principles; and that is disposed to suffer every kind of humiliation, provided it can satisfy both its sordid avarice and its projects of usurpation over the Floridas."

Scandalized at the rapid evaporation of American courage, Turreau could explain it only as due to the natural defects of "a motley people, that will never have true patriotism, because it has no object of common interest;" a nation which looked on the most shameless outrages of its own virtue as only "unfortunate events." Yet one point remained which, al-

[1] Turreau to Talleyrand, Sept. 4, 1807; Archives des Aff. Étr. MSS.

though to every American it seemed most natural, was incomprehensible to the Frenchman, whose anger with America was due not so much to the dependence of the United States on England, as to their independence of France.

"What will doubtless astonish those who know the Americans but imperfectly, and what has surprised me myself,—me, who have a very bad opinion of this people, and who believe it just,—is the aversion (*éloignement*)—and I soften the word—which it has preserved for the French at the very moment when everything should recall a glorious and useful memory. It is hardly to be believed, yet is the exact truth, that in perhaps five hundred banquets produced by the anniversary of July 4, and among ten thousand toasts, but one has been offered in favor of France; and even this was given at an obscure meeting, and was evidently dictated by Duane."

Even the Administration press, Turreau complained, had thought proper to repudiate the idea of a French alliance. From his complaints the truth could be easily understood. In spite of reason, and in defiance of every ordinary rule of politics, France possessed in America no friend, or influence. The conclusion to be drawn was inevitable. If the United States would not accept the only alliance which could answer their purpose, England had nothing to fear. "In this state of affairs and condition of minds, it appears to me difficult to believe that Congress will take measures vigorous enough to revenge the insult offered to the Union, and to prevent the renewal of outrages."

This conclusion was reached by Turreau September 4, while as early as September 1 the same opinion was expressed by Erskine, the British minister:[1]

"From all the consideration which I have been able to give to the present state of things in this country, I am confirmed most strongly in the opinion which I have ventured to express in my former despatches, that, although I fear it might be possible for this government to lead the people into a war with Great Britain on the point of

[1] Erskine to Canning, Sept. 1, 1807; MSS. British Archives.

searching her national armed ships, yet I do not believe that there are any other grounds which would be powerful enough to urge them to so dangerous a measure to the political existence perhaps, but certainly to the general prosperity of this country."

No two men in America were better informed or more directly interested than Turreau and Erskine, and they agreed in regarding America as passive in the hands of England.

During the month of September the news from Europe tended to show that while England would not sustain the attack on the "Chesapeake," she meant to cut off, for her own benefit, another share of American commerce. The report on the West Indian trade and the debates in Parliament foreshadowed the enforcement of the so-called Rule of 1756 or some harsher measure. That Congress must in some way resent this interference with neutral rights was evident, unless America were to become again a British province. Erskine knew the strength of British influence too well to fear war; but he warned his Government that no nation could be expected to endure without protest of some kind the indignities which the United States daily experienced:[1] —

"I am persuaded that more ill-will has been excited in this country toward Great Britain by a few trifling illegal captures immediately off this coast, and some instances of insulting behavior by some of his Majesty's naval commanders in the very harbors and waters of the United States, than by the most rigid enforcement of the maritime rights of Great Britain in other parts of the world. It may easily be conceived to be highly grating to the feelings of an independent nation to perceive that their whole coast is watched as closely as if it was blockaded, and every ship coming in or going out of their harbors examined rigorously in sight of the shore, by British squadrons stationed within their waters."

Erskine added that the causes of difference were so various as to make any good understanding improbable, and any commercial treaty impossible; that the Federalists thought

[1] Erskine to Canning, Oct. 5, 1807; MSS. British Archives.

even worse of Monroe's treaty than the Government did, which rejected it; and that a great sensation had been produced by the late Report on the West Indian trade: —

"This point, and his Majesty's Order in Council to prohibit all neutral trade from port to port of his Majesty's enemies, — which, as you would perceive by Mr. Madison's letters on the subject, which have been transmitted to you, has given great offence to this Government, — together with the other points of difference between the two countries, particularly that of the impressment of British seamen out of American ships, will be taken up by Congress upon their meeting at the close of the present month; and I am fully convinced that unless some amicable adjustment of these points of dispute should previously take place, or be in a train to be concluded, a system of commercial restrictions on the trade of Great Britain with this country will be immediately formed, and every step short of actual war taken to show their dissatisfaction."

Thus, on the eve of the session, the most careful critics agreed that Congress would avoid war, and would resist England, if at all, by commercial measures. The President and Madison, Turreau and Erskine, were united in expecting the same course of events. No one knew that Napoleon had enforced against American commerce the provisions of his Berlin Decree. France counted for nothing in the councils of America; but the conduct of England obliged Congress to offer some protest against aggression, — and the easiest form of protest was a refusal to buy what she had to sell. The moment for testing Jefferson's statesmanship had come; and at no time since he became President had his theories of peaceable coercion enjoyed so fair a prospect of success. Abroad, Napoleon had shut the whole Continent of Europe to English trade, which was henceforward limited to countries beyond the seas. If ever England could be coerced by peaceable means, this was the time; while at home, the prospect was equally favorable, for never in American history had the authority of the government been so absolute.

Jefferson's hope of annihilating domestic opposition was nearly gratified. In the three southernmost States he had never met with serious attack; beyond the Alleghanies, in Tennessee, Kentucky, and Ohio, his word was law; in Virginia, John Randolph grew weaker day by day, and even with Monroe's aid could not shake the President's popularity; Pennsylvania was torn by factions, but none of them troubled Jefferson; New York, purged of Burr, was divided between Clintons and Livingstons, who were united in matters of national policy. The greatest triumph of all was won in Massachusetts, where the election of April, 1807, after calling out 81,500 voters, resulted in the choice of the Democrat Sullivan over the head of Governor Strong by about 42,000 votes against 39,000, and in the return of a Democratic majority in the State legislature. Connecticut alone of the New England States held to her old conservative principles; but Connecticut was powerless without Massachusetts.

Still more decidedly the decline of organized opposition was shown in the character of the Tenth Congress, which was to meet October 26. Of the old Federalist senators, Plumer of New Hampshire had been succeeded by a Democrat; J. Q. Adams of Massachusetts had publicly pledged himself to support any measures of resistance to England; Tracy of Connecticut— a very able opponent—was dead. Only five senators could be rallied to partisan opposition on matters of foreign policy,—Timothy Pickering of Massachusetts; James Hillhouse and Chauncey Goodrich of Connecticut; James A. Bayard and Samuel White of Delaware. Pickering, who considered Plumer and Adams as deserters to the Administration, felt little confidence in Bayard; and the event proved him right. There were limits to Bayard's partisanship; but even had he been willing to abet Pickering, four or five senators could hope to effect little against a compact majority of twenty-nine.

In the House the whole strength of opposition could not control thirty votes, while Jefferson was supported by one hundred and ten members or more. The President was the stronger for Randolph's departure into decided opposition, where he could no longer divide and mislead the majority, but must act as a Federalist or alone. Of the twenty-four Federalist members, Josiah Quincy was probably the ablest speaker; but in the energy of his Federalism he was rivalled by two men,—Barent Gardenier of New York, and Philip Barton Key of Maryland,—who were likely to injure their cause more than they helped it.

In the country and in Congress, not only was Jefferson supreme, but his enemies were prostrate. Federalism in New England, for the first time, lay helpless under his feet; Burr and the "little band" in New York were crushed; the creoles in New Orleans, and the Western revolutionists, with Wilkinson at their head, were cowering before the outburst of patriotism which struck their projects dead. The hand of government rested heavily on them, and threatened nobler prey. Even Chief-Justice Marshall felt himself marked for punishment; while Monroe and Randolph were already under ban of the republic. These were triumphs which outweighed foreign disasters, and warranted Jefferson in self-confidence; but they were chiefly due to the undisputed success of his financial management. Jefferson and Madison, Dearborn and Robert Smith, might do what they would, so long as they left Gallatin free to control the results of their experiments; for Gallatin redeemed the mistakes of his party. Madison's foreign policy had brought only trouble to the government; Dearborn's army had shown itself to be more dangerous to the Union than to its enemies; Smith's gunboats were a laughing-stock; but Gallatin never failed to cover every weak spot in the Administration, and in October, 1807, the Treasury was profuse of prosperity. Congress might abolish the salt tax and Mediterranean Fund alike, and still the customs would yield fourteen millions a year; while the sales of public lands exceeded 284,000 acres and brought another half million into the Treasury. December 31, after providing for all payments of public debt, Gallatin had a balance of seven millions six hundred thousand dollars on hand. During the Presidency of Jefferson, twenty-five and a half millions had been paid to redeem the principal of the public debt, and only the restraints imposed by the law prevented more rapid redemption. Even in case of war, Gallatin offered to sustain it for a year without borrowing money or increasing taxes.

There was the secret of Jefferson's strength, of his vast popularity, and of the fate which, without direct act of his, never had failed to overwhelm his enemies. The American people pardoned everything except an empty Treasury. No foreign insults troubled them long, and no domestic incompetence roused their disgust; but they were sensitive to any taxation which they directly felt. Gallatin atoned for starving the government by making it rich; and if obliged to endure disgrace and robbery abroad, he gave the President popularity at home. Conscious of this reserved strength, the President cared the less for foreign aggressions. His was, according to theory, the strongest government on earth; and at worst he had but to withdraw from intercourse with foreign nations in order to become impregnable to assault. He had no misgivings as to the result. When he returned, about October 8, from Monticello to Washington, his only thought was to assert the strength he felt. Nothing had then been received from England in regard to the "Chesapeake" negotiation, except Canning's letter of August 3, promising to "make reparation for any alleged injury to the sovereignty of the United States, whenever it should be clearly shown that such injury has been actually sustained, and that such reparation is really due." The President justly thought that this letter, though it disavowed the pretension to search ships of war, held out no sufficient hope of reparation for the "Chesapeake" outrage; and in writing the first draft of his Message, he expressed strongly his irritation at the conduct of England. The draft was sent, as usual, to the members of his Cabinet, and called out a remonstrance from Gallatin:—

"Instead of being written in the style of the proclamation, which has been almost universally approved at home and abroad, the Message appears to me to be rather in the shape of a manifesto, issued against Great Britain on the eve of a war, than such as the existing undecided state of affairs seems to require. It may either be construed into a belief that justice will be denied,—a result not to be anticipated in an official communication,—or it may be distorted into an eagerness of seeing matters brought to issue by an appeal to arms."[1]

In truth, the draft rather showed that Jefferson was ready

[1] Gallatin to Jefferson, Oct. 21, 1807; Gallatin's Writings, i. 853.

to see matters brought to an issue, provided that the issue should not be an appeal to arms.

A few days later, after Congress met, Gallatin wrote to his wife:—

> "The President's speech was originally more warlike than was necessary; but I succeeded in getting it neutralized—this between us; but it was lucky, for Congress is certainly peaceably disposed."[1]

The situation lay in these few words. Not only Congress but also the Government and people were peaceably disposed; and between the attitude of Congress and that of the President was but the difference that the former knew not what to do, while the latter had a fixed policy to impose. "I observe among the members," wrote a non-partisan senator, "great embarrassment, alarm, anxiety, and confusion of mind, but no preparation for any measure of vigor, and an obvious strong disposition to yield all that Great Britain may require, to preserve peace under a thin external show of dignity and bravery."[2] In such a state of minds, and with such a reserve of popular authority, President Jefferson's power found no restraint.

[1] Adams's Gallatin, p. 363.
[2] Diary of J. Q. Adams, Nov. 17, 1807; i. 476.

Chapter VII

S UCH WAS the situation October 26, when Congress assembled in obedience to the President's call. An unusually large number of members attended on the opening day, when for the first time the House was installed in a chamber of its own. After seven years of residence at Washington, the government had so far completed the south wing of the Capitol as to open it for use. A covered way of rough boards still connected the Senate Chamber in the north wing with the Chamber of Representatives in the southern extension of the building, and no one could foresee the time when the central structure, with its intended dome, would be finished; but the new chamber gave proof that the task was not hopeless. With extraordinary agreement every one admitted that Jefferson's and Latrobe's combined genius had resulted in the construction of a room equal to any in the world for beauty and size. The oval hall, with its girdle of fluted sandstone columns draped with crimson curtains, its painted ceiling, with alternate squares of glass, produced an effect of magnificence which was long remembered. Unfortunately, this splendor had drawbacks. Many and bitter were Randolph's complaints of the echoes and acoustic defects which marred the usefulness of the chamber.

That Randolph should feel no love for it was natural. The first scene it witnessed was that of his overthrow. Macon, who for six years had filled the chair, retired without a contest, dragged down by Randolph's weight; and of the one hundred and seventeen members present, fifty-nine, a bare majority, elected Joseph Bradley Varnum of Massachusetts their Speaker; while the minority of fifty-eight scattered their votes among half-a-dozen candidates. Varnum, ignoring Randolph, appointed George Washington Campbell of Tennessee chairman of the Ways and Means Committee. Troublesome as the Virginia leader had been, he was still the only member competent to control the House, and his fall was greatly regretted by at least one member of the Cabinet. "Varnum has, much against my wishes, removed Randolph from the Ways and Means, and appointed Campbell of Tennessee," wrote

Gallatin.[1] "It was improper as related to the public business, and will give me additional labor."

October 27 the President's Message was read.

"The love of peace," it began, "so much cherished in the bosoms of our citizens, which has so long guided the proceedings of their public councils and induced forbearance under so many wrongs, may not insure our continuance in the quiet pursuits of industry."

An account of Monroe's negotiation and treaty followed this threatening preamble; and the warmest friends of Monroe and Pinkney could hardly find fault with the President's gentle comments on their conduct.

"After long and fruitless endeavors to effect the purposes of their mission, and to obtain arrangements within the limits of their instructions, they concluded to sign such as could be obtained, and to send them for consideration; candidly declaring to their other negotiators, at the same time, that they were acting against their instructions, and that their Government, therefore, could not be pledged for ratification."

The provisions of the proposed treaty proved to be, in certain points, "too highly disadvantageous," and the minister had been instructed to renew negotiation. The attack on the "Chesapeake" followed, aggravated by the defiant conduct of the British commanders at Norfolk. Lord Howick's Order in Council had swept away by seizures and condemnations the American trade in the Mediterranean. Spain, too, had issued a decree in conformity with Napoleon's decree of Berlin. Of France alone no complaint was made, and the President could even say that commerce and friendly intercourse had been maintained with her on their usual footing. He had not yet heard of the seizures made two months before, by Napoleon's order, in the ports of Holland.

In the face of these alarming events, it had been thought better to concentrate all defensive resources on New York, Charleston, and New Orleans; to purchase such military

[1] Adams's Gallatin, p. 363.

stores as were wanted in excess of the supply on hand; to call all the gunboats into service, and to warn the States to be ready with their quotas of militia. "Whether a regular army is to be raised, and to what extent, must depend on the information so shortly expected."

If this language had the meaning which in other times and countries would have been taken for granted, it implied a resort to measures of force against foreign aggressions; yet neither the President nor his party intended the use of force, except for self-defence in case of actual invasion. The Message was, in reality, silent in regard to peace and war. The time had not yet come for avowing a policy; but even had the crisis been actually at hand, Jefferson would not have assumed the responsibility of pointing out a policy to Congress. The influence he exerted could rarely be seen in his official and public language; it took shape in private, in the incessant talk that went on, without witnesses, at the White House.

More pointed than the allusion to England was the menace to Chief-Justice Marshall. The threat against the court, which the President made in the summer, reappeared in the Message as a distinct invitation to Congress.

"I shall think it my duty to lay before you the proceedings and the evidence publicly exhibited on the arraignment of the principal offenders before the Circuit Court of Virginia. You will be enabled to judge whether the defect was in the testimony or in the law, or in the administration of the law; and wherever it shall be found, the Legislature alone can apply or originate the remedy. The framers of our Constitution certainly supposed they had guarded as well their government against destruction by treason, as their citizens against oppression under pretence of it; and if these ends are not attained, it is important to inquire by what means more effectual they may be secured."

This strong hint was quickly followed up. Burr's trial at Richmond had hardly closed when the President sent this Message to Congress; and within another month, November 23, another Message was sent, conveying a copy of the evidence and judicial opinions given at the trial, on which Congressional action might be taken.

So far as concerned foreign relations, no one could say with certainty whether the Annual Message leaned toward war or toward peace; but Gallatin's Report, which followed November 5, could be understood only as an argument to show that if war was to be made at all, it should be made at once. The Treasury had a balance of seven or eight millions in specie; the national credit was intact; taxes were not yet reduced; the Bank was still in active existence; various incidental resources were within reach; the first year of war would require neither increase of debt nor of taxation, and for subsequent years loans, founded on increased customs duties, would suffice. Calmly and easily Gallatin yielded to the impulse of the time, and dropping the objects for which—as he said—he had been brought into office, took up again the heavy load of taxation and debt which his life had been devoted to lightening. No one could have supposed, from his language in 1807, that within only ten years he and his party had regarded debt as fatal to freedom and virtue.

"An addition to the debt is doubtless an evil," he informed Congress; "but experience having now shown with what rapid progress the revenue of the Union increases in time of peace, with what facility the debt formerly contracted has in a few years been reduced, a hope may confidently be entertained that all the evils of the war will be temporary and easily repaired, and that the return of peace will, without any effort, afford ample resources for reimbursing whatever may have been borrowed during the war."

If Gallatin was so willing to abandon his dogma, the Federalists might at least be forgiven for asking why he had taken it up. For what practical object had he left the country helpless and defenceless for six years in order to pay off in driblets the capital of a petty debt which, within much less than a century, could be paid in full from the surplus of a single year? The success of his policy depended on the correctness of Jefferson's doctrine, that foreign nations could be coerced by peaceable means into respect for neutral rights; but Gallatin seemed to have already abandoned the theory of peaceable coercion before it had been tried.

The same conflict of ideas was felt in Congress, which had nothing to do but to wait for news from Europe that did not arrive. The month of November was passed in purposeless debate. That the time had come when some policy must be adopted for defending the coasts and frontiers was conceded, but no policy could be contrived which satisfied at once the economical and the military wants of the country. In this chaos of opinions, Jefferson alone held fixed theories; and as usual his opinions prevailed. He preferred gunboats to other forms of armament, and he had his way.

The Cabinet had not adopted the gunboat policy without protest. When in the preceding month of February the President sent to Congress his Message recommending that two hundred gunboats should be built, at a cost, as Gallatin thought, of a million dollars, the secretary remonstrated. In his opinion not one third that number were needed in peace, while in case of war any required number could be built within thirty days. "Exclusively of the first expense of building and the interest of the capital thus laid out, I apprehend that, notwithstanding the care which may be taken, they will infallibly decay in a given number of years, and will be a perpetual bill of costs for repairs and maintenance."[1] The President overruled these objections, affirming that the necessary gunboats could not be built even in six months; that after the beginning of a war they could not be built in the seaports, "because they would be destroyed by the enemy on the stocks;" and the first act of the enemy " would be to sweep all our seaports of their vessels at least;" finally, the expense of building and preserving them would be trifling.[2] Gallatin did not persist in the argument. Jefferson was determined to have gunboats, and gunboats were built.

The "Chesapeake" disaster riveted the gunboat policy on the government. Nearly every one, except the Federalists, agreed in Randolph's unwillingness to vote money for the support of a "degraded and disgraced navy."[3] Robert Smith made no apparent attempt to counteract this prejudice; he sacrificed the frigates for gunboats. October 22, 1807, at a full

---

[1] Gallatin's Writings, i. 330.
[2] Jefferson to Gallatin, Feb. 9, 1807; Works, v. 42.
[3] Annals of Congress, 1807–1808, p. 823.

Cabinet meeting, according to Jefferson's memoranda, the following order was taken in regard to the frigates, in view of war with England:[1] —

"The 'Constitution' is to remain at Boston, having her men discharged; the 'Wasp' is to come to New York; the 'Chesapeake' to remain at Norfolk; and the sending the 'United States' frigate to New York is reserved for further consideration, inquiring in the mean time how early she could be ready to go. It is considered that in case of war these frigates would serve as receptacles for enlisting seamen, to fill the gunboats occasionally."

A government which could imagine no other use for its frigates than as receiving ships for gunboats in time of war naturally cared to build none. When Congress took up the subject of naval defence, gunboats alone were suggested by the department. November 8 Robert Smith wrote to Dr. Mitchill, chairman of the Senate Committee on defences, a letter asking for eight hundred and fifty thousand dollars to build one hundred and eighty-eight more gunboats in order to raise the whole number to two hundred and fifty-seven.[2] A bill was at once introduced, passed the Senate without a division, and went to the House, where the Federalists sharply assailed it. Randolph ridiculed the idea of expelling by such means even so small a squadron as that which at Lynnhaven Bay had all summer defied the power of the United States. Josiah Quincy declared that except for rivers and shallow waters these gunboats were a danger rather than a defence; and that at all times and places they were uncomfortable, unpopular in the service, and dangerous to handle and to fight. Imprisonment for weeks, months, or years in a ship of the line was no small hardship, but service in a coop not wide enough to lie straight in, with the certainty of oversetting or running ashore or being sunk, in case of bad weather or hostile attack, was a duty intolerable to good seamen and fatal to the navy.

All this and much more was true. Fulton's steamer, the

[1] Jefferson's Writings (Ford), i. 330.
[2] Robert Smith to S. L. Mitchill, Nov. 8, 1807; Annals of Congress, 1807–1808, p. 32.

"Clermont," with a single gun would have been more effective for harbor defence than all the gunboats in the service, and if supplemented by Fulton's torpedoes would have protected New York from any line-of-battle ship; but President Jefferson, lover of science and of paradox as he was, suggested no such experiment. By the enormous majority of 111 to 19, the House, December 11, passed the bill for additional gunboats. A million dollars were voted for fortifications. In all, an appropriation of one million eight hundred and fifty thousand dollars for defences was the work accomplished by Congress between October 26 and December 18, 1807. In face of a probable war with England, such action was equivalent to inaction; and in this sense the public accepted it.

While Congress wrangled about systems of defence almost equally inefficient,—gunboats and frigates, militia and volunteers, muskets, movable batteries, and fixed fortifications,—the country listened with drawn breath for news from England. Time dragged on, but still the "Revenge" did not return. About the end of November, despatches[1] dated October 10 arrived from Monroe, announcing that Canning refused to couple the "Chesapeake" affair with the impressment of merchant seamen, that he was about to send a special envoy to Washington with the exclusive object of settling the "Chesapeake" affair; that Monroe had taken his final audience of King George, and that William Pinkney was henceforward sole minister of the United States in London. Of the treaty not a hope seemed to exist. Monroe's return was ominous of failure.

Erskine, uneasy at hearing these reports, hastened to the White House, and without delay reported Jefferson's conversation to his Government:[2] —

"I found from my interview with the President that he was much disappointed at the result of the discussions which had taken place, and, as he expressed himself, greatly alarmed by some of the passages in your letters that a satisfactory redress of the injuries complained of was not likely

[1] Monroe to Madison, Oct. 10, 1807; State Papers, iii. 191.
[2] Erskine to Canning, Dec. 2, 1807; MSS. British Archives.

to be afforded to the United States. He informed me that the reasons which had induced him to instruct the American ministers to endeavor to obtain some arrangement upon the point of impressment of British seamen out of American ships, at the same time that a reparation for the attack on the 'Chesapeake' by his Majesty's ship 'Leopard' was demanded, were that he conceived that if a satisfactory security against the injuries arising to the United States from such impressments could have been obtained, a redress for the attack upon their national ship would have been much easier settled; but that if the point of honor was to be taken into consideration by itself, he foresaw greater difficulties in the way of an amicable adjustment of it. . . . The President further observed, however, that although he feared the separating the two subjects would increase the difficulty of the negotiation, and that he considered the determination of his Majesty's government to postpone the consideration of the point of impressment—which he said was the most serious ground of difference—as an unfavorable symptom of their ultimate intentions upon that subject, yet that he certainly would not refuse upon the ground of form only that the affair of the 'Chesapeake' should be first concluded; but expressed a hope that the minister who should be sent to this country to settle that subject of complaint should also be invested by his Majesty with powers to negotiate upon the point of impressment."

The sanguine temperament which challenged a duel accorded ill with the afterthought which shrank from it. Voluntarily, coolly, with mature reflection, Jefferson had invited Canning's blow; and when Canning struck, Jefferson recoiled. Monroe might well claim that such conditions as were imposed on him should never have been made, or should never have been withdrawn; that at moments of violent irritation no nation could afford to tease another with demands not meant to be enforced.

To increase the President's embarrassment, the Secretary of War Dearborn made a natural mistake. The original instructions to Monroe, decided in Cabinet meeting July 2,[1] did not connect the "Chesapeake" outrage with impressments of merchant seamen. Neither July 4 nor July 5, when full Cabinet meetings were held, did the subject come up.[2] The final instructions, dated July 6, changed the original demand by extending the required redress over all cases of impressment; but meanwhile General Dearborn had left Washington for New York, and was not told of the change.[3] So it happened that when in October the Federalist newspapers began to attack Jefferson, on the authority of the English press, for coupling the subject of general impressment with the attack on the "Chesapeake," Dearborn, who chanced to be in Massachusetts, denied the charge; and on his authority the Republican newspapers asserted that the alleged instructions had not been given. This denial created no little confusion among Republicans, who could not understand why the instructions had been changed, or on what ground the Administration meant to defend them.

In truth, the change had been an afterthought, founded on the idea that as abandonment of impressments was a *sine qua non* in the commercial negotiation, and a point on which the Government meant inflexibly to insist, it should properly be made a *sine qua non* in this or any other agreement.[4] This decision had been made in July, with knowledge that England would rather fight than yield a point so vital to her supposed interests. In December, on hearing that Canning refused to yield, the President told Erskine that the *sine qua non*, so formally adopted, would be abandoned.

That conduct in appearance so vacillating should perplex Jefferson's friends and irritate his enemies was natural; but in reality nothing vacillating was in the President's mind. These negotiations were but outpost skirmishes, and covered his steady retreat to the fortress which he believed to be impregnable. He meant to coerce Canning, but his method of coercion needed neither armies nor negotiators. While telling

[1] See p. 948.
[2] Jefferson's Writings (Ford), i. 325.
[3] Dearborn to Jefferson, Oct. 18, 1807; Jefferson MSS.
[4] R. Smith to Jefferson, July 17, 1807; Jefferson MSS.

Erskine that the *sine qua non* should not prevent a settlement of the "Chesapeake" affair, he set in motion the first of the series of measures which were intended to teach England to respect American rights.

December 14, against strong remonstrances from the merchants, the Non-importation Act of April 18, 1806, went into effect. The exact amount of British trade affected by that measure was not known. All articles of leather, silk, hemp, glass, silver, paper, woollen hosiery, ready-made clothing, millinery, malt liquors, pictures, prints, playing-cards, and so forth, if of English manufacture, were henceforward prohibited; and any person who had them in his possession incurred forfeiture and fine. The measure was in its nature coercive. The debates in Congress showed that no other object than that of coercion was in the mind of the American government; the history of the Republican party and the consistent language of Jefferson, Madison, and the Virginian school proclaimed that the policy of prohibition was their substitute for war. England was to be punished, by an annual fine of several million dollars, for interference with American trade to the continent of Europe.

Two days after this law went into effect Madison received from the British government a document which threw the Non-importation Act into the background, and made necessary some measure more energetic. The King's proclamation of October 17, requiring all British naval officers to exercise the right of impressment to its full extent over neutral merchant-vessels, was printed in the "National Intelligencer" of December 17; and if Sir William Scott's decision in the case of the "Essex" required the Non-importation Act as its counterpoise, the Impressment Proclamation could be fairly balanced only by a total cessation of relations.

In rapid succession the ships which had sailed a month before from Europe arrived in American harbors, after unusually quick voyages. Monroe, in the "Augustus," reached Norfolk December 13; the "Edward" arrived at Boston December 12; the "Brutus" got in at New York December 14, preceded December 12 by the "Revenge." All these ships brought news to the same effect. Armstrong's despatches by the "Revenge" announced Napoleon's enforcement of the

Berlin Decree. London newspapers of November 12 agreed in predicting some immediate and sweeping attack by the British government upon American commerce; and from Pinkney and Monroe came the official papers which put an end to all hope of a commercial treaty with England. Private letters bore out the worst public rumors. Among other persons who were best informed as to the intentions of the British government was Senator Pickering of Massachusetts, whose nephew Samuel Williams had been removed by Jefferson from the London consulate, and remained in that city as an American merchant, in connection with his brother Timothy Williams of Boston. December 12 Timothy Williams in Boston wrote to his uncle Senator Pickering at Washington,[1] —

"My brother writes me on the 9th of November 'that he was informed the Government would in a few days declare Cuba, Martinique, and Guadeloupe in a state of blockade, and restrict still more the trade of neutrals with the Continent.' The British no doubt had or would issue an Order above referred to, to counteract our friend Bonaparte's decree of Nov. 21, 1806. I cannot however think the intercourse with the Continent will be entirely cut off. The influence of the West Indian planters will procure the blockading of the enemy's islands, no doubt. What has not this country lost by the miserable policy of the Administration! Your prudence will know to whom you can or cannot communicate any of the above paragraphs."

"With much solicitude respecting the present state of things," Timothy Williams concluded this letter of warning; and his anxiety was shared by every one who read the newspapers which proclaimed the danger of war. At Washington the alarming news arrived December 17, at the heels of the Impressment Proclamation. The President instantly called his Cabinet together. Under less serious circumstances in 1794, Congress had imposed an embargo for thirty days, forbidding clearances to all foreign-bound vessels while the question of war or peace was deciding. By common consent an embargo was the proper measure to be taken in the face of an expected

[1] T. Williams to T. Pickering, Dec. 12, 1807; Pickering MSS.

attack on commerce. On reading the news from France and England, every one assumed that an embargo would be imposed until the exact nature of the French and British aggressions should be learned; but safe precedent required that the law should restrict its own operation within some reasonable limit of time. An embargo for thirty or sixty days, or even for three months, might be required before reaching some decision as to peace or war.

On a loose sheet of letter-paper, which happened to bear the address of General Mason, the President wrote a hasty draft of an embargo message to Congress.[1] After referring to Armstrong's despatch announcing the Emperor's decision to enforce the Berlin Decree, Jefferson's draft noticed the threatened orders of England:—

"The British regulations had before reduced us to a direct voyage to a single port of their enemies, and it is now believed they will interdict all commerce whatever with them. A proclamation, too, of that Government (not officially, indeed, communicated to us, yet so given out to the public as to become a rule of action with them) seems to have shut the door on all negotiation with us, except as to the single aggression on the 'Chesapeake.' The sum of these mutual enterprises on our national rights is that France and her allies, reserving for future consideration the prohibiting our carrying anything to the British territories, have virtually done it by restraining our bringing a return cargo from them; and Great Britain, after prohibiting a great proportion of our commerce with France and her allies, is now believed to have prohibited the whole. The whole world is thus laid under interdict by these two nations, and our vessels, their cargoes, and crews are to be taken by the one or the other for whatever place they may be destined out of our own limits. If, therefore, on leaving our harbors we are certainly to lose them, is it not better, as to vessels, cargoes, and seamen, to keep them at home? This is submitted to the wisdom of Congress, who alone are competent to provide a remedy."

[1] Jefferson to Gen. J. Mason; Works, v. 217. Cf. Jefferson to Madison, July 14, 1824; Works, vii. 373.

Unfortunately, no official document could be produced in proof of the expected British interdict, and mere newspaper paragraphs could not be used for the purpose. To avoid this difficulty Madison wrote, in pencil, another draft which omitted all direct mention of the expected British order. He proposed to send Congress the official letter in which the Grand Judge Regnier announced that the Berlin Decree would be enforced, and with this letter a copy of the British Impressment Proclamation as printed in the "National Intelligencer." On these two documents he founded his draft of a Message: —

> "The communications now made showing the great and increasing danger with which our merchandise, our vessels, and our seamen are threatened on the high seas and elsewhere by the belligerent Powers of Europe, and it being of the greatest importance to keep in safety these essential resources, I deem it my duty to recommend the subject to the consideration of Congress, who will doubtless perceive all the advantages which may be expected from an immediate inhibition of the departure of our vessels from the ports of the United States."[1]

The Cabinet, every member being present, unanimously concurred in the recommendation to Congress;[2] but at least one member would have preferred that the embargo should be limited in time. The Cabinet meeting was held in the afternoon or evening of December 17, and early the next morning Gallatin wrote to the President suggesting a slight change in the proposed measure, and adding a serious warning which Jefferson would have done well to regard: —

> "I also think," said Gallatin,[3] "that an embargo for a limited time will at this moment be preferable in itself and less objectionable in Congress. In every point of view—privations, sufferings, revenue, effect on the enemy, politics at home, etc.—I prefer war to a permanent embargo. Gov-

[1] Draft of Embargo Message, Jefferson MSS. Cf. Jefferson to Madison, July 14, 1824; Works, vii. 373.
[2] Jefferson to John G. Jackson, Oct. 13, 1808; Jefferson MSS.
[3] Gallatin to Jefferson, Dec. 18, 1807; Gallatin's Writings, i. 368.

ernmental prohibitions do always more mischief than had been calculated; and it is not without much hesitation that a statesman should hazard to regulate the concerns of individuals, as if he could do it better than themselves. The measure being of a doubtful policy, and hastily adopted on the first view of our foreign intelligence, I think that we had better recommend it with modifications, and at first for such a limited time as will afford us all time for reconsideration, and if we think proper, for an alteration in our course without appearing to retract. As to the hope that it may have an effect on the negotiation with Mr. Rose, or induce England to treat us better, I think it entirely groundless."

To this remarkable letter the President immediately replied by summoning the Cabinet together at ten o'clock in the morning.[1] No record of the consultation was preserved; but when the Senate met at noon the Message was read by the Vice-president as it had been shaped by Madison. The suggestion of Gallatin as to a limit of time had not been adopted. The Senate instantly referred the Message to a committee of five, with General Smith and J. Q. Adams at its head:—

"We immediately went into the committee-room," recorded Senator Adams in his Diary,[2] "and after some discussion, in which I suggested very strong doubts as to the propriety of the measure upon the papers sent with the President's Message, I finally acquiesced in it as a compliance with the special call for it in the Message. I inquired whether there were other reasons for it besides the diplomatic papers sent with the Message, as *they* appeared to me utterly inadequate to warrant such a measure. Smith, the chairman, said that the President wanted it to aid him in the negotiation with England upon which Mr. Rose is coming out, and that perhaps it might enable us to get rid of the Non-importation Act. I yielded. But I believe there are yet other reasons, which Smith did not tell. There was no other opposition in committee."

[1] Jefferson to Gallatin, Dec. 18, 1807; Gallatin's Writings, i. 369.
[2] Diary of J. Q. Adams, Dec. 18, 1807, i. 491.

Senator Adams was right in believing that other reasons existed; but although the "National Intelligencer" of the same morning had published the warnings of British newspapers,—doubtless in order to affect the action of Congress,—no one of the Republican senators seemed to rely on the expected British order as the cause of the embargo. In foreign affairs Jefferson maintained the reserve of a European monarch. He alone knew what had been done or was doing, and on him rested the whole responsibility of action. The deference paid by the Senate to the Executive in matters of foreign policy seemed patriotic, but it proved fatal to one senator at least, whose colleague had grievances to revenge. When the committee, after a short deliberation, reported an Embargo Bill, and some of the senators appealed for delay, Adams, who was chafing under the delays which had already lowered the self-respect of Government and people, broke into a strenuous appeal for energy. "The President has recommended the measure on his high responsibility. I would not consider, I would not deliberate; I would act!" The words were spoken in secret session, but Senator Pickering noted them for future use.[1] Among the antipathies and humors of New-England politics none was more characteristic than this personal antagonism, beginning a new conspiracy which was to shake the Union to its foundations.

The Senate agreed with the committee that if an embargo was to be laid it should be laid promptly; and the bill, probably drawn by the President, passed through its three stages on the same day, by a vote of twenty-two to six. At the second reading it was strongly opposed by Hillhouse, Pickering, and Sumter of South Carolina; while William H. Crawford, the new senator from Georgia, asked only time for consideration.[2] Within four or five hours after hearing the Message read, the Senate sent its Embargo Act to the House.

Meanwhile the House also had received the President's Message, and had, like the Senate, gone at once into secret session. No sooner was the Message read than John Randolph and Jacob Crowninshield sprang at the same moment

[1] Pickering's Letter to Governor Sullivan, April 22, 1808. Cf. New-England Federalism, p. 174, *n.*

[2] Diary of J. Q. Adams, i. 491, 492.

to their feet. The Speaker recognized Randolph, who instantly offered a Resolution, "that an embargo be laid on all shipping, the property of citizens of the United States, now in port, or which shall hereafter arrive." After some time passed in discussion, on receiving the Senate bill the House laid Randolph's Resolution aside, and in secret session began a long and warm debate, which continued all day, and was not concluded on Saturday, December 19, when the House adjourned over Sunday.

The loss of this debate was unfortunate; for no private citizen ever knew the reasons which Congress considered sufficient to warrant a strain of the Constitution so violent as a permanent embargo implied. The debate was certainly dramatic: it was not only the first great political crisis witnessed in the new scenery of the Representatives' Chamber, but it also brought John Randolph forward in an attitude which astonished even those who had witnessed the Virginian's growing eccentricity. On Friday Randolph "scrambled" with Crowninshield for the floor, eager to force on the House a policy of embargo which he had again and again recommended as the only proper measure of national defence. On Saturday he rose again, but only to denounce his own measure as one that crouched to the insolent mandates of Napoleon, and led to immediate war with England.[1] The cry of French influence, raised by him and by the Federalist members, began on that day, and echoed in louder and louder tones for years.

On Monday, December 21, the debate closed, and the House consumed the day in voting. Amendment after amendment was rejected. Most significant of all these votes was the list of yeas and nays on the question of limiting the embargo to the term of two months. Forty-six members voted in the affirmative; eighty-two in the negative. The New England and Pennsylvania Democrats obeyed the wishes of Jefferson, and riveted a permanent embargo on the people, without public discussion of the principle or explanation of the effect which was expected from a measure more trying than war

[1] Adams's Randolph, p. 227.

itself to patriotism. The bill then passed by a vote of eighty-two to forty-four.

So small a part was played in this debate by the expected Order in Council that members afterward disputed whether the subject was mentioned at all. Probably the Administration preferred silence in public, either for fear of prejudicing the expected negotiation with Rose, or of weakening the effect of arguments which without the order were sufficiently strong; but in private no such reticence was shown. The British minister on Monday, before the bill had become law, notified Canning not only that an embargo was about to be laid, but of the cause which produced the measure:[1] —

> "It has been confidentially communicated to me that an embargo on all the shipping in the United States has been proposed in Congress, and although it is strongly resisted, it is expected that it will be carried, on the ground of expecting that a proclamation by his Majesty will be issued declaring France and her dependencies in a state of blockade. I hasten to send you this letter for fear of the effect of an embargo."

The person from whom Erskine received this confidential communication was probably the Secretary of State; for two days afterward, when the British minister wrote to say that the embargo had been laid, he added:[2] —

> "I propose to send off his Majesty's packet-boat with this intelligence immediately, and avail myself of this opportunity by a private ship to inform you that the embargo is not intended, as this Government declares, as a measure of hostility against Great Britain, but only as a precaution against the risk of the capture of their ships in consequence of the decree of Bonaparte of Nov. 21, 1806, which they have just learned is to be rigorously enforced; and also from an apprehension of a retaliatory order by Great Britain."

[1] Erskine to Canning, Dec. 21, 1807; MSS. British Archives.
[2] Erskine to Canning, Dec. 23, 1807; MSS. British Archives.

Thus the embargo was imposed; and of all President Jefferson's feats of political management, this was probably the most dexterous. On his mere recommendation, without warning, discussion, or publicity, and in silence as to his true reasons and motives, he succeeded in fixing upon the country, beyond recall, the experiment of peaceable coercion. His triumph was almost a marvel; but no one could fail to see its risks. A free people required to know in advance the motives which actuated government, and the intended consequences of important laws. Large masses of intelligent men were slow to forgive what they might call deception. If Jefferson's permanent embargo should fail to coerce Europe, what would the people of America think of the process by which it had been fastened upon them? What would be said and believed of the President who had challenged so vast a responsibility?

Chapter VIII

DECEMBER 22 Jefferson signed the Embargo Act; four days afterward George Rose arrived at Norfolk. The avowed object of his mission was to offer satisfaction for the attack upon the "Chesapeake;" the true object could be seen only in the instructions with which he was furnished by Canning.[1]

These instructions, never yet published, began by directing that in case any attempt should be made to apply the President's proclamation of July 2 to Rose's frigate, the "Statira," he should make a formal protest, and if the answer of the American government should be unsatisfactory, or unreasonably delayed, he should forthwith return to England. Should no such difficulty occur, he was on arriving at Washington to request an audience of the President and Secretary of State, and to announce himself furnished with full powers to enter into negotiation on the "Chesapeake" affair, but forbidden to entertain any proposition on any other point.

"With respect to that object, you will express your conviction that the instructions under which you act would enable you to terminate your negotiation amicably and satisfactorily. But you will state that you are distinctly instructed, previously to entering into any negotiation, to require the recall of the proclamation of the President of the United States, and the discontinuance of the measures which have been adopted under it."

After explaining that the disavowal and recall of Admiral Berkeley had taken away the excuse for interdicting free communication with British ships, and that thenceforward the interdict became an aggression, Canning directed that if the request be refused, Rose should declare his mission at an end; but supposing the demand to be satisfied, he was to disavow at once the forcible attack on the "Chesapeake."

"You will state further that Admiral Berkeley has been recalled from his command for having acted in an affair of

[1] Instructions to G. H. Rose, Oct. 24, 1807; MSS. British Archives.

such importance without authority. You will add that his Majesty is prepared to discharge those men who were taken by this unauthorized act out of the American frigate; reserving to himself the right of reclaiming such of them as shall prove to have been deserters from his Majesty's service, or natural-born subjects of his Majesty; and further, that in order to repair as far as possible the consequences of an act which his Majesty disavows, his Majesty is ready to secure to the widows and orphans (if such there be) of such of the men who were unfortunately killed on board the 'Chesapeake' as shall be proved not to have been British subjects, a provision adequate to their respective situation and condition in life."

This disavowal, and the removal of Berkeley from command, were to be the limit of concession. The circumstances of provocation under which Berkeley had acted, greatly extenuated his procedure; "and his Majesty therefore commands me to instruct you peremptorily to reject any further mark of his Majesty's displeasure toward Admiral Berkeley."

The remainder of Canning's instructions admits of no abridgment:—

"You will next proceed to state that after this voluntary offer of reparation on his Majesty's part, his Majesty expects that the Government of the United States will be equally ready to remove those causes of just complaint which have led to this unfortunate transaction.

"His Majesty requires this, not only as a due return for the reparation which he has thus voluntarily tendered, but as indispensable to any well-founded expectation of the restoration and continuance of that harmony and good understanding between the two governments which it is equally the interest of both to cultivate and improve.

"However much his Majesty may regret the summary mode of redress which has been resorted to in the present instance, it cannot be supposed that his Majesty is prepared to acquiesce in an injury so grievous to his Majesty as the encouragement of desertion from his naval service.

"The extent to which this practice has been carried is too notorious to require illustration; but the instance of the

'Chesapeake' itself is sufficient to justify the demand of adequate satisfaction.

"The protestation of Commodore Barron is contradicted in the face of the world by the conviction and confession of one of those unhappy men who had been seduced from his allegiance to his Majesty, and to whom Commodore Barron had promised his protection.

"His Majesty, however, does not require any proceeding of severity against Commodore Barron; but he requires a formal disavowal of that officer's conduct in encouraging deserters from his Majesty's service, in retaining them on board his ship, and in denying the fact of their being there; and he requires that this disavowal shall be such as plainly to show that the American government did not countenance such proceedings, and to deter any officer in their service from similar misconduct in future.

"He requires a disavowal of other flagrant proceedings, —detailed in papers which have been communicated to you,—unauthorized, his Majesty has no doubt, but with respect to which it ought to be known to the world that the American government did not authorize and does not approve them.

"You will state that such disavowals, solemnly expressed, would afford to his Majesty a satisfactory pledge on the part of the American government that the recurrence of similar causes will not on any occasion impose on his Majesty the necessity of authorizing those means of force to which Admiral Berkeley has resorted without authority, but which the continued repetition of such provocations as unfortunately led to the attack upon the 'Chesapeake' might render necessary, as a just reprisal on the part of his Majesty.

"And you will observe, therefore, that if the American government is animated by an equally sincere desire with that which his Majesty entertains to preserve the relations of peace between the two countries from being violated by the repetition of such transactions, they can have no difficulty in consenting to make these disavowals.

"This consent is to be the express and indispensable condition of your agreeing to reduce into an authentic and official form the particulars of the reparation which you are instructed to offer."

Rose came, not to conciliate, but to terrify. His apology was a menace. So little was the President prepared for such severity, that from the moment of his consent to treat the "Chesapeake" affair by itself he rather regarded the mission and reparation as a formality. So completely had Monroe been beguiled by Canning's courteous manners, that no suspicion of the truth crossed his mind or crept into his despatches. No prominent American, except Giles, ventured to hint that this mission of peace and friendship was intended only to repeat the assertion of supremacy which had led to the original offence.

George Henry Rose was chiefly remembered as the father of Lord Strathnairn; but his merits were quite different from those of his son. Without the roughness which sometimes marked English character, Rose's manners betrayed a dignified and slightly patronizing courteousness,—a certain civil condescension,—impressive to Americans of that day, who rarely felt at ease in the presence of an Englishman, or were quite certain that an American gentleman knew the habits of European society. Benevolent superiority and quiet assumption, so studied as to be natural and simple, were the social weapons with which George Rose was to impose an unparalleled indignity on a government which, in professing contempt for forms, invited discourtesies. No man could have been chosen with qualities better suited for enforcing Canning's will on the yielding moods of Jefferson.

Rose's first act after arriving in Hampton Roads was to notify the President that he could not land until assured that the proclamation of July 2 would not be enforced against his ship. Canning had been already officially informed that the proclamation expressly excepted vessels on a service like that of the "Statira," as he might have seen for himself by a moment's inquiry; but his instructions were written to suit the temper of Tory constituents. Rose was obliged to wait from December 26 until January 9 before leaving his ship, while messengers carried explanations and notes between Norfolk and Washington.

Monroe, who sailed from England a day later than Rose, reached Washington December 22. Rose arrived only January 14. January 16 he was received by the President, and made no complaint of the mode of reception. In the four years that had passed since Merry's arrival, Jefferson had learned to be less strict in Republican etiquette; but although Rose suffered no indignity at the White House, he found much to disapprove in the government. January 17, in a despatch to Canning, he mentioned that Congress contained one tailor, one weaver, six or seven tavern-keepers, four notorious swindlers, one butcher, one grazier, one curer of hams, and several schoolmasters and Baptist preachers.[1]

The most aristocratic American of the twentieth century will probably agree with the most extreme socialist in admitting that Congress, in 1808, might with advantage have doubled its proportion of tailors, butchers, and swindlers, if by doing so it could have lessened the number of its conspirators. To the latter class belonged Senator Pickering, whose power for mischief and whose appetite for intrigue combined to make him a valuable ally for Rose. Within forty-eight hours after Rose's arrival, the senator from Massachusetts had fallen under the fascination of the British envoy's manners and conversation. January 18 he wrote to his nephew Timothy Williams,[2] —

"I now take up my pen merely to mention an unexpected interview with Mr. Rose. I met him last Saturday [January 16] at Georgetown, at the table of Mr. Peter, whose lovely wife is a granddaughter of Mrs. Washington. Mr. Rose's face is indicative of a placid temper, and his conversation confirms it. He possesses good sense and a disposition perfectly conciliatory. Such also is the disposition of the minister, Canning, by whom he was selected for this mission. Canning was his school-fellow and intimate friend. It seemed to me a sort of friendly compulsion that sent him hither. It was a sacrifice for a domestic man who left a wife and seven children behind him, and from whom he had never before been separated. Thus much I gathered from

[1] Rose to Canning, Jan. 17, 1808; MSS British Archives.
[2] Pickering to T. Williams, Jan. 18, 1808; Pickering MSS.

his conversation with me, which was marked with ease and candor; indeed with singular openness, as if I had been an old acquaintance. He expressed his surprise that the real state of the negotiation with Mr. Monroe had not become officially known to the people by an open communication to Congress. No minister of Great Britain, he observed, would have used such concealment as existed here. He manifested a solicitude even to anxiety for a pacific adjustment of all our differences. What our Government will demand as a reparation for the attack on the 'Chesapeake' I do not know, nor what Mr. Rose is authorized to concede; but I run no hazard in saying that nothing in reality will be denied, and that if after all a war with England should ensue, the fault will be our own."

In giving this account of Rose's singular openness and candor, Senator Pickering did not repeat his own remarks in the conversation; but they could be inferred from the rest of his letter.

"I wrote last week to Mr. Cabot that I had the best authority for saying that our Government had abandoned the ground taken in London,—to treat of the 'Chesapeake' affair only in connection with the old subjects of dispute. They have now determined to negotiate on this separately, and even say that it is an affair by itself and ought to be so treated. Perhaps they may demand that Admiral Berkeley be brought to a British court-martial,—that at any rate he be removed from command; and that the three rascals of deserters who remain unhung should be restored.

"*Confidence* now seems to be in Mr. Jefferson's hands as effectual in producing a compliance with his recommendations as soldiers in the hands of Bonaparte in procuring submission to his commands. With the like implicit, blind confidence which enacted the Embargo, the legislatures of Virginia and Maryland have approved it. To this day if you ask any member of Congress the cause and the object of the Embargo, he can give no answer which common-sense does not spurn at. I have reason to believe that Mr. Jefferson expected to get some credit for it by having it ready just in time to meet the retaliating order of England for

Napoleon's decree of Nov. 21, 1806. With much solicitude he, two or three weeks ago, expressed his wonder that it did not arrive, apparently desiring it as a material justification with the people for the Embargo. He will doubtless be utterly disappointed."

That Jefferson in recommending the Embargo had the Orders in Council in his mind was therefore known to Pickering,[1] and was the general talk of Federalists in Washington during the month which followed the Embargo Act; but the orders themselves reached America only the day after this letter was written, and were published in the "National Intelligencer" of January 22. In full view of the official command that American trade with Europe should pass through British ports and pay duty to the British Treasury, doubt as to the wisdom of an Embargo seemed at an end. No further dispute appeared possible except on the question whether or when the Embargo should be raised in order to declare war. Already, January 11, Senator Adams offered a Resolution for appointing a committee to consider and report when the Embargo could be taken off and vessels permitted to arm; but the Senate silently rejected the Resolution, January 21, by a vote of seventeen to ten.[2] Neither decision nor debate on so serious a point could be profitably undertaken before the result of Rose's diplomacy should be revealed.

Saturday, January 16, before meeting Senator Pickering at dinner, Rose had delicately explained to Madison that the President's "Chesapeake" proclamation was likely to prove a stumbling-block. In conversations which consumed another week he urged its withdrawal, while Madison replied that the exclusion of British ships was not a punishment but a precaution, that the "Leopard's" attack was but one of its causes, and that it was a measure taken in the interests of peace. Argument against Canning's positive instructions answered no purpose. Rose could not give way, and when he had been one week in Washington, January 21, the negotiation was already at a stand-still. There it would under any other Admin-

---

[1] Cf. Letters addressed to the People of the United States, by Col. Timothy Pickering. London (reprinted), 1811. Letter xiii. p. 96. Review of Cunningham Correspondence, by Timothy Pickering (Salem, 1824), pp. 56–58.

[2] Diary of J. Q. Adams, i. 504.

istration have been permitted to remain. Rose had come to offer an apology and to restore the captured seamen. He had only to do this and go home.

Rose, after an interview with the Secretary of State about January 21, waited until January 27 before writing to Canning. Then he resumed his story:[1] —

"Within a few hours after my last conference with Mr. Madison, an indirect and confidential communication was made to me from one of the members of the Government to the following purport: that the real difficulty as to the recall of the proclamation was that of finding grounds upon which the President could found his declared motives for such a measure without exposing himself to the charge of inconsistency and disregard of the national honor, and without compromising his own personal weight in the State; that it was earnestly wished that I could make, as it were, a bridge over which he might pass; and that I would develop just so much of the tenor of my instructions as to the conditions of reparation as might justify him in the course which I required should be taken; that should however this be impossible, and should the negotiation fail, the United States would not commence war with Great Britain, but would continue their Embargo, and adopting a sort of Chinese policy would shut themselves up from the rest of the world; that if we attacked them they would sally out just far enough to repel us, and would invade Canada. . . . Communications of a similar nature were repeated to me on subsequent days; and it did not seem advisable to address Mr. Madison in writing until the utmost point to which they would go was ascertained. At length I had a conversation with the gentleman in question. He avowed to me that what had passed was with the knowledge of the President, whose difficulty arose from the sacrifice of public opinion which he apprehended must follow from the abandonment of the proclamation. He said I must be aware how dear to Mr. Jefferson his popularity must be, and especially at the close of his political career, and that this consideration must be held particularly in view by him; and he

[1] Rose to Canning, Jan. 27, 1808; MSS. British Archives.

pressed me earnestly to take such steps as would conciliate the President's wish to give his Majesty satisfaction on the point in question and yet to maintain the possession of what was pre-eminently valuable to him. He expressed his own personal anxiety for the accommodation of the present difference,—an anxiety heightened by his knowledge that the United States had forever lost all hope of obtaining the Floridas, the negotiation for them having totally failed, and by his intimate persuasion that France is the dormant owner of them. He said, moreover, that since America could not obtain those provinces, he sincerely wished to see them in the hands of Great Britain, whose possession of them could never be anxious to the United States."

The supplications of this Cabinet minister were reinforced by entreaties from leading Federalists, who begged Rose not to follow a course which would aid the President in rousing popular feeling against England; but the British envoy could yield only so far as not to break the negotiation abruptly. January 26 he wrote to the Secretary a note, in courteous language announcing himself authorized to express the conviction—which he certainly could not have felt—that if the proclamation were withdrawn, he should be able "to termi nate the negotiation amicably and satisfactorily." Madison sent no answer to the note, but kept the negotiation alive by private interviews. January 29 Rose suggested the idea of his friendly return to England with a representation of the difficulty. Madison reported this suggestion to the President, who on the following Monday, February 1, decided against the idea, preferring to yield the point of dignity so far as to offer a recall of the proclamation, conditional upon an informal disclosure by Rose of the terms in which the atonement would be made.[1]

Throughout this tortuous affair Rose stood impassive. He made no advance, offered no suggestion of aid, showed no anxiety. Republicans and Federalists crowded about him with entreaties and advice. Rose listened in silence. Amateur diplomacy never showed its evils more plainly than in the negotiation with Rose; and when Madison allowed the President to

[1] Negotiations with Mr. Rose; Madison's Works, ii. 411.

take the affair into his own hands, employing another Cabinet officer to do what no Secretary of State could permit himself to undertake, the nuisance became a scandal. In the despatch of January 27 Rose concealed the name of the deputy Secretary of State; but in a despatch of February 6 he revealed it:—

"I should here add that a member of the Cabinet (the Secretary of the Navy), who informed me that all his communications with me were with the President's knowledge, assures me that a rupture with France is inevitable and at hand."

That Robert Smith acted in the matter as negotiator for the President was afterward made known by Jefferson himself.[1]

Jefferson clung with touching pathos to the love and respect of his fellow-citizens, who repaid his devotion with equal attachment; but many an American President who yearned no less passionately for the people's regard would have died an outcast rather than have trafficked in their dignity and his own self-respect in order to seek or save a personal popularity. Perhaps Jefferson never knew precisely what was said of him by his Secretary of the Navy,—a passing remark by such a man as Robert Smith, repeated through such a medium as George Rose, need count for little; but the truth must be admitted that in 1808—for the first and probably for the last time in history—a President of the United States begged for mercy from a British minister.

In obedience to the President's decision, Madison yielded to the British demand on condition that the Executive should not be exposed to the appearance of having yielded.[2] He arranged with Rose the "bridge" which Robert Smith had previously prepared for the President to cross. In a "secret and confidential" despatch dated Feb. 6, 1808, Rose explained to Canning, with evident uneasiness, the nature of the new proposal:[3] —

"The proposition made to me by Mr. Madison at the

[1] Jefferson to W. Wirt, May 2, 1811; Works, v. 593.
[2] Negotiations with Mr. Rose, Feb. 4, 1808; Madison's Works, ii. 12.
[3] Rose to Canning, Feb. 6, 1808; MSS. British Archives. Cf. Madison's Writings, ii. 413.

close of our conference of yesterday was that he should put
into my hands a proclamation recalling the original proclamation, sealed and signed by the President, bearing date on
the day of adjustment of differences, and conceived in such
terms as I should agree to; that on this being done we
should proceed to sign the instruments adjusting the reparation. I answered that positive as my instructions were to
the effect I had invariably stated to him, such was the
knowledge I had of the disposition of his Majesty's government to act with the utmost conciliation toward this country that I would attempt the experiment, but premising
distinctly that it must be made unofficially through the
whole of it, and with the assurance of our mutual good
faith to that effect; and that as it must be completely and
essentially informal,—for the purpose of getting over difficulties which appeared insuperable in any other way,—it
must be distinctly understood that if the attempt failed, the
regular and official communication must be resumed on my
explanatory note of January 26, and on that alone."

In the defence which Rose offered for thus disregarding his
instructions, the cause of his embarrassment was plain. Duty
required him to act as though England had hitherto endured
with magnanimity the wrongs inflicted by America, but
might find herself obliged soon to resent them. This attitude
could have been maintained against ordinary forms of diplomacy, but Rose found himself stifled in the embraces of men
whose hatred was necessary to warrant his instructions. He
would gladly have assumed that Madison's concessions and
Robert Smith's cajoleries were treacherous; but his Federalist
friends, whose interests were actively English, assured him
that if America could avoid a war with England, she would
inevitably drift into a war with France. The temptation to
show equal courtesy to that which was shown to him, the
instinctive shrinking from a harsh act, the impossibility of
obeying instructions without putting himself in the wrong,
and finally perhaps an incapacity to understand the full humiliation implied in his unrevealed demands,—led him to
give way, and to let Madison partially into the secret of Canning's instructions.

On the evening of February 5 Rose and Erskine went to the house of the Secretary, and a draft of the proposed proclamation was there offered to them and accepted. The next day, at the Department, Rose delicately began to reveal the further disavowals he was instructed to demand. Even then he seemed ashamed to betray the whole, but delayed and discussed, knowing that he had done too much or too little for the objects of his mission. Not until after repeated interviews did he at last, February 14, mention "with an apology for omitting it before, when he intended to do it," that a disavowal of Commodore Barron would be required.[1]

So cautious was Madison on his side that he offered to make a part of the required disavowals, provided these should be mutual. Rose declined this offer, but proposed nothing more, and seemed rather to invite a friendly failure of agreement. He ended the conversation of February 14 by addressing to Madison the usual words of rupture: "I will not dissemble that I leave you with the most painful impressions."[2] February 16 Madison closed these informal interviews with the dry remark that the United States could not be expected to "make as it were an expiatory sacrifice to obtain redress, or beg for reparation."[3]

The delay had strengthened Rose by weakening the President. The embargo was beginning to work. That the people should long submit to it was impossible, reported Rose; even North Carolina was turning against it. Monroe's influence made itself felt.

"I learn this day," wrote the British envoy February 17, "that Mr. Monroe has been indefatigable in representing through Virginia the contrasted systems of Great Britain and France in their true lights, the certain destruction which must result to America from the prevalence of the latter, and the necessity of uniting for existence with the former. He has undoubtedly acquired a very strong party in that State,—it is now said a decided majority in its legislature, and one entirely brought over to the views above enounced."

[1] Madison's Writings, ii. 416.
[2] Rose to Canning, Feb. 16, 1808; MSS. British Archives.
[3] Rose to Canning, Feb. 17, 1808; MSS. British Archives.

February 22, only a few days after the rupture of negotiation, the Milan Decree arrived, and was published in the "National Intelligencer." This violent act of Napoleon did much to divert popular indignation from England. Under the influence of this good fortune, Rose so little feared war as a consequence of his failure that he speculated rather as to the policy of accepting the United States as an ally:

"It would certainly be highly desirable," he wrote,[1] "that a rupture between France and America should take place; but the latter under its present Constitution and Administration could take but a very feeble part in the warfare, and I know not if it is to be wished that it should be roused to greater exertions, which must lead to a more efficient form of government, a knowledge of its strength, and the development of extensive views of ambition."

Nothing remained but to revert to Rose's note of January 26, and to close the affair by a formal correspondence. No further attempt was made to conciliate the British envoy, or to obtain concessions from him; but February 24 he was told by Madison of two steps to be taken by the Government which bore on his negotiation. The President would recommend to Congress an increase of the army to ten thousand men, and a levy of twenty-four thousand volunteers. Madison added that these were to be considered as "measures of preparation, but not as leading to war, or as directed against any particular nation." The Secretary added that an order had been issued to discharge all British subjects from national ships,—"an act of complaisance in its effects which he observed Great Britain could lay no claim to; which was done gratuitously, but from views of policy and fitness entertained by this Government."

March 5 Madison at last sent his reply to Rose's note of January 26. After repeating the reasons which forbade a withdrawal of the President's proclamation, the Secretary closed by informing Rose that the President "has authorized me, in the event of your disclosing the terms of reparation which you believe will be satisfactory, and on its appearing that they

---

[1] Rose to Canning, Feb. 27, 1808; MSS. British Archives.

are so, . . . to proceed to concert with you a revocation of that act."[1] Rose waited till March 17, as though hoping for some further overture, but finally replied, "It is with the most painful sensations of regret that I find myself . . . under the necessity of declining to enter into the terms of negotiation which by direction of the President you therein offer."[2]

Rose's professions of regret were doubtless sincere. Apart from the wish felt by every young diplomatist to avoid the appearance of failure, Rose could not but see that his Government must wish to be relieved of the three American seamen imprisoned at Halifax, whose detention, admitted to be an act of violence, must become a festering sore in the relations of the two countries. That the American government meant to profit by it was evident. By leaving the "Chesapeake" affair unsettled, Rose played into the hands of a national party. For the first time since 1794 language began to be used to a British minister in the United States which he could not hear without loss of dignity or sense of discredit. The word "war" was semi-officially pronounced.

When on Monday, March 21, Rose made his parting visits, he found the President silent; the Secretary of State studiously avoided all political topics, while if Rose's report was accurate, Gallatin and Robert Smith talked with intentional freedom.

"Mr. Gallatin, the Secretary of the Treasury, has little influence in the Government, though by far the ablest and best informed member of it; and he probably does not interfere materially beyond the limits of his own department; but his utility in that department, in which no adequate successor to him is contemplated, is such that, as they feel they cannot do without him, they are anxious to retain him at the head of it, and consequently are obliged to keep him informed of their proceedings. . . . Mr. Gallatin said at once and spontaneously that *nothing* of real difficulty remained between the two countries but his Majesty's Orders in Council. This he repeated twice, dwelling upon the word 'nothing' with particular emphasis. He added that if the

[1] Madison to Rose, March 5, 1808; State Papers, iii. 214.
[2] Rose to Madison, March 17, 1808; State Papers, iii. 217.

belligerent Powers persisted in enforcing their restrictions on the neutral commerce, the embargo must be continued until the end of the year, and that then America must take part in the war; that England had officially declared that she would revoke the restrictions she had imposed if her enemy would do the same; but that though France had professed as much, she had neither done it to the minister of the United States at Paris nor directly to this Government; neither had she made any communication to it of her restrictive edicts, or relative to them; and that this Government felt sensibly the difference of the conduct held toward it by those of Great Britain and France in those respects."[1]

Gallatin's assertion that if the Orders in Council were enforced America within a year must declare war, went far beyond any threat ever made before by President Jefferson or his party. The Secretary of the Navy held a somewhat different tone:—

"Mr. Smith told me that all would remain quiet if no new vexations were committed on their coast, and that the only measure which the Government would carry into effect would be the levy of the body of regulars to consist nominally of six thousand, but really of four thousand men."

Senator Giles and other Republican leaders avowed readiness for war with England. Before Rose's departure, the new policy had become defined. Its first object was to unite America in resisting England and France; the second, to maintain the embargo till the country should be ready for war.

With these ends in view, the Administration threw aside the "Chesapeake" affair as a matter which concerned England rather than America. Madison notified Erskine that the subject had lost its consequence, and that if England wished a settlement she must seek it.

"It will throw some light upon the views of this Government," wrote Rose in his last despatch,[2] "if I state that in

[1] Rose to Canning, March 22, 1808; MSS. British Archives.
[2] Rose to Canning, March 22, 1808; MSS. British Archives. Cf. Madison to Pinckney, April 4, 1808; State Papers, iii. 221.

a recent conversation with Mr. Erskine, Mr. Madison observed that since England has thus publicly disclaimed the
right of search of national ships for deserters, and Admiral
Berkeley has been recalled from command of the Halifax
squadron, although a more formal mode of terminating the
business would have been more acceptable to this Government, it would consider itself as satisfied on the restoration
of the seamen taken away by an act of force disavowed by
his Majesty; but that it would not again ask for reparation
upon this matter."

From that moment all eyes turned toward the embargo.
The President had chosen his ground. Unless his experiment
succeeded, he might yet be forced into the alternative of a
second submission or war.

Chapter IX

ALL WINTER Congress waited for the result of Rose's negotiation. The huge majority, without leadership, split by divergent interests, a mere mob guided from the White House, showed little energy except for debate, and no genius except for obedience.

The first political effect of the embargo was shown in the increased virulence of debate. The Act of December 22, passed on the spur of the moment, was powerless to prevent evasions in the seaports, and left untouched the trade with Canada and Florida. A supplementary Act was necessary; but to warrant a law for stopping all commerce by sea and land, the Government could no longer profess a temporary purpose of protecting ships, merchandise, and seamen, but must admit the more or less permanent nature of the embargo, and the policy of using it as a means of peaceable coercion. The first Supplementary Act passed Congress as early as January 8, but applied only to coasting and fishing vessels, which were put under heavy bonds and threatened with excessive penalties in case of entering a foreign port or trading in foreign merchandise. Finding that this measure was not effective, and that neither England nor France showed a sign of relaxing the so-called system of retaliation, Government was obliged to complete its restrictions. February 11 the House instructed its Committee of Commerce to inquire what further legislation was necessary "to prevent the exportation of goods, wares, and merchandise of foreign or domestic growth or manufacture to any foreign port or place." The committee instantly reported a bill; and as Rose's negotiation broke down, February 19 the House went into committee to debate a second supplementary Embargo Act, which was to stop by land and sea all commerce with the world.

The next day, February 20, Barent Gardenier of New York, who surpassed Josiah Quincy in hatred of the Administration, attacked the new bill in a speech which showed much rough power and more temper. He said with force that between the original embargo and this Supplementary Act no connection existed. The one was an embargo, the other was non-intercourse; and he charged that the original embargo was a fraud, intended to trick the country into a permanent system of non-intercourse:—

"The more the original measure develops itself, the more I am satisfied that my first view of it was correct; that it was a sly, cunning measure; that its real object was not merely to prevent our vessels from going out, but to effect a non-intercourse. Are the nation prepared for this? If you wish to try whether they are, tell them at once what is your object. Tell them what you mean. Tell them you mean to take part with the Grand Pacificator. Or else stop your present course. Do not go on forging chains to fasten us to the car of the Imperial Conqueror."

Interrupted by a dozen Republican members who leaped to their feet in anger, Gardenier for a time returned to his argument and dropped the assertion of subservience to Napoleon:—

"I ask the intelligent and candid men of this House whether to prevent the farmers of Vermont from selling their pigs in Canada is calculated to increase or diminish our essential resources; whether the object which the President professed to have in view is counteracted by a traffic of this kind. . . . I could wish gentlemen would, instead of bolting at me in the fulness of their rage, endeavor to satisfy my poor understanding by cool reasoning that they are right; that they would show me how this measure will prepare us for war; how the weakening by distressing every part of the country is to increase its strength and its vigor."

Had Gardenier stopped there, his argument would have admitted no answer; but he had the defect of a Federalist temper, and could not control his tongue.

"Sir, I cannot understand it. I am astonished,—indeed I am astonished and dismayed. I see effects, but I can trace them to no cause. Yes, sir, I do fear that there is an unseen hand which is guiding us to the most dreadful destinies,— unseen because it cannot endure the light. Darkness and mystery overshadow this House and this whole nation. We know nothing; we are permitted to know nothing; we sit here as mere automata; we legislate without knowing—nay, sir, without wishing to know—why or wherefore. We are told what we are to do, and the Council of Five Hundred do it. We move, but why or wherefore no man knows. We are put in motion, but how I for one cannot tell."

Gardenier was believed to be the author of a letter written during the secret session, December 19, and published in the "New York Evening Post," which began the cry of French influence.[1] His speech of February 20, insulting to the House, disorderly and seditious, resting on innuendo but carrying the weight of a positive assertion, outraged every member of the majority. Even John Randolph had never gone so far as to charge his opponents with being the willing and conscious tools of a foreign despot. The House was greatly exasperated, and at the next session, Monday, February 22, three members—Richard M. Johnson of Kentucky, George W. Campbell of Tennessee, and John Montgomery of Maryland—rose successively and declared that Gardenier's expressions were a slander, which if not supported by proof made their author an object of contempt. Gardenier challenged Campbell, and March 2 a duel took place at Bladensburg. Gardenier was severely wounded, but escaped with life, while the bitterness of party feeling became more violent than before.

Yet no member ventured fairly to avow and defend the policy of non-intercourse as a policy of coercion. Campbell, the leader of the majority, admitted that the embargo was intended to distress England and France, but treated it mainly as a measure of defence. No full and fair discussion of the subject was attempted; and the bill passed both Houses and was approved by the President March 12, without calling from the Government a hint in regard to the scope of its policy or the length of time during which the system of seclusion was to last. Even Jefferson kept silence upon what was uppermost in his mind, and defended the embargo on every ground except that which with him, if with no one else, was strongest. In private he said that the measure was intended to last until

[1] Annals of Congress, 1807–1808, p. 1251, *n.*

the return of peace in Europe, or as long as the orders and decrees of England and France should be maintained:—

> "Till they return to some sense of moral duty we keep within ourselves. This gives time. Time may produce peace in Europe; peace in Europe removes all causes of difference till another European war; and by that time our debt may be paid, our revenues clear, and our strength increased."[1]

With such reasoning the opponents of the embargo were far from pleased. Nevertheless, Jefferson carried his point, and could for the moment afford to disregard criticism. His experiment of peaceable coercion was sure of a trial. His control over Congress seemed absolute. Only twenty-two members voted against the Supplementary Embargo Act, and in the Senate no opposition was recorded.

With such influence Jefferson might promise himself success in any undertaking; and if he had at heart one object more momentous than the embargo, it was the punishment of Chief-Justice Marshall for his treatment of Burr. As early as Nov. 5, 1807, Senator Tiffin of Ohio began his career in the Senate by moving, as an amendment to the Constitution, that all judges of the United States should hold office for a term of years, and should be removed by the President on address by two-thirds of both Houses. Governor Tiffin's motion was not an isolated or personal act. The State legislatures were invoked. Vermont adopted the amendment. The House of Delegates in Virginia, both branches of the Pennsylvania legislature, the popular branch in Tennessee, and various other State governments, in whole or in part, adopted the principle and urged it upon Congress. In the House, George W. Campbell moved a similar amendment January 30, and from time to time other senators and members made attempts to bring the subject forward. In the Senate, Giles aided the attack by bringing in a bill for the punishment of treason. February 11 he spoke in support of his proposed measure, advancing doctrines which terrified Democrats as well as Federalists. Joseph Story was one of his audience, and wrote an account of this alarming speech:—

[1] Jefferson to John Taylor, Jan. 6, 1808; Works, v. 226.

"Giles exhibits in his appearance no marks of greatness; he has a dark complexion and retreating eyes, black hair, and robust form. His dress is remarkably plain and in the style of Virginia carelessness. Having broken his leg a year or two since, he uses a crutch, and perhaps this adds somewhat to the indifference or doubt with which you contemplate him. But when he speaks, your opinion immediately changes. . . . I heard him a day or two since in support of a bill to define treason, reported by himself. Never did I hear such all-unhinging and terrible doctrines. He laid the axe at the root of judicial power, and every stroke might be distinctly felt. His argument was very specious and forensic, sustained with many plausible principles and adorned with various political axioms, designed *ad captandum*. One of its objects was to prove the right of the Legislature to *define* treason. My dear friend, look at the Constitution of the United States and see if any such construction can possibly be allowed! . . . He attacked Chief-Justice Marshall with insidious warmth. Among other things he said, 'I have learned that judicial opinions on this subject are like changeable silks, which vary their colors as they are held up in political sunshine.' "[1]

Had Giles's proposed definition of treason become law, it would in another half-century have had singular interest for Virginians of his school. According to this bill any persons, without exception, "owing allegiance to the United States of America," who should assemble with intent forcibly to change the government of the United States, or to dismember them or any one of them, or to resist the general execution of any public law, should suffer death as a traitor; and even though not personally present at the assemblage or at the use of force, yet should any person aid or assist in doing any of the acts proscribed, such person should also suffer death as a traitor.[2] Fortunately for Southern theories the bill, although it passed the Senate by means of Southern votes, was lost in

[1] Story's Life and Letters of Joseph Story, i. 158–159.
[2] Bill for the Punishment of Treason and other crimes; Annals of Congress, 1807–1808, p. 108.

the House, where John Randolph had introduced a bill of his own more moderate in character.[1]

Although the attack on the Supreme Court was more persistent and was carried further than ever before, it met with passive resistance which foreshadowed failure, and probably for this reason was allowed to exhaust its strength in the committee-rooms of Congress. The chief-justice escaped without a wound. Under the shadow of the embargo he could watch in security the slow exhaustion of his antagonist. Jefferson had lost the last chance of reforming the Supreme Court. In another six months Congress would follow the will of some new Executive chief; and if in the full tide of Jefferson's power Marshall had repeatedly thwarted or defied him with impunity, the chance was small that another President would meet a happier fate.

The failure of his attack on the Supreme Court was not the only evidence that Jefferson's authority when put to the test was more apparent than real. If in the President's eyes Marshall deserved punishment, another offender merited it still more. Senator Smith of Ohio was deeply implicated in Burr's conspiracy. The dignity of the President and of Congress demanded inquiry, and an investigation was made. The evidence left no reasonable doubt that Smith had been privy to Burr's scheme; but the motion to expel him from the Senate failed by a vote of nineteen to ten, two thirds being required for this purpose. In the House, John Randolph brought charges against General Wilkinson which could neither be admitted nor met. The Administration was obliged to cover and ignore the military scandals brought to light by Burr's trial.

Even in regard to more serious matters the Government could hardly feel secure. In February, Sloan of New Jersey offered a motion that the seat of government should be removed from Washington to Philadelphia. The House, February 2, by a vote of sixty-eight to forty-seven, agreed to consider the resolution, and a debate followed which proved how far from stable the actual arrangement was supposed to be. Republicans and Federalists alike assailed the place in which they were condemned to live. Fifteen million dollars, it

[1] Annals of Congress, 1807–1808, p. 1717.

was said, had been spent upon it with no other result than to prove that a city could never be made to exist there. One day they were choked with dust; the next they were wallowing in mire. The climate was one of violent changes and piercing winds. Members sickened and died in greater numbers than ever before, but in case of illness they could find no physician except by sending to the navy yard some miles away. At the last session the House had been driven from its old hall by the wind breaking its windows. The new hall, however magnificent was unfit for its purpose, to hear was impossible; its ventilation was so bad as to have caused the illness of Jacob Crowninshield, one of its leading members, then lying at the point of death. The prices of everything in Washington were excessive. Butter was fifty cents a pound; a common turkey cost a dollar and a half; in Philadelphia members would save one hundred and fifty dollars a day in hack-hire alone. Even these objections were trifling compared with the inconvenience of governing from a wilderness where no machinery existed to make administration easy. As an example of the absurdities of such a system, members pointed to the navy yard, only to be reached by following the windings of the shallow Potomac, while the Navy Department was obliged at extravagant cost to bring every article of use from the seaboard, besides recruiting seamen at the commercial ports for every ship fitted out at Washington.

Sloan desisted from his motion only after the House had shown itself strongly inclined toward his opinion. On another point the divergence of ideas became more marked, and Jefferson found himself obliged to strain his influence.

In the Republican party any vote for a standing army had been hitherto considered a crime. The Federalists in 1801 had left a force of five thousand men; Jefferson reduced it to three thousand. The Republican party believed in a militia, but neglected it. Throughout the Southern States the militia was undisciplined and unarmed; but in Massachusetts, as President Jefferson was beginning to notice, the Federalists took much care of their State soldiery. The United States fort at Newport was garrisoned only by goats, and the strategic line of Lake Champlain and the Hudson River, which divided New England from the rest of the Union, lay open to an enemy. In view of war with England such negligence became wanton. Jefferson saw that an army must be raised; but many of his truest followers held that militia alone could be trusted, and that the risk of conquest from abroad was better than the risk of military despotism at home.

For a people naturally brave, Americans often showed themselves surprisingly unwilling to depend upon their own strength. To defy danger, to rush into competition with every foreign rival, to take risks without number, and to depend wholly on themselves were admitted characteristics of Americans as individuals; but the same man who, when left to his own resources, delighted in proving his skill and courage, when brought within the shadow of government never failed to clamor for protection. As a political body the American people shrank from tests of its own capacity. "American systems" of politics, whether domestic or foreign, were systems for evading competition. The American system in which the old Republican party believed was remarkable for avowing want of self-confidence as the foundation of domestic as well as of foreign policy. The Republican party stood alone in refusing, on principle, to protect national rights from foreign outrage; but it defied imitation when the sacrifice of national rights was justified by the argument that if American liberties were not abandoned to foreign nations they would be destroyed by the people themselves. War, which every other nation in history had looked upon as the first duty of a State, was in America a subject for dread, not so much because of possible defeat as of probable success. No truer Republican could be found in Virginia than John W. Eppes, one of Jefferson's sons-in-law; and when the House debated in February a Senate bill for adding two regiments to the regular army, Eppes declared the true Republican doctrine:[1] —

"If we have war, this increase of the army will be useless; if peace, I am opposed to it. I am in favor of putting arms into the hands of our citizens and then let them defend themselves. . . . If we depend on regular troops alone, the liberty of the country must finally be destroyed by that army which is raised to defend it. Is there an instance in

[1] Annals of Congress, Feb. 17, 1808; Thirteenth Congress, pp. 1627, 1631.

which a nation has lost its liberty by its own citizens in time of peace? It is by standing armies and very often by men raised on an emergency and professing virtuous feelings, but who eventually turned their arms against their country. . . . I never yet have voted for a regular army or soldier in time of peace. Whenever an opportunity has offered I have voted them down; and so help me God! I will as long as I live."

One week after Eppes spoke these words, President Jefferson sent to Congress a Message asking for an immediate addition of six thousand men to the regular army.[1] No such blow had ever been given to the established practices of Republican administration. Ten years before, every leader of the party had denounced the raising of twelve regiments at a time of actual hostilities with France, although the law limited their service to the term of the expected war. The eight regiments demanded by Jefferson were to be raised for five years in a time of peace. The Southern Republicans saw themselves required to walk, publicly and avowedly, in the footsteps of their monarchical predecessors; while John Randolph stood by and jeered at them.

The House waited until Rose had fairly sailed and the session drew near its end, with embargo fastened upon the country, and no alternative visible but war; then slowly and unwillingly began its recantations. April 4 John Clopton of Virginia[2] admitted that in 1798 he had voted against the army. His excuse for changing his vote was that in 1798 he thought there was no ground for fearing war, while in 1808 he saw little ground for hoping peace. Yet he voted for the new regiments only because they were so few; and even in the event of actual war "he could scarcely imagine that he could be induced to admit the expediency of increasing the regular forces to a number much greater than they would be" under the present bill. Clopton was answered by Randolph, who warmly opposed the new army for the same reasons which had led him to oppose the old one. Randolph was followed by George M. Troup of Georgia,—a young man not then so

[1] Message of Feb. 25, 1808; Annals of Congress, 1807–1808, p. 1691.
[2] Annals of Congress, 1807–1808, p. 1901.

prominent as he was destined to become, who declared that no one had more confidence than he felt in militia; but "it is well known that the present defective system of militia in our quarter of the country at least is good for nothing;" and a small standing army was not dangerous but necessary, because it would preserve peace by preparing for war.[1] Smilie of Pennsylvania added another reason. He argued that John Randolph had favored raising troops in the year 1805 to protect the Southern frontier "from Spanish inroad and insult." Smilie had then opposed the motion and the House had rejected it, but to Smilie the argument that Randolph had once favored an increase of the army, seemed decisive.

A much respected member from South Carolina—David R. Williams, one of Randolph's friends—then took the floor.[2] He could not bring himself to vote for the bill, because no half-way measure would answer. War would require not six but sixty thousand men; defensive armies were worse than none, either in war or peace. Williams's argument was so evidently weak that it failed to convince even Macon, who had voted against the twelve regiments in 1798, but meant to change his ground and believed himself able to prove his consistency. In contradiction to the bill itself he maintained that the new army was not a peace establishment; that if it were so he would not vote for it. He condemned the maxim that to preserve peace nations must be prepared for war, and asserted that no analogy existed between 1798 and 1808, for that in 1808 America was attacked by foreign powers, while in 1798 she attacked them.[3]

Discordant as these voices were, the debate was the next day enlivened by a discord more entertaining. Richard Stanford of North Carolina, one of the oldest members of the House, a close ally of Randolph, Macon, and Williams, made a speech which troubled the whole body of Southern Republicans.[4] Stanford voted for the twelve regiments in 1798, but like the majority of Republicans he did so in deference to a party caucus, in order to ward off the danger of a larger force.

[1] Annals of Congress, 1807–1808, p. 1916.
[2] Annals of Congress, 1807–1808, p. 1922.
[3] Annals of Congress, 1807–1808, p. 1937.
[4] Annals of Congress, 1807–1808, p. 1939.

He said it was the only Federalist vote he ever gave, and he promised his friends never again to be caught in the same mistake. With candor intended to irritate, he arrayed the occasions on which his party had refused to increase the military establishment: first, in a state of actual hostilities in 1798; again, when Spain defied and insulted the government in 1805; still again, on the brink of a Spanish war during Burr's conspiracy in 1806. He quoted Jefferson's first Inaugural Address, which counted among the essential principles of the government "a well-disciplined militia, our best reliance in peace and for the first moments of war till regulars may relieve them;" and the Annual Message of 1806, which said, "Were armies to be raised whenever a speck of war is visible in our horizon, we never should have been without them; our resources would have been exhausted on dangers which have never happened, instead of being reserved for what is really to take place." He quoted also pungent resolutions of 1798, speeches of Eppes and Wilson Cary Nicholas, of Varnum and Gallatin; he showed the amount of patronage once abolished but restored by this bill; and when at last he sat down, the Southern members were ruffled until even Macon lost his temper.

Soon John Randolph rose again, and if Stanford's speech was exasperating in its candor, Randolph's was stinging in its sarcasm.[1] He treated the new defensive system with ridicule. The Navy Department, he said, had dwindled to a Gunboat Department. Congress built gunboats to protect shipping and coasts, and built forts to protect gunboats. The army was equally feeble; and both were at odds with the embargo:—

> "When the great American tortoise draws in his head you do not see him trotting along; he lies motionless on the ground; it is when the fire is put on his back that he makes the best of his way, and not till then. The system of embargo is one system, withdrawing from every contest, quitting the arena, flying the pit. The system of raising troops and fleets of whatever sort is another and opposite to that dormant state. . . . They are at war with each other, and cannot go on together."

[1] Annals of Congress, 1807–1808, p. 1959.

Even if not inconsistent with the embargo, the army was still useless: —

"My worthy friend from Georgia has said that the tigress, prowling for food for her young, may steal upon you in the night. I would as soon attempt to fence a tiger out of my plantation with a four-railed fence as to fence out the British navy with this force."

Randolph ventured even to ridicule the State of Virginia which was said to demand an army: —

"My friend and worthy colleague tells us that the State of Virginia, so much opposed to armies, has now got to the war pitch so far as to want one regiment for the defence of half a million of souls and seventy thousand square miles. . . . Yes, sir; the legislature of Virginia, my parent State, of whom I cannot speak with disrespect, nor will I suffer any man worth my resentment to speak of her with disrespect in my hearing, has been carried away by the military mania, and they want one regiment!"

Yet Randolph approved the embargo as little as he liked the army and navy.

"I am not one of those who approve the embargo," he said in another speech.[1] "It gives up to Great Britain all the seamen and all the commerce, — their feet are not now upon your decks, for your vessels are all riding safely moored along your slips and wharves; and this measure absolutely gives Agriculture a blow which she cannot recover till the embargo is removed. What has become of your fisheries? Some gentleman has introduced a proposition for buying their fish to relieve the fishermen. Indeed, I would much sooner assent to buying their fish than to raising these troops, except indeed we are raising the troops to eat the fish."

Randolph broke into shrill laughter at his own joke, delighted with the idea of six thousand armed men paid to eat the fish that were rotting on the wharves at Gloucester and Marblehead.

[1] Annals of Congress, 1807–1808, p. 2037.

Keenly as Randolph enjoyed the pleasure of ridiculing his colleagues and friends, he could expect to gain no votes. George W. Campbell and the other Administration speakers admitted that the embargo might yield to war and that an army had become necessary. Even Eppes had the courage to defy ridicule, and in full recollection of having vowed to God February 17 that as long as he lived he would vote down a regular army, he rose April 7 to support the bill for raising eight regiments: —

> "I consider it as part of the system designed to meet the present crisis in our affairs. . . . The period must arrive when the embargo will be a greater evil than war. When that period shall arrive it will be taken off."[1]

On the same day the bill passed by a vote of ninety-five to sixteen, and the Republican party found itself poorer by the loss of one more traditional principle. Events were hurrying the Government toward dangers which the party had believed to be preventable under the system invented by Virginia and Pennsylvania. In 1804 Jefferson wrote to Madison: "It is impossible that France and England should combine to any purpose."[2] The impossible had happened, and every practice founded on the theory of mutual jealousy between European Powers became once more a subject of dispute. On the day of Rose's departure Jefferson, abandoning the secrecy in which until that moment he had wrapped his diplomacy, sent to Congress a mass of diplomatic correspondence with England and France, running back to the year 1804. A few days later, March 30, he sent a secret message accompanied by documents which gave to Congress, with little exception, everything of importance that had passed between the governments. Only one subject was kept back: — the tenebrous negotiation for Florida remained secret.

From these documents Congress could see that the time for talking of theories of peace and friendship or of ordinary commercial interests had passed. Violence and rapine marked every page of the latest correspondence. February 23 Erskine had at last notified the Government officially of the existence

[1] Annals of Congress, 1807–1808, p. 2049.
[2] Jefferson to Madison, Aug. 15, 1804; Works, iv. 557.

and purpose of the Orders in Council. His note repeated the words of Canning's instructions.[1] After asserting that America had submitted to the French Decrees, and had thereby warranted England in forbidding if she pleased all American commerce with France, Erskine pointed out that the Orders in Council, by not prohibiting but limiting this commerce, gave proof of his Majesty's amicable disposition. The Americans might still transport French and Spanish colonial produce to England, and re-export it to the continent of Europe under certain regulations:—

"The object of these regulations will be the establishment of such a protecting duty as shall prevent the enemy from obtaining the produce of his own colonies at a cheaper rate than that of the colonies of Great Britain. In this duty it is evident that America is no otherwise concerned than as being to make an advance to that amount, for which it is in her power amply to indemnify herself at the expense of the foreign consumer."

Further, the orders licensed the importation through England into France of all strictly American produce, except cotton, without paying duty in transit:—

"The reason why his Majesty could not feel himself at liberty, consistent with what was necessary for the execution of his purpose in any tolerable degree, to allow this relaxation to apply to cotton is to be found in the great extent to which France has pushed the manufacture of that article, and the consequent embarrassment upon her trade which a heavy import upon cotton as it passes through Great Britain to France must necessarily produce."

Erskine's note claimed credit for England because the orders were not abruptly enforced, but allowed time for neutrals to understand and conform to them. The concluding sentences were intended to soothe the suffering merchants:—

"The right of his Majesty to resort to retaliation cannot be questioned. The suffering occasioned to neutral parties is incidental, and not of his Majesty's seeking. In the exer-

[1] Erskine to Madison, Feb. 23, 1808; State Papers, iii. 209.

cise of this undoubted right, his Majesty has studiously endeavored to avoid aggravating unnecessarily the inconveniences suffered by the neutral; and I am commanded
by his Majesty especially to represent to the Government
of the United States the earnest desire of his Majesty to see
the commerce of the world restored once more to that freedom which is necessary for its prosperity; and his readiness
to abandon the system which has been forced upon him
whenever the enemy shall retract the principles which have
rendered it necessary."

From this note—a model of smooth-spoken outrage—
Congress could understand that until the King of England
should make other regulations American commerce was to be
treated as subject to the will and interest of Great Britain. At
the same moment Congress was obliged to read a letter from
Champagny to Armstrong, dated Jan. 15, 1808, in defence of
the Berlin and Milan Decrees.[1] Written in words dictated by
Napoleon, this letter asserted rude truths which irritated
Americans the more because they could not be denied:—

"The United States, more than any other Power, have to
complain of the aggressions of England. It has not been
enough for her to offend against the independence of their
flag,—nay, against that of their territory and of their
inhabitants,—by attacking them even in their ports, by
forcibly carrying away their crews; her decrees of the 11th
November have made a fresh attack on their commerce and
on their navigation as they have done on those of all other
Powers.

"In the situation in which England has placed the Continent, especially since her decrees of the 11th November,
his Majesty has no doubt of a declaration of war against
her by the United States. Whatever transient sacrifices war
may occasion, they will not believe it consistent either with
their interest or dignity to acknowledge the monstrous
principle and the anarchy which that government wishes to
establish on the seas. If it be useful and honorable for all
nations to cause the true maritime law of nations to be

[1] Champagny to Armstrong, Jan. 15, 1808; State Papers, iii. 248.

re-established, and to avenge the insults committed by England against every flag, it is indispensable for the United States, who from the extent of their commerce have oftener to complain of those violations. War exists then in fact between England and the United States; and his Majesty considers it as declared from the day on which England published her decrees."

Two such letters could hardly have been written to the chief of an independent people and submitted to a free legislature in Europe without producing a convulsion. Patient as Congress was, the temper excited by Champagny's letter obliged the President, April 2, to withdraw the injunction of secrecy after the House had twice rejected a motion to do so without his permission; but the motive of the Federalists in publishing Champagny's letter was not so much to resent it as to divert popular anger from England to France. No outburst of national self-respect followed the appearance of the two letters. During the next week the House debated and passed the bill for raising the army to ten thousand men, but on all sides the friends and opponents of the measure equally deprecated war. The report of a special committee in the Senate, April 16, expressed on that point the general feeling of Congress:[1] —

"With respect to a resort to war as a remedy for the evils experienced, the committee will offer no other reflection than that it is in itself so great an evil that the United States have wisely considered peace and honest neutrality as the best foundation of their general policy. It is not for the committee to say under what degree of aggravated injuries and sufferings a departure from this policy may become a duty, and the most pacific nation find itself compelled to exchange for the calamities of war the greater distresses of longer forbearance. In the present state of things the committee cannot recommend any departure from that policy which withholds our commercial and agricultural property from the licensed depredations of the great maritime belligerent Powers. They hope that an adherence to this policy

[1] Annals of Congress, 1807–1808, p. 364.

will eventually secure to us the blessings of peace without any sacrifice of our national rights; and they have no doubt that it will be supported by all the manly virtue which the good people of the United States have ever discovered on great and patriotic occasions."

The Senate passed a bill authorizing the President during the recess to suspend the embargo in whole or in part if in his judgment the conduct of the belligerent Powers should render suspension safe. After a hot debate, chiefly on the constitutionality of the measure, it passed the House, and April 22 became law. April 25 the session ended.

As the result of six months' labor, Congress could show besides the usual routine legislation a number of Acts which made an epoch in the history of the Republican party. First came the Embargo, its two Supplements, and the Act empowering the President to suspend it at will. Next came the series of appropriation Acts which authorized the President to spend in all four million dollars in excess of the ordinary expenditures,—for gunboats, eight hundred and fifty thousand dollars; for land fortifications, one million; for five new regiments of infantry, one of riflemen, one of light artillery, and one of light dragoons, two million dollars; and two hundred thousand dollars for arming the militia. Such progress toward energy was more rapid than could have been expected from a party like that which Jefferson had educated and which he still controlled.

Chapter X

"THIS SIX MONTHS' SESSION has worn me down to a state of almost total incapacity for business," wrote President Jefferson to his attorney-general.[1] "Congress will certainly rise to-morrow night, and I shall leave this for Monticello on the 5th of May, to be here again on the 8th of June." More earnestly than ever he longed for repose and good-will. "For myself," he said,[2] "I have nothing further to ask of the world than to preserve in retirement so much of their esteem as I may have fairly earned, and to be permitted to pass in tranquillity, in the bosom of my family and friends, the days which yet remain to me." He could not reasonably ask from the world more than he had already received from it; but a whole year remained, during which he must still meet whatever demand the world should make upon him. He had brought the country to a situation where war was impossible for want of weapons, and peace was only a name for passive war. He was bound to carry the government through the dangers he had braved; and for the first time in seven years American democracy, struck with sudden fear of failure, looked to him in doubt, and trembled for its hopes.

Fortunately for Jefferson's ease, no serious opposition was made in the Republican party to his choice of a successor. Giles and Nicholas, who managed Madison's canvass in Virginia, caused a caucus to be held, January 21, at Richmond, where one hundred and twenty-three members of the State legislature joined in nominating electors for Madison. Randolph's friends held another caucus, at which fifty-seven members of the same legislature joined in nominating electors for Monroe. To support the Virginia movement for Madison, a simultaneous caucus was held at Washington, where, January 20, Senator Bradley of Vermont issued a printed circular inviting the Republican members of both Houses to consult, January 23, respecting the next Presidential election. Bradley's authority was disputed by Monroe's partisans, and only Madison's friends, or indifferent persons, obeyed the call. Eighty-

[1] Jefferson to Rodney, April 24, 1808; Works, v. 275.
[2] Jefferson to Monroe, March 10, 1808; Works, v. 253.

nine senators and members attended; and on balloting, eighty-three votes were given for Madison as President, seventy-nine for George Clinton as Vice-President; but the names of the persons present were never published, and the caucus itself seemed afraid of its own action. About sixty Republican members or senators held aloof. John Randolph and sixteen of his friends published a protest against the caucus and its candidate:—

"We ask for energy, and we are told of his moderation. We ask for talents, and the reply is his unassuming merit. We ask what were his services in the cause of public liberty, and we are directed to the pages of the 'Federalist,' written in conjunction with Alexander Hamilton and John Jay, in which the most extravagant of their doctrines are maintained and propagated. We ask for consistency as a Republican, standing forth to stem the torrent of oppression which once threatened to overwhelm the liberties of the country. We ask for that high and honorable sense of duty which would at all times turn with loathing and abhorrence from any compromise with fraud and speculation. We ask in vain."[1]

Jefferson had commanded the warm and undisputed regard of his followers; Madison held no such pre-eminence. "Every able diplomatist is not fit to be President," said Macon. George Clinton, who had yielded unwillingly to Jefferson, held Madison in contempt. While Monroe set up a Virginia candidacy which the Republicans of Randolph's school supported, George Clinton set up a candidacy of his own, in New York, supported by Cheetham's "Watch-Tower," and by a portion of the country press. Before long, the public was treated to a curious spectacle. The regular party candidate for the Vice-presidency became the open rival of the regular candidate for the Presidency. Clinton's newspapers attacked Madison without mercy, while Madison's friends were electing Clinton as Madison's Vice-president.

In this state of things successful opposition to Madison depended upon the union of his enemies in support of a

[1] Address to the People of the United States, National Intelligencer, March 7, 1808.

common candidate. Not only must either Monroe or Clinton retire, but one must be able to transfer his votes to the other; and the whole Federalist party must be induced to accept the choice thus made. The Federalists were not unwilling; but while they waited for the politicians of Virginia and New York to arrange the plan of campaign, they busied themselves with recovering control of New England, where they had been partially driven from power. The embargo offered them almost a certainty of success.

From the first moment of the embargo, even during the secret debate of Dec. 19, 1807, its opponents raised the cry of French influence; and so positively and persistently was Jefferson charged with subservience to Napoleon, that while a single Federalist lived, this doctrine continued to be an article of his creed. In truth, Jefferson had never stood on worse terms with France than when he imposed the embargo. He acted in good faith when he enclosed Armstrong's letter and Regnier's decision in his Embargo Message. Turreau was annoyed at his conduct, thinking it intended to divert public anger from England to France in order to make easier the negotiation with Rose. Instead of dictating Jefferson's course, as the Federalists believed, Turreau was vexed and alarmed by it. He complained of Armstrong, Madison, and Jefferson himself. The Embargo Message, he said, exposed the Administration in flank to the Federalists, and gave the English envoy free play. "For me it was a useless proof—one proof the more—of the usual awkwardness of the Washington Cabinet, and of its falsity (*fausseté*) in regard to France."[1] His contempt involved equally people, Legislature, and Executive:—

"Faithful organs of the perverse intentions of the American people, its representatives came together before their usual time, in accordance with the President's views, and in their private conversation and in their public deliberations seemed entirely to forget the offences of England, or rather to have been never affected by them. This temper, common to the men of all parties, proved very evidently what was the state of popular opinion in regard to Great Britain, against whom no hostile project will ever enter into

[1] Turreau to Champagny, May 20, 1808; Archives des Aff. Étr. MSS.

an American's thoughts. The Annual Message was not calculated to inspire energy into the honorable Congress. All these political documents from the President's pen are cold and colorless."[1]

The result of Rose's negotiation confirmed Turreau's disgust:—

"It can be no longer doubtful that the United States, whatever insults they may have to endure, will never make war on Great Britain unless she attacks them. Every day I have been, and still am, met with the objection that the decrees of the French government have changed the disposition of the members of the Executive, and especially of members of Congress. Both have seized this incident as a pretext to color their cowardice (*lâcheté*), and extend it over their system of inaction; since it is evident that however severe the measures of the French government may have been, they weigh light in the balance when set in opposition to all the excesses, all the outrages, that England has permitted herself to inflict on the United States."[2]

During the winter and spring nothing occurred to soothe Turreau's feelings. On the contrary, his irritation was increased by the President's communication to Congress of Champagny's letter of January 15, and by the "inconceivable weakness" which made this letter public:—

"Although I could hardly have calculated on this new shock, which has considerably weakened our political credit in the United States, I well knew that we had lost greatly in the opinion of the Cabinet at Washington and of its chief. After Mr. Rose's departure,—that is to say, about three weeks before the end of the session,—I quitted the city for reasons of health, which were only too well founded. I had seen Mr. Jefferson only a week before I went to take leave of him. Perhaps I should tell your Excellency that I commonly see the President once a week, and always in the evening,—a time when I am sure of finding him at home, and nearly always alone. I never open upon

[1] Turreau to Champagny, May 20, 1808; Archives des Aff. Étr. MSS.
[2] Turreau to Champagny, May 20, 1808; Archives des Aff. Étr. MSS.

the chapter of politics, because it seems more proper for me to wait for him to begin this subject, and I never wait long. At the interview before the last I found him extremely cool in regard to the interests of Europe and the measures of the Powers coalesced against England. At the last interview he asked me if I had recent news from Europe. I told him—what was true—that I had nothing official since two months. 'You treat us badly,' he replied. 'The governments of Europe do not understand this government here. Even England, whose institutions have most analogy with ours, does not know the character of the American people and the spirit of its Administration,' etc. I answered that Great Britain having violated the law of nations in regard to every people in succession, the nature and the difference of their institutions mattered little to a Power which had abjured all principles. He interrupted me to say: 'When severe measures become necessary we shall know how to take them, but we do not want to be dragged into them (*y être entraînés*).' Although this was directly to the address of the minister of France, I thought best to avoid a retort, and contented myself with observing that generally France gave the example of respect for governments which sustained their dignity, and that the object of the coalition of all the European States against England was to constrain that Power to imitate her. The rest of the conversation was too vague and too insignificant to be worth remembering. Nevertheless, Mr. Jefferson repeated to me what he tells me at nearly every interview,—that he has much love for France."

Turreau drew the inference "that the federal government intends to-day more than ever to hold an equal balance between France and England." Erskine saw matters in the same light. Neither the Frenchman nor the Englishman, although most directly interested in the bias of President Jefferson, reported any word or act of his which showed a wish to serve Napoleon's ends.

The interests of the Federalists required them to assert the subservience of Jefferson to France. They did so in the most positive language, without proof, and without attempting to obtain proof. Had this been all, they would have done no worse than their opponents had done before them; but they also used the pretext of Jefferson's devotion to France in order to cover and justify their own devotion to England.

After the failure of Rose, in the month of February, to obtain further concessions from Madison, the British envoy cultivated more closely the friendship of Senator Pickering, and even followed his advice. As early as March 4 he wrote to his Government on the subject,[1] —

"It is apprehended, should this Government be desirous that hostilities should take place with England, it will not venture to commence them, but will endeavor to provoke her to strike the first blow. In such a case it would no doubt adopt highly irritating measures. On this head I beg leave, but with great diffidence, to submit the views which I have formed here, and which I find coincide completely with those of the best and most enlightened men of this country, and who consider her interests as completely identified with those of Great Britain. I conceive it to be of extreme importance in the present state of the public mind in this nation, and especially as operated upon by the embargo, such as I have endeavored to represent it in preceding despatches, to avoid if possible actual warfare, — should it be practicable consistently with the national honor, to do no more than retort upon America any measures of insolence and injury falling short of it which she may adopt. Such a line of conduct would, I am persuaded, render completely null the endeavors exerted to impress upon the public mind here the persuasion of the inveterate rancor with which Great Britain seeks the destruction of America, and would turn their whole animosity, — goaded on, as they would be, by the insults and injuries offered by France, and the self-inflicted annihilation of their own commerce, — against their own Government, and produce an entire change in the politics of the country. A war with Great Britain would, I have no doubt, prove ultimately fatal to this Government; but it is to be feared that the people would necessarily rally round it at the first moment and at

[1] Rose to Canning, March 4, 1808; MSS. British Archives.

the instant of danger; and an exasperation would be produced which it might be found impossible to eradicate for
a series of years. Their soundest statesmen express to me
the utmost anxiety that their fellow-citizens should be allowed to bear the whole burden of their own follies, and
suffer by evils originating with themselves; and they are
convinced that the effects of punishment inflicted by their
own hands must ere long bring them into co-operation
with Great Britain, whilst if inflicted by hers, it must turn
them perhaps irrevocably against her."

"The best and most enlightened men of the country,"—
who "considered her interests as completely identified with
those of Great Britain," and who thus concerted with Canning a policy intended to bring themselves into power as
agents of Spencer Perceval and Lord Castlereagh,—were Senator Pickering and his friends. To effect this coalition with the
British ministry Pickering exerted himself to the utmost. Not
only by word of mouth, but also by letter, he plied the British
envoy with argument and evidence. Although Rose, March 4,
wrote to Canning in the very words of the Massachusetts
senator, March 13 the senator wrote to Rose repeating his
opinion:[1]—

> "You know my solicitude to have peace preserved
> between the two nations, and I have therefore taken the
> liberty to express to you my opinion of the true point of
> policy to be observed by your Government toward the
> United States, in case your mission prove unsuccessful; that
> is, to let us alone; to bear patiently the wrongs we do our-
> selves. In one word, amidst the irritations engendered by
> hatred and folly, to maintain a dignified composure, and to
> abstain from war,—relying on this, that whatever disposi-
> tion exists to provoke, there is none to commence a war on
> the part of the United States."

To support his views Pickering enclosed a letter from Rufus
King. "I also know," he continued, "that in the present unexampled state of the world our own best citizens consider the
interests of the United States to be interwoven with those of

[1] Pickering to Rose, March 13, 1808; New England Federalism, p. 366.

Great Britain, and that our safety depends on hers. . . . Of the opinions and reasonings of such men I wish you to be possessed." He held out a confident hope that the embargo would end in an overthrow of the Administration, and that a change in the head of the government would alter its policy "in a manner propitious to the continuance of peace." A few days afterward he placed in Rose's hands two letters from George Cabot. Finally, on the eve of Rose's departure, March 22, he gave the British envoy a letter to Samuel Williams of London. "Let him, if you please, be the medium of whatever epistolary intercourse may take place between you and me."[1]

To these advances Rose replied in his usual tone of courteous superiority:—

> "I avail myself thankfully of your permission to keep that gentleman's [Rufus King's] letter, which I am sure will carry high authority where I can use it confidentially, and whither it is most important that what I conceive to be right impressions should be conveyed. It is not to you that I need protest that rancorous impressions of jealousy or ill-will have never existed there; but it is to be feared that at some time or another the extremest point of human forbearance may be reached. Yet at the present moment there is, I think, a peculiarity of circumstances most strange indeed, which enables the offended party to leave his antagonist to his own suicidal devices, unless, in his contortions under them, he may strike some blow which the other might not be able to dissemble."[2]

No senator of the United States could submit, without some overpowering motive, to such patronage. That Pickering should have invited it was the more startling because he knew better than any other man in America the criminality of his act. Ten years before, at a time when Pickering was himself Secretary of State, the Pennsylvania Quaker, Dr. Logan, attempted, with honest motives, to act as an amateur negotiator between the United States government and that of

[1] Pickering to G. H. Rose, March 22, 1808; New England Federalism, p. 368.

[2] G. H. Rose to Pickering, March 18, 1808; New England Federalism, p. 367.

France. In order to prevent such mischievous follies for the future, Congress, under the inspiration of Pickering, passed a law known as "Logan's Act," which still stood on the statute book:[1] —

> "Every citizen of the United States, whether actually resident or abiding within the same, or in any foreign country, who, without the permission or authority of the government, directly or indirectly commences or carries on any verbal or written correspondence or intercourse with any foreign government, or any officer or agent thereof, with an intent to influence the measures or conduct of any foreign government, or of any officer or agent thereof, in relation to any disputes or controversies with the United States, or to defeat the measures of the government of the United States; and every person . . . who counsels, advises, or assists in any such correspondence, with such intent, shall be punished by a fine of not more than five thousand dollars, and by imprisonment during not less than six months, nor more than three years."

When Pickering defied fine and imprisonment under his own law, in order to make a concert of political action with George Canning to keep the British government steady in aggression, he believed that his end justified his means; and he avowed his end to be the bringing of his friends into power. For this purpose he offered himself to Canning as the instrument for organizing what was in fact a British party in New England, asking in return only the persistence of Great Britain in a line of policy already adopted, which was sure to work against the Republican rule. Pickering knew that his conduct was illegal; but he had in his hands an excuse which justified him, as he chose to think, in disregarding the law. He persuaded himself that Jefferson was secretly bound by an engagement with Napoleon to effect the ruin of England.

Then came Pickering's master-stroke. The April election—which would decide the political control of Massachusetts for the coming year, and the choice of a senator in the place of J. Q. Adams—was close at hand. February 16, the day when

[1] Rev. Stat. sec. 5335. Cf. Act of Jan. 30, 1799; Annals of Congress, 1797–1799, p. 3795.

Rose's negotiation broke down, Pickering sent to Governor Sullivan of Massachusetts a letter intended for official communication to the State legislature.[1] "I may claim some share of attention and credit," he began,—"that share which is due to a man who defies the world to point, in the whole course of a long and public life, at one instance of deception, at a single departure from Truth." He entered into speculations upon the causes which had led Congress to impose the embargo. Omitting mention of the Orders in Council, he showed that the official reasons presented in the President's Embargo Message were not sufficient to justify the measure, and that some secret motive must lie hidden from public view:—

"Has the French Emperor declared that he will have no neutrals? Has he required that our ports, like those of his vassal States in Europe, be shut against British commerce? Is the embargo a substitute, a milder form of compliance, with that harsh demand, which if exhibited in its naked and insulting aspect the American spirit might yet resent? Are we still to be kept profoundly ignorant of the declarations and avowed designs of the French Emperor, although these may strike at our liberty and independence? And in the mean time are we, by a thousand irritations, by cherishing prejudices, and by exciting fresh resentments, to be drawn gradually into a war with Great Britain? Why amid the extreme anxiety of the public mind is it still kept on the rack of fearful expectation by the President's portentous silence respecting his French despatches? In this concealment there is danger. In this concealment must be wrapt up the real cause of the embargo. On any other supposition it is inexplicable."

Never was Jefferson's sleight-of-hand more dexterously turned against him than in this unscrupulous appeal to his own official language. In all Pickering's voluminous writings this letter stood out alone, stamped by a touch of genius.

"By false policy," he continued, "or by inordinate fears,

[1] Letter from the Hon. Timothy Pickering to His Excellency James Sullivan (Boston, 1808).

our country may be betrayed and subjugated to France as surely as by corruption. I trust, sir, that no one who knows me will charge it to vanity when I say that I have some knowledge of public men and of public affairs; and on that knowledge, and with solemnity, I declare to you that I have no confidence in the wisdom or correctness of our public measures; that our country is in imminent danger; that it is essential to the public safety that the blind confidence in our rulers should cease; that the State legislatures should know the facts and the reasons on which important general laws are founded; and especially that those States whose farms are on the ocean and whose harvests are gathered in every sea, should immediately and seriously consider how to preserve them."

To those Federalists leaders who had been acquainted with the plans of 1804, the meaning of this allusion to the commercial States could not be doubtful. Least of all could Pickering's colleague in the Senate, who had so strenuously resisted the disunion scheme, fail to understand the drift of Pickering's leadership. John Quincy Adams, at whose growing influence this letter struck, had been from his earliest recollection, through his father's experience or his own, closely connected with political interests. During forty years he had been the sport of public turbulence, and for forty years he was yet to undergo every vicissitude of political failure and success; but in the range of his chequered life he was subjected to no other trial so severe as that which Pickering forced him to meet. In the path of duty he might doubtless face social and political ostracism, even in a town such as Boston then was, and defy it. Men as good as he had done as much, in many times and places; but to do this in support of a President whom he disliked and distrusted, for the sake of a policy in which he had no faith, was enough to shatter a character of iron. Fortunately for him, his temper was not one to seek relief in half-way measures. He had made a mistake in voting for an embargo without limit of time; but since no measure of resistance to Europe more vigorous than the embargo could gain support from either party, he accepted and defended it. He attended the Republican caucus January 23, and voted for George Clinton as President; and when Pick ering flung down his challenge in the letter of February 16, Adams instantly took it up.

Governor Sullivan naturally declined to convey Senator Pickering's letter to the Legislature; but a copy had been sent to George Cabot, who caused it, March 9, to be published. The effect was violent. Passion took the place of reason, and swept the Federalists into Pickering's path. Governor Sullivan published a vigorous reply, but lost his temper in doing so, and became abusive where he should have been cool.[1] When Pickering's letter was received at Washington, Adams wrote an answer,[2] which reached Boston barely in time to be read before the election. He went over the history of the embargo; pointed out its relation to the Orders in Council; recapitulated the long list of English outrages; turned fiercely upon the British infatuation of Pickering's friends, and called upon them to make their choice between embargo and war: —

> "If any statesman can point out another alternative I am ready to hear him, and for any practicable expedient to lend him every possible assistance. But let not that expedient be submission to trade under British licenses and British taxation. We are told that even under these restrictions we may yet trade to the British dominions, to Africa and China, and with the colonies of France, Spain, and Holland. I ask not how much of this trade would be left when our intercourse with the whole continent of Europe being cut off would leave us no means of purchase and no market for sale. I ask not what trade we could enjoy with the colonies of nations with which we should be at war. I ask not how long Britain would leave open to us avenues of trade which even in these very Orders of Council she boasts of leaving open as a special indulgence. If we yield the principle, we abandon all pretence to national sovereignty."

Thus the issue between a British and American party was sharply drawn. Governor Sullivan charged Pickering with an attempt to excite sedition and rebellion, and to bring about a

[1] Interesting Correspondence (Boston, 1808).
[2] Letter to the Hon. Harrison Gray Otis, by John Quincy Adams (Boston, 1808).

dissolution of government. Adams made no mention of his colleague's name. In Massachusetts the modern canvass was unknown; newspapers and pamphlets took the place of speeches; the pulpit and tavern bar were the only hustings; and the public opinions of men in high official or social standing weighed heavily. The letters of Pickering, Sullivan, and Adams penetrated every part of the State, and on the issues raised by them the voters made their choice.

The result showed that Pickering's calculation on the embargo was sound. He failed to overthrow Governor Sullivan, who won his re-election by a majority of some twelve hundred in a total vote of about eighty-one thousand; but the Federalists gained in the new Legislature a decided majority, which immediately elected James Lloyd to succeed J. Q. Adams in the Senate, and adopted resolutions condemning the embargo. Adams instantly resigned his seat. The Legislature chose Lloyd to complete the unfinished term.

Thus the great State of Massachusetts fell back into Federalism. All, and more than all, that Jefferson's painful labors had gained, his embargo in a few weeks wasted. Had the evil stopped there no harm need have been feared; but the reaction went far beyond that point. The Federalists of 1801 were the national party of America; the Federalists of 1808 were a British faction in secret league with George Canning.

The British government watched closely these events. Rose's offensive and defensive alliance with Timothy Pickering and with the Washington representatives of the Essex Junto was not the only tie between Westminster and Boston. Of all British officials, the one most directly interested in American politics was Sir James Craig, then Governor of Lower Canada, who resided at Quebec, and had the strongest reason to guard against attack from the United States. In February, 1808, when the question of peace or war seemed hanging on the fate of Rose's mission, Sir James Craig was told by his secretary, H. W. Ryland, that an Englishman about to visit New England from Montreal would write back letters as he went, which might give valuable hints in regard to the probable conduct of the American government and people. The man's name was John Henry; and in reporting his letters to Lord Castlereagh as they arrived, Sir James Craig spoke highly of the writer. —

"Mr. Henry is a gentleman of considerable ability, and, I believe, well able to form a correct judgment on what he sees passing. He resided for some time in the United States, and is well acquainted with some of the leading people of Boston, to which place he was called very suddenly from Montreal, where he at present lives, by the intelligence he received that his agent there was among the sufferers by the recent measures of the American government. He has not the most distant idea that I should make this use of his correspondence, which therefore can certainly have no other view than that of an unreserved communication with his friend who is my secretary."[1]

Sir James Craig had something to learn in regard to volunteer diplomatists of Henry's type; but being in no way responsible for the man, he read the letters which came addressed to Ryland, but which were evidently meant for the Governor of Canada, and proved to be worth his reading. The first was written March 2, from Swanton in Vermont, ten miles from the Canada border: —

"You will have learned that Congress has passed a law prohibiting the transport of any American produce to Canada, and the collector at this frontier post expects by this day's mail instructions to carry it into rigorous execution. The sensibility excited by this measure among the inhabitants in the northern part of Vermont is inconceivable. The roads are covered with sleighs, and the whole country seems employed in conveying their produce beyond the line of separation. The clamor against the Government— and this measure particularly—is such that you may expect to hear of an engagement between the officers of government and the sovereign people on the first effort to stop the introduction of that vast quantity of lumber and produce which is prepared for the Montreal market."

From Windsor in Vermont, March 6, Henry wrote again,

[1] Sir J. H. Craig to Lord Castlereagh, April 10, 1808; MSS. British Archives.

announcing that the best-informed people believed war to be inevitable between the United States and England. From Windsor Henry went on to Boston, where he found himself at home. Acquainted with the best people, and admitted freely into society,[1] he heard all that was said. March 10, when he had been not more than a day or two in Boston, he wrote to Ryland, enclosing a Boston newspaper of the same morning, in which Senator Pickering's letter to Governor Sullivan appeared and the approaching departure of Rose was announced. Already he professed to be well-advised of what was passing in private Federalist councils.

"The men of talents, property, and influence in Boston are resolved to adopt without delay every expedient to avert the impending calamity, and to express their determination not to be at war with Great Britain in such a manner as to indicate resistance to the government in the last resort. . . . Very active, though secret, measures are taken to rouse the people from the lethargy which if long continued must end in their subjection to the modern Attila."

March 18 Henry wrote again, announcing that the fear of war had vanished, and that Jefferson meant to depend upon his embargo and a system of irritation:—

"It is, however, to be expected that the evil will produce its own cure, and that in a few months more of suffering and privation of all the benefits of commerce the people of the New England States will be ready to withdraw from the confederacy, establish a separate government, and adopt a policy congenial with their interests and happiness. For a measure of this sort the men of talents and property are now ready, and only wait until the continued distress of the multitude shall make them acquainted with the source of their misery, and point out an efficient remedy."

These letters, immediately on their receipt at Quebec, were enclosed by Sir James Craig to Lord Castlereagh in a letter marked "Private," dated April 10, and sent by the Halifax

---

[1] Quincy's Life of Josiah Quincy, p. 250.

mail, as the quickest mode of conveyance.[1] Meanwhile Henry completed his business in Boston and returned to Montreal, where he arrived April 11, and three days afterward wrote again to Ryland at Quebec: —

> "I attended a private meeting of several of the principal characters in Boston, where the questions of *immediate* and *ultimate* necessity were discussed. In the first, all agreed that memorials from all the towns (beginning with Boston) should be immediately transmitted to the Administration, and a firm determination expressed that they will not co-operate in a war against England. I distributed several copies of a memorial to that effect in some of the towns in Vermont on my return. The measure of ultimate necessity which I suggested I found in Boston some unwillingness to consider. It was 'that in case of a declaration of war the State of Massachusetts should treat separately for itself, and obtain from Great Britain a guaranty of its integrity.' Although it was not deemed necessary to decide on a measure of this sort at this moment, it was considered as a very probable step in the last resort. In fine, every man whose opinion I could ascertain was opposed to a war, and attached to the cause of England."

That Henry reported with reasonable truth the general character of Federalist conversation was proved by the nearly simultaneous letters of Pickering to Rose; but his activity did not stop there. In a final letter of April 25 he gave a more precise account of the measures to be taken: —

> "In my last I omitted to mention to you that among the details of the plan for averting from the Northern States the miseries of French alliance and friendship, individuals are selected in the several towns on the seaboard and throughout the country to correspond and act in concert with the superintending committee at Boston. The benefits of any organized plan over the distinct and desultory exertions of individuals are, I think, very apparent. Whether this confederacy of the men of talents and property be

[1] Sir James Craig to Lord Castlereagh, April 10, 1808; MSS. British Archives, Lower Canada, vol. cvii.

regarded as a diversion of the power of the nation, as an efficient means of resistance to the general government in the event of a war, or the nucleus of an English party that will soon be formidable enough to negotiate for the friendship of Great Britain, it is in all respects very important; and I have well-founded reason to hope that a few months more of suffering and the suspension of everything collateral to commerce will reconcile the multitude to any men and any system which will promise them relief."

May 5 the second part of Henry's correspondence was forwarded by Sir James Craig to Lord Castlereagh, who could compare its statements with those of Pickering, and with the reports of Rose. The alliance between the New England Federalists and the British Tories was made. Nothing remained but to concentrate against Jefferson the forces at their command.

Chapter XI

THE EMBARGO had lasted less than four months, when April 19 the President at Washington was obliged to issue a proclamation announcing that on Lake Champlain and in the adjacent country persons were combined for the purpose of forming insurrections against the laws, and that the military power of the government must aid in quelling such insurrections.[1] Immense rafts of lumber were collecting near the boundary line; and report said that one such raft, near half a mile long, carried a ball-proof fort, and was manned by five or six hundred armed men prepared to defy the custom-house officers. This raft was said to contain the surplus produce of Vermont for a year past,—wheat, potash, pork, and beef,—and to be worth upward of three hundred thousand dollars.[2] The governor of Vermont ordered out a detachment of militia to stop this traffic, and the governor of New York ordered another detachment to co-operate with that of Vermont. May 8 rumors of a battle were afloat, and of forty men killed or wounded.[3] The stories were untrue, but the rafts escaped, the customs officials not venturing to stop them.

Reports of this open defiance and insurrection on the Canada frontier reached Washington at the same time with other reports which revealed endless annoyances elsewhere. If the embargo was to coerce England or France, it must stop supplies to the West Indian colonies, and prevent the escape of cotton or corn for the artisans of Europe. The embargo aimed at driving England to desperation, but not at famishing America; yet the President found himself at a loss to do the one without doing the other. Nearly all commerce between the States was by coasting-vessels. If the coasting-trade should be left undisturbed, every schooner that sailed from an American port was sure to allege that by stress of weather or by the accidents of navigation it had been obliged to stop at some port of Nova Scotia or the West Indies, and there to leave its cargo. Only the absolute prohibition of the coasting-

[1] Proclamation of April 19, 1808; Annals of Congress, 1808–1809, p. 580.
[2] New York Evening Post, May, 1808
[3] National Intelligencer, May 23, 1808.

trade could prevent these evasions; but to prohibit the coast-ing-trade was to sever the Union. The political tie might re-main, but no other connection could survive. Without the coasting-trade New England would be deprived of bread, and her industries would perish; Charleston and New Orleans would stagnate in unapproachable solitude.

Jefferson proclaimed the existence of an insurrection on the Canadian frontier shortly before the adjournment of Con-gress. Immediately after the adjournment he took in hand the more serious difficulties of the coasting-trade. The experiment of peaceable coercion was at last to have full trial, and Jeffer-son turned to the task with energy that seemed to his friends excessive, but expressed the vital interest he felt in the success of a theory on which his credit as a statesman depended. The crisis was peculiarly his own; and he assumed the responsibil-ity for every detail of its management.

May 6 the President wrote to Gallatin a letter containing general directions to detain in port every coasting-vessel which could be regarded as suspicious. His orders were sweeping. The power of the embargo as a coercive weapon was to be learned.

"In the outset of the business of detentions," said the President,[1] "I think it impossible to form precise rules. Af-ter a number of cases shall have arisen, they may probably be thrown into groups and subjected to rules. The great leading object of the Legislature was, and ours in execution of it ought to be, to give complete effect to the embargo laws. They have bidden agriculture, commerce, navigation to bow before that object,—to be nothing when in com-petition with that. Finding all their endeavors at general rules to be evaded, they finally gave us the power of deten-tion as the panacea; and I am clear we ought to use it freely, that we may by a fair experiment know the power of this great weapon, the embargo."

A few days later Jefferson repeated the warning in stronger language: "I place immense value in the experiment being

[1] Jefferson to Gallatin, May 6, 1808; Works, v. 287.

fully made, how far an embargo may be an effectual weapon in future as well as on this occasion."[1]

"Where you are doubtful," continued the instructions to Gallatin, "consider me as voting for detention;" and every coasting-vessel was an object of doubt. On the same day with the letter of May 6 to the Secretary of the Treasury, the President wrote a circular to the governors of New Hampshire, Massachusetts, South Carolina, Georgia, and Orleans, —portions of the Union which consumed more wheat than they produced,—requesting them to issue certificates for such quantities of flour as were likely to be needed beyond their local supply. The certificates, directed to the collector of some port usually exporting flour, were to be issued to "any merchant in whom you have confidence."[2] All other shipments of produce were objects of suspicion. "I really think," wrote the President to Gallatin, "it would be well to recommend to every collector to consider every shipment of provisions, lumber, flaxseed, tar, cotton, tobacco, etc.,—enumerating the articles,—as sufficiently suspicious for detention and reference here." He framed new instructions to the governors on this idea: "We find it necessary to consider every vessel as suspicious which has on board any articles of domestic produce in demand at foreign markets, and most especially provisions."[3]

Gallatin, having early declared his want of faith in the embargo as a coercive measure, was the more bound to prove that his private opinion did not prevent him from giving full trial to the experiment which Executive and Legislature had ordered him to make. He set himself resolutely to the unpleasant task. Instead of following the President's plan of indiscriminate suspicion and detention, he preferred to limit the suspicious cargo in value, so that no vessel could carry provisions to the amount of more than one-eighth of the bond; but before he could put his system in force, new annoyances arose. Governor Sullivan of Massachusetts, under the President's circular, issued certificates before July 15 to the amount of fifty thousand barrels of flour and one hundred thousand bushels of corn, besides rice and rye. Gallatin complained to

[1] Jefferson to the Secretary of the Treasury, May 15, 1808; Works, v. 289.
[2] Jefferson to the Governors of Orleans, etc., May 6, 1808; Works, v. 285.
[3] Jefferson to Gallatin, May 16, 1808; Gallatin's Writings, i. 389.

the President,[1] who instantly wrote to the governor of Massachusetts an order to stop importing provisions:—

"As these supplies, although called for within the space of two months, will undoubtedly furnish the consumption of your State for a much longer time, I have thought advisable to ask the favor of your Excellency, after the receipt of this letter, to discontinue issuing any other certificates, that we may not unnecessarily administer facilities to the evasion of the embargo laws."[2]

That Massachusetts already on the brink of rebellion should tolerate such dictation could hardly be expected; and it was fortunate for Jefferson that the Federalists had failed to elect a governor of their own stripe. Even Sullivan, Democrat as he was, could not obey the President's request, and excused his disobedience in a letter which was intended to convince Jefferson that the people of Massachusetts were the best judges of the amount of food they needed.

"The seaport towns," Sullivan wrote,[3] "are supported almost entirely by bread from the Southern and Middle States. The interior of this State live on a mixture of Indian corn and rye in common regimen, but their fine bread and pastry depend on the importations from the southward, carted into the interior. The country towns consume more imported flour than is equivalent for all the grain they carry to market in the seaport towns. Their hogs and poultry consume much Indian corn. The rice imported here from the southward, since the Embargo Act, has been very inconsiderable. The Indian corn is in greater quantities, but that would not find a market in the British or French dominions if there was no embargo. This is an article of great demand here, not as bread, but as sustenance for carriage-horses, draft-horses, etc., and the quantity consumed is really astonishing."

Sullivan admitted that the habits of the Massachusetts people, contracted under the royal government and still

[1] Gallatin to Jefferson, July 15, 1808; Gallatin's Writings, i. 394.
[2] Jefferson to Sullivan, July 16, 1808; Works, v. 317.
[3] Sullivan to Jefferson, July 23, 1808; Jefferson MSS.

continued, led to the evasion of commercial laws; but he told the President what would be the result of an arbitrary interference with their supplies of food: —

"You may depend upon it that three weeks after these certificates shall be refused, an artificial and actual scarcity will involve this State in mobs, riots, and convulsions, pretendedly on account of the embargo. Your enemies will have an additional triumph, and your friends suffer new mortifications."[1]

Governor Sullivan was a man of ability and courage. Popular and successful, he had broken the long sway of Federalism in Massachusetts, and within a few months had carried his re-election against the utmost exertions of the Essex Junto; but he had seen John Quincy Adams fall a sacrifice to the embargo, and he had no wish to be himself the next victim of Jefferson's theories. His situation was most difficult, and he warned the President that the embargo was making it worse: —

"The embargo has been popular with what is denominated the Republican part of the State; but as it does not appear from anything that has taken place in the European Powers that it has had the expected effect there, it has begun to lose its support from the public opinion. . . . There are judicious men in this State who are friends to the present Administration, and who have been in favor of the embargo as a measure of expedience which ought to have been adopted by the government, but who now express great doubts as to the power of enforcing it much longer under present circumstances. They do not perceive any of the effects from it that the nation expected; they do not perceive foreign Powers influenced by it, as they anticipated. They are convinced, as they say, that the people of this State must soon be reduced to suffering and poverty. . . . These men consider the embargo as operating very forcibly to the subversion of the Republican interest here. Should the measure be much longer continued, and then fail of producing any important public good, I imagine

[1] Sullivan to Jefferson, July 21, 1808; Jefferson MSS.

it will be a decisive blow against the Republican interest now supported in this Commonwealth."[1]

Jefferson resented Sullivan's conduct. A few days afterward he wrote to General Dearborn, the Secretary of War, who was then in Maine, warning him to be ready to support the measure which Sullivan had declined to adopt.

"Yours of July 27 is received," Jefferson said.[2] "It confirms the accounts we receive from others that the infractions of the embargo in Maine and Massachusetts are open. I have removed Pope, of New Bedford, for worse than negligence. The collector of Sullivan is on the totter. The Tories of Boston openly threaten insurrection if their importation of flour is stopped. The next post will stop it. I fear your Governor [Sullivan] is not up to the tone of these parricides, and I hope on the first symptom of an open opposition of the law by force you will fly to the scene, and aid in suppressing any commotion."

Blood was soon shed, but Jefferson did not shrink. The new army was stationed along the Canada frontier. The gunboats and frigates patrolled the coast. On every side dangers and difficulties accumulated. "I did not expect a crop of so sudden and rank growth of fraud and open opposition by force could have grown up in the United States."[3] At Newburyport an armed mob on the wharf prevented the customhouse officers from detaining a vessel about to sail. The collectors and other officers were ill-disposed, or were harassed by suits at law for illegal detentions. Rebellion and disunion stared Jefferson in the face, but only caused him to challenge an outbreak and to invite violence.

"That the Federalists may attempt insurrection is possible," he wrote to Gallatin,[4] "and also that the governor would sink before it; but the Republican part of the State, and that portion of the Federalists who approve the embargo in their judgments, and at any rate would not court

---

[1] Sullivan to Jefferson, July 23, 1808; Jefferson MSS.
[2] Jefferson to Lincoln, Aug. 9, 1808; Works, v. 334.
[3] Jefferson to Gallatin, Aug. 11, 1808; Works, v. 336.
[4] Jefferson to Gallatin, Aug. 19, 1808; Works, v. 346.

mob law, would crush it in embryo. I have some time ago written to General Dearborn to be on the alert on such an occasion, and to take direction of the public authority on the spot. Such an incident will rally the whole body of Republicans of every shade to a single point,—that of supporting the public authority."

The Federalists knew when to rebel. Jefferson could teach them little on that subject. They meant first to overthrow Jefferson himself, and were in a fair way to gratify their wish; for the people of New England—Republican and Federalist alike—were rapidly rallying to common hatred of the President. As winter approached, the struggle between Jefferson and Massachusetts became on both sides vindictive. He put whole communities under his ban. He stopped the voyage of every vessel "in which any person is concerned, either in interest or in navigating her, who has ever been concerned in interest or in the navigation of a vessel which has at any time before entered a foreign port contrary to the views of the embargo laws, and under any pretended distress or duress whatever."[1] When a permit was asked for the schooner "Caroline," of Buckstown on the Penobscot, Jefferson replied,—

"This is the first time that the character of the place has been brought under consideration as an objection. Yet a general disobedience to the laws in any place must have weight toward refusing to give them any facilities to evade. In such a case we may fairly require positive proof that the individual of a town tainted with a general spirit of disobedience has never said or done anything himself to countenance that spirit."[2]

Jefferson went still further in his reply to a petition from the island of Nantucket for food. "Our opinion here is that that place has been so deeply concerned in smuggling, that if it wants it is because it has illegally sent away what it ought to have retained for its own consumption."[3]

Of all the old Republican arguments for a policy of peace,

[1] Jefferson to Gallatin, Dec. 7, 1808; Works, v. 396.
[2] Jefferson to Gallatin, Nov. 13, 1808; Works, v. 386.
[3] Jefferson to Levi Lincoln, Nov. 13, 1808; Works, v. 387.

the commonest was that a standing army would be dangerous, not to foreign enemies, but to popular liberties; yet the
first use of the new army and gunboats was against fellow-
citizens. New England was chiefly controlled by the navy; but
in New York the army was needed and was employed. Open
insurrection existed there. Besides forcible resistance offered
to the law, no one was ignorant that the collectors shut their
eyes to smuggling, and that juries, in defiance of court and
President, refused to indict rioters. Governor Tompkins announced that Oswego was in active insurrection, and called
on the President to issue a proclamation to that effect.[1] Jefferson replied by offering to take into the United States service the militia required to suppress the riots, and begged
Governor Tompkins to lead his troops in person. "I think it
so important in example to crush these audacious proceedings
and to make the offenders feel the consequences of individuals daring to oppose a law by force, that no effort should be
spared to compass this object."[2]

When permission was asked to establish a packet on Lake
Champlain, "I do not think this is a time," replied Jefferson,
"for opening new channels of intercourse with Canada and
multiplying the means of smuggling."[3] The people who lived
on the shores of Lake Champlain might object to such interference in their affairs, but could not deny the force of Jefferson's reasoning. Another application of a different kind was
rejected on grounds that seemed to give to the President general supervision over the diet of the people: —

"The declaration of the bakers of New York that their
citizens will be dissatisfied, under the present circumstances
of their country, to eat bread of the flour of their own
State, is equally a libel on the produce and citizens of the
State. . . . If this prevails, the next application will be for
vessels to go to New York for the pippins of that State,
because they are higher flavored than the same species of
apples growing in other States."[4]

[1] Gallatin to Jefferson, July 29, 1808; Gallatin's Writings, i. 396.
[2] Jefferson to Governor Tompkins, Aug. 15, 1808; Works, v. 343.
[3] Jefferson to the Secretary of the Treasury, Sept. 9, 1808; Works, v. 363.
[4] Jefferson to Gallatin, July 12, 1808; Works, v. 307.

The same sumptuary rule applied to Louisiana. "You know I have been averse to letting Atlantic flour go to New Orleans merely that they may have the *whitest* bread possible."[1]

The President seemed alone to feel this passionate earnestness on behalf of the embargo. His Cabinet looked on with alarm and disgust. Madison took no share in the task of enforcement. Robert Smith sent frigates and gunboats hither and thither, but made no concealment of his feelings. "Most fervently," he wrote to Gallatin, "ought we to pray to be relieved from the various embarrassments of this said embargo. Upon it there will in some of the States, in the course of the next two months, assuredly be engendered monsters. Would that we could be placed on proper ground for calling in this mischief-making busy-body."[2] Smith talked freely, while Gallatin, whose opinion was probably the same, said little, and labored to carry out the law, but seemed at times disposed to press on the President's attention the deformities of his favorite monster.

"I am perfectly satisfied," wrote Gallatin to the President July 29,[3] "that if the embargo must be persisted in any longer, two principles must necessarily be adopted in order to make it sufficient: First, that not a single vessel shall be permitted to move without the special permission of the Executive; Second, that the collectors be invested with the general power of seizing property anywhere, and taking the rudders, or otherwise effectually preventing the departure of any vessel in harbor, though ostensibly intended to remain there,—and that without being liable to personal suits. I am sensible that such arbitrary powers are equally dangerous and odious; but a restrictive measure of the nature of the embargo, applied to a nation under such circumstances as the United States, cannot be enforced without the assistance of means as strong as the measure itself. To that legal authority to prevent, seize, and detain, must be added a sufficient physical force to carry it into effect; and although I believe that in our seaports little

[1] Jefferson to Gallatin, Sept. 9, 1808; Works, v. 363.
[2] Smith to Gallatin, Aug. 1, 1808; Adams's Gallatin, p. 373.
[3] Gallatin to Jefferson, July 19, 1808; Gallatin's Writings, i. 396.

1108   SECOND ADMINISTRATION OF JEFFERSON

difficulty would be encountered, we must have a little army along the Lakes and British lines generally. . . . That in the present situation of the world every effort should be attempted to preserve the peace of this nation, cannot be doubted; but if the criminal party-rage of Federalists and Tories shall have so far succeeded as to defeat our endeavors to obtain that object by the only measure that could possibly have effected it, we must submit and prepare for war."

"I mean generally to express an opinion," continued the secretary, "founded on the experience of this summer, that Congress must either invest the Executive with the most arbitrary powers and sufficient force to carry the embargo into effect, or give it up altogether." That Jefferson should permit a member of his Cabinet to suggest the assumption of "the most arbitrary powers;" that he should tolerate the idea of using means "equally dangerous and odious,"—seemed incredible; but his reply showed no sign of offence. He instantly responded,—

> "I am satisfied with you that if Orders and Decrees are not repealed, and a continuance of the embargo is preferred to war (which sentiment is universal here), Congress must legalize all means which may be necessary to obtain its end."[1]

If repeated and menacing warnings from the people, the State authorities, and officers of the national government failed to produce an impression on the President's mind, he was little likely to regard what came from the Judiciary; yet the sharpest of his irritations was caused by a judge whom he had himself, in 1804, placed on the Supreme Bench to counteract Marshall's influence. Some merchants of Charleston, with consent of the collector and district-attorney, applied for a mandamus to oblige the collector of that town to clear certain ships for Baltimore. The collector admitted that he believed the voyage to be intended in good faith, and that under the Embargo Law he had no right of detention; but he laid Secretary Gallatin's instructions before the court. The case was submitted without argument, and Justice William John-

[1] Jefferson to Gallatin, Aug. 11, 1808; Works, v. 336.

son, of the South Carolina circuit,—a native of South Carolina, and a warm friend of the President,—decided that the
Act of Congress did not warrant detention, and that without
the sanction of law the collector was not justified by instructions from the Executive in increasing the restraints upon
commerce. The mandamus issued.

These proceedings troubled but did not check the President. "I saw them with great concern," he wrote to the governor of South Carolina,[1] "because of the quarter from
whence they came, and where they could not be ascribed to
any political waywardness." Rodney, the attorney-general,
undertook to overrule Justice Johnson's law, and wrote, under
the President's instructions, an official opinion that the court
had no power to issue a mandamus in such a case. This opinion was published in the newspapers at the end of July, "an
act unprecedented in the history of executive conduct," which
in a manner forced Justice Johnson into a newspaper controversy. The Judge's defence of his course was temperate and
apparently convincing to himself, although five years afterward he delivered an opinion[2] of the whole Supreme Court
in a similar case, "unquestionably inconsistent" with his embargo decision, which he then placed on technical ground.
He never regained Jefferson's confidence, and so effective was
the ban that in the following month of December the Georgia
grand-jury, in his own circuit, made him the object of a presentment for "improper interference with the Executive."

If the conduct of Justice Johnson only stimulated the President's exercise of power, the constitutional arguments of
Federalist lawyers and judges were unlikely to have any better
effect; yet to a Virginia Republican of 1798 no question could
have deeper interest than that of the constitutionality of the
embargo. The subject had already been discussed in Congress,
and had called out a difference of opinion. There, Randolph
argued against the constitutionality in a speech never reported, which turned on the distinction between regulating
commerce and destroying it; between a restriction limited
in time and scope, and an interdict absolute and permanent.
The opponents of the embargo system, both Federalists and

[1] Jefferson to Governor Pinckney, July 18, 1808; Works, v. 322.
[2] McIntyre v. Wood, March, 1813; 7 Cranch, p. 504.

Republicans, took the same ground. The Constitution, they said, empowered Congress "to *regulate* commerce with foreign nations, and among the several States, and with the Indian tribes;" but no one ever supposed it to grant Congress the power "to *prohibit* commerce with foreign nations, and among the several States, and with the Indian tribes." Had such words been employed, the Constitution could not have gained the vote of a single State.

History has nothing to do with law except to record the development of legal principles. The question whether the embargo was or was not Constitutional depended for an answer on the decision of Congress, President, and Judiciary, and the assent of the States. Whatever unanimous decision these political bodies might make, no matter how extravagant, was law until it should be reversed. No theory could control the meaning of the Constitution; but the relation between facts and theories was a political matter, and between the embargo and the old Virginia theory of the Constitution no relation could be imagined. Whatever else was doubtful, no one could doubt that under the doctrine of States-rights and the rules of strict construction the embargo was unconstitutional. Only by the widest theories of liberal construction could its constitutionality be sustained.

The arguments in its favor were arguments which had been once regarded as fatal to public liberty. The first was made by Richard M. Johnson of Kentucky: "If we have power to lay an embargo for one day, have we not the power to renew it at the end of that day? If for sixty days, have we not the power to renew it again? Would it not amount to the same thing? If we pass a law to expire within a limited term, we may renew it at the end of that term; and there is no difference between a power to do this, and a power to pass laws without specified limit."[1] This principle, if sound, might be applied to the right of habeas corpus or of free speech, to the protection of American manufactures or to the issue of paper money as a legal tender; and whenever such application should be made, the Union must submit to take its chance of the consequences sure to follow the removal of specified

[1] Annals of Congress, 1807–1808, p. 2091.

limits to power. Another argument was used by David R. Williams, a representative South Carolinian. "The embargo is not an annihilation but a suspension of commerce," he urged,[1] "to regain the advantages of which it has been robbed." If Congress had the right to regulate commerce for such a purpose in 1808, South Carolina seemed to have no excuse for questioning, twenty years later, the constitutionality of a protective system. Still another argument was used by George W. Campbell of Tennessee.

"A limited embargo," he said,[2] "can only mean an embargo that is to terminate at some given time; and the length of time, if a hundred years, will not change the character of the embargo,— it is still limited. If it be constitutional to lay it for one day, it must be equally so to lay it for ten days or a hundred days or as many years,— it would still be a limited embargo; and no one will, I presume, deny that an embargo laid for such a length of time, and one laid without limitation, would in reality and to all practical purposes be the same."

This reasoning was supported by an immense majority in both Houses of Congress; was accepted as sound by the Executive, and roused no protest from the legislature of any Southern State. So far as concerned all these high political authorities, the principle was thus settled that the Constitution, under the power to regulate commerce, conferred upon Congress the power to suspend foreign commerce forever; to suspend or otherwise regulate domestic and inter-state commerce; to subject all industry to governmental control, if such interference in the opinion of Congress was necessary or proper for carrying out its purpose; and finally, to vest in the President discretionary power to execute or to suspend the system, in whole or in part.

The Judiciary had still to be consulted. In the September Term, 1808, an embargo case was argued at Salem before John Davis, judge of the District Court for Massachusetts; and Samuel Dexter, the ablest lawyer in New England, urged the constitutional objections to the embargo with all the force

[1] Annals of Congress, 1807–1808, p. 2130.
[2] Annals of Congress, p. 2147.

that ability and conviction could give. No sounder Federalist than Judge Davis sat on the bench; but although the newspapers of his party were declaiming against the constitutionality of the law, and although Chief-Justice Parsons, of the Massachusetts Supreme Court, the most eminent legal authority in the State, lent his private influence on the same side, Judge Davis calmly laid down the old Federalist rule of broad construction. His opinion, elaborately argued and illustrated, was printed in every newspaper.

"Stress has been laid in argument," he said, "on the word 'regulate,' as implying in itself a limitation. Power to 'regulate,' it is said, cannot be understood to give a power to annihilate. To this it may be replied that the Acts under consideration, though of very ample extent, do not operate as a prohibition of all foreign commerce. It will be admitted that partial prohibitions are authorized by the expression; and how shall the degree or extent of the prohibition be adjusted but by the discretion of the national government, to whom the subject appears to be committed."

In the Federalist spirit the Judge invoked the "necessary and proper" clause, which had been the cloak for every assumption of doubtful powers; and then passed to the doctrine of "inherent sovereignty," the radical line of division between the party of President Washington and that of President Jefferson:—

"Further, the power to regulate commerce is not to be confined to the adoption of measures exclusively beneficial to commerce itself, or tending to its advancement; but in our national system, as in all modern sovereignties, it is also to be considered as an instrument for other purposes of general policy and interest. The mode of its management is a consideration of great delicacy and importance; but the national right or power to adapt regulations of commerce to other purposes than the mere advancement of commerce appears to me unquestionable."

After drawing these conclusions from the power to regulate commerce, the Judge went a step further, and summoned to his aid the spirits which haunted the dreams of every true Republican,—the power of war, and necessity of State:—

> "Congress has power to declare war. It of course has power to prepare for war; and the time, the manner, and the measure, in the application of constitutional means, seem to be left to its wisdom and discretion. Foreign intercourse becomes in such times a subject of peculiar interest, and its regulation forms an obvious and essential branch of federal administration. . . . It seems to have been admitted in the argument that State necessity might justify a limited embargo, or suspension of all foreign commerce; but if Congress have the power, for purposes of safety, of preparation, or counteraction, to suspend commercial intercourse with foreign nations, where do we find them limited as to the duration more than as to the manner and extent of the measure?"

Against this remarkable decision Dexter did not venture to appeal. Strong as his own convictions were, he knew the character of Chief-Justice Marshall's law too well to hope for success at Washington. One of Marshall's earliest constitutional decisions had deduced from the power of Congress to pay debts the right for government to assume a preference over all other creditors in satisfying its claims on the assets of a bankrupt.[1] Constructive power could hardly go further; and the habit of mind which led to such a conclusion would hardly shrink from sustaining Judge Davis's law.

Yet the embargo, in spite of Executive, Legislative, Judicial, and State authorities, rankled in the side of the Constitution. Even Joseph Story, though in after life a convert to Marshall's doctrines, could never wholly reconcile himself to the legislation of 1808.

> "I have ever," he wrote, "considered the embargo a measure which went to the utmost limit of constructive power under the Constitution. It stands upon the extreme verge of the Constitution, being in its very form and

[1] United States *v.* Fisher and others, February Term, 1805; Cranch's Reports, ii. 358–405.

terms an unlimited prohibition or suspension of foreign commerce."[1]

That President Jefferson should exercise "dangerous and odious" powers, carrying the extremest principles of his Federalist predecessors to their extremest results; that he should in doing so invite bloodshed, strain his military resources, quarrel with the State authorities of his own party and with judges whom he had himself made; that he should depend for constitutional law on Federalist judges whose doctrines he had hitherto believed fatal to liberty,—these were the first fruits of the embargo. After such an experience, if he or his party again raised the cry of States-rights, or of strict construction, the public might, with some foundation of reason, set such complaints aside as factious and frivolous, and even, in any other mouth than that of John Randolph, as treasonable.

[1] Story's Life of Story, i. 185.

Chapter XII

THE EMBARGO was an experiment in politics well worth making. In the scheme of President Jefferson's statesmanship, non-intercourse was the substitute for war,—the weapon of defence and coercion which saved the cost and danger of supporting army or navy, and spared America the brutalities of the Old World. Failure of the embargo meant in his mind not only a recurrence to the practice of war, but to every political and social evil that war had always brought in its train. In such a case the crimes and corruptions of Europe, which had been the object of his political fears, must, as he believed, sooner or later teem in the fat soil of America. To avert a disaster so vast, was a proper motive for statesmanship, and justified disregard for smaller interests. Jefferson understood better than his friends the importance of his experiment; and when in pursuing his object he trampled upon personal rights and public principles, he did so, as he avowed in the Louisiana purchase, because he believed that a higher public interest required the sacrifice:—

"My principle is, that the conveniences of our citizens shall yield reasonably, and their taste greatly, to the importance of giving the present experiment so fair a trial that on future occasions our legislators may know with certainty how far they may count on it as an engine for national purposes."[1]

Hence came his repeated entreaties for severity, even to the point of violence and bloodshed:—

"I do consider the severe enforcement of the embargo to be of an importance not to be measured by money, for our future government as well as present objects."[2]

Everywhere, on all occasions, he proclaimed that embargo was the alternative to war. The question next to be decided was brought by this means into the prominence it deserved.

[1] Jefferson to Gallatin, July 12, 1808; Works, v. 307.
[2] Jefferson to Robert Smith, July 16, 1808; Works, v. 316.

Of the two systems of statesmanship, which was the most costly,—which the most efficient?

The dread of war, radical in the Republican theory, sprang not so much from the supposed waste of life or resources as from the retroactive effects which war must exert upon the form of government; but the experience of a few months showed that the embargo as a system was rapidly leading to the same effects. Indeed, the embargo and the Louisiana purchase taken together were more destructive to the theory and practice of a Virginia republic than any foreign war was likely to be. Personal liberties and rights of property were more directly curtailed in the United States by embargo than in Great Britain by centuries of almost continuous foreign war. No one denied that a permanent embargo strained the Constitution to the uttermost tension; and even the Secretary of the Treasury and the President admitted that it required the exercise of most arbitrary, odious, and dangerous powers. From this point of view the system was quickly seen to have few advantages. If American liberties must perish, they might as well be destroyed by war as be stifled by non-intercourse.

While the constitutional cost of the two systems was not altogether unlike, the economical cost was a point not easily settled. No one could say what might be the financial expense of embargo as compared with war. Yet Jefferson himself in the end admitted that the embargo had no claim to respect as an economical measure. The Boston Federalists estimated that the net American loss of income, exclusive of that on freights, could not be less than ten per cent for interest and profit on the whole export of the country,—or ten million eight hundred thousand dollars on a total export value of one hundred and eight millions.[1] This estimate was extravagant, even if the embargo had been wholly responsible for cutting off American trade; it represented in fact the loss resulting to America from Napoleon's decrees, the British orders, and the embargo taken together. Yet at least the embargo was more destructive than war would have been to the interests of foreign commerce. Even in the worst of foreign wars American commerce could not be wholly stopped,—some outlet for

[1] Speech of Josiah Quincy, Nov. 28, 1808; Annals of Congress, 1808, 1809, p. 543.

American produce must always remain open, some inward bound ships would always escape the watch of a blockading squadron. Even in 1814, after two years of war, and when the coast was stringently blockaded, the American Treasury collected six million dollars from imports; but in 1808, after the embargo was in full effect, the customs yielded only a few thousand dollars on cargoes that happened to be imported for some special purpose. The difference was loss, to the disadvantage of embargo. To this must be added loss of freight, decay of ships and produce, besides enforced idleness to a corresponding extent; and finally the cost of a war if the embargo system should fail.

In other respects the system was still costly. The citizen was not killed, but he was partially paralyzed. Government did not waste money or life, but prevented both money and labor from having their former value. If long continued, embargo must bankrupt the government almost as certainly as war; if not long continued, the immediate shock to industry was more destructive than war would have been. The expense of war proved, five years afterward, to be about thirty million dollars a year, and of this sum much the larger portion was pure loss; but in 1808, owing to the condition of Europe, the expense need not have exceeded twenty millions, and the means at hand were greater. The effect of the embargo was certainly no greater than the effect of war in stimulating domestic industry. In either case the stimulus was temporary and ineffective; but the embargo cut off the resources of credit and capital, while war gave both an artificial expansion. The result was that while embargo saved perhaps twenty millions of dollars a year and some thousands of lives which war would have consumed, it was still an expensive system, and in some respects more destructive than war itself to national wealth.

The economical was less serious than the moral problem. The strongest objection to war was not its waste of money or even of life; for money and life in political economy were worth no more than they could be made to produce. A worse evil was the lasting harm caused by war to the morals of mankind, which no system of economy could calculate. The reign of brute force and brutal methods corrupted and debauched society, making it blind to its own vices and ambitious only for mischief. Yet even on that ground the embargo had few advantages. The peaceable coercion which Jefferson tried to substitute for war was less brutal, but hardly less mischievous, than the evil it displaced. The embargo opened the sluice-gates of social corruption. Every citizen was tempted to evade or defy the laws. At every point along the coast and frontier the civil, military, and naval services were brought in contact with corruption; while every man in private life was placed under strong motives to corrupt. Every article produced or consumed in the country became an object of speculation; every form of industry became a form of gambling. The rich could alone profit in the end; while the poor must sacrifice at any loss the little they could produce.

If war made men brutal, at least it made them strong; it called out the qualities best fitted to survive in the struggle for existence. To risk life for one's country was no mean act even when done for selfish motives; and to die that others might more happily live was the highest act of self-sacrifice to be reached by man. War, with all its horrors, could purify as well as debase; it dealt with high motives and vast interests; taught courage, discipline, and stern sense of duty. Jefferson must have asked himself in vain what lessons of heroism or duty were taught by his system of peaceable coercion, which turned every citizen into an enemy of the laws,—preaching the fear of war and of self-sacrifice, making many smugglers and traitors, but not a single hero.

If the cost of the embargo was extravagant in its effects on the Constitution, the economy, and the morals of the nation, its political cost to the party in power was ruinous. War could have worked no more violent revolution. The trial was too severe for human nature to endure. At a moment's notice, without avowing his true reasons, President Jefferson bade foreign commerce to cease. As the order was carried along the seacoast, every artisan dropped his tools, every merchant closed his doors, every ship was dismantled. American produce —wheat, timber, cotton, tobacco, rice—dropped in value or became unsalable; every imported article rose in price; wages stopped; swarms of debtors became bankrupt; thousands of sailors hung idle round the wharves trying to find employment on coasters, and escape to the West Indies or Nova

Scotia. A reign of idleness began; and the men who were not already ruined felt that their ruin was only a matter of time.

The British traveller, Lambert, who visited New York in 1808, described it as resembling a place ravaged by pestilence:[1] —

> "The port indeed was full of shipping, but they were dismantled and laid up; their decks were cleared, their hatches fastened down, and scarcely a sailor was to be found on board. Not a box, bale, cask, barrel, or package was to be seen upon the wharves. Many of the counting-houses were shut up, or advertised to be let; and the few solitary merchants, clerks, porters, and laborers that were to be seen were walking about with their hands in their pockets. The coffee-houses were almost empty; the streets, near the water-side, were almost deserted; the grass had begun to grow upon the wharves."

In New England, where the struggle of existence was keenest, the embargo struck like a thunderbolt, and society for a moment thought itself at an end. Foreign commerce and shipping were the life of the people, — the ocean, as Pickering said, was their farm. The outcry of suffering interests became every day more violent, as the public learned that this paralysis was not a matter of weeks, but of months or years. New Englanders as a class were a law-abiding people; but from the earliest moments of their history they had largely qualified their obedience to the law by the violence with which they abused and the ingenuity with which they evaded it. Against the embargo and Jefferson they concentrated the clamor and passion of their keen and earnest nature. Rich and poor, young and old, joined in the chorus; and one lad, barely in his teens, published what he called "The Embargo: a Satire," —a boyish libel on Jefferson, which the famous poet and Democrat would afterward have given much to recall: —

> "And thou, the scorn of every patriot name,
>   Thy country's ruin, and her councils' shame.
>
>   .   .   .   .
>
>   Go, wretch! Resign the Presidential chair,

[1] Lambert's Travels, ii. 64, 65.

Disclose thy secret measures, foul or fair;
Go search with curious eye for hornèd frogs
'Mid the wild waste of Louisiana bogs;
Or where Ohio rolls his turbid stream
Dig for huge bones, thy glory and thy theme."[1]

The belief that Jefferson, sold to France, wished to destroy American commerce and to strike a deadly blow at New and Old England at once, maddened the sensitive temper of the people. Immense losses, sweeping away their savings and spreading bankruptcy through every village, gave ample cause for their complaints. Yet in truth, New England was better able to defy the embargo than she was willing to suppose. She lost nothing except profits which the belligerents had in any case confiscated; her timber would not harm for keeping, and her fish were safe in the ocean. The embargo gave her almost a monopoly of the American market for domestic manufactures; no part of the country was so well situated or so well equipped for smuggling. Above all, she could easily economize. The New Englander knew better than any other American how to cut down his expenses to the uttermost point of parsimony; and even when he became bankrupt he had but to begin anew. His energy, shrewdness, and education were a capital which the embargo could not destroy, but rather helped to improve.

The growers of wheat and live stock in the Middle States were more hardly treated. Their wheat, reduced in value from two dollars to seventy-five cents a bushel, became practically unsalable. Debarred a market for their produce at a moment when every article of common use tended to rise in cost, they were reduced to the necessity of living on the produce of their farms; but the task was not then so difficult as in later times, and the cities still furnished local markets not to be despised. The manufacturers of Pennsylvania could not but feel the stimulus of the new demand; so violent a system of protection was never applied to them before or since. Probably for that reason the embargo was not so unpopular in Pennsylvania as elsewhere, and Jefferson had nothing to

[1] The Embargo; or Sketches of the Times. A Satire. By William Cullen Bryant. 1808.

fear from political revolution in this calm and plodding community.

The true burden of the embargo fell on the Southern States, but most severely upon the great State of Virginia. Slowly decaying, but still half patriarchal, Virginia society could neither economize nor liquidate. Tobacco was worthless; but four hundred thousand negro slaves must be clothed and fed, great establishments must be kept up, the social scale of living could not be reduced, and even bankruptcy could not clear a large landed estate without creating new encumbrances in a country where land and negroes were the only forms of property on which money could be raised. Stay-laws were tried, but served only to prolong the agony. With astonishing rapidity Virginia succumbed to ruin, while continuing to support the system that was draining her strength. No episode in American history was more touching than the generous devotion with which Virginia clung to the embargo, and drained the poison which her own President held obstinately to her lips. The cotton and rice States had less to lose, and could more easily bear bankruptcy; ruin was to them— except in Charleston—a word of little meaning; but the old society of Virginia could never be restored. Amid the harsh warnings of John Randolph it saw its agonies approach; and its last representative, heir to all its honors and dignities, President Jefferson himself woke from his long dream of power only to find his own fortunes buried in the ruin he had made.

Except in a state of society verging on primitive civilization, the stoppage of all foreign intercourse could not have been attempted by peaceable means. The attempt to deprive the laborer of sugar, salt, tea, coffee, molasses, and rum; to treble the price of every yard of coarse cottons and woollens; to reduce by one half the wages of labor, and to double its burdens,—this was a trial more severe than war; and even when attempted by the whole continent of Europe, with all the resources of manufactures and wealth which the civilization of a thousand years had supplied, the experiment required the despotic power of Napoleon and the united armies of France, Austria, and Russia to carry it into effect. Even then it failed. Jefferson, Madison, and the Southern Republicans had no idea of the economical difficulties their system created, and were surprised to find American society so complex even in their own Southern States that the failure of two successive crops to find a sale threatened beggary to every rich planter from the Delaware to the Sabine. During the first few months, while ships continued to arrive from abroad and old stores were consumed at home, the full pressure of the embargo was not felt; but as the summer of 1808 passed, the outcry became violent. In the Southern States, almost by common consent debts remained unpaid, and few men ventured to oppose a political system which was peculiarly a Southern invention; but in the Northern States, where the bankrupt laws were enforced and the habits of business were comparatively strict, the cost of the embargo was soon shown in the form of political revolution.

The relapse of Massachusetts to Federalism and the overthrow of Senator Adams in the spring of 1808 were the first signs of the political price which President Jefferson must pay for his passion of peace. In New York the prospect was little better. Governor Morgan Lewis, elected in 1804 over Aaron Burr by a combination of Clintons and Livingstons, was turned out of office in 1807 by the Clintons. Governor Daniel D. Tompkins, his successor, was supposed to be a representative of De Witt Clinton and Ambrose Spencer. To De Witt Clinton the State of New York seemed in 1807 a mere appendage,—a political property which he could control at will; and of all American politicians next to Aaron Burr none had shown such indifference to party as he. No one could predict his course, except that it would be shaped according to what seemed to be the interests of his ambition. He began by declaring himself against the embargo, and soon afterward declared himself for it. In truth, he was for or against it as the majority might decide; and in New York a majority could hardly fail to decide against the embargo. At the spring election of 1808, which took place about May 1, the Federalists made large gains in the legislature. The summer greatly increased their strength, until Madison's friends trembled for the result, and their language became despondent beyond reason. Gallatin, who knew best the difficulties created by the embargo, began to despair. June 29 he wrote: "From present appearances the Federalists will turn us out by 4th of March next." Ten days afterward he explained the reason of his fears: "I think that Vermont is lost; New Hampshire is in a bad neighborhood; and Pennsylvania is extremely doubtful." In August he thought the situation so serious that he warned the President: —

> "There is almost an equal chance that if propositions from Great Britain, or other events, do not put it in our power to raise the embargo before the 1st of October, we will lose the Presidential election. I think that at this moment the Western States, Virginia, South Carolina, and perhaps Georgia are the only sound States, and that we will have a doubtful contest in every other."[1]

Two causes saved Madison. In the first place, the opposition failed to concentrate its strength. Neither George Clinton nor James Monroe could control the whole body of opponents to the embargo. After waiting till the middle of August for some arrangement to be made, leading Federalists held a conference at New York, where they found themselves obliged, by the conduct of De Witt Clinton, to give up the hope of a coalition. Clinton decided not to risk his fortunes for the sake of his uncle the Vice President; and this decision obliged the Federalists to put a candidate of their own in the field. They named C. C. Pinckney of South Carolina for President, and Rufus King of New York for Vice-President, as in 1804.

From the moment his opponents divided themselves among three candidates, Madison had nothing to fear; but even without this good fortune he possessed an advantage that weighed decisively in his favor. The State legislatures had been chosen chiefly in the spring or summer, when the embargo was still comparatively popular; and in most cases, but particularly in New York, the legislature still chose Presidential electors. The people expressed no direct opinion on national politics, except in regard to Congressmen. State after State deserted to the Federalists without affecting the general election. Early in September Vermont elected a Federalist governor, but the swarm of rotten boroughs in the State

[1] Adams's Gallatin, 373, 374.

secured a Republican legislature, which immediately chose electors for Madison. The revolution in Vermont surrendered all New England to the Federalists. New Hampshire chose Presidential electors by popular vote; Rhode Island did the same,—and both States, by fair majorities, rejected Madison and voted for Pinckney. In Massachusetts and Connecticut the legislatures chose Federalist electors. Thus all New England declared against the Administration; and had Vermont been counted as she voted in September, the opposition would have received forty-five electoral votes from New England, where in 1804 it had received only nine. In New York the opponents of the embargo were very strong, and the nineteen electoral votes of that State might in a popular election have been taken from Madison. In this case Pennsylvania would have decided the result. Eighty-eight electoral votes were needed for a choice. New England, New York, and Delaware represented sixty-seven. Maryland and North Carolina were so doubtful that if Pennsylvania had deserted Madison, they would probably have followed her, and would have left the Republican party a wreck.

The choice of electors by the legislatures of Vermont and New York defeated all chance of overthrowing Madison; but apart from these accidents of management the result was already decided by the people of Pennsylvania. The wave of Federalist success and political revolution stopped short in New York, and once more the Democracy of Pennsylvania steadied and saved the Administration. At the October election of 1808,—old Governor McKean having at last retired,—Simon Snyder was chosen governor by a majority of more than twenty thousand votes. The new governor was the candidate of Duane and the extreme Democrats; his triumph stopped the current of Federalist success, and enabled Madison's friends to drive hesitating Republicans back to their party. In Virginia, Monroe was obliged to retire from the contest, and his supporters dwindled in numbers until only two or three thousand went to the polls. In New York, De Witt Clinton contented himself with taking from Madison six of the nineteen electoral votes and giving them to Vice-President Clinton. Thus the result showed comparatively little sign of the true Republican loss; yet in the electoral college where in 1804 Jefferson had received the voices of one hundred and sixty-two electors, Madison in 1808 received only one hundred and twenty-two votes. The Federalist minority rose from fourteen to forty-seven.

In the elections to Congress the same effects were shown. The Federalists doubled their number of Congressmen, but the huge Republican majority could well bear reduction. The true character of the Eleventh Congress could not be foretold by the party vote. Many Northern Republicans chosen to Congress were as hostile to the embargo as though they had been Federalists. Elected on the issue of embargo or anti-embargo, the Congress which was to last till March 5, 1811, was sure to be factious; but whether factious or united, it could have neither policy nor leader. The election decided its own issue. The true issue thenceforward was that of war; but on this point the people had not been asked to speak, and their representatives would not dare without their encouragement to act.

The Republican party by a supreme effort kept itself in office; but no one could fail to see that if nine months of embargo had so shattered Jefferson's power, another such year would shake the Union itself. The cost of this "engine for national purposes" exceeded all calculation. Financially, it emptied the Treasury, bankrupted the mercantile and agricultural class, and ground the poor beyond endurance. Constitutionally, it overrode every specified limit on arbitrary power and made Congress despotic, while it left no bounds to the authority which might be vested by Congress in the President. Morally, it sapped the nation's vital force, lowering its courage, paralyzing its energy, corrupting its principles, and arraying all the active elements of society in factious opposition to government or in secret paths of treason. Politically, it cost Jefferson the fruits of eight years painful labor for popularity, and brought the Union to the edge of a precipice.

Finally, frightful as the cost of this engine was, as a means of coercion the embargo evidently failed. The President complained of evasion, and declared that if the measure were faithfully executed it would produce the desired effect; but the people knew better. In truth, the law was faithfully executed. The price-lists of Liverpool and London, the published

returns from Jamaica and Havana, proved that American produce was no longer to be bought abroad. On the continent
of Europe commerce had ceased before the embargo was laid,
and its coercive effects were far exceeded by Napoleon's own
restrictions; yet not a sign came from Europe to show that
Napoleon meant to give way. From England came an answer
to the embargo, but not such as promised its success. On all
sides evidence accumulated that the embargo, as an engine of
coercion, needed a long period of time to produce a decided
effect. The law of physics could easily be applied to politics;
force could be converted only into its equivalent force. If the
embargo—an exertion of force less violent than war—was to
do the work of war, it must extend over a longer time the
development of an equivalent energy. Wars lasted for many
years, and the embargo must be calculated to last much
longer than any war; but meanwhile the morals, courage, and
political liberties of the American people must be perverted
or destroyed; agriculture and shipping must perish; the
Union itself could not be preserved.

Under the shock of these discoveries Jefferson's vast popularity vanished, and the labored fabric of his reputation fell in
sudden and general ruin. America began slowly to struggle,
under the consciousness of pain, toward a conviction that she
must bear the common burdens of humanity, and fight with
the weapons of other races in the same bloody arena; that she
could not much longer delude herself with hopes of evading
laws of Nature and instincts of life; and that her new statesmanship which made peace a passion could lead to no better
result than had been reached by the barbarous system which
made war a duty.

Chapter XIII

WHILE THE PEOPLE of the United States waited to see the effect of the embargo on Europe, Europe watched with breathless interest the death-throes of Spain.

The Emperor Napoleon, in December, 1807, hurried in triumphal progress from one ancient city to another, through his Italian kingdom, while his armies steadily crossed the Pyrenees, and spread over every road between Bayonne and Lisbon. From Madrid, Godoy saw that the end was near. Until that moment he had counted with certainty on the devotion of the Spanish people to their old King. In the last months of 1807 he learned that even Spanish loyalty could not survive the miseries of such a reign. Conspiracy appeared in the Escorial itself. Ferdinand, Prince of the Asturias, only son of Don Carlos IV., was discovered in a plot for dethroning his father by aid of Napoleon. Ferdinand was but twenty-three years old; yet even in the flower of youth he showed no social quality. Dull, obstinate, sullen, just shrewd enough to be suspicious, and with just enough passion to make him vindictive, Ferdinand was destined to become the last and worst of the Spanish Bourbon kings; yet in the year 1807 he had a strong bond of sympathy with the people, for he hated and feared his father and mother and the Prince of Peace. Public patience, exhausted by endless disaster, and outraged by the King's incompetence, the Queen's supposed amours, and Godoy's parade of royal rank and power, vanished at the news that Ferdinand shared in the popular disgust; and the Prince of Peace suddenly woke to find the old King already dethroned in his subjects' love, while the Prince of the Asturias, who was fitted only for confinement in an asylum, had become the popular ideal of virtue and reform.

Godoy stifled Ferdinand's intrigue, and took from Napoleon that pretext for interference; but he gained at most only a brief respite for King Charles. The pardon of Ferdinand was issued Nov. 5, 1807; December 23, Napoleon sent from Milan to his minister of war orders[1] to concentrate armies for occupying the whole peninsula, and to establish the magazines

---

[1] Napoleon to General Clarke, Dec. 23, 1807; Correspondance, xvi. 212.

necessary for their support. He was almost ready to act; and his return to Paris, Jan. 3, 1808, announced to those who were in the secret that the new drama would soon begin.

Among the most interested of his audience was General Armstrong, who had longed, since 1805, for a chance to meet the Emperor with his own weapons, and who knew that Napoleon's schemes required control of North and South America, which would warrant Jefferson in imposing rather than in receiving terms for Florida. Whatever these terms might be, Napoleon must grant them, or must yield the Americas to England's naval supremacy. The plan as Armstrong saw it was both safe and sure. Napoleon made no secret of his wants. Whatever finesse he may have used in the earlier stage of his policy was flung aside after his return to Paris, January 3. In reply to Armstrong's remonstrances against the Milan Decree, the Emperor ordered Champagny to use the language of command:[1] —

> "Answer Mr. Armstrong, that I am ashamed to discuss points of which the injustice is so evident; but that in the position in which England has put the Continent, I do not doubt of the United States declaring war against her, especially on account of her decree of November 11; that however great may be the evil resulting to America from war, every man of sense will prefer it to a recognition of the monstrous principles and of the anarchy which that Government wants to establish on the seas; that in my mind I regard war as declared between England and America from the day when England published her decrees; that, for the rest, I have ordered that the American vessels should remain sequestered, to be disposed of as shall be necessary according to circumstances."

No coarser methods were known to diplomacy than those which Napoleon commonly took whenever the moment for action came. Not only did he thus hold millions of American property sequestered as a pledge for the obedience of America, but he also offered a bribe to the United States government. January 28 he gave orders[2] for the occupation of

[1] Napoleon to Champagny, Jan. 12, 1808; Correspondance, xvi. 243.
[2] Napoleon to General Clarke, Jan. 28, 1808; Correspondance, xvi. 281, 282.

Barcelona and the Spanish frontier as far as the Ebro, and for pushing a division from Burgos to Aranda on the direct road to Madrid. These orders admitted of no disguise; they announced the annexation of Spain to France. A few days afterward, February 2, the Emperor began to dispose of Spanish territory as already his own.

"Let the American minister know verbally," he wrote to Champagny,[1] "that whenever war shall be declared between America and England, and whenever in consequence of this war the Americans shall send troops into the Floridas to help the Spaniards and repulse the English, I shall much approve of it. You will even let him perceive (*vous lui laisserez même entrevoir*) that in case America should be disposed to enter into a treaty of alliance, and make common cause with me, I shall not be unwilling (*éloigné*) to intervene with the court of Spain to obtain the cession of these same Floridas in favor of the Americans."

The next day Champagny sent for Armstrong and gave him a verbal message, which the American minister understood as follows:[2] —

"General, I have to communicate to you a message from the Emperor. I am instructed to say that the measure of taking the Floridas, to the exclusion of the British, meets entirely the approbation of his Majesty. I understand that you wish to purchase the Floridas. If such be your wish, I am further instructed to say that his Majesty will interest himself with Spain in such way as to obtain for you the Floridas, and, what is still more important, a convenient western boundary for Louisiana, on condition that the United States will enter into an alliance with France."

Weary of verbal and semi-official advances, Armstrong determined to put this overture on record, and in doing so, to tell the Emperor plainly the price of American friendship. February 5 he wrote to Champagny a note, embodying the

[1] Napoleon to Champagny, Feb. 2, 1808; Correspondance, xvi. 301.
[2] Armstrong to Madison, Feb. 15, 1808; MSS. State Department Archives.

message as he understood it, and promising to convey it to the President.[1]

"I should little deserve," he added, "and still less reciprocate the frankness of this declaration, were I to withhold from your Excellency my belief that the present conduct of France toward the commerce of the United States, so far from promoting the views of his Majesty, is directly calculated to contravene them. That the United States are at this moment on the eve of a war with Great Britain on account of certain outrages committed against their rights as a neutral nation is a fact abundantly and even generally known. Another fact, scarcely less known, is that under these circumstances France also has proceeded, in many instances and by various means, to violate these very rights. In both cases all the injunctions of public law have been equally forgotten; but between the two we cannot fail to remark a conspicuous difference. With Great Britain the United States could invoke no particular treaty providing rights supplementary to these injunctions; but such was not their situation with France. With her a treaty did exist, . . . a treaty sanctioned with the name and guaranteed by the promise of the Emperor 'that all its obligations should be inviolably preserved.' "

This was hardly the reply which the Emperor expected; but, temper for temper, Napoleon was not a man to be thus challenged by a mere diplomatist.

"You must write to the American minister," was his order to Champagny,[2] "that France has taken engagements with America, has made with her a treaty founded on the principle that the flag covers the goods, and that if this sacred principle had not been solemnly proclaimed, his Majesty would still proclaim it; that his Majesty treated with America independent, and not with America enslaved (*asservie*); that if she submits to the King of England's Decree of November 11, she renounces thereby the protection

[1] Armstrong to Champagny, Feb. 5, 1808; MSS. State Department Archives.
[2] Napoleon to Champagny, Feb. 11, 1808; Correspondance, xvi. 319.

of her flag; but that if the Americans, as his Majesty cannot doubt without wounding their honor, regard this act as one of hostility, the Emperor is ready to do justice in every respect."

In forwarding these documents to Washington, Armstrong expressed in plain language his opinion of Napoleon and Champagny. "With one hand they offer us the blessings of equal alliance against Great Britain; with the other they menace us with war if we do not accept this kindness; and with both they pick our pockets with all imaginable diligence, dexterity, and impudence." Armstrong's patience was exhausted. He besought the Government to select its enemy, either France or England; but "in either case do not suspend a moment the seizure of the Floridas."[1] A week afterward he wrote to Madison that "in a council of Administration held a few days past, when it was proposed to modify the operation of the Decrees of November, 1806, and December, 1807, though the proposition was supported by the whole weight of the council, the Emperor became highly indignant, and declared that these decrees should suffer no change, and that the Americans should be compelled to take the positive character either of allies or of enemies."[2]

These letters from Armstrong, enclosing Champagny's version of Napoleon's blunt words, were despatched to Washington during the month of February; and, as the story has already shown, President Jefferson roused a storm against France by communicating to Congress the Emperor's order that the United States government should regard itself as at war with England. Turreau felt the publication as a fatal blow to his influence; but even Turreau, soldier as he was, could never appreciate the genius of his master's audacity. Napoleon knew his ground. From the moment England adopted the Orders in Council the United States were necessarily a party in the war, and no process of evasion or delay could more than disguise their position. Napoleon told Jefferson this plain truth, and offered him the Floridas as a bribe to declare himself on the side of France. These advances were

[1] Armstrong to Madison, Feb. 15, 1808; MSS. State Department Archives.
[2] Armstrong to Madison, Feb. 22, 1808; State Papers, iii. 250.

made before the embargo system was fairly known or fully understood at Paris; and the policy of peaceable coercion, as applied to England, had not been considered in the Emperor's plans. Alliance or war seemed to him the necessary alternative, and from that point of view America had no reason or right to complain because he disregarded treaty stipulations which had become a dead letter.

All this while the Emperor held Spain in suspense, but February 21 he gave orders for securing the royal family. Murat was to occupy Madrid; Admiral Rosily, who commanded a French squadron at Cadiz, was to bar the way "if the Spanish Court, owing to events or a folly that can hardly be expected, should wish to renew the scene of Lisbon."[1] Godoy saw the impending blow, and ordered the Court to Cadiz, intending to carry the King even to Mexico if no other resource remained. He would perhaps have saved the King, and Admiral Rosily himself would have been the prisoner, had not the people risen in riot on hearing of the intended flight. March 17 a sudden mob sacked Godoy's house at Aranjuez, hunting him down like a wild beast, and barely failing to take his life; while by sheer terror Don Carlos IV. was made to abdicate the throne in favor of his son Ferdinand. March 19 the ancient Spanish empire crumbled away.

Owing to the skill with which Napoleon had sucked every drop of blood from the veins, and paralyzed every nerve in the limbs of the Spanish monarchy, the throne fell without apparent touch from him, and his army entered Madrid as though called to protect Carlos IV. from violence. When the news reached Paris the Emperor, April 2, hurried to Bordeaux and Bayonne, where he remained until August, regulating his new empire. To Bayonne were brought all the familiar figures of the old Spanish *régime*,—Carlos IV., Queen Luisa, Ferdinand, the Prince of Peace, Don Pedro Cevallos,—the last remnants of picturesque Spain; and Napoleon passed them in review with the curiosity which he might have shown in regarding a collection of rococo furniture. His victims always interested him, except when, as in the case of Tousaint

---

[1] Decrès to Rosily, Feb. 21, 1808; Thiers's Empire, viii. 669.

Louverture, they were not of noble birth. King Charles, he said,[1] looked a *bon et brave homme*.

"I do not know whether it is due to his position or to the circumstances, but he has the air of a patriarch, frank and good. The Queen carries her heart and history on her face; you need to know nothing more of her. The Prince of Peace has the air of a bull; something like Daru. He is beginning to recover his senses; he has been treated with unexampled barbarity. It is well to discharge him of every false imputation, but he must be left covered with a slight tinge of contempt."

This was a compliment to Godoy; for Napoleon made it his rule to throw contempt only upon persons—like the Queen of Prussia, or Mme. de Staël, or Toussaint—whose influence he feared. Of Ferdinand, Napoleon could make nothing, and became almost humorous in attempting to express the antipathy which this last Spanish Bourbon aroused.

"The King of Prussia is a hero in comparison with the Prince of the Asturias. He has not yet said a word to me; he is indifferent to everything; very material; eats four times a day, and has no ideas; . . . sullen and stupid."

Madrid and Aranjuez, the Escorial and La Granja were to know King Charles and his court no more. After showing themselves for a few days at Bayonne, these relics of the eighteenth century disappeared to Compiègne, to Valençay, to one refuge after another, until in 1814 unhappy Spain welcomed back the sullen and stupid Ferdinand, only to learn his true character; while old King Charles, beggared and forgotten, dragged out a melancholy existence in Italy, served to the last by Godoy with a loyalty that half excused his faults and vices. The Bourbon rubbish was swept from Madrid; Don Carlos had already abdicated; Ferdinand, entrapped and terrified, was set aside; the old palaces were garnished for newcomers; and after Lucien and Louis Bonaparte had refused the proffered throne, Napoleon sent to Naples for Joseph, who was crowned, June 15, King of Spain at Bayonne.

[1] Napoleon to Talleyrand, Correspondance, xvii. 39, 49, 65.

Meanwhile the Spanish people woke to consciousness that their ancient empire had become a province of France, and their exasperation broke into acts of wild revenge. May 2 Madrid rose in an insurrection which Murat suppressed by force. Several hundred lives on either side were lost; and although the affair itself was one of no great importance, it had results which made the day an epoch in modern history.

The gradual breaking up of the old European system of politics was marked by an anniversary among each of the Western nations. The English race dated from July 4, 1776, the beginning of a new era; the French celebrated July 14, 1789, the capture of the Bastille, as decisive of their destinies. For a time, Bonaparte's *coup d'état* of the 18th Brumaire in 1799 forced both France and England back on their steps; but the dethronement of Charles IV. began the process in a new direction. The Second of May—or as the Spaniards called it, the Dos de Maio—swept the vast Spanish empire into the vortex of dissolution. Each of the other anniversaries—that of July 4, 1776, and of July 14, 1789—had been followed by a long and bloody convulsion which ravaged large portions of the world; and the extent and violence of the convulsion which was to ravage the Spanish empire could be measured only by the vastness of Spanish dominion. So strangely had political forces been entangled by Napoleon's hand, that the explosion at Madrid roused the most incongruous interests into active sympathy and strange companionship. The Spaniards themselves, the least progressive people in Europe, became by necessity democratic; not only the people, but even the governments of Austria and Germany felt the movement, and yielded to it; the Tories of England joined with the Whigs and Democrats in cheering a revolution which could not but shake the foundations of Tory principles; confusion became chaos, and while all Europe, except France, joined hands in active or passive support of Spanish freedom, America, the stronghold of free government, drew back and threw her weight on the opposite side. The workings of human development were never more strikingly shown than in the helplessness with which the strongest political and social forces in the world followed or resisted at haphazard the necessities of a movement which they could not control or comprehend. Spain, France, Germany, England, were swept into a vast and bloody torrent which dragged America, from Montreal to Valparaiso, slowly into its movement; while the familiar figures of famous men,—Napoleon, Alexander, Canning, Godoy, Jefferson, Madison, Talleyrand; emperors, generals, presidents, conspirators, patriots, tyrants, and martyrs by the thousand,—were borne away by the stream, struggling, gesticulating, praying, murdering, robbing; each blind to everything but a selfish interest, and all helping more or less unconsciously to reach the new level which society was obliged to seek. Half a century of disorder failed to settle the problems raised by the Dos de Maio; but from the first even a child could see that in the ruin of a world like the empire of Spain, the only nation certain to find a splendid and inexhaustible booty was the Republic of the United States. To President Jefferson the Spanish revolution opened an endless vista of democratic ambition.

Yet at first the Dos de Maio seemed only to rivet Napoleon's power, and to strengthen the reaction begun on the 18th Brumaire. The Emperor expected local resistance, and was ready to suppress it. He had dealt effectually with such popular outbreaks in France, Italy, and Germany; he had been overcome in St. Domingo not by the people, but, as he believed, by the climate. If the Germans and Italians could be made obedient to his orders, the Spaniards could certainly offer no serious resistance. During the two or three months that followed the dethronement of the Bourbons, Napoleon stood at the summit of his hopes. If the letters he then wrote were not extant to prove the plans he had in mind, commonsense would refuse to believe that schemes so unsubstantial could have found lodgment in his brain. The English navy and English commerce were to be driven from the Mediterranean Sea, the Indian Ocean, and American waters, until the ruin of England should be accomplished, and the empire of the world should be secured. Order rapidly followed order for reconstructing the navies of France, Spain, and Portugal. Great expeditions were to occupy Ceuta, Egypt, Syria, Buenos Ayres, the Isle de France, and the East Indies.

"The concurrence of these operations," he wrote May

13,[1] "will throw London into a panic. A single one of them, that of India, will do horrible damage there. England will then have no means of annoying us or of disturbing America. I am resolved on this expedition."

For this purpose the Emperor required not only the submission of Spain, but also the support of Spanish America and of the United States. He acted as though he were already master of all these countries, which were not yet within his reach. Continuing to treat the United States as a dependent government, he issued April 17 a new order directing the seizure of all American vessels which should enter the ports of France, Italy, and the Hanse towns.[2] This measure, which became famous as the Bayonne Decree, surpassed the Decrees of Berlin and Milan in violence, and was gravely justified by Napoleon on the ground that, since the embargo, no vessel of the United States could navigate the seas without violating the law of its own government, and furnishing a presumption that it did so with false papers, on British account or in British connection. "This is very ingenious," wrote Armstrong in reporting the fact.[3] Yet it was hardly more arbitrary or unreasonable than the British "Rule of 1756," which declared that a neutral should practise no trade with a belligerent which it had not practised with the same nation during peace.

While these portentous events were passing rapidly before the eyes of Europe, no undue haste marked Madison's movements. Champagny's letter of Jan. 15, 1808, arrived and was sent to Congress toward the end of March; but although the United States quickly knew by heart Napoleon's phrase, "War exists in fact between England and the United States, and his Majesty considers it as declared from the day on which England published her decrees;" although Rose departed March 22, and the embargo was shaped into a system of coercion long before Rose's actual departure,—yet Congress waited until April 22 before authorizing the President to suspend the embargo, if he could succeed in persuading or compelling England or France to withdraw the belligerent decrees; and not

[1] Napoleon to Decrès, May 13, 1808; Correspondance, xvii. 112.
[2] Napoleon to Gaudin, April 17, 1808; Correspondance, xvii. 16.
[3] Armstrong to Madison, April 25, 1808; MSS. State Department Archives. Cf. State Papers, iii. 291.

until May 2—the famous Dos de Maio—did Madison send
to Armstrong instructions which were to guide that minister
through the dangers of Napoleonic diplomacy.

The Secretary began by noticing Champagny's letter of
January 15, which had assumed to declare war for the United
States government.

"That [letter]," said Madison,[1] ". . . has, as you will see
by the papers herewith sent, produced all the sensations
here which the spirit and style of it were calculated to excite
in minds alive to the interests and honor of the nation. To
present to the United States the alternative of bending to
the views of France against her enemy, or of incurring a
confiscation of all the property of their citizens carried into
the French prize courts, implied that they were susceptible
of impressions by which no independent and honorable nation can be guided; and to prejudge and pronounce for
them the effect which the conduct of another nation ought
to have on their councils and course of proceeding, had the
air at least of an assumed authority not less irritating to the
public feeling. In these lights the President makes it your
duty to present to the French government the contents of
Mr. Champagny's letter; taking care, as your discretion will
doubtless suggest, that while you make that Government
sensible of the offensive tone employed, you leave the way
open for friendly and respectful explanations, if there be a
disposition to offer them, and for a decision here on any
reply which may be of a different character."

While Armstrong waited for Napoleon's "friendly and respectful explanations," he was to study the Act of Congress
which vested in the President an authority to suspend the
embargo:—

"The conditions on which the suspending authority is to
be exercised will engage your particular attention. They appeal equally to the justice and the policy of the two great
belligerent Powers now emulating each other in violations
of both. The President counts on your best endeavors to
give to this appeal all the effect possible with the French

[1] Madison to Armstrong, May 2, 1808; State Papers, iii. 252.

government. Mr. Pinkney will be doing the same with that of Great Britain."

The Florida affair remained to be discussed. The President courteously acknowledged the Emperor's wishes "for an accession of the United States to the war against England, as an inducement to which his interposition would be employed with Spain to obtain for them the Floridas." Armstrong was told to say in reply "that the United States having chosen as the basis of their policy a fair and sincere neutrality among the contending Powers, they are disposed to adhere to it as long as their essential interests will permit, and are more particularly disinclined to become a party to the complicated and general warfare which agitates another quarter of the globe, for the purpose of obtaining a separate and particular object, however interesting to them; but," Madison added, "should circumstances demand from the United States a precautionary occupation against the hostile designs of Great Britain, it will be recollected with satisfaction that the measure has received his Majesty's approbation." Finally, Armstrong's advice to seize the Floridas without delay was answered only by the singular remark that the Emperor had given no reason to suppose he would approve the step. In private Jefferson gave other explanations, but perhaps he most nearly expressed his true feeling when he added that Armstrong wrote "so much in the buskin that he cannot give a naked fact in an intelligible form."[1]

Turreau, who stood nearer than any other man to the secrets of American foreign politics, attempted to draw the President from this defensive attitude. Turreau's instructions were such as to warrant him in using strong language. In a despatch dated February 15, Champagny repeated to his minister at Washington in still plainer words the substance of what had been said to Armstrong: "Some American ships have been seized, but the Emperor contents himself for the moment with holding them in sequestration. His conduct toward the Americans will depend on the conduct of the United

---

[1] Jefferson to Madison, Sept. 13, 1808; Writings, v. 367. Cf. Jefferson to Armstrong, March 5, 1809; Works, v. 433.

States toward England." As previously to Armstrong, so again to Turreau, the threat was supported by the bribe:—

"The Emperor, wishing on this occasion to establish a still more intimate union of interests between America and France, has authorized me to notify Mr. Armstrong verbally that if England should make any movement against the Floridas, he would not take it ill if the United States should move troops there for defence. You will be cautious in making use of this communication, which is purely conditional, and can take effect only in case the Floridas are attacked."[1]

Not until late in the month of June did Turreau find an opportunity to talk at his ease with the President and Secretary of State; but, as usual, his account of the conversation was interesting.[2] He began with Madison; and after listening with some impatience to the Secretary's long list of complaints, he brought forward the suggestion of alliance:—

"I watched the Secretary of State, and the experience I have in dealing with him made me easily perceive that my proposal embarrassed him; so he replied in an evasive manner. At last, finding himself too hard pressed, for a third time he said to me 'that the intention of the Federal government was to observe the most exact impartiality between France and England.' 'You have departed from it,' said I, 'when you place the two Powers on the same line relatively to their conduct toward you.' . . . 'Well,' said he, 'we must wait the decision of the next Congress with regard to the embargo; doubtless it will be raised in favor of the Power which shall first recall the measures that harass our commerce.'"

For three hours Turreau lectured the secretary on the iniquities of England, while the secretary doggedly repeated his phrases. Wearied but not satisfied, the French minister abandoned Madison and attacked the President. Jefferson entertained him with a long list of complaints against Spain, which Turreau had heard so often as to know them by memory.

[1] Champagny to Turreau, Feb. 15, 1808; Archives des Aff. Étr. MSS.
[2] Turreau to Champagny, June 28, 1808; Archives des Aff. Étr. MSS.

When at last the conversation had been brought to the subject of alliance against England, Jefferson took a new view of the situation, which hardly agreed with that taken by the Secretary of State.

"You have complained," replied the President, "that in consequence of our measures and of the proceedings of the last Congress, France has been put on a level with England in regard to the wrongs we allege against both Powers, while there was no kind of analogy either in the date or the gravity of their wrongs toward the Americans. I am going to prove to you generally that we never intended to admit any comparison in the conduct of these two Powers, by recalling to you the effect of the very measures you complain of. The embargo, which seems to strike at France and Great Britain equally, is in fact more prejudicial to the latter than to the former, by reason of the greater number of colonies which England possesses, and their inferiority in local resources."

After pursuing this line of argument Jefferson reverted to his own policy, and made an advance toward an understanding.

"It is possible," he said, "that Congress may repeal the embargo, the continuation of which would do us more harm than a state of war. For us in the present situation all is loss; whereas, however powerful the English may be, war would put us in a way of doing them much harm, because our people are enterprising. Yet as it is probable that Congress will favor raising the embargo if the Orders in Council are withdrawn, it would be necessary for your interests, if you are unwilling to withdraw your decrees, that at least you should promise their withdrawal on condition that the embargo be withdrawn in your favor. You will also observe that were the embargo withdrawn in favor of the English, this will not close our differences with them, because never—no, never—will there be an arrangement with them if they do not renounce the impressment of our seamen on our ships."

With this avowal, which Turreau understood as a sort of

pledge that Jefferson would lean toward war with England rather than with France, the French minister was obliged to content himself; while he pressed on his Government the assurance that both the President and the secretary wished more than all else to obtain the Floridas. Such reports were little calculated to change the Emperor's course. Human ingenuity discovered but one way to break Napoleon's will, and this single method was that of showing power to break his plans.

In due time Armstrong received his instructions of May 2, and wrote June 10 to Champagny a note declining the proposed alliance, and expressing the satisfaction which his Government felt at hearing the Emperor's approval of "a cautionary occupation of the Floridas." Napoleon, who was still at Bayonne in the flush of his power, no sooner read this reply than he wrote to Champagny,[1] —

> "Answer the American minister that you do not know what he means about the occupation of the Floridas; and that the Americans, being at peace with the Spaniards, cannot occupy the Floridas without the permission or the request of the King of Spain."

Armstrong, a few days afterward, was astonished by receiving from Champagny a note[2] denying positively that any suggestion had ever been made to warrant an American occupation of the Floridas without an express request from the King of Spain: "The Emperor has neither the right nor the wish to authorize an infraction of international law, contrary to the interests of an independent Power, his ally and his friend." When Napoleon chose to deny a fact, argument was thrown away; yet Armstrong could not do otherwise than recall Champagny's own words, which he did in a formal note, and there left the matter at rest, writing to his Government that the change in tone had "no doubt grown out of the new relations which the Floridas bear to this government since the abdication of Charles IV."[3]

For once Armstrong was too charitable. He might safely

[1] Napoleon to Champagny, June 21, 1808; Correspondance, xvii. 326.
[2] Champagny to Armstrong, June 22, 1808; MSS. State Department Archives.
[3] Armstrong to Madison, July 8, 1808; MSS. State Department Archives.

have assumed that Napoleon was also continuing the same coarse game he had played since April, 1803,—snatching away the lure he loved to dangle before Jefferson's eyes, punishing the Americans for refusing his offer of alliance, and making them feel the constant pressure of his will. They were fortunate if he did not at once confiscate the property he had sequestered. Indeed, not only did his seizures of American property continue even more rigorously than before,[1] but such French frigates as could keep at sea actually burned and sunk American ships that came in their way. The Bayonne Decree was enforced like a declaration of war. The Emperor tolerated no remonstrance. At Bayonne, July 6, he had an interview with one of the Livingstons, who was on his way to America as bearer of despatches.

"We are obliged to embargo your ships," said the Emperor;[2] "they keep up a trade with England; they come to Holland and elsewhere with English goods; England has made them tributary to her. This I will not suffer. Tell the President from me when you see him in America that if he can make a treaty with England, preserving his martime rights, it will be agreeable to me; but that I will make war upon the universe, should it support her unjust pretensions. I will not abate any part of my system."

Yet in one respect he made a concession. He no longer required a declaration of war from the United States. The embargo seemed to him, as to Jefferson, an act of hostility to England which answered the immediate wants of France. In the report on foreign relations, dated Sept. 1, 1808, Napoleon expressed publicly his approval of the embargo:—

"The Americans,—this people who placed their fortune, their prosperity, and almost their existence in commerce,— have given the example of a great and courageous sacrifice. By a general embargo they have interdicted all commerce, all exchange, rather than shamefully submit to that tribute which the English pretend to impose on the shipping of all nations."

[1] Napoleon to Champagny, July 11, 1808; Correspondance, xvii. 364.
[2] Armstrong to Jefferson, July 28, 1808; Jefferson MSS.

Armstrong, finding that his advice was not even considered at home, withdrew from affairs. After obeying his instructions of May 2, and recording the conventional protest against Napoleon's uncivil tone,[1] he secluded himself, early in August, at the baths of Bourbon l'Archambault, one hundred and fifty miles from Paris, and nursed his rheumatism till autumn. Thither followed him instructions from Madison, dated July 21,[2] directing him to present the case of the burned vessels "in terms which may awaken the French government to the nature of the injury and the demands of justice;" but the limit of Armstrong's patience was reached, and he flatly refused to obey. Any new experiment made at that moment, he said, would certainly be useless and perhaps injurious: —

"This opinion, formed with the utmost circumspection, is not only a regular inference from the ill success of my past endeavors, which have hitherto produced only palliations, and which have latterly failed to produce these, but a direct consequence of the most authentic information that the Emperor does not, on this subject and at this time, exercise even the small degree of patience proper to his character."[3]

Finally Armstrong summed up the results of Jefferson's policy so far as France was concerned, in a letter[4] dated August 30, which carried candor to the point of severity: —

"We have somewhat overrated our means of coercing the two great belligerents to a course of justice. The embargo is a measure calculated above any other to keep us whole and keep us in peace; but beyond this you must not count upon it. Here it is not felt, and in England . . . it is forgotten. I hope that unless France shall do us justice we will raise the embargo, and make in its stead the experiment of an armed commerce. Should she adhere to her wicked and foolish measures, we ought not to content ourselves with doing this. There is much, very much, besides that we can

[1] Armstrong to Champagny, July 4, 1808; State Papers, iii. 254.
[2] Madison to Armstrong, July 21, 1808; State Papers, iii. 254
[3] Armstrong to Madison, Aug. 28, 1808; MSS. State Department Archives.
[4] Armstrong to Madison, Aug. 30, 1808; State Papers, iii. 256.

do; and we ought not to omit doing all we can, because it is believed here that we cannot do much, and even that we will not do what we have the power of doing."

Fortunately for Jefferson, the answer made by Spain, May 2, to Napoleon's orders was not couched in the terms which the United States government used on the same day. Joseph Bonaparte, entering his new kingdom, found himself a king without subjects. Arriving July 20 at Madrid, Joseph heard nothing but news of rebellion and disaster. On that day some twenty thousand French troops under General Dupont, advancing on Seville and Cadiz, were surrounded in the Sierra Morena, and laid down their arms to a patriot Spanish force. A few days afterward the French fleet at Cadiz surrendered. A patriot Junta assumed the government of Spain. Quick escape from Madrid became Joseph's most pressing necessity if he were to save his life. During one July week he reigned over his gloomy capital, and fled, July 29, with all the French forces still uncaptured, to the provinces beyond the Ebro.

This disaster was quickly followed by another. Junot and his army, far beyond support at Lisbon, suddenly learned that a British force under Arthur Wellesley had landed, August 1, about one hundred miles to the north of Lisbon, and was marching on that city. Junot had no choice but to fight, and August 21 he lost the battle of Vimieiro. August 30, at Cintra, he consented to evacuate Portugal, on condition that he and his twenty-two thousand men should be conveyed by sea to France.

Never before in Napoleon's career had he received two simultaneous shocks so violent. The whole of Spain and Portugal, from Lisbon to Saragossa, by a spasmodic effort freed itself from Bonaparte or Bourbon; but this was nothing,—a single campaign would recover the peninsula. The real blow was in the loss of Cadiz and Lisbon, of the fleets and workshops that were to restore French power on the ocean. Most fatal stroke of all, the Spanish colonies were thenceforward beyond reach, and the dream of universal empire was already dissolved into ocean mist. Napoleon had found the limits of his range, and saw the power of England rise, more defiant than ever, over the ruin and desolation of Spain.

Chapter XIV

W̲HEN PARLIAMENT met Jan. 21, 1808, the paroxysm of
excitement which followed the "Chesapeake" affair and
the attack on Copenhagen had begun to subside. War with
America was less popular than it had been six months before.
The "Morning Post"[1] exhorted the British public to maintain
"that sublime pitch" from which all opposition was to be
crushed; but the Whigs came to Parliament eager for attack,
while Perceval and Canning had exhausted their energies, and
were thrown back on a wearisome defensive.

The session—which lasted from January 21 to July 4—was
remarkable chiefly for an obstinate struggle over the Orders
in Council. Against Perceval's commercial measures the
Whigs bent the full strength of their party; and this strength,
so far as intelligence was concerned, greatly outmatched that
of the Ministry. New men made reputations in the conflict.
In January, 1808, Alexander Baring—then about thirty-four
years of age, not yet in Parliament, but second to no English
merchant in standing—published a pamphlet, in reply to Stephen's "War in Disguise;" and his superior knowledge and
abilities gave, for the first time since 1776, solid ground of
support to American influence in British politics. Side by side
with Baring, a still younger man thrust himself into public
notice by force of qualities which for half a century were to
make him the object of mixed admiration and laughter. The
new American champion, Henry Brougham, a native of Edinburgh, thirty years of age, like many other Scotch lawyers had
come to seek and find at Westminster the great prize of his
profession. Like Baring, Brougham was not yet in Parliament;
but this obstacle—which would have seemed to most men
final—could not prevent him from speaking his mind, even
in presence of the House.

Lord Grenville began the attack, and Canning the defence,
on the first day of the session; but not until after January 27,
when news of the embargo arrived, and all immediate danger
of war vanished, did the situation become clear. February 5
the debate began. The Whigs found that Perceval met their

[1] The Morning Post, Jan. 16, 1808.

assaults on the character and policy of his orders by quotations from Lord Howick's Order, which the Whigs only twelve months before had issued and defended as an act of retaliation. Narrow as this personal rejoinder might be, it was fatal to the Whig argument. Baring and Brougham might criticise Spencer Perceval; but Lord Grenville and Lord Howick had enough to do in explaining their own words. The more vehement they became, the more obstinately their opponents persevered in holding them to this single point.

Yet the issue the Whigs wished to make was fairly met. Government showed remarkable candor in avowing the commercial object of the so-called retaliation. Admitting that even if Napoleon had issued no decrees England might have been obliged to enforce the Rule of 1756, Spencer Perceval declared that after the Berlin Decree a much stronger measure was necessary in order to protect British commerce. Lord Bathurst, Lord Hawkesbury, and Lord Castlereagh took the same tone. Their argument, carried to its ultimate conclusion, implied that Great Britain might lawfully forbid every other nation to trade with any country that imposed a prohibitive duty on British manufactures. Not even a state of war seemed essential to the soundness of the principle.

Already Lord Grenville had declared that "this principle of forcing trade into our markets would have disgraced the darkest ages of monopoly,"[1] when March 8 Lord Erskine spoke in support of a series of resolutions condemning the orders as contrary to the Constitution, the laws of the realm, and the rights of nations, and a violation of Magna Charta. With especial energy he declaimed against Perceval's favorite doctrine of retaliation as applied to the protection of British commerce. Lord Erskine, like Lord Grenville, never spared epithets.

"It is indeed quite astonishing," he said,[2] "to hear the word 'retaliation' twisted and perverted in a manner equally repugnant to grammar and common-sense. . . . It is a new application of the term, that if A strikes me, I may retaliate by striking B. . . . I cannot, my Lords, conceive anything more preposterous and senseless than the idea of

[1] Cobbett's Debates, x. 482, 483.
[2] Cobbett's Debates, x. 937, 938.

retaliation upon a neutral on whom the decree has never been executed, because it is only by its execution on him that we can be injured."

Erskine supported his positions by a long professional argument. Lord Chancellor Eldon replied by developing international law in a direction till then unexplored.[1]

"I would beg the House to consider what is meant by the law of nations," he began. "It is formed of an accumulation of the dicta of wise men in different ages, and applying to different circumstances, but none resembling in any respect such a state of things as at present exists in the face of the world. Indeed, none of the writers upon the subject of this law appear to have such a state in their contemplation. But yet nothing is to be found in their writings which does not fully warrant the right of self-defence and retaliation. Upon that right the present ministers acted in advising those Orders in Council, and upon the same right their predecessors issued the order of the 7th of January."

The doctrine that because international law wanted the sanction of a well-defined force it was, strictly speaking, no law at all, was naturally favored by the school of common law; but Lord Eldon's doctrine went further, for he created a sanction of one-sided force by which international law might supersede its own principles. His brother, Sir William Scott, carried out the theory by contending in the House of Commons that "even if the French Decree was not acted upon (which rested with the other party to prove), it was nevertheless an injury, because it was an insult to the country,"[2] —a dictum which could hardly find a parallel as the foundation for an attack on the rights and property of an innocent third party.

Erskine's Resolutions were of course rejected; but meanwhile the merchants of the chief cities began to protest. As the bill for carrying the orders into effect came to its engrossment, March 7, the resistance became hot. March 11 the bill passed the House by a vote of 168 to 68; but Brougham had

[1] Cobbett's Debates, x. 971.
[2] Cobbett's Debates, x. 1066.

yet to be heard, and no ordinary power was capable of suppressing Henry Brougham. As counsel for the American merchants of Liverpool, Manchester, and London, he appeared March 18 at the bar of the House, and for the next fortnight occupied most of its time in producing testimony to prove that the orders had ruinously affected the commercial interest. April 1 he summed up the evidence in a speech of three hours, which James Stephen thought pernicious and incendiary.[1] Perceval was obliged to produce witnesses on the other side; and Stephen, who had been brought into Parliament for the purpose, devoted himself to the task of proving that the orders had as yet been allowed no chance to produce any effect whatever, and that the commercial distress was due to the recent enforcement of the Berlin Decree. That much distress existed no one denied; but its causes might well be matter of dispute; and Parliament left the merchants to decide the point as they pleased. Brougham's inquiry had no other effect.

Pinkney's dealings with Canning were equally fruitless. January 26, when Pinkney received official news of the embargo, he went instantly to Canning, " who received my explanations with great apparent satisfaction, and took occasion to express the most friendly disposition toward our country."[2] Pinkney used this opportunity to remonstrate against the tax imposed on American cotton by the Orders in Council. A week afterward Canning sent for him, and gravely suggested a friendly arrangement. He wished to know Pinkney's private opinion whether the United States would prefer an absolute interdict to a prohibitory duty on cotton intended for the continent.[3] The sting of this inquiry rested not so much in the alternative thus presented as in the seriousness with which Canning insisted that his overture was a concession to America. With all his wit, as Lord Castlereagh soon had reason to learn, Canning could not quite acquire tact or understand the insults he offered. Pinkney tried, with much good temper, to make him aware that his offer was in bad taste; but nothing could stop him in the path of conciliation, and February 22 he addressed to Pinkney a note announcing that the British government

[1] Brougham to Grey, April 21, 1808; Brougham's Memoirs, i. 399.
[2] Pinkney to Madison, Jan. 26, 1808; State Papers, iii. 206.
[3] Pinkney to Madison, Feb. 2, 1808; State Papers, iii. 207.

meant to prohibit the export of American cotton to the continent of Europe.

"I flatter myself," he continued,[1] "that this alteration in the legislative regulations by which the Orders of Council are intended to be carried into execution, will be considered by you as a satisfactory evidence of the disposition of his Majesty's government to consult the feelings as well as the interests of the United States in any manner which may not impair the effect of that measure of commercial restriction to which the necessity of repelling the injustice of his enemies has compelled his Majesty reluctantly to have recourse."

"One object of all this is certainly to conciliate us," wrote Pinkney to Madison.[2] On the day of Canning's note Spencer Perceval carried out the promise by moving the House for leave to bring in a bill prohibiting the export of cotton, except by license. At the same time he extended the like prohibition to Jesuit's bark, or quinine. Impervious to indignation and ridicule,—caring as little for the laughter of Sydney Smith as for the wrath of Lord Grenville,—Perceval pushed all his measures through Parliament, and by the middle of April succeeded in riveting his restrictive system on the statute-book. No power short of a new political revolution could thenceforward shake his grasp on American commerce.

Yet Perceval felt and dreaded the effects of the embargo, which threatened to paralyze the healthiest industries of England. To escape the effects of this weapon Perceval would have made every possible concession short of abandoning his great scheme of restrictive statesmanship. March 26 he submitted to his colleagues a paper containing suggestions on this point.[3] "It must be admitted," he began, "that it is extremely desirable that America should relax her embargo at least as far as respects the intercourse with this country." The Americans submitted to it with reluctance, chiefly because they feared the seizure of their vessels in case England or

[1] Canning to Pinkney, Feb. 22, 1808; State Papers, iii. 208.

[2] Pinkney to Madison, Feb. 23, 1808; State Papers, iii. 208.

[3] Suggestions by S. P. for a Supplementary Order in Council, March 26, 1808; Perceval MSS.

France should declare war. To profit by this situation Perceval proposed a new order, which should guaranty the safety of every merchant-vessel, neutral or belligerent, on a voyage to or from a British port. The advantages of this step were political as well as commercial. The British ministry was disposed to meet the wishes of the Boston Federalists. Such an order, Perceval said, " would have the appearance of a friendly act on the part of this government toward America, and would increase the embarrassment and difficulties of that government in prevailing upon their subjects to submit to the embargo."

Lord Bathurst approved the suggestion; Lord Castlereagh opposed it, for reasons best given in his own words:[1] —

"If the only object to be aimed at in conducting ourselves toward America was to force the abrogation of the embargo, I agree with Mr. Perceval that the proposed measure would make it more difficult for the American government to sustain it; but in yielding so far to the popular feeling the governing party would still retain much of their credit, and they would continue to act on all the unsettled questions between the two countries in their past spirit of hostility to Great Britain and partiality to France. I think it better to leave them with the full measure of their own difficulties to lower and degrade them in the estimation of the American people. The continuance of the embargo for some time is the best chance of their being destroyed *as a party*; and I should prefer exposing them to the disgrace of rescinding their own measure at the demand of their own people than furnish them with any creditable pretext for doing so. I look upon the embargo as operating at present more forcibly in our favor than any measure of hostility we could call forth were war actually declared, and doubt the policy of exhibiting too great an impatience on our part of its continuance, which so strong a departure from our usual practice toward neutrals would indicate."

Secretary Canning wrote to his colleague in accord with Castlereagh's views.[2]

[1] Opinion of Lord Castlereagh, March–April, 1808; Perceval MSS.
[2] Opinion of Mr. Canning, March 28, 1808; Perceval MSS.

"It is so plain upon the face of this measure," began Canning, "that however comprehensive it may be made in words, it *in fact* refers to America *only*; and the embargo in America seems to be working so well for us, without our interference, that on that ground alone I confess I could wish that no new steps should be taken, at least till we have more certain information of the real issue of the present crisis in America. I have no apprehension whatever of a war with the United States. . . . Above all things I feel that *to do nothing now*, at this precise moment,—absolutely nothing,—is the wisest, safest, and most manful policy. The battle about the Orders in Council is just fought. They are established as a system. We have reason to hope that they are working much to good, and very little to mischief. Every day may be expected to bring additional proofs of this. But whether this be true to the extent that we hope or no, their effects, whatever they are, have been produced in America. Nothing that we now do can alter those effects; but an attempt to do something will perplex the view of them which we shall otherwise have to present to the country in so short a time, and which there is so much reason to believe will be highly satisfactory."

Perceval, was less certain than Canning that the country would feel high satisfaction with the effect of the orders; and he rejoined by an argument which overthrew opposition:—

"The reason which strongly urges me to continue the circulation of this paper, after having read Mr. Canning's paper, in addition to those already stated, is the apprehension I feel of the want of provision not only for Sweden, but for the West Indies; and therefore every possible facility or encouragement which we could give to prevail upon the American people either to evade the embargo by running their produce to the West Indian Islands, or to compel their government to relax it, would in my opinion be most wise."

The order was accordingly issued. Dated April 11, 1808,[1] it directed British naval commanders to molest no neutral vessel

[1] American State Papers, iii. 281.

on a voyage to the West Indies or South America, even though the vessel should have no regular clearances or papers, and "notwithstanding the present hostilities, or any future hostilities that may take place." No measure of the British government irritated Madison more keenly than this. "A more extraordinary experiment," he wrote to Pinkney,[1] "is perhaps not to be found in the annals of modern transactions." Certainly governments did not commonly invite citizens of friendly countries to violate their own laws; but one avowed object of the embargo was to distress the British people into resisting their government, and news that the negroes of Jamaica and the artisans of Yorkshire had broken into acts of lawless violence would have been grateful to the ears of Jefferson. So distinct was this object, and so real the danger, that Perceval asked Parliament[2] to restrict the consumption of grain in the distilleries in order to countervail the loss of American wheat and avert a famine. The price of wheat had risen from thirty-nine to seventy-two shillings a quarter, and every farmer hoped for a rise above one hundred shillings, as in 1795 and 1800. Disorders occurred; lives were lost; the embargo, as a coercive measure, pressed severely on British society; and Madison, with such a weapon in his hand, could not require Perceval to perceive the impropriety of inviting a friendly people to violate their own laws.

The exact cost of the embargo to England could not be known. The total value of British exports to America was supposed to be nearly fifty million dollars; but the Americans regularly re-exported to the West Indies merchandise to the value of ten or fifteen millions. The embargo threw this part of the trade back into British hands. The true consumption of the United States hardly exceeded thirty-five million dollars, and was partially compensated to England by the gain of freights, the recovery of seamen, and by smuggling consequent on the embargo. Napoleon's decrees must in any case have greatly reduced the purchasing power of America, and had in fact already done so. Perhaps twenty-five million dollars might be a reasonable estimate for the value of the remaining trade which the embargo stopped; and if the British

[1] Madison to Pinkney, July 18, 1808; State Papers, iii. 224.
[2] Cobbett's Debates, xi. 536.

manufacturers made a profit of twenty per cent on this trade, their loss in profits did not exceed five million dollars for the year,—a sum not immediately vital to English interests at a time when the annual expenditure reached three hundred and fifty million dollars, and when, as in 1807, the value of British exports was reckoned at nearly two hundred million dollars. Indeed, according to the returns, the exports of 1808 exceeded those of 1807 by about two millions.

Doubtless the embargo caused suffering. The West Indian negroes and the artisans of Staffordshire, Lancashire, and Yorkshire were reduced to the verge of famine; but the ship-owners rejoiced, and the country-gentleman and farmers were enriched. So ill balanced had the British people become in the excitement of their wars and industries that not only Cobbett but even a man so intelligent as William Spence undertook to prove[1] that foreign commerce was not a source of wealth to England, but that her prosperity and power were derived from her own resources, and would survive the annihilation of her foreign trade. James Mill replied[2] at great length to the eccentricities of Spence and Cobbett, which the common-sense of England would in ordinary times have noticed only with a laugh.

The population of England was about ten millions. Perhaps two millions were engaged in manufactures. The embargo by raising the price of grain affected them all, but it bore directly on about one tenth of them. The average sum expended on account of the poor was £4,268,000 in 1803 and 1804; it was £5,923,000 in 1811; and in 1813, 1814, and 1815, when the restrictive system had produced its full effect, the poor-rates averaged £6,130,000. The increase was probably due to the disturbance of trade and was accompanied by a state of society bordering on chronic disorder.

Probably at least five thousand families of working-men were reduced to pauperism by the embargo and the decrees of Napoleon; but these sufferers, who possessed not a vote among them and had been in no way party to the acts of either government, were the only real friends whom Jefferson could hope to find among the people of England; and his

[1] Britain Independent of Commerce, by William Spence (London), 1808.
[2] Commerce Defended, by James Mill (London), 1808.

embargo ground them in the dust in order to fatten the squires and ship-owners who had devised the Orders in Council. If the English laborers rioted, they were shot: if the West Indian slaves could not be fed, they died. The embargo served only to lower the wages and the moral standard of the laboring classes throughout the British empire, and to prove their helplessness.

Each government thus tried to overthrow the other; but that of England was for the moment the more successful. The uneducated force of democracy seemed about to break against the strength of an aristocratic system. When Parliament rose, July 4, domestic opposition was silenced, and nothing remained but to crush the resistance of America,—a task which all advices from the United States showed to be easy; while as though to make ministers invulnerable, Spain suddenly opened her arms to England, offering new markets that promised boundless wealth. At this unexpected good fortune England went well-nigh mad; and the Spanish revolution, which was in truth a gain to democracy, seemed to strike Jefferson a mortal blow. During the month of July, 1808, Canning and his colleagues exulted over Europe and America alike, looking down on Jefferson and his embargo with the disgust and horror which they might have felt for some monster of iniquity like the famous butcher of the Marrs, who was to rouse the shudders of England during these lurid years. According to Canning, Napoleon's system was already "broken up into fragments utterly harmless and contemptible."[1] According to Henry Brougham,[2] hardly ten men could be found in London who did not believe Bonaparte utterly broken, or think him worth paying one hundred pounds a year to live in retirement at Ajaccio the rest of his life. America was still more contemptible, and equally hated. Early in August, at a great dinner given at the London Tavern to the Spanish patriots, Sir Francis Baring, of the house of Baring Brothers,—a man who for a whole generation had stood at the head of British merchants,—proposed as chairman, among the regular toasts, the health of the President of the United States, and his voice was instantly drowned in hisses

[1] Canning to Pinkney, Sept. 23, 1808; State Papers, iii. 231.
[2] Brougham to Grey, July 2, 1808; Brougham's Memoirs, i. 405.

and protests. Jefferson, thanks to the slanders of Pickering and the Federalists, stood before England in the attitude of a foiled cutthroat, at the moment when by his order the American minister in London came to the British Foreign Office with a request that the Orders in Council should be withdrawn.

"That the Orders in Council did not produce the embargo, that they were not substantially known in America when the embargo took place,"[1] was the burden of Canning's and Castlereagh's constant charge against the United States government. Canning was one of six or eight men in the world who might with truth have said that they knew the orders to have produced the embargo. He alone could have proved it by publishing Erskine's official evidence;[2] but he preferred to support Timothy Pickering and Barent Gardenier in persuading the world that Jefferson's acts were dictated from Paris, and that their only motive was the assassination of England. "Nor, sir, do I think," continued Canning before the whole House of Commons, "that the Orders in Council themselves could have produced any irritation in America. . . . Since the return of Mr. Rose no communication has been made by the American government in the form of complaint, or remonstrance, or irritation, or of any description whatever." With infinite industry the assertions of Pickering and Gardenier, of John Randolph and of the Boston newspapers and pamphlets, were reprinted and circulated in London. "Your modesty would suffer," wrote Rose to Pickering,[3] "if you were aware of the sensation produced in this country by the publication of a letter from a senator of Massachusetts to his constituents."

Every American slander against Jefferson was welcomed in England, until Pinkney asked Madison in disgust, "Have you prohibited the exportation of all pamphlets which uphold our rights and honor?"[4] The English people could hardly be blamed if they became almost insane under the malice of these falsehoods, for no whisper of Iago was more poisonous than

[1] Speech of Mr. Canning, June 24, 1808; Cobbett's Debates, xi. 1050.
[2] See p. 1047.
[3] Rose to Pickering, May 8, 1808; New England Federalism, p. 371.
[4] Wheaton's Life of Pinkney, p. 91.

Canning's innuendoes. Believing Jefferson to be in secret league with Napoleon, they insisted that the United States should be punished for the treason Jefferson had planned. Joseph Marriatt, a prominent member of Parliament, in a pamphlet[1] published in August, reminded President Jefferson of the fate of the late Czar Paul. The feeling of society was so bitter that by tacit agreement America ceased to be talked about; no one ventured longer to defend her.

In June Pinkney received instructions, dated April 30,[2] authorizing him to offer a withdrawal of the embargo on condition that England should withdraw the Orders in Council. In the situation of English feeling such an offer was almost an invitation to insult, and Pinkney would have gladly left it untouched. He tried to evade the necessity of putting it in writing; but Canning was inexorable. From week to week Pinkney postponed the unpleasant task. Not until August 23 did he write the note which should have been written in June. No moment could have been more unfortunate; for only two days before, Arthur Wellesley had defeated Junot at Vimieiro; and August 30 Junot capitulated at Cintra. The delirium of England was higher than ever before or since.

September 23 Canning replied.[3] Beginning with a refusal to admit the President's advance, his note went on to discuss its propriety. "His Majesty," it said, "cannot consent to buy off that hostility which America ought not to have extended to him, at the expense of a concession made, not to America, but to France." Canning was a master of innuendo; and every sentence of his note hinted that he believed Jefferson to be a tool of Napoleon; but in one passage he passed the bounds of official propriety:—

"The Government of the United States is not to be informed that the Berlin Decree of Nov. 21, 1806, was the practical commencement of an attempt, not merely to check or impair the prosperity of Great Britain, but utterly to annihilate her political existence through the ruin of her commercial prosperity; that in this attempt almost all the

[1] Hints to both Parties (London), 1808, pp. 64, 65.
[2] Madison to Pinkney, April 30, 1808; State Papers, iii. 222.
[3] Canning to Pinkney, Sept. 23, 1808; State Papers, iii. 231.

Powers of the European continent have been compelled more or less to co-operate; and that the American embargo, though most assuredly not intended to that end, — for America can have no real interest in the subversion of the British power, and her rulers are too enlightened to act from any impulse against the real interests of their country, — but by some unfortunate concurrence of circumstances, without any hostile intention, the American embargo did come in aid of the 'blockade of the European continent' precisely at the very moment when if that blockade could have succeeded at all, this interposition of the American government would most effectually have contributed to its success."

Like his colleague Lord Castlereagh, Canning deliberately tried to "lower and degrade" the American government in the eyes of its own people. His defiance was even more emphatic than his sarcasm.

"To this universal combination," he continued, "his Majesty has opposed a temperate but a determined retaliation upon the enemy, — trusting that a firm resistance would defeat this project, but knowing that the smallest concession would infallibly encourage a perseverance in it.

"The struggle has been viewed by other Powers not without an apprehension that it might be fatal to this country. The British government has not disguised from itself that the trial of such an experiment might be arduous and long, though it has never doubted of the final issue. But if that issue, such as the British government confidently anticipated, has providentially arrived much sooner than could even have been hoped; if 'the blockade of the Continent,' as it has been triumphantly styled by the enemy, is raised even before it had been well established; and if that system, of which extent and continuity were the vital principles, is broken up into fragments utterly harmless and contemptible, — it is, nevertheless, important in the highest degree to the reputation of this country (a reputation which constitutes a great part of her power), that this disappointment of the hopes of her enemies should not have been purchased by any concession; that not a doubt should remain to distant times of her determination and of her ability to have continued her resistance; and that no step which could even mistakenly be construed into concession should be taken on her part while the smallest link of the confederacy remains undissolved, or while it can be a question whether the plan devised for her destruction has or has not either completely failed or been unequivocally abandoned."

With this sweeping assertion of British power Canning might well have stopped; but although he had said more than enough, he was not yet satisfied. His love of sarcasm dragged him on. He thought proper to disavow the wish to depress American prosperity, and his disavowal was couched in terms of condescension as galling as his irony; but in one paragraph he concentrated in peculiar force the worst faults of his character and taste: —

"His Majesty would not hesitate to contribute, in any manner in his power, to restore to the commerce of the United States its wonted activity; and if it were possible to make any sacrifice for the repeal of the embargo without appearing to deprecate it as a measure of hostility, he would gladly have facilitated its removal as a measure of inconvenient restriction upon the American people."

Earl Grey, although he approved of rejecting the American offer, wrote to Brougham that in this note Canning had outdone himself.[1] No doubt his irony betrayed too much of the cleverness which had been so greatly admired by Eton schoolboys; but it served the true purpose of satire, — it stung to the quick, and goaded Americans into life-long hatred of England. Pinkney, whose British sympathies had offered long resistance to maltreatment, fairly lost his temper over this note. "Insulting and insidious," he called it in his private correspondence with Madison.[2] He was the more annoyed because Canning wrote him an explanatory letter of the same date which gave a personal sting to the public insult.[3] "I feel

[1] Grey to Brougham, Jan. 3, 1809; Brougham's Memoirs, i. 397.
[2] Pinkney to Madison, Oct. 11, 1808; Wheaton's Pinkney, p. 412.
[3] Canning to Pinkney, Sept. 23, 1808; State Papers, iii. 230.

that it is not such a letter as I could have persuaded myself to write in similar circumstances," he complained.[1]

Pinkney's abilities were great. In the skirmish of words in which Canning delighted, Pinkney excelled; and in his later career at the bar, of which he was the most brilliant leader, and in the Senate, where he was heard with bated breath, he showed more than once a readiness to overbear opposition by methods too nearly resembling those of Canning; but as a diplomatist he contented himself with preserving the decorous courtesy which Canning lacked. He answered the explanatory letter of September 23 with so much skill and force that Canning was obliged to rejoin; and the rejoinder hardly raised the British secretary's reputation.[2]

With this exchange of notes, the diplomatic discussion ended for the season; and the packet set sail for America, bearing to Jefferson the news that his scheme of peaceable coercion had resulted in a double failure, which left no alternative but war or submission.

[1] Pinkney to Madison, Nov. 2, 1808; Wheaton's Pinkney, p. 416.

[2] Pinkney to Canning, Oct. 10, 1808; State Papers, iii. 233. Canning to Pinkney, Nov. 22, 1808; State Papers, iii. 237.

Chapter XV

ARLY IN AUGUST, at the time when public feeling against the embargo was beginning to turn into personal hatred of Jefferson, news of the Spanish outbreak reached America, and put a new weapon into Federalist hands. The embargo, in its effects upon Spain and her colonies was a powerful weapon to aid Napoleon in his assault on Spanish liberty and in his effort to gain mastery of the ocean. In an instant England appeared as the champion of human liberty, and America as an accomplice of despotism. Jefferson, in his pursuit of Florida, lost what was a thousand times more valuable to him than territory,—the moral leadership which belonged to the head of democracy. The New England Federalists seized their advantage, and proclaimed themselves the friends of Spain and freedom. Their press rang with denunciations of Napoleon, and of Jefferson his tool. For the first time in many years the Essex Junto stood forward as champions of popular liberty.

So deeply mired was Jefferson in the ruts of his Spanish policy and prejudices that he could not at once understand the revolution which had taken place. On hearing the earlier reports of Spanish resistance his first thought was selfish. "I am glad to see that Spain is likely to give Bonaparte employment. *Tant mieux pour nous!*"[1] To each member of his Cabinet he wrote his hopes:[2]—

> "Should England make up with us, while Bonaparte continues at war with Spain, a moment may occur when we may without danger of commitment with either France or England seize to our own limits of Louisiana as of right, and the residue of the Floridas as reprisals for spoliations. It is our duty to have an eye to this in rendezvousing and stationing our new recruits and our armed vessels, so as to be ready, if Congress authorizes it, to strike in a moment."

The victories at Bailen and Vimieiro, the flight of Joseph

[1] Jefferson to Robert Smith, Aug. 9, 1808; Writings, v. 335.
[2] Jefferson to Dearborn, Aug. 12, 1808; Writings, v. 338. Jefferson to Gallatin, v. 338. Jefferson to R. Smith, v. 337. Jefferson to Madison, v. 339.

from Madrid, the outburst of English enthusiasm for Spain, and the loud echo from New England, in the anxieties of a general election, brought the President to wider views. October 22 the Cabinet debated the subject, arriving at a new result, which Jefferson recorded in his memoranda:[1] —

"Unanimously agreed in the sentiments which should be unauthoritatively expressed by our agents to influential persons in Cuba and Mexico; to wit: 'If you remain under the dominion of the kingdom and family of Spain, we are contented; but we should be extremely unwilling to see you pass under the dominion or ascendency of France or England. In the latter case, should you choose to declare independence, we cannot now commit ourselves by saying we would make common cause with you, but must reserve ourselves to act according to the then existing circumstances; but in our proceedings we shall be influenced by friendship to you, by a firm feeling that our interests are intimately connected, and by the strongest repugnance to see you under subordination to either France or England, either politically or commercially.' "

No allusion to Florida was made in this outline of a new policy, and none was needed, for Florida would obviously fall to the United States. The Spanish patriots,—who were as little disposed as Don Carlos IV. and the Prince of Peace to see their empire dismembered, and who knew as well as Godoy and Cevallos the motives that controlled the United States government,—listened with only moderate confidence to the protests which Jefferson, through various agents, made at Havana, Mexico, and New Orleans.

"The truth is that the patriots of Spain have no warmer friends than the Administration of the United States," began the President's instructions to his agents;[2] "but it is our duty to say nothing and to do nothing for or against either. If they succeed, we shall be well satisfied to see Cuba and Mexico remain in their present dependence, but very unwilling to see them in that of France or England, politi-

[1] Cabinet Memoranda; Writings (Ford), i. 334.
[2] Jefferson to Claiborne, Oct. 29, 1808; Writings, v. 381.

cally or commercially. We consider their interests and ours as the same, and that the object of both must be to exclude all European influence from this hemisphere."

The patriotic junta at Cadiz, which represented the empire of Spain, could hardly believe in the warm friendship which admitted its object of excluding them from influence over their own colonies. In private, Jefferson avowed[1] that American interests rather required the failure of the Spanish insurrection. "Bonaparte, having Spain at his feet, will look immediately to the Spanish colonies, and think our neutrality cheaply purchased by a repeal of the illegal parts of his decrees, with perhaps the Floridas thrown into the bargain." In truth, Jefferson and the Southern interest cared nothing for Spanish patriotism; and their indifference was reflected in their press. The independence of the Spanish colonies was the chief object of American policy; and the patriots of Spain had no warmer friends than the Administration of the United States so far as they helped and hurried this great catastrophe; but beyond this purpose Jefferson did not look.

In the Eastern States the Democratic and Southern indifference toward the terrible struggle raging in Spain helped to stimulate the anger against Jefferson, which had already swept many firm Republicans into sympathy with Federalism. In their minds indifference to Spain meant submission to Napoleon and hatred of England; it proved the true motives which had induced the President to suppress Monroe's treaty and to impose the Non-importation Act and the embargo; it called for vehement, universal, decisive protest. The New England conscience, which had never submitted to the authority of Jefferson, rose with an outburst of fervor toward the Spaniards, and clung more energetically than ever to the cause of England,—which seemed at last, beyond the possibility of doubt, to have the sanction of freedom. Every day made Jefferson's position less defensible, and shook the confidence of his friends.

With the sanguine temper which had made him victorious in so many trials, the President hoped for another success. He still thought that England must yield under the grinding dep-

[1] Jefferson to Monroe, Jan. 28, 1809; Writings, v. 419.

rivations of the embargo, and he was firm in the intention to exact his own terms of repeal. Pinkney's earlier despatches offered a vague hope that Canning might withdraw the orders; and at this glimpse of sunshine Jefferson's spirits became buoyant.

> "If they repeal their orders, we must repeal our embargo; if they make satisfaction for the 'Chesapeake,' we must revoke our proclamation, and generalize its application by a law; if they keep up impressments, we must adhere to non-intercourse, manufactures, and a Navigation Act."[1]

Canning was not altogether wrong in thinking that concession by Great Britain would serve only to establish on a permanent footing the system of peaceable coercion.

The first blow to the President's confidence came from France. Armstrong's letters gave no hope that Napoleon would withdraw or even modify his decrees.

> "We must therefore look to England alone," wrote Madison September 14,[2] "for the chances of disembarrassment,—and look with the greater solicitude as it seems probable that nothing but some striking proof of the success of the embargo can arrest the successful perversion of it by its enemies, or rather the enemies of their country."

To England, accordingly, the President looked for some sign of successful coercion,—some proof that the embargo had been felt, or at least some encouragement to hold that its continuance might save him from the impending alternative of submission or war; and he had not long to wait. The "Hope," bringing Canning's letters of September 23, made so quick a voyage that Pinkney's despatches came to hand October 28, as the President was preparing his Annual Message to Congress for its special meeting November 7.

Had Canning chosen the moment when his defiance should have most effect, he would certainly have selected the instant when the elections showed that Jefferson's authority had reached its limit. Friends and enemies alike united in telling the President that his theory of statesmanship had failed, and

[1] Jefferson to Madison, Sept. 6, 1808; Writings, v. 361.
[2] Madison to Jefferson, Sept. 14, 1808; Jefferson MSS.

must be thrown aside. The rapid decline of his authority was measured by the private language of representative men, speaking opinions not meant for popular effect. In the whole Union no men could be found more distinctly representative than Wilson Cary Nicholas, James Monroe, John Marshall, and Rufus King. Of these, Nicholas was distinguished as being the President's warm and sympathetic friend, whose opinions had more weight, and whose relations with him were more confidential, than those of any other person not in the Cabinet; but even Nicholas thought himself required to prepare the President's mind for abandoning his favorite policy.

"If the embargo could be executed," wrote Nicholas October 20,[1] "and the people would submit to it, I have no doubt it is our wisest course; but if the complete execution of it and the support of the people cannot be counted upon, it will neither answer our purpose nor will it be practicable to retain it. Upon both these points I have the strongest doubts. . . . What the alternative ought to be, I cannot satisfy myself. I see such difficulties at every turn that I am disposed to cling to the embargo as long as there is anything to hope from it; and I am unwilling to form an opinion until I have the aid of friends upon whom I rely, and who are more in the way of information."

This admission of helplessness coming from the oldest Virginian Republicans betrayed the discouragement of all Jefferson's truest friends, and accorded with the language of Monroe, who whatever might be his personal jealousies was still Republican in spirit. After his return from England, at the moment when his attitude toward the Administration was most threatening, both Jefferson and Madison had made efforts, not without success, to soothe Monroe's irritation; and in the month of February Jefferson had even written to him a letter of friendly remonstrance, to which Monroe replied, admitting that he had been "deeply affected" by his recall, and had freely expressed his feelings. The correspondence, though long and not unfriendly, failed to prevent Monroe from

---

[1] W. C. Nicholas to Jefferson, Oct. 20, 1808; Jefferson MSS.

appearing as a rival candidate for the Presidency. One of his warmest supporters was Joseph H. Nicholson, to whom he wrote, September 24, a letter which in a different tone from that of Wilson Cary Nicholas betrayed the same helplessness of counsel:[1] —

"We seem now to be approaching a great crisis. Such is the state of our affairs, and such the compromitment of the Administration at home and abroad by its measures, that it seems likely that it will experience great difficulty in extricating itself. . . . We are invited with great earnestness to give the incumbents all the support we can, — by which is meant to give them our votes at the approaching election; but it is not certain that we could give effectual support to the person in whose favor it is requested, or that it would be advisable in any view to yield it. While we remain on independent ground, and give support where we think it is due, we preserve a resource in favor of free government within the limit of the Republican party. Compromit ourselves in the sense proposed, and that resource is gone. After what has passed, it has no right to suppose that we will, by a voluntary sacrifice, consent to bury ourselves in the same tomb with it."

If Wilson Cary Nicholas and James Monroe stood in such attitudes toward the Administration, admitting or proclaiming that its policy had failed, and that it could command no further confidence, what could be expected from the Federalists, who for eight years had foretold the failure? New England rang with cries for disunion. The Federalist leaders thought best to disavow treasonable intentions;[2] but they fell with their old bitterness on the personal character of President Jefferson, and trampled it deep in the mire. Many of the ablest and most liberal Federalist leaders had lagged behind or left the party, but the zealots of Pickering's class were stronger than ever. Pickering bent his energies to the task of proving that Jefferson was a tool of Napoleon, and that the embargo was laid in consequence of Napoleon's command. The success of this political delusion, both in England and

[1] Monroe to Joseph H. Nicholson, Sept. 24, 1808; Nicholson MSS.
[2] George Cabot to Pickering, Oct. 5, 1808; Lodge's Cabot, p. 308.

America, was astounding. Even a mind so vigorous and a judgment so calm as that of Chief-Justice Marshall bent under this popular imposture.

"Nothing can be more completely demonstrated," he wrote to Pickering,[1] "than the inefficacy of the embargo; yet that demonstration seems to be of no avail. I fear most seriously that the same spirit which so tenaciously maintains this measure will impel us to a war with the only power which protects any part of the civilized world from the despotism of that tyrant with whom we shall then be arranged. You have shown that the principle commonly called the Rule of 1756 is of much earlier date, and I fear have also shown to what influences the embargo is to be traced."

Chief-Justice Marshall had read Canning's insulting note of September 23 more than a month before this letter to Pickering was written; yet the idea of resenting it seemed not to enter his mind. Napoleon alone was the terror of Federalism; and this unreasoning fear exercised upon Marshall's calm judgment hardly less power than upon the imagination of Fisher Ames or the austerity of Timothy Pickering. Second only to Marshall, Rufus King was the foremost of Federalists; and the same horror of France which blinded Marshall, Ames, and Pickering to the conduct of England led King to hold the President responsible for Napoleon's violence. December 1, 1808, King wrote to Pickering a long letter containing views which in result differed little from those of Nicholas and Monroe. The Berlin Decree, he said, had violated treaty rights:[2]

"How dare then our Government with this document before them, to affirm and endeavor to impose upon the country so gross a misstatement as they have done in reference to this French Decree? The Berlin Decree, being an infringement of our rights, should have been resisted, as a similar decree of the Directory was resisted by the Federalists in 1798. Had we so done, there would have been no

[1] Marshall to Pickering, Dec. 19, 1808; Lodge's Cabot, p. 489.
[2] Rufus King to Pickering, Dec. 1, 1808; Pickering MSS.

Orders in Council, no embargo, and probably before this we should have been again in peace with France. . . . We are now told that the embargo must be continued or the country disgraced. Admitting the alternative, how shameful is it—how criminal rather, might I say—that the men who have brought the country to this condition should have the effrontery to make this declaration! The Administration will be disgraced by the repeal, and they deserve to be; perhaps they merit more than disgrace. But will the continuance of the embargo save the country from disgrace? As to its effect on France and England, we have sufficient evidence of its inefficacy. The longer it is continued, the deeper our disgrace when it is raised. It is earnestly to be hoped that the Federalists will leave to the Administration and its supporters all projects by way of substitute to the embargo. Having plunged the nation into its present embarrassment, let them bear the whole responsibility for their measures. The embargo must be repealed. That simple, unqualified measure must be adopted. It is high time to discard visionary experiments. For God's sake, let the Federalists abstain from any share in them!"

King was not only the ablest of the Northern Federalists, he was also the one who knew England best; and yet even he condescended to the excuse or palliation of England's conduct, as though Jefferson could have resisted the Berlin Decree without also resisting the previous robberies, impressments, and blockades of Great Britain. So deeply diseased was American opinion that patriotism vanished, and the best men in the Union took active part with Lord Castlereagh and George Canning in lowering and degrading their own government. Not even Rufus King could see the selfishness of that Tory reaction which, without regard to Napoleon's decrees, swept Great Britain into collision with the United States, and from which no act of Jefferson could have saved American interests. Though King were admitted to be right in thinking that the system of peaceable coercion, the "visionary experiments" of President Jefferson's statesmanship, the fretfulness of Madison's diplomacy, had invited or challenged insult, yet after these experiments had evidently failed and the failure was conceded, a modest share of patriotism might consent that some policy for the future should be indicated, and that some remnant of national dignity should be saved. No such sentimental weakness showed itself in the ranks of Federalism. Jefferson's friends and enemies alike foresaw that the embargo must be repealed; but neither friend nor enemy could or would suggest a remedy for national disgrace.

No record remains to show in what temper Jefferson received the letters of Canning and the warnings of Wilson Cary Nicholas. Had he in the course of his sorely tried political life ever given way to unrestrained violence of temper, he might fairly have flamed into passion on reading Canning's notes; but he seemed rather to deprecate them,—he made even an effort to persuade Canning that his innuendoes were unjust. A long memorandum in his own handwriting recorded an interview which took place November 9 between him and Erskine, the British minister.[4]

> "I told him I was going out of the Administration, and therefore might say to him things which I would not do were I to remain in. I wished to correct an error which I at first thought his Government above being led into from newspapers; but I apprehended they had adopted it. This was the supposed partiality of the Administration, and particularly myself, in favor of France and against England. I observed that when I came into the Administration there was nothing I so much desired as to be on a footing of intimate friendship with England; that I knew as long as she was our friend no enemy could hurt; that I would have sacrificed much to have effected it, and therefore wished Mr. King to have continued there as a favorable instrument; that if there had been an equal disposition on their part, I thought it might have been effected; for although the question of impressments was difficult on their side, and insuperable with us, yet had that been the sole question we might have shoved along in the hope of some compromise; . . . that he might judge from the communications now before Congress whether there had been any partiality to France, to whom he would see we had never made the

[1] Cabinet Memoranda; Writings (Ford), i. 336.

proposition to revoke the embargo immediately, which we did to England, and, again, that we had remonstrated strongly to them on the style of M. Champagny's letter, but had not to England on that of Canning, equally offensive; that the letter of Canning now reading to Congress, was written in the high ropes, and would be stinging to every American breast. . . . I told him in the course of the conversation that this country would never return to an intercourse with England while those Orders in Council were in force. In some part of it also I told him that Mr. Madison (who, it was now pretty well understood, would be my successor, to which he assented) had entertained the same cordial wishes as myself to be on a friendly footing with England."

Erskine reported this conversation to his Government;[1] and his report was worth comparing with that of Jefferson:—

"I collected from the general turn of his sentiments that he would prefer the alternative of embargo for a certain time, until the Congress should be enabled to come to some decided resolution as to the steps to be pursued. By this observation I believe he meant that he would wish to wait until March next, when the new Congress would be assembled, and the general sense of the people of the United States might be taken upon the state of their affairs. . . . He took an opportunity of observing in the course of his conversation that his Administration had been most wrongfully accused of partiality toward France; that for his own part he felt no scruple, as he was about to retire, to declare that he had been always highly desirous of an intimate connection with Great Britain; and that if any temporary arrangement on the subject of impressment could have been made, although he never would have consented to abandon the principle of immunity from impressment for the citizens of the United States, yet that the two countries might have shoved along (was his familiar expression) very well until some definite settlement could have taken place. He remarked also that these were, he knew,

[1] Erskine to Canning, Nov. 10, 1808; MSS. British Archives.

the sentiments of Mr. Madison, who would in all probability succeed him in his office. He hinted also that both had been long jealous of the ambitious views and tyrannical conduct of Bonaparte."

"These declarations," continued Erskine, "are so opposite to the general opinion of what their real sentiments have been that it is very difficult to reconcile them." In truth, the footing of intimate friendship with England so much desired by Jefferson demanded from England more concessions than she was yet ready to yield; but nothing could be truer or more characteristic than the President's remark that under his charge the two countries might have "shoved along very well," had peace depended only upon him. In this phrase lay both the defence and the criticism of his statesmanship.

In any event, nothing could be more certain than that the time for shoving along at all was past. The country had come to a stand-still; and some heroic resolution must be taken. The question pressing for an answer concerned Jefferson more directly than it concerned any one else. What did he mean to do? For eight years, in regard to foreign relations his will had been law. Except when the Senate, in 1806, with disastrous results, obliged him to send William Pinkney to negotiate a treaty with England, Congress had never crossed the President's foreign policy by wilful interference; and when this policy ended in admitted failure, his dignity and duty required him to stand by the government, and to take the responsibility that belonged to him. Yet the impression which Erskine drew from his words was correct. He had no other plan than to postpone further action until after March 4, 1809, when he should retire from control. With singular frankness he avowed this wish. After the meeting of Congress, November 7, when doubt and confusion required control, Jefferson drew himself aside, repeating without a pause the formula that embargo was the alternative to war.[1] "As yet the first seems most to prevail," he wrote,[2] a few days after his interview with Erskine; and no one doubted to which side he leaned, though as if it were a matter of course that he

[1] Jefferson to Governor Pinckney, Nov. 8, 1808; Writings, v. 383.
[2] Jefferson to Governor Lincoln, Nov. 13, 1808; Writings, v. 387.

should quit the government before his successor was even elected, he added. "On this occasion I think it is fair to leave to those who are to act on them the decisions they prefer, being to be myself but a spectator. I should not feel justified in directing measures which those who are to execute them would disapprove. Our situation is truly difficult. We have been pressed by the belligerents to the very wall, and all further retreat is impracticable."

Madison and Gallatin did not share Jefferson's notion of Executive duties, and they made an effort to bring the President back to a juster sense of what was due to himself and to the nation. November 15 Gallatin wrote a friendly letter to Jefferson, urging him to resume his functions.

"Both Mr. Madison and myself," wrote Gallatin,[1] "concur in the opinion that considering the temper of the Legislature it would be eligible to point out to them some precise and distinct course. As to what that should be we may not all perfectly agree, and perhaps the knowledge of the various feelings of the members, and of the apparent public opinion, may on consideration induce a revision of our own. I feel myself nearly as undetermined between enforcing the embargo or war as I was at our last meeting. But I think that we must, or rather you must, decide the question absolutely, so that we may point out a decisive course either way to our friends. Mr. Madison, being unwell, proposed that I should call on you, and suggest our wish that we might, with the other gentlemen, be called by you on that subject. Should you think that course proper, the sooner the better."

Jefferson's reply to this request was not recorded, but he persisted in considering himself as no longer responsible for the government. Although Madison could not become even President-elect before the first Wednesday in December, when the electors were to give their votes; and although the official declaration of this vote could not take place before the second Wednesday in February,—Jefferson insisted that his functions were merely formal from the moment when the name of his probable successor was known.

[1] Gallatin to Jefferson, Nov. 15, 1808; Gallatin's Writings, i. 420.

"I have thought it right," he wrote December 27,[1] "to take no part myself in proposing measures the execution of which will devolve on my successor. I am therefore chiefly an unmeddling listener to what others say. On the same ground, I shall make no new appointments which can be deferred till the fourth of March, thinking it fair to leave to my successor to select the agents for his own Administration. As the moment of my retirement approaches I become more anxious for its arrival, and to begin at length to pass what yet remains to me of life and health in the bosom of my family and neighbors, and in communication with my friends undisturbed by political concerns or passions."

So freely did he express this longing for escape that his enemies exulted in it as a fresh proof of their triumph. Josiah Quincy, his fear of the President vanishing into contempt,— "a dish of skim-milk curdling at the head of our nation,"— writing to the man whom eight years before Jefferson had driven from the White House, gave an account of the situation differing only in temper from Jefferson's description of himself:[2] —

"Fear of responsibility and love of popularity are now master-passions, and regulate all the movements. The policy is to keep things as they are, and wait for European events. It is hoped the chapter of accidents may present something favorable within the remaining three months; and if it does not, no great convulsion can happen during that period. The Presidential term will have expired, and then—away to Monticello, and let the Devil take the hindmost. I do believe that not a whit deeper project than this fills the august mind of your successor."

Had Jefferson strictly carried out his doctrine, and abstained from interference of any kind in the decision of a future policy, the confusion in Congress might have been less than it was, and the chance of agreement might have been greater; but while apparently refusing to interfere, in effect he

[1] Jefferson to Dr. Logan, Dec. 27, 1808; Writings, v. 404.
[2] Josiah Quincy to John Adams, Dec. 15, 1808; Quincy's Life of J. Quincy, p. 146.

exerted his influence to prevent change; and to prevent a change of measures was to maintain the embargo. In insisting that the whole matter should be left to the next Congress and President, Jefferson resisted the popular pressure for repeal, embarrassing his successor, distracting the Legislature, and destroying the remnants of his own popularity. Especially the Eastern Democrats, who had reason to believe that in New England the Union depended on repeal, were exasperated to find Jefferson, though declaring neutrality, yet privately exert ing his influence to postpone action until the meeting of another Congress. Among the Eastern members was Joseph Story, who had been elected to succeed Crowninshield, as a Republican, to represent Salem and Marblehead. Story took his seat Dec. 20, 1808, and instantly found himself in opposition to President Jefferson and the embargo: —

"I found that as a measure of retaliation the system had not only failed, but that Mr. Jefferson, from pride of opinion as well as from that visionary course of speculation which often misled his judgment, was absolutely bent upon maintaining it at all hazards. He professed a firm belief that Great Britain would abandon her Orders in Council if we persisted in the embargo; and having no other scheme to offer in case of the failure of this, he maintained in private conversation the indispensable necessity of closing the session of Congress without any attempt to limit the duration of the system."[1]

Josiah Quincy and Joseph Story were comparatively friendly in their views of Jefferson's conduct. The extreme Federalist opinion, represented by Timothy Pickering, placed the President in a light far more repulsive.

"It is scarcely conceivable," wrote Pickering[2] to Christopher Gore Jan. 8, 1809, "that Mr. Jefferson should so obstinately persevere in the odious measure of the embargo, which he cannot but see has impaired his popularity and hazards its destruction, if he were not under secret engagements to the French Emperor,—unless you can suppose

[1] Story's Life of Story, i. 184.
[2] Pickering to C. Gore, Jan. 8, 1809; Pickering MSS.

that he would run that hazard and the ruin of his country, rather than that a measure which he explicitly recommended should be pronounced unwise. . . . When we advert to the real character of Mr. Jefferson, there is no nefarious act of which we may not suppose him capable. *He would rather the United States should sink, than change the present system of measures.* This is not opinion, but history. I repeat it confidentially to you until I obtain permission to vouch it on evidence which I trust I can obtain."[1]

Pickering's hatred of Jefferson amounted to mania; but his language showed the influence which, whether intentionally or not, the President still exerted on the decisions of Congress. All accounts agreed that while refusing to act officially, the President resisted every attempt to change, during his time, the policy he had established. Canning's defiance and Napoleon's discipline reduced him to silence and helplessness; but even when prostrate and alone, he clung to the remnant of his system. Disaster upon disaster, mortification upon mortification, crowded fast upon the man whose triumphs had been so brilliant, but whose last hope was to escape a public censure more humiliating than any yet inflicted on a President of the United States. The interest attached to the history of his administration—an interest at all times singularly personal—centred at last upon the single point of his personality, all eyes fixing themselves upon the desperate malice with which his ancient enemies strove to drive him from his cover, and the painful efforts with which he still sought to escape their fangs.

[1] Cf. Pickering to S. P. Gardner; New England Federalism, p. 379.

Chapter XVI

NOVEMBER 8 President Jefferson sent to Congress his last Annual Message, and with it the correspondence of Pinkney and Armstrong. Intent as the public was upon foreign affairs alone, the Message had no further interest than as it dealt with the question of embargo; but Jefferson showed that he had lost none of his old dexterity, for he succeeded in giving to his words the appearance of conveying no opinion: —

"Under a continuance of the belligerent measures which, in defiance of laws which consecrate the rights of neutrals, overspread the ocean with danger, it will rest with the wisdom of Congress to decide on the course best adapted to such a state of things; and bringing with them as they do from every part of the Union the sentiments of our constituents, my confidence is strengthened that in forming this decision they will, with an unerring regard to the rights and interests of the nation, weigh and compare the painful alternatives out of which a choice is to be made. Nor should I do justice to the virtues which on other occasions have marked the character of our fellow-citizens, if I did not cherish an equal confidence that the alternative chosen, whatever it may be, will be maintained with all the fortitude and patriotism which the crisis ought to inspire."

The favorite assumption that Congress, not the Executive, directed the national policy served again to veil Jefferson's wishes, but in this instance with some reason; for no one was ignorant that a strong party in Congress meant if possible to take the decision out of the President's hands. Only by the phrase "painful alternatives" did he hint an opinion, for every one knew that by this phrase he aimed at narrowing the choice of Congress between embargo and war. One other paragraph suggested that his own choice would favor continued commercial restrictions: —

"The situation into which we have thus been forced has impelled us to apply a portion of our industry and capital to internal manufactures and improvements. The extent of this conversion is daily increasing, and little doubt remains that the establishments formed and forming will—under the auspices of cheaper material and subsistence, the freedom of labor from taxation with us, and of protecting duties and prohibitions—become permanent."

Not only the Message but also the language, still more emphatic, of private letters showed that Jefferson had become a convert to manufactures and protected industries. "My idea is that we should encourage home manufactures," he said,[1] "to the extent of our own consumption of everything of which we raise the raw material." This avowal did much to increase the ill-will of New England, where Jefferson's hostility to foreign commerce as a New England interest was believed to be inveterate and deadly; but the anger of Massachusetts and Connecticut at the wound thus threatened to their commerce and shipping could not exceed the perplexity of Southern Republicans, who remembered that Jefferson in 1801 promised them "a wise and frugal government, which shall restrain men from injuring one another; which shall leave them otherwise free to regulate their own pursuits of industry and improvement, and shall not take from the mouth of labor the bread it has earned." Not only manufactures but also internal improvements were to become a chief object of governmental regulation to an extent which no Federalist had ever suggested. The absolute prohibition of foreign manufactures was to go hand in hand with a magnificent scheme of public works. In the actual state of public affairs,—without revenue and on the verge of war with France and England,—Jefferson exposed himself to ridicule by alluding to a surplus; years were to pass before the employment of surplus revenue was to become a practical question in American politics, and long before it rose Jefferson had reverted to his old theories of "a wise and frugal government;" but in 1808, as President, he welcomed any diversion which enabled him to avoid the need of facing the spectre of war.

"The probable accumulation of the surpluses of reve-

[1] Jefferson to Colonel Humphreys, Jan. 20, 1809; to Mr. Leiper, Jan. 21, 1809; Works, v. 415, 416.

nue," he said, "whenever the freedom and safety of our commerce shall be restored, merits the consideration of Congress. Shall it lie unproductive in the public vaults? Shall the revenue be reduced? Or shall it not rather be appropriated to the improvements of roads, canals, rivers, education, and other great foundations of prosperity and union, under the powers which Congress may already possess, or such amendments of the Constitution as may be approved by the States?"

The whole meaning of this paragraph was explained by other documents. March 2, 1807, the Senate adopted a Resolution calling upon the President for a plan of internal improvements. April 4, 1808, Gallatin made an elaborate Report, which sketched a great scheme of public works. Canals were to be cut through Cape Cod, New Jersey, Delaware, and from Norfolk to Albemarle Sound, —thus creating an internal water-way nearly the whole length of the coast. Four great Eastern rivers—the Susquehanna, Potomac, James, and Santee, or Savannah—were to be opened to navigation from tide-water to the highest practicable points, and thence to be connected by roads with four corresponding Western rivers, —the Alleghany, Monongahela, Kanawha, and Tennessee,— wherever permanent navigation could be depended upon. Other canals were to connect Lake Champlain and Lake Ontario with the Hudson River; to pass round Niagara and the falls of the Ohio; and to connect other important points. A turnpike road was to be established from Maine to Georgia along the coast. To carry out these schemes Congress was to pledge two million dollars of the annual surplus for ten years in advance; and the twenty millions thus spent might be partly or wholly replaced by selling to private corporations the canals and turnpikes as they should become productive; or the public money might at the outset be loaned to private corporations for purposes of construction.

A national university was intended to crown a scheme so extensive in its scope that no European monarch, except perhaps the Czar, could have equalled its scale. Jefferson cherished it as his legacy to the nation,—the tangible result of his "visionary" statesmanship. Five years afterward he still spoke of it as "the fondest wish of his heart," and declared that "so enviable a state in prospect for our country induced me to temporize and to bear with national wrongs which under no other prospect ought ever to have been unresented or unresisted."[1] Even in the close presence of bankruptcy or war he could not lay aside his hopes, or abstain from pressing his plan upon the attention of Congress at the moment when the last chance of its success had vanished.

The contrast between the President's sanguine visions and the reality was made the more striking by Gallatin's Annual Report, sent to Congress a few days later. The President spoke for the Administration that was passing away, while Gallatin represented the Administration to come. That the secretary leaned toward war was notorious, and that he was Madison's chief adviser, perhaps to be the head of his Cabinet, was known or suspected by the men who stood nearest to the Secretary of State, and who studied Gallatin's Report as though it were Madison's first Annual Message. The more carefully it was studied, the more distinctly it took the character of a War Budget.

Receipts from customs had stopped, but the accrued revenue of 1807 had brought nearly eighteen million dollars into the Treasury; and sixteen millions would remain to supply the wants of Government at the close of the year 1808. Of this sum the ordinary annual appropriations would consume thirteen millions. Starting from this point, Gallatin discussed the financial effect of the alternatives which lay before Congress. The first was that of total or partial submission to the belligerents; "and as, in pursuing that humble path, means of defence will become unnecessary,—as there will be no occasion for either an army or a navy,—it is believed that there would be no difficulty in reducing the public expenditures to a rate corresponding with the fragments of impost which might still be collected." The second choice of measures was to continue the embargo without war; and in this case the government might be supported for two years with no greater effort than that of borrowing five million dollars. Finally, Congress might declare war against one or both of the belligerents, and

[1] Jefferson to Eppes, Sept. 11, 1813; Works, vi. 194.

in that event Gallatin asked only leave to contract loans. Persons familiar with the history of the Republican party, and with the career of its leaders when in opposition, could not but wonder that Gallatin should ask leave to create a new funded debt for purposes of war. To reconcile the inconsistency Gallatin once more argued that experience proved debt to be less dangerous than had ten years before been supposed: —

"The high price of public stocks and indeed of all species of stocks, the reduction of the public debt, the unimpaired credit of the general government, and the large amount of existing bank-stock in the United States leave no doubt of the practicability of obtaining the necessary loans on reasonable terms. The geographical situation of the United States, their history since the Revolution, and above all present events remove every apprehension of frequent wars It may therefore be confidently expected that a revenue derived solely from duties on importations, though necessarily impaired by war, will always be amply sufficient during long intervals of peace not only to defray current expenses, but also to reimburse the debt contracted during the few periods of war. No internal taxes, either direct or indirect, are therefore contemplated, even in the case of hostilities carried on against the two great belligerent Powers."

Such language was an invitation to war. Gallatin carried courage as far as the President carried caution. While Jefferson talked of surpluses and deprecated "painful alternatives," his Secretary of the Treasury invited Congress to declare war against the two greatest Powers in the world, and promised to support it without imposing a single internal tax.

Madison, upon whose decision even more than on that of Congress the future policy of the Government depended, would not express an emphatic opinion. A glimpse of the chaos that prevailed in the Executive Department was given in a letter from Macon to Nicholson,[1] written December 4, after Macon had offered Resolutions in the House looking to a persistence in the system of embargo and peaceable coercion: —

[1] Macon to Joseph H. Nicholson, Dec. 4, 1808; Adams's Gallatin, p. 384.

"Gallatin is most decidedly for war, and I think that the Vice-President [Clinton] and W. C. Nicholas are of the same opinion. It is said that the President [Jefferson] gives no opinion as to the measures that ought to be adopted. It is not known whether he be for war or peace. It is reported that Mr. Madison is for the plan which I have submitted, with the addition of high protecting duties to encourage the manufacturers of the United States. I am as much against war as Gallatin is in favor of it. Thus I have continued in Congress till there is not one of my old fellow-laborers that agrees with me in opinion."

Indecision ruled everywhere at Washington down to the close of the year. Jefferson would say nothing at all; Madison would say nothing decisive;[1] and Gallatin struggled in vain to give a show of character to the Government. December 29 one of the Massachusetts representatives wrote to a correspondent the details of the secretary's plan:[2] —

"Yesterday I spent an hour with Mr. Gallatin, when he unfolded to me his plan, — a plan which he thinks will finally prevail. It is this: That we immediately pass a non-intercourse Act to take effect, say, June 1 next; and as the bill now reads, that it become null toward that Power which may relax. Send out the Act forthwith to England and to France, together with an Act raising the embargo partially, say, at the same time, and arming, or granting letters of marque, etc. These being made known to Great Britain and France, it is expected that the obstinate Emperor will not alter his course, but it is expected that Great Britain, when she finds the stand we deliberately take, — that we have no rebellion; that Madison and a majority of Democrats are chosen; and that we shall be fighting a common enemy (France) with her, — and when she finds that we intend living without dishonorable purchases of her goods, etc., will study her interest and relax."

The same day Gallatin wrote confidentially to Nicholson, describing the extreme anxieties he felt:[3] —

[1] Madison to Pinkney, Dec. 5, 1808; Madison's Writings, ii. 427.
[2] Orchard Cook to J. Q. Adams, Dec. 29, 1808; Adams MSS.
[3] Gallatin to Nicholson, Dec. 29, 1808; Adams's Gallatin, p. 384.

"Never was I so overwhelmed with public business. That would be nothing if we went right; but a great confusion and perplexity reign in Congress. Mr. Madison is, as I always knew him, slow in taking his ground, but firm when the storm arises. What I had foreseen has taken place. A majority will not adhere to the embargo much longer, and if war be not speedily determined on, submission will soon ensue."

Joseph Story two days afterward wrote a more exact account of the distraction which prevailed at the White House.

"The Administration are desirous of peace," wrote Story,[1] in confidence, December 31. "They believe that we must suffer much from war; they are satisfied, even now, that if the embargo could be continued for one year our rights would be acknowledged were our own citizens only true to their own interests. They deem this continuance impracticable, and therefore are of opinion that after midsummer the plan must be abandoned; and war will then ensue unless the belligerents abandon their aggressions."

The chaos prevailing in the White House was order compared with the condition of Congress; and there again Gallatin was forced to guide. After listening November 8 to the President's serene Message, the House three days later referred the paragraphs concerning foreign Powers to a committee with G. W. Campbell at its head. Campbell probably consulted Madison, and his instance doubtless caused the fruitless appeal of November 15, through Gallatin, to Jefferson. Failing to obtain guidance from the President, Gallatin wrote a Report, which was probably approved by Madison, and which Campbell presented November 22 to the House. For clearness and calmness of statement this paper, famous in its day as "Campbell's Report,"[2] has never been surpassed in the political literature of the United States; but the rigorous logic of its conclusions terrified men who could not refute and would not accept them: —

"What course ought the United States to pursue? Your

[1] Joseph Story to Joseph White, Dec. 31, 1808; Story's Life of Story, i. 172.
[2] State Papers, iii. 259.

committee can perceive no other alternative but abject and degrading submission, war with both nations, or a continuance and enforcement of the present suspension of commerce.

"The first cannot require any discussion; but the pressure of the embargo, so sensibly felt, and the calamities inseparable from a state of war, naturally create a wish that some middle course might be discovered which should avoid the evils of both and not be inconsistent with national honor and independence. That illusion must be dissipated; and it is necessary that the people of the United States should fully understand the situation in which they are placed.

"There is no other alternative but war with both parties or a continuance of the present system. For war with one of the belligerents only would be submission to the edicts and will of the other; and a repeal, in whole or in part, of the embargo must necessarily be war or submission."

To Federalists these stern truths were not wholly unwelcome, since they brought to an issue the whole policy, domestic and foreign, which for eight years the Federalist party had never ceased to condemn; but to Republicans, who were equally responsible with the President for the policy which ended in Gallatin's alternative, the harshness of the choice was intolerable. They felt that the embargo must be abandoned; but they felt still more strongly that the double war was ruin. In vain Gallatin tried in his Treasury Report to persuade them that to fight the two nations was a practicable task. Congress writhed and rebelled.

Campbell's report closed by recommending three Resolutions as common ground on which all parties could take their stand, whether for war or embargo. The first declared that the United States could not, without a sacrifice of their rights, honor, and independence, submit to the edicts of Great Britain and France. The second declared the expediency of excluding from the United States the ships and the products of all Powers which maintained these edicts in force. The third recommended immediate preparations for defence.

The Federalists were eager for attack; and when, November 28, Campbell called up the first of his Resolutions for debate,

Josiah Quincy fell upon it with violence not easily forgotten, and doubtless meant to strengthen the general belief that New England would control her passions no longer.

"The course advocated in that Report is in my opinion loathsome," he said; "the spirit it breathes disgraceful; the temper it is likely to inspire neither calculated to regain the rights we have lost, nor to preserve those which remain to us."

Assuming that the Report was made in the interest of embargo, and that it foreshadowed the permanence of the anti-commercial system, he met it by threats of insurrection and civil war, expressed in the same breath with which they were disavowed: —

"Good Heavens! Mr. Chairman, are men mad? Is this House touched with that insanity which is the never-failing precursor of the intention of Heaven to destroy? The people of New England, after eleven months' deprivation of the ocean, to be commanded still longer to abandon it! for an undefined period to hold their unalienable rights at the tenure of the will of Britain or of Bonaparte! . . . I am lost in astonishment, Mr. Chairman. I have not words to express the matchless absurdity of this attempt. I have no tongue to express the swift and headlong destruction which a blind perseverance in such a system must bring upon this nation. . . . This embargo must be repealed. You cannot enforce it for any important period of time longer. When I speak of your inability to enforce this law, let not gentlemen misunderstand me. I mean not to intimate insurrection or open defiance of them; although it is impossible to foresee in what acts that oppression will finally terminate which, we are told, makes wise men mad." Nature gave the ocean to New England, "and among a people thus situated, thus educated, thus numerous, laws prohibiting them from the exercise of their natural rights will have a binding effect not one moment longer than the public sentiment supports them."

Always assuming that the talk of war covered the plan of retaining the embargo, Quincy allowed himself to encourage warlike ideas much more recklessly than suited some of his party friends. He ventured to goad the majority toward a decision which of all possible results was most disliked by the Federalists of New England: —

> "Take no counsel of fears. Your strength will increase with the trial, and prove greater than you are now aware. But I shall be told this may lead to war. I ask, Are we now at peace? Certainly not, unless retiring from insult be peace, unless shrinking under the lash be peace. The surest way to prevent war is not to fear it. The idea that nothing on earth is so dreadful as war is inculcated too studiously among us. Disgrace is worse. Abandonment of essential rights is worse."

Whatever Quincy might have been willing to accept, the party to which he belonged wanted no war except with France, while the Republicans were opposed to war in any shape. John Randolph did indeed hint at the use of force, but Randolph's opinion was never for two days the same. Philip Barton Key of Maryland, as vehement a Federalist as Quincy, also advised a policy which could lead only to war: —

> "I would let our vessels go out armed for resistance, and if they were interfered with I would make the *dernier* appeal. We are able and willing to resist; and when the moment arrives, there will be but one heart and one hand throughout the Union."

The sentiment was patriotic; but as though expressly to prove how little it could be trusted, Barent Gardenier rose to say, in emphatic and unqualified terms, that England was wholly in the right, and that from the first the American government had aimed at provoking war.[1] Gardenier's views were those of a majority of Federalists, and in the end were adopted by the party. Quincy's blindness to the serious danger of war cost him the confidence of more cautious conservatives.

On the opposite side, the Republicans seemed for the most part fairly cowed by the vigor with which the Federalists

[1] Annals of Congress, 1808–1809, p. 839.

defied the embargo and war at once. Nothing in American history offered a more interesting illustration of the first stage of the national character than the open avowals by Congress in 1808 of motives closely akin to fear. America as a nation could run no serious military peril, even though she declared war on England and France at once. The worst military disaster that could happen would be a bombardment or temporary occupation of some seaboard city; the most terrible punishment within the range of possibility was the burning of a few small wooden towns which could be rebuilt in three months, and whose destruction implied no necessary loss of life. Neither England nor France had armies to spare for permanent conquest in America; but so thoroughly had the theory of peaceable coercion taken possession of the national character that men of courage appealed to motives such as in a private dispute they would have thought degrading.

"The gentleman talked of resistance, and resistance on sea," said Willis Alston of North Carolina, in reply to Quincy.[1] "Did any one believe that he seriously meant meeting the powerful navy of Great Britain on the sea,— of that Britain who had been emphatically styled 'the mistress of the ocean,' and who was 'fighting for the liberties of the world and of mankind'? No, sir; nothing of the kind is meant. Submission to her orders would be the inevitable consequence of the gentleman's resistance, and finally a loss of everything dear to the American character,—a loss of our liberty and independence as a free people."

As though one such admission were not enough, Alston obstinately recurred to it. "An idea of that sort of resistance is too idle to merit serious consideration." That Willis Alston was a man of no great distinction might be true; but such expressions were not confined to him. Richard M. Johnson of Kentucky, as brave a man as lived, could not face the idea of war:—

"At the most alarming crisis that ever convulsed the political world, when empires and kingdoms have changed with the season, and America, buffeted on every side, has

[1] Annals of Congress, 1808–1809, p. 556.

maintained the ground of perfect neutrality, this nation should make a pause on this high eminence before they plunge into the dread conflict."

A nation which had never yet moved a muscle could hardly "make a pause;" but even if Colonel Johnson's figures had been more correct, the sentiment was in his mouth unexpected, for in Kentucky gentlemen "buffeted on every side" were not supposed to pause. Still more remarkable was the language of Troup of Georgia—"the hot-headed Georgian," as Jefferson afterward called him, who twenty years later challenged a civil war, but who in 1808 was even more anxious than Johnson to pause on the high eminence where he was buffeted on every side.

"Permission to arm," he said,[1] "is tantamount to a declaration of war; and the people of this country want peace as long as they can preserve it with honor. And do you think, sir, we are ready to plunge into a ruinous war, naked and unarmed, to gratify a few bankrupt commercial speculators? It is easy to declare war; it is more difficult under present circumstances to maintain peace; and it is most difficult of all to wage a successful war. Sir, beware! It is the object of the gentleman from Massachusetts and his friends to lead you step by step into a war, and if he can into an unpopular war, which the moment you cease to conduct with effect you are ruined, and he and his friends are exalted; . . . and, sir, the moment this party ceases to rule, republicanism is gone, and with it the hopes of all good men forever."

Apart from the picture of American jealousies, Troup's remarks offered an interesting example of the ideas then held in regard to national honor. No one made the obvious retort that a nation which preserved peace by tolerating insults like those inflicted by Champagny and Canning had best say nothing of its honor. The fiction of pride was still kept up, though members descended to appeals which seemed to imply physical fear. Madison's brother-in-law, John G. Jackson, admitted himself to be cowed by Canning's brutality.

[1] Annals of Congress, 1808–1809, p. 606.

"The fires lighted up in Copenhagen," said he,[1] "are scarcely extinguished; they are yet glowing before us in imagination at least. And we ought to recollect that if we do not submit, it is war; if we do submit, it is tribute; and if we have war, our towns will share the fate of fortified Copenhagen, unless we strengthen and fortify them."

On such reasoning, submission and tribute alone were possible, since fortifications which had failed to protect Copenhagen were little likely to protect Norfolk or New York. Macon joined in the same cry:

"We have enough of the necessaries of life to make us content, and there is no nation in the world at this time that enjoys more of the luxuries of Europe and of the East and West Indies than we do,—in a word, none that enjoys more of the good things of this world."

The spectacle of simple and hardy Speaker Macon in his homespun suit enjoying all the luxuries of Europe and the farthest East, while Pinkney and Armstrong paid for them in the spoils of American merchants, was quaintly humorous; but no one felt its sting of satire. Even the typical South Carolinian, David R. Williams,—a man second to none in courage and independence of character,—wished to hide behind the embargo for fear of war:—

"I see no other honorable course in which peace can be maintained. Take whatever other project has been hinted at and war inevitably results. While we can procrastinate the miseries of war, I am for procrastinating. We thereby gain the additional advantage of waiting the events in Europe. The true interests of this country can be found only in peace. Among many other important considerations, remember that the moment you go to war you may bid adieu to every prospect of discharging the national debt."[2]

The Secretary of the Treasury had only a month before officially asserted the contrary; but any excuse for avoiding war seemed to satisfy the House. From the beginning to the end

[1] Annals of Congress, 1808–1809, p. 657.
[2] Annals of Congress, 1808–1809, p. 797.

of this long and ardent debate not one member from any quarter of the Union ventured to say—what every man in the United States would have said ten years later—that after the formal and fixed decisions of France and England war existed in fact and should be declared in form.

With all John Randolph's waywardness and extravagance, he alone shone among this mass of mediocrities, and like the water-snakes in Coleridge's silent ocean his every track was a flash of golden fire. At moments he struck passionately at his own favorite companions—at Macon and Williams—as he struck at Jefferson. The steady decline of public spirit stung his pride. "It was in that fatal session of 1805–1806 that the policy of yielding to anything that might come in the shape of insult and aggression was commenced. The result was then foretold. It has happened."[1] Speaker after speaker revelled in narrating the long list of insults and outrages which America had endured in patience.

"The House will pardon me," said Randolph,[2] "if I forbear a minute recapitulation of the wrongs which we have received not only from the two great belligerents of Europe, but from the little belligerents also. I cannot, like Shylock, take a pleasure in saying, 'On such a day you called me dog; on such a day you spit upon my gabardine.'"

Yet Randolph himself fell naturally into the habits at which he sneered; and his wit alone raised him above the common level of Congressmen. However happily he might ridicule the timidity and awkwardness of others, he never advanced a positive opinion of his own without repudiating it the moment he was taken at his word. "I would scuffle for commerce," he said;[3] and the phrase was itself unworthy of a proud people like the Virginians; but when Campbell tried to force from him a pledge to stand by the Government in asserting the national rights, Randolph declined to gratify him.

Of all the speakers, George Washington Campbell—the reputed author of the Report—alone took a tone which might almost be called courageous; but even Campbell thought

[1] Annals of Congress, 1808–1809, p. 685.
[2] Annals of Congress, 1808–1809, p. 595.
[3] Annals of Congress, 1808–1809, pp. 687, 688.

more of tactics than of dignity. He admitted that the object of his Report was to unite the party on common ground; but he dared not say whether this common ground was to be embargo or war; he did not even say—what must have been in his mind—that the Government had exhausted alternatives. His chief effort seemed rather to be directed toward making a dilemma for the Federalists:—

"Are they determined to vindicate the rights and independence of their country? If they are, we wish to know in what manner. If they are not willing to pursue the measures of resistance we propose, of a total interdiction of intercourse with those Powers, will they assume a higher ground? Will they prefer war? If they do, this is one of the alternatives presented in the Report. We wish to know what measures they are willing to adopt for the safety of the nation. The crisis is awful. The time has come to unite the people of America. We join issue with the gentlemen as to a temporizing policy. We have not,—we will not now temporize. We say there is no middle course. We are in the first place for cutting off all intercourse with those Powers who trample on our rights. If that will not prove effectual, we say take the last alternative, war, with all its calamities, rather than submission or national degradation."

The most interesting part of Campbell's speech was his awkward admission that peaceable coercion had failed. Such an admission was equivalent to avowing that the Republican party had failed, but Campbell stumbled as he best could through this mortifying confession.

"We could not foresee," he said,[1] "that the Governments of those Powers would not regard the distress and sufferings of their own people; that France would suffer her West Indian colonies to be almost desolated with famine, and to be compelled to apply to their inveterate enemy to save them from actual starvation rather than revoke her decrees; nor could we know that the Government of Great Britain would be regardless of the complaints and representations of her manufacturers and a respectable portion of her

[1] Annals of Congress, 1808–1809, p. 747.

merchants; that it would lend a deaf ear to the hungry cries of the starving mechanics, and silence their just and loud complaints with the thunder of their murdering guns, and quench their hunger with a shower of balls instead of bread. We cannot be culpable for not anticipating such events."

Yet for twenty years the Federalists had wearied the country with prophecies of these disappointments which Campbell and his Republican friends said they could not be expected to foresee. Jefferson had persisted in acting on the theory that he could enforce national rights by peaceable means; had staked his reputation, after long and varied experience, on the soundness of this doctrine which his political opponents denied; and suddenly, on its failure, his followers pleaded that they could not be held culpable for failing to anticipate what their political opponents had steadily foretold. The confession of such an oversight was more fatal than all the sneers of Randolph and the taunts of Quincy.

There Congress for the moment stopped. The debate— which began November 28 and lasted till December 17— ended in the adoption of Campbell's first Resolution by a vote of one hundred and eighteen to two; of the second by eighty-four to thirty; and of the third without opposition. Nothing was decided; and the year closed leaving Congress, as Gallatin told his friend Nicholson, in "great confusion and perplexity."

Chapter XVII

B EHIND THE SCENES diplomacy was at work, actively seeking to disentangle or to embroil the plot of the culminating drama. Erskine, the British minister, sympathizing with his father Lord Erskine, in good will to America, hurried from one to another of the officials at Washington, trying to penetrate their thoughts,—an easy task,—and to find a bond of union between them and George Canning,—a problem as difficult as any that ever diplomacy solved. Besides his interview with Jefferson, he reported conversations with the Cabinet.

"I have had several interviews with Mr. Madison since the arrival of the 'Hope,' " he wrote November 5,[1] "and have often turned the conversation upon the points above mentioned, which he did not seem willing to discuss; but I could collect from what he did say that it was his own opinion that all intercourse ought to be broken off with the belligerents, and that some steps further—to use his expression—ought to be taken. . . . I will just communicate to you the hints which were thrown out by Mr. Smith, Secretary of the Navy, in a conversation which I had with him,—of an unofficial kind, indeed, but in which he expressed his sentiments unequivocally,—that in addition to the steps alluded to by Mr. Madison, he would wish that their ministers should be recalled from England and France, and that preparations should be immediately made for a state of hostility. Mr. Gallatin, the Secretary of the Treasury, would have preferred taking a decided part against one or other of those Powers before the embargo was first laid, but thinks that no other course can now be adopted. The Vice-President, Mr. Clinton, was and is strongly averse to the embargo system; and though he does not openly declare himself, it is well known that he is entirely opposed to the present Administration. . . . Indeed, in conversation with me yesterday he inveighed with great force against the conduct of Bonaparte toward Spain, and

[1] Erskine to Canning, Nov. 5, 1808; MSS. British Archives.

expressed his astonishment that any American should have *hesitated* to express such sentiments. He alluded to the conduct of this Government in not only withholding any approbation of the noble efforts of the Spaniards to resist that usurper's tyranny over them, but to the language held by their newspapers, and in private by themselves, of regret at these events as being likely to conduce to the interest and success of England. A different tone is now assumed upon that important subject; and the President said to me a few days ago that however he might doubt the eventual success of the Spanish cause, the feelings of a *tiger* could alone lead to an attempt to subjugate them through such torrents of blood and such devastation as must ensue if followed by success."

Erskine's report was nearly exact. In regard to Robert Smith, it was confirmed by a letter written at the same moment by Smith to the President;[1] and so far as concerned Madison, Gallatin, and George Clinton, it was not far wrong. A month then passed while Congress drifted toward a decision. At last, about December 1, Erskine roused himself to an effort. Doubtless Madison and Gallatin knew his purpose,— perhaps they inspired it; but in any case, Erskine acted rather in their interests than in the spirit or policy of Canning.

December 3 the British minister wrote to his Government the first of a series of despatches calculated to bring Canning to his senses.

"The Government and party in power," said he,[2] "unequivocally express their resolution not to remove the embargo, except by substituting war measures against both belligerents, unless either or both should relax their restrictions upon neutral commerce."

To reinforce this assertion Erskine reported an interview with Secretary Madison, who after reviewing the facts had ended by explicitly threatening a declaration of war. He said in substance—

[1] R. Smith to Jefferson, Nov. 1, 1808; Jefferson MSS.
[2] Erskine to Canning, Dec. 3, 1808; Cobbett's Debates, xvii., Appendix cxxxiv.

"That as the world must be convinced that America had in vain taken all the means in her power to obtain from Great Britain and France a just attention to their rights as a neutral Power by representations and remonstrances, that she would be fully justified in having recourse to hostilities with either belligerent, and that she only hesitated to do so from the difficulty of contending with both; but that she must be driven even to endeavor to maintain her rights against the two greatest Powers in the world, unless either of them should relax their restrictions upon neutral commerce,—in which case the United States would side with that Power against the other which might continue the aggression. Mr. Madison observed to me that it must be evident that the United States would enter upon measures of hostility with great reluctance, as he acknowledged that they are not at all prepared for war, much less with a Power so irresistibly strong as Great Britain; and that nothing would be thought to be too great a sacrifice to the preservation of peace, except their independence and their honor. He said that he did not believe that any Americans would be found willing to submit to (what he termed) the encroachments upon the liberty and the rights of the United States by the belligerents; and therefore the alternatives were, Embargo or War. He confessed that the people of this country were beginning to think the former alternative too passive, and would perhaps soon prefer the latter, as even less injurious to the interests, and more congenial with the spirit, of a free people."

In support of Madison's views Erskine reported December 4[1] a long conversation with Gallatin, which connected the action of Congress with the action of diplomacy. Gallatin and Robert Smith, according to the British minister, had not approved the embargo as a measure of defence, "and had thought that it had been better to have resorted to measures of a more decided nature at first; but that now they had no other means left but to continue it for a short time longer, and then in the event of no change taking place in the con-

[1] Erskine to Canning, Dec. 4, 1808; Cobbett's Debates, xvii., Appendix cxxxvii.

duct of the belligerents toward the United States, to endeavor to assert their rights against both Powers." Gallatin—acting as Madison's Secretary of State—sketched an ingenious and plausible project which Erskine was to suggest for Canning's use. His leading idea was simple. The total non-intercourse with both belligerents—the measure recommended by Campbell's Report, and about to become law—must remove two causes of dispute with England; for this non-intercourse superseded the President's "Chesapeake" proclamation and the Non-importation Act of April, 1806, against British man-ufactures. Henceforward England could not complain of American partiality to France, seeing that America impartially prohibited every kind of intercourse with both countries. This mode of conciliation was but a fair return for Canning's con-ciliatory prohibition of American cotton, and if carried one step further must end on both sides in a declaration of war in order to prove their wish for peace; but Canning could hardly object to his own style of reasoning. After thus evading two English grievances, Gallatin arrived at his third point,—that Congress meant to interdict the employment of foreign sea-men on American vessels, and thus put an end to all occasion for impressment. Finally, Erskine represented Gallatin as say-ing that the United States were ready to concede the Rule of 1756, and not to claim in time of war a trade prohibited in time of peace.

In the ease of private and friendly conversation the most cautious of men, even more than the most reckless, stood at the mercy of reporters. Gallatin was by temperament exces-sively cautious, and was evidently on his guard in talking with Erskine; but he could not prevent Erskine from misunder-standing his words, and still less from misconstruing his re-serve. The British minister afterward officially explained that the Secretary of the Treasury had offered no such concession as was implied by the Rule of 1756; he proposed only to yield the American claim, never yet seriously pressed, to the direct trade between the colonies of France and their mother coun-try;[1] but although Erskine's mistake on this point proved troublesome, it was not so embarrassing to Gallatin as the

---

[1] Erskine to Gallatin, Aug. 15, 1809; State Papers, iii. 307.

inference which the British minister drew from his reserve on a point of merely personal interest.

"I have no doubt," continued Erskine, "but these communications were made with a sincere desire that they might produce the effect of conciliation, because it is well known that Mr. Gallatin has long thought that the restrictive and jealous system of non-import laws, extra duties, and other modes of checking a free trade with Great Britain has been erroneous and highly injurious to the interests of America. He informed me distinctly that he had always entertained that opinion, and that he had uniformly endeavored to persuade the President to place the conduct of Great Britain and France in a fair light before the public. He seemed to check himself at the moment he was speaking upon that subject, and I could not get him to express himself more distinctly; but I could clearly collect from his manner, and from some slight insinuations, that he thought the President had acted with partiality toward France; for he turned the conversation immediately upon the character of Mr. Madison, and said that he could not be accused of having such a bias toward France, and remarked that Mr. Madison was known to be an admirer of the British Constitution, to be generally well disposed toward the nation, and to be entirely free from any enmity to its general prosperity. He appealed to me whether I had not observed that he frequently spoke with approbation of its institutions, its energy, and spirit, and that he was thoroughly well versed in its history, literature, and arts. These observations he made at that time for the purpose of contrasting the sentiments of Mr. Madison with those of the President, as he knew that I must have observed that Mr. Jefferson never spoke with approbation of anything that was British, and always took up French topics in his conversation, and always praised the people and country of France, and never lost an opportunity of showing his dislike to Great Britain."

When in course of time this despatch was printed, Gallatin felt himself obliged to make a public disavowal of Erskine's statements. That he had at first preferred measures more decided than the embargo was, he said, a mistake; and the inferences drawn in regard to President Jefferson were wholly erroneous:—

> "Eight years of the most intimate intercourse, during which not an act, nor hardly a thought, respecting the foreign relations of America was concealed, enable me confidently to say that Mr. Jefferson never had in that respect any other object in view but the protection of the rights of the United States against every foreign aggression or injury, from whatever nation it proceeded, and has in every instance observed toward all the belligerents the most strict justice and the most scrupulous impartiality."[1]

This denial was hardly necessary. The despatches themselves plainly showed that Erskine, having set his heart on effecting a treaty, used every argument that could have weight with Englishmen, and dwelt particularly upon the point—which he well knew to be a dogma of British politics—that President Jefferson had French sympathies, whereas Madison's sympathies were English. If Erskine had been a Tory, he would have known better than to suppose that Perceval's acts were in any way due to Jefferson or his prejudices; but the British minister wished to employ all the arguments that could aid his purpose; and to do him justice, he used without stint that argument which his British instincts told him would be most convincing,—the single word, War.

> "I ascertained from Mr. Madison," he wrote November 26,[2] "that . . . the Report of the Committee seemed distinctly to announce that the ULTIMATE and only effectual mode of resisting the aggressions of the belligerents would be by a *war*."

If Canning could be panic-struck by italics and capital letters, Erskine meant to excite his worst alarms. Perhaps Madison was a little the accomplice of these tactics; for at the moment when he threatened war in language the most menacing, the future President was trembling lest Congress

---

[1] Gallatin to the National Intelligencer, April 21, 1810; Gallatin's Writings, i. 475.

[2] Erskine to Canning, Nov. 26, 1808; MSS. British Archives.

should abjectly submit to British orders. Erskine's despatches early in December echoed the official words of Madison, Gallatin, and Robert Smith, but gave little idea of their difficulties. The same tactics marked his next letters. Jan. 1, 1809, he wrote to Canning[1] that the bill which was to carry into effect the Resolutions of Campbell's Report had been laid before the House: —

"You will observe, sir, that the provisions of this bill are exactly such as this Government informed me would be adopted, and which I detailed to you in my despatches by the last month's packet. On these measures, and a strict enforcement of the embargo, the Government and Congress have determined to rely for a short time, in the hope that some events in Europe may take place to enable them to extricate themselves from their present highly embarrassing situation. It is now universally acknowledged that the Embargo Act must be raised by next summer; and nearly all the members of the ruling party declare that unless the belligerent Powers should remove their restrictions upon neutral commerce before that time, it will be incumbent upon the United States to adopt measures of hostility toward such of those Powers as may continue their aggressions."

War was the incessant burden of Erskine's reports; and he spared no pains to convince his Government that Madison had both the power and the will to fight. The next House, he reported, would contain ninety-five Republicans to forty-seven Federalists: "This great majority (which may vary a few votes) would of course be strong enough to carry any measures they wished; and all their declarations and their whole conduct indicate a determination to adopt the line of conduct which I have before pointed out." Only three days earlier Gallatin had privately written to Nicholson that great confusion and perplexity reigned in Congress, that Madison was slow in taking his ground, and that if war were not speedily determined submission would soon ensue; but Erskine reported little of this pacific temper, while he sent cry after cry of alarm

[1] Erskine to Canning, Jan. 1, 1809 (No. 1); MSS. British Archives.

to London. Toward the end of December Congress took up a measure for raising fifty thousand troops. Erskine asked the Secretary of State for what purpose so large a force was needed; and Madison replied that the force was no greater than the state of relations with foreign Powers required.

"He added (to my great surprise) that if the United States thought proper, they might act as if war had been declared by any or all of them, and at any rate by Great Britain and France. When I pressed him for a further explanation of his meaning, he said that such had been the conduct of both those Powers toward the United States that they would be justified in proceeding to immediate hostilities. From his manner as well as from his conversation, I could perceive that he was greatly incensed; and it appeared to me that he wished that Great Britain might take offence at the conduct of the United States and commence hostilities upon them, so as to give this Government a strong ground of appeal to the people of this country to support them in a war,—unless indeed they could be extricated from their difficulties by Great Britain giving way and withdrawing her Orders in Council."[1]

Following one letter by another, in these varied tones of menace, Erskine ended by sending, Jan. 3, 1809, a Message from the President-elect which wanted nothing except a vote of Congress to make it a formal announcement of war:[2] —

"I have the honor to inform you that I had an interview with Mr. Madison yesterday, in which he declared that he had no hesitation in assuring me that in the event of the belligerent nations continuing their restrictions upon neutral commerce, it was intended by this Government to recommend to Congress to pass a law to allow merchant-ships to arm, and also to issue letters of marque and reprisal. The exact time when this course would be adopted, he said, might depend upon circumstances such as could not precisely be described; but he said that he was confident that if it was not taken before the expiration of the present

[1] Erskine to Canning, Jan. 1, 1809 (No. 2); MSS. British Archives.
[2] Erskine to Canning, Jan. 3, 1809; MSS. British Archives.

Congress, in March, it would be one of the first measures of the new Congress, which will be held early in May next."

Erskine added that the Federalists also thought Great Britain wrong in refusing the American offers, and that they too declared war to be necessary if these offers should still be rejected. He wrote to Sir James Craig to be on guard against sudden attack from the United States. These measures taken, the British minister at Washington waited the echo of his alarm-cries, and Madison left the matter in his hands. No instructions were sent to Pinkney, no impulse was given to the press; and the public obstinately refused to believe in war. Perhaps Erskine received some assurance that no decisive step would be taken before he should have obtained from London a reply to his despatches of December; but whether or not he had any tacit understanding with Madison, his ambition to reunite the two countries and to effect the diplomatic triumph of a treaty certainly led him to exaggerate the warlike ardor of America, and to cross by a virtuous intrigue what he thought the ruinous career of his own Government.

On the other hand, General Turreau flattered himself that the diplomatic triumph would fall not to Erskine, but to himself; and the hope of war upon England almost overcame for a sanguine moment his contempt for American character and courage. Turreau acquiesced in the embargo, since such was the Emperor's will,—but only as a choice of evils; for he knew better than Napoleon how deep a wound the embargo inflicted on Martinique and Guadeloupe. He consoled himself only by the hope that it injured Great Britain still more. "I have always considered," he said,[1] "that the embargo, rigorously executed, hurt us less than it hurt England, because our colonial interests are of small account in the balance against the colonial interests of the enemy." In his eyes a declaration of war against France was better suited than the embargo to French interests, provided it were joined with a like declaration against England; and he prepared his Government in advance for treating such a war as though it were an alliance.

"I believe that France ought not to take this declaration

[1] Turreau to Champagny, Jan. 15, 1809; Archives des Aff. Étr. MSS.

in its literal sense, because its apparent object would be only nominal, and not in the intention of the legislators. I know that such is now their disposition; and although it is conceded that the number of Federalists will be greater in the next Congress than in this, yet the Administration will always have a great majority in the House, and a still greater in the Senate. I am in such close relations with the greater number of senators as not to be deceived in regard to their intentions. But in this case, too, it would be necessary that France should not answer the challenge of war, and should wait until the first hostilities had taken place between England and the United States. Then I shall hope that the declaration against France will be immediately withdrawn. I have reason to believe that a declaration of war against France as well as against England will take place only with the intention of reaching this last Power without too much shocking public opinion, and in order to avoid the reproach of too much partiality toward the first. Your Excellency can, from this, form an idea of the weakness of Congress, and of the disposition of the American people."[1]

This despatch, written in the middle of January, completed the diplomatic manœuvres by which Madison hoped to unite his foreign with his domestic policy. The scheme was ingenious. Even if it should fail to wring concessions from Canning, hostilities would result only in a cheap warfare on the ocean, less wearisome than the embargo,—a war which, so far as concerned the continent of Europe, would rather benefit than injure commerce; but a policy like this, at once bold and delicate, required the steady support of a vigorous Congress. Neither Erskine nor Turreau told the full strength of the difficulties with which Madison and Gallatin struggled within their own party; or that while the new Administration was laboring to build up a new policy, the Federalists had already laid their hands on the material that the new policy needed for its use.

Whatever might be their differences in other respects, Jefferson, Madison, and Gallatin agreed on one common point.

[1] Turreau to Champagny, Jan. 15, 1809; Archives des Aff. Étr. MSS.

They held that until some decision should be reached in regard to peace or war, the embargo must be maintained and enforced. Neither the dignity nor the interests of the country permitted a sudden break with the policy which had been steadily followed during the eight years of their power. Abandonment of embargo without war was an act of submission to England and France which would certainly destroy whatever national self-respect might have survived the mortifications of the last three years; but if the embargo was to be maintained, it must be enforced, and without new legislation strict enforcement was impossible. This new legislation was demanded by Gallatin, in a letter of Nov. 24, 1808, addressed to Senator Giles of the Senate committee. December 8, Giles introduced a Bill conferring on Gallatin the "arbitrary" and "dangerous" powers he asked. The new measure answered Gallatin's description. Henceforward coasting-vessels were to give impossible bonds, to the amount of six times the value of vessel and cargo, before any cargo could even be put on board; collectors might refuse permission to load, even when such bonds were offered, "whenever in their opinion there is an intention to violate the embargo;" in suits on the bond, the defence was to be denied the right to plead capture, distress, or accident, except under conditions so stringent as to be practically useless; no ship-owner could sell a vessel without giving bond, to the amount of three hundred dollars for each ton, that such ship should not contravene any of the Embargo Acts; and by Section 9, the whole country was placed under the arbitrary will of government officials: "The collectors of all the districts of the United States shall . . . take into their custody specie or other articles of domestic growth, produce, or manufacture . . . when in vessels, carts, wagons, sleighs, or any other carriage, or in any manner apparently on their way toward the territory of a foreign nation or the vicinity thereof, or toward a place whence such articles are intended to be exported;" and after seizure the property could be recovered by the owner only on giving bonds for its transfer to some place " whence, in the opinion of the collector, there shall not be any danger of such articles being exported." The collectors not only received authority to seize at discretion all merchandise anywhere in transit, but were also declared to be not liable at law for their seizures, and were to be supported at need by the army, navy, and militia.

In vain did Giles[1] and the other stanch followers of Jefferson affirm that this bill contained no new principles of legislation; that it was but an extension of ordinary customs laws; and that its provisions were "necessary and proper" for carrying into effect the great constitutional object,—the embargo. Giles held so many opinions in the course of his public life that no Federalist cared to ask what might be his momentary theory of the Constitution; but whether as a matter of law he was right or wrong, he could hardly dispute what Gallatin in private admitted, that the powers conferred by his Enforcement Act were "most arbitrary," "equally dangerous and odious." The Senate knew well the nature of the work required to be done, but twenty senators voted for the passage of the bill, December 21, while only seven voted in the negative.

In pressing this measure at a moment so critical, Gallatin may have been bold, but was certainly not discreet. If he meant to break down the embargo, he chose the best means; if he meant to enforce it, he chose the worst. The Eastern congressmen made no secret that they hoped to resist the law by force.

> "This strong tone was held by many of the Eastern members in a large company where I was present," wrote the British minister to Canning Jan. 1, 1809; "and the gentlemen who so expressed themselves declared that they had no hesitation in avowing such opinions, and said that they would maintain them in their places in Congress."

They were as good as their word, and when the bill came before the House arguments and threats were closely intermingled; but the majority listened to neither, and January 5, in a night session, forced the bill to its passage by a vote of seventy-one to thirty-two. January 9 the Enforcement Act received the signature of President Jefferson.

Senator Pickering, of Massachusetts, alone profited by this audacious act of power; and his overwhelming triumph

[1] Annals of Congress, 1808–1809, p. 259.

became every day more imminent, as the conservative forces of New England arrayed themselves under his lead. Since the departure of Rose, in March, he had basked in the sunshine of success and flattery. Single-handed he had driven John Quincy Adams from public life, and had won the State of Massachusetts, for the first time, to the pure principles of the Essex Junto. That he felt, in his austere way, the full delight of repaying to the son the debt which for eight years he had owed to the father was not to be doubted; but a keener pleasure came to him from beyond the ocean. If the American of that day, and especially the New England Federalist, conceived of any applause as deciding the success of his career, he thought first of London and the society of England; although the imagination could scarcely invent a means by which an American could win the favor of a British public. This impossibility Pickering accomplished. His name and that of John Randolph were as familiar in London as in Philadelphia; and Rose maintained with him a correspondence calculated to make him think his success even greater than it was.

"In Professor Adams's downfall, at which I cannot but be amused," wrote Rose from London,[1] "I see but the forerunner of catastrophes of greater mark. This practical answer of your common constituents to his reply to you was the best possible. By his retreat he admits his conviction that you were the fitter representative of the State legislature. In the conversion of Massachusetts, I see the augury of all that is of good promise with you. Let me thank you cordially for your answer to Governor Sullivan. It was an unintentional kindness on his part thus to compel you to bring to the public eye the narrative of a life so interesting, so virtuous, and honorable. Receive the assurance of how anxiously I hope that though gratitude is not the virtue of republics, the remaining years of that life may receive from yours the tribute of honor and confidence it has so many claims to. In so wishing, I wish the prosperity of your country."

Flattery like this was rare in Pickering's toilsome career;

[1] Rose to Pickering, Aug. 4, 1808; New England Federalism, p. 372.

and man, almost in the full degree of his antipathy to dema-
gogy, yearns for the popular regard he will not seek. Pickering's ambition to be President was as evident to George Rose
as it had been to John Adams. "Under the simple appearance
of a bald head and straight hair," wrote the ex-President,[1]
"and under professions of profound republicanism, he con-
ceals an ardent ambition, envious of every superior, and impatient of obscurity." That Timothy Pickering could become
President over a Union which embraced Pennsylvania and
Virginia was an idea so extravagant as to be unsuited even to
coarsely flavored flattery; but that he should be the chief of a
New England Confederation was not an extravagant thought,
and toward a New England Confederation events were tending fast. The idea of combining the Eastern States against the
embargo,—which if carried out put an end to the Union under the actual Constitution,—belonged peculiarly to Pickering; and since he first suggested it in his famous embargo
letter, it had won its way until New England was ripe for the
scheme.

One by one, the Federalist leaders gave their adhesion to
the plan. Of all these gentlemen, the most cautious—or, as
his associates thought, the most timid—was Harrison Gray
Otis, President of the Massachusetts Senate. Never in the full
confidence of the Essex Junto, he was always a favorite orator
in Boston town-meeting, and a leader in Boston society; but
he followed impulses stronger than his own will, and when
he adopted an opinion his party might feel secure of popular
sympathy. Dec. 15, 1808, Otis wrote from Boston to Josiah
Quincy at Washington a letter which enrolled him under
Pickering's command.[2]

"It would be a great misfortune for us to justify the ob-
loquy of wishing to promote a separation of the States, and
of being solitary in that pursuit. . . . On the other hand,
to do nothing will seem to be a flash in the pan, and our
apostate representatives will be justified in the opinions
which they have doubtless inculcated of our want of union
and of nerve. What then shall we do? In other words, what

[1] Cunningham Letters, p. 56.
[2] H. G. Otis to Quincy, Dec. 15, 1808; Quincy's Life of Quincy, p. 164.

can Connecticut do? For we can and will come up to her tone. Is she ready to declare the embargo and its supplementary chains unconstitutional; to propose to their State the appointment of delegates to meet those from the other commercial States, in convention at Hartford or elsewhere, for the purpose of providing some mode of relief that may not be inconsistent with the Union of these States, to which we should adhere as long as possible? Shall New York be invited to join; and what shall be the proposed objects of such a convention?"

In thus adopting the project of Timothy Pickering for a New England convention, Otis was not less careful than Pickering himself to suggest that the new Union should be consistent with the old one. American constitutional lawyers never wholly succeeded in devising any form of secession which might not coexist with some conceivable form of Union, such as was recognized by the Declaration of July 4, 1776; but no form of secession ever yet devised could coexist with the Union as it was settled by the Constitution of 1789; and the project of a New England convention, if carried out, dissolved that Union as effectually as though it had no other object. "No State shall, without the consent of Congress, . . . enter into an agreement or compact with another State."[1] Such was the emphatic interdict of the Constitution, and its violation must either destroy the Union or give it new shape. Doubtless the Union had existed before the Constitution, and might survive it; but a convention of the New England States could not exist under the Union of 1789.

Another Boston Federalist, second to none in standing, who unlike Otis was implicitly trusted by the Essex Junto, wrote a letter to Senator Pickering, dated five days later:—

"Our Legislature will convene on January 24," began Christopher Gore,[2] "and what will be proper for us to do under the circumstances of our times is doubtful. To ascertain the most useful course to be pursued on this occasion fills our minds with deep and anxious solicitude. . . . By conversing with our friends from the other New England

[1] Constitution of the United States, Art. I. sect. 10.
[2] Gore to Pickering, Dec. 20, 1808; New England Federalism, p. 375.

States you might be able to know in what measures and to what extent they would be willing to co-operate with Massachusetts. The opposition, to be effectual of any change in our rulers, should comprehend all New England. These men, I fear, are too inflated with their own popularity to attend to any call short of this."

The action of Massachusetts was to be concerted with Connecticut; and the leading senator from Connecticut was Pickering's very intimate friend, James Hillhouse, whose amendments to the Constitution, proposed to the Senate in an elaborate speech April 12, 1808, were supposed by his enemies to be meant as the framework for a new confederacy, since they were obviously inconsistent with the actual Union. Hillhouse and Pickering stood in the most confidential relations. From their common chamber in the "Six Buildings" they carried on their joint campaign against the embargo;[1] and with this advantage, Pickering in due time wrote his reply to Christopher Gore for the guidance of the Massachusetts General Court: —

"New England must be united in whatever great measure shall be adopted. During the approaching session of our Legislature there may be such further advances in mischief as may distinctly point out the course proper to be adopted. A convention of delegates from those States, including Vermont, seems obviously proper and necessary. Massachusetts and Connecticut can appoint their delegates with regular authority. In the other States they must be appointed by county conventions. A strong and solemn address, stating as concisely as will consist with perspicuity the evil conduct of our Administration as manifested in their measures, ought to be prepared to be laid before our Legislature when they meet, to be sent forth by their authority, to the people. But the fast, which I have repeatedly heard mentioned here, I hope will be postponed till the very crisis of our affairs, if such a crisis should be suffered to arise. To proclaim a fast sooner would, I fear, have more the appearance of management than of religion."[2]

[1] Pickering to Hillhouse, Dec. 16, 1814; New England Federalism, p. 414.
[2] Pickering to C. Gore, Jan. 8, 1809; New England Federalism, p. 376.

Such action was not to be easily reconciled with the spirit of the Constitution, but Pickering attempted to show its accord; and in doing so he completed the revolution which for eight years had been in progress between the two political parties. He placed himself on the precise ground taken by Jefferson in the Kentucky Resolutions of 1798:—

"Pray look into the Constitution, and particularly to the tenth article of the Amendments. How are the powers reserved to the States respectively, or to the people, to be maintained, but by the respective States judging for themselves, and putting their negative on the usurpations of the general government."

That the States of Massachusetts and Connecticut meant to take the first step toward a change in the Federal compact was an open secret at Washington before the close of the year. As early as December 29 Gallatin wrote to his friend Nicholson a letter of alarm,[1] which showed that the plan was already known by the Administration:—

"I actually want time to give you more details, but I will only state that it is intended by the Essex Junto to prevail on the Massachusetts legislature, who meet in two or three weeks, to call a convention of the five New England States, to which they will try to add New York; and that something must be done to anticipate and defeat that nefarious plan."

[1] Adams's Gallatin, p. 384.

Chapter XVIII

AMONG THE FEDERALISTS were still a few moderate men who hoped that Jefferson might not be wholly sold to France, and who were inclined to ask for some new policy of peace or war before throwing aside the old one. Pickering's contempt for such allies echoed the old feuds of New England, and revived the root-and-branch politics of the Puritans:

> "Some *cautious* men here of the Federal party discovered an inclination to wait patiently till the first of June the promised repeal of the embargo. God forbid that such timid counsels should reach the Massachusetts legislature, or a single member of it! A million of such men would not save the nation. Defeat the accursed measure now, and you not only restore commerce, agriculture, and all sorts of business to activity, but you save the country from a British war. The power of the present miserable rulers—I mean their power to do material mischief—will then be anni-hilated."[1]

Pickering's instructions were exactly followed; his temper infused itself through every New England town. Once more, a popular delusion approaching frenzy,—a temporary insan-ity like the witchcraft and Quaker mania,—took possession of the mind of Massachusetts, and broke into acute expres-sion. Not for a full century had the old Puritan prejudice shown itself in a form so unreasoning and unreasonable; but although nearly one half the people held aloof and wondered at the madness of their own society, the whole history of Massachusetts, a succession of half-forgotten disputes and re-bellions, seemed to concentrate itself for the last time in a burst of expiring passions, mingled with hatred of Virginia and loathing for Jefferson, until the rest of America, perplexed at paroxysms so eccentric, wondered whether the spirit of Massachusetts liberty could ever have been sane. For the mo-ment Timothy Pickering was its genius.

The decision reached by the Federalists at Washington, on

[1] Pickering to S. P. Gardner; New England Federalism, p. 379.

or about December 21, when the Enforcement Bill passed the
Senate, was quickly known in Massachusetts, and without
further delay the crisis was begun. Hitherto the tone of remonstrance had been respectful; under cover of the Enforcement Act it rapidly became revolutionary. Dec. 27, 1808, a
town-meeting at Bath, in the district of Maine, set the movement on foot by adopting Resolutions[1] which called on the
general court, at its meeting January 25, to take "immediate
steps for relieving the people, either by themselves alone, or
in concert with other commercial States;" while at the same
time the town voted "that a committee of safety and correspondence be appointed, to correspond with committees of
other towns, . . . and to watch over the safety of the people
of this town, and to give immediate alarm so that a regular
meeting may be called whenever any infringement of their
rights shall be committed by any person or persons under
color and pretence of authority derived from any officer of
the United States." This extravagant measure, evidently intended to recall the memory of 1776, was quickly imitated by
the town of Gloucester, which, January 12,[2] formally approved the Resolutions passed at Bath, voted an address to
the general court, and appointed a committee of public safety.
These first steps went so far that other towns could not easily
keep pace with them, and were obliged to fall behind. The
scheme of appointing everywhere town-committees of public
safety to organize combined resistance to the national government, was laid aside, or fell to the ground; but the town-
meetings went on. In the county of Hampshire, a public
meeting of citizens, January 12,[3] announced "that causes are
continually occurring which tend to produce a most calamitous event,—a dissolution of the Union;" and January 20, a
meeting at Newburyport, in Senator Pickering's County of
Essex, voted—

"That we will not aid or assist in the execution of the
several embargo laws, especially the last, and that we consider all those who do as violators of the Constitution of

[1] New England Palladium, Jan. 3, 1809.
[2] New England Palladium, Jan. 17, 1809.
[3] New England Palladium, Jan. 20, 1809.

the United States and of this Commonwealth; and that they be considered as unworthy of the confidence and esteem of their fellow-citizens."

On the eve of the day fixed for the General Court to assemble, in the midst of town-meetings far and near, Boston called a meeting at Faneuil Hall. The town had grown to a population of more than thirty thousand, but old citizens could remember the Stamp Act and the Boston Port Bill; they had seen Samuel Adams and John Hancock defy, in Faneuil Hall, the power of Parliament; and the same town-meeting which had stood firm against King George, even to the point of armed rebellion, still existed unchanged, ready to resist the tyranny of a Virginia President. January 23 four thousand citizens swarmed to the hall famous for its Revolutionary associations; and in the minds of all, either as a hope or a terror, revolution was the absorbing thought.

Socially, nothing could be more respectable than the assembly. The names of the committee appointed to draft a petition to the general court included the best people of Boston. The list began with Thomas Handasyd Perkins, and included Samuel Dexter, John Warren, William Sullivan, Jonathan Mason, and Theodore Lyman,—members of a city aristocracy which still existed in vigor as robust as in the days when aristocracy was sustained by English example and patronage. Chief-Justice Parsons, who freely expressed his opinion that the embargo was unconstitutional, had no part in the proceedings; but on his privately given advice the meeting was to take its stand. The Essex Junto, willing to escape its own unpopularity, surrendered the apparent lead to a man who shared in few of the extreme opinions of Pickering, Parsons, and George Cabot,—a man who stood second to no Federalist in ability, but who had never sympathized with Alexander Hamilton's feuds, or with factious hostility either to Federalist or to Republican Presidents. Samuel Dexter, Secretary of War in 1800, Secretary of the Treasury in 1801, a lawyer of the highest standing, had been employed to argue against the constitutionality of the Embargo Act before Judge Davis in September, and although he lost his cause, he stoutly maintained the soundness of his argument. In truth, the question was still open; and since the trial at Salem, the Enforcement Act had greatly strengthened constitutional objections already strong. Dexter believed that his duty required him to join in protesting against such legislation, and accordingly he took an active part in drafting and defending the Resolutions and memorial reported by his committee, which appealed to the general court "for their interposition to save the people of this Commonwealth from the destructive consequences which they apprehend to their liberties and property from the continuance of the present system."

No measure reported by Samuel Dexter was likely to satisfy the hot temper of a town-meeting. The regular Resolutions were duly adopted, with little vigorous opposition, and the meeting adjourned till the next day; but when the citizens reassembled, January 24, they passed another resolve, offered by Daniel Sargent, which startled the law-abiding public of Massachusetts by formally declaring that " we will not voluntarily aid or assist in the execution" of the Enforcement Act; and that "all those who shall so assist in enforcing upon others the arbitrary and unconstitutional provisions of this Act, ought to be considered as enemies to the Constitution of the United States and of this State, and hostile to the liberties of this people."

Alarming as was the tone of Boston, Samuel Dexter and his associates avoided taking open part with the British government against their own. Elsewhere no such reticence was shown. Not only in private, in all places, at every table, did the bitterness of New England temper and the intensity of local prejudice allow themselves the freest expression, but the numerous town-meetings also showed a spirit rather British than American. Among many examples a few are worth recalling, to show the absence of national feeling, and the difficulties and dangers which stood in the nation's way.

January 24 the town of Beverly, in Essex County, voted[1] that—

"They have witnessed with regret too strong a propensity to palliate and overlook the unjust aggressions of one foreign nation, and to exaggerate and misrepresent the con-

[1] New England Palladium, Jan. 31, 1809.

duct of another; that the measures pursued are calculated and designed to force us into a war with Great Britain,—a war which would be extremely detrimental to our agriculture, fatal to our commerce, and which would probably deprive us forever of the Bank fishery,—and to unite us in alliance with France, whose embrace is death."

January 26 the town of Plymouth voted[1] —

"That by the partial and insidious management of our external relations, by a servile compliance with the views of one belligerent whose restless ambition is grasping at the subjugation of the civilized world, and by the unnecessary provocations offered to another, magnanimously contending for its own existence and the emancipation of the oppressed, our national peace is endangered, and our national dignity and good faith sacrificed on the altar of duplicity."

January 23 the town of Wells, in the district of Maine, voted[2] —

"That we deprecate that cringing sycophancy which has marked the conduct of our national government toward the tyrant of Europe, while we view with indignation and alarm its hostility toward Great Britain."

On the same day Gloucester spoke in language still more insulting to the national government:[3] —

"We see not only the purse-strings of our nation in the hands of a Frenchified Genevan, but all our naval forces and all our militia placed under the control of this same foreigner, whom we cannot but think a satellite of Bonaparte. . . . In our opinion the national Cabinet has given to this country and the world the most indubitable evidence of their insincerity; that their great study has been to involve this country in a war with Great Britain, and of course to form a coalition with France, regardless of consequences. Their pledges to France of their willingness to submit to the wishes or mandates of the Corsican have

[1] New England Palladium, Jan. 31, 1809.
[2] New England Palladium, Feb. 3, 1809.
[3] New England Palladium, Feb. 24, 1809.

been satisfactory. . . . We should deprecate a separation of the States, and would resort to every honorable means of redress before we would seek relief in a dissolution of the Union. . . . Our Administration can dissemble their real motives no longer; our dreadful forebodings prove realities; the expected blow has reached us, and by it has fled our liberty."

In quaint and pathetic phrases, the little town of Alfred, in Maine, sent to the general court a petition[1] which charged the national government with endeavoring "to provoke a ruinous and destructive war with England, to gratify the ambition and caprice, and augment the power, of the tyrant of France."

"We are the poor inhabitants of a small town," continued the Alfred petition, "rendered poorer by the wayward, inconsistent policy of the general government; but life and liberty are as dear to us as to our opulent brethren of the South, and we flatter ourselves that we have as much love of liberty and abhorrence of slavery as those who oppress us in the name of Republicanism. We love liberty in principle but better in practice. We cling to a union of the States as the rock of our salvation; and nothing but a fearful looking for of despotism would induce us to wish for a severance of the band that unites us. But oppression did sever us from the British empire; and what a long and continued repetition of similar acts of the government of the United States would effect, God only knows!"

These extracts showed the temper in which the Massachusetts legislature met. The Federalist leaders had more difficulty to restrain than to excite the people, and felt themselves strong enough to assume the air of cautious and conservative men. After an exchange of opinions between the Legislature and Levi Lincoln, who had become governor on the death of Sullivan shortly before, both Houses turned their attention to national affairs. The numerous petitions on the subject of the embargo were referred to committees. Without loss of time the Senate committee, February 1, made a Report recom-

[1] New England Palladium, Feb. 17, 1809.

mending an Act to secure the people of the State from "unreasonable, arbitrary, and unconstitutional searches in their dwelling-houses;" to which was added a series of four Resolutions, closing with a formal adoption of the step so long desired by Senator Pickering.

"*Resolved*, That the Legislature of this Commonwealth will zealously co-operate with any of the other States in all legal and constitutional measures for procuring such amendments to the Constitution of the United States as shall be judged necessary to obtain protection and defence for commerce, and to give to the commercial States their fair and just consideration in the government of the Union; and for affording permanent security, as well as present relief, from the oppressive measures under which they now suffer.

"*Resolved*, That the Honorable the President of the Senate, and the Honorable the Speaker of the House of Representatives, be requested to transmit a copy of this Report, and the Resolutions thereon, to the legislatures of such of our sister States as manifest a disposition to concur with us in measures to rescue our common country from impending ruin, and to preserve inviolate the union of the States."

These Resolutions proclaimed that a union of the Eastern States against the national government was the earnest wish of Massachusetts; and the advance thus made was instantly met by Connecticut, where Jonathan Trumbull, a Federalist of pure stock, who had for ten years filled the chair of governor, called a special meeting of the Legislature in pursuance of the arrangement concerted at Washington. The temper of Governor Trumbull could be judged from a letter written by him, February 4, to Secretary Dearborn, who had requested him to select militia officers on whom the collectors might call for military aid in enforcing the embargo.

"Conceiving as I do," replied Governor Trumbull, "and believing it to be the opinion of the great mass of citizens of this State, that the late law of Congress for a more rigorous enforcement of the embargo is unconstitutional in many of its provisions, interfering with the State sovereignties, and subversive of the rights, privileges, and immunities of the citizens of the United States, . . . my mind has been led to a serious and decided determination to decline a compliance with your request, and to have no agency in the appointments which the President has been pleased to refer to me."

In calling together the legislature of Connecticut, Governor Trumbull's concert with Massachusetts was evident, and his object of resisting the embargo was avowed. So bluntly did the Federalists proclaim their purpose, that when the Connecticut legislature met, February 23, the governor in his opening speech explained his action as though it were a matter of course that he should call upon the State to nullify an Act of Congress.

"Whenever our national legislature," he said, "is led to overleap the prescribed bounds of their constitutional powers, on the State legislatures in great emergencies devolves the arduous task,—it is their right, it becomes their duty,—to interpose their protecting shield between the rights and liberties of the people and the assumed power of the general government."

If Madison was not by that time weary of his own words,—if the Resolutions of 1798 and the fatal "interpose" of Virginia had not become hateful to his ears,—he might have found some amusement in the irony with which Trumbull flung the familiar phrases of Virginia back into her face; but serious as such conduct was, the mere defiance carried less alarm than was warranted by the signs of secret concert with England which the Federalists willingly betrayed. Trumbull and Hillhouse, Pickering and Otis, were not necessarily masters of the situation, even when at the head of all New England; but when they pointed significantly at the fleets and armies of Great Britain behind them, they carried terror to the heart of the Union. So little did they hide their attitude toward the British government that their organ, the "New England Palladium," published, January 6, Canning's personal letter of Sept. 23, 1808, to Pinkney, which Madison had suppressed. How it had been obtained, no one knew. The British

Foreign Office seemed to stand in direct communication with Boston, while the Boston Federalists exulted in a chance to swell what they thought the triumph of George Canning over their own Federalist friend, William Pinkney.

Tactics like these, unscrupulous though they might be, were effective. Jefferson and Madison had the best reason to know the force of such factiousness, for only ten years before, on less provocation, they had themselves led in Virginia and Kentucky a movement with a similar purpose; but although their history as leaders of an opposition implied agreement in principle with the doings of Massachusetts and Connecticut, their dignity and interest as Presidents of the United States required them to carry out the laws they had advised and approved. Whatever might be the personal wishes of a few men like Pickering, the great mass of Federalists wished at heart no more harm to the country than to overthrow and humiliate Jefferson, and to cripple Madison from the start; while the Administration, on its side, in struggling to escape a personal humiliation, was obliged to adopt any course that offered the best hope of success even though it should sacrifice the national character. As the last weeks of President Jefferson's Administration approached, this personal conflict—the bitterness of sixteen years—concentrated its virulence upon a single point, but that point vital to Jefferson's fame and popularity,—the embargo.

Rarely in American history has been seen a struggle more furious or less ennobling than that which took place at Washington in the months of January and February, 1809. With a bold face, but with small confidence, Madison and Gallatin pressed their measures. After passing the Enforcement Act on the morning of January 6, Congress turned at once to a matter even more serious. January 7 a Resolution was offered in the House providing for an early meeting of the next Congress, and in the short debate that followed, a distinct line began for the first time to divide the advocates of war from the partisans of peace. The extra session was avowedly to be called for the purpose of declaring war. Simultaneously a bill was introduced to raise, arm, and equip fifty thousand volunteers to serve for the term of two years; while the Senate sent down another bill ordering all the frigates and gunboats to be "fitted out, officered, manned, and employed as soon as may be." The fourth Monday in May was the date proposed for the extra session, and Congress at last found itself face to face with the naked issue of war.

The effect of the crisis upon Congress was immediate. Doubt, defiance, dismay, and disgust took possession of the Legislature, which swayed backward and forward from day to day, as courage or fear prevailed. The old Republicans, who could not yield their faith in the embargo, begged almost piteously for delay.

"A large portion of the people, the South almost unanimously," urged David R. Williams of South Carolina, "have expressed a wish that the Government should adhere to the embargo till it produces an effect, or the capacity to produce the effect be disproved. You are like to be driven out of the embargo by war? Why, sir, look at the sensation in New England and New York, and talk about going to war when you cannot maintain an embargo! . . . If you do not adopt war before the fourth Monday in May, will the nation be ruined if you postpone it still further?"[1]

Macon declared that the embargo was still the people's choice: —

"As to the people being tired of the embargo, whenever they want war in preference to it they will send their petitions here to that effect. . . . Let each man put the question to his neighbor whether he will have war or embargo, and there is no doubt but he will answer in favor of the latter."

Such reasoning, honest and true as it was in the mouths of men like Macon and Williams, gave a tone of weakness and irresolution to the debate, while it acted on the Federalists with the force of defiance, and drew from Josiah Quincy a speech which long remained famous, and which no Republican ever forgot or forgave.

That this strong, self-asserting Boston gentleman, gifted, ambitious, the embodiment of Massachusetts traditions and

[1] Annals of Congress, 1808–1809, p. 1100.

British prejudices, should feel deep contempt for the moral courage and the understanding of men whose motives were beyond the range of his sympathies and experience, was natural; for Josiah Quincy belonged to a class of Americans who cared so intensely for their own convictions that they could not care for a nation which did not represent them; and in his eyes Jefferson was a transparent fraud, his followers were dupes or ruffians, and the nation was hastening to a fatal crisis. Yet with all this to excuse him, his language still passed the bounds of license. He began by reaffirming that deception had been practised on the House when the President induced it to adopt the embargo without alluding to its coercive purpose:—

> "I do not think I state my position too strongly when I say that not a man in this House deemed the embargo intended chiefly as a measure of coercion on Great Britain; that it was to be made permanent at all hazards until it had effected that object, and that nothing else effectual was to be done for the support of our maritime rights. If any individual was influenced by such motives, certainly they were not those of a majority of this House. Now, sir, on my conscience, I do believe that these were the motives and intentions of the Administration when they recommended the embargo to the adoption of this House."

So far as concerned President Jefferson this charge was true; but every one knew that Jefferson habitually threw responsibility on Congress, and after the scandal made by John Randolph in the Spanish affair of 1805, the House alone was to blame if it incurred consequences which were evident on the face of its measures. Quincy next asserted a worse and more mischievous charge:—

> "Not only that embargo was resorted to as a means of coercion, but from the first it was never intended by the Administration to do anything else effectual for the support of our maritime rights. Sir, I am sick—sick to loathing—of this eternal clamor of 'war, war, war!' which has been kept up almost incessantly on this floor, now for more than two years. Sir, if I can help it, the old women of this

country shall not be frightened in this way any longer. I have been a long time a close observer of what has been done and said by the majority of this House, and for one I am satisfied that no insult, however gross, offered to us by either France or Great Britain, could force this majority into the declaration of war. To use a strong but common expression, it could not be kicked into such a declaration by either nation."[1]

Insults are pointless unless they have a foundation of truth or probability. The Parliament of Great Britain would have laughed at such a taunt; Napoleon would not have understood what it meant; but Congress drew a deep breath of dismay, for every member knew that openly and secretly, in public and in private, the single decisive argument against war had been and still was—fear. After four years of outrage such as would have made the blood of an Englishman or a French man turn to fire in his veins, not an American could be found, between Canada and Texas, who avowed the wish to fight. Quincy's speech produced a momentary outbreak of passion; hot retorts were made; the chamber rang with epithets of abuse, but still no one professed to want war. The House twisted and turned like a martyr on his bed of steel, but its torture was of painful doubt, not of passion.

So far as mere words affected the public mind, Josiah Quincy's taunt, not less than the sarcasms of Canning and the arrogance of Napoleon, stung Americans beyond endurance. In one sense Quincy did good service to his country; his statesmanship, if not refined, was effective; his argument, if somewhat brutal, was strong; and within four-and-twenty hours the House met it in the only way that could preserve the dignity of Congress and the Administration, by passing the bill for an extra session with eighty votes against twenty-six. This result was reached January 20, and seemed to prove that the Government had overcome its difficulties and mastered the situation; but nothing was further from the truth. Quincy knew what was passing behind the scenes. The Administration, so far from gaining strength, barely showed steadiness. At the moment when New England flung herself, with every

[1] Annals of Congress, 1808–1809, p. 1112.

sign of desperate rage, across the path of Government, faction within the Republican party struck Madison a severe blow before he had time for defence.

The first sign of Republican revolt appeared in unexpected favors lavished on the maltreated navy. Sixteen Republican senators combined with the Federalists to pass through the Senate a bill which ordered every armed vessel of the government, including gunboats, to be employed at once in active service. Gallatin saw in this measure only an intrigue of the Smiths and an attack upon the Treasury which would cost six million dollars without possible advantage to the public; but in fact the bill proved something more than an intrigue, for it showed the violence of New England reaction against the long starvation of the navy. Futile as was the scheme of manning gunboats in order to waste money which should have been spent on construction or magazines, New England was ready to join the Smiths or any other faction in any vote, however unreasonable, which promised employment for the seamen. Jefferson's system had shown its character most clearly in distrust and discouragement of the navy; and no one could wonder if the first sign of waning in his authority appeared in that department, or if Madison's first difficulties occurred in the weakest part of the old statesmanship.

Gallatin was taken by surprise, for the bill passed the Senate without serious opposition; but when it reached the House, January 10, the Treasury, through George W. Campbell, tried to strike out the clause which obliged the government to fit out and man all the vessels in the service without regard to the purpose of their employment. A number of Republican members, largely from New England, combining with the Federalists, defeated Campbell by a close vote of sixty-four to fifty-nine. In alarm at a measure which, before war was decided, threatened to take from the Treasury and throw into the ocean all the money reserved to support the first year of hostilities, Gallatin exerted himself to stop it. January 11, David R. Williams and the old Republicans came to his rescue with a motion to recommit, but they were again beaten by fifty-nine to fifty-eight. The next day John Montgomery of Maryland changed sides. By a vote of sixty-nine to fifty-three the bill was recommitted; January 13 the House in committee struck out the mandatory clause by fifty-three votes against forty-two; and January 16 the House accepted the amendment by sixty-eight votes against fifty-five. These divisions showed a considerable number of Republicans still acting with the Federalists; and in this respect the Senate was even less manageable than the House. Only after an obstinate struggle did the Senate give way so far that at last Congress agreed upon ordering four frigates to be fitted out, and as many gunboats as the public service might in the President's judgment require.

The reasons given by the Senate for persisting in its plan were proof that something remained untold; for they showed the hand and influence of the Smiths, rather than the interests of Madison's coming Administration. David R. Williams, who was a member of the Conference Committee, reported to the House that the managers for the Senate gave three reasons for insisting on their bill: —

"The first of them was that they wanted a pledge from this House that it was willing to come forward and defend the nation; another was that these [frigates] were necessary to defend the gunboats in their operations; and a third, that men could not be got to enlist for the service of the gunboats, and that to remedy this evil they might be enlisted to man the frigates, and afterwards transferred."[1]

A Navy Department which used its frigates to defend gunboats and decoy seamen was hardly fit to be trusted with unlimited credit on the Treasury. Gallatin lost his temper at finding his authority threatened with overthrow by an influence which he knew to be incompetent, and believed to be selfish and corrupt. Irritated by the vote of January 10, the Secretary of the Treasury studied the division-list to learn whence came the hostile influence which formed what he called[2] "the navy coalition of 1809, by whom were sacrificed forty Republican members, nine Republican States, the Republican cause itself, and the people of the United States, to a system of favoritism, extravagance, parade, and folly." He found the central point in the "Smith faction, or ruling

[1] Annals of Congress, 1808–1809, p. 1185.
[2] Adams's Gallatin, p. 387.

party," of which he declared Wilson Cary Nicholas to be file-leader in the House, with six votes. With these acted six New York followers of Vice-President Clinton, and five "scared Yankees." The others were merely misled Republicans or Federalists.

"The Smith faction, or ruling party," of which Wilson Cary Nicholas was file-leader in the House, and which never failed to make its influence felt in moments of trouble, had gained in the Senate an ally whose selfishness was equal to that of General Smith, and whose nature was far more malignant. Of all the enemies with whom Madison had to deal, only one in his own party was venomous. Old George Clinton, though openly hostile, possessed strong qualities, and in any event was too old for serious effort. Samuel Smith played the game of politics somewhat too much like a game of whist, in which he allowed his trumps to fall indifferently on his partners or on his opponents, whenever he saw the chance to insure a trick to his own hand; but Smith was still a man from whom in the last resort courage and energy might be expected, and in whom, selfishness apart, confidence could be placed. No such redeeming quality could be truthfully attributed to William Branch Giles, the senator from Virginia, the third member of the senatorial cabal who was about to place himself in the path of the Administration, and to apply his abilities and persistence to the deliberate task of blocking the wheels of government.

Giles had served his party long and well, and thought himself entitled to higher recognition than he had as yet received. In later times a safe seat in the Senate became almost the highest prize of politics,—men sometimes preferred it to a candidacy for the Presidential office itself; but in 1809 the Cabinet stood above the Senate, and Giles looked upon himself as entitled to the Department of State, and in due time to the Presidency. Madison, with a different view of the public good and of his own comfort, betrayed the intention of appointing Gallatin his Secretary of State; and Gallatin's fitness for the post was so evident as to make his appointment the best that could be suggested; but at the first rumor of the intention, Giles united with Smith in threatening to procure the rejection of Gallatin by the Senate. To deny the President the selection of his own Secretary of State was an act of factiousness which remained without a parallel; but Giles and Smith had both the will and the power to carry their point. Even Wilson Cary Nicholas remonstrated in vain.

"From the first," was the story told by Nicholas,[1] "Mr. Giles declared his determination to vote against Gallatin. I repeatedly urged and entreated him not to do it; for several days it was an object of discussion between us; there was no way which our long and intimate friendship would justify, consistent with my respect for him, in which I did not assail him. To all my arguments he replied that his duty to his country was to him paramount to every other consideration, and that he could not justify to himself permitting Gallatin to be Secretary of State, if his vote would prevent it."

Thus Gallatin's foreign birth—the only objection alleged against him—became the pretext for Giles to declare war against the coming Administration of President Madison. With the aid of Vice-President Clinton, Senator Samuel Smith, and the Federalists, Giles could control the Senate; and every factious interest which wished to force on Madison an object of its own was sure to ally itself with these intriguers until its object should be conceded. The Senate was already a hot-bed of intrigue, where William B. Giles, Timothy Pickering, George Clinton, and Samuel Smith held control; and unless Madison by some great effort of force or skill could crush Giles, in time not only the new Administration, but also the Union itself, might find a deadly danger in the venom of his selfishness.

At the close of January, affairs at Washington were trembling on a poise. The laws required for Madison's purpose were all passed save one; but the party was rent in pieces by faction. Discipline was at an end; the States of Massachusetts and Connecticut were openly adopting treasonable measures; and the great trial of strength—the decision of Congress on immediate repeal of the embargo—had not yet been reached.

[1] Adams's Gallatin p. 388.

Chapter XIX

EARLY IN JANUARY the intended policy of Madison became known. As the story has already told, Madison and Gallatin decided to retain the embargo until June, but to call the new Congress together May 22, and then to declare war, unless Erskine could make concessions. President Jefferson was chiefly interested in maintaining the embargo until after March 4, and the despotism he had so long maintained over Congress seemed still to exasperate his enemies. By common consent, attack upon the embargo was regarded as attack upon the President: and the Northern Democrats had so far lost respect for their old leader as to betray almost a passion for telling him unpleasant truths.

Joseph Story, who took the lead in this party rebellion, came to Congress determined to overthrow the embargo, and found Ezekiel Bacon—another Massachusetts member—equally determined with himself. In after years Justice Story told the tale as he remembered it:[1] —

"The whole influence of the Administration was directly brought to bear upon Mr. Ezekiel Bacon and myself to seduce us from what we considered a great duty to our country, and especially to New England. We were scolded, privately consulted, and argued with by the Administration and its friends on that occasion. I knew at the time that Mr. Jefferson had no ulterior measure in view, and was determined on protracting the embargo for an indefinite period, even for years. I was well satisfied that such a course would not and could not be borne by New England, and would bring on a direct rebellion. It would be ruin to the whole country. Yet Mr. Jefferson, with his usual visionary obstinacy, was determined to maintain it; and the New England Republicans were to be made the instruments. Mr. Bacon and myself resisted; and measures were concerted by us, with the aid of Pennsylvania, to compel him to abandon his mad scheme. For this he never forgave me."

[1] Story's Life of Story, i. 187.

Joseph Story, with very high and amiable qualities, was quick in temper; and in regard to Jefferson he let his temper master his memory.

"One thing I did learn while I was a member of Congress," he continued, "and that was that New England was expected, so far as the Republicans were concerned, to do everything and to have nothing. They were to obey, but not to be trusted. This, in my humble judgment, was the steady policy of Mr. Jefferson at all times. We were to be kept divided, and thus used to neutralize each other."

In this spirit toward his own President Story came to Washington, and joined hands with Timothy Pickering, John Randolph, and George Canning in the attempt "to lower and degrade" Jefferson in the eyes of his own people. Jefferson asked only to be spared the indignity of signing with his own hand the unconditional repeal of the embargo; while the single point on which Story, Bacon, Pickering, and Canning were agreed was that the repeal should be the act of the man who made the law. On one side Jefferson, Madison, Gallatin, and their friends entreated Congress to stand firm; to maintain the ground already solemnly taken; to leave the embargo until June, and then to declare war if they pleased. On the other hand, Pickering, Bacon, Story, the Clintons, and the Pennsylvanians demanded immediate repeal,—partly to pacify New England, but quite as much for the reason, which Pickering urged, that immediate repeal would prevent war. That it would in fact prevent war was obvious. Repeal was submission.

Story took no part in the public struggle, for he left Washington about January 20, and the great debate began ten days afterward; but although he held his peace in public, and his friends made no open display of their anger, the temper in which they acted was notorious, and the breach between them and Jefferson was never healed. They could not forgive him: that Jefferson should ever forget the wound they inflicted, required magnanimity beyond that of any philosopher known in politics.

As soon as the naval and military bills and the extra session for May 22 were at last fairly determined and every detail decided, Wilson Cary Nicholas took the lead of the House, and January 30 called up a Resolution intended to settle the policy of embargo and war. The words of this Resolve were too serious not to have received very careful attention:

"*Resolved*, As the opinion of this House, that the United States ought not to delay beyond the ——— day of ——— to resume, maintain, and defend the navigation of the high seas; and that provision ought to be made by law for repealing on the ——— day of ——— the several embargo laws, and for authorizing at the same time letters of marque and reprisal against Great Britain and France, provided on that day their Orders or Edicts violating the lawful commerce and neutral rights of the United States shall be in force; or against either of those nations having in force such Orders or Edicts."

Nicholas agreed to divide the Resolution so that a test vote might first be taken on the repeal of the embargo; and he then moved to fill the blank with the words, "the first day of June." The House was thus asked to pledge itself that on June 1 the embargo should cease. On this question the debate began.

David R. Williams was a typical Carolinian. With something of the overbearing temper which marked his class, he had also the independence and the honesty which went far to redeem their failings. He had stood for years, with his friend Macon, proof against the influence of patronage and power; he supported the embargo, and was not ashamed to avow his dread of war; but since his favorite measure was to be thrown aside, he stood by his character, and made an appeal to the House, giving at once to the debate an air of dignity which it never wholly lost:—

"Will you drive us to a repeal of the embargo, and make no resistance? Are you ready to lie down quietly under the impositions laid upon you? You have driven us from the embargo. The excitements in the East render it necessary that we should enforce the embargo with the bayonet or repeal it. I will repeal it,—and I could weep over it more than over a lost child. If you do not resist, you are no

longer a nation; you dare not call yourself so; you are the
merest vassals conceivable. . . . I appeal to the minority,
who hold the destinies of the nation in their grasp,—for
they can enforce embargo without the bayonet,—I beg
them, if they will not declare war, that they will do the best
they can for their country."

No one then wondered to see South Carolina almost on
her knees before Massachusetts, beseeching her, on her own
terms, for her own honor, to do the best she could for the
common country; but Massachusetts had no voice to re-
spond. Dryly, in the caustic tone of Connecticut austerity,
Samuel Dana replied that the days of ancient chivalry had not
yet returned. When Massachusetts at last found a spokesman,
she gave her answer through the mouth of Ezekiel Bacon,—
a man second to none in respectability, but not one whom,
in a moment of supreme crisis, the State would naturally have
chosen among all her citizens to pronounce her will. Bacon
had carefully collected advice from the men in his State who
were most competent to give counsel;[1] but in Massachusetts
affairs at Washington were little understood. Bent only on
saving the Union by forcing a repeal of the embargo, and
hampered by alliance with Federalists and Pennsylvanians, Bacon could not afford to show a sense of national self-respect.

He began by admitting that the discontents in New England made immediate repeal necessary:—

"It surely could not be sound policy, by adhering to this
system beyond the measure of absolute necessity, to risk in
the hands of any faction which might be disposed to wield
it an instrument by which they may endanger the union of
our country, and raise themselves to power on the ruins of
liberty and the Constitution."

Such a beginning, offering a reward for threats of disunion,
and conceding to traitors what would have been refused to
good citizens, was an evil augury; and the rest of Bacon's
speech carried out the promise. As he refused to prolong the
embargo, so he refused to vote for war. "In every point of

---

[1] Cf. J. Q. Adams to Ezekiel Bacon, Nov. 17 and Dec. 21, 1808; New England Federalism, pp, 127, 131.

view, the policy of declaring offensive war against any nation four months in advance is to me wholly objectionable." The conclusion was as feeble as was required by the premises; but only some demon of bad taste could have inspired an orator at such a moment to use the language of Falstaff;—

> "We choose not to take measures any more than to give reasons 'upon compulsion,' and we will not so take them. We will, however, I trust, defend ourselves against the depredations of both [belligerents]; and if they both or either choose to persevere in the execution of their lawless aggressions, we shall, it is hoped, become more united in our determination and our efforts to vindicate our rights, if they shall continue to be assailed. At any rate, I am for leaving it to the wisdom of the ensuing Congress, which is to meet at an early day, to determine upon that position which the nation shall take in relation to such a state of things as may grow out of the course which I propose."

Between the Federalists and the Republicans of Massachusetts Congress was left under no illusions. Bacon expressed in these vacillating phrases the true sense of the country. On the evening of February 2, after four days of debate, the committee, by seventy-three votes against forty, rejected Wilson Cary Nicholas's motion to fix June 1 as the date for removing the embargo; and the next day, by an affirmative vote of seventy, with no negatives, March 4 was fixed as the term.

Immediately after this decisive division John Randolph took the floor. Discord had become his single object in public life. The Federalists at least had a purpose in their seditiousness, and were honest in preferring the British government to their own; the Republicans of all shades, however weak in will or poor in motive, were earnest in their love of country; but Randolph was neither honest nor earnest, neither American nor English nor truly Virginian. Disappointed ambition had turned him into a mere egoist; his habits had already become intemperate, and his health was broken; but he could still charge upon Jefferson all the disasters of the country, and could delight in the overwhelming ruin which had fallen upon his former chief. Randolph's speech of February 3 was stale and tedious. Except on the single point of raising the embargo he was spiritless; and his only positive idea, borrowed from the Federalists, consisted in a motion that, instead of issuing letters of marque, Government should authorize merchant-vessels to arm and defend themselves from seizure. If the scheme had a meaning, it meant submission to the British Orders, and was suggested by the Federalists for no other object; but in Randolph's mind such a plan carried no definite consequence.

On Randolph's motion the debate continued until February 7. The Republicans, disconcerted and disheartened by the conduct of their friends from New England and New York, made little show of energy, and left to David R. Williams the task of expressing the whole ignominy of their defeat. Williams struggled manfully. Randolph's fears for the Constitution were answered by the South Carolinian in a few words, which condensed into a single paragraph the results of his party theories: —

"If the Constitution is made of such brittle stuff as not to stand a single war; if it is only to be preserved by submission to foreign taxation, — I shall very soon lose all solicitude for its preservation."

With more than Federalist bitterness he taunted the hesitation of the Democrats, — "contemptible cowardice," he called it. "It is time we should *assume*, if it is not in our natures, nerve enough to decide whether we will go to war or submit." The House replied by striking out the recommendation of reprisals, by a vote of fifty-seven to thirty-nine.

These two votes rendered the Administration for the moment powerless to make head against the sweeping Federalist victory. Josiah Quincy, who watched every symptom of democratic disaster, wrote as early as February 2, before the first defeat of the Administration:[1] "There is dreadful distraction in the enemy's camp on the subject of removing the embargo. Jefferson and his friends are obstinate. Bacon and the Northern Democrats are equally determined that it shall be raised in March." The next day Quincy added: "Jefferson is a host; and if the wand of that magician is not broken, he will yet defeat the attempt."

[1] Quincy's Life of Quincy, p. 185.

The contest had become personal; to break the "wand of the magician" was as much the object of Democrats as of Federalists, and neither Madison nor Gallatin could restore discipline. February 4 the Secretary of the Treasury wrote:[1] "As far as my information goes, everything grows more quiet in Massachusetts and Maine. All would be well if our friends remained firm here."

The attempt to hold the friends of the Administration firm brought only greater disaster. The vote in committee refusing to recommend reprisals took place February 7; and the next day Quincy wrote again: "Great caucusing is the order of the day and the night here. The Administration is determined to rally its friends, and postpone the removal of the embargo till May. But I think they cannot succeed. Bacon, I am told, stands firm and obstinate against all their solicitations and even almost denunciations. However, they had another caucus last night. The event is unknown. Jefferson has prevailed."

February 9 the result of the caucus was shown by a vote of the House discharging the Committee of the Whole, and referring the subject to the Committee of Foreign Relations, whose chairman was G. W. Campbell,—which amounted to a public admission that Madison's plan had failed, and that some new expedient for uniting the party must be invented. Ezekiel Bacon refused to obey the caucus, and voted with the Federalists against the reference.

President Jefferson, though his name was still a terror to his enemies, accepted whatever decision his Cabinet advised. Till the day of his death he never forgot the violence of these last weeks of his administration, or the outcry of the New England towns. "How powerfully did we feel the energy of this organization in the case of the embargo," he wrote long afterward.[2] "I felt the foundations of the government shaken under my feet by the New England townships." He showed the same lack of interest in February which had marked his conduct in November; not even the certainty of his own overthrow called out the familiar phrases of vexation. February 7 he wrote to his son-in-law, Thomas Mann Randolph,[3] —

[1] Adams's Gallatin, p. 386.
[2] Jefferson to J. C. Cabell, Feb. 2, 1816; Works, vi. 540.
[3] Works, v. 424.

"I thought Congress had taken their ground firmly for continuing their embargo till June, and then war. But a sudden and unaccountable revolution of opinion took place the last week, chiefly among the New England and New York members, and in a kind of panic they voted the 4th of March for removing the embargo, and by such a majority as gave all reason to believe they would not agree either to war or non-intercourse. This, too, was after we had become satisfied that the Essex Junto had found their expectation desperate, of inducing the people there either to separation or forcible opposition. The majority of Congress, however, has now rallied to the removing the embargo on the 4th March, non-intercourse with France and Great Britain, trade everywhere else, and continuing war preparations. The further details are not yet settled, but I believe it is perfectly certain that the embargo will be taken off the 4th of March."

As the President became more subdued, Senator Pickering became more vehement; his hatred for Jefferson resembled the hatred of Cotton Mather for a witch. February 4 he wrote to his nephew in Boston:[1] —

"I entertain no doubt that Jefferson stands pledged to Bonaparte to maintain the embargo until a non-intercourse or war shall succeed; and he dreads the explosion justly to be apprehended by him from the disappointment and passion of Bonaparte, should the embargo be removed without a substitute as well or better comporting with his views. Upon this aspect of things it behooves our State legislature to advance with a firm step in defence of the rights of our citizens and of the Constitution. The palatines tremble at their posts. The least relaxation or wavering in the councils of New England would give them fresh courage, and hazard the most disastrous consequences."

Another observer wrote comments, serious in a different sense. Erskine watched with extreme interest every detail of this complicated struggle, and reported to Canning both facts and speculations which could not fail to affect the British

---

[1] Pickering to T. Williams, Feb. 4, 1809; Pickering MSS.

government. Aware that Canning had won a brilliant success, Erskine labored to profit by his triumph, and to turn it in the interests of peace. A vast majority of Americans, he said,[1] wanted only some plausible excuse to justify them in resenting Napoleon's conduct; but "they naturally wish to be saved the complete humiliation of being obliged avowedly to recant all their violent declarations of their determination never to submit to the Orders in Council of Great Britain." He speculated "how far it might be possible still further to bend the spirit of that part of the people of the United States until they should be forced to single out France to be resisted as the original aggressors while his Majesty's Orders in Council continued to be enforced." After the repeal of the embargo and the refusal to make war, but one remnant of American protest against British aggressions remained. The Republican caucus, February 7, decided in favor of returning to Jefferson's pacific non-intercourse,—the system which had been, by common consent, thrown aside as insufficient even before the embargo. February 10 Erskine gave an account of the new measure, and of its probable effect on American politics:—

"It is true that a non-intercourse law may be considered by the Eastern States very objectionable; but as it would be rather a nominal prohibition than a rigorous enforcement, a resistance to it would be less likely to be made, and of less importance if it should take place. The ultimate consequences of such differences and jealousies arising between the Southern and Eastern States would inevitably tend to a dissolution of the Union, which has been for some time talked of, and has of late, as I have heard, been seriously contemplated by many of the leading people in the Eastern division."

The Non-intercourse Bill, which Erskine described February 10 as likely to be no more than a nominal prohibition of commerce, was reported February 11 to the House from the Committee of Foreign Relations. The bill excluded all public and private vessels of France and England from American waters; forbade under severe penalties the importation of British

[1] Erskine to Canning, Feb. 9, 1809; MSS. British Archives.

or French goods; repealed the embargo laws, "except so far as they relate to Great Britain or France or their colonies or dependencies, or places in the actual possession of either;" and gave the President authority to reopen by proclamation the trade with France or England in case either of these countries should cease to violate neutral rights. That the proposed non-intercourse was in truth submission to the Orders in Council, no one denied.

"I conceive that great advantages may be reaped from it by England," wrote Erskine,[1] "as she has the command of the seas, and can procure through neutrals any of the produce of this country, besides the immense quantity which will be brought direct to Great Britain under various pretences; whereas France will obtain but little, at a great expense and risk."

Such a non-intercourse merely sanctioned smuggling, and was intended for no other purpose. Gallatin in his disgust flung open the doors to illicit commerce. When Erskine went to him to ask what was meant by "France, England, and their dependencies," Gallatin replied that only places in actual possession of England and France were intended, that it was impossible to say what nations had decrees in force infringing neutral rights, but that even Holland would be considered an independent country.[2]

"The intention of this indefinite description," continued Erskine, "is undoubtedly to leave open as many places for their commerce as they can, consistently with keeping up an appearance of resistance to the belligerent restrictions; but it is thoroughly understood that the whole measure is a mere subterfuge to extricate themselves from the embarrassments of the embargo system, and is never intended to be enforced."

When this bill came before the House, another long debate arose. Hardly a trace of national pride remained. No one approved the bill, but no one struggled longer against submission. Josiah Quincy and many of the Federalists held that the

[1] Erskine to Canning, Feb. 10, 1809; MSS. British Archives.
[2] Erskine to Canning, Feb. 13, 1809; MSS. British Archives.

surrender was not yet complete enough, and that total submission to Great Britain must precede the return of Massachusetts to harmony with the Union, or to a share in measures of government. His words were worth noting:—

"He wished peace if possible; if war, union in that war. For this reason he wished a negotiation to be opened, unshackled with those impediments to it which now existed. As long as they remained, the people in the portion of country whence he came would not deem an unsuccessful attempt at negotiation to be cause for war. If they were removed, and an earnest attempt at negotiation was made, unimpeded with these restrictions, and should not meet with success, they would join heartily in a war."

Doubtless Quincy believed the truth of what he said; but as though to prove him mistaken in claiming even the modest amount of patriotism which he asserted for his party, Barent Gardenier immediately followed with a declaration that Great Britain was wholly in the right, and that America should not only submit to the Orders in Council, but should take pride in submission:—

"I do not say that the orders were lawful, or that they were not infringements of our rights as a neutral nation,— as it might offend the prejudices of the House. But I may be permitted to say that if they were unlawful, I have proved that they are not hurtful; that the British Orders in Council only supplied to that which our sense of honor would lead us to do, their sanction."[1]

Gardenier's views roused no longer much outward irritation. The war Republicans liked honest avowals better than sham patriotism; but John Randolph, unwilling to be embarrassed with allies so candid, rated Gardenier sharply:—

"I looked at the gentleman from New York at that moment with the sort of sensation which we feel in beholding a sprightly child meddling with edged tools,—every moment expecting, what actually happened, that he will cut his fingers. . . . The gentleman's friends, if any he have,—

[1] Annals of Congress, 1808–1809, p. 1460.

and I have no right to presume that he has none, but the contrary,—will do well to keep such dangerous implements out of his way for the future."

Randolph himself persisted in the scheme of withdrawing all restrictions on commerce, and allowing merchant-vessels to arm,—a measure which had the advantage of being warlike or pacific, according as he should prefer in the future to represent it. David R. Williams hit upon an idea more sensible, and likely to prove more effective. "If the embargo is to be taken off, and war not to be substituted,—if the nation is to submit,—I wish to do it profitably." He proposed to shut out the shipping of England and France, but to admit their manufactures, under a duty of fifty per cent when imported in American vessels. A number of Southern Republicans approved this plan.

Much the strongest speech against the bill was that of George W. Campbell, who made no attempt to hide his mortification at seeing the House desert him, its leader, and turn its back upon the pledge it had solemnly given in accepting his Report only two months before:—

"At the very time when your own people are rallying round the standard of their government; when they are about to shake off that timidity, that alarm, that restless disposition, which the first pressure occasioned by the suspension of commerce naturally produced; when they are, in almost every quarter of the Union, declaring their determination and solemnly pledging themselves to support your measures, to maintain the embargo, or go to war if necessary,—to do anything but submit: at that very moment, instead of being invited by a similar patriotic enthusiasm to throw yourselves in front, and to lead them on to the honorable contest, you abandon the ground you have already occupied, you check their generous enthusiasm, and leave them the mortification of seeing their country disgraced by a timid, temporizing policy that must, if persevered in, ruin the nation."

Although events had already proved that no appeal to self-respect called out a response from this Congress, Campbell might reasonably suppose that arguments of self-interest would be heard; and he pressed one objection to the bill which, in theory, should have been decisive:—

> "The non-intercourse would press most severely on the Southern and Western States, who depend chiefly on the immediate exchange of their productions for foreign goods, and would throw almost the whole commerce of the nation into the hands of the Eastern States, without competition, and also add a premium on their manufactures at the expense of the agricultural interest to the South and West. Foreign goods being excluded, the manufacturing States would furnish the rest of the Union with their manufactured goods at their own prices."

A moment's reflection must have satisfied the Republicans that this argument against the bill was fatal. Non-intercourse must ruin the South, in order to offer an immense bribe to the shipping and manufactures of New England as an inducement for New England to remain in the Union. The manufacturing interests never ventured to ask such extravagant protection as was thrust upon them in 1809 by the fears of the agricultural States; the greed of corporate capital never suggested the monopoly created for Eastern ships and factories by a measure which shut from America all ships and manufactures but theirs. Even if but partially enforced, such legislation was ruinous to agriculture.

Entreaty and argument were thrown away. The House lost discipline, self-respect, and party character. No one felt responsible for any result, no majority approved any suggestion. As the last days of the session drew near, the machinery of legislation broke down, and Congress became helpless. So strange and humiliating a spectacle had not before been seen. The nation seemed sinking into the weakness of dissolution.

The paralysis came in a form that could not be disguised. While the House disputed over one Non-intercourse Bill, the Senate passed another; and February 22 the House laid aside its own measure in order to take up that of the Senate, which contained the disputed clause authorizing letters of marque and reprisal against nations that should continue their unlawful edicts after repeal of the embargo. In pursuance of its vote of February 7, the House in committee promptly struck out the reprisal clause. Next it rejected David R. Williams's motion for discriminating duties. Ezekiel Bacon, perhaps somewhat scandalized at the legislation he had chiefly caused, suggested the Federalist plan of authorizing merchant-vessels to resist seizure; and February 25 a struggle occurred on the question of permitting forcible resistance by merchant-vessels. The minority was deeply agitated as the act of complete submission became imminent. David R. Williams cried that if the House could so abandon national rights, they deserved to be scoffed by all the world; John W. Eppes declared himself compelled to believe Josiah Quincy's assertion that the majority could not be kicked into a war; even the peaceable Macon moved a warlike amendment. Vote after vote was taken; again and again the ayes and noes were called on dilatory motions of adjournment; but every motion looking toward war was steadily voted down, and in the end, February 27, the Non-intercourse Bill in its most unresisting shape received the approval of the House. Not a speaker defended it; at the last moment the charge was freely made that the bill had not a single friend. The members who voted for it declared in doing so that the measure was a weak and wretched expedient, that they detested it, and took it merely as a choice of evils; but eighty-one members voted in its favor, and only forty in the negative. More extraordinary still, this non-intercourse, which bound the South to the feet of New England, was supported by forty-one Southern members, while but twelve New England representatives recorded their names in its favor.

Three months afterward, at a moment when the danger of war seemed to have vanished, John Randolph recalled the memory of this confused struggle, and claimed for President Jefferson and himself the credit for having prevented a declaration of war. He had voted against the non-intercourse, he said, because he had believed that he could get rid of the embargo on still better terms; others had voted against it because they thought it absolute disgrace:[1] —

"The fact is that nobody would advocate it; that though

[1] Annals of Congress, 1809-1810; part i. 149, 150.

it was carried by a majority of two to one, those who finally voted for it condemned it, and all parties seemed ashamed of it; and that . . . all the high-toned men and high-toned presses in this country denounced the majority of this House for passing that law, as having utterly disgraced themselves. . . . If the great leaders could have been gratified, according to their own showing they would have dragged this country into a war with Great Britain. . . . Now to be sure, sir, those persons who undertook to stop their wild career were composed of heterogeneous materials; . . . there were minority men, caucus men, protesters,—in fact, sir, all parties, Catholics, Protestants, Seceders,—and all were united in the effort to prevent the leaders of both Houses from plunging the nation into a war with one Power and knuckling to the other; from riveting the chains of French influence, perhaps of French alliance upon us. Thank God that their designs were proclaimed to the nation, that the President did not give his consent, which would have made us kick the beam. Yes, sir! Federalists, minority men, protesters, and all would have kicked the beam if it had ever emanated from the Cabinet that the President was for war."

If Randolph was right, the "wand of the magician" had not been broken; and other observers besides Randolph held the same opinion. "Jefferson has triumphed," wrote Josiah Quincy, February 27, immediately after the repeal; "his intrigues have prevailed."[1]

In a spirit widely different from that of Randolph and Quincy, Nathaniel Macon, February 28, wrote to his friend Nicholson,—

"Otis, the Secretary of the Senate, has this moment informed the House of Representatives that the Senate have agreed to the amendments made by the House to the Bill to repeal the embargo.

"The Lord, the mighty Lord, must come to our assistance, or I fear we are undone as a nation!"[2]

[1] Quincy's Life of Quincy, p. 185.
[2] Macon to Nicholson, Feb. 28, 1809; Nicholson MSS.

Chapter XX

THE REPEAL of the embargo, which received the President's signature March 1, closed the long reign of President Jefferson; and with but one exception the remark of John Randolph was destined to remain true, that "never has there been any Administration which went out of office and left the nation in a state so deplorable and calamitous." That the blame for this failure rested wholly upon Jefferson might be doubted; but no one felt more keenly than he the disappointment under which his old hopes and ambitions were crushed.

Loss of popularity was his bitterest trial. He who longed like a sensitive child for sympathy and love left office as strongly and almost as generally disliked as the least popular President who preceded or followed him. He had undertaken to create a government which should interfere in no way with private action, and he had created one which interfered directly in the concerns of every private citizen in the land. He had come into power as the champion of States-rights, and had driven States to the verge of armed resistance. He had begun by claiming credit for stern economy, and ended by exceeding the expenditure of his predecessors. He had invented a policy of peace, and his invention resulted in the necessity of fighting at once the two greatest Powers in the world.

The feelings of the New England Democrats have been described in their own words. Angry as Ezekiel Bacon and Joseph Story were, their bitterness against Jefferson was hardly so great as that of the Clintonians in New York; but the same irritation extended even into the compact democracy of Pennsylvania. In the preceding summer, before the Presidential election, A. J. Dallas said to Gallatin:[1] "I verily believe one year more of writing, speaking, and appointing would render Mr. Jefferson a more odious President, even to the Democrats, than John Adams." So far as could be judged from the conduct of the party, the prophecy became truth. The Southern Republicans, always loyal to a Southern President, would

[1] Dallas to Gallatin, July 30, 1808; Adams's Gallatin, p. 372.

not openly turn against their old leader, but the Northern Democrats made no disguise of their aversion.

Not even in 1798 had factiousness been so violent as in the last month of President Jefferson's power; in 1800 the country in comparison had been contented. Feb. 23, 1809, nearly three weeks after the disastrous overthrow of the embargo in Congress, the Connecticut legislature met in special session to "interpose" between the people and the national government. In a Report echoing the words of Governor Trumbull's speech, the House instantly approved his refusal to aid in carrying out the "unconstitutional and despotic" Enforcement Act, and pledged itself to join the legislature of Massachusetts in the measures proposed "to give to the commercial States their fair and just consideration in the Union."[1] The spirit in which Massachusetts meant to act was shown in a formal Address to the People issued by her Legislature March 1, bearing the official signatures of Harrison Gray Otis, President of the Senate, and Timothy Bigelow, Speaker of the House.

"Protesting in the sight of God the sincerity of their attachment to the Union of the States, and their determination to cherish and preserve it at every hazard until it shall fail to secure to them those blessings which alone give value to any form of government," the Massachusetts legislature laid before the people of the State certain Reports and measures adopted for the purpose of impeding the embargo laws, and apologized for having done no more, on the ground that more could not have been done " without authorizing a forcible resistance to Acts of Congress,—an ultimate resource so deeply to be deprecated that the cases which might justify it should not be trusted even to the imagination until they actually happen." Less than forty years before, Massachusetts had used much the same language in regard to Acts of Parliament, and the world knew what then followed; but even in the bitterest controversies over Stamp Act or Port Bill, the General Court of Massachusetts had never insulted King George as they insulted President Jefferson. The Address at great length asserted that his Government was laboring under "an habitual and impolitic predilection for France;" and even

[1] Report and Resolutions, National Intelligencer, March 10, 1809.

in making this assertion it apologized for England in terms which echoed the words of Canning and Castlereagh:—

"Without pretending to compare and adjust the respective injuries sustained from the two nations, it cannot be disguised that in some instances our nation has received from Great Britain compensation; in others offers of atonement, and in all the language of conciliation and respect."

On the other hand, war with England must lead to alliance with France; and that a connection with France "must be forever fatal to the liberty and independence of the nation is obvious to all who are not blinded by partiality and passion."

Such reasoning had the merits of its emphasis. The case of forcible resistance which could not be trusted to the imagination until it happened pointed designedly to a war with England, which, being equivalent to a connection with France, must be forever fatal to the liberty and independence of the United States. The dogma that a British war must dissolve the Union had become more than ever an article of Federalist faith. Even Rufus King, writing to Pickering, January 31, said:[1] "The embargo, as we are now told, is to give way to war. If the project be to unite with France against England, the Union cannot be preserved." To prevent war with England was to prevent a dissolution of the Union; and the legislature of Massachusetts, acting on that idea, closed what it called its "Patriotick Proceedings," by declaring to the people of the Commonwealth the measures by which alone the Union could be saved:—

"As the malady is deep, you will still be deceived by trusting to any temporary relief. You must realize and comprehend the nature of your peculiar interests, and by steady, persevering, and well-concerted efforts rise into an attitude to promote and preserve them. The farmer must remember that his prosperity is inseparable from that of the merchant; and that there is little affinity between his condition and habits and those of a Southern planter. The interests of New England must be defined, understood, and firmly represented. A perfect intelligence must be cultivated

[1] King's Life and Correspondence, v. 131.

among those States, and a united effort must be made and continued to acquire their just influence in the national government. For this purpose the Constitution should be amended, and the provision which gives to holders of slaves a representation equal to that of six hundred thousand free citizens should be abolished. Experience proves the injustice, and time will increase the inequality, of this principle, the original reason for which has entirely failed. Other amendments to secure commerce and navigation from a repetition of destructive and insidious theories are indispensable."

Such were the conditions on which Massachusetts must insist: —

"The Legislature are aware that their measures and sentiments will encourage their opponents in propagating the foul imputation of a design to dismember the Union. But when did party malice want a theme to excite popular prejudice? When did it have recourse to one more absurd and unfounded?"

The object of the Federalist majority was to strengthen the Union, — so they protested and so they doubtless believed; but in truth they insisted upon creating a new Union as a condition of their remaining in the old. The fatal word "must" ran through all their demands: —

"If the Southern States are disposed to avail themselves of the advantages resulting from our strength and resources for common defence, they must be willing to patronize the interests of navigation and commerce without which our strength will be weakness. If they wish to appropriate a portion of the public revenue toward roads, canals, or for the purchase of arms and the improvement of their militia, they must consent that you who purchase your own arms, and have already roads, canals, and militia in most excellent order, shall have another portion of it devoted to naval protection. If they in the spirit of chivalry are ready to rush into an unnecessary and ruinous war with one nation, they must suffer you to pause before you bid an eternal adieu to your independence by an alliance with another."

Union of New England against the national Union—an idea hitherto confined to the brain of Timothy Pickering—had become the avowed object of the Massachusetts and Connecticut legislatures. "Nothing less than a perfect union and intelligence among the Eastern States" could answer the objects of Pickering; but side by side with the perfect union of the Eastern States went a perfect intelligence between those States and the British government. On one side, Pickering maintained relations with Rose; on the other, Sir James Craig kept a secret agent at Boston. January 26, at the moment when the crisis of war or peace was about to be decided at Washington, Mr. Ryland at Quebec, on behalf of the Governor-General of Canada, sent for John Henry to undertake another winter journey through New England.[1] His instructions, dated February 6 and signed by Sir James Craig himself, enjoined the utmost secrecy, and restricted Henry to the task of ascertaining how far, in case of war, the Federalists of the Eastern States would look to England for assistance, or be disposed to enter into a connection with the British government.[2] Only in case the Federalist leaders should express a wish to that effect was Henry cautiously to avow his official character, and to receive any communication for transmittal. February 10 Henry started on this errand, but before he reached Boston the news that Congress had decided to repeal the embargo without declaring war left him little to do. He remained quietly in Boston, in familiar relations with the Federalist leaders,[3] without betraying his errand; and the substance of his reports to the governor-general amounted only to a decided opinion that the Federalists were not yet ready to act: "I can assure you that at this moment they do not freely entertain the project of withdrawing the Eastern States from the Union, finding it a very unpopular topic."[4] Until midsummer, when the last fear of war vanished, this accredited agent of the governor-general waited at Boston for events. "His manners being gentlemanly and his letters of introduction good," said Josiah Quincy, "he was admitted

[1] Ryland to John Henry, Jan. 26, 1809; State Papers, iii. 546.
[2] Sir James Craig to John Henry, Feb. 6, 1809; State Papers, iii. 546.
[3] Quincy's Life of Quincy, p. 250.
[4] Henry to Sir J. Craig, March 7, 1809; State Papers, iii. 549.

freely into society and heard the conversation at private tables."

Had Jefferson known that a British emissary was secretly waiting at Boston to profit by the result of eight years' Republican policy, he could not but have felt deep personal mortification mingled with his sense of wrong. Of all Jefferson's hopes, perhaps the warmest had been that of overthrowing the power of his New England enemies,—those whom he had once called the monarchical Federalists,—the clergy and the Essex Junto. Instead of overthrowing them he had given them, for the first time in their lives, unlimited power for mischief; he had overthrown only the moderate Federalists, who when forced to choose between treason and embargo submitted to the embargo and hated its author. The Essex Junto became supreme in New England; and behind it stood the power of Great Britain, ready to interpose, if necessary, for its defence.

Jefferson submitted in silence, and even with an air of approval, to the abrupt abandonment of his favorite measure. He admitted that the embargo had failed; he even exaggerated its evils, and described it as more costly than war. His language implied that the failure of peaceable coercion was no longer a matter of doubt in his mind.

"The belligerent edicts," he wrote to Armstrong,[1] "rendered our embargo necessary to call home our ships, our seamen, and property. We expected some effect, too, from the coercion of interest. Some it has had, but much less on account of evasions and domestic opposition to it. After fifteen months' continuance, it is now discontinued because, losing fifty million dollars of exports annually by it, it costs more than war, which might be carried on for a third of that, besides what might be got by reprisal."

To Dupont de Nemours Jefferson wrote in the same strain.[2] He signed without the betrayal of a protest the bill repealing the embargo, and talked of war as a necessary evil. Not until more than a year afterward did he admit the bitterness of his disappointment and mortification; but July 16,

[1] Jefferson to Armstrong, March 5, 1809; Works, v. 433.
[2] Jefferson to Dupont de Nemours, March 2, 1809; Works, v. 432.

1810, he wrote to his old Secretary of War a letter which expressed, in his familiar note of irritability, the feelings he had pent up:[1] —

"The Federalists during their short-lived ascendency have nevertheless, by forcing us from the embargo, inflicted a wound on our interests which can never be cured, and on our affections which will require time to cicatrize. I ascribe all this to one pseudo-Republican, — Story. He came on in place of Crowninshield, I believe, and stayed only a few days, — long enough, however, to get complete hold of Bacon, who, giving in to his representations, became panic-struck, and communicated the panic to his colleagues, and they to a majority of the sound members of Congress. They believed in the alternative of repeal or civil war, and produced the fatal measure of repeal. . . . I have ever been anxious to avoid a war with England unless forced by a situation more losing than war itself; but I did believe we could coerce her to justice by peaceable means; and the embargo, evaded as it was, proved it would have coerced her had it been honestly executed. The proof she exhibited on that occasion that she can exercise such an influence in this country as to control the will of its government and three fourths of its people is to me the most mortifying circumstance which has occurred since the establishment of our government."

In truth, the disaster was appalling; and Jefferson described it in moderate terms by admitting that the policy of peaceable coercion brought upon him mortification such as no other President ever suffered. So complete was his overthrow that his popular influence declined even in the South. Twenty years elapsed before his political authority recovered power over the Northern people; for not until the embargo and its memories faded from men's minds did the mighty shadow of Jefferson's Revolutionary name efface the ruin of his Presidency. Yet he clung with more and more tenacity to the faith that his theory of peaceable coercion was sound; and when within a few months of his death he alluded for the last time

[1] Jefferson to Dearborn, July 15, 1810; Works, v. 529.

to the embargo, he spoke of it as "a measure which, persevered in a little longer, we had subsequent and satisfactory assurance would have effected its object completely."[1]

A discomfiture so conspicuous could not fail to bring in its train a swarm of petty humiliations which for the moment were more painful than the great misfortune. Jefferson had hoped to make his country forever pure and free; to abolish war, with its train of debt, extravagance, corruption, and tyranny; to build up a government devoted only to useful and moral objects; to bring upon earth a new era of peace and good-will among men. Throughout the twistings and windings of his course as President he clung to this main idea; or if he seemed for a moment to forget it, he never failed to return and to persist with almost heroic obstinacy in enforcing its lessons. By repealing the embargo, Congress avowedly and even maliciously rejected and trampled upon the only part of Jefferson's statesmanship which claimed originality, or which in his own opinion entitled him to rank as a philosophic legislator. The mortification he felt was natural and extreme, but such as every great statesman might expect, and such as most of them experienced. The supreme bitterness of the moment lay rather in the sudden loss of respect and consideration which at all times marked the decline of power, but became most painful when the surrender of office followed a political defeat at the hands of supposed friends.

The last days of his authority were embittered by a personal slight which wounded him deeply. After the peace of Tilsit the Emperor Alexander of Russia expressed a wish to exchange ministers with the United States government. In every point of view America must gain by winning the friendship of Russia; and much as Jefferson disliked multiplying diplomatic offices, he could not but feel that at a time when his ministers were likely at any moment to be driven from France and England, nothing could be more useful than to secure a foothold at St. Petersburg. Without loss of time he created the mission, and appointed his old personal friend William Short to the new post. In August, 1808, during the recess of Congress, he sent Short to Europe, with orders to stop at

---

[1] Jefferson to W. B. Giles, Dec. 25, 1825; Works, vii. 424.

Paris until the Senate should confirm his appointment. For political reasons Jefferson waited till the close of the session, and then, February 24, made this appointment the subject of his last Message to the Senate, explaining the motives which had induced him to create a diplomatic agency at St. Petersburg, and announcing that Short had received his commission and had gone to Europe six months before on this errand.

No sooner had the Senate, on receiving this Message, gone into executive session than Senator Bradley of Vermont offered a Resolution that any intercourse with Russia, such as the President suggested, might "be carried on with equal facility and effect by other public agents of the United States without the expense of a permanent minister plenipotentiary;" or in case of sudden negotiations for peace in Europe, "the permanent minister at any of the Courts thereof may be instructed to attend on the same;" and that for these reasons the proposed appointment was at present inexpedient and unnecessary. After much secret debate, Senator Bradley, February 27, withdrew his motion, and the Senate then abruptly and unanimously rejected Short's nomination.

The discourtesy was flagrant. As a matter of policy the new mission might fairly be subject for argument; and the Senate had a right, if it chose, to follow its own opinions on such a subject. Unreasonable as was the idea of sending hither and thither the American ministers "at any of the Courts of Europe," when every senator knew that on the continent of Europe America had but one minister, and even he was on the verge of dismissal or recall; ill-judged as was the assertion that a consular agent could carry on "with equal facility and effect" at a Court like that of St. Petersburg a diplomatic intercourse which would need every resource of public and private influence; narrow as was the policy of refusing "the expense of a permanent minister plenipotentiary" to the only nation in the world which offered her friendship at a moment when England and France were doing their utmost to spare America the expense of legations at London and Paris,—yet these objections to Jefferson's wish were such as the Senate might naturally make, for they were the established creed of the Republican party, and no one had done more than Jefferson himself to erect them into a party dogma. Dislike of diplomacy was a relic of the old colonial status when America had been dependent on Europe,—a prejudice rising chiefly from an uneasy sense of social disadvantage. Whenever America should become strong and self-confident, these petty jealousies were sure to disappear, and her relations with other Powers would be controlled solely by her wants; but meanwhile the Senate in every emergency might be expected to embarrass the relations of the Executive with foreign governments, and to give untenable reasons for its conduct. That the Senate should object, could have been no surprise to Jefferson; but that it should without even a private explanation reject abruptly and unanimously the last personal favor asked by a President for whom every Republican senator professed friendship, and from whom most had received innumerable favors, seemed an unpardonable insult. So Jefferson felt it. He wrote to Short in accents of undisguised mortification:—

"It is with much concern I inform you that the Senate has negatived your appointment. We thought it best to keep back the nomination to the close of the session, that the mission might remain secret as long as possible, which you know was our purpose from the beginning. It was then sent in with an explanation of its object and motives. We took for granted, if any hesitation should arise, that the Senate would take time, and that our friends in that body would make inquiries of us and give us the opportunity of explaining and removing objections; but to our great surprise and with an unexampled precipitancy they rejected it at once. This reception of the last of my official communications to them could not be unfelt."[1]

Senators attempted explanations: Short had been too long in the diplomatic service or resident abroad; the diplomatic connections of the United States with Europe were already too extensive, and rather than send more ministers those actually abroad should be recalled; "riveted to the system of unentanglement with Europe," the Senate, though sensible of "the great virtues, the high character, the powerful influence, and valuable friendship of the Emperor," declined the honor

[1] Jefferson to W. Short, March 8, 1809; Works, v. 435.

of relations with him. Yet these reasons showed only that the Senate felt as little regard for Jefferson's opinions and feelings as for those of the Czar. The manner of the rejection, even more than the rejection itself, proved the willingness of the President's oldest friends to inflict what they knew to be a painful wound on the self-respect of a fallen leader.

These mortifications, which rapidly followed each other in the last days of February, were endured by Jefferson with dignity and in silence. Perhaps senators would have better understood and might have more respected a vigorous burst of anger, even at some cost of dignity, than they did the self-restraint of the sensitive gentleman who had no longer a wish but to escape from Washington and seek peace in the calm of Monticello. He could with only a pang of mortified pride write his excuses to the Emperor Alexander and to William Short, and dismiss the matter forever from his mind. Public annoyances were for him nearly at an end, and could never recur; but unfortunately these public trials came upon him at a moment when his private anxieties were extreme.

In his style of life as President, Jefferson had indulged in such easy and liberal expenses as suited the place he held. Far from showing extravagance, the White House and its surroundings had in his time the outward look of a Virginia plantation. The President was required to pay the expenses of the house and grounds. In consequence, the grounds were uncared for, the palings broken or wanting, the paths undefined, and the place a waste, running imperceptibly into the barren fields about it. Within, the house was as simple as without, after the usual style of Virginia houses, where the scale was often extravagant but the details plain. Only in his table did Jefferson spend an unusual amount of money with excellent results for his political influence, for no President ever understood better than Jefferson the art of entertaining; yet his table cost him no excessive sums. For the best champagne he paid less than a dollar a bottle; for the best Bordeaux he paid a dollar; and the Madeira which was drunk in pipes at the White House cost between fifty and sixty cents a bottle. His French cook and cook's assistant were paid about four hundred dollars a year. On such a scale his salary of twenty-five thousand dollars was equivalent to fully sixty thousand dollars of modern money; and his accounts showed that for the first and probably the most expensive year of his Presidency he spent only $16,800 which could properly be charged to his public and official character.[1] A mode of life so simple and so easily controlled should in a village like Washington have left no opening for arrears of debt; but when Jefferson, about to quit the White House forever, attempted to settle his accounts, he discovered that he had exceeded his income. Not his expenses as President, but his expenses as planter dragged him down. At first he thought that his debts would reach seven or eight thousand dollars, which must be discharged from a private estate hardly exceeding two hundred thousand dollars in value at the best of times, and rendered almost worthless by neglect and by the embargo. The sudden demand for this sum of money, coming at the moment of his political mortifications, wrung from him cries of genuine distress such as no public disaster had called out. He wrote to his commission-merchant entreating him to borrow the money: —

"Since I have become sensible of this deficit I have been under an agony of mortification, and therefore must solicit as much urgency in the negotiation as the case will admit. My intervening nights will be almost sleepless, as nothing could be more distressing to me than to leave debts here unpaid, if indeed I should be permitted to depart with them unpaid, of which I am by no means certain."[2]

Large as it was, this estimate of the debt fell far short of the reality. The arrears amounted in truth to twenty thousand dollars.[3] Nothing but immediate and rigid economy could restore the loss, and even with every advantage Jefferson could never hope to live again upon his old scale without incurring bankruptcy; he must cease to be a *grand seigneur*, or drag his family into the ruin which seemed to be the fate of every Virginian.

Under the weight of these troubles, public and private, Jefferson's longing to escape became intense; and his letters re-

[1] Jefferson's Financial Diary. Harper's Magazine, March, 1885, pp. 534–542.
[2] Domestic Life of Thomas Jefferson, p. 400.
[3] Randall's Jefferson, iii. 326.

peated, in accents more and more earnest, the single wish that
filled his mind.

"I shall within a few days," he wrote February 25,[1] "divest myself of the anxieties and the labors with which I
have been oppressed, and retire with inexpressible delight
to my family, my friends, my farms, and books. There I
may indulge at length in that tranquillity and those pursuits
from which I have been divorced by the character of the
times in which I have lived, and which have forced me into
the line of political life under a sense of duty and against a
great and constant aversion to it."

March 2 he wrote to Dupont de Nemours,[2] in stronger
terms of weariness and disgust: "Never did a prisoner released
from his chains feel such relief as I shall on shaking off the
shackles of power. Nature intended me for the tranquil pursuits of science by rendering them my supreme delight."
March 4 he rode once more on horseback to the Capitol, and
stood by the side of Madison while John Marshall administered the oath of office. The weight of administration was at
last removed, but the longing for home became only the
greater. March 5 he wrote to Armstrong:[3] "Within two or
three days I retire from scenes of difficulty, anxiety, and of
contending passions, to the elysium of domestic affections
and the irresponsible direction of my own affairs." A week
afterward Jefferson quitted Washington forever. On horseback, over roads impassable to wheels, through snow and
storm, he hurried back to Monticello to recover in the quiet
of home the peace of mind he had lost in the disappointments
of his statesmanship. He arrived at Monticello March 15, and
never again passed beyond the bounds of a few adjacent
counties.

With a sigh of relief which seemed as sincere and deep as
his own, the Northern people saw him turn his back on the
White House and disappear from the arena in which he had
for sixteen years challenged every comer. In the Northern
States few regrets were wasted upon his departure, for every

[1] Jefferson to Warden, Feb. 25, 1809; Jefferson MSS.
[2] Jefferson to Dupont de Nemours, March 2, 1809; Works, v. 432.
[3] Jefferson to Armstrong, March 5, 1809; Works, v. 434.

mind was intent on profiting by the overthrow of his system; but Virginia was still loyal to him, and the citizens of his own county of Albemarle welcomed with an affectionate address his final return. His reply, dignified and full of grateful feeling, seemed intended as an answer to the attacks of partisan grossness and a challenge to the judgment of mankind: —

"The anxieties you express to administer to my happiness do of themselves confer that happiness; and the measure will be complete if my endeavors to fulfil my duties in the several public stations to which I have been called have obtained for me the approbation of my country. The part which I have acted on the theatre of public life has been before them, and to their sentence I submit it; but the testimony of my native county, of the individuals who have known me in private life, to my conduct in its various duties and relations is the more grateful as proceeding from eye-witnesses and observers, from triers of the vicinage. Of you, then, my neighbors, I may ask in the face of the world, 'Whose ox have I taken, or whom have I defrauded? Whom have I oppressed, or of whose hand have I received a bribe to blind mine eyes therewith?' On your verdict I rest with conscious security."

Index

Chronology

1838 Born in Boston, Massachusetts, on February 16, third son of Charles Francis Adams and Abigail Brooks Adams, great-grandson of President John Adams, and grandson of President John Quincy Adams, at whose home in Quincy he is a frequent summer visitor as a boy.

1854–58 Enters Harvard College. Contributes to the *Harvard Magazine* and is active in theatricals. Graduates as Class Orator.

1858 Sails, September 29, with several fellow graduates, for the traditional Grand Tour of Europe. Arrives at Liverpool on October 9. Attends the university as a student of civil law in Berlin after his arrival on October 22. Transfers to a German secondary school and writes an article on his winter's experience there (published in *American Historical Review*, Oct. 1947).

1859 In April resumes study of civil law in Dresden, where he lives until April 1, 1860. During intervals tours Austria and Germany and travels in northern Italy with his sister Louisa Kuhn before going on to Rome.

1860–61 Travels in Italy and Sicily until June. Interviews the Italian patriot Garibaldi just after the surrender of the Bourbon troops. Publishes his Italian travel letters in the *Boston Daily Courier*. Returns to Quincy, Massachusetts, in October. In December accompanies his father, who had been reelected to Congress, to Washington as his private secretary. December to mid-March 1861, serves as Washington correspondent of the *Boston Daily Advertiser*. Prepares "The Great Secession Winter, 1860–1861" (published in *Proceedings*, Massachusetts Historical Society, 1909–10).

1861–63 Sails for England, May 1. Serves as private secretary to his father, whom Lincoln has appointed as minister to Great Britain, until his father's resignation in May 1868. As London correspondent of *The New York Times* from June 1861 to January 1862, Adams reports British reaction to the American Civil War. His father sends Adams as a special messenger to the King of Denmark, December 1862. Tours Scotland and the Isle of Skye in August 1863 with his fifteen-year-old brother, Brooks.

1864–66   Grows restless with London society. Travels with mother, sister, and younger brother on the Continent. Returns to London; publishes unsigned scholarly articles.

1867   Publishes "Captaine John Smith" in the *North American Review*, demonstrating that that idol of Virginians had invented the tale of his rescue by Pocahontas. Also publishes "British Finance in 1816" and "The Bank of England Restriction," the latter illustrating the futility of issuing inconvertible paper money.

1868   Publishes a long review article on Sir Charles Lyell's tenth edition of his *Principles of Geology* in the *North American Review*, challenging current theories of glaciation and Darwin's theory of evolution as "in its nature incapable of proof." Returns to America in July with his parents and begins work in Washington as a free-lance political journalist and lobbyist in favor of currency reform, free trade, and the establishment of civil service, contributing occasional pieces to the New York *Nation* toward the end of the year.

1869   Attacks the subservience of Congress to special interests and its reliance on the spoils system in "The Session" and "Civil Service Reform," articles published in the *North American Review*. Publishes "American Finance, 1865–1869," an article critical of the financial expedients of the period, in the *Edinburgh Review*. Continues brief contributions to the *Nation* into 1870.

1870   Publishes "The Legal-Tender Act" (with the assistance of Francis A. Walker), vigorously attacking that legislation and its sponsor, Elbridge G. Spaulding, and a second "Session" critical of Congress in the *North American Review*. Adams makes a holiday visit to England, but he is shortly summoned to his sister Louisa's bedside at Bagni di Lucca, where on July 13 she dies of tetanus, leaving Adams with a lasting impression of Nature's indifference to human suffering. Is appointed assistant professor of history by Charles W. Eliot, the new president of Harvard College. Begins teaching courses in medieval English and European history; later adds courses in American history. Assumes editorship of the *North American Review*, to which he contributes two articles and over twenty reviews over the next seven years. Finally places his sensational exposé, "The New York Gold Conspiracy," in the *Westminster Review*. Drops the use of his middle name, Brooks.

1871   Publishes with his brother Charles Francis Adams, Jr., *Chapters of Erie*, a collection of some of their previously published articles. Travels to the Far West where he meets Clarence King of the United States Geological Survey. King soon afterward brings him into the circle of scientists connected with the Survey and the Smithsonian Institution.

1872–73 On June 27, Adams marries Marian (Clover) Hooper, daughter of the retired physician Dr. Robert William Hooper, a prominent Bostonian and a long-time widower. They sail July 9 on a wedding journey to England, the Continent, and Egypt. Adams renews friendships with Sir Robert Cunliffe, Charles Milnes Gaskell, Francis Palgrave, and Thomas Woolner, and consults European and English scholars such as Heinrich von Sybel, Ernst Curtius, Heinrich von Gneist, Georg H. Pertz, Theodor Mommsen, William Stubbs, John Richard Green, Sir Henry Maine, Robert Laing, and Benjamin Jowett. Returns to Boston August 1873.

1876   Publishes *Essays in Anglo-Saxon Law*, which includes his own essay "Anglo-Saxon Courts of Law" and three essays written by his doctoral candidates—Henry Cabot Lodge, Ernest Young, and James Lawrence Laughlin. Publishes "The Independents in the Canvass" in the *North American Review*, urging Republicans to break away from the conservative regular party. The article offends the publisher and leads to Adams' ending his connection with the *Review*. In December, Adams delivers his Lowell Institute lecture, "Primitive Rights of Women."

1877   Resigns from Harvard after accepting an invitation to work on the papers of Albert Gallatin, Thomas Jefferson's Secretary of the Treasury. As a friend of Secretary of State Evarts, Adams is given full access to the State Department archives. Publishes *Documents Relating to New England Federalism* in defense of the anti-Federalist policy of John Quincy Adams.

1879   Publishes *The Life of Albert Gallatin* and *The Writings of Albert Gallatin*. Forms friendships with Senator James D. Cameron and his wife, Elizabeth, and with John Hay, former private secretary of Abraham Lincoln. An inner circle of intimate friends is established of "The Five of Hearts"—the Adamses, John and Clara Hay, and Clarence King. Adams' wife presides over exclusive salon, which attracts friends such as Secretary of the Interior Carl Schurz, Attorney General Charles Devens, Senator Lucius Lamar of Mississippi, Congressman Abram Hewitt, Turkish minister Aristarchi Bey, and a procession of diplomats and foreign visitors. Adams begins acquaintance with a long succession of American presidents.

1879–80   Travels in Europe researching archives of London, Paris, and Madrid for his projected history of the administrations of Jefferson and Madison.

1880   Anonymously publishes *Democracy: An American Novel*, widely read in the United States and England for its depiction of political corruption in Washington.

1882   Publishes *John Randolph* in the American Statesmen Series.

1884   Under the pseudonym Frances Snow Compton, publishes *Esther: A Novel*. Adams and Hay begin construction of their residences on H Street facing Lafayette Square in Washington. The houses were designed by Adams' college mate, Henry Hobson Richardson. Circulates six copies, privately printed, of the first section of his *History of the United States during the Administrations of Thomas Jefferson and James Madison* to a few intimates for criticism.

1885   Circulates six copies of the second section of the *History*. Dr. Hooper, Adams' father-in-law, dies in April. On December 6, Adams' wife, Marian, commits suicide. Shortly afterward moves into the just-completed house at 1603 H Street.

1886   Commissions bronze figure to be executed by American sculptor Augustus Saint-Gaudens for the gravesite of Marian Adams in Rock Creek Cemetery. June to October, Adams tours Japan with artist John La Farge. November 21, Adams' father dies at Quincy at age seventy-nine.

1888   Circulates six copies of the third section of the *History*. (The fourth section was set directly from manuscript.) Adams makes his first visit to Cuba. Makes a circle tour of the Far West with his English friend Robert Cunliffe.

1889   Charles Scribner's Sons publishes the first two volumes of the trade edition of the *History* (four more volumes are published in 1890; the final three volumes and the volume of *Historical Essays* are published in 1891). June 6, Adams' mother dies at Quincy at age eighty-one. Adams becomes increasingly dependent on his friendship with Elizabeth Cameron.

1890–92 Adams travels with John La Farge to Hawaii, Samoa, Tahiti, Fiji, Australia, and Ceylon from August 1890 to September 1891. Writes poem "Buddha and Brahma" aboard ship en route from Ceylon (published in *The Yale Review*, Oct. 1915). Has a reunion with Elizabeth Cameron in France. Leaves England for America February 3, 1892.

1893   Commences intellectual collaboration with his brother Brooks, whose radical *Law of Civilization and Decay* will appear in 1895. Privately prints *Memoirs of Marau Taaroa, Last Queen of Tahiti*. Twice visits the World Columbian Exposition in Chicago, whose buildings seem to him to promise a renaissance in art and architecture.

1894   In December, sends his presidential address predicting the development of scientific history to the annual meeting of the American Historical Association to be delivered in absentia ("The Tendency of History," published in *Annual Report of the American Historical Association for the Year 1894*). Tours Cuba with Clarence King, February to March; travels to the Yellowstone and the Tetons with John Hay, July to September; tours Mexico and the Caribbean Islands with Chandler Hale, December 1894 to April 1895.

1895   Adams makes his first systematic study of the Gothic architecture of Normandy cathedrals and Mont-Saint-Michel in the company of Henry and Anna Cabot Lodge.

1896   Prepares "Recognition of Cuban Independence" for Senator Cameron, printed in the Senate Report. In April, travels to Mexico with the Camerons. Tours Europe with the Hays, May to October.

1897–98   Prolonged stay abroad is spent in London, Paris, Egypt (with the Hays), Turkey, Greece, the Balkans, Vienna, and Paris. Is in England, June to November. While visiting with Adams at Surrenden Dering in England, Hay is appointed U.S. Secretary of State, having served as ambassador to England since March 1897.

1899   Tours Italy and Sicily with the Lodges. Resides in Paris, June to January 1900. (Until 1911, in Paris for part of each year; from 1908 as member of Edith Wharton's circle.)

1900   Visits the Paris Exposition and is especially impressed by the Hall of Dynamos. Composes the poem "Prayer to the Virgin of Chartres," which includes a "Prayer to the Dynamo" (published 1920, in Mabel La Farge, *Letters to a Niece*).

1901   Revises and enlarges the Tahiti memoir as *Memoirs of Arii Taimai* for private distribution. Travels with the Lodges during July and August to Bayreuth, Vienna, Warsaw, Moscow, and St. Petersburg, then alone during September to Sweden and Norway.

1904   Privately prints *Mont Saint Michel and Chartres*. Contributes chapter on Clarence King in *Clarence King Memoirs*. In the spring, accompanies Secretary of State John Hay to the opening of the St. Louis Exposition.

1907   In February, issues the private edition of *The Education of Henry Adams*, containing the first formulation of his Dynamic Theory of History and his Law of Acceleration. Circulates the volume for correction to persons it comments on, including his brothers, Henry Cabot Lodge, Charles Gaskell, Theodore Roosevelt, Charles William Eliot, and Speck von Sternburg.

1908   Edits the *Letters of John Hay and Extracts from Diary*, but Adams surrenders completion to Hay's widow, who reduces the names to initials.

1909   Writes "The Rule of Phase Applied to History," in which he reformulates his theory of scientific history, now basing it on an analogy to Josiah Willard Gibbs's "Rule of Phase" contained in Gibbs's "On the Equilibrium of Heterogeneous Substances."

1910   Prints and distributes to university libraries and history professors the small volume *A Letter to American Teachers of History* proposing a theory of history based on the Second Law of Thermodynamics and the principle of entropy.

1911   Publishes *The Life of George Cabot Lodge*, prepared at the instance of the Lodges.

1912   Issues a second private edition, slightly revised, of *Mont Saint Michel and Chartres*. Is partially paralyzed by a cerebral thrombosis, April to late July.

1913   Authorizes the American Institute of Architects to publish a trade edition of the *Chartres*, edited by Ralph Adams Cram and issued through Houghton Mifflin Company. The advance sale breaks the publisher's records.

1913–14   Spends summers again in France, first at the Chateau Marivault in the countryside north of Paris and subsequently at the Chateau Coubertin. Engages Aileen Tone, a musician, as secretary-companion and becomes engrossed in the study and performance of medieval *chansons*.

1914–18   Presides at his noontime breakfast table at 1603 H Street during the war years, entertaining nieces and "nieces in wish" and visiting dignitaries such as Arthur Balfour, Henri Bergson, and French Ambassador Jusserand.

1918   Dies in Washington March 27 at the age of eighty. Buried beside his wife in Rock Creek Cemetery. First trade publication of *The Education of Henry Adams*. "Tendency of History," "Rule of Phase Applied to History," and "A Letter to American Teachers" are included by Brooks Adams in *The Degradation of the Democratic Dogma* (1919). The Pulitzer Prize is awarded posthumously in 1919 for *The Education*.

Note on the Texts

In the fall of 1879, with *The Life of Albert Gallatin* recently published, Henry Adams left America for London, Paris, Madrid, and Seville to do research in government archives. Adams wrote that he was in "pursuit of the larger subject, for which the Gallatin is only a preliminary study." This larger subject, a "History of the United States from 1801 to 1815," as he then called it, " will be an affair of at least ten years work, and will exhaust all that I have to say in this world, I hope. To compress this into three volumes and to expunge every unnecessary syllable, will be my great labor for several years. To make it readable is the great hope of my life."

As he continued to examine hitherto secret documents, his collection of relevant materials grew. In 1880, after taking stock of his European documents and beginning to write, Adams expressed a hope to publish in 1886; he gradually realized, however, that he would need more time—and more space—than he had planned. The history of Jefferson's two presidential administrations took shape during the early 1880s, and by the end of 1884 these first two parts of the *History* were written—and indeed were in print in private editions of six copies each for circulation among friends. Adams' progress in these years was rapid; in addition to this work on the *History*, he published the biography *John Randolph* and the novels *Democracy* and *Esther*. That progress was slowed, however, first by fatigue and then by the suicide of his wife, Marian, in December 1885.

Adams returned from a restorative trip to Japan in the summer of 1886 with a new resolve to finish his history. Working sometimes ten hours a day, he moved ahead on the history of Madison's administrations while continuing to fill gaps in the first two parts. By 1888, after Adams had spent nearly a decade researching, writing, and expanding, the *History* had grown to a size that he thought would require eight published volumes—two for each of the four presidential administrations that his work considered. (Madison's second administration, combined with a long, detailed general index, eventually filled three volumes instead of two, bringing the trade edition to nine volumes.)

In June 1888 Adams' assistant, Theodore Dwight, a former State Department librarian, wrote to arrange for publication with Charles Scribner's Sons. Adams requested as printer the Cambridge, Massachusetts, firm of John Wilson & Son, which set type and prepared the stereotype plates that would be used for all subsequent printings during Adams' lifetime. Through the rest of 1888 and 1889, Adams supplied copy to Wilson, worked on proofs, and rewrote the later portions of the *History*. He also negotiated with Charles Scribner on nearly every aspect of production and design— binding, thickness of paper, page design, typography, reproduction of maps and plans, and indexing—and on subjects such as whether or not to have chapter titles and what system to use in running heads. The nine volumes of *History of the United States* (New York: Charles Scribner's Sons, 1889–91) were issued in a ten-volume set with Adams' *Historical Essays*. He himself was not at home to receive copies of his final volumes; after sending the last revised proofs to Wilson, he set off for Polynesia in August 1890, leaving Dwight in charge of final details.

Adams believed he was writing the *History* for "a continent of a hundred million people fifty years hence," as he told an English friend, and he strove to improve the work by constant revision and incorporation of new information. As late as September 1889, he was in Ottawa gathering material about the War of 1812, and in early 1890 he was still working in new documents arriving from England.

Revision did not end with publication. Adams knew, as he complained in one letter, "how impossible it is to make a first edition accurate in its statements and reasoning, to say nothing of its style." He returned to the French archives after his Polynesian trip, and he revised parts of the *History* at various times throughout the 1890s.

In January 1899, Adams requested Scribner's to "be so kind as to send me a set of my History for revision and correction, so that in future my absence may not interfere with your requests." In February he told his friend Elizabeth Cameron that he was enjoying reading his own work, "which I am correcting in case of further editions"; and by March he returned the set to Scribner's "with a list of the pages on which corrections are to be made." These final revisions were cut into the plates and appeared in new printings of parts of the *History* as Scribner's required more copies.

This Library of America volume contains the first two parts of Adams' work, *History of the United States of America during the First Administration of Thomas Jefferson* and *History of the United States of America during the Second Administration of Thomas Jefferson*. The companion volume contains the last two parts covering James Madison's two administrations. In each case, the text is that of the last printing containing new revisions by Adams.

History of the United States of America during the First Administration of Thomas Jefferson was largely drafted and revised over the years 1881 to 1883. In March 1883, Adams wrote that he was "going next summer to put a twice-written volume of history into type, in order to rewrite it before publication." Adams had this "draft" volume privately printed by John Wilson & Son, in an edition of six copies, not only to have a clean text to revise for publication; he also wanted to safeguard his work, establish the priority of his scholarship, and elicit comments and criticism from colleagues—including his brother Charles Francis Adams and the historian George Bancroft. Printed in late 1883 and distributed in early 1884, the text of this private edition was divided into five "books"—an organization that was dropped in the trade edition.

Adams had initially planned to publish the trade edition in 1885 or 1886 along with the history of Jefferson's second administration. He later decided to publish his entire four-part work together, at roughly six-month intervals, and so delayed publication until the parts of Madison's administrations were nearly finished. When Dwight arranged for publication with Scribner's in June 1888, Adams called in the copies of the private printings, so that any annotations in them could be used in preparing printer's copy—his third major revision of the text. Scribner was assured that Adams would be "exceptionally careful in proof-reading," since "everyone criticizes first volumes," and warned not to "feel uneasy if I seem at first over-fussy in requiring revisions."

The trade edition, set from a copy of the privately printed draft volume with Adams' revisions, was published in two volumes on October 22, 1889, in a printing of 1500 copies. Two weeks later, Dwight was busy preparing a list of errata for the next impression despite Adams' exceptionally careful proofreading. Some of Dwight's letters mention a "corrected" edition of these two volumes, apparently issued some time in 1890 and containing only a few alterations.

The Second Administration of Thomas Jefferson was prepared in much the same way. A draft was finished in August 1884, and a private edition of six copies printed by Wilson in the fall of that year and distributed for comment and criticism. The Scribner's trade edition was set from a marked copy of the privately printed draft volume and published in two volumes on February 8, 1890, in a printing of 1500. By the end of the year another 500 copies were in print, perhaps incorporating the "few small corrections" that Adams mentions in an 1890 letter to Scribner.

From this point forward, the four volumes covering Jefferson's two administrations have identical careers. New printings of these volumes, incorporating revisions, appeared in 1898. For the most part, the changes involved the correction of typographical errors, minor stylistic revisions, and the correction of misspelled names: "Lyttleton" Tazewell was changed to "Littleton," and 22 occurrences of "Breckenridge" were corrected to "Breckinridge." Substantive changes were also made. Among others, two passages regarding Napoleon's policy in the West Indies were rewritten to incorporate additional facts. One of these (264.21–38) replaced a passage assessing Toussaint L'Ouverture's motives with a factual recital of the events leading up to the invasion of Hispaniola. This change continued Adams' pre-publication practice of revising toward a more objective, "scientific" style.

In January 1899, Adams made his final set of revisions, which were cut into the plates and appeared in new printings of each volume as Scribner's required more copies. It was in 1903 that the revised texts of the four volumes covering the history of Jefferson's administrations first appeared. Certain systematic changes were made throughout. Paul Leicester Ford's edition of *The Writings of Thomas Jefferson* (10 volumes,

1892–99) had by this time been published in its entirety, and
Adams (or Dwight working at Adams' direction) struck out
references to Jefferson manuscripts and cited Ford's edition
wherever possible. Numerous alterations in the quotations
drawn from Jefferson were also made, probably correcting
copyists' errors or Adams' misreading of the copyists' handwriting. Adams also systematically changed the "State-rights"
of earlier printings to "States-rights."

Of the other revisions, a few were stylistic. An ironic reference to a "modest compliment" that Jefferson payed to
himself in a pseudonymous article (357.30–31), for example,
was changed to the neutral "inserted compliment." The great
majority of the revisions, however, involved using more accurate information to alter or qualify assertions of fact. The
early printings' "a mail thrice a week to New York," for example, became "six mail-coaches a week to New York"
(18.15–16). In one case (562.27) an assertion was reversed:
where the early printings stated that Rufus King, American
minister in London, "knew of the Louisiana cession" when
signing a treaty, the new printing claims instead that "King
had not known" of the cession at that time.

This Library of America volume presents the texts of the
1903 printings of History of the United States of America during
the First Administration of Thomas Jefferson and History of the
United States of America during the Second Administration of
Thomas Jefferson, which incorporate Adams' final revisions in
those works. Adams' large general index (which he himself
assembled by reworking and expanding the indexes to the
first three parts and adding entries for the fourth) has been
separated into two indexes corresponding to this edition's
two-volume format, and entries have been corrected where
necessary. Maps and plans are reproduced from the History by
courtesy of The Massachusetts Historical Society.

Adams treated the four administrations as distinct units,
and he insisted on four different title pages with four sets of
volume numbers—"I" and "II" for each of the first three
units and "I," "II," and "III" for the fourth. He compromised
with Charles Scribner's desire for a series format, however,
by allowing the spines of the volumes to bear the series title
"History of the United States," inclusive dates, and consecu-

tive volume numbers 1 through 9. The Library of America has followed an analogous practice in the present edition: different title pages for the two volumes, with the series title and dates stamped on the binding.

This volume is concerned with presenting the texts of the 1903 printings; it does not attempt to reproduce features of the typographic design, such as the display capitalization of chapter openings. The texts are reproduced without change, except for the correction of typographical errors. Spelling, punctuation, and capitalization often are expressive features, and they are not altered, even when inconsistent or irregular. The following is a list of the typographical errors, cited by page and line number: 55.3, obligarchy; 155.39, Works.; 174.1, State-rights; 176.14, State-rights; 189.15, Breckenridge; 232.40, Etr.; 238.38, Correspondence; 247.33, MSS; 374.5, war"; 438.28, the Construction; 471.27, Breckenridge; 487.37, Papers.; 512.22, Only; 533.17, "I; 536.38, 1802:; 559.17, Breckenridge; 562.27, known the; 589.29, repress; 615.20, State-rights; 627.39, 7.; 646.38, Works; 671.38, 1805:; 705.39, 1805;; 744.35, Mr; 755.15, Breckenridge; 758.38, MSS; 788.37, Breckenridge; 872.27, Papers; 951.39, v; 1059.24, them; 1090.25, power; 1106.36, i,; 1125.3, hnndred; 1136.9, reach.

Notes

For more detailed notes, references to other studies, and further bio-graphical background, see Ernest Samuels' *The Young Henry Adams*, *Henry Adams: The Middle Years*, and *Henry Adams: The Major Phase* (Cambridge, Mass.: The Belknap Press of Harvard University Press, 1967, 1958, 1964); Earl N. Harbert's "Henry Adams" in *Fifteen American Authors Before 1900: Bibliographical Essays on Research and Criticism* (Madison, Wis.: University of Wisconsin Press, 1984), edited by Harbert and Robert A. Rees; and *The Letters of Henry Adams*, 3 vols. (Cambridge, Mass.: The Belknap Press of Harvard University Press, 1982; volumes 4–6 forthcoming), edited by J. C. Levenson, Ernest Samuels, Charles Vandersee, and Viola Hopkins Winner. In the notes below, the numbers refer to the page and line of the present volume (the line count includes chapter titles). No note is made for material included in a standard desk-reference book. Notes printed at the foot of pages within the text are Adams' own.

5.3   ACCORDING . . . 1800]   In December 1888, Adams wrote to Charles Scribner: "My only doubt regards the introductory chapters which will be eight in number, and will fill near half a volume. Ought these chapters to be set apart and headed Introduction, or ought they to run directly into the narrative? The question has greatly perplexed me. I do not fancy Introductions. I see that most of the historians had the same feeling. Gibbon ran his introductory chapters into his narrative, and Macaulay actually broke off his narrative to insert his introductory chapter. On the other hand I admit that my first seven or eight chapters are wholly introductory, not only to my sixteen years but also to the century. They ought to stand by themselves." He added, "I will follow your opinion if you have a decided one either way."

14.9–11   Between . . . Petersburg]   Previous printings read: "Between New York and Petersburg in Virginia was a daily service; between New York and Boston, and also between Petersburg", etc.

18.15–16   six . . . week]   In previous printings, "a mail thrice a week".

89.9   Connecticut]   "New Haven" in the first printing.

154.15   disdain . . . shall]   Omitted from previous printings. This and other quotations were corrected for the 1903 printing, while the citations were changed from various sources to Paul Leicester Ford's edition of *The Writings of Thomas Jefferson*, 10 vols. (New York: G. P. Putnam's Sons, 1892–99).

238.26–30   In October . . . Louisiana,]   This replaced the following passage in the first printing: "In Talleyrand's new colonial scheme lay the germ of the ideas and measures which were to occupy his life. From first to last, he had the great purpose of restoring France to a career of sound and conservative development. France had never ceased to regret the loss of Louisiana." The extract from Bonaparte's letter was added to provide "proof that Talleyrand had indoctrinated Bonaparte with his scheme" (Adams' note in his copy of the first printing).

264.18–38   that . . . opposition."]   This passage first appeared in the 1898 printing to replace the following: "Bonaparte's acts as well as his professions showed that he was bent on crushing democratic ideas, and that he regarded St. Domingo as an outpost of American republicanism, although Toussaint had made a rule as arbitrary as that of Bonaparte himself. 'The liberty of the blacks,' the letter continued, 'once recognized at St. Domingo and legitimated by the government, would be for all time a point of support for the republic in the New World.' The republic which Bonaparte had served and betrayed in Europe, and was about to pursue to St. Domingo and Louisiana, was the republic in its cosmopolitan sense, of which the President of the United States was the only representative; and by a strange confusion of events Toussaint Louverture, because he was a negro, became the champion of republican principles, with which he had nothing but the instinct of personal freedom in common. Toussaint's government was less republican than that of Bonaparte; he was doing by necessity in St. Domingo what Bonaparte was doing by choice in France."

322.28–29   Marbois . . . Livingston]   On February 27, 1883, Adams wrote to his friend Daniel C. Gilman about Gilman's biography of James Monroe for the American Statesmen Series: "I have just read your Monroe and have to thank you for a decided increase of my stock of information. . . . I . . . want to know where you found (p. 82) that 'ten days later,' &c, Marbois laid his project before Livingston, &c. I have hunted in vain hitherto to find a date for anything in this mysterious negotiation which never had a protocol or any of the ordinary forms. Please tell me where to look!" On March 2 he wrote again: "I must have a copy of that memorandum. If it be in the State Dept., I can get it; if you have one, please let me copy it, and instruct me all you can, for I labor ignorantly and history is more lie than truth."

357.30   inserted]   In earlier printings, "modest".

425.5–8   No . . . said[1]]   In earlier printings, this passage read: "No sooner did Griswold reach that city, a week afterward, on his way from Washington to Connecticut, than he kept his engagement with Burr, and the conversation strengthened him in his policy.[1] Burr was cautious, but said", etc. Adams added a citation to Charles R. King's *The Life and Correspondence of Rufus King* (6 vols., 1894–1900), one of the new sources consulted for the revisions of 1903.

549.18   A month . . . Code]   Earlier printings had: "Either before or
soon after Merry's arrival the President wrote the rules", etc.

549.39   ²King . . . Archives.]   Added in 1903.

562.27   King . . . known]   In earlier printings, this sentence stated that
King "knew of" the Louisiana cession when he signed the treaty.

718.10–11   when . . . Circuit,]   In the first printing, this read " when the
President offered him a seat"; Adams penciled the changes into his copy of
the first printing and also inserted the "Sixth" before "Maryland Circuit".

718.20–21   Nicholson escaped]   Earlier printings had "lifting Nicholson"
here.

721.10–11   ¹Cf. . . . 434.]   Handwritten in Adams' copy of the first printing and added in 1903.

934.23–25   company . . . sickness]   The first printing stated that the
ship's company " was short of its full complement, but she carried about
three hundred and seventy-five men and boys, all told. Much sickness", etc.

Cataloging Information

Adams, Henry, 1838–1918.
    History of the United States of America during the administrations of Thomas Jefferson and James Madison. 2 vols.
        Vol. 1 History of the United States of America during the administrations of Thomas Jefferson
        Vol. 2 History of the United States of America during the administrations of James Madison
    Edited by Earl N. Harbert.

    (The Library of America ; 31, 32)
    Includes indexes.
1. United States—Politics and government—1801–1809.
2. United States—Politics and government—1809–1817.
I. Title.   II. Series.
E331.A192   1986   973.4'6'0924
ISBN 0–940450–34–8 (v. 1)
ISBN 0–940450–35–6 (v. 2)

This book is set in 10 point Linotron Galliard,
a face designed for photocomposition by Matthew Carter
and based on the sixteenth-century face Granjon. The paper
is acid-free Ecusta Nyalite and meets the requirements for permanence of the American National Standards Institute. The binding
material is Brillianta, a 100% woven rayon cloth made by
Van Heek-Scholco Textielfabrieken, Holland. The composition is by Haddon Craftsmen, Inc., and The
Clarinda Company. Printing and binding
by R. R. Donnelley & Sons Company.
Designed by Bruce Campbell.